AMERICA'S TOP JOBS® FOR COLLEGE GRADUATES

Detailed Information on 112 Major Jobs
Requiring Four-Year and Higher Degrees

Third Edition

This newly revised edition includes the following:

- ✥ 112 revised and updated job descriptions
- ✥ Thorough career planning and job search advice
- ✥ New sections on the "best jobs," 500 major occupations, industry trends, and print and Internet information resources
- ✥ Easy-to-use format

J. Michael Farr

America's Top Jobs® for College Graduates, Third Edition
Detailed Information on 112 Major Jobs Requiring Four-Year and Higher Degrees

© 1999 by J. Michael Farr

Some other books by J. Michael Farr:	**Other books in the America's Top Jobs® series:**
■ *The Very Quick Job Search*	■ *America's Fastest Growing Jobs*
■ *America's Top Resumes for America's Top Jobs®*	■ *America's Top Federal Jobs*
■ *The Quick Resume & Cover Letter Book*	■ *America's Top Medical, Education & Human Services Jobs*
■ *How to Get a Job Now!*	■ *America's Top White-Collar Jobs*
■ *The Quick Interview & Salary Negotiation Book*	■ *America's Top Jobs® for People Without a Four-Year Degree*
■ *Getting the Job You Really Want*	■ *America's Top 300 Jobs*
	■ *Career Guide to America's Top Industries*

Several pages at the back of this book present some of our many career-related products. Please look there for additional resources and for ordering information. These and other JIST books can also be ordered from your bookstore.

Published by JIST Works, Inc.
720 N. Park Avenue
Indianapolis, IN 46202-3490
Phone: 317-264-3720   Fax: 317-264-3709   E-mail: jistworks@aol.com
World Wide Web Address: http://www.jist.com

Editors: Susan Pines, Sherri W. Emmons
Interior design: Aleata Howard
Interior layout: Carolyn J. Newland
Cover design: Michael Nolan
Proofreader: Chuck Hutchinson

Printed in the United States of America

03 02 01 00 99   5 4 3 2 1

3 2280 00661 0562

We have been careful to provide accurate information throughout this book, but it is possible that errors and omissions have been introduced. Please consider this in making any career plans or other important decisions. Trust your own judgment above all else and in all things.

ISBN 1-56370-493-5

RELAX—YOU DON'T HAVE TO READ THIS WHOLE BOOK!

This is a big book, but you don't need to read it all. I've organized it into easy-to-use sections so you can browse just the information you want. To get started, simply turn the page and check over the Table of Contents. I provide brief explanations there of the major sections of this book, plus a list of the jobs whose descriptions are in Section Two.

Who Should Use This Book

This is more than just a book of job descriptions. It has been compiled to be of great use for people in a variety of situations, including the following.

- ❖ **Those exploring career options:** The job descriptions in this book give a wealth of information on many of the most desirable jobs in the labor market.

- ❖ **People considering additional education or training:** Avoid costly mistakes in choosing a career or in obtaining additional training or education—and increase your chances of planning a bright future.

- ❖ **Job seekers:** The Section Two descriptions will help you identify new job targets, prepare for interviews, and write targeted resumes. Section Three, which provides career planning and job search advice, has been proven to cut job search time in half.

- ❖ **Counselors:** The substantial information in this book makes it a valuable source of information on jobs and trends.

Major Improvements in This Edition

I've made substantial changes in this edition, and I think it is the best yet. Of course, I am being completely objective. The changes include the following:

- ❖ **A shorter introduction.** I want to encourage more people to read it.

- ❖ **New "top job" lists:** Section One lists the best jobs organized in a variety of interesting ways such as highest paying, fastest growing, and by different education levels.

- ❖ **More job descriptions:** Section Two offers updated descriptions for 112 jobs, including all major jobs that typically require four years or more of college, plus all major jobs that do not require degrees but that employ high percentages of college grads.

- ❖ **Revised Section Three:** I've enhanced the career planning and job search advice to include information on using the Internet.

- ❖ **New trends and earnings information:** Sections Four and Five provide useful information on employment trends, including employment and earnings by college major, growth trends for major occupations and industries, and much more.

- ❖ **New bibliography:** This is a new feature that I hope you will find useful. It lists books and Web sites providing good information on careers and education.

As with previous editions, the occupational descriptions come from the good people at the U.S. Department of Labor, as published in the most recent edition of a book titled the *Occupational Outlook Handbook*. The *OOH* is considered by many to be the best source of career information available anywhere, and the updated descriptions include the latest data on earnings and other details. Information in the other sections comes from a variety of other Department of Labor publications and is among the most accurate and up-to-date available.

I hope you learn some interesting things from this book.

Regards,

Mike Farr

Mike Farr

TABLE OF CONTENTS

Summary of Major Sections

Introduction: This brief introduction provides an overview of trends and earnings for college graduates; tips on using the book for career or educational planning; and other useful tidbits. It's short, so consider reading it. *Begins on page 1.*

Section One: The Top Jobs Lists. This material offers very interesting lists of jobs, including those with the fastest growth, highest pay, and largest number of openings. It also includes lists of the best jobs (highest combined scores for pay, growth, and openings) at different levels of education, for young and older workers, for part-time and self-employment, and more. Most interesting. *Begins on page 9.*

Section Two: Descriptions of the 112 Top Jobs for College Graduates. This is the book's main section, with thorough descriptions for all major jobs requiring a four-year college degree or above. You will also find descriptions of jobs often held by grads but that do not require a degree. Descriptions include substantial information on working conditions, skills required, growth projections, training and education required, typical earnings, and other facts. *Begins on page 33.*

Section Three: Career Planning and Job Search Advice. Learn results-oriented career planning and job search techniques. This section includes tips on exploring career options, defining your ideal job, writing resumes, getting two interviews a day, how to answer problem questions, surviving unemployment, and more. *Begins on page 363.*

Section Four: Good Articles for College Graduates and Those Considering College. Read seven information-packed articles: "The Outlook for College Graduates Through 2006"; "Trends in College Degrees and Majors"; "Earnings of College Graduates in All Major Occupations"; "Earnings of College Graduates—Women Compared with Men"; "The Employment Status of New Graduates—One Year After Graduation"; "The Job Market for Ph.D.'s"; and "Occupations and Earnings of Workers with Some College but No Degree." *Begins on page 395.*

Section Five: Important Labor Market Trends and Details on All Major Industries and Jobs. This section features an excellent article titled "Tomorrow's Jobs." In addition are two boring tables that provide lots of useful information. The second article provides data on 500 major jobs, including earnings, growth, education needed, unemployment, and other details. The last article reviews growth and trends in all major industries. *Begins on page 453.*

Bibliography of Useful Career Resources and Internet Sites: This excellent review lists hundreds of career-related books, software, and Internet sites. *Begins on page 503.*

The 112 Top Jobs for College Graduates— Organized by Degree and Experience Required

The list that follows organizes 112 major jobs that typically require a four-year college degree or more. Descriptions for each are included in Section Two. You can go through the list and select jobs that interest you, then read more about them in Section Two. It's that easy, although I suggest you read the introduction and browse the other sections of this book as well.

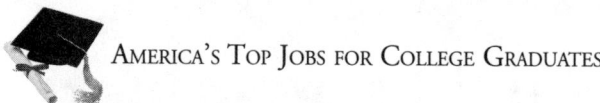
Jobs Typically Requiring a Bachelor's Degree

Jobs That Do Not Require a Bachelor's Degree but Are Often Held by College Graduates

© 1999 • J. Michael Farr • JIST Works, Inc. • Indianapolis, IN

College graduates make up about 25 percent of our workforce, and many of the highest-paying and fastest-growing jobs require a college degree. If you already have a four-year college degree, this book will give you lots of information on your job options. It offers information about how others with similar majors have done in the job market. This is important knowledge to have as you consider your options for the future. If you are considering more education—such as additional course work, a college degree, or an advanced degree—you'll find this book helpful as well.

But this book is not just about choosing a college major or a job, it's about improving your life. The job you hold has an enormous impact on how you live your life. Today's labor market is more competitive than ever, and earning good pay is not as easy as it once was. More training typically is required to get better jobs now, and good career planning and job-seeking skills are essential for long-term career success.

It is clear that jobs requiring more training or education pay off. For example, high school graduates working in jobs that require at least some training make an average of $7,500 more a year than those working in jobs requiring no training. College graduates earn about twice what high school graduates earn. That's a lot of money; over the years, that earnings difference can have a big effect on your lifestyle. But averages can be misleading. Some jobs—and some self-employment options—can pay quite well, even for those without advanced degrees.

The time you spend planning your career can pay off for you in more than just higher earnings. Being satisfied with your work—and with your life—can be even more important than how much you earn. This book can help you explore a variety of options to find the work best suited to you.

Major Trends for College Graduates

The labor market has rewarded those with college degrees for many years, and the projections for the future remain positive. While more detailed information is presented later in this book, here are a few of the major trends for college graduates.

More Demand

The labor market is projected to grow by about 14 percent between now and 2006, adding millions of new positions to the workforce. A closer look reveals that the projected demand for jobs requiring college degrees is almost twice that for those without: 23 percent versus 12 percent.

Higher Pay

While some high-paying jobs do not require a college degree—such as blue-collar supervisors, carpenters, registered nurses, and police detectives—most jobs with higher pay do. Average earnings for college graduates are considerably higher than for those without. College graduates earn an average of $35,768 a year—about 72 percent more than the average high school graduate and $10,000 more than the average for all workers. Over time, this difference in earning power has enormous implications on lifestyle.

College graduates also tend to marry college graduates—and women with degrees are more likely to work—resulting in substantially higher family incomes.

Lower Unemployment Rates

High school graduates have an unemployment rate about three times the current 2.5 percent average rate for all college graduates. The unemployment percentages change with the overall rates of unemployment, but the data clearly indicates that, on average, college graduates find jobs more quickly and lose them less often.

Unemployment Rates for Persons of Various Education Levels

Education Level	Unemployment Rate
Professional degree	1%
Ph.D. degree	1%
Master's degree	3%
Bachelor's degree	4%
High school graduate	8%

Your Situation May Not Be "Average"

While general trends for college graduates are positive, averages do not hold true for everyone. For example, new graduates often have trouble finding jobs related to their degrees. Many end up taking positions for which they feel overqualified. The unemployment rate for bachelor's degree holders ages 20 to 24 is 7 percent—almost twice the average for all graduates—and another 36 percent are "underemployed"—that is, working in jobs not typically requiring a college degree. While this can be discouraging, most graduates eventually do end up in jobs requiring a degree, although it may take a few years to get there. In addition, college graduates who lose their jobs to "downsizing" probably will find no consolation in knowing that the average unemployment rate for graduates is quite low.

Average earnings for college graduates can be quite misleading as well. For example, earnings for workers one year after graduation averaged about $24,000 in 1996—not the higher average noted earlier, which included those with substantially more experience. Overall, about 16 percent of college graduates earn less than the average high school graduate.

My point is this: Your situation probably is not average. Some people do better than others. Earnings vary enormously by region, occupation, and industry. But you can do many things to get ahead in the labor market. Finding solid information is a good place to start. Good information will give you a solid foundation for making good decisions.

What Degree or Job Should You Pursue?

If I could answer this question for you, I would be successful indeed. Unfortunately, to find the answer, you must consider a variety of conflicting options—and probably then settle on the best compromise.

One temptation is to look only at jobs that are projected to be in high demand or that have high earnings. For example, if you look at the following chart, you might come to the conclusion that education and humanities are "bad" majors, while engineering, computer science, and business are "good" ones. While it is probably a good idea to think about potential earnings when you choose a college major, it is only one thing to consider. Many people have majored in fields projected to have high earnings only to find a scarcity of job openings in their regions—and lower earnings as a result. Others have majored in high-paying fields only to find they hate the jobs they trained for. This is not a good way to achieve success.

Earnings of New Graduates by College Major

College Major	Average Annual Earnings
All graduates	$24,200
Biological sciences	$22,800
Business and management	$27,100
Education	$19,300
Engineering	$30,900
Health professions	$31,300
History	$21,000
Humanities	$21,300
Math, computer, and physical science	$24,400
Psychology	$19,500
Public affairs/social services	$22,000
Social science	$22,100

From a report on new graduates' earnings published in the Department of Labor's 1998 Occupational Outlook Quarterly. The entire article can be found in Section Four.

Education or Training	Average Annual Earnings	Premium Over High School Graduates
Professional degree	$55,111	166%
Ph.D. degree	$44,162	113%
Master's degree	$35,559	71%
Bachelor's plus experience	$40,982	98%
Bachelor's degree	$35,768	72%
Associate degree	$33,317	61%
On-the-job training	$20,699	
Average for all workers	**$25,183**	

Planning your career options is not a simple process and there are no shortcuts. I hope this book helps. It includes lots of information on jobs, and Section Three provides career planning and job search advice. Sections Four and Five have additional information on trends, earnings, and employment outcomes by major.

Four Labor Market Trends That Will Affect Your Career

The U.S. economy has changed in dramatic ways, with profound effects on how we work and live. Here are four labor market trends you simply *must* consider in your career plans.

1. Education and Earnings Are Related

It should come as no surprise that people with higher levels of education and training have higher average earnings. The data that follow are from the Department of Labor's Bulletin 2502, published in February 1998. The data reflect a new way of measuring earnings based on the education or training typically required for employment. High school graduates with no technical training and high school dropouts typically hold jobs that require on-the-job training or experience. I used the earnings of these jobs to calculate the premium in earnings for those with additional education.

The average earnings difference between a college graduate and someone with a high school education is more than $15,000 a year—enough to buy a nice car or a month's vacation for two in Europe. Over a lifetime, this earnings difference has an enormous impact.

And what is more, jobs that require a four-year college degree are projected to grow about twice as fast as jobs that do not. Note, however, that many rapidly growing and good-paying jobs do not require a four-year college degree. Many of the jobs listed in Section One don't require such a degree, but most of the better-paying jobs do require training beyond high school or substantial work experience.

2. Computer Knowledge Is Increasingly Important

As you look over the list of the most rapidly growing jobs in Section One, you will notice that many require computer or technical skills. Even jobs that don't appear to be "technical" now require computer literacy. Managers, for example, typically are expected to understand and use computer software for things like spreadsheets, word processing, and databases. Most clerical workers cannot find employment without appropriate computer skills. Factory workers, auto mechanics, and many others need technical training to handle increasingly complex jobs. Those who do not have these skills often have a more difficult time finding good jobs.

3. Ongoing Education and Training Are Essential

It used to be that school and work were separate activities. Most people did not go back to school once they began working. But with rapid changes in technology, most people must continue to learn throughout their work lives. Jobs are being continually upgraded, and many of today's jobs cannot be handled with skills learned only five years ago. What this means is that you should plan on upgrading your job skills throughout your working life. This may include taking formal courses, doing after-work reading, taking on-the-job training, and pursuing other forms of adult education. Continual upgrading of your work-related skills is no longer optional for most jobs, and you ignore it at your peril.

4. Good Career Planning Is Critical

Most people spend more time watching TV in a week than they spend on career planning in an entire year. Yet most people will change jobs many times during their work lives; today's workers are projected to make major career changes five to seven times.

The information on occupations in this book will help in your career planning. Section Three has career-planning and job-seeking advice, and Section Five gives information on major labor market trends. I urge you to read these and other career planning materials, because career-planning and job-seeking skills are adult survival skills in this new economy.

Section One: The Top Job Lists

Section One provides lists of jobs arranged in a variety of useful ways. For example, there are lists for the fastest-growing jobs, the ones with the highest pay, lists of the "best" jobs at various levels of education, and other interesting lists. Use the lists as another way to identify jobs you want to explore in more detail.

Section Two: Descriptions of the 112 Top Jobs for College Graduates

This section is the largest of the book, providing thorough descriptions for 112 major jobs typically held by people with college degrees. The jobs are listed in the Table of Contents (and in Section Two) under five major headings:

Jobs Typically Requiring a Professional or Doctoral Degree. This includes such jobs as dentists, physicians, lawyers, and veterinarians.

Jobs Typically Requiring a Master's Degree. Jobs such as psychologists, librarians, and management analysts are included in this section.

Jobs Typically Requiring a Bachelor's Degree or Higher, Plus Work Experience. This includes jobs such as education administrators, general managers, architects, and mathematicians.

Jobs Typically Requiring a Bachelor's Degree. In this section are jobs such as accountants, computer programmers, and designers.

Jobs That Do Not Require a Bachelor's Degree but Are Often Held by College Graduates. Jobs such as aircraft pilots, actors, insurance agents, and police detectives are in this section.

I used new data from the U.S. Department of Labor to identify the jobs typically held by college graduates and categorized them into the preceding groupings. The last grouping is new for this book, and while many jobs in that grouping do not require a four-year college degree, they are included because many people who work in these jobs have degrees—and many employers require such degrees for new hires.

What Each Job Description Provides

Each job description presents similar information and uses a standard format. Most are only two or three pages long, and each is packed with useful information, including the following.

- ❖ **Job Title:** This is the job title used by the *Occupational Outlook Handbook*, a book published by the Department of Labor.

- ❖ *Dictionary of Occupational Titles* **Codes:** The numbers in parentheses that appear just below each job title are from the *Dictionary of Occupational Titles (DOT), Fourth Edition*, a U.S. Department of Labor publication. *DOT* numbers are used by state employment service offices to classify applicants and job openings. They are included because some career information centers and libraries use them for filing occupational information. The Department of Labor has recently replaced the *DOT* with the O*NET—the Occupational Information Network. JIST publishes *The O*NET Dictionary of Occupational Titles™*, which provides descriptions for each O*NET occupation as well as other information related to the new O*NET system.

- ❖ **Significant Points:** This section provides highlights of key occupational characteristics for each job.

- ❖ **Nature of the Work:** Here you will find a variety of information, including the following:

  - What workers do, the equipment they use, and how closely they are supervised

  - How the duties of workers vary by industry, establishment, and size of firm

  - How the responsibilities of entry-level workers differ from those of experienced, supervisory, or self-employed workers

- How technological innovations are affecting what workers do and how they do it

- Emerging specialties

❖ **Working Conditions:** This section describes typical working and environmental conditions for workers in that occupation, including the following information:

- Typical hours worked

- The workplace environment

- Susceptibility to injury, illness, and job-related stress

- Necessary protective clothing and safety equipment

- Physical activities required

- Extent of travel required

❖ **Employment:** Here you will find information on who is working in the occupation, where they are employed, and other details such as the following:

- The number of people working in the job

- Key industries employing workers in the occupation

- Geographic distribution of jobs

- The proportion of part-time (fewer than 35 hours a week) and self-employed workers in the occupation

❖ **Training, Other Qualifications, and Advancement:** What kind of training will you need to perform a job? Where can you receive that training? What is the typical route of advancement? Those and other questions are answered here. This section includes information on the following:

- Most significant sources of training, typical length of training, and training preferred by employers

- Whether workers acquire skills through previous work experience, informal on-the-job training, formal training (including apprenticeships), the armed forces, home study, or hobbies and other activities

- Formal educational requirements (high school, postsecondary vocational or technical training, college, or graduate or professional education)

- Desirable skills, aptitudes, and personal characteristics

- Certification, examination, or licensing required for entry into the field, advancement, or independent practice

- Continuing education or skill improvement requirements

- Advancement opportunities

❖ **Job Outlook:** Where will the occupation be in the future? This valuable section gives projections, including the following:

- Forces that will result in growth or decline in the number of jobs

- Relative number of job openings an occupation provides (Large occupations with high turnover rates generally provide the most job openings—reflecting the need to replace workers who transfer to other occupations or stop working.)

- Degree of competition for jobs (Is there a surplus or shortage of job seekers compared to the number of openings? Do opportunities vary by industry, size of firm, or geographic location? Even in overcrowded fields, job openings exist, and good students or well-qualified individuals should not be deterred from undertaking training or seeking entry.)

- Susceptibility to layoffs due to imports, slowdowns in economic activity, technological advancements, or budget cuts

❖ **Earnings:** Here's an issue that's on everyone's mind: How much money will you make? This section includes the following information:

- Typical earnings of workers in the occupation

- How earnings vary with experience, location, and tenure

- Whether workers are compensated through annual salaries, hourly wages, commissions, piece rates, tips, or bonuses

- Earnings of wage and salary workers compared to self-employed persons

- Benefits, including health insurance, pensions, paid vacation and sick leave, family leave, child care or elder care, employee assistance programs, summers off, sabbaticals, tuition for dependents, discounted airfare or merchandise, stock options, profit-sharing plans, savings plans, and expense accounts

❖ **Related Occupations:** This section can point you to other jobs involving similar aptitudes, interests, education, and training.

❖ **Sources of Additional Information:** So you've found a job that looks interesting. How can you find out more? This section includes the following:

– Addresses for associations, government agencies, unions, and other organizations that provide useful occupational information. In some cases, toll-free phone numbers, Internet home page addresses, FAX numbers, and electronic mail addresses are included.

– Free or inexpensive publications offering more information, some of which are available in libraries, school career centers, and guidance offices.

Key Phrases Used in the Descriptions

The Department of Labor's Office of Employment Projections uses some key phrases to describe projected changes in employment and the relationship between the supply of and demand for workers in a particular occupation. But how do you interpret those phrases?

If the statement reads:	Employment is projected to:
Grow much faster than average	increase 36 percent or more
Grow faster than average	increase 21 to 35 percent
Grow about as fast as average	increase 10 to 20 percent
Grow more slowly than average or little or no change	decrease 0 to 9 percent
Decline	decrease 1 percent or more

If the statement reads:	Job openings compared to job seekers may be:
Very good to excellent opportunities	More numerous
Good or favorable opportunities	In rough balance
May face keen competition or can expect keen competition	Fewer

Tips for Exploring Career, Education, or Training Alternatives

This book is an excellent resource for anyone exploring career, education, or training alternatives. Many people take career interest tests to identify their career options, but this book can perform a similar function. If you do not have a good idea of what you want to do in your career—or if you are considering additional training or education but don't

know what sort you should pursue—there are several ways this book can help.

Review the List of Jobs

First of all, trust yourself. Many studies indicate that your interests are your best guide to career options. Begin by looking over the list of occupations in the Table of Contents. If others will be using this book, please don't mark it. Instead, make a photocopy of the Table of Contents; then check each job title that sounds interesting to you. Look at all the occupations, since you may identify job possibilities you have previously overlooked.

The next step is to read the job descriptions that most interest you. A quick review often will eliminate one or more of these jobs based on earnings, education required, or other considerations. Once you have identified the three or four jobs that are most interesting, research each one more thoroughly before making any important decisions.

Consider Additional Training or Education

Too often people pursue training or education without knowing much about the jobs related to that training. Reviewing the descriptions in this book is one way to learn more about an occupation before you enroll in an education or training program. If you are currently a student, the job descriptions can also help you decide on a major course of study or tell you about the jobs for which your studies are preparing you.

Don't eliminate a job that interests you too quickly. If a job requires more education or training than you have, there are many ways you can pursue the training you need.

Section Three: Career Planning and Job Search Advice

I know that most people who read this book do so because they want to improve themselves or because they need to find a job. For the past 20 years, I have been interested in helping people find better jobs in less time. So I have included advice on career planning and job seeking in this book. Section Three is short, but it gives you the basics you need to plan your career and reduce the time it takes to get a job.

Many people resist completing the activities in this section, but consider this: Often, it is not the best person who gets the job, but the best job seeker. Those who do their homework often get jobs over those with better credentials. People who have spent time planning their careers and who know how to conduct effective job searches have some distinct advantages over those who don't, including these:

1. **They get more interviews.** In fact, they get interviews for jobs that are never advertised.

2. **They do better in interviews.** They know how to present their skills, and they can answer problem questions. This can mean the difference between getting a job offer or sitting at home.

So please spend some time reading Section Three and completing the activities. It *can* make a difference.

Sections Four and Five: Articles with Good Information

Sections Four and Five contain articles from a variety of publications from the U.S. Department of Labor. Section Four provides specific information on the earnings and trends for those with college degrees. Section Five offers an article on major trends in the labor market as well as detailed information on all major jobs and industries. All of this information can be helpful in making good career decisions. Here are the titles of the various articles:

Section Four—Good Articles for College Graduates and Those Considering College

❖ "The Outlook for College Graduates Through 2006"

❖ "Trends in College Degrees and Majors"

❖ "Earnings of College Graduates in All Major Occupations"

❖ "Earnings of College Graduates—Women Compared with Men"

❖ "The Employment Status of New Graduates—One Year After Graduation"

❖ "The Job Market for Ph.D.'s"

❖ "Occupations and Earnings of Workers with Some College but No Degree"

Section Five—Important Labor Market Trends and Details on All Major Industries and Jobs

❖ "Tomorrow's Jobs: Important Labor Market Trends through the Year 2006"

❖ "Details on the Top 500 Jobs: Earnings, Projected Growth, Education Required, Unemployment Rates, and Other Details"

❖ "Employment Trends within Major Industries"

Bibliography: Useful Career Resources and Internet Sites

I've included a list of books and other resources on career planning, job seeking, and related topics. This list includes many resources you can find in a library and on the Internet.

Keep in mind that this is simply a beginning in your search for information. What matters most is that you include elements of meaning and fun into your career and life plans. Otherwise, why bother?

Sources of Information Used in This Book

The best source of data on labor market trends is the U.S. Department of Labor; the department's information is as reliable as it gets. I have used this information as a basis for the occupational descriptions in Section Two as well as for the content of Sections Four and Five. The information in Section Three is mine, as are the book's concept, introduction, and other elements. So I think it's fair to say this is a joint government and private project. America! Isn't this a great place?

Please note that data in this book come from information collected and reported at different times. I have included some recent data (the job descriptions, for example, were first available in 1998) and some based on earlier information. In all cases, I have tried to find the most recent information available; I have included previously published data because of its value.

THE TOP JOB LISTS

One step in creating this book was to research the data on earnings and projected job growth for major jobs. This information is available from government sources, but it needs to be reorganized so that it makes sense. This reorganization is an essential step in choosing which job descriptions to include in this book.

The jobs described in this book typically require or are held by people with four-year college degrees. In Section Two, those jobs are arranged by education required, but jobs can be organized in other ways. In this section, I have organized jobs by useful lists. I hope you find these lists helpful. Many but not all jobs included in the lists are described in this book.

The "Best Jobs"

LaVerne Ludden and I recently completed work on a book titled *Best Jobs for the 21st Century* (JIST Works, 1999). It was an interesting project, because it was one of the first books to use data from the Occupational Information Network (O*NET), a new database of occupational information released by the U.S. Department of Labor. Designed to replace the older data systems, the O*NET allowed us to analyze and sort jobs in some useful ways that previously had been difficult. The O*NET also listed the most recent earnings, growth projections, and other job-related information.

The lists that follow are some of the many in *Best Jobs for the 21st Century*. All are based on the new O*NET information. One problem with these tables is that the O*NET uses some job titles that differ from the titles used in Section Two. The job descriptions in Section Two also use different data sources for earnings and projected growth, so you'll see some differences between the following tables and the Section Two job descriptions. Even so, the information is useful, and you should be able—for the most part—to find a corresponding description (with a closely related title) in Section Two.

We began these lists with almost 1,200 jobs from the O*NET database. We cut that number to include only the 279 jobs that met our criteria for high pay, fast growth, or large numbers of openings. We then sorted the 279 jobs into lists in order of highest pay, fastest growth, and largest number of openings. The occupation with the highest pay was given a score of 279; the one with the next highest pay, 278; and so on. We continued this process for all criteria on each occupation, until we arrived at a total score for each. Then we created a new list based on these scores. "Systems analysts" was the occupation with the highest combined score, so it is at the top of the first list that follows. The other occupations follow in descending order, based on their total scores.

Because of space limitations, we could not include all the "best jobs" lists here. You can find the complete set (for all levels of education, younger and older workers, men and women, by interests, and so on) in *Best Jobs for the 21st Century*, or on JIST's Web site at www.JIST.com. Lists that do not include "best" in the title come from other Department of Labor sources.

© 1999 • J. Michael Farr • JIST Works, Inc. • Indianapolis, IN

TABLE 1

Best Jobs for the 21st Century—Jobs with the Best Combination of High Pay, Fast Growth, and Large Number of Openings

Of all O*NET jobs, the jobs in Table 1 are those with the highest combined scores. This is the list that most people want to know about, and here are some observations:

◆ Among the top 50 occupations, there are jobs in most major occupational groups and industries, including the arts, education, health care and other helping professions, business, and management.

◆ Many of these jobs are in the service and information industries. Contrary to what we often hear, these are not "dead end" jobs with low pay and status.

◆ While pay is only one factor determining which jobs were included in this list, about 80 percent of the jobs here pay more than the average for all workers (which is just above $26,000 a year), and 42 percent pay $40,000 or more per year.

◆ This list illustrates that many opportunities exist for jobs with good pay in the twenty-first century. In order to get them, you may need to learn new skills and continue to update your skills in the future.

I expect that many people will turn to this list first. I know I would. Like most people, you probably consider earnings an important factor in choosing a career.

But keep in mind that the earnings here reflect the national average for all workers in the occupation. This is an important consideration, because starting pay in any job is usually less than the average. Earnings also vary significantly by region of the country, so actual pay in your area could be substantially different.

Occupation	Annual Earnings	Annual Job Openings	Percentage Growth through 2006
Systems analysts	$48,360	87,318	103
Computer engineers	$54,912	34,884	109
Engineering, mathematical, and natural science managers	$65,686	37,494	45
Securities and financial services sales workers	$59,634	40,568	38
Marketing, advertising, and public relations managers	$53,602	54,600	29
Computer scientists	$48,630	26,732	118
Service managers	$48,339	171,229	21
Physical therapists	$52,811	19,122	71
Special education teachers	$37,104	49,029	59
General managers and top executives	$58,344	288,825	15
Computer programmers	$48,360	58,990	23
Management support workers	$35,339	154,129	26

(continued)

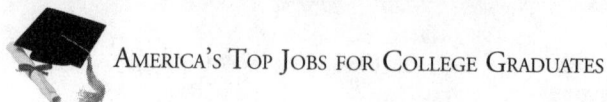

TABLE 1 (CONTINUED)
Best Jobs for the 21st Century—Jobs with the Best Combination of High Pay, Fast Growth, and Large Number of Openings

Occupation	Annual Earnings	Annual Job Openings	Percentage Growth through 2006
Registered nurses	$40,310	165,362	21
Lawyers	$70,117	45,929	19
Secondary school teachers	$36,784	168,392	22
Electrical and electronics engineers	$53,227	19,098	29
Physicians	$96,637	29,681	21
Financial managers	$54,392	74,297	18
Social workers	$31,221	75,554	32
College and university faculty	$44,800	126,584	19
Dental hygienists	$42,432	18,373	48
Management analysts	$48,194	46,026	21
Management support specialists	$38,251	124,342	20
Occupational therapists	$46,779	9,543	66
Speech-language pathologists and audiologists	$42,702	12,202	51
Musicians	$30,888	49,350	33
Artists and commercial artists	$33,114	46,893	28
Vocational education and training instructors	$33,800	82,354	23
Loan officers and counselors	$37,419	29,989	28
Paralegals	$32,032	21,705	68
Sales specialists and support workers	$24,502	765,025	23
Correction officers	$28,787	48,102	32
Writers and editors	$38,355	41,449	21
Sports instructors and coaches	$22,901	82,035	41
Food service and lodging managers	$26,562	68,207	29
Adjustment clerks	$22,422	80,643	46
Clerical supervisors and managers	$31,013	143,806	19
Designers	$30,867	42,478	26
Health care support specialists	$31,054	45,719	24
Home health aides	$16,286	156,127	77
Bill and account collectors	$22,402	68,308	42
Receptionists and information clerks	$18,075	336,852	30
Teacher aides and educational assistants	$15,974	353,119	38
Insurance adjusters, examiners, and investigators	$38,230	21,662	23
Customer service representatives	$27,061	29,751	36
Flight attendants	$36,442	9,844	35
Physician assistants	$40,414	5,090	47
Personal service workers	$17,202	279,051	31
Physical and corrective therapy assistants	$23,587	26,479	79
Respiratory therapists	$32,781	9,453	46

TABLE 2
Highest-Paying Jobs

The highest-paying job in this table is physicians, with average annual earnings of $96,636. All of the top 25 jobs here have average annual earnings greater than $52,000. The average annual earnings for all workers is slightly more than $26,000, so the top 25 jobs on this list earn more than double the national average.

Most of the best-paying jobs require at least a four-year degree. This isn't surprising since the lifetime earnings of the average college graduate is more than double that of the average high school graduate. Six of the 10 best-paying jobs require a professional degree, which normally takes three or more years of education beyond a bachelor's degree. Workers with professional degrees have lifetime earnings about four times greater than those of high school graduates. While it is clear that higher levels of education and training often are required for jobs with high earnings, opportunities remain for higher-than-average pay at all levels of education.

Occupation	Average Annual Earnings
Physicians	$96,636
Dentists	$85,508
Podiatrists	$85,134
Lawyers	$70,116
Aircraft pilots and flight engineers	$69,097
Petroleum engineers	$68,224
Actuaries	$66,352
Engineering, mathematical, and natural science managers	$65,686
Optometrists	$64,209
Chiropractors	$63,211
Physicists and astronomers	$62,774
Aerospace engineers	$59,633
Securities and financial services sales workers	$59,633
General managers and top executives	$58,344
Nuclear engineers	$57,740
Medical scientists	$56,659
Chemical engineers	$55,764
Pharmacists	$55,328
Computer engineers	$54,912
Financial managers	$54,392
Production engineers	$54,329
Marketing, advertising, and public relations managers	$53,601
Electrical and electronics engineers	$53,227
Veterinarians and veterinary inspectors	$52,936
Physical therapists	$52,811

TABLE 3
Fastest-Growing Jobs

I created the list in this table by sorting the 250 jobs described in the current edition of the *Occupational Outlook Handbook* (published by the U.S. Department of Labor) by percentage of growth rate projected through the year 2006. Of these 250 jobs, 111 had average (14 percent) or higher projected growth rates. These 111 jobs appear next.

The second column shows the projected percentage increase in employment for each job. The third shows how many people are currently employed in the job. The final column shows how many new positions are projected by the year 2006.

Note that 6 of the 10 most rapidly growing jobs are in the medical field. Also notice that 9 of the 10 fastest-growing jobs require technical training beyond high school. Only the occupation "homemaker-home health aides" can be learned in a few months. While job opportunities exist at all levels of education and training, many better-paying ones require education or training beyond high school.

Occupation	Percentage Growth through 2006	Number Employed	New Openings through 2006
Computer scientists, computer engineers, and systems analysts	108	933,000	1,004,000
Physical and corrective therapy assistants and aides	79	84,000	66,000
Homemaker-home health aides	79	697,000	550,000
Medical assistants	74	225,000	166,000
Physical therapists	71	115,000	81,000
Occupational therapy assistants and aides	69	16,000	11,000
Paralegals	68	113,000	76,000
Occupational therapists	66	57,000	38,000
Special education teachers	59	407,000	241,000
Services sales representatives	57	694,000	39,300
Social and human services assistants	55	178,000	98,000
Speech-language pathologists and audiologists	51	87,000	44,000
Health information technicians	51	87,000	44,000
Dental hygienists	48	133,000	64,000
Physician assistants	47	64,000	30,000
Respiratory therapists	46	82,000	37,000
Emergency medical technicians	45	150,000	67,000

(continued)

© 1999 • J. Michael Farr • JIST Works, Inc. • Indianapolis, IN

TABLE 3 (CONTINUED)
Fastest-Growing Jobs

Occupation	Percentage Growth through 2006	Number Employed	New Openings through 2006
Engineering, science, and computer systems managers	45	343,000	155,000
Dental assistants	38	202,000	77,000
Securities and financial services sales representatives	38	263,000	100,000
Teacher aides	38	981,000	370,000
Computer and office machine repairers	37	141,000	53,000
Flight attendants	35	132,000	46,000
Restaurant and food service managers	34	493,000	166,000
Musicians	33	274,000	92,000
Surgical technologists	32	49,000	15,000
Correctional officers	32	320,000	103,000
Social workers	32	585,000	188,000
Preschool teachers and child-care workers	32	1,172,000	379,000
Receptionists	30	1,074,000	318,000
Radiologic technologists	29	174,000	50,000
Electrical and electronics engineers	29	367,000	105,000
Marketing, advertising, and public relations managers	29	482,000	138,000
Dancers and choreographers	28	23,000	6,500
Library technicians	28	78,000	22,000
Loan officers and counselors	28	209,000	59,000
Visual artists	28	276,000	78,000
Health services managers	28	329,000	93,000
Chiropractors	27	44,000	12,000
Public relations specialists	27	110,000	30,000
Designers	26	342,000	89,000
Biological and medical scientists	25	118,000	29,000
Adjusters, investigators, and collectors	25	1,340,000	335,000
Electroneurodiagnostic technologists	24	6,500	1,500
Actors, directors, and producers	24	105,000	25,000
Travel agents	24	142,000	34,000
Nursing aides and psychiatric aides	24	1,415,000	342,000
Veterinarians	23	58,000	13,000

(continued)

TABLE 3 (CONTINUED)
Fastest-Growing Jobs

Occupation	Percentage Growth through 2006	Number Employed	New Openings through 2006
Water and wastewater treatment plant operators	23	98,000	23,000
Veterinary assistants and nonfarm animal caretakers	23	163,000	37,000
Counter and rental clerks	23	374,000	84,000
Computer programmers	23	568,000	129,000
Guards	23	955,000	221,000
Information clerks	23	1,591,000	366,000
Recreation workers	22	233,000	52,000
Adult education teachers	22	559,000	123,000
Landscape architects	21	17,000	3,500
Recreational therapists	21	38,000	8,000
Hotel and motel desk clerks	21	144,000	30,000
Management analysts and consultants	21	244,000	52,000
Writers and editors	21	286,000	61,000
Physicians	21	560,000	118,000
Licensed practical nurses	21	699,000	148,000
Registered nurses	21	1,971,000	411,000
Agricultural scientists	20	24,000	4,800
Architects	20	94,000	18,000
Bus drivers	20	592,000	117,000
Landscaping, groundskeeping, nursery, greenhouse, and lawn service occupations	20	925,000	180,000
Economists and marketing research analysts	19	51,000	9,400
Insulation workers	19	65,000	13,000
Counselors	19	175,000	33,000
College and university faculty	19	864,000	162,000
Clerical supervisors and managers	19	1,369,000	262,000
Dietitians and nutritionists	18	58,000	11,000
Private detectives and investigators	18	58,000	11,000
Chemists	18	91,000	17,000
Civil engineers	18	196,000	35,000
Construction managers	18	249,000	45,000
Human resources specialists and managers	18	544,000	97,000

(continued)

© 1999 • J. Michael Farr • JIST Works, Inc. • Indianapolis, IN

TABLE 3 (CONTINUED)
Fastest-Growing Jobs

Occupation	Percentage Growth through 2006	Number Employed	New Openings through 2006
Financial managers	18	800,000	146,000
General maintenance mechanics	18	1,362,000	246,000
Engineers	18	1,382,000	250,000
Foresters and conservation scientists	17	37,000	6,400
Photographers and camera operators	17	154,000	26,000
Heating, air-conditioning, and refrigeration technicians	17	256,000	44,000
Lawyers and judges	17	699,000	120,000
Cashiers	17	3,146,000	530,000
Chefs, cooks, and other kitchen workers	17	3,402,000	583,000
Property managers	16	271,000	44,000
Employment interviewers	16	87,000	14,000
Cost estimators	16	188,000	29,000
Mechanical engineers	16	228,000	36,000
Kindergarten, elementary, and secondary school teachers	16	3,053,000	483,000
Archivists and curators	15	20,000	2,900
Geologists and geophysicists	15	47,000	6,900
Broadcast technicians	15	46,000	6,900
Chemical engineers	15	49,000	7,400
Library assistants and bookmobile drivers	15	125,000	19,000
Clinical laboratory technologists and technicians	15	285,000	42,000
Painters and paperhangers	15	444,000	66,000
Truck drivers	15	3,050,000	442,000
General managers and top executives	15	3,210,000	467,000
Dispensing opticians	14	67,000	9,400
Construction and building inspectors	14	66,000	10,000
Brokerage clerks and statement clerks	14	102,000	14,000
Aircraft pilots	14	110,000	15,000
Industrial engineers	14	115,000	16,000
Bricklayers and stonemasons	14	142,000	19,000
Line installers and cable splicers	14	309,000	44,000
Manufacturers' and wholesale sales representatives	14	1,557,000	211,000
Handlers, equipment cleaners, helpers, and laborers	14	4,975,000	679,000

TABLE 4
Highest-Growth Industries

This table shows the 20 industries with the highest growth rates projected through the year 2006. All are in the services sector rather than in manufacturing. While most people think more about occupations in planning their careers, the industry you work in can have an important effect on your earnings and job satisfaction.

Industry	Percentage Growth Projected through 2006
Computer and data processing services	108
Home health care services	90
Automotive services, except repair	80
Water supply and sanitary services	66
Management and public relations	60
Residential care	59
Freight transportation arrangement	56
Personnel supply services	53
Individual and miscellaneous social services	50
Offices of physicians, including osteopaths	46
Medical service and health insurance	40
School buses	38
Public warehousing and storage	38
Nursing and personal care facilities	37
Security and commodity brokers and dealers	36
Producers, orchestras, and entertainers	35
Offices and clinics of dentists	34
Mortgage bankers and brokers	34
Motion picture production and distribution	33
Passenger transportation arrangement	30

TABLE 5
Jobs with Largest Number of Annual Openings

Occupations with a large number of annual openings provide easier entry for new workers and afford the ability to move from one job to another with relative ease. Such jobs are attractive to people reentering the labor market, part-time job seekers, and workers who want to move from one employer to another. Many of the jobs listed in Table 5 are "second jobs" held by people who want to supplement their income.

Note that just because an occupation has large numbers of openings does not mean it is high paying. For example, the top 25 occupations on this list pay an average of under $20,000 a year—less than the $26,500-a-year average paid to all workers. And the average growth rate of these jobs is less than 16 percent, a bit higher than the 14 percent growth rate projected for all occupations through the year 2006.

Occupation	Number of Annual Openings
Retail salespersons	1,236,273
Cashiers	1,109,571
Janitors, cleaners, and maids	818,941
Sales specialists and support workers	765,025
Food counter and fountain workers	727,389
Waiters and waitresses	714,482
General office clerks	661,333
Helpers and laborers	586,697
Food preparation workers	573,079
Secretaries	433,901
Teacher aides and educational assistants	353,119
Stock clerks	346,772
Truck drivers, light and heavy	346,612
Receptionists and information clerks	336,852
Child care workers	328,078
Bookkeeping, accounting, and auditing clerks	327,125
Marketing and sales worker supervisors	305,545
Nursing aides, orderlies, and attendants	304,868
General managers and top executives	288,825
Guards	283,077
Personal service workers	279,051
Hand packers and packagers	271,086
Hand workers	267,301
Short-order and fast-food cooks	237,301
Freight, stock, and material movers	232,034

TABLE 6
Best Jobs Requiring a Graduate or Professional Degree

Jobs requiring a degree beyond a bachelor's have been combined in this list. The education levels include the following:

◆ **Professional degree**. This degree typically requires at least two years of education beyond the bachelor's degree. Physicians and attorneys require a professional degree.

◆ **Doctoral degree**. This degree typically requires at least three years of full-time academic work beyond the bachelor's degree. Medical scientists and college faculty require a doctoral degree.

◆ **Master's degree**. This degree typically requires one to two years of full-time study beyond the bachelor's degree. Urban and regional planners and librarians require a master's degree.

There are 21 jobs whose scores were high enough to be included in this group. The average earnings for the group is $54,069; the average rate of growth through the year 2006 is 16 percent; and the average number of job openings annually is 16,638.

Occupation	Education Level	Annual Earnings	Percentage Growth through 2006	Annual Number of Openings
Physicians	Professional	$96,637	21	29,681
Lawyers	Professional	$70,117	19	45,929
Management analysts	Master's	$48,194	21	46,026
Chiropractors	Professional	$63,211	27	2,595
College and university faculty	Doctorate	$44,800	19	126,584
Speech-language pathologists and audiologists	Master's	$42,702	51	12,202
Medical scientists	Doctorate	$56,659	25	3,333
Dentists	Professional	$85,509	8	5,073
Veterinarians and veterinary inspectors	Professional	$52,936	23	2,381
Biological scientists	Doctorate	$41,829	25	7,110
Counselors	Master's	$36,566	19	27,181
Optometrists	Professional	$64,210	12	1,630
Psychologists	Master's	$48,090	8	10,914
Podiatrists	Professional	$85,134	10	616
Clergy	Professional	$28,870	13	14,514
Operations research analysts	Master's	$45,760	8	5,316
Physicists and astronomers	Doctorate	$62,774	-2	1,073
Mathematicians	Doctorate	$46,342	9	960
Curators, archivists, museum technicians, and restorers	Master's	$30,035	15	2,367
Urban and regional planners	Master's	$40,934	5	3,856
Life scientists	Doctorate	$44,138	-3	53

TABLE 7
Best Jobs Requiring a Bachelor's Degree Plus Experience

Jobs in this category often are management positions and require experience in a related nonmanagerial position. Because of the experience requirements for entry, many of these jobs pay better than those requiring a bachelor's degree alone. The average earnings for the 12 jobs in this group is $49,793; the average growth rate through the year 2006 is 19 percent; and the average number of job openings annually is 65,285.

Occupation	Annual Earnings	Percentage Growth through 2006	Annual Number of Openings
Engineering, mathematical, and natural science managers	$65,686	45	37,494
General managers and top executives	$58,344	15	288,825
Marketing, advertising, and public relations managers	$53,602	29	54,600
Financial managers	$54,392	18	74,297
Service managers	$48,339	21	171,229
Artists and commercial artists	$33,114	28	46,893
Education administrators	$52,437	12	39,333
Personnel, training, and labor relations managers	$45,989	18	20,995
Communication, transportation, and utilities managers	$48,818	15	10,840
Administrative services managers	$44,200	11	24,605
Judges and magistrates	$51,667	2	3,558
Purchasing managers	$40,934	8	10,746

TABLE 8
Best Jobs Requiring a Bachelor's Degree

The bachelor's degree typically requires four to five years of full-time academic work beyond high school. Sixty O*NET jobs requiring a bachelor's degree had scores high enough to be included on this list. The average earnings for the group is $42,245; the average growth rate through the year 2006 is 24 percent; and the average job openings annually is 30,946.

Occupation	Annual Earnings	Percentage Growth through 2006	Annual Number of Openings
Computer engineers	$54,912	109	34,884
Systems analysts	$48,360	103	87,318
Physical therapists	$52,811	71	19,122
Computer scientists	$48,630	118	26,732
Electrical and electronics engineers	$53,227	29	19,098
Computer programmers	$48,360	23	58,990
Special education teachers	$37,104	59	49,029
Secondary school teachers	$36,784	22	168,392
Management support workers	$35,339	26	154,129
Management support specialists	$38,251	20	124,342
Loan officers and counselors	$37,419	28	29,989
Occupational therapists	$46,779	66	9,543
Writers and editors	$38,355	21	41,449
Social workers	$31,221	32	75,554
Civil engineers	$49,920	18	15,979
Economists	$50,544	19	11,343
Production engineers	$54,330	14	19,706
Physical scientists	$47,632	28	4,131
Physician assistants	$40,414	47	5,090
Residential counselors	$19,261	41	38,516
Construction managers	$46,301	18	22,043
Designers	$30,867	26	42,478
Pharmacists	$55,328	13	13,826
Mechanical engineers	$48,901	16	14,290
Architects	$46,883	20	10,404
Public relations specialists and publicity writers	$33,862	27	17,954
Insurance claims examiners	$41,142	22	7,281

(continued)

TABLE 8 (CONTINUED)
Best Jobs Requiring a Bachelor's Degree

Occupation	Annual Earnings	Percentage Growth through 2006	Annual Number of Openings
Accountants and auditors	$38,168	12	118,375
Personnel, training, and labor relations specialists	$36,566	18	36,049
Preschool and kindergarten teachers	$23,216	20	77,151
Chemists	$43,306	18	10,572
Elementary teachers	$35,280	10	164,163
Industrial production managers	$50,710	-3	14,917
Therapeutic services and administration	$31,866	67	4,767
Director of religious education and activities	$24,170	36	10,781
Aerospace engineers	$59,634	8	3,771
Chemical engineers	$55,765	15	1,434
Recreation workers	$17,139	22	29,880
Interior designers	$32,094	28	9,238
Tutors and instructors	$26,000	15	149,064
Industrial engineers	$51,064	14	3,554
Geologists, geophysicists, and oceanographers	$52,083	15	1,687
Property and real estate managers	$33,114	16	29,483
Landscape architects	$38,875	21	1,593
Actuaries	$66,352	0	1,165
Nuclear engineers	$57,741	5	715
Budget analysts	$42,058	12	8,204
Credit analysts	$36,962	16	5,454
Clinical laboratory technologists	$30,805	15	23,944
Petroleum engineers	$68,224	-14	549
Employment interviewers	$35,090	16	10,430
Agricultural and food scientists	$35,942	20	2,016
Foresters and conservation scientists	$36,650	17	3,200
Materials engineers	$49,566	7	933
Recreational therapists	$26,770	21	3,414
Dietitians and nutritionists	$32,406	18	4,079
Farm and home management advisors	$48,506	-38	3,078
Meteorologists	$47,674	8	421
Mining engineers	$49,837	-13	130
Statisticians	$47,507	1	93

TABLE 9
Best Jobs for Younger Workers

We sorted the list of O*NET occupations to find those with the highest percentage of workers (30 percent or more) ages 16 to 24—who constitute about 16 percent of the total U.S. workforce.

While young workers are employed in all major occupations, most work in entry-level, part-time, seasonal, or service jobs. Many of these jobs pay the minimum wage. These low-paying jobs are referred to as *entry-level jobs* because they offer inexperienced workers an opportunity to enter the labor market.

While these jobs employ the highest percentage of young workers, other fields may provide jobs with higher long-term earnings, opportunities for advancement, and other career advantages.

Occupation	Percentage Ages 16 to 24	Annual Earnings	Percentage Growth through 2006	Annual Number of Openings
Helpers and laborers	30	$20,509	16	586,697
Short-order and fast-food cooks	38	$18,491	22	237,301
Cashiers	52	$17,472	17	1,109,571
Retail salespersons	33	$19,302	10	1,236,273
Amusement and recreation attendants	46	$17,222	48	130,390
Food preparation workers	40	$17,181	19	573,079
Bread and pastry bakers	38	$19,178	26	61,382
Freight, stock, and material movers	46	$18,678	5	232,034
Restaurant cooks	38	$17,118	15	224,725
Specialty food workers	39	$16,536	27	82,637
Counter and rental clerks	45	$15,496	23	129,889
Food counter and fountain workers	51	$14,643	14	727,389
Vehicle washers and equipment cleaners	39	$16,078	25	103,946
Construction trades helpers	44	$18,075	9	137,805
Ski patrol workers and lifeguards	76	$17,202	17	53,969
Waiters and waitresses	47	$13,998	11	714,482
Veterinary assistants	31	$14,685	28	7,248
Sprayer applicators	30	$16,182	21	5,889
Gardeners and groundskeepers	30	$15,038	0	188,023
Ushers, lobby attendants, and ticket takers	46	$13,354	28	25,394

TABLE 10
Best Jobs for Older Workers

This table lists O*NET occupations that employ a high percentage (at least 15 percent) of workers who are 55 or older. These workers account for approximately 12.5 percent of the workforce. Participation in the workforce for people 55 or older is less than that of other age groups as workers begin to retire.

This list can help you if you are changing careers or approaching retirement. Some occupations are listed because they are attractive to older workers who want part-time work to supplement their retirement income. For example, "lawn service manager" pays fairly well, can be held part-time, offers a flexible schedule, and lends itself to self-employment. Other occupations on the list—such as clergy, physicians, and musicians—take years of training and experience.

Occupation	Percentage 55 and Older	Annual Earnings	Percentage Growth through 2006	Annual Number of Openings
Chiropractors	17	$63,211	27	2,595
Veterinarians and veterinary inspectors	17	$52,936	23	2,381
Physicians	18	$96,637	21	29,681
Musicians	19	$30,888	33	49,350
Director of religious education activities	17	$24,170	36	10,781
Human services workers	22	$21,112	55	42,907
Management analysts	22	$48,194	21	46,026
Personal and home care aides	22	$13,832	85	58,134
Lawn service managers	35	$25,917	22	4,637
College and university faculty	19	$44,800	19	126,584
Civil engineers	17	$49,920	18	15,979
Pest controllers and assistants	18	$21,507	22	16,835
Guards	22	$16,640	23	283,077
Nursery and greenhouse managers	35	$26,104	19	2,575
Recreation workers	17	$17,139	22	29,880
Dietitians and nutritionists	15	$32,406	18	4,079
Property and real estate managers	27	$33,114	16	29,483
Construction and building inspectors	15	$35,381	15	5,878
Private detectives	22	$24,648	19	17,441
Optometrists	17	$64,210	12	1,630

TABLE 11
Best Jobs for Part-Time Workers

Many people prefer working part-time—others end up doing so because they can't find full-time jobs. For example, a person who is going to school or has young children may prefer part-time work in order to attend classes or spend time with family. Still others work a second job to supplement their income.

If you want to work part-time, Table 11 will show you where others are finding opportunities for this kind of work. Many of these jobs can be learned quickly, offer flexible work schedules, and are easy to obtain.

While many people think of part-time jobs as requiring low skill and having low pay, this is not always the case. For example, 5 of the 10 best-paying, part-time jobs require professional credentials or substantial experience (such as university faculty and musicians), and 6 of the 20 best-paying, part-time jobs are in teaching and education.

The occupations in this table are those in which 30 percent or more of the workforce is part-time. Note that this is the only table in which hourly earnings (as opposed to yearly earnings) are reported.

Occupation	Percentage Part-Time	Hourly Wages	Percentage Growth through 2006	Annual Number of Openings
Receptionists and information clerks	35	$8.69	30	336,852
Sports instructors and coaches	43	$11.01	41	82,035
Teacher aides and educational assistants	47	$7.68	38	353,119
Personal service workers	40	$8.27	31	279,051
College and university faculty	32	$21.54	19	126,584
Vocational education and training instructors	43	$16.25	23	82,354
Musicians	54	$14.85	33	49,350
Physical and corrective therapy assistants	35	$11.34	79	26,479
Tutors and instructors	40	$12.50	15	149,064
Human services workers	42	$10.15	55	42,907
Dental assistants	40	$10.37	38	45,487
Adult education instructors	43	$13.16	21	81,219
Childcare workers	43	$6.73	36	328,078
Flight attendants	46	$17.52	35	9,844
Retail salespersons	40	$8.26	10	1,236,273
General office clerks	31	$9.27	7	661,333
Preschool and kindergarten teachers	32	$11.16	20	77,151
Amusement and recreation attendants	49	$6.42	48	130,390
Travel agents	32	$10.56	24	38,234
Bookkeeping, accounting, and auditing clerks	33	$10.95	-5	327,125

Opportunities and Earnings for Workers with and without College Degrees

The average annual wage for all workers, at all levels of education, is about $25,000 a year. Those with four-year degrees earn more, on average. But averages can be misleading, and some people with less than a four-year degree do quite well.

The information that follows shows how the earnings of workers with different levels of education compare with the average earnings of all workers. The first column presents the level of education attained. The second and third columns present the percentage of these workers whose earnings are higher than the average earnings for all workers and for four-year college graduates.

As you can see, many people without four-year degrees have relatively high earnings.

Education Level of Worker	Percent Earning More Than the Average of All Workers	Percent Earning More Than the Average of Workers with Four-Year Degree
Less than high school	19.4	6.8
High school	37	14.5
Some college, no degree	48.4	23.1
Associate degree	55.6	27.8

In looking at occupations, you need to realize that many jobs employ people with a variety of educational backgrounds. For example, columns three, four, and five of the information that follows present major occupational groups along with the percentage of people employed in these groups based on their level of education. This information shows that, for example, while the largest percentage of executives, administrators, and managers have four or more years of college, more than half do not.

While I am a strong believer in the value of education, my point here is that there are many paths to upward mobility. A four-year college degree makes lots of sense, but so could shorter technical training.

Educational Attainment of Workers

Occupation	Percentage Growth through 2006	High School Graduate	1 to 3 Years of College	4+ Years of College	Average Weekly Earnings
Executives, administrators, and managers	26	25	27	48	$652
Professional specialty	37	9	19	72	596
Technicians and related support	32	26	45	29	489
Marketing and sales	21	46	32	22	346
Administrative support and clerical	13	50	37	13	341
Service workers	33	68	26	6	232
Agriculture, forestry, fishing, and related	4	75	17	8	258
Precision production, craft, and repair	13	68	26	6	470
Operators, fabricators, and laborers	10	80	17	3	331
Averages	22	50	27	23	406

TABLE 12
Percentage of Workers Not Having a Four-Year Degree

Here is another table that shows that there are exceptions among many occupations that typically require a four-year college degree. But also note that those who do not have such a degree may face stiff competition from those who do.

Occupation	Number Employed (in Thousands)	Percentage Not Having a Degree
Accountants and auditors	313	28
Administrators and officials, public administration	215	42
Assemblers	845	96
Automobile mechanics	480	96
Bus, truck, and stationary engine mechanics	274	98
Carpenters	606	93
Computer operators	367	82
Computer programmers	197	40
Computer system analysts and scientists	190	31
Correctional institution officers	261	91
Designers	154	53
Electrical and electronic engineers	121	26
Electrical and electronic equipment repairers, except telephone	271	87
Electrical and electronic technicians	212	83
Electrical power installers and repairers	101	96
Electricians	475	95
Financial managers	203	42
Fire-fighting occupations	155	90
Health technologists and technicians	808	79
Industrial, mechanical, and all other engineers	274	27
Industrial machinery repairers	487	96
Insurance sales occupations	200	55
Investigators and adjusters, insurance and other	673	75
Machine operators and tenders, except precision	3,667	96
Machinists and precision metalworking occupations	669	96
Mail carriers and postal clerks	513	89

(continued)

© 1999 • J. Michael Farr • JIST Works, Inc. • Indianapolis, IN

TABLE 12 (CONTINUED)
Percentage of Workers Not Having a Four-Year Degree

Occupation	Number Employed (in Thousands)	Percentage Not Having a Degree
Managers, marketing, advertising, and public relations	181	41
Managers, properties and real estate	201	65
Managers, food service and lodging establishments	469	78
Managers and administrators not elsewhere classified	2,065	57
Other financial officers	249	43
Personnel, training, and labor relations specialists	164	47
Plumbers, pipefitters, and steamfitters	287	96
Police and detectives	353	75
Purchasing agents and buyers	260	66
Rail transportation occupations	95	94
Real estate sales occupations	168	54
Registered nurses	656	51
Sales occupations, other business services	190	53
Sales representatives, mining and manufacturing and wholesale	635	56
Science and engineering technicians	287	75
Secretaries	2,326	90
Stationary engineers and other plant and system operators	230	91
Supervisors, police and fire fighting	92	71
Supervisors, mechanics and repairers	181	89
Supervisors, construction occupations	419	88
Supervisors, production occupations	1,010	87
Supervisors, administrative support occupations	519	73
Supervisors and proprietors, sales occupations	1,658	72
Telephone and telephone line installers and repairers	211	95
Truck drivers	2,000	96
Welders and cutters	438	98
All other occupations	26,021	70

TABLE 13
High-Wage Jobs Not Requiring a Degree

This table lists occupations with earnings averaging over $700 a week in which significant percentages of those employed do not have college degrees. New entrants into some of these jobs often are required to have a college degree, but many now employed in these fields were hired before these requirements were standard.

Occupation	Percentage Not Having a Degree
Accountants and auditors	28
Administrators and officials, public administration	42
Assemblers	96
Automobile mechanics	96
Bus, truck, and stationary engine mechanics	98
Carpenters	93
Computer operators	82
Computer programmers	40
Computer scientists and system analysts	31
Correctional officers	91
Designers	53
Electrical and electronic engineers	26
Electrical and electronic equipment repairers, except telephone	87
Electrical and electronic technicians	83
Electrical power installers and repairers	96
Electricians	95
Financial managers	42
Fire-fighting occupations	90
Health technologists and technicians	79
Industrial machinery repairers	96
Insurance sales occupations	55
Investigators and adjusters, insurance and other	75
Machine operators and tenders, except precision	96
Machinists and precision metalworking occupations	96
Postal clerk and mail carriers	89
Marketing, advertising, and public relations managers	41

(continued)

TABLE 13 (CONTINUED)
High-Wage Jobs Not Requiring a Degree

Occupation	Percentage Not Having a Degree
Property and real estate managers	65
Food service managers	78
Managers and administrators	57
Personnel, training, and labor relations specialists and managers	47
Plumbers and pipefitters	96
Police and detectives	75
Purchasers and buyers	66
Rail transportation workers	data not available
Real estate agents, brokers, and appraisers	54
Registered nurses	51
Sales occupations	53
Manufacturers' and wholesale sales representatives	56
Engineering technicians	75
Secretaries	90
Stationary engineers and other plant and system operators	91
Supervisors, various occupations	data not available
Telephone installers and repairers	95
Truck drivers	96
Welders, cutters, and welding machine operators	98

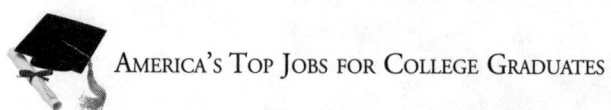

TABLE 14
Occupations with High Percentages of Self-Employed Workers

Many occupations provide opportunities for self-employment. About 11 percent of all working people are self-employed, a sizable portion of the U.S. workforce. Table 14 lists occupations that meet some interesting criteria. Each is projected to have fast growth and low unemployment— and each has at least 20 percent self-employed and family workers (family members who work in small family-owned businesses). While many jobs provide opportunities for self-employment, most opportunities are in fields requiring creativity, artistic ability, or design skills. All but one job in this list require a bachelor's degree. Thousands of new positions are projected to be created by the year 2006.

Occupation	Projected Self-Employment Growth through 2006
Food service and lodging managers	167.7%
Lawyers	118.4%
Securities and financial services sales workers	99.6%
Artists and commercial artists	78.2%
Designers, except interior designers	71.8%
Writers and editors, including technical writers	60.7%
Management analysts	51.7%
Adult education instructors (nonvocational)	51.1%
Property and real estate managers	44.3%
Photographers	23.2%
Architects, except landscape and marine	18.5%
Interior designers	17.3%
Veterinarians and veterinarian inspectors	13.2%
Chiropractors	11.8%
Economists	9.4%
Recreational therapists	8.0%
Locksmiths and safe repairers	3.7%
Landscape architects	3.5%
Camera and photographic equipment repairers	4.4%

DESCRIPTIONS OF THE 112 TOP JOBS FOR COLLEGE GRADUATES

This is the book's major section. It contains descriptions for 112 major occupations, arranged in alphabetic order within groupings based on education and experience required. Refer to the table of contents for a list of the jobs and the page numbers where specific descriptions begin.

The introduction to this book provides information on the content of each description, along with other details. If you are not a person who reads introductions, the descriptions in this section are easy to understand and well written, so feel free to jump in and begin reading.

A good way to identify job descriptions that you want to explore is to use the table of contents as a checklist. If you are interested in technical jobs, for example, you can go through the table of contents and quickly find the jobs you want to learn more about. If you look at all the job titles, you will identify other jobs that might be interesting—and you should consider these as well. Section One provides jobs listed in a variety of ways that may interest you. For example, one list puts jobs in order of highest growth percentage. Another lists jobs with high earnings, and another organizes jobs by education and training required.

Of course, there is more to selecting and learning about career options than reading job descriptions. For this reason, I suggest that you read Section Three, which provides advice on planning your career and on getting a good job. Sections Four and Five offer a great deal of useful information to help you make good decisions.

When reading the descriptions, keep in mind that they present information that is the average for the country. Conditions in your area and with specific employers may be quite different. For example, pay may be higher or lower than average, and the same job is often in great demand in one location and hard to obtain in another. People just entering a job will typically earn considerably less than the pay of a more experienced worker. These are just several examples of how the "average" situation may not fit your own.

Jobs Typically Requiring a Professional or Doctoral Degree

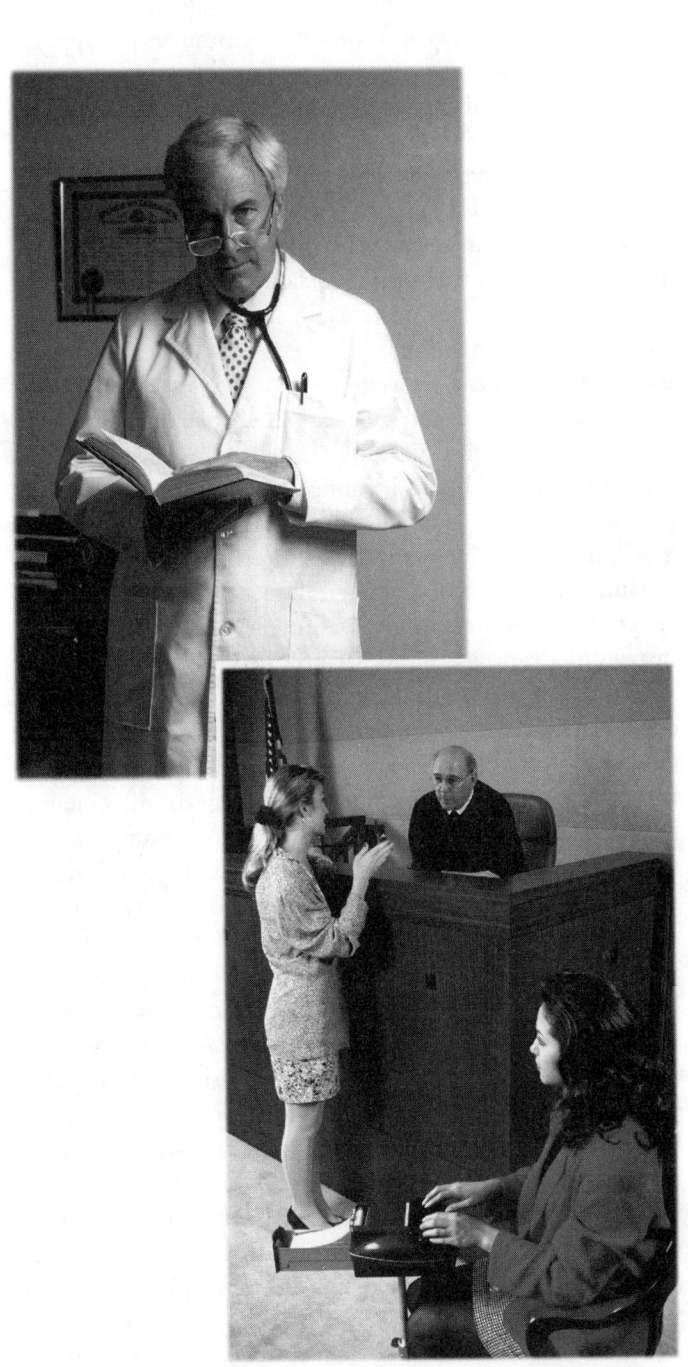

Included are the following jobs:
   Biological and Medical Scientists
   Chiropractors
   College and University Faculty
   Dentists
   Lawyers and Judges
   Optometrists
   Physicians
   Physicists and Astronomers
   Podiatrists
   Veterinarians

Biological and Medical Scientists

(*D.O.T.* 022.081-010; 041.061, except -014, -018, -046, and -082; 041.067-010; 041.261-010)

Significant Points

* *For biological scientists, a Ph.D. degree is generally required for independent research; a master's degree is sufficient for some jobs in applied research or product development; a bachelor's degree is adequate for some nonresearch jobs.*

* *For medical scientists, the Ph.D. degree in a biological science is required; some need a medical degree.*

* *Doctoral degree holders face considerable competition for independent research positions; those with a bachelor's or master's degree in biological science can expect better opportunities for nonresearch positions.*

Nature of the Work

Biological and medical scientists study living organisms and their relationship to their environment. Most specialize in some area of biology such as zoology (the study of animals) or microbiology (the study of microscopic organisms).

Many biological scientists and virtually all medical scientists work in research and development. Some conduct basic research to advance knowledge of living organisms, including viruses, bacteria, and other infectious agents. Past research has resulted in the development of vaccines, medicines, and treatments for cancer and other diseases. Basic biological and medical research continues to provide the building blocks necessary to develop solutions to human health problems and to preserve and repair the natural environment. Biological and medical scientists may work independently in private industry, university, or government laboratories, often exploring new areas of research or expanding on specialized research started in graduate school. Those who are not wage and salary workers in private industry typically submit grant proposals to obtain funding for their projects. Colleges and universities, private industry, and federal government agencies, such as the National Institutes of Health and the National Science Foundation, contribute to the support of scientists whose research proposals are determined to be financially feasible and have the potential to advance new ideas or processes.

Biological and medical scientists who work in applied research or product development use knowledge provided by basic research to develop new drugs and medical treatments, increase crop yields, and protect and clean up the environment. They usually have less autonomy than basic researchers to choose the emphasis of their research, relying instead on market-driven directions based on the firm's products and goals. Biological and medical scientists doing applied research and product development in private industry may be required to express their research plans or results to nonscientists who are in a position to veto or approve their ideas, and they must understand the business impact of their work. Scientists are increasingly working as part of teams, interacting with engineers, scientists of other disciplines, business managers, and technicians. They may also work with customers or suppliers, and manage budgets.

Biological and medical scientists who conduct research usually work in laboratories and use electron microscopes, computers, thermal cyclers, or a wide variety of other equipment. Some conduct experiments using laboratory animals or greenhouse plants. For some biological scientists, a good deal of research is performed outside of laboratories. For example, a botanist may do research in tropical rain forests to see what plants grow there, or an ecologist may study how a forest area recovers after a fire.

Some biological and medical scientists work in managerial or administrative positions, usually after spending some time doing research and learning about the firm, agency, or project. They may plan and administer programs for testing foods and drugs, for example, or direct activities at zoos or botanical gardens. Some biological scientists work as consultants to business firms or to government, while others test and inspect foods, drugs, and other products.

In the 1980s, swift advances in basic biological knowledge related to genetics and molecules spurred growth in the field of biotechnology. Biological and medical scientists using this technology manipulate the genetic material of animals or plants, attempting to make organisms more productive or resistant to disease. Research using biotechnology techniques, such as recombining DNA, has led to the discovery of important drugs, including human insulin and growth hormone. Many other substances not previously available in large quantities are starting to be produced by biotechnological means; some may be useful in treating cancer and other diseases. Today, many biological and medical scientists are involved in biotechnology, including those who work on the Human Genome project, isolating, identifying, and sequencing human genes. This work continues to lead to the discovery of the genes associated with specific diseases and inherited traits, such as certain types of cancer or obesity. These advances in biotechnology have opened up research opportunities in

almost all areas of biology, including commercial applications in agriculture, environmental remediation, and the food and chemical industries.

Most biological scientists who come under the broad category of biologist are further classified by the type of organism they study or by the specific activity they perform, although recent advances in the understanding of basic life processes at the molecular and cellular levels have blurred some traditional classifications.

Aquatic biologists study plants and animals living in water. Marine biologists study salt water organisms and limnologists study fresh water organisms. Marine biologists are sometimes erroneously called oceanographers, but oceanography is the study of the physical characteristics of oceans and the ocean floor.

Biochemists study the chemical composition of living things. They try to understand the complex chemical combinations and reactions involved in metabolism, reproduction, growth, and heredity. Much of the work in biotechnology is done by biochemists and molecular biologists because this technology involves understanding the complex chemistry of life.

Botanists study plants and their environment. Some study all aspects of plant life; others specialize in areas such as identification and classification of plants, the structure and function of plant parts, the biochemistry of plant processes, the causes and cures of plant diseases, and the geological record of plants.

Microbiologists investigate the growth and characteristics of microscopic organisms such as bacteria, algae, or fungi. Medical microbiologists study the relationship between organisms and disease or the effect of antibiotics on microorganisms. Other microbiologists may specialize in environmental, food, agricultural, or industrial microbiology, virology (the study of viruses), or immunology (the study of mechanisms that fight infections). Many microbiologists use biotechnology to advance knowledge of cell reproduction and human disease.

Physiologists study life functions of plants and animals, both in the whole organism and at the cellular or molecular level, under normal and abnormal conditions. Physiologists may specialize in functions such as growth, reproduction, photosynthesis, respiration, or movement, or in the physiology of a certain area or system of the organism.

Zoologists study animals—their origin, behavior, diseases, and life processes. Some experiment with live animals in controlled or natural surroundings, while others dissect dead animals to study their structure. Zoologists are usually identified by the animal group studied—ornithologists (birds), mammalogists (mammals), herpetologists (reptiles), and ichthyologists (fish).

Ecologists study the relationship among organisms and between organisms and their environments and the effects of influences such as population size, pollutants, rainfall, temperature, and altitude.

Biological scientists who do biomedical research are usually called medical scientists. Medical scientists working on basic research into normal biological systems often do so to understand the causes of and to discover treatment for disease and other health problems. Medical scientists may try to identify the kinds of changes in a cell, chromosome, or even gene that signal the development of medical problems, such as different types of cancer. After identifying structures of or changes in organisms that provide clues to health problems, medical scientists may then work on the treatment of problems. For example, a medical scientist involved in cancer research might try to formulate a combination of drugs which will lessen the effects of the disease. Medical scientists who have a medical degree might then administer the drugs to patients in clinical trials, monitor their reactions, and observe the results. (Medical scientists who do not have a medical degree normally collaborate with a medical doctor who deals directly with patients.) The medical scientist might then return to the laboratory to examine the results and, if necessary, adjust the dosage levels to reduce negative side effects or to try to induce even better results. In addition to using basic research to develop treatments for health problems, medical scientists attempt to discover ways to prevent health problems from developing, such as affirming the link between smoking and increased risk of lung cancer, or alcoholism and liver disease.

Working Conditions

Biological and medical scientists generally work regular hours in offices or laboratories and usually are not exposed to unsafe or unhealthy conditions. Those who work with dangerous organisms or toxic substances in the laboratory must follow strict safety procedures to avoid contamination. Medical scientists also spend time working in clinics and hospitals administering drugs and treatments to patients in clinical trials. Many biological scientists such as botanists, ecologists, and zoologists take field trips which involve strenuous physical activity and primitive living conditions.

Biological and medical scientists who depend on grant money to support their research may be under pressure to meet deadlines and conform to rigid grant-writing specifications when preparing proposals to seek new or extended funding.

Employment

Biological and medical scientists held about 118,000 jobs in 1996. Almost one in four biological scientists were employed by federal, state, and local governments. Federal biological scientists worked mainly in the U.S. Departments of Agriculture, the Interior, and Defense, and in the National Institutes of Health. Most of the rest worked in the drug industry, which includes pharmaceutical and biotechnology establishments; hospitals; or research and testing laboratories. About one in five medical scientists worked in state government, with most of the remainder found in research and testing laboratories, educational institutions, the drug industry, and hospitals.

In addition, many biological and medical scientists held biology faculty positions in colleges and universities.

Training, Other Qualifications, and Advancement

For biological scientists, the Ph.D. degree generally is required for independent research and for advancement to administrative positions. A master's degree is sufficient for some jobs in applied research or product development and for jobs in management, inspection, sales, and service. The bachelor's degree is adequate for some nonresearch jobs. Some graduates with a bachelor's degree start as biological scientists in testing and inspection, or get jobs related to biological science such as technical sales or service representatives. In some cases, graduates with a bachelor's degree are able to work in a laboratory environment on their own projects, but this is unusual. Some may work as research assistants. Others become biological technicians, medical laboratory technologists or, with courses in education, high school biology teachers. Many with a bachelor's degree in biology enter medical, dental, veterinary, or other health profession schools. Some enter a wide range of occupations with little or no connection to biology.

Most colleges and universities offer bachelor's degrees in biological science and many offer advanced degrees. Curriculums for advanced degrees often emphasize a subfield such as microbiology or botany, but not all universities offer all curriculums. Advanced degree programs include classroom and field work, laboratory research, and a thesis or dissertation. Biological scientists who have advanced degrees often take temporary postdoctoral research positions which provide specialized research experience. In private industry, some may become managers or administrators within biology; others leave biology for nontechnical managerial, administrative, or sales jobs.

Biological scientists should be able to work independently or as part of a team and be able to communicate clearly and concisely, both orally and in writing. Those in private industry, especially those who aspire to management or administrative positions, should possess strong business and communication skills and be familiar with regulatory issues and marketing and management techniques. Those doing field research in remote areas must have physical stamina.

The Ph.D. degree in a biological science is the minimum education required for prospective medical scientists because the work of medical scientists is almost entirely research oriented. A Ph.D. degree qualifies one to do research on basic life processes or on particular medical problems or diseases, and to analyze and interpret the results of experiments on patients. Medical scientists who administer drug or gene therapy to human patients, or who otherwise interact medically with patients—such as drawing blood, excising tissue, or performing other invasive procedures—must have a medical degree. It is particularly helpful for medical scientists to earn both Ph.D. and medical degrees.

In addition to the formal education, medical scientists are usually expected to spend several years in a postdoctoral position before they are offered permanent jobs. Postdoctoral work provides valuable laboratory experience, including experience in specific processes and techniques, such as gene splicing, which are transferable to other research projects. In some institutions, the postdoctoral position can lead to a permanent position.

Job Outlook

Despite prospects of faster-than-average job growth over the 1996–2006 period, biological and medical scientists can expect to face considerable competition for coveted basic research positions. Much research and development, including many areas of medical research, is funded by the federal government. Recent budget tightening has led to smaller increases in research and development expenditures, further limiting the dollar amount of each grant and slowing the growth of the number of grants awarded to researchers. At the same time, the number of newly trained scientists has continued to increase at a steady rate, so both new and established scientists have experienced greater difficulty winning and renewing research grants. If the number of advanced degrees awarded continues to grow unabated, this competitive scenario is likely to persist. Additionally, applied research positions in private industry may become more difficult if more scientists seek jobs in private industry than in the past due to the competitive job market for college and university faculty.

Opportunities for those with a bachelor's or master's degree in biological science are expected to be better. The number of science-related jobs in sales, marketing, and research management, for which non-Ph.D.s generally qualify, are expected to be more plentiful than independent research positions. They may also fill positions as science or engineering technicians or

health technologists and technicians. Some become high school biology teachers, while those with a doctorate in biological science may become college and university faculty.

Biological and medical scientists enjoyed very rapid gains in employment between the mid-1980s and mid-1990s, in part reflecting increased staffing requirements in new biotechnology companies. Employment growth should slow as increases in the number of new biotechnology firms slows and existing firms merge or are absorbed into larger ones. However, much of the basic biological research done in recent years has resulted in new knowledge, including the isolation and identification of new genes. Biological and medical scientists will be needed to take this knowledge to the next stage, which is the understanding of how certain genes function within an entire organism so that gene therapies can be developed to treat diseases. Even pharmaceutical and other firms not solely engaged in biotechnology are expected to increasingly use biotechnology techniques, spurring employment increases for biological and medical scientists. In addition, efforts to discover new and improved ways to clean up and preserve the environment will continue to add to growth. More biological scientists will be needed to determine the environmental impact of industry and government actions and to prevent or correct environmental problems. Expected expansion in research related to health issues—such as AIDS, cancer, and Alzheimer's disease—should also result in growth.

Biological and medical scientists are less likely to lose their jobs during recessions than those in many other occupations because many are employed on long-term research projects. However, a recession could further influence the amount of money allocated to new research and development efforts, particularly in areas of risky or innovative research. A recession could also limit the possibility of extension or renewal of existing projects.

Earnings

According to the National Association of Colleges and Employers, beginning salary offers in private industry in 1997 averaged $25,400 a year for bachelor's degree recipients in biological science; about $26,900 for master's degree recipients; and about $52,400 for doctoral degree recipients.

Median annual earnings for biological and life scientists were about $36,300 in 1996; the middle 50 percent earned between $28,400 and $50,900. Ten percent earned less than $22,000, and 10 percent earned over $66,000. For medical scientists, median annual earnings were about $34,300; the middle 50 percent earned between $25,200 and $52,200. Ten percent earned less than $18,700, and 10 percent earned over $74,000.

In the federal government in 1997, general biological scientists in nonsupervisory, supervisory, and managerial positions earned an average salary of $52,100; microbiologists, $58,700; ecologists, $52,700; physiologists, $65,900; and geneticists, $62,700.

Related Occupations

Many other occupations deal with living organisms and require a level of training similar to that of biological and medical scientists. These include the conservation occupations of forester, range manager, and soil conservationist; animal breeders, horticulturists, soil scientists, and most other agricultural scientists. Many health occupations are also related to those in the biological sciences, such as medical doctors, dentists, and veterinarians.

Sources of Additional Information

For information on careers in the biological sciences, contact:

❑ American Institute of Biological Sciences, Suite 200, 1444 I St. NW, Washington, DC 20005. Homepage: http://www.aibs.org

For information on careers in physiology, contact:

❑ American Physiological Society, Education Office, 9650 Rockville Pike, Bethesda, MD 20814. Homepage: http://www.faseb.org/aps

For information on careers in biotechnology, contact:

❑ Biotechnology Industry Organization, 1625 K St. NW, Suite 1100, Washington, DC 20006.

For information on careers in biochemistry, contact:

❑ American Society for Biochemistry and Molecular Biology, 9650 Rockville Pike, Bethesda, MD 20814.

For information on careers in biophysics, contact:

❑ Biophysical Society, 9650 Rockville Pike, Room 0512, Bethesda, MD 20814.

For information on careers in botany, contact:

❑ Botanical Society of America, Business Office, 1735 Neil Ave., Columbus, OH 43210-1293. Homepage: http://www.botany.org

For information on careers in microbiology, contact:

❑ American Society for Microbiology, Office of Education and Training—Career Information, 1325 Massachusetts Ave. NW, Washington, DC 20005. Homepage: http://www.asmusa.org

Information on acquiring a job as a biological or medical scientist with the federal government may be obtained from the Office of Personnel Management through a telephone-based system. Consult your telephone directory under U.S. government for a local number or call (912) 757-3000 (TDD 912 744-2299). That number is not toll-free and charges may result. Information also is available from their Internet site: http://www.usajobs.opm.gov

Chiropractors

(D.O.T. 079.101-010)

Significant Points

* *Employment of chiropractors is expected to increase rapidly and job prospects should be good.*
* *Chiropractic treatment of back, neck, extremities, and other joint damage has become more accepted as a result of recent research and changing attitudes.*
* *In chiropractic, as in other types of independent practice, earnings are relatively low in the beginning, and increase as the practice grows.*

Nature of the Work

Chiropractors, also known as doctors of chiropractic or chiropractic physicians, diagnose and treat patients whose health problems are associated with the body's muscular, nervous, and skeletal systems, especially the spine. Chiropractors believe interference with these systems impairs normal functions and lowers resistance to disease. They also hold that spinal or vertebral dysfunction alters many important body functions by affecting the nervous system, and that skeletal imbalance through joint or articular dysfunction, especially in the spine, can cause pain.

The chiropractic approach to health care is holistic, stressing the patient's overall well-being. It recognizes that many factors affect health, including exercise, diet, rest, environment, and heredity. Chiropractors use natural, drugless, nonsurgical health treatments, and rely on the body's inherent recuperative abilities. They also recommend lifestyle changes—in eating, exercise, and sleeping habits, for example—to their patients. When appropriate, chiropractors consult with and refer patients to other health practitioners.

Like other health practitioners, chiropractors follow a standard routine to secure the information needed for diagnosis and treatment: They take the patient's medical history, conduct physical, neurological, and orthopedic examinations, and may order laboratory tests. X rays and other diagnostic images are important tools because of the emphasis on the spine and its proper function. Chiropractors also employ a postural and spinal analysis common to chiropractic diagnosis.

In cases in which difficulties can be traced to involvement of musculoskeletal structures, chiropractors manually manipulate or adjust the spinal column. Many chiropractors also use water, light, massage, ultrasound, electric, and heat therapy and may apply supports such as straps, tapes, and braces. They may also counsel patients about wellness concepts such as nutrition, exercise, lifestyle changes, and stress management, but do not prescribe drugs or perform surgery.

Some chiropractors specialize in sports injuries, neurology, orthopedics, nutrition, internal disorders, or diagnostic imaging.

Many chiropractors are solo or group practitioners who also have the administrative responsibilities of running a practice. In larger offices, chiropractors delegate these tasks to office managers and chiropractic assistants. Chiropractors in private practice are responsible for developing a patient base, hiring employees, and keeping records.

Working Conditions

Chiropractors work in clean, comfortable offices. The average workweek is about 42 hours, although longer hours are not uncommon. Solo practitioners set their own hours, but may work evenings or weekends to accommodate patients.

Chiropractors who take x rays employ appropriate precautions against the dangers of repeated exposure to radiation.

Employment

Chiropractors held about 44,000 jobs in 1996. About 70 percent of active chiropractors are in solo practice. The remainder are in group practice or work for other chiropractors. A small number teach, conduct research at chiropractic institutions, or work in hospitals and clinics.

Many chiropractors are located in small communities. There are geographic imbalances in the distribution of chiropractors, in part because many establish practices close to chiropractic institutions.

Training, Other Qualifications, and Advancement

All states and the District of Columbia regulate the practice of chiropractic and grant licenses to chiropractors who meet educational requirements and pass a state board examination. Chiropractors can only practice in states where they are licensed. Some states have agreements that permit chiropractors licensed in one state to obtain a license in another without further examination.

Most state licensing boards require completion of a four-year chiropractic college course following at least two years of undergraduate education, although a few states require a bachelor's degree. All state boards recognize academic training in chiropractic programs and institutions accredited by the Council on Chiropractic Education.

For licensure, most state boards recognize either all or part of the four-part test administered by the National Board

of Chiropractic Examiners. State examinations may supplement the National Board tests, depending on state requirements.

To maintain licensure, almost all states require completion of a specified number of hours of continuing education each year. Continuing education programs are offered by accredited chiropractic programs and institutions, and chiropractic associations. Special councils within some chiropractic associations also offer programs leading to clinical specialty certification, called "diplomate" certification, in areas such as orthopedics, neurology, sports injuries, occupational and industrial health, nutrition, diagnostic imaging, thermography, and internal disorders.

In 1997, there were 16 chiropractic programs and institutions in the United States accredited by the Council on Chiropractic Education. All required applicants to have at least 60 semester hours of undergraduate study leading toward a bachelor's degree, including courses in English, the social sciences or humanities, organic and inorganic chemistry, biology, physics, and psychology. Many applicants have a bachelor's degree, which may eventually become the minimum entry requirement. Several chiropractic colleges offer prechiropractic study, as well as a bachelor's degree program.

During the first two years, most chiropractic programs emphasize classroom and laboratory work in basic science subjects such as anatomy, physiology, public health, microbiology, pathology, and biochemistry. The last two years stress courses in manipulation and spinal adjustments, and provide clinical experience in physical and laboratory diagnosis, neurology, orthopedics, geriatrics, physiotherapy, and nutrition. Chiropractic programs and institutions grant the degree of Doctor of Chiropractic (DC).

Chiropractic requires keen observation to detect physical abnormalities. It also takes considerable hand dexterity to perform manipulations, but not unusual strength or endurance. Chiropractors should be able to work independently and handle responsibility. As in other health-related occupations, empathy, understanding, and the desire to help others are good qualities for dealing effectively with patients.

Newly licensed chiropractors can set up a new practice, purchase an established one, or enter into partnership with an established practitioner. They may also take a salaried position with an established chiropractor, a group practice, or a health care facility.

Job Outlook

Job prospects are expected to be good for persons who enter the practice of chiropractic. Employment of chiropractors is expected to grow faster than the average for all occupations through the year 2006 as consumer demand for alternative medicine grows. Chiropractors emphasize the importance of healthy lifestyles and do not prescribe drugs or perform surgery. As a result, chiropractic care is appealing to many health-conscious Americans. Chiropractic treatment of back, neck, extremities, and other joint damage has become more accepted as a result of recent research and changing attitudes. The rapidly expanding older population, with their increased likelihood of mechanical and structural problems, will also increase demand.

Demand for chiropractic treatment is also related to the ability of patients to pay, either directly or through health insurance. Although more insurance plans now cover chiropractic services, details of such coverage vary among plans. Increasingly, chiropractors must educate communities about the benefits of chiropractic care, in order to establish a successful practice.

In this occupation, replacement needs arise almost entirely from retirements. Chiropractors generally remain in the occupation until they retire; few transfer to other occupations. Establishing a new practice will be easiest in areas with a low concentration of chiropractors.

Earnings

In 1995, median income for chiropractors was about $80,000, after expenses, according to the American Chiropractic Association. In chiropractic, as in other types of independent practice, earnings are relatively low in the beginning, and increase as the practice grows. In 1995, the lowest 10 percent of chiropractors had median net incomes of $30,000 or less, and the highest 10 percent earned $170,000 or more. Earnings are also influenced by the characteristics and qualifications of the practitioner, and geographic location. Self-employed chiropractors must provide for their own health insurance and retirement.

Related Occupations

Chiropractors treat and work to prevent bodily disorders and injuries. So do physicians, dentists, optometrists, podiatrists, veterinarians, occupational therapists, and physical therapists.

Sources of Additional Information

General information on chiropractic as a career is available from:

- ❏ American Chiropractic Association, 1701 Clarendon Blvd., Arlington, VA 22209.
- ❏ International Chiropractors Association, 1110 North Glebe Rd., Suite 1000, Arlington, VA 22201.

❑ World Chiropractic Alliance, 2950 N. Dobson Rd., Suite 1, Chandler, AZ 85224-1802.

For a list of chiropractic programs and institutions, as well as general information on chiropractic education, contact:

❑ Council on Chiropractic Education, 7975 North Hayden Rd., Suite A-210, Scottsdale, AZ 85258.

For information on state education and licensure requirements, contact:

❑ Federation of Chiropractic Licensing Boards, 901 54th Ave., Suite 101, Greeley, CO 80634.

For information on requirements for admission to a specific chiropractic college, as well as scholarship and loan information, contact the admissions office of the individual college.

College and University Faculty

(D.O.T. 090.227-010)

Significant Points

* *A Ph.D. is generally required for full-time positions in four-year colleges and universities; in two-year institutions, master's degree holders may qualify.*

* *Applicants for full-time college faculty positions face keen competition because many colleges and universities, in an effort to cut costs, will hire more part-time faculty.*

* *Job prospects will continue to be better in certain fields—computer science, engineering, and business, for example—that offer attractive nonacademic job opportunities and attract fewer applicants for academic positions.*

Nature of the Work

College and university faculty teach and advise nearly 15 million full- and part-time college students and perform a significant part of our nation's research. They also study and meet with colleagues to keep up with developments in their field and consult with government, business, nonprofit, and community organizations.

Faculty generally are organized into departments or divisions, based on subject or field. They usually teach several different courses in their department—algebra, calculus, and statistics, for example. They may instruct undergraduate or graduate students, or both. College and university faculty may give lectures to several hundred students in large halls, lead small seminars, or supervise students in laboratories. They prepare lectures, exercises, and laboratory experiments, grade exams and papers, and advise and work with students individually. In universities, they also counsel, advise, teach, and supervise graduate student teaching and research. College faculty work with an increasingly varied student population made up of growing shares of part-time, older, and culturally and racially diverse students.

Faculty keep abreast of developments in their field by reading current literature, talking with colleagues, and participating in professional conferences. They also do their own research to expand knowledge in their field. They experiment, collect and analyze data, and examine original documents, literature, and other source material. From this, they develop hypotheses, arrive at conclusions, and publish their findings in scholarly journals, books, and electronic media.

College and university faculty increasingly use technology in all areas of their work. In the classroom, they may use computers—including the Internet; electronic mail; software programs, such as statistical packages; and CD-ROMs—as teaching aids. Some professors teach "satellite" courses that are broadcast to students at off-campus sites through closed-circuit or cable television. Faculty also use computers to do their own research, participate in discussion groups in their field, or publicize their professional research papers.

Most faculty members serve on academic or administrative committees which deal with the policies of their institution, departmental matters, academic issues, curricula, budgets, equipment purchases, and hiring. Some work with student as well as community organizations. Department chairpersons are faculty members who usually teach some courses but generally have heavier administrative responsibilities.

The proportion of time spent on research, teaching, administrative, and other duties varies by individual circumstance and type of institution. Faculty members at universities generally spend a significant part of their time doing research; those in four-year colleges, somewhat less; and those in two-year colleges, relatively little. However, the teaching load usually is heavier in two-year colleges and somewhat lower at four-year institutions. Full professors at all types of institutions usually spend a larger portion of their time conducting research than assistant professors, instructors, and lecturers.

Working Conditions

College faculty generally have flexible schedules. They must be present for classes, usually 12 to 16 hours a week, and for faculty and committee meetings. Most establish regular office hours for student consultations, usually three to six hours per week. Otherwise, faculty are free to decide when and where they will work, and how much time to devote to

course preparation, grading papers and exams, study, research, graduate student supervision, and other activities. Initial adjustment to these responsibilities can be challenging as new faculty adapt to switching roles from student to teacher. This adjustment may be even more difficult as class size grows in response to faculty and budget cutbacks, increasing an instructor's workload. Also, many institutions are increasing their reliance on part-time faculty, who generally have limited administrative and student advising duties, which leaves the declining number of full-time faculty with a heavier workload.

Some faculty members work staggered hours and teach classes at night and on weekends. This is particularly true for faculty who teach at two-year community colleges or institutions with large enrollments of older students with full-time jobs or family responsibilities on weekdays. Most faculty are employed on a nine-month contract, which allows them the time to teach, do research, travel, or pursue nonacademic interests during the summer and school holidays. Most colleges and universities have funds to support faculty research or other professional development needs, including travel to conferences and research sites.

Faculty may experience a conflict between their responsibilities to teach students and the pressure to do research and publish their findings. This may be a particular problem for young faculty seeking advancement in four-year research universities. Increasing emphasis on undergraduate teaching performance in tenure decisions may alleviate some of this pressure, however.

Part-time faculty generally spend little time on campus, because they usually don't have an office. In addition, they may teach at more than one college, requiring travel between their various places of employment, earning the name "gypsy faculty." Part-time faculty are usually not eligible for tenure. Dealing with this lack of job security can be stressful.

Employment

College and university faculty held about 864,000 jobs in 1996, mostly in public institutions.

About four out of ten college and university faculty worked part-time in 1996. Some part-timers, known as "adjunct faculty," have primary jobs outside of academia—in government, private industry, or in nonprofit research—and teach "on the side." Others seek full-time jobs but are unable to obtain them due to intense competition for available openings. Some work part-time in more than one institution.

Training, Other Qualifications, and Advancement

Most college and university faculty are in four academic ranks: Professor, associate professor, assistant professor, and instructor. These positions are usually considered to be tenure-track positions. A small number of faculty, called lecturers, usually are not on the tenure track.

Most faculty members are hired as instructors or assistant professors. Four-year colleges and universities generally only consider doctoral degree holders for full-time, tenure-track positions, but may hire master's degree holders or doctoral candidates for certain disciplines, such as the arts, or for part-time and temporary jobs. In two-year colleges, master's degree holders often qualify for full-time positions. However, with increasing competition for available jobs, institutions can be more selective in their hiring practices. Master's degree holders may find it increasingly difficult to obtain employment as they are passed over in favor of candidates holding a Ph.D.

Doctoral programs, including time spent completing a master's degree and a dissertation, take an average of six to eight years of full-time study beyond the bachelor's degree. Some programs, such as the humanities, take longer to complete; others, such as engineering, generally are shorter. Candidates usually specialize in a subfield of a discipline—for example, organic chemistry, counseling psychology, or European history—but also take courses covering the entire discipline. Programs include 20 or more increasingly specialized courses and seminars plus comprehensive examinations on all major areas of the field. Candidates also must complete a dissertation—a written report on original research in the candidate's major field of study. The dissertation sets forth an original hypothesis or proposes a model and tests it. Students in the natural sciences and engineering usually do laboratory work; in the humanities, they study original documents and other published material. The dissertation, done under the guidance of one or more faculty advisors, usually takes one or two years of full-time work.

In some fields, particularly the natural sciences, some students spend an additional two years on postdoctoral research and study before taking a faculty position. Some Ph.D.s extend or take new postdoctoral appointments if they are unable to find a faculty job. Most of these appointments offer a nominal salary.

A major step in the traditional academic career is attaining tenure. New tenure-track faculty are usually hired as instructors or assistant professors, and must serve a certain period (usually seven years) under term contracts. At the end of the contract period, their record of teaching, research, and overall contribution to the institution is reviewed; tenure is granted if the review is favorable. According to the American Association of University Professors, in 1995–96 about 65 percent of all full-time faculty held tenure, while 88 percent were in tenure-track positions. Those denied tenure usually must leave the institution. Tenured professors cannot be fired without just cause and due process. Tenure protects the faculty's academic freedom—the ability to teach and conduct research without fear of being fired for advocating unpopular ideas. It also gives both faculty and institutions the stability needed for effective research and teaching, and provides financial security for faculty. Some institutions have adopted post-tenure review policies to encourage ongoing evaluation of tenured faculty.

The number of tenure-track positions is expected to decline as institutions rely more heavily on less costly part-time faculty who do not hold tenure-track positions. Consequently, increased reliance on part-time faculty is expected to shrink the total pool of faculty who hold tenure. Some institutions have placed caps on the percentage of faculty who can be tenured. Other institutions offer prospective faculty limited term contracts—typically two-, three-, or five-year, full-time contracts—in an effort to adapt to changes in the budget and the size of the student body. These contracts may be terminated or extended at the end of the period. Institutions are not obligated to grant tenure to these contract holders.

Some faculty—based on teaching experience, research, publication, and service on campus committees and task forces—move into administrative and managerial positions, such as departmental chairperson, dean, and president. At four-year institutions, such advancement requires a doctoral degree. At two-year colleges, a doctorate is helpful but not generally required, except for advancement to some top administrative positions.

College faculty should have inquiring and analytical minds, and a strong desire to pursue and disseminate knowledge. They must be able to communicate clearly and logically, both orally and in writing. They should be able to establish rapport with students and, as models for them, be dedicated to the principles of academic integrity and intellectual honesty. Additionally, they must be self-motivated and able to work in an environment where they receive little direct supervision.

Job Outlook

Employment of college and university faculty is expected to increase about as fast as the average for all occupations through the year 2006 as enrollments in higher education increase. Many additional openings will arise as faculty members retire. Faculty retirements should increase significantly from the late 1990s through 2006 as a large number of faculty who entered the profession during the 1950s and 1960s reach retirement age. Most faculty members likely to retire are full-time tenured professors. However, in an effort to cut

costs, some institutions are expected to either leave these positions vacant or hire part-time, non-tenured faculty as replacements. Prospective job applicants should be prepared to face keen competition for available jobs as growing numbers of Ph.D. graduates, including foreign-born Ph.D.s, vie for fewer full-time openings. As more and more Ph.D.s compete for openings, master's degree holders may find competition for jobs even more intense.

Enrollments in institutions of higher education increased in the mid-1980s through the early 1990s despite a decline in the traditional college-age (18-to-24) population. This resulted from a higher proportion of 18- to 24-year-olds attending college, along with a growing number of part-time, female, and older students. Between 1996 and 2006, the traditional college-age population will begin to grow again, spurred by the leading edge of the baby-boom "echo" generation (children of the baby-boomers) reaching college age. College enrollment is projected to rise from 14 million in 1996 to 16 million in 2006, an increase of 14 percent.

In the past two decades, keen competition for faculty jobs forced some applicants to accept part-time or short-term academic appointments that offered little hope of tenure, and others to seek nonacademic positions. This trend of hiring adjunct or part-time faculty is likely to continue due to financial difficulties faced by colleges and universities. Many colleges, faced with reduced state funding for higher education, have increased the hiring of part-time faculty to save money on pay and benefits. Public two-year colleges employ a significantly higher number of part-time faculty as a percentage of their total staff than public four-year colleges and universities, but all institutions have increased their part-time hiring. With uncertainty over future funding, many colleges and universities are continuing to cut costs by eliminating some academic programs, increasing class size, and closely monitoring all expenses.

Once enrollments and retirements start increasing at a faster pace in the late 1990s, opportunities for college faculty may begin to improve somewhat. Growing numbers of students will necessitate hiring more faculty to teach. At the same time, many faculty will be retiring, opening up even more positions. Job prospects will continue to be better in certain fields—business, engineering, health science, and computer science, for example—that offer attractive nonacademic job opportunities and attract fewer applicants for academic positions.

Employment of college faculty is affected by the nonacademic job market. Excellent job prospects in a field—for example, computer science from the late 1970s to the mid-1980s—cause more students to enroll, increasing faculty needs

in that field. On the other hand, poor job prospects in a field, such as history in recent years, discourages students and reduces demand for faculty.

Earnings

Earnings vary according to faculty rank and type of institution, geographic area, and field. According to a 1995–96 survey by the American Association of University Professors, salaries for full-time faculty averaged $51,000. By rank, the average for professors was $65,400; associate professors, $48,300; assistant professors, $40,100; instructors, $30,800; and lecturers, $33,700. Faculty in four-year institutions earn higher salaries, on the average, than those in two-year schools. Average salaries for faculty in public institutions—$50,400— were lower in 1995–96 than those for private independent institutions—$57,500—but higher than those for religion-affiliated private institutions—$45,200. In fields with high-paying nonacademic alternatives—notably medicine and law but also engineering and business, among others—earnings exceed these averages. In others—such as the humanities and education—they are lower.

Most faculty members have significant earnings in addition to their base salary, from consulting, teaching additional courses, research, writing for publication, or other employment, both during the academic year and the summer.

Most college and university faculty enjoy some unique benefits, including access to campus facilities, tuition waivers for dependents, housing and travel allowances, and paid sabbatical leaves. Part-time faculty have fewer benefits than full-time faculty, and usually do not receive health insurance, retirement benefits, or sabbatical leave.

Related Occupations

College and university faculty function both as teachers and researchers. They communicate information and ideas. Related occupations include elementary and secondary school teachers, librarians, writers, consultants, lobbyists, trainers and employee development specialists, and policy analysts. Faculty research activities often are similar to those of scientists, as well as managers and administrators in industry, government, and nonprofit research organizations.

Sources of Additional Information

Professional societies generally provide information on academic and nonacademic employment opportunities in their fields.

Special publications on higher education, available in libraries, such as *The Chronicle of Higher Education*, list specific employment opportunities for faculty.

Dentists

(*D.O.T.* 072, except .117)

Significant Points

✳ *Most dentists have at least eight years of education beyond high school but they have very high earnings.*

✳ *Employment of dentists is expected to grow slower than the average as the middle-aged and elderly population requires more dental care, but young people are troubled less by tooth decay.*

✳ *If the number of dentists being trained increases significantly above present levels, job seekers may face competition.*

Nature of the Work

Dentists diagnose, prevent, and treat problems of the teeth and tissues of the mouth. They remove decay, fill cavities, examine x rays, place protective plastic sealants on children's teeth, straighten teeth, and repair fractured teeth. They also perform corrective surgery of the gums and supporting bones to treat gum diseases. Dentists extract teeth and make molds and measurements for dentures to replace missing teeth. Dentists provide instruction in diet, brushing, flossing, the use of fluorides, and other aspects of dental care, as well. They also administer anesthetics and write prescriptions for antibiotics and other medications.

Dentists use a variety of equipment, including x-ray machines, drills, and instruments such as mouth mirrors, probes, forceps, brushes, and scalpels.

Dentists in private practice oversee a variety of administrative tasks, including bookkeeping, and buying equipment and supplies. They may employ and supervise dental hygienists, dental assistants, dental laboratory technicians, and receptionists.

Most dentists are general practitioners, handling a wide variety of dental needs. Other dentists practice in one of eight specialty areas. Orthodontists, the largest group of specialists, straighten teeth. The next largest group, oral and maxillofacial surgeons, operate on the mouth and jaws. The remainder specialize in pediatric dentistry (dentistry for children); periodontics (treating the gums and the bone supporting the teeth); prosthodontics (making artificial teeth or dentures); endodontics (root canal therapy); dental public health; and oral pathology (studying diseases of the mouth).

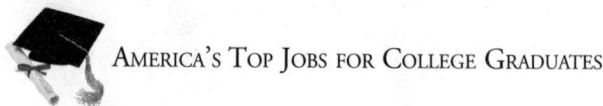

Working Conditions

Most dentists work four or five days a week. Some work evenings and weekends to meet their patients' needs. Most full-time dentists work about 40 hours a week, but others work more. Younger dentists may work more hours as they establish their practice; older dentists often work fewer hours. A considerable number continue in part-time practice well beyond the usual retirement age.

Most dentists are solo practitioners, meaning they own their own businesses and work alone or with a small staff. Some dentists have partners, and a few work for other dentists as associate dentists.

Dentists wear masks, gloves, and safety glasses to protect themselves and their patients from infectious diseases, such as hepatitis.

Employment

Dentists held about 162,000 jobs in 1996. About nine out of ten dentists are in private practice. Others work in private and public hospitals and clinics, and in dental research.

Training, Other Qualifications, and Advancement

All 50 states and the District of Columbia require dentists to be licensed. To qualify for a license in most states, a candidate must graduate from a dental school accredited by the American Dental Association's Commission on Dental Accreditation, and pass written and practical examinations. Candidates may fulfill the written part of the state licensing by passing the National Board Dental Examinations. Individual states or regional testing agencies give the written and/ or practical examinations.

Currently, about 17 states require dentists to obtain a specialty license before practicing as a specialist. Requirements include two to four years of post graduate education and, in some cases, completion of a special state examination. Most state licenses permit dentists to engage in both general and specialized practice. Dentists who want to teach or do research usually spend an additional two to five years in advanced dental training, in programs operated by dental schools or hospitals.

Dental schools require a minimum of two years of college-level predental education. However, most dental students have at least a bachelor's degree. Predental education emphasizes course work in the sciences.

All dental schools require applicants to take the Dental Admissions Test (DAT). They consider scores earned on the DAT, the applicants' overall grade point average (GPA), science course GPA, and information gathered through recommendations and interviews when selecting students.

Dental school generally lasts four academic years. Studies begin with classroom instruction and laboratory work in basic sciences including anatomy, microbiology, biochemistry, and physiology. Beginning courses in clinical sciences, including laboratory technique courses, are also provided at this time. During the last two years, students treat patients, usually in dental clinics, under the supervision of licensed dentists.

Most dental schools award the degree of Doctor of Dental Surgery (DDS). The rest award an equivalent degree, Doctor of Dental Medicine (DMD).

Dentistry requires diagnostic ability and manual skills. Dentists should have good visual memory, excellent judgment of space and shape, a high degree of manual dexterity, and scientific ability. Good business sense, self-discipline, and communication skills are helpful for success in private practice. High school students who want to become dentists should take courses in biology, chemistry, physics, health, and mathematics.

Some recent dental school graduates work for established dentists as associates for a year or two in order to gain experience and save money to equip an office of their own. Most dental school graduates, however, purchase an established practice or open a new practice immediately after graduation. Each year about one-fourth to one-third of new graduates enroll in postgraduate training programs to prepare for a dental specialty.

Job Outlook

Employment of dentists is expected to grow slower than the average for all occupations through the year 2006. While employment growth will provide some job opportunities, most jobs will result from the need to replace the large number of dentists projected to retire. Job prospects should be good if the number of dental school graduates does not grow significantly, thus keeping the supply of newly qualified dentists near current levels. There is cause for some concern about the outlook, however, because the number of first-year enrollees in dental school programs has increased over enrollment in the late 1980s. If the number of enrollees continues to increase, there will be a larger pool of dentists, and job seekers may face competition.

Demand for dental care should grow substantially through 2006. As members of the baby-boom generation advance into middle age, a large number will need maintenance on complicated dental work, such as bridges. In addition, elderly people are more likely to retain their teeth than their predecessors, so they will require much more care than in the past. The younger generation will continue to need preventive check-ups despite treatments such as fluoridation of the water supply, which decreases the incidence of tooth decay.

However, the employment of dentists is not expected to grow as rapidly as the demand for dental services. As their practices expand, dentists are likely to hire more dental hygienists and dental assistants to handle routine services they now perform themselves.

Earnings

According to the American Dental Association, median net income of dentists in private practice was about $120,000 a year in 1995. Median net income for those in specialty practice was about $175,000 a year, and for those in general practice, about $109,000 a year. Dentists in the beginning years of their practice often earn less, while those in mid-careers earn more.

A relatively large proportion of dentists are self-employed. Like other business owners, these dentists must provide their own health insurance, life insurance, and retirement benefits.

Related Occupations

Dentists examine, diagnose, prevent, and treat diseases and abnormalities. So do clinical psychologists, optometrists, physicians, chiropractors, veterinarians, and podiatrists.

Sources of Additional Information

For information on dentistry as a career and a list of accredited dental schools, contact:

❏ American Dental Association, Commission on Dental Accreditation, 211 E. Chicago Ave., Chicago, IL 60611.

❏ American Association of Dental Schools, 1625 Massachusetts Ave. NW, Washington, DC 20036. Homepage: http://www.ada.org

The American Dental Association will also furnish a list of state boards of dental examiners. Persons interested in practicing dentistry should obtain the requirements for licensure from the board of dental examiners of the state in which they plan to work.

Prospective dental students should contact the office of student financial aid at the schools to which they apply, for information on scholarships, grants, and loans, including federal financial aid.

Lawyers and Judges

(*D.O.T.* 110; 111; 119.107, .117, .167-010, .267-014; 169.267-010)

Significant Points

✷ *Formal educational requirements usually include a four-year college degree, followed by three years in law*

school. After that, all states require applicants for admission to the bar to pass a written bar examination.

✷ *Competition for admission to many law schools is intense, as the number of applicants greatly exceeds the number that may be admitted.*

✷ *Aspiring lawyers or judges should encounter keen competition for jobs.*

Nature of the Work

Lawyers. Lawyers, also called attorneys, act as both advocates and advisors in our society. As advocates, they represent one of the parties in criminal and civil trials by presenting evidence in court supporting their client. As advisors, lawyers counsel their clients as to their legal rights and obligations, and suggest particular courses of action in business and personal matters. Whether acting as advocates or advisors, all attorneys interpret the law and apply it to specific situations.

Lawyers research the purposes behind laws and judicial decisions that have been applied to circumstances similar to those faced by their client. While all lawyers continue to use law libraries to prepare cases, some supplement their search of conventional printed sources with computer sources. Software can be used to search legal literature automatically, and to identify legal texts relevant to a specific case. In litigation involving many supporting documents, lawyers may use computers to organize and index material. Tax lawyers use computers for making tax computations and exploring alternative tax strategies for clients.

Lawyers increasingly use the Internet for research and to advertise their services. Ethical standards for advertising on the Internet are still evolving. Lawyers also use electronic filing, videoconferencing, and voice-recognition technology. Electronic filing promotes the sharing of information by providing all parties in a case access to a database with all official filings, briefs, and other court documents; these technologies also save time and reduce legal costs.

Lawyers communicate the information obtained through research to others. They advise clients and draw up legal documents, such as wills and contracts. Lawyers may not disclose matters discussed in confidence with clients. They hold positions of great responsibility, and are obligated to adhere to a strict code of ethics.

The more detailed aspects of a lawyer's job depend upon his or her field of specialization and position. While all lawyers are licensed to represent parties in court, some appear in court more frequently than others; some lawyers specialize in trial work. Their ability to think quickly and speak with ease and authority as well as their familiarity with courtroom rules and strategy are particularly important in trial work. However, trial lawyers still spend most of their time outside the courtroom conducting research, interviewing clients and witnesses, and handling other details in preparation for trial.

Besides trials, lawyers may specialize in other areas, such as bankruptcy, probate, or international law. Environmental lawyers, for example, may represent public interest groups, waste disposal companies, or construction firms in their dealings with the Environmental Protection Agency (EPA) and other state and federal agencies. They help clients prepare and file for licenses and applications for approval before certain activities may occur. They also represent clients' interests in administrative adjudications.

Some lawyers concentrate in the growing field of intellectual property. These lawyers help protect clients' claims to copyrights, art work under contract, product designs, and computer programs. Still other lawyers advise insurance companies about the legality of insurance transactions. They write insurance policies to conform with the law and to protect companies from unwarranted claims. They review claims filed against insurance companies and represent the companies in court.

The majority of lawyers are in private practice, where they concentrate on criminal or civil law. In criminal law, lawyers represent individuals who have been charged with crimes and argue their cases in courts of law. In civil law, attorneys assist clients with litigation, wills, trusts, contracts, mortgages, titles, and leases. Others handle only public interest cases—civil or criminal—which may have a potential impact extending well beyond the individual client.

Lawyers are sometimes employed full-time by a single client. If the client is a corporation, the lawyer is known as "house counsel," and usually advises the company concerning legal issues related to its business activities. These issues might involve patents, government regulations, contracts with other companies, property interests, or collective bargaining agreements with unions.

A significant number of attorneys are employed at the various levels of government. Lawyers who work for state attorneys general, prosecutors, public defenders, and courts play a key role in the criminal justice system. At the federal level, attorneys investigate cases for the Department of Justice or other agencies. Government lawyers also help develop programs, draft and interpret laws and legislation, establish enforcement procedures, and argue civil and criminal cases on behalf of the government.

Other lawyers work for legal aid societies—private, nonprofit organizations established to serve disadvantaged people. These lawyers generally handle civil, rather than criminal cases.

A relatively small number of trained attorneys work in law schools. Most are faculty members who specialize in one or more subjects, and others serve as administrators. Some work full-time in nonacademic settings and teach part-time. Some lawyers become judges.

Judges. Judges apply the law and oversee the legal process in courts according to local, state, and federal statutes. They preside over cases concerning every aspect of society, from traffic offenses to disputes over management of professional sports, or from the rights of huge corporations to questions of disconnecting life support equipment for terminally ill persons. They must ensure trials and hearings are conducted fairly, and the court administers justice in a manner safeguarding the legal rights of all parties involved.

Judges preside over trials or hearings and listen as attorneys representing the parties present and argue their cases. They rule on the admissibility of evidence and methods of conducting testimony, and settle disputes between the opposing attorneys. They ensure rules and procedures are followed, and if unusual circumstances arise for which standard procedures have not been established, judges direct how the trial will proceed based on their knowledge of the law.

Judges often hold pretrial hearings for cases. They listen to allegations and, based on the evidence presented, determine whether there is enough merit for a trial to be held. In criminal cases, judges may decide that persons charged with crimes should be held in jail pending their trial, or may set conditions for release through the trial. In civil cases, judges may impose restrictions upon the parties until a trial is held.

When trials are held, juries are often selected to decide cases, including guilt or innocence in criminal cases, and the liability and the amount of compensation in civil cases. In these cases, judges instruct juries on applicable laws, direct them to deduce the facts from the evidence presented, and hear their verdict. However, judges decide cases when the law does not require a jury trial, or when the parties waive their right to a jury. In the absence of a jury, the judge determines guilt and imposes sentences in a criminal case; in civil cases, the judge rewards relief—such as compensation for damages—to the parties in the lawsuit (also called litigants).

Judges also work outside the courtroom "in chambers." In their private offices, judges read documents on pleadings and motions, research legal issues, write opinions, and oversee the court's operations. Running a court is like running a small business, and judges also manage their courts' administrative and clerical staff.

Judges' duties vary according to the extent of their jurisdictions and powers. General trial court judges of the federal

and state court systems have jurisdiction over any case in their system. They generally try civil cases transcending the jurisdiction of lower courts, and all cases involving felony offenses. Federal and state appellate court judges, although few in number, have the power to overrule decisions made by trial court or administrative law judges if they determine that legal errors were made in a case, or if legal precedent does not support the judgment of the lower court. They rule on fewer cases and rarely have direct contacts with litigants. Instead, they usually base their decisions on lower court records and written and oral arguments by lawyers.

Many state court judges preside in courts in which jurisdiction is limited by law to certain types of cases. A variety of titles are assigned to these judges, but among the most common are municipal court judge, county court judge, magistrate, or justice of the peace. Traffic violations, misdemeanors, small claims cases, and pretrial hearings constitute the bulk of the work of these judges, but some states allow them to handle cases involving domestic relations, probate, contracts, and other selected areas of the law.

Administrative law judges, formerly called hearing officers, are employed by government agencies to make determinations for administrative agencies. They make decisions on a person's eligibility for various Social Security benefits or worker's compensation, protection of the environment, enforcement of health and safety regulations, employment discrimination, and compliance with economic regulatory requirements.

Working Conditions

Lawyers and judges do most of their work in offices, law libraries, and courtrooms. Lawyers sometimes meet in clients' homes or places of business and, when necessary, in hospitals or prisons. They may travel to attend meetings, gather evidence, and appear before courts, legislative bodies, and other authorities.

Salaried lawyers generally have structured work schedules. Lawyers in private practice may work irregular hours while conducting research, conferring with clients, or preparing briefs during nonoffice hours. Lawyers often work long hours, and about half regularly work 50 hours or more per week. They are under particularly heavy pressure, for example, when a case is being tried. Preparation for court includes keeping abreast of the latest laws and judicial decisions.

Although work is not generally seasonal, the work of tax lawyers and other specialists may be an exception. Because lawyers in private practice can often determine their own workload and when they will retire, many stay in practice well beyond the usual retirement age.

Many judges work a standard 40-hour week, but a third of all judges work over 50 hours per week. Some judges with limited jurisdiction are employed part-time and divide their time between their judicial responsibilities and other careers.

Employment

Lawyers held about 622,000 jobs in 1996; judges, about 78,000. About seven out of ten lawyers practiced privately, either in law firms or in solo practices. Most of the remaining lawyers held positions in government, the greatest number at the local level. In the federal government, lawyers work for many different agencies but are concentrated in the Departments of Justice, Treasury, and Defense. Other lawyers are employed as house counsel by public utilities, banks, insurance companies, real estate agencies, manufacturing firms, welfare and religious organizations, and other business firms and nonprofit organizations. Some salaried lawyers also have part-time independent practices; others work as lawyers part-time while working full-time in another occupation.

All judges, magistrates, and other judicial workers were employed by federal, state, or local governments, with about four out of ten holding positions in the federal government.

Law professors also hold law degrees, as well as other professionals such as politicians, managers, and administrators.

Training, Other Qualifications, and Advancement

Lawyers. To practice law in the courts of any state or other jurisdiction, a person must be licensed, or admitted to its bar, under rules established by the jurisdiction's highest court. All require that applicants for admission to the bar pass a written bar examination; most jurisdictions also require applicants to pass a separate written ethics examination. Lawyers who have been admitted to the bar in one jurisdiction may occasionally be admitted to the bar in another without taking an examination if they meet that jurisdiction's standards of good moral character, and have a specified period of legal experience. Federal courts and agencies set their own qualifications for those practicing before them.

To qualify for the bar examination in most states, an applicant must usually obtain a college degree and graduate from a law school accredited by the American Bar Association (ABA) or the proper state authorities. (ABA accreditation signifies that the law school—particularly its library and faculty—meets certain standards developed to promote quality legal education.) ABA currently accredits 179 law schools. Others are approved by state authorities only. With certain exceptions, graduates of schools not approved by the ABA are restricted to taking the bar examination and practicing in the state or other jurisdiction in which the school is located; most of these schools are in California. In 1997, seven states accepted the study of law in a law office or in combination with study in a law school; only California accepts the study of law by correspondence as qualifying for taking the bar examination. Several states require registration and approval of students by the state Board of Law Examiners, either before they enter law school or during the early years of legal study.

Although there is no nationwide bar examination, 47 states, the District of Columbia, Guam, the Northern Mariana Islands, and the Virgin Islands require the six-hour Multistate Bar Examination (MBE) as part of the bar examination; the MBE is not required in Indiana, Louisiana, Washington, and Puerto Rico. The MBE covers issues of broad interest, and is sometimes given in addition to a locally prepared state bar examination. The three-hour Multistate Essay Examination (MEE) is used as part of the state bar examination in a few states. States vary in their use of MBE and MEE scores.

Performance examinations to test practical skills of beginning lawyers are required by eight states. This program has been well received and more states are expected to require performance testing in the future. Requirements vary by state, although the test usually is taken at the same time as the bar exam, and is a one-time requirement.

The required college and law school education usually takes seven years of full-time study after high school—four years of undergraduate study followed by three years in law school. Although some law schools accept a very small number of students after three years of college, most require applicants to have a bachelor's degree. To meet the needs of students who can attend only part-time, a number of law schools have night or part-time divisions which usually require four years of study; about one in ten graduates from ABA-approved schools attends part-time.

Although there is no recommended prelaw major, prospective lawyers should develop proficiency in writing and speaking, reading, researching, analyzing, and thinking logically—skills needed to succeed both in law school and in the profession. Whatever the major, a multidisciplinary background is recommended. Courses in English, foreign language, public speaking, government, philosophy, history, economics, mathematics, and computer science, among others, are useful.

Students interested in a particular aspect of law may find related courses helpful. For example, prospective patent lawyers need a strong background in engineering or science, and future tax lawyers must have extensive knowledge of accounting.

Acceptance by most law schools depends on the applicant's ability to demonstrate an aptitude for the study of law, usually through good undergraduate grades, the Law School Admission Test (LSAT), the quality of the applicant's undergraduate school, any prior work experience, and sometimes a personal interview. However, law schools vary in the weight they place on each of these and other factors.

All law schools approved by the ABA, except for those in Puerto Rico, require applicants to take the LSAT. Nearly all law schools require applicants to have certified transcripts sent to the Law School Data Assembly Service, which then sends applicants' LSAT scores and their standardized records of college grades to the law schools of their choice. Both this service and the LSAT are administered by the Law School Admission Council.

Competition for admission to many law schools is intense. Enrollments in these schools rose very rapidly during the 1970s, with applicants far outnumbering available seats. The number of applicants decreased markedly in the 1990s, easing competition slightly; however, the number of applicants to most law schools still greatly exceeds the number that can be admitted. Competition for admission to the more prestigious law schools is always keen.

During the first year or year and a half of law school, students generally study fundamental courses such as constitutional law, contracts, property law, torts, civil procedure, and legal writing. In the remaining time, they may elect specialized courses in fields such as tax, labor, or corporation law. Law students often acquire practical experience by participation in school sponsored legal clinic activities, in the school's moot court competitions in which students conduct appellate arguments, in practice trials under the supervision of experienced lawyers and judges, and through research and writing on legal issues for the school's law journal.

In 1997, law students in 48 states were required to pass the Multistate Professional Responsibility Examination (MPRE), which tests their knowledge of the ABA codes on professional responsibility and judicial conduct. In some states, the MPRE may be taken during law school, usually after completing a course on legal ethics.

A number of law schools have clinical programs in which students gain legal experience through practice trials and law school projects under the supervision of practicing lawyers and law school faculty. Law school clinical programs might include work in legal aid clinics, for example, or on the staff of legislative committees. Part-time or summer clerkships in law firms, government agencies, and corporate legal departments also provide valuable experience. Such training can provide references or lead directly to a job after graduation,

and can help students decide what kind of practice best suits them. Clerkships may also be an important source of financial aid.

Graduates receive the degree of juris doctor (J.D.) as the first professional degree. Advanced law degrees may be desirable for those planning to specialize, do research, or teach. Some law students pursue joint degree programs, which generally require an additional semester or year. Joint degree programs are offered in a number of areas, including law and business administration or public administration.

After graduation, lawyers must keep informed about legal and nonlegal developments that affect their practice. Currently, 37 states and jurisdictions mandate Continuing Legal Education (CLE). Many law schools and state and local bar associations provide continuing education courses that help lawyers stay abreast of recent developments. Some states allow CLE credits to be obtained through participation in seminars on the Internet.

The practice of law involves a great deal of responsibility. Individuals planning careers in law should like to work with people, and be able to win the respect and confidence of their clients, associates, and the public. Perseverance and reasoning ability are essential to analyze complex cases and reach sound conclusions. Lawyers also need creativity when handling new and unique legal problems.

Most beginning lawyers start in salaried positions. Newly hired salaried attorneys usually start as associates and work with more experienced lawyers or judges. After several years of progressively more responsible salaried employment, some lawyers are admitted to partnership in their firm, or go into practice for themselves. Some lawyers, after several years of practice, become full-time law school faculty or administrators; a growing number have advanced degrees in other fields as well.

Some attorneys use their legal training in administrative or managerial positions in various departments of large corporations. A transfer from a corporation's legal department to another department often is viewed as a way to gain administrative experience and rise in the ranks of management.

Judges. Most judges have first been lawyers. Federal and state judges are generally required to be lawyers. About 40 states allow nonlawyers to hold limited jurisdiction judgeships, but opportunities are better with law experience. Federal administrative law judges must be lawyers and pass a competitive examination administered by the U.S. Office of Personnel Management. Some state administrative law judges and other hearing officials are not required to be lawyers, but law degrees are preferred for most positions.

Federal judges are appointed for life by the President, with the consent of the Senate. Federal administrative law judges are appointed by the various federal agencies with virtually lifetime tenure. About half of all state judges are appointed, while the remainder are elected in partisan or nonpartisan state elections. Many state and local judges serve fixed renewable terms, which range from four or six years for some trial court judgeships, to as long as 14 years or life for other trial or appellate court judges. Judicial nominating commissions, composed of members of the bar and the public, are used to screen candidates for judgeships in many states, as well as for some federal judgeships.

All states have some type of orientation for newly elected or appointed judges. The Federal Judicial Center, ABA, National Judicial College, and National Center for State Courts provide judicial education and training for judges and other judicial branch personnel. General and continuing education courses usually run from a couple of days to three weeks in length. Over half of the states, including Puerto Rico, require judges to enroll in continuing education courses while serving on the bench.

Job Outlook

Individuals interested in pursuing careers as lawyers or judges should encounter keen competition through the year 2006. The number of law school graduates is expected to continue to strain the economy's capacity to absorb them. As for judges, the prestige associated with serving on the bench should ensure continued, intense competition for openings.

Lawyers. Employment of lawyers grew very rapidly from the early 1970s through the early 1990s, but has started to level off in the last several years. Employment is expected to grow about as fast as the average for all occupations through the year 2006. Continuing demand for lawyers will result from growth in the population and the general level of business activities. Demand will also be spurred by growth of legal action in such areas as health care, intellectual property, international law, elder law, sexual harassment, and the environment. The wider availability and affordability of legal clinics and prepaid legal service programs should result in increased use of legal services by middle-income people.

Employment growth should be slower than in the past. In an effort to reduce the money spent on legal fees, many businesses are turning to large accounting firms to provide employee benefit counseling, process documents, and handle other services previously performed by law firms. Also, mediation and dispute resolution are increasingly used as alternatives to litigation.

Competition for job openings should continue to be keen because of the large numbers graduating from law school each year. During the 1970s, the annual number of law school graduates more than doubled, outpacing the rapid growth of jobs. Growth in the yearly number of law school graduates slowed during the early to mid-1980s, but increased again in the late 1980s to early 1990s. Although graduates with superior academic records from well-regarded law schools will have more job opportunities, most graduates will encounter stiff competition for jobs. As in the past, some graduates may have to accept positions in areas outside their field of interest or for which they feel overqualified. They may choose to enter jobs for which legal training is an asset, but not normally a requirement—for example, administrative, managerial, and business positions in banks, insurance firms, real estate companies, government agencies, and other organizations.

Some recent law school graduates who are unable to find permanent positions are turning to the growing number of legal temporary staffing firms, which place attorneys in short-term jobs until they are able to secure full-time positions. This service allows companies to hire lawyers on an "as needed" basis and allows beginning lawyers to develop practical skills while looking for permanent positions.

Due to the competition for jobs, a law graduate's geographic mobility and work experience assume greater importance. The willingness to relocate may be an advantage in getting a job, but to be licensed in a new state, a lawyer may have to take an additional state bar examination. In addition, employers increasingly seek graduates who have advanced law degrees and experience in a specialty such as tax, patent, or admiralty law.

Employment growth for lawyers will continue to be concentrated in salaried jobs, as businesses and all levels of government employ a growing number of staff attorneys, and as employment in the legal services industry grows in larger law firms. Most salaried positions are in urban areas where government agencies, law firms, and big corporations are concentrated. The number of self-employed lawyers is expected to increase slowly, reflecting the difficulty of establishing a profitable new practice in the face of competition from larger, established law firms. Also, the growing complexity of law, which encourages specialization, along with the cost of maintaining up-to-date legal research materials, favor larger firms.

For lawyers who wish to work independently, establishing a new practice will probably be easiest in small towns and expanding suburban areas, as long as an active market for legal services exists. In such communities, competition from larger established law firms is likely to be less than in big cit-

ies, and new lawyers may find it easier to become known to potential clients.

Some lawyers are adversely affected by cyclical swings in the economy. During recessions, the demand declines for some discretionary legal services, such as planning estates, drafting wills, and handling real estate transactions. Also, corporations are less likely to litigate cases when declining sales and profits result in budgetary restrictions. Some corporations and law firms will not hire new attorneys until business improves or may cut staff to contain costs. Several factors, however, mitigate the overall impact of recessions on lawyers. During recessions, individuals and corporations face other legal problems, such as bankruptcies, foreclosures, and divorces requiring legal action.

Judges. Employment of judges is expected to grow more slowly than the average for all occupations. Contradictory social forces affect the demand for judges. Growing public concerns about crime, safety, and efficient administration of justice should spur demand; on the other hand, tight public funding should slow job growth.

Competition for judgeships should remain keen. Most job openings will arise as judges retire. Traditionally, many judges have held their positions until late in life. Now, early retirement is becoming more common, creating more job openings. However, becoming a judge will still be difficult. Besides competing with other qualified people, judicial candidates must gain political support in order to be elected or appointed.

Earnings

Median salaries of lawyers six months after graduation from law school in 1996 varied by type of work, as indicated by table 1.

Salaries of experienced attorneys also vary widely according to the type, size, and location of their employer. The median annual salary of all lawyers was about $60,000 in 1996. General attorneys in the federal government averaged around $72,700 a year in 1997; the relatively small number of patent attorneys in the federal government averaged around $81,600.

Table 1. Median salaries of lawyers six months after graduation, 1996

All graduates	$40,000
Private practice	50,000
Business/industry	45,000
Academe	35,000
Judicial clerkship	35,000
Government	34,500
Public interest	30,000

SOURCE: National Association for Law Placement

Lawyers who practice alone usually earn less than those who are partners in law firms. Lawyers starting their own practice may need to work part-time in other occupations to supplement their income until their practice is well-established.

According to the Administrative Office of the U.S. Courts, federal district court judges had salaries of $133,600 in 1997, as did judges in the Court of Federal Claims; circuit court judges earned $141,700 a year. Federal judges with limited jurisdiction, such as magistrates and bankruptcy court judges, had salaries of $122,900. Full-time federal administrative law judges had average salaries of $94,800. The Chief Justice of the United States Supreme Court earned $171,500, and the Associate Justices earned $164,100.

According to a survey by the National Center for State Courts, annual salaries of associate justices of states' highest courts averaged $101,800 in 1997, and ranged from about $68,900 to $133,600. Salaries of state intermediate appellate court judges averaged $91,000, and ranged from $79,400 to $124,200. Salaries of state judges with limited jurisdiction vary widely; some salaries are set locally.

Most salaried lawyers and judges are provided health and life insurance, and contributions are made on their behalf to retirement plans. Lawyers who practice independently are only covered if they arrange and pay for such benefits themselves.

Related Occupations

Legal training is useful in many other occupations. Some of these are arbitrator, mediator, journalist, patent agent, title examiner, legislative assistant, lobbyist, FBI special agent, political office holder, and corporate executive.

Sources of Additional Information

Information on law schools and law as a career may be obtained from:

❏ American Bar Association, 750 North Lake Shore Dr., Chicago, IL 60611.

Information on the LSAT, the Law School Data Assembly Service, applying to law school, and financial aid for law students may be obtained from:

❏ Law School Admission Council, P.O. Box 40, Newtown, PA 18940. Homepage: http://www.lsac.org

Information on acquiring a job as a lawyer with the federal government may be obtained from the Office of Personnel Management through a telephone-based system. Consult your telephone directory under U.S. government for a local number or call (912) 757-3000 (TDD 912 744-2299). That number is not toll-free and charges may result. Information also is available from their Internet site: http://www.usajobs.opm.gov

The specific requirements for admission to the bar in a particular state or other jurisdiction may also be obtained at the state capital from the clerk of the Supreme Court or the administrator of the State Board of Bar Examiners.

Optometrists

(D.O.T. 079.101-018)

Significant Points

✱ *All states and the District of Columbia require that optometrists be licensed. Applicants for a license must have a Doctor of Optometry degree from an accredited optometry school and pass both a written and a clinical state board examination.*

✱ *Although many optometrists practice alone, a growing number are in a partnership or group practice.*

✱ *Because optometrists generally remain in practice until they retire, the number of job openings arising from the need to replace optometrists who leave the occupation is low.*

Nature of the Work

Over half the people in the United States wear glasses or contact lenses. Optometrists (doctors of optometry, also known as ODs) provide most of the primary vision care people need.

Optometrists examine people's eyes to diagnose vision problems and eye diseases. They use instruments and observation to examine eye health and to test patients' visual acuity, depth and color perception, and their ability to focus and coordinate the eyes. They analyze test results and develop a treatment plan. Optometrists prescribe eyeglasses and contact lenses, and provide vision therapy and low vision rehabilitation. They use drugs for diagnosis of eye vision problems and prescribe drugs to treat some eye diseases. Optometrists often provide pre- and post-operative care to cataract and other eye surgery patients. They also diagnose conditions due to systemic diseases such as diabetes and high blood pressure, and refer patients to other health practitioners as needed.

Optometrists should not be confused with ophthalmologists or dispensing opticians. Ophthalmologists are physicians who perform eye surgery, and diagnose and treat eye diseases and injuries. Like optometrists, they also examine eyes and prescribe eyeglasses and contact lenses. Dispensing opticians fit and adjust eyeglasses and in some states may fit contact lenses according to prescriptions written by ophthalmologists or optometrists.

Most optometrists are in general practice. Some specialize in work with the elderly, children, or partially sighted persons who need specialized visual devices to improve their vision. Others develop and implement ways to protect workers' eyes from on-the-job strain or injury. Some specialize in contact lenses, sports vision, or vision therapy. A few teach optometry, do research, or consult.

Most optometrists are private practitioners who also handle the business aspects of running an office, such as developing a patient base, hiring employees, keeping records, and ordering equipment and supplies. Optometrists who operate franchise optical stores may also have some of these duties.

Working Conditions

Optometrists work in places—usually their own offices—that are clean, well lighted, and comfortable. The work requires attention to detail and good manual dexterity. Most full-time optometrists work about 40 hours a week, but a substantial number work more than 50 hours a week. Many work Saturdays and evenings to suit the needs of patients, but emergency calls are rare.

Employment

Optometrists held about 41,000 jobs in 1996. The number of jobs is greater than the number of practicing optometrists because some optometrists hold two or more jobs. For example, an optometrist may have a private practice, but also work in another practice, clinic, or vision care center. According to the American Optometric Association, about two-thirds of practicing optometrists are in private practice.

Although many optometrists practice alone, a growing number are in a partnership or group practice. Some optometrists work as salaried employees of other optometrists or of ophthalmologists, hospitals, health maintenance organizations (HMOs), or retail optical stores. A small number of optometrists are consultants for industrial safety programs, insurance companies, manufacturers of ophthalmic products, HMOs, and others.

Training, Other Qualifications, and Advancement

All states and the District of Columbia require that optometrists be licensed. Applicants for a license must have a Doctor of Optometry degree from an accredited optometry school and pass both a written and a clinical state board examination. In many states, applicants can substitute the examinations of the National Board of Examiners in Optometry, usually taken during the student's academic career, for part or all of the written examination. Licenses are renewed every one to three years and in all states, continuing education credits are needed for renewal.

The Doctor of Optometry degree requires completion of a four-year program at an accredited optometry school preceded by at least three years of preoptometric study at an accredited college or university (most optometry students hold a bachelor's degree). In 1997, 17 U.S. schools and colleges of optometry held an accredited status with the Council on Optometric Education of the American Optometric Association.

Requirements for admission to schools of optometry include courses in English, mathematics, physics, chemistry, and biology. A few schools require or recommend courses in psychology, history, sociology, speech, or business. Applicants must take the Optometry Admissions Test, which measures academic ability and scientific comprehension. Most applicants take the test after their sophomore or junior year. Competition for admission is keen.

Optometry programs include classroom and laboratory study of health and visual sciences, as well as clinical training in the diagnosis and treatment of eye disorders. Included are courses in pharmacology, optics, vision science, biochemistry, and systemic disease.

Business ability, self-discipline, and the ability to deal tactfully with patients are important for success.

Optometrists wishing to teach or do research may study for a master's or Ph.D. degree in visual science, physiological optics, neurophysiology, public health, health administration, health information and communication, or health education. One-year postgraduate clinical residency programs are available for optometrists who wish to specialize in family practice optometry, pediatric optometry, geriatric optometry, vision therapy, contact lenses, hospital based optometry, primary care optometry, or ocular disease.

Job Outlook

Employment of optometrists is expected to grow about as fast as the average for all occupations through the year 2006 in response to the vision care needs of a growing and aging population. As baby boomers age, they will be more likely to visit optometrists and ophthalmologists because of the onset of vision problems in middle age, including computer-related vision problems. The demand for optometric services will also increase because of growth in the oldest age group, with their increased likelihood of cataracts, glaucoma, diabetes, and hypertension. Employment of optometrists will also grow due to greater recognition of the importance of vision care, rising personal incomes, and growth in employee vision care plans.

Employment of optometrists would grow more rapidly were it not for anticipated productivity gains which will allow each optometrist to see more patients. These gains will result from greater use of optometric assistants and other support personnel, and the introduction of new equipment and procedures. New surgical procedures using lasers are available that can correct some vision problems, but they remain expensive.

In addition to growth, the need to replace optometrists who leave the occupation will create employment opportunities. Relatively few opportunities from this source are expected, however, because most optometrists continue to practice until they retire; few transfer to other occupations.

Earnings

According to the American Optometric Association, new optometry graduates in their first year of practice earned median net incomes of $57,500 in 1996. Overall, optometrists earned median net incomes of $80,000.

Incomes vary depending upon location, specialization, and other factors. Salaried optometrists tend to earn more initially than optometrists who set up their own independent practice. In the long run, those in private practice generally earn more.

Related Occupations

Workers in other occupations who apply scientific knowledge to prevent, diagnose, and treat disorders and injuries are chiropractors, dentists, physicians, podiatrists, veterinarians, speech-language pathologists, and audiologists.

Sources of Additional Information

For information on optometry as a career and a listing of accredited optometric educational institutions, as well as required preoptometry courses, contact:

❏ American Optometric Association, Educational Services, 243 North Lindbergh Blvd., St. Louis, MO 63141-7881. Homepage: http://www.aoanet.org/aoanet

❏ Association of Schools and Colleges of Optometry, 6110 Executive Blvd., Suite 510, Rockville, MD 20852. Homepage: http://www.opted.org

The Board of Optometry in each state can supply information on licensing requirements.

For information on specific admission requirements and sources of financial aid, contact the admissions officer of individual optometry schools.

Physicians

(*D.O.T.* 070 and 071)

Significant Points

✱ *Amid reports of an oversupply of physicians, opportunities will be best in primary care fields of general and family medicine, internal medicine, and general pediatrics.*

✱ *Physicians are much more likely to work as salaried employees of group medical practices, clinics, or health care networks than in the past.*

✱ *It takes many years of education and training to become a physician, but earnings are among the highest of any occupation.*

Nature of the Work

Physicians serve a fundamental role in our society and have an effect upon all our lives. They diagnose illnesses and prescribe and administer treatment for people suffering from injury or disease. Physicians examine patients, obtain medical histories, and order, perform, and interpret diagnostic tests. They counsel patients on diet, hygiene, and preventive health care.

There are two types of physicians: MD—Doctor of Medicine—and the DO—Doctor of Osteopathic Medicine. MDs are also known as allopathic physicians. While MDs and DOs may use all accepted methods of treatment, including drugs and surgery, DOs place special emphasis on the body's musculoskeletal system, preventive medicine, and holistic patient care.

About one-third of MDs are primary care physicians. They practice general and family medicine, general internal medicine, or general pediatrics and are usually the first health professionals patients consult. Primary care physicians tend to see the same patients on a regular basis for preventive care and to treat a variety of ailments. General and family practitioners emphasize comprehensive health care for patients of all ages and for the family as a group. Those in general internal medicine provide care mainly for adults who have a wide range of problems associated with the body's organs. General pediatricians focus on children's health. When appropriate, primary care physicians refer patients to specialists, who are experts in medical fields such as obstetrics and gynecology, cardiology, psychiatry, or surgery (see table 1). DOs are more likely to be primary care providers than allopathic physicians, although they can be found in all specialties.

Table 1. Percentage distribution of MDs by specialty, 1995

	Percentage
Total	100.0
Primary care	
General internal medicine	16.0
General and family medicine	10.5
General pediatrics	7.0
Medical specialties	
Allergy	.5
Cardiovascular diseases	2.6
Dermatology	1.2
Gastroenterology	1.3
Obstetrics and gynecology	5.2
Pediatric cardiology	.2
Pulmonary diseases	1.0
Surgical specialties	
Colon and rectal surgery	.1
General surgery	5.2
Neurological surgery	.7
Ophthalmology	2.4
Orthopedic surgery	3.1
Otalaryngology	1.3
Plastic surgery	.8
Thoracic surgery	.3
Urological surgery	1.4
Other specialties	
Aerospace medicine	.1
Anesthesiology	4.6
Child psychiatry	.8
Diagnostic radiology	2.7
Emergency medicine	2.7
Forensic pathology	.1
General preventive medicine	.2
Neurology	1.6
Nuclear medicine	.2
Occupational medicine	.4
Pathology	2.5
Physical medicine and rehabilitation	.8
Psychiatry	5.3
Public health	.2
Radiology	1.1
Radiation oncology	.5
Other specialty	1.0
Unspecified/unknown/inactive	14.4

SOURCE: American Medical Association

Working Conditions

Many physicians work long, irregular hours. About one-third of all full-time physicians worked 60 hours or more a week in 1996. They must travel frequently between office and hospital to care for their patients. Increasingly, physicians practice in groups or health care organizations that provide back-up coverage and allow for more time off. These physicians work as part of a team that coordinates care for a population of patients; they are less independent than solo practitioners of the past. Physicians who are on-call deal with many patients' concerns over the phone, and may make emergency visits to hospitals.

Employment

Physicians (MDs and DOs) held about 560,000 jobs in 1996. About seven out of ten were in office-based practice, including clinics and HMOs; about two out of ten were employed by hospitals. Others practiced in the federal government, most in Department of Veterans Affairs hospitals and clinics or in the Public Health Service of the Department of Health and Human Services.

A growing number of physicians are partners or salaried employees of group practices. Organized as clinics or as groups of physicians, medical groups can afford expensive medical equipment and realize other business advantages. Also, hospitals are integrating physician practices into health care networks that provide a continuum of care both inside and outside of the hospital setting.

The northeastern and western states have the highest ratio of physicians to population; the southcentral states, the lowest. DOs are more likely than MDs to practice in small cities and towns and in rural areas. MDs tend to locate in urban areas, close to hospital and educational centers.

Osteopathic physicians locate chiefly in states that have osteopathic schools and hospitals. In 1997, about one-half of active DOs practiced in six states: Pennsylvania, Michigan, Ohio, Florida, New Jersey, and Texas.

Training, Other Qualifications, and Advancement

It takes many years of education and training to become a physician: four years of undergraduate school, four years of medical school, and three to eight years of internship and residency, depending on the specialty selected. A few medical schools offer a combined undergraduate and medical school program that lasts six years instead of the customary eight years.

Premedical students must complete undergraduate work in physics, biology, mathematics, English, and inorganic and organic chemistry. Students also take courses in the humanities and the social sciences. Some students also volunteer at local hospitals or clinics to gain practical experience in the health professions.

The minimum educational requirement for entry to a medical or osteopathic school is three years of college; most applicants, however, have at least a bachelor's degree, and many have advanced degrees. There are 142 medical schools in the United States—125 teach allopathic medicine and award a Doctor of Medicine (MD); 17 teach osteopathic medicine

and award the Doctor of Osteopathy (DO). Acceptance to medical school is very competitive. Applicants must submit transcripts, scores from the Medical College Admission Test, and letters of recommendation. Schools also consider character, personality, leadership qualities, and participation in extracurricular activities. Most schools require an interview with members of the admissions committee.

Students spend most of the first two years of medical school in laboratories and classrooms taking courses such as anatomy, biochemistry, physiology, pharmacology, psychology, microbiology, pathology, medical ethics, and laws governing medicine. They also learn to take medical histories, examine patients, and diagnose illness. During the last two years, students work with patients under the supervision of experienced physicians in hospitals and clinics to learn acute, chronic, preventive, and rehabilitative care. Through rotations in internal medicine, family practice, obstetrics and gynecology, pediatrics, psychiatry, and surgery, they gain experience in the diagnosis and treatment of illness.

Following medical school, almost all MDs enter a residency—graduate medical education in a specialty that takes the form of paid on-the-job training, usually in a hospital. Most DOs serve a 12-month rotating internship after graduation before entering a residency which may last two to six years. Physicians may benefit from residencies in managed care settings by gaining experience with this increasingly common type of medical practice.

All states, the District of Columbia, and U.S. territories license physicians. To be licensed, physicians must graduate from an accredited medical school, pass a licensing examination, and complete one to seven years of graduate medical education. Although physicians licensed in one state can usually get a license to practice in another without further examination, some states limit reciprocity. Graduates of foreign medical schools can qualify for licensure after passing an examination and completing a U.S. residency.

MDs and DOs seeking board certification in a specialty may spend up to seven years—depending on the specialty—in residency training. A final examination immediately after residency, or after one or two years of practice, is also necessary for board certification by the American Board of Medical Specialists (ABMS) or the American Osteopathic Association (AOA). There are 24 specialty boards, ranging from allergy and immunology to urology. For certification in a subspecialty, physicians usually need another one to two years of residency.

A physician's training is costly. While education costs have increased, student financial assistance has not. Over 80 percent of medical students borrow money to cover their expenses.

People who wish to become physicians must have a desire to serve patients, be self-motivated, and be able to survive the pressures and long hours of medical education and practice. Physicians must also have a good bedside manner, emotional stability, and the ability to make decisions in emergencies. Prospective physicians must be willing to study throughout their career to keep up with medical advances. They will also need to be flexible to respond to the changing demands of a rapidly evolving health care system.

Job Outlook

Employment of physicians will grow faster than the average for all occupations through the year 2006 due to continued expansion of the health care industries. The growing and aging population will drive overall growth in the number of physicians. In addition, new technologies permit more intensive care: Physicians can do more tests, perform more procedures, and treat conditions previously regarded as untreatable. Job prospects will be best for primary care physicians such as general and family practitioners, general pediatricians, and general internists; and for geriatric and preventive care specialists.

Because of efforts to control health care costs and increased reliance on utilization guidelines that often limit the use of specialty services, a lower percentage of specialists will be in demand. At the same time, the number of specialists continues to grow. Competition for jobs among specialists will be especially keen in large urban and suburban areas, and for those who work directly for hospitals, such as anesthesiologists and radiologists.

A number of prestigious organizations, including the National Academy of Sciences Institute of Medicine and the Pew Health Professions Commission, have found a current oversupply of physicians. They suggest that measures should be taken to reduce the number being trained through such means as a reduction in the number of residency slots. If successful, a reduction in the number of new physicians entering the workforce will help to alleviate the effects of any physician oversupply.

A physician oversupply may not substantially limit the ability of physicians to find employment. However, it could result in physicians working fewer hours, having lower earnings, and having to practice in underserved areas. Opportunities should be good in some rural and low income areas, because some physicians find these areas unattractive due to lower earnings potential, isolation from medical colleagues, or other reasons. It is also possible that physicians trained in specialties will provide primary care services as well as specialty care.

Unlike their predecessors, newly trained physicians face radically different choices of where and how to practice. New physicians are much less likely to enter solo practice and more likely to take salaried jobs in group medical practices, clinics, and health care networks.

Earnings

Physicians have among the highest earnings of any occupation. According to the American Medical Association, median income, after expenses, for allopathic physicians was about $160,000 in 1995. The middle 50 percent earned between $115,000 and $238,000. Self-employed physicians—those who own or are part owners of their medical practice—had higher median incomes than salaried physicians. Earnings vary according to number of years in practice; geographic region; hours worked; and skill, personality, and professional reputation. As shown in table 2, median income of allopathic physicians, after expenses, also varies by specialty.

Average salaries of medical residents ranged from $32,789 in 1996–97 for those in their first year of residency to $40,849 for those in their sixth year, according to the Association of American Medical Colleges.

Table 2. Median net income of MDs after expenses, 1995

All physicians	$160,000
Radiology	230,000
Surgery	225,000
Anesthesiology	203,000
Obstetrics/gynecology	200,000
Pathology	185,000
Emergency medicine	170,000
General internal medicine	138,000
Pediatrics	129,000
Psychiatry	124,000
General/family practice	124,000

SOURCE: American Medical Association

Related Occupations

Physicians work to prevent, diagnose, and treat diseases, disorders, and injuries. Professionals in other occupations that require similar kinds of skill and critical judgment include acupuncturists, audiologists, chiropractors, dentists, nurse practitioners, optometrists, physician assistants, podiatrists, speech pathologists, and veterinarians.

Sources of Additional Information

For a list of allopathic medical schools and residency programs, as well as general information on premedical education, financial aid, and medicine as a career, contact:

❏ American Medical Association, 515 N. State St., Chicago, IL 60610.

❏ Association of American Medical Colleges, Section for Student Services, 2450 N St. NW, Washington, DC 20037-1131. Homepage: http://www.aamc.org

For general information on osteopathic medicine as a career, contact:

❏ American Osteopathic Association, Department of Public Relations, 142 East Ontario St., Chicago, IL 60611. Homepage: http://www.am-osteo-assn.org

❏ American Association of Colleges of Osteopathic Medicine, 5550 Friendship Blvd., Suite 310, Chevy Chase, MD 20815-7321. Homepage: http://www.aacom.org

Information on federal scholarships and loans is available from the directors of student financial aid at schools of allopathic and osteopathic medicine.

Information on licensing is available from state boards of examiners.

Physicists and Astronomers

D.O.T. 015.021-010; 021.067-010; 023.061-010, -014, and .067; 079.021-014)

Significant Points

✴ *A doctoral degree is the usual educational requirement because most jobs are in basic research and development; a master's degree is sufficient for some jobs in applied research and development; a bachelor's degree is adequate for some nonresearch jobs.*

✴ *Ph.D.s face competition for jobs as funding for research declines, and as the large pool of postdoctoral workers adds to the supply of new graduates.*

Nature of the Work

Physicists explore and identify basic principles governing the structure and behavior of matter, the generation and transfer of energy, and the interaction of matter and energy. Some physicists use these principles in theoretical areas, such as the nature of time and the origin of the universe; others apply their physics knowledge to practical areas such as the development of advanced materials, electronic and optical devices, and medical equipment.

Physicists design and perform experiments with lasers, cyclotrons, telescopes, mass spectrometers, and other equipment. Based on observations and analysis, they attempt to discover laws describing the forces of nature, such as gravity, electromagnetism, and nuclear interactions. They also find ways to apply physical laws and theories to problems in nuclear

energy, electronics, optics, materials, communications, aerospace technology, navigation equipment, and medical instrumentation.

Astronomy is sometimes considered a subfield of physics. Astronomers use the principles of physics and mathematics to learn about the fundamental nature of the universe, including the sun, moon, planets, stars, and galaxies. They also apply their knowledge to problems in navigation and space flight, and to develop the instrumentation and techniques used to observe and collect astronomical data.

Most physicists work in research and development. Some do basic research to increase scientific knowledge. Physicists who conduct applied research build upon the discoveries made through basic research, and work to develop new devices, products, and processes. For instance, basic research in solid-state physics led to the development of transistors and then to the integrated circuits used in computers.

Physicists also design research equipment. This equipment often has additional unanticipated uses. For example, lasers are used in surgery; microwave devices are used for ovens; and measuring instruments can analyze blood or the chemical content of foods. A small number work in inspection, testing, quality control, and other production-related jobs in industry.

Much physics research is done in small or medium-size laboratories. However, experiments in plasma, nuclear, high energy, and some other areas of physics require extremely large, expensive equipment such as particle accelerators. Physicists in these subfields often work in large teams. Although physics research may require extensive experimentation in laboratories, research physicists still spend time in offices planning, recording, analyzing, and reporting on research.

Almost all astronomers do research. Some are theoreticians, working on the laws governing the structure and evolution of astronomical objects. Others analyze large quantities of data gathered by observatories and satellites, and write scientific papers or reports on their findings. Astronomers may spend only a few weeks each year making observations with optical telescopes, radio telescopes, and other instruments. For many years, satellites and other space-based instruments have provided tremendous amounts of astronomical data. New technology resulting in improvements in analytical techniques and instruments, such as computers and optical telescopes and mounts, is leading to a resurgence in ground-based research. A small number of astronomers work in museums housing planetariums. These astronomers develop and revise the programs presented to the public, and may also direct operations.

Physicists generally specialize in one of many subfields— elementary particle physics; nuclear physics; atomic and molecular physics; physics of condensed matter (solid-state physics); optics; acoustics; space physics; plasma physics; or the physics of fluids. Some specialize in a subdivision of one of these subfields; for example, within condensed matter physics, specialties include superconductivity, crystallography, and semiconductors. However, all physics involves the same fundamental principles, so specialties may overlap, and physicists may switch from one subfield to another. Also, growing numbers of physicists work in combined fields such as biophysics, chemical physics, and geophysics.

Working Conditions

Physicists often work regular hours in laboratories and offices. At times, however, those who are deeply involved in research may work long or irregular hours. Most do not encounter unusual hazards in their work. Some physicists temporarily work away from home at national or international facilities with unique equipment such as particle accelerators. Astronomers who make observations may spend long periods of time in observatories; this work usually involves travel to remote locations. Long hours, including routine night work, may create temporarily stressful conditions.

Physicists and astronomers whose work is dependent on grant money are often under pressure to write grant proposals to keep their work funded.

Employment

Physicists and astronomers held nearly 18,000 jobs in 1996. About three in ten nonfaculty physicists and astronomers worked for commercial or noncommercial research, development, and testing laboratories. The federal government employed almost two in ten, mostly in the Department of Defense, but also in the Departments of Commerce, Health and Human Services, and Energy, and the National Aeronautics and Space Administration. Others worked in colleges and universities in nonfaculty positions, and for state governments, drug companies, and electronic equipment manufacturers.

Besides the jobs described above, many physicists held faculty positions in colleges and universities.

Although physicists and astronomers are employed in all parts of the country, most work in areas in which universities, large research and development laboratories, or observatories are located.

Training, Other Qualifications, and Advancement

A doctoral degree is the usual educational requirement for physicists and astronomers, because most jobs are in basic research and development. Additional experience and training in a postdoctoral research assignment, although not required, is helpful in preparing physicists and astronomers for permanent research positions. Many physics and astronomy Ph.D. holders ultimately teach at the college or university level.

Master's degree holders usually do not qualify for basic research positions, but do qualify for many kinds of jobs requiring a physics background, including positions in applied research and development, and manufacturing. Physics departments in some colleges and universities are creating professional master's degree programs to specifically prepare students for physics-related research which does not require a Ph.D. in private industry. A master's degree may suffice for teaching jobs in two-year colleges. Those having bachelor's degrees in physics are rarely qualified to fill positions as research or teaching physicists. They are, however, usually qualified to work in an engineering-related area or other scientific fields, to work as technicians, or to assist in setting up laboratories. Some may qualify for applied research jobs in private industry or nonresearch positions in the federal government. Some become science teachers in secondary schools. Astronomy bachelor's or master's degree holders often enter a field unrelated to astronomy, but they are also qualified to work in planetariums running science shows or to assist astronomers doing research.

Over 500 colleges and universities offer a bachelor's degree in physics. The undergraduate program provides a broad background in the natural sciences and mathematics. Typical physics courses include mechanics, electromagnetism, optics, thermodynamics, atomic physics, and quantum mechanics.

About 180 colleges and universities have departments offering Ph.D.s in physics. Graduate students usually concentrate in a subfield of physics, such as elementary particles or condensed matter. Many begin studying for their doctorate immediately after receiving their bachelor's degree.

About 80 universities offer the master's or Ph.D. in astronomy, either through an astronomy, a physics, or combined physics/astronomy department. Applicants to astronomy doctoral programs face keen competition for available slots. Those planning a career in astronomy should have a very strong physics background. In fact, an undergraduate degree in either physics or astronomy is excellent preparation, followed by a Ph.D. in astronomy.

Mathematical ability, computer skills, an inquisitive mind, imagination, and the ability to work independently are important traits for anyone planning a career in physics or astronomy. Prospective physicists who hope to work in industrial laboratories applying physics knowledge to practical problems should broaden their educational background to include courses outside of physics, such as economics, computer technology, and business management. Good oral and written communication skills are also important because many physicists work as part of a team or have contact with clients or customers with non-physics backgrounds.

Most physics and astronomy Ph.D.s begin their careers in a postdoctoral research position, where they may work with experienced physicists as they continue to learn about their specialty and develop ideas and results to be used in later work. The initial work may be under the close supervision of senior scientists. After some experience, they perform increasingly complex tasks and work more independently. Physicists who develop new products or processes sometimes form their own companies or join new firms to exploit their own ideas.

Job Outlook

Historically, many physicists and astronomers have been employed on research projects—often defense-related. Further reductions in defense-related research and a continued slowdown in the growth of civilian physics-related research will result in a small decline in employment of physicists and astronomers through the year 2006. The need to replace physicists and astronomers who retire will account for almost all expected job openings. Proposed employment cutbacks and overall budget tightening in the federal government will also affect employment of physicists, especially those dependent on federal research grants. The federal government funds numerous noncommercial research and development facilities; the government's plan to balance the federal budget may limit funding and, consequently, the scope of research in these facilities.

The number of doctorates granted in physics has been much greater than the number of openings for physicists for several years, resulting in keen competition, particularly for research positions in colleges and universities and research and development centers. Competitive conditions may ease slightly when the number of degrees awarded begins to drop midway between 1996 and 2006, following recent declines in enrollment. However, job applicants should still expect to face competition from the large pool of postdoctoral workers who will add to the supply of new graduates. Also, more prospective researchers will likely compete for less grant money.

Although research and development budgets in private industry will continue to grow, many research laboratories in private industry are expected to reduce basic research, which includes much physics research, in favor of applied or manufacturing research and product and software development. Although many physicists and astronomers will be eligible for retirement over the next decade, it is possible not all of them will be replaced when they retire.

Opportunities may be more numerous for those with a master's degree, particularly graduates from programs preparing students for applied research and development, product design, and manufacturing positions in industry. Many of these positions, however, will have titles other than physicist, such as engineer or computer scientist.

Persons with only a bachelor's degree in physics or astronomy are not qualified to enter most physicist or astronomer jobs, but may qualify for a wide range of positions in engineering, technician, mathematics, and computer- and environment-related occupations. Those who meet state certification requirements may become high school physics teachers, an occupation reportedly in strong demand in many school districts. Despite strong competition for traditional physics and astronomy research jobs, individuals with a physics degree at any level will find their skills useful for entry to many other occupations.

Earnings

According to a 1997 National Association of Colleges and Employers survey, the average starting salary offer to physics doctoral degree candidates was $34,700.

The American Institute of Physics reported a median salary of $65,000 in 1996 for its members with Ph.D.s; with master's degrees, $55,000; and with bachelor's degrees, $50,000. Those working in temporary postdoctoral positions earned significantly less.

Average earnings for physicists in nonsupervisory, supervisory, and managerial positions in the federal government in 1997 were about $71,800 a year, and for astronomy and space scientists, $77,400.

Related Occupations

The work of physicists and astronomers relates closely to that of engineers, chemists, meteorologists, geophysicists, computer scientists, computer programmers, and mathematicians.

Sources of Additional Information

General information on career opportunities in physics is available from:

❏ American Institute of Physics, Career Planning and Placement, One Physics Ellipse, College Park, MD 20740-3843. Homepage: http://www.aip.org

❏ The American Physical Society, Education Department, One Physics Ellipse, College Park, MD 20740-3844. Homepage: http://www.aps.org

For a pamphlet containing information on careers in astronomy, send your request to:

❏ American Astronomical Society, Education Office, Adler Planetarium and Astronomy Museum, 1300 S. Lake Shore Dr., Chicago IL 60605. Homepage: http://www.aas.org

Podiatrists

(D.O.T. 079.101-022)

Significant Points

✴ *A limited number of job openings for podiatrists is expected because the occupation is small and most podiatrists remain in the occupation until they retire.*

✴ *Most podiatrists are solo practitioners, although more are entering partnerships and multi-specialty group practices.*

✴ *Podiatrists enjoy very high earnings.*

Nature of the Work

The human foot is a complex structure. It contains 26 bones—plus muscles, nerves, ligaments, and blood vessels—and is designed for balance and mobility. The 52 bones in your feet make up about one fourth of all the bones in your body. Podiatrists, also known as doctors of podiatric medicine (DPMs), diagnose and treat disorders, diseases, and injuries of the foot and lower leg to keep this part of the body working properly.

Podiatrists treat corns, calluses, ingrown toenails, bunions, heel spurs, and arch problems; ankle and foot injuries, deformities and infections; and foot complaints associated with diseases such as diabetes. To treat these problems, podiatrists prescribe drugs, order physical therapy, set fractures, and perform surgery. They also fit corrective inserts called orthotics, design plaster casts and strappings to correct deformities, and design custom-made shoes. Podiatrists may use a force plate to help design the orthotics. Patients walk across a plate connected to a computer that "reads" the patients' feet. From the computer readout, podiatrists order the correct design.

To diagnose a foot problem, podiatrists order x rays and laboratory tests. The foot may be the first area to show signs of serious conditions such as arthritis, diabetes, and heart disease. For example, diabetics are prone to foot ulcers and infections due to poor circulation. Podiatrists consult with and refer patients to other health practitioners when they detect symptoms of these disorders.

Most podiatrists have a general practice. Some specialize in surgery, orthopedics, primary care, or public health. Besides these board-certified specialties, podiatrists may practice a subspecialty such as sports medicine, pediatrics, dermatology, radiology, geriatrics, or diabetic foot care. Podiatrists generally are in private practice, which means they run a small business. They may hire employees, order supplies, and keep records.

Working Conditions

Podiatrists usually work independently in their own offices. They may also spend time visiting patients in nursing homes or performing surgery at a hospital, but generally have fewer after-hours emergencies than other doctors. Those with private practices set their own hours, but to meet the needs of their patients, they may work evenings and weekends.

Employment

Podiatrists held about 11,000 jobs in 1996. Most podiatrists are solo practitioners, although more are entering partnerships and multi-specialty group practices. Others are employed in hospitals, nursing homes, the U.S. Public Health Service, and the Department of Veterans Affairs.

Training, Other Qualifications, and Advancement

All states and the District of Columbia require a license for the practice of podiatric medicine. Each defines its own licensing requirements. Generally, the applicant must be a graduate of an accredited college of podiatric medicine and pass written and oral examinations. Some states permit applicants to substitute the examination of the National Board of Podiatric Examiners, given in the second and fourth years of podiatric medical college, for part or all of the written state examination. Most states also require completion of a postdoctoral residency program. Most states grant reciprocity to podiatrists who are licensed in another state. Most states require continuing education for licensure renewal.

Prerequisites for admission to a college of podiatric medicine include the completion of at least 90 semester hours of undergraduate study, an acceptable grade point average, and suitable scores on the Medical College Admission Test (MCAT). All require eight semester hours each of biology, inorganic chemistry, organic chemistry, and physics, and six hours of English. The science courses should be those designed for pre-medical students. Potential podiatric medical students may also be evaluated on the basis of extracurricular and community activities, personal interviews, and letters of recommendation. Over 90 percent of podiatric students have at least a bachelor's degree.

Colleges of podiatric medicine offer a four-year program whose core curriculum is similar to that in other schools of medicine. During the first two years, students receive classroom instruction in basic sciences, including anatomy, chemistry, pathology, and pharmacology. Third- and fourth-year students have clinical rotations in private practices, hospitals, and clinics. During these rotations, they learn how to take general and podiatric histories, perform routine physical examinations, interpret tests and findings, make diagnoses, and perform therapeutic procedures. Graduates receive the doctor of podiatric medicine (DPM) degree.

Most graduates complete a hospital residency program after receiving a DPM. Residency programs last from one to three years. Residents receive advanced training in podiatric medicine and surgery and serve clinical rotations in anesthesiology, internal medicine, pathology, radiology, emergency medicine, and orthopedic and general surgery. Residencies lasting more than one year provide more extensive training in specialty areas.

There are a number of certifying boards for the podiatric specialties of orthopedics, primary medicine, or surgery. Certification means that the DPM meets higher standards than those required for licensure. Each board requires advanced training, completion of written and oral examinations, and experience as a practicing podiatrist. Most managed care organizations prefer board-certified podiatrists.

People planning a career in podiatry should have scientific aptitude, manual dexterity, interpersonal skills, and good business sense.

Podiatrists may advance to become professors at colleges of podiatric medicine, department chiefs of hospitals, or general health administrators.

Job Outlook

Employment of podiatrists is expected to grow about as fast as the average for all occupations through the year 2006. More people will turn to podiatrists for foot care as the elderly population grows. The elderly have more years of wear and tear on their feet and legs than most younger people, so they are more prone to foot ailments. Injuries sustained by an increasing number of men and women of all ages leading active lifestyles will also spur demand for podiatric care.

In addition to growth, the need to replace podiatrists who leave the occupation will create employment opportunities. Relatively few opportunities from this source are expected, however, because most podiatrists continue to practice until they retire; few transfer to other occupations. Even when combined, the number of job openings resulting from both growth and replacement needs is very low because the occupation is small.

Medicare and most private health insurance programs cover acute medical and surgical foot services, as well as diagnostic x rays and leg braces. Details of such coverage vary among plans. However, routine foot care—including the removal of corns and calluses—is ordinarily not covered, unless the patient has a systemic condition that has resulted in severe circulatory problems or areas of desensitization in the

legs or feet. Like dental services, podiatric care is more dependent on disposable income than other medical services.

Employment of podiatrists would grow even faster were it not for continued emphasis on controlling the costs of specialty health care. Insurers will balance the cost of sending patients to podiatrists against the cost and availability of substitute practitioners, such as physicians and physical therapists. Opportunities will be better for board-certified podiatrists, because many managed care organizations require board-certification. Opportunities for newly trained podiatrists will be better in group medical practices, clinics, and health networks than in a traditional solo practice. Establishing a practice will be most difficult in the areas surrounding colleges of podiatric medicine because podiatrists are concentrated in these locations.

Earnings

According to a survey by Podiatry Management, median net income of podiatrists was about $91,400 in 1996. Earnings vary according to practice size and location, and years of experience.

According to a survey by the American Podiatric Medical Association, average net income for podiatrists in private practice was $108,156 in 1995. Those practicing for less than two years earned an average of $44,662; those practicing 16 to 30 years earned an average of $141,135.

Related Occupations

Workers in other occupations who apply scientific knowledge to prevent, diagnose, and treat disorders and injuries are chiropractors, dentists, optometrists, physicians, and veterinarians.

Sources of Additional Information

For information on podiatric medicine as a career, contact:

❏ American Podiatric Medical Association, 9312 Old Georgetown Rd., Bethesda, MD 20814-1621. Homepage: http://www.apma.org

Information on colleges of podiatric medicine, entrance requirements, curriculums, and student financial aid is available from:

❏ American Association of Colleges of Podiatric Medicine, 1350 Piccard Dr., Suite 322, Rockville, MD 20850-4307. Homepage: HYPERLINK http://www.aacpm.org

Veterinarians

(D.O.T. 073.)

Significant Points

★ *Graduation from an accredited college of veterinary medicine and a license to practice are required.*

★ *Competition for admission to veterinary school is keen.*

★ *Job prospects may be better for those who specialize in farm animals than for small animal practitioners because fewer graduates have a desire to work in rural and isolated areas.*

Nature of the Work

Veterinarians play a major role in the health care of pets, livestock, and zoo, sporting, and laboratory animals. Veterinarians also use their skills to protect humans against diseases carried by animals, and conduct clinical research on human and animal health problems.

Most veterinarians perform clinical work in private practices. About one-half of these veterinarians predominately or exclusively treat small animals. Small animal practitioners usually care for companion animals, such as dogs and cats, but also treat birds, reptiles, rabbits, and other animals that may be kept as pets. Some veterinarians work in mixed animal practices, where they see pigs, goats, sheep, and some nondomestic animals, in addition to companion animals. Veterinarians in clinical practice diagnose animal health problems, vaccinate against diseases such as distemper and rabies, medicate animals with infections or illnesses, treat and dress wounds, set fractures, perform surgery, and advise owners about feeding, behavior, and breeding.

A smaller number of private practice veterinarians work exclusively with large animals, focusing mostly on horses or cows, but may care for all kinds of food animals. These veterinarians usually drive to farms or ranches to provide veterinary services for herds or individual animals. Much of their work involves preventive care in order to maintain the health of food animals. They test for and vaccinate against diseases, and consult with farm or ranch owners and managers on production, feeding, and housing issues. They also treat and dress wounds, set fractures, perform surgery—including cesarean sections on birthing animals—and do artificial insemination. Veterinarians also euthanize animals when necessary.

Veterinarians who treat animals use surgical instruments; medical equipment, such as stethoscopes; and diagnostic equipment, such as radiology machines.

Veterinarians contribute to human as well as animal health. A number of veterinarians work with physicians and scientists as they research better ways to prevent and treat human health problems such as cancer, AIDS, and alcohol or drug abuse. Some test the effects of drug therapies, antibiotics, or new surgical techniques on animals. Veterinarians who are livestock inspectors check animals for transmissible diseases, advise owners on treatment, and may quarantine animals. Veterinarians who are meat, poultry, or egg product inspectors examine slaughtering and processing plants, check live animals and carcasses for disease, and enforce government regulations regarding food purity and sanitation. Some veterinarians care for zoo or aquarium animals, or for laboratory animals.

Working Conditions

Veterinarians often work long hours, with nearly half spending 50 or more hours on the job. Those in group practices may take turns being on call for evening, night, or weekend work, and solo practitioners may work extended and weekend hours responding to emergencies and squeezing in unexpected appointments.

Veterinarians in large animal practice also spend time driving between office and farm or ranch. They work outdoors in all kinds of weather, and may have to treat animals or perform surgery under less-than-sanitary conditions. When working with animals that are frightened or in pain, veterinarians risk being bitten, kicked, or scratched.

Employment

Veterinarians held about 58,000 jobs in 1996. About a third were self-employed, in solo or group practices. Most others were employees of a practice. The federal government employed about 2,000 civilian veterinarians, chiefly in the U.S. Department of Agriculture, and about 500 military veterinarians in the U.S. Army and U.S. Air Force. Other employers of veterinarians are state and local governments, colleges of veterinary medicine, medical schools, research laboratories, animal food companies, and pharmaceutical companies. A few veterinarians work for zoos. Most veterinarians caring for zoo animals are private practitioners who contract with zoos to provide services, usually on a part-time basis.

Although veterinarians are located in every state, in 1996 about three out of ten establishments providing veterinary services were located in just four states: California, Florida, New York, and Texas.

Training, Other Qualifications, and Advancement

Prospective veterinarians must graduate from a four-year program at an accredited college of veterinary medicine with a Doctor of Veterinary Medicine (DVM or VMD) degree and obtain a license to practice. There are 27 colleges in 26 states that meet accreditation standards set by the Council on Edu-

cation of the American Veterinary Medical Association. The prerequisites for admission vary by veterinary medical college. Many do not actually require a bachelor's degree for entrance, but all require a significant number of credit hours at the undergraduate level, ranging from 45 to 90 semester hours. Preveterinary courses emphasize the sciences, and veterinary medical colleges typically require classes in organic and inorganic chemistry, physics, biochemistry, general biology, animal biology, animal nutrition, genetics, vertebrate embryology, cell or microbiology, zoology, and systemic physiology. Some programs require calculus; some require only statistics, college algebra and trigonometry, or precalculus; and others require no math at all. Most veterinary medical colleges also require some core courses, including English or literature, social science, and the humanities. Although a bachelor's degree is generally not required for entry to veterinary medical school, most of the students admitted have completed an undergraduate program.

Most veterinary medical colleges will only consider applicants who have a minimum grade point average (GPA). The required GPA varies by school from a low of 2.5 to a high of 3.2, based on a maximum GPA of 4.0. However, the average GPA of candidates at most schools is higher than these minimums. Those who receive offers of admission usually have a GPA of 3.0 or better.

In addition to satisfying preveterinary course requirements, applicants must also submit test scores from the Graduate Record Examination (GRE), the Veterinary College Admission Test (VCAT), or the Medical College Admission Test (MCAT), depending on the preference of each college.

Veterinary medical colleges also weigh heavily a candidate's veterinary and animal experience in the admissions process. Formal experience, such as work with veterinarians or scientists in clinics, agribusiness, research, or in some area of health science, is particularly advantageous. Less formal experience, such as working with animals on a farm, ranch, stable, or animal shelter, is also helpful. Students must demonstrate ambition and eagerness to work with animals.

Competition for admission to veterinary school is keen. The number of accredited veterinary colleges has remained at 27 since 1983, while the number of applicants has risen. About one in three applicants was accepted in 1996. Most veterinary medical colleges are public, state-supported institutions, and reserve the majority of their openings for in-state residents. Twenty states that do not have a veterinary medical college agree to pay a fee or subsidy to help cover the cost of veterinary education for a limited number of their residents at one or more out-of-state colleges. Nonresident students who are admitted under such a contract arrangement may have to

pay out-of-state tuition, or they may have to repay their state of residency all or part of the subsidy that was provided to the contracting college. Residents of the remaining four states and the District of Columbia may apply to any of the 27 veterinary medical colleges as an at-large applicant. The number of positions available to at-large applicants is very limited at most schools, making admission difficult.

While in veterinary medical college, students receive additional academic instruction and are exposed to clinical procedures such as diagnosing and treating animal diseases and performing surgery. They also do laboratory work in anatomy, biochemistry, and other scientific and medical subjects. At most veterinary medical colleges, students who plan a career in research can earn both a DVM and a Doctor of Philosophy (Ph.D.) degree at the same time.

Veterinary graduates who plan to work with specific types of animals or specialize in a clinical area, such as pathology, surgery, radiology, or laboratory animal medicine, usually complete a one-year internship. Interns receive only a small salary, but usually find that their internship experience leads to higher starting salaries relative to other starting veterinarians. Veterinarians who seek board certification in a specialty must also complete a two- to three-year residency program which provides intensive training in one of the following areas: Internal medicine, oncology, radiology, surgery, dermatology, anesthesiology, neurology, cardiology, ophthalmology, or exotic small animal medicine.

All states and the District of Columbia require that veterinarians be licensed before they can practice. The only exemptions are for veterinarians working for some federal agencies and some state governments. Licensing is controlled by the states and is not strictly uniform, although all states require successful completion of the D.V.M. degree—or equivalent education—and passage of a national board examination. The Educational Commission for Foreign Veterinary Graduates (ECFVG) grants certification to individuals trained outside the U.S. who demonstrate that they meet specified English language and clinical proficiency requirements. ECFVG certification fulfills the educational requirement for licensure in all states except Nebraska.

Applicants for licensure satisfy the examination requirement by passing the National Board Examination (NBE) and the Clinical Competency Test (CCT). The NBE comprises 400 multiple choice questions covering all aspects of veterinary medicine and takes one day to complete. The CCT is a half-day examination consisting of 14 problems covering real-life situations in which the candidate is given a set of facts and must choose the correct course of action for the patient. Many states permit candidates to take the NBE in their third year of veterinary school, but those who pass must still graduate with the D.V.M. before they can be licensed.

The majority of states also require candidates to pass a state jurisprudence examination, covering state laws and regulations. Some states also do additional testing on clinical competency. There are very few reciprocal agreements between states, making it difficult for a veterinarian to practice in a new state without first taking another state examination.

Thirty-nine states have continuing education requirements for licensed veterinarians. Requirements differ by state, and may involve attending a class or otherwise demonstrating knowledge of recent medical and veterinary advances.

Most veterinarians begin as employees or partners in established practices. Despite the substantial financial investment in equipment, office space, and staff, many veterinarians with experience set up their own practice or purchase an established one.

Newly trained veterinarians may become U.S. government meat and poultry inspectors, disease-control workers, epidemiologists, research assistants, or commissioned officers in the U.S. Public Health Service, U.S. Army, or U.S. Air Force. A state license may be required.

Prospective veterinarians must have good manual dexterity. They should have an affinity for animals and the ability to get along with animal owners. They must also be able to make decisions in emergencies.

Job Outlook

Employment of veterinarians is expected to grow faster than the average for all occupations through the year 2006. Job openings stemming from the need to replace veterinarians who retire or otherwise leave the labor force will be almost as numerous as new jobs resulting from employment growth over the 1996–2006 period.

Most veterinarians practice in animal hospitals or clinics, many of whom care primarily for companion animals. The number of pets is expected to increase more slowly during the projection period than in the previous decade, partly because the large baby-boom generation is aging and will acquire fewer dogs and cats. Slower pet population growth may curtail the demand for veterinarians who specialize in small animals. Nevertheless, new technologies and medical advancements will permit veterinarians to offer more and better care to animals. Pet owners are becoming more aware of the availability of advanced care. They may increasingly take advantage of nontraditional veterinary services such as preventive dental care, and more willingly pay for intensive care than in the past. Veterinarians who enter small animal practice may face competition. Large numbers of new graduates continue to be attracted to small animal medicine because they prefer to deal with pets, and live and work near or in populated areas. However, an oversupply does not necessarily limit the ability of veterinarians to find employment or set up and maintain a practice. It could result in more veterinarians taking positions requiring much evening or weekend work to accommodate the extended hours of operation which more practices are offering. Others could take salaried positions in retail stores offering limited veterinary services. Self-employed veterinarians may have to work harder and longer to build a sufficient clientele.

The number of jobs for large animal veterinarians is expected to grow slowly because productivity gains in the agricultural production industry mean demand for fewer veterinarians to treat food animals. Nevertheless, job prospects may be better for veterinarians who specialize in farm animals than for small animal practitioners because fewer veterinary medical college graduates have the desire to work in rural or isolated areas.

Continued support for public health and food safety, disease control programs, and biomedical research on human health problems will contribute to the demand for veterinarians, although such positions are relatively few in number. Also, anticipated budget tightening in the federal government may lead to lower funding levels for some programs, limiting job growth. Veterinarians with training in public health and epidemiology should have the best opportunities for a career in the federal government.

Earnings

Average starting salaries of 1995 veterinary medical college graduates varied by type of practice or employing industry, as indicated by table 1.

Table 1. Average starting salaries of veterinary medical college graduates, 1995

All graduates	$29,900
Large animal, exclusive	39,500
Large animal, predominate	34,300
Mixed animal	31,900
Small animal, exclusive	31,900
Small animal, predominate	31,000
Equine	27,500
Industry	
Industry/commercial	44,500
Uniformed services	41,100
State/local government	40,000
Not-for-profit	36,000
Federal government	32,800
University	19,700
Other public or corporate	34,000

SOURCE: American Veterinary Medical Association

The average income of veterinarians in private practice was $57,500 in 1995. New veterinary medical college graduates who enter the federal government usually start at $35,800. Beginning salaries were slightly higher in selected areas where the prevailing local pay level was higher. The average annual salary for veterinarians in the federal government in nonsupervisory, supervisory, and managerial positions was $57,600 in 1997.

Related Occupations

Veterinarians prevent, diagnose, and treat diseases, disorders, and injuries in animals. Those who do similar work for humans include chiropractors, dentists, optometrists, physicians, and podiatrists. Veterinarians also have extensive training in physical and life sciences, and some do scientific and medical research, closely paralleling occupations such as biological, medical, and animal scientists.

Animal trainers, animal breeders, and veterinary technicians work extensively with animals. Like veterinarians, they must have patience and feel comfortable with animals. However, the level of training required for these occupations is substantially less than that needed by veterinarians.

Sources of Additional Information

For more information on careers in veterinary medicine and a list of U.S. schools and colleges of veterinary medicine, send a letter-size, self-addressed, stamped envelope to:

❑ American Veterinary Medical Association, 1931 N. Meacham Rd., Suite 100, Schaumburg, IL 60173-4360.

For information on scholarships, grants, and loans, contact the financial aid officer at the veterinary schools to which you wish to apply.

For information on veterinary education, write to:

❑ Association of American Veterinary Medical Colleges, 1101 Vermont Ave. NW, Suite 710, Washington, DC 20005.

For information on the federal agencies that employ veterinarians and a list of addresses for each agency, write to:

❑ National Association of Federal Veterinarians, 1101 Vermont Ave. NW, Suite 710, Washington, DC 20005.

Jobs Typically Requiring a Master's Degree

Included are the following jobs:

- **Archivists and Curators**
- **Counselors**
- **Economists and Marketing Research Analysts**
- **Librarians**
- **Management Analysts and Consultants**
- **Operations Research Analysts**
- **Psychologists**
- **Speech-Language Pathologists and Audiologists**
- **Urban and Regional Planners**

Archivists and Curators

(*D.O.T.* 099.167-030; 101; 102 except .261-014 and .367-010; 109.067-014, .267-010, .281, .361, .364; 979.361)

Significant Points

✱ *Employment generally requires graduate education and substantial work experience.*

✱ *Competition for jobs is expected to be keen as qualified applicants outnumber job openings.*

Nature of the Work

Archivists, curators, museum and archives technicians, and conservators search for, acquire, appraise, analyze, describe, arrange, catalogue, restore, preserve, exhibit, maintain, and store items of lasting value so that they can be used by researchers or for exhibitions, publications, broadcasting, and other educational programs. Depending on the occupation, these items may consist of historical documents, audiovisual materials, institutional records, works of art, coins, stamps, minerals, clothing, maps, living and preserved plants and animals, buildings, computer records, or historic sites.

Archivists and curators plan and oversee the arrangement, cataloguing, and exhibition of collections and, along with technicians and conservators, maintain collections. Archivists and curators may coordinate educational and public outreach programs, such as tours, workshops, lectures, and classes, and may work with the boards of institutions to administer plans and policies. They also may conduct research on topics or items relevant to their collections. Although some duties of archivists and curators are similar, the types of items they deal with differ. Curators usually handle objects found in cultural, biological, or historical collections, such as sculptures, textiles, and paintings, while archivists mainly handle valuable records, documents, or objects that are retained because they originally accompanied and relate specifically to the document.

Archivists determine what portion of the vast amount of records maintained by various organizations, such as government agencies, corporations, or educational institutions, or by families and individuals, should be made part of permanent historical holdings, and which of these records should be put on exhibit. They maintain records in their original arrangement according to the creator's organizational scheme, and describe records to facilitate retrieval. Records may be saved on any medium, including paper, film, videotape, audiotape, electronic disk, or computer. They also may be copied onto some other format to protect the original from repeated handling, and to make them more accessible to researchers who use the records. As computers and various storage media evolve, archivists must keep abreast of technological advances in electronic information storage.

Archives may be part of a library, museum, or historical society, or may exist as a distinct archival unit within an organization or company. Archivists consider any medium containing recorded information as documents, including letters, books, and other paper documents, photographs, blueprints, audiovisual materials, and computer records. Any document which reflects organizational transactions, hierarchy, or procedures can be considered a record. Archivists often specialize in an area of history or technology so they can better determine what records in that area qualify for retention and should become part of the archives. Archivists also may work with specialized forms of records, such as manuscripts, electronic records, photographs, cartographic records, motion pictures, and sound recordings.

Computers are increasingly used to generate and maintain archival records. Professional standards for use of computers in handling archival records are still evolving. However, use of computers is expected to transform many aspects of archival collections as computer capabilities, including multimedia and worldwide web use, expand and allow more records to be stored electronically.

Curators oversee collections in museums, zoos, aquariums, botanic gardens, nature centers, and historic sites. They acquire items through purchases, gifts, field exploration, intermuseum exchanges, or, in the case of some plants and animals, reproduction. Curators also plan and prepare exhibits. In natural history museums, curators collect and observe specimens in their natural habitat. Their work involves describing and classifying species, while specially trained collection managers and technicians provide hands-on care of natural history collections. Most curators use computer databases to catalogue and organize their collections. Many also use the Internet to make information available to other curators and the public. Increasingly, curators are expected to participate in grant writing and fund raising to support their projects.

Most curators specialize in a specific field, such as botany, art, paleontology, or history. Those working in large institutions may be highly specialized. A large natural history museum, for example, would employ specialists in birds, fishes, insects, and mollusks. Some curators maintain the collection, others do research, and others perform administrative tasks. Registrars, for example, keep track of and move objects in the collection. In small institutions, with only one or a few cura-

tors, one curator may be responsible for multiple tasks, from maintaining collections to directing the affairs of museums.

Conservators manage, care for, preserve, treat, and document works of art, artifacts, and specimens. This may require substantial historical, scientific, and archaeological research. They use x rays, chemical testing, microscopes, special lights, and other laboratory equipment and techniques to examine objects and determine their condition, the need for treatment or restoration, and the appropriate method for preservation. They then document their findings and treat items to minimize deterioration or restore items to their original state. Conservators usually specialize in a particular material or group of objects, such as documents and books, paintings, decorative arts, textiles, metals, or architectural material.

Museum directors formulate policies, plan budgets, and raise funds for their museums. They coordinate activities of their staff to establish and maintain collections. As their role has evolved, museum directors increasingly need business backgrounds in addition to an understanding and empathy for the subject matter of their collections.

Museum technicians assist curators and conservators by performing various preparatory and maintenance tasks on museum items. Some museum technicians may also assist curators with research. Archives technicians help archivists organize, maintain, and provide access to historical documentary materials.

Working Conditions

The working conditions of archivists and curators vary. Some spend most of their time working with the public, providing reference assistance and educational services. Others perform research or process records, which often means working alone or in offices with only a few people. Those who restore and install exhibits or work with bulky, heavy record containers may climb, stretch, or lift. Those in zoos, botanical gardens, and other outdoor museums or historic sites frequently walk great distances.

Curators who work in large institutions may travel extensively to evaluate potential additions to the collection, organize exhibitions, and conduct research in their area of expertise. However, in small institutions, travel for curators is rare.

Employment

Archivists and curators held about 20,000 jobs in 1996. About a quarter were employed in museums, botanical gardens, and zoos, and approximately two in ten worked in educational services, mainly in college and university libraries. About four in ten worked in federal, state, and local government. Most federal archivists work for the National

Archives and Records Administration; others manage military archives in the Department of Defense. Most federal government curators work at the Smithsonian Institution, in the military museums of the Department of Defense, and in archaeological and other museums managed by the Department of Interior. All state governments have archival or historical records sections employing archivists. State and local governments have numerous historical museums, parks, libraries, and zoos employing curators.

Some large corporations have archives or records centers, employing archivists to manage the growing volume of records created or maintained as required by law or necessary to the firms' operations. Religious and fraternal organizations, professional associations, conservation organizations, major private collectors, and research firms also employ archivists and curators.

Conservators may work under contract to treat particular items, rather than as a regular employee of a museum or other institution. These conservators may work on their own as private contractors, or as an employee of a conservation laboratory or regional conservation center which contracts their services to museums.

Training, Other Qualifications, and Advancement

Employment as an archivist, conservator, or curator generally requires graduate education and substantial work experience. Many archivists and curators work in archives or museums while completing their formal education, to gain the hands-on experience that many employers seek when hiring.

Employers generally look for archivists with undergraduate and graduate degrees in history or library science, with courses in archival science. Some positions may require knowledge of the discipline related to the collection, such as business or medicine. An increasing number of archivists have a double master's degree in history and library science. There are currently no programs offering a bachelor's or master's degree in archival science. However, approximately 65 colleges and universities offer courses or practical training in archival science as part of history, library science, or another discipline. The Academy of Certified Archivists offers voluntary certification for archivists. Certification requires the applicant to have experience in the field and to pass an examination offered by the Academy.

Archivists need research and analytical ability to understand the content of documents and the context in which they were created, and to decipher deteriorated or poor quality printed matter, handwritten manuscripts, or photographs and films. A background in preservation management is often required of archivists since they are responsible for taking proper care of their records. Archivists also must be able to organize large amounts of information and write clear instructions for its retrieval and use. In addition, computer skills and the ability to work with electronic records and databases are increasingly important.

Many archives are very small, including one-person shops, with limited promotion opportunities. Archivists typically advance by transferring to a larger unit with supervisory positions. A doctorate in history, library science, or a related field may be needed for some advanced positions, such as director of a state archives.

In most museums, a master's degree in an appropriate discipline of the museum's specialty—for example, art, history, or archaeology—or museum studies is required for employment as a curator. Many employers prefer a doctoral degree, particularly for curators in natural history or science museums. Earning two graduate degrees—in museum studies (museology) and a specialized subject—gives a candidate a distinct advantage in this competitive job market. In small museums, curatorial positions may be available to individuals with a bachelor's degree. For some positions, an internship of full-time museum work supplemented by courses in museum practices is needed.

Curatorial positions often require knowledge in a number of fields. For historic and artistic conservation, courses in chemistry, physics, and art are desirable. Since curators—particularly those in small museums—may have administrative and managerial responsibilities, courses in business administration, public relations, marketing, and fundraising also are recommended. Similar to archivists, curators need computer skills and the ability to work with electronic databases. Curators also need to be familiar with digital imaging, scanning technology, and copyright infringement, since many are responsible for posting information on the Internet.

Curators must be flexible because of their wide variety of duties. They need an aesthetic sense to design and present exhibits and, in small museums, manual dexterity to erect exhibits or restore objects. Leadership ability and business skills are important for museum directors, while marketing skills are valuable for increasing museum attendance and fund raising.

In large museums, curators may advance through several levels of responsibility, eventually to museum director. Curators in smaller museums often advance to larger ones. Individual research and publications are important for advancement in larger institutions.

Museum technicians generally need a bachelor's degree in an appropriate discipline of the museum's specialty, museum studies training, or previous museum work experience, particularly in exhibit design. Similarly, archives technicians generally need a bachelor's degree in library science or history, or relevant work experience. Technician positions often serve as a stepping stone for individuals interested in archival and curatorial work. With the exception of small museums, a master's degree is needed for advancement.

When hiring conservators, employers look for a master's degree in conservation, or in a closely related field, and substantial experience. There are only a few graduate programs in museum conservation techniques in the United States. Competition for entry to these programs is keen; to qualify, a student must have a background in chemistry, archaeology or studio art, and art history, as well as work experience. For some programs, knowledge of a foreign language is also helpful. Conservation apprenticeships or internships as an undergraduate can also enhance one's admission prospects. Graduate programs last two to four years; the latter years include internship training. A few individuals enter conservation through apprenticeships with museums, nonprofit organizations, and conservators in private practice. Apprenticeships should be supplemented with courses in chemistry, studio art, and history. Apprenticeship training, although accepted, generally is a more difficult route into the conservation profession.

Relatively few schools grant a bachelor's degree in museum studies. More common are undergraduate minors or tracks of study that are part of an undergraduate degree in a related field, such as art history, history, or archaeology. Students interested in further study may obtain a master's degree in museum studies. Colleges and universities throughout the country offer master's degrees in museum studies. However, many employers feel that, while museum studies are helpful, a thorough knowledge of the museum's specialty and museum work experience are more important.

Continuing education, which enables archivists, curators, conservators, and museum technicians to keep up with developments in the field, is available through meetings, conferences, and workshops sponsored by archival, historical, and museum associations. Some larger organizations, such as the National Archives, offer such training in-house.

Job Outlook

Competition for jobs as archivists and curators is expected to be keen as qualified applicants outnumber job openings. Graduates with highly specialized training, such as master's degrees in both library science and history, with a concentration in archives or records management, and extensive computer skills should have the best opportunities for jobs as

archivists. A job as a curator is attractive to many people, and many applicants have the necessary training and subject knowledge; yet there are only a few openings. Consequently, candidates may have to work part-time, as an intern, or even as a volunteer assistant curator or research associate after completing their formal education. Substantial work experience in collection management, exhibit design, or restoration, as well as database management skills, will be necessary for permanent status. Job opportunities for curators should be best in art and history museums, since these are the largest employers in the museum industry.

The job outlook for conservators may be more favorable, particularly for graduates of conservation programs. However, competition is stiff for the limited number of openings in these programs, and applicants need a technical background. Students who qualify and successfully complete the program, have knowledge of a foreign language, and are willing to relocate will have an advantage over less qualified candidates in obtaining a position.

Employment of archivists and curators is expected to increase about as fast as the average for all occupations through the year 2006. Jobs are expected to grow as public and private organizations put more emphasis on establishing archives and organizing records and information, and as public interest in science, art, history, and technology increases. However, museums and other cultural institutions are often subject to funding cuts during recessions or periods of budget tightening, reducing demand for archivists and curators during these times. Although the rate of turnover among archivists and curators is relatively low, the need to replace workers who leave the occupation or stop working will create some additional job openings.

Earnings

Earnings of archivists and curators vary considerably by type and size of employer, and often by specialty. Average salaries in the federal government, for example, are generally higher than those in religious organizations. Salaries of curators in large, well-funded museums may be several times higher than those in small ones.

The average annual salary for all museum curators in the federal government in nonsupervisory, supervisory, and managerial positions was about $55,000 in 1997. Archivists averaged $53,600; museum specialists and technicians, $36,300; and archives technicians, $31,200.

According to a survey by the Association of Art Museum Directors, median salaries for selected workers in larger art museums in 1996 were as follows:

Director	$103,000
Curator	50,000
Senior conservator	48,500
Curatorial assistant	22,600

Related Occupations

Archivists' and curators' skills in preserving, organizing, and displaying objects or information of historical interest are shared by anthropologists, arborists, archaeologists, artifacts conservators, botanists, ethnologists, folklorists, genealogists, historians, horticulturists, information specialists, librarians, paintings restorers, records managers, and zoologists.

Sources of Additional Information

For information on archivists and on schools offering courses in archival studies, contact:

❏ Society of American Archivists, 600 South Federal St., Suite 504, Chicago, IL 60605.

For general information about careers as a curator and schools offering courses in museum studies, contact:

❏ American Association of Museums, 1575 I St. NW, Suite 400, Washington, DC 20005.

For information about conservation and preservation careers and education programs, contact:

❏ American Institute for Conservation of Historic and Artistic Works, 1717 K St. NW, Suite 301, Washington, DC 20006.

Counselors

(*D.O.T.* 045.107-010, -014, -018, -038, -042 -050, -054, -058, .117; 090.107; 094.107-010; and 169.267-026)

Significant Points

★ *About six out of ten counselors have a master's degree.*

★ *Rapid job growth is expected among rehabilitation and mental health counselors; however, budgetary con-straints may limit growth among school counselors, and employment counselors working in government.*

Nature of the Work

Counselors assist people with personal, family, educational, mental health, and career decisions and problems. Their duties depend on the individuals they serve and the settings in which they work.

School and college counselors—who work at the elementary, middle, secondary, and postsecondary school levels—help students evaluate their abilities, interests, talents, and personality characteristics so that students can develop realistic academic and career goals. Counselors use interviews, counseling sessions, tests, or other methods when evaluating and advising students. They may operate career information centers and career education programs. High school counselors advise on college majors, admission requirements, entrance exams, and financial aid, and on trade, technical school, and apprenticeship programs. They help students develop job finding skills such as resume writing and interviewing techniques. College career planning and placement counselors assist alumni or students with career development and job hunting techniques.

Elementary school counselors observe younger children during classroom and play activities and confer with their teachers and parents to evaluate their strengths, problems, or special needs. They also help students develop good study habits. They do less vocational and academic counseling than secondary school counselors.

School counselors at all levels help students understand and deal with their social, behavioral, and personal problems. They emphasize preventive and developmental counseling to provide students with the life skills needed to deal with problems before they occur, and to enhance personal, social, and academic growth. Counselors provide special services, including alcohol and drug prevention programs, and classes that teach students to handle conflicts without resorting to violence. Counselors also try to identify cases involving domestic abuse and other family problems that can affect a student's development. Counselors work with students individually, in small groups, or with entire classes. They consult and work with parents, teachers, school administrators, school psychologists, school nurses, and social workers.

Rehabilitation counselors help people deal with the personal, social, and vocational effects of their disabilities. They may counsel people with disabilities resulting from birth defects, illness or disease, accidents, or the stress of daily life. They evaluate the strengths and limitations of individuals, provide personal and vocational counseling, and may arrange for medical care, vocational training, and job placement. Rehabilitation counselors interview individuals with disabilities and their families, evaluate school and medical reports, and confer and plan with physicians, psychologists, occupational therapists, and employers to determine the capabilities and skills of the individual. Conferring with the client, they develop a rehabilitation program, which may include training to help the person develop job skills. They also work toward increasing the client's capacity to live independently.

Employment counselors help individuals make wise career decisions. They explore and evaluate the client's education, training, work history, interests, skills, and personal traits, and may arrange for aptitude and achievement tests. They also work with individuals to develop job-seeking skills and assist clients in locating and applying for jobs.

Mental health counselors emphasize prevention and work with individuals and groups to promote optimum mental health. They help individuals deal with addictions and substance abuse, suicide, stress management, problems with self-esteem, issues associated with aging, job and career concerns, educational decisions, issues of mental and emotional health, and family, parenting, and marital problems. Mental health counselors work closely with other mental health specialists, including psychiatrists, psychologists, clinical social workers, psychiatric nurses, and school counselors.

Other counseling specialties include marriage and family, multicultural, or gerontological counseling. A gerontological counselor provides services to elderly persons who face changing lifestyles due to health problems, and helps families cope with these changes. A multicultural counselor helps employers adjust to an increasingly diverse workforce.

Working Conditions

Most school counselors work the traditional nine- to ten-month school year with a two- to three-month vacation, although an increasing number are employed on 10½- or 11-month contracts. They generally have the same hours as teachers. College career planning and placement counselors may work long and irregular hours during recruiting periods.

Rehabilitation and employment counselors generally work a standard 40-hour week. Self-employed counselors and those working in mental health and community agencies often work evenings to counsel clients who work during the day.

Counselors must possess high physical and emotional energy to handle the array of problems they address. Dealing with these day-to-day problems can cause stress and emotional burnout.

Since privacy is essential for confidential and frank discussions with clients, counselors usually have private offices.

Employment

Counselors held about 175,000 jobs in 1996. (This estimate includes only vocational and educational counselors; employment data are not available for other counselors discussed in this statement, such as rehabilitation and mental health counselors.)

In addition to elementary and secondary schools and colleges and universities, counselors work in a wide variety of

public and private establishments. These include health care facilities; job training, career development, and vocational rehabilitation centers; social agencies; correctional institutions; and residential care facilities, such as halfway houses for criminal offenders and group homes for children, the aged, and the disabled. Counselors also work in organizations engaged in community improvement and social change, as well as drug and alcohol rehabilitation programs and state and local government agencies. A growing number of counselors work in health maintenance organizations, insurance companies, group practice, and private practice. This growth has been spurred by laws allowing counselors to receive payments from insurance companies, and requiring employers to provide rehabilitation and counseling services to employees.

Training, Other Qualifications, and Advancement

Recent data indicate that six out of ten counselors have a master's degree; fields of study include college student affairs, elementary or secondary school counseling, education, gerontological counseling, marriage and family counseling, substance abuse counseling, rehabilitation counseling, agency or community counseling, clinical mental health counseling, counseling psychology, career counseling, or a related field.

Graduate-level counselor education programs in colleges and universities usually are in departments of education or psychology.

Courses are grouped into eight core areas: Human growth and development; social and cultural foundations; helping relationships; groups; lifestyle and career development; appraisal; research and evaluation; and professional orientation. In an accredited program, 48 to 60 semester hours of graduate study, including a period of supervised clinical experience in counseling, are required for a master's degree. In 1996, 111 institutions offered programs in counselor education, including career, community, gerontological, mental health, school, student affairs, and marriage and family counseling, accredited by the Council for Accreditation of Counseling and Related Educational Programs (CACREP).

In 1997, 42 states and the District of Columbia had some form of counselor credentialing legislation, licensure, certification, or registry for practice outside schools. Requirements vary from state to state. In some states, credentialing is mandatory; in others, voluntary.

Many counselors elect to be nationally certified by the National Board for Certified Counselors (NBCC), which grants the general practice credential, "National Certified Counselor." To be certified, a counselor must hold a master's degree in counseling from a regionally accredited institution,

have at least two years of supervised professional counseling experience, and pass NBCC's National Counselor Examination for Licensure and Certification. This national certification is voluntary and distinct from state certification. However, in some states those who pass the national exam are exempt from taking a state certification exam. NBCC also offers specialty certification in career, gerontological, school, clinical mental health, and addictions counseling. To maintain their certification, counselors must complete 100 hours of acceptable continuing education credit every five years.

All states require school counselors to hold state school counseling certification; however, certification requirements vary from state to state. Some states require public school counselors to have both counseling and teaching certificates. Depending on the state, a master's degree in counseling and two to five years of teaching experience may be required for a counseling certificate.

Vocational and related rehabilitation agencies generally require a master's degree in rehabilitation counseling, counseling and guidance, or counseling psychology for rehabilitation counselor jobs. Some, however, may accept applicants with a bachelor's degree in rehabilitation services, counseling, psychology, sociology, or related fields. A bachelor's degree may qualify a person to work as a counseling aide, rehabilitation aide, or social service worker. Experience in employment counseling, job development, psychology, education, or social work may be helpful.

The Council on Rehabilitation Education (CORE) accredits graduate programs in rehabilitation counseling. A minimum of two years of study—including 600 hours of supervised clinical internship experience—are required for the master's degree.

In most state vocational rehabilitation agencies, applicants must pass a written examination and be evaluated by a board of examiners to obtain licensure. In addition, many employers require rehabilitation counselors to be nationally certified. To become certified by the Commission on Rehabilitation Counselor Certification, counselors must graduate from an accredited educational program, complete an internship, and pass a written examination. They are then designated as "Certified Rehabilitation Counselors." To maintain their certification, counselors must complete 100 hours of acceptable continuing education credit every five years.

Some states require counselors in public employment offices to have a master's degree; others accept a bachelor's degree with appropriate counseling courses.

Clinical mental health counselors generally have a master's degree in mental health counseling, another area of counseling, or in psychology or social work. They are voluntarily certified by the National Board for Certified Counselors. Generally, to receive certification as a clinical mental health counselor, a counselor must have a master's degree in counseling, two years of post-master's experience, a period of supervised clinical experience, a taped sample of clinical work, and a passing grade on a written examination.

Some employers provide training for newly hired counselors. Many have work-study programs so that employed counselors can earn graduate degrees. Counselors must participate in graduate studies, workshops, institutes, and personal studies to maintain their certificates and licenses.

Persons interested in counseling should have a strong interest in helping others and the ability to inspire respect, trust, and confidence. They should be able to work independently or as part of a team. Counselors follow the code of ethics associated with their respective certifications and licenses.

Prospects for advancement vary by counseling field. School counselors may move to a larger school; become directors or supervisors of counseling, guidance, or pupil personnel services; or, usually with further graduate education, become counselor educators, counseling psychologists, or school administrators. Some counselors also may advance to work at the state department of education.

Rehabilitation, mental health, and employment counselors may become supervisors or administrators in their agencies. Some counselors move into research, consulting, or college teaching, or go into private or group practice.

Job Outlook

Overall employment of counselors is expected to grow about as fast as the average for all occupations through the year 2006. In addition, replacement needs should increase significantly as a large number of counselors reach retirement age.

Employment of school and vocational counselors is expected to grow as a result of increasing enrollments, particularly in secondary and postsecondary schools, state legislation requiring counselors in elementary schools, and the expanded responsibilities of counselors. Counselors are becoming more involved in crisis and preventive counseling, helping students deal with issues ranging from drug and alcohol abuse to death and suicide. Also, the growing diversity of student populations is presenting challenges to counselors in dealing with multicultural issues. Job growth among counselors, however, may be dampened by budgetary constraints. High student-to-counselor ratios in many schools could increase even more as student enrollments grow. When funding is tight, schools usually prefer to hire new teachers before adding counselors in an effort to keep classroom sizes at acceptable levels.

Rapid job growth is expected among rehabilitation and mental health counselors. Under managed care systems, insurance companies increasingly provide for reimbursement of counselors, enabling many counselors to move from schools and government agencies to private practice. Counselors are also forming group practices to receive expanded insurance coverage. The number of people who need rehabilitation services will rise as advances in medical technology continue to save lives that only a few years ago would have been lost. In addition, legislation requiring equal employment rights for people with disabilities will spur demand for counselors. Counselors not only will help individuals with disabilities with their transition into the work force, but also will help companies comply with the law. Employers are also increasingly offering employee assistance programs which provide mental health and alcohol and drug abuse services. A growing number of people are expected to use these services as the elderly population grows, and as society focuses on ways of developing mental well-being, such as controlling stress associated with job and family responsibilities.

As with other government jobs, the number of employment counselors, who work primarily for state and local government, could be limited by budgetary constraints. However, demand for government employment counseling may grow as new welfare laws require welfare recipients to find jobs. Opportunities for employment counselors working in private job training services should grow as counselors provide skill training and other services to laid-off workers, experienced workers seeking a new or second career, full-time homemakers seeking to enter or reenter the workforce, and workers who want to upgrade their skills.

Earnings

Median earnings for full-time educational and vocational counselors were about $35,800 a year in 1996. The middle 50 percent earned between $25,600 and $48,500 a year. The bottom 10 percent earned less than $18,600 a year, while the top 10 percent earned over $60,100 a year.

According to the Educational Research Service, the average salary of public school counselors in the 1995–96 academic year was about $44,100. Many school counselors are compensated on the same pay scale as teachers. School counselors can earn additional income working summers in the school system or in other jobs.

Self-employed counselors who have well-established practices, as well as counselors employed in group practices, generally have the highest earnings, as do some counselors working for private firms, such as insurance companies and private rehabilitation companies.

Related Occupations

Counselors help people evaluate their interests, abilities, and disabilities, and deal with personal, social, academic, and career problems. Others who help people in similar ways include college and student affairs workers, teachers, personnel workers and managers, human services workers, social workers, psychologists, psychiatrists, psychiatric nurses, members of the clergy, occupational therapists, training and employee development specialists, and equal employment opportunity/affirmative action specialists.

Sources of Additional Information

For general information about counseling, as well as information on specialties such as school, college, mental health, rehabilitation, multicultural, career, marriage and family, and gerontological counseling, contact:

❏ American Counseling Association, 5999 Stevenson Ave., Alexandria, VA 22304.

For information on accredited counseling and related training programs, contact:

❏ Council for Accreditation of Counseling and Related Educational Programs, American Counseling Association, 5999 Stevenson Ave., Alexandria, VA 22304.

For information on national certification requirements for counselors, contact:

❏ National Board for Certified Counselors, 3 Terrace Way, Suite D, Greensboro, NC 27403. Homepage: http://www.nbcc.org/

For information on certification requirements for rehabilitation counselors and a list of accredited rehabilitation education programs, contact:

❏ Council on Rehabilitation Counselor Certification, 1835 Rohlwing Rd., Suite E, Rolling Meadows, IL 60008.

State departments of education can supply information on colleges and universities that offer approved guidance and counseling training for state certification and licensure requirements.

State employment service offices have information about job opportunities and entrance requirements for counselors.

Economists and Marketing Research Analysts

(*D.O.T.* 050.067)

Significant Points

✶ *Demand for qualified marketing research analysts should be strong.*

✶ *Candidates who hold a master's degree in economics have much better employment prospects than bachelor's degree holders.*

Nature of the Work

Economists. Economists study the ways society distributes scarce resources such as land, labor, raw materials, and machinery to produce goods and services. They conduct research, collect and analyze data, monitor economic trends, and develop forecasts. They research issues such as energy costs, inflation, interest rates, imports, or employment levels.

Most economists are concerned with practical applications of economic policy in a particular area. They use their understanding of economic relationships to advise businesses and other organizations, including insurance companies, banks, securities firms, industry and trade associations, labor unions, and government agencies. Economists use mathematical models to develop programs predicting answers to questions such as the nature and length of business cycles, the effects of a specific rate of inflation on the economy, or the effects of tax legislation on unemployment levels.

Economists devise methods and procedures for obtaining the data they need. For example, sampling techniques may be used to conduct a survey, and various mathematical modeling techniques may be used to develop forecasts. Preparing reports on the results of their research is an important part of the economist's job. Relevant data must be reviewed and analyzed, applicable tables and charts prepared, and the results presented in clear, concise language that can be understood by non-economists. Presenting economic and statistical concepts in a meaningful way is particularly important for economists whose research is directed toward making policies for an organization.

Economists who work for government agencies may assess economic conditions in the United States or abroad, in order to estimate the economic effects of specific changes in legislation or public policy. They may study areas such as how the dollar's fluctuation against foreign currencies affects import and export levels. The majority of government economists work in the area of agriculture, labor, or quantitative analysis; some economists work in almost every area of government. For example, some economists in the U.S. Department of Commerce study production, distribution, and consumption of commodities produced overseas, while economists employed with the Bureau of Labor Statistics analyze data on the domestic economy such as prices, wages, employment, productivity, and safety and health. An economist working in state or local government might analyze data on the growth of school-aged populations, prison growth, and employment and unemployment rates, in order to project spending needs for future years.

Marketing Research Analysts. Marketing research analysts are concerned with the potential sales of a product or service. They analyze statistical data on past sales to predict future sales. They gather data on competitors and analyze prices, sales, and methods of marketing and distribution. Like economists, marketing research analysts devise methods and procedures for obtaining the data they need. They often design telephone, personal, or mail interview surveys to assess consumer preferences. The surveys are usually conducted by trained interviewers under the marketing research analyst's direction. Once the data are compiled, marketing research analysts evaluate it. They then make recommendations to their client or employer based upon their findings. They provide a company's management with information needed to make decisions on the promotion, distribution, design, and pricing of company products or services, or to determine the advisability of adding new lines of merchandise, opening new branches, or otherwise diversifying the company's operations. Analysts may conduct opinion research to determine public attitudes on various issues. This can help political or business leaders and others assess public support for their electoral prospects or advertising policies.

Working Conditions

Economists and marketing research analysts have structured work schedules. They often work alone, writing reports, preparing statistical charts, and using computers, but they may also be an integral part of a research team. Most work under pressure of deadlines and tight schedules, and sometimes must work overtime. Their routine may be interrupted by special requests for data, as well as by the need to attend meetings or conferences; regular travel may be necessary to do this.

Employment

Economists and marketing research analysts held about 51,000 jobs in 1996. Private industry, particularly economic and marketing research firms, management consulting firms, banks, securities and commodities brokers, and computer and data processing companies, employed about three out of four salaried workers. The remainder, primarily economists, were employed by a wide range of government agencies, primarily in the state government. The Departments of Labor, Agriculture, and Commerce are the largest federal employers of economists. A number of economists and marketing research analysts combine a full-time job in government, academia, or business with part-time or consulting work in another setting.

Employment of economists and marketing research analysts is concentrated in large cities. Some economists work abroad for companies with major international operations, for U.S. government agencies, and for international organizations like the World Bank and the United Nations.

Besides the jobs described above, many economists and marketing research analysts held economics and marketing faculty positions in colleges and universities. Economics and marketing faculty have flexible work schedules, and may divide their time among teaching, research, consulting, and administration.

Training, Other Qualifications, and Advancement

Graduate training is required for most private sector economist and marketing research analyst jobs, and for advancement to more responsible positions. Economics includes many specialties at the graduate level, such as advanced economic theory, econometrics, international economics, and labor economics. Students should select graduate schools strong in specialties in which they are interested. Marketing research analysts may earn advanced degrees in economics, business administration, marketing, statistics, or some closely related discipline. Some schools help graduate students find internships or part-time employment in government agencies, economic consulting firms, financial institutions, or marketing research firms prior to graduation.

In the federal government, candidates for entry-level economist positions must have a bachelor's degree with a minimum of 21 semester hours of economics and three hours of statistics, accounting, or calculus. Competition is keen for those positions which require only a bachelor's degree, however, and additional education or superior academic performance is likely to be required to gain employment.

For a job as an instructor in many junior and some community colleges, a master's degree is the minimum requirement. In most colleges and universities, however, a Ph.D. is necessary for appointment as an instructor. A Ph.D. and extensive publications in academic journals are required for a professorship, tenure, and promotion.

Whether working in government, industry, research organizations, marketing, or consulting firms, economists and marketing research analysts who have a graduate degree usually qualify for more responsible research and administrative positions. A Ph.D. is necessary for top economist or marketing positions in many organizations. Many corporation and government executives have a strong background in economics or marketing.

A bachelor's degree with a major in economics or marketing is generally not sufficient to obtain positions as economist or marketing analyst, but is excellent preparation for many entry-level positions as a research assistant, administrative or management trainee, marketing interviewer, or any of a number of professional sales jobs.

Economics majors can choose from a variety of courses, ranging from those which are intensely mathematical such as microeconomics, macroeconomics, and econometrics, to more philosophical courses such as the history of economic thought.

In addition to courses in business, marketing, and consumer behavior, marketing majors should take other liberal arts and social science courses, including economics, psychology, English, and sociology. Because of the importance of quantitative skills to economists and marketing researchers, courses in mathematics, statistics, econometrics, sampling theory and survey design, and computer science are extremely helpful.

Aspiring economists and marketing research analysts should gain experience gathering and analyzing data, conducting interviews or surveys, and writing reports on their findings while in college. This experience can prove invaluable later in obtaining a full-time position in the field, since much of their work, in the beginning, may center around these duties. With experience, economists and marketing research analysts eventually are assigned their own research projects.

Those considering careers as economists or marketing research analysts should be able to work accurately because much time is spent on data analysis. Patience and persistence are necessary qualities since economists and marketing research analysts must spend long hours on independent study and problem solving. At the same time, they must work well with others, especially marketing research analysts, who often oversee interviews for a wide variety of individuals. Economists and marketing research analysts must be able to present their findings, both orally and in writing, in a clear, meaningful way.

Job Outlook

Employment of economists and marketing research analysts is expected to grow about as fast as the average for all occupations through the year 2006. Most job openings, however, are likely to result from the need to replace experienced workers who transfer to other occupations, retire, or leave the labor force for other reasons.

Opportunities for economists should be best in private industry, especially in research, testing, and consulting firms, as more companies contract out for economic research services. Competition, the growing complexity of the global economy, and increased reliance on quantitative methods for analyzing the current value of future funds, business trends, sales, and purchasing should spur demand for economists. The growing need for economic analyses in virtually every industry should result in additional jobs for economists. Employment of economists in the federal government should decline more slowly than the rate projected for the entire federal workforce. Average employment growth is expected among economists in state and local government.

An advanced degree coupled with a strong background in economic theory, mathematics, statistics, and econometrics provides the basis for acquiring any specialty within the field. Those skilled in quantitative techniques and their application to economic modeling and forecasting, using computers, coupled with good communications skills, should have the best job opportunities.

Those who graduate with a bachelor's degree in economics through the year 2006 will face keen competition for the limited number of economist positions for which they qualify. They will qualify for a number of other positions, however, where they can take advantage of their economic knowledge in conducting research, developing surveys, or analyzing data. Many graduates with bachelor's degrees will find good jobs in industry and business as management or sales trainees, or administrative assistants. Economists with good quantitative skills are qualified for research assistant positions in a broad range of fields. Those who meet state certification requirements may become high school economics teachers. The demand for secondary school economics teachers is expected to grow as economics becomes an increasingly important and popular course.

Candidates who hold a master's degree in economics have much better employment prospects than bachelor's degree holders. Many businesses, research and consulting firms, and government agencies seek master's degree holders who have strong computer and quantitative skills and can perform complex research, but do not command the higher salary of a Ph.D. Ph.D. holders are likely to face competition for teaching positions in colleges and universities.

Demand for qualified marketing research analysts should be strong due to an increasingly competitive economy. Marketing research provides organizations valuable feedback from purchasers, allowing companies to evaluate consumer satisfaction and more effectively plan for the future. As companies seek to expand their market and consumers become better informed, the need for marketing professionals is increasing. Opportunities for marketing research analysts with graduate degrees should be good in a wide range of employment settings, particularly in marketing research firms, as companies find it more profitable to contract out for marketing research services rather than support their own marketing department. Other organizations, including financial services organizations, health care institutions, advertising firms, manufacturing firms producing consumer goods, and insurance companies may offer job opportunities for marketing research analysts.

A strong background in marketing, mathematics, statistics, and econometrics provides the basis for acquiring any specialty within the field. Those skilled in quantitative techniques and their application to marketing research using computers should have the best job opportunities. Like economists, marketing research graduates with related work experience in a closely related business field or industry should have the best job opportunities.

Those with only a bachelor's degree but who have a strong background in mathematics, statistics, survey design, and computer science may be hired by private firms as research assistants or interviewers.

Earnings

According to a 1997 salary survey by the National Association of Colleges and Employers, persons with a bachelor's degree in economics received offers averaging $31,300 a year; for those with a bachelor's degrees in marketing, $27,900.

The median base salary of business economists in 1996 was $73,000, according to a survey by the National Association of Business Economists. The median entry-level salary was about $35,000, with most new entrants' possessing a masters degree. Ninety-three percent of the respondents held advanced degrees. The highest salaries were reported by those who had a Ph.D., with a median salary of $85,000. Master's degree holders earned a median salary of $65,500, while bachelor's degree holders earned $60,000. The highest paid business economists were in the securities and investment industry, which reported a median income of $100,000, followed by banking and mining at $93,000 and the nondurable manufacturing industry at $87,000. The lowest paid were in government and nonprofit research.

The federal government recognizes education and experience in certifying applicants for entry level positions. The entrance salary for economists having a bachelor's degree was about $19,500 a year in 1997; however, those with superior academic records could begin at $24,200. Those having a master's degree could qualify for positions at an annual salary of $29,600. Those with a Ph.D. could begin at $35,800, while some individuals with experience and an advanced degree could start at $42,900. Starting salaries were slightly higher in selected areas where the prevailing local pay was higher. The average annual salary for economists employed by the federal government was $63,870 a year in early 1997.

Related Occupations

Economists are concerned with understanding and interpreting financial matters, among other subjects. Other jobs in this area include financial managers, financial analysts, underwriters, actuaries, credit analysts, loan officers, and budget officers.

Marketing research analysts do research to find out how well products or services are received by the market. This may include the planning, implementation, and analysis of surveys to determine people's needs and preferences. Other jobs using these skills include psychologists, sociologists, and urban and regional planners.

Sources of Additional Information

For information on careers in economics and business, contact:

❑ National Association of Business Economists, 1233 20th St. NW, Suite 505, Washington, DC 20036.

For information about careers and salaries in marketing research, contact:

❑ Marketing Research Association, 2189 Silas Deane Hwy., Suite 5, Rocky Hill, CT 06067.

❑ Council of American Survey Research Organizations, 3 Upper Devon, Port Jefferson, NY 11777.

Information on obtaining a job with the federal government may be obtained from the Office of Personnel Management through a telephone-based system. Consult your telephone directory under U.S. government for a local number or call (912) 757-3000 (TDD 912 744-2299). That number is not toll-free and charges may result. Information also is available from their Internet site: http://www.usajobs.opm.gov

Librarians

(D.O.T. 100 except .367-018; 109.267-014)

Significant Points

✴ *A master's degree in library science is usually required; special librarians may need an additional graduate or professional degree.*

✴ *Slow employment growth, coupled with an increasing number of master of library science graduates, will result in more applicants competing for fewer jobs.*

✴ *Applicants for librarian jobs in large cities or suburban areas will face competition, while those willing to work in rural areas should have better job prospects.*

Nature of the Work

The traditional concept of a library is being redefined, from a place to access paper records or books, to one which also houses the most advanced media, including CD-ROM, the Internet, virtual libraries, and remote access to a wide range of resources. Consequently, librarians are increasingly combining traditional duties with tasks involving quickly changing technology. Librarians assist people in finding information and using it effectively in their personal and professional lives. They must have knowledge of a wide variety of scholarly and public information sources, and follow trends related to publishing, computers, and the media to effectively oversee the selection and organization of library materials. Librarians manage staff and develop and direct information programs and systems for the public, to ensure information is organized to meet users' needs.

There are generally three aspects of library work—user services, technical services, and administrative services; most librarian positions incorporate all three aspects. Even librarians specializing in one of these areas may perform other responsibilities. Librarians in user services, such as reference and children's librarians, work with the public to help them find the information they need. This may involve analyzing users' needs to determine what information is appropriate, and searching for, acquiring, and providing information. It also includes an instructional role, such as showing users how to access information. For example, librarians commonly help users navigate the Internet, showing them how to most efficiently search for relevant information. Librarians in technical services, such as acquisitions and cataloguing, acquire and prepare materials for use and may not deal directly with the public. Librarians in administrative services oversee the management and planning of libraries, negotiate contracts for services, materials, and equipment, supervise library employees, perform public relations and fundraising duties, prepare budgets, and direct activities to ensure that everything functions properly.

In small libraries or information centers, librarians generally handle all aspects of the work. They read book reviews, publishers' announcements, and catalogues to keep up with current literature and other available resources, and select and purchase materials from publishers, wholesalers, and distributors. Librarians prepare new materials for use by classifying them by subject matter, and describe books and other library materials in a way users can easily find them. They supervise assistants who prepare cards, computer records, or other access tools that direct users to resources. In large libraries, librarians may specialize in a single area, such as acquisitions, cataloguing, bibliography, reference, special collections, or ad-ministration. Teamwork is increasingly important to ensure quality service to the public.

Librarians also compile lists of books, periodicals, articles, and audiovisual materials on particular subjects, analyze collections, and recommend materials to be acquired. They may collect and organize books, pamphlets, manuscripts, and other materials in a specific field, such as rare books, genealogy, or music. In addition, they coordinate programs such as storytelling for children, and literacy skills and book talks for adults; conduct classes on Internet use and other topics; publicize services; provide reference help; supervise staff; prepare budgets; write grants; and oversee other administrative matters.

Librarians may be classified according to the type of library in which they work—public libraries, school library media centers, academic libraries, and special libraries. They may work with specific groups, such as children, young adults, adults, or the disadvantaged. In school library media centers, librarians help teachers develop curricula, acquire materials for classroom instruction, and sometimes team teach.

Librarians may also work in information centers or libraries maintained by government agencies, corporations, law firms, advertising agencies, museums, professional associations, medical centers, hospitals, religious organizations, and research laboratories. They build and arrange the organization's information resources, usually limited to subjects of special interest to the organization. These special librarians can provide vital information services by preparing abstracts and indexes of current periodicals, organizing bibliographies, or analyzing background information and preparing reports on areas of particular interest. For instance, a special librarian working for a corporation may provide the sales department with information on competitors or new developments affecting their field.

Many libraries have access to remote databases, as well as maintaining their own computerized databases. The widespread use of automation in libraries makes database searching skills important to librarians. Librarians develop and index databases and act as trainers to help users develop searching skills to obtain the information they need. Some libraries are forming consortiums with other libraries through electronic mail (e-mail). This allows patrons to submit information requests to several libraries at once. Use of the Internet and other worldwide computer systems is also expanding the amount of available reference information. Librarians must be aware of how to use these resources to locate information.

Librarians with appropriate computer and information systems skills may work as automated systems librarians, planning and operating computer systems, and information science librarians, designing information storage and retrieval systems and developing procedures for collecting, organizing, interpreting, and classifying information. These librarians may analyze and plan for future information needs. The increased use of automated information systems enables librarians to focus on administrative and budgeting responsibilities, grant writing, and specialized research requests, while delegating more technical and user services responsibilities to technicians.

Increasingly, librarians apply their information management and research skills to arenas outside of libraries—for example, database development, reference tool development, information systems, publishing, Internet coordination, marketing, and training of database users. Entrepreneurial librarians may start their own consulting practices, acting as free-lance librarians or information brokers and providing services to other libraries, businesses, or government agencies.

Working Conditions

Assisting users in obtaining information for their jobs, recreational purposes, and other needs can be challenging and satisfying; working with users under deadlines may be demanding and stressful. Selecting and ordering new materials can be stimulating and rewarding. However, librarians also spend a significant portion of time at their desks or in front of computer terminals; extended work at video display terminals may cause eyestrain and headaches.

More than three out of ten librarians work part-time. Public and college librarians often work weekends and evenings, and may have to work some holidays. School librarians generally have the same workday schedule as classroom teachers and similar vacation schedules. Special librarians may work normal business hours, but in fast-paced industries, such as advertising or legal services, may work longer hours during peak times.

Employment

Librarians held about 154,000 jobs in 1996. Most were in school and academic libraries; others were in public and special libraries. A small number of librarians worked for hospitals and religious organizations. Others worked for governments at all levels.

Training, Other Qualifications, and Advancement

A master's degree in library science (MLS) is necessary for librarian positions in most public, academic, and special libraries, and in some school libraries. In the federal government, an MLS or the equivalent in education and experience is required. Many colleges and universities offer MLS programs, but employers often prefer graduates of the approximately 50 schools accredited by the American Library Association. Most MLS programs require a bachelor's degree; any liberal arts major is appropriate.

Most MLS programs take one year to complete; others take two. A typical graduate program includes courses in the foundations of library and information science, including the history of books and printing, intellectual freedom and censorship, and the role of libraries and information in society. Other basic courses cover material selection and processing; the organization of information; reference tools and strategies; and user services. Courses are adapted to educate librarians to use new resources brought about by advancing technology such as on-line reference systems, Internet search methods, and automated circulation systems. Course options can include resources for children or young adults; classification, cataloguing, indexing, and abstracting; library administration; and library automation.

An MLS provides general preparation for library work, but some individuals specialize in a particular area such as reference, technical services, or children's services. A Ph.D. in library and information science is advantageous for a college teaching position, or a top administrative job in a college or university library or large library system.

In special libraries, an MLS is usually required. In addition, most special librarians supplement their education with knowledge of the subject specialization, sometimes earning a master's, doctoral, or professional degree in the subject. Subject specializations include medicine, law, business, engineering, and the natural and social sciences. For example, a librarian working for a law firm may also be a licensed attorney, holding both library science and law degrees. In some jobs, knowledge of a foreign language is needed.

State certification requirements for public school librarians vary widely. Most states require that school librarians, often called library media specialists, be certified as teachers and have courses in library science. In some cases, an MLS, perhaps with a library media specialization, or a master's in education with a specialty in school library media or educational media, is needed. Some states require certification of public librarians employed in municipal, county, or regional library systems.

Librarians participate in continuing training once they are on the job, to keep abreast of new information systems brought about by changing technology.

Experienced librarians may advance to administrative positions, such as department head, library director, or chief information officer.

Job Outlook

Slow employment growth, coupled with an increasing number of MLS graduates, will result in more applicants competing for fewer jobs. Applicants for librarian jobs in large cities or suburban areas, where most graduates prefer to work, will face competition; those willing to work in rural areas should have better job prospects.

Some job openings for librarians will stem from projected slower-than-average employment growth through the year 2006, reflecting budgetary constraints in school, public, and college and university libraries. Additional job openings will arise from replacement needs over the next decade, as many librarians reach retirement age. In an effort to reduce costs, however, libraries are reluctant to add new positions and may even reduce staff.

The increasing use of computerized information storage and retrieval systems may contribute to reduced demand for librarians. Computerized systems make cataloguing easier, and this task can now be handled by library technicians. In addition, many libraries are equipped for users to access library computers directly from their homes or offices. These systems allow users to bypass librarians and conduct research on their own. However, librarians are needed to manage staff, help users develop database searching techniques, address complicated reference requests, and define users' needs.

Opportunities will be best for librarians outside traditional settings. Nontraditional library settings include information brokers, private corporations, and consulting firms. Many companies are turning to librarians because of their research and organizational skills, and knowledge of computer databases and library automation systems. Librarians can review the vast amount of information that is available and analyze, evaluate, and organize it according to a company's specific needs. Librarians are also hired by organizations to set up information on the Internet. Librarians working in these settings may be classified as systems analysts, database specialists and trainers, webmasters or web developers, or LAN (local area network) coordinators.

Earnings

Salaries of librarians vary by the individual's qualifications and the type, size, and location of the library.

According to a survey by the American Library Association, the average salary of children's librarians in academic and public libraries was $34,600 in 1996; reference/information librarians averaged $35,800; and cataloguers and classifiers earned $36,600. Beginning librarians with a master's degree but no professional experience averaged $28,700 in 1996.

According to the Special Libraries Association, salaries for special librarians with two years or less of library experience averaged $33,100 in 1996, while those with three to five years of experience averaged $37,400. Salaries for special librarians with primarily administrative responsibilities averaged $58,400.

Salaries for medical librarians with one year or less experience averaged $25,900 in 1995, according to the Medical Library Association. The average salary for all medical librarians was $40,800.

The average annual salary for all librarians in the federal government in nonsupervisory, supervisory, and managerial positions was $50,400 in 1997.

Related Occupations

Librarians play an important role in the transfer of knowledge and ideas by providing people with access to the information they need and want. Jobs requiring similar analytical, organizational, and communicative skills include archivists, information scientists, museum curators, publishers' representatives, research analysts, information brokers, and records managers. The management aspect of a librarian's work is similar to the work of managers in a variety of business and government settings. School librarians have many duties similar to those of school teachers. Other jobs requiring the computer skills of some librarians include webmasters or web developers, database specialists, and systems analysts.

Sources of Additional Information

Information on librarianship, including information on scholarships or loans, is available from the American Library Association. For a listing of accredited library education programs, check their homepage:

❑ American Library Association, Office for Library Personnel Resources, 50 East Huron St., Chicago, IL 60611. Homepage: http://www.ala.org/

For information on a career as a special librarian, write to:

❑ Special Libraries Association, 1700 18th St. NW, Washington, DC 20009.

Material about a career in information science is available from:

❑ American Society for Information Science, 8720 Georgia Ave., Suite 501, Silver Spring, MD 20910.

Information on graduate schools of library and information science can be obtained from:

❑ Association for Library and Information Science Education, P.O. Box 7640, Arlington, VA 22207. Homepage: http://www.sils.umich.edu/ALISE/

For information on a career as a law librarian, scholarship information, and a list of ALA-accredited schools offering programs in law librarianship, contact:

> ❑ American Association of Law Libraries, 53 West Jackson Blvd., Suite 940, Chicago, IL 60604.

For information on employment opportunities as a health sciences librarian, scholarship information, credentialing information, and a list of MLA-accredited schools offering programs in health sciences librarianship, contact:

> ❑ Medical Library Association, 6 N. Michigan Ave., Suite 300, Chicago, IL 60602.

Information on acquiring a job as a librarian with the federal government may be obtained from the Office of Personnel Management through a telephone-based system. Consult your telephone directory under U.S. government for a local number or call (912) 757-3000 (TDD 912 744-2299). That number is not toll-free and charges may result. Information also is available from their Internet site: http://www.usajobs.opm.gov

Information concerning requirements and application procedures for positions in the Library of Congress may be obtained directly from:

> ❑ Personnel Office, Library of Congress, 101 Independence Ave. SE., Washington, DC 20540.

State library agencies can furnish information on scholarships available through their offices, requirements for certification, and general information about career prospects in the state. Several of these agencies maintain job hotlines reporting openings for librarians.

State departments of education can furnish information on certification requirements and job opportunities for school librarians.

Many library science schools offer career placement services to their alumni and current students. Some allow nonaffiliated students and job seekers to use their services.

Management Analysts and Consultants

(*D.O.T.* 100.117-014; 161.117-014, .167-010, -014, -018, and -022, .267 except -014 and -030; 169.167-074; 184.267; and 310.267-010)

Significant Points

* *About 45 percent of these workers were self-employed, almost three times the average for other executive, administrative, and managerial occupations.*

* *A master's degree and at least five years' specialized experience generally are required for jobs in the private sector.*

Nature of the Work

Management analysts and consultants analyze and suggest solutions to management problems. For example, a rapidly growing small company may need help in designing a better system of control over inventories and expenses and decides to engage a consultant who is an expert in just-in-time inventory management. In another case, a large company which realizes its corporate structure must be reorganized after acquiring a new division brings in management experts to restructure the company and eliminate duplicate and nonessential managerial positions. These are just some of the many organizational problems that management analysts, as they are called in government agencies, and consultants, as business firms refer to them, help solve.

The work of management analysts and consultants varies with each client or employer and from project to project. For example, some projects require a team of consultants, each specializing in one area; at other times, consultants work independently with the organization's managers. In general, analysts and consultants first collect, review, and analyze information. They then make recommendations to management and may assist in the implementation of their proposal.

Both public and private organizations use consultants for a variety of reasons. Some don't have the internal resources needed to handle a project, while others need a consultant's expertise to determine what resources will be required, and what problems may be encountered, if they pursue a particular opportunity.

Firms providing consulting services range in size from a single practitioner to large international organizations employing many thousands of consultants. Some analysts and consultants specialize in a specific industry, while others specialize by type of business function, such as human resources or information systems. In government, management analysts tend to specialize by type of agency. Consulting services often are provided on a contract basis. To engage a consultant, a company first solicits proposals from a number of consulting firms specializing in the area in which it needs assistance. These proposals include the estimated cost and scope of the project, staffing requirements, references from a number of previous clients, and a completion deadline. The company then selects the best proposal for its needs.

Upon getting an assignment or contract, consultants or management analysts define the nature and extent of the problem. During this phase of the job, they analyze pertinent data such as annual revenues, employment, or expenditures and interview managers and employees while observing their operations.

The analyst or consultant develops solutions to the problem. In the course of preparing their recommendations, they take into account the nature of the organization, the relationship it has with others in that industry, and its internal organization and culture. Insight into the problem may be gained by building and solving mathematical models.

Once they have decided on a course of action, consultants report their findings and recommendations to the client, often in writing. In addition, they generally make oral presentations regarding their findings. For some projects, this is all that is required. For others, consultants assist in the implementation of their suggestions.

Management analysts in government agencies use the same skills as their private-sector colleagues to advise managers on many types of issues, most of which are similar to the problems faced by private firms. For example, if an agency is planning to purchase personal computers, it must first determine which type to buy, given its budget and data processing needs. Management analysts would assess the various types of machines available by price range and determine which best meets their department's needs.

Working Conditions

Management analysts and consultants usually divide their time between their offices and their client's site. Although much of their time is spent indoors in clean, well-lighted offices, they may experience a great deal of stress as a result of trying to meet a client's demands, often on a tight schedule.

Typically, analysts and consultants work at least 40 hours a week. Uncompensated overtime is common, especially when project deadlines are near. Since they must spend a significant portion of their time with clients, they travel frequently.

Self-employed consultants can set their workload and hours and work at home. On the other hand, their livelihood depends on their ability to maintain and expand their client base. Salaried consultants also must impress potential clients to get and keep clients for their company.

Employment

Management analysts and consultants held about 244,000 jobs in 1996. Around 45 percent of these workers were self-employed. Most of the rest worked in financial and management consulting firms and for federal, state, and local governments. The majority of those working for the federal government were found in the Department of Defense.

Management analysts and consultants are found throughout the country, but employment is concentrated in large metropolitan areas.

Training, Other Qualifications, and Advancement

Educational requirements for entry-level jobs in this field vary widely between private industry and government. Employers in private industry generally seek individuals with a master's degree in business administration or a related discipline and at least five years of experience in the field in which they hope to consult. Most government agencies hire people with a bachelor's degree and no work experience as entry-level management analysts.

Many fields of study provide a suitable educational background for this occupation because of the wide range of problem areas addressed by management analysts and consultants. These include most areas of business and management, as well as computer and information sciences and engineering.

Most entrants to this occupation have, in addition to the appropriate formal education, years of experience in management, human resources, inventory control, or other specialties. The value of this experience enables many to land consultant positions, since most prospective clients now demand experience in the area where they feel they need help.

Management analysts and consultants often work with little or no supervision, so they should be self-motivated and disciplined. Analytical skills, the ability to get along with a wide range of people, strong oral and written communication skills, good judgment, the ability to manage time well, and creativity in developing solutions to problems are other desirable qualities for prospective management analysts and consultants.

Consulting teams are becoming more common. The team is responsible for the entire project and each consultant on the team is assigned to a particular area.

As consultants gain experience, they often become solely responsible for a specific project full-time, taking on more responsibility and managing their own hours. At the senior level, consultants may supervise lower-level workers and become increasingly involved in seeking out new business. Those with exceptional skills may eventually become a partner or principal in the firm. Others with entrepreneurial ambition may open their own firm.

Analysts and consultants routinely attend conferences to keep abreast of current developments in their field.

A high percentage of management consultants are self-employed, partly because business start-up costs are low. Self-employed consultants also can share office space, administrative help, and other resources with other self-employed consultants or small consulting firms—thus reducing overhead costs. Many such firms fail, however, because of an inability to acquire and maintain a profitable client base.

The Institute of Management Consultants (a division of the Council of Consulting Organizations, Inc.) offers the Certified Management Consultant (CMC) designation to those who pass an examination and meet minimum levels of education and experience. Certification is not mandatory for management consultants to practice, but it may give a job seeker a competitive advantage.

Job Outlook

Employment of management analysts and consultants is expected to grow faster than the average for all occupations through the year 2006 as industry and government increasingly rely on outside expertise to improve the performance of their organizations. Growth is expected in very large consulting firms, but also in smaller niche consulting firms whose consultants specialize in specific areas of expertise. For example, some consultants specialize in biotechnology, pharmacy, engineering, or telecommunications. Clients increasingly demand a team approach, which enables examination of a variety of different areas within the organization; this development may hinder individual practitioners.

Increased competition has forced American industry to take a closer look at its operations. As international and domestic markets become more competitive, firms must use resources more efficiently. Management consultants are being increasingly relied upon to help reduce costs, streamline operations, and develop marketing strategies. As businesses downsize, opportunities will be created for consultants to perform duties that were previously handled internally. Businesses attempting to expand, particularly into world markets, frequently need the skills of management consultants to help with organizational, administrative, and other issues. Continuing changes in the business environment also are expected to lead the demand for consultants to incorporate new technologies, and to adapt to a changing labor force. As businesses rely more on technology, there are increasing roles for consultants with a technical background, such as engineering or biotechnology, particularly when combined with an MBA.

Federal, state, and local agencies also are expected to expand their use of management analysts. Analysts' skills at identifying problems and implementing cost reduction measures are expected to become increasingly important.

Despite projected rapid employment growth, competition for jobs as management analysts and consultants is expected to be keen. Because management consultants can come from such diverse educational backgrounds, the pool of applicants from which employers can hire is quite large.

Additionally, the independent and challenging nature of the work, combined with high earnings potential, makes this occupation attractive to many. Job opportunities are expected to be best for those with a graduate degree, a talent for salesmanship and public relations, and industry expertise.

Because many small consulting firms fail each year for lack of managerial expertise and clients, those interested in opening their own firm must have good organizational and marketing skills and several years of consulting experience.

Earnings

Salaries for management analysts and consultants vary widely by experience, education, and employer. In 1996, those who were full-time wage and salary workers had median annual earnings of about $39,500. The middle 50 percent earned between $30,200 and $61,300, and the top 10 percent earned more than $81,500.

In 1996, according to the Association of Management Consulting Firms, earnings—including bonuses and/or profit sharing—for research associates in member firms averaged $32,400; for entry level consultants, $35,200; for management consultants, $50,500; for senior consultants, $74,300; for junior partners, $91,100; and for senior partners, $167,100.

The average annual salary for management analysts in the federal government in nonsupervisory, supervisory, and managerial positions was $55,240 in 1997.

Typical benefits for salaried analysts and consultants include health and life insurance, a retirement plan, vacation and sick leave, profit sharing, and bonuses for outstanding work. In addition, all travel expenses usually are reimbursed by the employer. Self-employed consultants have to maintain their own office and provide their own benefits.

Related Occupations

Management analysts and consultants collect, review, and analyze data; make recommendations; and assist in the implementation of their ideas. Others who use similar skills are managers, computer systems analysts, operations research analysts, economists, and financial analysts. Researchers prepare data and reports for consultants to use in their recommendations.

Sources of Additional Information

Information about career opportunities in management consulting is available from:

❑ The Association of Management Consulting Firms, 521 Fifth Ave., 35th Floor, New York, NY 10175-3598.

For information about a career as a state or local government management analyst, contact your state or local employment service.

Information on obtaining a management analyst position with the federal government may be obtained from the Office of Personnel Management through a telephone-based system. Consult your telephone directory under U.S. government for a local number or call (912) 757-3000 (TDD 912 744-2299). That number is not toll-free and charges may result. Information also is available from their Internet site: http:// www.usajobs.opm.gov

Operations Research Analysts

(D.O.T. 020.067-018)

Significant Points

* *Individuals with a master's or Ph.D. degree in management science or operations research should find good job prospects through the year 2006, despite projected slower than average employment growth.*

* *Skills acquired by operations research analysts are useful for higher-level management jobs.*

Nature of the Work

Efficiently running a complex organization such as a manufacturing plant or an airline requires the precise coordination of materials, equipment, and people. Operations research analysts help organizations coordinate and operate in the most efficient manner by applying mathematical principles to organizational problems. Managers then evaluate alternatives and choose the course of action that best meets their goals.

Operations research analysts tackle a whole host of problems facing large business and government organizations, including strategy, forecasting, resource allocation, facilities layout, inventory control, personnel schedules, and distribution systems. Their methods generally use a mathematical model consisting of a set of equations that describe how things happen within the organization. Use of models enables the analyst to break down problems into their component parts, assign numerical values to different components, and determine the mathematical relationships between them. These values can be altered to examine what will happen to the system under different circumstances. The situation under consideration determines the mathematical method used. Some of the methods available include simulation, linear optimization, networks, waiting lines, and game theory.

Operations research analysts use computers extensively in their work. They are typically highly proficient in database collection and management, programming, and in the development and use of sophisticated software programs. Many of the models employed in operations research are so complicated that only a computer can solve them efficiently.

The type of problem they handle varies by industry. For example, a civilian analyst for the Armed Forces may coordinate flight and maintenance schedules to produce an optimal schedule for the safe deployment of troops and material. An analyst employed by a hospital concentrates on a different set of factors, such as scheduling admissions, managing patient flow, assigning shifts, monitoring use of pharmacy and laboratory services, and forecasting demand for hospital services.

The duties of the operations research analyst vary according to the structure and management philosophy of the employer or client. Some firms centralize operations research in one department, while others use operations research in all divisions. Firms may contract out operations research services to a consulting firm. Some operations research analysts specialize in one type of application, whereas others are generalists, especially at the beginning of their careers. In addition, economists, systems analysts, mathematicians, industrial engineers, and others may also apply operations research techniques to address problem areas within their respective fields.

The degree of supervision varies by organizational structure and experience. In some organizations, analysts have a great deal of professional autonomy, while in others, analysts are more closely supervised. Operations research analysts work closely with senior managers, who have a wide variety of support needs. Analysts must adapt their work to reflect these requirements.

Regardless of the industry or structure of the organization, operations research entails a similar set of procedures. Managers begin the process by describing the symptoms of a problem to the analyst, who then formally defines the problem. For example, an operations research analyst for an auto manufacturer may be asked to determine the best inventory level for each of the materials for a new production line or, more specifically, to determine how many windshields should be kept in inventory.

Analysts study the problem and then break it into its component parts. Then they gather information about each of these parts. Usually this involves consulting a wide variety of sources of information. To determine the most efficient amount of inventory to be kept on hand, for example, operations research analysts might talk with engineers about production levels, discuss purchasing arrangements with buyers, and examine data on storage costs provided by the

With this information in hand, the analyst is ready to select the most appropriate analytical technique. There may be several techniques that could be used, but all techniques involve the construction of a mathematical model that explains the system and solves the problem. In almost all cases, the computer program used to solve the model must be modified repeatedly to reflect different solutions.

A model for airline flight scheduling, for example, might include variables for the cities to be connected, amount of fuel required to fly the routes, projected levels of passenger demand, varying ticket and fuel prices, pilot scheduling, and maintenance costs. The analyst then chooses values for these variables, enters them into a computer which is then programmed to solve the calculations, and runs the program to produce the best flight schedule consistent with various sets of assumptions.

At this point, the operations research analyst presents the final work to management along with recommendations based on the results of the analysis. Additional computer runs based on different assumptions may be needed to help in making the final decision between various options. Once a decision has been reached by management, the analyst may work with others in the organization to ensure the plan's successful implementation.

Working Conditions

Operations research analysts generally work regular hours in an office environment. Because they work on projects that are of immediate interest to management, analysts often are under pressure to meet deadlines and often work more than a 40-hour week.

Employment

Operations research analysts held about 50,000 jobs in 1996. They are employed in most industries. Major employers include telecommunication companies, air carriers, computer and data processing services, financial institutions, insurance carriers, engineering and management services firms, and the federal government. About one out of five analysts work for management, research, public relations, and testing agencies that do operations research consulting.

Most operations research analysts in the federal government work for the Armed Forces. In addition, many operations research analysts in private industry work directly or indirectly on national defense.

Training, Other Qualifications, and Advancement

Employers generally prefer applicants with at least a master's degree in operations research, industrial engineering, or management science, coupled with a bachelor's degree in computer science or one of the quantitative disciplines like economics, mathematics, or statistics.

Employers often sponsor skills-improvement training for experienced workers, helping them keep up with new developments in operations research techniques as well as advances in computer science. Some analysts attend advanced university classes on these subjects at their employer's expense.

Operations research analysts must be able to think logically and work well with people, so employers prefer workers with good oral and written communication skills. The computer is the most important tool for quantitative analysis, and both training and experience in programming are a must.

Beginning analysts usually do routine work under the supervision of more experienced analysts. As they gain knowledge and experience, they are assigned more complex tasks, with greater autonomy to design models and solve problems. Operations research analysts advance by assuming positions as technical specialists or supervisors. The skills acquired by operations research analysts are useful for higher-level management jobs, and experienced analysts may leave the field to assume nontechnical managerial or administrative positions.

Job Outlook

Individuals seeking employment as operations research or management science analysts who hold master's or Ph.D. degrees in management science or operations research should find good opportunities through the year 2006 because the number of openings generated each year as a result of the slower than average employment growth expected and the need to replace those leaving the occupation is expected to exceed the number of persons graduating with these credentials. Graduates with only a bachelor's degree in operations research or management science should find opportunities as research assistants in a variety of related fields which allow them to use their quantitative abilities. Organizations are expected to use operations research and management science techniques to improve productivity and quality and to reduce costs. This reflects an acceptance of a systematic approach to decision making by top managers. This should result in a steady demand for workers knowledgeable in operations research techniques in the years ahead.

The importance of quantitative analysis in decision making ensures that training in operations research will continue to be valuable in obtaining employment. Employment opportunities will occur in the transportation, manufacturing, finance, and services sectors, where the use of quantitative analysis can achieve dramatic improvements in operating efficiency and profitability.

Earnings

In 1996, the median salary of operations and systems researchers and analysts was about $42,400 a year. The middle 50 percent earned between about $33,100 and $55,500; the lowest 10 percent were paid less than $24,300, while the highest 10 percent earned over $65,500 a year.

The average annual salary for operations research analysts in the federal government in nonsupervisory, supervisory, and managerial positions was $66,760 in 1997.

Related Occupations

Operations research analysts apply mathematical principles to large, complicated problems. Workers in other occupations that stress quantitative analysis include computer scientists, engineers, mathematicians, statisticians, and economists. Because its goal is improved organizational efficiency, operations research is closely allied to managerial occupations.

Sources of Additional Information

Information on career opportunities for operations research analysts is available from:

❑ The Institute for Operations Research and the Management Sciences, 901 Elkridge Landing Rd., Suite 400, Linthicum, MD 21090.

For information on careers in the Armed Forces and Department of Defense, contact:

❑ Military Operations Research Society, 101 South Whiting St., Suite 202, Alexandria, VA 22304.

Psychologists

(*D.O.T.* 045.061, .067, .107-022, -026, -030, -034, and -046)

Significant Points

✴ *Over 40 percent of all psychologists are self-employed, about five times the average for all professional workers.*

✴ *A doctoral degree generally is required for employment as a licensed clinical or counseling psychologist.*

✴ *Opportunities for employment in psychology for those with only a bachelor's degree are severely limited.*

Nature of the Work

Psychologists study the human mind and human behavior. Research psychologists investigate the physical, cognitive, emotional, or social aspects of human behavior. Psychologists in applied fields provide mental health care in hospitals, clinics, schools, or private settings.

Like other social scientists, psychologists formulate hypotheses and collect data to test their validity. Research methods may vary depending on the topic under study. Psychologists sometimes gather information through controlled laboratory experiments, as well as through administering personality, performance, aptitude, and intelligence tests. Other methods include observation, interviews, questionnaires, clinical studies, and surveys.

Psychologists apply their knowledge to a wide range of endeavors, including health and human services, management, education, law, and sports. In addition to a variety of work settings, psychologists generally specialize in one of a number of different areas.

Clinical psychologists—who constitute the largest specialty—generally work in counseling centers, independent or group practices, or in health maintenance organizations, hospitals, or clinics. They assist mentally or emotionally disturbed clients adjust to life and may help medical and surgical patients deal with their illnesses or injuries. Some work in physical rehabilitation settings, treating patients with spinal cord injuries, chronic pain or illness, stroke, arthritis, and neurologic conditions such as multiple sclerosis. Others help people deal with times of personal crisis, such as divorce or the death of a loved one. Clinical psychologists often interview patients and give diagnostic tests. They may provide individual, family, and group psychotherapy, and design and implement behavior modification programs. Some clinical psychologists collaborate with physicians and other specialists to develop and implement treatment and intervention programs that patients can understand and comply with. Other clinical psychologists work in universities and medical schools, where they train graduate students in the delivery of mental health and behavioral medicine services. Some administer community mental health programs.

Some areas of specialization within clinical psychology include health psychology, neuropsychology, and geropsychology. *Health psychologists* promote good health through health maintenance counseling programs that are designed to help people achieve goals such as to stop smoking or lose weight. *Neuropsychologists* study the relation between the brain and behavior. They often work in stroke and head injury programs. *Geropsychologists* deal with the special problems faced by the elderly. The emergence and growth of these specialties reflects the increasing participation of psychologists in providing direct services to special patient populations.

Cognitive psychologists deal with memory, thinking, and perceptions. Some conduct research related to computer programming and artificial intelligence.

Counseling psychologists use various techniques, including interviewing and testing, to advise people on how to deal with problems of everyday living. They work in settings such as university counseling centers, hospitals, and individual or group practices.

Developmental psychologists study the physiological development that takes place throughout life. Some specialize in behavior during infancy, childhood, and adolescence, changes that take place during maturity or old age, or developmental disabilities and their effects. Increasingly, research is developing ways to help elderly people stay as independent as possible.

Experimental or research psychologists work in university and private research centers, and in business, nonprofit, and governmental organizations. They study behavior processes with human beings and animals such as rats, monkeys, and pigeons. Prominent areas of study in experimental research include motivation, thinking, attention, learning and memory, sensory and perceptual processes, effects of substance abuse, and genetic and neurological factors affecting behavior.

Industrial-organizational psychologists (I/O) apply psychological principles and research methods to the workplace in the interest of improving productivity and the quality of worklife. They also are involved in research into management and marketing problems. They conduct applicant screening, training and development, counseling, and organizational development and analysis. An industrial psychologist might work with management to reorganize the work setting to improve productivity or quality of life in the workplace. They frequently act as consultants, brought in by management in order to solve a particular problem.

School psychologists work in elementary and secondary schools or school district offices with students, teachers, parents, and administrators to resolve students' learning and behavior problems. They collaborate with teachers, parents, and school personnel to improve classroom management strategies or parenting skills, counter substance abuse, work with students with disabilities or gifted and talented students, and improve teaching and learning strategies. They may evaluate the effectiveness of academic programs, behavior management procedures, and other services provided in the school setting.

Social psychologists examine people's interactions with others and with the social environment. They work in organizational consultation, marketing research, systems design or other applied psychology fields. Prominent areas of study include group behavior, leadership, attitudes, and perception.

Working Conditions

A psychologist's specialty and place of employment determine working conditions. Clinical, school, and counseling psychologists in private practice have their own offices and set their own hours. However, they often must offer evening and weekend hours to accommodate their clients. Those employed in hospitals, nursing homes, and other health facilities may work shifts including evenings and weekends, while those who work in schools and clinics generally work regular hours. Psychologists employed as faculty by colleges and universities divide their time between teaching and research, and some have administrative responsibilities as well. Many have part-time consulting practices. Most psychologists in government and industry have structured schedules. Increasingly, psychologists work as part of a team and consult with other psychologists and professionals. Many experience pressures due to deadlines, tight schedules, and overtime work. Their routine may be interrupted frequently. Travel is required to attend conferences or conduct research.

Employment

Psychologists held about 143,000 jobs in 1996. Educational institutions employed nearly four out of ten salaried psychologists in positions other than teaching, such as counseling, testing, research, and administration. Three out of ten were employed in health services, primarily in hospitals, mental health clinics, rehabilitation centers, nursing homes, and other health facilities. Government agencies at the federal, state, and local levels employed about 16 percent. Government employs psychologists in hospitals, clinics, correctional facilities, and other settings. The Department of Veterans Affairs and the Department of Defense employ about 80 percent of the psychologists working for federal agencies. Some psychologists work in social service organizations, research organizations, management consulting firms, marketing research firms, and other businesses.

After several years of experience, some psychologists—usually those with doctoral degrees—enter private practice or set up their own research or consulting firms. Over 40 percent of all psychologists are self-employed.

In addition to the jobs described above, many held positions as psychology faculty at colleges and universities, and as high school psychology teachers.

Training, Other Qualifications, and Advancement

A doctoral degree is generally required for employment as a licensed clinical or counseling psychologist. Psychologists with a Ph.D. qualify for a wide range of teaching, research, clinical, and counseling positions in universities, elementary and secondary schools, private industry, and government. Psychologists with a Psy.D.—Doctor of Psychology—generally

work in clinical positions. Persons with a master's degree in psychology often work as school or industrial-organizational psychologists. Others work as psychological assistants, under the supervision of doctoral-level psychologists, and conduct research or psychological evaluations.

A bachelor's degree in psychology qualifies a person to assist psychologists and other professionals in community mental health centers, vocational rehabilitation offices, and correctional programs. They may work as research or administrative assistants or become sales or management trainees in business. Some work as technicians in related fields such as marketing research. However, without additional academic training, their opportunities in psychology are severely limited.

In the federal government, candidates having at least 24 semester hours in psychology and one course in statistics qualify for entry-level positions. Because this is one of the few areas in which one can work as a psychologist without an advanced degree, competition for these jobs is keen.

Clinical psychologists generally must have completed the Ph.D. or Psy.D. requirements and served an internship. Vocational and guidance counselors usually need two years of graduate study in counseling and one year of counseling experience. School psychology requires a master's degree followed by a one-year internship.

Most students need at least two years of full-time graduate study to earn a master's degree in psychology. Requirements usually include practical experience in an applied setting and a master's thesis based on an original research project.

A doctoral degree usually requires five to seven years of graduate study. The Ph.D. degree culminates in a dissertation based on original research. Courses in quantitative research methods, which include the use of computer-based analysis, are an integral part of graduate study and are necessary to complete the dissertation. The Psy.D. may be based on practical work and examinations rather than a dissertation. In clinical or counseling psychology, the requirements for the doctoral degree generally include a year or more of internship.

Competition for admission into graduate programs is keen. Some universities require an undergraduate major in psychology. Others prefer only course work in basic psychology with courses in the biological, physical, and social sciences, statistics, and mathematics.

Most colleges and universities offer a bachelor's degree in psychology. Over 650 departments offer either a master's or a full Ph.D. program. A smaller number of professional schools of psychology offer the Psy.D.

The American Psychological Association (APA) presently accredits doctoral training programs in clinical, counseling, and school psychology. The National Council for Accreditation of Teacher Education, with the assistance of the National Association of School Psychologists, also is involved in the accreditation of advanced degree programs in school psychology. The APA also accredits institutions that provide internships for doctoral students in school, clinical, and counseling psychology.

Psychologists in independent practice or those who offer any type of patient care, including clinical, counseling, and school psychologists, must meet certification or licensing requirements in all states and the District of Columbia. Licensing laws vary by state and by type of position. Clinical and counseling psychologists generally require a doctorate in psychology, completion of an approved internship, and one to two years of professional experience. In addition, all states require that applicants pass an examination. Most state boards administer a standardized test and many supplement that with additional oral or essay questions. Most states certify those with a master's degree as school psychologists after completion of an internship. Some states require continuing education for license renewal.

Most states require that licensed or certified psychologists limit their practice to areas in which they have developed professional competence through training and experience.

The American Board of Professional Psychology recognizes professional achievement by awarding certification, primarily in clinical psychology, clinical neuropsychology, counseling, forensic, industrial-organizational, and school psychology. Candidates for APA certification need a doctorate in psychology, five years of experience, professional endorsements, and a passing grade on an examination.

Aspiring psychologists who are interested in direct patient care must be emotionally stable, mature, and able to deal effectively with people. Sensitivity, compassion, and the ability to lead and inspire others are particularly important qualities for clinical work and counseling. Research psychologists should be able to do detailed work independently and as part of a team. Excellent communications skills are necessary to succeed in research. Patience and perseverance are vital qualities because results from psychological treatment of patients or from research usually take a long time.

Job Outlook

Employment of psychologists is expected to grow more slowly than the average for all occupations through the year 2006. Job opportunities in health care should increase slightly in health care provider networks, such as health maintenance and preferred provider organizations, and in nursing homes and alcohol and drug abuse programs. More job opportunities will arise in businesses, nonprofit organizations, and research and computer firms for psychologists working as consultants. Companies will use psychologists' expertise in survey design, analysis, and research to provide marketing evaluation and statistical analysis. The increase in employee assistance programs, which offer employees help with personal problems, should also spur job growth.

Opportunities for people holding doctorates from leading universities in areas with an applied emphasis, such as clinical, counseling, health, and educational psychology, should have particularly good prospects. Psychologists with extensive training in quantitative research methods and computer science may have a competitive edge over applicants without this background.

Graduates with a master's degree in psychology are qualified for positions in school and industrial-organizational psychology. Graduates of master's degree programs in school psychology should have the best job prospects, as schools are expected to increase student counseling and mental health services. Masters' degree holders with several years of industrial experience can obtain jobs in consulting and marketing research. Other master's degree holders may find jobs as psychological assistants in the community mental health field, which often requires direct supervision by a licensed psychologist. Still others may find jobs involving research and data collection and analysis in universities, government, or private companies.

Bachelor's degree holders can expect very few opportunities directly related to psychology. Some may find jobs as assistants in rehabilitation centers, or in other jobs involving data collection and analysis. Those who meet state certification requirements may become high school psychology teachers.

Earnings

According to a 1995 survey by the American Psychological Association, the median salary of psychologists with a doctoral degree and five to nine years of experience was $55,000 in counseling psychology in individual private practice; $54,500 in private research organizations; $51,000 as clinical psychologists in public psychiatric hospitals; and $59,000 in school psychology. The median annual salary of master's degree holders was $38,000 in counseling psychology; $43,000 in clinical psychology; $41,500 in research positions; $60,000 in school psychology, and $55,000 in industrial-organizational psychology. Some psychologists have much higher earnings, particularly those in private practice.

The federal government recognizes education and experience in certifying applicants for entry-level positions. In general, the starting salary for psychologists having a bachelor's degree was about $19,500 a year in 1997; those with superior academic records could begin at $24,200. Psychologists with a master's degree and one year of experience could start at $29,600. Psychologists having a Ph.D. or Psy.D. degree and one year of internship could start at $35,800, and some individuals with experience could start at $42,900. Beginning salaries were slightly higher in selected areas of the country where the prevailing local pay level was higher. The average salary for psychologists in the federal government in nonsupervisory, supervisory, and managerial positions was about $62,120 a year in 1997.

Related Occupations

Psychologists are trained to conduct research and teach, evaluate, counsel, and advise individuals and groups with special needs. Others who do this kind of work include marketing research analysts, advertising and public relations managers, clinical social workers, physicians, sociologists, clergy, special education teachers, and counselors.

Sources of Additional Information

For information on careers, educational requirements, financial assistance, and licensing in all fields of psychology, contact:

❏ American Psychological Association, Research Office and Education in Psychology and Accreditation Offices, 750 1st St. NE., Washington, DC 20002. Information is also available from their Internet site: http://www.apa.org/

For information on careers, educational requirements, and licensing of school psychologists, contact:

❏ National Association of School Psychologists, 4030 East West Highway, Suite 402, Bethesda, MD 20814.

Information about state licensing requirements is available from:

❏ Association of State and Provincial Psychology Boards, P.O. Box 4389, Montgomery, AL 36103-4389.

Information on obtaining a job with the federal government may be obtained from the Office of Personnel Management through a telephone-based system. Consult your telephone directory under U.S. government for a local number or call (912) 757-3000 (TDD 912 744-2299). That number is not toll-free and charges may result. Information also is available from their Internet site: http://www.usajobs.opm.gov

Speech-Language Pathologists and Audiologists

(D.O.T. 076.101-010, .104-010, and .107-010)

Significant Points

✷ *About half work in schools, and most others are employed by health care facilities.*

✷ *A master's degree in speech-language pathology or audiology is the standard credential.*

✷ *Projected much-faster-than-average employment growth reflects the increasing number of people who will need speech-language pathology and audiology services.*

Nature of the Work

Speech-language pathologists assess, treat, and help to prevent speech, language, cognitive communication, voice, swallowing, fluency, and other related disorders; audiologists identify, assess, and manage auditory, balance, and other neural systems.

Speech-language pathologists work with people who cannot make speech sounds, or cannot make them clearly; those with speech rhythm and fluency problems, such as stuttering; people with voice quality problems, such as inappropriate pitch or harsh voice; those with problems understanding and producing language; and those with cognitive communication impairments, such as attention, memory, and problem solving disorders. They may also work with people who have oral motor problems causing eating and swallowing difficulties.

Speech and language problems can result from hearing loss, brain injury or deterioration, cerebral palsy, stroke, cleft palate, voice pathology, mental retardation, or emotional problems. Problems can be congenital, developmental, or acquired. Speech-language pathologists use written and oral tests, as well as special instruments, to diagnose the nature and extent of impairment and to record and analyze speech, language, and swallowing irregularities. Speech-language pathologists develop an individualized plan of care, tailored to each patient's needs. For individuals with little or no speech capability, speech-language pathologists select augmentative alternative communication methods, including automated devices and sign language, and teach their use. They teach these individuals how to make sounds, improve their voices, or increase their language skills to communicate more effectively. Speech-language pathologists help patients develop, or recover, reliable communication skills so patients can fulfill their educational, vocational, and social roles.

Most speech-language pathologists provide direct clinical services to individuals with communication disorders. In speech and language clinics, they may independently develop and carry out treatment programs. In medical facilities, they may work with physicians, social workers, psychologists, and other therapists to develop and execute treatment plans. Speech-language pathologists in schools develop individual or group programs, counsel parents, and may assist teachers with classroom activities.

Speech-language pathologists keep records on the initial evaluation, progress, and discharge of clients. This helps pinpoint problems, tracks client progress, and justifies the cost of treatment when applying for reimbursement. They counsel individuals and their families concerning communication disorders and how to cope with the stress and misunderstanding that often accompany them. They also work with family members to recognize and change behavior patterns that impede communication and treatment and show them communication-enhancing techniques to use at home.

Some speech-language pathologists conduct research on how people communicate. Others design and develop equipment or techniques for diagnosing and treating speech problems.

Audiologists work with people who have hearing, balance, and related problems. They use audiometers and other testing devices to measure the loudness at which a person begins to hear sounds, the ability to distinguish between sounds, and the nature and extent of hearing loss. Audiologists interpret these results and may coordinate them with medical, educational, and psychological information to make a diagnosis and determine a course of treatment.

Hearing disorders can result from trauma at birth, viral infections, genetic disorders, or exposure to loud noise. Treatment may include examining and cleaning the ear canal, fitting and dispensing a hearing aid or other assistive device, and audiologic rehabilitation (including auditory training or instruction in speech or lip reading). Audiologists may recommend, fit, and dispense personal or large area amplification systems, such as hearing aids and alerting devices. Audiologists provide fitting and tuning of cochlear implants and provide the necessary rehabilitation for adjustment to listening with implant amplification systems. They also test noise levels in workplaces and conduct hearing protection programs in industry, as well as in schools and communities.

Audiologists provide direct clinical services to individuals with hearing or balance disorders. In audiology (hearing) clinics, they may independently develop and carry out treatment programs. Audiologists, in a variety of settings, work as members of interdisciplinary professional teams in planning and implementing service delivery for children and adults, from birth to old age. Similar to speech-language pathologists, audiologists keep records on the initial evaluation, progress, and discharge of clients. These records help pinpoint problems, track client progress, and justify the cost of treatment, when applying for reimbursement.

Audiologists may conduct research on types of, and treatment for, hearing, balance, and related disorders. Others design and develop equipment or techniques for diagnosing and treating these disorders.

Working Conditions

Speech-language pathologists and audiologists usually work at a desk or table in clean comfortable surroundings. The job is not physically demanding but does require attention to detail and intense concentration. The emotional needs of clients and their families may be demanding. Most full-time speech-language pathologists and audiologists work about 40 hours per week; some work part-time. Those who work on a contract basis may spend a substantial amount of time traveling between facilities.

Employment

Speech-language pathologists and audiologists held about 87,000 jobs in 1996. About one-half provided services in preschools, elementary and secondary schools, or colleges and universities. More than one in ten were in hospitals. Others were in offices of physicians; offices of speech-language pathologists and audiologists; speech, language, and hearing centers; home health care agencies; or other facilities. Some were in private practice, working either as solo practitioners or in a group practice. Some speech-language pathologists and audiologists contract to provide services in schools, hospitals, or nursing homes, or work as consultants to industry. Audiologists are more likely to be employed in independent health care offices, while speech-language pathologists are more likely to work in school settings.

Training, Other Qualifications, and Advancement

Of the states that regulate licensing (44 for speech-language pathologists and 47 for audiologists), almost all require a master's degree or equivalent. Other requirements are 300 to 375 hours of supervised clinical experience, a passing score on a national examination, and nine months of postgraduate professional clinical experience. Thirty-four states have continuing education requirements for licensure renewal. Medicaid, Medicare, and private health insurers generally require a practitioner to be licensed to qualify for reimbursement.

About 230 colleges and universities offer graduate programs in speech-language pathology. Courses cover anatomy and physiology of the areas of the body involved in speech, language, and hearing; the development of normal speech, language, and hearing; the nature of disorders; acoustics; and psychological aspects of communication. Graduate students also learn to evaluate and treat speech, language, and hearing disorders and receive supervised clinical training in communication disorders.

About 120 colleges and universities offer graduate programs in audiology in the United States. Course work includes anatomy; physiology; basic science; math; physics; genetics; normal and abnormal communication development; auditory, balance and neural systems assessment and treatment; audiologic rehabilitation; and ethics.

Speech-language pathologists can acquire the Certificate of Clinical Competence in Speech-Language Pathology (CCC-SLP) offered by the American Speech-Language-Hearing Association, and audiologists can earn the Certificate of Clinical Competence in Audiology (CCC-A). To earn a CCC, a person must have a graduate degree and 375 hours of supervised clinical experience, complete a 36-week postgraduate clinical fellowship, and pass a written examination.

Speech-language pathologists and audiologists should be able to effectively communicate diagnostic test results, diagnoses, and proposed treatment in a manner easily understood by their clients. They must be able to approach problems objectively and provide support to clients and their families. Because a client's progress may be slow, patience, compassion, and good listening skills are necessary.

Speech-language pathologists and audiologists may work in a variety of settings, including schools, hospitals, health departments, clinics, and private practices. Some members of these professions also serve as clinical supervisors for student clinicians, professors in universities and colleges, or conduct research.

Job Outlook

Employment of speech-language pathologists and audiologists is expected to increase much faster than the average for all occupations through the year 2006. Employment in health and rehabilitation services will increase as a result of advances in medical technology and growth in the elderly population. Because hearing loss is strongly associated with aging, rapid growth in the population age 55 and over will cause the number of persons with hearing impairment to increase markedly. In addition, baby boomers are now entering middle age, when the possibility of neurological disorders and associated speech, language, and hearing impairments

increases. Medical advances are also improving the survival rate of premature infants and trauma and stroke victims, who then need assessment and possible treatment.

Employment in schools will increase along with growth in elementary and secondary school enrollments, including enrollment of special education students. Federal law guarantees special education and related services to all eligible children with disabilities. Greater awareness of the importance of early identification and diagnosis of speech, language, and hearing disorders will also increase employment.

The number of speech-language pathologists and audiologists in private practice, though small, is likely to rise sharply due to the increasing use of contract services by managed care, hospitals, schools, and nursing homes. In addition to job openings stemming from rapid job growth over the 1996–2006 period, some openings for speech-language pathologists and audiologists will arise from the need to replace those who leave the occupation.

Earnings

Median weekly earnings of full-time salaried speech-language pathologists and audiologists were about $690 in 1996. The middle 50 percent earned between $560 and $880. The lowest 10 percent earned less than $440 and the top 10 percent more than $1,160.

According to a 1997 survey by the American Speech-Language-Hearing Association, the median annual salary for full-time certified speech-language pathologists was $44,000; for audiologists, $43,000. Certified speech-language pathologists with one to three years of experience earned a median annual salary of $38,000; licensed audiologists with one to three years of experience earned $32,000. Speech-language pathologists with 22 years' experience earned a median annual salary of $52,000, while audiologists with comparable experience earned about $55,000. Salaries also vary according to geographic location and type of employment facility.

Related Occupations

Speech-language pathologists specialize in the prevention, diagnosis, and treatment of speech and language problems. Workers in related occupations include occupational therapists, optometrists, physical therapists, psychologists, recreational therapists, and rehabilitation counselors.

Audiologists specialize in the prevention, diagnosis, and treatment of hearing problems. Workers in related occupations include neurologists, neonatologists, acoustical engineers, industrial hygienists, and other rehabilitation professionals.

Sources of Additional Information

State licensing boards in each state can provide information on licensure requirements. State departments of education can supply information on certification requirements for those who wish to work in public schools.

General information on careers in speech-language pathology and audiology is available from:

❏ American Speech-Language-Hearing Association, 10801 Rockville Pike, Rockville, MD 20852. Homepage: http://www.asha.org

Information on a career in audiology is also available from:

❏ American Academy of Audiology, 8201 Greensboro Dr., Suite 300, McLean, VA 22102.

Urban and Regional Planners

(*D.O.T.* 188.167-110 and 199.167-014)

Significant Points

✱ *Most entry-level jobs require a master's degree in urban or regional planning or urban design, landscape architecture, or the equivalent in work experience.*

✱ *Most new jobs will arise in more affluent, rapidly growing communities.*

Nature of the Work

Urban and regional planners are often referred to as community, county, or city planners because the majority are employed by local governments. They develop long and short-term land use plans to provide for growth and revitalization of urban, suburban, and rural communities, while helping local officials make decisions concerning social, economic, and environmental problems.

Planners promote the best use of a community's land and resources for residential, commercial, and recreational purposes. Planners may be involved in various other activities, including decisions on alternative public transportation system plans, resource development, and protection of ecologically sensitive regions. They address issues such as traffic congestion, air pollution, and the effect of growth and change on a community. They may formulate master plans relating to the construction of new school buildings, public housing, or other infrastructure. Some planners are involved in environmental issues ranging from pollution control to wetland preservation, forest conservation, or the location of new landfills. Planners also may be involved with drafting legislation on environmental, social, and economic issues, such as sheltering the homeless, planning a new park, or meeting the demand for new correctional facilities.

Planners examine proposed community facilities such as schools to be sure these facilities will meet the demands placed upon them over time by population growth. They keep abreast of the economic and legal issues involved in zoning codes, building codes, and environmental regulations. They ensure that builders and developers follow these codes and regulations. Planners also deal with land use issues created by population movements. For example, as suburban growth and economic development create more new jobs outside cities, the need for public transportation that enables urban workers to get to jobs in the suburbs increases. In response, planners develop transportation models for possible implementation and explain their details to planning boards and the general public.

Before preparing plans for community development, planners report on the current use of land for residential, business, and community purposes. These reports include information on the location and capacity of streets, highways, water and sewer lines, schools, libraries, and cultural and recreational sites, and provide data on the types of industries in the community, characteristics of the population, and employment and economic trends. With this information, along with input from citizens' advisory committees, planners design the layout of buildings and other facilities such as subway lines and stations, and prepare reports showing how their programs can be carried out and what they will cost.

Planners use computers to record and analyze information, and to prepare reports and recommendations for government executives and others. Computer databases, spreadsheets, and analytical techniques are widely used to project program costs and forecast future trends in employment, housing, transportation, or population. Computerized geographic information systems enable planners to map land areas and overlay maps with geographic variables, such as population density, as well as to combine and manipulate geographic information to produce alternative plans for land use or development.

Urban and regional planners often confer with land developers, civic leaders, and public officials. They may function as mediators in community disputes and present alternatives that are acceptable to opposing parties. Planners may prepare material for community relations programs, speak at civic meetings, and appear before legislative committees and elected officials to explain and defend their proposals.

In large organizations, planners usually specialize in a single area such as transportation, demography, housing, historic preservation, urban design, environmental and regulatory issues, or economic development. In small organizations, planners must be generalists, available to do various kinds of planning.

Working Conditions

Urban and regional planners periodically travel to and personally inspect the features of land under consideration for development or regulation, including its current use and the types of structures on it. Some local government planners involved in site development inspections spend most of their time in the field. Although most planners have a scheduled 40-hour workweek, they frequently attend evening or weekend meetings or public hearings with citizens' groups. Planners may experience the pressure of deadlines and tight work schedules, as well as political pressure generated by interest groups affected by their land use proposals.

Employment

Urban and regional planners held about 29,000 jobs in 1996, and about two out of three were employed by local governments. An increasing proportion of planners work in the private sector for companies involved with research and testing or management and public relations. Others are employed in state agencies dealing with housing, transportation, or environmental protection, and a small number work for the federal government.

Training, Other Qualifications, and Advancement

Employers prefer workers who have advanced training. Most entry-level jobs in federal, state, and local government agencies require a master's degree in urban or regional planning or urban design, geography, or the equivalent in work experience. A bachelor's degree from an accredited planning program, coupled with a master's degree in architecture, landscape architecture, or civil engineering, is good preparation for entry-level planning jobs in areas such as urban design, traffic, or the environment. A master's degree from an accredited planning program provides the best training for a number of planning fields. Although graduates from one of the limited number of accredited bachelor's degree programs qualify for many beginning positions, their advancement opportunities are often limited unless they acquire an advanced degree. Courses in related disciplines such as architecture, law, earth sciences, demography, economics, finance, health administration, geographic information systems, and management are highly recommended. In addition, familiarity with computer models and statistical techniques is necessary.

In 1997, about 80 colleges and universities offered an accredited master's degree program, and about 10 offered an accredited bachelor's degree program in urban or regional planning. These programs are accredited by the Planning Accreditation Board, which consists of representatives of the American Institute of Certified Planners, the American Planning Association, and the Association of Collegiate Schools of Planning. Most graduate programs in planning require a minimum of two years.

Specializations most commonly offered by planning schools are environmental planning, land use and comprehensive planning, economic development, and housing. Other popular offerings include community development, transportation, and urban design. Graduate students spend considerable time in studios, workshops, and laboratory courses learning to analyze and solve planning problems. They are often required to work in a planning office part-time or during the summer. Local government planning offices frequently offer students internships, providing experience that proves invaluable in obtaining a full-time planning position after graduation.

The American Institute of Certified Planners (AICP), a professional institute within the American Planning Association (APA), grants certification to individuals who have the appropriate combination of education and professional experience and who pass an examination. Certification may be helpful for promotion.

Planners must be able to think in terms of spatial relationships and visualize the effects of their plans and designs. Planners should be flexible and able to reconcile different viewpoints and to make constructive policy recommendations. The ability to communicate effectively, both orally and in writing, is necessary for anyone interested in this field.

After a few years of experience, planners may advance to assignments requiring a high degree of independent judgment, such as designing the physical layout of a large development or recommending policy and budget options. Some public sector planners are promoted to community planning director and spend a great deal of time meeting with officials, speaking to civic groups, and supervising a staff. Further advancement occurs through a transfer to a larger jurisdiction with more complex problems and greater responsibilities, or into related occupations, such as director of community or economic development.

Job Outlook

Employment of urban and regional planners is expected to grow more slowly than the average for all occupations through the year 2006. Factors contributing to the limited job growth expected in this sector include the need for governments to do more with less while still providing services such as regulation of commercial development, the environment, transportation, housing, and land use and development, and for the private sector to comply with such regulations. Nongovernmental initiatives such as historic preservation and central city redevelopment will provide additional openings. Most job openings, however, are expected to arise from the need to replace experienced planners who transfer to other occupations, retire, or leave the labor force for other reasons.

Most planners work in local government, many of which have limited resources and many demands for services. When communities need to cut expenditures, planning services may be cut before more basic services such as police or education. The number of openings in private industry for consulting positions is expected to grow more rapidly than the number of openings in government.

Most new jobs for urban and regional planners will arise in more affluent, rapidly expanding communities. Local governments need planners to address an array of problems associated with population growth. For example, new housing developments require roads, sewer systems, fire stations, schools, libraries, and recreation facilities that must be planned while considering budgetary constraints. Small town chambers of commerce, economic development authorities, and tourism bureaus may hire planners, preferring candidates with some background in marketing and public relations.

Earnings

Salaries of planners vary by educational attainment, type of employer, experience, size of community in which they work, and geographic location. According to a report by the American Planning Association (APA), in 1995, urban and regional planners with less than five years' experience earned median annual salaries of $30,000. Planners with between five and ten years' experience earned median salaries of $39,900. Those with more than ten years' experience earned median annual salaries of $55,000. The APA reports the median annual salary for all planners was $45,300. Salaries of community planners employed by the federal government in nonsupervisory, supervisory, and managerial positions averaged about $57,620 a year in early 1997.

Related Occupations

Urban and regional planners develop plans for the orderly growth of urban and rural communities. Others whose work is similar to the work of planners include architects,

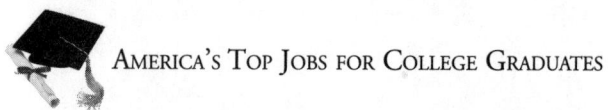

landscape architects, city managers, civil engineers, environmental engineers, directors of community or economic development, and geographers.

Sources of Additional Information

Information on careers, salaries, and certification in urban and regional planning is available from:

❑ American Planning Association, Education Division, 122 South Michigan Avenue, Suite 1600, Chicago, IL 60630-6107.

Jobs Typically Requiring a Bachelor's Degree or Higher, Plus Work Experience

Included are the following jobs:

- **Administrative Services Managers**
- **Agricultural Scientists**
- **Architects**
- **Education Administrators**
- **Engineering, Science, and Computer Systems Managers**
- **Farmers and Farm Managers**
- **Financial Managers**
- **General Managers and Top Executives**
- **Government Chief Executives and Legislators**
- **Marketing, Advertising, and Public Relations Managers**
- **Mathematicians**
- **Pharmacists**
- **Protestant Ministers**
- **Rabbis**
- **Roman Catholic Priests**
- **Statisticians**

Administrative Services Managers

(D.O.T. 163.167-026; 169.167-034; 188.117-122, .167-106)

Significant Points

* Many advance to these jobs by acquiring work experience in various administrative positions.

* Keen competition is expected due to low turnover and an ample supply of competent, experienced workers seeking managerial jobs.

Nature of the Work

Administrative services managers are employed throughout the American economy, and their range of duties is broad. They coordinate and direct support services, which may include secretarial and reception; administration; payroll; conference planning and travel; information and data processing; mail; facilities management; materials scheduling and distribution; printing and reproduction; records management; telecommunications management; personal property procurement, supply, and disposal; security; and parking.

In small organizations, a single administrative services manager may oversee all support services. In larger ones, however, first-line administrative services managers report to mid-level supervisors who, in turn, report to proprietors or top-level managers.

First-line administrative services managers directly oversee a staff that performs various support services. Mid-level managers develop departmental plans, set goals and deadlines, develop procedures to improve productivity and customer service, and define the responsibilities of supervisory-level managers. They are often involved in the hiring and dismissal of employees, but generally have no role in the formulation of personnel policy.

As the size of the firm increases, administrative services managers are more likely to specialize in one or more support activities. For example, some administrative services managers work primarily as facilities managers, office managers, property managers, or unclaimed property officers. In many cases, the duties of these administrative services managers are quite similar to those of other managers and supervisors.

Administrative services managers who specialize in facilities management or planning may oversee the purchase, sale, or lease of facilities; redesign work areas to be more efficient and user-friendly; ensure that facilities comply with government regulations; and supervise maintenance, grounds, and custodial staffs. In some firms, they are called facilities managers.

Some mid-level administrative services managers oversee first-line supervisors from various departments, including the clerical staff. In small firms, however, clerical supervisors perform this function.

Property management is divided into the following functions: Management and use of personal property such as office supplies, administrative services management, and real property management. Personal property managers acquire, distribute, and store supplies, and may sell or dispose of surplus property. Other property managers are engaged solely in surplus property disposal, which involves the resale of scraps, rejects, and surplus or unneeded supplies and machinery. This is an increasingly important source of revenue for many commercial organizations. In government, surplus property officers may receive surplus from various departments and agencies, and then sell or dispose of it to the public or other agencies.

Some administrative services managers oversee unclaimed property disposal. In government, this activity may entail auctioning off unclaimed liquid assets such as stocks, bonds, the contents of safe deposit boxes, or personal property such as motor vehicles, after attempts to locate their rightful owners have failed.

Working Conditions

Administrative services managers generally work in comfortable offices. In smaller organizations, they may work alongside the people they supervise and the office may be crowded and noisy.

The work of administrative services managers can be stressful, as they attempt to schedule work to meet deadlines. Although the 40-hour week is standard, uncompensated overtime is often required to resolve problems. Managers involved in personal property procurement, use, and disposal may travel extensively between their home office, branch offices, vendors' offices, and property sales sites. Facilities managers who are responsible for the design of work spaces may spend time at construction sites and may travel between different facilities while monitoring the work of maintenance, grounds, and custodial staffs.

Employment

Administrative services managers held about 291,000 jobs in 1996. Over half worked in service industries, including management, business, social, and health services organizations. Others were found in virtually every other industry.

Training, Other Qualifications, and Advancement

Many administrative services managers advance through the ranks in their organization, acquiring work experience in various administrative positions before assuming first-line supervisory duties. All managers who oversee departmental supervisors should be familiar with office procedures and equipment. Facilities managers may have a background in architecture, engineering, construction, interior design, or real estate, in addition to managerial experience. Managers of personal property acquisition and disposal need experience in purchasing and sales, and knowledge of a wide variety of supplies, machinery, and equipment. Managers concerned with supply, inventory, and distribution must be experienced in receiving, warehousing, packaging, shipping, transportation, and related operations. Managers of unclaimed property often have experience in insurance claims analysis and records management.

Educational requirements for these managers vary widely, depending on the size and complexity of the organization. In small organizations, experience may be the only requirement needed to enter a position as office manager. When an opening in administrative services management occurs, the office manager may be promoted to the position based on past performance. In large organizations, however, administrative services managers are normally hired from outside, and each position has formal requirements concerning education and experience. For first-line administrative services managers of secretarial, mail room, and related support activities, many employers prefer an associate degree in business or management, although a high school diploma may suffice when combined with appropriate experience. For managers of audiovisual, graphics, and other technical activities, postsecondary technical school training is preferred. For managers of highly complex services, a bachelor's degree in business, human resources, or finance is often required. The curriculum should include courses in office technology, accounting, business mathematics, computer applications, human resources, and business law. Similarly, facilities managers may need a bachelor's degree in engineering, architecture, or business administration, although some have an associate degree in a technical specialty. Some administrative services managers have advanced degrees. Whatever the manager's educational background, it must be accompanied by related work experience reflecting demonstrated ability.

Persons interested in becoming administrative services managers should have good communication skills and be able to establish effective working relationships with many different people, ranging from managers, supervisors, and professionals, to clerks and blue-collar workers. They should be analytical, detail oriented, flexible, and decisive. The ability to coordinate several activities at once and quickly analyze and resolve specific problems is important. Ability to work under pressure and cope with deadlines is also important.

Advancement in small organizations is normally achieved by moving to other management positions or to a larger organization. Advancement is easier in large firms employing several levels of administrative services managers. Attainment of the Certified Administrative Manager (CAM) designation, through work experience and successful completion of examinations offered by the Institute of Certified Professional Managers, can increase one's advancement potential. A bachelor's degree enhances a first-level manager's opportunities to advance to a mid-level management position, such as director of administrative services, and eventually to a top-level management position, such as executive vice president for administrative services. Those with the required capital and experience can establish their own management consulting firm.

Job Outlook

Employment of administrative services managers is expected to grow about as fast as the average for all occupations through the year 2006. Like other managerial occupations, this occupation is characterized by low turnover. These factors, coupled with the ample supply of competent, experienced workers seeking managerial jobs, should result in keen competition for administrative services management positions in the coming years.

Many firms are increasingly contracting out administrative services positions and otherwise streamlining these functions in an effort to cut costs. Corporate restructuring has reduced the number of administrative services manager positions in recent years, and this trend is expected to continue.

As it becomes more common for firms and governments at all levels to contract out administrative services, demand for administrative services managers will increase in the management services, management consulting, and facilities support services firms providing these services.

Earnings

Earnings of administrative services managers vary greatly depending on their employer, specialty, and geographic area in which they work. According to a 1996 survey conducted by the AMS Foundation, building services/facilities managers earned about $53,800 a year in 1996; office/administrative services managers earned about $41,400; and records managers about $37,900.

In the federal government, facilities managers in nonsupervisory, supervisory, and managerial positions averaged $49,140 a year in early 1997; miscellaneous administrative and program officers, $53,330; industrial property managers, $47,930; property disposal specialists, $43,460; administrative officers $49,070, and support services administrators, $39,700.

Related Occupations

Administrative services managers direct and coordinate support services and oversee the purchase, use, and disposal of personal property. Occupations with similar functions include administrative assistants, appraisers, buyers, clerical supervisors, contract specialists, cost estimators, procurement services managers, property and real estate managers, purchasing managers, and personnel managers.

Sources of Additional Information

For information about careers in facilities management, contact:

❏ International Facility Management Association, 1 East Greenway Plaza, Suite 1100, Houston, TX 77046-0194 Homepage: http:// www.IFMA.org

For information about the certified administrative manager designation, contact:

❏ Institute of Certified Professional Managers, James Madison University, College of Business, Harrisonburg, VA 22807.

For information about compensation of administrative managers, contact:

❏ AMS Foundation, 350 W. Jackson Boulevard, Suite 360, Chicago, IL 60661.

Agricultural Scientists

(*D.O.T.* 040.061-010, -014, -018, -038, -042, and -058; 041.061-014, -018, -046, and -082; and 041.081)

Significant Points

★ *A large proportion, about 30 percent, work for federal, state, and local governments.*

★ *A bachelor's degree in agricultural science is sufficient for some jobs in applied research; a master's or doctoral degree is required for basic research.*

★ *Those with advanced degrees have the best prospects; however, competition may be keen for some basic research jobs if federal and state funding for these positions is cut.*

Nature of the Work

The work agricultural scientists do plays an important part in maintaining and increasing the nation's agricultural productivity. Agricultural scientists study farm crops and animals and develop ways of improving their quantity and quality. They look for ways to improve crop yield and quality with less labor, control pests and weeds more safely and effectively, and conserve soil and water. They research methods of converting raw agricultural commodities into attractive and healthy food products for consumers.

Agricultural science is closely related to biological science, and agricultural scientists use the principles of biology, chemistry, physics, mathematics, and other sciences to solve problems in agriculture. They often work with biological scientists on basic biological research and in applying to agriculture the advances in knowledge brought about by biotechnology.

Many agricultural scientists work in basic or applied research and development. Others manage or administer research and development programs or manage marketing or production operations in companies that produce food products or agricultural chemicals, supplies, and machinery. Some agricultural scientists are consultants to business firms, private clients, or to government.

Depending on the agricultural scientist's area of specialization, the nature of the work performed varies.

Food science. Food scientists or technologists are usually employed in the food processing industry, universities, or the federal government, and help meet consumer demand for food products that are healthful, safe, palatable, and convenient. To do this, they use their knowledge of chemistry, microbiology, and other sciences to develop new or better ways of preserving, processing, packaging, storing, and delivering foods. Some engage in basic research, discovering new food sources; analyzing food content to determine levels of vitamins, fat, sugar, or protein; or searching for substitutes for harmful or undesirable additives, such as nitrites. Many food technologists work in product development. Others enforce government regulations, inspecting food processing areas and ensuring that sanitation, safety, quality, and waste management standards are met.

Plant science. Agronomy, crop science, entomology, and plant breeding are included in plant science. Scientists in these dis-

ciplines study plants and their growth in soils, helping producers of food, feed, and fiber crops to continue to feed a growing population while conserving natural resources and maintaining the environment. Agronomists and crop scientists not only help increase productivity, but also study ways to improve the nutritional value of crops and the quality of seed. Some crop scientists study the breeding, physiology, and management of crops and use genetic engineering to develop crops resistant to pests and drought. Entomologists conduct research to develop new technologies to control or eliminate pests in infested areas and prevent the spread of harmful pests to new areas, and which are compatible with the environment. They also do research or engage in oversight activities aimed at halting the spread of insect-borne disease.

Soil science. These workers study the chemical, physical, biological, and mineralogical composition of soils as they relate to plant or crop growth. They study the responses of various soil types to fertilizers, tillage practices, and crop rotation. Many soil scientists who work for the federal government conduct soil surveys, classifying and mapping soils. They provide information and recommendations to farmers and other landowners regarding the best use of land and how to avoid or correct problems such as erosion. They may also consult with engineers and other technical personnel working on construction projects about the effects of, and solutions to, soil problems. Since soil science is closely related to environmental science, persons trained in soil science also apply their knowledge to ensure environmental quality and effective land use.

Animal science. Developing better, more efficient ways of producing and processing meat, poultry, eggs, and milk is the work of animal scientists. Dairy scientists, poultry scientists, animal breeders, and other related scientists study the genetics, nutrition, reproduction, growth, and development of domestic farm animals. Some animal scientists inspect and grade livestock food products, purchase livestock, or work in technical sales or marketing. As extension agents or consultants, animal scientists advise agricultural producers on how to upgrade animal housing facilities properly, lower mortality rates, or increase production of animal products, such as milk or eggs.

Working Conditions

Agricultural scientists involved in management or basic research tend to work regular hours in offices and laboratories. The working environment for those engaged in applied research or product development varies, depending on the discipline of agricultural science and the type of employer. For example, food scientists in private industry may work in test kitchens while investigating new processing techniques.

Animal scientists working for federal, state, or university research stations may spend part of their time at dairies, farrowing houses, feedlots, farm animal facilities, or outdoors conducting research associated with livestock. Soil and crop scientists also spend time outdoors conducting research on farms or agricultural research stations. Entomologists work in laboratories, insectories, or agricultural research stations, and may also spend time outdoors studying or collecting insects in their natural habitat.

Employment

Agricultural scientists held about 24,000 jobs in 1996. In addition, several thousand persons held agricultural science faculty positions in colleges and universities.

About 30 percent of all nonfaculty agricultural scientists work for federal, state, or local governments. Nearly one out of five worked for the federal government in 1996, mostly in the Department of Agriculture. In addition, large numbers worked for state governments at state agricultural colleges or agricultural research stations. Some worked for agricultural service companies; others worked for commercial research and development laboratories, seed companies, pharmaceutical companies, wholesale distributors, and food products companies. About 2,000 agricultural scientists were self-employed in 1996, mainly as consultants.

Training, Other Qualifications, and Advancement

Training requirements for agricultural scientists depend on their specialty and the type of work they perform. A bachelor's degree in agricultural science is sufficient for some jobs in applied research or for assisting in basic research, but a master's or doctoral degree is required for basic research. A Ph.D. degree in agricultural science is usually needed for college teaching and for advancement to administrative research positions. Degrees in related sciences such as biology, chemistry, or physics or in related engineering specialties also may qualify persons for some agricultural science jobs.

All states have a land-grant college which offers agricultural science degrees. Many other colleges and universities also offer agricultural science degrees or some agricultural science courses. However, not every school offers all specialties. A typical undergraduate agricultural science curriculum includes communications, economics, business, and physical and life sciences courses, in addition to a wide variety of technical agricultural science courses. For prospective animal scientists, these technical agricultural science courses might include animal breeding, reproductive physiology, nutrition, and meats and muscle biology; students preparing as food scientists take courses such as food chemistry, food analysis, food microbiology, and food processing operations; and those preparing as crop or soil scientists take courses in plant pathology, soil chemistry, entomology, plant physiology, and biochemistry, among others. Advanced degree programs include classroom and fieldwork, laboratory research, and a thesis or dissertation based on independent research.

Agricultural scientists should be able to work independently or as part of a team and be able to communicate clearly and concisely, both orally and in writing. Most agricultural scientists also need an understanding of basic business principles.

The American Society of Agronomy offers certification in agronomy, crop science, soil science, soil classification, horticulture, plant pathology, and weed science. To become certified, applicants must meet certain examination, education, and professional work experience standards.

Agricultural scientists who have advanced degrees usually begin in research or teaching. With experience, they may advance to jobs such as supervisors of research programs or managers of other agriculture-related activities.

Job Outlook

Employment of agricultural scientists is expected to grow about as fast as the average for all occupations through the year 2006. Additionally, the need to replace agricultural scientists who retire or otherwise leave the occupation permanently will account for many more job openings than projected growth.

Past agricultural research has resulted in the development of higher-yielding crops, crops with better resistance to pests and plant pathogens, and chemically-based fertilizers and pesticides. Further research is necessary as insects and diseases continue to adapt to pesticides, and as soil fertility and water quality deteriorate. Agricultural scientists will be needed to balance increased agricultural output with protection and preservation of the soil, water, and ecosystems. They will practice "sustainable agriculture" by developing and implementing plans to manage pests, crops, soil fertility and erosion, and animal waste in ways that reduce the use of harmful chemicals and do little damage to the natural environment. Products developed using biotechnology methods will assist in these challenges. Also, an expanding population and a public increasingly focused on diet, health, and food safety will result in growing opportunities for agricultural scientists to work in food science and technology.

Generally speaking, those with advanced degrees will be in the best position to enter jobs as agricultural scientists. However, competition may be keen for teaching positions in colleges or universities and for some basic research jobs, even for doctoral holders. Federal and state budget cuts may limit funding for these positions through the year 2006.

Bachelor's degree holders can work in some applied research and product development positions, but usually only in certain subfields, such as food science and technology. Also, the federal government hires bachelor's degree holders to work as soil scientists. Despite the more limited opportunities for those with only a bachelor's degree to obtain jobs as agricultural scientists, a bachelor's degree in agricultural science is useful for managerial jobs in businesses that deal with ranchers and farmers, such as feed, fertilizer, seed, and farm equipment manufacturers; retailers or wholesalers; and farm credit institutions. Four-year degrees may also help persons enter occupations such as farmer or farm or ranch manager, cooperative extension service agent, agricultural products inspector, or purchasing or sales agent for agricultural commodity or farm supply companies.

Earnings

According to the National Association of Colleges and Employers, beginning salary offers in 1997 for graduates with a bachelor's degree in animal science averaged about $24,900 a year, and for graduates in plant science, $24,000.

The median salary for full-time food scientists or technologists was $55,200, according to a 1995 salary survey by the Institute of Food Technologists.

Average federal salaries for employees in nonsupervisory, supervisory, and managerial positions in certain agricultural science specialties in 1997 were as follows: Animal science, $65,500; agronomy, $52,000; soil science, $49,400; horticulture, $50,400; and entomology, $62,200.

Related Occupations

The work of agricultural scientists is closely related to that of biologists and other natural scientists such as chemists, foresters, and conservation scientists. It is also related to agricultural production occupations such as farmer and farm manager and cooperative extension service agent. Certain specialties of agricultural science are also related to other occupations. For example, the work of animal scientists is related to that of veterinarians; horticulturists, to landscape architects; and soil scientists, to soil conservationists.

Sources of Additional Information

Information on careers in agricultural science is available from:

❑ American Society of Agronomy, Crop Science Society of America, Soil Science Society of America, 677 S. Segoe Rd., Madison, WI 53711-1086.

❏ Food and Agricultural Careers for Tomorrow, Purdue University, 1140 Agricultural Administration Bldg., West Lafayette, IN 47907-1140.

For information on careers in food technology, write to:

❏ Institute of Food Technologists, Suite 300, 221 N. LaSalle St., Chicago IL 60601.

For information on careers in entomology, contact:

❏ Entomological Society of America, 9301 Annapolis Rd., Lanham, MD 20706. Attn: Public Relations Coordinator.

Information on acquiring a job as an agricultural scientist with the federal government may be obtained from the Office of Personnel Management through a telephone-based system. Consult your telephone directory under U.S. government for a local number, or call (912) 757-3000 (TDD 912-744-2299). That number is not toll-free and charges may result. Information also is available from their Internet site: http://www.usajobs.opm.gov

Architects

(*D.O.T.* 001.061-010 and .167-010)

Significant Points

* *Nearly 30 percent—over three times the proportion for all professionals—are self-employed, practicing as partners in architecture firms or on their own.*

* *Licensure requirements include a professional degree in architecture, a period of practical training or internship, and passage of all sections of the Architect Registration Examination.*

* *Prospective architects may face competition, especially for jobs in the most prestigious firms; those who complete at least one summer internship while in school and know computer-aided design and drafting technology may have a distinct advantage in the job market.*

Nature of the Work

Architects design buildings and other structures. The design of a building involves far more than its appearance. Buildings must also be functional, safe, and economical, and must suit the needs of the people who use them. Architects take all these things into consideration when they design buildings and other structures.

Architects provide a wide variety of professional services to individuals and organizations planning a construction project. They may be involved in all phases of development, from the initial discussion of general ideas with the client through the entire life of the facility. Their duties require a number of skills—design, engineering, managerial, communication, and supervisory.

The architect and client first discuss the purposes, requirements, and budget of a project. In some cases, architects provide various predesign services—conducting feasibility and environmental impact studies, selecting a site, or specifying the requirements the design must meet. For example, they may determine space requirements by researching the number and type of potential users of a building. The architect then prepares drawings and a report presenting ideas for the client to review.

After the initial proposals are discussed and accepted, architects develop final construction plans. These plans show the building's appearance and details for its construction. Accompanying these are drawings of the structural system; air-conditioning, heating, and ventilating systems; electrical systems; plumbing; and possibly site and landscape plans. They also specify the building materials and, in some cases, the interior furnishings. In developing designs, architects follow building codes, zoning laws, fire regulations, and other ordinances, such as those requiring easy access by disabled persons. Throughout the planning stage, they make necessary changes. Although they have traditionally used pencil and paper to produce design and construction drawings, architects are increasingly turning to computer-aided design and drafting (CADD) technology for these important tasks.

Architects may also assist the client in obtaining construction bids, selecting a contractor, and negotiating the construction contract. As construction proceeds, they may visit the building site to ensure the contractor is following the design, adhering to the schedule, using the specified materials, and meeting quality work standards. The job is not complete until all construction is finished, required tests are made, and construction costs are paid. Sometimes, architects also provide postconstruction services, such as facilities management. They advise on energy efficiency measures, evaluate how well the building design adapts to the needs of occupants, and make necessary improvements.

Architects design a wide variety of buildings, such as office and apartment buildings, schools, churches, factories, hospitals, houses, and airport terminals. They also design multibuilding complexes such as urban centers, college campuses, industrial parks, and entire communities. In addition to designing buildings, they may advise on the selection of building sites, prepare cost analysis and land-use studies, and do long-range planning for land development.

Architects sometimes specialize in one phase of work. Some specialize in the design of one type of building—for example, hospitals, schools, or housing. Others focus on planning and predesign services or construction management, and do little design work. They often work with engineers, urban planners, interior designers, landscape architects, and others.

During a training period leading up to licensure as architects, entry-level workers are called intern-architects. This training period gives them practical work experience while they prepare for the Architect Registration Examination (ARE). Typical duties may include preparing construction drawings on CADD, or assisting in the design of one part of a project.

Working Conditions

Architects generally work in a comfortable environment. Most of their time is spent in offices advising clients, developing reports and drawings, and working with other architects and engineers. However, they often visit construction sites to review the progress of projects.

Architects may occasionally be under great stress, working nights and weekends to meet deadlines. In 1996, about two out of five architects worked more than 40 hours a week, in contrast to one in four workers in all occupations combined.

Employment

Architects held about 94,000 jobs in 1996. The majority of jobs were in architecture firms—most of which employ fewer than five workers. A few worked for builders, real estate developers, and for government agencies responsible for housing, planning, or community development, such as the U.S. Departments of Defense and Interior, and the General Services Administration. Nearly three in ten architects are self-employed, practicing as partners in architecture firms or on their own.

Training, Other Qualifications, and Advancement

All states and the District of Columbia require individuals to be licensed (registered) before they may call themselves architects or contract to provide architectural services. Many architecture school graduates work in the field even though they are not licensed. However, a licensed architect is required to take legal responsibility for all work. Licensure requirements include a professional degree in architecture, a period of practical training or internship, and passage of all sections of the ARE.

In many states, the professional degree in architecture must be from one of the 105 schools of architecture with programs accredited by the National Architectural Accrediting Board (NAAB). However, state architectural registration boards set their own standards, so graduation from a non-NAAB-

accredited program may meet the education requirement for licensure in some states. There are several types of professional degrees in architecture. The majority of all architecture degrees are from five-year Bachelor of Architecture programs, intended for students entering from high school or with no previous architecture training. Some schools offer a two-year Master of Architecture program for students with a preprofessional undergraduate degree in architecture or a related area, or a three- or four-year Master of Architecture program for students with a degree in another discipline. In addition, there are many combinations and variations of these degree programs.

The choice of degree type depends upon each individual's preference and educational background. Prospective architecture students should carefully consider the available options before committing to a program. For example, although the five-year Bachelor of Architecture program offers the fastest route to the professional degree, courses are specialized and, if the student does not complete the program, moving to a nonarchitecture program may be difficult. A typical program includes courses in architectural history and theory, building design, professional practice, math, physical sciences, and liberal arts. Central to most architecture programs is the design studio, where students put into practice the skills and concepts learned in the classroom. During the final semester of many programs, students devote their studio time to creating an architectural project from beginning to end, culminating in a three-dimensional model of their design.

Many architecture schools also offer graduate education for those who already have a bachelor's or master's degree in architecture or other areas. Although graduate education beyond the professional degree is not required for practicing architects, it is normally required for research, teaching, and certain specialties.

Architects must be able to visually communicate their ideas to clients. Artistic and drawing ability is very helpful in doing this, but not essential. More important is a visual orientation and the ability to conceptualize and understand spatial relationships. Good communication skills, the ability to work independently or as part of a team, and creativity are important qualities for anyone interested in becoming an architect. Computer literacy is also required as most firms use computers for specifications writing, two- and three-dimensional drafting, and financial management. A knowledge of computer-aided design and drafting (CADD) is helpful and will become more important as architecture firms continue to adopt this technology.

All state architectural registration boards require a training period before candidates may sit for the ARE and become

licensed. Many states have adopted the training standards established by the Intern Development Program, a branch of the American Institute of Architects and the National Council of Architectural Registration Boards. These standards stipulate broad and diversified training under the supervision of a licensed architect over a three-year period. New graduates usually begin as intern-architects in architecture firms, where they assist in preparing architectural documents or drawings. They may also do research on building codes and materials, or write specifications for building materials, installation criteria, the quality of finishes, and other related details. Graduates with degrees in architecture also enter related fields such as graphic, interior, or industrial design; urban planning; real estate development; civil engineering; or construction management. In such cases, an architectural license, and thus the internship period, is not required.

After completing the internship period, intern-architects are eligible to sit for the ARE. The examination tests candidates on a broad body of architectural knowledge, and is given in sections throughout the year. Candidates who pass the ARE and meet all standards established by their state board are licensed to practice in that state.

After becoming licensed and gaining experience, architects take on increasingly responsible duties, eventually managing entire projects. In large firms, architects may advance to supervisory or managerial positions. Some architects become partners in established firms; others set up their own practice.

Several states require continuing education to maintain licensure, and many more states are expected to adopt mandatory continuing education. Requirements vary by state, but usually involve the completion of a certain number of credits every year or two through seminars, workshops, formal university classes, conferences, self-study courses, or other sources.

Job Outlook

Despite projected average employment growth coupled with job openings stemming from the need to replace architects who retire or leave the labor force for other reasons, prospective architects may face competition, especially if the number of architecture degrees awarded remains at, or above, current levels. Many individuals are attracted to this occupation, and the number of applicants often exceeds the number of available jobs, especially in the most prestigious firms. Prospective architects who complete at least one summer internship—either paid or unpaid—while in school and know CADD technology may have a distinct advantage in getting an intern-architect position after graduation.

Because construction—particularly office and retail—is sensitive to cyclical changes in the economy, architects will face particularly strong competition for jobs or clients during recessions, and layoffs may occur. Those involved in the design of institutional buildings such as schools, hospitals, nursing homes, and correctional facilities will be less affected by fluctuations in the economy.

Even in times of overall good job opportunities, however, there may be areas of the country with poor opportunities. Architects who are licensed to practice in one state must meet the licensing requirements of other states before practicing. These requirements are becoming more standardized, however, facilitating movement to other states.

Employment of architects is strongly tied to the level of local construction, particularly nonresidential structures such as office buildings, shopping centers, schools, and health care facilities. The boom in nonresidential construction during the 1980s resulted in high vacancy rates and a slowdown in this type of construction during the first half of the 1990s. Although this sector of the construction industry is beginning to recover, slower labor force growth, rapid increases in telecommuting and flexiplace work, and the earlier overbuilding are expected to continue to suppress demand for new office space between 1996 and 2006. Nevertheless, employment of architects is expected to grow about as fast as the average for all occupations during this period.

As the stock of buildings ages, demand for remodeling and repair work should grow considerably. The needed renovation and rehabilitation of old buildings, particularly in urban areas where space for new buildings is becoming limited, are expected to provide many job opportunities for architects. In addition, demographic trends and changes in health care delivery are influencing the demand for certain institutional structures, and should also provide more jobs for architects in the future. For example, increases in the school-age population will result in new school construction and additions to existing schools. And, growth is expected in the number of adult care centers, assisted-living facilities, and community health clinics, all of which are preferable, less costly alternatives to hospitals and nursing homes.

Earnings

According to The American Institute of Architects, the median compensation, including bonuses, for intern-architects in architecture firms was $27,000 in 1996. Licensed architects with three to five of years experience had median earnings of $33,000; licensed architects with eight to ten years of experience, but who were not managers or principals of a firm, earned $45,000. Principals or partners of firms earned

$75–100,000 in 1996, although partners in some large practices earned considerably more. Similar to other industries, small architecture firms (fewer than five employees) are less likely than larger firms to provide employee benefits.

Earnings of partners in established architecture firms may fluctuate due to changing business conditions. Some architects may have difficulty establishing their own practices, and may go through a period when their expenses are greater than their income, requiring substantial financial resources.

Related Occupations

Architects design and construct buildings and related structures. Others who engage in similar work are landscape architects, building contractors, civil engineers, urban planners, interior designers, industrial designers, and graphic designers.

Sources of Additional Information

Information about education and careers in architecture can be obtained from:

❏ Careers in Architecture Program, The American Institute of Architects, 1735 New York Ave. NW, Washington, DC 20006. Homepage: http://www.aiaonline.com

❏ Society of American Registered Architects, Nathan Kolodny Consultants, Suite 2A, 100 Pinewood Rd., Hartsdale, NY 10530.

Education Administrators

(*D.O.T.* 075.117-010, -018, -030; 090.117 except -034, .167; 091.107; 092.167; 094.117-010, .167-014; 096.167; 097.167; 099.117 except -022, .167-034; 100.117-010; 169.267-022; 239.137-010)

Significant Points

✳ *Most jobs require experience in a related occupation, such as teacher or admissions counselor, and a master's or doctoral degree.*

✳ *Competition will be keen for jobs in higher education, but will be much less intense for jobs at the elementary and secondary school level.*

Nature of the Work

Smooth operation of an educational institution requires competent administrators. Education administrators provide direction, leadership, and day-to-day management of educational activities in schools, colleges and universities, businesses, correctional institutions, museums, and job training and community service organizations. Education administrators set educational standards and goals and establish the policies and procedures to carry them out. They develop academic programs; monitor students' educational progress; train and motivate teachers and other staff; manage guidance and other student services; administer recordkeeping; prepare budgets; handle relations with parents, prospective and current students, employers, and the community; and perform many other duties.

Education administrators also supervise managers, support staff, teachers, counselors, librarians, coaches, and others. In an organization such as a small daycare center, one administrator may handle all these functions. In universities or large school systems, responsibilities are divided among many administrators, each with a specific function.

Those who manage elementary and secondary schools are called principals. They set the academic tone, hire teachers and other staff, help them improve their skills, and evaluate them. Principals confer with staff—advising, explaining, or answering procedural questions. They visit classrooms, observe teaching methods, review instructional objectives, and examine learning materials. They actively work with teachers to develop and maintain high curriculum standards, develop mission statements, and set performance goals and objectives. Principals must ensure they use clear, objective guidelines for teacher appraisals, since pay is often based on performance ratings.

Principals also meet and interact with other administrators, students, parents, and representatives of community organizations. Decision-making authority has shifted from school district central offices to individual schools. Thus, parents, teachers, and other members of the community play an important role in setting school policies and goals. Principals must pay attention to the concerns of these groups when making administrative decisions.

Budgets and reports on various subjects, including finances and attendance, are prepared by principals, who also oversee the requisitioning and allocation of supplies. As school budgets become tighter, many principals are more involved in public relations and fund raising to secure financial support for their schools from local businesses and the community.

Principals must take an active role to ensure that students meet national academic standards. Many principals develop school/business partnerships and school-to-work transition programs for students. Increasingly, principals must be sensitive to the needs of the rising number of non-English speaking and culturally diverse students. Growing enrollments, which are leading to overcrowding at many existing schools, are also a cause for concern. When addressing problems of inadequate available resources, administrators serve as advocates to build new schools or repair existing ones.

Schools continue to be involved with students' emotional welfare as well as their academic achievement. As a result, principals face responsibilities outside the academic realm. For example, in response to the growing number of dual-income and single-parent families and teenage parents, schools have established before- and after-school child-care programs or family resource centers, which also may offer parenting classes and social service referrals. With the help of community organizations, some principals have established programs to combat the increase in crime, drug and alcohol abuse, and sexually transmitted disease among students.

Assistant principals aid the principal in the overall administration of the school. Some assistant principals hold this position for several years to prepare for advancement to principal; others are career assistant principals. Depending on the number of students, the number of assistant principals a school employs may vary. They are responsible for programming student classes, ordering textbooks and supplies, and coordinating transportation, custodial, cafeteria, and other support services. They usually handle discipline, attendance, social and recreational programs, and health and safety. They also may counsel students on personal, educational, or vocational matters. With site-based management, assistant principals play a greater role in developing curriculum, evaluating teachers, and school-community relations, responsibilities previously assumed solely by the principal.

Administrators in school district central offices manage public schools under their jurisdiction. This group includes those who direct subject area programs such as English, music, vocational education, special education, and mathematics. They plan, evaluate, standardize, and improve curriculums and teaching techniques, and help teachers improve their skills and learn about new methods and materials. They oversee career counseling programs, and testing which measures students' abilities and helps place them in appropriate classes. Central office administrators also include directors of programs such as guidance, school psychology, athletics, curriculum and instruction, and professional development. With site-based management, principals and assistant principals, along with teachers and other staff, have primary responsibility for many of these programs in their individual schools.

In colleges and universities, academic deans, deans of faculty, provosts, and university deans assist presidents and develop budgets and academic policies and programs. They direct and coordinate activities of deans of individual colleges and chairpersons of academic departments.

College or university department heads or chairpersons are in charge of departments such as English, biological science, or mathematics. In addition to teaching, they coordinate schedules of classes and teaching assignments; propose budgets; recruit, interview, and hire applicants for teaching positions; evaluate faculty members; encourage faculty development; and perform other administrative duties. In overseeing their departments, chairpersons must consider and balance the concerns of faculty, administrators, and students.

Higher education administrators also provide student services. Vice presidents of student affairs or student life, deans of students, and directors of student services may direct and coordinate admissions, foreign student services, health and counseling services, career services, financial aid, and housing and residential life, as well as social, recreational, and related programs. In small colleges, they may counsel students. Registrars are custodians of students' records. They register students, prepare student transcripts, evaluate academic records, assess and collect tuition and fees, plan and implement commencement, oversee the preparation of college catalogs and schedules of classes, and analyze enrollment and demographic statistics. Directors of admissions manage the process of recruiting, evaluating, and admitting students, and work closely with financial aid directors, who oversee scholarship, fellowship, and loan programs. Registrars and admissions officers must adapt to technological innovations in student information systems. For example, for those whose institutions present information—such as college catalogs and schedules—on the Internet, knowledge of on-line resources, imaging, and other computer skills is important. Directors of student activities plan and arrange social, cultural, and recreational activities, assist student-run organizations, and may orient new students. Athletic directors plan and direct intramural and intercollegiate athletic activities, including publicity for athletic events, preparation of budgets, and supervision of coaches.

Working Conditions

Education administrators hold management positions with significant responsibility. Coordinating and interacting with faculty, parents, and students can be fast-paced and stimulating, but also stressful and demanding. Some jobs include travel. Principals and assistant principals whose main duty often is discipline may find working with difficult students frustrating, but challenging. The number of school-age children is rising, and some school systems have hired assistant principals when a school's population increased significantly. In other school systems, principals may manage larger student bodies, which can also be stressful.

Most education administrators work more than 40 hours a week, including many nights and weekends when they oversee school activities. Many administrators work 10 or 11 months a year, while others work year round.

Employment

Education administrators held about 386,000 jobs in 1996. About nine out of ten were in educational services—in elementary, secondary, and technical schools and colleges and universities. The rest worked in child daycare centers, religious organizations, job training centers, state departments of education, and businesses and other organizations that provide training for their employees.

Training, Other Qualifications, and Advancement

Most education administrators begin their careers in related occupations, and prepare for a job in education administration by completing a master's or doctoral degree. Because of the diversity of duties and levels of responsibility, their educational backgrounds and experience vary considerably. Principals, assistant principals, central office administrators, and academic deans usually have held teaching positions before moving into administration. Some teachers move directly into principal positions; others first become assistant principals, or gain experience in other central office administrative jobs at either the school or district level in positions such as department head, curriculum specialist, or subject matter advisor. In some cases, administrators move up from related staff jobs such as recruiter, guidance counselor, librarian, residence hall director, or financial aid or admissions counselor.

To be considered for education administrator positions, workers must first prove themselves in their current jobs. In evaluating candidates, supervisors look for determination, confidence, innovativeness, motivation, leadership, and managerial attributes, such as ability to make sound decisions and organize and coordinate work efficiently. Since much of an administrator's job involves interacting with others, from students to parents to teachers, they must have strong interpersonal skills and be effective communicators and motivators. Knowledge of management principles and practices, gained through work experience and formal education, is important.

In most public schools, principals, assistant principals, and school administrators in central offices need a master's degree in education administration or educational supervision. Some principals and central office administrators have a doctorate or specialized degree in education administration. Most states require principals to be licensed as school administrators. Requirements for licensure vary by state. National standards for school leaders, including principals and supervisors, were recently developed by the Interstate School Leaders

Licensure Consortium. States may use these national standards as guidelines for licensure requirements, or for activities such as mentoring, professional development, or accreditation of training programs. In private schools, which are not subject to state certification requirements, some principals and assistant principals hold only a bachelor's degree; however, the majority have a master's or doctoral degree.

Academic deans and chairpersons usually have a doctorate in their specialty. Most have held a professorship in their department before advancing. Admissions, student affairs, and financial aid directors and registrars sometimes start in related staff jobs with bachelor's degrees—any field usually is acceptable—and obtain advanced degrees in college student affairs or higher education administration. A Ph.D. or Ed.D. usually is necessary for top student affairs positions. Computer literacy and a background in mathematics or statistics may be assets in admissions, records, and financial work.

Advanced degrees in higher education administration, educational supervision, and college student affairs are offered in many colleges and universities. The National Council for Accreditation of Teacher Education accredits programs. Education administration degree programs include courses in school management, school law, school finance and budgeting, curriculum development and evaluation, research design and data analysis, community relations, politics in education, counseling, and leadership. Educational supervision degree programs include courses in supervision of instruction and curriculum, human relations, curriculum development, research, and advanced pedagogy courses.

Education administrators advance by moving up an administrative ladder or transferring to larger schools or systems. They also may become superintendent of a school system or president of an educational institution.

Job Outlook

Substantial competition is expected for prestigious jobs as higher education administrators. Many faculty and other staff meet the education and experience requirements for these jobs, and seek promotion. However, the number of openings is relatively small; only the most highly qualified are selected. Candidates who have the most formal education and who are willing to relocate should have the best job prospects.

On the other hand, it is becoming more difficult to attract candidates for principal, vice principal, and administration jobs at the elementary and secondary school level—competition for these jobs is declining. Many teachers no longer have an incentive to move into these positions since the pay is not significantly higher and does not compensate for the added workload and responsibility of the position.

Also, site-based management has given teachers more decision-making responsibility in recent years, possibly satisfying their desire to move into administration.

Employment of education administrators is expected to grow about as fast as the average for all occupations over the 1996–2006 period. However, most job openings will result from the need to replace administrators who retire or transfer to other occupations.

School enrollments at the elementary, secondary, and postsecondary level are all expected to grow over the projection period. Rather than opening new schools, many existing school populations will expand, spurring demand for assistant principals to help with the increased workload. Employment of education administrators will also grow as more services are provided to students and as efforts to improve the quality of education continue.

However, budget constraints are expected to moderate growth in this profession. At the postsecondary level, some institutions have been reducing administrative staffs to contain costs. Some colleges are consolidating administrative jobs and contracting with other providers for some administrative functions.

Earnings

Salaries of education administrators vary according to position, level of responsibility and experience, and the size and location of the institution. Generally, principals employed in public schools earn higher salaries than those in private schools.

According to a survey of public schools, conducted by the Educational Research Service, average salaries for principals and assistant principals in the 1996–97 school year were as follows:

Principals:	
Elementary school	$62,900
Junior high/middle school	66,900
Senior high school	72,400
Assistant principals:	
Elementary school	$52,300
Junior high/middle school	56,500
Senior high school	59,700
Directors, managers, coordinators, and	
supervisors of instructional services	70,800

In 1995–96, according to the College and University Personnel Association, median annual salaries for selected administrators in higher education were as follows:

Academic deans:	
Medicine	$201,200
Law	141,400
Engineering	112,800
Arts and sciences	82,500
Business	81,000
Education	80,000
Social sciences	61,800
Mathematics	59,900
Student services directors:	
Admissions and registrar	$50,700
Student financial aid	45,400
Student activities	34,500

Related Occupations

Education administrators apply organizational and leadership skills to provide services to individuals. Workers in related occupations include health services administrators, social service agency administrators, recreation and park managers, museum directors, library directors, and professional and membership organization executives. Since principals and assistant principals generally have extensive teaching experience, their backgrounds are similar to those of teachers and many school counselors.

Sources of Additional Information

For information on elementary and secondary school principals, assistant principals, and central office administrators, contact:

❑ American Federation of School Administrators, 1729 21st St. NW, Washington, DC 20009.

❑ American Association of School Administrators, 1801 North Moore St., Arlington, VA 22209.

For information on elementary school principals and assistant principals, contact:

❑ The National Association of Elementary School Principals, 1615 Duke St., Alexandria, VA 22314-3483.

For information on secondary school principals and assistant principals, contact:

❑ The National Association of Secondary School Principals, 1904 Association Dr., Reston, VA 20191.

For information on college student affairs administrators, contact:

❑ National Association of Student Personnel Administrators, 1875 Connecticut Ave. NW, Suite 418, Washington, DC 20009-5728.

For information on collegiate registrars and admissions officers, contact:

❑ American Association of Collegiate Registrars and Admissions Officers, One Dupont Circle NW, Suite 330, Washington, DC 20036-1171.

Engineering, Science, and Computer Systems Managers

(*D.O.T.* 002.167-018; 003.167-034 and -070; 005.167-010 and -022; 007.167-014; 008.167-010; 010.161-010, -014, and .167-018; 011.161-010; 012.167-058 and -062; 018.167-022; 019.167-014; 022.161-010; 024.167-010; 029.167-014; 162.117-030; 169.167-030 and -082; and 189.117-014)

Significant Points

★ *The majority of growth in these managerial occupations is caused by the rapid expansion of employment in computer-related occupations.*

★ *These managers need the specialized technical skills possessed by their staff to perform effectively.*

Nature of the Work

Engineering, science, and computer systems managers plan, coordinate, and direct research, development, design, production, and computer-related activities. They supervise a staff which may include engineers, scientists, technicians, computer specialists, and information technology workers, along with support personnel.

Engineering, science, and computer systems managers determine scientific and technical goals within broad outlines provided by top management. These goals may include the redesigning of an aircraft, improvements in manufacturing processes, the development of a large computer program, or advances in scientific research. Managers make detailed plans for the accomplishment of these goals—for example, working with their staff, they may develop the overall concepts of new products or identify problems standing in the way of project completion. They determine the cost of and equipment and personnel needed for projects and programs. They hire and assign scientists, engineers, technicians, computer specialists, information technology workers, and support personnel to carry out specific parts of the projects. The managers supervise these employees' work, and review their designs, programs, and reports. They present ideas and projects to top management for approval or when seeking additional funds for development.

Managers coordinate the activities of their unit with other units or organizations. They confer with higher levels of management; with financial, industrial production, marketing, and other managers; and with contractors and equipment and materials suppliers. They also establish working and administrative procedures and policies.

Engineering managers supervise people who design and develop machinery, products, systems, and processes; or direct and coordinate production, operations, quality assurance, testing, or maintenance in industrial plants. Many are plant engineers, who direct and coordinate the design, installation, operation, and maintenance of equipment and machinery in industrial plants. Others manage research and development teams that produce new products and processes or improve existing ones.

Science managers oversee activities in agricultural science, chemistry, biology, geology, meteorology, or physics. They manage research and development projects and direct and coordinate experimentation, testing, quality control, and production in research institutes and industrial plants. Science managers are often involved in their own research in addition to managing the work of others.

Computer systems managers direct and plan programming, computer operations, and data processing, and coordinate the development of computer hardware, systems design, and software. Top-level managers direct all computer-related activities in an organization. They analyze the computer and data information requirements of their organization and assign, schedule, and review the work of systems analysts, computer programmers, and computer operators. They determine personnel and computer hardware requirements, evaluate equipment options, and make purchasing decisions.

Some engineering, science, and computer systems managers head a section of scientists, engineers, or computer professionals and support staff. Above them are heads of divisions composed of a number of sections. A few are directors of research or of large laboratories.

Working Conditions

Engineering, science, and computer systems managers spend most of their time in an office. Some managers, however, may also work in laboratories or industrial plants, where they are normally exposed to the same conditions as research scientists and may occasionally be exposed to the same conditions as production workers. Most managers work at least 40 hours a week and may work much longer on occasion if meeting project deadlines. Some may experience considerable pressure in meeting technical or scientific goals within a short time or a tight budget.

Employment

Engineering, science, and computer systems managers held about 343,000 jobs in 1996. Although these managers are found in almost all industries, about 38 percent are em-

ployed in manufacturing, especially in the industrial machinery and equipment, electrical and electronic equipment, instruments, chemicals, and transportation equipment industries. However, the two industries employing the greatest number of these managers were engineering and architectural services and computer and data processing services; each employed about one in ten in 1996. The majority are most likely engineering managers, often managing industrial research, development, and design projects. Others work for government agencies, research and testing services, communications and utilities companies, financial and insurance firms, and management and public relations services companies.

Training, Other Qualifications, and Advancement

It is essential that engineering, science, and computer systems managers have a base of technical knowledge that allows them to understand and guide the work of their subordinates and to explain the work in non-technical terms to senior management and potential customers. Therefore, experience as an engineer, mathematician, scientist, or computer professional is usually required to become an engineering, science, or computer systems manager. Educational requirements are consequently similar to those for scientists, engineers, and computer professionals.

Engineering managers first start as engineers. A bachelor's degree in engineering from an accredited engineering program is acceptable for beginning engineering jobs, but many engineers increase their chances for promotion to a managerial position by obtaining a master's degree in engineering, engineering management, or business administration. A degree in business administration or engineering management is especially useful for becoming a general manager, because these degree programs teach engineers about managing personnel and technical and financial resources.

Science managers usually start as a chemist, physicist, biologist, or other natural scientist. Most scientists engaged in basic research have a Ph.D. degree. Some in applied research and other activities may have lesser degrees. First-level science managers are usually specialists in the work they supervise. For example, the manager of a group of physicists doing optical research is almost always a physicist who is an expert in optics. Many scientific research firms are started and managed by scientists who obtain funding to build a staff and purchase technology to pursue their research agenda, with the goal of eventually developing a commercially successful product.

Most computer systems managers have been systems analysts, although some may have experience as computer engineers, programmers, operators, or other computer specialties. There is no universally accepted way of preparing for a job as a systems analyst. Many have degrees in computer or information science, computer information systems, or data processing and have experience as computer programmers. A bachelor's degree is usually required and a graduate degree is often preferred by employers. However, a few computer systems managers have associate degrees. A typical career advancement progression in a large organization would be from programmer to programmer/analyst, to systems analyst, and then to project leader or senior analyst. The first real managerial position might be as project manager, programming supervisor, systems supervisor, or software manager.

In addition to educational requirements, scientists, engineers, or computer specialists must demonstrate above-average technical skills to be considered for a promotion to manager. Superiors also look for leadership and communication skills, as well as managerial attributes such as the ability to make rational decisions, to manage time well, organize and coordinate work effectively, establish good working and personal relationships, and motivate others. Also, a successful manager must have the desire to perform management functions. Many scientists, engineers, and computer specialists want to be promoted but actually prefer doing technical work.

Some scientists and engineers become managers in marketing, personnel, purchasing, or other areas, or become general managers.

Job Outlook

Employment of engineering, science, and computer systems managers is expected to increase much faster than the average for all occupations through the year 2006. Underlying much of the growth of managers in science and engineering are competitive pressures and advancing technologies which force companies to update and improve products more frequently. Research and investment in plants and equipment to expand output of goods and services and to raise productivity will also add to employment requirements for science and engineering managers involved in research and development, design, and the operation and maintenance of production facilities.

Employment of computer systems managers will increase rapidly due to the fast-paced expansion of the computer and data processing services industry and the increased employment of computer systems analysts. Large computer centers are consolidating or closing as small computers become more powerful, resulting in fewer opportunities for computer systems managers at these centers. As the economy expands and as advances in technology lead to broader applications for computers, however, opportunities will increase and employment should grow rapidly.

Opportunities for those who wish to become engineering, science, and computer systems managers should be closely related to the growth of the occupations they supervise and the industries in which they are found. Because many engineers, natural scientists, and computer specialists are eligible for management and seek promotion, there may be substantial competition for these openings.

Many of the industries which employ engineers and scientists derive a large portion of their business from defense contracts. Because defense expenditures are being reduced, employment has declined and the job outlook for managers is not as favorable in these industries, compared to less defense-oriented industries.

Earnings

Earnings for engineering, science, and computer systems managers vary by specialty and level of management. According to 1996 data, science and engineering managers had average salaries that ranged from $41,000 to well over $100,000 for the most senior managers in large organizations. According to Robert Half International, computer systems managers earned salaries ranging from $33,000 to well over $100,000, depending on establishment size. Managers often earn about 15 to 25 percent more than those they directly supervise, although there are cases in which some employees are paid more than the manager who supervises them. This is especially true in research fields.

According to a survey of workplaces in 160 metropolitan areas, lower-level engineering managers had median annual earnings of $84,200 in 1995, with the middle half earning between $76,300 and $92,800. The highest-level engineering managers had median annual earnings of $117,000, with the middle half earning between $104,000 and $133,000. Beginning systems analysts managers had median annual earnings of $60,900, with the middle half earning between $55,100 and $67,000. The most senior systems analysts managers had median annual earnings of $84,200, with the middle half earning between $76,200 and $92,000.

In addition, engineering, science, and computer systems managers, especially those at higher levels, often are provided with more benefits (such as expense accounts, stock option plans, and bonuses) than non-managerial workers in their organizations.

Related Occupations

The work of engineering, science, and computer systems managers is closely related to that of engineers, natural scientists, computer personnel, and mathematicians. It is also related to the work of other managers, especially general managers and top executives.

Sources of Additional Information

For information about a career as an engineering, science, or computer systems manager, contact the sources of additional information for engineers, natural scientists, and computer occupations.

Farmers and Farm Managers

(*D.O.T.* 180.117, .161, and .167-018, -026 through -046, -058, and -066; 401.161; 402.161; 403.161; 404.161; 405.161; 407.161; 410.161; 411.161; 412.161; 413.161; 421.161; and 446.161)

Significant Points

* *Modern farming requires work experience, sometimes acquired through growing up on a farm, and formal education, preferably a bachelor's degree in agriculture or in business with a concentration in agriculture.*

* *Overall employment is projected to decline due to increasing productivity and consolidation in the highly efficient agricultural production industry.*

Nature of the Work

American farmers and farm managers direct the activities of one of the world's largest and most productive agricultural sectors. They produce enough food and fiber to meet the needs of our nation, and to export huge quantities to countries around the world.

Farmers may be farmer-owners or tenant farmers, who rent the use of land. Their specific tasks are determined by the type of farm they operate. On crop farms—farms growing grain, cotton and other fibers, fruit, and vegetables—farmers are responsible for planning, tilling, planting, fertilizing, cultivating, spraying, and harvesting. After the harvest, they make sure the crops are properly packaged, stored or marketed. On livestock, dairy, and poultry farms, farmers must feed, and plan and care for the animals and keep barns, pens, coops, and other farm buildings clean and in good condition. They also oversee breeding and marketing activities. On horticultural specialty farms, farmers oversee the production of ornamental plants, nursery products—such as flowers, bulbs, shrubbery, and sod—and fruits and vegetables grown in greenhouses. On aquaculture farms, farmers raise fish and shellfish in marine, brackish, or fresh water, usually in ponds,

floating net pens, raceways, or recirculating systems. They stock, feed, protect, and otherwise manage aquatic life sold for consumption or used for recreational fishing.

Farmers must make many managerial decisions. Their farm output is strongly influenced by the weather, disease, fluctuations in prices of domestic and foreign farm products, and federal farm programs. In a crop operation, farmers usually determine the best time to plant seed, apply fertilizer and chemicals, harvest, and market. They carefully plan the combination of crops they grow so if the price of one crop drops, they will have sufficient income from another to make up for the loss. Crop and livestock prices change frequently from one month to another. Farmers who plan ahead may be able to store their crops or keep their livestock to take advantage of better prices later in the year. Those who participate in the futures market—where contracts and options on futures contracts on commodities are traded through stock brokers—try to anticipate or track changes in the supply of and demand for agricultural commodities, and thus changes in the prices of farm products. By buying or selling futures contracts, or by pricing their products in advance of future sales, they attempt to either limit their risk or reap greater profits than would normally be realized. They may have to secure loans from credit agencies to finance the purchase of machinery, fertilizer, livestock, and feed. Farming operations have become more complex in recent years, so many farmers use computers to keep their extensive financial and inventory records. They also use computer databases and spreadsheets to manage breeding, dairy, and other farm operations.

Farmers perform tasks ranging from caring for livestock, to operating machinery and maintaining equipment and facilities. The size of the farm often determines which of these tasks farmers will handle themselves. Operators of large farms have employees who do much of the physical work that small-farm operators do themselves. Farmers are responsible for training workers in the use of equipment, and supervising them in the performance of their work. Although employment on most farms is limited to the farmer and one or two family workers or hired employees, some large farms have 100 or more full-time and seasonal workers. Some of these employees are in nonfarm occupations, working as truck drivers, sales representatives, bookkeepers, and computer specialists.

Farm managers guide and assist farmers and ranchers in maximizing the financial returns to their land by managing the day-to-day activities. Their duties and responsibilities vary widely. For example, the owner of a very large livestock farm may employ a farm manager to oversee a single activity, such as feeding livestock. When managing a small crop farm for an absentee owner, on the other hand, a farm manager may assume responsibility for all functions, from selecting the crops to participating in planting and harvesting. Farm management firms and corporations involved in agriculture employ highly trained professional farm managers who may manage farm operations or oversee tenant operators of several farms. In these cases, farm managers may establish output goals; determine financial constraints; monitor production and marketing; hire, assign, and supervise workers; determine crop transportation and storage requirements; and oversee maintenance of the property and equipment.

Working Conditions

The work of farmers and farm managers is often strenuous, their work hours are frequently long, and their days off are sometimes infrequent. Of those who work full time, more than half work 60 or more hours a week. Nevertheless, to those who enter farming, these disadvantages are outweighed by the opportunities for living in a rural area, working outdoors, being self-employed, and making a living working the land.

Farmers and farm managers on crop farms usually work from sunrise to sunset during the planting and harvesting seasons. During the rest of the year they plan next season's crops, market their output, and repair machinery; some may earn additional income by working a second job off the farm.

On livestock producing farms, work goes on throughout the year. Animals must be fed and watered every day, unless they are grazing, and dairy cows must be milked two or three times a day. Farmers rarely get the chance to get away unless they hire an assistant or arrange for a temporary substitute.

Farm work can be hazardous. The proper operation of equipment and handling of chemicals are required to ensure a safe working environment.

On very large farms, farmers spend substantial time meeting with farm managers or farm supervisors in charge of various activities. Professional farm managers overseeing several farms may divide their time between traveling to meet farmers or landowners and planning the farm operations in their offices. As farming practices and agricultural technology become more sophisticated, farmers and farm managers are spending more time in offices and at computers, where they electronically manage many aspects of the business.

Employment

Farmers and farm managers held nearly 1.3 million jobs in 1996. About 85 percent were self-employed farmers. Most managed crop production activities, while others managed livestock and dairy production. A relatively small number were involved in agricultural services, such as contract harvesting and farm labor contracting.

The soil, topography of the land, and the climate of an area generally determine the type of farming done. For example, wheat, corn, and other grains are most efficiently grown on large farms on level land where large, complex machinery can be used. Thus, these crops are prevalent on the prairies and plains of Iowa, Illinois, Indiana, Nebraska, Ohio, Kansas, and southern Minnesota and Wisconsin. Crops requiring longer growing seasons, such as cotton, tobacco, and peanuts, are grown chiefly in the South. Most of the country's fruits and vegetables come from California, Texas, and Florida. Many dairy herds are found in the areas with good pasture land, such as Wisconsin, New York, and Minnesota. However, in recent years dairy farming has expanded rapidly in California, Arizona, and Texas.

Training, Other Qualifications, and Advancement

Growing up on a family farm and participating in agricultural programs for young people sponsored by the National Future Farmers of America Organization or the 4-H youth educational programs are important sources of training for those interested in pursuing agriculture as a career. However, modern farming requires increasingly complex scientific, business, and financial decisions. Therefore, even people who were raised on farms must acquire the appropriate education. High school training should include courses in mathematics and the sciences. Completion of a two-year and preferably a four-year bachelor's degree program in a college of agriculture is becoming increasingly important.

Not all future farm managers grow up on farms. For these people, a bachelor's degree in business with a concentration in agriculture is important. In addition to formal education, they will need several years' work experience in the different aspects of farm operations in order to qualify for a farm manager position.

Students should select the college most appropriate to their specific interests and location. In the United States, all state university systems have one land-grant university with a school of agriculture. Common programs of study include agronomy, dairy science, agricultural economics and business, horticulture, crop and fruit science, and animal science. For students interested in aquaculture, formal programs are available, and include course work in fisheries biology, fish culture, hatchery management and maintenance, and hydrology. Whatever one's interest, the college curriculum should include courses in agricultural production, finance, and economics.

Professional status can be enhanced through voluntary certification as an Accredited Farm Manager (AFM) by the American Society of Farm Managers and Rural Appraisers.

Certification requires several years of farm management experience and the appropriate academic background—a bachelor's degree or preferably a master's degree in a field of agricultural science—and passing courses and examinations relating to business, financial, and legal aspects of farm management.

Farmers and farm managers need to keep abreast of continuing advances in farming methods both in the United States and abroad. They should be willing to try new processes and adapt to constantly changing technologies to produce their crops or raise their livestock more efficiently. Farmers must also have enough technical knowledge of crops, growing conditions, and plant and animal diseases to make decisions ensuring the successful operation of their farms. Knowledge of the relationship between farm operations—for example, the use of pesticides—and environmental conditions is essential. Mechanical aptitude and the ability to work with tools of all kinds are also valuable skills for the operator of a small farm, who often maintains and repairs machinery or farm structures.

Farmers and farm managers must have the managerial skills necessary to organize and operate a business. A basic knowledge of accounting and bookkeeping can be helpful in keeping financial records, and a knowledge of credit sources is essential. They must also be familiar with complex safety regulations and requirements of government agricultural support programs. Computer skills are increasingly important, especially on large farms, where computers are widely used for recordkeeping and business analysis. For example, some farmers use personal computers to get the latest information on prices of farm products and other agricultural news.

Job Outlook

Employment of farmers and farm managers is expected to continue to decline through the year 2006. The expanding world population is increasing the demand for food and fiber. In particular, improving economies and increasing personal income in developing nations have resulted in better diets and stronger demand for beef, poultry, pork, and feed grain. However, increasing productivity in the highly efficient agricultural production industry is expected to meet domestic and export requirements with fewer farmers and farm managers. The overwhelming majority of job openings will result from the need to replace farmers who retire or leave the occupation for economic or other reasons.

The long-term trend toward fewer and larger farms is expected to continue during the 1996–2006 period, as consolidation takes place in response to market pressures, further reducing the number of jobs for farmers and farm managers. Some farmers acquire farms by inheritance; how-

ever, purchasing a farm or additional land is expensive and requires substantial capital. In addition, sufficient funds are required to withstand the adverse effects of climate and price fluctuations upon farm output and income and to cover operating costs—livestock, feed, seed, and fuel. Also, the complexity of modern farming and keen competition among farmers leave little room for the marginally successful farmer.

Despite the projected decline in overall employment of farmers and farm managers, aquaculture should continue to provide new employment opportunities over the 1996–2006 period. Overfishing has resulted in reduced ocean catch, and the growing demand for certain seafood items—such as shrimp, salmon, and catfish—has spurred the growth of aquaculture farms. Aquaculture output increased strongly between 1983 and the mid-1990s. Over 700,000 pounds of fish were produced in 1994. Efforts to produce more farm-raised fish and shellfish should continue in response to demand.

Earnings

Farmers' incomes vary greatly from year to year, because prices of farm products fluctuate depending upon weather conditions and other factors that influence the amount and quality of farm output and the demand for those products. A farm that shows a large profit in one year may show a loss in the following year. Under the 1996 Farm Act, federal government subsidy payments, which have traditionally shielded some grain producers from the ups and downs of the market, are fixed regardless of yields or prices. Consequently, these farmers may experience more income variability from year to year than in the past. The Act also phases out price supports for dairy farmers, and may result in lower incomes for dairy producers. Many farmers—primarily operators of small farms—have income from off-farm business activities, often greater than that of their farm income.

Farm income also varies greatly depending upon the type and size of farm. For example, vegetable and cotton farms, and nurseries and greenhouses generally produce the highest income; fruit, nut, corn, and peanut farms produce more moderate income; and beef and hog farms generate relatively low income. Generally, large farms generate more income than small farms. Exceptions include some low volume specialty farms producing high value horticultural and fruit products.

Full-time, salaried farm managers, with the exception of horticultural managers, had median earnings of $485 a week in 1996. The middle half earned between $325 and $650 a week. The highest paid 10 percent earned about $760 a week in 1996, while the lowest paid 10 percent made less than $205 a week. Horticultural specialty farm managers generally earn considerably more.

Farmers and self-employed farm managers make their own provisions for benefits. As members of farm organizations, they may derive benefits such as group discounts on health and life insurance premiums. Salaried farm managers may receive housing and usual organizational benefits.

Related Occupations

Farmers and farm managers strive to improve the quality of agricultural products and the efficiency of farms. Workers with similar functions include agricultural engineers, animal breeders, animal scientists, county agricultural agents, dairy scientists, extension service specialists, feed and farm management advisors, horticulturists, plant breeders, and poultry scientists.

Sources of Additional Information

For general information about farming and agricultural occupations, contact:

❏ American Farm Bureau Federation, 225 Touhy Ave., Park Ridge, IL 60068. Homepage: http://www.fb.com

For information about certification as an accredited farm manager, contact:

❏ American Society of Farm Managers and Rural Appraisers, 950 South Cherry St., Suite 508, Denver, CO 80222. Homepage: http://www.agriassociations.org

For general information about farm occupations, opportunities, and 4-H activities, contact your local county extension service office.

Financial Managers

(*D.O.T.* 160.167-058; 161.117-018; 169.167-086; 186.117-066, -070, -078, -086; .167-054, -086; 189.117-038)

Significant Points

★ *A bachelor's degree in finance or a related field is the minimum academic preparation, but many employers increasingly seek graduates with a master's degree and a strong analytical background.*

★ *The need for skilled financial management will spur average employment growth; however, the number of applicants is expected to exceed the number of openings, resulting in competition for jobs.*

Nature of the Work

Practically every firm has one or more financial managers. Among them are chief financial officers, vice presidents of finance, treasurers, controllers, credit managers, and cash managers; they prepare the financial reports required by the firm to conduct its operations and to ensure that the firm satisfies tax and regulatory requirements. Financial managers also oversee the flow of cash and financial instruments, monitor the extension of credit, assess the risk of transactions, raise capital, analyze investments, develop information to assess the present and future financial status of the firm, and communicate with stock holders and other investors.

In small firms, chief financial officers usually handle all financial management functions. In large firms, these officers oversee financial management departments and help top managers develop financial and economic policy, establish procedures, delegate authority, and oversee the implementation of these policies.

Highly trained and experienced financial managers head each financial department. Controllers direct the preparation of all financial reports—income statements, balance sheets, and special reports, such as depreciation schedules. They oversee the accounting, audit, or budget departments. Cash and credit managers monitor and control the flow of cash receipts and disbursements to meet the business and investment needs of the firm. For example, cash flow projections are needed to determine whether loans must be obtained to meet cash requirements, or whether surplus cash may be invested in interest-bearing instruments. Risk and insurance managers oversee programs to minimize risks and losses that may arise from financial transactions and business operations undertaken by the institution. Credit operations managers establish credit rating criteria, determine credit ceilings, and monitor their institution's extension of credit. Reserve officers review their institution's financial statements and direct the purchase and sale of bonds and other securities to maintain the asset-liability ratio required by law. Managers specializing in international finance develop financial and accounting systems for the banking transactions of multinational organizations. A working knowledge of the financial systems of foreign countries is essential.

Financial institutions—such as banks, savings and loan associations, credit unions, personal credit institutions, and finance companies—may serve as depositories for cash and financial instruments and offer loans, investment counseling, consumer credit, trust management, and other financial services. Some specialize in specific financial services. Financial managers in financial institutions include vice presidents, bank branch managers, savings and loan association managers, consumer credit managers, and credit union managers. These managers make decisions in accordance with policy set by the institution's board of directors and federal and state laws and regulations.

Due to changing regulations and increased government scrutiny, financial managers in financial institutions must place greater emphasis on accurate reporting of financial data. They must have detailed knowledge of industries allied to banking—such as insurance, real estate, and securities—and a broad knowledge of business and industrial activities. With growing domestic and foreign competition, financial managers must keep abreast of an expanding and increasingly complex variety of financial products and services. Besides supervising financial services, financial managers in banks and other financial institutions may advise individuals and businesses on financial planning.

Working Conditions

Financial managers are provided with comfortable offices, often close to top managers and to departments which develop the financial data these managers need. Financial managers typically work 40 hours a week, but many work longer hours. They are often required to attend meetings of financial and economic associations, and may travel to visit subsidiary firms or meet customers.

Employment

Financial managers held about 800,000 jobs in 1996. Although these managers are found in virtually every industry, more than a third were employed by services industries, including business, health, social, and management services. Nearly three out of ten were employed by financial institutions—banks, savings institutions, finance companies, credit unions, insurance companies, securities dealers, and real estate firms, for example.

Training, Other Qualifications, and Advancement

A bachelor's degree in finance, accounting, economics, or business administration is the minimum academic preparation for financial managers. However, many employers increasingly seek graduates with a master's degree, preferably in business administration, economics, finance, or risk management. These academic programs develop analytical skills, and provide knowledge of the latest financial analysis methods and information and technology management techniques, widely used in this field.

Experience may be more important than formal education for some financial manager positions—notably branch managers in banks. Banks typically fill branch manager positions by promoting experienced loan officers and other professionals who excel at their jobs.

Continuing education is vital for financial managers, reflecting the growing complexity of global trade, shifting federal and state laws and regulations, and a proliferation of new, complex financial instruments. Firms often provide opportunities for workers to broaden their knowledge and skills, and encourage employees to take graduate courses at colleges and universities or attend conferences relating to their specialty. Financial management, banking, and credit union associations, often in cooperation with colleges and universities, sponsor numerous national or local training programs. Persons enrolled prepare extensively at home and then attend sessions on subjects such as accounting management, budget management, corporate cash management, financial analysis, international banking, and information systems. Many firms pay all or part of the costs for those who successfully complete courses. Although experience, ability, and leadership are emphasized for promotion, advancement may be accelerated by this type of special study.

In some cases, financial managers may also broaden their skills and exhibit their competency in specialized fields by attaining professional certification. For example, the Association for Investment Management and Research confers the Chartered Financial Analyst designation to investment professionals who have a bachelor's degree, pass three test levels, and meet work experience requirements. The National Association of Credit Management administers a three-part certification program for business credit professionals. Through a combination of experience and examinations, these financial managers pass through the level of Credit Business Associate, to Credit Business Fellow, to Certified Credit Executive. The Treasury Management Association confers the Certified Cash Manager credential on those who have two years of relevant experience and pass an exam, and the Certified Treasury Executive designation on those more senior in treasury management who meet experience and continuing education requirements.

Persons interested in becoming financial managers should enjoy working independently, dealing with people, and analyzing detailed account information. The ability to communicate effectively, both orally and in writing, is also important. They also need tact, good judgment, and the ability to establish effective personal relationships to oversee staff.

Because financial management is critical for efficient business operations, well-trained, experienced financial managers who display a strong grasp of the operations of various departments within their organization are prime candidates for promotion to top management positions. Some financial managers transfer to closely related positions in other industries. Those with extensive experience and access to sufficient capital may start their own consulting firms.

Job Outlook

Like other managerial occupations, the number of applicants for financial management positions is expected to exceed the number of openings, resulting in competition for jobs. Those with lending experience, and familiarity with the latest lending regulations and financial products and services, should enjoy the best opportunities for branch management jobs in banks. Those with a graduate degree, a strong analytical background, and knowledge of various aspects of financial management, such as asset management and information and technology management, should enjoy the best opportunities for other financial management positions. Developing expertise in a rapidly growing industry, such as health care, could also be an advantage in the job market.

Employment of financial managers is expected to increase about as fast as the average for all occupations through the year 2006. The need for skilled financial management will increase due to the demands of global trade, the proliferation of complex financial instruments, and changing federal and state laws and regulations. Many firms have reduced the ranks of middle managers in an effort to be more efficient and competitive, but much of the downsizing and restructuring is complete. The banking industry, on the other hand, is still undergoing mergers and consolidation, and may eliminate some financial management positions as a result.

Earnings

The median annual salary of financial managers was $40,700 in 1996. The lowest 10 percent earned $21,800 or less, while the top 10 percent earned over $81,100.

According to a 1997 survey by Robert Half International, a staffing services firm specializing in accounting and finance, salaries of assistant controllers range from $41,000 in the smallest firms, to $81,000 in the largest firms; controllers, $47,000 to $138,000; and chief financial officers/treasurers, $62,000 to $307,000.

The results of the Treasury Management Association's 1997 compensation survey are presented in table 1. The earnings listed in the table represent total compensation, including bonuses. The survey also found that financial managers with a master's degree in business administration average $10,900 more than managers with a bachelor's degree.

Table 1. Annual earnings for selected financial managers, 1997

Chief financial officer	$142,900
Vice president of finance	138,000
Treasurer	122,500
Assistant treasurer	88,400
Controller	85,100
Treasury manager	66,900
Assistant controller	56,200
Senior analyst	55,600
Cash manager	51,600
Analyst	40,500
Assistant cash manager	38,800

SOURCE: Treasury Management Association

Salary level depends upon the manager's experience and the size and location of the organization, and is likely to be higher in larger organizations and cities. Many financial managers in private industry receive additional compensation in the form of bonuses, which also vary substantially by the size of the firm.

Related Occupations

Financial managers combine formal education with experience in one or more areas of finance, such as asset management, lending, credit operations, securities investment, or insurance risk and loss control. Workers in other occupations requiring similar training and ability include accountants and auditors, budget officers, credit analysts, loan officers, insurance consultants, portfolio managers, pension consultants, real estate advisors, securities analysts and underwriters.

Sources of Additional Information

For information about financial management careers, contact:

❏ American Bankers Association, 1120 Connecticut Ave. NW, Washington, DC 20036.

❏ Financial Management Association, International, College of Business Administration, University of South Florida, Tampa, FL 33620-5500.

For information about financial careers in business credit management; the Credit Business Associate, Credit Business Fellow, and Certified Credit Executive programs; and institutions offering graduate courses in credit and financial management, contact:

❏ National Association of Credit Management (NACM), Credit Research Foundation, 8815 Centre Park Dr., Columbia, MD 21045-2117. E-mail address: nacm@nacm.org Homepage: http://www.nacm.org/

For information about careers in treasury management from entry level to chief financial officer, and the Certified Cash Manager and Certified Treasury Executive programs, contact:

❏ Treasury Management Association, 7315 Wisconsin Ave., Suite 600 West, Bethesda, MD 20814.

For information about the Chartered Financial Analyst program, contact:

❏ Association for Investment Management and Research, 5 Boar's Head Lane, P.O. Box 3668, Charlottesville, VA 22903. Homepage: http://www.aimr.com/

For information about financial management careers in the health care industry, contact:

❏ Healthcare Financial Management Association, Two Westbrook Corporate Center, Suite 700, Westchester, IL 60154.

State bankers' associations can furnish specific information about job opportunities in their respective states, or write directly to a particular bank to inquire about job openings. For the names and addresses of banks and savings and related institutions, as well as the names of their principal officers, consult the following directories.

❏ *The American Financial Directory* (Norcross, GA, McFadden Business Publications).

❏ *The U.S. Savings and Loan Directory* (Chicago, Rand McNally & Co.).

❏ *Rand McNally Credit Union Directory* (Chicago, Rand McNally & Co.).

❏ *Polk's World Bank Directory* (Nashville, R.L. Polk & Co.).

General Managers and Top Executives

(*D.O.T.* codes are too numerous to list.)

Significant Points

✴ *This group is among the highest paid workers in the nation, but long hours and substantial travel often are required.*

✴ *Competition for top managerial jobs will be keen because of the large number of qualified applicants seeking jobs.*

Nature of the Work

Chief executive officer, president, executive vice president, owner, partner, brokerage office manager, school superintendent, and police chief—each is a general manager or top executive—the individual who formulates the policies and directs the operations of businesses and corporations, nonprofit institutions, and government agencies.

The fundamental objective of private for-profit companies is to make a profit for their owners, or in corporations, to increase shareholder value. Nonprofit organizations and

government agencies implement programs that further their policies within budgetary constraints. General managers and top executives set strategies and try to ensure that their organizations' objectives are met.

A corporation's general goals and policies are established by the chief executive officer in collaboration with other top executives, who are overseen by a board of directors. In a large corporation, the chief executive officer meets frequently with subordinate executives to ensure that operations are being carried out in accordance with these policies. Although the chief executive officer of a corporation retains overall accountability, a chief operating officer may be delegated the authority to oversee the executives who direct the activities of various departments and are responsible for implementing the organization's policies on a day-to-day basis. In publicly-held corporations, it is the board of directors that is ultimately accountable for the success or failure of the enterprise; the chief executive officer reports to the board. In nonprofit corporations, the board of trustees or board of directors fulfills the same role.

The scope of other high level executive's responsibilities depends upon the size of the organization. In large organizations, their duties are highly specialized. Managers of cost and profit centers are responsible for the overall performance of one aspect of the organization, such as manufacturing, marketing, sales, purchasing, finance, personnel, training, administrative services, electronic data processing, property management, transportation, or the legal services department. In smaller firms, the chief executive or general manager might be responsible for all or a number of these functions.

Working Conditions

Top executives are generally provided with spacious offices and secretarial and support staff. General managers in large firms or non-profit organizations are usually provided with comfortable offices close to the top executives to whom they report. Long hours, including evenings and weekends, are the rule for most top executives and general managers, though their schedules may be flexible.

Substantial travel often is required of managers and executives, who may travel between national, regional, and local offices, or overseas, to monitor operations and meet with customers, staff, and other executives. Many managers and executives attend meetings and conferences sponsored by associations. The conferences provide an opportunity to meet with prospective donors, customers, or government officials and contractors, and allow managers and executives to keep abreast of technological and managerial innovations.

In large organizations, frequent job transfers between local offices or subsidiaries are common. General managers and top executives are under intense pressure to earn ever higher profits, provide better service, or attain fundraising and charitable goals. Executives in charge of poorly performing organizations or departments generally find their jobs in jeopardy.

Employment

General managers and top executives held over 3.2 million jobs in 1996. They are found in every industry, but wholesale, retail, and services industries employ over eight out of ten.

Training, Other Qualifications, and Advancement

The educational background of managers and top executives varies as widely as the nature of their responsibilities. Many general managers and top executives have a bachelor's degree or higher in liberal arts or business administration. Their major often is related to the departments they direct—for example, accounting for a manager of finance or computer science for a manager of information systems. Graduate and professional degrees are common. Many managers in administrative, marketing, financial, and manufacturing activities have a master's degree in business administration. Managers in highly technical manufacturing and research activities often have a master's degree in engineering or a doctoral degree in a scientific discipline. A law degree is mandatory for managers of legal departments; hospital administrators generally have a master's degree in health services administration or business administration. College presidents and school superintendents generally have an advanced degree, the former, a doctorate in the field they originally taught, and the latter, often a master's degree in education administration. On the other hand, in industries such as retail trade or transportation, it is possible for individuals without a college degree to work their way up within the company and become managers.

In the public sector, many managers have liberal arts degrees in public administration or one of the social sciences. Park superintendents, for example, often have liberal arts degrees, while police chiefs are generally graduates of law enforcement academies and hold degrees in criminal justice or a related field.

Since many general manager and top executive positions are filled by promoting experienced, lower level managers when an opening occurs, many are promoted from within the organization. Some companies prefer that their top executives have specialized backgrounds and hire individuals who are managers in other organizations. Qualities critical for success include leadership, self-confidence, motivation, decisiveness, flexibility, the ability to communicate effectively, sound business judgment, and stamina.

Advancement may be accelerated by participation in company training programs to gain a broader knowledge of company policy and operations. Through attendance at national or local training programs sponsored by various industry and trade associations and by continuing their education, normally at company expense, managers can become familiar with the latest developments in management techniques and improve their chances of promotion. Every year, thousands of senior managers, who often have experience in a particular field, such as accounting or engineering, attend executive development programs to facilitate their promotion to general managers. Participation in conferences and seminars can expand knowledge of national and international issues influencing the organization and can help develop a network of useful contacts.

General managers and top executives must have highly developed personal skills. An analytical mind able to quickly assess large amounts of information and data is very important, as is the ability to consider and evaluate the interrelationships of numerous factors; they must also be able to communicate clearly and persuasively, and need highly developed interpersonal skills.

General managers may advance to top executive positions, such as executive vice president, in their own firm or they may take a corresponding position in another firm. They may even advance to peak corporate positions such as chief operating officer or chief executive officer. Chief executive officers often become members of the board of directors of one or more firms, typically as a director of their own firm and often as chair of its board of directors. Some general managers and top executives go on to establish their own firms or become independent consultants.

Job Outlook

Employment of general managers and top executives is expected to grow about as fast as the average for all occupations through the year 2006. Because this is a large occupation, many openings will occur each year as executives transfer to other positions, start their own businesses, or retire. Nonetheless, competition for top managerial jobs will be keen. Many executives who leave their jobs transfer to other executive or managerial positions, limiting openings for new entrants.

Projected employment growth of general managers and top executives varies widely among industries. For example,

employment growth is expected to be faster than average in all services industries combined, but only about as fast as average in all finance, insurance, and real estate industry subgroups. Employment of general managers and top executives is projected to decline in manufacturing industries overall.

Experienced managers whose accomplishments reflect strong leadership qualities and the ability to improve the efficiency or competitive position of an organization will have the best opportunities. In an increasingly global economy, certain types of experience, such as international economics, marketing, information systems, and knowledge of several languages, may also help.

Earnings

General managers and top executives are among the highest paid workers in the nation. However, salary levels vary substantially depending upon the level of managerial responsibility, length of service, and type, size, and location of the firm.

At the highest level, chief executive officers (CEOs) of medium and large corporations are extremely well paid. Salaries often are related to the size of the corporation—a top manager in a very large corporation can earn significantly more than a counterpart in a small firm. Total compensation often includes stock options, dividends, and other performance bonuses, in addition to salaries.

Salaries also vary substantially by type and level of responsibilities and by industry. According to a salary survey by Robert Half International, senior vice presidents/heads of lending in banks with $1 billion or more in assets earned about $200,000 to $215,000 in 1997. Executive Compensation Reports, a division of Harcourt Brace & Company, reports that the median salary for CEOs of public companies from the fiscal year 1995 Fortune 500 list was approximately $714,000, with three-quarters making less than about $900,000. In the nonprofit sector, three quarters of the CEOs make under $135,000 in 1996, according to a survey by Abbott, Langer, & Associates.

Company-paid insurance premiums and physical examinations, the use of executive dining rooms and company cars, and expense allowances are among benefits commonly enjoyed by general managers and top executives in private industry. CEOs often enjoy company-paid club memberships, a limousine with driver, and other amenities. CEOs of very large corporations may have the use of private aircraft.

Related Occupations

General managers and top executives plan, organize, direct, control, and coordinate the operations of an organization

and its major departments or programs. The members of the board of directors and supervisory managers are also involved in these activities. Related occupations in government with similar functions are President, governor, mayor, commissioner, and legislator.

Sources of Additional Information

For a wide variety of information on general managers and top executives, including educational programs and job listings, contact:

❏ American Management Association, 1601 Broadway, New York, NY 10019-7420.

❏ National Management Association, 2210 Arbor Blvd., Dayton, OH 45439.

Government Chief Executives and Legislators

Significant Points

✱ *Over eight out of ten government chief executives and legislators work in local government, while the rest work primarily in state governments.*

✱ *Many jobs at the local and even state level are part time and pay little.*

✱ *Few long-term career opportunities are available.*

Nature of the Work

Chief executives and legislators at the federal, state, and local level direct government activities and pass laws that affect each of us. Chief executives run the governmental bodies that formulate and enforce laws. These officials include the President and Vice President of the United States, state governors and lieutenant governors, county executives, town and township officials, mayors, and city, county, town, township, and special district managers. All except appointed government managers are elected by their constituents. Non-elected managers are hired by a local government council or commission.

Government chief executives, like their counterparts in the private sector, have overall responsibility for the performance of their organizations. Working in conjunction with legislators, they set goals and then organize programs to attain them. They appoint department heads who oversee the work of the civil servants who carry out programs and enforce laws enacted by their legislative bodies. They oversee budgets specifying how government resources will be used, and ensure that resources are used properly and programs are carried out as planned.

Chief executives meet with legislators and constituents to discuss proposed programs and determine their level of support. They frequently confer with leaders of other governments to solve mutual problems. Chief executives nominate citizens to boards and commissions, solicit bids from and select contractors to do work for the government, encourage business investment and economic development in their jurisdictions, and seek federal or state funds. Chief executives of large jurisdictions rely on a staff of aides and assistants, but those in small jurisdictions often must do much of the work themselves.

Legislators are the elected officials who pass or amend laws. They include U.S. Senators and Representatives, state senators and representatives, county legislators, and city and town council members.

Legislators may introduce bills in the legislative body and examine and vote on bills introduced by other legislators. In preparing legislation, they read staff reports and may work with constituents, representatives of interest groups, members of boards and commissions, the chief executive and department heads, and others with an interest in the legislation. They generally must approve budgets and the appointments of department heads and commission members submitted by the chief executive. In some jurisdictions, the legislative body appoints a city, town, or county manager. Many legislators, especially at the state and federal levels, have a staff to perform research, prepare legislation, and help resolve constituents' problems.

Both chief executives and legislators perform many ceremonial duties such as opening new buildings, making proclamations, welcoming visitors, and leading celebrations.

Working Conditions

The working conditions of chief executives and legislators vary with the size and budget of the governmental unit. Time spent at work ranges from meeting once a month for a local council member to 60 or more hours per week for a U.S. Senator. U.S. Senators and Representatives, governors and lieutenant governors, and chief executives and legislators in large local jurisdictions usually work full time year round, as do county and city managers. Many state legislators work full time while legislatures are in session (usually for two to six months a year), and part time the rest of the year. Local elected officials in many jurisdictions work a schedule that is officially designated part time, but actually is the equivalent of a full-time schedule when unpaid duties are taken into account. In addition to their regular schedules, chief executives are on call at all hours to handle emergencies.

Some jobs require occasional out-of-town travel, but others involve long periods away from home to attend sessions of the legislature.

Employment

Chief executives and legislators held about 93,000 jobs in 1996. About eight out of ten worked in local government, while the rest worked primarily in state governments. Chief executives and legislators in the federal government include the 535 Senators and Representatives and the President and Vice President. State governors, legislators and other managers, as well as executives, managers, and council members for local governments made up the remainder.

Chief executives and legislators who do not hold full-time, year-round positions often work in a second occupation as well. This is commonly the one they held before being elected.

Training, Other Qualifications, and Advancement

Voters seek to elect the individual believed to be most qualified from among a number of candidates who meet the minimum age, residency, and citizenship requirements. Successful candidates usually have a strong record of accomplishment in paid and unpaid work in their district. Some have business, teaching, or legal experience, but others come from a wide variety of occupations. In addition, many have experience as members of boards or commissions. Some candidates become well-known for their work with charities, political action groups, political campaigns, or with religious, fraternal, and social organizations.

Management-level work experience and public service help develop the planning, organizing, negotiating, motivating, fund-raising, budgeting, public speaking, and problem-solving skills needed to run an effective political campaign. Candidates must make decisions quickly, sometimes on the basis of limited or contradictory information. They must inspire and motivate their constituents and their staff. They should appear sincere and candid, presenting their views thoughtfully and convincingly. Additionally, they must know how to hammer out compromises and satisfy the demands of constituents. National and statewide campaigns require massive amounts of energy and stamina, as well as superior fund-raising skills.

Town, city, and county managers are generally hired by a council or commission. Managers come from a variety of educational backgrounds. A master's degree in public administration, including courses such as public financial management and legal issues in public administration, is widely recommended. Virtually all town, city, and county managers have at least a bachelor's degree and the majority hold a master's degree. Working in management support positions in government is a prime source of the experience and personal contacts required in eventually securing a manager position.

Generally, a town, city, or county manager in a smaller jurisdiction is required to have expertise in a wide variety of areas. Those who work for larger jurisdictions specialize in financial, administrative, and personnel matters. For all managers, communication skills and the ability to get along with others are essential.

Advancement opportunities for elected public officials are not clearly defined. Because elected positions normally require a period of residency and local public support is critical, officials can usually advance to other offices only in the jurisdictions where they live. For example, council members may run for mayor or for a position in the state government, and state legislators may run for governor or for Congress. Many officials are not politically ambitious, however, and do not seek advancement. Others lose their bids for reelection or voluntarily leave the occupation. A lifetime career as a government chief executive or legislator is rare except for those who reach the national level.

Town, city, and county managers have a better defined career path. They generally obtain a master's degree in public administration and then gain experience as management analysts or assistants in government departments working for committees, councils, or chief executives. They learn about planning, budgeting, civil engineering, and other aspects of running a government. With sufficient experience, they may be hired to manage a small government and often move on to manage progressively larger governments over time.

Job Outlook

Little, if any, growth is expected in the number of state or federal government chief executives and legislators through the year 2006. Few new governments at any level are likely to form, and the number of chief executives and legislators in existing governments rarely changes. Some increase will occur at the local level as counties, cities, and towns take on new responsibilities. New positions will develop as cities and counties turn to professional management to deal with growth, federal regulations, and long-range planning, and volunteer positions are converted to paid positions.

Elections give newcomers the chance to unseat incumbents or to fill vacated positions. In many elections, there is substantial competition, although the level of competition varies from jurisdiction to jurisdiction and from year to year.

Generally, there is less competition in small jurisdictions, which have part-time positions offering relatively low salaries and little or no staff to help with routine work, than in large jurisdictions, which have full-time positions offering higher salaries, more staff, and greater status.

Earnings

Earnings of public administrators vary widely, depending on the size of the government unit and on whether the job is part time, full time and year round, or full time for only a few months a year. Salaries range from little or nothing for a small town council member to $200,000 a year for the President of the United States.

According to the International City/County Management Association, the average annual salary of chief elected county officials in 1996 was $25,600, while chief elected city officials was about $12,200. ICMA data indicate that the average salary for city managers was about $70,600 in 1996, while that of county managers was about $86,700.

According to the National Conference of State Legislatures, the salary for legislators in the 40 states that paid an annual salary ranged from about $10,000 to $47,000 per year. In six states, legislators received a daily salary plus an allowance for expenses while legislatures were in session. Two states paid no expenses and only nominal daily salaries, while two states paid no salary at all but did pay a daily expense allowance. Salaries and the expense allowance were generally higher in the larger states.

Data from Book of the States, 1996–97 indicate that gubernatorial annual salaries ranged from $60,000 in Arkansas to $130,000 in New York. In addition to a salary, most governors received perquisites such as transportation and an official residence.

In 1997, U.S. Senators and Representatives earned $133,600, the Senate and House Majority and Minority leaders $148,400, and the Vice President $171,500.

Related Occupations

Related occupations include managerial positions that require a broad range of skills in addition to administrative expertise, such as corporate chief executives and board members, and high ranking officers in the military.

Sources of Additional Information

Information on appointed officials in local government can be obtained from:
- ❏ International City/County Management Association, 777 North Capitol St. NE, Suite 500, Washington, DC 20002.

Marketing, Advertising, and Public Relations Managers

(*D.O.T.* 096.161-010; 141.137-010; 159.167-022; 163.117-014, -018, -022, -026, .167-010, -014, -018, -022, .267-010; 164.117-010, -014, -018, .167-010; 165.117-010, -014; 185.157-014, .167-042; 187.167-162, -170; 189.117-018)

Significant Points

- ✶ *Employment is projected to increase rapidly, but competition is expected to be intense.*
- ✶ *Marketing, advertising, and public relations managers have high earnings, but substantial travel and long hours, including evenings and weekends, are common.*
- ✶ *A college degree with almost any major is suitable for entering this occupation, but most people enter these jobs after acquiring experience in related, less responsible positions.*

Nature of the Work

The objective of any firm is to market its products or services profitably. In small firms, all marketing responsibilities may be assumed by the owner or chief executive officer. In large firms, which may offer numerous products and services nationally or even worldwide, experienced marketing, advertising, and public relations managers coordinate these and related activities.

In large firms an executive vice president directs the overall marketing policy—including market research, marketing strategy, sales, advertising, promotion, pricing, product development, and public relations activities. Middle and supervisory managers oversee and supervise staffs of professionals and technicians.

Marketing managers develop the firm's detailed marketing strategy. With the help of subordinates, including product development managers and market research managers, they determine the demand for products and services offered by the firm and its competitors and identify potential consumers—for example, business firms, wholesalers, retailers, government, or the general public. Mass markets are further categorized according to various factors such as region, age, income, and lifestyle. Marketing managers develop pricing strategy with an eye towards maximizing the firm's share of the market and its profits while ensuring that the firm's customers are satisfied. In collaboration with sales, product development, and other managers, they monitor trends that indicate the need for new products and services and oversee product development. Marketing managers work with advertising and promotion managers to best promote the firm's products and services and to attract potential users.

Sales managers direct the firm's sales program. They assign sales territories and goals and establish training programs for their sales representatives. Managers advise their sales representatives on ways to improve their sales performance. In large, multiproduct firms, they oversee regional and local sales managers and their staffs. Sales managers maintain contact with dealers and distributors. They analyze sales statistics gathered by their staffs to determine sales potential and inventory requirements and monitor the preferences of customers. Such information is vital to develop products and maximize profits.

Except in the largest firms, advertising and promotion staffs generally are small and serve as a liaison between the firm and the advertising or promotion agency to which many advertising or promotional functions are contracted out. Advertising managers oversee the account services, creative services, and media services departments. The account services department is managed by account executives, who assess the need for advertising and, in advertising agencies, maintain the accounts of clients. The creative services department develops the subject matter and presentation of advertising. This department is supervised by a creative director, who oversees the copy chief and art director and their staffs. The media services department is supervised by the media director, who oversees planning groups that select the communication media—for example, radio, television, newspapers, magazines, or outdoor signs—to disseminate the advertising.

Promotion managers supervise staffs of promotion specialists. They direct promotion programs combining advertising with purchase incentives to increase sales. In an effort to establish closer contact with purchasers—dealers, distributors, or consumers—promotion programs may involve direct mail, telemarketing, television or radio advertising, catalogs, exhibits, inserts in newspapers, in-store displays and product endorsements, and special events. Purchase incentives may include discounts, samples, gifts, rebates, coupons, sweepstakes, and contests.

Public relations managers supervise public relations specialists. These managers direct publicity programs to a targeted public. They use any necessary communication media in their effort to maintain the support of the specific group upon whom their organization's success depends, such as consumers, stockholders, or the general public. For example, public relations managers may clarify or justify the firm's point of view on health or environmental issues to community or special interest groups. They evaluate advertising and promotion programs for compatibility with public relations efforts, and, in effect,

serve as the eyes and ears of top management. They observe social, economic, and political trends that might ultimately have an effect upon the firm, and make recommendations to enhance the firm's image based on those trends. Public relations managers may confer with labor relations managers to produce internal company communications—such as news about employee-management relations—and with financial managers to produce company reports. They assist company executives in drafting speeches, arranging interviews, and other forms of public contact; oversee company archives; and respond to information requests. In addition, some handle special events such as sponsorship of races, parties introducing new products, or other activities the firm supports in order to gain public attention through the press without advertising directly.

Working Conditions

Marketing, advertising, and public relations managers are provided with offices close to top managers. Long hours, including evenings and weekends, are common. Almost 45 percent of marketing, advertising, and public relations managers worked 50 hours or more a week, compared to 20 percent for all occupations. Working under pressure is unavoidable as schedules change, problems arise, and deadlines and goals must be met. Marketing, advertising, and public relations managers meet frequently with other managers; some meet with the public and government officials.

Substantial travel may be involved. For example, attendance at meetings sponsored by associations or industries is often mandatory. Sales managers travel to national, regional, and local offices and to various dealers and distributors. Advertising and promotion managers may travel to meet with clients or representatives of communications media. At times, public relations managers travel to meet with special interest groups or government officials. Job transfers between headquarters and regional offices are common—particularly among sales managers—and can disrupt family life.

Employment

Marketing, advertising, and public relations managers held about 482,000 jobs in 1996. They are found in virtually every industry. Industries employing them in significant numbers include motor vehicle dealers, printing and publishing, advertising, department stores, computer and data processing services, and management and public relations.

Training, Other Qualifications, and Advancement

A wide range of educational backgrounds is suitable for

entry into marketing, advertising, and public relations managerial jobs, but many employers prefer a broad liberal arts background. A bachelor's degree in sociology, psychology, literature, or philosophy, among other subjects, is acceptable. However, requirements vary depending upon the particular job.

For marketing, sales, and promotion management positions, some employers prefer a bachelor's or master's degree in business administration with an emphasis on marketing. Courses in business law, economics, accounting, finance, mathematics, and statistics are also highly recommended. In highly technical industries, such as computer and electronics manufacturing, a bachelor's degree in engineering or science combined with a master's degree in business administration is preferred. For advertising management positions, some employers prefer a bachelor's degree in advertising or journalism. A course of study should include courses in marketing, consumer behavior, market research, sales, communications methods and technology, and visual arts—for example, art history and photography. For public relations management positions, some employers prefer a bachelor's or master's degree in public relations or journalism. The individual's curriculum should include courses in advertising, business administration, public affairs, political science, and creative and technical writing. For all these specialties, courses in management and completion of an internship while in school are highly recommended. Familiarity with word processing and database applications also is important for many marketing, advertising, and public relations management positions. Today interactive marketing, product promotion, and advertising experience are increasingly important, and computer skills are very important.

Most marketing, advertising, and public relations management positions are filled by promoting experienced staff or related professional or technical personnel, for example, sales representatives, purchasing agents, buyers, product or brand specialists, advertising specialists, promotion specialists, and public relations specialists. In small firms, where the number of positions is limited, advancement to a management position generally comes slowly. In large firms, promotion may occur more quickly.

Although experience, ability, and leadership are emphasized for promotion, advancement can be accelerated by participation in management training programs conducted by many large firms. Many firms also provide their employees with continuing education opportunities, either in-house or at local colleges and universities, and encourage employee participation in seminars and conferences, often provided by professional societies. Often in collaboration with colleges and universities, numerous marketing and related associations sponsor national or local management training programs. Courses include brand and product management, international marketing, sales management evaluation, telemarketing and direct sales, promotion, marketing communication, market research, organizational communication, and data processing systems procedures and management. Many firms pay all or part of the cost for those who successfully complete courses.

Some associations (listed under Sources of Additional Information) offer certification programs for marketing, advertising, and public relations managers. Certification is a sign of competence and achievement in this field that is particularly important in a competitive job market. While relatively few marketing, advertising, and public relations managers currently are certified, the number of managers who seek certification is expected to grow. For example, Sales and Marketing Executives International offers a management certification program based on education and job performance. The Public Relations Society of America offers an accreditation program for public relations practitioners based on years of experience and an examination. The International Association of Business Communicators offers an accreditation program for the manager or the person ready to move into communication management. The American Marketing Association is developing a certification program for marketing managers.

Persons interested in becoming marketing, advertising, and public relations managers should be mature, creative, highly motivated, resistant to stress, and flexible, yet decisive. The ability to communicate persuasively, both orally and in writing, with other managers, staff, and the public is vital. Marketing, advertising, and public relations managers also need tact, good judgment, and exceptional ability to establish and maintain effective personal relationships with supervisory and professional staff members and client firms.

Because of the importance and high visibility of their jobs, marketing, advertising, and public relations managers often are prime candidates for advancement. Well-trained, experienced, successful managers may be promoted to higher positions in their own or other firms. Some become top executives. Managers with extensive experience and sufficient capital may open their own businesses.

Job Outlook

Marketing, advertising, and public relations manager jobs are highly coveted and will be sought by other managers or highly experienced professional and technical personnel, resulting in substantial job competition. College graduates with extensive experience, a high level of creativity, and strong communication skills should have the best job opportunities. Those who have new media and interactive marketing skills will be particularly sought after.

Employment of marketing, advertising, and public relations managers is expected to increase faster than the average for all occupations through the year 2006. Increasingly intense domestic and global competition in products and services offered to consumers should require greater marketing, promotional, and public relations efforts by managers. Management and public relations firms may experience particularly rapid growth as businesses increasingly hire contractors for these services rather than support additional full-time staff.

Projected employment growth varies by industry. For example, employment of marketing, advertising, and public relations managers is expected to grow much faster than average in most business services industries, such as computer and data processing, and management and public relations firms, while average growth is projected in manufacturing industries overall. Many companies that eliminated in-house marketing and advertising departments during downsizing in recent years are now relying on firms which specialize in promotion, marketing, and advertising activities to provide these services.

Earnings

According to a National Association of Colleges and Employers survey, starting salaries for marketing majors graduating in 1997 averaged about $29,000; advertising majors, about $27,000.

The median annual salary of marketing, advertising, and public relations managers was $46,000 in 1996. The lowest 10 percent earned $23,000 or less, while the top 10 percent earned $97,000 or more. Many earn bonuses equal to 10 percent or more of their salaries. Surveys show that salary levels vary substantially depending upon the level of managerial responsibility, length of service, education, and the employer's size, location, and industry. For example, manufacturing firms generally pay marketing, advertising, and public relations managers higher salaries than nonmanufacturing firms. For sales managers, the size of their sales territory is another important determinant of salary.

According to a 1996 survey by *Advertising Age Magazine*, the average annual salary of a vice president brand manager was $79,000; vice president product manager, $105,000; vice president advertising, $130,000; and vice president marketing, $133,000.

According to a 1996 survey by the Public Relations Society of America, senior public relations managers earned an average of $76,790.

Related Occupations

Marketing, advertising, and public relations managers direct the sale of products and services offered by their firms and the communication of information about their firms' activities. Other personnel involved with marketing, advertising, and public relations include art directors, commercial and graphic artists, copy chiefs, copywriters, editors, lobbyists, marketing research analysts, public relations specialists, promotion specialists, sales representatives, and technical writers.

Sources of Additional Information

For information about careers in sales and marketing management, contact:

❑ American Marketing Association, 250 S. Wacker Dr., Chicago, IL 60606.

❑ Sales and Marketing Executives International, 458 Statler Office Tower, Cleveland, OH 44115.

For information about careers in advertising management, contact:

❑ American Advertising Federation, Education Services Department, 1101 Vermont Ave. NW, Suite 500, Washington, DC 20005.

Information about careers in promotion management is available from:

❑ Association of Promotion and Marketing Agencies Worldwide (APMA), 750 Summer St., Stamford, CT 06901.

❑ Promotion Marketing Association of America, Inc., 322 Eighth Ave., Suite 1201, New York, NY 10001.

Information about careers in public relations management is available from:

❑ Public Relations Society of America, 33 Irving Place, New York, NY 10003-2376.

Information on accreditation for business communicators is available from:

❑ International Association of Business Communicators, One Hallidie Plaza, Suite 600, San Francisco, CA 94102.

Mathematicians

(*D.O.T.* 020.067-014, .167-030; 199.267-014)

Significant Points

✴ *Employment is expected to grow more slowly than the average as civilian and defense-related research activities face limited expansion.*

✴ *Bachelor's degree holders with a strong background in computer science, electrical or mechanical engineering, or operations research should have good opportunities in related occupations.*

Nature of the Work

Mathematics is one of the oldest and most fundamental sciences. Mathematicians create new mathematical theories and techniques involving the latest technology and solve economic, scientific, engineering, and business problems using mathematical knowledge and computational tools.

Mathematics falls into two broad classes: theoretical (pure) mathematics and applied mathematics. However, these classes are not sharply defined and often overlap.

Theoretical mathematicians advance mathematical knowledge by developing new principles and recognizing previously unknown relationships between existing principles of mathematics. Although they seek to increase basic knowledge without necessarily considering its practical use, such pure and abstract knowledge has been instrumental in producing or furthering many scientific and engineering achievements.

Applied mathematicians use theories and techniques, such as mathematical modeling and computational methods, to formulate and solve practical problems in business, government, engineering, and the physical, life, and social sciences. For example, they may analyze the most efficient way to schedule airline routes between cities, the effects of new drugs on disease, the aerodynamic characteristics of an experimental aircraft, or the distribution costs or manufacturing processes of businesses. Applied mathematicians working in industrial research and development may develop or enhance mathematical methods when confronted with difficult problems. Some mathematicians, called cryptanalysts, analyze and decipher encryption systems designed to transmit military, political, financial, or law enforcement-related information.

Mathematicians use computers extensively to analyze relationships among variables, solve complex problems, develop models, and process large amounts of data.

Much work in applied mathematics, however, is carried on by persons with titles other than mathematician. In fact, because mathematics is the foundation upon which so many other academic disciplines are built, the number of workers using mathematical techniques is many times greater than the number actually designated as mathematicians. Engineers, computer scientists, physicists, and economists are among those who use mathematics extensively but have job titles other than mathematician. Some workers, such as statisticians, actuaries, and operations research analysts, actually are specialists in a particular branch of mathematics.

Working Conditions

Mathematicians working for government agencies or private firms usually have structured work schedules. They generally work as an integral part of an interdisciplinary team that may include engineers, computer scientists, physicists, technicians, and others. Deadlines, overtime work, special rush requests for information or analysis, and prolonged travel to attend seminars or conferences may be part of their jobs.

Employment

Mathematicians held about 16,000 jobs in 1996. In addition, about 20,000 persons held mathematics faculty positions in colleges and universities in 1995, according to the American Mathematical Society.

Many nonfaculty mathematicians work for either federal or state governments. The Department of Defense is the primary federal employer of mathematicians, employing almost three-fourths of the mathematicians employed by the federal government. In the private sector, major employers include research and testing services, educational services, security and commodity exchanges, and management and public relations services. Within manufacturing, the drug industry is the key employer. Some mathematicians also work for banks, insurance companies, and public utilities.

Training, Other Qualifications, and Advancement

A bachelor's degree in mathematics is the minimum education needed for prospective mathematicians. In the federal government, entry-level job candidates usually must have a four-year degree with a major in mathematics or a four-year degree with the equivalent of a mathematics major—24 semester hours of mathematics courses.

In private industry, job candidates generally need a master's or a Ph.D. degree to obtain jobs as mathematicians. Most of the positions designated for mathematicians are in research and development laboratories as part of technical teams. These research scientists engage in either pure mathematical, or basic, research; or in applied research focusing on developing or improving specific products or processes. The majority of those with a bachelor's or master's degree in mathematics who work in private industry do so not as mathematicians, but in related fields such as computer science, where they have titles such as computer programmers, systems analysts, or systems engineers.

A bachelor's degree in mathematics is offered by most colleges and universities. Mathematics courses usually required for this degree are calculus, differential equations, and linear and abstract algebra. Additional courses might include probability theory and statistics, mathematical analysis, numerical analysis, topology, discrete mathematics, and mathematical logic. Many colleges and universities urge or even require students majoring in mathematics to take several courses in a field that uses or is closely related to mathematics, such as computer science, engineering, operations research, a physical science, statistics, or economics. A double major in mathematics and another discipline such as computer science, economics, or one of the sciences is particularly desirable to many employers. A prospective college mathematics major should take as many mathematics courses as possible while in high school.

In 1996, about 240 colleges and universities offered a master's degree as the highest degree in either pure or applied mathematics; 195 offered a Ph.D. in pure or applied mathematics. In graduate school, students conduct research and take advanced courses, usually specializing in a subfield of mathematics. Some areas of concentration are algebra, number theory, real or complex analysis, geometry, topology, logic, and applied mathematics.

For work in applied mathematics, training in the field in which the mathematics will be used is very important. Fields in which applied mathematics is used extensively include physics, actuarial science, engineering, and operations research; of increasing importance are computer and information science, business and industrial management, economics, statistics, chemistry, geology life sciences, and the behavioral sciences.

Mathematicians should have substantial knowledge of computer programming because most complex mathematical computation and much mathematical modeling is done by computer.

Mathematicians need good reasoning ability and persistence in order to identify, analyze, and apply basic principles to technical problems. Communication skills are also important, as mathematicians must be able to interact with others, including nonmathematicians, and discuss proposed solutions to problems.

Job Outlook

Employment of mathematicians is expected to increase more slowly than the average for all occupations through the year 2006. The number of jobs available for workers whose educational background is solely mathematics is not expected to increase significantly. Many firms engaged in civilian research and development that use mathematicians are not planning to expand their research departments much, and, in some cases, may reduce them. Expected reductions in defense-related research and development will also affect mathematicians' employment, especially in the federal government. Those whose educational background includes the study of a related discipline will have better job opportunities. However, as advancements in technology lead to expanding applications of mathematics, more workers with a knowledge of mathematics

will be required. Many of these workers have job titles which reflect the end product of their work rather than the discipline of mathematics used in that work.

Bachelor's degree holders in mathematics are usually not qualified for most jobs as mathematicians. However, those with a strong background in computer science, electrical or mechanical engineering, or operations research should have good opportunities in industry. Bachelor's degree holders who meet state certification requirements may become high school mathematics teachers.

Holders of a master's degree in mathematics will face very strong competition for jobs in theoretical research. However, job opportunities in applied mathematics and related areas such as computer programming, operations research, and engineering design in industry and government will be more numerous.

Earnings

According to a 1997 survey by the National Association of Colleges and Employers, starting salary offers for mathematics graduates with a bachelor's degree averaged about $31,800 a year and for those with a master's degree, $38,300.

In the federal government in 1997, the average annual salary for mathematicians in supervisory, nonsupervisory, and managerial positions was $62,000; for mathematical statisticians, $65,660; and for cryptanalysts, $56,160.

Benefits for mathematicians tend to be similar to those offered to most professionals who work in office settings: vacation and sick leave, health and life insurance, and a retirement plan, among others.

Related Occupations

Other occupations that require a degree in or extensive knowledge of mathematics include actuary, statistician, computer programmer, systems analyst, systems engineer, and operations research analyst. In addition, a strong background in mathematics facilitates employment in fields such as engineering, economics, finance, and physics.

Sources of Additional Information

For more information about the field of mathematics, including career opportunities and professional training, contact:

❑ American Mathematical Society, Department of Professional Programs and Services, P.O. Box 6248, Providence, RI 02940-6248.

❑ Mathematical Association of America, 1529 18th St. NW, Washington, DC 20036.

For a 1996 resource guide on careers in mathematical sciences, contact:

❑ Conference Board of the Mathematical Sciences, 1529 18th St. NW, Washington, DC 20036.

For specific information on careers in applied mathematics, contact:

❑ Society for Industrial and Applied Mathematics, 3600 University City Science Center, Philadelphia, PA 19104-2688.

Information on obtaining a mathematician position with the federal government may be obtained from the Office of Personnel Management through a telephone-based system. Consult your telephone directory under U.S. government for a local number or call (912) 757-3000 (TDD 912 744-2299). That number is not toll-free and charges may result. Information also is available from their Internet site: http://www.usajobs.opm.gov

Pharmacists

(D.O.T. 074.161-010 and -014)

Significant Points

✶ *Pharmacists are stepping beyond the traditional delivery of prescriptions to become more involved in drug therapy decision-making and patient counseling.*

✶ *Earnings are very high, but some pharmacists work long hours.*

Nature of the Work

Pharmacists dispense drugs prescribed by physicians and other health practitioners and provide information to patients about medications and their use. They advise physicians and other health practitioners on the selection, dosages, interactions, and side effects of medications. Pharmacists must understand the use, composition, and effects of drugs. Compounding—the actual mixing of ingredients to form powders, tablets, capsules, ointments, and solutions—is only a small part of a pharmacist's practice, because most medicines are produced by pharmaceutical companies in a standard dosage and form.

Pharmacists in community (retail) pharmacies counsel patients, as well as answer questions about prescription drugs, such as possible adverse reactions and interactions. They provide information about over-the-counter drugs and make recommendations after asking a series of health questions, such as whether the customer is taking any other medications. They also give advice about durable medical equipment and home health care supplies. Those who own or manage community pharmacies may buy and sell nonhealth-related merchandise, hire and supervise personnel, and oversee the general opera-

tion of the pharmacy. Some community pharmacists offer specialized disease state management services for conditions such as diabetes, asthma, smoking cessation, or high blood pressure.

Pharmacists in hospitals and clinics dispense medications and advise the medical staff on the selection and effects of drugs. They may make sterile solutions and buy medical supplies. They also assess, plan, and monitor drug regimens. They counsel patients on the use of drugs while in the hospital, and on their use at home when they are discharged. Pharmacists may also evaluate drug use patterns and outcomes in the hospital or in a patient population.

Pharmacists who work in home health care prepare infusions (solutions that are injected into patients) and other medications for use in the home, and monitor drug therapy.

Most pharmacists keep computerized records of patients' drug therapies to ensure that harmful drug interactions do not occur. They frequently teach pharmacy students serving as externs in preparation for graduation and licensure.

Some pharmacists specialize in specific areas, such as drugs for psychiatric disorders, intravenous nutrition support, oncology, nuclear pharmacy, or pharmacotherapy.

Working Conditions

Pharmacists usually work in clean, well-lighted, and well-ventilated areas. Many pharmacists spend most of their time on their feet. When working with sterile or potentially dangerous pharmaceutical products, pharmacists wear gloves and masks and work with special protective equipment. Many community and hospital pharmacies are open extended hours or around the clock, so pharmacists may work evenings, nights, weekends, and holidays. Consultant pharmacists may travel to nursing homes or other facilities to monitor people's drug therapy.

About one out of five pharmacists worked part-time in 1996. Most full-time salaried pharmacists worked about 40 hours a week. Some, including most self-employed pharmacists, worked more than 50 hours a week.

Employment

Pharmacists held about 172,000 jobs in 1996. About three out of five worked in community pharmacies, either independently owned, part of a drug store chain, or part of a grocery store, department store, or mass merchandiser. Most community pharmacists were salaried employees, but some were self-employed owners. About one-quarter worked in hospitals, and others worked in clinics, mail-order pharmacies, pharmaceutical wholesalers, home health care agencies, or the federal government.

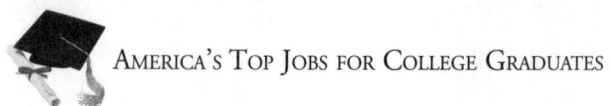

Some pharmacists hold more than one job. They may work a standard week in their primary work setting, and also work part-time.

Training, Other Qualifications, and Advancement

A license to practice pharmacy is required in all states, the District of Columbia, and U.S. territories. To obtain a license, one must graduate from an accredited college of pharmacy, pass a state examination, and serve an internship under a licensed pharmacist. Most states grant a license without extensive reexamination to qualified pharmacists already licensed by another state (check with state boards of pharmacy for details). Many pharmacists are licensed to practice in more than one state. Most states require continuing education for license renewal.

At least five years of study beyond high school are required to graduate from programs accredited by the American Council on Pharmaceutical Education. A Bachelor of Science (B.S.) in Pharmacy, the degree received by most graduates, takes five years. A Doctor of Pharmacy (Pharm.D.) normally requires at least six years, during which an intervening bachelor's degree is usually not awarded. Those who already hold the bachelor's degree may enter Pharm.D. programs, but the combined period of study is usually longer than six years. In 1997, 79 colleges of pharmacy conferred degrees. The number of schools offering the Pharm.D. as the only professional degree increased to 41, and the number offering the B.S. in Pharmacy as the only professional degree continued to decline, reaching four.

Requirements for admission to colleges of pharmacy vary. A few colleges admit students directly from high school. Most colleges of pharmacy, however, require one or two years of college-level prepharmacy education. Entry requirements usually include mathematics and basic sciences, such as chemistry, biology, and physics, as well as courses in the humanities and social sciences. Some colleges require the applicant to take the Pharmacy College Admissions Test.

All colleges of pharmacy offer courses in pharmacy practice, designed to teach students to dispense prescriptions, communicate with patients and other health professionals, and to strengthen their understanding of professional ethics and practice management responsibilities. Pharmacists' training increasingly emphasizes direct patient care, as well as consultative services to other health professionals.

Recently, pharmacy schools voted to move toward offering the Pharm.D. as the only professional degree in pharmacy. However, some schools continue to offer the B.S. in Pharmacy. All accredited pharmacy schools are expected to graduate their last B.S. class by the year 2004. Either degree currently fulfills the requirements to take the licensure examination of a state board of pharmacy.

The bachelor's degree in pharmacy is generally acceptable for most positions in community pharmacies, at least in the foreseeable future. A growing number of hospital employers prefer that a pharmacist have a Pharm.D. degree. A master's or Ph.D. degree in pharmacy or a related field usually is required to do research, and a Pharm.D. with additional residency or fellowship training, master's, or Ph.D. usually is necessary for faculty positions.

In 1996–97, 60 colleges of pharmacy awarded the Master of Science degree or the Ph.D. degree. Although a number of pharmacy graduates interested in further training pursue an advanced degree in pharmacy, there are other options. Some enter one- or two-year residency programs or fellowships. Pharmacy residencies are organized, directed, postgraduate training programs in pharmacy practice. Pharmacy fellowships are directed, highly individualized programs designed to prepare participants to work in research laboratories.

Areas of graduate study include pharmaceutics and pharmaceutical chemistry (physical and chemical properties of drugs and dosage forms), pharmacology (effects of drugs on the body), and pharmacy administration, including pharmacoeconomics and social-behavioral aspects of patient care.

Prospective pharmacists should have scientific aptitude, good communication skills, and a desire to help others. They must also be conscientious and pay close attention to detail, because the decisions they make affect human lives.

In community pharmacies, pharmacists usually begin at the staff level. After they gain experience and secure the necessary capital, many become owners or part owners of pharmacies. Pharmacists in chain drug stores may be promoted to pharmacy supervisor or manager at the store level and then at the district or regional level, and later to an executive position within the chain's headquarters.

Hospital pharmacists may advance to supervisory or administrative positions. Pharmacists in the pharmaceutical industry may advance in marketing, sales, research, quality control, production, packaging, and other areas.

Job Outlook

Employment of pharmacists is expected to grow as fast as the average for all occupations through the year 2006, due to the increased pharmaceutical needs of a larger and older population, and greater use of medication. Cost-conscious insurers and health systems will continue to emphasize the role of pharmacists in primary and preventive health services. They realize

that the expense of using medication to treat diseases and conditions is often considerably less than the potential costs for patients whose conditions go untreated, and pharmacists can also play an important role in reducing the expenses resulting from unexpected complications due to allergic reactions or medication interactions.

The increased number of middle aged and elderly people will spur demand for pharmacists in all practice settings. The number of prescriptions influences the demand for pharmacists, and the middle-aged and elderly population uses more prescription drugs, on average, than younger people.

Other factors likely to increase the demand for pharmacists through the year 2006 include the likelihood of scientific advances that will make more drug products available, new developments in administering medication, and increasingly sophisticated consumers seeking more information about drugs.

Employment in hospitals is expected to grow slowly, as hospitals reduce inpatient stays, downsize, and consolidate departments. Pharmacy services are shifting to long-term, ambulatory, and home care settings, where opportunities for pharmacists will be best. New opportunities for pharmacists are emerging in managed care organizations, where pharmacists analyze trends and patterns in medication use for their populations of patients. Fast growth is also expected for pharmacists employed in research, disease management, and pharmacoeconomics—determining the costs and benefits of different drug therapies.

Because of efforts to control prescription drug costs, retail pharmacies are taking steps to increase their prescription volume to make up for declining dispensing fees. Automation of drug dispensing and greater use of pharmacy technicians will help them dispense more prescriptions. The number of community pharmacists needed in the future will depend on the expansion rate of chain drug stores and the willingness of insurers to reimburse pharmacists for providing clinical services to patients taking prescription drugs. With its emphasis on cost control, managed care has encouraged the growth of lower-cost distributors of prescription drugs such as mail-order firms. Slower employment growth is expected in traditional chain and independent pharmacies.

Earnings

Median weekly earnings of full-time, salaried pharmacists were $992 in 1996. Half earned between $827 and $1,177. The lowest 10 percent earned less than $554 and the top 10 percent more than $1,422.

According to a survey by *Drug Topics* magazine, published by Medical Economics Inc., average base salaries of full-time,

salaried pharmacists were $59,276 per year in 1996. Pharmacists working in chain drug stores had an average base salary of $61,735 per year, while pharmacists working in independent drug stores averaged $52,189, and hospital pharmacists averaged $61,317. Overall, salaries for pharmacists were highest in the West and second highest in the East. Many pharmacists also receive compensation in the form of bonuses, overtime, and profit-sharing.

Related Occupations

Persons in other professions who may work with pharmaceutical compounds are pharmaceutical chemists, pharmacologists, medical scientists, and biological technicians.

Sources of Additional Information

For information on pharmacy as a career, preprofessional and professional requirements, programs offered by all the colleges of pharmacy, and student financial aid, contact:

❏ American Association of Colleges of Pharmacy, 1426 Prince St., Alexandria, VA 22314.

Information on requirements for licensure in a particular state is available from the state board of pharmacy.

Information on specific college entrance requirements, curriculums, and financial aid is available from the dean of any college of pharmacy.

Protestant Ministers

(*D.O.T.* 120.107-010)

Significant Points

✳ *Entry requirements vary greatly; many denominations require a bachelor's degree followed by study at a theological school, while other denominations have no formal educational requirements.*

✳ *Competition for positions is expected because of the large number of qualified candidates; the degree of competition will vary among denominations and geographic regions.*

Nature of the Work

Protestant ministers lead their congregations in worship services and administer the various rites of the church, such as baptism, confirmation, and Holy Communion. The services ministers conduct differ among the numerous Protestant denominations, and even among congregations within a denomination. In many denominations, ministers follow a traditional order of worship; in others, they adapt the services to the needs of youth and other groups within the congregation. Most services include Bible reading, hymn singing, prayers, and a sermon. In some denominations, Bible reading by a member of the congregation and individual testimonials may constitute a large part of the service. In addition to these duties, ministers officiate at weddings, funerals, and other occasions.

Each Protestant denomination has its own hierarchical structure. Some ministers are responsible only to the congregation they serve, while others are assigned duties by elder ministers, or by the bishops of the diocese they serve. In some denominations, ministers are reassigned to a new pastorate by a central governing body or diocese every few years.

Ministers serving small congregations generally work personally with parishioners. Those serving large congregations may share specific aspects of the ministry with one or more associates or assistants, such as a minister of education who assists in educational programs for different age groups, or a minister of music.

Working Conditions

Protestant ministers typically work long and irregular hours. In 1996, about one in four full-time clergy worked 60 or more hours a week, compared to only one in 14 workers in all professional specialty occupations. Although many of their activities are sedentary and intellectual in nature, they are frequently called upon at short notice to visit the sick, comfort the dying and their families, and provide counseling to those in need. Involvement in community, administrative, and educational activities may require clergy to work evenings, early mornings, holidays, and weekends.

Employment

According to the National Council of Churches, there were over 300,000 Protestant ministers in 1996, including those who served without a regular congregation or worked in closely related fields, such as chaplains in hospitals, the Armed Forces, universities, and correctional institutions. While there are many denominations, most ministers are employed by the five largest Protestant bodies—Baptist, Episcopalian, Lutheran, Methodist, and Presbyterian.

Although most ministers are located in urban areas, many serve two or more small congregations in less densely populated areas. Some small churches increasingly are employing part-time ministers who may be seminary students, retired ministers, or holders of secular jobs. Unpaid pastors serve other churches with meager funds. Some churches employ specially trained members of the laity to conduct nonliturgical functions.

Training, Other Qualifications, and Advancement

Educational requirements for entry into the Protestant ministry vary greatly. Many denominations require, or at least strongly prefer, a bachelor's degree followed by study at a theological school. However, some denominations have no formal educational requirements, and others ordain persons having various types of training in Bible colleges or institutes, or liberal arts colleges. Many denominations now allow women to be ordained, but others do not. Persons considering a career in the ministry should first verify the entrance requirements with their particular denomination.

In general, each large denomination has its own schools of theology that reflect its particular doctrine, interests, and needs. However, many of these schools are open to students from other denominations. Several interdenominational schools associated with universities give both undergraduate and graduate training covering a wide range of theological points of view.

In 1996, about 150 American Protestant theological schools were accredited by the Association of Theological Schools in the United States and Canada. These only admit students who have received a bachelor's degree or its equivalent in liberal arts from an accredited college. After college graduation, many denominations require a three-year course of professional study in one of these accredited schools, or seminaries for the degree of Master of Divinity.

The standard curriculum for accredited theological schools consists of four major categories: Biblical, historical, theological, and practical. Courses of a practical nature include pastoral care, preaching, religious education, and administration. Many accredited schools require that students work under the supervision of a faculty member or experienced minister. Some institutions offer Doctor of Ministry degrees to students who have completed additional study, usually two or more years, and served at least two years as a minister. Scholarships and loans are often available for students of theological institutions.

Persons who have denominational qualifications for the ministry usually are ordained after graduation from a seminary or after serving a probationary pastoral period. Denominations that do not require seminary training ordain clergy at various appointed times. Some evangelical churches may ordain ministers with only a high school education.

Men and women entering the clergy often begin their careers as pastors of small congregations or as assistant pastors in large churches. Pastor positions in large metropolitan areas or in large congregations often require many years of experience.

Job Outlook

Competition is expected to continue for paid Protestant ministers through the year 2006, reflecting slow growth of church membership and the large number of qualified candidates. Graduates of theological schools should have the best prospects. The degree of competition for paid positions will vary among denominations and geographic regions. For example, relatively favorable prospects are expected for ministers in evangelical churches. Competition will still be keen for more responsible positions serving large, urban congregations. Ministers willing to work part-time or for smaller, rural congregations should have better opportunities. Most job openings will stem from the need to replace ministers who retire, die, or leave the ministry.

Employment alternatives for newly ordained Protestant ministers who are unable to find positions in parishes include working in youth counseling, family relations, and welfare organizations; teaching in religious educational institutions; and serving as chaplains in the Armed Forces, hospitals, universities, and correctional institutions.

Earnings

Salaries of Protestant clergy vary substantially, depending on experience, denomination, size and wealth of congregation, and geographic location. Based on limited information, the estimated average annual income of Protestant ministers was about $30,000 in 1996. In large, wealthier denominations, ministers often earned significantly higher salaries. Ministers with modest salaries typically earn additional income from employment in secular occupations.

Sources of Additional Information

Persons who are interested in entering the Protestant ministry should seek the counsel of a minister or church guidance worker. Theological schools can supply information on admission requirements. Prospective ministers should also contact the ordination supervision body of their particular denomination for information on special requirements for ordination.

Rabbis

(D.O.T. 120.107-010)

Significant Points

* ✴ *Ordination usually requires completion of a college degree followed by a four- or five-year program at a Jewish seminary.*

* ✴ *Graduates of Jewish seminaries have good job prospects, reflecting current unmet needs for rabbis and the need to replace the many rabbis approaching retirement age.*

Nature of the Work

Rabbis serve either Orthodox, Conservative, Reform, or Reconstructionist Jewish congregations. Regardless of their particular point of view, all preserve the substance of Jewish religious worship. Congregations differ in the extent to which they follow the traditional form of worship—for example, in the wearing of head coverings, the use of Hebrew as the language of prayer, or the use of instrumental music or a choir. The format of the worship service and, therefore, the ritual that the rabbi uses may vary even among congregations belonging to the same branch of Judaism.

Rabbis are more independent than other clergy, because there is no formal hierarchy in Judaism. Rabbis are only responsible to the Board of Trustees of the congregation they serve. Those serving large congregations may spend considerable time in administrative duties, working with their staffs and committees. Large congregations frequently have associate or assistant rabbis, who often serve as educational directors.

Rabbis also may write for religious and lay publications, and teach in theological seminaries, colleges, and universities.

Working Conditions

Rabbis typically work long and irregular hours. In 1996, about one in four full-time rabbis worked 60 or more hours a week, compared to only one in 14 workers in all professional specialty occupations. Although many of their activities are sedentary and intellectual in nature, they are frequently called upon at short notice to visit the sick, comfort the dying and their families, and provide counseling to those in need. Involvement in community, administrative, and educational activities may require rabbis to work evenings, early mornings, holidays, and weekends.

Employment

Based on information from organizations representing the four major branches of Judaism, there were approximately 1,800 Reform, 1,250 Conservative, 1,000 Orthodox, and 250 Reconstructionist rabbis in 1996. Although the majority served congregations, many rabbis functioned in other settings. Some taught in Jewish studies programs at colleges and universities, while others served as chaplains in the military, hospitals, colleges, or one of the many Jewish community service agencies.

Although rabbis serve Jewish communities throughout the nation, they are concentrated in major metropolitan areas with large Jewish populations.

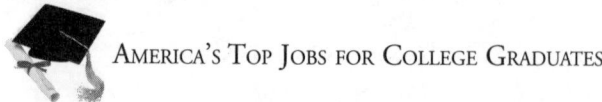

Training, Other Qualifications, and Advancement

To become eligible for ordination as a rabbi, a student must complete a course of study in a seminary. Entrance requirements and the curriculum depend upon the branch of Judaism with which the seminary is associated. Most seminaries require applicants to be college graduates.

Jewish seminaries typically take five years for completion of studies, with an additional preparatory year required for students without sufficient grounding in Hebrew and Jewish studies. In addition to the core academic program, training generally includes field work and internships providing hands-on experience and, in some cases, study in Jerusalem. Seminary graduates are awarded the title Rabbi and the Master of Arts in Hebrew Letters degree; after more advanced study, some earn the Doctor of Hebrew Letters degree.

In general, the curriculums of Jewish theological seminaries provide students with a comprehensive knowledge of the Bible, Talmud, Rabbinic literature, Jewish history, theology, and courses in education, pastoral psychology, and public speaking. Students receive extensive practical training in dealing with social problems in the community. Training for alternatives to the pulpit, such as leadership in community services and religious education, is increasingly stressed. Some seminaries grant advanced academic degrees in such fields as Biblical and Talmudic research. All Jewish theological seminaries make scholarships and loans available.

About 35 seminaries educate and ordain Orthodox rabbis. The Rabbi Isaac Elchanan Theological Seminary and the Beth Medrash Govoha Seminary are representative of the two basic kinds of Orthodox seminaries. The former requires a bachelor's degree for entry and has a formal four-year ordination program. The latter has no formal admission requirements but may require more years of study for ordination. The training is rigorous. When students have become sufficiently learned in the Talmud, the Bible, and other religious studies, they may be ordained with the approval of an authorized rabbi, acting either independently or as a representative of a rabbinical seminary.

Other major rabbinical seminaries include the Jewish Theological Seminary of America, which educates rabbis for the Conservative branch; the Hebrew Union College—Jewish Institute of Religion, which educates rabbis for the Reform branch; and the Reconstructionist Rabbinical College, which educates rabbis in the newest branch of Judaism.

Newly ordained rabbis usually begin as spiritual leaders of small congregations, assistants to experienced rabbis, directors of Hillel Foundations on college campuses, teachers in educational institutions, or chaplains in the Armed Forces. As a rule, experienced rabbis fill the pulpits of large and well-established Jewish congregations.

Job Outlook

Job opportunities for rabbis are expected to be favorable in the four major branches of Judaism through the year 2006, reflecting current unmet needs for rabbis together with the need to replace the many rabbis approaching retirement age. Rabbis willing to work in small communities should have particularly good prospects.

Graduates of Orthodox seminaries who seek pulpits should have good opportunities as growth in enrollments slows, and many graduates seek alternatives to the pulpit. Reconstructionist rabbis are expected to have very good employment opportunities as membership expands rapidly. Conservative and Reform rabbis are also expected to have good job opportunities serving congregations or in other settings.

Earnings

Based on limited information, annual average earnings of rabbis generally ranged from $45,000 to $75,000 in 1997, including benefits. Benefits may include housing, health insurance, and a retirement plan. Income varies widely, depending on the size and financial status of the congregation, as well as its denominational branch and geographic location. Rabbis may earn additional income from gifts or fees for officiating at ceremonies such as bar mitzvahs and weddings.

Sources of Additional Information

Persons who are interested in becoming rabbis should discuss their plans for a vocation with a practicing rabbi. Information on the work of rabbis and allied occupations can be obtained from:

❑ Rabbinical Council of America, 305 7th Ave., New York, NY 10001. (Orthodox)

❑ The Jewish Theological Seminary of America, 3080 Broadway, New York, NY 10027. (Conservative) Homepage: http://www.jtsa.edu

❑ Rabbinical Placement Commission, 192 Lexington Ave., New York, NY 10016. (Reform)

❑ Reconstructionist Rabbinical College, 1299 Church Rd., Wyncote, PA 19095.

Roman Catholic Priests

(D.O.T. 120.107-010)

Significant Points

* *Preparation generally requires eight years of study beyond high school, usually including a college degree followed by four years at a seminary.*

* *The shortage of Roman Catholic priests is expected to continue, resulting in a very favorable outlook.*

Nature of the Work

Roman Catholic priests attend to the spiritual, pastoral, moral, and educational needs of the members of their church. A priest's day usually begins with morning meditation and mass and may end with an individual counseling session or an evening visit to a hospital or home. Many priests direct and serve on church committees, work in civic and charitable organizations, and assist in community projects. Some counsel parishioners preparing for marriage or the birth of a child.

Priests in the Catholic church belong to one of two groups—diocesan or religious. Both types of priests have the same powers, acquired through ordination by a bishop. Their differences lie in their way of life, their type of work, and the church authority to whom they are responsible. Diocesan priests commit their lives to serving the people of a diocese, a church administrative region, and generally work in parishes assigned by the bishop of their diocese. Diocesan priests make promises of celibacy and obedience. Religious priests belong to a religious order, such as the Jesuits, Dominicans, or Franciscans. Religious priests are assigned duties by their superiors in their respective religious orders. Some religious priests specialize in teaching, while others serve as missionaries in foreign countries, where they may live under difficult and primitive conditions. Others live a communal life in monasteries, where they devote their lives to prayer, study, and assigned work. Religious priests take vows of chastity, poverty, and obedience.

Both religious and diocesan priests hold teaching and administrative posts in Catholic seminaries, colleges and universities, and high schools. Priests attached to religious orders staff a large proportion of the church's institutions of higher education and many high schools, whereas diocesan priests are usually concerned with the parochial schools attached to parish churches and with diocesan high schools. The members of religious orders do most of the missionary work conducted by the Catholic Church in this country and abroad.

Working Conditions

Priests typically work long and irregular hours. In 1996, about one in four full-time clergy worked 60 or more hours a week, compared to only one in 14 workers in all professional specialty occupations. Although many of their activities are sedentary and intellectual in nature, they are frequently called upon at short notice to visit the sick, comfort the dying and their families, and provide counseling to those in need. Involvement in community, administrative, and educational activities may require clergy to work evenings, early mornings, holidays, and weekends.

Employment

According to the Official Catholic Directory, there were approximately 49,000 priests in 1996; about two-thirds were diocesan priests. There are priests in nearly every city and town and in many rural communities; however, the majority are in metropolitan areas, where most Catholics reside. Large numbers of priests are located in communities near Catholic schools, hospitals, social service agencies, and other institutions.

Training, Other Qualifications, and Advancement

Preparation for the priesthood generally requires eight years of study beyond high school, usually including a college degree followed by four years at a seminary. There are 198 seminaries—72 for diocesan priests and 126 for religious priests. Priests commit themselves to celibacy, remaining unmarried. Only men are ordained as priests; women serve in other church positions that do not require priestly ordination.

Preparatory study for the priesthood may begin either in the first year of high school, at the college level, or in theological seminaries after college graduation. Today, most candidates for the priesthood take a four-year degree program at a conventional college or university. After graduation from college, candidates generally receive one or two years of preparatory study (philosophy, religious studies, and prayer) before entering the seminary. Theology course work in the seminary includes sacred scripture; dogmatic, moral, and pastoral theology; homiletics (art of preaching); church history; liturgy (sacraments); and canon (church) law. Fieldwork experience is usually required; in recent years, this aspect of a priest's training has been emphasized. Diocesan and religious priests attend different major seminaries, where slight variations in the training reflect the differences in their duties.

According to the U.S. Bishops Conference, ten high school seminaries provided a college preparatory program in 1996. Programs emphasize English grammar, speech, literature, and social studies. Latin may be required, and modern languages are encouraged. In Hispanic communities, knowledge of Spanish is mandatory.

Young men are never denied entry into seminaries because of lack of funds. In seminaries for secular priests, scholarships or loans are available. Those in religious seminaries are financed by contributions of benefactors and the Catholic Church.

Postgraduate work in theology is offered at a number of American Catholic universities or at ecclesiastical universities around the world, particularly in Rome. Also, many priests do graduate work in fields unrelated to theology. Priests are encouraged by the Catholic Church to continue their studies, at least informally, after ordination. In recent years, continuing education for ordained priests has stressed social sciences, such as sociology and psychology.

A newly ordained secular priest usually works as an assistant pastor. Newly ordained priests of religious orders are assigned to the specialized duties for which they are trained. Depending on the talents, interests, and experience of the individual, many opportunities for greater responsibility exist within the church.

Job Outlook

The shortage of Roman Catholic priests is expected to continue, resulting in a very favorable job outlook through the year 2006. Many priests will be needed in the years ahead to provide for the spiritual, educational, and social needs of the increasing number of Catholics. In recent years, the number of ordained priests has been insufficient to fill the needs of newly established parishes and other Catholic institutions, and to replace priests who retire, die, or leave the priesthood. This situation is likely to continue—even if the recent modest increase in seminary enrollments continues—as an increasing proportion of priests approaches retirement age.

In response to the shortage of priests, certain traditional functions increasingly are being performed by permanent deacons and by teams of clergy and laity. Throughout most of the country, permanent deacons have been ordained to preach and perform liturgical functions such as baptisms, marriages, and funerals, and provide service to the community. Deacons are not authorized to celebrate Mass, nor administer the Sacraments of Reconciliation and the Anointing of the Sick. Teams of clergy and laity undertake some liturgical and nonliturgical functions such as hospital visits and religious teaching.

Earnings

Diocesan priests' salaries vary from diocese to diocese. Based on limited information, salaries averaged about $11,000 in 1996. In addition to a salary, diocesan priests receive a package of benefits which may include a car allowance, room and board in the parish rectory, health insurance, and a retirement plan.

Priests who do special work related to the church, such as teaching, usually receive a partial salary which is less than a lay person in the same position would receive. The difference between the usual salary for these jobs and the salary that the priest receives is called "contributed service." In some of these situations, housing and related expenses may be provided; in other cases, the priest must make his own arrangements. Some priests doing special work receive the same compensation that a lay person would receive.

Religious priests take a vow of poverty and are supported by their religious order. Any personal earnings are given to the order. Their vow of poverty is recognized by the Internal Revenue Service, which exempts them from paying federal income tax.

Sources of Additional Information

Young men interested in entering the priesthood should seek the guidance and counsel of their parish priests and diocesan vocational office. For information regarding the different religious orders and the diocesan priesthood, as well as a list of the seminaries which prepare students for the priesthood, contact the diocesan director of vocations through the office of the local pastor or bishop.

Individuals seeking additional information about careers in the Catholic Ministry should contact their local diocese.

Statisticians

(*D.O.T.* 020.067-022, .167-026)

Significant Points

* *Many with bachelors and master's degrees in statistics enter jobs in which they do not have the title of statistician.*

* *In private industry and colleges and universities, many positions require a graduate degree, often a doctorate, in statistics.*

Nature of the Work

Statistics is a science, applying mathematical tools, involved with the collection, analysis, interpretation, and presentation of numerical data. Many applications—including predicting population growth or economic conditions, providing quality control tests for manufactured products, and helping business managers and government officials make decisions—benefit from statistical techniques. Statisticians are the individuals who design surveys and experiments, collect

data, and interpret the results. In doing so, they often apply their knowledge of statistical methods to a particular subject area, such as biology, economics, engineering, medicine, or psychology. Some statisticians develop new statistical methods.

Statisticians typically work with professionals in other fields to solve practical problems. For example, biostatisticians involved in clinical research have developed sequential procedures that minimize patients' exposure to harmful treatment and make beneficial treatments more rapidly accessible.

Often statisticians are able to obtain information about a group of people or things by surveying a small portion, called a sample, of the group. For example, to determine the size of the total audience for particular programs, television rating services ask only a few thousand families, rather than all viewers, which programs they watch. Statisticians decide where and how to gather the data, determine the type and size of the sample group, and develop the survey questionnaire or reporting form. They also prepare instructions for workers who will collect and tabulate the data. Finally, statisticians analyze, interpret, and summarize the data, usually using sophisticated statistical computer software.

In manufacturing industries, statisticians play an important role in the area of quality improvement. For example, a statistician in an automobile manufacturing company might design experiments using statistical models to estimate the failure time of an engine exposed to extreme weather conditions and to identify factors that can lead to improved performance. In chemical companies, statisticians might design experiments to determine what combination of chemicals would produce the best product for a specific purpose.

Because statistics are used in so many areas, specialists in other fields who use statistics often have other designations. For example, a person using statistical methods on economic data may have the title of econometrician.

Working Conditions

Statisticians usually work regular hours in offices. Some statisticians travel to provide advice on research projects, supervise or set up surveys, or to gather statistical data. Some may have fairly repetitive tasks, while others may have a variety of tasks, such as designing experiments.

Employment

Statisticians held about 14,000 jobs in 1996. Over one-fourth of these jobs were in the federal government, where statisticians were concentrated in the Departments of Commerce, Agriculture, and Health and Human Services. Most of the remaining jobs were in private industry, especially in the

biopharmaceutical industry. In addition, many statisticians work in academia.

Training, Other Qualifications, and Advancement

A bachelor's degree with a major in statistics or mathematics is the minimum educational requirement for some beginning jobs in statistics. The training required for employment as an entry level statistician in the federal government is a college degree including at least 15 semester hours of statistics—or a combination of 15 hours of mathematics and statistics if at least six semester hours are in statistics. An additional nine semester hours in another academic discipline, such as economics, physical or biological science, medicine, education, engineering, or social science, are also required. To qualify as a mathematical statistician in the federal government requires 24 semester hours of mathematics and statistics with a minimum of six semester hours in statistics and 12 semester hours in advanced mathematics, such as calculus, differential equations, or vector analysis. Research positions in institutions of higher education and many positions in private industry require a graduate degree, often a doctorate, in statistics.

About 80 colleges and universities offered bachelor's degrees in statistics in 1996. Many other schools also offered degrees in mathematics, operations research, and other fields which included a sufficient number of courses in statistics to qualify graduates for some beginning positions, particularly in the federal government. Required subjects for statistics majors include differential and integral calculus, statistical methods, mathematical modeling, and probability theory. Additional courses that undergraduates should take include linear algebra, design and analysis of experiments, applied multivariate analysis, and mathematical statistics. Because computers are used extensively for statistical applications, a strong background in computer science is highly recommended. For positions involving quality and productivity improvement, training in engineering or physical science is useful. A background in biological, chemical, or health science is important for positions involving the preparation and testing of pharmaceutical or agricultural products. For many jobs in market research, business analysis, and forecasting, courses in economics and business administration are helpful.

In 1996, approximately 110 universities offered a master's degree program in statistics, and 58 had statistics departments which offered a doctoral degree program. Many other schools also offered graduate-level courses in applied statistics for students majoring in biology, business, economics, education, engineering, psychology, and other fields. Acceptance into graduate statistics programs does not require an undergraduate degree in statistics although a good mathematics background is essential.

Good communications skills are important for prospective statisticians, not only for those who plan to teach, but also to qualify for many positions in industry, where the need to explain technical processes to those who are not statisticians is common. A solid understanding of business and the economy is important for those who plan to work in private industry.

Beginning statisticians who have only the bachelor's degree often spend much of their time doing routine work supervised by an experienced statistician. With experience, they may advance to positions of greater technical and supervisory responsibility. However, opportunities for promotion are best for those with advanced degrees. Master's and Ph.D. degree holders enjoy greater independence in their work and are qualified to engage in research, to develop statistical methods, or, after a number of years of experience in a particular area, to become statistical consultants.

Job Outlook

Although employment of statisticians is expected to grow little through the year 2006, job opportunities should remain favorable for individuals with statistical training. Many individuals at the bachelor's degree level, and some at the master's degree level, will find positions in which they do not have the title of statistician. This is especially true for those involved in analyzing and interpreting data from other disciplines such as economics, biological science, psychology, or engineering.

Among graduates with a bachelor's degree in statistics, those with a strong background in mathematics, engineering, or computer science should have the best prospects of finding jobs related to their field of study. Federal government agencies will need statisticians in fields such as demography, agriculture, consumer and producer surveys, Social Security, health care, education, energy conservation, and environmental quality. However, competition for entry level positions in the federal government is expected to be strong for those just meeting the minimum qualification standards for statisticians. Those who meet state certification requirements may become high school statistics teachers, a newly emerging field.

Private industry will continue to require statisticians, especially at the master's and Ph.D. degree levels, to monitor and improve productivity and quality in the manufacture of various products including pharmaceuticals, motor vehicles, chemicals, and food products. For example, pharmaceutical firms will need statisticians to assess the safety and effectiveness of the rapidly expanding number of drugs. To counter stiff competition, motor vehicle manufacturers will need statisticians to improve the quality of automobiles, trucks, and their components by developing and testing new designs. Some statisticians with a knowledge of engineering and the physical sciences will find jobs in research and development, working with teams of scientists and engineers to help improve design and production processes in order to ensure consistent quality of newly developed products. Business firms will rely more heavily on workers with a background in statistics to forecast sales, analyze business conditions, and help solve management problems. In addition, sophisticated statistical services will increasingly be contracted out to consulting firms.

Earnings

The average annual salary for statisticians in the federal government in nonsupervisory, supervisory, and managerial positions was $61,030 in 1997; mathematical statisticians averaged $65,660.

Statisticians who hold advanced degrees generally earn higher starting salaries.

Benefits for statisticians tend to resemble those offered most professionals: Vacation and sick leave, health and life insurance, and a retirement plan, among others.

Related Occupations

People in numerous occupations work with statistics. Among them are actuaries, mathematicians, operations research analysts, computer programmers, computer systems analysts, engineers, economists, financial analysts, information scientists, life scientists, physical scientists, and social scientists.

Sources of Additional Information

For information about career opportunities in statistics, contact:

❑ American Statistical Association, 1429 Duke St., Alexandria, VA 22314.

Information on obtaining a statistician position with the federal government may be obtained from the Office of Personnel Management through a telephone-based system. Consult your telephone directory under U.S. government for a local number or call (912) 757-3000 (TDD 912 744-2299). That number is not toll-free and charges may result. Information also is available from their Internet site: http://www.usajobs.opm.gov

Jobs Typically Requiring a Bachelor's Degree

Included are the following jobs:

Accountants and Auditors
Actuaries
Adult Education Teachers
Aerospace Engineers
Budget Analysts
Chemical Engineers
Chemists
Civil Engineers
Clinical Laboratory Technologists and Technicians
Computer Programmers
Computer Scientists, Computer Engineers, and Systems Analysts
Construction Managers

Designers
Dietitians and Nutritionists
Electrical and Electronics Engineers
Foresters and Conservation Scientists
Geologists and Geophysicists
Health Services Managers
Human Resources Specialists and Managers
Industrial Engineers
Industrial Production Managers
Insurance Underwriters
Landscape Architects
Loan Officers and Counselors
Mechanical Engineers
Metallurgical, Ceramic, and Materials Engineers
Meteorologists
Mining Engineers
Nuclear Engineers
Occupational Therapists
Petroleum Engineers
Physical Therapists
Physician Assistants
Property Managers
Public Relations Specialists
Purchasers and Buyers
Recreational Therapists
Reporters and Correspondents
School Teachers, Kindergarten, Elementary, and Secondary
Social Workers
Special Education Teachers
Surveyors and Mapping Scientists
Writers and Editors

Accountants and Auditors

(D.O.T. 160 through .167-042, -054, .267-014)

Significant Points

* *Most jobs require at least a bachelor's degree in accounting or a related field.*

* *Professional recognition through certification or licensure, a master's degree, familiarity with accounting and auditing computer software, or specialized expertise provide an advantage in the job market.*

* *Competition will remain keen for the most prestigious jobs—those with major accounting and business firms.*

Nature of the Work

Accountants and auditors prepare, analyze, and verify financial reports and taxes, and monitor information systems that furnish this information to managers in business, industry, and government.

The major fields of accounting are public, management, and government accounting, and internal auditing. Public accountants have their own businesses or work for public accounting firms. They perform a broad range of accounting, auditing, tax, and consulting activities for their clients, who may be corporations, governments, nonprofit organizations, or individuals. Management accountants—also called industrial, corporate, or private accountants—record and analyze the financial information of the companies for which they work. Other responsibilities include budgeting, performance evaluation, cost management, and asset management. They are usually part of executive teams involved in strategic planning or new product development. Internal auditors verify the accuracy of their organization's records and check for mismanagement, waste, or fraud. Government accountants and auditors maintain and examine the records of government agencies, and audit private businesses and individuals whose activities are subject to government regulations or taxation.

Within each field, accountants often concentrate on one aspect of accounting. For example, many public accountants concentrate on tax matters, such as preparing individual income tax returns and advising companies of the tax advantages and disadvantages of certain business decisions. Others concentrate on consulting and offer advice on matters such as compensation or employee health care benefits; the design of accounting and data processing systems; and controls to safeguard assets. Some specialize in forensic accounting—investigating and interpreting bankruptcies and other complex financial transactions. Still others work primarily in auditing—examining a client's financial statements and reporting to investors and authorities that they have been prepared and reported correctly. However, accounting firms are performing less auditing relative to consulting services, which are more profitable.

Increasing numbers of accounting graduates are working in private corporations. Management accountants analyze and interpret the financial information corporate executives need to make sound business decisions. They also prepare financial reports for nonmanagement groups, including stockholders, creditors, regulatory agencies, and tax authorities. Within accounting departments, they may work in financial analysis, planning and budgeting, cost accounting, and other areas.

Internal auditing is increasingly important. As computer systems make information more timely, top management can base its decisions on actual data, rather than personal observation. Internal auditors examine and evaluate their firms' financial and information systems, management procedures, and internal controls to ensure that records are accurate and controls are adequate to protect against fraud and waste. They also review company operations—evaluating their efficiency, effectiveness, and compliance with corporate policies and procedures, laws, and government regulations. There are many types of highly specialized auditors, such as electronic data processing, environmental, engineering, legal, insurance premium, bank, and health care auditors.

Accountants employed by federal, state, and local governments see that revenues are received and expenditures are made in accordance with laws and regulations. Many persons with an accounting background work for the federal government as Internal Revenue Service agents or in financial management, financial institution examination, and budget analysis and administration.

Computers are widely used in accounting and auditing. With the aid of special software packages, accountants summarize transactions in standard formats for financial records, or organize data in special formats for financial analysis. These accounting packages greatly reduce the amount of tedious manual work associated with data and records; some packages require few specialized computer skills, while others require formal training. Personal and laptop computers enable accountants and auditors in all fields to use their clients' computer system and to extract information from large mainframe computers. Internal auditors may recommend controls for their organization's computer system to ensure the reliability of the system and the integrity of the data. A growing

number of accountants and auditors have extensive computer skills and specialize in correcting problems with software or developing software to meet unique data needs.

Working Conditions

Accountants and auditors work in a normal office setting. Self-employed accountants may be able to do part of their work at home. Accountants and auditors employed by public accounting firms and government agencies may travel frequently to perform audits at clients' places of business, branches of their firm, or government facilities.

Most accountants and auditors generally work a standard 40-hour week, but many work longer, particularly if they are self-employed and free to take on the work of as many clients as they choose. Tax specialists often work long hours during the tax season.

Employment

Accountants and auditors held over a million jobs in 1996. They worked throughout private industry and government, but about one-third worked on salary for accounting, auditing, and bookkeeping firms, or were self-employed.

Many accountants and auditors were unlicensed management accountants, internal auditors, or government accountants and auditors. However, many are state-licensed Certified Public Accountants (CPAs), Public Accountants (PAs), Registered Public Accountants (RPAs), and Accounting Practitioners (APs).

Most accountants and auditors work in urban areas, in which public accounting firms and central or regional offices of businesses are concentrated.

Many individuals with backgrounds in accounting and auditing are full-time college and university faculty; others teach part time while working as self-employed accountants, or as salaried accountants for private industry or government.

Training, Other Qualifications, and Advancement

Most accountant and internal auditor positions require at least a bachelor's degree in accounting or a related field. Based on recommendations made by the American Institute of Certified Public Accountants, a small number of states currently require CPA candidates to complete 150 semester hours of college course work—an additional 30 hours beyond the usual four-year bachelor's degree—and many more states are expected to introduce this requirement in the future. Most schools have altered their curricula accordingly, and prospective accounting majors should carefully research accounting curricula and the requirements for any states in which they

hope to become licensed before enrolling. Some employers prefer applicants with a master's degree in accounting, or a master's degree in business administration with a concentration in accounting. Most employers also prefer applicants who are familiar with computers and their applications in accounting and internal auditing.

For beginning accounting and auditing positions in the federal government, four years of college (including 24 semester hours in accounting or auditing) or an equivalent combination of education and experience is required.

Previous experience in accounting or auditing can help an applicant get a job. Many colleges offer students an opportunity to gain experience through summer or part-time internship programs conducted by public accounting or business firms. Such training is advantageous in gaining permanent employment in the field.

Professional recognition through certification or licensure provides a distinct advantage in the job market. All CPAs must have a certificate and the partners in their firm must have a license issued by a state board of accountancy. The vast majority of states require CPA candidates to be college graduates, but a few states substitute a certain number of years of public accounting experience for the educational requirement. As indicated earlier, a growing number of states require 150 hours of course work; the composition of the additional 30 hours is unspecified by most states.

All states use the four-part Uniform CPA Examination prepared by the American Institute of Certified Public Accountants. The two-day CPA examination is rigorous, and only about one-quarter of those who take it each year pass each part they attempt. Candidates are not required to pass all four parts at once, although most states require candidates to pass at least two parts for partial credit. Many states require all sections of the test to be passed within a certain period of time. Most states also require applicants for a CPA certificate to have some accounting experience.

The designations PA or RPA are also recognized by most states, and several states continue to issue these licenses. With the growth in the number of CPAs, however, the majority of states are phasing out non-CPA designations—PA, RPA, and AP—by not issuing any more new licenses. Accountants who hold PA or RPA designations have similar legal rights, duties, and obligations as CPAs, but their qualifications for licensure are less stringent. The AP designation requires less formal training and covers a more limited scope of practice than the CPA.

Nearly all states require CPAs and other public accountants to complete a certain number of hours of continuing professional education before their licenses can be renewed. The professional associations representing accountants sponsor numerous courses, seminars, group study programs, and other forms of continuing education.

Professional societies bestow other forms of credentials on a voluntary basis. Voluntary certification can attest to professional competence in a specialized field of accounting and auditing. It can also certify that a recognized level of professional competence has been achieved by accountants and auditors who acquired some skills on the job, without the formal education or public accounting work experience needed to meet the rigorous standards required to take the CPA examination. Employers are increasingly seeking applicants with these credentials.

The Institute of Management Accountants (IMA) confers the Certified Management Accountant (CMA) designation upon applicants who complete a bachelor's degree, although a minimum score on specified graduate school entrance exams can be substituted for a bachelor's degree; pass a four-part examination; agree to meet continuing education requirements; comply with standards of professional conduct; and have at least two years' work in management accounting. The CMA program is administered through the Institute of Certified Management Accountants, an affiliate of the IMA.

The Institute of Internal Auditors confers the designation Certified Internal Auditor (CIA) to graduates from accredited colleges and universities who have completed two years' work in internal auditing, and who have passed a four-part examination. The Information Systems Audit and Control Association confers the designation Certified Information Systems Auditor (CISA) upon candidates who pass an examination, and who have five years of experience in auditing electronic data processing systems. However, auditing or data processing experience and college education may be substituted for up to three years. The Accreditation Council for Accountancy and Taxation, a satellite organization of the National Society of Public Accountants, confers three designations—Accredited in Accountancy (AA), Accredited Tax Advisor (ATA), and Accredited Tax Preparer (ATP). Candidates for the AA must pass an exam, while candidates for the ATA and ATP must complete the required course work and pass an exam. Other organizations, such as the National Association of Certified Fraud Examiners and the Bank Administration Institute, confer specialized auditing designations. It is not uncommon for a practitioner to hold multiple licenses and designations. For instance, an internal auditor might be a CPA, CIA, and CISA.

Persons planning a career in accounting should have an aptitude for mathematics; be able to analyze, compare, and interpret facts and figures quickly; and make sound judgments based on this knowledge. They must be able to clearly communicate the results of their work, orally and in writing, to clients and management.

Accountants and auditors must be good at working with people as well as with business systems and computers. Accuracy and the ability to handle responsibility with limited supervision are important. Perhaps most important, because millions of financial statement users rely on their services, accountants and auditors should have high standards of integrity.

Capable accountants and auditors should advance rapidly; those having inadequate academic preparation may be assigned routine jobs and find promotion difficult. Many graduates of junior colleges and business and correspondence schools, as well as bookkeepers and accounting clerks who meet the education and experience requirements set by their employers, can obtain junior accounting positions and advance to more responsible positions by demonstrating their accounting skills on the job.

Beginning public accountants usually start by assisting with work for several clients. They may advance to positions with more responsibility in one or two years, and to senior positions within another few years. Those who excel may become supervisors, managers, partners, open their own public accounting firms, or transfer to executive positions in management accounting or internal auditing in private firms.

Beginning management accountants often start as cost accountants, junior internal auditors, or as trainees for other accounting positions. As they rise through the organization, they may advance to accounting manager, chief cost accountant, budget director, or manager of internal auditing. Some become controllers, treasurers, financial vice presidents, chief financial officers, or corporation presidents. Many senior corporation executives have a background in accounting, internal auditing, or finance.

There is a large degree of mobility among public accountants, management accountants, and internal auditors. Practitioners often shift into management accounting or internal auditing from public accounting, or between internal auditing and management accounting. However, it is less common for accountants and auditors to move from either management accounting or internal auditing into public accounting.

Job Outlook

Accountants and auditors who have earned professional recognition through certification or licensure should have the best job prospects. For example, CPAs should continue to enjoy a wide range of job opportunities, especially as more states enact the 150-hour requirement, making it more difficult to obtain this certification. Similarly, CMAs should be in

demand as their management advice is increasingly sought. Applicants with a master's degree in accounting, or a master's degree in business administration with a concentration in accounting, may also have an advantage in the job market. Familiarity with accounting and auditing computer software, or expertise in specialized areas such as international business, specific industries, or current legislation, may also be helpful in landing certain accounting and auditing jobs. In addition, employers increasingly seek well-rounded applicants with strong interpersonal and communication skills. Regardless of one's qualifications, however, competition will remain keen for the most prestigious jobs—those with major accounting and business firms.

Employment of accountants and auditors is expected to grow about as fast as the average for all occupations through the year 2006. The need to replace accountants and auditors who retire or transfer to other occupations will produce thousands of additional job openings annually, reflecting the large size of this occupation.

As the economy grows, the number of business establishments increases, requiring more accountants and auditors to set up their books, prepare their taxes, and provide management advice. As these businesses grow, the volume and complexity of information developed by accountants and auditors on costs, expenditures, and taxes will increase as well. More complex requirements for accountants and auditors also arise from changes in legislation related to taxes, financial reporting standards, business investments, mergers, and other financial matters. In addition, businesses will increasingly need quick, accurate, and individually tailored financial information due to the demands of growing international competition.

The changing role of accountants and auditors also will spur job growth. Accountants will perform less auditing work due to potential liability and relatively low profits, and less tax work due to growing competition from tax preparation firms, but they will offer more management and consulting services in response to market demand. Accountants will continue to take on a greater advisory role as they develop more sophisticated and flexible accounting systems, and focus more on analyzing operations rather than just providing financial data. Internal auditors will be increasingly needed to discover and eliminate waste and fraud.

Earnings

According to a salary survey conducted by the National Association of Colleges and Employers, bachelor's degree candidates in accounting received starting offers averaging $29,400 a year in 1996; master's degree candidates in accounting, $33,000.

According to a survey of workplaces in 160 metropolitan areas, accountants with limited experience had median earnings of $26,000 in 1995, with the middle half earning between $23,300 and $29,400. The most experienced accountants had median earnings of $87,400, with the middle half earning between $77,600 and $98,000. Public accountants—employed by public accounting firms—with limited experience had median earnings of $29,400, with the middle half earning between $28,200 and $32,000. The most experienced public accountants had median earnings of $48,700, with the middle half earning between $44,500 and $54,000. Many owners and partners of firms earned considerably more.

According to a salary survey conducted by Robert Half International, a staffing services firm specializing in accounting and finance, accountants and auditors with up to one year of experience earned between $25,000 and $39,400 in 1997. Those with one to three years of experience earned between $27,000 and $46,600. Senior accountants and auditors earned between $34,300 and $57,800; managers earned between $40,000 and $81,900; and directors of accounting and auditing earned between $54,800 and $109,800 a year. The variation in salaries reflects differences in size of firm, location, level of education, and professional credentials.

In the federal government, the starting annual salary for junior accountants and auditors was about $19,500 in 1997. Candidates who had a superior academic record might start at $24,200, while applicants with a master's degree or two years of professional experience might begin at $29,600. Beginning salaries were slightly higher in selected areas where the prevailing local pay level was higher. Accountants employed by the federal government in nonsupervisory, supervisory, and managerial positions averaged about $54,000 a year in 1997; auditors averaged $57,900.

Related Occupations

Accountants and auditors design internal control systems and analyze financial data. Others for whom training in accounting is invaluable include appraisers, budget officers, loan officers, financial analysts and managers, bank officers, actuaries, underwriters, tax collectors and revenue agents, FBI special agents, securities sales representatives, and purchasing agents.

Sources of Additional Information

Information about careers in certified public accounting and about CPA standards and examinations may be obtained from:

❏ American Institute of Certified Public Accountants, Harborside Financial Center, 201 Plaza III, Jersey City, NJ 07311-3881. Homepage: http://www.aicpa.org

Information on careers in management accounting and the CMA designation may be obtained from:

❏ Institute of Management Accountants, 10 Paragon Dr., Montvale, NJ. Homepage: http://www.imanet.org

Information on the Accredited in Accountancy/Accredited Business Accountant, Accredited Tax Advisor, or Accredited Tax Preparer designations may be obtained from:

❏ National Society of Accountants and the Accreditation Council for Accountancy and Taxation, 1010 North Fairfax St., Alexandria, VA 22314. Homepage: http://www.nspa.org

Information on careers in internal auditing and the CIA designation may be obtained from:

❏ The Institute of Internal Auditors, 249 Maitland Ave., Altamonte Springs, FL 32701-4201. Homepage: http://www.theiia.org

Information on careers in information systems auditing and the CISA designation may be obtained from:

❏ The Information Systems Audit and Control Association, 3701 Algonquin Rd., Suite 1010, Rolling Meadows, IL 60008. Homepage: http://www.isaca.org

For information on accredited programs in accounting and business, contact:

❏ American Assembly of Collegiate Schools of Business, 605 Old Ballas Rd., Suite 220, St. Louis, MO 63141. Homepage: http://www.aacsb.edu

Actuaries

(D.O.T. 020.167-010)

Significant Points

✶ *A strong background in mathematics is essential for persons interested in a career as an actuary.*

✶ *Competition for jobs is expected due to relatively high earnings, the small size of the occupation, and downsizing and merger activity in the insurance industry.*

Nature of the Work

Actuaries answer questions about future risk, make pricing decisions, and formulate investment strategies. Some design insurance, financial, and pension plans and ensure that these plans are maintained on a sound financial basis. Most actuaries specialize in life, health, or property and casualty insurance; others specialize in pension plans.

Actuaries assemble and analyze data to estimate probabilities of death, sickness, injury, disability, retirement income level, property loss, or return on investment. They use this information to estimate how much an insurance company will have to pay out in claims, or to make other business decisions. For example, actuaries may calculate the expected amount of claims due to automobile accidents, which can vary depending on the insured's age, sex, driving history, type of car, and other factors. Actuaries ensure that the price charged for such insurance, or premium, will enable the company to cover claims and expenses as they incur. Finally, this premium charged must be profitable and yet be competitive with other insurance companies. The actuary calculates premium rates and determines policy contract provisions for each type of insurance offered.

To perform their duties effectively, actuaries must keep informed about general economic and social trends and legislation, as well as developments in health, business, finance, and economics that may affect insurance or investment practices. Using their broad knowledge of business and mathematics, actuaries may work in investment, risk classification, or pension planning.

Actuaries in executive positions help determine company policy. In that role, they may be called upon to explain complex technical matters to other company executives, government officials, shareholders, policyholders, and the public in general. They may testify before public agencies on proposed legislation affecting their businesses or explain changes in contract provisions to customers. They also may help companies develop plans to enter new lines of business.

A small but growing group of actuaries work in the financial services industry, where they manage credit, prepayment, and other risks, and help price corporate securities offerings.

Consulting actuaries provide advice to various clients on a fee basis. Their clients include insurance companies, corporations, hospitals and other health care providers, labor unions, government agencies, and attorneys. Some consulting actuaries design pension and welfare plans, calculate future benefits, and determine the amount of employer contributions. Others provide advice to health care plans or financial services firms. Consultants may be called upon to testify in court regarding the value of potential lifetime earnings lost by a person who has been disabled or killed in an accident, the current value of future pension benefits in divorce cases, or the calculation of insurance rates. Pension actuaries enrolled under the provisions of the Employee Retirement Income Security Act of 1974 (ERISA) evaluate the pension plans covered by that act and report on their financial soundness to plan members, sponsors, and federal regulators.

Working Conditions

Actuaries have desk jobs that require little physical activ-

ity, and their offices are generally comfortable and pleasant. They usually work at least 40 hours a week. Some actuaries, particularly consulting actuaries, often travel to meet with clients. Consulting actuaries may also be expected to work more than 40 hours per week.

Employment

Actuaries held about 16,000 jobs in 1996. Some were self-employed. In addition, some actuaries held faculty positions in colleges and universities.

Almost one-half of the actuaries who were wage and salary workers were employed in the insurance industry. Most worked for life insurance companies; others worked for property, casualty, and health insurance companies, pension funds, and insurance agents and brokers. Most of the remaining actuaries worked for firms providing services, especially management and public relations, and actuarial consulting services. A relatively small number of actuaries worked for security and commodity brokers or government agencies. Some are employed developing computer software for actuarial calculations.

Training, Other Qualifications, and Advancement

A good educational background for a beginning job in a large life or casualty company is a bachelor's degree in mathematics, actuarial science, or statistics, or a business-related discipline, such as economics, finance, or accounting. Some companies hire applicants without specifying a major, provided the applicant has a working knowledge of mathematics, including calculus, probability, and statistics, and who has demonstrated this ability by passing at least the beginning actuarial exams required for professional designation. Courses in economics, accounting, computer science, and insurance are also useful. Companies increasingly prefer well-rounded individuals who, in addition to a strong technical background, have some training in liberal arts and business. Good communication and interpersonal skills are important, particularly for prospective consulting actuaries. About 55 colleges and universities offer an actuarial science program, and most colleges and universities offer a degree in mathematics or statistics.

A strong background in mathematics is essential for persons interested in a career as an actuary. It is an advantage to pass, while still in school, two or more of the examinations offered by professional actuarial societies. Two professional societies sponsor programs leading to full professional status in their specialty. The Society of Actuaries (SOA) administers a series of actuarial examinations for life and health insurance, pension, and finance and investment fields. The Casualty

Actuarial Society (CAS) gives a series of examinations for the property and casualty field, which include fire, accident, medical malpractice, workers' compensation, and personal injury liability. Because the first parts of the examination series of each society are jointly sponsored and cover the same material, students need not commit themselves to a specialty until they have taken the initial examinations. These examinations test an individual's competence in subjects such as linear algebra, probability, calculus, statistics, risk theory, and actuarial mathematics. The first few examinations help students evaluate their potential as actuaries. Those who pass one or more examinations have better opportunities for employment and higher starting salaries than those who do not.

Actuaries are encouraged to complete the entire series of examinations as soon as possible, advancing first to the Associate level, and then to the Fellowship level. Completion of the examination process generally takes from five to ten years. Examinations are given twice each year, in May and November. Although many companies allot time to their employees for study, extensive home study is required to pass the examinations; many actuaries study for months to prepare for each examination. Most reach Associateship within four to six years. Fellowship candidates usually have several years of experience. Most actuaries complete the Fellowship exams a few years after reaching Associateship. Both levels of examinations are extremely difficult.

Pension actuaries who verify the financial status of defined benefit pension plans to the federal government must be enrolled by the Joint Board for the Enrollment of Actuaries. To qualify for enrollment, applicants must meet certain experience and examination requirements, as stipulated by the Joint Board.

Beginning actuaries often rotate between jobs to learn various actuarial operations and phases of insurance work, such as marketing, underwriting, or product development. At first, they prepare data for actuarial projects or perform other simple tasks. As they gain experience, actuaries may supervise clerks, prepare correspondence and reports, and do research. They may move from one company to another in their early careers, as they move up to progressively more responsible positions.

Advancement depends largely on job performance and the number of actuarial examinations passed. Actuaries with a broad knowledge of the insurance, pension, investment, or employee benefits fields can advance to administrative and executive positions in their companies. Actuaries with supervisory ability may advance to management positions in other areas, such as underwriting, accounting, data processing, marketing, or advertising.

Job Outlook

Prospective actuaries who have passed the beginning actuarial exams will face competition for jobs, since the number of openings each year is limited by the relatively small size of the occupation.

Employment of actuaries is expected to grow more slowly than the average for all occupations through the year 2006, due to expected slower growth in the insurance industry. Anticipated downsizing and merger activity in the insurance industry is likely to have the greatest negative effect on those actuaries with the least experience. The expected growth in managed health plans in the health services industry should provide better prospects for actuaries, however.

Employment growth of consulting actuaries is expected to be faster than employment growth of actuaries in insurance carriers—traditionally the leading employer of actuaries. As many companies seek to boost profitability by streamlining operations, actuarial employment may be cut back by insurance carriers. Investment firms and large corporations may increasingly turn to consultants to provide actuarial services formerly performed in-house.

The liability of companies for damage resulting from their products has received much attention in recent years. Casualty actuaries will continue to be involved in the development of product liability insurance, medical malpractice and workers' compensation coverage, and self-insurance, which may involve internal reserve funds established by some large corporations. The growing need to evaluate catastrophic risks such as earthquakes and calculate prices for insuring facilities against such risks, which may involve huge losses, will be an increasing source of demand for property and casualty actuaries. So is planning for the systematic financing of environmental risks, such as toxic waste clean-up.

Earnings

In 1996, starting salaries for actuaries averaged about $37,600 for those with a bachelor's degree, according to the National Association of Colleges and Employers. New college graduates entering the actuarial field without having passed any actuarial exams averaged slightly lower salaries.

Insurance companies and consulting firms give merit increases to actuaries as they gain experience and pass examinations. Some companies also offer cash bonuses for each professional designation achieved. A 1996 salary survey of insurance and financial services companies, conducted by the Life Office Management Association, Inc., indicated that the average base salary for an entry-level actuary was about $36,500. Associate Actuaries, who direct and provide leadership in the design and pricing of products received a salary of

about $78,600. Actuaries with additional experience earned an average of $93,500.

Actuaries typically receive other benefits including vacation and sick leave, health and life insurance, and pension plans.

Related Occupations

Actuaries determine the probability of income or loss from various risk factors. Other workers whose jobs involve related skills include accountants, economists, financial analysts, mathematicians, and statisticians.

Sources of Additional Information

For facts about actuarial careers, contact:
- ❏ American Academy of Actuaries, 1100 17th St. NW, 7th Floor, Washington, DC 20036.

For information about actuarial careers in life and health insurance, employee benefits and pensions, and finance and investments, contact:
- ❏ Society of Actuaries, 475 N. Martingale Rd., Suite 800, Schaumburg, IL 60173-2226.

For information about actuarial careers in property and casualty insurance, contact:
- ❏ Casualty Actuarial Society, 1100 N. Glebe Rd., Suite 600, Arlington, VA 22201. Homepage: http://www.casact.org

Career information on actuaries specializing in pensions is available from:
- ❏ American Society of Pension Actuaries, 4350 N. Fairfax Dr., Suite 820, Arlington, VA 22203.

Adult Education Teachers

(*D.O.T.* 075.127-010; 090.222, .227-018; 097.221, .227; 099.223, .224-014, .227-014, -018, -026, -030, -038; 149.021; 150.027-014; 151.027-014; 152.021; 153.227-014; 159.227; 166.221, .227; 239.227; 375.227; 522.264; 621.221; 683.222; 689.324; 715.221; 740.221; 788.222; 789.222; 919.223; and 955.222)

Significant Points

* *About half work part-time; many also hold other jobs—often involving work related to the subject they teach.*

* *A graduate degree may be required to teach nonvocational courses, whereas practical experience is often all that is needed to teach vocational courses.*

* *Rising demand for adult education courses for career advancement, skills upgrading, or personal enrichment and enjoyment will spur faster-than-average employment growth; opportunities should be best for part-time positions.*

Nature of the Work

Adult education teachers work in four main areas—adult vocational-technical education, adult remedial education, adult continuing education, and prebaccalaureate training. Adult vocational-technical education teachers provide instruction for occupations that do not require a college degree, such as welder, dental hygienist, automated systems manager, x-ray technician, auto mechanic, and cosmetologist. Other instructors help people update their job skills or adapt to technological advances. For example, an adult education teacher may train students how to use new computer software programs. Adult remedial education teachers provide instruction in basic education courses for school dropouts or others who need to upgrade their skills to find a job. Adult continuing education teachers teach courses which students take for personal enrichment, such as cooking, dancing, writing, exercise and physical fitness, photography, and finance. Some adult education teachers in junior or community colleges prepare students for a four-year degree program, teaching classes for credit that can be applied toward that degree.

Adult education teachers may lecture in classrooms or work in an industry or laboratory setting to give students hands-on experience. Increasingly, adult vocational-technical education teachers integrate academic and vocational curriculums so that students obtain a variety of skills that can be applied to the real world. For example, an electronics student may be required to take courses in principles of mathematics and science in conjunction with hands-on electronics skills. Generally, teachers demonstrate techniques, have students apply them, and critique the students' work. For example, welding instructors show students various welding techniques, including the use of tools and equipment, watch them use the techniques, and have them repeat procedures until specific standards required by the trade are met.

Increasingly, minimum standards of proficiency are being established for students in various vocational-technical fields. Adult education teachers must be aware of new standards and develop lesson plans to ensure that students meet basic criteria. Also, adult education teachers and community colleges are assuming a greater role in students' transition from school to work, by helping establish internships and providing information about prospective employers.

Businesses also are increasingly providing their employees with work-related training to keep up with changing technology. Training is often provided through contractors, professional associations, or community colleges.

Adult education teachers who instruct in adult basic education programs may work with students who do not speak English; teach adults reading, writing, and mathematics up to the 8th-grade level; or teach adults through the 12th-grade level in preparation for the General Educational Development tests (GED). The GED offers the equivalent of a high school diploma. These teachers may refer students for counseling or job placement. Because many people who need adult basic education are reluctant to seek it, teachers also may recruit participants.

Adult education teachers also prepare lessons and assignments, grade papers and do related paperwork, attend faculty and professional meetings, and stay abreast of developments in their field.

Working Conditions

Since adult education teachers work with adult students, they do not encounter some of the behavioral or social problems sometimes found when teaching younger students. The adults are there by choice, are highly motivated, and bring years of experience to the classroom—attributes that can make teaching these students rewarding and satisfying. However, teachers in adult basic education deal with students at different levels of development who may lack effective study skills and self-confidence, and who may require more attention and patience than other students.

About one out of two adult education teachers works part-time. To accommodate students who may have job or family responsibilities, many institutions offer courses at night or on weekends, which range from two- to four-hour workshops and one-day mini-sessions to semester-long courses. Some adult education teachers have several part-time teaching assignments or work a full-time job in addition to their part-time teaching job, leading to long hours and a hectic schedule.

Although most adult education teachers work in a classroom setting, some are consultants to a business and teach classes at the job site.

Employment

Adult education teachers held about 559,000 jobs in 1996. Many adult education teachers are self-employed.

Adult education teachers are employed by public school systems; community and junior colleges; universities; businesses that provide formal education and training for their employees; automotive repair, bartending, business, computer, electronics, medical technology, and similar schools and institutes; dance studios; health clubs; job training centers; community organizations; labor unions; and religious organizations.

Training, Other Qualifications, and Advancement

Training requirements vary by state and by subject. In general, teachers need work or other experience in their field, and a license or certificate in fields where these usually are required for full professional status. In some cases, particularly at educational institutions, a master's or doctoral degree is required to teach nonvocational courses which can be applied toward a four-year degree program. Many vocational teachers in junior or community colleges do not have a master's or doctoral degree but draw on their work experience and knowledge, bringing practical experience to the classroom. For general adult education classes that are taken for interest or enjoyment, an acceptable portfolio of work is required. For example, to secure a job teaching a photography course, an applicant would need to show examples of previous work.

Most states and the District of Columbia require adult basic education teachers and adult literacy instructors to have a bachelor's degree from an approved teacher training program, and some require teacher certification.

Adult education teachers update their skills through continuing education to maintain certification—requirements vary among institutions. Teachers may take part in seminars, conferences, or graduate courses in adult education or training and development, or may return to work in business or industry for a limited time. Businesses are playing a growing role in adult education, forming consortiums with training institutions and junior colleges and providing input to curriculum development. Adult education teachers maintain an ongoing dialogue with businesses to determine the most current skills required in the workplace.

Adult education teachers should communicate and relate well with students, enjoy working with them, and be able to motivate them. Adult basic education instructors, in particular, must be patient, understanding, and supportive to make students comfortable, develop trust, and help them better understand concepts.

Some teachers advance to administrative positions in departments of education, colleges and universities, and corporate training departments. These positions often require advanced degrees, such as a doctorate in adult and continuing education.

Job Outlook

Employment of adult education teachers is expected to grow faster than the average for all occupations through the year 2006 period as the demand for adult education programs continues to rise. Opportunities should be best for part-time positions, especially in fields such as computer technology, automotive mechanics, and medical technology, which offer very attractive, and often higher-paying, job opportunities outside of teaching.

An estimated four out of ten adults participated in some form of adult education in 1995. Participation in continuing education grows as the educational attainment of the population increases. Both employers and employees are realizing that life-long learning is important for success. To keep abreast of changes in their fields and advances in technology, an increasing number of adults are taking courses—often subsidized or funded entirely by employers—for career advancement or to upgrade their skills. Also, an increasing number of adults are participating in classes for personal enrichment and enjoyment. Enrollment in adult basic education and literacy programs is increasing because of changes in immigration policy that require basic competency in English and civics. And, more employers are demanding higher levels of basic academic skills—reading, writing, and arithmetic—which is increasing enrollment in remedial education and GED preparation classes.

Employment growth of adult vocational-technical education teachers will result from the need to train young adults for entry-level jobs. Experienced workers who want to switch fields or whose jobs have been eliminated due to changing technology or business reorganization also require training. Businesses are finding it essential to provide training to their workers to remain productive and globally competitive. Cooperation between businesses and educational institutions continues to increase to ensure that students are taught the skills employers desire. This should result in greater demand for adult education teachers, particularly at community and junior colleges. Since adult education programs receive state and federal funding, employment growth may be affected by government budgets.

Additional job openings for adult education teachers will stem from the need to replace persons who leave the occupation. Many teach part-time and move into and out of the occupation for other jobs, family responsibilities, or to retire.

Earnings

In 1996, salaried adult education teachers who usually worked full-time had median earnings around $31,300 a year. The middle 50 percent earned between $19,200 and $44,800. The lowest 10 percent earned about $13,100, while the top 10 percent earned more than $56,600. Earnings varied widely by subject, academic credentials, experience, and region of the country. Part-time instructors generally are paid hourly wages and do not receive benefits or pay for preparation time outside of class.

Related Occupations

Adult education teaching requires a wide variety of skills and aptitudes, including the ability to influence, motivate, train, and teach; organizational, administrative, and communication skills; and creativity. Workers in other occupations that require these aptitudes include other teachers, counselors, school administrators, public relations specialists, employee development specialists, and social workers.

Sources of Additional Information

Information on adult basic education programs and teacher certification requirements is available from state departments of education and local school districts.

For information about adult vocational-technical education teaching positions, contact state departments of vocational-technical education.

For information on adult continuing education teaching positions, contact departments of local government, state adult education departments, schools, colleges and universities, religious organizations, and a wide range of businesses that provide formal training for their employees.

General information on adult education is available from:

- ❏ American Association for Adult and Continuing Education, 1200 19th St. NW, Suite 300, Washington, DC 20036.
- ❏ American Vocational Association, 1410 King St., Alexandria, VA 22314.
- ❏ ERIC Clearinghouse on Adult, Career, and Vocational Education, 1900 Kenny Rd., Columbus, OH 43210-1090.

Aerospace Engineers

(D.O.T. 002.061 and .167)

Significant Points

- ✴ *A bachelor's degree in engineering is almost always required for beginning aerospace engineering jobs. Good employment opportunities are expected for new graduates.*
- ✴ *Starting salaries for aerospace engineers are significantly higher than those of bachelor's degree graduates in other fields.*
- ✴ *Knowledge of technological advances must be acquired through continued study and education.*

Nature of the Work

Aerospace engineers design, develop, and test missile, spacecraft, and commercial and military aircraft, and super-

vise manufacturing of these products. They develop new technologies for use in commercial aviation, defense systems, and space exploration, often specializing in areas like structural design, guidance, navigation and control, instrumentation and communication, or production methods. They also may specialize in a particular type of aerospace product, such as commercial transports, helicopters, spacecraft, or rockets. Aerospace engineers may be experts in aerodynamics, propulsion, thermodynamics, structures, celestial mechanics, acoustics, or guidance and control systems.

Working Conditions

Most aerospace engineers work in office buildings, laboratories, or industrial plants. Some engineers travel extensively to plants or work sites.

Most aerospace engineers work a standard 40-hour week. At times, deadlines or design standards may bring extra pressure to a job. When this happens, aerospace engineers may work long hours and experience considerable stress.

Employment

Aerospace engineers held about 53,000 jobs in 1996. More than two-fifths worked in the aircraft and parts and guided missile and space vehicle manufacturing industries. Federal government agencies, primarily the Department of Defense and the National Aeronautics and Space Administration, provided more than one out of seven jobs. Business services, engineering and architectural services, research and testing services, and electrical and electronics manufacturing firms accounted for most of the remaining jobs.

California, Washington, Texas, and Florida—states with large aerospace manufacturers—have the most aerospace engineers.

Training, Other Qualifications, and Advancement

A bachelor's degree in engineering is usually required for beginning engineering jobs. College graduates with a degree in a physical science or mathematics may occasionally qualify for some engineering jobs, especially in engineering specialties in high demand. Most engineering degrees are granted in electrical, mechanical, or civil engineering. However, engineers trained in one branch may work in related branches; for example, many aerospace engineers have training in mechanical engineering. This flexibility allows employers to meet staffing needs in new technologies and specialties in which engineers are in short supply. It also allows engineers to shift to fields with better employment prospects, or to ones that match their interests more closely.

In addition to the standard engineering degree, many colleges offer degrees in engineering technology, which are offered as either two- or four-year programs. These programs prepare students for practical design and production work rather than for jobs that require more theoretical, scientific and mathematical knowledge. Graduates of four-year technology programs may get jobs similar to those obtained by graduates with a bachelor's degree in engineering. Some employers regard them as having skills between those of a technician and an engineer.

Graduate training is essential for engineering faculty positions, but is not required for the majority of entry-level engineering jobs. Many engineers obtain graduate degrees in engineering or business administration to learn new technology, broaden their education, and enhance promotion opportunities. Many high-level executives in government and industry began their careers as engineers.

About 320 colleges and universities offer bachelor's degree programs in engineering that are accredited by the Accreditation Board for Engineering and Technology (ABET), and about 250 colleges offer accredited bachelor's degree programs in engineering technology. ABET accreditation is based on an examination of an engineering program's faculty, curricular content, facilities, and admissions standards. Although most institutions offer programs in the major branches of engineering, only a few offer some of the smaller specialties. Also, programs of the same title may vary in content. For example, some emphasize industrial practices, preparing students for a job in industry, while others are more theoretical and are better for students preparing to take graduate work. Therefore, students should investigate curricula and check accreditations carefully before selecting a college. Admissions requirements for undergraduate engineering schools include a solid background in mathematics (algebra, geometry, trigonometry, and calculus), sciences (biology, chemistry, and physics), and courses in English, social studies, humanities, and computers.

Bachelor's degree programs in engineering are typically designed to last four years, but many students find that it takes between four and five years to complete their studies. In a typical four-year college curriculum, the first two years are spent studying mathematics, basic sciences, introductory engineering, humanities, and social sciences. In the last two years, most courses are in engineering, usually with a concentration in one branch. For example, the last two years of an aerospace program might include courses such as fluid mechanics, heat transfer, applied aerodynamics, analytical mechanics, flight vehicle design, trajectory dynamics, and aerospace propulsion systems. Some programs offer a general engineering curriculum; students then specialize in graduate school or on the job.

Some engineering schools and two-year colleges have agreements whereby the two-year college provides the initial engineering education and the engineering school automatically admits students for their last two years. In addition, a few engineering schools have arrangements whereby a student spends three years in a liberal arts college studying pre-engineering subjects and two years in the engineering school, and receives a bachelor's degree from each. Some colleges and universities offer five-year master's degree programs. Some five- or even six-year cooperative plans combine classroom study and practical work, permitting students to gain valuable experience and finance part of their education.

All 50 states and the District of Columbia require registration for engineers whose work may affect life, health, or property, or who offer their services to the public. Registration generally requires a degree from an ABET-accredited engineering program, four years of relevant work experience, and passing a state examination. Some states will not register people with degrees in engineering technology. Engineers may be registered in several states.

Engineers should be creative, inquisitive, analytical, and detail-oriented. They should be able to work as part of a team and be able to communicate well, both orally and in writing.

Beginning engineering graduates usually work under the supervision of experienced engineers and, in larger companies, may also receive formal classroom or seminar-type training. As they gain knowledge and experience, they are assigned more difficult projects with greater independence to develop designs, solve problems, and make decisions. Engineers may advance to become technical specialists or to supervise a staff or team of engineers and technicians. Some eventually become engineering managers or enter other managerial, management support, or sales jobs.

Job Outlook

Those seeking employment as aerospace engineers are likely to face competition. The decline in Defense Department expenditures for military aircraft, missiles, and other aerospace systems has caused mergers and acquisitions among defense contractors. Federal government funding for research and development of new systems has also declined. Growth in the civilian sector is projected to increase due to orders from domestic and foreign airlines that need more aircraft to accommodate increasing passenger traffic, and to replace the present fleet of airliners with quieter and more fuel-efficient aircraft. Consequently, employment of aerospace engineers is expected to grow more slowly than the average through the year 2006. Future growth of employment in this field could be moderate because a higher proportion of engineers in

aerospace manufacturing may come from the materials, mechanical, or electrical engineering fields. Most job openings will result from the need to replace aerospace engineers who transfer to other occupations or leave the labor force.

Earnings

Starting salaries for aerospace engineers with the bachelor's degree are significantly higher than starting salaries of bachelor's degree graduates in other fields. According to the National Association of Colleges and Employers, starting salaries for those with the bachelor's degree were about $37,957 in 1996.

The median annual salary for all aerospace engineers who worked full-time was about $57,000 in 1996.

The average annual salary for engineers in the federal government in nonsupervisory, supervisory, and managerial positions was $61,950 in 1997.

Related Occupations

Aerospace engineers apply the principles of physical science and mathematics in their work. Other workers who use scientific and mathematical principles include engineering, science, and computer systems managers; physical, life, and computer scientists; mathematicians; engineering and science technicians; and architects.

Sources of Additional Information

High school students interested in obtaining general information on a variety of engineering disciplines should contact the Junior Engineering Technical Society by sending a self-addressed business-size envelope, with six first-class stamps affixed, to:

❑ JETS-Guidance, 1420 King St., Suite 405, Alexandria, VA 22314-2794. Homepage: http://www.asee.org/jets

High school students interested in obtaining information on ABET accredited engineering programs should contact:

❑ The Accreditation Board for Engineering and Technology, Inc., 111 Market Place, Suite 1050, Baltimore, MD 21202-4012. Homepage: http://www.abet.ba.md.us

Non-high school students and those wanting more detailed information should send $3 to:

❑ American Institute of Aeronautics and Astronautics, Inc., Suite 500, 1801 Alexander Bell Drive, Reston, VA 20191-4344.

Budget Analysts

(*D.O.T.* 161.117-010, .267-030)

Significant Points

✷ *Federal, state, and local governments employ one out of three budget analysts.*

✷ *A bachelor's degree generally is the minimum educational requirement; however, some employers require a master's degree.*

✷ *Competition for jobs should remain keen because of the substantial number of qualified applicants; those with a master's degree should enjoy the best job prospects.*

Nature of the Work

Budget analysts play a primary role in the development, analysis, and execution of budgets. Budgets are financial plans used to estimate future requirements and organize and allocate operating and capital resources effectively. The analysis of spending behavior and the planning of future operations are an integral part of the decision-making process in most corporations and government agencies.

Budget analysts work in private industry, nonprofit organizations, and the public sector. In private industry, a budget analyst examines, analyzes, and seeks new ways to improve efficiency and increase profits. Although analysts working in government generally are not concerned with profits, they too are interested in finding the most efficient distribution of funds and other resources among various departments and programs.

A major responsibility of budget analysts is to provide advice and technical assistance in the preparation of annual budgets. At the beginning of the budget cycle, managers and department heads submit proposed operating and financial plans to budget analysts for review. These plans outline expected programs, including proposed program increases and new initiatives; estimated costs and expenses; and capital expenditures needed to finance these programs.

Analysts begin by examining the budget estimates or proposals for completeness, accuracy, and conformance with established procedures, regulations, and organizational objectives. Sometimes they review financial requests by employing cost-benefit analysis, assessing program trade-offs, and exploring alternative funding methods. They also examine past and current budgets, and research economic and financial developments that affect the organization's spending. This process allows analysts to evaluate proposals in terms of the organization's priorities and financial resources.

After this review process, budget analysts consolidate the individual department budgets into operating and capital budget summaries. The analysts submit preliminary budgets to senior management, or sometimes, as is often the case in local and state governments, to appointed or elected officials, with comments and supporting statements that justify or deny funding requests. By reviewing different departments' operating plans, analysts gain insight into an organization's overall operations. This generally proves useful when they interpret and offer technical assistance to officials approving the budget. At this point in the budget process, budget analysts help the chief operating officer, agency head, or other top managers analyze the proposed plan and devise possible alternatives if the projected results are unsatisfactory. The final decision to approve the budget, however, is usually made by the organization head in a private firm or elected officials in government, such as the state legislative body.

Throughout the rest of the year, analysts periodically monitor the budget by reviewing reports and accounting records to determine if allocated funds have been spent as specified. If deviations appear between the approved budget and actual performance, budget analysts may write a report explaining the causes of the variations along with recommendations for new or revised budget procedures. They suggest reallocation of excess funds or recommend program cuts to avoid or alleviate deficits. They also inform program managers and others within their organization of the status and availability of funds in different budget accounts. Before any changes are made to an existing program or a new one is started, a budget analyst assesses its efficiency and effectiveness. Analysts also may project budget needs for long-range planning.

The budget analyst's role has broadened as limited funding has led to downsizing and restructuring throughout private industry and government. In addition to developing guidelines and policies governing the formulation and maintenance of the budget, analysts may measure organizational performance, assessing the effect of various programs and policies on the budget, and help draft budget-related legislation. Budget analysts sometimes conduct training sessions for company or government agency personnel on new budget procedures.

Working Conditions

Budget analysts work in a normal office setting, generally 40 hours per week. However, during the initial development and mid-year and final reviews of budgets, they often experience the pressure of deadlines and tight work schedules. The work during these periods can be extremely stressful, and analysts are usually required to work more than the routine 40 hours a week.

Budget analysts spend the majority of their time working independently, compiling and analyzing data and preparing budget proposals. Nevertheless, their routine schedule can be interrupted by special budget requests, meetings, and training sessions. Others may travel to obtain budget details and explanations of various programs from coworkers, and to personally observe what funding is being used for in the field.

Employment

Budget analysts held about 66,000 jobs throughout private industry and government in 1996. Federal, state, and local governments are major employers, accounting for one-third of budget analyst jobs. The Department of Defense employed seven of every ten budget analysts working for the federal government. Other major employers of budget analysts are schools, hospitals, banks; and manufacturers of transportation equipment, chemicals and allied products, electrical and electronic machinery, and industrial machines.

Training, Other Qualifications, and Advancement

Private firms and government agencies generally require candidates for budget analyst positions to have at least a bachelor's degree. Within the federal government, a bachelor's degree in any field is sufficient background for an entry-level budget analyst position. State and local governments have varying requirements, but a bachelor's degree in one of many areas—accounting, finance, business or public administration, economics, political science, planning, statistics, or a social science such as sociology—may qualify one for entry into the occupation. Sometimes, a field closely related to the employing industry or organization within an industry, such as engineering, may be preferred. An increasing number of states and other employers require a candidate to possess a master's degree to ensure adequate analytical and communication skills. Some firms prefer candidates with business backgrounds because business courses emphasize quantitative analytical skills. Budget and financial experience can occasionally be substituted for formal education when applying for a budget analyst position.

Because developing a budget involves manipulating numbers and requires strong analytical skills, courses in statistics or accounting are helpful, regardless of the prospective budget analyst's major field of study. Financial analysis in most organizations is automated, and requires familiarity with word processing and the financial software packages used in budget analysis. Software packages commonly used by budget analysts include electronic spreadsheets and database and graphics software. Employers generally prefer job candidates who already possess these computer skills over those who need to be trained.

In addition to analytical and computer skills, those seeking a career as a budget analyst must also be able to work under strict time constraints. Strong oral and written communication skills are essential for analysts to prepare, present, and defend budget proposals to decision makers.

Entry-level budget analysts may receive some formal training when they begin their jobs. However, most employers feel that the best training is obtained by working through one complete budget cycle. During the cycle, analysts become familiar with all the steps involved in the budgeting process.

The federal government, on the other hand, offers extensive on-the-job and classroom training for entry-level analysts, who are initially called trainees. Analysts are encouraged to participate in the various classes offered throughout their careers.

Beginning analysts usually work under close supervision. Capable entry-level analysts can be promoted into intermediate-level positions within one to two years, and then into senior positions within a few more years. Progressing to a higher level means added budgetary responsibility and can lead to a supervisory role.

In the federal government, for example, beginning budget analysts compare projected costs with prior expenditures; consolidate and enter data prepared by others; and assist higher grade analysts by doing research. As analysts progress, they begin to develop and formulate budget estimates and justification statements; perform in-depth analyses of budget requests; write statements supporting funding requests; advise program managers and others on the status and availability of funds in different budget activities; and present and defend budget proposals to senior managers.

Because of the importance and high visibility of their jobs, senior budget analysts are prime candidates for promotion to management positions in various parts of the organization.

Job Outlook

Despite the increase in demand for budget analysts, competition for jobs should remain keen because of the substantial number of qualified applicants. Job opportunities are generally best for candidates with a master's degree. In some cases, budget and financial experience can offset a lack of formal education. A working knowledge of computer financial software packages can also enhance one's employment prospects in this field.

Employment of budget analysts is expected to grow about as fast as the average for all occupations through the year 2006. In addition to employment growth, many job openings will result from the need to replace experienced budget analysts who transfer to other occupations or leave the labor force.

Planning and financial control demand more attention because of the growing complexity of business and the increasing specialization within organizations. Many companies will continue to rely heavily on budget analysts to examine, analyze, and develop budgets to determine capital require-

ments and to allocate labor and other resources efficiently among all parts of the organization. Managers will continue to use budgets as a vehicle to plan, coordinate, control, and evaluate activities within their organizations more effectively.

Expanding automation continues to make budget analysts more productive, allowing them to process more data in less time. Also, computers are increasingly used to organize, summarize, and disseminate data to top-level managers, thereby centralizing decision-making and reducing the need for middle managers in many organizations. However, any computer-induced effects on employment of budget analysts may be offset by growing demand for information and analysis. Easier manipulation of and accessibility to data provide management with more considerations on which to base decisions.

The financial work performed by budget analysts is an important function in every organization. Financial and budget reports must be completed during periods of economic growth and slowdowns. Therefore, budget analysts generally are less subject to layoffs during economic downturns than many other workers.

Earnings

Salaries of budget analysts vary widely by experience, education, and employer. According to a survey conducted by Robert Half International, a staffing services firm specializing in accounting and finance, starting salaries of budget and other financial analysts in small firms ranged from $24,000 to $33,200 in 1997; in large organizations, from $28,000 to $38,700. In small firms, analysts with one to three years of experience earned from $28,000 to $43,100; in large companies, from $31,000 to $51,300. Senior analysts in small firms earned from $34,500 to $50,000; in large firms, from $39,000 to $60,600. Earnings of managers in this field ranged from $40,000 to $65,000 a year in small firms, while managers in large organizations earned between $47,000 and $83,800.

A survey of workplaces in 160 metropolitan areas reported that inexperienced budget analysts had median annual earnings of about $30,100 in 1995, with the middle half earning between $26,200 and $35,500 a year.

In the federal government, budget analysts generally started as trainees earning $19,500 or $24,200 a year in 1997. Candidates with a master's degree might begin at $29,600. Beginning salaries were slightly higher in selected areas where the prevailing local pay level was higher. The average annual salary for budget analysts employed by the federal government in nonsupervisory, supervisory, and managerial positions was $48,600 in 1997.

Related Occupations

Budget analysts review, analyze, and interpret financial data; make recommendations for the future; and assist in the implementation of new ideas. Workers who use these skills in other occupations include accountants and auditors, economists, financial analysts, financial managers, and loan officers.

Sources of Additional Information

Information about career opportunities as a budget analyst may be available from your state or local employment service.

Information on acquiring a job as a budget analyst with the federal government may be obtained from the Office of Personnel Management through a telephone-based system. Consult your telephone directory under U.S. government for a local number, or call (912) 757-3000 (TDD 912 744-2299). That number is not toll-free and charges may result. Information also is available from their Internet site: http://www.usajobs.opm.gov

Chemical Engineers

(*D.O.T.* 008.061)

Significant Points

* *A bachelor's degree in chemical engineering is almost always required for beginning jobs. Good employment opportunities are expected for new graduates.*

* *Starting salaries for chemical engineers are significantly higher than those of bachelor's degree graduates in other fields.*

* *Knowledge of technological advances must be acquired through continued study and education.*

Nature of the Work

Chemical engineers apply the principles of chemistry and engineering to solve problems involving the production or use of chemicals. They design equipment and develop processes for large scale chemical manufacturing, plan and test methods of manufacturing the products and treating the by-products, and supervise production. Chemical engineers also work in industries other than chemical manufacturing such as electronics or photographic equipment. Because the knowledge and duties of chemical engineers cut across many fields, they apply principles of chemistry, physics, mathematics, and mechanical and electrical engineering in their work. They frequently specialize in a particular operation such as oxidation or polymerization. Others specialize in a particular area such as pollution control or the production of specific products such as automotive plastics or chlorine bleach. Chemical engineers are increasingly using computer technology to optimize all phases of production, and therefore need to understand how to apply computer skills to process analysis, computer control systems, and statistical quality control.

Working Conditions

Most chemical engineers work in office buildings, laboratories, or industrial plants. Some chemical engineers travel extensively to plants or work sites.

Most chemical engineers work a standard 40-hour week. At times, deadlines or design standards may bring extra pressure to a job. When this happens, chemical engineers may work long hours and experience considerable stress.

Employment

Chemical engineers held over 49,000 jobs in 1996. Manufacturing industries employed two-thirds of all employees, primarily in the chemical, petroleum refining, paper, and related industries. Most of the rest worked for engineering services, research and testing services, or consulting firms that design chemical plants. Still others worked on a contract basis, for government agencies or as independent consultants.

Training, Other Qualifications, and Advancement

A bachelor's degree in engineering is usually required for beginning engineering jobs. College graduates with a degree in a physical science or mathematics may occasionally qualify for some engineering jobs, especially in engineering specialties in high demand. Most engineering degrees are granted in electrical, mechanical, or civil engineering. However, engineers trained in one branch may work in related branches; for example, many aerospace engineers have training in mechanical engineering. This flexibility allows employers to meet staffing needs in new technologies and specialties in which engineers are in short supply. It also allows engineers to shift to fields with better employment prospects, or to ones that match their interests more closely.

In addition to the standard engineering degree, many colleges offer degrees in engineering technology, which are offered as either two- or four-year programs. These programs prepare students for practical design and production work rather than for jobs that require more theoretical, scientific, and mathematical knowledge. Graduates of four-year technology programs may get jobs similar to those obtained by graduates with a bachelor's degree in engineering. Some

employers regard them as having skills between those of a technician and an engineer.

Graduate training is essential for engineering faculty positions, but is not required for the majority of entry-level engineering jobs. Many engineers obtain graduate degrees in engineering or business administration to learn new technology, broaden their education, and enhance promotion opportunities. Many high-level executives in government and industry began their careers as engineers.

About 320 colleges and universities offer bachelor's degree programs in engineering that are accredited by the Accreditation Board for Engineering and Technology (ABET), and about 250 colleges offer accredited bachelor's degree programs in engineering technology. ABET accreditation is based on an examination of an engineering program's faculty, curricular content, facilities, and admissions standards. Although most institutions offer programs in the major branches of engineering, only a few offer some of the smaller specialties. Also, programs of the same title may vary in content. For example, some emphasize industrial practices, preparing students for a job in industry, while others are more theoretical and are better for students preparing to take graduate work. Therefore, students should investigate curricula and check accreditations carefully before selecting a college. Admissions requirements for undergraduate engineering schools include a solid background in mathematics (algebra, geometry, trigonometry, and calculus), sciences (biology, chemistry, and physics), and courses in English, social studies, humanities, and computers.

Bachelor's degree programs in engineering are typically designed to last four years, but many students find that it takes between four and five years to complete their studies. In a typical four-year college curriculum, the first two years are spent studying mathematics, basic sciences, introductory engineering, humanities, and social sciences. In the last two years, most courses are in engineering, usually with a concentration in one branch. For example, the last two years of an aerospace program might include courses such as fluid mechanics, heat transfer, applied aerodynamics, analytical mechanics, flight vehicle design, trajectory dynamics, and aerospace propulsion systems. Some programs offer a general engineering curriculum; students then specialize in graduate school or on the job.

Some engineering schools and two-year colleges have agreements whereby the two-year college provides the initial engineering education and the engineering school automatically admits students for their last two years. In addition, a few engineering schools have arrangements whereby a student spends three years in a liberal arts college studying pre-engineering subjects and two years in the engineering

school, and receives a bachelor's degree from each. Some colleges and universities offer five-year master's degree programs. Some five- or even six-year cooperative plans combine classroom study and practical work, permitting students to gain valuable experience and finance part of their education.

All 50 states and the District of Columbia require registration for engineers whose work may affect life, health, or property, or who offer their services to the public. Registration generally requires a degree from an ABET-accredited engineering program, four years of relevant work experience, and passing a state examination. Some states will not register people with degrees in engineering technology. Engineers may be registered in several states.

Engineers should be creative, inquisitive, analytical, and detail-oriented. They should be able to work as part of a team and be able to communicate well, both orally and in writing.

Beginning engineering graduates usually work under the supervision of experienced engineers and, in larger companies, may also receive formal classroom or seminar-type training. As they gain knowledge and experience, they are assigned more difficult projects with greater independence to develop designs, solve problems, and make decisions. Engineers may advance to become technical specialists or to supervise a staff or team of engineers and technicians. Some eventually become engineering managers or enter other managerial, management support, or sales jobs.

Job Outlook

Although employment in the chemical manufacturing industry is projected to grow slowly through 2006, employment of chemical engineers should increase about as fast as the average for all occupations as chemical companies research and develop new chemicals and more efficient processes to increase output of existing chemicals. Much of the projected growth in employment, however, will be in nonmanufacturing industries, especially service industries. Chemical engineering graduates may face competition for jobs as the number of openings is projected to be lower than the number of graduates. Areas relating to the production of specialty chemicals, pharmaceuticals, and plastics materials may provide better opportunities than other portions of the chemical industry.

Earnings

Starting salaries for chemical engineers with the bachelor's degree are significantly higher than starting salaries of bachelor's degree graduates in other fields. According to the National Association of Colleges and Employers, starting salaries for those with the bachelor's degree in 1996 were about $42,817 in 1996.

The median annual salary for all chemical engineers who worked full-time in 1996 was $52,600.

The average annual salary for engineers in the federal government in nonsupervisory, supervisory, and managerial positions was $61,950 in 1997.

Related Occupations

Chemical engineers apply the principles of physical science and mathematics in their work. Other workers who use scientific and mathematical principles include engineering, science, and computer systems managers; physical, life, and computer scientists; mathematicians; engineering and science technicians; and architects.

Sources of Additional Information

High school students interested in obtaining general information on a variety of engineering disciplines should contact the Junior Engineering Technical Society by sending a self-addressed business-size envelope, with six first-class stamps affixed, to:

❑ JETS-Guidance, 1420 King St., Suite 405, Alexandria, VA 22314-2794. Homepage: http://www.asee.org/jets

High school students interested in obtaining information on ABET accredited engineering programs should contact:

❑ The Accreditation Board for Engineering and Technology, Inc., 111 Market Place, Suite 1050, Baltimore, MD 21202-4012. Homepage: http://www.abet.ba.md.us

Non-high school students and those wanting more detailed information should contact:

❑ American Institute of Chemical Engineers, 345 East 47th St., New York, NY 10017-2395.

❑ American Chemical Society, Department of Career Services, 1155 16th St. NW, Washington, DC 20036.

Chemists

(*D.O.T.* 022.061-010, -014, and .137-010)

Significant Points

✶ *A bachelor's degree in chemistry or a related discipline is usually the minimum educational requirement; however, many research jobs require a Ph.D. degree.*

✶ *Job growth will be concentrated in drug manufacturing and research, development, and testing services firms.*

Nature of the Work

Everything in our physical environment, whether naturally occurring or of human design, is composed of chemicals. Chemists search for and put to practical use new knowledge about chemicals. Chemical research has led to the discovery and development of new and improved synthetic fibers, paints, adhesives, drugs, cosmetics, electronic components, lubricants, and thousands of other products. Chemists also develop processes which save energy and reduce pollution, such as improved oil refining and petrochemical processing methods. Research on the chemistry of living things spurs advances in medicine, agriculture, food processing, and other fields.

Chemists can apply their knowledge of chemistry to various purposes. Many work in research and development (R&D). In basic research, chemists investigate the properties, composition, and structure of matter and the laws that govern the combination of elements and reactions of substances. In applied research and development, they create new products and processes or improve existing ones, often using knowledge gained from basic research. For example, synthetic rubber and plastics resulted from research on small molecules uniting to form large ones, a process called polymerization. R&D chemists use computers and a wide variety of sophisticated laboratory instrumentation. They also spend time documenting and analyzing the results of their work and writing formal reports.

Chemists also work in production and quality control in chemical manufacturing plants. They prepare instructions for plant workers which specify ingredients, mixing times, and temperatures for each stage in the process. They also monitor automated processes to ensure proper product yield, and they test samples of raw materials or finished products to ensure they meet industry and government standards, including the regulations governing pollution. Chemists also record and report on test results, and improve existing or develop new test methods.

Chemists often specialize in a subfield. Analytical chemists determine the structure, composition, and nature of substances by examining and identifying the various elements or compounds that make up a substance. They study the relations and interactions of the parts and develop analytical techniques. They also identify the presence and concentration of chemical pollutants in air, water, and soil. Organic chemists study the chemistry of the vast number of carbon compounds which make up all living things. Many commercial products, such as drugs, plastics, and elastomers (elastic substances similar to rubber), have been developed by organic chemists who synthesize elements or simple compounds to create new compounds or substances that have different properties and applications. Inorganic chemists study compounds consisting mainly of elements other than carbon, such as those in electronic components. Physical chemists study the physical characteristics of atoms and molecules and investigate how

chemical reactions work. Their research may result in new and better energy sources.

Working Conditions

Chemists usually work regular hours in offices and laboratories. Research chemists spend much time in laboratories, but also work in offices when they do theoretical research or plan, record, and report on their lab research. Although some laboratories are small, others are large and may incorporate prototype chemical manufacturing facilities as well as advanced equipment. Chemists may also do some of their work in a chemical plant or outdoors—while gathering water samples to test for pollutants, for example. Some chemists are exposed to health or safety hazards when handling certain chemicals, but there is little risk if proper procedures are followed.

Employment

Chemists held about 91,000 jobs in 1996. Nearly half of chemists are employed in manufacturing firms—mostly in the chemical manufacturing industry, which includes firms that produce plastics and synthetic materials, drugs, soaps and cleaners, paints, industrial organic chemicals, and other miscellaneous chemical products. Chemists also work for state and local governments, and for federal agencies. Health and Human Services, which includes the Food and Drug Administration, the National Institutes of Health, and the Center for Disease Control, is the major federal employer of chemists. The Departments of Defense and Agriculture, and the Environmental Protection Agency, also employ chemists. Other chemists work for research, development, and testing services. In addition, thousands of persons held chemistry faculty positions in colleges and universities.

Chemists are employed in all parts of the country, but they are mainly concentrated in large industrial areas.

Training, Other Qualifications, and Advancement

A bachelor's degree in chemistry or a related discipline is usually the minimum educational requirement for entry-level chemist jobs. However, many research jobs require a Ph.D.

Many colleges and universities offer a bachelor's degree program in chemistry, about 620 of which are approved by the American Chemical Society (ACS). Several hundred colleges and universities also offer advanced degree programs in chemistry; around 320 master's programs, and about 190 doctoral programs are ACS-approved.

Students planning careers as chemists should enjoy studying science and mathematics, and should like working with their hands building scientific apparatus and performing experiments. Perseverance, curiosity, and the ability to concentrate on detail and to work independently are essential. In addition to required courses in analytical, inorganic, organic, and physical chemistry, undergraduate chemistry majors usually study biological sciences, mathematics, and physics. Those who are interested in the environmental field should take courses in environmental studies and become familiar with current legislation and regulations. Computer courses are essential, as employers increasingly prefer job applicants who are able to apply computer skills to modeling and simulation tasks and operate computerized laboratory equipment.

Because research and development chemists are increasingly expected to work on interdisciplinary teams, some understanding of other disciplines, including business and marketing or economics, is desirable, along with leadership ability and good oral and written communication skills. Experience, either in academic laboratories or through internships or co-op programs in industry, also is useful. Some employers of research chemists, particularly in the pharmaceutical industry, prefer to hire individuals with several years of postdoctoral experience.

Graduate students typically specialize in a subfield of chemistry, such as analytical chemistry or polymer chemistry, depending on their interests and the kind of work they wish to do. For example, those interested in doing drug research in the pharmaceutical industry usually develop a strong background in synthetic organic chemistry. However, students normally need not specialize at the undergraduate level. In fact, undergraduates who are broadly trained have more flexibility when job hunting or changing jobs than if they narrowly define their interests. Most employers provide new bachelor's degree chemists with additional training or education.

In government or industry, beginning chemists with a bachelor's degree work in quality control, analytical testing, or assist senior chemists in research and development laboratories. Many employers prefer chemists with a Ph.D. or at least a master's degree to lead basic and applied research. A Ph.D. is also often preferred for advancement to many administrative positions.

Job Outlook

Employment of chemists is expected to grow about as fast as the average for all occupations through the year 2006. Job growth will be concentrated in drug manufacturing and research, development, and testing services firms. The chemical industry, the major employer of chemists, should face continued demand for goods such as new and better pharmaceuticals and personal care products, as well as more specialty chemicals designed to address specific problems or applications. To meet these demands, chemical firms will continue to devote money to research and development—through in-house teams or outside contractors—spurring employment growth of chemists.

Within the chemical industry, job opportunities are expected to be most plentiful in pharmaceutical and biotechnology firms. Stronger competition among drug companies and an aging population are contributing to the need for innovative and improved drugs discovered through scientific research. Chemical firms that develop and manufacture personal products such as toiletries and cosmetics also must continually innovate and develop new and better products to remain competitive. Additionally, as the population grows and becomes better informed, the demand for different or improved grooming products—including vegetable-based products, products with milder formulas, treatments for aging skin, and products that have been developed using more benign chemical processes than in the past—will remain strong, spurring the need for chemists.

In the remaining segments of the chemical industry, employment growth is expected to be much slower than in drug manufacturing, and in some cases, may decline as companies downsize and turn to outside contractors to provide specialized services. Nevertheless, some job openings will result from the need to replace chemists who retire or otherwise leave the labor force. Quality control will continue to be an important issue in the chemical and other industries that use chemicals in their manufacturing processes. Chemists will also be needed to develop and improve the technologies and processes used to produce chemicals for all purposes, and to monitor and measure air and water pollutants to ensure compliance with local, state, and federal environmental regulations.

Outside the chemical industry, firms that provide research, development, and testing services are expected to be the source of numerous job opportunities between 1996 and 2006. Chemical companies, including drug manufacturers, are increasingly turning to these services to perform specialized research and other work formerly done by in-house chemists. Chemists will also be needed to work in research and testing firms that focus on environmental testing and cleanup.

During periods of economic recession, layoffs of chemists may occur—especially in the industrial chemicals industry. This industry provides many of the raw materials to the auto manufacturing and construction industries, both of which are vulnerable to temporary slowdowns during recessions.

Earnings

A survey by the American Chemical Society reports that the median salary of all their members with a bachelor's de-gree was $49,400 a year in 1997; with a master's degree, $56,200; and with a Ph.D., $71,000. Median salaries were highest for those working in private industry; those in academia earned the least. According to an ACS survey of recent graduates, inexperienced chemistry graduates with a bachelor's degree earned a median starting salary of $25,000 in 1996; with a master's degree, $31,100; and with a Ph.D., $45,000. Among bachelor's degree graduates, those who had completed internships or had other work experience while in school commanded the highest starting salaries.

In 1997, chemists in nonsupervisory, supervisory, and managerial positions in the federal government earned an average salary of $60,000.

Related Occupations

The work of chemical engineers, agricultural scientists, biological scientists, and chemical technicians is closely related to the work done by chemists. The work of other physical and life science occupations, such as physicists and medical scientists, may also be similar to that of chemists.

Sources of Additional Information

General information on career opportunities and earnings for chemists is available from:

❑ American Chemical Society, Education Division, 1155 16th St. NW, Washington, DC 20036.

Information on acquiring a job as a chemist with the federal government may be obtained from the Office of Personnel Management through a telephone-based system. Consult your telephone directory under U.S. government for a local number, or call (912) 757-3000 (TDD 912-744-2299). That number is not toll-free and charges may result. Information also is available from their Internet site: http://www.usajobs

Civil Engineers

(*D.O.T.* 005.061 except-042, .167-014 and -018; and 019.167-018)

Significant Points

* *A bachelor's degree in civil engineering is almost always required for beginning jobs. Good employment opportunities are expected for new graduates.*

* *Starting salaries for civil engineers are significantly higher than those of bachelor's degree graduates in other fields.*

* *Knowledge of technological advances must be acquired through continued study and education.*

Nature of the Work

Civil engineers work in the oldest branch of engineering, designing and supervising the construction of roads, buildings, airports, tunnels, bridges, and water supply and sewage systems. Major specialties within civil engineering are structural, water resources, environmental, construction, transportation, and geotechnical engineering.

Many civil engineers hold supervisory or administrative positions, ranging from supervisor of a construction site to city engineer. Others may work in design, construction, research, and teaching.

Working Conditions

Most civil engineers work in office buildings, laboratories, or industrial plants. Some civil engineers travel extensively to plants or work sites.

Most civil engineers work a standard 40-hour week. At times, deadlines or design standards may bring extra pressure to a job. When this happens, civil engineers may work long hours and experience considerable stress.

Employment

Civil engineers held about 196,000 jobs in 1996. Almost 47 percent were in firms providing engineering consulting services, primarily developing designs for new construction projects. Another 39 percent of the jobs were in federal, state, and local government agencies. The construction industry, public utilities, transportation, and manufacturing industries accounted for most of the rest. About 13,000 civil engineers were self-employed, many as consultants.

Civil engineers usually work near major industrial and commercial centers, often at construction sites. Some projects are situated in remote areas or in foreign countries. In some jobs, civil engineers move from place to place to work on different projects.

Training, Other Qualifications, and Advancement

A bachelor's degree in engineering is usually required for beginning engineering jobs. College graduates with a degree in a physical science or mathematics may occasionally qualify for some engineering jobs, especially in engineering specialties in high demand. Most engineering degrees are granted in electrical, mechanical, or civil engineering. However, engineers trained in one branch may work in related branches; for example, many aerospace engineers have training in mechanical engineering. This flexibility allows employers to meet staffing needs in new technologies and specialties in which engineers are in short supply. It also allows engineers to shift to fields with better employment prospects, or to ones that match their interests more closely.

In addition to the standard engineering degree, many colleges offer degrees in engineering technology, which are offered as either two- or four-year programs. These programs prepare students for practical design and production work rather than for jobs that require more theoretical, scientific and mathematical knowledge. Graduates of four-year technology programs may get jobs similar to those obtained by graduates with a bachelor's degree in engineering. Some employers regard them as having skills between those of a technician and an engineer.

Graduate training is essential for engineering faculty positions, but is not required for the majority of entry-level engineering jobs. Many engineers obtain graduate degrees in engineering or business administration to learn new technology, broaden their education, and enhance promotion opportunities. Many high-level executives in government and industry began their careers as engineers.

About 320 colleges and universities offer bachelor's degree programs in engineering that are accredited by the Accreditation Board for Engineering and Technology (ABET), and about 250 colleges offer accredited bachelor's degree programs in engineering technology. ABET accreditation is based on an examination of an engineering program's faculty, curricular content, facilities, and admissions standards. Although most institutions offer programs in the major branches of engineering, only a few offer some of the smaller specialties. Also, programs of the same title may vary in content. For example, some emphasize industrial practices, preparing students for a job in industry, while others are more theoretical and are better for students preparing to take graduate work. Therefore, students should investigate curricula and check accreditations carefully before selecting a college. Admissions requirements for undergraduate engineering schools include a solid background in mathematics (algebra, geometry, trigonometry, and calculus), sciences (biology, chemistry, and physics), and courses in English, social studies, humanities, and computers.

Bachelor's degree programs in engineering are typically designed to last four years, but many students find that it takes between four and five years to complete their studies. In a typical four-year college curriculum, the first two years are spent studying mathematics, basic sciences, introductory engineering, humanities, and social sciences. In the last two years, most courses are in engineering, usually with a concentration in one branch. For example, the last two years of an aerospace program might include courses such as fluid mechanics, heat transfer, applied aerodynamics, analytical mechanics, flight vehicle design, trajectory dynamics, and aerospace propulsion systems. Some programs offer a general engineering curriculum; students then specialize in graduate school or on the job.

Some engineering schools and two-year colleges have agreements whereby the two-year college provides the initial engineering education and the engineering school automatically admits students for their last two years. In addition, a few engineering schools have arrangements whereby a student spends three years in a liberal arts college studying pre-engineering subjects and two years in the engineering school, and receives a bachelor's degree from each. Some colleges and universities offer five-year master's degree programs. Some five- or even six-year cooperative plans combine classroom study and practical work, permitting students to gain valuable experience and finance part of their education.

All 50 states and the District of Columbia require registration for engineers whose work may affect life, health, or property, or who offer their services to the public. Registration generally requires a degree from an ABET-accredited engineering program, four years of relevant work experience, and passing a state examination. Some states will not register people with degrees in engineering technology. Engineers may be registered in several states.

Engineers should be creative, inquisitive, analytical, and detail-oriented. They should be able to work as part of a team and be able to communicate well, both orally and in writing.

Beginning engineering graduates usually work under the supervision of experienced engineers and, in larger companies, may also receive formal classroom or seminar-type training. As they gain knowledge and experience, they are assigned more difficult projects with greater independence to develop designs, solve problems, and make decisions. Engineers may advance to become technical specialists or to supervise a staff or team of engineers and technicians. Some eventually become engineering managers or enter other managerial, management support, or sales jobs.

Job Outlook

Employment of civil engineers is expected to increase about as fast as the average for all occupations through the year 2006. Graduates of civil engineering programs should find favorable opportunities. Spurred by general population growth and an expanding economy, more civil engineers will be needed to design and construct higher capacity transportation, water supply, and pollution control systems; large buildings and building complexes; and to repair or replace existing roads, bridges, and other public structures. Most job openings, however, will result from the need to replace civil engineers who transfer to other occupations or leave the labor force.

Because construction and related industries—including those providing design services—employ many civil engineers, employment opportunities will vary by geographic area and may decrease during economic slowdowns, when construction is often curtailed.

Earnings

Starting salaries for civil engineers with the bachelor's degree are significantly higher than starting salaries of bachelor's degree graduates in other fields. According to the National Association of Colleges and Employers, starting salaries for those with the bachelor's degree were about $33,119 in 1996.

The median annual salary for all civil engineers who worked full-time in 1996 was $46,000.

The average annual salary for engineers in the federal government in nonsupervisory, supervisory, and managerial positions was $61,950 in 1997.

Related Occupations

Civil engineers apply the principles of physical science and mathematics in their work. Other workers who use scientific and mathematical principles include engineering, science, and computer systems managers; physical, life, and computer scientists; mathematicians; engineering and science technicians; and architects.

Sources of Additional Information

High school students interested in obtaining general information on a variety of engineering disciplines should contact the Junior Engineering Technical Society by sending a self-addressed business-size envelope, with six first-class stamps affixed, to:

❑ JETS-Guidance, 1420 King St., Suite 405, Alexandria, VA 22314-2794. Homepage: http://www.asee.org/jets

High school students interested in obtaining information on ABET accredited engineering programs should contact:

❑ The Accreditation Board for Engineering and Technology, Inc., 111 Market Place, Suite 1050, Baltimore, MD 21202-4012. Homepage: http://www.abet.ba.md.us

Non-high school students and those wanting more detailed information should contact:

❑ American Society of Civil Engineers, 1801 Alexander Bell Drive, Reston, VA 20191-4400.

Clinical Laboratory Technologists and Technicians

(*D.O.T.* 078.221-010, .261-010, -014, -026, -030, and -038, .281-010, .381-014, .687-010, and 559.361-010)

Significant Points

✶ *Medical and clinical laboratory technologists usually have a bachelor's degree with a major in medical technology or in one of the life sciences; medical and clinical laboratory technicians typically need either an associate degree or a certificate.*

✶ *Competition for jobs has increased and individuals may now have to look longer to find employment than in the past.*

Nature of the Work

Clinical laboratory testing plays a crucial role in the detection, diagnosis, and treatment of disease. Clinical laboratory technologists and technicians, also known as medical technologists and technicians, perform most of these tests.

Clinical laboratory personnel examine and analyze body fluids, tissues, and cells. They look for bacteria, parasites, or other micro-organisms; analyze the chemical content of fluids; match blood for transfusions, and test for drug levels in the blood to show how a patient is responding to treatment. They also prepare specimens for examination, count cells, and look for abnormal cells. They use automated equipment and instruments that perform a number of tests simultaneously, as well as microscopes, cell counters, and other kinds of sophisticated laboratory equipment to perform tests. Then they analyze the results and relay them to physicians.

The complexity of tests performed, the level of judgment needed, and the amount of responsibility workers assume depend largely on the amount of education and experience they have.

Medical and clinical laboratory technologists generally have a bachelor's degree in medical technology or in one of the life sciences, or have a combination of formal training and work experience. They perform complex chemical, biological, hematological, immunologic, microscopic, and bacteriological tests. Technologists microscopically examine blood, tissue, and other body substances. They make cultures of body fluid or tissue samples to determine the presence of bacteria, fungi, parasites, or other micro-organisms. They analyze samples for chemical content or reaction and determine blood glucose or cholesterol levels. They also type and cross-match blood samples for transfusions.

Medical and clinical laboratory technologists may evaluate test results, develop and modify procedures, and establish and monitor programs to ensure the accuracy of tests. Some medical and clinical laboratory technologists supervise medical and clinical laboratory technicians.

Technologists in small laboratories perform many types of tests, while those in large laboratories generally specialize. Technologists who prepare specimens and analyze the chemical and hormonal contents of body fluids are clinical chemistry technologists. Those who examine and identify bacteria and other micro-organisms are microbiology technologists. Blood bank technologists collect, type, and prepare blood and its components for transfusions. Immunology technologists examine elements and responses of the human immune system to foreign bodies. Cytotechnologists prepare slides of body cells and microscopically examine these cells for abnormalities which may signal the beginning of a cancerous growth.

Medical and clinical laboratory technicians perform less complex tests and laboratory procedures than technologists. Technicians may prepare specimens and operate automatic analyzers, for example, or they may perform manual tests following detailed instructions. Like technologists, they may work in several areas of the clinical laboratory or specialize in just one. Histology technicians cut and stain tissue specimens for microscopic examination by pathologists, and phlebotomists draw and test blood. They usually work under the supervision of medical and clinical laboratory technologists or laboratory managers.

Working Conditions

Hours and other working conditions vary according to the size and type of employment setting. In large hospitals or in independent laboratories that operate continuously, personnel usually work the day, evening, or night shift, and may work weekends and holidays. Laboratory personnel in small facilities may work on rotating shifts rather than on a regular shift. In some facilities, laboratory personnel are on call, available in case of an emergency, several nights a week or on weekends.

Clinical laboratory personnel are trained to work with infectious specimens. When proper methods of infection control and sterilization are followed, few hazards exist.

Laboratories generally are well lighted and clean; however, specimens, solutions, and reagents used in the laboratory sometimes produce odors. Laboratory workers may spend a great deal of time on their feet.

Employment

Clinical laboratory technologists and technicians held about 285,000 jobs in 1996. More than half worked in hospitals. Most others worked in medical laboratories and offices and clinics of physicians. Some worked in blood banks, research and testing laboratories, and in the federal government—at Department of Veterans Affairs hospitals and U.S.

Public Health Service facilities. About one laboratory worker in six worked part-time.

Training, Other Qualifications, and Advancement

The usual requirement for an entry level position as a medical or clinical laboratory technologist is a bachelor's degree with a major in medical technology or in one of the life sciences. Universities and hospitals offer medical technology programs. It is also possible to qualify through a combination of on-the-job and specialized training.

Bachelor's degree programs in medical technology include courses in chemistry, biological sciences, microbiology, and mathematics, and specialized courses devoted to knowledge and skills used in the clinical laboratory. Many programs also offer or require courses in management, business, and computer applications.

Master's degrees in medical technology and related clinical laboratory sciences provide training for specialized areas of laboratory work or teaching, administration, or research.

The Clinical Laboratory Improvement Act (CLIA) requires technologists who perform certain highly complex tests to have at least an associate degree.

Medical and clinical laboratory technicians generally have either an associate degree from a community or junior college, or a certificate from a hospital, vocational or technical school, or from one of the Armed Forces. A few technicians learn on the job.

Nationally recognized accrediting agencies in the clinical laboratory science include the National Accrediting Agency for Clinical Laboratory Sciences, and the Accrediting Bureau of Health Education Schools (ABHES). National Accrediting Agency for Clinical Laboratory Sciences fully accredits 621, and approves 72 programs that provide education for medical and clinical laboratory technologists, cytotechnologists, histologic technicians, specialists in blood bank technology, and medical and clinical laboratory technicians. ABHES accredits training programs for medical and clinical laboratory technicians.

Some states require laboratory personnel to be licensed or registered. Information on licensure is available from state departments of health or boards of occupational licensing. Certification is a voluntary process by which a nongovernmental organization such as a professional society or certifying agency grants recognition to an individual whose professional competence meets prescribed standards. Widely accepted by employers in the health industry, certification is a prerequisite for most jobs and often is necessary for advancement. Agencies that certify medical and clinical laboratory technolo-

gists and technicians include the Board of Registry of the American Society of Clinical Pathologists, the American Medical Technologists, the American Society for Clinical Laboratory Science, and the Credentialing Commission of the International Society for Clinical Laboratory Technology. These agencies have different requirements for certification and different organizational sponsors.

Clinical laboratory personnel need analytical judgment and the ability to work under pressure. Close attention to detail is essential because small differences or changes in test substances or numerical readouts can be crucial for patient care. Manual dexterity and normal color vision are highly desirable. With the widespread use of automated laboratory equipment, computer skills are important. In addition, technologists in particular are expected to be good at problem solving.

Technologists may advance to supervisory positions in laboratory work or become chief medical or clinical laboratory technologists or laboratory managers in hospitals. Manufacturers of home diagnostic testing kits and laboratory equipment and supplies seek experienced technologists to work in product development, marketing, and sales. Graduate education in medical technology, one of the biological sciences, chemistry, management, or education usually speeds advancement. A doctorate is sometimes needed to become a laboratory director. However, federal regulation allows directors of moderate complexity laboratories to have either a master's degree or a bachelor's degree combined with the appropriate amount of training and experience. Technicians can become technologists through additional education and experience.

Job Outlook

Employment of clinical laboratory workers is expected to grow about as fast as the average for all occupations through the year 2006 as the volume of laboratory tests increases with population growth and the development of new types of tests. Hospitals and independent laboratories have recently undergone considerable consolidation and restructuring that has boosted productivity and allowed the same number of personnel to perform more tests than previously possible. As a result, competition for jobs has increased and individuals may now have to look longer to find employment than in the past.

Technological advances will continue to have two opposing effects on employment through 2006. New, more powerful diagnostic tests will encourage more testing and spur employment. However, advances in laboratory automation and simpler tests, which make it possible for each worker to perform more tests, should slow growth. Research and development efforts are targeted at simplifying routine testing procedures so that nonlaboratory personnel, physicians

and patients in particular, can perform tests now done in laboratories. Also, robots may prepare specimens, a job done now by technologists and technicians.

Although significant, growth will not be the only source of opportunities. As in most occupations, many openings will result from the need to replace workers who transfer to other occupations, retire, or stop working for some other reason.

Earnings

Median weekly earnings of full-time, salaried clinical laboratory technologists and technicians were $520 in 1996. Half earned between $403 and $706. The lowest 10 percent earned less than $298 and the top 10 percent more than $852.

According to a Hay Group survey of acute care hospitals, the median annual base salary of full-time laboratory technicians was $26,500 in January 1997. The middle 50 percent earned between $23,700 and $29,500. Full-time salaried staff medical laboratory technologists earned about $35,100; the middle 50 percent earned between $32,500 and $37,900.

The average annual salary for medical technologists employed by the federal government was $40,680 in early 1997. Medical technicians earned an average of $26,130.

Related Occupations

Clinical laboratory technologists and technicians analyze body fluids, tissue, and other substances using a variety of tests. Similar or related procedures are performed by analytical, water purification, and other chemists; science technicians; crime laboratory analysts; food testers; and veterinary laboratory technicians.

Sources of Additional Information

Career and certification information is available from:
- ❑ American Society of Clinical Pathologists, Board of Registry, P.O. Box 12277, Chicago, IL 60612.
- ❑ American Medical Technologists, 710 Higgins Rd., Park Ridge, IL 60068.
- ❑ American Society of Cytopathology, 400 West 9th St., Suite 201, Wilmington, DE 19801.
- ❑ American Society for Clinical Laboratory Science, 7910 Woodmont Ave., Suite 530, Bethesda, MD 20814.
- ❑ International Society for Clinical Laboratory Technology, 917 Locust St., Suite 1100, St. Louis, MO 63101-1413.

For more career information, write to:
- ❑ American Association of Blood Banks, 8101 Glenbrook Rd., Bethesda, MD 20814-2749.

For a list of accredited and approved educational programs for clinical laboratory personnel, write to:
- ❑ National Accrediting Agency for Clinical Laboratory Sciences, 8410 W. Bryn Mawr Ave., Suite 670, Chicago, IL 60631.

For a list of training programs for medical and clinical laboratory technicians accredited by the Accrediting Bureau of Health Education Schools, write to:
- ❑ Secretary-ABHES, 2700 S. Quincy St., Suite 210, Arlington, VA 22206.

For information about a career as a medical and clinical laboratory technician and schools offering training, contact:
- ❑ National Association of Health Career Schools, 750 First St. NE., Suite 940, Washington, DC 20002. FAX: (202) 842-1565 E-mail: NAHCS@aol.com

Computer Programmers

(*D.O.T.* 030.162-010, -018, -022, and .167-010)

Significant Points

★ *The level of education and quality of training required by employers have been rising due to the increasing complexity of programming tasks.*

★ *A growing number of computer programmers are employed on a temporary or contract basis.*

Nature of the Work

Computer programmers write, test, and maintain the detailed instructions—called *programs* or *software*—that list in a logical order the steps computers must execute to perform their functions. Programmers often are categorized as technicians, distinct from the higher level of theoretical expertise characteristic of computer scientists, computer engineers, and systems analysts. However, many technical innovations in programming—advanced computing technologies and sophisticated new languages and programming tools—have redefined the role of a programmer and elevated much of the programming work done today. It is becoming much more difficult to distinguish different computer specialists—including programmers—since job titles shift so rapidly, reflecting new areas of specialization or changes in technology. Job titles and descriptions also may vary depending on the organization. In this statement, "computer programmer" refers to individuals whose main job function is programming; this group has a wide range of responsibilities and educational backgrounds.

Computer programs tell the computer what to do, such as which information to identify and access, how to process it, and what equipment to use. Programs vary widely depending upon the type of information to be accessed or generated. For example, the instructions involved in updating financial records are very different from those required to duplicate conditions on board an aircraft for pilots training in a flight simulator. Although simple programs can be written in a few hours, programs that use complex mathematical formulas, whose solutions can only be approximated, or that draw data from many existing systems require more than a year of work. In most cases, several programmers work together as a team under a senior programmer's supervision.

Programmers write specific programs by breaking down each step into a logical series of instructions the computer can follow. They then code these instructions in a conventional programming language, such as C and FORTRAN; an artificial intelligence language, such as LISP or Prolog; or one of the more advanced function-oriented or object-oriented languages, such as UML, Java, C++, Visual Basic, or Ada. Programmers usually know more than one programming language and since many languages are alike, they can often learn new languages relatively easily. In practice, programmers are often referred to by the language they know or the type of environment they generally work in such as mainframe programmer, object-oriented programmer, or Internet or World Wide Web programmer. In many large organizations, programmers follow descriptions that have been prepared by software engineers or systems analysts. These descriptions list the input required, the steps the computer must follow to process data, and the desired arrangement of the output.

Many programmers are involved in updating, repairing, modifying, and expanding existing programs. When making changes to a section of code, called a "routine," programmers need to make other users aware of the task the routine is to perform. They do this by inserting comments in the coded instructions so others can understand the program. Innovations such as Computer-Aided Software Engineering (CASE) tools enable a programmer to concentrate on writing the unique parts of the program because the tools automate various pieces of the program being built. CASE tools generate whole sections of code automatically, rather than line by line. This also yields more reliable and consistent programs and increases programmers' productivity by eliminating some of the routine steps.

Programmers test a program by running it to ensure the instructions are correct and it produces the desired information. If errors do occur, the programmer must make the appropriate change and recheck the program until it produces the correct results, a process called *debugging*. Programmers working in a mainframe environment may still prepare instructions for a computer operator who will run the program. They may also contribute to a user's manual for the program.

Programmers often are grouped into two broad types: applications programmers and systems programmers. Applications programmers usually are oriented toward business, engineering, or science. They write software to handle specific jobs within an organization, such as a program used in an inventory control system. They may also work alone to revise existing packaged software. Systems programmers, on the other hand, maintain and control the use of computer systems software. These workers make changes in the sets of instructions that determine how the network, workstations, and central processing unit of the system handle the various jobs they have been given and how they communicate with peripheral equipment, such as terminals, printers, and disk drives. Because of their knowledge of the entire computer system, systems programmers often help applications programmers determine the source of problems that may occur with their programs.

In some organizations, particularly smaller ones, workers more commonly referred to as programmer-analysts are responsible for both the systems analysis and the actual programming work. Advanced programming languages and new object-oriented programming capabilities are increasing the efficiency and productivity of both programmers and users. The transition from a mainframe environment to a primarily PC-based environment has blurred the once rigid distinction between the programmer and the user. Increasingly, adept users are taking over many of the tasks previously performed by programmers. For example, the growing use of packaged software, like spreadsheet and database management software packages, allows users to write simple programs to access data and perform calculations.

Programmers in software development companies may work directly with experts from various fields to create software—either programs designed for specific clients or packaged software for general use—ranging from games and educational software to programs for desktop publishing, financial planning, and spreadsheets. Much of this type of programming is in the preparation of packaged software, which comprises one of the most rapidly growing segments of the computer services industry.

Working Conditions

Programmers generally work in offices in comfortable surroundings. Although they usually work about 40 hours a week, programmers may work longer hours or weekends in order to meet deadlines or fix critical problems that occur during off hours. Given the technology available, telecommuting is becoming more common for a wider range of computer professionals—including computer programmers. Programmers can access a system directly, but from remote locations, to make corrections or fix problems.

Like other workers who spend long periods of time in front of a computer terminal typing at a keyboard, they are susceptible to eyestrain, back discomfort, and hand and wrist problems such as carpal tunnel syndrome or cumulative trauma disorder.

Employment

Computer programmers held about 568,000 jobs in 1996. Programmers are employed in almost every industry, but the largest concentration is in the computer and data processing services industry which includes firms that write and sell software. Large numbers of programmers can also be found working for firms that provide engineering and management services, manufacturers of computer and office equipment, financial institutions, insurance carriers, educational institutions, and government agencies.

A growing number of computer programmers are employed on a temporary or contract basis or work as independent consultants as companies demand expertise with newer programming languages or more specialized areas of application. Rather than hiring programmers as permanent employees and then laying them off after a job is completed, employers can contract with temporary help agencies, consulting firms, or directly with programmers themselves. A marketing firm, for example, may only require the services of several programmers to write and "debug" the software necessary to get a new database management system running. This practice also enables companies to bring in people with a specific set of skills, usually in one of the latest technologies as it applies to their business needs. Bringing in an independent contractor or consultant with a certain level of experience in a new or advanced programming language, for example, enables an establishment to complete a particular job without having to retrain existing workers. Such jobs may last anywhere from several weeks to a year or longer. There were 20,000 self-employed computer programmers in 1996 and this number is expected to increase.

Training, Other Qualifications, and Advancement

While there are many training paths available for programmers, mainly because employers' needs are so varied, the level of education and quality of training employers seek have been rising due to the growth in the number of qualified applicants and the increasing complexity of some programming tasks. Bachelor's degrees are now commonly required, although some programmers qualify with two-year degrees or certificates. College graduates who are interested in changing careers or developing an area of expertise also may return to a two-

year community college or technical school for additional training. In the absence of a degree, substantial specialized experience or expertise may be needed. Even with a degree, employers appear to be placing more emphasis on previous experience for all types of programmers.

The majority of computer programmers—almost 60 percent—had a bachelor's degree or higher in 1996 (see table 1). Of these, some hold a B.A. or B.S. in computer science, mathematics, or information systems, while others have taken special courses in computer programming to supplement their study in fields such as accounting, inventory control, or other business areas. As the level of education and training required by employers continues to rise, this percentage should increase in the future.

Table 1. Percent distribution of highest level of school completed or degree received, computer programmers, 1996

	Percentage
High school graduate or equivalent or less	10.0
Some college, no degree	20.9
Associate degree	9.6
Bachelor's degree	45.2
Graduate degree	14.2

Most systems programmers hold a four-year degree in computer science. Extensive knowledge of a variety of operating systems is essential. This includes being able to configure the operating system to work with different types of hardware, and adapting the operating system to best meet the needs of the particular organization. They must also be able to work with database systems such as DB2, Oracle, or Sybase, for example.

When hiring programmers, employers look for people with the necessary programming skills who can think logically and pay close attention to detail. The job calls for patience, persistence, and the ability to work on exacting analytical work, especially under pressure. Ingenuity and imagination are also particularly important when programmers design solutions and test their work for potential failures. The ability to work with abstract concepts and do technical analysis is especially important for systems programmers because they work with the software that controls the computer's operation. Since programmers are expected to work in teams and interact directly with users, employers want programmers who are able to communicate with non-technical personnel.

Beginning programmers may work alone on simple assignments after some initial instruction, or on a team with more experienced programmers. Either way, beginning programmers generally must work under close supervision.

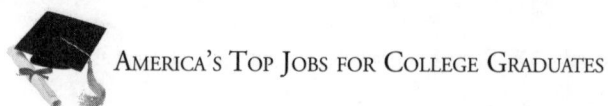

Because technology changes so rapidly, programmers must continuously update their training by taking courses sponsored by their employer or software vendors.

For skilled workers who keep up to date with the latest technology, the prospects for advancement are good. In large organizations, they may be promoted to lead programmer and be given supervisory responsibilities. Some applications programmers may move into systems programming after they gain experience and take courses in systems software. With general business experience, programmers may become programmer-analysts or systems analysts, or be promoted to a managerial position. Other programmers, with specialized knowledge and experience with a language or operating system, may work in research and development areas such as multimedia or Internet technology. As employers increasingly contract out programming jobs, more opportunities should arise for experienced programmers with expertise in a specific area to work as consultants.

Technical or professional certification is becoming more common as a way for employers to ensure a level of competency or quality in all areas. Many product vendors offer certification or may even require certification of technicians and professionals who work with their products. The number of voluntary certificate or certification programs is also growing and this type of certification is available through organizations such as the Institute for Certification of Computing Professionals (ICCP). ICCP confers the designation Certified Computing Professional (CCP) to those who have at least four years of experience or two years of experience and a college degree. To qualify, individuals must pass a core examination plus exams in two specialty areas, or an exam in one specialty area and two computing languages. Those with little or no experience may be tested for certification as an Associate Computer Professional (ACP). Certification is not mandatory, but it may give a job-seeker a competitive advantage.

Job Outlook

Employment of programmers is expected to grow faster than the average through the year 2006. Jobs for both systems and applications programmers should remain plentiful in data processing service firms, software houses, and computer consulting businesses. These types of establishments are part of one of the fastest growing industries—computer and data processing services, which is projected to be the fastest growing industry. As companies attempt to control costs and keep up with changing technology, they will maintain a need for programmers to assist in conversions to new languages and from one system to the next. In addition, a majority of the

job openings for programmers will still result from the need to replace programmers who move to other occupations or leave the labor force. Most programmers who leave transfer to other occupations, such as manager or systems analyst.

Despite numerous openings, however, the consolidation and centralization of systems and applications should continue to moderate growth, as will developments in packaged software, advanced programming languages and tools, and the growing ability of users to design, write, and implement more of their own programs to meet their changing needs. As the level of technological innovation and sophistication increases, programmers should continue to face increasing competition from programming businesses overseas where more of the routine work can be outsourced at a lower cost.

As programming tasks become more complex and increasingly sophisticated skills and experience are demanded by employers, graduates of two-year programs, and people with less than a two-year degree or its equivalent in work experience, should face stronger competition for programming jobs. Competition for entry-level positions, however, can even affect applicants with a bachelor's degree. Although demand fluctuates as employers' needs change with technology, prospects should be best for college graduates with knowledge of and experience working with a variety of programming languages and tools, particularly C++ and other object-oriented languages—such as Smalltalk, Visual Basic, Ada, and Java—as well as newer, domain-specific languages that apply to computer networking, database management, and Internet applications. In order to remain competitive, college graduates should keep up to date with the latest skills and technologies.

Many employers prefer to hire applicants with previous experience in the field. Employers are increasingly interested in programmers who can combine areas of technical expertise or who are adaptable and able to learn and incorporate new skills. Therefore, individuals who want to become programmers can enhance their chances of doing so by combining the appropriate formal training with practical work experience. Students should try to gain experience by participating in a college work-study program, or undertaking an internship. Students also can greatly improve their employment prospects by taking courses such as accounting, management, engineering, or science—allied fields in which applications programmers are in demand.

With the expansion of client/server environments, employers will continue to look for programmers with strong technical skills who understand their business and its programming needs. Businesses also look for programmers who develop a technical specialization in areas such as client/server

programming, multimedia technology, graphic user interface (GUI), and fourth- and fifth-generation programming tools. Programmers will be creating and maintaining expert systems and embedding these technologies in more and more products. Other areas of progress include data communications and the business application of Internet technologies. Networking computers so they can communicate with each other is necessary to achieve the greater efficiency organizations require to remain competitive. Demand for programmers with strong object-oriented programming capabilities and experience should arise from the expansion of Intranets, extranets, and World Wide Web applications.

Earnings

Median earnings of programmers who worked full-time in 1996 were about $40,100 a year. The middle 50 percent earned between $30,700 and $52,000 a year. The lowest 10 percent earned less than $22,700; the highest 10 percent earned more than $65,200. Starting salary offers for graduates with a bachelor's degree in the area of computer programming averaged about $35,167 a year in private industry in 1997, according to the National Association of Colleges and Employers. Programmers working in the West and Northeast earned somewhat more than those working in the South and Midwest. On average, systems programmers earn more than applications programmers.

A survey of workplaces in 160 metropolitan areas reported that beginning programmers had median annual earnings of about $27,000 in 1995. Experienced mid-level programmers with some supervisory responsibilities had median annual earnings of about $40,000. Median annual earnings for programmers at the supervisory or team leader level were about $55,000.

According to Robert Half International, Inc., starting salaries ranged from $32,500 to $39,000 for programmers and $47,500 to $60,000 for systems programmers in large establishments in 1997. Starting salaries for programmers in small establishments ranged from $28,000 to $37,000.

In the federal government, the entrance salary for programmers with a college degree or qualifying experience was about $19,520 a year in early 1997; for those with a superior academic record, $24,180.

Related Occupations

Programmers must pay great attention to detail as they write and debug programs. Other professional workers who must be detail-oriented include computer scientists, computer engineers, and systems analysts, statisticians, mathematicians, engineers, financial analysts, accountants, auditors, actuaries, and operations research analysts.

Sources of Additional Information

State employment service offices can provide information about job openings for computer programmers. Also check with your city's chamber of commerce for information on the area's largest employers.

For information about certification as a computing professional, contact:

❏ Institute for Certification of Computing Professionals (ICCP), 2200 East Devon Ave., Suite 268, Des Plaines, IL 60018. Homepage: http://www.iccp.org

Further information about computer careers is available from:

The Association for Computing (ACM), 1515 Broadway, New York, NY 10036.

❏ IEEE Computer Society, Headquarters Office, 1730 Massachusetts Ave., NW, Washington, DC 20036-1992.

Computer Scientists, Computer Engineers, and Systems Analysts

(D.O.T. 030.062-010, .162-014, .167-014; 031; 032; 033; 039; and 109.067-010)

Significant Points

✴ *Expected to be the top three fastest growing occupations and among the top twenty in the number of new jobs as computer applications continue to expand throughout the economy.*

✴ *A bachelor's degree is virtually a prerequisite for most employers. Relevant work experience also is very important. For some of the more complex jobs, persons with graduate degrees are preferred.*

Nature of the Work

The rapid spread of computers has generated a need for highly trained workers to design and develop new hardware and software systems and to incorporate technological advances into new or existing systems. The *OOH* refers to this group of professionals as computer scientists, computer engineers, and systems analysts, but in reality this group includes a wide range of professional computer-related occupations. Job titles used to describe this broad category of workers evolve rapidly, reflecting new areas of specialization or changes in technology as well as the preferences and practices of employers. Although many narrow specializations exist, the professional specialty group is commonly referred to as computer scientists, computer engineers, and systems analysts.

The title computer scientist can be applied to a wide range of computer professionals who generally design computers and the software that runs them, develop information technologies, and develop and adapt principles for applying computers to new uses. Computer scientists perform many of the same duties as other computer professionals throughout a normal workday, but their jobs are distinguished by the higher level of theoretical expertise and innovation they apply to complex problems and the creation or application of new technology.

Computer scientists can work as theorists, researchers, or inventors. Those employed by academic institutions work in areas ranging from complexity theory, to hardware, to programming language design. Some work on multi-discipline projects, such as developing and advancing uses of virtual reality in robotics. Their counterparts in private industry work in areas such as applying theory, developing specialized languages or information technologies, or designing programming tools, knowledge-based systems, or even computer games.

Computer engineers also work with the hardware and software aspects of systems design and development. Whereas computer scientists emphasize the application of theory, computer engineers emphasize the building of prototypes, although there is much crossover. Computer engineers generally apply the theories and principles of science and mathematics to the design of hardware, software, networks, and processes to solve technical problems. They often work as part of a team that designs new computing devices or computer-related equipment, systems, or software. Computer hardware engineers generally design, develop, test, and supervise the manufacture of computer hardware—for example, chips or device controllers. Software engineers, on the other hand, are involved in the design and development of software systems for control and automation of manufacturing, business, and management processes. Software engineers or software developers also may design and develop both packaged and systems software or be involved in creating custom software applications for clients. These professionals also possess strong programming skills, but they are more concerned with analyzing and solving programming problems than with simply writing the code for the programs.

Far more numerous, systems analysts use their knowledge and skills to solve computer problems and enable computer technology to meet the individual needs of an organization. They study business, scientific, or engineering data processing problems and design new solutions using computers. This process may include planning and developing new computer systems or devising ways to apply existing systems' resources to additional operations. Systems analysts may design entirely new systems, including both hardware and software, or add a single new software application to harness more of the computer's power. They work to help an organization realize the maximum benefit from its investment in equipment, personnel, and business processes. Most systems analysts generally work with a specific type of system depending on the type of organization they work for—for example, business, accounting or financial systems, or scientific and engineering systems. Companies generally seek business systems analysts who specialize in the type of systems they use.

Analysts begin an assignment by discussing the systems problem with managers and users to determine its exact nature. Much time is devoted to clearly defining the goals of the system and understanding the individual steps used to achieve them so that the problem can be broken down into separate programmable procedures. Analysts then use techniques such as structured analysis, data modeling, information engineering, mathematical model building, sampling, and cost accounting to plan the system. Analysts must specify the inputs to be accessed by the system, design the processing steps, and format the output to meet the users' needs. Once the design has been developed, systems analysts prepare charts and diagrams that describe it in terms that managers and other users can understand. They may prepare cost-benefit and return-on-investment analyses to help management decide whether implementing the proposed system will be financially feasible.

When a system is accepted, analysts determine what computer hardware and software will be needed to set it up. They coordinate tests and observe initial use of the system to ensure it performs as planned. They prepare specifications, work diagrams, and structure charts for computer programmers to follow and then work with them to "debug," or eliminate errors from the system.

In some organizations a single worker called a programmer-analyst is responsible for both systems analysis and programming. As this becomes more commonplace, these analysts will increasingly work with Computer Aided Software Engineering (CASE) tools and object-oriented programming languages, as well as client/server applications development, and multimedia and Internet technology.

One obstacle associated with expanding computer use is the inability of different computer systems to communicate with each other. Because maintaining up-to-date information—accounting records, sales figures, or budget projections, for example—is important in modern organizations, systems analysts may be instructed to make the computer systems in

each department compatible so that information can be shared. Many systems analysts are involved with "networking" or connecting all the computers in an individual office, department, or establishment. A primary goal of networking is to allow users to retrieve data from a mainframe computer or a server and use it on their machine. This connection also allows data to be entered into the mainframe from a personal computer. Analysts must design the hardware and software to allow free exchange of data, custom applications, and the computer power to process it all. They study the seemingly incompatible pieces and create ways to link them so users can access information from any part of the system. Networks come in many variations and network systems and data communications analysts design, test, and evaluate systems such as Local Area Networks (LAN), Wide Area Networks (WAN), Internet, and Intranet and other data communications systems. These analysts perform network modeling, analysis and planning, and even research and recommend necessary hardware and software.

Other computer professionals include database administrators and computer support specialists. Database administrators work with database management systems software, coordinating changes to, testing, and implementing computer databases. Since they also may be responsible for design implementation and system security, database administrators plan and coordinate security measures. Computer support specialists provide assistance and advice to users. They interpret problems and provide technical support for hardware, software, and systems. Support specialists may work within an organization or directly for a computer or software vendor. Increasingly, these technical professionals work for help-desk or support services firms, providing customer support on a contract basis to clients as more of this type of work is outsourced.

Many others specialize in analysis, application, or design of a particular system or piece of the system. Network or systems administrators, for example, may install, configure, and support an organization's systems or portion of a system. Telecommunications specialists generally are involved with the interfacing of computer and communications equipment. Computer security specialists are responsible for planning, coordinating, and implementing an organization's information security measures. These and other growing specialty occupations reflect the increasing emphasis on client/server applications, the growth of the Internet, the expansion of World Wide Web applications and Intranets, and the demand for more end-user support. An example of this is the growing number of job titles relating to the Internet and World Wide Web such as Internet and Web developers, or Webmasters.

Working Conditions

Computer scientists, computer engineers, and systems analysts normally work in offices or laboratories in comfortable surroundings. They usually work about 40 hours a week—the same as many other professional or office workers. However, evening or weekend work may be necessary to meet deadlines or solve specific problems. Given the technology available today, telecommuting is becoming more common for computer professionals. More work, including technical support, can be done from remote locations using modems, laptops, electronic mail, and even through the Internet. It is now possible for technical personnel, such as computer support specialists, to tap into a customer's computer remotely to identify and fix problems.

Like other workers who spend long periods of time in front of a computer terminal typing on a keyboard, computer scientists, engineers, and systems analysts are susceptible to eye strain, back discomfort, and hand and wrist problems such as carpal tunnel syndrome or cumulative trauma disorder.

Employment

Computer scientists, computer engineers, and systems analysts held about 933,000 jobs in 1996, including about 58,000 who were self-employed. About 216,000 were computer engineers, about 506,000 were computer systems analysts, and about 212,000 were database administrators, computer support specialists, and all other computer scientists.

Although they are employed in most industries, the greatest concentration is in the computer and data processing services industry. This industry includes firms providing nearly every service related to commercial computer use on a contract basis. Services include customized computer programming services and applications and systems software design; the design, development, and production of prepackaged computer software; systems integration, networking, and reengineering services; data processing and preparation services; information retrieval services including on-line databases and Internet services; on-site computer facilities management; the development and management of databases; and a variety of specialized consulting services. Many others work for government agencies, manufacturers of computer and related electronic equipment, insurance companies, financial institutions, and universities.

A growing number of computer professionals are employed on a temporary or contract basis—many of whom are self-employed, working independently as contractors or self-employed consultants. For example, a company installing a new computer system may need the services of several systems analysts just to get the system running. Because not all of them would be needed once the system is functioning, the company might contract directly with the systems analysts themselves or with a temporary help agency or consulting firm. Such jobs may last from several months up to two years or more. This growing practice enables companies to bring in people with the exact skills they need to complete a particular project, rather than having to spend time or money training or retraining existing workers. Often, experienced consultants then train a company's in-house staff as a project develops.

Training, Other Qualifications, and Advancement

While there is no universally accepted way to prepare for a job as a computer professional because employers' preferences depend on the work to be done, a bachelor's degree is virtually a prerequisite for most employers. Relevant work experience also is very important. For some of the more complex jobs, persons with graduate degrees are preferred.

Computer hardware engineers generally require a bachelor's degree in computer engineering or electrical engineering, whereas software engineers are more likely to need a degree in computer science. For systems analyst or even database administrator positions, many employers seek applicants who have a bachelor's degree in computer science, information science, computer information systems, or data processing. Computer support specialists may also need a bachelor's degree in a computer-related field, as well as significant experience working with computers, including programming skills. Generally, a Ph.D., or at least a master's degree in computer science or engineering, is required for computer scientist jobs in research laboratories or academic institutions.

Many people develop advanced computer skills in other occupations in which they work extensively with computers, and then transfer into computer occupations. For example, an accountant may become a systems analyst or computer support specialist specializing in accounting systems development, or an individual may move into a systems analyst job after working as a computer programmer.

Regardless of college major, employers generally look for people who are familiar with programming languages and have broad knowledge of and experience with computer systems and technologies, strong problem-solving and analysis skills, and good interpersonal skills. Courses in computer programming or systems design offer good preparation for a job in this field. For jobs in a business environment, employers usually want systems analysts to have a background in business management or a closely related field, while a background in the physical sciences, applied mathematics, or engineering is preferred for work in scientifically oriented organizations. Since employers generally look for experience, entry-level employees enhance their employment opportunities by participating in internship or co-op programs offered through their schools. A related background in the industry in which the job is located, such as financial services, banking, or accounting, can also give an applicant an edge.

Computer scientists, computer engineers, and systems analysts must be able to think logically and have good communication skills. They often deal with a number of tasks simultaneously; the ability to concentrate and pay close attention to detail is important. Although many computer specialists sometimes work independently, they often work in teams on large projects. They must be able to communicate effectively with computer personnel, such as programmers and managers, as well as with users or other staff who may have no technical computer background.

Systems analysts may be promoted to senior or lead systems analysts with experience. Those who show leadership ability also can advance to management positions, such as manager of information systems or chief information officer.

Computer engineers and scientists employed in industry may eventually advance into managerial or project leadership positions. Those employed in academic institutions can become heads of research departments or published authorities in their field. Computer professionals with several years of experience and considerable expertise in a particular subject area or application may find lucrative opportunities as independent consultants or choose to start their own computer consulting firms.

Technological advances come so rapidly in the computer field that continuous study is necessary to keep skills up to date. Continuing education is usually offered by employers, hardware and software vendors, colleges and universities, or private training institutions. Additional training may come from professional development seminars offered by professional computing societies.

As technology becomes more sophisticated and complex, a higher level of skill and expertise is demanded by employers in all areas. Technical or professional certification is becoming a more common way to ensure employers of a level of competency or quality in a prospective employee. Many product vendors offer and may even require professionals who work with their products to be certified. Voluntary certification is also available through organizations such as the Institute for Certification of Computing Professionals (ICCP). ICCP offers the designation Certified Computing Professional (CCP) to those who have at least four years of work experience as a

computer professional, or at least two years experience and a college degree. Candidates must pass a core examination testing general knowledge, plus exams in two specialty areas, or in one specialty area and two computer programming languages. The Quality Assurance Institute (QAI) awards the designation Certified Quality Analyst (CQA) to those who meet education and experience requirements, pass an exam, and endorse a code of ethics. Neither designation is mandatory, but professional certification may provide a job seeker a competitive advantage.

Job Outlook

Computer scientists, computer engineers, and systems analysts are expected to be the three fastest growing occupations through the year 2006. Employment of computing professionals is expected to increase much faster than average as technology becomes more sophisticated and organizations continue to adopt and integrate these technologies, making for plentiful job openings. Growth will be driven by very rapid growth in the computer and data processing services industry, which is projected to be the fastest growing industry. In addition, thousands of job openings will result annually from the need to replace workers who move into managerial positions or other occupations or who leave the labor force.

Nevertheless, computer scientists, computer engineers, and systems analysts will need to continually upgrade their technical expertise and improve their ability to interact with users as the sophistication and complexity of technology advances. As more computing power is made available to the individual user and users develop more sophisticated knowledge of computers, they become more aware of the machine's potential and better able to suggest how computers could be used to increase their own productivity and that of the organization. Increasingly, users are able to design and implement more of their own applications and programs. The result is a growing demand for computer support specialists, help desk personnel, and technical consultants.

The demand for *networking* to facilitate the sharing of information, the expansion of client/server environments, and the need for specialists to use their knowledge and skills in a problem-solving capacity will be a major factor in the rising demand for systems analysts. Falling prices of computer hardware and software should continue to induce more businesses to expand computerized operations and integrate new technologies. In order to maintain a competitive edge and operate more cost effectively, firms will continue to demand computer professionals who are knowledgeable about the latest technologies and able to apply them to meet the needs of businesses.

New growth areas generally arise from the development of new technologies. Therefore, it is important for computer professionals at all levels to keep their skills up to date. The expanding integration of Internet technologies by businesses, for example, has resulted in a rising demand for a variety of skilled professionals who can develop and support Internet, Intranet, and World Wide Web applications. Growth in these areas is also expected to create demand for computer scientists, computer engineers, and systems analysts knowledgeable about network, data, and communications security.

Since employers look for the most qualified applicants possessing a high level of technical expertise, individuals with an advanced degree in computer science, management information systems (MIS), computer engineering, or an MBA with a concentration in information systems should enjoy very favorable employment prospects. College graduates with a bachelor's degree in computer science, computer engineering, information science, or information systems should also enjoy favorable prospects, very particularly if they have supplemented their formal education with some level of practical experience. College graduates with non-computer science majors who have had courses in computer programming, systems analysis, and other data processing areas, as well as training or experience in an applied field, should also be able to find jobs as computer professionals. Those who are familiar with client/server environments, CASE tools and object-oriented programming, Internet, Intranet, and multimedia technology will have an even greater advantage, as will individuals with significant networking, database, and systems experience. Employers will continue to seek computer professionals who can combine strong programming and traditional systems analysis skills with good interpersonal and business skills.

Earnings

Median annual earnings of computer systems analysts and scientists who worked full-time in 1996 were about $46,300. The middle 50 percent earned between $34,000 and $59,900. The lowest 10 percent earned less than $24,800 and the highest tenth, more than $76,200. Computer scientists with advanced degrees generally earn more than systems analysts.

Starting salaries for computer scientists or computer engineers with a bachelor's degree can be significantly higher than starting salaries of bachelor's degree graduates in many other fields. According to the National Association of Colleges and Employers, starting salary offers for graduates with a bachelor's degree in computer engineering averaged about $39,722 a year in 1997; those with a master's degree, $44,734 a year; and those with a Ph.D., $63,367. Starting offers for

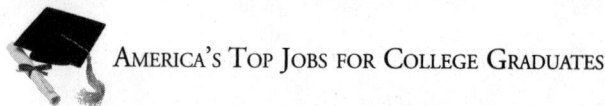
graduates with a bachelor's degree in computer science averaged about $36,597 a year; in information sciences, about $35,407 a year; and in systems analysis, about $43,800 a year in 1997. Offers for those with the bachelor's degree vary by functional area for all types of employers, as shown in the following tabulation.

Computer programming	$35,167
Information systems	34,689
Systems analysis and design	36,261
Software design and development	39,190
Hardware design and development	41,237

Offers for graduates with a master's degree in computer science in 1997 averaged $45,853 a year; and those with a Ph.D. in computer and information sciences, $61,306.

According to Robert Half International, Inc., starting salaries in 1997 for systems analysts employed by large establishments employing more than 50 staff members ranged from $46,000 to $57,500. Salaries for those employed in small establishments ranged from $38,000 to $48,000. Salaries for programmer-analysts ranged from $39,000 to $50,000 in large establishments and $33,500 to $43,000 in small establishments. Starting salaries ranged from $54,000 to $67,500 for database administrators, from $36,000 to $55,000 for network administrators, from $25,000 to $36,500 for help desk support technicians, and from $49,000 to $67,500 for software development specialists.

In the federal government, the entrance salary for systems analysts who are recent college graduates with a bachelor's degree was about $19,520 a year in early 1997; for those with a superior academic record, $24,180. The average annual salary for computer engineers employed by the federal government in nonsupervisory, supervisory, and managerial positions was $62,900 in early 1997.

Related Occupations

Other workers who use research, logic, and creativity to solve business problems are computer programmers, financial analysts, urban planners, engineers, mathematicians, statisticians, operations research analysts, management analysts, and actuaries.

Sources of Additional Information

Further information about computer careers is available from:

❑ Association for Computing (ACM), 1515 Broadway, New York, NY 10036.

❑ IEEE Computer Society, Headquarters Office, 1730 Massachusetts Ave., NW, Washington, DC 20036-1992.

Information about the designation Certified Computing Professional is available from:

❑ Institute for Certification of Computing Professionals (ICCP), 2200 East Devon Ave., Suite 268, Des Plaines, IL 60018. Homepage: http://www.iccp.org

Information about the designation Certified Quality Analyst is available from:

❑ Quality Assurance Institute, 7575 Dr. Phillips Blvd., Suite 350, Orlando, FL 32819.

Construction Managers

(D.O.T. 182.167-010, -018, -026, -030, and -034)

Significant Points

* Construction managers make decisions regarding daily construction activities at the job site.

* Good employment opportunities are expected because the increasing complexity of construction projects should increase demand for management-level personnel.

* More and more employers—particularly, large construction firms—seek to hire individuals who combine industry work experience with a bachelor's degree in construction or building science or construction management.

Nature of the Work

Construction managers plan and direct construction projects. They may hold a variety of job titles, such as construction superintendent, general superintendent, project engineer, project manager, general construction manager, or executive construction manager. Construction managers may be owners or salaried employees of a construction management or contracting firm, or may work under contract or as a salaried employee of the owner, developer, contractor, or management firm overseeing the construction project. The OOH uses the term "construction manager" to describe all salaried or self-employed managers of construction who oversee construction supervisors and workers.

In contrast with the OOH definition, the term "construction manager" is used more narrowly within the construction industry to denote a management firm, or an individual employed by such a firm, involved in management oversight of a construction project. Under this narrower definition, construction managers generally act as representatives of the owner or developer with other participants throughout the life of a project. Although they generally play no direct role in the

actual construction of a structure, they typically schedule and coordinate all design and construction processes including the selection, hiring, and oversight of specialty subcontractors.

Managers and other professionals who work in the construction industry, such as general managers, project engineers, cost estimators, and others, are increasingly referred to as constructors. This term refers to a broad group of professionals in construction who, through education and experience, are capable of managing, coordinating, and supervising the construction process from conceptual development through final construction on a timely and economical basis. Given designs for buildings, roads, bridges, or other projects, constructors oversee the organization, scheduling, and implementation of the project to execute those designs. They are responsible for coordinating and managing people, materials, and equipment; budgets, schedules, and contracts; and the safety of employees and the general public.

On large projects, construction managers may work for a general contractor—the firm with overall responsibility for all activities. There they oversee the completion of all construction in accordance with the engineer or architect's drawings and specifications and prevailing building codes. They arrange for subcontractors to perform specialized craft work or other specified construction work. On small projects, such as remodeling a home, a self-employed construction manager or skilled trades worker who directs and oversees employees is often referred to as the construction "contractor."

Large construction projects, such as an office building or industrial complex, are too complicated for one person to manage. These projects are divided into many segments: site preparation, including land clearing and earth moving; sewage systems; landscaping and road construction; building construction, including excavation and laying foundations, erection of structural framework, floors, walls, and roofs; and building systems, including fire protection, electrical, plumbing, air-conditioning, and heating. Construction managers may work as part of a team or be in charge of one or more of these activities.

Construction managers evaluate various construction methods and determine the most cost-effective plan and schedule. They determine the appropriate construction methods and schedule all required construction site activities into logical, specific steps, budgeting the time required to meet established deadlines. This may require sophisticated estimating and scheduling techniques, and use of computers with specialized software. This also involves the selection and coordination of subcontractors hired to complete specific pieces of the project—which could include everything from structural metalworking and plumbing, to painting and carpet installation. Construction managers determine the labor requirements and, in some cases, supervise or monitor the hiring and dismissal of workers. They oversee the performance of all trade contractors and are responsible for ensuring all work is completed on schedule.

Managers direct and monitor the progress of construction activities, at times through other construction supervisors. This includes the delivery and use of materials, tools, and equipment; the quality of construction, worker productivity, and safety. They are responsible for obtaining all necessary permits and licenses and, depending upon the contractual arrangements, direct or monitor compliance with building and safety codes and other regulations. They may have several subordinates, such as assistant managers or superintendents, field engineers, or crew supervisors, reporting to them.

Construction managers regularly review engineering and architectural drawings and specifications to monitor progress and ensure compliance with plans and specifications. They track and control construction costs to avoid cost overruns. Based upon direct observation and reports by subordinate supervisors, managers may prepare daily reports of progress and requirements for labor, material, and machinery and equipment at the construction site. They meet regularly with owners, subcontractors, architects, and other design professionals to monitor and coordinate all phases of the construction project.

Working Conditions

Construction managers work out of a main office from which the overall construction project is monitored or out of a field office at the construction site. Management decisions regarding daily construction activities are usually made at the job site. Managers usually travel when the construction site is in another state or when they are responsible for activities at two or more sites. Management of overseas construction projects usually entails temporary residence in another country.

Construction managers must be on call to deal with delays, bad weather, or emergencies at the site. Most work more than a standard 40-hour week because construction may proceed around-the-clock. This type of work schedule can go on for days, even weeks, to meet special project deadlines, especially if there are delays.

Although the work generally is not considered dangerous, construction managers must be careful while touring construction sites. Managers must be able to establish priorities and assign duties. They need to observe job conditions and to be alert to changes and potential problems, particularly involving safety on the job site and adherence to regulations.

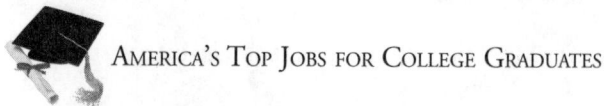

Employment

Construction managers held about 249,000 jobs in 1996. Around 40,000 were self-employed. Over 85 percent were employed in the construction industry, primarily by specialty trade contractors—for example, plumbing, heating and air-conditioning, and electrical contractors—and general building contractors. Others were employed by engineering, architectural, surveying, and construction management services firms, as well as local governments, educational institutions, and real estate developers.

Training, Other Qualifications, and Advancement

Persons interested in becoming a construction manager need a solid background in building science, business, and management, as well as related work experience within the construction industry. They need to be able to understand contracts, plans, and specifications, and to be knowledgeable about construction methods, materials, and regulations. Familiarity with computers and software programs for job costing, scheduling, and estimating is increasingly important.

Traditionally, persons advanced to construction management positions after having substantial experience as construction craft workers—for example, as carpenters, masons, plumbers, or electricians—or after having worked as construction supervisors or as owners of independent specialty contracting firms overseeing workers in one or more construction trades. However, more and more employers—particularly, large construction firms—seek to hire individuals who combine industry work experience with a bachelor's degree in construction or building science or construction management.

Construction managers should be adaptable and be able to work effectively in a fast-paced environment. They should be decisive and able to work well under pressure, particularly when faced with unexpected occurrences or delays. The ability to coordinate several major activities at once, while analyzing and resolving specific problems, is essential, as is understanding engineering, architectural, and other construction drawings. Good oral and written communication skills are also important. Managers must be able to establish a good working relationship with many different people including owners, other managers, design professionals, supervisors, and craft workers.

Advancement opportunities for construction managers vary depending upon the size and type of company for which they work. Within large firms, managers may eventually become top-level managers or executives. Highly experienced individuals may become independent consultants; some serve as expert witnesses in court or as arbitrators in disputes. Those

with the required capital may establish their own construction management services or general contracting firm.

In 1996, over 100 colleges and universities offered four-year degree programs in construction management or construction science. These programs include courses in project control and development, site planning, design, construction methods, construction materials, value analysis, cost estimating, scheduling, contract administration, accounting, business and financial management, building codes and standards, inspection procedures, engineering and architectural sciences, mathematics, statistics, and information technology. Graduates from four-year degree programs are usually hired as assistants to project managers, field engineers, schedulers, or cost estimators. An increasing number of graduates in related fields—engineering or architecture, for example—also enter construction management, often after having had substantial experience on construction projects or after completing graduate studies in construction management or building science.

Around 30 colleges and universities offer a master's degree program in construction management or construction science, and at least two offer a Ph.D. in the field. Master's degree recipients, especially those with work experience in construction, typically become construction managers in very large construction or construction management companies. Often, individuals who hold a bachelor's degree in an unrelated field seek a master's degree in order to work in the construction industry. Doctoral degree recipients generally become college professors or work in an area of research.

Many individuals also attend training and educational programs sponsored by industry associations, often in collaboration with postsecondary institutions. A number of two-year colleges throughout the country offer construction management or construction technology programs.

Both the American Institute of Constructors (AIC) and the Construction Management Association of America (CMA) have established voluntary certification programs for construction professionals. Both programs' requirements combine written examinations with verification of professional experience. AIC awards the designations Associate Constructor (AC) and Certified Professional Constructor (CPC) to candidates who meet the requirements and pass appropriate construction examinations. CMA awards the designation Certified Construction Manager (CCM) to practitioners who meet the requirements, complete a professional construction management "capstone" course, and pass a technical examination. Although certification is not required to work in the construction industry, voluntary certification can be valuable because it provides evidence of competence and experience.

Job Outlook

Employment of construction managers is expected to increase as fast as the average for all occupations through the year 2006, as the level of construction activity and complexity of construction projects continues to grow. Prospects in construction management, engineering and architectural services, and construction contracting firms should be particularly favorable for persons with a bachelor's degree or higher in construction science, construction management, or construction engineering who have worked in construction. Employers prefer applicants with previous construction work experience who can combine a strong background in building technology with proven supervisory or managerial skills. In addition, many job openings should result annually from the need to replace workers who transfer to other occupations or leave the labor force.

The increasing complexity of construction projects should increase demand for management level personnel within the construction industry, as sophisticated technology and the proliferation of laws setting standards for buildings and construction materials, worker safety, energy efficiency, and environmental protection have further complicated the construction process. Advances in building materials and construction methods and the growing number of multipurpose buildings, electronically operated "smart" buildings, and energy-efficient structures will further add to the demand for more construction managers. However, employment of construction managers can be sensitive to the short-term nature of many construction projects and cyclical fluctuations in construction activity.

Earnings

Earnings of salaried construction managers and incomes of self-employed independent construction contractors vary depending upon the size and nature of the construction project, its geographic location, and economic conditions. According to a 1997 salary survey by the National Association of Colleges and Employers, bachelor's degree candidates with degrees in the field of construction management received offers averaging $28,060 a year. Bachelor's degree candidates with degrees in the field of construction science received offers averaging $31,949 a year. Based on the limited information available, the average salary for experienced construction managers in 1996 ranged from around $40,000 to $100,000 annually. Many salaried construction managers receive benefits such as bonuses, use of company motor vehicles, paid vacations, and life and health insurance.

Related Occupations

Construction managers participate in the conceptual development of a construction project and oversee its organization, scheduling, and implementation. Occupations in which similar functions are performed include architects, civil engineers, construction supervisors, cost engineers, cost estimators, developers, electrical engineers, industrial engineers, landscape architects, and mechanical engineers.

Sources of Additional Information

For information about career opportunities in the construction industry, contact:

❏ Associated Builders and Contractors, 1300 North 17th St., Rosslyn, VA 22209. Homepage: http://www.abc.org

❏ Associated General Contractors of America, 1957 E St. NW, Washington, DC 20006-5199. Homepage: http://www.agc.org

For information about constructor certification and professional career opportunities in the construction industry, contact:

❏ American Institute of Constructors, 466 94th Ave. North, St. Petersburg, FL 33702. E-mail address: aicnatl@aol.com Homepage: http://www.aicnet.org

For information about construction management and construction manager certification, contact:

❏ Construction Management Association of America, 7918 Jones Branch Dr., Suite 540, McLean, VA 22102. Homepage: http://www.access.digex.net/~cmaa

Information on accredited construction science and management programs and accreditation requirements is available from:

❏ American Council for Construction Education, 1300 Hudson Lane, Suite 3, Monroe, LA 71201-6054. E-mail address: acce@iamerica.net

Designers

(*D.O.T.* 141.051, .061, .067; 142 except .061-030, -054)

Significant Points

✴ *Nearly 40 percent are self-employed, almost five times the proportion in all professional occupations.*

✴ *Creativity is crucial in all design occupations; formal education requirements range from a high school diploma for floral designers to a bachelor's degree for industrial designers.*

✴ *Despite projected faster than average employment growth, keen competition is expected for most jobs because many talented individuals are attracted to careers as designers.*

Nature of the Work

Designers organize and design articles, products, and materials so they serve the purpose for which they were intended and are visually pleasing. Pleasant surroundings, beautiful clothes, and floral arrangements can boost our spirits, and products and packaging that are eye-catching are more likely to attract buyers than those that are not.

Many designers specialize in a particular area of design, such as automobiles, clothing, furniture, home appliances, industrial equipment, interiors of homes and office buildings, exhibits, movie and theater sets, packaging, or floral arrangements. Others work in more than one design field. The first step in developing a new design or altering an existing one is to determine the needs of the client. The designer then considers various factors, including the size, shape, weight, and color of the product; materials used; and the product functions. The ease of use, safety, and cost of the design are additional factors. Designers offer suggestions to their clients; some ideas are more practical, while others are more aesthetically appealing. The designers develop by hand, or with the aid of a computer, sketches of several design concepts they present for final selection to a client, an art or design director, a product development team, or producer of a play, film, or television production. The designer then makes a model, a prototype, or detailed plans drawn to scale. Designers in some specialties increasingly use computer-aided design (CAD) tools to create and better visualize a final product. Computers greatly reduce the cost and time necessary to create a model or prototype, which gives a real idea of what the product will look like. Industrial designers use computer-aided industrial design (CAID) to create designs and to communicate them to automated production tools.

Designers may supervise assistants who carry out their designs. Those who run their own businesses may also devote a considerable amount of time to developing new business contacts and to administrative tasks, such as reviewing catalogs and ordering samples.

Design encompasses a number of different fields. Industrial designers develop and design countless manufactured products including cars, home appliances, children's toys, computer equipment, and medical, office, or recreational equipment. They combine artistic talent with research on product use, marketing, materials, and production methods to create the most functional and appealing design and to make the product competitive with others in the marketplace.

Furniture designers design furniture for manufacture, according to knowledge of design trends, competitors' products, production costs, capability of production facilities, and characteristics of a company's market. They may also prepare detailed drawings of fixtures, forms, or tools required to be used in production of furniture, along with designing custom pieces or styles according to a specific period or country. They must be strongly involved with the fashion industry and aware of current trends and styles.

Interior designers plan the space and furnish the interiors of private homes, public buildings, and commercial establishments, such as offices, restaurants, hospitals, hotels, and theaters. They also may plan additions and renovations. With a client's tastes, needs, and budget in mind, they develop designs and prepare working drawings and specifications for interior construction, furnishings, lighting, and finishes. Increasingly, designers use computers to plan layouts that can be changed easily to include ideas received from the client. They also design lighting and architectural details such as crown molding, coordinate colors, and select furniture, floor coverings, and curtains. Interior designers must design space in accordance with federal, state, and local laws, including building codes. Increasingly, they plan spaces that meet accessibility standards for the disabled and elderly.

Set designers design movie, television, and theater sets. They study scripts, confer with directors, and conduct research to determine appropriate architectural styles.

Fashion designers design clothing and accessories. Some high-fashion designers are self-employed and design for individual clients. They make fashion news by establishing the "line," colors, and kinds of materials that will be worn each season. Other high-fashion designers cater to specialty stores or high-fashion department stores. They design original garments, as well as follow the established fashion trends. Most fashion designers, however, work for apparel manufacturers, adapting men's, women's, and children's fashions for the mass market.

Textile designers design fabric for garments, upholstery, rugs, and other products, using their knowledge of textile materials and fashion trends. Computers are widely used in pattern design and grading; intelligent pattern engineering (IPE) systems enable even greater automation in generating patterns.

Floral designers cut and arrange live, dried, or artificial flowers and foliage into designs to express the sentiments of the customer. They trim flowers and arrange bouquets, sprays, wreaths, dish gardens, and terrariums. They usually work from a written order indicating the occasion, customer preference for color and type of flower, price, and the date, time, and place the floral arrangement or plant is to be delivered. The variety of duties performed by a floral designer depends on the size of the shop and number of designers employed. In a small operation, the floral designer may own the shop and do almost everything from growing flowers to keeping books.

Working Conditions

Working conditions and places of employment vary. Designers employed by manufacturing establishments or design firms generally work regular hours in well-lighted and comfortable settings. Self-employed designers tend to work longer hours—especially at first, when they are trying to establish themselves and cannot afford to hire assistants or clerical help.

Designers frequently adjust their workday to suit their clients, meeting with them in the evenings, or on weekends when necessary. They may transact business in their own offices, clients' homes or offices, or may travel to other locations such as showrooms or manufacturing facilities.

Industrial designers usually work regular hours but occasionally work overtime to meet deadlines. In contrast, set designers, especially those in television broadcasting, often work long and irregular hours. The pace of television production is very fast, and set designers are often under pressure to make rapid changes in the sets. Fashion designers who work in the apparel industry usually have regular hours. During production deadlines or before fashion shows, however, they may be required to put in overtime. In addition, fashion designers may be required to travel to production sites overseas and across the United States. Interior designers generally work under deadlines and often work overtime to finish a job. Floral designers usually work regular hours in a pleasant work environment, except during holidays when overtime usually is required.

All designers face frustration at times, when their designs are rejected or when they cannot be as creative as they wish. Independent consultants, who are paid by the assignment, are under pressure to please clients and to find new ones to maintain their incomes.

Employment

Designers held about 342,000 jobs in 1996. Nearly four out of ten were self-employed, compared to less than one out of ten workers in all occupations.

Salaried designers work in a number of different industries, depending on their design specialty. Most industrial designers, for example, work for consulting firms or for large corporations. Interior designers usually work for design or architectural firms, department stores and home furnishing stores, or hotel and restaurant chains. Many do freelance work—full-time, part-time, or in addition to a salaried job in another occupation.

Set designers work for theater companies and film and television production companies. Fashion designers generally work for textile, apparel, and pattern manufacturers, or for fashion salons, high-fashion department stores, and specialty shops. Some work in the entertainment industry, designing costumes for theater, dance, television, and movies. Most floral designers work for retail flower shops, but a growing number work in floral departments of grocery stores.

Training, Other Qualifications, and Advancement

Creativity is crucial in all design occupations. People in this field must have a strong sense of color, an eye for detail, a sense of balance and proportion, and sensitivity to beauty. Sketching ability is especially important for fashion designers. A good portfolio—a collection of examples of a person's best work—is often the deciding factor in getting a job. However, formal preparation in design is important in all fields with the exception of floral design.

Educational requirements for entry-level positions vary. Some design occupations, notably industrial design, require a bachelor's degree. Interior designers also generally need a college education because few clients—especially commercial clients—are willing to entrust responsibility for designing living and working space to a designer with no formal credentials. Interior designers must also be knowledgeable about federal, state, and local codes, and toxicity and flammability standards for furniture and furnishings.

Interior design is the only design field subject to government regulation. According to a 1997 survey from the American Society for Interior Designers, 22 states required interior designers to be licensed. Because licensing is not mandatory in all states, membership in a professional association is universally recognized as a mark of achievement for interior designers. Professional membership usually requires the completion of three or four years of postsecondary education in design, at least two years of practical experience in the field, and completion of the National Council for Interior Design qualification examination.

In fashion design, some formal career preparation, such as a two- or four-year degree, is usually needed to enter the field. Employers seek individuals who are knowledgeable in the areas of textiles, fabrics, and ornamentation, as well as trends in the fashion world. Similarly, furniture designers must keep abreast of trends in fashion and style, in addition to methods and tools used in furniture production. Several universities and schools of design offer degrees in furniture design.

In contrast to the other design occupations, a high school diploma ordinarily suffices for floral design jobs. Most floral designers learn their skills on the job. When they hire trainees, employers generally look for high school graduates who have a flair for color and a desire to learn. However, completion of formal training is an asset for floral designers, particularly for advancement to the chief floral designer level. Vocational and technical schools offer programs in floral design usually lasting less than a year, while two- and four-year programs in floriculture, horticulture, floral design, or ornamental horticulture are offered by community and junior colleges, and colleges and universities.

Formal training for some design professions is also available in two- and three-year professional schools which award certificates or associate degrees in design. Graduates of two-year programs generally qualify as assistants to designers. The Bachelor of Fine Arts degree is granted at four-year colleges and universities. The curriculum in these schools includes art and art history, principles of design, designing and sketching, and specialized studies for each of the individual design disciplines such as garment construction, textiles, mechanical and architectural drawing, computerized design, sculpture, architecture, and basic engineering. A liberal arts education, with courses in merchandising, business administration, marketing, and psychology, along with training in art, is also a good background for most design fields. Persons with training or experience in architecture also qualify for some design occupations, particularly interior design.

Computer-aided design (CAD) courses are very useful. CAD is used in various areas of design, and many employers expect new designers to be familiar with the use of the computer as a design tool. For example, industrial designers extensively use computers in the aerospace, automotive, and electronics industries. Interior designers are using computers to create numerous versions of space designs. Images can be inserted, edited, or replaced—making it possible for a client to see and choose among several designs. In furniture design, a chair's basic shape and structure may be duplicated and updated by applying new upholstery styles and fabrics with the use of computers.

In 1997, the National Association of Schools of Art and Design accredited about 200 postsecondary institutions with programs in art and design; most of these schools award a degree in art. Some award degrees in industrial, interior, textile, graphic, or fashion design. Many schools do not allow formal entry into a bachelor's degree program until a student has successfully finished a year of basic art and design courses. Applicants may be required to submit sketches and other examples of their artistic ability.

The Foundation for Interior Design Education Research accredits interior design programs and schools. Currently, there are over 120 accredited programs in the United States and Canada, located in schools of art, architecture, and home economics.

Individuals in the design field must be creative, imaginative, persistent, and able to communicate their ideas both visually and verbally. Because tastes in style and fashion can change quickly, designers need to be open to new ideas and influences. Problem-solving skills and the ability to work independently are important traits. People in this field need self-discipline to start projects on their own, budget their time, and meet deadlines and production schedules. Business sense and sales ability are also important for those who are freelancers or run their own businesses.

Beginning designers usually receive on-the-job training, and normally need one to three years of training before they advance to higher-level positions. Experienced designers in large firms may advance to chief designer, design department head, or other supervisory positions. Some experienced designers open their own firms.

Job Outlook

Despite projected faster than average employment growth, designers in most fields—with the exception of floral and furniture design—are expected to face competition for available positions because many talented individuals are attracted to careers as designers. Individuals with little or no formal education in design who lack creativity and perseverance will find it very difficult to establish and maintain a career in design.

Finding a job as a floral designer should be relatively easy due to the relatively low pay and limited opportunities for advancement.

Overall, the employment of designers is expected to grow faster than the average for all occupations through the year 2006. Demand for industrial designers will stem from continued emphasis on product quality and safety; design of new products that are easy and comfortable to use; high-technology products in medicine, transportation, and other fields; and increasing global competition among businesses. Rising demand for professional design of private homes, office space, restaurants and other retail establishments, and institutions that care for the rapidly growing elderly population should spur employment growth among interior designers. Floral design should experience healthy growth with the addition of floral departments in many grocery and department stores. Demand for fashion, textile, and furniture designers should rise as consumers become more concerned with fashion and style. In addition to employment growth, many job openings will result from the need to replace designers who leave the field.

Earnings

Full-time designers in all specialties combined had median weekly earnings of about $590 in 1996. The middle 50

percent earned between $380 and $890 a week. The bottom 10 percent earned less than $280, while the top 10 percent earned over $1,300.

Earnings of floral designers were lower than most types of designers. According to a survey conducted by Floral Finance, Inc., beginning floral designers had average earnings of $5.85 an hour in 1996. Designers with one to three years of experience earned $6.94, while designers with over three years of experience averaged $8.17. Managers had average earnings of $10.10 per hour in 1996.

According to the Industrial Designers Society of America, the average base salary for an entry-level industrial designer with one to two years of experience was about $27,000 in 1996. Staff designers with five years of experience earned $35,000, while senior designers with eight years of experience earned $45,000. Industrial designers in managerial or executive positions earned substantially more—up to $140,000 annually.

Related Occupations

Workers in other occupations who design or arrange objects, materials, or interiors to improve their appearance and function include visual artists, architects, landscape architects, engineers, photographers, interior decorators, and merchandise displayers. Some computer-related occupations, including Internet page designer and webmaster, require design skills.

Sources of Additional Information

For a list of accredited schools of art and design, contact:
❏ National Association of Schools of Art and Design, 11250 Roger Bacon Dr., Suite 21, Reston, VA 20190.

For information on careers and a list of academic programs in industrial design, write to:
❏ Industrial Designers Society of America, 1142-E Walker Rd., Great Falls, VA 22066. Homepage: http://www.idsa.org

For information on degree, continuing education, and licensure programs in interior design, contact:
❏ American Society for Interior Designers, 608 Massachusetts Ave. NE, Washington, DC 20002-6006.

For a list of accredited programs in interior design, contact:
❏ Foundation for Interior Design Education Research, 60 Monroe Center NW, Grand Rapids, MI 49503. Homepage: http://www.fider.org

For information about careers in floral design, contact:
❏ Society of American Florists, 1601 Duke St., Alexandria, VA 22314.

For a list of schools with accredited programs in furniture design, contact:
❏ American Society of Furniture Designers, P.O. Box 2688, High Point, NC 27261.

Dietitians and Nutritionists

(*D.O.T.* 077 except .117-010 and .124-010)

Significant Points

✳ *Employment of dietitians is expected to grow about as fast as the average for all occupations through the year 2006 due to increased emphasis on the prevention of disease by improved health habits.*

✳ *The basic educational requirement for dietitians and nutritionists is a bachelor's degree with a major in dietetics, foods and nutrition, food service systems management, or a related area.*

Nature of the Work

Dietitians and nutritionists plan nutrition programs and supervise the preparation and serving of meals. They help prevent and treat illnesses by promoting healthy eating habits, scientifically evaluating clients' diets, and suggesting diet modifications, such as less salt for those with high blood pressure or reduced fat and sugar intake for those who are overweight.

Dietitians run food service systems for institutions such as hospitals and schools, promote sound eating habits through education, and conduct research. Major areas of practice are clinical, community, management, and consultant dietetics.

Clinical dietitians provide nutritional services for patients in institutions such as hospitals and nursing homes. They assess patients' nutritional needs, develop and implement nutrition programs, and evaluate and report the results. They also confer with doctors and other health care professionals in order to coordinate medical and nutritional needs. Some clinical dietitians specialize in the management of overweight patients, care of the critically ill, or care of renal (kidney) and diabetic patients. In addition, clinical dietitians in nursing homes or small hospitals may also manage the food service department.

Community dietitians counsel individuals and groups on nutritional practices designed to prevent disease and promote good health. Working in such places as public health clinics, home health agencies, and health maintenance organizations, they evaluate individual needs, develop nutritional care plans, and instruct individuals and their families. Dietitians working in home health agencies may provide instruction on grocery shopping and food preparation to the elderly, or patients with AIDS, cancer, or diabetes.

Popular interest in nutrition has led to opportunities in food manufacturing, advertising, and marketing, in which dietitians analyze foods, prepare literature for distribution, or report on issues such as the nutritional content of recipes, dietary fiber, or vitamin supplements.

Management dietitians oversee large-scale meal planning and preparation in such places as health care facilities, company cafeterias, prisons, and schools. They hire, train, and direct other dietitians and food service workers; budget for and purchase food, equipment, and supplies; enforce sanitary and safety regulations; and prepare records and reports.

Consultant dietitians work under contract with health care facilities or in their own private practice. They perform nutrition screening for their clients, and offer advice on diet-related concerns such as weight loss or cholesterol reduction. Some work for wellness programs, sports teams, supermarkets, and other nutrition-related businesses. They may consult with food service managers, providing expertise in sanitation, safety procedures, budgeting, and planning.

Working Conditions

Most dietitians work a regular 40-hour week, although some work weekends. Many dietitians work part-time.

Dietitians and nutritionists spend much of their time in clean, well-lighted, and well-ventilated areas. However, some dietitians spend time in hot, steamy kitchens. Dietitians and nutritionists may be on their feet for most of the workday.

Employment

Dietitians and nutritionists held about 58,000 jobs in 1996. Over half were in hospitals, nursing homes, or offices and clinics of physicians.

State and local governments provided about one job in six—mostly in health departments and other public health related areas. Other jobs were in restaurants, social service agencies, residential care facilities, diet workshops, physical fitness facilities, school systems, colleges and universities, and the federal government—mostly in the Department of Veterans Affairs. Others were employed by firms that provide food services on contract to such facilities as colleges and universities, airlines, and company cafeterias.

Some dietitians were self-employed, working as consultants to facilities such as hospitals and nursing homes, and seeing individual clients.

Training, Other Qualifications, and Advancement

The basic educational requirement for dietitians and nutritionists is a bachelor's degree with a major in dietetics, foods and nutrition, food service systems management, or a related area. Students take courses in foods, nutrition, institution management, chemistry, biology, microbiology, and physiology. Other suggested courses include business, mathematics, statistics, computer science, psychology, sociology, and economics.

Of the 40 states having laws governing dietetics, 27 require licensure, 12 require certification, and one requires registration. The Commission on Dietetic Registration of the American Dietetic Association (ADA) awards the Registered Dietitian credential to those who pass a certification exam after completing their academic education and supervised experience.

As of 1997, there were 231 ADA-approved bachelor's degree programs. Supervised practice experience can be acquired in two ways. There are 49 ADA-accredited coordinated programs combining academic and supervised practice experience in a four-year program. The second option requires completion of 900 hours of supervised practice experience, either in one of the 190 ADA-accredited internships or in one of the 64 ADA-approved preprofessional practice programs. Internships and preprofessional practice programs may be full-time programs lasting 9 to 12 months, or part-time programs lasting two years. Students interested in research, advanced clinical positions, or public health should get a graduate degree.

Recommended high school courses include biology, chemistry, mathematics, health, and home economics.

Experienced dietitians may advance to assistant, associate, or director of a dietetic department, or become self-employed. Some dietitians specialize in areas such as renal or pediatric dietetics. Others may leave the occupation to become sales representatives for equipment or food manufacturers.

Job Outlook

Employment of dietitians is expected to grow about as fast as the average for all occupations through the year 2006 due to increased emphasis on the prevention of disease by improved health habits. A growing and aging population will increase demand for meals and nutritional counseling in nursing homes, schools, prisons, community health programs, and home health care agencies. Public interest in nutrition and the emphasis on health education and prudent lifestyles will also spur demand. Besides employment growth, job openings will also result from the need to replace experienced workers who leave the occupation.

Employment of dietitians in hospitals is expected to decline because of anticipated slow growth in the number of inpatients, and as hospitals contract out food service operations. On the other hand, faster than average growth in employment is expected in nursing homes as the number of elderly people rises sharply, in contract providers of food

services, in residential care facilities, in offices and clinics of physicians, and in other social services.

Employment growth for dietitians and nutritionists may be somewhat constrained by some employers substituting other workers such as nurses, health educators, food service managers, and dietetic technicians. Growth would be faster but there are limitations on insurance reimbursement for dietetic services.

Earnings

According to a Hay Group survey of acute care hospitals, the median annual base salary of full-time staff dietitians was $34,400 in January 1997. The middle 50 percent earned between $31,300 and $37,200.

According to the American Dietetic Association, median annual income for registered dietitians in 1995 varied by practice area as follows: clinical nutrition, $34,131; food and nutrition management, $42,964; community nutrition, $33,902; consultation and business, $43,374; and education and research, $42,784. Salaries also vary by years in practice, educational level, geographic region, and size of community.

Related Occupations

Dietitians and nutritionists apply the principles of nutrition in a variety of situations. Workers with duties similar to those of management dietitians include home economists and food service managers. Nurses and health educators often provide services related to those of community dietitians.

Sources of Additional Information

For a list of academic programs, scholarships, and other information about dietetics, contact:

❏ The American Dietetic Association, 216 West Jackson Blvd., Suite 800, Chicago, IL 60606-6995. Homepage: http://www.eatright.org

Electrical and Electronics Engineers

(*D.O.T.* 003.061, .167 except -034 and -070, and .187)

Significant Points

✴ *A bachelor's degree in engineering is almost always required for beginning electrical and electronics engineering jobs. Good employment opportunities are expected for new graduates.*

✴ *Starting salaries are significantly higher than those of bachelor's degree graduates in other fields.*

✴ *Knowledge of technological advances must be acquired through continued study and education.*

Nature of the Work

Electrical and electronics engineers design, develop, test, and supervise the manufacture of electrical and electronic equipment. Electrical equipment includes power generating and transmission equipment used by electric utilities, and electric motors, machinery controls, and lighting and wiring in buildings, automobiles, and aircraft. Electronic equipment includes radar, computer hardware, and communications and video equipment.

The specialties of electrical and electronics engineers include several major areas—such as power generation, transmission, and distribution; communications; computer electronics; and electrical equipment manufacturing—or a subdivision of these areas—industrial robot control systems or aviation electronics, for example. Electrical and electronics engineers design new products, write performance requirements, and develop maintenance schedules. They also test equipment, solve operating problems, and estimate the time and cost of engineering projects.

Working Conditions

Most electrical and electronics engineers work in office buildings, laboratories, or industrial plants. Others spend a considerable amount of time outdoors at construction sites, where they monitor or direct operations or solve onsite problems. Some electrical and electronic engineers travel extensively to plants or worksites.

Most electrical and electronic engineers work a standard 40-hour week. At times, deadlines or design standards may bring extra pressure to a job. When this happens, engineers may work long hours and experience considerable stress.

Employment

Electrical and electronics engineers held about 367,000 jobs in 1996, making it the largest branch of engineering. Most jobs were in engineering and business consulting firms, manufacturers of electrical and electronic equipment, industrial machinery manufacturers, professional and scientific instruments, and government agencies. Communications and utilities firms, manufacturers of aircraft and guided missiles, and computer and data processing services firms accounted for most of the remaining jobs.

Training, Other Qualifications, and Advancement

A bachelor's degree in engineering is usually required for beginning engineering jobs. College graduates with a degree in a physical science or mathematics may occasionally qualify for some engineering jobs, especially in engineering specialties in high demand. Most engineering degrees are granted in electrical, mechanical, or civil engineering. However, engineers trained in one branch may work in related branches; for example, many aerospace engineers have training in mechanical engineering. This flexibility allows employers to meet staffing needs in new technologies and specialties in which engineers are in short supply. It also allows engineers to shift to fields with better employment prospects, or to ones that match their interests more closely.

In addition to the standard engineering degree, many colleges offer degrees in engineering technology, which are offered as either two- or four-year programs. These programs prepare students for practical design and production work rather than for jobs that require more theoretical, scientific, and mathematical knowledge. Graduates of four-year technology programs may get jobs similar to those obtained by graduates with a bachelor's degree in engineering. Some employers regard them as having skills between those of a technician and an engineer.

Graduate training is essential for engineering faculty positions, but is not required for the majority of entry-level engineering jobs. Many engineers obtain graduate degrees in engineering or business administration to learn new technology, broaden their education, and enhance promotion opportunities. Many high-level executives in government and industry began their careers as engineers.

About 320 colleges and universities offer bachelor's degree programs in engineering that are accredited by the Accreditation Board for Engineering and Technology (ABET), and about 250 colleges offer accredited bachelor's degree programs in engineering technology. ABET accreditation is based on an examination of an engineering program's faculty, curricular content, facilities, and admissions standards. Although most institutions offer programs in the major branches of engineering, only a few offer some of the smaller specialties. Also, programs of the same title may vary in content. For example, some emphasize industrial practices, preparing students for a job in industry, while others are more theoretical and are better for students preparing to take graduate work. Therefore, students should investigate curricula and check accreditations carefully before selecting a college. Admissions requirements for undergraduate engineering schools include a solid background in mathematics (algebra, geometry, trigonometry, and calculus), sciences (biology, chemistry, and physics), and courses in English, social studies, humanities, and computers.

Bachelor's degree programs in engineering are typically designed to last four years, but many students find that it takes between four and five years to complete their studies. In a typical four-year college curriculum, the first two years are spent studying mathematics, basic sciences, introductory engineering, humanities, and social sciences. In the last two years, most courses are in engineering, usually with a concentration in one branch. For example, the last two years of an aerospace program might include courses such as fluid mechanics, heat transfer, applied aerodynamics, analytical mechanics, flight vehicle design, trajectory dynamics, and aerospace propulsion systems. Some programs offer a general engineering curriculum; students then specialize in graduate school or on the job.

Some engineering schools and two-year colleges have agreements whereby the two-year college provides the initial engineering education and the engineering school automatically admits students for their last two years. In addition, a few engineering schools have arrangements whereby a student spends three years in a liberal arts college studying pre-engineering subjects and two years in the engineering school, and receives a bachelor's degree from each. Some colleges and universities offer five-year master's degree programs. Some five- or even six-year cooperative plans combine classroom study and practical work, permitting students to gain valuable experience and finance part of their education.

All 50 states and the District of Columbia require registration for engineers whose work may affect life, health, or property, or who offer their services to the public. Registration generally requires a degree from an ABET-accredited engineering program, four years of relevant work experience, and passing a state examination. Some states will not register people with degrees in engineering technology. Engineers may be registered in several states.

Engineers should be creative, inquisitive, analytical, and detail-oriented. They should be able to work as part of a team and be able to communicate well, both orally and in writing.

Beginning engineering graduates usually work under the supervision of experienced engineers and, in larger companies, may also receive formal classroom or seminar-type training. As they gain knowledge and experience, they are assigned more difficult projects with greater independence to develop designs, solve problems, and make decisions. Engineers may advance to become technical specialists or to supervise a staff or team of engineers and technicians. Some eventually become engineering managers or enter other managerial, management support, or sales jobs.

Job Outlook

Job openings resulting from job growth and the need to replace electrical engineers who transfer to other occupations or leave the labor force should be sufficient to absorb the

number of new graduates and other entrants, making for good employment opportunities through 2006. Employment of electrical and electronics engineers is expected to increase faster than the average for all occupations. The need for electronics manufacturers to invest heavily in research and development to remain competitive will provide openings for graduates who have learned the latest technologies. Increased demand by businesses and government for improved computers and communications equipment is expected to account for much of the projected employment growth. Consumer demand for electrical and electronic goods should create additional jobs. Job growth is expected to be fastest in non-manufacturing industries, however, because firms are increasingly getting electronic engineering expertise from consulting and service companies.

Engineers who fail to keep up with the rapid changes in technology in some specialties risk technological obsolescence, which makes them more susceptible to layoffs or, at a minimum, more likely to be passed over for advancement. Opportunities for electronics engineers in defense-related firms may improve as the trend shifts to upgrading existing aircraft and weapons systems with improved navigation, control, guidance, and targeting systems.

Earnings

Starting salaries for electrical and electronics engineers with the bachelor's degree are significantly higher than starting salaries of bachelor's degree graduates in other fields. According to the National Association of Colleges and Employers, starting salaries for those with the bachelor's degree in 1996 were about $39,513 in 1996.

The median annual salary for all electrical and electronics engineers who worked full-time in 1996 was $51,700.

The average annual salary for engineers in the federal government in nonsupervisory, supervisory, and managerial positions was $61,950 in 1997.

Related Occupations

Electrical and electronics engineers apply the principles of physical science and mathematics in their work. Other workers who use scientific and mathematical principles include engineering, science, and computer systems managers; physical, life, and computer scientists; mathematicians; engineering and science technicians; and architects.

Sources of Additional Information

High school students interested in obtaining general information on a variety of engineering disciplines should contact the Junior Engineering Technical Society by sending a self-addressed business-size envelope, with six first-class stamps affixed, to:

❑ JETS-Guidance, 1420 King St., Suite 405, Alexandria, VA 22314-2794. Homepage: http://www.asee.org/jets

High school students interested in obtaining information on ABET accredited engineering programs should contact:

❑ The Accreditation Board for Engineering and Technology, Inc., 111 Market Place, Suite 1050, Baltimore, MD 21202-4012. Homepage: http://www.abet.ba.md.us

Non-high school students and those wanting more detailed information should contact:

❑ Institute of Electrical and Electronics Engineers, 1828 L St. NW, Suite 1202, Washington, DC 20036.

Foresters and Conservation Scientists

(*D.O.T.* 040.061-030, -046, -050, -054, and -062; .167-010; 049.127)

Significant Points

* *About two out of three work for federal, state, or local governments.*

* *A bachelor's degree in forestry, range management, or a related field is generally the minimum educational requirement.*

* *Projected average employment growth will stem from continuing emphasis on environmental protection and responsible land management.*

Nature of the Work

Forests and rangelands serve a variety of needs. They supply wood products, livestock forage, minerals, and water; serve as sites for recreational activities; and provide habitats for wildlife. Foresters and conservation scientists manage, develop, use, and help protect these and other natural resources.

Foresters manage forested lands for a variety of purposes. Those working in private industry may procure timber from private landowners. To do this, foresters contact local forest owners and gain permission to take inventory of the type, amount, and location of all standing timber on the property, a process known as timber cruising. Foresters then appraise the timber's worth, negotiate the purchase of timber, and draw up a contract for procurement. Next, they subcontract with loggers or pulpwood cutters for tree removal, aid in road layout, and maintain close contact with the subcontractor's workers and the landowner to ensure that the work meets the landowner's requirements, as well as federal, state, and local environmental specifications. Forestry consultants often act as agents for the forest owner, performing the above duties and negotiating timber sales with industrial procurement foresters.

Throughout the process, foresters consider the economics of the purchase as well as the environmental impact on natural resources, a function which has taken on added importance in recent years. To do this, they determine how best to conserve wildlife habitats, creek beds, water quality, and soil stability and how best to comply with environmental regulations. Foresters must balance the desire to conserve forested ecosystems for future generations with the need to use forest resources for recreational or economic purposes.

Through a process called regeneration, foresters also supervise the planting and growing of new trees. They choose and prepare the site, using controlled burning, bulldozers, or herbicides to clear weeds, brush, and logging debris. They advise on the type, number, and placement of trees to be planted. Foresters then monitor the seedlings to ensure healthy growth and to determine the best time for harvesting. If they detect signs of disease or harmful insects, they decide on the best course of treatment to prevent contamination or infestation of healthy trees.

Foresters who work for state and federal governments manage public forests and parks and also work with private landowners to protect and manage forest land outside of the public domain. They may also design campgrounds and recreation areas.

Foresters use a number of tools to perform their jobs: Clinometers measure the heights, diameter tapes measure the diameter, and increment borers and bark gauges measure the growth of trees so that timber volumes can be computed and future growth estimated. Photogrammetry and remote sensing (aerial photographs and other imagery taken from airplanes and satellites) often are used for mapping large forest areas and for detecting widespread trends of forest and land use. Computers are used extensively, both in the office and in the field, for the storage, retrieval, and analysis of information required to manage the forest land and its resources.

Range managers, also called range conservationists, range ecologists, or range scientists, manage, improve, and protect rangelands to maximize their use without damaging the environment. Rangelands cover about one billion acres of the United States, mostly in the western states and Alaska. They contain many natural resources, including grass and shrubs for animal grazing, wildlife habitats, water from vast watersheds, recreation facilities, and valuable mineral and energy resources. Range managers help ranchers attain optimum livestock production by determining the number and kind of animals to graze, the grazing system to use, and the best sea-

son for grazing. At the same time, however, they maintain soil stability and vegetation for other uses such as wildlife habitats and outdoor recreation. They also plan and implement revegetation of disturbed sites.

Soil conservationists provide technical assistance to farmers, ranchers, state and local governments, and others concerned with the conservation of soil, water, and related natural resources. They develop programs designed to get the most productive use of land without damaging it. Conservationists visit areas with erosion problems, find the source of the problem, and help landowners and managers develop management practices to combat it.

Foresters and conservation scientists often specialize in one area such as forest resource management, urban forestry, wood technology, or forest economics.

Working Conditions

Working conditions vary considerably. Although some of the work is solitary, foresters and conservation scientists also deal regularly with landowners, loggers, forestry technicians and aides, farmers, ranchers, government officials, special interest groups, and the public in general. Some work regular hours in offices or labs. Others may split their time between field work and office work, while some—especially independent consultants or less experienced workers—spend the majority of their time outdoors overseeing or participating in hands-on work.

The work can be physically demanding. Foresters and conservation scientists who work outdoors do so in all kinds of weather, sometimes in isolated areas. Some foresters may need to walk long distances through densely wooded land to carry out their work. Foresters also may work long hours fighting fires. Conservation scientists often are called in to prevent erosion after a forest fire, and they provide emergency help after floods, mudslides, and tropical storms.

Employment

Foresters and conservation scientists held about 37,000 jobs in 1996. Nearly three out of ten salaried workers were in the federal government, mostly in the U.S. Department of Agriculture (USDA). Foresters were concentrated in the USDA's Forest Service; soil conservationists in the USDA's Natural Resource Conservation Service. Most range managers worked in the Department of the Interior's Bureau of Land Management or in the USDA's Natural Resource Conservation Service. Nearly another three out of ten foresters and conservation scientists worked for state governments, and nearly one out of ten worked for local governments. The remainder worked in private industry, mainly in the forestry industry, logging and lumber companies and sawmills, and

© 1999 • J. Michael Farr • JIST Works, Inc. • Indianapolis, IN

research and testing services. Some were self-employed as consultants for private landowners, state and federal governments, and forestry-related businesses.

Although foresters and conservation scientists work in every state, employment of foresters is concentrated in the western and southeastern states, where many national and private forests and parks, and most of the lumber and pulpwood-producing forests, are located. Range managers work almost entirely in the western states, where most of the rangeland is located. Soil conservationists, on the other hand, are employed in almost every county in the country.

Training, Other Qualifications, and Advancement

A bachelor's degree in forestry is the minimum educational requirement for professional careers in forestry. In the federal government, a combination of experience and appropriate education occasionally may substitute for a four-year forestry degree, but job competition makes this difficult.

Fifteen states have mandatory licensing or voluntary registration requirements which a forester must meet in order to acquire the title "professional forester" and practice forestry in the state. Licensing or registration requirements vary by state, but usually entail completing a four-year degree in forestry, a minimum period of training time, and passing an exam.

Foresters who wish to perform specialized research or teach should have an advanced degree, preferably a Ph.D.

Most land-grant colleges and universities offer bachelor's or higher degrees in forestry; 48 of these programs are accredited by the Society of American Foresters. Curriculums stress science, mathematics, communications skills, and computer science, as well as technical forestry subjects. Courses in forest economics and business administration supplement the student's scientific and technical knowledge. Forestry curricula increasingly include courses on best management practices, wetlands analysis, water and soil quality, and wildlife conservation, in response to the growing focus on protecting forested lands during timber harvesting operations. Prospective foresters should have a strong grasp on policy issues and on the increasingly numerous and complex environmental regulations which affect many forestry-related activities. Many colleges require students to complete a field session either in a camp operated by the college or in a cooperative work-study program with a federal or state agency or private industry. All schools encourage students to take summer jobs that provide experience in forestry or conservation work.

A bachelor's degree in range management or range science is the usual minimum educational requirement for range managers; graduate degrees generally are required for teaching and research positions. In 1996, about 30 colleges and universities offered degrees in range management or range science or in a closely related discipline with a range management or range science option. A number of other schools offered some courses in range management or range science. Specialized range management courses combine plant, animal, and soil sciences with principles of ecology and resource management. Desirable electives include economics, forestry, hydrology, agronomy, wildlife, animal husbandry, computer science, and recreation.

Very few colleges and universities offer degrees in soil conservation. Most soil conservationists have degrees in environmental studies, agronomy, general agriculture, hydrology, or crop or soil science; a few have degrees in related fields such as wildlife biology, forestry, and range management. Programs of study generally include 30 semester hours in natural resources or agriculture, including at least three hours in soil science. The Soil and Water Conservation Society sponsors a certification program based on education, experience, and testing. Upon completion of the program, individuals are designated as Certified Professional Erosion and Sediment Control specialist.

In addition to meeting the demands of forestry and conservation research and analysis, foresters and conservation scientists generally must enjoy working outdoors, be physically hardy, and be willing to move to where the jobs are. They must also work well with people and have good communications skills.

Recent forestry and range management graduates usually work under the supervision of experienced foresters or range managers. After gaining experience, they may advance to more responsible positions. In the federal government, most entry-level foresters work in forest resource management. An experienced federal forester may supervise a ranger district, and may advance to forest supervisor, regional forester, or to a top administrative position in the national headquarters. In private industry, foresters start by learning the practical and administrative aspects of the business and acquiring comprehensive technical training. They are then introduced to contract writing, timber harvesting, and decision making. Some foresters work their way up to top managerial positions within their companies. Foresters in management usually leave the field work behind, spending more of their time in an office, working with teams to develop management plans and supervising others. After gaining several years of experience, some foresters may become consulting foresters, working alone or with one or several partners. They contract with state or local governments, private landowners, private industry, or other forestry consulting groups.

Soil conservationists usually begin working within one county or conservation district and with experience may advance to the area, state, regional, or national level. Also, soil conservationists can transfer to related occupations such as farm or ranch management advisor or land appraiser.

Job Outlook

Employment of foresters and conservation scientists is expected to grow about as fast as the average for all occupations through the year 2006. Growth should be strongest in state and local governments, where demand will be spurred by a continuing emphasis on environmental protection and responsible land management. For example, the nationwide Stewardship Incentive Program, funded by the federal government, provides money to the states to encourage landowners to practice multiple-use forest management. Foresters will continue to be needed to help landowners manage their forested property. However, job opportunities are expected to be best for soil conservationists as government regulations, such as those regarding the management of storm water and coastlines, has created demand for persons knowledgeable about erosion on farms and in cities and suburbs. Soil and water quality experts will also be needed as states attempt to improve water quality by preventing pollution by agricultural producers and industrial plants.

Fewer opportunities for foresters and conservation scientists are expected in the federal government, partly due to budgetary constraints. Also, federal land management agencies, such as the Forest Service, are deemphasizing their timber programs and increasingly focusing on wildlife, recreation, and sustaining ecosystems, thereby increasing demand for other life and social scientists relative to foresters. However, a large number of foresters is expected to retire or leave the government for other reasons, resulting in some job openings between 1996 and 2006. In addition, the need for range and soil conservationists to provide technical assistance, through the Natural Resource Conservation Service, to owners of grazing land may lead to a small number of new jobs.

The recent reductions in timber harvesting on public lands, most of which are located in the Northwest and California, also will dampen job growth for private industry foresters in these regions. Opportunities will be better for foresters in the Southeast, where much forested land is privately owned. Rising demand for timber on private lands will increase the need for forest management plans which maximize production while sustaining the environment for future growth. Salaried foresters working for private industry—such as paper companies, sawmills, and pulp wood mills—and consulting foresters will be needed to provide technical assistance

and management plans to landowners.

Research and testing firms have increased their hiring of foresters and conservation scientists in recent years in response to demand for professionals to prepare environmental impact statements and erosion and sediment control plans, monitor water quality near logging sites, and advise on tree harvesting practices required by federal, state, or local regulations. Hiring in these firms should continue during the 1996–2006 period, though at a slower rate.

Earnings

In 1997, most graduates entering the federal government as foresters, range managers, or soil conservationists with a bachelor's degree started at $19,500 or $24,200 a year, depending on academic achievement. Those with a master's degree could start at $24,200 or $29,600. Holders of doctorates could start at $35,800 or, in research positions, at $42,900. Beginning salaries were slightly higher in selected areas where the prevailing local pay level was higher. In 1997, the average federal salary for foresters in nonsupervisory, supervisory, and managerial positions was $47,600; for soil conservationists, $45,200; for rangeland managers, $43,100, and for forest products technologists, $62,000.

According to the National Association of Colleges and Employers, graduates with a bachelor's degree in natural resources received an average starting salary offer of $24,800 in 1997.

In private industry, starting salaries for students with a bachelor's degree were comparable to starting salaries in the federal government, but starting salaries in state and local governments were generally lower.

Foresters and conservation scientists who work for federal, state, and local governments and large private firms generally receive more generous benefits than those working for smaller firms.

Related Occupations

Foresters and conservation scientists manage, develop, and protect natural resources. They are aided by range, soil conservation, and forestry technicians. Other workers with similar responsibilities include agricultural scientists, agricultural engineers, biological scientists, environmental scientists and engineers, farm and ranch managers, soil scientists, and wildlife managers.

Sources of Additional Information

For information about the forestry profession and lists of schools offering education in forestry, send a self-addressed, stamped business envelope to:

❏ Society of American Foresters, 5400 Grosvenor Ln., Bethesda, MD 20814. Homepage: http://www.safnet.org

For information about career opportunities in forestry in the federal government, contact:

❏ Chief, U.S. Forest Service, U.S. Department of Agriculture, P.O. Box 96090, SW, Washington, DC 20090-6090.

For information about a career in state forestry organizations, contact:

❏ National Association of State Foresters, 444 N. Capitol St. NW, Suite 540, Washington, DC 20001.

Information about a career as a range manager as well as a list of schools offering training is available from:

❏ Society for Range Management, 1839 York St., Denver, CO 80206.

Information about a career in conservation science is available from:

❏ Soil and Water Conservation Society, 7515 Northeast Ankeny Rd., RR #1, Ankeny, IA 50021-9764.

Geologists and Geophysicists

(D.O.T. 024.061 except -014, and .161)

Significant Points

✴ *Work at remote field sites is common.*

✴ *A bachelor's degree in geology or geophysics is adequate for entry-level jobs; better jobs with good advancement potential usually require at least a master's degree; and a Ph.D. is required for most research positions in colleges and universities, and for some research jobs in government.*

✴ *Job opportunities are expected to be good in the petroleum and related industries, reflecting increasing demand for energy coupled with fewer degrees awarded in geology in recent years.*

Nature of the Work

Geologists and geophysicists, also known as geological scientists or geoscientists, study the physical aspects and history of the Earth. They identify and examine rocks, study information collected by remote sensing instruments in satellites, conduct geological surveys, construct field maps, and use instruments to measure the Earth's gravity and magnetic field. They also analyze information collected through seismic studies, which involves bouncing energy waves off buried rock layers. Many geologists and geophysicists search for oil, natural gas, minerals, and groundwater.

Other geological scientists play an important role in preserving and cleaning up the environment. Their activities include designing and monitoring waste disposal sites, preserving water supplies, and reclaiming contaminated land and water to comply with federal environmental regulations. They also help locate safe sites for hazardous waste facilities and landfills.

Geologists and geophysicists examine chemical and physical properties of specimens in laboratories. They study fossil remains of animal and plant life, or experiment with the flow of water and oil through rocks. Some geoscientists use two- or three-dimensional computer modeling to portray water layers and the flow of water or other fluids through rock cracks and porous materials. They use a variety of sophisticated laboratory instruments, including x-ray diffractometers, which determine the crystal structure of minerals, and petrographic microscopes, for the study of rock and sediment samples. Geoscientists also use seismographs, instruments which measure energy waves resulting from movements in the Earth's crust, to determine the locations and intensities of earthquakes.

Geoscientists working in metal mining or the oil and gas industry sometimes process and interpret the maps produced by remote sensing satellites to help identify potential new mineral, oil, or gas deposits. Seismic technology is also an important exploration tool. Seismic waves are used to develop three-dimensional computer models of underground or underwater rock formations. Seismic reflection technology may also reveal unusual underground features which sometimes indicate accumulations of natural gas or petroleum, facilitating exploration and reducing the risks associated with drilling in previously unexplored areas.

Geologists and geophysicists also apply geological knowledge to engineering problems in constructing large buildings, dams, tunnels, and highways. Some administer and manage research and exploration programs; others become general managers in petroleum and mining companies.

Geology and geophysics are closely related fields, but there are major differences. Geologists study the composition, structure, and history of the Earth's crust. They try to find out how rocks were formed and what has happened to them since formation. Geophysicists use the principles of physics, mathematics, and chemistry to study not only the Earth's surface, but its internal composition, ground and surface waters, atmosphere, oceans, and its magnetic, electrical, and gravitational forces. Both, however, commonly apply their skills and knowledge to the search for natural resources and to solve environmental problems.

There are numerous subdisciplines or specialties falling under the two major disciplines of geology and geophysics which further differentiate the type of work geoscientists do. For example, petroleum geologists explore for oil and gas deposits by studying and mapping the subsurface of the ocean or land. They use sophisticated geophysical instrumentation, well log data, and computers to collect information. Mineralogists analyze and classify minerals and precious stones according to composition and structure. Paleontologists study fossils found in geological formations to trace the evolution of plant and animal life and the geologic history of the Earth. Stratigraphers help to locate minerals by studying the distribution and arrangement of sedimentary rock layers and by examining the fossil and mineral content of such layers. Those who study marine geology are usually called oceanographers or marine geologists. They study and map the ocean floor, and collect information using remote sensing devices aboard surface ships or underwater research craft.

Geophysicists may specialize in areas such as geodesy, seismology, or marine geophysics, also known as physical oceanography. Geodesists study the size and shape of the Earth, its gravitational field, tides, polar motion, and rotation. Seismologists interpret data from seismographs and other geophysical instruments to detect earthquakes and locate earthquake-related faults. Volcanologists, geochemists, and petrologists study the chemical and physical evolution of rocks and minerals, particularly igneous and metamorphic rocks. Geomagnetists measure the Earth's magnetic field and use measurements taken over the past few centuries to devise theoretical models to explain its origin. Paleomagnetists interpret fossil magnetization in rocks and sediments from the continents and oceans, which record the spreading of the sea floor, the wandering of the continents, and the many reversals of polarity that the Earth's magnetic field has undergone through time. Physical oceanographers study the physical aspects of oceans such as currents and the interaction of the surface of the sea with the atmosphere. Other geophysicists study atmospheric sciences and space physics.

Hydrology is a discipline closely related to geology and geophysics. Hydrologists study the distribution, circulation, and physical properties of underground and surface waters. They study the form and intensity of precipitation, its rate of infiltration into the soil, movement through the Earth, and its return to the ocean and atmosphere. The work they do is particularly important in environmental preservation and remediation.

Working Conditions

Some geoscientists spend the majority of their time in an office, but many others divide their time between fieldwork and office or laboratory work. Geologists often travel to remote field sites by helicopter or four-wheel drive vehicles, and cover large areas on foot. Exploration geologists and geophysi-

cists often work overseas or in isolated areas, leading to job relocation. Many exploration geologists travel to meet with prospective clients or investors. Marine geologists and oceanographers may spend considerable time at sea on academic research ships.

Geoscientists in positions funded by federal government agencies may be under pressure to design programs and write grant proposals in order to continue their data collection and research. Geoscientists in consulting jobs may face similar pressures to market their skills and write proposals to maintain steady work.

Employment

Geologists and geophysicists held about 47,000 jobs in 1996. Many more individuals held geology, geophysics, and oceanography faculty positions in colleges and universities, but they are considered college and university faculty.

Among salaried geologists and geophysicists, nearly four in ten were employed in engineering and management services, and two in ten worked for oil and gas extraction companies or metal mining companies. About one geoscientist in seven was self-employed; most were consultants to industry or government.

The federal government employed about 5,800 geologists, geophysicists, oceanographers, and hydrologists in 1996. Over half worked for the Department of the Interior, mostly within the U.S. Geological Survey (USGS). Others worked for the Departments of Defense, Agriculture, Commerce, and Energy, and the Environmental Protection Agency. Over 3,000 worked for state agencies such as state geological surveys and state departments of conservation.

Training, Other Qualifications, and Advancement

A bachelor's degree in geology or geophysics is adequate for entry-level jobs, but better jobs with good advancement potential usually require at least a master's degree in geology or geophysics. Persons with degrees in physics, chemistry, mathematics, or computer science may also qualify for some geophysics or geology jobs if their course work included study in geology. A Ph.D. is required for most research positions in colleges and universities, and is also important for work in federal agencies and some state geological surveys involving basic research.

Hundreds of colleges and universities offer a bachelor's degree in geology; fewer schools offer programs in geophysics, oceanography, or other geosciences. Other programs offering related training for beginning geological scientists include geophysical technology, geophysical engineering, geophysical

prospecting, engineering geology, petroleum geology, hydrology, and geochemistry. In addition, several hundred more universities award advanced degrees in geology or geophysics.

Traditional geoscience courses emphasizing classical geologic methods and topics (such as mineralogy, paleontology, stratigraphy, and structural geology) are important for all geoscientists. Those students interested in working in the environmental or regulatory fields, either in environmental consulting firms or federal or state government, should take courses in hydrology, hazardous waste management, environmental legislation, chemistry, fluid mechanics, and geologic logging. An understanding of environmental regulations and government permit issues is also valuable for those planning to work in mining and oil and gas extraction. Computer skills are becoming essential for prospective geoscientists; students who have some experience with computer modeling, data analysis and integration, digital mapping, remote sensing, and geographic information systems (GIS) will be the most prepared entering the job market. A knowledge of the Global Positioning System (GPS) is very helpful. Some employers seek applicants with field experience, so a summer internship may be beneficial to prospective geoscientists.

Geologists and geophysicists must be able to work as part of a team. Strong oral and written communication skills are important, as well as the ability to think independently and creatively. Those involved in fieldwork must have physical stamina.

Geologists and geophysicists often begin their careers in field exploration or as research assistants in laboratories or offices. They are given more difficult assignments as they gain experience. Eventually, they may be promoted to project leader, program manager, or another management and research position.

Job Outlook

Many jobs for geologists and geophysicists are in or related to the petroleum industry, especially the exploration for oil and gas. This industry is subject to cyclical fluctuations. During the 1980s and the early 1990s, low oil prices, higher production costs, improvements in energy efficiency, shrinking oil reserves, and restrictions on potential drilling sites caused exploration activities to be curtailed in the United States; this limited the number of job openings for geoscientists in the petroleum and related industries. As a result of generally poor job prospects, the number of graduates in geology and geophysics, especially in petroleum geology, dropped considerably during the last decade.

Recently, a growing worldwide demand for oil and gas, and new exploration and recovery techniques, have returned stability to the petroleum industry and increased the demand for geologists and geophysicists. Growing populations, stronger economies in the United States and abroad, and continuing industrialization of developing countries are driving the need for more energy. At the same time, the oil and gas and related industries—such as petroleum engineering services—are taking advantage of new technologies that lower costs and facilitate exploration and recovery of natural gas and oil, particularly in deep water and other previously inaccessible sites. Because of the lower number of degrees awarded in geology recently and the significant number of geoscientists who left the industry during earlier periods of downsizing, job opportunities in the petroleum and related industries are expected to be good. Employment prospects will be best for job seekers who hold a master's degree and are familiar with advanced technologies, such as computer modeling and GPS, which are increasingly used to locate new oil and gas fields or pinpoint hidden deposits in existing fields. Because of the cyclical nature of the oil and gas industry, hiring on a contractual basis is common.

Employment of geologists and geophysicists is expected to grow about as fast as the average for all occupations through the year 2006, due in part to the generally improved outlook in the oil and gas industry. Geologists and geophysicists will also continue to be needed to work in areas of environmental protection and reclamation. Some will help clean up contaminated sites in the United States, and others will help private companies and government comply with numerous and complex environmental regulations. However, job opportunities in state and federal government and in environmental consulting firms are expected to be fewer in number than in the previous decade and, in some cases, may be limited to replacing retirees or those who leave geoscience jobs for other reasons. The USGS, the primary employer of geologists in the federal government, has recently faced cutbacks. Hiring should continue to be very limited in the USGS and other agencies, as the federal government attempts to balance its budget during the 1996–2006 projection period. Oceanographers, whose work is often research-oriented and dependent on grants from federal agencies, are expected to face strong competition. Budget constraints are expected to continue to limit hiring in state government as well.

Earnings

Surveys by the National Association of Colleges and Employers indicate that graduates with bachelor's degrees in geology and the geological sciences received an average starting salary offer of about $30,900 a year in 1997. However, starting salaries can vary widely depending on the employing industry. For example, according to a 1996 American

Association of Petroleum Geologists survey, the average salary in the oil and gas industry for geoscientists with less than two years of experience was about $48,400.

The petroleum, mineral, and mining industries offer higher salaries, but less job security, than other industries. These industries are vulnerable to recessions and changes in oil and gas prices, among other factors, and usually release workers when exploration and drilling slow down.

In 1997, the federal government's average salary for geologists in managerial, supervisory, and nonsupervisory positions was $59,700; for geophysicists, $67,100; for hydrologists, $54,800; and for oceanographers, $62,700.

Related Occupations

Many geologists and geophysicists work in the petroleum and natural gas industry. This industry also employs many other workers in the scientific and technical aspects of petroleum and natural gas exploration and extraction, including engineering technicians, science technicians, petroleum engineers, and surveyors. Also, some life scientists, physicists, chemists, and meteorologists—as well as mathematicians, computer scientists, soil scientists, and mapping scientists—perform related work in both petroleum and natural gas exploration and extraction, and in environment-related activities.

Sources of Additional Information

Information on training and career opportunities for geologists is available from:

❏ American Geological Institute, 4220 King St., Alexandria, VA 22302-1502. Homepage: http://www.agiweb.org

❏ Geological Society of America, P.O. Box 9140, Boulder, CO 80301-9140. Homepage: http://www.geosociety.org

❏ American Association of Petroleum Geologists, Communications Department, P.O. Box 979, Tulsa, OK 74101.

Information on training and career opportunities for geophysicists is available from:

❏ American Geophysical Union, 2000 Florida Ave. NW, Washington, DC 20009.

A list of education and training programs in oceanography and related fields is available from:

❏ Marine Technology Society, 1828 L St. NW, Suite 906, Washington, DC 20036.

Information on acquiring a job as a geologist, geophysicist, hydrologist, or oceanographer with the federal government may be obtained from the Office of Personnel Management through a telephone-based system. Consult your telephone directory under U.S. government for a local number or call (912) 757-3000 (TDD 912 744-2299). That number is not toll-free and charges may result. Information also is available from its Internet site: http://www.usajobs.opm.gov

Health Services Managers

(D.O.T. 072.117-010; 074.167-010, 075.117-014, -022, -026, -030 and -034, .167-010 and -014; 076.117-010; 077.117-010; 078.131-010, .161-010 and -014, .162-010; 079.117-010, .131-010, .151-010, and .167-014; 187.117-010, -058, -062, and .167-034, and -090; 188.117-082

Significant Points

★ *Earnings of health services managers are high, but long weekly work hours are common.*

★ *Most are employed by hospitals, but the fastest employment growth will be in home health care agencies, long-term care facilities, and practitioners' offices and clinics.*

Nature of the Work

Health care is a business, albeit a special one. Like every other business, it needs good management to keep it running smoothly, especially during times of change. The term "health services manager" encompasses individuals in many different positions who plan, organize, coordinate, and supervise the delivery of health care. Health services managers include both generalists—administrators who manage or help to manage an entire facility or system—and health specialists—managers in charge of specific clinical departments or services found only in the health industry.

The structure and financing of health care is changing rapidly. Future health services managers must be prepared to deal with evolving integrated health care delivery systems, restructuring of work, technological innovations, and an increased focus on preventive care. They will be called upon to improve efficiency in all health care facilities, while continually improving quality of the health care provided. Increasingly, health services managers work in organizations in which they must optimize efficiency of a variety of interrelated services, ranging from inpatient care to outpatient follow-up care, for example.

The top administrator or chief executive officer (CEO) and the assistant administrators without specific titles are health care generalists, who set the overall direction of the organization. They concentrate on such areas as community outreach, planning, marketing, human resources, finance, and complying with government regulations. Their range of knowledge is broad, including developments in the clinical departments as well as in the business arena. They often speak before civic groups, promote public participation in health programs, and coordinate the activities of the organization with those of government or community agencies. CEOs make long-term institutional plans by assessing the need for services, person-

nel, facilities, and equipment and recommending changes such as opening a home health service. CEOs need leadership ability, as well as technical skills, to provide quality health care while satisfying demand for financial viability, cost containment, and public and professional accountability.

Larger facilities typically have several assistant administrators to aid the top administrator and to handle day-to-day decisions. They may direct activities in clinical areas such as nursing, surgery, therapy, food service, and medical records; or the activities in nonhealth areas such as finance, housekeeping, human resources, and information management. (Because the nonhealth departments are not directly related to health care, these managers are not included in this statement.) In smaller facilities, top administrators may handle more of the details of day-to-day operations. For example, many nursing home administrators directly manage personnel, finance, operations, admissions, and have a larger role in resident care.

Clinical managers have more narrowly defined responsibilities than generalists, and have training and/or experience in a specific clinical area. For example, directors of physical therapy are experienced physical therapists, and most health information administrators have a bachelor's degree in health information administration. These managers establish and implement policies, objectives, and procedures for their departments; evaluate personnel and work; develop reports and budgets; and coordinate activities with other managers.

In group practices, managers work closely with the physician owners. While an office manager may handle business affairs in small medical groups, leaving policy decisions to the physicians themselves, larger groups generally employ a full-time administrator to advise on business strategies and coordinate day-to-day business.

A small group of 10 or 15 physicians might employ a single administrator to oversee personnel matters, billing and collection, budgeting, planning, equipment outlays, and patient flow. A large practice of 40 or 50 physicians may have a chief administrator and several assistants, each responsible for different areas.

Health services managers in health maintenance organizations (HMOs) and other managed care settings perform functions similar to those in large group practices, except their staffs may be larger. Also, they may do more work in the areas of community outreach and preventive care than managers of a group practice. The size of the administrative staff in HMOs varies according to the size and type of HMO.

Some health services managers oversee the activities of a number of facilities in multifacility health organizations.

Working Conditions

Most health services managers work long hours. Facilities such as nursing homes and hospitals operate around the clock, and administrators and managers may be called at all hours to deal with problems. They may also travel to attend meetings or inspect satellite facilities.

Employment

Health services managers held about 329,000 jobs in 1996. Over one-half of all jobs were in hospitals. About one in four were in nursing and personal care facilities or offices and clinics of physicians. The remainder worked in home health agencies, medical and dental laboratories, offices of dentists and other practitioners, and other health and allied services.

Training, Other Qualifications, and Advancement

Health services managers must be familiar with management principles and practices. Some learn from work experience. However, formal education is usually necessary for advancement. Most CEO positions require a graduate degree in health services administration, nursing administration, public health, or business administration. For some generalist positions, employers seek applicants with clinical experience (as nurses or therapists, for example) as well as academic preparation in business or health services administration.

Bachelor's, master's, and doctoral degree programs in health administration are offered by colleges, universities, and schools of public health, medicine, allied health, public administration, and business administration. There are also some certificate or diploma programs, generally lasting less than one year, in health services administration and in medical office management. A master's degree—in health services administration, long-term care administration, health sciences, public health, public administration, or business administration—is the standard credential for most generalist positions in this field. However, a bachelor's degree is adequate for some entry-level positions in smaller operations. A bachelor's degree is required to work in some settings, such as nursing homes, and for entry-level positions at the departmental level within health care organizations. Physicians' offices and some other facilities may substitute on-the-job experience for formal education. For clinical department heads, a degree in the appropriate field and work experience may be sufficient, but a master's degree in health services administration usually is required to advance.

In 1997, 67 schools had accredited programs leading to the master's degree in health services administration, according to the Accrediting Commission on Education for Health Services Administration.

Some graduate programs seek students with undergraduate degrees in business or health administration; however, many programs prefer students with a liberal arts or health professions background. Competition for entry to these programs is keen, and applicants need above-average grades to gain admission. The programs generally last between two and three years. They may include up to one year of supervised administrative experience, and course work in areas such as hospital organization and management, marketing, accounting and budgeting, human resources administration, strategic planning, health economics, and health information systems. Some programs allow students to specialize in one type of facility—hospitals; nursing homes; mental health facilities; HMOs; or outpatient care facilities, including medical groups. Other programs encourage a generalist approach to health administration education.

New graduates with master's degrees in health services administration may start as department managers or in staff positions. The level of the starting position varies with the experience of the applicant and size of the organization. Postgraduate residencies and fellowships are offered by hospitals and other health facilities; these are usually staff positions. Graduates from master's degree programs also take jobs in HMOs, large group medical practices, clinics, mental health facilities, and multifacility nursing home corporations.

Graduates with bachelor's degrees in health administration usually begin as administrative assistants or assistant department heads in larger hospitals, or as department heads or assistant administrators in small hospitals or nursing homes.

A Ph.D. degree may be required to teach, consult, or do research. Nursing service administrators are usually chosen from among supervisory registered nurses with administrative abilities and a graduate degree in nursing or health services administration.

Most states and the District of Columbia require nursing home administrators to have a bachelor's degree, pass a licensing examination, complete a state-approved training program, and pursue continuing education. A license is not required in other areas of health services management.

Health services managers are often responsible for millions of dollars of facilities and equipment and hundreds of employees. To make effective decisions, they need to be open to different opinions and good at analyzing contradictory information. They must understand finance and information systems, and be able to interpret data. Motivating others to implement their decisions requires strong leadership abilities. Tact, diplomacy, flexibility, and communication skills are essential because health services managers spend much of their time interacting with others.

Health services managers advance by moving into more responsible and higher paying positions, such as assistant or associate administrator, or by moving to larger facilities.

Job Outlook

Employment of health services managers is expected to grow faster than the average for all occupations through the year 2006 as health services continue to expand and diversify. Opportunities for health services managers should be closely related to growth in the industry in which they are employed. Opportunities will be good in home health care, long-term care, and nontraditional health organizations such as managed care operations, particularly for health services managers with work experience in the health care field and strong business and management skills.

Hospitals will continue to employ the most managers, although the number of jobs will grow slowly compared to other areas. As hospitals continue to consolidate, centralize, and diversify functions, competition will increase at all job levels.

Employment will grow the fastest in home health agencies, offices of physicians and other health practitioners, and nursing and personal care facilities due to an increased number of elderly individuals who will need care. In addition, many services previously provided in hospitals will be shifted to these sectors, especially as medical technologies improve. Demand in medical group practice management will grow as medical group practices become larger and more complex. Health services managers will need to deal with the pressures of cost containment and financial accountability, as well as the increased focus on preventive and primary care. They will have more responsibility for improving the health of populations and communities.

Health services managers will also be employed by health care management companies who provide management services to hospitals and other organizations, as well as specific departments such as emergency, information management systems, managed care contract negotiations, and physician recruiting.

Earnings

Earnings of health services managers vary by type and size of the facility, as well as by level of responsibility. For example, the Medical Group Management Association reported that the median salary for administrators in small group

practices—with fewer than seven physicians—was about $56,000 in 1996; for those in larger group practices—with more than seven physicians—77,000.

According to a 1997 survey by Modern Healthcare magazine, half of all hospital CEOs earned total compensation of $190,500 or more. Salaries varied according to size of facility and geographic region. Clinical department heads' salaries varied also. Median total compensation in 1997 for heads of the following clinical departments were: respiratory therapy, $54,500; home health care, $62,000; clinical laboratory, $63,700; radiology, $64,000; physical therapy, $64,900; ambulatory/outpatient services, $68,500, rehabilitation services, $70,400; and nursing services, $97,000.

According to the Buck Survey conducted by the American Health Care Association in 1996, nursing home administrators had median annual compensation of about $49,500. The middle 50 percent earned between $42,100 and $57,300. Assistant administrators earned about $32,000, with the middle 50 percent earning between $26,200 and $40,000.

Executives often receive bonuses based on performance outcomes such as cost containment, quality assurance, and patient satisfaction.

Related Occupations

Health services managers have training or experience in both health and management. Other occupations requiring knowledge of both fields are public health directors, social welfare administrators, directors of voluntary health agencies and health professional associations, and underwriters in health insurance companies.

Sources of Additional Information

General information about health administration is available from:

❑ American College of Healthcare Executives, One North Franklin St., Suite 1700, Chicago, IL 60606. Homepage: http://www.ache.org

Information about undergraduate and graduate academic programs in this field is available from:

❑ Association of University Programs in Health Administration, 1911 North Fort Myer Dr., Suite 503, Arlington, VA 22209. Homepage: http://www.aupha.org

For a list of accredited graduate programs in health services administration, contact:

❑ Accrediting Commission on Education for Health Services Administration, 1911 North Fort Myer Dr., Suite 503, Arlington, VA 22209.

For information about career opportunities in long-term care administration, contact:

❑ American College of Health Care Administrators, 325 S. Patrick St., Alexandria, VA 22314.

For information about career opportunities in medical group practices and ambulatory care management, contact:

❑ Medical Group Management Association, 104 Inverness Terrace East, Englewood, CO 80112.

Human Resources Specialists and Managers

(D.O.T. 079.127; 099.167-010; 166.067, .117, .167 except -046, .257, .267-014 through -046; 169.107, .167-062, .207; 188.117-010, -086, .217)

Significant Points

✱ *Employers generally seek college graduates for entry level jobs. Depending on the job duties, a strong background in human resources, business, technical, or liberal arts subjects is preferred.*

✱ *The job market is likely to remain competitive in view of the abundant supply of qualified college graduates and experienced workers.*

Nature of the Work

Attracting the most qualified employees available and matching them to the jobs for which they are best suited is important for the success of any organization. However, many enterprises are too large to permit close contact between top management and employees. Human resources specialists and managers provide this link. These individuals recruit and interview employees, and advise on hiring decisions in accordance with policies and requirements that have been established in conjunction with top management. In an effort to improve morale and productivity and limit job turnover, they also help their firms effectively use employees' skills, provide training opportunities to enhance those skills, and boost employees' satisfaction with their jobs and working conditions. Although some jobs in the human resources field require only limited contact with people outside the office, most involve frequent contact. Dealing with people is an essential part of the job.

In a small organization, a human resources generalist may handle many, or all, aspects of human resources work, requiring a broad range of knowledge. The responsibilities of human resources generalists can vary widely, depending on their employer's needs. In a large corporation, the top human resources executive usually develops and coordinates personnel programs and policies. These policies are usually implemented by a director or manager of human resources and, in some cases, a director of industrial relations.

The director of human resources may oversee several departments, each headed by an experienced manager, who most likely specializes in one personnel activity such as employment, compensation, benefits, training and development, or employee relations.

Employment and placement managers oversee the hiring and separation of employees and supervise various workers, including equal employment opportunity specialists and recruitment specialists.

Recruiters maintain contacts within the community and may travel extensively, often to college campuses, to search for promising job applicants. Recruiters screen, interview, and test applicants. They may also check references and extend offers of employment to qualified candidates. These workers must be thoroughly familiar with the organization and its personnel policies to discuss wages, working conditions, and promotional opportunities with prospective employees. They must also keep informed about equal employment opportunity (EEO) and affirmative action guidelines and laws, such as the Americans With Disabilities Act.

EEO representatives or affirmative action coordinators handle this area in large organizations. They investigate and resolve EEO grievances, examine corporate practices for possible violations, and compile and submit EEO statistical reports.

Employer relations representatives—who usually work in government agencies—maintain working relationships with local employers and promote the use of public employment programs and services. Similarly, employment interviewers—whose many job titles include personnel consultants, personnel development specialists, and human resources coordinators—help match job seekers with employers.

Job analysts, sometimes called position classifiers, perform very exacting work. They collect and examine detailed information about job duties to prepare job descriptions. These descriptions explain the duties, training, and skills each job requires. Whenever a large organization introduces a new job or reviews existing jobs, it calls upon the expert knowledge of the job analyst.

Occupational analysts conduct research, generally in large firms. They are concerned with occupational classification systems and study the effects of industry and occupational trends upon worker relationships. They may serve as technical liaison between the firm and industry, government, and labor unions.

Establishing and maintaining a firm's pay system is the principal job of the compensation manager. Assisted by staff specialists, compensation managers devise ways to ensure fair and equitable pay rates. They may conduct surveys to see how their rates compare with others and to see that the firm's pay scale complies with changing laws and regulations. In addition, compensation managers often oversee their firm's performance evaluation system, and they may design reward systems such as pay-for-performance plans.

Employee benefits managers handle the company's employee benefits program, notably its health insurance and pension plans. Expertise in designing and administering benefits programs continues to gain importance as employer-provided benefits account for a growing proportion of overall compensation costs, and as benefit plans increase in number and complexity. For example, pension benefits might include savings and thrift, profit-sharing, and stock ownership plans; health benefits may include long-term catastrophic illness insurance and dental insurance. Familiarity with health benefits is a top priority at present, as more firms struggle to cope with the rising cost of health care for employees and retirees. In addition to health insurance and pension coverage, some firms offer their employees life and accidental death and dismemberment insurance, disability insurance, and relatively new benefits designed to meet the needs of a changing workforce, such as parental leave, child care and elder care, long-term nursing home care insurance, employee assistance and wellness programs, and flexible benefits plans. Benefits managers must keep abreast of changing federal and state regulations and legislation that may affect employee benefits.

Employee assistance plan managers—also called employee welfare managers—are responsible for a wide array of programs covering occupational safety and health standards and practices; health promotion and physical fitness, medical examinations, and minor health treatment, such as first aid; plant security; publications; food service and recreation activities; car pooling; employee suggestion systems; child care and elder care; and counseling services. Child care and elder care are increasingly important due to growth in the number of dual-income households and the elderly population. Counseling may help employees deal with emotional disorders, alcoholism, or marital, family, consumer, legal, and financial problems. Some employers offer career counseling as well. In large firms, some of these programs—such as security and safety—are in separate departments headed by other managers.

Training is supervised by training and development managers. Increasingly, management recognizes that training offers a way of developing skills, enhancing productivity and quality of work, and building loyalty to the firm. Training is widely accepted as a method of improving employee morale, but this is only one of the reasons for its growing importance. Other factors include the complexity of the work environment, the

rapid pace of organizational and technological change, and the growing number of jobs in fields that constantly generate new knowledge. In addition, advances in learning theory have provided insights into how adults learn, and how training can be organized most effectively for them.

Training specialists plan, organize, and direct a wide range of training activities. Trainers conduct orientation sessions and arrange on-the-job training for new employees. They help rank-and-file workers maintain and improve their job skills, and possibly prepare for jobs requiring greater skill. They help supervisors improve their interpersonal skills in order to deal effectively with employees. They may set up individualized training plans to strengthen an employee's existing skills or to teach new ones. Training specialists in some companies set up programs to develop executive potential among employees in lower-level positions. In government-supported training programs, training specialists function as case managers. They first assess the training needs of clients and then guide them through the most appropriate training method. After training, clients may either be referred to employer relations representatives or receive job placement assistance.

Planning and program development is an important part of the training specialist's job. In order to identify and assess training needs within the firm, trainers may confer with managers and supervisors or conduct surveys. They also periodically evaluate training effectiveness.

Depending on the size, goals, and nature of the organization, trainers may differ considerably in their responsibilities and in the methods they use. Training methods include on-the-job training; schools in which shop conditions are duplicated for trainees prior to putting them on the shop floor; apprenticeship training; classroom training; programmed instruction, which may involve interactive videos, videodiscs, and other computer-aided instructional technologies; simulators; conferences; and workshops.

The director of industrial relations forms labor policy, oversees industrial labor relations, negotiates collective bargaining agreements, and coordinates grievance procedures to handle complaints resulting from disputes under the contract for firms with unionized employees. The director of industrial relations also advises and collaborates with the director of human resources, other managers, and members of their staff, because all aspects of personnel policy—such as wages, benefits, pensions, and work practices—may be involved in drawing up a new or revised contract.

Industrial labor relations programs are implemented by labor relations managers and their staff. When a collective bargaining agreement is up for negotiation, labor relations specialists prepare information for management to use during negotiation, which requires familiarity with economic and wage data as well as extensive knowledge of labor law and collective bargaining trends. The labor relations staff interprets and administers the contract with respect to grievances, wages and salaries, employee welfare, health care, pensions, union and management practices, and other contractual stipulations. As union membership is continuing to decline in most industries, industrial relations personnel are working more with employees who are not members of a labor union.

Dispute resolution—attaining tacit or contractual agreements—has become increasingly important as parties to a dispute attempt to avoid costly litigation, strikes, or other disruptions. Dispute resolution also has become more complex, involving employees, management, unions, other firms, and government agencies. Specialists involved in dispute resolution must be highly knowledgeable and experienced, and often report to the director of industrial relations. Conciliators, or mediators, advise and counsel labor and management to prevent and, when necessary, resolve disputes over labor agreements or other labor relations issues. Arbitrators, sometimes called umpires or referees, decide disputes that bind both labor and management to specific terms and conditions of labor contracts. Labor relations specialists who work for unions perform many of the same functions on behalf of the union and its members.

Other emerging specialists include international human resources managers, who handle human resources issues related to a company's foreign operations, and human resources information system specialists, who develop and apply computer programs to process personnel information, match job seekers with job openings, and handle other personnel matters.

Working Conditions

Personnel work generally takes place in clean, pleasant, and comfortable office settings. Arbitrators and mediators may work out of their homes. Many human resources specialists and managers work a standard 35- to 40-hour week. However, longer hours might be necessary for some workers—for example, labor relations specialists and managers, arbitrators, and mediators—when contract agreements are being prepared and negotiated.

Although most human resources specialists and managers work in the office, some travel extensively. For example, recruiters regularly attend professional meetings and visit college campuses to interview prospective employees; arbitrators and mediators often must travel to the site chosen for negotiations.

Employment

Human resources specialists and managers held about 544,000 jobs in 1996. They were employed in virtually every industry. Specialists accounted for three out of five positions; managers, two out of five. About 15,000 specialists were self-employed, working as consultants to public and private employers.

The private sector accounted for about 86 percent of salaried jobs. Among these salaried jobs, services industries—including business, health, social, management, and educational services—accounted for four out of ten jobs; labor organizations, the largest employer among specific industries, accounted for one out of ten. Manufacturing industries accounted for two out of ten jobs, while finance, insurance, and real estate firms accounted for about one out of ten.

Federal, state, and local governments employed about 14 percent of salaried human resources specialists and managers. They handled the recruitment, interviewing, job classification, training, salary administration, benefits, employee relations, and related matters of the nation's public employees.

Training, Other Qualifications, and Advancement

Because of the diversity of duties and level of responsibility, the educational backgrounds of human resources specialists and managers vary considerably. In filling entry-level jobs, employers generally seek college graduates. Some employers prefer applicants who have majored in human resources, personnel administration, or industrial and labor relations; others look for college graduates with a technical or business background; and still others feel that a well-rounded liberal arts education is best.

Many colleges and universities have programs leading to a degree in personnel, human resources, or labor relations. Some offer degree programs in personnel administration or human resources management, training and development, or compensation and benefits. Depending on the school, courses leading to a career in human resources management may be found in departments of business administration, education, instructional technology, organizational development, human services, communication, or public administration, or within a separate human resources institution or department.

Because an interdisciplinary background is appropriate in this field, a combination of courses in the social sciences, business, and behavioral sciences is useful. Some jobs may require a more technical or specialized background in engineering, science, finance, or law, for example. Most prospective human resources specialists should take courses in compensation, recruitment, training and development, and performance appraisal, as well as courses in principles of management, organizational structure, and industrial psychology. Other relevant courses include business administration, public administration, psychology, sociology, political science, economics, and statistics. Courses in labor law, collective bargaining, labor economics, labor history, and industrial psychology also provide a valuable background for the prospective labor relations specialist. As in many other fields, knowledge of computers and information systems is useful.

An advanced degree is increasingly important for some jobs. Many labor relations jobs require graduate study in industrial or labor relations. A strong background in industrial relations and law is highly desirable for contract negotiators, mediators, and arbitrators; in fact, many people in these specialties are lawyers. A background in law is also desirable for employee benefits managers and others who must interpret the growing number of laws and regulations. A master's degree in human resources, or labor relations, or in business administration with a concentration in human resources management is highly recommended for those seeking general and top management positions.

For many specialized jobs in the human resources field, previous experience is an asset; for more advanced positions including managers as well as arbitrators and mediators, it is essential. Many employers prefer entry-level workers who have gained some experience through an internship or work-study program while in school. Personnel administration and human resources development require the ability to work with individuals as well as a commitment to organizational goals. This field also demands other skills people may develop elsewhere—using computers, selling, teaching, supervising, and volunteering, among others. This field offers clerical workers opportunities for advancement to professional positions. Responsible positions are sometimes filled by experienced individuals from other fields, including business, government, education, social services administration, and the military.

The human resources field demands a range of personal qualities and skills. Human resources specialists and managers must speak and write effectively; work with or supervise people having various cultural backgrounds, levels of education, and experience; cope with conflicting points of view, and the unexpected and unusual; function under pressure; and demonstrate integrity, fair-mindedness, and a persuasive, congenial personality.

Entry-level workers often enter formal or on-the-job training programs in which they learn how to classify jobs, interview

applicants, or administer employee benefits. They then are assigned to specific areas in the personnel department to gain experience. Later, they may advance to a managerial position, overseeing a major element of the personnel program—compensation or training, for example.

Exceptional human resources workers may be promoted to director of personnel or industrial relations, which can eventually lead to a top managerial or executive position. Others may join a consulting firm or open their own business. A Ph.D. is an asset for teaching, writing, or consulting work.

Most organizations specializing in human resources offer classes intended to enhance the marketable skills of their members. Some organizations offer certification programs, which are signs of competence and can enhance one's advancement opportunities. For example, the International Foundation of Employee Benefits Plans confers the Certified Employee Benefits Specialist certification to persons who complete a series of college-level courses and pass exams covering employee benefit plans. The Society for Human Resources Management has two levels of certification—Professional in Human Resources, and Senior Professional in Human Resources—both of which require experience and a comprehensive exam.

Job Outlook

The job market for human resources specialists and managers is likely to remain competitive through 2006, due to an abundant supply of qualified college graduates and experienced workers, despite large numbers of annual job openings that will stem from the need to replace workers who transfer to other jobs, retire, or stop working for other reasons coupled with projected average employment growth.

New jobs will stem from increasing efforts throughout industry to recruit and retain quality employees; employers are expected to devote greater resources to job-specific training programs in response to the increasing complexity of many jobs, the aging of the workforce, and technological advances that can leave employees with obsolete skills. In addition, legislation and court rulings setting standards in occupational safety and health, equal employment opportunity, wages, and health, pension, family leave, and other benefits will increase demand for experts in these areas. Rising health care costs, in particular, should spur demand for specialists to develop creative compensation and benefits packages that firms can offer prospective employees. Employment of labor relations staff, including arbitrators and mediators, should grow as firms become more involved in labor relations, and attempt to resolve potentially costly labor-management disputes out of court. Additional job growth may stem from increasing de-

mand for specialists in international human resources management and human resources information systems.

Employment demand should be strong among firms involved in management, consulting, and personnel supply, as businesses increasingly contract out personnel functions or hire personnel specialists on a temporary basis to meet the increasing cost and complexity of training and development programs. Demand should also increase in firms that develop and administer complex employee benefits and compensation packages for other organizations.

Demand for human resources specialists and managers is also governed by the staffing needs of the firms for which they work. A rapidly expanding business is likely to hire additional human resources workers—either as permanent employees or consultants—while a business that has experienced a merger or a reduction in its workforce will require fewer human resources workers. Also, as human resources management becomes increasingly important to the success of an organization, some small and medium-size businesses that do not have a human resources department may assign employees various human resources duties together with other unrelated responsibilities. In any particular firm, the size and the job duties of the human resources staff are determined by a variety of factors, including the firm's organizational philosophy and goals, the skills of its workforce, the pace of technological change, government regulations, collective bargaining agreements, standards of professional practice, and labor market conditions.

Job growth could be limited by the widespread use of computerized human resources information systems that make workers more productive. Similar to other workers, employment of human resources specialists and managers, particularly in larger firms, may be adversely affected by corporate downsizing and restructuring.

Earnings

According to a salary survey conducted by the National Association of Colleges and Employers, bachelor's degree candidates majoring in human resources, including labor relations, received starting offers averaging $25,300 a year in 1996; master's degree candidates, $39,900.

According to a 1996 survey of compensation in the human resources field, conducted by Abbott, Langer, and Associates of Crete, Illinois, the median total cash compensation for selected personnel and labor relations occupations were:

Industrial/labor relations directors	$106,100
Divisional human resources directors	91,300
Compensation and benefits directors	90,500
Employee/community relations directors	87,500
Training and organizational directors	86,600
Benefits directors	80,500
Plant/location human resources managers	64,400
Recruitment and interviewing managers	63,800
Compensation supervisors	53,400
Training generalists	49,900
Employment interviewing supervisors	42,800
Safety specialists	42,500
Job evaluation specialists	39,600
Employee assistance/employee counseling specialists	39,000
Human resources information systems specialists	38,800
Benefits specialists	38,300
E.E.O./affirmative action specialists	38,200
Training material development specialists	37,200
Employee services/employee recreation specialists	35,000

According to a survey of workplaces in 160 metropolitan areas, personnel specialists with limited experience had median earnings of $25,700 a year in 1995; the middle half earned between $23,700 and $28,500 a year. Personnel supervisors/managers with limited experience had median earnings of $59,000 a year. The middle half earned between $54,000 and $65,200 a year.

In the federal government in 1997, persons with a bachelor's degree or three years' general experience in the personnel field generally started at $19,500 a year. Those with a superior academic record or an additional year of specialized experience started at $24,200 a year. Those with a master's degree may start at $29,600, and those with a doctorate in a personnel field may start at $35,800. Beginning salaries were slightly higher in areas where the prevailing local pay level was higher. There are no formal entry-level requirements for managerial positions. Applicants must possess a suitable combination of educational attainment, experience, and record of accomplishment.

Personnel specialists in the federal government averaged $52,900 a year in 1997; personnel managers, $55,400.

Related Occupations

All human resources occupations are closely related. Other workers with skills and expertise in interpersonal relations include employment, rehabilitation, and college career planning and placement counselors; lawyers; psychologists; sociologists; social workers; public relations specialists; and teachers.

Sources of Additional Information

For information about careers in employee training and development, contact:

❏ American Society for Training and Development, 1640 King St., Box 1443, Alexandria, VA 22313.

For information about careers and certification in employee compensation and benefits, contact:

❏ American Compensation Association, 14040 Northsight Blvd., Scottsdale, AZ 85260.

Information about careers and certification in employee benefits is available from:

❏ International Foundation of Employee Benefit Plans, 18700 W. Bluemound Rd., Brookfield, WI 53045.

For information about careers in arbitration and other aspects of dispute resolution, contact:

❏ American Arbitration Association, 140 West 51st St., New York, NY 10020. Phone: (800) 778-7879

For information about academic programs in industrial relations, write to:

❏ Industrial Relations Research Association, University of Wisconsin, 7226 Social Science Bldg., 1180 Observatory Dr., Madison, WI 53706.

Information about personnel careers in the health care industry is available from:

❏ American Society for Healthcare Human Resources Administration, One North Franklin, 31st Floor, Chicago, IL 60606.

Industrial Engineers

(D.O.T. 005.167-026; 012.061 -018, .067, .167 except -022, -026, -034, -058, and -062, and .187)

Significant Points

★ *A bachelor's degree in industrial engineering is almost always required for beginning engineering jobs. Good employment opportunities are expected for new graduates.*

★ *Starting salaries for industrial engineers are significantly higher than those of bachelor's degree graduates in other fields.*

★ *Knowledge of technological advances must be acquired through continued study and education.*

Nature of the Work

Industrial engineers determine the most effective ways for an organization to use the basic factors of production—people, machines, materials, information, and energy—to make or process a product or produce a service. They are the bridge between management goals and operational performance. They are more concerned with increasing productivity through

the management of people, methods of business organization, and technology than are engineers in other specialties, who generally work more with products or processes.

To solve organizational, production, and related problems most efficiently, industrial engineers carefully study the product and its requirements, use mathematical methods such as operations research to meet those requirements, and design manufacturing and information systems. They develop management control systems to aid in financial planning and cost analysis, design production planning and control systems to coordinate activities and control product quality, and design or improve systems for the physical distribution of goods and services. Industrial engineers determine which plant location has the best combination of raw materials availability, transportation, and costs. They also develop wage and salary administration systems and job evaluation programs. Many industrial engineers move into management positions because the work is closely related.

Working Conditions

Most industrial engineers work in office buildings, laboratories, or industrial plants. Some travel extensively to plants or work sites.

Most industrial engineers work a standard 40-hour week. At times, deadlines or design standards may bring extra pressure to a job. When this happens, industrial engineers may work long hours and experience considerable stress.

Employment

Industrial engineers held about 115,000 jobs in 1996. About 73 percent of these jobs were in manufacturing industries. Because their skills can be used in almost any type of organization, industrial engineers are more widely distributed among manufacturing industries than other engineers.

Their skills can be readily applied outside manufacturing as well. Some work in engineering and management services, utilities, and business services; others work for government agencies or as independent consultants.

Training, Other Qualifications, and Advancement

A bachelor's degree in engineering is usually required for beginning engineering jobs. College graduates with a degree in a physical science or mathematics may occasionally qualify for some engineering jobs, especially in engineering specialties in high demand. Most engineering degrees are granted in electrical, mechanical, or civil engineering. However, engineers trained in one branch may work in related branches; for example, many aerospace engineers have training in

mechanical engineering. This flexibility allows employers to meet staffing needs in new technologies and specialties in which engineers are in short supply. It also allows engineers to shift to fields with better employment prospects, or to ones that match their interests more closely.

In addition to the standard engineering degree, many colleges offer degrees in engineering technology, which are offered as either two- or four-year programs. These programs prepare students for practical design and production work rather than for jobs that require more theoretical, scientific, and mathematical knowledge. Graduates of four-year technology programs may get jobs similar to those obtained by graduates with a bachelor's degree in engineering. Some employers regard them as having skills between those of a technician and an engineer.

Graduate training is essential for engineering faculty positions, but is not required for the majority of entry-level engineering jobs. Many engineers obtain graduate degrees in engineering or business administration to learn new technology, broaden their education, and enhance promotion opportunities. Many high-level executives in government and industry began their careers as engineers.

About 320 colleges and universities offer bachelor's degree programs in engineering that are accredited by the Accreditation Board for Engineering and Technology (ABET), and about 250 colleges offer accredited bachelor's degree programs in engineering technology. ABET accreditation is based on an examination of an engineering program's faculty, curricular content, facilities, and admissions standards. Although most institutions offer programs in the major branches of engineering, only a few offer some of the smaller specialties. Also, programs of the same title may vary in content. For example, some emphasize industrial practices, preparing students for a job in industry, while others are more theoretical and are better for students preparing to take graduate work. Therefore, students should investigate curricula and check accreditations carefully before selecting a college. Admissions requirements for undergraduate engineering schools include a solid background in mathematics (algebra, geometry, trigonometry, and calculus), sciences (biology, chemistry, and physics), and courses in English, social studies, humanities, and computers.

Bachelor's degree programs in engineering are typically designed to last four years, but many students find that it takes between four and five years to complete their studies. In a typical four-year college curriculum, the first two years are spent studying mathematics, basic sciences, introductory engineering, humanities, and social sciences. In the last two years, most courses are in engineering, usually with a concentration in one branch. For example, the last two years of an aerospace program might include courses such as fluid mechanics, heat transfer, applied aerodynamics, analytical mechanics, flight vehicle design, trajectory dynamics, and aerospace propulsion systems. Some programs offer a general engineering curriculum; students then specialize in graduate school or on the job.

Some engineering schools and two-year colleges have agreements whereby the two-year college provides the initial engineering education and the engineering school automatically admits students for their last two years. In addition, a few engineering schools have arrangements whereby a student spends three years in a liberal arts college studying pre-engineering subjects and two years in the engineering school, and receives a bachelor's degree from each. Some colleges and universities offer five-year master's degree programs. Some five- or even six-year cooperative plans combine classroom study and practical work, permitting students to gain valuable experience and finance part of their education.

All 50 states and the District of Columbia require registration for engineers whose work may affect life, health, or property, or who offer their services to the public. Registration generally requires a degree from an ABET-accredited engineering program, four years of relevant work experience, and passing a state examination. Some states will not register people with degrees in engineering technology. Engineers may be registered in several states.

Engineers should be creative, inquisitive, analytical, and detail-oriented. They should be able to work as part of a team and be able to communicate well, both orally and in writing.

Beginning engineering graduates usually work under the supervision of experienced engineers and, in larger companies, may also receive formal classroom or seminar-type training. As they gain knowledge and experience, they are assigned more difficult projects with greater independence to develop designs, solve problems, and make decisions. Engineers may advance to become technical specialists or to supervise a staff or team of engineers and technicians. Some eventually become engineering managers or enter other managerial, management support, or sales jobs.

Job Outlook

Employment of industrial engineers is expected to grow about as fast as the average for all occupations through the year 2006, making for favorable opportunities. Industrial growth, more complex business operations, and the greater use of automation in factories and in offices underlie the projected employment growth. Because the main function of industrial engineers is to make a higher quality product as efficiently as possible, their services should be in demand in the manufacturing sector as firms seek to reduce costs and increase productivity through scientific management and safety engineering. Most job openings, however, will result from the need to replace industrial engineers who transfer to other occupations or leave the labor force.

Earnings

Starting salaries for industrial engineers with the bachelor's degree are significantly higher than starting salaries of bachelor's degree graduates in other fields. According to the National Association of Colleges and Employers, starting salaries for those with the bachelor's degree were about $38,026 in 1996.

The median annual salary for all industrial engineers who worked full-time in 1996 was $43,700.

The average annual salary for engineers in the federal government in nonsupervisory, supervisory, and managerial positions was $61,950 in 1997.

Related Occupations

Industrial engineers apply the principles of physical science and mathematics in their work. Other workers who use scientific and mathematical principles include engineering, science, and computer systems managers; physical, life, and computer scientists; mathematicians; engineering and science technicians; and architects.

Sources of Additional Information

High school students interested in obtaining general information on a variety of engineering disciplines should contact the Junior Engineering Technical Society by sending a self-addressed business-size envelope, with six first-class stamps affixed, to:

❑ JETS-Guidance, 1420 King St., Suite 405, Alexandria, VA 22314-2794. Homepage: http://www.asee.org/jets

High school students interested in obtaining information on ABET accredited engineering programs should contact:

❑ The Accreditation Board for Engineering and Technology, Inc., 111 Market Place, Suite 1050, Baltimore, MD 21202-4012. Homepage: http://www.abet.ba.md.us

Non-high school students and those wanting more detailed information should contact:

❑ Institute of Industrial Engineers, Inc., 25 Technology Park/Atlanta, Norcross, GA 30092. Homepage: http://www.iienet.org

Industrial Production Managers

(*D.O.T.* 180.167-054; 181.117-010; 182.167-022; 183.117-010, -014, .161-014, .167-010, -014, -018, -022, -026, -034, -038; 188.167-094; 189.117-042, .167-042, -046)

Significant Points

* The projected decline in employment reflects growing productivity and organizational restructuring.
* Applicants with college degrees in industrial engineering or business administration, and particularly those with MBAs and undergraduate engineering degrees, have the best job prospects.

Nature of the Work

Industrial production managers coordinate the resources and activities required to produce millions of goods every year in the United States. Although their duties vary from plant to plant, industrial production managers share many of the same major functions. These functions include responsibility for production scheduling, staffing, equipment, quality control, inventory control, and the coordination of production activities with those of other departments.

The primary mission of industrial production managers is planning the production schedule within budgetary limitations and time constraints. This entails analyzing the plant's personnel and capital resources to select the best way of meeting the production quota. Industrial production managers determine which machines will be used, whether overtime or extra shifts are necessary, and the sequence of production. They also monitor the production run to make sure that it stays on schedule and correct any problems that may arise.

Industrial production managers must also monitor product standards. When quality drops below the established standard, they must determine why standards aren't being maintained and how to improve the product. If the problem is poor work, the manager may implement better training programs, reorganize the manufacturing process, or institute employee suggestion or involvement programs. If the cause is substandard materials, the manager works with the purchasing department to improve the quality of the product's components.

Because the work of many departments is interrelated, managers work closely with heads of other departments such as sales, purchasing, and traffic to plan and implement company goals, policies, and procedures. For example, the production manager works with the purchasing department to ensure that plant inventories are maintained at their optimal level. This is vital to a firm's operation because maintaining the inventory of materials necessary for production ties up the firm's financial resources, yet insufficient quantities cause delays in production. A breakdown in communications between the production manager and the purchasing department can cause slowdowns and a failure to meet production schedules. Computers are coming to play a more important role not only in this coordination, but also in providing up-to-date data on inventory, work-in-progress, and quality standards.

Production managers usually report to the plant manager or the vice president for manufacturing, and may act as liaison between executives and first-line supervisors. In many plants, one production manager is responsible for all aspects of production. In large plants with several operations—aircraft assembly, for example—there are managers in charge of each operation, such as machining, assembly, or finishing.

Working Conditions

Most industrial production managers divide their time between the shop floor and their offices. While on the floor, they must follow established health and safety practices and wear the required protective clothing and equipment. The time in the office, which is often located on or near the production floor, is usually spent meeting with subordinates or other department managers, analyzing production data, and writing and reviewing reports.

Most industrial production managers work more than 40 hours a week, especially when production deadlines must be met. In facilities that operate around the clock, managers often work late shifts and may be called at any hour to deal with emergencies. This could mean going to the plant to resolve the problem, regardless of the hour, and staying until the situation is under control. Dealing with production workers as well as superiors when working under the pressure of production deadlines or emergency situations can be stressful. This stress has been compounded by restructuring that has eliminated levels of management and support staff, shifting more responsibilities to production managers.

Employment

Industrial production managers held about 207,000 jobs in 1996. Although employed throughout the manufacturing sector, about one-half are employed in firms that produce industrial machinery and equipment, transportation equipment, electronic and electrical equipment, fabricated metal products, instruments and related products, and food products. Production managers work in all parts of the country, but jobs are most plentiful in areas where manufacturing is concentrated.

Training, Other Qualifications, and Advancement

Because of the diversity of manufacturing operations and job requirements, there is no standard preparation for this occupation. Many industrial production managers have a college degree in business administration or industrial engineering. Some have a master's degree in business administration (MBA). Others are former production line supervisors who have been promoted. Although many employers prefer candidates to have a degree in business or engineering, some companies hire liberal arts graduates.

As production operations become more sophisticated, an increasing number of employers are looking for candidates with MBAs. Combined with an undergraduate degree in engineering, this is considered particularly good preparation. Companies also are placing greater importance on a candidate's personality. Because the job requires the ability to compromise, persuade, and negotiate, successful production managers must be well-rounded and have excellent communication skills.

The few who enter the field directly from college or graduate school often are unfamiliar with the firm's production process. As a result, they may spend their first few months on the job in the company's training program. These programs familiarize trainees with the production line, company policies, and the requirements of the job. In larger companies, they may also include assignments to other departments, such as purchasing and accounting. A number of companies hire college graduates as blue-collar worker supervisors and later promote them.

Some industrial production managers have worked their way up the ranks, perhaps after having worked as blue-collar worker supervisors. These workers already have an intimate knowledge of the production process and the firm's organization. To be selected for promotion, they must have demonstrated leadership qualities and usually have taken company-sponsored courses in management skills and communication techniques.

In addition to formal training, industrial production managers must closely follow new production technologies and management practices. To do this, they belong to professional organizations and attend trade shows where new equipment is displayed; they also attend industry conferences and conventions where changes in production methods and technological advances are discussed.

Industrial production managers with a proven record of superior performance may advance to plant manager or vice president for manufacturing. Others transfer to jobs at larger firms with more responsibilities. Opportunities also exist as consultants.

Job Outlook

Employment of industrial production managers is expected to decline slightly through the year 2006. However, a number of job openings will stem from the need to replace workers who transfer to other occupations or leave the labor force. Applicants with college degrees in industrial engineering or business administration, and particularly those with MBAs and undergraduate engineering degrees, will be in the best position to fill these openings. Employers also are likely to seek candidates who have excellent communication skills, and who are personable, flexible, and eager to participate in ongoing training.

Although manufacturing output is projected to rise, growing productivity among production managers and organizational restructuring will limit the demand for these workers. Productivity gains will result from the widening use of computers for scheduling, planning, and coordination. In addition, just-in-time manufacturing eases scheduling demands, and a growing emphasis on building quality inspection into the production process has redistributed some of the production manager's oversight responsibilities. Because production managers are so integral to the efficient operation of a plant, they have not been greatly affected by recent efforts to flatten management structures. Nevertheless, this trend has led production managers to assume more responsibilities and has discouraged the creation of more employment opportunities.

Earnings

Salaries of industrial production managers vary significantly by industry and plant size. According to Abbott, Langer, and Associates, the average salary for all production managers was $60,000 in 1996. In addition to salary, industrial production managers may receive bonuses based on job performance.

Related Occupations

Industrial production managers oversee production staff and equipment, ensure that production goals and quality standards are being met, and implement company policies. Individuals with similar functions include materials, operations, purchasing, and traffic managers. Other occupations requiring similar training and skills are sales engineer, manufacturer's sales representative, and industrial engineer.

Sources of Additional Information

Information on industrial production management can be obtained from:

❑ National Management Association, 2210 Arbor Blvd., Dayton, OH 45439.

❑ American Management Association, 1601 Broadway, New York, NY 10019.

Insurance Underwriters

(D.O.T. 169.267-046)

Significant Points

✷ *Most large insurance companies prefer college graduates who have a degree in business administration or finance, with courses or experience in accounting.*

✷ *Employment is projected to grow more slowly than average as insurance companies use "smart" underwriting software systems that automatically analyze and rate insurance applications, and as more businesses self-insure.*

Nature of the Work

Insurance companies protect individuals and organizations from financial loss by assuming billions of dollars in risks each year. Underwriters identify and analyze the risk of loss from their policyholders, establish appropriate premium rates, and write policies that cover that risk. An insurance company may lose business to competitors if the underwriter appraises risks too conservatively, or it may have to pay more claims if the underwriting actions are too liberal.

Technology plays an increasingly important role in an underwriter's job. Underwriters use computer applications called "smart systems" to manage risks more efficiently and accurately. They enter into the computer various information relating to a person or organization whose application for insurance is pending. These systems automatically analyze and rate insurance applications and then recommend acceptance or denial of the risk, or they adjust the premium rate in accordance with the risk. Underwriters are then better equipped to make sound decisions in an effort to avoid excessive losses in the future.

With the aid of computers, underwriters analyze information in insurance applications, reports from loss control consultants, medical reports, and actuarial studies—reports that describe the probability of insured loss. They then decide whether to issue a policy and outline the terms of the contract, including the amount of the premium. Underwriters sometimes correspond with policyholders, agents, and managers about policy cancellations or other matters. On rare occasions, they accompany sales representatives on appointments with prospective clients. (Life insurance agents and brokers are increasingly called "life underwriters.")

Most underwriters specialize in one of three major categories of insurance—life, property and casualty, or health. They further specialize in group or individual policies. Property and casualty underwriters often specialize by type of risk insured, such as fire, homeowners, automobile, marine, property, liability, or workers' compensation. In cases where casualty companies insure in a single "package" policy, covering various types of risks, the underwriter must be familiar with different lines of insurance. Some underwriters, called commercial account underwriters, handle business insurance exclusively. They often evaluate a firm's entire operation in appraising its application for insurance.

An increasing proportion of insurance sales, particularly in life and health insurance, are being made through group contracts. A standard group policy insures everyone in a specified group through a single contract at a standard premium rate. The group underwriter analyzes the overall composition of the group to assure that the total risk is not excessive. Another type of group policy provides members of a group—a labor union, for example—with individual policies reflecting their needs. These generally are casualty policies, such as those covering automobiles. The casualty underwriter analyzes the application of each group member and makes individual appraisals. Some group underwriters meet with union or employer representatives to discuss the types of policies available to their group.

Working Conditions

Underwriters have desk jobs that require no unusual physical activity. Their offices generally are comfortable and pleasant. Although overtime may be required, underwriters generally work from 35 to 40 hours a week. They occasionally attend meetings away from home for several days. Construction and marine underwriters often travel to inspect work sites and assess risks.

Employment

Insurance underwriters held about 95,000 jobs in 1996. The following tabulation shows the percent distribution of employment by industry in 1996.

Fire, marine, and casualty insurance carriers	37
Insurance agents, brokers, and service	33
Life insurance carriers	15
Pension funds and miscellaneous insurance carriers	4
Medical service and health insurance carriers	4
Other industries	7

Most underwriters worked for insurance companies, often called "carriers." Most of the remaining underwriters worked in independent insurance agencies (firms which represent one or more insurance companies) and brokers (firms which may deal with any insurance company and represent the interests of the buyers of insurance, known as "insureds.") A small number of underwriters worked in agencies owned and operated by banks, mortgage companies, and real estate firms.

Office underwriters in the life insurance industry are most likely to work in an insurance company's home office. In some large general agencies, underwriters help life insurance agents, or "producers," determine if the risk will be accepted or rejected by the home office. However, most local life insurance offices deal predominantly with sales, not underwriting. Property and casualty underwriters also work in home offices, but more work for agencies or regional branch offices, where they have the authority to underwrite risks and determine an appropriate rating without consulting the home office.

Training, Other Qualifications, and Advancement

For beginning underwriting jobs, most large insurance companies prefer college graduates who have a degree in business administration or finance, with courses or experience in accounting. However, a bachelor's degree in almost any field—plus courses in business law and accounting—provides a good general background and may be sufficient to qualify. Computer knowledge is essential.

Beginners typically start as underwriter trainees or assistant underwriters. They may help collect information on applicants and evaluate routine applications under the supervision of an experienced risk analyst. Property and casualty trainees may study claim files to become familiar with factors associated with certain types of losses. Many larger insurers offer a training program, lasting from a few months to a year, that combines study with work. As trainees gain experience, they are assigned policy applications that are more complex and cover greater risks. These require the use of computers for more efficient analysis and processing.

Continuing education is necessary for advancement. Insurance companies generally pay tuition for underwriting courses that their trainees successfully complete; some also offer salary incentives. Independent study programs for experienced property and casualty underwriters are also available. The Insurance Institute of America offers a program called "Introduction to Underwriting" for beginning underwriters, and the specialty designation, AU, or Associate Underwriting, the second formal step in developing a career in underwriting. To earn the AU designation, underwriters complete a series of courses and examinations; it usually takes about two years to earn the AU designation. The American Institute for Chartered Property Casualty Underwriters awards the designation, CPCU, or Chartered Property and Casualty Underwriter, the third and final stage of development for an underwriter. Earning the more advanced CPCU designation generally takes about five years, and requires passing ten examinations covering personal and commercial insurance, risk management, business and insurance law, accounting, finance, management, economics, and ethics. Although CPCUs may be underwriters, the CPCU is intended for everyone working in all aspects of property and casualty insurance. The American Society of Chartered Life Underwriters provides the Chartered Life Underwriter (CLU) designation, intended for underwriters working in life insurance.

Underwriting can be a satisfying career for people who enjoy working with detail and analyzing information. In addition, underwriters must possess good judgment in order to make sound decisions. They must also be imaginative and aggressive, especially when they have to obtain information from many outside sources.

Experienced underwriters who complete courses of study may advance to senior underwriter or underwriting manager positions. Some underwriting managers are promoted to senior managerial jobs. Others are attracted to the earnings potential of sales and obtain state licensing to sell insurance and insurance products as agents or brokers.

Job Outlook

Employment of underwriters is expected to increase more slowly than the average for all occupations through the year 2006. Most job openings are expected to result from the need to replace underwriters who transfer to other occupations or stop working altogether.

A number of factors underlie the continuing need for underwriters. As people acquire assets and take on family responsibilities, the need for life, health, and property and casualty insurance grows. For example, concerns for financial security and liability contribute to demands for more insurance protection for homes, automobiles, pleasure craft, and other valuables. Expanding long-term health care and pension benefits for retirees—who are an increasing proportion of the population—also will increase underwriting opportunities. And, new or expanding businesses will need protection for new factories and equipment, and product liability, workers' compensation, and employee benefits insurance.

Employment of underwriters, however, is not expected to keep pace with growth in demand for insurance. Increased use of underwriting software systems will slow the demand

for new underwriters. As more businesses self-insure—by setting a rate for their own company and paying premiums into a contingency fund—demand for some property and casualty underwriters will decline. Additionally, many property and casualty companies are forgoing personal lines of insurance—especially automobile and homeowners—and are concentrating on commercial lines of business.

Underwriters specializing in certain lines of insurance may find it difficult to transfer to another type of insurance if their jobs are threatened by corporate downsizing. Because insurance is usually regarded as a necessity, regardless of economic conditions, underwriters are unlikely to be laid off because of a recession.

Earnings

Median annual earnings of full-time wage and salary underwriters were about $31,400 in 1996. The middle 50 percent earned between $24,000 and $41,000 a year. The lowest 10 percent earned less than $18,400; the top 10 percent, more than $52,400.

In addition to typical benefits, almost all insurance companies provide employer-financed group life, health, and retirement plans.

Related Occupations

Underwriters make decisions on the basis of financial data. Other workers with the same type of responsibility include auditors, budget analysts, financial advisers, loan officers, credit managers, real estate appraisers, and risk managers.

Sources of Additional Information

General information about a career as an insurance underwriter is available from the home offices of many life insurance and property-liability insurance companies. Information about the insurance business in general and the underwriting function in particular also may be obtained from:

❏ The American Institute for Chartered Property and Casualty Underwriters, and the Insurance Institute of America, 720 Providence Rd., P.O. Box 3016, Malvern, PA 19355-0716.

Landscape Architects

(D.O.T. 001.061-018)

Significant Points

* *Nearly 30 percent—over three times the proportion for all professionals—are self-employed.*

* *A bachelor's degree in landscape architecture is the minimum requirement for entry-level jobs; many employers prefer to hire landscape architects who have completed at least one internship.*

* *Because many landscape architects work for small firms or are self-employed, benefits tend to be less generous than those provided to workers in large organizations.*

Nature of the Work

Everyone enjoys attractively designed residential areas, public parks and playgrounds, college campuses, shopping centers, golf courses, parkways, and industrial parks. Landscape architects design these areas so that they are not only functional but beautiful and compatible with the natural environment as well. They may plan the location of buildings, roads, and walkways and the arrangement of flowers, shrubs, and trees. Historic preservation and natural resource conservation and reclamation are other important objectives to which landscape architects may apply their knowledge of the environment as well as their design and artistic talents.

Many types of organizations—from real estate development firms starting new projects to municipalities constructing airports or parks—hire landscape architects, who are often involved with the development of a site from its conception. Working with architects, surveyors, and engineers, landscape architects help determine the best arrangement of roads and buildings. They also collaborate with environmental scientists, foresters, and other professionals to find the best way to conserve or restore natural resources. Once these decisions are made, landscape architects create detailed plans indicating new topography, vegetation, walkways, and other landscaping details, such as fountains and decorative features.

In planning a site, landscape architects first consider the nature and purpose of the project and the funds available. They analyze the natural elements of the site, such as the climate, soil, slope of the land, drainage, and vegetation; observe where sunlight falls on the site at different times of the day and examine the site from various angles; and assess the effect of existing buildings, roads, walkways, and utilities on the project.

After studying and analyzing the site, they prepare a preliminary design. To account for the needs of the client as well as the conditions at the site, they may have to make many changes before a final design is approved. They must also take into account any local, state, or federal regulations such as those protecting wetlands or historic resources. Computer-aided design (CAD) has become an essential tool for most landscape architects in preparing designs. Many landscape architects also use video simulation to help clients envision the proposed ideas and plans. For larger scale site planning, landscape architects also use geographic information systems technology, a computer mapping system.

Throughout all phases of the planning and design, landscape architects consult with other professionals involved in the project. Once the design is complete, they prepare a proposal for the client. They produce detailed plans of the site, including written reports, sketches, models, photographs, land-use studies, and cost estimates, and submit them for approval by the client and by regulatory agencies. If the plans are approved, landscape architects prepare working drawings showing all existing and proposed features. They also outline in detail the methods of construction and draw up a list of necessary materials.

Although many landscape architects supervise the installation of their design, some are involved in the construction of the site. However, this usually is done by the developer or landscape contractor.

Some landscape architects work on a wide variety of projects. Others specialize in a particular area, such as residential development, historic landscape restoration, waterfront improvement projects, parks and playgrounds, or shopping centers. Still others work in regional planning and resource management; feasibility, environmental impact, and cost studies; or site construction.

Although most landscape architects do at least some residential work, relatively few limit their practice to landscape design for individual homeowners because most residential landscape design projects are too small to provide suitable income compared with larger commercial or multiunit residential projects. Some nurseries offer residential landscape design services, but these services often are performed by lesser qualified landscape designers or others with training and experience in related areas.

Landscape architects who work for government agencies do site and landscape design for government buildings, parks, and other public lands, as well as park and recreation planning in national parks and forests. In addition, they may prepare environmental impact statements and studies on environmental issues such as public land-use planning. Some are involved in efforts to restore degraded land, such as mines or landfills.

Working Conditions

Landscape architects spend most of their time in offices creating plans and designs, preparing models and cost estimates, doing research, or attending meetings with clients and other professionals involved in a design or planning project.

The remainder of their time is spent at the site. During the design and planning stage, landscape architects visit and analyze the site to verify that the design can be incorporated into the landscape. After the plans and specifications are completed, they may spend additional time at the site observing or supervising the construction. Those who work in large firms may spend considerably more time out of the office because of travel to sites outside the local area.

Salaried employees in both government and landscape architectural firms usually work regular hours; however, they may work overtime, sometimes 60 or more hours a week, to meet a project deadline. Hours of self-employed landscape architects may vary.

Employment

Landscape architects held about 17,000 jobs in 1996. About two out of five worked for firms that provide landscape architecture services. Most of the rest were employed by architectural firms. The federal government also employs these workers, primarily in the U.S. Departments of Agriculture, Defense, and Interior. About three of every ten landscape architects were self-employed.

Employment of landscape architects is concentrated in urban and suburban areas throughout the country. Some landscape architects work in rural areas, particularly those in the federal government who plan and design parks and recreation areas.

Training, Other Qualifications, and Advancement

A bachelor's or master's degree in landscape architecture is usually necessary for entry into the profession. The bachelor's degree in landscape architecture takes four or five years to complete. There are two types of accredited master's degree programs. The master's degree as a first professional degree is a three-year program designed for students with an undergraduate degree in another discipline; this is the most common type. The master's degree as the second professional degree is a two-year program for students who have a bachelor's degree in landscape architecture and wish to teach or specialize in some aspect of landscape architecture, such as regional planning or golf course design.

In 1996, 54 colleges and universities offered 70 undergraduate and graduate programs in landscape architecture that were accredited by the Landscape Architecture Accreditation Board of the American Society of Landscape Architects.

College courses required in this field usually include technical subjects such as surveying, landscape design and construction, landscape ecology, site design, and urban and

regional planning. Other courses include history of landscape architecture, plant and soil science, geology, professional practice, and general management. Many landscape architecture programs are adding courses which address environmental issues. In addition, most students at the undergraduate level take a year of prerequisite courses such as English, mathematics, and social and physical science. The design studio is an important aspect of many landscape architecture curriculums. Whenever possible, students are assigned real projects, providing them with valuable hands-on experience. While working on these projects, students may become more proficient in the use of technologies such as computer-aided design, geographic information systems, and video simulation.

In 1996, 45 states required landscape architects to be licensed or registered. Licensing is based on the Landscape Architect Registration Examination (L.A.R.E.), sponsored by the Council of Landscape Architectural Registration Boards and administered over a three-day period. Admission to the exam usually requires a degree from an accredited school plus one to four years of work experience, although standards vary from state to state. Currently, 18 states require the passage of a state examination in addition to the L.A.R.E. to satisfy registration requirements. State examinations, which are usually one hour in length and completed at the end of the L.A.R.E., focus on laws, environmental regulations, plants, soils, climate, and any other characteristics unique to the state.

Because state requirements for licensure are not uniform, landscape architects may not find it easy to transfer their registration from one state to another. However, those who meet the national standards of graduating from an accredited program, serving three years of internship under the supervision of a registered landscape architect, and passing the L.A.R.E. can satisfy requirements in most states.

In the federal government, candidates for entry positions should have a bachelor's or master's degree in landscape architecture. The federal government does not require its landscape architects to be licensed.

Persons planning a career in landscape architecture should appreciate nature and enjoy working with their hands. Creative vision and artistic talent are desirable qualities, but they are not essential to success as a landscape architect. Good oral communication skills are important, because these workers must be able to convey their ideas to other professionals and clients and to make presentations before large groups. Strong writing skills are also valuable, as is knowledge of computer applications of all kinds, including word processing, desktop publishing, and spreadsheets. Landscape architects use these tools to develop presentations, proposals, reports, and land impact studies for clients, colleagues, and superiors. The ability to draft and design using CAD software is essential. Many employers recommend that prospective landscape architects complete at least one summer internship with a landscape architecture firm in order to gain an understanding of the day-to-day operations of a small business, including how to win clients, generate fees, and work within a budget.

In states where licensure is required, new hires may be called apprentices or intern landscape architects until they become licensed. Their duties vary depending on the type and size of employing firm. They may do project research or prepare working drawings, construction documents, or base maps of the area to be landscaped. Some are allowed to participate in the actual design of a project. However, interns must perform all work under the supervision of a licensed landscape architect. Additionally, all drawings and specifications must be signed and sealed by the licensed landscape architect, who takes legal responsibility for the work. After gaining experience and becoming licensed, landscape architects usually can carry a design through all stages of development. After several years, they may become project managers, taking on the responsibility for meeting schedules and budgets, in addition to overseeing the project design; and later, associates or partners, with a proprietary interest in the business.

Many landscape architects are self-employed because start-up costs, after an initial investment in CAD software, are relatively low. Self-discipline, business acumen, and good marketing skills are important qualities for those who choose to open their own business. Even with these qualities, however, some may struggle while building a client base.

Those with landscape architecture training also qualify for jobs closely related to landscape architecture, and may, after gaining some experience, become construction supervisors, land or environmental planners, or landscape consultants.

Job Outlook

Employment of landscape architects is expected to increase faster than the average for all occupations through the year 2006. The level of new construction plays an important role in determining demand for landscape architects. Overall, anticipated growth in construction is expected to increase demand for landscape architectural services over the long run. However, opportunities will vary from year to year and by geographic region, depending on local economic conditions. During a recession, when real estate sales and construction slow down, landscape architects may face layoffs and greater competition for jobs. The need to replace landscape architects who retire or leave the labor force for other reasons is expected to produce nearly as many job openings as new openings stemming from job growth.

An increasing proportion of office and other commercial and industrial development will occur outside cities. These projects are typically located on larger sites with more surrounding land which needs to be designed, in contrast to urban development, which often includes little or no surrounding land. Also, as the cost of land rises, the importance of good site planning and landscape design grows. Increasingly, new development is contingent upon compliance with environmental regulations and land use zoning, spurring demand for landscape architects to help plan sites and integrate man-made structures with the natural environment in the least disruptive way.

Increased development of open space into recreation areas, wildlife refuges, and parks will also require the skills of landscape architects. However, budget tightening in the federal government may restrict funding for such initiatives in the Forest Service and the National Park Service, agencies which traditionally employ many landscape architects.

In addition to the work related to new development and construction, landscape architects are expected to be involved in historic preservation, land reclamation, and refurbishment of existing sites, although these activities are expected to account for only a small proportion of new jobs.

New graduates can expect to face competition for jobs in the largest and most prestigious landscape architecture firms. The number of professional degrees awarded in landscape architecture has remained steady over the years, even during times of fluctuating demand due to economic conditions. Opportunities will be best for landscape architects who develop strong technical and communication skills and a knowledge of environmental codes and regulations. Those with additional training or experience in urban planning increase their opportunities for employment in landscape architecture firms that specialize in site planning as well as landscape design. Many employers prefer to hire entry-level landscape architects who have internship experience, which significantly reduces training time.

Earnings

Median annual earnings for all architects, including landscape architects, were about $39,500 in 1996. The middle 50 percent earned between $30,200 and $53,900; 10 percent earned less than $23,900; and 10 percent earned over $65,800. In 1997, the average annual salary for all landscape architects in the federal government in nonsupervisory, supervisory, and managerial positions was about $53,300.

Because many landscape architects work for small firms or are self-employed, benefits tend to be less generous than those provided to workers in large organizations.

Related Occupations

Landscape architects use their knowledge of design, construction, land-use planning, and environmental issues to develop a landscape project. Others whose work requires similar skills are architects, surveyors, civil engineers, soil conservationists, and urban and regional planners. Landscape architects also know how to grow and use plants in the landscape. Botanists, who study plants in general, and horticulturists, who study ornamental plants as well as fruit, vegetable, greenhouse, and nursery crops, do similar work.

Sources of Additional Information

Additional information, including a list of colleges and universities offering accredited programs in landscape architecture, is available from:

❏ American Society of Landscape Architects, Career Information, 4401 Connecticut Ave. NW, Suite 500, Washington, DC 20008.

General information on registration or licensing requirements is available from:

❏ Council of Landscape Architectural Registration Boards, 12700 Fair Lakes Circle, Suite 110, Fairfax, VA 22033. FAX (703) 818-1309. E-mail address: clarb2@aol.com

Loan Officers and Counselors

(D.O.T. 186.167-078, .267-018, -022, -026)

Significant Points

* *Loan officer positions generally require a bachelor's degree in finance, economics, or a related field; for commercial or mortgage loan officers, training or experience in sales is advantageous.*

* *Faster than average employment growth will stem from increases in the number and complexity of loans and in the importance of loan officers to the success of banks and other lending institutions.*

Nature of the Work

Banks and other financial institutions need up-to-date information on companies and individuals applying for loans and credit. Customers and clients provide this information to the financial institution's loan officers, generally the first employees to be seen by them. Loan officers prepare, analyze, and verify loan applications, make decisions regarding the extension of credit, and help borrowers fill out loan applications. Loan counselors, also called loan collection officers, contact

borrowers who have delinquent accounts and help them find a method of repayment to avoid a default on the loan.

Loan officers usually specialize in commercial, consumer, or mortgage loans. Commercial or business loans help companies pay for new equipment or expand operations. Consumer loans include home equity, automobile, and personal loans. Mortgage loans are made to purchase real estate or to refinance an existing mortgage.

Consumer loan officers attempt to lower their firm's risk by receiving collateral—property pledged as security for the payment of a loan. For example, when lending money for a college education, the bank may insist that the borrower offer his or her home as collateral. If the borrower were ever unable to repay the loan, the borrower would have to sell the home to raise the necessary money.

Commercial and mortgage loan officers behave as sales people who actively seek out potential customers. Commercial loan officers contact firms that may or may not have accounts with their bank. They find out if their potential client is planning any projects for which they may need a loan; if so, loan officers try to establish a relationship with the firm so that the firm will contact them when the loan is needed. Similarly, mortgage loan officers try to develop relationships with commercial or residential real estate agencies; when an individual or firm buys a property, the real estate agent might recommend contacting that loan officer for financing.

Banks and other lenders are offering a growing variety of loans. Loan officers must keep abreast of new types of loans and other financial products and services so they can meet their customers' needs.

Loan officers meet with customers to gather basic information about the loan request, and explain the different types of loans that are available to the applicant. Often customers will not fully understand the information requested, and will call the loan officer for clarification. Once the customer completes the financial forms, the loan officer begins to process them. The loan officer verifies that the customer has correctly identified the type and purpose of the loan. The loan officer then requests a credit report from one or more of the major credit reporting agencies. This information, along with comments from the loan officer, is included in a loan file, and is compared to the lending institution's requirements. Banks and other lenders have established requirements for the maximum percentage of income that can safely go to repay loans. At this point, the loan officer, in consultation with his or her manager, decides whether or not to grant the loan. A loan that would otherwise be denied may be approved if the customer can provide the lender appropriate collateral. The loan officer also informs the borrower if the loan is approved or denied.

Loan counselors contact holders of delinquent accounts in an effort to develop a repayment plan. If a repayment plan cannot be developed, the loan counselor initiates collateral liquidation, in which case the collateral used to secure the loan—a home or car, for example—is seized by the lender and sold to repay the loan.

Working Conditions

Commercial and mortgage loan officers frequently work away from their offices, relying on laptop computers, cellular phones, and pagers to keep in contact with their offices and clients. Mortgage loan officers frequently work out of their home or car, often visiting offices or homes of clients while completing the loan application. Commercial loan officers may travel to other cities to prepare complex loan agreements. Consumer loan officers and loan counselors are likely to spend most of their time in an office.

Most loan officers and counselors work a standard 40-hour week, but may work longer, particularly mortgage loan officers who are free to take on as many customers as they choose. Loan officers usually carry a heavy caseload and sometimes cannot accept new clients until they complete current cases. They are especially busy when interest rates are low, triggering a surge in loan applications.

Employment

Loan officers and counselors held about 209,000 jobs in 1996. About three out of five are employed by commercial banks, savings institutions, and credit unions. Others are employed by nonbank financial institutions, such as mortgage brokerage firms and personal credit firms. Loan officers are concentrated in urban and suburban areas. In rural areas, the loan application process is often handled by the branch or assistant manager.

Training, Other Qualifications, and Advancement

Loan officer positions generally require a bachelor's degree in finance, economics, or a related field. Most employers also prefer applicants who are familiar with computers and their applications in banking. For commercial or mortgage loan officer jobs, training or experience in sales is highly valued by potential employers. A small number of loan officers advance through the ranks in an organization, acquiring several years of work experience in various other occupations, such as teller or customer service representative.

Persons planning a career as a loan officer or counselor should be capable of developing effective working relationships with others, confident in their abilities, and highly motivated. Loan officers must be willing to attend community events as a representative of their employer.

The American Institute of Banking, which is affiliated with the American Bankers Association, offers courses through correspondence and in some colleges and universities for students and others interested in lending, as well as for experienced loan officers. Completion of these courses and programs enhances one's employment and advancement opportunities.

Capable loan officers and counselors may advance to larger branches of the firm or to a managerial position, while less capable workers and those having inadequate academic preparation may be assigned to smaller branches and find promotion difficult. Advancement from a loan officer position usually includes becoming a supervisor over other loan officers and clerical staff.

Job Outlook

While employment in banks—where most loan officers and counselors are found—is projected to decline, employment of loan officers and counselors is expected to grow faster than the average for all occupations through the year 2006. As the population and economy grow, applications for commercial, consumer, and mortgage loans will increase, spurring demand for loan officers and counselors. Growth in the variety and complexity of loans, and the importance of loan officers to the success of banks and other lending institutions, also should assure employment growth. Although increased demand will generate many new jobs, most openings will result from the need to replace workers who leave the occupation or retire. College graduates and those with banking, lending, or sales experience should have the best job prospects.

Loan officers and counselors are less likely to lose their jobs than other workers in banks and other lending institutions during economic downturns. Because loans are the major source of income for banks, loan officers are fundamental to the success of their organizations. Also, many loan officers are compensated in part on a commission basis. Loan counselors are likely to see an increase in the number of delinquent loans during difficult economic times.

Earnings

The form of compensation for loan officers varies, depending on the lending institution. Some banks offer salary plus commission as an incentive to increase the number of loans processed, while others pay only salaries.

According to a salary survey conducted by Robert Half International, a staffing services firm specializing in accounting and finance, residential real estate mortgage loan officers earned between $30,600 and $45,000 in 1997; commercial

real estate mortgage loan officers, between $45,100 and $73,000; consumer loan officers, between $28,900 and $48,000; and commercial lenders, between $37,400 and $85,000. Smaller banks generally paid 15 percent less than larger banks. Loan officers who are paid on a commission basis generally earn more than those on salary only.

Banks and other lenders sometimes offer their loan officers free checking privileges and somewhat lower interest rates on personal loans.

Related Occupations

Loan officers help the public manage financial assets and secure loans. Occupations that involve similar functions include securities and financial services sales representatives, financial aid officers, real estate agents and brokers, and insurance agents and brokers.

Sources of Additional Information

Information about a career as a loan officer or counselor may be obtained from:

❏ American Bankers Association, 1120 Connecticut Ave. NW, Washington, DC 20036.

State bankers' associations can furnish specific information about job opportunities in their state. Or, contact individual banks to inquire about job openings, and for more details about the activities, responsibilities, and preferred qualifications of their loan officers. For the names and addresses of banks and savings and related institutions, as well as the names of their principal officers, consult one of the following directories.

❏ *The American Financial Directory* (Norcross, GA, McFadden Business Publications).

❏ *Polk's World Bank Directory* (Nashville, R.L. Polk & Co.).

❏ *Rand McNally Bankers Directory* (Chicago, Rand McNally & Co.).

❏ *The U.S. Savings and Loan Directory* (Chicago, Rand McNally & Co.).

❏ *Rand McNally Credit Union Directory* (Chicago, Rand McNally & Co.).

Mechanical Engineers

(*D.O.T.* 007.061, .161-022, -034, and -038, and .267-010)

Significant Points

✴ *A bachelor's degree in mechanical engineering is almost always required for beginning jobs. Good employment opportunities are expected for new graduates.*

✶ *Starting salaries for mechanical engineers are significantly higher than those of bachelor's degree graduates in other fields.*

✶ *Knowledge of technological advances must be acquired through continued study and education.*

Nature of the Work

Mechanical engineers plan and design tools, engines, machines, and other mechanical equipment. They design and develop power-producing machines such as internal combustion engines, steam and gas turbines, and jet and rocket engines. They also design and develop power-using machines such as refrigeration and air-conditioning equipment, robots, machine tools, materials handling systems, and industrial production equipment.

The work of mechanical engineers varies by industry and function. Specialties include, among others, applied mechanics, design, energy systems, pressure vessels and piping, and heating, refrigeration, and air conditioning systems. Mechanical engineers design tools needed by other engineers for their work.

Mechanical engineering is the broadest engineering discipline, extending across many interdependent specialties. Mechanical engineers may work in production operations, maintenance, or technical sales; many are administrators or managers.

Working Conditions

Most mechanical engineers work in office buildings, laboratories, or industrial plants. Engineers travel extensively to plants or work sites.

Most mechanical engineers work a standard 40-hour week. At times, deadlines or design standards may bring extra pressure to a job. When this happens, engineers may work long hours and experience considerable stress.

Employment

Mechanical engineers held about 228,000 jobs in 1996. Almost six out of ten jobs were in manufacturing—of these, most were in the machinery, transportation equipment, electrical equipment, instruments, and fabricated metal products industries. Business and engineering consulting services and federal government agencies provided most of the remaining jobs.

Training, Other Qualifications, and Advancement

A bachelor's degree in engineering is usually required for beginning engineering jobs. College graduates with a degree in a physical science or mathematics may occasionally qualify for some engineering jobs, especially in engineering specialties in high demand. Most engineering degrees are granted in electrical, mechanical, or civil engineering. However, engineers trained in one branch may work in related branches; for example, many aerospace engineers have training in mechanical engineering. This flexibility allows employers to meet staffing needs in new technologies and specialties in which engineers are in short supply. It also allows engineers to shift to fields with better employment prospects, or to ones that match their interests more closely.

In addition to the standard engineering degree, many colleges offer degrees in engineering technology, which are offered as either two- or four-year programs. These programs prepare students for practical design and production work rather than for jobs that require more theoretical, scientific and mathematical knowledge. Graduates of four-year technology programs may get jobs similar to those obtained by graduates with a bachelor's degree in engineering. Some employers regard them as having skills between those of a technician and an engineer.

Graduate training is essential for engineering faculty positions, but is not required for the majority of entry-level engineering jobs. Many engineers obtain graduate degrees in engineering or business administration to learn new technology, broaden their education, and enhance promotion opportunities. Many high-level executives in government and industry began their careers as engineers.

About 320 colleges and universities offer bachelor's degree programs in engineering that are accredited by the Accreditation Board for Engineering and Technology (ABET), and about 250 colleges offer accredited bachelor's degree programs in engineering technology. ABET accreditation is based on an examination of an engineering program's faculty, curricular content, facilities, and admissions standards. Although most institutions offer programs in the major branches of engineering, only a few offer some of the smaller specialties. Also, programs of the same title may vary in content. For example, some emphasize industrial practices, preparing students for a job in industry, while others are more theoretical and are better for students preparing to take graduate work. Therefore, students should investigate curricula and check accreditations carefully before selecting a college. Admissions requirements for undergraduate engineering schools include a solid background in mathematics (algebra, geometry, trigonometry, and calculus), sciences (biology, chemistry, and physics), and courses in English, social studies, humanities, and computers.

Bachelor's degree programs in engineering are typically designed to last four years, but many students find that it takes between four and five years to complete their studies. In a typical four-year college curriculum, the first two years are spent studying mathematics, basic sciences, introductory engineering, humanities, and social sciences. In the last two years, most courses are in engineering, usually with a concentration in one branch. For example, the last two years of an aerospace program might include courses such as fluid mechanics, heat transfer, applied aerodynamics, analytical mechanics, flight vehicle design, trajectory dynamics, and aerospace propulsion systems. Some programs offer a general engineering curriculum; students then specialize in graduate school or on the job.

Some engineering schools and two-year colleges have agreements whereby the two-year college provides the initial engineering education and the engineering school automatically admits students for their last two years. In addition, a few engineering schools have arrangements whereby a student spends three years in a liberal arts college studying pre-engineering subjects and two years in the engineering school, and receives a bachelor's degree from each. Some colleges and universities offer five-year master's degree programs. Some five- or even six-year cooperative plans combine classroom study and practical work, permitting students to gain valuable experience and finance part of their education.

All 50 states and the District of Columbia require registration for engineers whose work may affect life, health, or property, or who offer their services to the public. Registration generally requires a degree from an ABET-accredited engineering program, four years of relevant work experience, and passing a state examination. Some states will not register people with degrees in engineering technology. Engineers may be registered in several states.

Engineers should be creative, inquisitive, analytical, and detail-oriented. They should be able to work as part of a team and be able to communicate well, both orally and in writing.

Beginning engineering graduates usually work under the supervision of experienced engineers and, in larger companies, may also receive formal classroom or seminar-type training. As they gain knowledge and experience, they are assigned more difficult projects with greater independence to develop designs, solve problems, and make decisions. Engineers may advance to become technical specialists or to supervise a staff or team of engineers and technicians. Some eventually become engineering managers or enter other managerial, management support, or sales jobs.

Job Outlook

Employment of mechanical engineers is expected to grow about as fast as the average for all occupations through the year 2006. Graduates of mechanical engineering programs should have favorable job opportunities. Most of the expected job openings, resulting from both employment growth and the need to replace those who will leave the occupation, should be sufficient to absorb the supply of new graduates and other entrants.

Although overall employment in manufacturing is expected to decline, employment of mechanical engineers in manufacturing should increase as the demand for improved machinery and machine tools grows and industrial machinery and processes become increasingly complex. Employment of mechanical engineers in business and engineering services firms is expected to grow faster than average as other industries in the economy increasingly contract out to these firms to solve engineering problems.

Earnings

Starting salaries for mechanical engineers with the bachelor's degree are significantly higher than starting salaries of bachelor's degree graduates in other fields. According to the National Association of Colleges and Employers, starting salaries for those with the bachelor's degree were about $38,113 in 1996.

The median annual salary for all mechanical engineers who worked full-time was in 1996 was $49,700.

The average annual salary for engineers in the federal government in nonsupervisory, supervisory, and managerial positions was $61,950 in 1997.

Related Occupations

Mechanical engineers apply the principles of physical science and mathematics in their work. Other workers who use scientific and mathematical principles include engineering, science, and computer systems managers; physical, life, and computer scientists; mathematicians; engineering and science technicians; and architects.

Sources of Additional Information

High school students interested in obtaining general information on a variety of engineering disciplines should contact the Junior Engineering Technical Society by sending a self-addressed business-size envelope, with six first-class stamps affixed, to:

❑ JETS-Guidance, 1420 King St., Suite 405, Alexandria, VA 22314-2794. Homepage: http://www.asee.org/jets

High school students interested in obtaining information on ABET accredited engineering programs should contact:

❑ The Accreditation Board for Engineering and Technology, Inc., 111 Market Place, Suite 1050, Baltimore, MD 21202-4012. Homepage: http://www.abet.ba.md.us

Non-high school students and those wanting more detailed information should contact:

❏ The American Society of Mechanical Engineers, 345 E. 47th St., New York, NY 10017.

❏ American Society of Heating, Refrigerating, and Air-Conditioning Engineers, Inc., 1791 Tullie Circle NE, Atlanta, GA 30329. Homepage://www.ashrae.org

Metallurgical, Ceramic, and Materials Engineers

(*D.O.T.* 006.061; 011.061; and 019.061-014)

Significant Points

✷ *A bachelor's degree in engineering is almost always required for beginning metallurgical, ceramic, and materials engineering jobs. Good employment opportunities are expected for new graduates.*

✷ *Starting salaries are significantly higher than those of bachelor's degree graduates in other fields.*

✷ *Knowledge of technological advances must be acquired through continued study and education.*

Nature of the Work

Metallurgical, ceramic, and materials engineers develop new types of metal alloys, ceramics, plastics, composites, and other materials, and adapt existing materials to new uses. Engineers manipulate the atomic and molecular structure of materials in controlled manufacturing environments, selecting materials with desirable mechanical, electrical, magnetic, chemical, and heat-transfer properties which meet special performance requirements. Examples are graphite golf club shafts that are light but stiff, ceramic tiles on the space shuttle that protect it from burning up during reentry into the atmosphere, and the alloy turbine blades in a jet engine.

Most metallurgical engineers work in one of the three main branches of metallurgy—extractive or chemical, physical, and mechanical or process. Extractive metallurgists are concerned with removing metals from ores and refining and alloying them to obtain useful metal. Physical metallurgists study the nature, structure, and physical properties of metals and their alloys, and methods of processing them into final products. Mechanical metallurgists develop and improve metalworking processes such as casting, forging, rolling, and drawing.

Ceramic engineers develop new ceramic materials and methods for making ceramic materials into useful products.

Ceramics include all nonmetallic, inorganic materials which require high temperatures in their processing. Ceramic engineers work on products as diverse as glassware, semiconductors, automobile and aircraft engine components, fiber-optic phone lines, tile, and electric power line insulators.

Materials engineers evaluate technical requirements and material specifications to develop materials that can be used, for example, to reduce the weight, but not the strength of an object. Materials engineers also test and evaluate materials and develop new materials, such as the composite materials now being used in "stealth" aircraft.

Working Conditions

Most metallurgical, ceramic, and materials engineers work in office buildings, laboratories, or industrial plants. Others spend a considerable amount of time outdoors at construction sites, mines, and oil and gas exploration sites, where they monitor or direct operations or solve onsite problems. Some travel extensively to plants or worksites.

Most metallurgical, ceramic, and materials engineers work a standard 40-hour week. At times, deadlines or design standards may bring extra pressure to a job. When this happens, engineers may work long hours and experience considerable stress.

Employment

Metallurgical, ceramic, and materials engineers held about 18,000 jobs in 1996. One-fourth worked in metal-producing and processing industries. They also worked in aircraft manufacturing; research and testing services; federal government agencies; industries that manufacture machinery and electrical equipment; stone, clay, and glass products manufacturing; and engineering consulting firms.

Training, Other Qualifications, and Advancement

A bachelor's degree in engineering is usually required for beginning engineering jobs. College graduates with a degree in a physical science or mathematics may occasionally qualify for some engineering jobs, especially in engineering specialties in high demand. Most engineering degrees are granted in electrical, mechanical, or civil engineering. However, engineers trained in one branch may work in related branches; for example, many aerospace engineers have training in mechanical engineering. This flexibility allows employers to meet staffing needs in new technologies and specialties in which engineers are in short supply. It also allows engineers to shift to fields with better employment prospects, or to ones that match their interests more closely.

In addition to the standard engineering degree, many colleges offer degrees in engineering technology, which are offered as either two- or four-year programs. These programs prepare students for practical design and production work rather than for jobs that require more theoretical, scientific, and mathematical knowledge. Graduates of four-year technology programs may get jobs similar to those obtained by graduates with a bachelor's degree in engineering. Some employers regard them as having skills between those of a technician and an engineer.

Graduate training is essential for engineering faculty positions, but is not required for the majority of entry-level engineering jobs. Many engineers obtain graduate degrees in engineering or business administration to learn new technology, broaden their education, and enhance promotion opportunities. Many high-level executives in government and industry began their careers as engineers.

About 320 colleges and universities offer bachelor's degree programs in engineering that are accredited by the Accreditation Board for Engineering and Technology (ABET), and about 250 colleges offer accredited bachelor's degree programs in engineering technology. ABET accreditation is based on an examination of an engineering program's faculty, curricular content, facilities, and admissions standards. Although most institutions offer programs in the major branches of engineering, only a few offer some of the smaller specialties. Also, programs of the same title may vary in content. For example, some emphasize industrial practices, preparing students for a job in industry, while others are more theoretical and are better for students preparing to take graduate work. Therefore, students should investigate curricula and check accreditations carefully before selecting a college. Admissions requirements for undergraduate engineering schools include a solid background in mathematics (algebra, geometry, trigonometry, and calculus), sciences (biology, chemistry, and physics), and courses in English, social studies, humanities, and computers.

Bachelor's degree programs in engineering are typically designed to last four years, but many students find that it takes between four and five years to complete their studies. In a typical four-year college curriculum, the first two years are spent studying mathematics, basic sciences, introductory engineering, humanities, and social sciences. In the last two years, most courses are in engineering, usually with a concentration in one branch. For example, the last two years of an aerospace program might include courses such as fluid mechanics, heat transfer, applied aerodynamics, analytical mechanics, flight vehicle design, trajectory dynamics, and aerospace propulsion systems. Some programs offer a general engineering curriculum; students then specialize in graduate school or on the job.

Some engineering schools and two-year colleges have agreements whereby the two-year college provides the initial engineering education and the engineering school automatically admits students for their last two years. In addition, a few engineering schools have arrangements whereby a student spends three years in a liberal arts college studying pre-engineering subjects and two years in the engineering school, and receives a bachelor's degree from each. Some colleges and universities offer five-year master's degree programs. Some five- or even six-year cooperative plans combine classroom study and practical work, permitting students to gain valuable experience and finance part of their education.

All 50 states and the District of Columbia require registration for engineers whose work may affect life, health, or property, or who offer their services to the public. Registration generally requires a degree from an ABET-accredited engineering program, four years of relevant work experience, and passing a state examination. Some states will not register people with degrees in engineering technology. Engineers may be registered in several states.

Engineers should be creative, inquisitive, analytical, and detail-oriented. They should be able to work as part of a team and be able to communicate well, both orally and in writing.

Beginning engineering graduates usually work under the supervision of experienced engineers and, in larger companies, may also receive formal classroom or seminar-type training. As they gain knowledge and experience, they are assigned more difficult projects with greater independence to develop designs, solve problems, and make decisions. Engineers may advance to become technical specialists or to supervise a staff or team of engineers and technicians. Some eventually become engineering managers or enter other managerial, management support, or sales jobs.

Job Outlook

Individuals seeking employment as metallurgical, ceramic, and materials engineers should find good opportunities as the number of anticipated job openings should be sufficient to absorb the low number of new graduates relative to those in other engineering disciplines. Employment of metallurgical, ceramic, and materials engineers is expected to increase more slowly than the average for all occupations through the year 2006.

Many of the industries in which these engineers are concentrated, such as stone, clay, and glass products; primary metals; fabricated metal products; and transportation equipment industries, are expected to experience little if any employment growth through the year 2006. Anticipated employment growth in service industries, such as research and

Non-high school students and those wanting more detailed information should contact:

- ❏ The American Society of Mechanical Engineers, 345 E. 47th St., New York, NY 10017.

- ❏ American Society of Heating, Refrigerating, and Air-Conditioning Engineers, Inc., 1791 Tullie Circle NE, Atlanta, GA 30329. Homepage://www.ashrae.org

Metallurgical, Ceramic, and Materials Engineers

(D.O.T. 006.061; 011.061; and 019.061-014)

Significant Points

✳ *A bachelor's degree in engineering is almost always required for beginning metallurgical, ceramic, and materials engineering jobs. Good employment opportunities are expected for new graduates.*

✳ *Starting salaries are significantly higher than those of bachelor's degree graduates in other fields.*

✳ *Knowledge of technological advances must be acquired through continued study and education.*

Nature of the Work

Metallurgical, ceramic, and materials engineers develop new types of metal alloys, ceramics, plastics, composites, and other materials, and adapt existing materials to new uses. Engineers manipulate the atomic and molecular structure of materials in controlled manufacturing environments, selecting materials with desirable mechanical, electrical, magnetic, chemical, and heat-transfer properties which meet special performance requirements. Examples are graphite golf club shafts that are light but stiff, ceramic tiles on the space shuttle that protect it from burning up during reentry into the atmosphere, and the alloy turbine blades in a jet engine.

Most metallurgical engineers work in one of the three main branches of metallurgy—extractive or chemical, physical, and mechanical or process. Extractive metallurgists are concerned with removing metals from ores and refining and alloying them to obtain useful metal. Physical metallurgists study the nature, structure, and physical properties of metals and their alloys, and methods of processing them into final products. Mechanical metallurgists develop and improve metalworking processes such as casting, forging, rolling, and drawing.

Ceramic engineers develop new ceramic materials and methods for making ceramic materials into useful products.

Ceramics include all nonmetallic, inorganic materials which require high temperatures in their processing. Ceramic engineers work on products as diverse as glassware, semiconductors, automobile and aircraft engine components, fiber-optic phone lines, tile, and electric power line insulators.

Materials engineers evaluate technical requirements and material specifications to develop materials that can be used, for example, to reduce the weight, but not the strength of an object. Materials engineers also test and evaluate materials and develop new materials, such as the composite materials now being used in "stealth" aircraft.

Working Conditions

Most metallurgical, ceramic, and materials engineers work in office buildings, laboratories, or industrial plants. Others spend a considerable amount of time outdoors at construction sites, mines, and oil and gas exploration sites, where they monitor or direct operations or solve onsite problems. Some travel extensively to plants or worksites.

Most metallurgical, ceramic, and materials engineers work a standard 40-hour week. At times, deadlines or design standards may bring extra pressure to a job. When this happens, engineers may work long hours and experience considerable stress.

Employment

Metallurgical, ceramic, and materials engineers held about 18,000 jobs in 1996. One-fourth worked in metal-producing and processing industries. They also worked in aircraft manufacturing; research and testing services; federal government agencies; industries that manufacture machinery and electrical equipment; stone, clay, and glass products manufacturing; and engineering consulting firms.

Training, Other Qualifications, and Advancement

A bachelor's degree in engineering is usually required for beginning engineering jobs. College graduates with a degree in a physical science or mathematics may occasionally qualify for some engineering jobs, especially in engineering specialties in high demand. Most engineering degrees are granted in electrical, mechanical, or civil engineering. However, engineers trained in one branch may work in related branches; for example, many aerospace engineers have training in mechanical engineering. This flexibility allows employers to meet staffing needs in new technologies and specialties in which engineers are in short supply. It also allows engineers to shift to fields with better employment prospects, or to ones that match their interests more closely.

In addition to the standard engineering degree, many colleges offer degrees in engineering technology, which are offered as either two- or four-year programs. These programs prepare students for practical design and production work rather than for jobs that require more theoretical, scientific, and mathematical knowledge. Graduates of four-year technology programs may get jobs similar to those obtained by graduates with a bachelor's degree in engineering. Some employers regard them as having skills between those of a technician and an engineer.

Graduate training is essential for engineering faculty positions, but is not required for the majority of entry-level engineering jobs. Many engineers obtain graduate degrees in engineering or business administration to learn new technology, broaden their education, and enhance promotion opportunities. Many high-level executives in government and industry began their careers as engineers.

About 320 colleges and universities offer bachelor's degree programs in engineering that are accredited by the Accreditation Board for Engineering and Technology (ABET), and about 250 colleges offer accredited bachelor's degree programs in engineering technology. ABET accreditation is based on an examination of an engineering program's faculty, curricular content, facilities, and admissions standards. Although most institutions offer programs in the major branches of engineering, only a few offer some of the smaller specialties. Also, programs of the same title may vary in content. For example, some emphasize industrial practices, preparing students for a job in industry, while others are more theoretical and are better for students preparing to take graduate work. Therefore, students should investigate curricula and check accreditations carefully before selecting a college. Admissions requirements for undergraduate engineering schools include a solid background in mathematics (algebra, geometry, trigonometry, and calculus), sciences (biology, chemistry, and physics), and courses in English, social studies, humanities, and computers.

Bachelor's degree programs in engineering are typically designed to last four years, but many students find that it takes between four and five years to complete their studies. In a typical four-year college curriculum, the first two years are spent studying mathematics, basic sciences, introductory engineering, humanities, and social sciences. In the last two years, most courses are in engineering, usually with a concentration in one branch. For example, the last two years of an aerospace program might include courses such as fluid mechanics, heat transfer, applied aerodynamics, analytical mechanics, flight vehicle design, trajectory dynamics, and aerospace propulsion systems. Some programs offer a general engineering curriculum; students then specialize in graduate school or on the job.

Some engineering schools and two-year colleges have agreements whereby the two-year college provides the initial engineering education and the engineering school automatically admits students for their last two years. In addition, a few engineering schools have arrangements whereby a student spends three years in a liberal arts college studying pre-engineering subjects and two years in the engineering school, and receives a bachelor's degree from each. Some colleges and universities offer five-year master's degree programs. Some five- or even six-year cooperative plans combine classroom study and practical work, permitting students to gain valuable experience and finance part of their education.

All 50 states and the District of Columbia require registration for engineers whose work may affect life, health, or property, or who offer their services to the public. Registration generally requires a degree from an ABET-accredited engineering program, four years of relevant work experience, and passing a state examination. Some states will not register people with degrees in engineering technology. Engineers may be registered in several states.

Engineers should be creative, inquisitive, analytical, and detail-oriented. They should be able to work as part of a team and be able to communicate well, both orally and in writing.

Beginning engineering graduates usually work under the supervision of experienced engineers and, in larger companies, may also receive formal classroom or seminar-type training. As they gain knowledge and experience, they are assigned more difficult projects with greater independence to develop designs, solve problems, and make decisions. Engineers may advance to become technical specialists or to supervise a staff or team of engineers and technicians. Some eventually become engineering managers or enter other managerial, management support, or sales jobs.

Job Outlook

Individuals seeking employment as metallurgical, ceramic, and materials engineers should find good opportunities as the number of anticipated job openings should be sufficient to absorb the low number of new graduates relative to those in other engineering disciplines. Employment of metallurgical, ceramic, and materials engineers is expected to increase more slowly than the average for all occupations through the year 2006.

Many of the industries in which these engineers are concentrated, such as stone, clay, and glass products; primary metals; fabricated metal products; and transportation equipment industries, are expected to experience little if any employment growth through the year 2006. Anticipated employment growth in service industries, such as research and

testing services and engineering and architectural services, however, should provide significant job openings as these firms are hired to develop improved materials for their industrial customers.

Earnings

Starting salaries for metallurgical, ceramic, and materials engineers with the bachelor's degree are significantly higher than starting salaries of bachelor's degree graduates in other fields. According to the National Association of Colleges and Employers, starting salaries for those with the bachelor's degree were about $38,550 in 1996.

The average annual salary for engineers in the federal government in nonsupervisory, supervisory, and managerial positions was $61,950 in 1997.

Related Occupations

Metallurgical, ceramic, and materials engineers apply the principles of physical science and mathematics in their work. Other workers who use scientific and mathematical principles include engineering, science, and computer systems managers; physical, life, and computer scientists; mathematicians; engineering and science technicians; and architects.

Sources of Additional Information

High school students interested in obtaining general information on a variety of engineering disciplines should contact the Junior Engineering Technical Society by sending a self-addressed business-size envelope, with six first-class stamps affixed, to:

❏ JETS-Guidance, 1420 King St., Suite 405, Alexandria, VA 22314-2794. Homepage: http://www.asee.org/jets

High school students interested in obtaining information on ABET accredited engineering programs should contact:

❏ The Accreditation Board for Engineering and Technology, Inc., 111 Market Place, Suite 1050, Baltimore, MD 21202-4012. Homepage: http://www.abet.ba.md.us

Non-high school students and those wanting more detailed information should contact:

❏ The Minerals, Metals, & Materials Society, 420 Commonwealth Dr., Warrendale, PA 15086-7514. Homepage: http://www.tms.org

❏ ASM International, Student Outreach Program, Materials Park, OH 44073-0002.

Meteorologists

(D.O.T. 025.062-010)

Significant Points

★ *The federal government employs about four out of ten meteorologists and is the largest employer of these workers.*

★ *A bachelor's degree in meteorology, or in a closely related field with courses in meteorology, is the minimum educational requirement; a master's degree or Ph.D. is required for research positions.*

★ *With slower-than-average employment growth expected through the year 2006, applicants may face competition if the number of degrees awarded in atmospheric science and meteorology remain near current levels.*

Nature of the Work

Meteorology is the study of the atmosphere—the blanket of air covering the Earth. Meteorologists study the atmosphere's physical characteristics, motions, and processes, and the way it affects the rest of our environment. The best known application of this knowledge is in forecasting the weather. However, weather information and meteorological research are also applied in air-pollution control, agriculture, air and sea transportation, defense, and the study of trends in Earth's climate such as global warming or ozone depletion.

Meteorologists who forecast the weather, known professionally as operational meteorologists, are the largest group of specialists. They study information on air pressure, temperature, humidity, and wind velocity, and apply physical and mathematical relationships to make short- and long-range weather forecasts. Their data come from weather satellites, weather radar, and remote sensors and observers in many parts of the world. Meteorologists use sophisticated computer models of the world's atmosphere to make long-term, short-term, and local-area forecasts. These forecasts inform not only the general public, but also those who need accurate weather information for both economic and safety reasons, as in the shipping, air transportation, agriculture, fishing, and utilities industries.

The use of weather balloons, launched several times a day, to measure wind, temperature, and humidity in the upper atmosphere, is currently supplemented by sophisticated weather equipment that transmits data as frequently as every few minutes. Doppler radar, for example, can detect air flow patterns in violent storm systems—allowing forecasters to better predict tornadoes and other hazardous winds, as well as monitoring the storm's direction and intensity. Combined radar and satellite observations allow meteorologists to predict flash floods.

Some meteorologists work in research. Physical meteorologists, for example, study the atmosphere's chemical and physical properties; the transmission of light, sound, and radio waves; and the transfer of energy in the atmosphere. They also study factors affecting the formation of clouds, rain, snow, and other weather phenomena, such as severe storms. Synoptic meteorologists develop new tools for weather forecasting using computers and sophisticated mathematical models. Climatologists collect, analyze, and interpret past records of wind, rainfall, sunshine, and temperature in specific areas or regions. Their studies are used to design buildings, plan heating and cooling systems, and aid in effective land use and in agricultural production. Other research meteorologists examine the most effective ways to control or diminish air pollution.

Working Conditions

Most weather stations operate around the clock seven days a week. Jobs in such facilities often involve night, weekend, and holiday work with rotating shifts. During times of weather emergencies, such as hurricanes, operational meteorologists may work overtime. Operational meteorologists are also often under pressure to meet forecast deadlines. Weather stations are found all over the country—at airports, in or near cities, and in isolated and remote areas. Some meteorologists also spend time observing weather conditions and collecting data from aircraft. Weather forecasters who work for radio or television stations broadcast their reports from station studios, and may work evenings and weekends. Meteorologists in smaller weather offices often work alone; in larger ones, they work as part of a team. Meteorologists not involved in forecasting work regular hours, usually in offices. Those who work for private consulting firms or for companies analyzing and monitoring emissions to improve air quality usually work with other scientists or engineers.

Employment

Meteorologists held about 7,300 jobs in 1996. The federal government is the largest employer of civilian meteorologists. The National Oceanic and Atmospheric Administration (NOAA) employed about 2,700 meteorologists; nearly 90 percent worked in the National Weather Service at stations throughout the nation. The remainder of NOAA's meteorologists worked mainly in research or management. The Department of Defense employed about 280 civilian meteorologists. Others worked for private weather consulting services, research and testing services, and computer and data processing services.

Although hundreds of people teach meteorology and related courses in college and university departments of meteorology or atmospheric science, physics, earth science, and geophysics, these individuals are classified as college or university faculty, rather than meteorologists.

In addition to civilian meteorologists, hundreds of members of the Armed Forces are involved in forecasting and other meteorological work.

Training, Other Qualifications, and Advancement

A bachelor's degree with a major in meteorology, or in a closely related field with courses in meteorology, is generally the minimum educational requirement for a beginning job as a meteorologist.

The preferred educational requirement for entry-level meteorologists in the federal government is a bachelor's degree—not necessarily in meteorology—with at least 24 semester hours of meteorology courses, including six hours in the analysis and prediction of weather systems and two hours of remote sensing of the atmosphere or instrumentation. Other required courses include differential and integral calculus, differential equations, six hours of college physics, and at least nine hours of courses appropriate for a physical science major—such as statistics, computer science, chemistry, physical oceanography, or physical climatology. Sometimes, a combination of experience and education may be substituted for a degree.

Although positions in operational meteorology are available for those with only a bachelor's degree, obtaining a graduate degree enhances advancement potential. A master's degree is usually necessary for conducting research and development, and a Ph.D. is required for most basic research positions. Students who plan a career in research and development need not necessarily major in meteorology as an undergraduate. In fact, a bachelor's degree in mathematics, physics, or engineering provides excellent preparation for graduate study in meteorology.

Because meteorology is a small field, relatively few colleges and universities offer degrees in meteorology or atmospheric science, although many departments of physics, earth science, geography, and geophysics offer atmospheric science and related courses. Prospective students should make certain that courses required by the National Weather Service and other employers are offered at the college they are considering. Computer science courses, additional meteorology courses, a strong background in mathematics and physics, and good communication skills are important to prospective employers. Many programs combine the study of meteorology with another field, such as agriculture, engineering, or physics. For example, hydrometeorology is the blending of

hydrology (the science of Earth's water) and meteorology, and is the field concerned with the effect of precipitation on the hydrologic cycle and the environment. Students who wish to become broadcast meteorologists for radio or television stations should develop excellent communication skills through courses in speech, journalism, and related fields. Those interested in air quality work should supplement their technical training with course work in policy or government affairs.

Beginning meteorologists often do routine data collection, computation, or analysis, and some basic forecasting. Entry-level operational meteorologists in the federal government are usually placed in intern positions for training and experience. During this period, they learn about the Weather Service's forecasting equipment and procedures, and rotate to different offices to learn about various weather systems. After completing the training period, they are assigned a permanent duty station. Experienced meteorologists may advance to supervisory or administrative jobs, or may handle more complex forecasting jobs. After several years of experience, some meteorologists establish their own weather consulting services.

The American Meteorological Society offers professional certification of consulting meteorologists, administered by a Board of Certified Consulting Meteorologists. Applicants must meet formal education requirements (though not necessarily a college degree), pass an examination to demonstrate thorough meteorological knowledge, have a minimum of five years of experience or a combination of experience plus an advanced degree, and provide character references from fellow professionals.

Job Outlook

Prospective meteorologists may face competition if the number of degrees awarded in atmospheric science and meteorology remain near current levels, coupled with projected slower-than-average employment growth through the year 2006. The National Weather Service (NWS) recently completed an extensive modernization of its weather forecasting equipment and all hiring of meteorologists needed to staff the upgraded stations. The NWS has no plans to increase the number of weather stations or the number of meteorologists in existing stations for many years. Employment of meteorologists in other federal agencies is expected to decline slightly as the federal government attempts to balance its budget.

On the other hand, private industry is expected to create a small number of new jobs for meteorologists over the 1996–2006 period. As research leads to continuing improvements in weather forecasting, the demand may grow for private weather consulting firms to provide more detailed informa-

tion than has formerly been available, especially to weather-sensitive industries. Farmers, commodity investors, radio and television stations, and utilities, transportation, and construction firms can greatly benefit from additional weather information more closely targeted to their needs than the general information provided by the National Weather Service. Additionally, if research on seasonal and other long-range forecasting yields positive results, more meteorologists may be needed to interpret these forecasts and advise weather-sensitive industries. However, because many customers for private weather services are in industries sensitive to fluctuations in the economy, the sales and growth of private weather services depend on the health of the economy.

There will continue to be demand for meteorologists to analyze and monitor the dispersion of pollutants into the air to ensure compliance with federal environmental regulations outlined in the Clean Air Act of 1990, but employment increases are expected to be small.

Earnings

The average salary for meteorologists in nonsupervisory, supervisory, and managerial positions employed by the federal government was about $57,000 in 1997. Meteorologists in the federal government with a bachelor's degree and no experience received a starting salary of $19,500 or $24,200 a year, depending on their college grades. Those with a master's degree could start at $24,200 or $29,600; those with the Ph.D. degree, at $35,800 or $42,900. Beginning salaries for all degree levels are slightly higher in selected areas of the country where the prevailing local pay level is higher.

Related Occupations

Workers in other occupations concerned with the physical environment include oceanographers, geologists and geophysicists, hydrologists, physicists, mathematicians, and civil, chemical, and environmental engineers.

Sources of Additional Information

Information about careers in meteorology is available from:

❑ American Meteorological Society, 45 Beacon St., Boston, MA 02108. Homepage: http://www.ametsoc.org/AMS

Information on acquiring a job as a meteorologist with the federal government may be obtained from the Office of Personnel Management through a telephone-based system. Consult your telephone directory under U.S. government for a local number or call (912) 757-3000 (TDD 912 744-2299). That number is not toll-free and charges may result. Information also is available from their Internet site: http://www.usajobs.opm.gov

Mining Engineers

(*D.O.T.* 010.061 except -018)

Significant Points

* ✶ *A bachelor's degree in engineering is almost always required for beginning mining engineering jobs. Good employment opportunities are expected for new graduates.*

* ✶ *Starting salaries for mining engineers are significantly higher than those of bachelor's degree graduates in other fields.*

* ✶ *Knowledge of technological advances must be acquired through continued study and education.*

Nature of the Work

Mining engineers find, extract, and prepare coal, metals, and minerals for use by manufacturing industries and utilities. They design open pit and underground mines, supervise the construction of mine shafts and tunnels in underground operations, and devise methods for transporting minerals to processing plants. Mining engineers are responsible for the safe, economical, and environmentally sound operation of mines. Some mining engineers work with geologists and metallurgical engineers to locate and appraise new ore deposits. Others develop new mining equipment or direct mineral processing operations to separate minerals from the dirt, rock, and other materials with which they are mixed. Mining engineers frequently specialize in the mining of one mineral or metal, such as coal or gold. With increased emphasis on protecting the environment, many mining engineers work to solve problems related to land reclamation and water and air pollution.

Working Conditions

Most mining engineers spend a considerable amount of time outdoors at mines and oil and gas exploration sites, where they monitor or direct operations or solve onsite problems. Some travel extensively to work sites.

Most mining engineers work a standard 40-hour week. At times, deadlines or design standards may bring extra pressure to a job. When this happens, engineers may work long hours and experience considerable stress.

Employment

Mining engineers held about 3,100 jobs in 1996. While two-thirds worked in the mining industry, other mining engineers worked in government agencies, manufacturing industries, or engineering consulting firms.

Mining engineers are usually employed at the location of mineral deposits, often near small communities, and sometimes outside the United States. Those in research and development, management, consulting, or sales, however, are often are located in metropolitan areas.

Training, Other Qualifications, and Advancement

A bachelor's degree in engineering is usually required for beginning engineering jobs. College graduates with a degree in a physical science or mathematics may occasionally qualify for some engineering jobs, especially in engineering specialties in high demand. Most engineering degrees are granted in electrical, mechanical, or civil engineering. However, engineers trained in one branch may work in related branches; for example, many aerospace engineers have training in mechanical engineering. This flexibility allows employers to meet staffing needs in new technologies and specialties in which engineers are in short supply. It also allows engineers to shift to fields with better employment prospects, or to ones that match their interests more closely.

In addition to the standard engineering degree, many colleges offer degrees in engineering technology, which are offered as either two- or four-year programs. These programs prepare students for practical design and production work rather than for jobs that require more theoretical, scientific, and mathematical knowledge. Graduates of four-year technology programs may get jobs similar to those obtained by graduates with a bachelor's degree in engineering. Some employers regard them as having skills between those of a technician and an engineer.

Graduate training is essential for engineering faculty positions, but is not required for the majority of entry-level engineering jobs. Many engineers obtain graduate degrees in engineering or business administration to learn new technology, broaden their education, and enhance promotion opportunities. Many high-level executives in government and industry began their careers as engineers.

About 320 colleges and universities offer bachelor's degree programs in engineering that are accredited by the Accreditation Board for Engineering and Technology (ABET), and about 250 colleges offer accredited bachelor's degree programs in engineering technology. ABET accreditation is based on an examination of an engineering program's faculty, curricular content, facilities, and admissions standards. Although most institutions offer programs in the major branches of engineering, only a few offer some of the smaller specialties.

Also, programs of the same title may vary in content. For example, some emphasize industrial practices, preparing students for a job in industry, while others are more theoretical and are better for students preparing to take graduate work. Therefore, students should investigate curricula and check accreditations carefully before selecting a college. Admissions requirements for undergraduate engineering schools include a solid background in mathematics (algebra, geometry, trigonometry, and calculus), sciences (biology, chemistry, and physics), and courses in English, social studies, humanities, and computers.

Bachelor's degree programs in engineering are typically designed to last four years, but many students find that it takes between four and five years to complete their studies. In a typical four-year college curriculum, the first two years are spent studying mathematics, basic sciences, introductory engineering, humanities, and social sciences. In the last two years, most courses are in engineering, usually with a concentration in one branch. For example, the last two years of an aerospace program might include courses such as fluid mechanics, heat transfer, applied aerodynamics, analytical mechanics, flight vehicle design, trajectory dynamics, and aerospace propulsion systems. Some programs offer a general engineering curriculum; students then specialize in graduate school or on the job.

Some engineering schools and two-year colleges have agreements whereby the two-year college provides the initial engineering education and the engineering school automatically admits students for their last two years. In addition, a few engineering schools have arrangements whereby a student spends three years in a liberal arts college studying pre-engineering subjects and two years in the engineering school, and receives a bachelor's degree from each. Some colleges and universities offer five-year master's degree programs. Some five- or even six-year cooperative plans combine classroom study and practical work, permitting students to gain valuable experience and finance part of their education.

All 50 states and the District of Columbia require registration for engineers whose work may affect life, health, or property, or who offer their services to the public. Registration generally requires a degree from an ABET-accredited engineering program, four years of relevant work experience, and passing a state examination. Some states will not register people with degrees in engineering technology. Engineers may be registered in several states.

Engineers should be creative, inquisitive, analytical, and detail-oriented. They should be able to work as part of a team and be able to communicate well, both orally and in writing.

Beginning engineering graduates usually work under the supervision of experienced engineers and, in larger companies, may also receive formal classroom or seminar-type training. As they gain knowledge and experience, they are assigned more difficult projects with greater independence to develop designs, solve problems, and make decisions. Engineers may advance to become technical specialists or to supervise a staff or team of engineers and technicians. Some eventually become engineering managers or enter other managerial, management support, or sales jobs.

Job Outlook

The mining industry traditionally has few openings. In fact, employment in the mining industry and of mining engineers is expected to decline through the year 2006. Therefore, graduates in mining engineering will face competition despite their low number.

Opportunities in the mining industry are closely related to the price of the metals and minerals they produce. If the price of these products is high, it makes it worthwhile for a mining company to invest the millions of dollars in material moving equipment and ore processing technology necessary to operate a mine. Although prices for mined products have been unstable, the increasing activity of auto manufacturing and expanded development and repair of the nation's roadways will help provide demand for metals and minerals.

The long-term business environment for mining is generally perceived to be favorable, but because a mine takes years of research, planning, and development to become fully operational, it may not contribute to expansion in employment opportunities for mining engineers. Also, because mining operations around the world recruit graduates of U.S. mining engineering programs, opportunities may be better worldwide than within the United States.

Earnings

Starting salaries for mining engineers with the bachelor's degree are significantly higher than starting salaries of bachelor's degree graduates in other fields. According to the National Association of Colleges and Employers, starting salaries for those with the bachelor's degree were about $36,724 in 1996.

The average annual salary for engineers in the federal government in nonsupervisory, supervisory, and managerial positions was $61,950 in 1997.

Related Occupations

Mining engineers apply the principles of physical science and mathematics in their work. Other workers who use scientific and mathematical principles include engineering, science, and computer systems managers; physical, life, and computer scientists; mathematicians; engineering and science technicians; and architects.

Sources of Additional Information

High school students interested in obtaining general information on a variety of engineering disciplines should contact the Junior Engineering Technical Society by sending a self-addressed business-size envelope, with six first-class stamps affixed, to:

❑ JETS-Guidance, 1420 King St., Suite 405, Alexandria, VA 22314-2794. Homepage: http://www.asee.org/jets

High school students interested in obtaining information on ABET accredited engineering programs should contact:

❑ The Accreditation Board for Engineering and Technology, Inc., 111 Market Place, Suite 1050, Baltimore, MD 21202-4012. Homepage: http://www.abet.ba.md.us

Non-high school students and those wanting more detailed information should contact:

❑ The Society for Mining, Metallurgy, and Exploration, Inc., P.O. Box 625002, Littleton, CO 80162-5002.

Nuclear Engineers

(*D.O.T.* 005.061-042; 015.061, .067, .137, and .167)

Significant Points

✱ *A bachelor's degree in engineering is almost always required for beginning nuclear engineering jobs. Good employment opportunities are expected for new graduates.*

✱ *Starting salaries for nuclear engineers are significantly higher than those of bachelor's degree graduates in other fields.*

✱ *Knowledge of technological advances must be acquired through continued study and education.*

Nature of the Work

Nuclear engineers research and develop the processes, instruments, and systems used to derive benefits from nuclear energy and radiation. They design, develop, monitor, and operate nuclear power plants used to generate electricity and power Navy ships. They may work on the nuclear fuel cycle—the production, handling, and use of nuclear fuel and the safe disposal of waste produced by nuclear energy—or on fusion energy. Some specialize in the development of nuclear power sources for spacecraft; others develop industrial and medical uses for radioactive materials, such as equipment to diagnose and treat medical problems.

Working Conditions

Most nuclear engineers work in office buildings, laboratories, or industrial plants. Some travel extensively to plants or work sites.

Most nuclear engineers work a standard 40-hour week. At times, deadlines or design standards may bring extra pressure to a job. When this happens, engineers may work long hours and experience considerable stress.

Employment

Nuclear engineers held about 14,000 jobs in 1996. About 20 percent each were in utilities, the federal government, and engineering consulting firms. Another 12 percent were in research and testing services. More than half of all federally employed nuclear engineers were civilian employees of the Navy, and most of the rest worked for the Nuclear Regulatory Commission, the Department of Energy, or the Tennessee Valley Authority. Most nonfederally employed nuclear engineers worked for public utilities or engineering consulting companies. Some worked for defense manufacturers or manufacturers of nuclear power equipment.

Training, Other Qualifications, and Advancement

A bachelor's degree in engineering is usually required for beginning engineering jobs. College graduates with a degree in a physical science or mathematics may occasionally qualify for some engineering jobs, especially in engineering specialties in high demand. Most engineering degrees are granted in electrical, mechanical, or civil engineering. However, engineers trained in one branch may work in related branches; for example, many aerospace engineers have training in mechanical engineering. This flexibility allows employers to meet staffing needs in new technologies and specialties in which engineers are in short supply. It also allows engineers to shift to fields with better employment prospects, or to ones that match their interests more closely.

In addition to the standard engineering degree, many colleges offer degrees in engineering technology, which are offered as either two- or four-year programs. These programs prepare students for practical design and production work rather than for jobs that require more theoretical, scientific, and mathematical knowledge. Graduates of four-year technology programs may get jobs similar to those obtained by graduates with a bachelor's degree in engineering. Some employers regard them as having skills between those of a technician and an engineer.

Graduate training is essential for engineering faculty positions, but is not required for the majority of entry-level

engineering jobs. Many engineers obtain graduate degrees in engineering or business administration to learn new technology, broaden their education, and enhance promotion opportunities. Many high-level executives in government and industry began their careers as engineers.

About 320 colleges and universities offer bachelor's degree programs in engineering that are accredited by the Accreditation Board for Engineering and Technology (ABET), and about 250 colleges offer accredited bachelor's degree programs in engineering technology. ABET accreditation is based on an examination of an engineering program's faculty, curricular content, facilities, and admissions standards. Although most institutions offer programs in the major branches of engineering, only a few offer some of the smaller specialties. Also, programs of the same title may vary in content. For example, some emphasize industrial practices, preparing students for a job in industry, while others are more theoretical and are better for students preparing to take graduate work. Therefore, students should investigate curricula and check accreditations carefully before selecting a college. Admissions requirements for undergraduate engineering schools include a solid background in mathematics (algebra, geometry, trigonometry, and calculus), sciences (biology, chemistry, and physics), and courses in English, social studies, humanities, and computers.

Bachelor's degree programs in engineering are typically designed to last four years, but many students find that it takes between four and five years to complete their studies. In a typical four-year college curriculum, the first two years are spent studying mathematics, basic sciences, introductory engineering, humanities, and social sciences. In the last two years, most courses are in engineering, usually with a concentration in one branch. For example, the last two years of an aerospace program might include courses such as fluid mechanics, heat transfer, applied aerodynamics, analytical mechanics, flight vehicle design, trajectory dynamics, and aerospace propulsion systems. Some programs offer a general engineering curriculum; students then specialize in graduate school or on the job.

Some engineering schools and two-year colleges have agreements whereby the two-year college provides the initial engineering education and the engineering school automatically admits students for their last two years. In addition, a few engineering schools have arrangements whereby a student spends three years in a liberal arts college studying pre-engineering subjects and two years in the engineering school, and receives a bachelor's degree from each. Some colleges and universities offer five-year master's degree programs. Some five- or even six-year cooperative plans combine class-

room study and practical work, permitting students to gain valuable experience and finance part of their education.

All 50 states and the District of Columbia require registration for engineers whose work may affect life, health, or property, or who offer their services to the public. Registration generally requires a degree from an ABET-accredited engineering program, four years of relevant work experience, and passing a state examination. Some states will not register people with degrees in engineering technology. Engineers may be registered in several states.

Engineers should be creative, inquisitive, analytical, and detail-oriented. They should be able to work as part of a team and be able to communicate well, both orally and in writing.

Beginning engineering graduates usually work under the supervision of experienced engineers and, in larger companies, may also receive formal classroom or seminar-type training. As they gain knowledge and experience, they are assigned more difficult projects with greater independence to develop designs, solve problems, and make decisions. Engineers may advance to become technical specialists or to supervise a staff or team of engineers and technicians. Some eventually become engineering managers or enter other managerial, management support, or sales jobs.

Job Outlook

Employment of nuclear engineers is expected to grow more slowly than the average for all occupations through the year 2006. Because this is a small occupation, it will translate into few growth-related opportunities. Most openings will arise as nuclear engineers transfer to other occupations or leave the labor force. However, good opportunities for nuclear engineers should still exist since the small number of nuclear engineering graduates is likely to be in balance with the number of job openings.

Due to public concerns over the cost and safety of nuclear power, there are only a small number of nuclear power plants under construction in the United States, and it is possible some older plants will shut down. Nevertheless, nuclear engineers will be needed to operate existing plants. In addition, nuclear engineers will be needed to work in defense-related areas, to develop nuclear medical technology, and to improve and enforce waste management and safety standards.

Earnings

Starting salaries for nuclear engineers with the bachelor's degree are significantly higher than starting salaries of bachelor's degree graduates in other fields. According to the National Association of Colleges and Employers, starting salaries for those with the bachelor's degree were about $37,194 in 1996.

The average annual salary for engineers in the federal government in nonsupervisory, supervisory, and managerial positions was $61,950 in 1997.

Related Occupations

Nuclear engineers apply the principles of physical science and mathematics in their work. Other workers who use scientific and mathematical principles include engineering, science, and computer systems managers; physical, life, and computer scientists; mathematicians; engineering and science technicians; and architects.

Sources of Additional Information

High school students interested in obtaining general information on a variety of engineering disciplines should contact the Junior Engineering Technical Society by sending a self-addressed business-size envelope, with six first-class stamps affixed, to:

❏ JETS-Guidance, 1420 King St., Suite 405, Alexandria, VA 22314-2794. Homepage: http://www.asee.org/jets

High school students interested in obtaining information on ABET accredited engineering programs should contact:

❏ The Accreditation Board for Engineering and Technology, Inc., 111 Market Place, Suite 1050, Baltimore, MD 21202-4012. Homepage: http://www.abet.ba.md.us

Non-high school students and those wanting more detailed information should contact:

❏ American Nuclear Society, 555 North Kensington Ave., LaGrange Park, IL 60525.

Occupational Therapists

(D.O.T. 076.121-010 and 076.l67-010)

Significant Points

★ *Occupational therapy offers good job opportunities and high pay.*

★ *Occupational therapists will be among the fastest growing occupations, as rapid growth in the number of middle-aged and elderly individuals increases the demand for therapeutic services.*

★ *Additional demand will result from medical advances that allow more patients with critical problems to survive and require rehabilitation.*

Nature of the Work

Occupational therapists work with individuals who have conditions that are mentally, physically, developmentally, or emotionally disabling, and help them to develop, recover, or maintain daily living and work skills. They not only help clients improve basic motor functions and reasoning abilities, but also compensate for permanent loss of function. Their goal is to help clients have independent, productive, and satisfying lives.

Occupational therapists assist clients in performing activities of all types, ranging from using a computer, to caring for daily needs such as dressing, cooking, and eating. Physical exercises may be used to increase strength and dexterity, while paper and pencil exercises may be chosen to improve visual acuity and the ability to discern patterns. A client with short-term memory loss, for instance, might be encouraged to make lists to aid recall. One with coordination problems might be assigned exercises to improve hand-eye coordination. Occupational therapists also use computer programs to help clients improve decision making, abstract reasoning, problem solving, and perceptual skills, as well as memory, sequencing, and coordination—all of which are important for independent living.

For those with permanent functional disabilities, such as spinal cord injuries, cerebral palsy, or muscular dystrophy, therapists instruct in the use of adaptive equipment such as wheelchairs, splints, and aids for eating and dressing. They also design or make special equipment needed at home or at work. Therapists develop and teach clients with severe limitations to operate computer-aided adaptive equipment that helps them to communicate, and control other aspects of their environment.

Some occupational therapists, called industrial therapists, treat individuals whose ability to function in a work environment has been impaired. They arrange employment, plan work activities, and evaluate the client's progress.

Occupational therapists may work exclusively with individuals in a particular age group, or with particular disabilities. In schools, for example, they evaluate children's abilities, recommend and provide therapy, modify classroom equipment, and in general, help children participate as fully as possible in school programs and activities.

Occupational therapists in mental health settings treat individuals who are mentally ill, mentally retarded, or emotionally disturbed. To treat these problems, therapists choose activities that help people learn to cope with daily life. Activities include time management skills, budgeting, shopping, homemaking, and use of public transportation. They may also work with individuals who are dealing with alcoholism, drug abuse, depression, eating disorders, or stress-related disorders.

Recording a client's activities and progress is an important part of an occupational therapist's job. Accurate records are essential for evaluating clients, billing, and reporting to physicians and others.

Working Conditions

Occupational therapists in hospitals and other health care and community settings generally work a 40-hour week. Those in schools may also participate in meetings and other activities, during and after the school day. Almost one-third of occupational therapists work part-time. In large rehabilitation centers, therapists may work in spacious rooms equipped with machines, tools, and other devices generating noise. The job can be tiring, because therapists are on their feet much of the time. Those providing home health care may spend several hours a day driving from appointment to appointment. Therapists also face hazards, such as backstrain from lifting and moving clients and equipment.

Therapists are increasingly taking on supervisory roles. Due to rising health care costs, third-party payers are beginning to encourage occupational therapy assistants and aides to take more hands-on responsibility. By having assistants and aides work more closely with clients under the guidance of a therapist, the cost of therapy should be more modest.

Employment

Occupational therapists held about 57,000 jobs in 1996. The largest number of jobs was in hospitals, including many in rehabilitation and psychiatric hospitals. Other major employers include offices and clinics of occupational therapists and other health practitioners, school systems, home health care services, nursing homes, community mental health centers, adult daycare programs, job training services, and residential care facilities.

A small number of occupational therapists are in private practice. Some are solo practitioners, while others are in group practices. They see clients referred by physicians or other health professionals, or provide contract or consulting services to nursing homes, schools, adult daycare programs, and home health agencies.

Training, Other Qualifications, and Advancement

A bachelor's degree in occupational therapy is the minimal requirement for entry into this field. All states, Puerto Rico, and the District of Columbia regulate occupational therapy. To obtain a license, applicants must graduate from an accredited educational program, and pass a national certi-

fication examination. Those who pass the test are awarded the title of registered occupational therapist.

In 1996, entry-level education was offered in 84 bachelor's degree programs; 15 post-bachelor's certificate programs for students with a degree other than occupational therapy; and 29 entry-level master's degree programs. Ten programs offered a combined bachelor's and master's degree. Most schools have full-time programs, although a growing number also offer weekend or part-time programs.

Occupational therapy course work includes physical, biological, and behavioral sciences, and the application of occupational therapy theory and skills. Completion of six months of supervised fieldwork is also required.

Persons considering this profession should take high school courses in biology, chemistry, physics, health, art, and the social sciences. College admissions offices also look with favor on paid or volunteer experience in the health care field.

Occupational therapists need patience and strong interpersonal skills to inspire trust and respect in their clients. Ingenuity and imagination in adapting activities to individual needs are assets. Those working in home health care must be able to successfully adapt to a variety of settings.

Job Outlook

Job opportunities for occupational therapists are expected to continue to be good. Employment of occupational therapists is expected to increase much faster than the average for all occupations through the year 2006, due to anticipated growth in demand for rehabilitation and long-term care services. The baby-boom generation's move into middle age, a period during which the incidence of heart attack and stroke increases, will increase the demand for therapeutic services. Additional services will also be demanded by the population 75 years of age and above, a rapidly growing age group that suffers from a very high incidence of disabling conditions.

Medical advances are now making it possible for more patients with critical problems to survive. These patients, however, may need extensive therapy. Finally, additional therapists will be needed to help children with disabilities prepare to enter special education programs, as required by federal legislation.

Due to industry growth and more intensive care, hospitals will continue to employ a large number of occupational therapists. Hospitals will also need occupational therapists to staff their growing home health care and outpatient rehabilitation programs.

Fast employment growth in schools will result from expansion of the school-age population and extended services for disabled students. Employment of occupational therapists in the home health field is also expected to grow very fast.

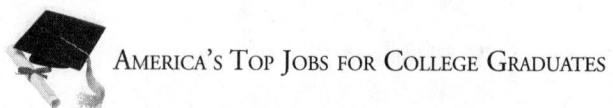

The rapidly growing number of people age 75 and older who are more likely to need home health care, and the greater use of at-home follow-up care, will encourage this growth.

Earnings

Median weekly earnings of full-time salaried occupational therapists were $780 in 1996. The middle 50 percent earned between $622 and $982. The lowest 10 percent earned less than $479; the top 10 percent earned more than $1,116.

According to a Hay Group survey of acute care hospitals, the median annual base salary of full-time occupational therapists was $42,700 in January 1997. The middle 50 percent earned between $39,100 and $46,100.

Related Occupations

Occupational therapists use specialized knowledge to help individuals perform daily living skills and achieve maximum independence. Other workers performing similar duties include orthotists, prosthetists, physical therapists, chiropractors, speech pathologists, audiologists, rehabilitation counselors, and recreational therapists.

Sources of Additional Information

For more information on occupational therapy as a career and a list of education programs, send a self-addressed label and $5 to:

❏ The American Occupational Therapy Association, 4720 Montgomery Ln., P.O. Box 31220, Bethesda, MD 20824-1220. Homepage: http://www.aota.org

Petroleum Engineers

(*D.O.T.* 010.061 except -014 and -026, .161-010, and .167-010 and -014)

Significant Points

* *A bachelor's degree in engineering is almost always required for beginning petroleum engineering jobs. Good employment opportunities are expected for new graduates.*

* *Starting salaries are significantly higher than those of bachelor's degree graduates in other fields.*

* *Knowledge of technological advances must be acquired through continued study and education.*

Nature of the Work

Petroleum engineers search the world for underground reservoirs containing oil or natural gas. When one is discovered, petroleum engineers work with geologists and other specialists to understand the geologic formation and properties of the rock containing the reservoir, determine the drilling methods to be used, and monitor drilling and production operations. They design equipment and processes to achieve the maximum profitable recovery of oil and gas, sometimes using computer models to simulate reservoir performance using different recovery techniques.

Because only a small proportion of the oil and gas in a reservoir will flow out under natural forces, petroleum engineers develop and use various enhanced recovery methods. These include injecting water, chemicals, gases, or steam into an oil reservoir to force more of the oil out, and computer-controlled drilling or fracturing to connect a larger area of a reservoir to a single well. Since even the best techniques in use today recover only a portion of the oil and gas in a reservoir, petroleum engineers research and develop technology and methods to increase this proportion and lower the cost of drilling and production operations.

Working Conditions

Most petroleum engineers work in office buildings, laboratories, or industrial plants. They spend a considerable amount of time outdoors at oil and gas exploration sites, where they monitor or direct operations or solve onsite problems. Some travel extensively to plants or work sites.

Most petroleum engineers work a standard 40-hour week. At times, deadlines or design standards may bring extra pressure to a job. When this happens, engineers may work long hours and experience considerable stress.

Employment

Petroleum engineers held over 13,000 jobs in 1996, mostly in the petroleum industry and closely allied fields. Employers include major oil companies and hundreds of smaller, independent oil exploration, production, and service companies. Engineering consulting firms, government agencies, oil field services, and equipment suppliers also employ petroleum engineers. Others work as independent consultants.

Most petroleum engineers work where oil and gas are found. Large numbers are employed in Texas, Oklahoma, Louisiana, Colorado, and California, including offshore sites. Many American petroleum engineers also work overseas in oil-producing countries. Because petroleum engineers specialize in the discovery and production of oil and gas, relatively few are employed in the refining, transportation, and retail sectors of the oil and gas industry.

Training, Other Qualifications, and Advancement

A bachelor's degree in engineering is usually required for beginning engineering jobs. College graduates with a degree in a physical science or mathematics may occasionally qualify for some engineering jobs, especially in engineering specialties in high demand. Most engineering degrees are granted in electrical, mechanical, or civil engineering. However, engineers trained in one branch may work in related branches; for example, many aerospace engineers have training in mechanical engineering. This flexibility allows employers to meet staffing needs in new technologies and specialties in which engineers are in short supply. It also allows engineers to shift to fields with better employment prospects, or to ones that match their interests more closely.

In addition to the standard engineering degree, many colleges offer degrees in engineering technology, which are offered as either two- or four-year programs. These programs prepare students for practical design and production work rather than for jobs that require more theoretical, scientific, and mathematical knowledge. Graduates of four-year technology programs may get jobs similar to those obtained by graduates with a bachelor's degree in engineering. Some employers regard them as having skills between those of a technician and an engineer.

Graduate training is essential for engineering faculty positions, but is not required for the majority of entry-level engineering jobs. Many engineers obtain graduate degrees in engineering or business administration to learn new technology, broaden their education, and enhance promotion opportunities. Many high-level executives in government and industry began their careers as engineers.

About 320 colleges and universities offer bachelor's degree programs in engineering that are accredited by the Accreditation Board for Engineering and Technology (ABET), and about 250 colleges offer accredited bachelor's degree programs in engineering technology. ABET accreditation is based on an examination of an engineering program's faculty, curricular content, facilities, and admissions standards. Although most institutions offer programs in the major branches of engineering, only a few offer some of the smaller specialties. Also, programs of the same title may vary in content. For example, some emphasize industrial practices, preparing students for a job in industry, while others are more theoretical and are better for students preparing to take graduate work. Therefore, students should investigate curricula and check accreditations carefully before selecting a college. Admissions requirements for undergraduate engineering schools include a solid background in mathematics (algebra, geometry, trigonometry, and calculus), sciences (biology, chemistry, and physics), and courses in English, social studies, humanities, and computers.

Bachelor's degree programs in engineering are typically designed to last four years, but many students find that it takes between four and five years to complete their studies. In a typical four-year college curriculum, the first two years are spent studying mathematics, basic sciences, introductory engineering, humanities, and social sciences. In the last two years, most courses are in engineering, usually with a concentration in one branch. For example, the last two years of an aerospace program might include courses such as fluid mechanics, heat transfer, applied aerodynamics, analytical mechanics, flight vehicle design, trajectory dynamics, and aerospace propulsion systems. Some programs offer a general engineering curriculum; students then specialize in graduate school or on the job.

Some engineering schools and two-year colleges have agreements whereby the two-year college provides the initial engineering education and the engineering school automatically admits students for their last two years. In addition, a few engineering schools have arrangements whereby a student spends three years in a liberal arts college studying pre-engineering subjects and two years in the engineering school, and receives a bachelor's degree from each. Some colleges and universities offer five-year master's degree programs. Some five- or even six-year cooperative plans combine classroom study and practical work, permitting students to gain valuable experience and finance part of their education.

All 50 states and the District of Columbia require registration for engineers whose work may affect life, health, or property, or who offer their services to the public. Registration generally requires a degree from an ABET-accredited engineering program, four years of relevant work experience, and passing a state examination. Some states will not register people with degrees in engineering technology. Engineers may be registered in several states.

Engineers should be creative, inquisitive, analytical, and detail-oriented. They should be able to work as part of a team and be able to communicate well, both orally and in writing.

Beginning engineering graduates usually work under the supervision of experienced engineers and, in larger companies, may also receive formal classroom or seminar-type training. As they gain knowledge and experience, they are assigned more difficult projects with greater independence to develop designs, solve problems, and make decisions. Engineers may advance to become technical specialists or to supervise a staff or team of engineers and technicians. Some eventually become engineering managers or enter other managerial, management support, or sales jobs.

Job Outlook

Employment of petroleum engineers is expected to decline through the year 2006 unless oil and gas prices unexpectedly rise enough to encourage increased exploration for oil in this country. In spite of this, employment opportunities for petroleum engineers should be favorable because the number of degrees granted in petroleum engineering has traditionally been low. Therefore, new graduates are not likely to significantly exceed the number of job openings arising as petroleum engineers transfer to other occupations or leave the labor force. Also, petroleum engineers work around the globe, and many employers seek U.S.-trained petroleum engineers for jobs in other countries.

The price of oil has a major effect on the level of employment opportunities for petroleum engineers in the United States. A high price of oil and gas makes it profitable for oil exploration and production firms to seek oil and gas reservoirs, and they will hire petroleum engineers to do so. With low oil prices, however, it is cheaper to purchase needed oil from other countries, such as Saudi Arabia, which have vast oil reserves. Also, the best exploration opportunities are in other countries because many of the most likely petroleum-producing areas in the United States have already been explored. However, the implementation of new technologies that expand drilling possibilities and improve the performance of reservoirs in the U.S. and the Gulf of Mexico may create new opportunities.

Earnings

Starting salaries for petroleum engineers with the bachelor's degree are significantly higher than starting salaries of bachelor's degree graduates in other fields. According to the National Association of Colleges and Employers, starting salaries for those with the bachelor's degree were about $43,674 in 1996.

The average annual salary for engineers in the federal government in nonsupervisory, supervisory, and managerial positions was $61,950 in 1997.

Related Occupations

Petroleum engineers apply the principles of physical science and mathematics in their work. Other workers who use scientific and mathematical principles include engineering, science, and computer systems managers; physical, life, and computer scientists; mathematicians; engineering and science technicians; and architects.

Sources of Additional Information

High school students interested in obtaining general information on a variety of engineering disciplines should contact the Junior Engineering Technical Society by sending a self-addressed business-size envelope, with six first-class stamps affixed, to:

❏ JETS-Guidance, 1420 King St., Suite 405, Alexandria, VA 22314-2794. Homepage: http://www.asee.org/jets

High school students interested in obtaining information on ABET accredited engineering programs should contact:

❏ The Accreditation Board for Engineering and Technology, Inc., 111 Market Place, Suite 1050, Baltimore, MD 21202-4012. Homepage: http://www.abet.ba.md.us

Non-high school students and those wanting more detailed information should contact:

❏ Society of Petroleum Engineers, P.O. Box 833836, Richardson, TX 75083-3836.

Physical Therapists

(D.O.T. 076.121-014)

Significant Points

✶ *Physical therapy offers very good job opportunities and high pay.*

✶ *Physical therapists will be among the fastest growing occupations, as growth in the number of individuals with disabilities or limited function increases the demand for physical therapy services.*

Nature of the Work

Physical therapists provide services that help restore function, improve mobility, relieve pain, and prevent or limit permanent physical disabilities of patients suffering from injuries or disease. They restore, maintain, and promote overall fitness and health. Their patients include accident victims and individuals with disabling conditions such as low back pain, arthritis, heart disease, fractures, head injuries, and cerebral palsy.

Therapists examine patients' medical histories and then test and measure their strength, range of motion, balance and coordination, posture, muscle performance, respiration, and motor function. They also determine patients' ability to be independent and reintegrate into the community or workplace after injury or illness. Next, they develop treatment plans describing the treatment strategy, its purpose, and the anticipated outcome. After devising a treatment strategy, physical therapists often delegate specific procedures to physical therapist assistants and aides. Therapists are increasingly taking on supervisory roles.

Treatment often includes exercise for patients who have been immobilized and lack flexibility, strength, or endurance. They encourage patients to use their own muscles to further increase flexibility and range of motion before finally advancing to other exercises improving strength, balance, coordination, and endurance. Their goal is to improve how an individual functions at work and home.

Physical therapists also use electrical stimulation, hot packs or cold compresses, and ultrasound to relieve pain and reduce swelling. They may use traction or deep-tissue massage to relieve pain. Therapists also teach patients to use assisting and adaptive devices such as crutches, prostheses, and wheelchairs. They may show patients exercises to do at home to expedite their recovery.

As treatment continues, physical therapists document progress, conduct periodic examinations, and modify treatments when necessary. Such documentation is used to track the patient's progress, and identify areas requiring more or less attention.

Physical therapists often consult and practice with a variety of other professionals, such as physicians, dentists, nurses, educators, social workers, occupational therapists, speech-language pathologists, and audiologists.

Some physical therapists treat a wide range of ailments; others specialize in areas such as pediatrics, geriatrics, orthopedics, sports medicine, neurology, and cardiopulmonary physical therapy.

Working Conditions

Physical therapists practice in hospitals, clinics, and private offices that have specially equipped facilities or they treat patients in hospital rooms, homes, or schools.

Most physical therapists work a 40-hour week, which may include some evenings and weekends. The job can be physically demanding because therapists often have to stoop, kneel, crouch, lift, and stand for long periods of time. In addition, physical therapists move heavy equipment and lift patients or help them turn, stand, or walk.

Employment

Physical therapists held about 115,000 jobs in 1996; about one in four worked part-time. Almost two-thirds were employed in either hospitals or offices of physical therapists. Other jobs were in home health agencies, outpatient rehabilitation centers, offices and clinics of physicians, and nursing homes. Some physical therapists are self-employed in private practices. They may provide services to individual patients or contract to provide services in hospitals, rehabilitation centers, nursing homes, home health agencies, adult daycare

programs, and schools. They may be in solo practice or be part of a consulting group. Physical therapists also teach in academic institutions and conduct research.

Training, Other Qualifications, and Advancement

All states require physical therapists to pass a licensure exam after graduating from an accredited physical therapist educational program before they can practice.

According to the American Physical Therapy Association, there were 173 accredited physical therapist programs as of July, 1997. Of the accredited programs, 46 offered bachelor's degrees and 116 were master's degree programs. By the year 2001, all accredited physical therapy programs will be at the master's degree level and above. Currently, the bachelor's degree curriculum starts with basic science courses such as biology, chemistry, and physics, and then introduces specialized courses such as biomechanics, neuroanatomy, human growth and development, manifestations of disease, examination techniques, and therapeutic procedures. Besides classroom and laboratory instruction, students receive supervised clinical experience. Individuals who have a four-year degree in another field and want to be a physical therapist, should enroll in a master's or a doctoral level physical therapist educational program.

Competition for entrance into physical therapist educational programs is very intense, so interested students should attain superior grades in high school and college, especially in science courses. Courses useful when applying to physical therapist educational programs include anatomy, biology, chemistry, social science, mathematics, and physics. Before granting admission, many professional education programs require experience as a volunteer in a physical therapy department of a hospital or clinic.

Physical therapists should have strong interpersonal skills to successfully educate patients about their physical therapy treatments. They should also be compassionate and posses a desire to help patients. Similar traits are also needed to interact with the patient's family.

Physical therapists are expected to continue professional development by participating in continuing education courses and workshops. A number of states require continuing education to maintain licensure.

Job Outlook

Anecdotal reports about shortages of physical therapists that existed in recent years are no longer common. The number of physical therapist educational programs has increased and more graduates have moved into the labor force. Nevertheless, job prospects are expected to continue to be very good.

Physical therapists are expected to be among the fastest growing occupations through the year 2006 as the demand for physical therapy services grows. The rapidly growing elderly population is particularly vulnerable to chronic and debilitating conditions that require therapeutic services. Also, the baby-boom generation is entering the prime age for heart attacks and strokes, increasing the demand for cardiac and physical rehabilitation. More young people will need physical therapy as technological advances save the lives of a larger proportion of newborns with severe birth defects. Future medical developments will also permit a higher percentage of trauma victims to survive, creating additional demand for rehabilitative care. Growth may also result from advances in medical technology which permit treatment of more disabling conditions.

Widespread interest in health promotion should also increase demand for physical therapy services. A growing number of employers are using physical therapists to evaluate work sites, develop exercise programs, and teach safe work habits to employees in the hope of reducing injuries.

Employment of physical therapists would grow even faster were it not for continued emphasis on controlling health care costs by limiting the use of therapeutic services in some instances.

Earnings

In 1996, median weekly earnings of salaried physical therapists who usually work full-time were $757. The middle 50 percent earned between $577 and $1,055. The top 10 percent earned at least $1,294 and the bottom 10 percent earned less than $400.

According to the American Physical Therapy Association's survey of physical therapists practicing in hospital settings, the median annual base salary of full-time physical therapists was $48,000 in 1996. The middle 50 percent earned between $42,000 and $57,000.

Related Occupations

Physical therapists rehabilitate persons with physical disabilities. Others who work in the rehabilitation field include occupational therapists, speech pathologists, audiologists, orthotists, prosthetists, and respiratory therapists.

Sources of Additional Information

Additional information on a career as a physical therapist and a list of accredited educational programs in physical therapy are available from:

❏ American Physical Therapy Association, 1111 North Fairfax St., Alexandria, VA 22314-1488. Homepage: http://www.apta.org/

Physician Assistants

(*D.O.T.* 079.364-018)

Significant Points

✴ *The typical physician assistant program lasts about two years and generally requires at least two years of college and some health care experience for admission.*

✴ *Earnings are high and job opportunities are expected to be excellent.*

Nature of the Work

Physician assistants (PAs) provide health care services with supervision by physicians. They should not be confused with medical assistants, who perform routine clinical and clerical tasks. PAs are formally trained to provide diagnostic, therapeutic, and preventive health care services under the direction of a physician. Working as members of the health care team, they take medical histories, examine patients, order and interpret laboratory tests and x rays, and make diagnoses. They also treat minor injuries by suturing, splinting, and casting. PAs record progress notes, instruct and counsel patients, and order or carry out therapy. In 39 states and the District of Columbia, physician assistants may prescribe medications. PAs may also have managerial duties. Some order medical and laboratory supplies and equipment, while others supervise technicians and assistants.

Physician assistants always work under the supervision of a physician. The extent of supervision, however, depends upon state law. For example, a PA may provide care in rural or inner city clinics where a physician is present for only one or two days each week, conferring with the supervising physician and other medical professionals as needed or required by law. PAs may also make house calls or go to hospitals and nursing homes to check on patients and report back to the physician.

In some states, the duties of a physician assistant are determined by the supervising physician; in others, they are determined by the state's regulatory agency. Aspiring PAs should investigate the laws and regulations in the states where they wish to practice.

Many PAs work in primary care areas such as general internal medicine, pediatrics, and family practice. Others work in specialty areas, such as general and thoracic surgery, emer-

gency medicine, orthopedics, and geriatrics. PAs specializing in surgery provide pre- and post-operative care and may work as first or second assistants during major surgery.

Working Conditions

Although PAs generally work in a comfortable, well-lighted environment, those in surgery often stand for long periods, and others do considerable walking. Schedules vary according to practice setting and often depend on the hours of the supervising physician. The workweek of PAs in physicians' offices may include weekends, night hours, or early morning hospital rounds to visit patients. They may also be on-call. PAs in clinics usually work a five-day, 40-hour week.

Employment

Physician assistants held about 64,000 jobs in 1996. Sixty-six percent were in the offices and clinics of physicians, dentists, or other health practitioners. Almost 20 percent were in hospitals. The rest were mostly in public health clinics, nursing homes, prisons, home health care agencies, and the Department of Veterans Affairs.

According to the American Academy of Physician Assistants, about one-third of all PAs provide health care to communities having fewer than 50,000 residents where physicians may be in limited supply.

Training, Other Qualifications, and Advancement

Almost all states require that new PAs complete an accredited, formal education program. In 1997, there were 96 such educational programs for physician assistants; 53 of these programs offered a baccalaureate degree or a degree option. The rest offered either a certificate, an associate degree, or a master's degree. Most PA graduates have at least a bachelor's degree.

Admission requirements vary, but many programs require two years of college and some work experience in the health care field. Students should take courses in biology, English, chemistry, math, psychology, and social sciences. More than half of all applicants hold a bachelor's or master's degree. Many applicants are former emergency medical technicians, other allied health professionals, or nurses.

PA programs generally last two years. Most programs are in schools of allied health, academic health centers, medical schools, or four-year colleges; a few are in community colleges, the military, or hospitals. Many accredited PA programs have clinical teaching affiliations with medical schools.

PA education includes classroom instruction in biochemistry, nutrition, human anatomy, physiology, microbiology, clinical pharmacology, clinical medicine, geriatric and home health care, disease prevention, and medical ethics. Students obtain supervised clinical training in several areas, including primary care medicine, inpatient medicine, surgery, obstetrics and gynecology, geriatrics, emergency medicine, psychiatry, and pediatrics. Sometimes, PA students serve one or more of these rotations under the supervision of a physician who is seeking to hire a PA. These rotations often lead to permanent employment.

As of 1997, 49 states and the District of Columbia had legislation governing the qualifications or practice of physician assistants. Mississippi did not. Forty-nine states required physician assistants to pass the Physician Assistants National Certifying Examination that is only open to graduates of an accredited educational program. Only those successfully completing the examination may use the credential "Physician Assistant-Certified (PA-C)." In order to remain certified, PAs must complete 100 hours of continuing medical education every two years. Every six years, they must pass a recertification examination or complete an alternate program combining learning experiences and a take-home examination.

Although they are not accredited, PA postgraduate residency training programs are available in gynecology, geriatrics, surgery, pediatrics, neonatology, and occupational medicine. Candidates must be graduates of an accredited program and be certified by the National Commission on Certification of Physician Assistants.

Physician assistants need leadership skills, self-confidence, and emotional stability. They must be willing to continue studying throughout their career to keep up with medical advances.

Some PAs pursue additional education in order to practice in a specialty area such as surgery, neonatology, or emergency medicine. Others, as they attain greater clinical knowledge and experience, advance to added responsibilities and higher earnings. However, by the very nature of the profession, individual PAs are usually supervised by physicians.

Job Outlook

Employment opportunities are expected to be excellent for physician assistants, particularly in areas or settings that have difficulty attracting physicians, such as rural and inner city clinics. Employment of PAs is expected to grow much faster than the average for all occupations through the year 2006 due to anticipated expansion of the health services industry and an emphasis on cost containment. Physicians and institutions are expected to employ more PAs to provide primary care and assist with medical and surgical procedures, because PAs are cost-effective and productive members of the health care team. Physician assistants can relieve physicians of routine duties and procedures. Telemedicine (using technology to facilitate interactive consultations between physicians and physician assistants) will also expand the use of physician assistants. Besides the traditional office-based setting, PAs should find a growing number of jobs in institutional settings such as hospitals, academic medical centers, public clinics, and prisons. Additional PAs may be needed to augment medical staffing in inpatient teaching hospital settings if the number of physician residents is reduced. In addition, state-imposed legal limitations on the numbers of hours worked by physician residents are increasingly common and encourage hospitals to use PAs to supply some physician resident services. Opportunities will be best in states that allow PAs a wider scope of practice, such as the ability to prescribe medication.

Earnings

According to the American Academy of Physician Assistants, the median income for physician assistants in full-time clinical practice in 1996 was $60,687; median income for first year graduates was $52,116. Income varies by specialty, practice setting, geographical location, and years of experience.

According to a Hay Group survey of HMOs, group practices, and hospital-based clinics, the median annual base salary of full-time physician assistants was $54,100 in May 1996. The middle 50 percent earned between $49,100 and $60,000.

The average annual salary for physician assistants employed by the federal government was $48,670 in early 1997.

Related Occupations

Other health workers who provide direct patient care that requires a similar level of skill and training include nurse practitioners, physical therapists, occupational therapists, clinical psychologists, speech-language pathologists, and audiologists.

Sources of Additional Information

For information on a career as a physician assistant, contact:

❏ American Academy of Physician Assistants Information Center, 950 North Washington St., Alexandria, VA 22314-1552. Homepage: http://www.aapa.org

For a list of accredited programs and a catalog of individual PA training programs, contact:

❏ Association of Physician Assistant Programs, 950 North Washington St., Alexandria, VA 22314-1552.

For eligibility requirements and a description of the Physician Assistant National Certifying Examination, write to:

❏ National Commission on Certification of Physician Assistants, Inc., 6849-B2 Peachtree Dunwoody Rd., Atlanta, GA 30328.

Property Managers

(*D.O.T.* 186.117-042, -046, -058, and -062, .167-018, -030, -038, -042, -046, -062, -066, and -090; 187.167-190; 191.117-046 and -050)

Significant Points

★ *Most persons enter the occupation as an on-site manager of an apartment complex, condominium, or community association, or as an assistant manager at a large property management company. Opportunities should be best for persons with college degrees in business administration and related fields.*

★ *About 40 percent were self-employed, over twice the average for other executive, administrative, and managerial occupations.*

Nature of the Work

Many people own real estate in the form of a home. To businesses and investors, however, properly managed real estate is a potential source of income and profits rather than simply a place for shelter. For this reason, property managers perform an important function in increasing and maintaining the value of real estate investments for investors. In general, property managers oversee the performance of income-producing commercial and residential properties or manage the communal property and services of condominium and community associations.

Most property managers work in the field of property management. When owners of apartments, office buildings, retail, or industrial properties lack the time or expertise needed for the day-to-day management of their real estate investments, they often hire a property manager, either directly or by contracting with a property management company.

Property managers handle the financial operations of the property, seeing to it that mortgages, taxes, insurance premiums, payroll, and maintenance bills are paid on time. They also supervise the preparation of financial statements and periodically report to the owners on the status of the property, occupancy rates, dates of lease expirations, and other matters.

If necessary, property managers negotiate contracts for janitorial, security, groundskeeping, trash removal, and other services. When contracts are awarded competitively, managers must solicit bids from several contractors and recommend to the owners which bid to accept. They monitor the performance of the contractors, and investigate and resolve complaints from residents and tenants when services are not properly provided. Managers also purchase supplies and

equipment needed for the property, and make arrangements with specialists for any repairs that cannot be handled by the regular property maintenance staff.

On top of these duties, property managers must understand the provisions of legislation, such as the Americans With Disabilities Act and the Federal Fair Housing Amendment Act, as well as local fair housing laws, to be sure their renting and advertising practices are not discriminatory.

On-site property managers are responsible for the day-to-day operations for one piece of property, such as an office building, shopping center, or apartment complex. To ensure the property is safe and being maintained properly, on-site managers routinely inspect the grounds, facilities, and equipment to determine what repairs are needed. They meet not only with current residents (when handling requests for repairs or trying to resolve complaints, for example), but also show vacant apartments or office space to prospective residents or tenants and explain the occupancy terms. On-site managers are also responsible for enforcing the terms of the rental or lease agreement, such as rent collection, parking and pet restrictions, and termination-of-lease procedures.

Other important duties of on-site managers include keeping accurate, up-to-date records of income and expenditures from property operations and the submission of regular expense reports to the property manager or owners.

The work of property managers who do not work on-site is similar to that of on-site managers, except that most of these managers are responsible for multiple properties and supervise on-site personnel. They act as a liaison between the on-site manager and the owner. They also market vacant space to prospective tenants through the use of a leasing agent, advertising, or by other means, and establish rental rates in accordance with prevailing local conditions.

Some property managers, termed real estate asset managers, act as the property owners' agent and adviser for the property. They plan and direct the purchase, development, and disposition of real estate on behalf of businesses and investors. These managers are involved in long-term strategic financial planning rather than the day-to-day operations of the property.

When looking to acquire property, real estate asset managers take several factors into consideration, such as property values, taxes, zoning, population growth, and traffic volume and patterns. Once a site is selected, they negotiate contracts for the purchase or lease of the property, securing the most beneficial terms.

Real estate asset managers periodically review their company's real estate holdings, identifying properties that are no longer commercially attractive. They then negotiate the sale or termination of the lease of properties selected for disposal.

The work of property managers employed by condominium and homeowner associations, often known as community association managers, is different than that of other property managers. Instead of renters, they interact on a daily basis with homeowners—members of the community association that employs the manager. Hired by the volunteer board of directors of the association, the community association manager administers daily affairs and oversees the maintenance of property and facilities that the homeowners own and use jointly through the association. Smaller community associations usually cannot afford professional management, but managers of larger condominiums or homeowner associations have many of the same responsibilities as the managers of large apartment complexes. Some homeowner associations encompass thousands of homes, and, in addition to administering the associations' financial records and budget, their managers are responsible for the operation of community pools, golf courses, community centers, and the maintenance of landscaping, parking areas, and streets. Other responsibilities usually include meeting with the elected boards of directors to discuss and solve legal and environmental issues and aiding in resolving disputes between neighbors.

Property managers who work for land development companies acquire land and plan the construction of shopping centers, houses and apartments, office buildings, or industrial parks. They negotiate with representatives of local government, other businesses, community and public interest groups, and public utilities to eliminate obstacles to the development of the land and gain support for the planned project. It sometimes takes years to win approval for a project, and in the process managers may have to modify the plans for the project many times. Once they are free to proceed with a project, managers negotiate short-term loans to finance the construction of the project, and later negotiate long-term permanent mortgage loans. They then contract with architectural firms to draw up detailed plans, and with construction companies to build the project.

Working Conditions

Offices of most property managers are clean, modern, and well-lighted. Many spend a major portion of their time away from their desks, however. On-site managers in particular may spend a large portion of their workday away from their office visiting the building engineer in the boiler room, showcasing apartments, checking on the janitorial and maintenance staff, or investigating problems reported by tenants. Property managers frequently visit the properties they oversee, sometimes on a daily basis when contractors are doing major repair or renovation work. Real estate asset managers may spend time away from home while traveling to company real estate holdings or searching for properties that might be acquired.

Property managers often must attend meetings in the evening with residents, property owners, community association boards of directors, or civic groups. Not surprisingly, many property managers put in long work weeks. Some apartment managers are required to live in the apartment complexes where they work so they are available to handle any emergency that occurs while they are off duty. They usually receive compensatory time off, however, for working at night or on weekends. Many apartment managers receive time off during the week so that they are available on weekends to show apartments to prospective residents.

Employment

Property managers held about 271,000 jobs in 1996. Most worked for real estate operators and lessors or for property management firms. Others worked for real estate development companies, government agencies that manage public buildings, and corporations with extensive holdings of commercial properties. About four out of ten property managers were self-employed, and over a quarter worked part time.

Training, Other Qualifications, and Advancement

Most employers prefer to hire college graduates for property management positions. Degrees in business administration, finance, real estate, public administration, or related fields are preferred, but persons with degrees in the liberal arts are often accepted. Good speaking, writing, and financial skills, as well as an ability to deal tactfully with people, are essential in all areas of property management.

Most persons enter property management as an on-site manager of an apartment complex, condominium, or community association, or as an assistant manager at a large property management company. As they acquire experience working under the direction of a property manager, they may advance to positions with greater responsibility at larger properties. Persons who excel as on-site managers often transfer to assistant property manager positions where they can acquire experience handling a broader range of property management responsibilities.

Previous employment as a real estate agent may be an asset to on-site managers because it provides experience useful in showing apartments or office space and dealing with people, as well as an understanding that an attractive, well-maintained property can command higher rental rates and result in lower turnover among tenants. In the past, many persons with backgrounds in building maintenance have advanced to on-site manager positions on the strength of their knowledge of building mechanical systems, but this is becoming less common as employers are placing greater emphasis on administrative, financial, and communication abilities for managerial jobs.

Although most persons who enter jobs as assistant property managers do so on the strength of on-site management experience, employers are increasingly hiring inexperienced college graduates with bachelor's or master's degrees in business administration, finance, or real estate for these jobs. Assistants work closely with a property manager and acquire experience performing a variety of management tasks, such as preparing the budget, analyzing insurance coverage and risk options, marketing the property to prospective tenants, and collecting overdue rent payments. In time, many assistants advance to property manager positions.

The responsibilities and compensation of property managers increase as they manage larger properties. Most property managers are responsible for several properties at a time, and as their careers advance they are gradually entrusted with properties that are larger or whose management is more complex. Many specialize in the management of one type of property, such as apartments, office buildings, condominiums, cooperatives, homeowner associations, or retail properties. Managers who excel at marketing properties to tenants may specialize in managing new properties, while those who are particularly knowledgeable about buildings and their mechanical systems might specialize in the management of older properties that require renovation or more frequent repairs. Some experienced property managers open their own property management firms.

Persons most commonly enter real estate asset manager jobs by transferring from positions as property managers or real estate brokers. Real estate asset managers must be good negotiators, adept at persuading and handling people, and good at analyzing data to assess the fair market value of property or its development potential. Resourcefulness and creativity in arranging financing are essential for managers who specialize in land development.

Attendance at short-term formal training programs conducted by various professional and trade associations active in the real estate field is often encouraged. Employers send managers to these programs to improve their management skills and expand their knowledge of specialized subjects, such as the operation and maintenance of building mechanical systems, enhancing property values, insurance and risk management, personnel management, business and real estate law,

resident/tenant relations, communications, and accounting and financial concepts. Managers also participate in these programs to prepare themselves for positions of greater responsibility in property management. Completion of these programs, together with meeting job experience standards and achieving a satisfactory score on a written examination, leads to certification, or the formal award of a professional designation, by the sponsoring association. In addition to these qualifications, some associations require their members to adhere to a specific code of ethics. Some of the organizations that offer such programs are listed at the end of this statement.

Managers of public housing subsidized by the federal government are required to be certified, but many property managers who work with all types of property choose to earn a professional designation voluntarily because it represents formal industry recognition of their achievements and status in the occupation.

Job Outlook

Employment of property managers is projected to increase as fast as the average for all occupations through the year 2006. In addition to rising demand for these workers, many job openings are expected to occur as property managers transfer to other occupations or leave the labor force. Opportunities should be best for persons with college degrees in business administration, real estate, and related fields, as well as those who attain professional designations.

Growth in the demand for property managers will be evident in several areas. In commercial real estate, the demand for managers is expected to coincide with the projected expansion in wholesale and retail trade; finance, insurance, and real estate; and services. Some additional employment growth will come from adding on to existing buildings.

An increase in the nation's stock of apartments and houses also should require more property managers. Developments of new homes are increasingly being organized with community or homeowner associations that provide community services and oversee jointly owned common areas, requiring professional management. To help properties become more profitable, more commercial and multi-unit residential property owners are expected to place their investments in the hands of professional managers.

Growth in demand should also arise as a result of the changing demographic composition of the population. The number of older people will increase during the projection period, creating a need for various types of suitable housing, such as assisted living arrangements and retirement communities. Accordingly, there will be a need for property managers

to operate these facilities, especially those who have a background in the operation and administrative aspects of running a health unit.

Earnings

Median annual earnings of all property managers were $28,500 in 1996. The middle 50 percent earned between $19,000 and $39,800. Ten percent earned less than $12,000 and 10 percent earned more than $60,700 annually.

Community association managers received compensation comparable to on-site and property managers employed by other types of properties. Many resident apartment managers receive the use of an apartment as part of their compensation package. Property managers often are given the use of a company automobile, and managers employed in land development often receive a small percentage of ownership in projects they develop.

Related Occupations

Property managers plan, organize, staff, and manage the real estate operations of businesses. Workers who perform similar functions in other fields include restaurant and food service managers, hotel and resort managers, facilities managers, health services managers, education administrators, and city managers.

Sources of Additional Information

General information about careers in property management and programs leading to the award of a professional designation in the field is available from:

❑ Institute of Real Estate Management, 430 N. Michigan Ave., Chicago, IL 60611. Homepage: http://www.irem.org

For information on careers and certification programs in commercial property management, contact:

❑ Building Owners and Managers Association International, 1201 New York Ave. NW, Suite 300, Washington, DC 20005. Homepage: http://www.boma.org

❑ Building Owners and Managers Institute (BOMI) International, 1521 Ritchie Hwy., Arnold, MD 21012. Homepage: http://www.bomi-edu.org

For information on careers and certification programs in residential property management, contact:

❑ Community Associations Institute, 1630 Duke St., Alexandria, VA 22314. Homepage: http://www.caionline.org

❑ National Apartment Association, Education Department, 201 N. Union St., Suite 200, Alexandria, VA 22314.

❑ National Association of Home Builders, 1201 15th St. NW, Washington, DC 20005. Homepage: http://www.nahb.com/multi.html

❑ National Association of Residential Property Managers, 35 E. Wacker Dr., Suite 500, Chicago, IL 60601.

Public Relations Specialists

(D.O.T. 165.017 and .167)

Significant Points

* *Employment of public relations specialists is expected to increase rapidly, while keen competition is expected for entry-level jobs.*

* *Opportunities should be best for college graduates with degrees in journalism, public relations, advertising, or other communications-related fields.*

* *Public relations work experience gained as an intern is an asset in competing for entry-level jobs.*

Nature of the Work

An organization's reputation, profitability, and even its continued existence can depend on the degree to which its goals and policies are supported by its targeted "publics." Public relations specialists serve as advocates for businesses, governments, universities, hospitals, schools, and other organizations, and strive to build and maintain positive relationships with the public. As managers recognize the growing importance of good public relations to the success of their organizations, they increasingly rely on public relations specialists for advice on strategy and policy of such programs.

Public relations specialists handle such organizational functions as media, community, consumer, and governmental relations; political campaigns; interest-group representation; conflict mediation; or employee and investor relations. However, public relations is not only "telling the organization's story." Understanding the attitudes and concerns of consumers, employees, and various other groups is also a vital part of the job. To improve communications, public relations specialists establish and maintain cooperative relationships with representatives of community, consumer, employee, and public interest groups and those in print and broadcast journalism.

Public relations specialists put together information that keeps the general public, interest groups, and stockholders aware of an organization's policies, activities, and accomplishments. Their work keeps management aware of public attitudes and concerns of the many groups and organizations with which it must deal.

Public relations specialists prepare press releases and contact people in the media who might print or broadcast their material. Many radio or television special reports, newspaper stories, and magazine articles start at the desks of public relations specialists. Sometimes the subject is an organization and its policies toward its employees or its role in the community. Often the subject is a public issue, such as health, nutrition, energy, or the environment.

Public relations specialists also arrange and conduct programs for contact between organization representatives and the public. For example, they set up speaking engagements and often prepare the speeches for company officials. These specialists represent employers at community projects; make film, slide, or other visual presentations at meetings and school assemblies; and plan conventions. In addition, they are responsible for preparing annual reports and writing proposals for various projects.

In government, public relations specialists—who may be called press secretaries, information officers, public affairs specialists, or communications specialists—keep the public informed about the activities of government agencies and officials. For example, public affairs specialists in the Department of Energy keep the public informed about the proposed lease of offshore land for oil exploration. A press secretary for a member of Congress keeps constituents aware of their elected representative's accomplishments.

In large organizations, the key public relations executive, who is often a vice president, may develop overall plans and policies with other executives. In addition, public relations departments employ public relations specialists to write, do research, prepare materials, maintain contacts, and respond to inquiries.

People who handle publicity for an individual or who direct public relations for a small organization may deal with all aspects of the job. They contact people, plan and do research, and prepare material for distribution. They may also handle advertising or sales promotion work to support marketing.

Working Conditions

Some public relations specialists work a standard 35- to 40-hour week, but unpaid overtime is common. In addition, schedules often have to be rearranged to meet deadlines, deliver speeches, attend meetings and community activities, and travel out of town. Occasionally they have to be at the job or on call around the clock, especially if there is an emergency or crisis.

Employment

Public relations specialists held about 110,000 jobs in 1996. About two-thirds worked in services industries—management and public relations firms, educational institutions, membership organizations, health care organizations, social service agencies, and advertising agencies, for example.

Others worked for a wide range of employers, including manufacturing firms, financial institutions, and government agencies. A few were self-employed.

Public relations specialists are concentrated in large cities in which press services and other communications facilities are readily available, and many businesses and trade associations have their headquarters. Many public relations consulting firms, for example, are in New York, Los Angeles, Chicago, and Washington, DC. There is a trend, however, for public relations jobs to be dispersed throughout the nation.

Training, Other Qualifications, and Advancement

Although there are no defined standards for entry into a public relations career, a college degree combined with public relations experience, usually gained through an internship, is considered excellent preparation for public relations work. The ability to write and speak well is essential. Many beginners have a college major in public relations, journalism, advertising, or communications. Some firms seek college graduates who have worked in electronic or print journalism. Other employers seek applicants with demonstrated communications skills and training or experience in a field related to the firm's business—science, engineering, sales, or finance, for example.

In 1996, well over 200 colleges and about 100 graduate schools offered degree programs or special curricula in public relations, usually in a journalism or communications department. In addition, many other colleges offered at least one course in this field. The Accrediting Council on Education in Journalism and Mass Communications is the only agency authorized to accredit schools or department in public relations. A commonly used public relations sequence includes the following courses: Public relations principles and techniques; public relations management and administration, including organizational development; writing, emphasizing news releases, proposals, annual reports, scripts, speeches, and related items; visual communications, including desktop publishing and computer graphics; and research, emphasizing social science research and survey design and implementation. Courses in advertising, journalism, business administration, political science, psychology, sociology, and creative writing also are helpful, as is familiarity with word processing and other computer applications. Specialties are offered in public relations for business, government, or nonprofit organizations.

Many colleges help students gain part-time internships in public relations that provide valuable experience and training. The Armed Forces can also be an excellent place to gain training and experience. Membership in local chapters of the Public Relations Student Society of America or the Interna-

tional Association of Business Communicators provides an opportunity for students to exchange views with public relations specialists and to make professional contacts who may help them find a full-time job in the field. A portfolio of published articles, television or radio programs, slide presentations, and other work is an asset in finding a job. Writing for a school publication or television or radio station provides valuable experience and material for one's portfolio.

Creativity, initiative, good judgment, and the ability to express thoughts clearly and simply are essential. Decision making, problem solving, and research skills are also important.

People who choose public relations as a career need an outgoing personality, self-confidence, an understanding of human psychology, and an enthusiasm for motivating people. They should be competitive, yet flexible and able to function as part of a team.

Some organizations, particularly those with large public relations staffs, have formal training programs for new employees. In smaller organizations, new employees work under the guidance of experienced staff members. Beginners often maintain files of material about company activities, scan newspapers and magazines for appropriate articles to clip, and assemble information for speeches and pamphlets. After gaining experience, they write news releases, speeches, and articles for publication, or design and carry out public relations programs. Public relations specialists in smaller firms generally get all-around experience, whereas those in larger firms tend to be more specialized.

The Public Relations Society of America accredits public relations specialists who have at least five years of experience in the field and have passed a comprehensive six-hour examination (five hours written, one hour oral). The International Association of Business Communicators also has an accreditation program for professionals in the communications field, including public relations specialists. Those who meet all the requirements of the program earn the designation, Accredited Business Communicator. Candidates must have at least five years of experience in a communication field and pass a written and oral examination. They also must submit a portfolio of work samples demonstrating involvement in a range of communication projects and a thorough understanding of communication planning. Employers consider professional recognition through accreditation a sign of competence in this field, and it may be especially helpful in a competitive job market.

Promotion to supervisory jobs may come as public relations specialists show they can handle more demanding managerial assignments. In public relations firms, a beginner may be hired as a research assistant or account assistant and be promoted to account executive, account supervisor, vice president, and eventually senior vice president. A similar career path is followed in corporate public relations, although the titles may differ. Some experienced public relations specialists start their own consulting firms.

Job Outlook

Keen competition for public relations jobs will likely continue among recent college graduates with a degree in communications—journalism, public relations, advertising, or a related field—as the number of applicants is expected to exceed the number of job openings. People without the appropriate educational background or work experience will face the toughest obstacles in finding a public relations job.

Employment of public relations specialists is expected to increase faster than the average for all occupations through the year 2006. Recognition of the need for good public relations in an increasingly competitive business environment should spur demand for public relations specialists in organizations of all sizes. Employment in public relations firms should grow as firms hire contractors to provide public relations services rather than support full-time staff. The vast majority of job opportunities should result from the need to replace public relations specialists who leave the occupation to take another job, retire, or for other reasons.

Earnings

Median annual earnings for salaried public relations specialists who usually worked full-time were about $34,000 in 1996. The middle 50 percent earned between $25,000 and $54,000 annually; the lowest 10 percent earned less than $16,000, and the top 10 percent earned more than $75,000.

According to a 1995 salary survey conducted for the Public Relations Society of America, the overall median salary in public relations was $49,070. Salaries in public relations ranged from less than $15,000 to more than $150,000. There was little difference between the median salaries in public relations firms and corporations, $51,340 and $50,770, respectively. However, practitioners working for government, health care, or non-profit organizations had a considerably lower median salary of $43,260.

Public affairs specialists in the federal government in nonsupervisory, supervisory, and managerial positions averaged about $52,540 a year in 1996.

Related Occupations

Public relations specialists create favorable attitudes among various organizations, special interest groups, and the public through effective communication. Other workers with similar jobs include fund raisers, lobbyists, promotion managers, advertising managers, and police officers involved in community relations.

Sources of Additional Information

A comprehensive directory of schools offering degree programs or a sequence of study in public relations, a brochure on careers in public relations, and a $5 brochure entitled "Where Shall I Go to Study Advertising and Public Relations" are available from:

❑ Public Relations Society of America, Inc., 33 Irving Place, New York, NY 10003-2376.

Career information on public relations in hospitals and other health care settings is available from:

❑ The Society for Health Care Strategy and Market Development, One North Franklin St., Suite 3100S, Chicago, IL 60606.

For a list of schools with accredited programs in public relations in their journalism departments, send a stamped self-addressed envelope to:

❑ Accrediting Council on Education in Journalism and Mass Communications, University of Kansas School of Journalism, Stauffer Flint Hall, Lawrence, KS 66045.

For information on accreditation for public relations specialists, contact:

❑ International Association of Business Communicators, One Hallidie Plaza, Suite 600, San Francisco, CA 94102.

Purchasers and Buyers

(*D.O.T.* 162.117-014 and -018, .157-018, -022, -030, -034, and -038, .167-022, and -030; 163.117-010; 169.167-054; 184.117-078; and 185.167-034)

Significant Points

∗ *Computerization has reduced the demand for lower-level buyers.*

∗ *About one-half were employed in wholesale or retail trade.*

Nature of the Work

Purchasers and buyers seek to obtain the highest quality merchandise at the lowest possible purchase cost for their employers. (In general, purchasers buy goods and services for the use of their company or organization, whereas buyers buy items for resale.) They determine which commodities or services are best, choose the suppliers of the product or service, negotiate the lowest price, and award contracts that ensure the correct amount of the product or service is received at the appropriate time. In order to accomplish these tasks success-

fully, purchasers and buyers study sales records and inventory levels of current stock, identify foreign and domestic suppliers, and keep abreast of changes affecting both the supply of and demand for products and materials for which they are responsible.

Purchasers and buyers evaluate suppliers based upon price, quality, service support, availability, reliability, and selection. To assist them in their search, they review listings in catalogs, industry periodicals, directories, and trade journals, research the reputation and history of the suppliers, and advertise anticipated purchase actions in order to solicit bids. Also, meetings, trade shows, conferences, and visits to suppliers' plants and distribution centers provide opportunities for purchasers and buyers to examine products, assess a supplier's production and distribution capabilities, as well as discuss other technical and business considerations that influence the purchasing decision. Once all the necessary information on suppliers is gathered, orders are placed and contracts are awarded to those suppliers who meet the purchasers' needs. Other specific job duties and responsibilities vary by employer and by the type of commodities or services to be purchased.

Purchasing professionals employed by government agencies or manufacturing firms are usually called purchasing directors, managers, or agents; buyers or industrial buyers; or contract specialists. These workers acquire product materials, intermediate goods, machines, supplies, services, and other materials used in the production of a final product. Some purchasing managers specialize in negotiating and supervising supply contracts and are called contract or supply managers. Purchasing agents and managers obtain items ranging from raw materials, fabricated parts, machinery, and office supplies to construction services and airline tickets. The flow of work—or even the entire production process—can be slowed or halted if the right materials, supplies, or equipment are not on hand when needed. In order to be effective, purchasers and buyers must have a working technical knowledge of the goods or services to be purchased.

In large industrial organizations, a distinction often is drawn between the work of a buyer or purchasing agent and that of a purchasing manager. Purchasing agents and buyers typically focus on routine purchasing tasks, often specializing in a commodity or group of related commodities—for example, steel, lumber, cotton, fabricated metal products, or petroleum products. This usually requires the purchaser to track such things as market conditions, price trends, or futures markets. Purchasing managers usually handle the more complex or critical purchases and may supervise a group of purchasing agents handling other goods and services. Whether a person is titled purchasing agent, buyer, or manager depends more on specific industry and employer practices than on specific job duties.

Changing business practices have altered the traditional roles of purchasing professionals in many industries. For example, manufacturing companies increasingly involve purchasing professionals at most stages of product development because of their ability to forecast a part's or material's cost, availability, and suitability for its intended purpose. Furthermore, potential problems with the supply of materials may be avoided by consulting the purchasing department in the early stages of product design.

Another new practice is for businesses to enter into integrated supply contracts. These contracts increase the importance of supplier selection because agreements are larger in scope and longer in duration. A major responsibility of most purchasers is to work out problems that may occur with a supplier because the success of the relationship directly affects the buying firm's performance.

Purchasing professionals often work closely with other employees in their own organization when deciding on purchases, an arrangement sometimes called team buying. For example, they may discuss the design of custom-made products with company design engineers, quality problems in purchased goods with quality assurance engineers and production supervisors, or shipment problems with managers in the receiving department before submitting an order.

Contract specialists and managers in various levels of government award contracts for an array of items, including office and building supplies, services for the public, and construction projects. They typically use sealed bids, but sometimes use negotiated agreements for complex items. Increasingly, purchasing professionals in government are placing solicitations for and accepting bids through the Internet. Government purchasing agents and managers must follow strict laws and regulations in their work. These legal requirements occasionally are changed, so agents and contract specialists must stay informed about the latest regulations and their applications.

Other professionals, who buy finished goods for resale, are employed by wholesale and retail establishments where they commonly are referred to as "buyers" or "merchandise managers." Wholesale and retail buyers are an integral part of a complex system of distribution and merchandising that caters to the vast array of consumer needs and desires. Wholesale buyers purchase goods directly from manufacturers or from other wholesale firms for resale to retail firms, commercial establishments, institutions, and other organizations. In retail firms, buyers purchase goods from wholesale firms or directly from manufacturers for resale to the public. Buyers largely determine which products their establishment will sell. Therefore, it is essential that they have the ability to accurately predict what will appeal to consumers. They must constantly stay informed of the latest trends because failure to do so could jeopardize profits and the reputation of their company. Buyers also follow ads in newspapers and other media to check competitors' sales activities and watch general economic conditions to anticipate consumer buying patterns. Buyers working for large and medium-sized firms usually specialize in acquiring one or two lines of merchandise, whereas buyers working for small stores may purchase their complete inventory.

The use of private-label merchandise and the consolidation of buying departments have increased the responsibilities of retail buyers. Private-label merchandise, produced for a particular retailer, requires buyers to work closely with vendors to develop and obtain the desired product. The downsizing and consolidation of buying departments is also increasing the demands placed on buyers because, although the amount of work remains unchanged, there are fewer people needed to accomplish it. The result is an increase in the workloads and levels of responsibility.

Many merchandise managers assist in the planning and implementation of sales promotion programs. Working with merchandising executives, they determine the nature of the sale and purchase accordingly. They also work with advertising personnel to create the ad campaign. For example, they may determine the media in which the advertisement will be placed—newspapers, direct mail, television, or some combination of these. In addition, merchandising managers often visit the selling floor to ensure that the goods are properly displayed. Often, assistant buyers are responsible for placing orders and checking shipments.

Computers are having a major effect on the jobs of purchasers and buyers. In manufacturing and service industries, computers handle most of the more routine tasks—enabling purchasing professionals to concentrate mainly on the analytical aspects of the job. Computers are used to obtain up-to-date product and price listings, to track inventory levels, process routine orders, and help determine when to make purchases. Computers also maintain bidders' lists, record the history of supplier performance, and issue purchase orders.

Computerized systems have dramatically simplified many of the routine buying functions and improved the efficiency of determining which products are selling. For example, cash registers connected to computers, known as point-of-sale terminals, allow organizations to maintain centralized, up-to-date sales and inventory records. This information can then be used to produce weekly sales reports that reflect the types of products in demand. Buyers also use computers to gain instant access to the specifications for thousands of commodities, inventory records, and their customers' purchase records. Some firms are linked with manufacturers or wholesalers by electronic purchasing systems. These systems speed selection and ordering and provide information on availability and shipment, allowing buyers to better concentrate on the selection of goods and suppliers.

Working Conditions

Most purchasers and buyers work in comfortable, well-lighted offices at stores, corporate headquarters, or production or service facilities. They frequently work more than a 40-hour week because of special sales, conferences, or production deadlines. Evening and weekend work is common. For those working in retail trade, this is especially true prior to holiday seasons. Consequently, many retail firms discourage the use of vacation time from late November until early January.

Buyers and merchandise managers often work under great pressure because wholesale and retail stores are so competitive; buyers need physical stamina to keep up with the fast-paced nature of their work.

Many purchasers and buyers spend at least several days a month traveling. Purchasers for worldwide manufacturing companies and large retailers, and buyers of high fashion, may travel outside the United States.

Employment

Purchasers and buyers held about 639,000 jobs in 1996. Purchasing agents and purchasing managers each accounted for slightly more than one-third of the total, while buyers accounted for the remainder.

About one-half of all purchasers and buyers worked in wholesale and retail trade establishments such as grocery or department stores, and another one-fourth worked in manufacturing. The remainder worked mostly in service establishments or different levels of government.

Training, Other Qualifications, and Advancement

Qualified persons usually begin as trainees, purchasing clerks, expediters, junior buyers, or assistant buyers. Retail and wholesale firms prefer to hire applicants who are familiar with the merchandise they sell as well as with wholesaling and retailing practices. Some retail firms promote qualified employees to assistant buyer positions; others recruit and train college graduates as assistant buyers. Most employers use a combination of methods.

Educational requirements tend to vary with the size of the organization. Large stores and distributors, especially those in wholesale and retail trade, prefer applicants who have completed a bachelor's degree program with a business emphasis. Many manufacturing firms prefer applicants with a bachelor's or master's degree in business, economics, or technical training such as engineering or one of the applied sciences and tend to put a greater emphasis on formal training.

Regardless of academic preparation, new employees must learn the specifics of their employers' business. Training periods vary in length, with most lasting one to five years. In wholesale and retail establishments, most trainees begin by selling merchandise, supervising sales workers, checking invoices on material received, and keeping track of stock on hand, although widespread use of computers has simplified some of these tasks. As they progress, retail trainees are given more buying-related responsibilities. In manufacturing, new purchasing employees often are enrolled in company training programs and spend a considerable amount of time learning about company operations and purchasing practices. They work with experienced purchasers to learn about commodities, prices, suppliers, and markets. In addition, they may be assigned to the production planning department to learn about the material requirements system and the inventory system the company uses to keep production and replenishment functions working smoothly.

Because the procurement process is becoming more automated, it is extremely important for purchasers and buyers to be computer literate, including knowing how to use word processing and spreadsheet software. Other important qualities include the ability to analyze technical data in suppliers' proposals, good communicating, negotiating, and math skills, knowledge of supply chain management, and the ability to perform financial analyses.

Persons who wish to become wholesale or retail buyers should be good at planning and decision making and have an interest in merchandising. Anticipating consumer preferences and ensuring that goods are in stock when they are needed require resourcefulness, good judgment, and self-confidence. Buyers must be able to make decisions quickly and take risks. Marketing skills and the ability to identify products that will sell are also very important. Employers often look for leadership ability because buyers spend a large portion of their time supervising assistant buyers and dealing with manufacturers' representatives and store executives.

Experienced buyers may advance by moving to a department that manages a larger volume or by becoming a merchandise manager. Others may go to work in sales for a manufacturer or wholesaler.

An experienced purchasing agent or buyer may become an assistant purchasing manager in charge of a group of purchasing professionals before advancing to purchasing manager, supply manager, or director of materials management. At the top levels, duties may overlap into other management functions such as production, planning, and marketing.

Regardless of industry, continuing education is essential for advancement. Many purchasers participate in seminars offered by professional societies and take college courses in purchasing. Although no national standard exists, professional certification is becoming increasingly important.

In private industry, the recognized marks of experience and professional competence are the designations Accredited Purchasing Practitioner (APP) and Certified Purchasing Manager (CPM), conferred by the National Association of Purchasing Management, and Certified Purchasing Professional (CPP), conferred by the American Purchasing Society. In federal, state, and local government, the indications of professional competence are the designations Certified Professional Public Buyer (CPPB) and Certified Public Purchasing Officer (CPPO), conferred by the National Institute of Governmental Purchasing.

As more materials purchasing is conducted on a long-term basis, both private and public purchasing professionals are specializing in the contractual aspects of purchasing. The National Contract Management Association confers the designations Simplified Acquisition Specialists (SAS), Certified Associate Contract Manager (CACM), and Certified Professional Contract Manager (CPCM). These designations primarily apply to contract managers in the federal government and its suppliers.

Most designations are awarded only after work-related experience and education requirements are met, and written or oral exams are completed successfully.

Job Outlook

Employment of purchasers and buyers is expected to increase more slowly than the average for all occupations through the year 2006. Demand for these workers will not keep pace with the rising level of economic activity because the increasing use of computers has allowed much of the paperwork typically involved in ordering and procuring supplies to be eliminated, reducing the demand for lower-level buyers who traditionally performed these duties. Also, limited sourcing and long-term contracting have allowed companies to negotiate with fewer suppliers less frequently. Consequently, most job openings will result from the need to replace workers who transfer to other occupations or leave the labor force.

In retail trade, mergers and acquisitions have forced the consolidation of buying departments, eliminating jobs. In addition, larger retail stores are removing their buying departments from geographic markets and centralizing them at their headquarters, eliminating more jobs.

The increased use of credit cards by some employees to purchase supplies without using the services of the procurement or purchasing office, combined with the growing number of buys being made electronically, will restrict demand of purchasing agents within governments and many manufacturing firms.

Persons who have a bachelor's degree in business should have the best chance of obtaining a buyer job in wholesale or retail trade or within government. A bachelor's degree, combined with industry experience and/or knowledge of a technical field, will be an advantage for those interested in working for a manufacturing or industrial company. A master's degree in business or public administration is usually required by government agencies and larger companies for top-level purchasing positions.

Earnings

Median annual earnings of purchasers and buyers were $33,200 in 1996. The middle 50 percent earned between $23,300 and $45,900. The lowest 10 percent earned less than $18,400, while the top 10 percent earned more than $63,000. Merchandise managers and purchasing managers generally earned higher salaries than buyers or agents. As a general rule, those with the most education in their field have the highest incomes.

The average annual salaries for purchasing agents and contract specialists in the federal government in early 1997 were about $28,700 and $51,110, respectively.

Purchasers and buyers receive the same benefits package as their coworkers, frequently including vacations, sick leave, life and health insurance, and pension plans. In addition to standard benefits, retail buyers often earn cash bonuses based on their performance and may receive discounts on merchandise bought from the employer.

Related Occupations

Workers in other occupations who need a knowledge of marketing and the ability to assess demand are retail sales workers, sales managers, marketing and advertising managers, manufacturers' and wholesale sales representatives, insurance sales agents, services sales representatives, and procurement services, materials, and traffic managers.

Sources of Additional Information

Further information about education, training, and/or certification for purchasing careers is available from:

❑ American Purchasing Society, 30 W. Downer Pl., Aurora, IL 60506. Homepage: http://www.american-purchasing.com

❑ National Association of Purchasing Management, Customer Service, 2055 East Centennial Circle, P.O. Box 22160, Tempe, AZ 85285. Homepage: http://www.napm.org

❑ National Institute of Governmental Purchasing, Inc., 11800 Sunrise Valley Dr., Suite 1050, Reston, VA 20191-5302. Homepage: http://www.nigp.org

❑ National Contract Management Association, 1912 Woodford Rd., Vienna, VA 22182. Homepage: http://www.ncmahq.org

❑ Federal Acquisition Institute (MVI), Office of Acquisition Policy, General Services Administration, 18th & F Streets NW, Room 4019, Washington, DC 20405. Homepage: http://www.gsa.gov/staff/v/mvi/key.htm

General information on buying careers in retail establishments is available from:

❑ National Retail Federation, 325 7th St. NW, Suite 1000, Washington, DC 20004. Homepage: http://www.nrf.com http://www.nrf.com

Recreational Therapists

(D.O.T. 076.124-014)

Significant Points

★ *Employment of recreational therapists is expected to increase rapidly as demand grows for physical and psychiatric rehabilitative services and for services for people with disabilities.*

★ *Opportunities should generally be good for persons with a bachelor's degree in therapeutic recreation or in recreation with an option in therapeutic recreation.*

Nature of the Work

Recreational therapists provide treatment services and recreation activities to individuals with illnesses or disabling conditions. They use a variety of techniques to treat or maintain the physical, mental, and emotional well-being of clients. Treatments may include the use of arts and crafts, animals, sports, games, dance and movement, drama, music, and community outings. Therapists help individuals reduce depression, stress, and anxiety. They help individuals recover their basic motor functioning and reasoning abilities, build confidence, and socialize more effectively to allow them to be more

independent, as well as reduce or eliminate the effects of illness or disability. Their focus is to help integrate people with disabilities into the community by helping them use community resources and recreational activities. Recreational therapists should not be confused with recreation workers, who organize recreational activities primarily for enjoyment.

In acute health care settings, such as hospitals and rehabilitation centers, recreational therapists treat and rehabilitate individuals with specific health conditions, usually in conjunction or collaboration with physicians, nurses, psychologists, social workers, and physical and occupational therapists. In long-term care facilities and residential facilities, they use leisure activities—especially structured group programs—to maintain general health and well-being. They may also treat clients and provide interventions to prevent further medical problems and secondary complications related to illness and disabilities. In these settings they may be called activity directors or therapeutic recreation specialists.

Recreational therapists assess clients based on information from standardized assessments, observations, medical records, medical staff, family, and clients themselves. They then develop and carry out therapeutic interventions consistent with patient needs and interests. For instance, clients isolated from others may be encouraged to play games with others; a right-handed person with a right-side paralysis may be instructed in adaptation and compensatory strategies to use his or her non-affected left side to throw a ball or swing a racket. Recreational therapists may instruct patients in relaxation techniques to reduce stress and tension, in correct stretching and limbering exercises, in proper body mechanics for participation in recreation activities, in pacing and energy conservation techniques, and in individual as well as team activities.

Community-based recreational therapists work in park and recreation departments, special education programs for school districts, or programs for older adults and people with disabilities. In these programs, therapists help clients develop leisure activities and provide them with opportunities for exercise, mental stimulation, creativity, and fun.

In schools, recreational therapists help counselors, parents, and special education teachers address the special needs of students. They are especially important in helping to ease the transition phase into adult life for the disabled. The transition phase extends from age 14 until high school graduation. Recreational therapists provide assistance in teaching the student about recreational activities and how to use community resources. The primary responsibility for these therapists is to integrate students into the community.

Recreational therapists observe and record patients' participation, reactions, and progress. These records are used by the medical staff and others, to monitor progress, to justify changes or end treatment, and for billing.

Working Conditions

Recreational therapists provide services in special activity rooms, but also must plan events and keep records in offices. When working with clients during community integration programs, they may travel locally to instruct clients on the accessibility of public transportation and other public areas, such as parks, playgrounds, swimming pools, restaurants, and theaters.

Therapists often lift and carry equipment as well as lead recreational activities. Recreational therapists generally work a 40-hour week, which may include some evenings, weekends, and holidays.

Employment

Recreational therapists held about 38,000 jobs in 1996. About 42 percent of salaried jobs for therapists were in hospitals and 38 percent were in nursing homes. Others worked in residential facilities, community mental health centers, adult day care programs, correctional facilities, community programs for people with disabilities, and substance abuse centers. About one out of four therapists was self-employed, generally contracting with long-term care facilities or community agencies to develop and oversee programs.

Training, Other Qualifications, and Advancement

A bachelor's degree in therapeutic recreation (or in recreation with an option in therapeutic recreation) is the usual requirement for entry-level positions. Persons may qualify for paraprofessional positions with an associate degree in recreational therapy or a health care-related field. An associates degree in recreational therapy; training in art, drama, or music therapy; or qualifying work experience may also be sufficient for activity director positions in nursing homes.

Most employers prefer to hire candidates who are certified therapeutic recreation specialists (CTRS). The National Council for Therapeutic Recreation Certification (NCTRC) certifies therapeutic recreation specialists. To become certified, specialists must have a bachelor's degree, pass a written certification examination, and complete an internship of at least 360 hours under the supervision of a certified therapeutic recreation specialist. A few colleges or agencies may require 600 hours of internship.

There are about 130 programs that prepare recreational therapists. Most offer bachelor's degrees, although some offer associates, master's, or doctoral degrees. As of 1996, there were fewer than 50 recreation programs with options in therapeutic recreation that were accredited by the National Council on Accreditation.

In addition to therapeutic recreation course work in assessment, treatment and program planning, and intervention design and evaluation, students study human anatomy, physiology, abnormal psychology, medical and psychiatric terminology, characteristics of illnesses and disabilities, and the concepts of inclusion and normalization. Courses cover professional ethics, assessment and referral procedures, interdisciplinary teamwork, management, and the use of assistive devices and technology.

Recreational therapists should be comfortable working with persons who are ill or have disabilities. Therapists must be patient, tactful, and persuasive when working with people who have a variety of special needs. Ingenuity, a good sense of humor, and a strong imagination are needed to adapt activities to individual needs, and good physical coordination is necessary to demonstrate or participate in recreational events.

Therapists can advance to supervisory or administrative positions. Some teach, conduct research, or perform contract consulting work.

Job Outlook

Employment of recreational therapists is expected to grow faster than the average for all occupations through the year 2006, because of anticipated expansion in long-term care, physical and psychiatric rehabilitation, and services for people with disabilities. Job prospects are expected to be favorable for those with a strong health care background.

Health care facilities will provide a large number of recreational therapy jobs through the year 2006. A growing number of these will be in hospital-based adult day care and outpatient programs, or in units offering short-term mental health and alcohol or drug abuse services. Long-term rehabilitation, home-health care, transitional programs, and psychiatric facilities will provide additional jobs.

The rapidly growing number of older adults is expected to spur job growth for activity directors and recreational therapy paraprofessionals in nursing homes, assisted living facilities, adult day care programs, and social service agencies. Continued growth is expected in community residential facilities as well as day care programs for individuals with disabilities.

Earnings

According to a survey by the American Therapeutic Recreation Association, the average salary for recreational therapists was about $33,000 in 1996. The average annual salary for consultants, supervisors, administrators, and educators was about $42,000 in 1996. The average for all recreational therapists in the federal government in non-supervisory, supervisory, and managerial positions was about $39,400 in 1997.

Related Occupations

Recreational therapists design activities to help people with disabilities lead more fulfilling and independent lives. Other workers who have similar jobs are recreational therapy paraprofessionals, orientation therapists for persons who are blind or have visual impairments, art therapists, drama therapists, dance therapists, music therapists, occupational therapists, physical therapists, and rehabilitation counselors.

Sources of Additional Information

For information on how to order materials describing careers and academic programs in recreational therapy, write to:

❏ American Therapeutic Recreation Association, P.O. Box 15215, Hattiesburg, MS 39402-5215. Homepage: http://www.atra-tr.org.

❏ National Therapeutic Recreation Society, 22377 Belmont Ridge Rd., Ashburn, VA 20148 or by e-mail: NTRSNRPA@aol.com.

Certification information may be obtained from:

❏ National Council for Therapeutic Recreation Certification, P.O. Box 479, Thiells, NY 10984-0479.

Reporters and Correspondents

(*D.O.T.* 131.262-018)

Significant Points

✸ *Employment is expected to decline and there should be keen competition for job openings.*

✸ *Less competition is expected for jobs with suburban and weekly newspapers.*

✸ *Jobs are often stressful due to irregular hours, frequent night and weekend work, and pressure to meet deadlines.*

Nature of the Work

Reporters and correspondents play a key role in our society. They gather information and prepare stories that inform

us about local, state, national, and international events; present points of view on current issues; and report on the actions of public officials, corporate executives, special interest groups, and others who exercise power. In covering a story, they investigate leads and news tips, look at documents, observe on-the-scene, and interview people. Reporters take notes and may also take photographs or shoot videos. At their office, they organize the material, determine their focus or emphasis, write their stories, and may also edit videos. Many enter information or write stories on portable computers and then submit them to their offices using a telephone modem. In some cases, news writers write the story from information collected and submitted by the reporter.

Radio and television reporters often compose stories and report live from the scene. Later, they may tape a commentary in the studio.

General assignment reporters write up news as assigned, such as an accident, a political rally, the visit of a celebrity, or a company going out of business. Large newspapers and radio and television stations assign reporters to gather news about specific news categories such as crime or education. Some reporters specialize in fields such as health, politics, foreign affairs, sports, theater, consumer affairs, social events, science, business, and religion. Investigative reporters cover stories that take many days or weeks of information gathering.

News correspondents are stationed, and report on news occurring in large U.S. and foreign cities. Reporters on small publications cover all aspects of the news: They take photographs, write headlines, lay out pages, edit wire service copy, and write editorials. They also may solicit advertisements, sell subscriptions, and perform general office work.

Working Conditions

The work of reporters and correspondents is usually hectic. They are under great pressure to meet deadlines. Some reporters work in comfortable, private offices; others work in large rooms filled with the sound of keyboards and computer printers, as well as the voices of other reporters. Those reporting from the scene for radio and television may be distracted by curious onlookers, police, or other emergency workers. Covering wars, political uprisings, fires, floods, and similar events is often dangerous.

Working hours vary. Reporters on morning papers often work from late afternoon until midnight. Those on afternoon or evening papers generally work from early morning until early or mid-afternoon. Radio and television reporters are usually assigned to a day or evening shift. Magazine reporters generally work during the day. Reporters may have to change their work hours to meet a deadline, or to follow late-breaking developments. Their work demands long hours, irregular schedules, and some travel.

Employment

Reporters and correspondents held about 60,000 jobs in 1996. About seven of every ten worked for newspapers, either large city dailies or suburban and small town dailies or weeklies. Almost two in ten worked in radio and television broadcasting, and others worked for magazines and wire services.

Training, Other Qualifications, and Advancement

Most employers prefer individuals with a bachelor's degree in journalism, but some hire graduates with other majors. They look for experience on school newspapers or broadcasting stations and internships with news organizations. Large city newspapers and stations may also prefer candidates with a degree in a subject-matter specialty such as economics, political science, or business. Large newspapers and broadcasters also require a minimum of three to five years experience as a reporter.

Bachelor's degree programs in journalism are available in over 410 colleges. About three-fourths of the courses in a typical curriculum are in liberal arts; the remainder are in journalism. Journalism courses include introductory mass media, basic reporting and copy editing, history of journalism, and press law and ethics. Students planning a career in broadcasting take courses in radio and television newscasting and production. Those planning newspaper or magazine careers usually specialize in news-editorial journalism. Those planning careers in new media, such as online newspapers or magazines, require a merging of traditional and new journalism skills. To create a story for multimedia presentation, they need to know how to use computer software to combine online story text with graphics, audio and video elements, and even 3-D animation.

Many community and junior colleges offer journalism courses or programs; credits may be transferable to four-year journalism programs.

A master's degree in journalism was offered by over 157 schools in 1996; about 32 schools offered a Ph.D. degree. Some graduate programs are intended primarily as preparation for news careers, while others prepare journalism teachers, researchers and theorists, and advertising and public relations workers.

High school courses in English, journalism, and social studies provide a good foundation for college programs. Useful college liberal arts courses include English with an emphasis on writing, sociology, political science, economics, history, and psychology. Courses in computer science, business, and speech are useful as well. Fluency in a foreign language is necessary in some jobs.

Reporters need good word processing skills, and computer graphics and desktop publishing skills are useful. A knowledge of news photography is valuable for entry-level positions for combination reporter/camera operator or reporter/photographer.

Experience in a part-time or summer job or an internship with a news organization is important. The Dow Jones Newspaper Fund and newspapers, magazines, and broadcast news organizations offer summer reporting and editing internships. Work on high school and college newspapers and broadcasting stations, community papers, and Armed Forces publications also helps. In addition, more than 3,200 journalism scholarships, fellowships, and assistantships were awarded to college journalism students by universities, newspapers, foundations, and professional organizations in 1996.

Experience as a *stringer*, a part-time reporter who is paid only for stories printed, is also helpful.

Reporters should be dedicated to providing accurate and impartial news. Accuracy is important both to serve the public and because untrue or libelous statements can lead to costly lawsuits. A "nose for news," persistence, initiative, poise, resourcefulness, a good memory, and physical stamina are important, as well as the emotional stability to deal with pressing deadlines, irregular hours, and dangerous assignments. Broadcast reporters must be comfortable on camera. All reporters must be at ease in unfamiliar places and with a variety of people.

Most reporters start at small publications or broadcast stations as general assignment reporters or copy editors. Large publications and stations hire very few recent graduates; they generally require new reporters to have several years of experience.

Beginning reporters cover court proceedings and civic and club meetings, summarize speeches, and write obituaries. With experience, they report more difficult assignments, cover an assigned beat, or specialize in a particular field.

Some reporters may advance by moving to larger papers or stations. A few experienced reporters become columnists, correspondents, writers, announcers, or public relations specialists. Others become editors in print journalism or program managers in broadcast journalism, who supervise reporters. Some eventually become broadcasting or publications industry managers.

Job Outlook

Competition will continue to be keen for reporting jobs on large metropolitan newspapers and broadcast stations and on national magazines. Small town and suburban newspapers will continue to offer better opportunities for beginners. Many openings arise on small publications as reporters become editors or reporters on larger publications or they leave the field. Talented writers who can handle highly specialized scientific or technical subjects have an advantage. Also, stringers and freelancers are being hired by more newspapers. In addition, online newspapers and magazines should continue to grow very fast and create numerous job opportunities.

Employment of reporters and correspondents is expected to decline through the year 2006—the result of mergers, consolidations and closures of newspapers, decreased circulations, increased expenses, and a decline in advertising profits. Some growth is expected in radio and television stations, and fast growth will occur in new online media areas.

Most job openings will arise from the need to replace reporters and correspondents who leave the occupation. Turnover is relatively high in this occupation—some may find the work too stressful and hectic, or may not like the lifestyle and transfer to other occupations where their skills are valuable. Journalism graduates have the background for work in such closely related fields as advertising and public relations, and many take jobs in these fields. Other graduates may accept sales, managerial, and other nonmedia positions, because of the difficulty related to finding media jobs.

The newspaper and broadcasting industries are sensitive to economic ups and downs. During recessions, few new reporters are hired and some reporters lose their jobs.

Earnings

The Newspaper Guild negotiates with individual newspapers on minimum salaries for both starting reporters, and those still on the job after three to six years. The median minimum salary for reporters was about $448 a week as of December 1, 1996. Of these contracts, 10 percent called for minimums of $342 or less; another 10 percent, $698 or more. The median minimum weekly salary for reporters after three to six years on the job was about $742 a week. Of these contracts, 10 percent called for top minimums of $484 or less; another 10 percent, $1,000 or more.

According to a survey conducted by the National Association of Broadcasters in 1996, annual average salaries of radio reporters ranged from $20,217 in the smallest stations, to $38,541 in the largest stations. For all stations, the median salary was $32,356. Salaries of television reporters ranged from

© 1999 • J. Michael Farr • JIST Works, Inc. • Indianapolis, IN

$17,435 in the smallest stations, to $79,637 in the largest ones. For all stations, the median salary was $31,235.

Related Occupations

Reporters and correspondents must write clearly and effectively to succeed in their profession. Others for whom writing ability is essential include technical writers, advertising copy writers, public relations workers, educational writers, fiction writers, biographers, screen writers, and editors.

Sources of Additional Information

Career information, including pamphlets titled "Newspaper Career Guide," and "Newspaper: What's In It For Me?" is available from:

❏ Newspaper Association of America, 1921 Gallows Rd., Suite 600, Vienna, VA 22182.

Information on careers in journalism, colleges and universities offering degree programs in journalism or communications, and journalism scholarships and internships may be obtained from:

❏ The Dow Jones Newspaper Fund, Inc., P.O. Box 300, Princeton, NJ 08543-0300.

Information on union wage rates for newspaper and magazine reporters is available from:

❏ The Newspaper Guild, Research and Information Department, 8611 Second Ave., Silver Spring, MD 20910.

For a list of schools with accredited programs in journalism, send a stamped, self-addressed envelope to:

❏ Accrediting Council on Education in Journalism and Mass Communications, University of Kansas School of Journalism, Stauffer-Flint Hall, Lawrence, KS 66045.

For general information about careers in journalism, contact:

❏ Association For Education in Journalism and Mass Communication, University of South Carolina, LeConte College, Room 121, Columbia, SC 29208-0251.

A pamphlet titled "Newspaper Careers and Challenges for the Next Century" can be obtained from:

❏ National Newspaper Association, 1525 Wilson Blvd., Suite 550, Arlington, VA 22209.

Names and locations of newspapers and a list of schools and departments of journalism are published in the Editor and Publisher International Year Book, available in most public libraries and newspaper offices.

School Teachers—Kindergarten, Elementary, and Secondary

(D.O.T. 091.221, .227; 092.227-010, -014; 099.224-010, .227-022)

Significant Points

✱ *Public school teachers must have a bachelor's degree, complete an approved teacher education program, and be licensed; some states require a master's degree.*

✱ *Many states offer alternative licensure programs to attract people into teaching and to fill certain jobs.*

✱ *Employment growth for secondary school teachers will be more rapid than for kindergarten and elementary school teachers due to student enrollments, but job outlook will vary by geographic area and by subject specialty.*

Nature of the Work

Teachers act as facilitators or coaches, using interactive discussions and hands-on learning to help students learn and apply concepts in subjects such as science, mathematics, or English. As teachers move away from the traditional repetitive drill approaches and rote memorization, they are using more "props" or "manipulatives" to help children understand abstract concepts, solve problems, and develop critical thought processes. For example, they teach the concepts of numbers or adding and subtracting by playing board games. As children get older, they use more sophisticated materials such as tape recorders, science apparatus, cameras, or computers.

Many classes are becoming less structured, with students working in groups to discuss and solve problems together. Preparing students for the future workforce is the major stimulus generating the changes in education. To be prepared, students must be able to interact with others, adapt to new technology, and logically think through problems. Teachers provide the tools and environment for their students to develop these skills.

Kindergarten and elementary school teachers play a vital role in the development of children. What children learn and experience during their early years can shape their views of themselves and the world, and affect later success or failure in school, work, and their personal lives. Kindergarten and elementary school teachers introduce children to numbers, language, science, and social studies. They use games, music, artwork, films, slides, computers, and other tools to teach basic skills.

Most elementary school teachers instruct one class of children in several subjects. In some schools, two or more teachers work as a team and are jointly responsible for a group of students in at least one subject. In other schools, a teacher may teach one special subject—usually music, art, reading, science, arithmetic, or physical education—to a number of classes. A small but growing number of teachers instruct multilevel classrooms, with students at several different learning levels.

Secondary school teachers help students delve more deeply into subjects introduced in elementary school and expose them to more information about the world and themselves. Secondary school teachers specialize in a specific subject, such as English, Spanish, mathematics, history, or biology. They teach a variety of related courses—for example, American history, contemporary American problems, and world geography.

Special education teachers—who instruct elementary and secondary school students who have a variety of disabilities—are discussed separately.

Teachers may use films, slides, overhead projectors, and the latest technology in teaching, including computers, telecommunication systems, and video discs. Use of computer resources, such as educational software and the Internet, exposes students to a vast range of experiences and promotes interactive learning. Through the Internet, American students can communicate with students in other countries to share personal experiences. Students also use the Internet for individual research projects and information gathering. Computers are used in other classroom activities as well, from helping students solve math problems to learning English as a second language. Teachers may also use computers to record grades and for other administrative and clerical duties. Teachers must continually update their skills to use the latest technology in the classroom.

Teachers often work with students from varied ethnic, racial, and religious backgrounds. With growing minority populations in many parts of the country, it is important for teachers to establish rapport with a diverse student population. Accordingly, some schools offer training to help teachers enhance their awareness and understanding of different cultures. Teachers may also include multicultural programming in their lesson plans to address the needs of all students, regardless of their cultural background.

Classroom presentations are designed by teachers to meet student needs and abilities. They also work with students individually. Teachers plan, evaluate, and assign lessons; prepare, administer, and grade tests; listen to oral presentations; and maintain classroom discipline. They observe and evaluate a student's performance and potential, and increasingly use new assessment methods. For example, teachers may examine a portfolio of a student's artwork or writing at the end of a learning period to judge the student's overall progress. They then provide additional assistance in areas where a student needs help. Teachers also grade papers, prepare report cards, and meet with parents and school staff to discuss a student's academic progress or personal problems.

In addition to classroom activities, teachers oversee study halls and homerooms and supervise extracurricular activities. They identify physical or mental problems and refer students to the proper resource or agency for diagnosis and treatment. Secondary school teachers occasionally assist students in choosing courses, colleges, and careers. Teachers also participate in education conferences and workshops.

In recent years, site-based management, which allows teachers and parents to participate actively in management decisions, has gained popularity. In many schools, teachers are increasingly involved in making decisions regarding the budget, personnel, textbook choices, curriculum design, and teaching methods.

Working Conditions

Seeing students develop new skills and gain an appreciation of knowledge and learning can be very rewarding. However, teaching may be frustrating when dealing with unmotivated and disrespectful students. Teachers may also experience stress when dealing with large classes, students from disadvantaged or multicultural backgrounds, and heavy workloads.

Teachers face isolation from their colleagues since they often work alone in a classroom of students. However, this autonomy provides teachers considerable freedom to choose their own teaching styles and methods.

Including school duties performed outside the classroom, many teachers work more than 40 hours a week. Most teachers work the traditional ten-month school year with a two-month vacation during the summer. Those on the ten-month schedule may teach in summer sessions, take other jobs, travel, or pursue other personal interests. Many enroll in college courses or workshops to continue their education. Teachers in districts with a year-round schedule typically work eight weeks, are on vacation for one week, and have a five-week midwinter break.

Most states have tenure laws that prevent teachers from being fired without just cause and due process. Teachers may obtain tenure after they have satisfactorily completed a probationary period of teaching, normally three years. Tenure does not absolutely guarantee a job, but it does provide some security.

Employment

Teachers held about 3.1 million jobs in 1996. Of those, about 1.7 million were kindergarten and elementary school teachers, and 1.4 million were secondary school teachers. Employment is distributed geographically, much the same as the population.

Training, Other Qualifications, and Advancement

All 50 states and the District of Columbia require public school teachers to be licensed. Licensure is not required for teachers in private schools. Usually licensure is granted by the state board of education or a licensure advisory committee. Teachers may be licensed to teach the early childhood grades (usually nursery school through grade 3); the elementary grades (grades 1 through 6 or 8); the middle grades (grades 5 through 8); a secondary education subject area (usually grades 7 through 12); or a special subject, such as reading or music (usually grades K through 12).

Requirements for regular licenses vary by state. However, all states require a bachelor's degree and completion of an approved teacher training program with a prescribed number of subject and education credits and supervised practice teaching. Some states require specific minimum grade point averages for teacher licensure. Some states require teachers to obtain a master's degree in education, which involves at least one year of additional course work beyond the bachelor's degree with a specialization in a particular subject.

Almost all states require applicants for teacher licensure to be tested for competency in basic skills such as reading and writing, teaching skills, or subject matter proficiency. Most states require continuing education for renewal of the teacher's license. Many states have reciprocity agreements that make it easier for teachers licensed in one state to become licensed in another.

Increasingly, many states are moving toward implementing performance-based standards for licensure, which require passing a rigorous comprehensive teaching examination to obtain provisional licensure, and then demonstrating satisfactory teaching performance over an extended period of time to obtain full licensure.

Many states offer alternative teacher licensure programs for people who have bachelor's degrees in the subject they will teach, but lack the necessary education courses required for a regular license. Alternative licensure programs were originally designed to ease teacher shortages in certain subjects, such as mathematics and science. The programs have expanded to attract other people into teaching, including recent college graduates and midcareer changers. In some programs, individuals begin teaching quickly under provisional licensure. After working under the close supervision of experienced educators for one or two years while taking education courses outside school hours, they receive regular licensure if they have progressed satisfactorily. Under other programs, college graduates who do not meet licensure requirements take only those courses that they lack, and then become licensed. This may

take one or two semesters of full-time study. States may issue emergency licenses to individuals who do not meet requirements for a regular license when schools cannot attract enough qualified teachers to fill positions. Teachers who need licensure may enter programs that grant a master's degree in education, as well as licensure.

In recent years, the National Board for Professional Teaching Standards began offering voluntary national certification for teachers. To become nationally certified, teachers must prove their aptitude by compiling a portfolio showing their work in the classroom, and by passing a written assessment and evaluation of their teaching knowledge. A teacher who is nationally certified may find it easier to obtain employment in another state. Certified teachers may also earn higher salaries, have more senior titles, and be eligible for more bonuses than noncertified teachers. While all states recognize national certification, however, many states have not established policies on specific benefits of holding national certification, such as salary differentials or reimbursement of certification fees.

The National Council for Accreditation of Teacher Education currently accredits over 500 teacher education programs across the United States. Generally, four-year colleges require students to wait until their sophomore year before applying for admission to teacher education programs. Traditional education programs for kindergarten and elementary school teachers include courses—designed specifically for those preparing to teach—in mathematics, physical science, social science, music, art, and literature, as well as prescribed professional education courses, such as philosophy of education, psychology of learning, and teaching methods. Aspiring secondary school teachers either major in the subject they plan to teach while also taking education courses, or major in education and take subject courses. Teacher education programs are now required to include classes in the use of computers and other technologies to maintain accreditation. Most programs require students to perform student teaching.

Many states now offer professional development schools, which are partnerships between universities and elementary or secondary schools. Students enter these one-year programs after completion of their bachelor's degree. Professional development schools merge theory with practice and allow the student to experience a year of teaching first-hand, with professional guidance.

In addition to being knowledgeable in their subject, the ability to communicate, inspire trust and confidence, and motivate students, as well as understand their educational and emotional needs, is essential for teachers. Teachers must be able to recognize and respond to individual differences in students, and employ different teaching methods that will result in high student achievement. They also should be organized, dependable, patient, and creative. Teachers must also be able to work cooperatively and communicate effectively with other teaching staff, support staff, parents, and other members of the community.

With additional preparation, teachers may move into positions as school librarians, reading specialists, curriculum specialists, or guidance counselors. Teachers may become administrators or supervisors, although the number of these positions is limited and competition for these desirable positions can be intense. In some systems, highly qualified, experienced teachers can become senior or mentor teachers, with higher pay and additional responsibilities. They guide and assist less experienced teachers while keeping most of their teaching responsibilities.

Job Outlook

The job market for teachers varies widely by geographic area and by subject specialty. Many inner cities—characterized by high crime rates, high poverty rates, and overcrowded conditions—and rural areas—characterized by their remote location and relatively low salaries—have difficulty attracting enough teachers, so job prospects should continue to be better in these areas than in suburban districts. Currently, many school districts have difficulty hiring qualified teachers in some subjects—mathematics, science (especially chemistry and physics), bilingual education, and computer science. Specialties that currently have an abundance of qualified teachers include general elementary education, English, art, physical education, and social studies. Teachers who are geographically mobile and who obtain licensure in more than one subject should have a distinct advantage in finding a job. With enrollments of minorities increasing, coupled with a shortage of minority teachers, efforts to recruit minority teachers should intensify. Also, the number of non-English speaking students has grown dramatically, especially in California and Florida which have large Spanish-speaking student populations, creating demand for bilingual teachers and those who speak English as a second language (ESL).

Overall employment of kindergarten, elementary, and secondary school teachers is expected to increase about as fast as the average for all occupations through the year 2006. The expected retirement of a large number of teachers currently in their 40s and 50s should open up many additional jobs. However, projected employment growth varies among individual teaching occupations.

Employment of secondary school teachers is expected to grow faster than the average for all occupations through the year 2006, while average employment growth is projected for kindergarten and elementary school teachers. Assuming relatively little change in average class size, employment growth of teachers depends on population growth rates and corresponding student enrollments. Enrollment of 14- to 17-year-olds is expected to grow through the year 2006. Enrollment of 5- to 13-year-olds also is projected to increase, but at a slower rate, through the year 2002, and then decline.

The number of teachers employed is also dependent on state and local expenditures for education. Pressures from taxpayers to limit spending could result in fewer teachers than projected; pressures to spend more to improve the quality of education could increase the teacher workforce.

The supply of teachers also is expected to increase in response to reports of improved job prospects, more teacher involvement in school policy, and greater public interest in education. In recent years, the total number of bachelor's and master's degrees granted in education has steadily increased. In addition, more teachers will be drawn from a reserve pool of career changers, substitute teachers, and teachers completing alternative certification programs, relocating to different schools, and reentering the workforce.

Earnings

According to the National Education Association, the estimated average salary of all public elementary and secondary school teachers in the 1995–96 school year was $37,900. Public secondary school teachers averaged about $38,600 a year, while public elementary school teachers averaged $37,300. Private school teachers generally earn less than public school teachers.

In 1996, over half of all public school teachers belonged to unions—mainly the American Federation of Teachers and the National Education Association—that bargain with school systems over wages, hours, and the terms and conditions of employment.

In some schools, teachers receive extra pay for coaching sports and working with students in extracurricular activities. Some teachers earn extra income during the summer working in the school system or in other jobs.

Related Occupations

Kindergarten, elementary, and secondary school teaching requires a wide variety of skills and aptitudes, including a talent for working with children; organizational, administrative, and record keeping abilities; research and communication skills; the power to influence, motivate, and train others; patience; and creativity. Workers in other occupations requiring some of these aptitudes include college and university faculty, counselors, education administrators, employment interview-

ers, librarians, preschool teachers, public relations specialists, sales representatives, social workers, and trainers and employee development specialists.

Sources of Additional Information

Information on licensure or certification requirements and approved teacher training institutions is available from local school systems and state departments of education.

Information on teachers' unions and education-related issues may be obtained from:

❏ American Federation of Teachers, 555 New Jersey Ave. NW, Washington, DC 20001.

❏ National Education Association, 1201 16th St. NW, Washington, DC 20036.

A list of institutions with accredited teacher education programs can be obtained from:

❏ National Council for Accreditation of Teacher Education, 2010 Massachusetts Ave. NW, Suite 500, Washington, DC 20036.

For information on voluntary national teacher certification requirements, contact:

❏ National Board for Professional Teaching Standards, 26555 Evergreen Rd., Suite 400, Southfield, MI 48076.

Social Workers

(*D.O.T.* 189.267-010; 195.107, .137, .164, .167-010, -014, .267-018, -022, and .367-026)

Significant Points

✴ *A bachelor's degree is the minimum requirement for many entry-level jobs; however, a master's degree in social work (MSW) is generally required for advancement.*

✴ *Employment is projected to grow faster than average.*

✴ *Competition for jobs is stronger in cities where training programs for social workers are prevalent; rural areas often find it difficult to attract and retain qualified staff.*

Nature of the Work

Social work is a profession for those with a strong desire to help people. Social workers help people deal with their relationships with others; solve their personal, family, and community problems; and grow and develop as they learn to cope with or shape the social and environmental forces affecting daily life. Social workers often encounter clients facing a life-threatening disease or a social problem requiring a quick solution. These situations may include inadequate housing,

unemployment, lack of job skills, financial distress, serious illness or disability, substance abuse, unwanted pregnancy, or antisocial behavior. They also assist families that have serious conflicts, including those involving child or spousal abuse.

Social workers practice in a variety of settings, including hospitals, from the obstetrics unit to the intensive care unit; in schools, helping children, teachers, and parents cope with problems; in mental health clinics and psychiatric hospitals; and in public agencies, from the employment office to the public welfare department. Through direct counseling, social workers help clients identify their concerns, consider solutions, and find resources. Often, they refer clients to specialists in various areas, including debt counseling, child care or elder care, public assistance or other benefits, or alcohol or drug rehabilitation programs. Social workers typically arrange for services in consultation with clients, following through to assure the services are helpful. They may review eligibility requirements, fill out forms and applications, arrange for services, visit clients on a regular basis, and provide support during crises.

Most social workers specialize—for example, in child welfare and family services, mental health, or school social work. Clinical social workers offer psychotherapy or counseling and a range of services in public agencies and clinics, and in private practice. Other social workers are employed in community organization, administration, or research.

Those specializing in child welfare or family services may counsel children and youths who have difficulty adjusting socially, advise parents on how to care for disabled children, or arrange for homemaker services during a parent's illness. If children have serious problems in school, child welfare workers may consult with parents, teachers, and counselors to identify underlying causes and develop plans for treatment. Some social workers assist single parents, arrange adoptions, and help find foster homes for neglected, abandoned, or abused children. Child welfare workers also work in residential institutions for children and adolescents.

Social workers in child or adult protective services investigate reports of abuse and neglect and intervene if necessary. They may institute legal action to remove children from homes and place them temporarily in an emergency shelter or with a foster family.

Mental health social workers provide services for persons with mental or emotional problems, such as individual and group therapy, outreach, crisis intervention, social rehabilitation, and training in skills of everyday living. They may also help plan for supportive services to ease patients' return to the community. (Counselors and psychologists may provide similar services.)

Health care social workers help patients and their families cope with chronic, acute, or terminal illnesses and handle problems that may stand in the way of recovery or rehabilitation. They may organize support groups for families of patients suffering from cancer, AIDS, Alzheimer's disease, or other illnesses. They also advise family caregivers, counsel patients, and help plan for their needs after discharge by arranging for at-home services—from meals-on-wheels to oxygen equipment. Some work on interdisciplinary teams that evaluate certain kinds of patients—geriatric or organ transplant patients, for example.

School social workers diagnose students' problems and arrange needed services, counsel children in trouble, and help integrate disabled students into the general school population. School social workers deal with problems such as student pregnancy, misbehavior in class, and excessive absences. They also advise teachers on how to deal with problem students.

Criminal justice social workers make recommendations to courts, prepare pre-sentencing assessments, and provide services for prison inmates and their families. Probation and parole officers provide similar services to individuals sentenced by a court to parole or probation.

Occupational social workers generally work in a corporation's personnel department or health unit. Through employee assistance programs, they help workers cope with job-related pressures or personal problems that affect the quality of their work. They often offer direct counseling to employees whose performance is hindered by emotional or family problems or substance abuse. They also develop education programs and refer workers to specialized community programs.

Some social workers specialize in gerontological services. They run support groups for family caregivers or for the adult children of aging parents; advise elderly people or family members about the choices in such areas as housing, transportation, and long-term care; and coordinate and monitor services.

Social workers also focus on policy and planning. They help develop programs to address such issues as child abuse, homelessness, substance abuse, poverty, and violence. These workers research and analyze policies, programs, and regulations. They identify social problems and suggest legislative and other solutions. They may help raise funds or write grants to support these programs.

Working Conditions

Although some social workers work a standard 40-hour week, many work some evenings and weekends to meet with clients, attend community meetings, and handle emergencies. Some, particularly in voluntary nonprofit agencies, work part-time. They may spend most of their time in an office or residential facility, but may also travel locally to visit clients or meet with service providers. Some have several offices within a local area.

The work, while satisfying, can be emotionally draining. Understaffing and large caseloads add to the pressure in some agencies.

Employment

Social workers held about 585,000 jobs in 1996. About four out of ten jobs were in state, county, or municipal government agencies, primarily in departments of health and human resources, mental health, social services, child welfare, housing, education, and corrections. As government increasingly contracts out social services, many jobs are likely to shift from government to private organizations in the future. Most jobs in the private sector were in social service agencies, community and religious organizations, hospitals, nursing homes, or home health agencies.

Although most social workers are employed in cities or suburbs, some work in rural areas.

Training, Other Qualifications, and Advancement

A bachelor's degree is the minimum requirement for many entry-level jobs. Besides the bachelor's in social work (BSW), undergraduate majors in psychology, sociology, and related fields satisfy hiring requirements in some agencies, especially small community agencies. A master's degree in social work (MSW) is generally necessary for positions in health and mental health settings. Jobs in public agencies may also require an MSW. Supervisory, administrative, and staff training positions usually require at least an MSW. College and university teaching positions and most research appointments normally require a doctorate in social work.

In 1996, the Council on Social Work Education accredited over 430 BSW programs and over 130 MSW programs. There were 55 doctoral programs for Ph.D.s in social work and DSWs (Doctor of Social Work). BSW programs prepare graduates for direct service positions such as case worker or group worker. They include courses in social work practice, social welfare policies, human behavior and the social environment, and social research methods. Accredited BSW programs require at least 400 hours of supervised field experience.

An MSW degree prepares graduates to perform assessments, manage cases, and supervise other workers. Master's programs usually last two years and include 900 hours of supervised field instruction, or internship. Entry into an MSW program does not require a bachelor's in social work, but

courses in psychology, biology, sociology, economics, political science, history, social anthropology, urban studies, and social work are recommended. In addition, a second language can be very helpful. Some schools offer an accelerated MSW program for those with a BSW.

Since 1993, all states and the District of Columbia have had licensing, certification, or registration laws regarding social work practice and the use of professional titles. Standards for licensing vary by state. In addition, voluntary certification is offered by the National Association of Social Workers (NASW), which grants the title ACSW (Academy of Certified Social Worker) or ACBSW (Academy of Certified Baccalaureate Social Worker) to those who qualify. For clinical social workers, who are granted the title QCSW (Qualified Clinical Social Worker), professional credentials include listing in the NASW Register of Clinical Social Workers. Advanced credentials include the NASW Diplomate in Clinical Social Work, and School Social Work Specialist. An advanced credential is also offered by the Directory of American Board of Examiners in Clinical Social Work. Credentials are particularly important for those in private practice; some health insurance providers require them for reimbursement.

Social workers should be emotionally mature, objective, and sensitive to people and their problems. They must be able to handle responsibility, work independently, and maintain good working relationships with clients and coworkers. Volunteer or paid jobs as a social work aide offer ways of testing one's interest in this field.

Advancement to supervisor, program manager, assistant director, or executive director of a social service agency or department is possible but generally requires an MSW degree and related work experience. Although some social workers with a BSW may be promoted to these positions after gaining experience, some employers choose to hire managers directly from MSW programs that focus specifically on management. These graduates often have little work experience but have an understanding of management through their education and training. Other career options for social workers include teaching, research, and consulting. Some help formulate government policies by analyzing and advocating policy positions in government agencies, in research institutions, and on legislators' staffs.

Some social workers go into private practice. Most private practitioners are clinical social workers who provide psychotherapy, usually paid through health insurance. Private practitioners must have an MSW and a period of supervised work experience. A network of contacts for referrals is also essential.

Job Outlook

Employment of social workers is expected to increase faster than the average for all occupations through the year 2006. The number of older people, who are more likely to need social services, is increasing rapidly. In addition, growing concern about crime, juvenile delinquency, and services for the mentally ill, the mentally retarded, AIDS patients, and individuals and families in crisis will spur demand for social workers. Many job openings will also stem from the need to replace social workers who leave the occupation.

As hospitals increasingly emphasize early discharge of patients in an effort to control costs, more social workers will be needed to ensure that the necessary medical and social services are in place when individuals leave the hospital. Social worker employment in home health care services is growing, not only because hospitals are releasing patients earlier, but because a large and growing number of people have impairments or disabilities that make it difficult to live at home without some form of assistance.

Employment of social workers in private social service agencies will grow, but not as rapidly as demand for their services. Agencies will increasingly restructure services and hire more lower-paid human services workers instead of social workers. Employment in government may grow in response to increasing needs for public welfare and family services; however, many of these jobs will be contracted out to private agencies. Additionally, employment levels will depend on government funding for various social service programs.

Employment of school social workers is expected to grow, due to expanded efforts to respond to rising rates of teen pregnancy and to the adjustment problems of immigrants and children from single-parent families. Moreover, continued emphasis on integrating disabled children into the general school population will lead to more jobs. Availability of state and local funding will dictate the actual job growth in schools, however.

Opportunities for social workers in private practice will expand because of the anticipated availability of funding from health insurance and public-sector contracts. Also, with increasing affluence, people will be better able to pay for professional help to deal with personal problems. The growing popularity of employee assistance programs is also expected to spur demand for private practitioners, some of whom provide social work services to corporations on a contractual basis.

Competition for social worker jobs is stronger in cities where training programs for social workers are prevalent; rural areas often find it difficult to attract and retain qualified staff.

Earnings

Based on limited information, social workers with an MSW had median earnings of about $35,000 in 1997, while social workers with a BSW earned about $25,000.

According to a Hay Group survey of acute care hospitals, the median annual salary of full-time social workers with a master's degree was $35,000 in 1997. The middle 50 percent earned between $32,300 and $38,700.

The average annual salary for all social workers in the federal government in nonsupervisory, supervisory, and managerial positions was about $46,900 in 1997.

Related Occupations

Through direct counseling or referral to other services, social workers help people solve a range of personal problems. Workers in occupations with similar duties include the clergy, mental health counselors, counseling psychologists, and human services workers.

Sources of Additional Information

For information about career opportunities in social work, contact:

❏ National Association of Social Workers, Career Information, 750 First St. NE., Suite 700, Washington, DC 20002-4241.

❏ National Network For Social Work Managers, Inc., 1316 New Hampshire Ave. NW, Suite 602, Washington, DC 20036.

An annual Directory of Accredited BSW and MSW Programs is available for a nominal charge from:

❏ Council on Social Work Education, 1600 Duke St., Alexandria, VA 22314-3421.

Special Education Teachers

(*D.O.T.* 094.107, .224, .227, .267; 099.227-042; 195.227-018)

Significant Points

✷ *A bachelor's degree, completion of an approved teacher preparation program, and a license are required; many states require a master's degree.*

✷ *Many states offer alternative licensure programs to attract people into special education teaching jobs.*

✷ *Job openings arising from rapid employment growth and job turnover, coupled with a declining number of graduates from special education teaching programs, mean excellent job prospects; many school districts report shortages of qualified teachers.*

Nature of the Work

Special education teachers work with children and youth who have a variety of disabilities. Most special education teachers instruct students at the elementary, middle, and secondary school level, although some teachers work with infants and toddlers. Special education teachers design and modify instruction to meet a student's special needs. Teachers also work with students who have other special instructional needs, including those who are gifted and talented.

The various types of disabilities delineated in government special education programs include specific learning disabilities, mental retardation, speech or language impairment, serious emotional disturbance, visual and hearing impairment, orthopedic impairment, autism, traumatic brain injury, and multiple disabilities. Students are classified under one of the categories, and special education teachers are prepared to work with specific groups.

Special education teachers use various techniques to promote learning. Depending on the disability, teaching methods can include individualized instruction, problem-solving assignments, and group or individual work. Special education teachers are legally required to help develop an Individualized Education Program (IEP) for each special education student. The IEP sets personalized goals for each student and is tailored to a student's individual learning style and ability. This program includes a transition plan outlining specific steps to prepare special education students for middle school or high school, or in the case of older students, a job or postsecondary study. Teachers review the IEP with the student's parents, school administrators, and often the student's general education teacher. Teachers work closely with parents to inform them of their child's progress and suggest techniques to promote learning at home.

Teachers design curricula, assign work geared toward each student's ability, and grade papers and homework assignments. Special education teachers are involved in a student's behavioral as well as academic development. They help special education students develop emotionally, be comfortable in social situations, and be aware of socially acceptable behavior. Preparing special education students for daily life after graduation is an important aspect of the job. Teachers may help students with routine skills, such as balancing a checkbook, or provide them with career counseling.

As schools have become more inclusive, special education teachers and general education teachers increasingly work together in general education classrooms. Special education teachers help general educators adapt curriculum materials and teaching techniques to meet the needs of students with disabilities.

Special education teachers work in a variety of settings. Some have their own classrooms and teach classes comprised entirely of special education students; others work as special education resource teachers and offer individualized help to students in general education classrooms; and others teach along with general education teachers in classes composed of both general and special education students. Some teachers work in a resource room, where special education students work several hours a day, separate from their general education classroom. A significantly smaller proportion of special education teachers work in residential facilities or tutor students in homebound or hospital environments. Special education teachers who work with infants usually travel to the child's home to work with the child and his or her parents.

A large part of a special education teacher's job involves interacting with others. They communicate frequently with parents, social workers, school psychologists, occupational and physical therapists, school administrators, and other teachers.

Early identification of a child with special needs is another important part of a special education teacher's job. Early intervention is essential in educating these children.

Technology is playing an increasingly important role in special education. Special education teachers use specialized equipment such as computers with synthesized speech, interactive educational software programs, and audio tapes.

Working Conditions

Helping students with disabilities achieve goals, and making a difference in their lives can be highly rewarding. Special education teachers enjoy the challenge of working with these students and the opportunity to establish meaningful relationships. However, the work can also be emotionally and physically draining. Special education teachers are under considerable stress due to heavy workloads and tedious administrative tasks. They must produce a substantial amount of paperwork documenting each student's progress. Exacerbating this stress is the threat of litigation by students' parents if correct procedures are not followed, or if the parent feels their child is not receiving an adequate education. Some special educators feel they are not adequately supported by school administrators, and feel isolated from general education teachers. The physical and emotional demands of the job result in a high "burnout" rate.

Many schools offer year-round education for special education students, but most special education teachers work the traditional ten-month school year with a two-month vacation during the summer.

Employment

Special education teachers held about 407,000 jobs in 1996. The majority of special education teachers were employed in elementary, middle, and secondary public schools. The rest worked in separate educational facilities—public or private—residential facilities, or in homebound or hospital environments.

Training, Other Qualifications, and Advancement

All 50 states and the District of Columbia require special education teachers to be licensed. Special education licensure varies by state. In many states, special education teachers receive a general education credential to teach kindergarten through grade 12. These teachers train in a specialty, such as learning disabilities or behavioral disorders. Some states offer general special education licensure, others license several different specialties within special education, while others require teachers to first obtain general education licensure and then additional licensure in special education. Usually licensure is granted by the state board of education or a licensure advisory committee.

All states require a bachelor's degree and completion of an approved teacher preparation program with a prescribed number of subject and education credits and supervised practice teaching. Many states require special education teachers to obtain a master's degree in special education, involving at least one year of additional course work, including a specialization, beyond the bachelor's degree.

Some states have reciprocity agreements allowing special education teachers to transfer their licensure from one state to another, but many still require special education teachers to pass licensure requirements for that state. National certification standards for special education teachers are currently being developed by the National Board for Professional Teaching Standards.

About 700 colleges and universities across the United States offer programs in special education, including undergraduate, master's, and doctoral programs. Special education teachers usually undergo longer periods of training than general education teachers. Most bachelor's degree programs are four-year programs including general and specialized courses in special education. However, an increasing number of institutions require a fifth year or other post-baccalaureate preparation. Courses include educational psychology, legal issues of special education, child growth and development, and knowledge and skills needed for teaching students with disabilities. Some programs require a specialization. Others offer generalized special education degrees, or study in several specialized areas. The last year of the program is usually spent student teaching in a classroom supervised by a certified teacher.

Alternative and emergency licensure is available in many states, due to the need to fill special education teaching positions. Alternative licensure is designed to bring college graduates and those changing careers into teaching more quickly. Requirements for alternative licensure may be less stringent than for regular licensure and vary by state. In some programs, individuals begin teaching quickly under provisional licensure. They can obtain regular licensure by teaching under the supervision of licensed teachers for a period of one to two years while taking education courses. Emergency licensure is enacted when states are having difficulty finding licensed special education teachers to fill positions.

Special education teachers must be patient, able to motivate students, understanding of their students' special needs, and accepting of differences in others. Teachers must be creative and apply different types of teaching methods to reach students who are having difficulty. Communication and cooperation are essential traits because special education teachers spend a great deal of time interacting with others, including students, parents, and school faculty and administrators.

Special education teachers can advance to become supervisors or administrators. They may also earn advanced degrees and become instructors in colleges that prepare others for special education teaching. In some school systems, highly experienced teachers can become mentor teachers to less experienced ones; they provide guidance to these teachers while maintaining a light teaching load.

Job Outlook

Special education teachers have excellent job prospects, as many school districts report shortages of qualified teachers. Job outlook varies by geographic area and specialty. Positions in rural areas and inner cities are more plentiful than job openings in suburban or wealthy urban areas. Also, job opportunities may be better in certain specialties—such as speech or language impairments, and learning disabilities—due to the considerable shortages of teachers in these fields. Recent legislation encouraging early intervention and special education for infants, toddlers, and preschoolers has created a need for early childhood special education teachers. Special education teachers who are bilingual or have multicultural experience are also needed to work with an increasingly diverse student population.

Employment of special education teachers is expected to increase much faster than the average for all occupations through the year 2006, spurred by continued growth in the number of special education students needing services, legislation emphasizing training and employment for individuals with disabilities, growing public interest in individuals with special needs, and educational reform. The high burnout rate will lead to many additional job openings as special education teachers switch to general education or change careers altogether. Rapid employment growth and job turnover, coupled with a declining number of graduates from special education teaching programs, should result in a very favorable job market.

The number of students requiring special education services has been steadily increasing. This trend is expected to continue due to legislation which expanded the age range of children receiving special education services to include those from birth to age 21; medical advances resulting in more survivors of accidents and illness; the postponement of childbirth by more women, resulting in a greater number of premature births and children born with birth defects; and growth in the general population.

The growing use of inclusive school settings, which integrate special education students into general education settings, will also lead to more reliance on special education teachers. The role of these teachers is expanding to include acting as a consultant to general education teachers, in addition to teaching special education students in resource rooms, general education classrooms, and separate classrooms made up entirely of special education students.

Earnings

Salaries of special education teachers follow the same scale as those for general education teachers. According to the National Education Association, the estimated average salary of all public elementary and secondary school teachers in the 1995–96 school year was $37,900. Public secondary school teachers averaged about $38,600 a year, while public elementary school teachers averaged $37,300. Private school teachers generally earn less than public school teachers.

In 1996, over half of all public school teachers belonged to unions—mainly the American Federation of Teachers and the National Education Association—that bargain with school systems over wages, hours, and the terms and conditions of employment.

In some schools, teachers receive extra pay for coaching sports and working with students in extracurricular activities. Some teachers earn extra income during the summer, working in the school system or in other jobs.

Related Occupations

Special education teachers work with students who have disabilities and special needs. Other occupations involved with the identification, evaluation, and development of students with disabilities include school psychologists, social workers, speech pathologists, rehabilitation counselors, adapted physical education teachers, special education technology specialists, and occupational, physical, creative arts, and recreational therapists.

Sources of Additional Information

For information on a career as a special education teacher, a list of accredited schools, financial aid information, and general information on special education-related personnel issues, contact:

❏ National Clearinghouse for Professions in Special Education, Council for Exceptional Children, 1920 Association Dr., Reston, VA 20191. Homepage: http://www.cec.sped.org

To learn more about the special education teacher certification and licensing requirements in your state, contact your state's department of education.

Surveyors and Mapping Scientists

(*D.O.T.* 018 except .167-022, and 024.061-014)

Significant Points

✴ *One of the few professional occupations in which employment is expected to decline.*

✴ *More than eight out of ten are employed in engineering services and government.*

✴ *Skill in the use of new technologies. enhances employment opportunities.*

Nature of the Work

Measuring and mapping the earth's surface are the responsibility of several different types of workers. Traditional land surveyors establish official land, air space, and water boundaries. They write descriptions of land for deeds, leases, and other legal documents; define air space for airports; and measure construction and mineral sites. Other surveyors provide data relevant to the shape, contour, location, elevation, or dimension of land or land features. Survey technicians assist land surveyors by operating survey instruments and collecting information. Mapping scientists compile geographic information and prepare maps of large areas.

Land surveyors manage survey parties that measure distances, directions, and angles between points and elevations of points, lines, and contours on the earth's surface. They plan the fieldwork, select known survey reference points, and determine the precise location of important features in the survey area. Surveyors research legal records and look for evidence of previous boundaries. They record the results of the survey, verify the accuracy of data, and prepare plots, maps, and reports. Surveyors who establish boundaries must be licensed by the state in which they work.

The information needed by the land surveyor is gathered by a survey party. A typical survey party is made up of a party chief and several survey technicians and helpers. The party chief, who may be either a land surveyor or a senior survey technician, leads the day-to-day work activities. The party chief is assisted by survey technicians, who adjust and operate surveying instruments, such as the theodolite (used to measure horizontal and vertical angles) and electronic distance-measuring equipment. Survey technicians or assistants position and hold the vertical rods or targets that the theodolite operator sights on to measure angles, distances, or elevations. They may also hold measuring tapes, if electronic distance-measuring equipment is not used. Survey technicians compile notes, make sketches, and enter the data obtained from these instruments into computers. Survey parties may include laborers or helpers who perform less skilled duties, such as clearing brush from sight lines, driving stakes, or carrying equipment.

New technology is changing the nature of the work of surveyors and survey technicians. For larger projects, surveyors are increasingly using the Global Positioning System (GPS), a satellite system that precisely locates points on the earth using radio signals transmitted by satellites. To use this system, a surveyor places a satellite signal receiver—a small instrument mounted on a tripod—on a desired point. The receiver simultaneously collects information from several satellites to locate a precise position. The receiver can also be placed in a vehicle for uses such as tracing out road systems. Since receivers now come in different sizes and shapes and the cost of the receivers has fallen, much more surveying work is being done by GPS.

Mapping scientists measure, map, and chart the earth's surface, which involves everything from geographical research and data compilation to actual map production. They collect, analyze, and interpret both spatial data—such as latitude, longitude, elevation, and distance—and nonspatial data—such as population density, land use patterns, annual precipitation levels, and demographic characteristics. Cartographers prepare maps in both digital or graphic form, using information provided by geodetic surveys, aerial photographs, and satellite data. Photogrammetrists prepare detailed maps and drawings from aerial photographs, usually of areas that are inaccessible or difficult to survey by other methods. Map editors develop and verify map contents from aerial photographs and other reference sources.

Some surveyors perform specialized functions which are closer to those of a mapping scientist than a traditional surveyor. For example, geodetic surveyors use high-accuracy techniques, including satellite observations, to measure large areas of the earth's surface. Geophysical prospecting surveyors mark sites for subsurface exploration, usually petroleum related. Marine surveyors survey harbors, rivers, and other bodies of water to determine shorelines, topography of the bottom, water depth, and other features.

The work of surveyors and mapping scientists is changing due to advancements in technology. These advancements include not only the GPS, but also new earth resources data satellites, improved aerial photography, and geographic information systems (GIS)—which are computerized data banks of spatial data. From the older specialties of photogrammetrist and cartographer, a new type of mapping scientist is emerging. The geographic information specialist combines the functions of mapping science and surveying into a broader field concerned with the collection and analysis of geographic information.

Working Conditions

Surveyors usually work an eight-hour day, five days a week, and may spend a lot of time outdoors. Sometimes they work longer hours during the summer, when weather and light conditions are most suitable for fieldwork.

Land surveyors and technicians do active and sometimes strenuous work. They often stand for long periods, walk considerable distances, and climb hills with heavy packs of instruments and other equipment. They can also be exposed to all types of weather. Occasionally, they may commute long distances, stay overnight, or temporarily relocate near a survey site.

Although surveyors can spend considerable time inside, planning surveys, analyzing data, and preparing reports and maps, mapping scientists, on the other hand, spend virtually all their time in offices and seldom visit the sites they are mapping.

Employment

Surveyors and mapping scientists held about 101,000 jobs in 1996. Engineering and architectural services firms employed about three-fifths of these workers. Federal, state, and local governmental agencies employed an additional quarter.

Major federal governmental employers are the U.S. Geological Survey, the Bureau of Land Management, the Army Corps of Engineers, the Forest Service, the National Oceanic and Atmospheric Administration, and the National Imagery and Mapping Agency (NIMA), formerly the Defense Mapping Agency. Most surveyors in state and local government work for highway departments and urban planning and redevelopment agencies. Construction firms, mining and oil and gas extraction companies, and public utilities also employ surveyors and mapping scientists. About 8,000 were self-employed in 1996.

Training, Other Qualifications, and Advancement

Most people prepare for a career as a licensed surveyor by combining postsecondary school courses in surveying with extensive on-the-job training. However, as technology advances, a four-year degree is becoming more of a prerequisite. About 25 universities now offer four-year programs leading to a B.S. degree in surveying. Junior and community colleges, technical institutes, and vocational schools offer one-, two-, and three-year programs in both surveying and surveying technology.

All 50 states license land surveyors. For licensure, most state licensing boards require that individuals pass two written examinations, one prepared by the state and one given by the National Council of Examiners for Engineering and Surveying. In addition, they must meet varying standards of formal education and work experience in the field. In the past, many individuals started as members of survey crews and worked their way up to become licensed surveyors with little formal training in surveying. However, due to advancing technology and an increase in licensing standards, formal education requirements are increasing. At present, most states require some formal post-high school education course work and 10 to 12 years of surveying experience to gain licensure. However, requirements vary among states. Generally, the quickest route to licensure is a combination of four years of college, two to four years of experience, and passing the licensing examinations. An increasing number of states require a bachelor's degree in surveying or in a closely related field, such as civil engineering or forestry (with courses in surveying) regardless of the number of years of experience.

High school students interested in surveying should take courses in algebra, geometry, trigonometry, drafting, mechanical drawing, and computer science. High school graduates with no formal training in surveying usually start as an apprentice. Beginners with postsecondary school training in surveying can generally start as technicians or assistants. With on-the-job experience and formal training in surveying—

either in an institutional program or from a correspondence school—workers may advance to senior survey technician, then to party chief, and in some cases, to licensed surveyor (depending on state licensing requirements).

The American Congress on Surveying and Mapping has a voluntary certification program for survey technicians. Technicians are certified at four levels requiring progressive amounts of experience, in addition to passing written examinations. Although not required for state licensure, many employers require certification for promotion to positions with greater responsibilities.

Surveyors should have the ability to visualize objects, distances, sizes, and abstract forms. They must work with precision and accuracy because mistakes can be costly. Members of a survey party must be in good physical condition, because they work outdoors and often carry equipment over difficult terrain. They need good eyesight, coordination, and hearing to communicate verbally and via hand signals. Surveying is a cooperative process, so good interpersonal skills and the ability to work as part of a team are important. Leadership qualities are important for party chief and other supervisory positions.

Mapping scientists, such as cartographers and photogrammetrists, usually have a bachelor's degree in a field such as engineering, forestry, geography, or a physical science. Although it is possible to enter these positions through previous experience as a photogrammetric or cartographic technician, most cartographic and photogrammetric technicians now have had some specialized postsecondary school training. With the development of Geographic Information Systems, cartographers, photogrammetrists, and other mapping scientists need additional education and stronger technical skills, including more experience with computers than in the past.

The American Society for Photogrammetry and Remote Sensing has voluntary certification programs for photogrammetrists and mapping scientists. To qualify for these professional distinctions, individuals must meet work experience standards and pass an oral or written examination.

Job Outlook

Employment of surveyors and mapping scientists is expected to decline slightly through the year 2006, as the widespread availability and use of advanced technologies, such as the Global Positioning System, Geographic Information Systems, and remote sensing, are increasing both the accuracy and productivity of survey and mapping work. Job openings, however, will continue to result from the need to replace workers who transfer to other occupations or leave the labor force altogether.

As a result of trends toward more complex technologies, opportunities will be best for surveyors and mapping scientists who have at least a bachelor's degree and strong technical skills. Increasing demand for geographic data, as opposed to traditional surveying services, will mean better opportunities for mapping scientists involved in the development and use of geographic and land information systems. New technologies, such as GPS and GIS may also enhance employment opportunities for surveyors and survey technicians who have the educational background enabling them to use these systems, but upgraded licensing requirements will continue to limit opportunities for those with less education.

Even as demand is increasing in nontraditional areas such as urban planning and natural resource exploration and mapping, opportunities for surveyors and mapping scientists should remain concentrated in engineering, architectural, and surveying services firms. Growth in construction through the year 2006 should require surveyors to lay out streets, shopping centers, housing developments, factories, office buildings, and recreation areas. However, employment may fluctuate from year to year along with construction activity. In addition, employment of mapping scientists and surveyors by private firms and the federal government will continue to be affected by budget cutbacks and technological efficiency.

Earnings

The median weekly earnings for surveyors and mapping scientists were about $694 a week in 1996. The middle 50 percent earned between $547 and $849 a week; 10 percent earned less than $446 a week; 10 percent earned more than $1000 a week.

The median weekly earnings for survey technicians were about $461 a week in 1996. The middle 50 percent earned between $378 and $725 a week; 10 percent earned less than $294 a week; 10 percent earned more than $942 a week.

In 1997, the federal government hired high school graduates with little or no training or experience at salaries of about $14,240 annually for entry level jobs on survey crews. Those with one year of related postsecondary training earned about $15,540 a year. Those with an associate degree that included course work in surveying generally started as instrument assistants with an annual salary of about $17,450. In 1997, entry level land surveyors or cartographers with the federal government earned about $19,520, $24,180, or $29,580 a year, depending on their qualifications. The average annual salary for federal land surveyors in early 1997 was about $47,850; for cartographers, about $52,500; and for geodesists, about $62,760. The average annual salary for federal surveying technicians was about $28,600; for cartographic technicians, about

$34,840; and for geodetic technicians, about $45,050.

Related Occupations

Surveying is related to the work of civil engineers and architects, since an accurate survey is the first step in land development and construction projects. Mapping science and geodetic surveying are related to the work of geologists and geophysicists, who study the earth's internal composition, surface, and atmosphere. Mapping science is also related to the work of geographers and urban planners, who study and decide how the earth's surface is used.

Sources of Additional Information

Information about career opportunities, licensure requirements, and the survey technician certification program is available from:

❑ American Congress on Surveying and Mapping, 5410 Grosvenor Lane, Suite 100, Bethesda, MD 20814-2122.

General information on careers in photogrammetry is available from:

❑ American Society for Photogrammetry and Remote Sensing, 5410 Grosvenor Lane, Suite 210, Bethesda, MD 20814.

Writers and Editors

(*D.O.T.* 052.067-010; 131 except .262-010 and -018; 132; and 203.362-026)

Significant Points

* *Most jobs require a college degree in the liberal arts—communications, journalism, and English are preferred—or a technical subject for technical writing positions.*

* *Less competition is expected for lower paying jobs at small daily and weekly newspapers, trade publication, and radio and television broadcasting stations in small communities.*

* *Persons who fail to gain better paying jobs or earn enough as independent writers are usually able to readily transfer to communications-related jobs in other occupations.*

Nature of the Work

Writers and editors communicate through the written word. Writers develop original fiction and nonfiction for books, magazines and trade journals, newspapers, technical reports, company newsletters, radio and television broadcasts, movies, and advertisements. Editors select and prepare material for publication or broadcasting and supervise writers.

Writers first select a topic or are assigned one by an editor. They then gather information through personal observation, library research, and interviews. Writers select and organize the material and put it into words, effectively conveying it to the reader, and often revise or rewrite sections, searching for the best organization of the material or the right phrasing.

News writers prepare news items for newspapers or news broadcasts, based on information supplied by reporters or wire services. Columnists analyze news and write commentaries, based on personal knowledge and experience. Editorial writers write comments to stimulate or mold public opinion, in accordance with their publication's viewpoint. Columnists and editorial writers are able to take sides on issues, be subjective, and express their opinions, while other news writers must be objective and neutral in their coverage.

Technical writers make scientific and technical information easily understandable to a nontechnical audience. They prepare operating and maintenance manuals, catalogs, parts lists, assembly instructions, sales promotion materials, and project proposals. They also plan and edit technical reports and oversee preparation of illustrations, photographs, diagrams, and charts.

Copy writers write advertising copy for use by publication or broadcast media, to promote the sale of goods and services.

Established writers may work on a freelance basis; they sell their work to publishers or publication units, manufacturing firms, and public relations and advertising departments or agencies. They sometimes contract to complete specific assignments such as writing about a new product or technique.

Editors frequently write and almost always review, rewrite, and edit the work of writers. However, their primary duties are to plan the contents of books, magazines, or newspapers and to supervise their preparation. They decide what will appeal to readers, assign topics to reporters and writers, and oversee the production of the publications. In small organizations, a single editor may do everything. In larger ones, an executive editor oversees associate or assistant editors who have responsibility for particular subjects, such as fiction, local news, international news, or sports, or who edit one or a few publications. Editors hire writers, reporters, or other employees; plan budgets; and negotiate contracts with freelance writers. In broadcasting companies, program directors have similar responsibilities.

Editors and program directors often have assistants, with the title of assistant editor, editorial assistant, copy editor, or production assistant. Many assistants hold entry-level jobs. They review copy for errors in grammar, punctuation, and spelling. They check manuscripts for readability, style, and agreement with editorial policy. They add and rearrange sentences to improve clarity or delete incorrect and unnecessary material. Editorial assistants do research for writers and verify facts, dates, and statistics. Assistants may also arrange page layouts of articles, photographs, and advertising. They may compose headlines, prepare copy for printing, and proofread printer's galleys. Some editorial assistants read and evaluate manuscripts submitted by freelance writers or answer letters about published or broadcast material. Production assistants on small papers or in radio stations clip stories that come over the wire services' printers, answer phones, and make photocopies. Most writers and editors use personal computers or word processors; many use desktop or electronic publishing systems.

Working Conditions

Some writers and editors work in comfortable, private offices; others work in noisy rooms filled with the sound of keyboards and computer printers as well as the voices of other writers tracking down information over the telephone. The search for information sometimes requires travel and visits to diverse workplaces, such as factories, offices, laboratories, the ballpark, or the theater, but many have to be content with telephone interviews and the library.

The workweek usually runs 35 to 40 hours. Those who prepare morning or weekend publications and broadcasts, work nights and/or weekends. Writers may work overtime to meet deadlines or to cover late-developing stories. They often face pressure to meet deadlines. On some jobs, deadlines are part of the daily routine.

Employment

Writers and editors held about 286,000 jobs in 1996. Nearly a third of salaried writers and editors work for newspapers, magazines, and book publishers. Substantial numbers also work in advertising agencies, in radio and television broadcasting, in public relations firms, and on journals and newsletters published by business and nonprofit organizations, such as professional associations, labor unions, and religious organizations. Others develop publications for government agencies or write for motion picture companies.

Many technical writers work for computer software firms or manufacturers of aircraft, chemicals, pharmaceuticals, and computers and other electronic equipment.

Jobs with major book publishers, magazines, broadcasting companies, advertising agencies and public relations firms, and the federal government are concentrated in New York, Chicago, Los Angeles, Boston, Philadelphia, San Francisco, and Washington, DC. Jobs with newspapers; and professional, religious, business, technical, and trade union magazines or journals are more widely dispersed throughout the country. Technical writers are employed throughout the country, but the largest concentrations are in the Northeast, Texas, and California.

Thousands of other individuals work as freelancers, earning some income from their articles, books, and less commonly, television and movie scripts. Most support themselves primarily with income derived from other sources.

Training, Other Qualifications, and Advancement

A college degree generally is required for a position as a writer or editor. Although some employers look for a broad liberal arts background, most prefer to hire people with degrees in communications, journalism, or English.

Technical writing requires a degree in, or some knowledge about a specialized field—engineering, business, or one of the sciences, for example. In many cases, people with good writing skills can learn specialized knowledge on the job. Some transfer from jobs as technicians, scientists, or engineers. Others begin as research assistants, editorial assistants, or trainees in a technical information department, develop technical communication skills, and then assume writing duties.

Writers and editors must be able to express ideas clearly and logically and should love to write. Creativity, curiosity, a broad range of knowledge, self-motivation, and perseverance are also valuable. For some jobs, the ability to concentrate amid confusion, and to work under pressure is essential. Familiarity with electronic publishing, graphics, and video production equipment is increasingly needed. Online newspapers and magazines require knowledge of computer software used to combine online text with graphics, audio, video, and 3-D animation. Editors must have good judgment in deciding what material to accept and what to reject. They need tact and the ability to guide and encourage others in their work.

High school and college newspapers, literary magazines, and community newspapers and radio and television stations all provide valuable, but sometimes unpaid, practical writing experience. Many magazines, newspapers, and broadcast stations have internships for students. Interns write short pieces, conduct research and interviews, and learn about the publishing or broadcasting business.

In small firms, beginning writers and editors may not only work as editorial or production assistants, but also write or edit material right away. They often advance by moving to other firms. In larger firms, jobs usually are more formally structured. Beginners generally do research, fact checking, or copy editing. They take on full-scale writing or editing duties less rapidly than do the employees of small companies. Advancement comes as they are assigned more important articles.

Job Outlook

Through the year 2006, the outlook for most writing and editing jobs is expected to continue to be competitive, because so many people are attracted to the field. However, opportunities will be good for technical writers because of the more limited number of writers who can handle technical material. Online publications and services, which are relatively new, will continue to grow and require an increased number of writers and editors. Opportunities should be better on small daily and weekly newspapers, and in small radio and television stations, where the pay is low. Some small publications are hiring freelance copy editors as back-up for their staff editors, or for additional help with special projects. Persons preparing to be writers and editors should also have academic preparation in another field as well, either to qualify them as writers specializing in that field, or to enter that field if they are unable to get a job in writing.

Employment of writers and editors is expected to increase faster than the average for all occupations through the year 2006. Employment of salaried writers and editors by newspapers, periodicals, book publishers, and nonprofit organizations is expected to increase with growing demand for their publications. Growth of advertising and public relations agencies should also be a source of new jobs. Demand for technical writers is expected to increase because of the continuing expansion of scientific and technical information, and the continued need to communicate it. Many job openings will also occur as experienced workers transfer to other occupations or leave the labor force. Turnover is relatively high in this occupation—many freelancers leave because they cannot earn enough money.

Earnings

In 1996, beginning salaries for writers and editorial assistants averaged $21,000 annually, according to the Dow Jones Newspaper Fund. According to the Newspaper Guild those who had at least five years experience averaged more than $30,000 and senior editors at the largest newspapers earned over $67,000 a year.

According to the 1996 Technical Communicator's Salary Survey, the median annual salary for technical writers was $44,000 annually.

The average annual salary for technical writers and editors in the federal government in nonsupervisory, supervisory, and managerial positions was about $47,440 in 1996; other writers and editors averaged about $46,590.

Related Occupations

Writers and editors communicate ideas and information. Other communications occupations include newspaper reporters and correspondents, radio and television announcers, advertising and public relations workers, and teachers.

Sources of Additional Information

For a guide to journalism careers and scholarships, contact:

❏ The Dow Jones Newspaper Fund, P.O. Box 300, Princeton, NJ 08540.

For information on college internships in magazine editing, contact:

❏ American Society of Magazine Editors, 919 3rd. Ave., New York, NY 10022.

For information on careers in technical writing, contact:

❏ Society for Technical Communication, Inc., 901 N. Stuart St., Suite 904, Arlington, VA 22203.

For information on union wage rates for newspaper and magazine editors, contact:

❏ The Newspaper Guild, Research and Information Department, 8611 Second Ave., Silver Spring, MD 20910.

For career information and a pamphlet titled "Newspaper Careers and Challenges for the Next Century" contact:

❏ National Newspaper Association, 1525 Wilson Blvd., Suite 550, Arlington, VA 22209.

Jobs That Do Not Require a Bachelor's Degree but Are Often Held by College Graduates

Engineering Technicians

Funeral Directors

Hotel Managers and Assistants

Inspectors and Compliance Officers, Except Construction

Insurance Agents and Brokers

Manufacturers' and Wholesale Sales Representatives

Musicians

Nuclear Medicine Technologists

Paralegals

Photographers and Camera Operators

Police, Detectives, and Special Agents

Radio and Television Announcers and Newscasters

Radiologic Technologists

Real Estate Agents, Brokers, and Appraisers

Recreation Workers

Registered Nurses

Respiratory Therapists

Restaurant and Food Service Managers

Science Technicians

Securities and Financial Services Sales Representatives

Social and Human Service Assistants

Visual Artists

Included are the following jobs:

Actors, Directors, and Producers

Adjusters, Investigators, and Collectors

Aircraft Pilots

Broadcast Technicians

Cardiovascular Technologists and Technicians

Computer and Office Machine Repairers

Construction and Building Inspectors

Cost Estimators

Court Reporters, Medical Transcriptionists, and Stenographers

Dental Hygienists

Drafters

Employment Interviewers

Actors, Directors, and Producers

(*D.O.T.* 139.167; 150 except .027-014; 159.041, .044, .047, .067, .117, .167-010 through -022, .267, .341, .344-010, -014, .347 except -010, .367, .647 except -018; 184.117-010, .162, .167-014, -022, -034; 187.167-174, -178, -182; 961.364, .667-014; 962.162-010, .167-014)

Significant Points

* ★ *Aspiring actors face frequent rejections when auditioning for work and long periods of unemployment between jobs; competition for roles is extremely keen because the glamour associated with this profession attracts large numbers of individuals.*
* ★ *While formal training is helpful, experience and talent are more critical for success.*

Nature of the Work

Actors, directors, and producers include stage and screen actors; narrators; magicians; clowns; comedians; impersonators; acrobats; jugglers; equestrians; amusement park entertainers; stunt, rodeo, and aquatic performers; casting, stage, news, sports, and public service directors; production, stage, and artist and repertoire managers; and producers and their assistants. This statement focuses on actors, directors, and producers.

Actors, directors, and producers express ideas and create images, based on a script, in theaters, film, television, and radio. They make the words come alive for their audiences.

Actors entertain and communicate with people through their interpretation of dramatic roles. However, only a few actors ever achieve recognition as stars—whether on stage, in motion pictures, or on television. A somewhat larger number are well-known, experienced performers, who frequently are cast in supporting roles. Most actors struggle for a toehold in the profession and pick up parts wherever they can. Although actors often prefer a certain type of role, experience is so critical to success in this field that even established actors continue to accept small roles, including commercials and product endorsements. Other actors work as extras, who have small parts with no lines to deliver; still others work for theater companies, teaching acting courses to the public.

Directors interpret plays or scripts. In addition, they audition and select cast members, conduct rehearsals, and direct the work of the cast and crew. Directors use their knowledge of acting, voice, and movement to achieve the best possible performance and usually approve the scenery, costumes, choreography, and music.

Producers are entrepreneurs. They select plays or scripts, arrange financing, and decide on the size and content of the production and its budget. They hire directors, principal members of the cast, and key production staff members, and negotiate contracts with artistic personnel, often in accordance with collective bargaining agreements. Producers also coordinate the activities of writers, directors, managers, and other personnel. Producers must have a working knowledge of new technologies as they relate to creating special effects.

Working Conditions

Acting demands patience and total commitment, because there are often rejections when auditioning for work and long periods of unemployment between jobs. Actors typically work long, irregular hours, sometimes under adverse weather conditions that may exist on location, and must travel when shows are on the road. Coupled with the heat of stage or studio lights and heavy costumes, these factors require stamina. Evening work is a regular part of a stage actor's life as several performances are often held on one day. Flawless performances require tedious memorizing of lines and repetitive rehearsals. On television, actors must deliver a good performance with very little preparation.

Actors working on Broadway productions often work long hours during rehearsals. However, once the show opens, they have more regular hours, working about 30 hours a week.

Directors and producers often work under stress as they try to meet schedules, stay within budgets, and resolve personnel problems while putting together a production. Directors must be aware of union rules and how they affect production schedules. For example, actors must be paid a minimum salary and can work no more than a set number of hours, depending on their contract.

Employment

In 1996, actors, directors, and producers held an average of about 105,000 jobs in motion pictures, stage plays, television, and radio. Many others were between jobs, so that the total number of people actually employed as actors, directors, and producers over the year was higher. In winter, most employment opportunities on stage are in New York and other large cities, many of which have established professional regional theaters. In summer, stock companies in suburban and resort areas also provide employment. Cruise lines and amusement parks also provide opportunities. In addition, many cities have small nonprofit professional companies such as "little theaters," repertory companies, and dinner theaters, which provide opportunities for local amateur talent as well as for professional entertainers. Normally, casts are selected in New York City for shows that go on the road.

Employment in motion pictures and films for television is centered in Hollywood and New York City. However, studios are also located in Florida, Seattle, and other parts of the country. In addition, many films are shot on location and may employ local professionals and nonprofessionals as day players and extras if the union contract allows. In television, opportunities are at the network entertainment centers in New York, Los Angeles, and Atlanta, and at local television stations around the country.

Training, Other Qualifications, and Advancement

For experience, aspiring actors and directors should take part in high school and college plays, or work with little theaters and other acting groups. Most actors and directors try to work their way up to major productions, although few succeed, due to the intense competition.

Formal dramatic training or acting experience is generally necessary, although some people enter the field without it. Most people take college courses in theater, arts, drama, and dramatic literature. Many experienced actors get additional formal training to learn new skills and improve old ones. Training can be obtained at dramatic arts schools in New York and Los Angeles, and at colleges and universities throughout the country offering bachelor's or higher degrees in dramatic and theater arts. College drama curriculums usually include courses in liberal arts, stage speech and movement, directing, play writing, play production, design, and history of the drama, as well as practical courses in acting.

The best way to start is to use local opportunities and build on them. Local and regional theater experience may help in obtaining work in New York or Los Angeles. Modeling experience may also be helpful. Actors need talent, creative ability, and training that will enable them to portray different characters. Training in singing and dancing is especially useful for stage work. Actors must have poise, stage presence, the capability to affect an audience, plus the ability to follow directions. Physical appearance is often a deciding factor in being selected for particular roles.

Many professional actors rely on agents or managers to find work, negotiate contracts, and plan their careers. Agents generally earn a percentage of an actor's contract. Other actors rely solely on attending open auditions for parts. Trade publications list the time, date, and location of these auditions—referred to as "cattle calls" in this industry.

To become a movie extra, one must usually be listed by a casting agency, such as Central Casting, a no-fee agency that supplies all extras to the major movie studios in Hollywood. Applicants are accepted only when the number of persons of a particular type on the list—for example, athletic young women, old men, or small children—is below the foreseeable need. In recent years, only a very small proportion of the applicants have succeeded in being listed.

There are no specific training requirements for directors and producers. However, talent, experience, and business acumen are very important. Directors and producers come from different backgrounds. Actors, writers, film editors, and business managers often enter these fields. Producers often start in the industry working behind the scenes with successful directors. Additionally, formal training in directing and producing is available at some colleges and universities.

As actors', directors', and producers' reputations grow, they are able to work on larger productions or in more prestigious theaters. Actors may also advance to lead or specialized roles. A few actors move into acting-related jobs, as drama coaches or directors of stage, television, radio, or motion picture productions. Some teach drama in colleges and universities. Many actors find that they must take a second job to support themselves.

The length of a performer's working life depends largely on training, skill, versatility, and perseverance. Some actors, directors, and producers continue working throughout their lives; however, many leave the occupation after a short time because they cannot find enough work to make a living.

Job Outlook

The glamour of actor, director, and producer jobs attracts a large number of people; this supply of potential workers, coupled with the lack of formal entry requirements, will continue to produce keen competition for these jobs. Only the most talented will find regular employment.

Employment of actors, directors, and producers is expected to grow faster than the average for all occupations through the year 2006. Rising foreign demand for American productions, combined with a growing domestic market—fueled by the growth of cable television, satellite television, home movie rentals, and television syndications—should stimulate demand for actors and other production personnel. Growth of opportunities in recorded media should be accompanied by increasing jobs in live productions. Growing numbers of people who enjoy live theatrical entertainment for excitement and aesthetics will attend stage productions. Touring productions of Broadway plays and other large shows are providing new opportunities for actors and directors. However, employment may be somewhat affected by government funding for the arts—a decline in funding could dampen future employment growth. Workers leaving the field will continue to create most job openings.

Earnings

Minimum salaries, hours of work, and other conditions of employment are covered in collective bargaining agreements between producers of shows and unions representing workers in this field. The Actors' Equity Association represents stage actors; the Screen Actors Guild and the Screen Extras Guild cover actors in motion pictures, including television, commercials, and films; and the American Federation of Television and Radio Artists (AFTRA) represents television and radio performers. Most stage directors belong to the Society of Stage Directors and Choreographers, and film and television directors belong to the Directors Guild of America. Of course, any actor or director may negotiate for a salary higher than the minimum.

According to Actors Equity Association, minimum weekly salary for actors in Broadway stage productions was $1,040 per week in 1997. Those in small "off-Broadway" theaters received minimums ranging from $400 to $625 a week, depending on the seating capacity of the theater. Smaller regional theaters pay $375 to $600 per week. For shows on the road, actors receive about $100 per day more for living expenses. However, less than 15 percent of dues-paying members work during any given week. In 1996, less than half worked on a stage production. Average earnings for those able to find employment were $13,700 in 1996.

According to the Screen Actors Guild, motion picture and television actors with speaking parts earned a minimum daily rate of $559, or $1,942 for a five-day week, in 1997. Actors also receive contributions to their health and pension plans and additional compensation for reruns and foreign telecasts.

Earnings from acting are low, because employment is so erratic. The Screen Actors Guild also reports that the average income its members earn from acting is less than $5,000 a year. Therefore, most actors must supplement their incomes by holding jobs in other fields.

Some well-known actors have salary rates well above the minimums, and the salaries of the few top stars are many times the figures cited, creating the false impression that all actors are highly paid.

Many actors who work more than a set number of weeks per year are covered by a union health, welfare, and pension fund, including hospitalization insurance, to which employers contribute. Under some employment conditions, Actors' Equity and AFTRA members have paid vacations and sick leave.

Earnings of stage directors vary greatly. According to the Society of Stage Directors and Choreographers, summer theaters offer compensation, including "royalties" (based on the number of performances), usually ranging from $2,500 to $8,000 for a three- to four-week run of a production. Directing a production at a dinner theater will usually pay less than a summer theater but has more potential for royalties. Regional theaters may hire directors for longer periods of time, increasing compensation accordingly. The highest paid directors work on Broadway productions, typically earning $80,000 plus royalties.

Producers seldom get a set fee; instead, they get a percentage of a show's earnings or ticket sales.

Related Occupations

People who work in occupations requiring acting skills include dancers, choreographers, disc jockeys, drama teachers or coaches, and radio and television announcers. Others working in occupations related to acting are playwrights, scriptwriters, stage managers, costume designers, makeup artists, hair stylists, lighting designers, and set designers. Workers in occupations involved with the business aspects of theater productions include managing directors, company managers, booking managers, publicists, and agents for actors, directors, and playwrights.

Sources of Additional Information

Information about opportunities in regional theaters may be obtained from:

❏ Theatre Communications Group, Inc., 355 Lexington Ave., New York, NY 10017.

A directory of theatrical programs may be purchased from:

❏ National Association of Schools of Theater, 11250 Roger Bacon Dr., Suite 21, Reston, VA 22090.

For general information on actors, directors, and producers, contact:

❏ Screen Actors Guild, 5757 Wilshire Blvd., Los Angeles CA 90036-3600.

❏ Association of Independent Video and Filmmakers, 304 Hudson Street, 6th Floor, New York, NY 10013.

❏ American Federation of Television and Radio Artists—Screen Actors Guild, 4340 East-West Hwy., Suite 204, Bethesda, MD 20814-4411.

Adjusters, Investigators, and Collectors

(*D.O.T.* 168.267-014 and -038; 191.167-022; 195.267-010; 203.382-014; 205.367-018, -034 and -046; 209.382-014 and .687-018; 219.362-042, and -050, .367-014, and .482-014; 241.217, .267-014, -018, -030, and -034, .357, .362, .367-010, -014, -022, and -034, and .387; and 249.367-030)

Significant Points

* *A high school education is sufficient to qualify for most positions, but a bachelor's degree is preferred for most claim representative positions.*

* *Projected employment change varies widely by occupation—for example, adjustment clerks are expected to grow much faster than average as businesses emphasize good customer relations, while policy processing clerks decline as their duties are increasingly computerized and assumed by other workers.*

Nature of the Work

Organizations must deal smoothly and efficiently with a variety of problems to maintain good relations with their customers. Handling complaints, interpreting and explaining policies or regulations, resolving billing disputes, collecting delinquent accounts, and determining eligibility for governmental assistance are just a few examples. Organizations like insurance companies, department stores, banks, and government social services agencies employ adjusters, investigators, and collectors to act as intermediaries with the public in these situations. The following is a discussion of occupations that comprise this group of workers.

Claim Representatives. Claim representatives at insurance companies investigate claims, negotiate settlements, and authorize payments to claimants. When a policyholder files a claim for damage or a loss, the claim adjuster, claim examiner, or claim investigator must initially determine whether the customer's insurance policy covers the loss and the amount of the loss covered.

Minor claims filed by automobile or homeowner policyholders are frequently handled by "inside adjusters" or "telephone adjusters." These workers contact claimants by telephone or by mail to get information on repair costs, medical expenses, or other details the company requires. Many companies centralize this operation in a drive-in claims center, where the cost of repair is determined and a check is issued immediately.

More complex cases are referred to an "independent adjuster" or "insurance company adjuster." Claim adjusters plan and schedule the work required to process a claim. They investigate claims by interviewing the claimant and witnesses, consulting police and hospital records, and inspecting property damage to determine the extent of the company's liability. They make photographs, take written or taped statements, and maintain computer files of information obtained from witnesses, and then prepare reports of their findings. When the policyholder's claim is legitimate, the claim adjuster

negotiates with the claimant and settles the claim. When claims are contested, adjusters may testify in court.

Some adjusters work with multiple lines of insurance. Others specialize in claims associated with fire damage, marine loss, automotive damage, product liability, or workers' compensation. Material damage adjusters inspect automobile damage and use the latest computerized estimating equipment to prepare estimates of the damage.

In life and health insurance companies, the counterpart of the claim adjuster is the claim examiner. In property and casualty insurance companies, the claim examiner may supervise claim adjusters. In both cases, they investigate questionable claims or authorize payment for those exceeding a designated amount. Larger claims are referred to senior examiners. Examiners may check claim applications for completeness and accuracy, interview medical specialists, consult policy files to verify information on a claim, or calculate benefit payments. They also maintain records of settled claims and prepare reports to be submitted to their company's data processing department.

Claim representatives are making greater use of computers to keep records of clients and actions taken in various claims. Most have computer terminals on their desks, and many use portable laptop computers to enter or access information when they are on assignment outside the office.

Insurance Processing Clerks. Policy processing clerks use computers to process new insurance policies, modifications to existing policies, and claims. They begin the new policy process by reviewing the insurance application to ensure that all the questions have been answered. After an application has been reviewed by underwriters and the company determines that it will issue a policy, a policy processing clerk prepares the necessary forms and informs the insurance sales agent of an application's processing status. Policy processing clerks also update existing policies—such as a change in beneficiary, amount of coverage, or type of insurance—and recalculate premiums. They mail correspondence notices regarding changes to the sales agent and to the policyholder. Policy processing clerks maintain computer files for each policyholder, including policies that are to be reinstated or canceled.

Claim clerks, also called claim interviewers, obtain information from policyholders regarding claims. Claims may concern various types of loss, such as fire damage, personal injury, or an automobile accident. They prepare reports and review insurance claim forms and related documents for completeness. They call or write the insured or other party involved for missing information to update claim files. They may transmit routine claims for payment or advise the claim supervisor if further investigation is needed.

Like policy processing clerks, claim clerks use computers extensively in their work. Most spend a large part of their time creating and updating records at a personal computer or terminal.

Adjustment Clerks. Adjustment clerks investigate and resolve customers' complaints about merchandise, service, billing, or credit rating. They may work for banks, department stores, utility companies, and other large organizations selling products and services to the public. Sometimes they are referred to as customer service representatives, customer complaint clerks, or adjustment correspondents.

Adjustment clerks examine all pertinent information to determine if a customer's complaint is valid. In a department store, this may mean checking sales slips or warranties, as well as the merchandise in question. In a bank, it could mean reviewing records and videotapes of automated teller machine transactions. In a utility company, they review meter books, microfilm, computer printouts, and machine accounting records. Regardless of the setting, these clerks get information—in person, by telephone, or through written correspondence—from all parties involved.

After an investigation and evaluation of the facts, adjustment clerks report their findings, adjustments, and recommendations. These may include exchanging merchandise, refunding money, crediting customers' accounts, or adjusting customers' bills. Adjustment clerks ensure that the appropriate changes are set in motion and follow up on the recommendations to ensure customer satisfaction. To prevent similar complaints in the future, they may recommend to management improvements in product, packaging, shipping methods, service, or billing methods and procedures. Adjustment clerks keep records of all relevant matters, using them to prepare reports for their supervisors.

Adjustment clerks also respond to inquiries from customers. Clerks frequently can answer these inquiries with a form letter, but other times they must compose a letter themselves. Upon request, adjustment clerks issue duplicate or additional credit cards for banks and department stores.

Bill and Account Collectors. Bill and account collectors, sometimes called collection correspondents, are responsible for ensuring customers pay their overdue accounts. Some are employed by third-party collection agencies, while others, known as "in-house collectors," work directly for the original creditors, like department stores, hospitals, or banks.

Many companies automatically notify customers by mail if their account is overdue. When customers do not respond, collectors are called on to locate and notify them of the delinquent account, usually over the telephone, sometimes by letter.

When customers move without leaving a forwarding address, collectors may check with the post office, telephone companies, credit bureaus, or former neighbors to obtain their new address. This is called "skip-tracing."

Once collectors find the debtor, they inform them of the overdue account and solicit payment. If necessary, they review the terms of the sale, service, or credit contract with the customer. Collectors may attempt to learn the cause of the delay in payment. Where feasible, they offer the customer advice and counsel on how to pay off the debts, such as by taking out a bill consolidation loan. However, the collector's objective is always to ensure that the customer first pays the debt in question.

If customers agree to pay, collectors note that for the record and check later to verify that the payment was indeed made. Collectors may have authority to grant an extension of time if customers ask for one. If customers fail to respond at all, collectors prepare a statement to that effect for the credit department of the establishment. In more extreme cases, collectors may initiate repossession proceedings or service disconnections, or hand the account over to an attorney for legal action.

Most collectors handle other administrative functions for the accounts assigned to them. This may include recording changes of addresses, and purging the records of the deceased. Bill and account collectors keep records of the amounts collected and the status of the accounts. Some fill out daily reports to keep their supervisors apprised of their progress. In some organizations, inside collectors receive payments and post the amounts to the customers' account. In most operations, however, the posting and receiving are done by other clerical workers. Collectors employed by collection agencies do not receive payments; rather, their primary responsibility is to get customers to pay their obligation.

Collectors use computers and a variety of automated systems to keep track of overdue accounts. Typically, collectors work at video display terminals that are linked to computers. In sophisticated predicted dialer systems, the computer dials the telephone automatically and the collector speaks only when a connection has been made. Such systems eliminate time spent calling busy or nonanswering numbers. Many collectors use regular telephones; some wear headsets like those used by telephone operators. Occasionally, supervisors may listen in on collectors' conversations with customers to evaluate their job performance.

Welfare Eligibility Workers and Interviewers. Welfare eligibility workers and interviewers—sometimes referred to as intake workers, eligibility determination workers, eligibil-

ity specialists, family investment counselors, or income maintenance specialists—determine who can receive welfare and other types of social assistance. They interview and investigate applicants and recipients; based on the personal and financial information they obtain and the rules and regulations of each program, they initiate procedures to grant, modify, deny, or terminate individuals' eligibility for various aid programs. This information is recorded and evaluated to determine the amounts of the grants.

Welfare eligibility workers and interviewers work with various public assistance programs. The best-known are Aid to Families with Dependent Children, Medicaid, Food Stamps, and the Work Incentive Program. Depending on local circumstances, there may be other programs, such as those for public housing, refugee assistance, and fuel assistance.

Many welfare eligibility workers and interviewers specialize in an area such as housing, but most are responsible for several areas. They may assist social workers by informing them of pertinent information they have gathered during their interviews with applicants. In some areas, particularly rural ones, eligibility workers may also perform other welfare duties.

These workers often provide information to applicants and current recipients. For example, they may explain and interpret eligibility rules and regulations or identify other resources available in the community for financial or social welfare assistance. More experienced workers may help train new workers. In addition, they may be assigned to special units whose responsibility is to detect fraud.

An increasing number of jurisdictions are using computers to increase worker productivity and to reduce the incidence of welfare fraud. In these settings, welfare eligibility workers and interviewers sit in front of computer terminals when they interview applicants and recipients. Welfare eligibility workers then enter the information provided. In the most advanced systems, the computer terminal prompts them with a variety of questions to ask during an interview.

Although these workers usually interview applicants and recipients who visit their offices, they may make occasional home visits, especially if the applicant or recipient is elderly or disabled. They may also check with employers or other references to verify answers and get further information.

The authority of welfare eligibility workers and interviewers varies from one jurisdiction to another. In some places, these workers are authorized to decide on an applicant's eligibility, subject to review by their supervisor. In other places, however, they can only make recommendations to their supervisors, who in turn make the ultimate decision.

Working Conditions

Most claim examiners have desk jobs that require no unusual physical activity. They typically work a standard five-day, 40-hour week. Claim examiners may work longer hours during peak periods or when quarterly and annual statements are prepared. Sometimes they travel to obtain information by personal interview.

Many claim adjusters work outside the office, visiting and inspecting damaged buildings, for example. Occasionally, experienced adjusters are away from home for days when they travel to the scene of a disaster—such as a tornado, hurricane, or flood—to work with local adjusters and government officials. Some adjusters are on emergency call in the case of such incidents. Material damage adjusters work at local claim centers where policyholders take their cars for estimates of damage.

Adjusters generally have the flexibility to arrange their work schedule to accommodate evening and weekend appointments with clients. Some report to the office every morning to get their assignments, while others simply call from home and spend their days traveling to claim sites. This enables some adjusters to work independently.

Most insurance processing clerks work 40 hours a week in an office. Much of the work is routine and requires remaining at work stations for extended periods of time. Because most insurance information is stored in computers, many of these workers sit at video display terminals and enter or access information while the customer is on the phone. Because most companies provide 24-hour claim service to their policyholders, some claim clerks work evenings and weekends. Many claim clerks work part-time.

Adjustment clerks, bill and account collectors, and welfare eligibility workers and interviewers work in offices, usually during regular business hours. Some work part-time. Many bill and account collectors work as temporaries for collection agencies. From their offices, they deal with customers, clients, or applicants, either by telephone or in person. Dealing with upset or angry clients is often part of the daily routine in these jobs, making the work stressful at times.

Some welfare eligibility workers and interviewers may be hired on a seasonal basis to help administer a specific program. For example, some states hire these workers for the winter to help run emergency fuel-assistance programs.

Employment

Adjusters, investigators, and collectors held about 1.3 million jobs in 1996. The following tabulation shows the percent distribution of employment by detailed occupation in 1996.

Adjustment clerks	30
Bill and account collectors	20
Insurance policy processing clerks	14
Insurance adjusters, examiners, and investigators	12
Insurance claims clerks	9
Welfare eligibility workers and interviewers	8
Claims examiners, property and casualty insurance	4
All other adjusters and investigators	3

Insurance companies employ the vast majority of claim adjusters, examiners, investigators, property and casualty insurance claim examiners, policy processing clerks, and claim clerks. The remainder are employed by real estate firms and government agencies.

Nearly two out of ten adjustment clerks are employed by department stores, grocery stores, or catalog and mail order houses. Manufacturing firms, banks and other financial institutions, and telephone companies are other major employers of these workers.

About one in six bill and account collectors works for a credit reporting and collection agency. Many others work in banks, department stores, and other institutions that extend credit.

Around nine of every ten welfare eligibility workers and interviewers work for state or local government agencies. In many states, these workers are employed exclusively by the state government. In the remainder, they are employed by the county or municipal government. Most of those not employed by government work for private social service agencies.

Training, Other Qualifications, and Advancement

Training and entry requirements vary widely for adjuster, investigator, and collector jobs. A high school education is sufficient to qualify for most insurance processing clerk, adjustment clerk, and bill and account collector positions, while a bachelor's degree is preferred for most claim representative positions. While some college education is preferred for positions as adjuster or welfare eligibility worker or interviewer, many people qualify for these positions on the strength of related prior work experience. Because a significant and growing proportion of adjusters, investigators, and collectors use computers, word processing skills are recommended. Employers view experience with computers as an asset.

Claim Representatives. Most companies prefer to hire college graduates for claim representative positions. Entry-level workers may be hired without college course work if they have specialized experience. For example, people with knowledge of automobile mechanics or body repair may qualify as material damage adjusters and those with extensive clerical experience might be hired as inside adjusters. Both adjusters and examiners should be observant and enjoy working with details.

No specific college major is recommended as the best preparation for these occupations. Although courses in insurance, economics, or other business subjects are helpful, a degree in almost any field is adequate. An adjuster who has a business or an accounting background might specialize in claims of financial loss due to strikes, breakdowns in equipment, or damage to merchandise. College training in engineering is helpful in adjusting industrial claims, such as damage from fires and other accidents. A legal background is most helpful to those handling workers' compensation and product liability cases. Knowledge of computer applications is extremely important.

Many states require adjusters to be licensed. Applicants usually must comply with one or more of the following: pass a licensing examination covering the fundamentals of adjusting; complete an approved course in insurance or loss adjusting; furnish character references; be at least 20 or 21 years of age and a resident of the state; and file a surety bond.

Because they often work closely with claimants, witnesses, and other insurance professionals, claim representatives must be able to communicate effectively with others. Some companies require applicants to pass a battery of written aptitude tests designed to measure communication, analytical, and general mathematical skills. Examiners must understand federal and state insurance laws and regulations.

Some large insurance companies provide on-the-job training and home-study courses for entry-level claim adjusters and examiners. For example, material damage adjusters would learn about automobile body construction, analysis of collision data, and repair cost estimation, including computerized estimating equipment. They also learn how to deal with customers.

Workers may receive their training through courses offered by the Insurance Institute of America, a nonprofit organization offering educational programs and professional certification to persons in the property-liability insurance industry. The Insurance Institute of America offers an Associate in Claims designation upon successful completion of four essay examinations. Adjusters can prepare for the examination by independent home study or through company or public classes. The Institute also offers a certificate upon successful completion of the Introduction to Claims program and an examination.

The International Claim Association offers a program on life and health insurance claim administration. Completion of the six-examination program leads to the professional designation, Associate, Life and Health Claims.

The Life Office Management Association (LOMA) offers a comprehensive ten-course life and health insurance educational program that leads to the professional designation, Fellow, Life Management Institute (FLMI). LOMA also offers the Master Fellow Program that is designed specifically to meet the continuing education needs of life and health insurance professionals. Students can prepare for FLMI exams through independent home study or through insurance company or FLMI Society classes.

Beginning adjusters and examiners work on small claims under the supervision of an experienced worker. As they learn more about claim investigation and settlement, they are assigned larger, more complex claims. Trainees are promoted as they demonstrate competence in handling assignments and as they progress in their course work. Because of the complexity of insurance regulations and claim procedures, workers who lack formal academic training tend to advance more slowly than those with additional education. Employees who demonstrate competence in claim work or administrative skills may be promoted to department supervisor in a field office or to a managerial position in the home office. Other claim examiners are promoted to investigators, whose role is to detect fraud.

Insurance Processing Clerks. High school graduation is considered adequate preparation for most insurance processing clerk positions. Courses in typing and word processing, and business arithmetic are desirable. Employers view favorably previous office experience and familiarity with computers. Most new workers begin as file clerks and move into insurance processing positions as they demonstrate their ability. However, people with considerable clerical experience may begin processing insurance policies immediately.

A few experienced insurance processing clerks may be promoted to a clerical supervisor position. Advancement to a claim representative or an underwriting technician position is possible for clerks who demonstrate potential, have college course work, or have taken specialized courses in insurance. Many companies offer home-study courses for their employees so they can acquire the knowledge necessary to advance.

Adjustment Clerks. Many employers do not require any formal education for adjustment clerk positions. Instead, they look for people who can read and write well and who possess good communication and interpersonal skills. Word processing ability is also viewed favorably.

Adjustment clerk is an entry-level position in some, but not all, organizations. Depending on their assignment, new adjustment clerks may receive training on the job from a supervisor or an experienced coworker, or they may enter a formal training course offered by the organization. Training covers such topics as how to use computers, what standard forms to use, whom to contact in other departments of the organization, and how to deal with customers. Some employers provide more advanced training for experienced adjustment clerks. This training may be offered in-house or from trade associations or local colleges.

Bill and Account Collectors. While high school graduation sometimes is required by employers when they hire bill and account collectors, formal education beyond high school is not stressed. Previous work experience as a collector is particularly valuable. Experience in the field of telemarketing or as a telephone operator also is helpful, as is knowledge of the billing process. Employers seek individuals who speak well and who are persistent and detail-oriented.

Employers normally provide training to new bill and account collectors. This training, which may last up to a couple of months, is usually conducted in a classroom or on the job. Although not required by law, many employers also require their collectors to get certified through the American Collectors Association (ACA). ACA seminars concentrate on current state and federal compliance laws. Since most states recognize these credentials, ACA-certified collectors have greater career mobility. In training seminars, employers use videotapes, computer programs, role-playing, and hands-on experience. Novice collectors learn about skip-tracing, billing procedures, and most importantly, communications and negotiating. Learning to use the firm's computer and telephone systems is also an integral part of their training.

Successful bill and account collectors may become supervisors. Some even start their own collection agencies.

Welfare Eligibility Workers and Interviewers. Hiring requirements for welfare eligibility workers and interviewers vary widely. Depending on the jurisdiction, applicants may need a high school diploma, associate degree, or bachelor's degree. Work experience in a closely related field—such as employment interviewing, social work, or insurance claims—may also qualify one for this job. In parts of the country with a high concentration of non-English speaking people, fluency in a foreign language may be an advantage.

Because they deal with people who are in difficult economic circumstances, welfare eligibility workers and interviewers should be compassionate and empathetic. Attention to detail is important because there are many procedures and regulations that must be observed.

After they are hired, eligibility workers are given training, sometimes in a formal classroom setting, other times in a more informal manner. They are taught the policies, procedures, and program regulations that they are expected to use to determine eligibility. If a formal training program is selected, it generally is followed by on-the-job training provided by the supervisor.

Advancement to the job of social worker is possible, although additional formal education, such as a bachelor's or master's degree, usually is needed.

Job Outlook

Overall employment of adjusters, investigators, and collectors is expected to grow faster than the average for all occupations over the 1996–2006 period. Most job openings, however, will result from the need to replace workers who transfer to other occupations or leave the labor force.

Growth rates will vary considerably by occupation. Employment of insurance claim examiners is expected to grow faster than the average as the increasing volume of insurance results in more insurance claims. As people accumulate assets and take on family responsibilities, the need for insurance—including life, health, home, and automobile—will increase. Also, new or expanding businesses will need protection for new plants and equipment and for insurance covering their employees' health and safety. Opportunities should be particularly good for claim representatives who specialize in complex business insurance such as marine cargo, workers' compensation, and product and pollution liability.

Employment of adjustment clerks is expected to grow much faster than average as business establishments place an increased emphasis on maintaining good customer relations. An important aspect of good customer service is resolving customers' complaints in a friendly and timely fashion. Because much of their work involves direct communication with customers, demand for adjustment clerks is expected to keep pace with growth in the number of customers.

Bill and account collector jobs also are expected to grow much faster than average as the level of consumer debt rises. As the economy expands, firms will strive to increase the efficiency of their debt collection to keep losses at a minimum. Contrary to the pattern in most occupations, employment of bill and account collectors tends to rise during recessions, reflecting the difficulty that many people have in meeting their financial obligations.

Overall employment of insurance claims and policy processing occupations is expected to grow about as fast as the average for all occupations. Within this group, employment of adjusters and claim clerks will increase faster than average because their work requires much interpersonal contact, which cannot be automated. However, employment of policy processing clerks will decline as their duties are increasingly computerized and assumed by other workers.

Employment of welfare eligibility workers and interviewers is expected to decline as many people move from welfare to work, and as state and local governments attempt to curb the growth in their expenditures for public assistance.

Earnings

Earnings of adjusters, investigators, and collectors vary significantly. For adjusters and investigators, the median weekly earnings in 1996 were $440. The middle 50 percent earned between about $340 and $590 a week. Adjusters are also furnished a company car or are reimbursed for use of their own vehicle for business purposes.

Specific information on earnings of insurance processing clerks is not available. However, median weekly earnings for records clerks, a category that includes policy processing clerks, were $390 in 1996. Interviewers, whose work is similar to that of claim clerks, also had median weekly earnings of $390.

Median weekly earnings of full-time bill and account collectors were $410 in 1996; the middle 50 percent earned between $330 and $510 a week. Ten percent earned less than $280 and 10 percent earned more than $660. Some bill and account collectors receive a base salary and work on commission beyond that.

Median weekly earnings of full-time welfare eligibility workers and interviewers were about $450 in 1996; the middle 50 percent earned between $360 and $590 a week. The lowest 10 percent earned less than $290 and the top 10 percent earned more than $670.

Welfare eligibility workers and interviewers are twice as likely to belong to unions than workers in all occupations. In 1996, about 26 percent of all welfare eligibility workers and interviewers were union members, compared to 13 for all occupations. The two principal unions representing these workers are the American Federation of State, County, and Municipal Employees, and the Service Employees International Union.

Related Occupations

Insurance adjusters and examiners investigate, analyze, and determine the validity of their firm's liability concerning personal, casualty, or property loss or damages, and settle with claimants. Workers in other occupations that require similar skills include cost estimators, budget analysts, and private investigators.

The work of insurance processing clerks and adjustment clerks is similar to that of other workers who compile, review, or maintain records—including title searchers and coding, contract, auditing, and reservation clerks.

The work of bill and account collectors is related to that of customer service representatives, telemarketers, telephone interviewers, and other workers who deal with the public over the telephone.

The work of welfare eligibility workers is similar to that of social and human service assistants, financial aid counselors, loan and credit counselors, probation officers, and other workers who interview customers or clients.

Sources of Additional Information

General information about a career as a claim representative or an insurance processing clerk is available from the home offices of many life and property and liability insurance companies.

Information about career opportunities in these occupations may be obtained from:

❏ Insurance Information Institute, 110 William St., New York, NY 10038.

❏ Alliance of American Insurers, 1501 Woodfield Rd., Suite 400 West, Schaumburg, IL 60173-4980.

Information about licensing requirements for claim adjusters may be obtained from the department of insurance in each state.

For information about the designation, Associate in Claims (AIC), or the Introduction to Claims program, contact:

❏ Insurance Institute of America, 720 Providence Rd., P.O. Box 3016, Malvern, PA 19355-0716.

Information on the Associate, Life and Health Claims, and the Fellow, Life Management Institute designations can be obtained from:

❏ Life Office Management Association, 2300 Windy Ridge Pkwy., Atlanta, GA 30327-4308.

Career information on bill and account collectors is available from:

❏ American Collectors Association, Inc., P.O. Box 39106, Minneapolis, MN 55439-0106. Homepage: http//www.collector.com/consumer/careers.html

Employment information on welfare eligibility workers and interviewers is available at social service offices of municipal, county, and state governments.

Aircraft Pilots

(*D.O.T.* 196, except .163 and .167-014 and 621.261-018)

Significant Points

★ *Competition is expected for jobs because aircraft pilots have very high earnings, especially those employed by airlines.*

★ *Pilots usually start with smaller commuter and regional airlines to acquire the experience needed to qualify for higher paying jobs with national airlines.*

★ *Most pilots have traditionally learned to fly in the military, but growing numbers are entering from civilian FAA-certified pilot training schools.*

Nature of the Work

Pilots are highly trained professionals who fly airplanes and helicopters to carry out a wide variety of tasks. Although most pilots transport passengers and cargo, others are involved in more unusual tasks, such as dusting crops, spreading seed for reforestation, testing aircraft, directing fire fighting efforts, tracking criminals, monitoring traffic, and rescuing and evacuating injured persons.

Except on small aircraft, two pilots usually make up the cockpit crew. Generally, the most experienced pilot, the captain, is in command and supervises all other crew members. The pilot and copilot split flying and other duties, such as communicating with air traffic controllers and monitoring the instruments. Some large aircraft still have a third pilot in the cockpit—the flight engineer—who assists the other pilots by monitoring and operating many of the instruments and systems, making minor inflight repairs, and watching for other aircraft. New technology can perform many flight tasks, however, and virtually all new aircraft now fly with only two pilots, who rely more heavily on computerized controls. Flight engineer jobs will be completely eliminated in the future.

Before departure, pilots plan their flights carefully. They thoroughly check their aircraft to make sure that the engines, controls, instruments, and other systems are functioning properly. They also make sure that baggage or cargo has been loaded correctly. They confer with flight dispatchers and aviation weather forecasters to find out about weather conditions en route and at their destination. Based on this information, they choose a route, altitude, and speed that should provide the fastest, safest, and smoothest flight. When flying under instrument flight rules—procedures governing the operation of the aircraft when there is poor visibility—the pilot in command, or the company dispatcher, normally files an instrument flight plan with air traffic control so that the flight can be coordinated with other air traffic.

Takeoff and landing are the most difficult parts of the flight and require close coordination between the pilot and first officer. For example, as the plane accelerates for takeoff, the pilot concentrates on the runway while the first officer scans the instrument panel. To calculate the speed they must attain to become airborne, pilots consider the altitude of the airport, outside temperature, weight of the plane, and the speed and direction of the wind. The moment the plane reaches takeoff speed, the first officer informs the pilot, who then pulls back on the controls to raise the nose of the plane.

Unless the weather is bad, the actual flight is relatively easy. Airplane pilots, with the assistance of autopilot and the flight management computer, steer the plane along their planned route and are monitored by the air traffic control stations they pass along the way. They regularly scan the instrument panel to check their fuel supply, the condition of their engines, and the air-conditioning, hydraulic, and other systems. Pilots may request a change in altitude or route if circumstances dictate. For example, if the ride is rougher than expected, they may ask air traffic control if pilots flying at other altitudes have reported better conditions. If so, they may request a change. This procedure also may be used to find a stronger tailwind or a weaker headwind to save fuel and increase speed.

In contrast, helicopters are used for short trips at relatively low altitude, so pilots must be constantly on the lookout for trees, bridges, power lines, transmission towers, and other dangerous obstacles. Regardless of the type of aircraft, all pilots must monitor warning devices designed to help detect sudden shifts in wind conditions that can cause crashes.

If visibility is poor, pilots must rely completely on their instruments. Using the altimeter readings, they know how high above ground they are and whether or not they can fly safely over mountains and other obstacles. Special navigation radios give pilots precise information which, with the help of special maps, tell them their exact position. Other very sophisticated equipment provides directions to a point just above the end of a runway and enables pilots to land completely "blind."

Once on the ground, pilots must complete records on their flight for their organization and the Federal Aviation Administration (FAA).

The number of nonflying duties that pilots have depends on the employment setting. Airline pilots have the services of large support staffs, and consequently, perform few nonflying duties. Pilots employed by other organizations such as charter operators or businesses have many other duties. They may load the aircraft, handle all passenger luggage to ensure a balanced load, and supervise refueling; other nonflying responsibilities include keeping records, scheduling flights, arranging for major maintenance, and performing minor aircraft maintenance and repair work.

Some pilots are instructors. They teach their students the principles of flight in ground-school classes and demonstrate how to operate aircraft in dual-controlled planes and helicop-

ters. A few specially trained pilots are "examiners" or "check pilots." They periodically fly with other pilots or pilot's license applicants to make sure that they are proficient.

Working Conditions

By law, airline pilots cannot fly more than 100 hours a month or more than 1,000 hours a year. Most airline pilots fly an average of 75 hours a month and work an additional 75 hours a month performing nonflying duties. Fifty percent of all pilots work more than 40 hours a week. Most spend a considerable amount of time away from home because the majority of flights involve overnight layovers. When pilots are away from home, the airlines provide hotel accommodations, transportation between the hotel and airport, and an allowance for meals and other expenses. Airlines operate flights at all hours of the day and night, so work schedules often are irregular. Flight assignments are based on seniority.

Those pilots not employed by the airlines often have irregular schedules as well; they may fly 30 hours one month and 90 hours the next. Because these pilots frequently have many nonflying responsibilities, they have much less free time than airline pilots. Except for business pilots, most do not remain away from home overnight. They may work odd hours. Flight instructors may have irregular and seasonal work schedules depending on their students' available time and the weather and often give lessons at night or on weekends.

Airline pilots, especially those on international routes, often suffer jet lag—fatigue caused by many hours of flying through different time zones. The work of test pilots, who check the flight performance of new and experimental planes, may be dangerous. Pilots who are crop dusters may be exposed to toxic chemicals and seldom have the benefit of a regular landing strip. Helicopter pilots involved in police work may be subject to personal injury.

Although flying does not involve much physical effort, the mental stress of being responsible for a safe flight, no matter what the weather, can be tiring. Particularly during takeoff and landing, pilots must be alert and quick to react if something goes wrong.

Employment

Civilian pilots held about 110,000 jobs in 1996. Three-fifths worked for airlines. Many others worked as flight instructors at local airports or for large businesses that fly company cargo and executives in their own airplanes or helicopters. Some pilots flew small planes for air taxi companies, usually to or from lightly traveled airports not served by the airlines. Others worked for a variety of businesses performing tasks such as crop dusting, inspecting pipelines, or conducting

sightseeing trips. Federal, state, and local governments also employed pilots. A few pilots were self-employed.

The employment of airplane pilots is not distributed like the population. Pilots are more concentrated in the states of California, Texas, Georgia, Washington, Nevada, Hawaii, and Alaska, which have a higher amount of flying activity relative to their population.

Training, Other Qualifications, and Advancement

All pilots who are paid to transport passengers or cargo must have a commercial pilot's license with an instrument rating issued by the FAA. Helicopter pilots must hold a commercial pilot's certificate with a helicopter rating. To qualify for these licenses, applicants must be at least 18 years old and have at least 250 hours of flight experience. The time can be reduced through participation in certain flight school curricula approved by the FAA. They also must pass a strict physical examination to make sure that they are in good health and have 20/20 vision with or without glasses, good hearing, and no physical handicaps that could impair their performance. Applicants must pass a written test that includes questions on the principles of safe flight, navigation techniques, and FAA regulations. They also must demonstrate their flying ability to FAA or designated examiners.

To fly in periods of low visibility, pilots must be rated by the FAA to fly by instruments. Pilots may qualify for this rating by having a total of 105 hours of flight experience, including 40 hours of experience in flying by instruments; they also must pass a written examination on procedures and FAA regulations covering instrument flying and demonstrate to an examiner their ability to fly by instruments.

Airline pilots must fulfill additional requirements. Those hired as flight engineers must pass FAA written and flight examinations to earn a flight engineer's license. Captains and first officers must have an airline transport pilot's license. Applicants for this license must be at least 23 years old and have a minimum of 1,500 hours of flying experience, including night and instrument flying. Usually they also have one or more advanced ratings, such as multi-engine aircraft or aircraft type ratings dependent upon the requirements of their particular flying jobs. Because pilots must be able to make quick decisions and accurate judgments under pressure, many airline companies reject applicants who do not pass required psychological and aptitude tests.

All licenses are valid as long as a pilot can pass the periodic physical examinations and tests of flying skills required by government and company regulations.

The Armed Forces have always been an important source of trained pilots for civilian jobs. Military pilots gain valuable experience on jet aircraft and helicopters, and persons with this experience are generally preferred for civilian pilot jobs. This primarily reflects the extensive flying time military pilots receive. Persons without armed forces training also become pilots by attending flight schools. The FAA has certified about 600 civilian flying schools, including some colleges and universities that offer degree credit for pilot training. Over the projected period, federal budget reductions are expected to reduce military pilot training. As a result, FAA certified schools will train a larger share of pilots than in the past.

Although some small airlines will hire high school graduates, most airlines require at least two years of college and prefer to hire college graduates; almost 90 percent of all pilots have completed some college. In fact, most entrants to this occupation have a college degree. If the number of college-educated applicants continues to increase, employers may make a college degree an educational requirement.

Depending on the type of aircraft in use, new airline pilots start as first officers or flight engineers. Although some airlines favor applicants who already have a flight engineer's license, they may provide flight engineer training for those who have only the commercial license. Many pilots begin with smaller regional or commuter airlines where they obtain vital experience flying passengers on scheduled flights into busy airports in all weather conditions. These jobs are often a stepping-stone to higher-paying jobs with the bigger national airlines.

Initial training for pilots includes a week of company indoctrination, three to six weeks of ground school and simulator training, and 25 hours of initial operating experience, including a check-ride with an FAA aviation safety inspector. Once trained and "on the line" pilots are required to attend recurrent training and simulator checks periodically throughout their employment. Recurrent training is required twice a year.

Organizations other than airlines generally require less flying experience. However, a commercial pilot's license is a minimum requirement, and employers prefer applicants who have experience in the type of craft they will be flying. New employees usually start as first officers, or fly less sophisticated equipment. Test pilots often are required to have an engineering degree.

Advancement for all pilots generally is limited to other flying jobs. Many pilots start as flight instructors, building up their flying hours while they earn money teaching. As they become more experienced, these pilots occasionally fly charter planes or perhaps get jobs with small air transportation firms, such as air taxi companies. Some advance to business flying jobs. A small number get flight engineer jobs with the airlines.

In the airlines, advancement usually depends on seniority provisions of union contracts. After one to five years, flight engineers advance according to seniority to first officer and, after 5 to 15 years, to captain. Seniority also determines which pilots get the more desirable routes. In a nonairline job, a first officer may advance to pilot and, in large companies, to chief pilot or director of aviation in charge of aircraft scheduling, maintenance, and flight procedures.

Job Outlook

Pilots are expected to face considerable competition for jobs through the year 2006 because the number of applicants for new positions is expected to exceed the number of job openings. Competition will be especially keen early in the projection period due to a temporary increase in the pool of qualified pilots seeking jobs. Mergers and bankruptcies during the recent restructuring of the industry caused a large number of airline pilots to lose their jobs. Also, federal budget reductions resulted in many pilots leaving the Armed Forces. These and other qualified pilots seek jobs in this occupation because it offers very high earnings, glamour, prestige, and free or low cost travel benefits. As time passes, some pilots will fail to maintain their qualifications and the number of applicants competing for each opening should decline. Factors affecting demand, however, are not expected to ease that competition.

Relatively few jobs will be created from rising demand for pilots as employment is expected to increase about as fast as average for all occupations through the year 2006. The expected growth in airline passenger and cargo traffic will create a need for more airliners, pilots, and flight instructors. However, computerized flight management systems on new aircraft will eliminate the need for flight engineers on those planes, thus restricting the growth of pilot employment. In addition, the trend toward using larger planes in the airline industry will increase pilot productivity. Future business travel could also be adversely affected by advances in teleconferencing and facsimile mail and the elimination of many middle management positions in corporate downsizing. Employment of business pilots is expected to grow more slowly than in the past as more businesses opt to fly with regional and smaller airlines serving their area rather than buy and operate their own aircraft. On the other hand, helicopter pilots are expected to grow more rapidly as the demand expands for the type of services helicopters can offer.

Job openings resulting from the need to replace pilots who retire or leave the occupation traditionally have been very low. Aircraft pilots understandably have an extremely strong attachment to their occupation because it requires a substantial investment in specialized training that is not transferable to other fields and it generally offers very high earnings. However, many of the pilots who were hired in the late 1960s during the last major industry boom are approaching the age for mandatory retirement, so during the projected period, retirements of pilots are expected to increase and generate several thousand job openings each year.

Pilots who have logged the greatest number of flying hours in the more sophisticated equipment generally have the best prospects. This is the reason military pilots usually have an advantage over other applicants. Job seekers with the most FAA licenses will also have a competitive advantage. Opportunities for pilots in the regional commuter airlines and international service are expected to be more favorable as these segments are expected to grow faster than other segments of the industry.

Employment of pilots is sensitive to cyclical swings in the economy. During recessions, when a decline in the demand for air travel forces airlines to curtail the number of flights, airlines may temporarily furlough some pilots. Commercial and corporate flying, flight instruction, and testing of new aircraft also decline during recessions, adversely affecting pilots employed in those areas.

Earnings

Earnings of airline pilots are among the highest in the nation. According to the Future Aviation Professionals of America (FAPA), the 1996 average starting salary for airline pilots ranged from about $15,000 at the smaller turboprop airlines to $26,290 at the larger major airlines. Average earnings for experienced pilots with six years of experience ranged from $28,100 at the turboprop airlines to almost $76,800 at the largest airlines. Some senior captains on the largest aircraft earned as much as $200,000 a year. Earnings depend on factors such as the type, size, and maximum speed of the plane, and the number of hours and miles flown. Extra pay may be given for night and international flights. Generally, pilots working outside the airlines earn lower salaries. Usually, pilots who fly jet aircraft earn higher salaries than non-jet pilots.

Data from the Future Aviation Professionals of America for 1996 show that commercial helicopter pilots averaged from $33,700 to $59,900 a year. Average pay for corporate helicopter pilots ranged from $47,900 to $72,500. Some helicopter pilots earned over $100,000 a year.

Airline pilots generally are eligible for life and health insurance plans financed by the airlines. They also receive retirement benefits and if they fail the FAA physical examination at some point in their careers, they get disability payments. In addition, pilots receive an expense allowance, or per diem, for every hour they are away from home. Per diem can represent up to $500 each month in addition to their salary. Some airlines also provide allowances to pilots for purchasing and cleaning their uniforms. As an additional benefit, pilots and their immediate families usually are entitled to free or reduced fare transportation on their own and other airlines.

Most airline pilots are members of unions. Most airline pilots are members of the Airline Pilots Association, International, but those employed by one major airline are members of the Allied Pilots Association. Some flight engineers are members of the Flight Engineers' International Association.

Related Occupations

Although they are not in the cockpit, air traffic controllers and dispatchers also play an important role in making sure flights are safe and on schedule, and participate in many of the decisions pilots must make.

Sources of Additional Information

Information about job opportunities, salaries for a particular airline and the qualifications required may be obtained by writing to the personnel manager of the airline.

For information on airline pilots, contact:
❑ Airline Pilots Association, 1625 Massachusetts Ave. NW, Washington, DC 20036.
❑ Air Transport Association of America, 1301 Pennsylvania Ave. NW, Suite 1110, Washington, DC 20006.

For information on helicopter pilots, contact:
❑ Helicopter Association International, 1619 Duke St., Alexandria, VA 22314.

For a copy of List of Certificated Pilot Schools, write to:
❑ Superintendent of Documents, U.S. Government Printing Office, Washington, DC 20402.

For information about job opportunities in companies other than airlines, consult the classified section of aviation trade magazines and apply to companies that operate aircraft at local airports.

Broadcast Technicians

(D.O.T. 193.167-014, .262-018, and -038; 194.062, .122, .262-010, -014, -018, -022, .282, .362, and .382-014, -018, 962.167-010, and .382-010)

Significant Points

★ *Competition is expected for the better paying jobs at radio and television stations serving large cities.*

★ *Beginners need formal training in broadcast technology to obtain their first job at a smaller station.*

★ *Evening, weekend, and holiday work is common.*

Nature of the Work

Broadcast technicians install, test, repair, set up, and operate the electronic equipment used to record and transmit radio and television programs. They work with television cameras, microphones, tape recorders, light and sound effects, transmitters, antennas, and other equipment. Some broadcast technicians develop movie sound tracks in motion picture production studios.

In the control room of a radio or television broadcasting studio, these technicians operate equipment that regulates the signal strength, clarity, and range of sounds and colors of recordings or broadcasts. They also operate control panels to select the source of the material. Technicians may switch from one camera or studio to another, from film to live programming, or from network to local programs. By means of hand signals and, in television, telephone headsets, they give technical directions to other studio personnel.

Broadcast technicians in small stations perform a variety of duties. In large stations and at the networks, technicians are more specialized, although job assignments may change from day to day. The terms "operator," "engineer," and "technician" often are used interchangeably to describe these jobs. Transmitter operators monitor and log outgoing signals and operate transmitters. Maintenance technicians set up, adjust, service, and repair electronic broadcasting equipment. Audio control engineers regulate sound pickup, transmission, and switching of television pictures, while video control engineers regulate their quality, brightness, and contrast. Recording engineers operate and maintain video and sound recording equipment. They may operate equipment designed to produce special effects, such as the illusions of a bolt of lightning or a police siren. Field technicians set up and operate broadcasting portable field transmission equipment outside the studio.

Television news coverage requires so much electronic equipment, and the technology is changing so fast, that many stations assign technicians exclusively to news. Chief engineers, transmission engineers, and broadcast field supervisors supervise the technicians who operate and maintain broadcasting equipment.

Technicians in the motion picture industry are called sound mixers or rerecording mixers. Mixers produce the sound track of a movie, using a process called dubbing. They sit at sound consoles facing the screen and fade in and fade out each sound and regulate its volume. Each technician is responsible for certain sounds. Technicians follow a script that tells at precisely what moment, as the film runs through the projector, each of the sounds must be faded in and out. All the sounds for each shot are thus blended on a master sound track.

Working Conditions

Broadcast technicians generally work indoors in pleasant surroundings. However, those who broadcast from disaster areas or crime scenes may work under unfavorable conditions. Technicians doing maintenance may climb poles or antenna towers, while those setting up equipment do heavy lifting.

Technicians in large stations and the networks usually work a 40-hour week, but may occasionally work overtime, under great pressure to meet broadcast deadlines. Technicians in small stations routinely work more than 40 hours a week. Evening, weekend, and holiday work is usual, because most stations are on the air 18 to 24 hours a day, seven days a week.

Those who work on motion pictures may be on a tight schedule to finish according to contract agreements.

Employment

Broadcast technicians held about 46,000 jobs in 1996. About seven out of ten broadcast technicians were in radio and television broadcasting. Almost two in ten worked in the motion picture industry. About 8 percent worked for cable and other pay television services. A few were self-employed. Television stations employ, on average, many more technicians than do radio stations. Some broadcast technicians are employed in other industries, producing employee communications, sales, and training programs. Technician jobs in television are located in virtually all cities, while jobs in radio are also found in many small towns. The highest paying and most specialized jobs are concentrated in New York City, Los Angeles, Chicago, and Washington, DC—the originating centers for most of network programs. Motion picture production jobs are concentrated in Los Angeles and New York City.

Training, Other Qualifications, and Advancement

The best way to prepare for a broadcast technician job in radio or television is to obtain technical school, community college, or college training in broadcast technology or in engineering or electronics. This is particularly true for those who hope to advance to supervisory positions or jobs at large stations or the networks. On the other hand, there is no formal training for jobs in the motion picture industry. People are hired as apprentice editorial assistants and work their way up to more skilled jobs. Employers in the motion picture industry usually hire freelance technicians on a picture-by-picture basis. Reputation, determination, and luck are important in getting jobs.

Beginners learn skills on the job from experienced technicians and supervisors. They generally begin their careers in small stations and, once experienced, move on to larger ones. Large stations generally only hire technicians with experience. Many employers pay tuition and expenses for courses or seminars to help technicians keep abreast of developments in the field.

The Federal Communications Commission no longer requires the licensing of broadcast technicians, as the Telecommunications Act of 1996 eliminated this licensing requirement. Certification by the Society of Broadcast Engineers is a mark of competence and experience. The certificate is issued to experienced technicians who pass an examination. By offering the Radio Operator and the Television Operator levels of certification, the Society of Broadcast Engineers has filled the void left by the elimination of the FCC license.

Prospective technicians should take high school courses in math, physics, and electronics. Building electronic equipment from hobby kits and operating a "ham," or amateur radio, are good experience, as is work in college radio and television stations.

Broadcast technicians must have manual dexterity and an aptitude for working with electrical, electronic, and mechanical systems and equipment.

Experienced technicians may become supervisory technicians or chief engineers. A college degree in engineering is needed to become chief engineer at a large TV station.

Job Outlook

People seeking beginning jobs as radio and television broadcast technicians are expected to face strong competition in major metropolitan areas, where the number of qualified job seekers greatly exceeds the number of openings. There, stations seek highly experienced personnel. Prospects for entry level positions generally are better in small cities and towns for people with appropriate training.

The overall employment of broadcast technicians is expected to grow about as fast as the average through the year 2006. Growth in the number of new radio and television stations and an increase in the number of programming hours should require additional technicians. However, employment growth in radio and television broadcasting may be tempered

somewhat because of labor-saving technical advances, such as computer-controlled programming and remote control of transmitters.

Employment in the cable industry should grow because of new products coming to market, such as cable modems, which deliver high speed Internet access to PCs, and digital set-top boxes, which transmit better sound and pictures, allowing cable operators to offer many more channels than in the past. These new products should cause traditional cable subscribers to sign up for additional services. Also, employment in the cable industry should grow, as today's young people establish their own households, for they are more accustomed to the idea of paying for TV than their parents.

Employment in the motion picture industry will grow faster than the average for all occupations. Job prospects are expected to remain competitive, because of the large number of people attracted to this relatively small field.

Virtually all job openings will result from the need to replace experienced technicians who leave the occupation. Turnover is relatively high for broadcast technicians. Many leave the occupation for electronic jobs in other areas, such as computer technology or commercial and industrial repair.

Earnings

Television stations usually pay higher salaries than radio stations; commercial broadcasting usually pays more than educational broadcasting; and stations in large markets pay more than those in small ones.

According to a survey conducted by the National Association of Broadcasters and the Broadcast Cable Financial Management Association, average earnings for technicians at radio stations were $30,251 a year in 1996. For chief engineer, average earnings were $46,602; and salaries ranged from $34,714 in the smallest markets to $46,602 in the largest markets. In television, average earnings for operator technicians were $24,260 a year and salaries ranged from $16,422 to $45,158; for technical directors, average earnings were $25,962 a year and the range was $18,444 to $44,531; for maintenance technicians, average earnings were $32,533 a year and the range was $24,210 to $50,235; and for chief engineers, the average earnings were $53,655 a year and salaries ranged from $38,178 in the smallest markets to $91,051 in the largest.

Earnings in the motion picture industry depend on skill and reputation and, based on limited information, range from $20,000 to $100,000 a year.

Related Occupations

Broadcast technicians need the electronics training and hand coordination necessary to operate technical equipment,

and they generally complete specialized postsecondary programs. Others with similar jobs and training include drafters, engineering and science technicians, surveyors, air traffic controllers, radiologic technologists, respiratory therapy workers, cardiovascular technologists and technicians, electroneurodiagnostic technicians, and clinical laboratory technologists and technicians.

Sources of Additional Information

For information on careers for broadcast technicians, write to:

❏ National Association of Broadcasters Employment Clearinghouse, 1771 N St. NW, Washington, DC 20036.

For a list of schools that offer programs or courses in broadcasting, contact:

❏ Broadcast Education Association, National Association of Broadcasters, 1771 N St. NW, Washington, DC 20036.

For information on certification, contact:

❏ Society of Broadcast Engineers, 8445 Keystone Crossing, Suite 140, Indianapolis, IN 46240.

For information on careers in the motion picture and television industry, contact:

❏ Society of Motion Picture and Television Engineers (SMPTE), 595 W. Hartsdale Ave., White Plains, NY 10607.

Cardiovascular Technologists and Technicians

(*D.O.T.* 078.264-010, .362-018, -030, -050, -062, .364-014, and .367-010)

Significant Points

✴ *Employment will grow as fast as the average, but the number of job openings created will be low because the occupation is small.*

✴ *More than nine out of ten jobs are in hospitals, in both inpatient and outpatient settings.*

Nature of the Work

Cardiovascular technologists and technicians assist physicians in diagnosing and treating cardiac (heart) and peripheral vascular (blood vessel) ailments.

Cardiovascular technicians who obtain electro- (electrical) cardio- (heart) grams (records) are known as electrocardiograph (abbreviated EKG or ECG) technicians. To take a basic EKG, which traces electrical impulses transmitted by the heart, technicians attach electrodes to the patient's chest, arms, and legs, and then manipulate switches on an electrocardiograph machine to obtain the reading. The test is done before most kinds of surgery and as part of a routine physical examination, especially for persons who have reached middle age or have a history of cardiovascular problems.

More skilled EKG technicians perform Holter monitor and stress testing. For a Holter monitoring, technicians place electrodes on the patient's chest and attach a portable EKG monitor to the patient's belt. Following 24–48 hours of normal routine for the patient, the technician removes a cassette tape from the monitor and places it in a scanner. After checking the quality of the recorded impulses on an electronic screen, the technician prints the information from the tape so it can be interpreted later. The printed output from the scanner is eventually used by a physician to diagnose heart ailments.

For a treadmill stress test, EKG technicians document the patient's medical history, explain the procedure, connect the patient to an EKG monitor, and obtain a baseline reading and resting blood pressure. Next, they monitor the heart's performance while the patient is walking on a treadmill, gradually increasing the treadmill's speed to observe the effect of increased exertion. Those cardiovascular technicians who perform EKG and stress tests are known as "noninvasive" technicians because the techniques they use do not require the insertion of probes or other instruments into the patient's body.

Cardiovascular technologists who specialize in cardiac catheterization procedures are called cardiology technologists. They assist physicians with invasive procedures in which a small tube, or catheter, is wound through a patient's blood vessel from a spot on the patient's leg into the heart to determine if a blockage exists or for other diagnostic purposes. In balloon angioplasty, a procedure used to treat blockages of blood vessels, technologists assist physicians who insert a catheter with a balloon on the end to the point of the obstruction. Technologists may prepare patients for these procedures by positioning them on an examining table and then shaving, cleaning, and administering anesthesia to the top of the patient's leg near the groin. During the procedures, they monitor patients' blood pressure and heart rate using EKG equipment, and notify the physician if something appears wrong. Technologists may also prepare and monitor patients during open heart surgery and the implantation of pacemakers.

Cardiovascular technologists and technicians may also specialize in noninvasive peripheral vascular tests. Those who assist physicians in the diagnosis of disorders affecting circulation are known as vascular technologists. Vascular technologists use ultrasound instrumentation, such as Doppler ultrasound, to noninvasively record information on the vessels such as blood pressure, limb volume changes, oxygen saturation, cerebral circulation, peripheral circulation, and abdominal circulation. Many of these tests are performed during or immediately after surgery. Technologists and technicians who use ultrasound on the heart are referred to as echocardiographers. They use ultrasound equipment that transmits sound waves and then collects the echoes to form an image on a screen.

Some cardiovascular technologists and technicians schedule appointments, type doctor's interpretations, maintain patient's files, and care for equipment.

Working Conditions

Technologists and technicians generally work a five-day, 40-hour week, which may include weekends. Those in catheterization labs tend to work longer hours and may work evenings. They may also be on call during the night and on weekends.

Cardiovascular technologists and technicians spend a lot of time walking and standing. Those who work in catheterization labs may face stressful working conditions, because they are in close contact with patients who have serious heart ailments. Some patients, for example, may encounter complications from time to time that have life or death implications.

Employment

Cardiovascular technologists and technicians held about 32,000 jobs in 1996. Most worked in hospital cardiology departments, while some worked in cardiologists' offices, cardiac rehabilitation centers, or ambulatory surgery centers. About one-half were EKG technicians.

Training, Other Qualifications, and Advancement

For basic EKGs, Holter monitoring, and stress testing, one-year certificate programs exist, although most EKG technicians are still trained on the job by an EKG supervisor or a cardiologist. On-the-job training usually lasts about 8 to 16 weeks, and applicants must be high school graduates. Most employers prefer to train people already in the health care field—nursing aides, for example. Some EKG technicians are students who are enrolled in two-year programs to become technologists, but work part-time to gain experience and make contact with employers.

Although some cardiovascular technologists, vascular technologists, and echocardiographers are currently trained on the job, more are being trained in two- to four-year programs. Cardiology technologists complete a two-year junior or community college program. One year is dedicated to core courses followed by a year of specialized instruction in either invasive, noninvasive, or noninvasive peripheral cardiology. Those who

© 1999 • J. Michael Farr • JIST Works, Inc. • Indianapolis, IN

are qualified in a related allied health profession only need to complete the year of specialized instruction. Graduates from programs accredited by the Joint Review Committee on Education in Cardiovascular Technology are eligible to register as professional technologists with the American Registry of Diagnostic Medical Sonographers or Cardiovascular Credentialing International.

Cardiovascular technologists and technicians must be reliable, have mechanical aptitude, and be able to follow detailed instructions. A pleasant, relaxed manner for putting patients at ease is an asset.

Job Outlook

Employment of cardiovascular technologists and technicians is expected to grow more slowly than the average for all occupations through the year 2006, with technologists and technicians experiencing different patterns of employment change. Employment of cardiology technologists is expected to grow faster than the average for all occupations. Growth will occur as the population ages, because older people have a higher incidence of heart problems. Likewise, employment of vascular technologists will grow faster than the average, as advances in vascular technology reduce the need for more costly and invasive procedures. In contrast, employment of EKG technicians is expected to decline as hospitals train registered nurses and others to perform basic EKG procedures. Individuals trained in Holter monitoring and stress testing are expected to have more favorable job prospects than those who can only perform a basic EKG.

Most job openings for cardiovascular technologists and technicians will arise from replacement needs as individuals transfer to other jobs or leave the labor force. Relatively few job openings due to both growth and replacement needs are expected, however, because the occupation is small.

Earnings

According to a Hay Group survey of acute care hospitals, the median annual base salary of full-time EKG technicians was $20,200 in January 1997. The middle 50 percent earned between $17,100 and $23,800 a year.

Based on limited information, the average salary for cardiovascular technologists was about $33,600 in 1996.

Related Occupations

Cardiovascular technologists and technicians operate sophisticated equipment that helps physicians and other health practitioners diagnose and treat patients. So do nuclear medicine technologists, radiologic technologists, diagnostic medical

sonographers, electroencephalographic technologists, perfusionists, and respiratory therapists.

Sources of Additional Information

Local hospitals can supply information about employment opportunities.

For general information about a career in cardiovascular technology, contact:

❑ Alliance of Cardiovascular Professionals, 910 Charles St., Fredericksburg, VA 22401.

For a list of accredited programs in cardiovascular technology, contact:

❑ Joint Review Committee on Education in Cardiovascular Technology, 3525 Ellicott Mills Dr., Suite N, Ellicott City, MD 21043-4547.

For information on vascular technology, contact:

❑ The Society of Vascular Technology, 4601 Presidents Dr., Suite 260, Lanham, MD 20706-4365.

For information on echocardiography, contact:

❑ American Society of Echocardiography, 4101 Lake Boone Trail, Suite 201, Raleigh, NC 27607.

For information regarding registration and certification contact:

❑ Cardiovascular Credentialing International, 4456 Corporation Lane, Suite 110, Virginia Beach, VA 23462.

❑ American Registry of Diagnostic Medical Sonographers, 600 Jefferson Plaza, Suite 360, Rockville, MD 20852-1150.

Computer and Office Machine Repairers

(*D.O.T.* 633.261-014, .281; 706.381-010 and -030)

Significant Points

✴ *Most employers prefer to hire persons who have completed one- or two-year formal training programs in electronics.*

✴ *Overall employment of computer and office machine repairers should increase rapidly.*

Nature of the Work

Computer and office machine repairers install equipment, do preventive maintenance, and correct problems. Computer repairers work on computers (mainframes, minis, and micros), peripheral equipment, and word processing systems, while office machine repairers work on photocopiers, cash registers, mail processing equipment, fax machines, and typewriters. Some repairers service both computer and office equipment. They also make cable and wiring connections when installing equipment, and work closely with electricians who install the wiring.

Even with preventive maintenance, computers and other machines break down. Repairers run diagnostic programs to locate malfunctions. Although some of the most modern and sophisticated computers have a self-diagnosing capacity that identifies problems, computer repairers must know enough about systems software to determine if the malfunction is in the hardware or in the software.

Working Conditions

Some computer and office machine repairers work shifts, including weekends and holidays, to service equipment in computer centers, manufacturing plants, hospitals, and telephone companies operating round the clock. Shifts are generally assigned on the basis of seniority. Repairers may also be on call at any time to handle equipment failure.

Computer and office machine repairers generally work in clean, well-lighted, air-conditioned surroundings. However, some may be exposed to heat, grease, and noise on factory floors. Some may occasionally have to work in cramped spaces.

The work of most computer and office machine repairers involves lifting, reaching, stooping, crouching, and crawling. Adherence to safety precautions is essential to guard against work hazards such as minor burns and electrical shock.

Employment

Computer and office machine repairers held about 141,000 jobs in 1996. Approximately 80,000 worked mainly on computer equipment, and the other 61,000 repaired mainly office machines. About three of every five were employed by wholesalers of computers and other office equipment, including the wholesaling divisions of equipment manufacturers, and by firms that provide maintenance services for a fee. Others worked for retail establishments and some with organizations that serviced their own equipment.

Repairers work throughout the country, even in relatively small communities. Most repairers, however, work in large cities, where computer and office equipment is concentrated.

Training, Other Qualifications, and Advancement

Most employers prefer applicants with formal training in electronics. Electronic training is offered by public post secondary vocational-technical schools, private vocational schools and technical institutes, junior and community colleges, and some high schools and correspondence schools. Programs take one to two years. The military services also offer formal training and work experience.

Training includes general courses in mathematics, physics, electricity, electronics, schematic reading, and troubleshooting. Students also choose courses which prepare them for a specialty, such as computers, commercial and industrial equipment, or home entertainment equipment. A few repairers complete formal apprenticeship programs sponsored jointly by employers and local chapters of the International Brotherhood of Electrical Workers.

Applicants for entry-level jobs may have to pass tests measuring mechanical aptitude, knowledge of electricity or electronics, manual dexterity, and general intelligence. Newly hired repairers, even those with formal training, usually receive some training from their employer. They may study electronics and circuit theory and math. They also get hands-on experience with equipment, doing basic maintenance and using diagnostic programs to locate malfunctions. Training may be in a classroom or it may be self-instruction, consisting of videotapes, programmed computer software, or workbooks that allow trainees to learn at their own pace.

Experienced computer and office machine repairers attend training sessions and read manuals to keep up with design changes and revised service procedures. Many also take advanced training in a particular system or type of repair.

Good eyesight and color vision are needed to inspect and work on small, delicate parts and good hearing to detect malfunctions revealed by sound. Because field repairers usually handle jobs alone, they must be able to work without close supervision. For those who have frequent contact with customers, a pleasant personality, neat appearance, and good communications skills are important. Computer and office machine repairers must also be trustworthy, because they may be exposed to money and other valuables in places such as banks and securities offices, and some employers require that they be bonded. A security clearance may be required for those who repair equipment or service machines in areas in which people are engaged in activities related to national security.

The International Society of Certified Electronics Technicians and the Electronics Technicians Association each administer a voluntary certification program. In both, an electronics repairer with four years of experience may become a Certified Electronics Technician. Certification, which is by examination, is offered in computer, radio-TV, industrial and commercial equipment, audio, avionics, wireless communications, video distribution, satellite, and radar systems repair. An Associate Level Test, covering basic electronics, is offered for students or repairers with less than four years of experience. An A+ certification is now desired for computer technicians. This certification is awarded by the Computing

Technology Industry Association (CompTIA) and requires knowledge of specific products manufactured by the vendor.

Experienced computer and office machine repairers with advanced training may become specialists or troubleshooters who help other repairers diagnose difficult problems, or work with engineers in designing equipment and developing maintenance procedures.

Because of their familiarity with equipment, computer and office machine repairers are particularly well qualified to become manufacturers' sales workers. Workers with leadership ability also may become maintenance supervisors or service managers. Some experienced workers open their own repair services or shops, or become wholesalers or retailers of electronic equipment.

Job Outlook

Employment of computer and office machine repairers is expected to grow much faster than the average for all occupations through the year 2006. However, employment of repairers will grow less rapidly than the anticipated increase in the amount of equipment because of the improved reliability of computer and office machines and ease of repair. Applicants for computer repairer positions will have the most favorable job prospects.

Employment of those who repair computers is expected to grow much faster than the average for all occupations. Demand for computer repairers will increase as the amount of computer equipment increases—organizations throughout the economy should continue to automate in search of greater productivity and improved service. The development of new computer applications and lower computer prices will also spur demand. More repairers will be needed to install new equipment coming on the market and upgrade existing systems.

Employment of those who repair office machines is expected to grow about as fast the average for all occupations. Slower growth in the amount of non-computer-based office equipment will somewhat dampen the demand for these repairers.

Earnings

In 1996, median weekly earnings of full-time computer and office machine repairers were $582.

According to a survey of workplaces in 160 metropolitan areas, beginning maintenance electronics technicians had median earnings of $11.50 an hour in 1995, with the middle half earning between $10.50 and $13.25 an hour. The most experienced repairers had median earnings of $20.13 an hour, with the middle half earning between $18.24 and $22.12 an hour.

Related Occupations

Workers in other occupations who repair and maintain the circuits and mechanical parts of electronic equipment include appliance and power tool repairers, automotive electricians, broadcast technicians, electronic organ technicians, and vending machine repairers. Electronics engineering technicians may also repair electronic equipment as part of their duties.

Sources of Additional Information

For career, and certification information, contact:
❏ The International Society of Certified Electronics Technicians, 2708 West Berry St., Fort Worth, TX 76109.

For certification, career, and placement information, contact:
❏ Electronics Technicians Association, 602 North Jackson, Greencastle, IN 46135.

For information on electronic equipment repairers in the telephone industry, write to:
❏ Communications Workers of America, Department of Apprenticeships, Benefits, and Employment, 501 3rd St. NW, Washington, DC 20001.

Construction and Building Inspectors

(*D.O.T.* 168.167-030, -034, -038, -046, and -050; .267-010, -102; 182.267; 850.387, .467)

Significant Points

✳ *Over 50 percent are employed by local governments, primarily municipal or county building departments.*

✳ *Construction and building inspectors tend to be older, more experienced workers who have spent years working in other related occupations.*

Nature of the Work

Construction and building inspectors examine the construction, alteration, or repair of buildings, highways and streets, sewer and water systems, dams, bridges, and other structures to ensure compliance with building codes and ordinances, zoning regulations, and contract specifications. Throughout the country, building codes and standards are the primary means by which building construction is regulated to assure the health and safety of the general public. Inspectors make an initial inspection during the first phase of construction, and follow-up inspections throughout the construction project to monitor compliance with regulations.

However, no inspection is ever exactly the same. In areas where certain types of severe weather or natural disasters are more common, inspectors monitor compliance with additional safety regulations designed to protect structures and occupants in these events.

Building inspectors inspect the structural quality and general safety of buildings. Some specialize—for example, in structural steel or reinforced concrete structures. Before construction begins, plan examiners determine whether the plans for the building or other structure comply with building code regulations, and if they are suited to the engineering and environmental demands of the building site. Inspectors visit the work site before the foundation is poured to inspect the soil condition and positioning and depth of the footings. Later, they return to the site to inspect the foundation after it has been completed. The size and type of structure and the rate of completion determine the number of other site visits they must make. Upon completion of the entire project, they make a final comprehensive inspection.

In addition to structural characteristics, a primary concern of building inspectors is fire safety. They inspect structure's fire sprinklers, alarms, and smoke control systems, as well as fire doors and exits. Inspectors assess the type of construction, building contents, adequacy of fire protection equipment, and risks posed by adjoining buildings.

There are many types of inspections and inspectors. Electrical inspectors examine the installation of electrical systems and equipment to ensure they function properly and comply with electrical codes and standards. They visit work sites to inspect new and existing sound and security systems, wiring, lighting, motors, and generating equipment. They also inspect the installation of the electrical wiring for heating and air-conditioning systems, appliances, and other components.

Elevator inspectors examine lifting and conveying devices such as elevators, escalators, moving sidewalks, lifts and hoists, inclined railways, ski lifts, and amusement rides.

Mechanical inspectors inspect the installation of the mechanical components of commercial kitchen appliances, heating and air-conditioning equipment, gasoline and butane tanks, gas and oil piping, and gas-fired and oil-fired appliances. Some specialize in boilers or ventilating equipment as well.

Plumbing inspectors examine plumbing systems, including private disposal systems, water supply and distribution systems, plumbing fixtures and traps, and drain, waste, and vent lines.

Public works inspectors ensure that federal, state, and local government construction of water and sewer systems, highways, streets, bridges, and dams conforms to detailed contract specifications. They inspect excavation and fill operations, the placement of forms for concrete, concrete mixing and pouring, asphalt paving, and grading operations. They record the work and materials used so contract payments can be calculated. Public works inspectors may specialize in highways, structural steel, reinforced concrete, or ditches. Others specialize in dredging operations required for bridges and dams or for harbors.

Home inspectors generally conduct inspections of newly built or previously owned homes. Increasingly, prospective home buyers hire home inspectors to inspect and report the condition of a home's major systems, components, and structure. They are typically hired either immediately prior to a purchase offer on a home, or as a contingency to a sales contract. In addition to structural quality, home inspectors must be able to inspect all home systems and features, from plumbing, electrical, and heating or cooling systems to roofing.

Specification inspectors are employed by the owner of a building or structure under construction to ensure work is done according to design specifications. They represent the owners' interests, not the general public. These inspectors may also be utilized by insurance companies or financial institutions.

Details concerning construction projects, building and occupancy permits, and other documentation are generally stored on computers so they can easily be retrieved and kept accurate and up to date. For example, inspectors may use laptop computers to record their findings while inspecting a site. Most inspectors use computers to help them monitor the status of construction inspection activities and keep track of issued permits.

Although inspections are primarily visual, most inspectors, except home inspectors, may use tape measures, survey instruments, metering devices, and test equipment such as concrete strength measurers. They keep a log of their work, take photographs, file reports, and, if necessary, act on their findings. For example, construction inspectors notify the construction contractor, superintendent, or supervisor when they discover a code or ordinance violation or something that does not comply with the contract specifications or approved plans. If the problem is not corrected within a reasonable or specified period of time, government inspectors have authority to issue a "stop-work" order.

Many inspectors also investigate construction or alterations being done without proper permits. Inspectors who are employees of municipalities enforce laws pertaining to the proper design, construction, and use of buildings. They direct violators of permit laws to obtain permits and submit to inspection.

Working Conditions

Construction and building inspectors usually work alone. However, several may be assigned to large, complex projects, particularly because inspectors tend to specialize in different areas of construction. Though they spend considerable time inspecting construction work sites, inspectors may spend much of their time in a field office reviewing blueprints, answering letters or telephone calls, writing reports, and scheduling inspections.

Inspection sites are dirty and may be cluttered with tools, materials, or debris. Inspectors may have to climb ladders or many flights of stairs, or may have to crawl around in tight spaces. Although their work is not generally considered hazardous, inspectors, like other construction workers, wear hard hats and adhere to other safety requirements while at a construction site.

Inspectors normally work regular hours. However, if an accident occurs at a construction site, inspectors must respond immediately and may work additional hours to complete their report.

Employment

Construction and building inspectors held about 66,000 jobs in 1996. Over 50 percent worked for local governments, primarily municipal or county building departments. Employment of local government inspectors is concentrated in cities and in suburban areas undergoing rapid growth. Local governments employ large inspection staffs, including many plan examiners or inspectors who specialize in structural steel, reinforced concrete, boiler, electrical, and elevator inspection.

Another 19 percent of all construction and building inspectors worked for engineering and architectural services firms, conducting inspections for a fee or on a contract basis. Most of the remaining inspectors were employed by the federal and state governments. Many construction inspectors employed by the federal government work for the U.S. Army Corps of Engineers. Other federal employers include the Tennessee Valley Authority and the Departments of Agriculture, Housing and Urban Development, and Interior.

Training, Other Qualifications, and Advancement

Although requirements vary considerably depending upon where one is employed, individuals who want to become construction and building inspectors should have a thorough knowledge of construction materials and practices in either a general area, such as structural or heavy construction, or in a specialized area, such as electrical or plumbing systems, reinforced concrete, or structural steel. Construction or building inspectors need several years of experience as a manager, supervisor, or craft worker before becoming inspectors. Many previously worked as carpenters, electricians, plumbers, or pipefitters.

Because inspectors need to posses the right mix of technical knowledge, experience, and education, employers prefer to hire inspectors who have formal training, as well as experience. Most require at least a high school diploma or equivalent even for those with considerable experience. More often, employers look for persons who have studied engineering or architecture, or who have a degree from a community or junior college, with courses in construction technology, drafting, mathematics, and building inspection. Many community colleges offer certificate or associate degree programs in building inspection technology. Courses in blueprint reading, algebra, geometry, and English are also useful.

Construction and building inspectors must be in good physical condition in order to walk and climb about construction sites. They must also have a driver's license. In addition, federal, state, and many local governments may require that inspectors pass a civil service examination.

Construction and building inspectors usually receive much of their training on the job, although they must often learn building codes and standards on their own. Working with an experienced inspector, they learn about inspection techniques; codes, ordinances, and regulations; contract specifications; and record keeping and reporting duties. They may begin by inspecting less complex types of construction, such as residential buildings, and then progress to more difficult assignments. An engineering or architectural degree is often required for advancement to supervisory positions.

Because they advise builders and the general public on building codes, construction practices, and technical developments, construction and building inspectors must keep abreast of changes in these areas. Continuing education is imperative in this ever-changing field. Many employers provide formal training programs to broaden inspectors' knowledge of construction materials, practices, and techniques. Inspectors who work for small agencies or firms that do not conduct training programs can expand their knowledge and upgrade their skills by attending state-sponsored training programs, by taking college or correspondence courses, or by attending seminars sponsored by various related organizations such as model code organizations.

Most states and cities require some type of certification for employment and, even if not required, certification can enhance an inspector's opportunities for employment and advancement to more responsible positions. To become certified, inspectors with substantial experience and education must pass stringent examinations on code requirements, construction techniques, and materials. The three major model code organizations offer voluntary certification as do other professional membership associations. In most cases, there are no education or experience prerequisites, and certification consists of passing an examination in a designated field. Many categories of certification are awarded for inspectors and plan examiners in a variety of disciplines, including the designation *CBO*, Certified Building Official.

Job Outlook

Employment of construction and building inspectors is expected to grow as fast as the average for all occupations through the year 2006. Growing concern for public safety and improvements in the quality of construction should continue to stimulate demand for construction and building inspectors. Despite the expected employment growth, most job openings will arise from the need to replace inspectors who transfer to other occupations or leave the labor force. Construction and building inspectors tend to be older, more experienced workers who have spent years working in other occupations.

Opportunities should be best for highly experienced supervisors and craft workers who have some college education, engineering or architectural training, or who are certified as inspectors or plan examiners. Thorough knowledge of construction practices and skills in areas such as reading and evaluating blueprints and plans are essential. However, inspectors are involved in all phases of construction, including maintenance and repair work, and are therefore less likely to lose jobs during recessionary periods when new construction slows. As the population grows and the volume of real estate transactions increases, greater emphasis on home inspections should result in rapid growth in employment of home inspectors. In addition, there should be good opportunities in engineering, architectural, and management services firms due to the tendency of governments—particularly the federal and state—to contract out inspection work, as well as expected growth in private inspection services.

Earnings

The median annual salary of construction and building inspectors was about $33,700 in 1996. The middle 50 percent earned between $26,500 and $45,800. The lowest 10 percent earned less than $21,600 and the highest 10 percent earned more than $55,800 a year. Generally, building inspectors, including plan examiners, earn the highest salaries. Salaries in large metropolitan areas are substantially higher than those in small local jurisdictions.

Related Occupations

Construction and building inspectors combine a knowledge of construction principles and law with an ability to coordinate data, diagnose problems, and communicate with people. Workers in other occupations using a similar combination of skills include engineers, drafters, estimators, industrial engineering technicians, surveyors, architects, and construction managers.

Sources of Additional Information

Information about certification and a career as a construction or building inspector is available from the following model code organizations:

❏ International Conference of Building Officials, 5360 Workman Mill Rd., Whittier, CA 90601-2298. Homepage: http://www.icbo.org

❏ Building Officials and Code Administrators International, Inc., 4051 West Flossmoor Rd., Country Club Hills, IL 60478. Homepage: http://www.bocai.org

❏ Southern Building Code Congress International, Inc., 900 Montclair Rd., Birmingham, AL 35213.

Information about a career as a home inspector is available from:

❏ American Society of Home Inspectors, Inc., 85 West Algonquin Rd., Arlington Heights, IL 60005. Homepage: http://www.ashi.com

For information about a career as a state or local government construction or building inspector, contact your state or local employment service.

Cost Estimators

(*D.O.T.* 169.267-038; 221.362-018, and .367-014)

Significant Points

✱ *Growth of the construction industry, where over 60 percent of all cost estimators are employed, will be the driving force behind the demand for these workers.*

✱ *Job prospects in construction should be best for those workers with a degree in construction management or construction science, engineering, or architectural drafting, who have experience in various phases of construction or a specialty craft area.*

Nature of the Work

Accurately predicting the cost of future projects is vital to the survival of any business. Cost estimators develop cost information for owners or managers to use in determining

resource and material quantities, making bids for contracts, determining if a new product will be profitable, or determining which products are making a profit for a firm.

Regardless of the industry in which they work, estimators compile and analyze data on all the factors that can influence costs—such as materials, labor, location, and special machinery requirements, including computer hardware and software. Job duties vary widely depending upon the type and size of the project. Those with an engineering background who apply scientific principles and methods to undertake feasibility studies, value engineering, and life-cycle costing may be referred to as cost engineers.

The methods of and motivations for estimating costs can vary greatly, depending on the industry. On a large construction project, for example, the estimating process begins with the decision to submit a bid. After reviewing the architect's drawings and specifications, the estimator visits the site of the proposed project. The estimator needs to gather information on access to the site and availability of electricity, water, and other services, as well as surface topography and drainage. The information developed during the site visit generally is recorded in a signed report that is made part of the final project estimate.

After the site visit is completed, the estimator determines the quantity of materials and labor the firm will have to furnish. This process, called the quantity survey or "takeoff," involves completing standard estimating forms, filling in dimensions, number of units, and other information. A cost estimator working for a general contractor, for example, will estimate the costs of all items the contractor must provide. Although subcontractors will estimate their costs as part of their own bidding process, the general contractor's cost estimator often analyzes bids made by subcontractors as well. Also during the takeoff process, the estimator must make decisions concerning equipment needs, sequence of operations, and crew size. Allowances for the waste of materials, inclement weather, shipping delays, and other factors that may increase costs must also be incorporated in the takeoff.

On completion of the quantity surveys, the chief estimator prepares a total project cost summary, including the costs of labor, equipment, materials, subcontracts, overhead, taxes, insurance, markup, and any other costs that may affect the project. The chief estimator then prepares the bid proposal for submission to the developer.

Construction cost estimators may also be employed by the project's architect or owner to estimate costs or track actual costs relative to bid specifications as the project develops. In large construction companies employing more than one estimator, it is common practice for estimators to specialize.

For instance, one may estimate only electrical work and another may concentrate on excavation, concrete, and forms.

In manufacturing and other firms, cost estimators generally are assigned to the engineering, cost, or pricing departments. The estimators' goal in manufacturing is to accurately estimate the costs associated with making products. The job may begin when management requests an estimate of the costs associated with a major redesign of an existing product or the development of a new product or production process. When estimating the cost of developing a new product, for example, the estimator works with engineers, first reviewing blueprints or conceptual drawings to determine the machining operations, tools, gauges, and materials that would be required for the job. The estimator then prepares a parts list and determines whether it is more efficient to produce or to purchase the parts. To do this, the estimator must initiate inquiries for price information from potential suppliers. The next step is to determine the cost of manufacturing each component of the product. Some high technology products require a tremendous amount of computer programming during the design phase. The cost of software development is one of the fastest growing and most difficult activities to estimate. Some cost estimators now specialize in only estimating computer software development and related costs.

The cost estimator then prepares time-phase charts and learning curves. Time-phase charts indicate the time required for tool design and fabrication, tool debugging—finding and correcting all problems—manufacturing of parts, assembly, and testing. Learning curves graphically represent the rate at which performance improves with practice. These curves are commonly called "cost reduction" curves because many problems—such as engineering changes, rework, parts shortages, and lack of operator skills—diminish as the number of parts produced increases, resulting in lower unit costs.

Using all of this information, the estimator then calculates the standard labor hours necessary to produce a predetermined number of units. Standard labor hours are then converted to dollar values, to which are added factors for waste, overhead, and profit to yield the unit cost in dollars. The estimator then compares the cost of purchasing parts with the firm's cost of manufacturing them to determine which is cheaper.

Computers play an integral role in cost estimating today, because estimating may involve complex mathematical calculations and require advanced mathematical techniques. For example, to undertake a parametric analysis, a process used to estimate project costs on a per unit basis subject to the specific requirements of a project, cost estimators use a computer database containing information on costs and conditions of many other similar projects. Although computers cannot be used for the entire estimating process, they can relieve estimators of much of the drudgery associated with routine, repetitive, and time-consuming calculations. Computers are also used to produce all of the necessary documentation with the help of basic word-processing and spreadsheet software. This leaves estimators with more time to study and analyze projects and can lead to more accurate estimates.

Working Conditions

Although estimators spend most of their time in an office, construction estimators must make frequent visits to project work sites that are dirty and cluttered with debris. Likewise, estimators in manufacturing must spend time on the factory floor where it also can be noisy and dirty. In some industries, frequent travel between a firm's headquarters and its subsidiaries or subcontractors also may be required.

Although estimators normally work a 40-hour week, overtime is common. Cost estimators usually operate under pressure, especially when facing deadlines. Inaccurate estimating can cause a firm to lose out on a bid or lose money on a job that proves to be unprofitable.

Employment

Cost estimators held about 188,000 jobs in 1996, over 60 percent of which were in the construction industry. Another 26 percent were employed in manufacturing industries. The remainder worked for engineering and architectural services firms, business services firms, and throughout a wide range of other industries. Operations research, production control, cost, and price analysts who work for government agencies may also do significant amounts of cost estimating in the course of their regular duties. In addition, the duties of construction managers may also include estimating costs.

Cost estimators work throughout the country, usually in or near major industrial, commercial, and government centers, and in cities and suburban areas undergoing rapid change or development.

Training, Other Qualifications, and Advancement

Entry requirements for cost estimators vary by industry. In the construction industry, employers increasingly prefer individuals with a degree in building construction, construction management, construction science, civil engineering, or architectural drafting. However, most construction estimators also have considerable construction experience. Applicants with a thorough knowledge of construction materials, costs, and procedures in areas ranging from heavy construction to electrical work, plumbing systems, or masonry work have a competitive edge.

In manufacturing industries, employers prefer to hire individuals with a degree in engineering, physical science, operations research, mathematics, or statistics, or in accounting, finance, business, economics, or a related subject. In most industries, great emphasis is placed on experience involving quantitative techniques.

Cost estimators should have an aptitude for mathematics, be able to quickly analyze, compare, and interpret detailed and sometimes poorly defined information, and be able to make sound and accurate judgments based on this knowledge. Assertiveness and self-confidence in presenting and supporting their conclusions are important, as are strong communications and interpersonal skills, because estimators may work as part of a project team alongside other managers as well as owners, engineers, and design professionals. Cost estimators also need to be at ease with computers and their application in the estimating process, including word-processing and spreadsheet packages used to produce necessary documentation. In some instances, familiarity with special estimation software or programming skills may be required.

Regardless of their background, estimators receive much training on the job; almost every company has its own way of handling estimates. Working with an experienced estimator, they become familiar with each step in the process. Those with no experience reading construction specifications or blueprints first learn that aspect of the work. They then may accompany an experienced estimator to the construction site or shop floor where they observe the work being done, take measurements, or perform other routine tasks. As they become more knowledgeable, estimators learn how to tabulate quantities and dimensions from drawings and how to select the appropriate material prices.

For most estimators, advancement takes the form of higher pay and prestige. Some move into management positions, such as project manager for a construction firm or manager of the industrial engineering department for a manufacturer. Others may go into business for themselves as consultants, providing estimating services for a fee to government or construction and manufacturing firms.

Many colleges and universities include cost estimating as part of bachelor and associate degree-level curriculums in civil engineering, industrial engineering, and construction management or construction engineering technology. In addition, cost estimating is a significant part of master's degree programs in construction science or construction management offered by many colleges and universities. Organizations representing cost estimators, such as American Association of Cost

Engineers (AACE) International and the Society of Cost Estimating and Analysis, also sponsor educational and professional development programs. These programs help students, estimators-in-training, and experienced estimators stay abreast of changes affecting the profession. Specialized courses and programs in cost estimating techniques and procedures are also offered by many technical schools, community colleges, and universities.

Voluntary certification can be valuable to cost estimators, because it provides professional recognition of the estimator's competence and experience. In some instances, individual employers may even require professional certification for employment. Both AACE International and the Society of Cost Estimating and Analysis administer certification programs. To become certified, estimators generally must have between three and seven years of estimating experience and must pass both a written and an oral examination. In addition, certification requirements may include publication of at least one article or paper in the field.

Job Outlook

Overall employment of cost estimators is expected to grow about as fast as average for all occupations through the year 2006. Given the fact that no new projects in construction, manufacturing, or other industries are undertaken without careful analysis and estimation of the costs involved, job opportunities should remain favorable. Even when construction and manufacturing activity decline, there should always remain a demand for cost estimators. In addition to openings created by growth, some job openings will also arise from the need to replace workers who transfer to other occupations or leave the labor force.

Growth of the construction industry, where over 60 percent of all cost estimators are employed, will be the driving force behind the demand for these workers. The fastest growing sectors of the construction industry are expected to be special trade contractors and those associated with heavy construction and spending on the nation's infrastructure. Construction and repair of highways and streets, bridges, and construction of more subway systems, airports, water and sewage systems, and electric power plants and transmission lines will stimulate demand for many more cost estimators. Job prospects in construction should be best for those workers with a degree in construction management or construction science, engineering, or architectural drafting, who have experience in various phases of construction or a specialty craft area.

Employment of cost estimators in manufacturing should remain relatively stable as firms continue to use their services to identify and control their operating costs. Experienced estimators with degrees in engineering, science, mathematics, business administration, or economics and who have computer expertise should have the best job prospects in manufacturing.

Earnings

Salaries of cost estimators vary widely by experience, education, size of firm, and industry. According to limited available data, most starting salaries in the construction industry for cost estimators with limited training were between about $20,000 and $30,000 a year in 1996. College graduates with degrees in fields such as engineering or construction management that provide a strong background in cost estimating could start at a higher level. According to a 1997 salary survey by the National Association of Colleges and Employers, bachelor's degree candidates with degrees in construction science received offers averaging $31,949 a year. Bachelor's degree candidates with degrees in construction management received offers averaging $28,060 a year. Highly experienced cost estimators earned $75,000 a year or more. Starting salaries and annual earnings in the manufacturing sector were usually somewhat higher.

Related Occupations

Other workers who quantitatively analyze information in a similar capacity include appraisers, cost accountants, auditors, budget analysts, cost engineers, economists, financial analysts, loan officers, operations research analysts, underwriters, and value engineers. In addition, the duties of production managers and construction managers may also involve analyzing costs.

Sources of Additional Information

Information about career opportunities, certification, educational programs, and cost estimating techniques may be obtained from:

❏ AACE International, 209 Prairie Ave., Suite 100, Morgantown, WV 26505. Homepage: http://www.aacei.org

❏ Professional Construction Estimators Association of America, P.O. Box 11626, Charlotte, NC 28220-1626.

❏ Society of Cost Estimating and Analysis, 101 S. Whiting St., Suite 201, Alexandria, VA 22304. Homepage: http://www.erols.com/scea/ http://www.erols.com/scea/

Court Reporters, Medical Transcriptionists, and Stenographers

(D.O.T. 202.362, .382-010, and 203.582-058)

Significant Points

* A high school diploma is sufficient for stenographers; employers prefer medical transcriptionists who have completed a vocational school or community college program; and court reporters generally complete a two- or four-year postsecondary school program.

* Overall employment is projected to grow more slowly than average, as growth among medical transcriptionists is offset by the decline among stenographers. Certified medical transcriptionists and court reporters should have the best prospects.

* Court reporters generally earn higher salaries than stenographers or medical transcriptionists.

Nature of the Work

Court reporters and stenographers take verbatim reports of speeches, conversations, legal proceedings, meetings, or other events when written accounts of spoken words are necessary for correspondence, records, or legal proof. Medical transcriptionists translate and edit recorded dictation by physicians and other healthcare providers regarding patient assessment and treatment.

Court reporters document all statements made in an official proceeding using a stenotype machine, and present their record as the official transcript. Because there is only one person creating an official transcript, accuracy is vitally important.

Although many court reporters record official proceedings in the courtroom, most court reporters work outside the courtroom. Freelance reporters take depositions for attorneys in offices, and document proceedings of meetings, conventions, and other private activities. Others capture the proceedings in the U.S. Congress, state and local governing bodies, and government agencies at all levels.

Court reporters use stenotype machines, which allow them to press more than one key at a time to record combinations of letters representing sounds, words, or phrases. The symbols are then recorded on computer disks. The disks are loaded into a computer that translates and displays the symbols in English—this is called computer-aided transcription. Stenotype machines that link directly to the computer are used for

real-time captioning. That is, as the reporter keys in the symbols, they are instantly transcribed by the computer. This is used for closed captioning for the deaf or hearing-impaired on television, or in courts, classrooms, or meetings. Court reporters who specialize in captioning live television programming are commonly known as stenocaptioners, and work for television networks or cable stations captioning news, emergency broadcasts, sporting events, and other programming.

Using a transcribing machine with headset and foot pedal, medical transcriptionists listen to recordings by physicians and other health care professionals dictating a variety of medical reports such as emergency room visits, diagnostic imaging studies, operations, chart reviews, and final summaries. To understand and accurately transcribe dictated reports into a format that is clear and comprehensible for the reader, the medical transcriptionist must understand the language of medicine, anatomy and physiology, diagnostic procedures, and treatment, and must be able to translate medical jargon and abbreviations into their expanded forms. Editing as necessary for grammar and clarity, the medical transcriptionist transcribes the dictated reports and returns them in either printed or electronic form to the dictator for review and signature, or correction. These reports eventually become a part of the patient's permanent file. (Medical secretaries may also transcribe as part of their jobs.)

Stenographers take dictation and then transcribe their notes on a word processor or onto a computer diskette. They may take dictation using either shorthand or a stenotype machine, which prints shorthand symbols. General stenographers, including most beginners, take routine dictation and perform other office tasks such as typing, filing, answering telephones, and operating office machines. Experienced and highly skilled stenographers take more difficult dictation. For example, they attend staff meetings and provide word-for-word records or summary reports of the proceedings to the participants. They also supervise other stenographers, typists, and clerical workers. Some experienced stenographers take dictation in foreign languages; others work as public stenographers serving traveling business people and others. Technical stenographers must know the medical, legal, engineering, or scientific terminology used in a particular profession.

Working Conditions

Court reporters work in the offices of attorneys, courtrooms, legislatures, and conventions. Transcriptionists work in hospitals, doctors' offices, or medical transcription services. An increasing number of court reporters and medical transcriptionists work from home-based offices as subcontractors for law firms, hospitals, and transcription services. Stenogra-

© 1999 • J. Michael Farr • JIST Works, Inc. • Indianapolis, IN

phers usually work in clean, well-lighted offices. Sitting in the same position for long periods can be tiring, and workers can suffer wrist, back, neck, or eye problems due to strain, and risk repetitive motion injuries such as carpal tunnel syndrome. The pressure to be accurate and fast can also be stressful.

Many court reporters, medical transcriptionists, and stenographers work a standard 40-hour week, although about one in four works part-time. A substantial number of court reporters and medical transcriptionists, however, are self-employed, which may result in irregular working hours.

Employment

Court reporters, medical transcriptionists, and stenographers held 98,000 jobs in 1996. More than one in four was self-employed. Of those who worked for a wage or salary, about one-third worked for state and local governments, a reflection of the large number of court reporters working in courts, legislatures, and various agencies. About one-fourth worked for hospitals and physicians' offices. Other stenographers and court reporters worked for colleges and universities, secretarial and court reporting services, temporary help supply services, and law firms.

Training, Other Qualifications, and Advancement

Court reporters generally complete a two- or four-year training program, offered by about 300 postsecondary vocational and technical schools and colleges. About 110 programs have been approved by the National Court Reporters Association (NCRA), all of which teach computer-aided transcription and real-time reporting. NCRA-approved programs require students to capture 225 words per minute. Court reporters in the federal government generally must capture at least 205 words a minute.

Some states require court reporters to be notary publics, or to be a Certified Court Reporter (CCR); reporters must pass a state certification test administered by a board of examiners to earn this designation. The National Court Reporters Association confers the designation, Registered Professional Reporter (RPR), upon those who pass a two-part examination and participate in continuing education programs. Although voluntary, the RPR designation is recognized as a mark of distinction in this field.

For medical transcriptionist jobs, understanding medical terminology is essential. Good English grammar and punctuation skills are required, as well as familiarity with personal computers and word processing software. Good listening skills are also necessary, because some doctors and health care professionals speak English as a second language.

Employers prefer to hire transcriptionists who have completed postsecondary training in medical transcription, offered by many vocational schools and community colleges. Completion of a two-year associate degree program—including course work in anatomy, medical terminology, medicolegal issues, and English grammar and punctuation—is highly recommended. Many of these programs include supervised on-the-job experience. The American Association for Medical Transcription awards the voluntary designation Certified Medical Transcriptionist (CMT) to those who earn passing scores on written and practical examinations. As in many other fields, certification is recognized as a sign of competence in medical transcription. To retain this credential, CMTs must obtain at least 30 continuing education credits every three years.

Stenographic skills are taught in high schools, vocational schools, community colleges, and proprietary business schools. For stenographer jobs, employers prefer to hire high school graduates, and seldom have a preference among the many different shorthand methods. Although requirements vary in private firms, applicants with the best speed and accuracy usually receive first consideration in hiring. To qualify for jobs in the federal government, stenographers must be able to take dictation at a minimum of 80 words per minute and type at least 40 words per minute. Workers must achieve higher rates to advance to more responsible positions.

Stenographers can advance to more responsible secretarial positions, especially if they develop their interpersonal and communication skills. Some stenographers complete the necessary education to become court reporters.

Job Outlook

Overall employment of court reporters, medical transcriptionists, and stenographers is projected to grow more slowly than the average for all occupations. Employment growth among medical transcriptionists should be offset by the decline among stenographers, and the number of court reporters should remain fairly stable.

Demand for medical transcriptionists is expected to increase with growth in the need for health care and the industries that provide it. Growing numbers of medical transcriptionists will be needed to amend patients' records, edit for grammar, and discover discrepancies in medical records. Those who earn an associate degree or American Association for Medical Transcription certification should have favorable job prospects.

Employment of court reporters should be stable. The growing number of conventions, conferences, depositions, seminars, and similar meetings in which proceedings are recorded should create demand for court reporters. Although many of these events are videotaped, a written transcript must still be created for legal purposes or if the proceedings are to be published. Also, the trend to provide instantaneous written captions for the deaf and hearing impaired should strengthen demand for stenocaptioners. In addition, demand should grow for court reporters willing to freelance or take depositions for court reporting service bureaus. However, budget constraints should limit the ability of federal, state, and local courts to expand, even in the face of rising numbers of criminal court cases and civil lawsuits. Competition for entry-level jobs is increasing, as more workers are attracted to the occupation. Opportunities should be best for those who earn National Court Reporters Association certification.

The widespread use of dictation machines has greatly reduced the need for office stenographers. The traditional "steno pool" is almost a thing of the past. Audio recording equipment and the use of personal computers by managers and other professionals should continue to greatly decrease the demand for these workers.

Earnings

Court reporters, medical transcriptionists, and stenographers had median earnings of about $410 a week in 1996. The middle 50 percent earned between $340 and $550; the lowest paid 10 percent earned less than $280; and the highest paid 10 percent earned over $840 a week.

Court reporters generally earn higher salaries than stenographers or medical transcriptionists, and many supplement their income by doing additional freelance work. According to a National Court Reporters Association survey of its members, average earnings for court reporters were about $1,080 per week in 1995. According to a 1996 survey by the American Association for Medical Transcription, over four out of ten members earned less than $25,000 a year, more than three out of ten earned between $25,000 and $35,000, and over two out of ten earned over $35,000. Regardless of specialty, earnings depend on education, experience, and geographic location.

Related Occupations

A number of other workers type, record information, and process paperwork. Among these are bookkeepers, receptionists, secretaries, personnel clerks, administrative assistants, and medical assistants.

Sources of Additional Information

For information about careers, training, and certification in court reporting, contact:

❏ National Court Reporters Association, 8224 Old Courthouse Rd., Vienna, VA 22182. Homepage: http://www.verbatimreporters.com

For information on a career as a medical transcriptionist, visit AAMT's Internet site or send a self-addressed, stamped envelope to:

❏ American Association for Medical Transcription, P.O. Box 576187, Modesto, CA 95357. Homepage: http://www.aamt.org/aamt

For information about job openings for stenographers, contact state employment service offices.

Dental Hygienists

(D.O.T. 078.361-010)

Significant Points

✳ *Dental hygienists are projected to be one of the 20 fastest growing occupations.*

✳ *Job opportunities should continue to be good if graduates of dental hygiene programs do not increase greatly in number.*

✳ *Part-time work and flexible schedules are common.*

Nature of the Work

Dental hygienists clean teeth and provide other preventive dental care, as well as teach patients how to practice good oral hygiene. Hygienists examine patients' teeth and gums, recording the presence of diseases or abnormalities. They remove calculus, stains, and plaque from teeth; take and develop dental x rays; and apply cavity preventive agents such as fluorides and pit and fissure sealants. In some states, hygienists administer local anesthetics and anesthetic gas; place and carve filling materials, temporary fillings, and periodontal dressings; remove sutures; and smooth and polish metal restorations.

Dental hygienists also help patients develop and maintain good oral health. For example, they may explain the relationship between diet and oral health, inform patients how to select toothbrushes, and show patients how to brush and floss their teeth.

Dental hygienists use hand and rotary instruments to clean teeth, x-ray machines to take dental pictures, syringes with needles to administer local anesthetics, and models of teeth to explain oral hygiene.

Working Conditions

Flexible scheduling is a distinctive feature of this job. Full-time, part-time, evening, and weekend work is widely available.

Dentists frequently hire hygienists to work only two or three days a week, so hygienists may hold jobs in more than one dental office.

Dental hygienists work in clean, well-lighted offices. Important health safeguards include strict adherence to proper radiological procedures, and use of appropriate protective devices when administering anesthetic gas. Dental hygienists also wear safety glasses, surgical masks and gloves to protect themselves from infectious diseases, such as hepatitis.

Employment

Dental hygienists held about 133,000 jobs in 1996. Because multiple job holding is common in this field, the number of jobs greatly exceeds the number of hygienists. More than half of all dental hygienists worked part-time—less than 35 hours a week.

Almost all dental hygienists work in private dental offices. Some work in public health agencies, hospitals, and clinics.

Training, Other Qualifications, and Advancement

Dental hygienists must be licensed by the state in which they practice. To qualify for licensure, a candidate must graduate from an accredited dental hygiene school and pass both a written and clinical examination. The American Dental Association Joint Commission on National Dental Examinations administers the written examination that is accepted by all states and the District of Columbia. State or regional testing agencies administer the clinical examination. In addition, examinations on legal aspects of dental hygiene practice are required by most states. Alabama allows candidates to take its examination if they have been trained through a state-regulated on-the-job program in a dentist's office.

In 1997, 230 programs in dental hygiene were accredited by the Commission on Dental Accreditation. Although some programs lead to a bachelor's degree, most grant an associate degree. Twelve universities offer master's degree programs in dental hygiene or a related area.

An associate degree is sufficient for practice in a private dental office. A bachelor's or master's degree is usually required for research, teaching, or clinical practice in public or school health programs.

About half of the dental hygiene programs prefer applicants who have completed at least one year of college. Some of the bachelor's degree programs require applicants to have completed two years. However, requirements vary from school to school. These schools offer laboratory, clinical, and classroom instruction in subjects such as anatomy, physiology,

chemistry, microbiology, pharmacology, nutrition, radiography, histology (the study of tissue structure), periodontology (the study of gum diseases), pathology, dental materials, clinical dental hygiene, and social and behavioral sciences.

Dental hygienists should work well with others and must have good manual dexterity because they use dental instruments with little room for error within a patient's mouth. Recommended high school courses for aspiring dental hygienists include biology, chemistry, and mathematics.

Job Outlook

Employment of dental hygienists is expected to grow much faster than the average for all occupations through the year 2006, in response to increasing demand for dental care and the greater substitution of hygienists for services previously performed by dentists. Job prospects are expected to remain very good unless the number of dental hygienist program graduates grows much faster than during the last decade, and results in a much larger pool of qualified applicants.

Demand will be stimulated by population growth, and greater retention of natural teeth by the larger number of middle-aged and elderly people. Also, dentists are likely to employ more hygienists for several reasons. Older dentists, who are less likely to employ dental hygienists, will leave and be replaced by recent graduates, who are more likely to do so. In addition, as dentists' workloads increase, they are expected to hire more hygienists to perform preventive dental care such as cleaning, so they may devote their own time to more profitable procedures.

Earnings

Earnings of dental hygienists are affected by geographic location, employment setting, and education and experience. Dental hygienists who work in private dental offices may be paid on an hourly, daily, salary, or commission basis.

According to the American Dental Association, experienced dental hygienists who worked 32 hours a week or more in a private practice averaged about $759 a week in 1995.

Benefits vary substantially by practice setting, and may be contingent upon full-time employment. Dental hygienists who work for school systems, public health agencies, the federal government, or state agencies usually have substantial benefits.

Related Occupations

Workers in other occupations supporting health practitioners in an office setting include dental assistants, ophthalmic medical assistants, podiatric medical assistants, office nurses, medical assistants, physician assistants, physical therapy assistants, and occupational therapy assistants.

Sources of Additional Information

For information on a career in dental hygiene and the educational requirements to enter this occupation, contact:

❏ Division of Professional Development, American Dental Hygienists' Association, 444 N. Michigan Ave., Suite 3400, Chicago, IL 60611. Homepage: http://www.adha.org

For information about accredited programs and educational requirements, contact:

❏ Commission on Dental Accreditation, American Dental Association, 211 E. Chicago Ave., Suite 1814, Chicago, IL 60611. Homepage: http://www.ada.org

The State Board of Dental Examiners in each state can supply information on licensing requirements.

Drafters

(*D.O.T.* 001.261; 002.261; 003.131, .261 except -010, .281; 005.281; 007.161-010, -014, and -018, .261, and .281; 010.281 except -022; 014.281; 017 except .261-010 and .684; 019.161-010, .261-014; and 726.364-014)

Significant Points

* *Demand for particular drafting specializations varies geographically, depending on the needs of local industry.*

* *Little change in employment is expected through the year 2006.*

* *Opportunities should be best for individuals who have at least two years of training in a technically strong drafting program and who have considerable skill and experience using computer-aided drafting (CAD) systems.*

Nature of the Work

Drafters prepare technical drawings and plans used by production and construction workers to build everything from manufactured products such as spacecraft or industrial machinery to structures such as office buildings or oil and gas pipelines. Their drawings provide visual guidelines, showing the technical details of the products and structures, specifying dimensions, materials to be used, and procedures and processes to be followed. Drafters fill in technical details, using drawings, rough sketches, specifications, codes, and calculations previously made by engineers, surveyors, architects, or scientists. For example, they use their knowledge of standardized building techniques to draw in the details of a structure. Some drafters employ a knowledge of engineering and manufacturing theory and standards to draw the parts of a machine in order to determine design elements such as the number and kind of fasteners needed to assemble it. To do this, they use technical handbooks, tables, calculators, and computers.

Traditionally, drafters sat at drawing boards and used compasses, dividers, protractors, triangles, and other drafting devices to prepare a drawing manually. Most drafters now use computer-aided drafting (CAD) systems to prepare drawings. These systems employ computer work stations which create a drawing on a video screen. The drawings are stored electronically so that revisions and/or duplications can be made easily. These systems also permit drafters to easily and quickly prepare variations of a design. Although this equipment has become easier to operate, CAD is only a tool. Persons who produce technical drawings using CAD still function as a drafter, and need most of the knowledge of traditional drafters—relating to drafting skills and standards—as well as CAD skills.

As CAD technology advances and the cost of the systems continues to fall, it is likely that almost all drafters will use CAD systems regularly in the future. However, manual drafting may still be used in certain applications, especially in specialty firms that produce many one-of-a-kind drawings with little repetition.

Drafting work has many specializations and titles may denote a particular discipline of design or drafting. Architectural drafters draw architectural and structural features of buildings and other structures. They may specialize by the type of structure, such as residential or commercial, or by material used, such as reinforced concrete, masonry, steel, or timber.

Aeronautical drafters prepare engineering drawings detailing plans and specifications used for the manufacture of aircraft, missiles, and parts.

Electrical drafters prepare wiring and layout diagrams used by workers who erect, install, and repair electrical equipment and wiring in communication centers, power plants, electrical distribution systems, and buildings.

Electronic drafters draw wiring diagrams, circuit board assembly diagrams, schematics, and layout drawings used in the manufacture, installation, and repair of electronic devices and components.

Civil drafters prepare drawings and topographical and relief maps used in major construction or civil engineering projects such as highways, bridges, pipelines, flood control projects, and water and sewage systems.

Mechanical drafters prepare detail and assembly drawings of a wide variety of machinery and mechanical devices, indicating dimensions, fastening methods, and other requirements.

Process piping or pipeline drafters prepare drawings used for layout, construction, and operation of oil and gas fields, refineries, chemical plants, and process piping systems.

Working Conditions

Drafters usually work in comfortable offices furnished to accommodate their tasks. They may sit at adjustable drawing boards or drafting tables when doing manual drawings, although most drafters work at computer terminals much of the time. Like other workers who spend long periods of time in front of a computer terminals doing detailed work, drafters may be susceptible to eyestrain, back discomfort, and hand and wrist problems.

Employment

Drafters held about 310,000 jobs in 1996. Over 32 percent of all drafters worked in engineering and architectural services firms that design construction projects or do other engineering work on a contract basis for organizations in other parts of the economy. Another 29 percent worked in durable goods manufacturing industries, such as machinery, electrical equipment, and fabricated metals. The remainder were mostly employed in the construction, communications, utilities, and personnel supply services industries. About 5,000 were self-employed in 1996.

Training, Other Qualifications, and Advancement

Employers prefer applicants for drafting positions who have completed post-high school training in drafting, which is offered by technical institutes, junior and community colleges, and some colleges and universities. Employers are most interested in applicants who have well-developed drafting and mechanical drawing skills; a knowledge of standards, mathematics, science, and engineering technology; and a solid background in computer-aided drafting and design techniques. In addition, communication and problem-solving skills are required.

Individuals planning careers in drafting should take courses in math, science, computer technology, design or computer graphics, and any high school drafting courses available. Mechanical and visual aptitude are also important. Prospective drafters should be able to draw freehand, three-dimensional objects and do detailed work accurately and neatly. Artistic ability is helpful in some specialized fields, as is knowledge of manufacturing and construction methods. In addition, prospective drafters should have good interpersonal skills because they work closely with engineers, surveyors, architects, and other professionals.

Entry level or junior drafters usually do routine work under close supervision. After gaining experience, intermediate-level drafters progress to more difficult work with less supervision. They may be required to exercise more judg-

ment and perform calculations when preparing and modifying drawings. Drafters may eventually advance to senior drafter, designer, or supervisor. Many employers pay for continuing education, and with appropriate college degrees, drafters may go on to become engineering technicians, engineers, or architects.

Many types of publicly and privately operated schools provide some form of drafting training. The kind and quality of programs can vary considerably. Therefore, prospective students should be careful in selecting a program. They should contact prospective employers regarding their preferences and ask schools to provide information about the kinds of jobs obtained by graduates, type and condition of instructional facilities and equipment, and faculty qualifications.

Technical institutes offer intensive technical training but less of the general education than do junior and community colleges. Some award certificates or diplomas based on completion of a certain number of course hours. Many offer two-year associate degree programs, which are similar to or part of the programs offered by community colleges or state university systems. Other technical institutes are run by private, often for-profit, organizations, sometimes called proprietary schools. Their programs vary considerably in both length and types of courses offered.

Junior and community colleges offer curriculums similar to those in technical institutes but include more courses on theory and liberal arts. Often there is little or no difference between technical institute and community college programs. However, courses taken at junior or community colleges are more likely to be accepted for credit at four-year colleges than those at technical institutes. After completing a two-year associate degree program, graduates may obtain jobs as drafters or continue their education in a related field at four-year colleges. Four-year colleges usually do not offer drafting training, but college courses in engineering, architecture, and mathematics are useful for obtaining a job as a drafter.

Area vocational-technical schools are postsecondary public institutions that serve local students and emphasize training needed by local employers. Many offer introductory drafting instruction. Most require a high school diploma or its equivalent for admission.

Technical training obtained in the Armed Forces can also be applied in civilian drafting jobs. Some additional training may be necessary, depending on the technical area or military specialty, but often this can be gained on the job.

The American Design Drafting Association (ADDA) has established a certification program for drafters. Although drafters are not generally required to be certified by employers, certification demonstrates that nationally recognized standards have been met. Individuals who wish to become certified must pass the Drafter Certification Test, which is administered periodically at ADDA-authorized test sites. Applicants are tested on their knowledge and understanding of basic drafting concepts such as geometric construction, working drawings, and architectural terms and standards.

Job Outlook

Employment of drafters is expected to change little through the year 2006. Although industrial growth and increasingly complex design problems associated with new products and manufacturing will increase the demand for drafting services, greater use of CAD equipment by architects and engineers, as well as drafters, should offset this growth in demand. Many job openings, however, are expected to arise as drafters move to other occupations or leave the labor force.

Opportunities should be best for individuals who have at least two years of training in a technically strong drafting program and who have considerable skill and experience using CAD systems. CAD has become a powerful tool, simplifying many traditional drafting tasks. It has increased the complexity of drafting applications while enhancing the productivity of drafters. As technology continues to advance, employers will look for drafters who can combine a strong background in fundamental drafting principles with a higher level of technical sophistication and an ability to apply this knowledge to a broader range of responsibilities.

Demand for particular drafting specializations varies throughout the country because employment is generally contingent upon the needs of local industry. Employment of drafters remains highly concentrated in industries that are sensitive to cyclical changes in the economy, such as engineering and architectural services and durable goods manufacturing. During recessions, drafters may be laid off. A growing number of drafters should continue to be employed on a temporary or contract basis, as more companies turn to the personnel supply services industry to meet their changing needs.

Earnings

Median annual earnings of drafters who worked year round, full-time were about $31,250 in 1996; the middle 50 percent earned between $23,400 and $41,500 annually. The top 10 percent earned more than $50,750, while the bottom 10 percent earned less than $19,000.

According to a survey of workplaces in 160 metropolitan areas, beginning drafters had median annual earnings of about $20,700 a year in 1995, with the middle half earning between about $18,600 and $22,400 a year. The most experienced drafters had median earnings of about $40,900 a year in 1996,

with the middle half earning between about $36,100 and $45,800 a year.

Related Occupations

Other workers who prepare or analyze detailed drawings and make precise calculations and measurements include architects, landscape architects, designers, engineers, engineering technicians, science technicians, cartographers, and surveyors.

Sources of Additional Information

Information on schools offering programs in drafting and related areas is available from:

❑ Accrediting Commission of Career Schools and Colleges of Technology, 2101 Wilson Blvd., Suite 302, Arlington, VA 22201.

Employment Interviewers

(D.O.T. 166.267-010)

Significant Points

✶ *Sales ability is required to succeed in personnel supply services firms, where most employment interviewers are found.*

✶ *Employment growth reflects expansion of personnel supply, particularly in temporary help firms.*

Nature of the Work

Whether you are looking for a job or trying to fill one, you could find yourself turning to an employment interviewer for help. Sometimes called personnel consultants, human resources coordinators, personnel development specialists, or employment brokers, among other job titles, these workers help job seekers find employment and help employers find qualified employees.

Working largely in private personnel supply firms or state employment security offices (also known as job or employment service centers), employment interviewers act as brokers, putting together the best combination of applicant and job. To accomplish this, they obtain information from employers as well as job seekers.

A private industry employment interviewer is a salesperson. Counselors pool together a group of qualified applicants and try to sell them to many different companies. Often a consultant will call a company that has never been a client (cold-calling) with the aim of filling their employment needs.

Employers generally pay private (but not public) agencies to recruit workers. The employer places a "job order" with the agency describing the opening and listing requirements such as education, licenses or credentials, and experience. Employment interviewers often contact the employer to determine their exact personnel needs. Job seekers are asked to fill out forms or present resumes that detail their education, experience, and other qualifications. They may be interviewed or tested and have their background, references, and credentials checked. The employment interviewer then reviews the job requirements and the job seeker qualifications to determine the best possible match of position and applicant. Although computers are increasingly used to keep records and match employers with job seekers, personal contact with an employment interviewer remains an essential part of an applicant's job search.

Maintaining good relations with employers is an important part of the employment interviewer's job because this helps assure a steady flow of job orders. Being prepared to fill an opening quickly with a qualified applicant impresses employers most and keeps them as clients.

Besides helping firms fill job openings, employment interviewers help individuals find jobs. The services they provide depend upon the company or type of agency they work for and the clientele it serves.

Employment interviewers in personnel supply firms who place permanent employees are generally called counselors. They usually place job applicants who have the right qualifications but lack knowledge of the job market for their desired position. Counselors in these firms offer tips on personal appearance, suggestions on presenting a positive image of oneself, background on the company with which an interview is scheduled, and recommendations about interviewing techniques. Many firms specialize in placing applicants in particular kinds of jobs—for example, secretarial, word processing, computer programming and computer systems analysis, engineering, accounting, law, or health. Counselors in such firms usually have three to five years of experience in the field into which they are placing applicants.

Some employment interviewers work in temporary help services companies. These companies send out their own employees to firms that need temporary help. Employment interviewers take job orders from client firms and match their requests against a list of available workers. Employment interviewers select the best qualified workers available and assign them to the firms requiring assistance. Sometimes employees placed with companies as temporaries are later hired as permanent employees.

Traditionally, firms that placed permanent employees usually dealt with highly skilled applicants, such as lawyers or accountants, and those placing temporary employees dealt with less skilled workers, such as secretaries or data entry operators. However, temporary help services increasingly place workers with a wide range of educational backgrounds and work experience; businesses are turning to temporary employees to fill all types of positions—from clerical to managerial, professional, and technical—to reduce costs of pay and benefits associated with hiring permanent employees.

Regular evaluation of employee job skills is an important part of the job for those interviewers working in temporary help services companies. Initially, interviewers evaluate or test new employees' skills to determine their abilities and weaknesses. The results, which are kept on file, are referred to when filling job orders. In some cases, the temporary help company will train employees to improve their skills. Periodically, the interviewer may reevaluate or retest employees to identify any new skills they may have developed.

The duties of employment interviewers in job service centers differ somewhat because applicants may lack marketable skills. In these centers, job seekers present resumes and fill out forms that ask about educational attainment, job history, skills, awards, certificates, and licenses. An employment interviewer reviews these forms and asks the applicant about the type of job sought and salary range desired. Applicants sometimes have exaggerated expectations. Employment interviewers must be tactful, but persuasive, if an applicant's job or salary requests are unreasonable.

Applicants may need help identifying the kind of work for which they are best suited. The employment interviewer evaluates the applicant's qualifications and either chooses an appropriate occupation or class of occupations, or refers the applicant for vocational testing.

After identifying an appropriate job type, the employment interviewer searches the file of job orders seeking a possible job match, and refers the applicant to the employer if a match is found. If no match is found, the interviewer shows the applicant how to use listings of available jobs.

Some applicants are high school dropouts or have poor English language skills, a history of drug or alcohol dependency, or a prison record, among other problems. The amount and nature of special help for such applicants vary from state to state. In some states, it is the employment interviewer's responsibility to counsel hard-to-place applicants and refer them elsewhere for literacy or language instruction, vocational training, transportation assistance, child care, and other services. In other states, specially trained counselors perform this task.

Working Conditions

Employment interviewers usually work in comfortable, well-lighted offices, often using a computer to match information about employers and job seekers. Some interviewers, however, may spend much of their time out of the office interviewing. The work can prove hectic, especially in temporary help service companies which supply clients with immediate help for short periods of time. Some overtime may be required, and temporary workers may need their own transportation to make employer visits. The private placement industry is competitive, so counselors feel pressed to give their client companies the best service.

Employment

Employment interviewers held about 87,000 jobs in 1996. About four out of five worked in the private sector for personnel supply services, generally for employment placement firms or temporary help services companies. About one out of five worked for state or local government. Others were employed by organizations that provide various services, such as job training and vocational rehabilitation.

Employees of career consulting or outplacement firms are not included in these estimates. Workers in these firms help clients market themselves; they do not act as job brokers, nor do they match individuals with particular vacancies.

Training, Other Qualifications, and Advancement

Although most public and private agencies prefer to hire college graduates for interviewer jobs, a degree is not always necessary. Hiring requirements in the private sector reflect a firm's management approach as well as the placements in which its interviewers specialize. Those that place highly trained individuals such as accountants, lawyers, engineers, physicians, or managers generally have some training or experience in the field in which they are placing workers. Thus, a bachelor's, master's, or even a doctoral degree may be a prerequisite for some interviewers. Even with the right education, however, sales ability is still required to succeed in the private sector.

Educational requirements play a lesser role for interviewers placing clerks or laborers—a high school diploma may be sufficient. In these positions, qualities such as energy level, telephone voice, and sales ability take precedence over educational attainment.

Entry-level employment interviewer positions in the public sector are generally filled by college graduates, even though the positions do not always require a bachelor's degree. Some states allow substitution of suitable work experience for col-

lege education. Suitable work experience is generally defined as public contact work or time spent at other jobs (including clerical jobs) in a job service office. In states that permit employment interviewers to engage in counseling, course work in counseling may be required.

Most states and many large city and county governments use some form of merit system for hiring interviewers. Applicants may take a written exam, undergo a preliminary interview, or submit records of their education and experience for evaluation. Those who meet the standards are placed on a list from which the top-ranked candidates are selected for later interviews and possible hiring.

Other desirable qualifications for employment interviewers include good communications skills, a desire to help people, office skills, and adaptability. A friendly, confidence-winning manner is an asset because personal interaction plays a large role in this occupation. Increasingly, employment interviewers use computers as a tool; thus, basic knowledge of computers is helpful.

Advancement as an employment interviewer in the public sector is often based on a system providing regular promotions and salary increases for those meeting established standards. Advancement to supervisory positions is highly competitive. In personnel supply firms, advancement often depends on one's success in placing workers and generally takes the form of greater responsibility and higher income. Successful individuals may form their own businesses.

Job Outlook

Employment in this occupation is expected to grow about as fast as the average for all occupations through the year 2006. The majority of new jobs will arise in personnel supply firms, especially those specializing in temporary help. Job growth is not anticipated in state job service offices because of budgetary problems and the growing use of computerized job matching and information systems, and as states increasingly contract out employment services to private firms. Other openings will stem from the need to replace experienced interviewers who transfer to other occupations, retire, or stop working for other reasons.

Rapid expansion of firms supplying temporary help will be responsible for much of the growth in this occupation. Businesses of all types are turning to temporary help services companies for additional workers for handling short-term assignments or one-time projects, for launching new programs, and to reduce costs of pay and benefits associated with hiring permanent employees.

Expansion of the personnel supply industry, in general, will also spur job growth. Job orders will increase as the

economy expands and new businesses are formed; this is expected to heighten demand for employment interviewers. Firms that lack the time or resources to develop their own screening procedures will likely turn to personnel firms.

Employment opportunities should be better in private placement firms than in state job service centers. Entry to this occupation is relatively easy for college graduates, or people who have had some college courses, except in those positions specializing in placement of workers with highly specialized training, such as lawyers, doctors, and engineers.

Employment interviewers who place permanent workers may lose their jobs during recessions because employers reduce or eliminate hiring for permanent positions during downturns in the economy. State job service employment interviewers are less susceptible to layoffs than those who place permanent or temporary personnel in the private sector.

Earnings

Earnings in private firms vary, in part, because the basis for compensation varies. Workers in personnel supply firms tend to be paid on a commission basis; those in temporary help service companies receive a salary.

When workers are paid on a commission basis (or salary plus commission), total earnings depend on how much business they bring in. This is usually based on the type as well as the number of placements. Those who place more highly skilled or hard-to-find employees earn more. An interviewer or counselor working strictly on a commission basis often makes around 30 percent of what he or she bills the client, although this varies widely from firm to firm. Some work on a salary-plus-commission basis because they fill difficult or highly specialized positions requiring long periods of search. The salary, usually small by normal standards, guarantees these individuals security through slow times. The commission provides the incentive and opportunity for higher earnings.

Some personnel supply firms employ new workers for a two- to three-month probationary period during which they draw a regular salary. This gives new workers time to develop their skills and acquire some clients. At the end of the probationary period, the new employees are evaluated, and they are either let go or switched to a commission basis.

Related Occupations

Employment interviewers serve as intermediaries for job seekers and employers. Workers in several other occupations do similar jobs.

Personnel officers screen and help hire new employees, but they concern themselves mainly with the hiring needs of the firm; they never represent individual job seekers. Personnel officers may also have additional duties in areas such as payroll or benefits management.

Career counselors help students and alumni find jobs, but they primarily emphasize career counseling and decision making, not placement.

Counselors in community organizations and vocational rehabilitation facilities help clients find jobs, but they also assist with drug or alcohol dependencies, housing, transportation, child care, and other problems that stand in the way of finding and keeping a job.

Sources of Additional Information

For information on a career as an employment interviewer/counselor, contact:

❏ National Association of Personnel Services, 3133 Mt. Vernon Ave., Alexandria, VA 22305.

❏ National Association of Temporary Staffing Services, 119 S. Saint Asaph St., Alexandria, VA 22314. Homepage: http://www.natss.org

For information on a career as an employment interviewer in state employment security offices, contact offices of the state government for which you are interested in working.

Engineering Technicians

(*D.O.T.* 002.261-014, .262-010; 003.161, .261-010, .362; 005.261; 006.261; 007.161-026 and -030, .167-010, .181 and .267-014; 008.261; 010.261-010 and -026; 011.261-010, -014, -018, and -022, .281, .361; 012.261-014, .267; 013.161; 017.261-010; 017.684; 019.161-014, .261-018, -022, -026, and -034, .267, .281; 194.381, .382-010; 199.261-014; 726.261-010 and -014; 806.281-014; 761.281-014; 828.261-018; and 869.261-026)

Significant Points

✴ *About 43 percent of all engineering technicians employed in 1996 were electrical and electronic engineering technicians.*

✴ *Most employers prefer those with an associate degree in engineering technology.*

Nature of the Work

Engineering technicians use the principles and theories of science, engineering, and mathematics to solve technical problems in research and development, manufacturing, sales, construction, inspection, and maintenance. Their work is more limited in scope and more practically oriented than that of scientists and engineers. Many engineering technicians assist engineers and scientists, especially in research and development. Others work in quality control—inspecting products and processes, conducting tests, or collecting data.

In manufacturing, they may assist in product design and development, process design, or production.

Engineering technicians who work in research and development, build or set up equipment, prepare and conduct experiments, calculate or record the results, and help engineers in other ways. Some make prototype versions of newly designed equipment. They also assist in design work, often using computer-aided design equipment.

Engineering technicians who work in manufacturing support the work of engineers. They may prepare specifications for materials, devise and run tests to ensure product quality, or study ways to improve manufacturing efficiency. They may also supervise production workers to make sure they follow prescribed procedures.

Most engineering technicians specialize in certain areas, learning skills and working in the same disciplines as engineers. Occupational titles, therefore, tend to follow the same structure as engineers. Chemical engineering technicians are usually employed in industries producing pharmaceuticals, chemicals, and petroleum products, among others. They work in laboratories as well as processing plants. They help develop new chemical products and processes, test processing equipment and instrumentation, monitor quality, and operate chemical manufacturing facilities.

Civil engineering technicians help civil engineers plan and build highways, buildings, bridges, dams, wastewater treatment systems, and other structures, and perform related surveys and studies. Some inspect water and wastewater treatment systems to ensure pollution control requirements are met. Others estimate construction costs and specify materials to be used. Some may even prepare drawings or perform land surveying duties.

Electrical and electronics engineering technicians help design, develop, test, and manufacture electrical and electronic equipment such as radios, radar, sonar, television, industrial and medical measuring or control devices, navigational equipment, and computers. They may work in product evaluation and testing, using measuring and diagnostic devices to adjust, test, and repair equipment. Workers who only repair electrical and electronic equipment are mechanics, installers, and repairers. Many of these repairers are often referred to as electronics technicians.

Electrical and electronic engineering technology is also applied to a wide variety of systems such as communications and process controls. Electromechanical engineering technicians combine fundamental principles of mechanical engineering technology with knowledge of electrical and electronic circuits to design, develop, test, and manufacture electrical and computer-controlled mechanical systems.

Industrial engineering technicians study the efficient use of personnel, materials, and machines in factories, stores, repair shops, and offices. They prepare layouts of machinery and equipment, plan the flow of work, make statistical studies, and analyze production costs.

Mechanical engineering technicians help engineers design, develop, test, and manufacture industrial machinery, mechanical parts, and other equipment. They may assist in the testing of a guided missile, or in the planning and design of an electric power generation plant. They make sketches and rough layouts, record data, make computations, analyze results, and write reports. When planning production, mechanical engineering technicians prepare layouts and drawings of the assembly process and of parts to be manufactured. They estimate labor costs, equipment life, and plant space. Some test and inspect machines and equipment in manufacturing departments or work with engineers to eliminate production problems.

Working Conditions

Most engineering technicians work 40 hours a week in a laboratory, office, manufacturing or industrial plant, or on a construction site. Some may be exposed to hazards from equipment, chemicals, or toxic materials.

Employment

Engineering technicians held about 698,000 jobs in 1996. Almost 298,000 of these were electrical and electronics engineering technicians. About 33 percent of all engineering technicians worked in durable goods manufacturing, mainly in the electrical and electronic machinery and equipment, industrial machinery and equipment, instruments and related products, and transportation equipment industries. Another 25 percent worked in service industries, mostly in engineering or business services companies that do engineering work on contract for government, manufacturing, or other organizations.

In 1996, the federal government employed about 42,000 engineering technicians. The major employer was the Department of Defense, followed by the Departments of Transportation, Agriculture, and the Interior, the Tennessee Valley Authority, and the National Aeronautics and Space Administration. State governments employed about 37,000 and local governments about 27,000.

Training, Other Qualifications, and Advancement

Although it is possible to qualify for some engineering technician jobs with no formal training, most employers prefer to hire someone with at least a two-year degree in

engineering technology. Training is available at technical institutes, junior and community colleges, extension divisions of colleges and universities, public and private vocational-technical schools, and through some technical training programs in the Armed Forces. Persons with college courses in science, engineering, and mathematics may also qualify for some positions but may need additional specialized training and experience.

Prospective engineering technicians should take as many high school science and math courses as possible to prepare for postsecondary programs in engineering technology. Most two-year associate programs accredited by the Accreditation Board for Engineering and Technology (ABET) require, at a minimum, college algebra and trigonometry, and one or two basic science courses. More math or science may be required depending on the area of specialty. The type of technical courses required also varies depending on the area of specialty. For example, prospective mechanical engineering technicians may take courses in fluid mechanics, thermodynamics, and mechanical design; electrical engineering technicians may take classes in electric circuits, microprocessors, and digital electronics; and those preparing to work in environmental engineering technology need courses in environmental regulations and safe handling of hazardous materials. Because many engineering technicians may become involved in design work, creativity is desirable. Good communication skills and the ability to work well with others is also important since they are often part of a team of engineers and other technicians.

Engineering technicians usually begin by performing routine duties under the close supervision of an experienced technician, technologist, engineer, or scientist. As they gain experience, they are given more difficult assignments with only general supervision. Some engineering technicians eventually become supervisors.

Many publicly and privately operated schools provide technical training; the type and quality of programs vary considerably. Therefore, prospective students should be careful in selecting a program. They should contact prospective employers regarding their preferences and ask schools to provide information about the kinds of jobs obtained by graduates, instructional facilities and equipment, and faculty qualifications. Graduates of ABET-accredited programs are generally recognized to have achieved an acceptable level of competence in the mathematics, science, and technical courses required for this occupation.

Technical institutes offer intensive technical training, but less theory and general education than junior and community colleges. Many offer two-year associate degree programs, and are similar to or part of a community college or state university system. Other technical institutes are run by private, often for-profit, organizations, sometimes called proprietary schools. Their programs vary considerably in length and types of courses offered, although some are two-year associate degree programs.

Junior and community colleges offer curriculums similar to those in technical institutes but may include more theory and liberal arts. Often there may be little or no difference between technical institute and community college programs, as both offer associate degrees. After completing the two-year program, some graduates get jobs as engineering technicians, while others continue their education at four-year colleges. However, there is a difference between an associate degree in pre-engineering and one in engineering technology. Students who enroll in a two-year pre-engineering program may find it very difficult to find work as an engineering technician should they decide not to enter a four-year engineering program, because pre-engineering programs usually focus less on hands-on applications and more on academic preparatory work. Conversely, graduates of two-year engineering technology programs may not receive credit for many of the courses they have taken if they choose to transfer to a four-year engineering program. Colleges with these four-year programs usually do not offer engineering technician training, but college courses in science, engineering, and mathematics are useful for obtaining a job as an engineering technician. Many four-year colleges offer bachelor's degrees in engineering technology, but graduates of these programs are often hired to work as technologists or applied engineers, not technicians.

Area vocational-technical schools include postsecondary public institutions that serve local students and emphasize training needed by local employers. Most require a high school diploma or its equivalent for admission.

Other training in technical areas may be obtained in the Armed Forces. Many military technical training programs are highly regarded by employers. However, skills acquired in military programs often are narrowly focused, so they are not necessarily transferable to civilian industry, which often requires broader training. Therefore, some additional training may be needed, depending on the acquired skills and the kind of job.

The National Institute for Certification in Engineering Technologies (NICET) has established a voluntary certification program for engineering technicians. Although engineering technicians are not generally required to be certified by employers, certification may provide job seekers a competitive advantage. Certification is available at various levels, each level combining a written examination in one of over 30 specialty fields with a certain amount of job related experience.

Job Outlook

Overall, employment of engineering technicians is expected to increase as fast as the average for all occupations through the year 2006. However, the growing availability and use of advanced technologies, such as computer-aided design and drafting and computer simulation, will continue to increase productivity and impact employment growth. Opportunities should be best for individuals who have completed a two-year program in engineering technology. As technology becomes more sophisticated, employers continue to look for technicians who are skilled in new technology and require a minimum of additional job training. In addition to growth, many job openings will be created to replace technicians who retire or leave the labor force for other reasons.

As production of technical products continues to grow, competitive pressures will force companies to improve and update manufacturing facilities and product designs more rapidly than in the past. Like engineers, employment of engineering technicians is influenced by local and national economic conditions. As a result, the employment outlook varies with area of specialization and industry. Employment of some types of engineering technicians, such as civil engineering and aeronautical engineering technicians, experience greater cyclical fluctuations than others. Technicians whose jobs are defense-related may experience fewer opportunities because of recent defense cutbacks. On the other hand, employment of the largest specialty group—electrical and electronics engineering technicians—is expected to grow slightly faster than the overall rate for all engineering technicians. Increasing demand for more sophisticated electrical and electronic products, as well as the expansion of these products and systems into all areas of industry and manufacturing processes, will contribute to stronger employment growth in this specialty area.

Earnings

According to a survey of workplaces in 160 metropolitan areas, engineering technicians at the most junior level had median earnings of about $20,200 in 1995, with the middle half earning between $17,700 and $22,800 a year. Engineering technicians with more experience and the ability to work with little supervision had median earnings of about $32,700, and those in supervisory or most senior level positions earned about $54,800.

In the federal government, engineering technicians started at about $15,500, $17,400, or $19,500 in early 1997, depending on their education and experience. Beginning salaries were slightly higher in selected areas of the country where the prevailing local pay level was higher. The average annual salary for engineering technicians in supervisory, non-supervisory, and management positions in the federal government in 1997 was $42,710; for electronics technicians, $46,040; and for industrial engineering technicians, $43,510.

Related Occupations

Engineering technicians apply scientific and engineering principles usually acquired in postsecondary programs below the baccalaureate level. Similar occupations include science technicians, drafters, surveyors, broadcast technicians, and health technologists and technicians.

Sources of Additional Information

For a small fee, information on a variety of engineering technician and technology careers is available from:

❏ The Junior Engineering Technical Society (JETS), at 1420 King St., Suite 405, Alexandria, VA 22314-2794. Enclose $3.50 to obtain a full package of guidance materials and information. Brochures are available free on JETS homepage: http://www.asee.org/jets

Information on ABET-accredited engineering technology programs is available from:

❏ Accreditation Board for Engineering and Technology, Inc. 111 Market Place, Suite 1050, Baltimore, MD 21202. Homepage: http://www.abet.ba.md.us

Funeral Directors

(D.O.T. 187.167-030)

Significant Points

★ *Job opportunities should be excellent because the number of mortuary science graduates is expected to be insufficient to meet demand.*

★ *Funeral directors must be licensed by the states that set the education and training requirements needed for entry.*

Nature of the Work

Since the earliest of times, most peoples have held funeral ceremonies. The dead have ritually been interred in pyramids, cremated on burning pyres, and sunk beneath the oceans' waves. Even today, funeral practices and rites vary greatly among various cultures and religions. Among the many diverse groups in the United States, funeral practices generally share some common elements: removal of the remains of the deceased to a mortuary, preparation of the remains, performance of a ceremony that honors the deceased and addresses the spiritual needs of the living as well as the dead, and the

burial or destruction of the remains. To unburden themselves of arranging and directing these tasks, grieving families turn to funeral directors.

Funeral directors are also called morticians or undertakers. Although this career does not appeal to everyone, the men and women who work as funeral directors take great pride in their ability to provide efficient and appropriate services that give comfort to their customers.

Funeral directors interview the family to learn what they desire with regard to the nature of the funeral, the clergy members or other persons who will officiate, and the final disposition of the remains; sometimes the deceased leave detailed instructions for their own funerals. Together with the family, directors establish the location, dates, and times of wakes, memorial services, and burials. They also send a hearse to carry the body to the funeral home or mortuary.

Burial in a casket is the most common method of disposing of remains in this country, although entombments also occur. Cremation, which is the burning of the body in a special furnace, is increasingly selected because it can be more convenient and less costly. Cremations are appealing because the remains can be shipped easily, kept at home, buried, or scattered. Memorials can be held anywhere, and at any time, sometimes months later when all relatives and friends can get together. Even when remains are cremated, many people still want a funeral service.

A funeral service followed by cremation need not be any different from a funeral service followed by a burial. Usually cremated remains are placed in some type of permanent receptacle, referred to as an urn, before being committed to a final resting place. The urn may be buried, placed in an indoor or outdoor mausoleum or columbarium, or interred in a special urn garden that many cemeteries provide for cremated remains.

Directors arrange the details and handle the logistics of funerals. They prepare obituary notices and have them placed in newspapers, arrange for pallbearers and clergy, schedule with the cemetery the opening and closing of a grave, decorate and prepare the sites of all services, and provide for the transportation of the remains, mourners, and flowers between sites. They also direct preparation and shipment of remains for out-of-state burial.

Funeral services may take place in the home, a house of worship, or the funeral home and at the grave site or crematory. Services may be nonreligious, but often they reflect the religion of the family, so funeral directors must be familiar with the funeral and burial customs of many faiths, ethnic groups, and fraternal organizations. For example, members of some religions seldom have the bodies of the deceased embalmed or cremated.

Funeral directors also prearrange funerals. They are increasingly arranging funerals in advance of need to provide a peace of mind that the client's wishes will be taken care of in a way that is satisfying to the person and to those who will survive.

Most funeral directors are also trained, licensed, and practicing embalmers. Embalming is a sanitary, cosmetic, and preservative process through which the body is prepared for interment. If more than 24 hours or so elapses between death and interment, state laws usually require that remains be refrigerated or embalmed. The embalmer washes the body with germicidal soap and replaces the blood with embalming fluid to preserve the body. Embalmers may reshape and reconstruct disfigured or maimed bodies using materials, such as clay, cotton, plaster of Paris, and wax. They also may apply cosmetics to provide a natural appearance, and then dress the body and place it in a casket. Embalmers maintain records such as embalming reports, and itemized lists of clothing or valuables delivered with the body. In large funeral homes, an embalming staff of two or more embalmers, plus several apprentices, may be employed.

Funeral directors also handle the paperwork involved with the person's death. They may help family members apply for veterans' burial benefits, notify the Social Security Administration of the death, apply on behalf of survivors for the transfer of any pensions, insurance policies, or annuities, and submit papers to state authorities so that a formal certificate of death may be issued and copies distributed to heirs.

Funeral directors are also responsible for the success and the profitability of their businesses. Directors keep records on expenses, purchases, and services rendered; prepare and send invoices for services; prepare and submit reports for unemployment insurance; prepare federal, state, and local tax forms; and prepare itemized bills for customers. Directors also strive to foster a cooperative spirit and friendly attitude among employees and a compassionate demeanor toward the families. A growing number of funeral directors are also involved in helping individuals adapt to changes in their lives following a death through post-death counseling and support group activities.

Most funeral homes have a chapel, one or more viewing rooms, a casket-selection room, and a preparation room. An increasing number also have a crematory on the premises. Equipment may include a hearse, a flower car, limousines, and sometimes an ambulance. They usually stock a selection of caskets and urns for families to purchase or rent.

Working Conditions

Funeral directors often work long, irregular hours. Shift work is sometimes necessary because funeral home hours include evenings and weekends. In smaller funeral homes, working hours vary, but in larger homes employees generally work eight hours a day, five or six days a week.

Funeral directors occasionally come into contact with the remains of persons who had contagious diseases, but the possibility of infection is remote if strict health regulations are followed.

To show proper respect and consideration for the families and the dead, funeral directors must dress appropriately. The profession usually requires short, neat haircuts and trimmed beards, if any, for men. Suits, ties, and dresses are customary for a conservative look.

Employment

Funeral directors held about 33,000 jobs in 1996. Almost one in four was self-employed. Nearly all worked in the funeral service and crematory industry, but a few worked for the federal government.

Training, Other Qualifications, and Advancement

Funeral directors must be licensed in all but one state, Colorado. Licensing laws vary from state to state, but most require applicants to be 21 years old, have a high school diploma, complete some college training in mortuary science, and serve an apprenticeship. After passing a state board licensing examination, new funeral directors may join the staff of a funeral home. Embalmers are required to be licensed in all states, and some states issue a single license for both funeral directors and embalmers. In states that have separate licensing and apprenticeship requirements for the two positions, most people in the field obtain both licenses. Persons interested in a career as a funeral director should contact their state board for specific state requirements.

College programs in mortuary science usually last from two to four years, depending on the school. There were 47 mortuary science programs accredited by the American Board of Funeral Service Education in 1996. Two-year programs are offered by a small number of community and junior colleges, and a few colleges and universities offer both two- and four-year programs. Mortuary science programs include courses in anatomy, physiology, embalming techniques, restorative art, business management, accounting and use of computers in funeral home management, and client services. They also include courses in the social sciences and legal, ethical, and regulatory subjects, such as psychology, grief counseling, oral and written communication, funeral service law, business law, and ethics.

The National Funeral Directors Association Educational Foundation offers a continuing education program designed for active practitioners in the field. It is a three-week program in communications, counseling, and management. Over 25 states have continuing education requirements that funeral directors must meet before a license can be renewed.

Apprenticeships must be completed under an experienced and licensed funeral director or embalmer. Depending on state regulations, apprenticeships last from one to two years and may be served before, during, or after mortuary school. They provide practical experience in all facets of the funeral service from embalming to transporting remains.

State board licensing examinations vary, but they usually consist of written and oral parts and include a demonstration of practical skills. Persons who want to work in another state may have to pass the examination for that state, although many states will grant licenses to funeral directors from another state without further examination.

High school students can start preparing for a career as a funeral director by taking courses in biology and chemistry and participating in public speaking or debating clubs. Part-time or summer jobs in funeral homes consist mostly of maintenance and clean-up tasks, such as washing and polishing limousines and hearses, but these tasks can help students become familiar with the operation of funeral homes.

Important personal traits for funeral directors are composure, tact, and the ability to communicate easily with the public. They also should have the desire and ability to comfort people in their time of sorrow.

Advancement opportunities are best in large funeral homes at which directors may earn promotions to higher paying positions such as branch manager or general manager. Some directors eventually acquire enough money and experience to establish their own funeral businesses.

Job Outlook

Employment opportunities for funeral directors are expected to be excellent, because the number of graduates in mortuary science is likely to continue to be lower than the number of job openings in the field. Although funeral directors are highly attached to their jobs, more openings will occur because more funeral directors are 55 years old and over compared to workers in other areas.

Employment of funeral directors is expected to increase slower than the average for all occupations through the year 2006. Demand for funeral services will rise as the population grows, and with it the number of deaths. The population is projected to become older because the number of persons age

55 and over is expected to increase significantly faster than the population as a whole. However, employment growth will be slowed by the number of people going into the field; this type of work is not attractive to many people.

Earnings

Median weekly earnings of full-time salaried funeral directors were $590 in 1996. The middle 50 percent earned between $447 and $849. The lowest 10 percent earned less than $356 and the top 10 percent more than $1,072.

Salaries of funeral directors depend on the number of years of experience in funeral services, the number of services performed, the number of facilities operated, the area of the country, the size of the community, and the formal education of the funeral director. A 1995 survey conducted by the National Funeral Directors Association found that the median salary, including bonus, for funeral directors ranged from a low of $21,775 annually for those with less than five years in the funeral service business and who performed fewer than 100 services a year to a high of $106,200 for an owner/manager who operated more than three facilities. Those funeral directors who had bachelor's degrees tended to earn more than those with just a high school education. Those who were located in large cities earned more than those in small towns and rural areas. Salaries were higher in New England than in the South.

Related Occupations

The job of a funeral director requires tact, discretion, and compassion when dealing with grieving people. Others who need these qualities include members of the clergy, social workers, psychologists, psychiatrists, and other health care professionals.

Sources of Additional Information

For a list of accredited mortuary science programs and information on the funeral service profession, write to:

❑ The National Funeral Directors Association, 11121 West Oklahoma Ave., Milwaukee, WI 53227-4096.

For information about college programs in mortuary science, scholarships, and funeral service as a career, contact:

❑ The American Board of Funeral Service Education, P.O. Box 1305, Brunswick, ME 04011.

For information on continuing education programs in funeral service, contact:

❑ The National Funeral Directors Association Educational Foundation, 11121 W. Oklahoma Ave., Milwaukee, WI 53227-4096.

For information on programs, publications, and statistics on cremations, write to:

❑ The Cremation Association of North America, 401 N. Michigan, Chicago, IL 60611.

Hotel Managers and Assistants

(*D.O.T.* 187.117-038, .137-018; .167-046, -078, -106, -122; and 320)

Significant Points

* *Long hours and the stress of dealing with hotel patrons result in high turnover.*

* *College graduates with degrees in hotel or restaurant management should have good job opportunities.*

Nature of the Work

A comfortable room, good food, and a helpful hotel staff can make being away from home an enjoyable experience for both vacationing families and business travelers. Hotel managers and assistant managers strive to ensure their guests will have a pleasant stay by providing many of the comforts of home, including cable television, fitness equipment, and voice mail. For business travelers, hotel managers make available meeting rooms and various equipment, including slide projectors and fax machines.

Hotel managers are responsible for the efficient and profitable operation of their establishments. In a small hotel, motel, or inn with a limited staff, a single manager may direct all aspects of operations. However, large hotels may employ hundreds of workers, and the general manager may be aided by a number of assistant managers assigned to the various departments of the operation. Assistant managers must ensure that the day-to-day operations of their departments meet the standards set by the general manager.

Computers are used extensively by hotel managers and their assistants, to keep track of the guest's bill, reservations, room assignments, meetings, and special events; order food, beverages, and housekeeping and other supplies; and prepare reports for hotel owners and top-level managers. Managers work with computer specialists to ensure that the hotel's computer system functions properly. Should the hotel's computer system fail, managers must ensure that guests' needs continue to be met.

The general manager has overall responsibility for the operation of the hotel. Within guidelines established by the owners of the hotel or executives of the hotel chain, the general manager sets room rates, allocates funds to departments, approves expenditures, and establishes standards for service to guests, decor, housekeeping, food quality, and banquet operations. Managers who work for chains also may be assigned to organize and staff a newly built hotel, refurbish an older hotel, or reorganize a hotel or motel that is not operating successfully. In order to fill some low-paying service and clerical jobs in hotels, some managers attend career fairs.

Resident managers live in hotels and are on call 24 hours a day to resolve problems or emergencies. However, they typically work an eight-hour day, while overseeing the day-to-day operations of the hotel. In many hotels, the general manager also serves as the resident manager.

Executive housekeepers are responsible for ensuring guest rooms, meeting and banquet rooms, and public areas are clean, orderly, and well maintained. They train, schedule, and supervise the work of housekeepers; inspect rooms; and order cleaning supplies.

Front office managers coordinate reservations and room assignments as well as train and direct the hotel's front desk staff. They ensure guests are treated courteously, complaints and problems are resolved, and requests for special services are carried out. Front office managers often have authorization to adjust charges posted on a customer's bill.

Food and beverage managers direct the food service operations of hotels. They oversee the hotels' restaurants, cocktail lounges, and banquet facilities. They supervise and schedule food and beverage preparation and service workers, plan menus, estimate costs, and deal with food suppliers.

Convention services managers coordinate the activities of large hotels' various departments for meetings, conventions, and special events. They meet with representatives of groups or organizations to plan the number of rooms to reserve, the desired configuration of hotel meeting space, and any banquet services needed. During the meeting or event, they resolve unexpected problems and monitor activities to check that hotel operations conform to the expectations of the group.

Other assistant managers are responsible for personnel, accounting and office administration, marketing and sales, purchasing, security, maintenance, and recreational facilities.

Working Conditions

Because hotels are open around the clock, night and weekend work is common. Many hotel managers work considerably more than 40 hours per week. Managers who live in the hotel usually have regular work schedules, but they may be called to work at any time. Some employees of resort hotels are managers during the busy season and have other duties during the rest of the year.

Hotel managers sometimes experience the pressures of coordinating a wide range of functions. Conventions and large groups of tourists may present unusual problems. Dealing with irate patrons can be stressful. The job can be particularly hectic for front office managers around check-in and check-out time. Computer failures can further complicate an already busy time.

Employment

Hotel managers and assistant managers held about 175,000 jobs in 1996. A significant number of these jobs were held by self-employed managers—primarily owners of small hotels and motels. Some managers were employed by companies that manage hotels and motels under contract.

Training, Other Qualifications, and Advancement

Postsecondary training in hotel or restaurant management is preferred for most hotel management positions, although a college liberal arts degree may be sufficient when coupled with related hotel experience. In the past, many managers were promoted from the ranks of front desk clerks, housekeepers, waiters and chefs, and hotel sales workers. Although some employees still advance to hotel management positions without the benefit of education or training beyond high school, postsecondary education is preferred.

Restaurant management training or experience is also a good background for entering hotel management because the success of a hotel's food service and beverage operations is often of great importance to the profitability of the entire establishment.

Internships or part-time or summer work while in school is an asset to anyone seeking a career in hotel management. The experience gained and the contacts made with employers can greatly benefit students when they seek full-time employment after graduation. Most bachelor's degree programs include work-study opportunities. A bachelor's degree in hotel and restaurant administration provides particularly strong preparation for a career in hotel management. In 1996, over 160 colleges and universities offered bachelor's and graduate programs in this field. More than 800 community and junior colleges, technical institutes, vocational and trade schools, and other academic institutions also have programs leading to an associate degree or other formal recognition in hotel or restaurant management. For example, many colleges and universities have certification programs in executive housekeeping; these programs typically cover a wide variety of topics, including environmental and workplace safety as well as federal, state, and local safety requirements. Graduates of hotel or restaurant management programs usually start as trainee assistant managers, or at least advance to such positions more quickly.

Hotel management programs include instruction in hotel administration, accounting, economics, marketing, housekeeping, food service management and catering, and hotel maintenance engineering. Computer training is an integral part of hotel management training due to the widespread use of computers in reservations, billing, and housekeeping management.

Hotel managers must be able to get along with all kinds of people, even in stressful situations. They must be able to solve problems and concentrate on details. Initiative, self-discipline, the ability to organize and direct the work of others, and effective communication skills are essential for managers at all levels.

Sometimes large hotels sponsor specialized on-the-job management training programs which allow trainees to rotate among various departments and gain a thorough knowledge of the hotel's operation. Other hotels may help finance formal training in hotel management for outstanding employees.

Most hotels promote employees who have proven their ability and completed formal education in hotel management. Newly built hotels, particularly those without well-established on-the-job training programs, often prefer experienced personnel for managerial positions. Large hotel and motel chains may offer better opportunities for advancement than small, independently owned establishments, but relocation every several years often is necessary for advancement. The large chains have more extensive career ladder programs and offer managers the opportunity to transfer to another hotel or motel in the chain or to the central office if an opening occurs. Career advancement can be accelerated by completion of certification programs offered by the associations listed below. These programs generally require a combination of course work, examinations, and experience.

Job Outlook

Employment of hotel managers is expected to grow about as fast as the average for all occupations through the year 2006. However, long hours and stressful working conditions result in high turnover in this field, with most job openings expected to occur as experienced managers transfer to other occupations, retire, or stop working for other reasons. Job opportunities in hotel management are expected to be good for persons with college degrees in hotel or restaurant management.

Business travel will continue to grow, and increased domestic and foreign tourism will also create demand for additional hotels and motels. However, manager jobs are not expected to grow as rapidly as the hotel industry due to consolidation, with chains and franchises acquiring independently owned establishments. In addition, front desk clerks are increasingly assuming some responsibilities previously reserved for managers. Also, to accommodate bargain-conscious guests, hotel chains are increasing the number of economy-class rooms. Economy hotels offer clean, comfortable rooms and front desk services without costly extras like restaurants and room service. Because there are not as many departments in each hotel, fewer managers are needed. Economy-class hotels have a general manager, and regional offices of the hotel management company employ department managers, such as executive housekeepers, to oversee several hotels.

Demand may also increase for suite hotels as some guests, especially business customers, are willing to pay higher prices for rooms with kitchens and suites that provide the space needed to conduct meetings. In addition to job growth in suite hotels and economy-class hotels, large full-service hotels—offering restaurants, fitness centers, large meeting rooms, and play areas for children, among other amenities—will continue to offer many trainee and managerial opportunities.

Earnings

Salaries of hotel managers vary greatly according to their responsibilities and the segment of the hotel industry in which they are employed. In 1996, annual salaries of assistant hotel managers averaged around $40,000, based on a hospitality industry survey conducted by Roth Young Personnel of Oklahoma City. Salaries of assistant managers also varied because of differences in duties and responsibilities. For example, food and beverage directors averaged $43,000, whereas front office managers averaged $28,000. The manager's level of experience is also an important factor.

In 1996, salaries of general managers averaged nearly $54,000, according to the Roth Young survey. Their salaries ranged from $39,000 to $81,000, depending on the size and type of establishment. Based on limited information, managers may earn bonuses up to 25 percent of their basic salary in some hotels. In addition, managers and their families may be furnished with lodging, meals, parking, laundry, and other services.

In addition to typical benefits, some hotels offer profit-sharing plans and educational assistance to their employees.

Related Occupations

Hotel managers and assistants are not the only workers concerned with organizing and directing a business where customer service is the cornerstone of their success. Other occupations sharing similar responsibilities include restaurant managers, apartment building managers, retail store managers, and office managers.

Sources of Additional Information

For information on careers and scholarships in hotel management, contact:

❑ The American Hotel and Motel Association (AH&MA), Information Center, 1201 New York Ave. NW, Washington, DC 20005-3931.

For information on educational programs, including correspondence courses, in hotel and restaurant management, write to:

❑ Council on Hotel, Restaurant, and Institutional Education, 1200 17th St. NW, Washington, DC 20036-3097.

Information on careers in housekeeping management may be obtained from:

❑ National Executive Housekeepers Association, Inc., 1001 Eastwind Dr., Suite 301, Westerville, OH 43081. Phone: (800) 200-6342.

General career information and a directory of accredited private trade and technical schools offering programs in hotel-motel management may be obtained from:

❑ Accrediting Commission of Career Schools and Colleges of Technology, 2101 Wilson Blvd., Suite 302, Arlington, VA 22201.

Inspectors and Compliance Officers, Except Construction

(D.O.T. codes are too numerous to list.)

Significant Points

✴ *Over 80 percent of the jobs are in federal, state, and local government agencies that inspect and enforce rules on matters such as health, safety, food, licensing, or finance.*

✴ *Because responsibilities vary, ranging from those of aviation safety inspectors to food inspectors, for example, training requirements and working conditions vary greatly.*

Nature of the Work

Inspectors and compliance officers enforce a wide range of laws, regulations, policies, or procedures. They inspect and enforce rules on matters such as health, safety, food, licensing, or finance. Inspectors' and compliance officers' duties vary widely.

Agricultural commodity graders apply quality standards to aid the buying and selling of commodities, and to ensure that retailers and consumers know the quality of the products they purchase. Although this grading is not required by law, buyers may not be willing to purchase ungraded commodities. Graders usually specialize in an area such as eggs, meat, poultry, processed or fresh fruits and vegetables, grain, tobacco, cotton, or dairy products. They examine product samples to determine quality and grade, and issue official grading certificates. To maintain sanitation standards, graders may inspect the plant and equipment used in processing.

Attendance officers investigate continued absences of pupils from public schools.

Aviation safety inspectors ensure that Federal Aviation Administration (FAA) regulations that govern the quality, performance, and safety of aircraft equipment, aircraft operations, and personnel are adhered to. Aviation safety inspectors may inspect aircraft and equipment manufacturing, maintenance and repair, or flight procedures. They may work in the areas of flight operations, maintenance, or avionics, and usually specialize in either commercial or general aviation aircraft. They also examine and certify aircraft pilots, pilot examiners, flight instructors, repair stations, schools, and instructional materials.

Bank examiners investigate financial institutions to enforce federal or state laws and regulations governing the institution's operations and solvency. Examiners schedule audits, determine actions protecting the institution's solvency and the interests of shareholders and depositors, and recommend acceptance or rejection of applications for mergers, acquisitions, or establishment of a new institution.

Consumer safety inspectors and officers inspect food, feeds, pesticides, weights and measures, biological products, cosmetics, drugs, medical equipment, and radiation emitting products. Some are proficient in several areas. Working individually or in teams under a senior inspector, they check on firms that produce, handle, store, or market the products they regulate. They ensure that standards are maintained and respond to consumer complaints by questioning employees, vendors, and others to obtain evidence. Inspectors look for inaccurate product labeling, and for decomposition or chemical or bacteriological contamination that could result in a product becoming harmful to health. They may use portable scales, cameras, ultraviolet lights, thermometers, chemical testing kits, radiation monitors, or other equipment to find violations. They may send product samples, collected as part of their examinations, to laboratories for analysis.

After completing their inspection, inspectors discuss their observations with plant managers or officials, and point out areas where corrective measures are needed. They write reports of their findings and, when necessary, compile evidence for use in court if legal action must be taken.

Customs inspectors enforce laws governing imports and exports. Stationed in the United States and overseas at air-

ports, seaports, and border crossing points, they examine, count, weigh, gauge, measure, and sample commercial and noncommercial cargoes entering and leaving the United States, to determine admissibility and the amount of duties that must be paid. They ensure that all cargo is properly described on accompanying importers' declarations to determine the proper duty and interdict contraband. They inspect baggage and articles carried by passengers and crew members to ensure that all merchandise is declared, proper duties are paid, and contraband is not present. They also ensure that people, ships, planes, and anything used to import or export cargo comply with all appropriate entrance and clearance requirements.

Dealer compliance representatives inspect franchised establishments, such as motels and fast food restaurants, to ensure compliance with the franchiser's policies and procedures. They may suggest changes in financial or other operations which, if not followed, can result in loss of the franchise.

Environmental health inspectors, who work primarily for state and local governments, ensure that food, water, and air meet government standards. They check the cleanliness and safety of food and beverages produced in dairies and processing plants, or served in restaurants, hospitals, and other institutions. They often examine the handling, processing, and serving of food for compliance with sanitation rules and regulations, and oversee the treatment and disposal of sewage, refuse, and garbage. In addition, inspectors may visit pollution sources and test for pollutants by collecting air, water, or waste samples for analysis. They try to determine the nature and cause of pollution and initiate action to stop it.

In large local and state health or agriculture departments, environmental health inspectors may specialize in the areas of milk and dairy products, food sanitation, waste control, air pollution, water pollution, institutional sanitation, or occupational health. In rural areas and small towns, they may be responsible for a wide range of environmental health activities.

Equal opportunity representatives ascertain and correct unfair employment practices through consultation with and mediation between employers and minority groups.

Federal and state laws require food inspectors to inspect meat, poultry, their byproducts, and egg products to ensure they are safe for public consumption. Working onsite, frequently as part of a team, they inspect meat and poultry slaughtering, processing, and packaging operations, as well as egg products operations. They also check for correct product labeling and proper sanitation.

Immigration inspectors interview and examine people seeking entrance to the United States and its territories. They inspect passports to determine whether people are legally eligible to enter and verify their citizenship status and identity. Immigration inspectors also prepare reports, maintain records, and process applications and petitions for immigration or temporary residence in the United States.

Logging operations inspectors review contract logging operations. They prepare reports and issue remedial instructions for violations of contractual agreements and of fire and safety regulations.

Mine safety and health inspectors work to ensure the health and safety of miners. They visit mines and related facilities to obtain information on health and safety conditions and to enforce safety laws and regulations. They discuss their findings with the management of the mine and issue citations describing violations and hazards that must be corrected. Mine inspectors also investigate and report on mine accidents and may direct rescue and fire fighting operations when fires or explosions occur.

Motor vehicle inspectors verify the compliance of automobiles and trucks with state requirements for safe operation and emissions. They inspect truck cargoes to assure compliance with legal limitations on gross weight and hazardous cargoes.

Occupational safety and health inspectors visit places of employment to detect unsafe machinery and equipment, or unhealthy working conditions. They discuss their findings with the employer or plant manager and order that violations be promptly corrected in accordance with federal, state, or local government safety standards and regulations. They interview supervisors and employees in response to complaints or accidents, and may order suspension of activity posing threats to workers.

Park rangers enforce laws and regulations in state and national parks. Their duties range from registering vehicles and visitors, collecting fees, and providing information regarding park use and points of interest, to patrolling areas to prevent fire, participating in first aid and rescue activities, and training and supervising other park workers. Some rangers specialize in snow safety and avalanche control. With increasing numbers of visitors to our national parks, some rangers specialize as law enforcement officers.

Postal inspectors observe the functioning of the postal system and enforce laws and regulations. As law enforcement agents, postal inspectors have statutory powers of arrest and the authority to carry firearms. They investigate criminal activities such as theft and misuse of the mail. In instances of suspected mismanagement or fraud, inspectors conduct management or financial audits. They also collaborate with other government agencies, such as the Internal Revenue Service, as members of special task forces.

Railroad inspectors verify the compliance of railroad systems and equipment with federal safety regulations. They investigate accidents and review railroads' operating practices.

Revenue officers investigate and collect delinquent tax returns from individuals or businesses. They investigate leads from various sources. They attempt to resolve tax problems with taxpayers and recommend penalties, collection actions, and recommend criminal prosecutions when necessary.

Securities compliance examiners implement regulations concerning securities and real estate transactions. They investigate applications for registration of securities sales and complaints of irregular securities transactions, and recommend legal action when necessary.

Travel accommodations raters inspect hotels, motels, restaurants, campgrounds, and vacation resorts. They evaluate travel and tourist accommodations for travel guide publishers and organizations such as tourism promoters and automobile clubs.

Other inspectors and compliance officers include coroners, code inspectors, mortician investigators, and dealer-compliance representatives. Closely related work is done by construction and building inspectors.

Working Conditions

Inspectors and compliance officers meet all kinds of people and work in a variety of environments. Their jobs often involve considerable field work, and some inspectors travel frequently. They are generally furnished with an automobile or are reimbursed for travel expenses.

Inspectors may experience unpleasant, stressful, and dangerous working conditions. For example, mine safety and health inspectors are exposed to the same hazards as miners. Some food inspectors examine and inspect the livestock slaughtering process in slaughterhouses and frequently come in contact with unpleasant conditions. Postal inspectors have to put up with the stress inherent in all law enforcement work, in addition to the danger inherent in making occasional arrests. Park rangers often work outdoors—in many cases, on rugged terrain—in very hot or bitterly cold weather for extended periods.

Many inspectors work long and often irregular hours. Even those inspectors not engaged in some form of law enforcement may find themselves in adversarial roles when the organization or individual being inspected objects to the inspection.

Employment

Inspectors and compliance officers held about 163,000 jobs in 1996. State governments employed 34 percent, the federal government—chiefly the Departments of Defense, Labor, Treasury, and Agriculture—employed 31 percent, and local governments employed 18 percent. The remaining 17 percent were employed throughout the private sector—primarily in education, hospitals, insurance companies, labor unions, and manufacturing firms.

Some consumer safety inspectors work for the U.S. Food and Drug Administration, but the majority of these inspectors work for state governments. Most food inspectors and agricultural commodity graders are employed by the U.S. Department of Agriculture. Many health inspectors work for state and local governments. Compliance inspectors are employed primarily by the Treasury and Labor departments on the federal level, as well as by state and local governments. The Department of Defense employs the most quality assurance inspectors. The states and the Treasury Department employ internal revenue officers. Aviation safety inspectors work for the Federal Aviation Administration. The Environmental Protection Agency employs inspectors to verify compliance with pollution control and other laws. The U.S. Department of Labor and many state governments employ occupational safety and health inspectors, equal-opportunity officers, and mine safety and health inspectors. The U.S. Department of Interior employs park rangers. Department of the Treasury customs inspectors work in the United States and overseas at airports, seaports, and border crossing points.

Training, Other Qualifications, and Advancement

Because of the diversity of the functions they perform, qualifications for inspector and compliance officer jobs differ greatly. Requirements include a combination of education, experience, and often a passing grade on a written examination. Employers may require college training, including courses related to the job. The following examples illustrate the range of qualifications for various inspector jobs.

Postal inspectors must have a bachelor's degree and one year's work experience. It is desirable that they have one of several professional certifications, such as that of certified public accountant. They also must pass a background suitability investigation, meet certain health requirements, undergo a drug screening test, possess a valid state driver's license, and be a U.S. citizen between 21 and 36 years of age when hired.

Aviation safety inspectors working in operations must be pilots with varying certificates, ratings, and numbers of flight hours to their credit. In addition, FAA medical certificates are required. Some also are required to have an FAA flight instructor rating. Maintenance and avionics inspectors must have

© 1999 • J. Michael Farr • JIST Works, Inc. • Indianapolis, IN

considerable experience in aviation maintenance and knowledge of industry standards and relevant federal laws. Many aviation safety inspectors have had flight and maintenance training in the Armed Forces. No written examination is required.

Applicants for positions as mine safety and health inspectors generally must have experience in mine safety, management, or supervision. Some may possess a skill such as that of an electrician (for mine electrical inspectors). Applicants must meet strict medical requirements and be physically able to perform arduous duties efficiently. Many mine safety inspectors are former miners.

Applicants for internal revenue officer jobs must be a U.S. citizen and have a bachelor's degree or three years of experience in business, legal, financial, or investigative practices.

Park rangers need at least two years of college with at least 12 credits in science and criminal justice, although some start as part-time, seasonal workers with the U.S. Forest Service. Most positions require a bachelor's degree.

Environmental health inspectors, called sanitarians in many states, sometimes must have a bachelor's degree in environmental health or in the physical or biological sciences. In most states, they are licensed by examining boards.

All inspectors and compliance officers are trained in the applicable laws or inspection procedures through some combination of classroom and on-the-job training. In general, people who want to enter this occupation should be responsible and like detailed work. Inspectors and compliance officers should be neat and personable, and able to communicate well orally and in writing.

Federal government inspectors and compliance officers whose job performance is satisfactory advance through their career ladder to a specified full performance level. For positions above this level (usually supervisory positions), advancement is competitive, based on agency needs and individual merit. Advancement opportunities in state and local governments and the private sector are often similar to those in the federal government.

Some civil service specifications, including those for mine inspectors, aviation safety inspectors, and agricultural commodity graders, rate applicants solely on their experience and education. Others require a written examination.

Job Outlook

Slower than average growth in employment of inspectors and compliance officers is expected through the year 2006, reflecting a balance of continuing public demand for a safe environment and quality products against the desire for smaller government and fewer regulations. Job openings will arise primarily from the need to replace those who transfer to other occupations, retire, or leave the labor force for other reasons. In private industry, employment growth will reflect industry growth, due to continuing self-enforcement of government and company regulations and policies, particularly among franchise operations in various industries.

Employment of inspectors and compliance officers is seldom affected by general economic fluctuations. Federal, state, and local governments—which employ most inspectors—provide workers with considerable job security.

Earnings

The median weekly salary of inspectors and compliance officers, except construction, was about $695 in 1996. The lowest 10 percent earned less than $381; the highest 10 percent earned over $1,215. In the federal government, the annual starting salaries for inspectors varied from $24,200 to $29,600 depending upon the nature of the inspection or compliance activity. Beginning salaries were slightly higher in selected areas where the prevailing local pay level was higher. The following tabulation presents 1997 average salaries for selected inspectors and compliance officers in the federal government in nonsupervisory, supervisory, and managerial positions.

Air safety investigators	$66,110
Highway safety inspectors	64,190
Mine safety and health inspectors	58,000
Railroad safety inspectors	55,910
Internal revenue agent	55,730
Equal employment opportunity officials	54,180
Environmental protection specialists	52,940
Safety and occupational health managers	50,070
Import specialists	49,370
Quality assurance inspectors	47,020
Customs inspectors	40,020
Securities compliance examiners	39,490
Agricultural commodity graders	39,080
Immigration inspectors	35,010
Consumer safety inspectors	34,360
Food inspectors	32,870
Environmental protection assistants	29,090

Most inspectors and compliance officers work for federal, state, and local governments and in large private firms, all of which generally offer more generous benefits than do smaller firms.

Related Occupations

Inspectors and compliance officers are responsible for seeing that laws and regulations are obeyed. Construction and building inspectors; fire marshals; federal, state, and local law enforcement professionals; corrections officers; and fish and game wardens also enforce laws and regulations.

Sources of Additional Information

Information on obtaining a job with the federal government may be obtained from the Office of Personnel Management through a telephone-based system. Consult your telephone directory under U.S. government for a local number or call (912) 757-3000 (TDD (912) 744-2299). The number is not toll-free and charges may result. Information also is available from their Internet site: http://www.usajobs.opm.gov

For information on a career as a specific type of federal inspector or compliance officer, a federal department or agency that employs them may also be contacted directly.

Information about state and local government jobs is available from state civil service commissions, usually located in each state capital, or from local government offices.

Information about jobs in private industry is available from the State Employment Service, which is listed under "Job Service" or "Employment" in the state government section of local telephone directories.

Insurance Agents and Brokers

(*D.O.T.* 169.167-050, 239.267-010, and 250.257-010)

Significant Points

* *Employers prefer to hire college graduates and persons with proven sales ability or success in other occupations.*

* *Employment is projected to grow more slowly than average as the increasing use of computers allows agents to handle more sales.*

* *Many beginners find it difficult to establish a sufficiently large clientele in this highly competitive business; consequently, many eventually leave for other jobs.*

Nature of the Work

Most people have their first contact with an insurance company through an insurance agent or broker. These professionals sell insurance policies to individuals and businesses to provide protection against financial loss. Insurance agents and brokers help individuals, families, and businesses select the policy that provides the best insurance protection for their lives and health, as well as for their automobiles, jewelry, personal valuables, furniture, household items, businesses, and other properties. Agents and brokers prepare reports, maintain records, and, in the event of a loss, help policyholders settle insurance claims. Some agents may help an employer

provide employees the opportunity to buy insurance through payroll deductions. Insurance agents may work for one insurance company or as "independent agents" selling for several companies. Insurance brokers do not sell for a particular company, but place insurance policies for their clients with the company that offers the best rate and coverage.

Insurance agents sell one or more of several types of insurance—life, property and casualty, health, disability, and long-term care. Life insurance agents specialize in selling policies that pay beneficiaries when a policyholder dies. Depending on the policyholder's circumstances, a whole-life policy can be designed to provide retirement income, funds for the education of children, or other benefits. Life insurance agents and brokers are sometimes referred to as life underwriters.

Property and casualty insurance agents and brokers sell policies that protect individuals and businesses from financial loss as a result of automobile accidents, fire or theft, storms, and other events that can damage property. For businesses, property and casualty insurance can also cover injured workers' compensation, product liability claims, or medical malpractice claims. Many life and property and casualty insurance agents also sell health insurance policies covering the costs of medical care and loss of income due to illness or injury.

An increasing number of insurance agents and brokers offer comprehensive financial planning services to their clients such as retirement planning counseling. As a result, many insurance agents and brokers are involved in "cross-selling" or "total account development"—besides insurance, these agents may become licensed to sell mutual funds, annuities, and other securities.

Since insurance sales agents obtain many new accounts through referrals, it is important that agents maintain regular contact with their clients to ensure their financial needs are being met as personal and business needs change. Developing a satisfied clientele who will recommend an agent's services to other potential customers is a key to success in this field. Some insurance agents and brokers are also using the Internet to advertise and describe the financial products and services that they provide.

Working Conditions

Most insurance agents and brokers work in small offices, contacting clients and providing insurance policy information. However, most of their time is spent outside their offices, traveling locally to meet with clients and close sales. They generally arrange their own hours of work, and often schedule evening and weekend appointments for the convenience of clients. Although the majority of agents and brokers work

no more than 40 hours a week, some work as much as 60 hours a week or even longer.

Employment

Insurance agents and brokers held about 409,000 jobs in 1996. About three out of ten agents and brokers were self-employed. While most insurance agents specialize in life insurance, a growing number of "multiline agents" offer life, property/casualty, and health and disability policies. The following tabulation shows the percent distribution of wage and salary jobs by industry in 1996.

Insurance agents, brokers, and services	44
Life insurance carriers	35
Fire, marine, and casualty insurance carriers	12
Medical service and health insurance carriers	4
Pension funds and miscellaneous insurance carriers	1
Other industries	4

Agents and brokers are employed in cities and towns throughout the country, but most work in or near large population centers. Some insurance agents and brokers are employed in the headquarters of insurance companies, but the majority work out of local company offices or independent agencies.

Training, Other Qualifications, and Advancement

For jobs selling insurance, most companies and independent agencies prefer to hire college graduates—particularly those who have majored in business or economics. Some hire high school graduates with potential or proven sales ability or who have been successful in other types of work. In fact, most entrants to agent and broker jobs transfer from other occupations. As a result, agents and brokers tend to be older than the entrants in many other occupations.

College training may help agents or brokers grasp the technical aspects of insurance policies and the fundamentals and procedures of selling insurance. Many colleges and universities offer courses in insurance, and a few schools offer a bachelor's degree in insurance. College courses in finance, mathematics, accounting, economics, business law, government, and business administration enable insurance agents or brokers to understand how social, marketing, and economic conditions relate to the insurance industry. It is important for insurance agents and brokers to keep up to date with issues concerning clients. Changes in tax laws, government benefit programs, and other state and federal regulations can affect the insurance needs of clients and how agents conduct business. Courses in psychology, sociology, and public speaking can prove useful in improving sales techniques. In addition,

familiarity with computers and popular software packages is very important. The use of computers to provide instantaneous information on a wide variety of financial products has greatly improved agents' and brokers' efficiency and enabled them to devote more time to clients' needs.

Insurance agents and brokers must obtain a license in the states where they plan to sell insurance. By law in most states, licenses are issued only to applicants who complete specified courses and then pass state examinations covering insurance fundamentals and the state insurance laws. Agents and brokers who plan to sell mutual funds and other securities must also obtain a separate securities license. New agents usually receive training in a classroom setting at pre-licensing schools conducted by state insurance agents' associations or at the home or branch offices of the insurance company. Often they attend company-sponsored classes to prepare for examinations. Others study on their own and accompany experienced agents when they call on prospective clients.

As the diversity of financial products sold by insurance agents and brokers increases, employers are placing greater emphasis on continuing professional education. Agents and brokers can enhance their selling skills and broaden their knowledge of insurance and other financial services by taking courses at colleges and universities and attending institutes, conferences, and seminars sponsored by insurance organizations. Most states have mandatory continuing education requirements focusing on insurance laws, consumer protection, and the technical details of various insurance policies.

A number of organizations offer professional designation programs which certify expertise in specialties such as life, health, property, and casualty insurance, or financial consulting. Although voluntary, professional designation assures clients and employers that an agent has a thorough understanding of the relevant specialty. Many professional societies now require agents to commit to continuing education in order to retain their designation.

Insurance agents and brokers should be enthusiastic, outgoing, self-confident, disciplined, hard working, and able to communicate effectively. They should be able to inspire customer confidence. Because they usually work without supervision, agents and brokers must be able to plan their time well and have the initiative to locate new clients.

An insurance agent who shows sales ability and leadership may become a sales manager in a local office. A few advance to agency superintendent or executive positions. However, many who have built up a good clientele prefer to remain in sales work. Some, particularly in the property/casualty field, establish their own independent agencies or brokerage firms.

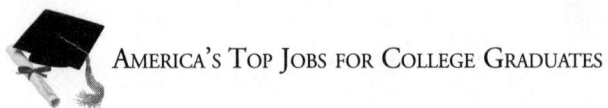

Job Outlook

Employment of insurance agents and brokers is expected to grow more slowly than the average for all occupations through the year 2006. Most job openings are expected to result from the need to replace agents and brokers who leave the occupation. Many beginners find it difficult to establish a sufficiently large clientele in this highly competitive business; consequently, many eventually leave for other jobs. Opportunities should be best for ambitious people who enjoy competitive sales work, and who have developed expertise and can advise people in a wide range of insurance and financial services.

Future demand for agents and brokers depends on the volume of sales of insurance and other financial products. The growing number of working women should increase insurance sales. Rising incomes as well as a concern for financial security should stimulate sales of mutual funds, variable annuities, and other financial products and services. Growing demand for long-term health care and pension benefits for retirees—an increasing proportion of the population—should spur insurance sales. Sales of property and casualty insurance should rise as more people seek coverage not only for their homes, cars, and valuables, but also for expensive, advanced technology products such as home computers. As new businesses emerge and existing firms expand coverage, sales of commercial insurance should increase. In addition, complex types of commercial coverage such as product liability, workers' compensation, employee benefits, and pollution liability insurance are increasingly in demand.

Employment of agents and brokers will not keep pace with the rising level of insurance sales, however. Using computers, agents can access an abundance of information on potential clients, allowing them to save time and money by carefully crafting individually tailored plans. Consequently, agents will be able to handle a greater volume of sales. Many companies and agencies are diversifying their marketing techniques to include some direct mail or telephone sales, as well as using the Internet to provide information on their product lines. These innovations reduce the time agents must spend developing sales leads, allowing them to concentrate on following up on potential clients. In some cases, clients can purchase certain policies without consultation from an agent. Also, customer service representatives are increasingly assuming some sales functions, such as expanding accounts and, occasionally, generating new accounts by offering additional financial products to interested clients. Trends toward multiline agents, group policies, and self-insurance, as more businesses set rates for their own exposure to risks and pay premiums into a reserve fund, will also contribute to employment rising

slower than the volume of insurance sales. In addition, large firms may increasingly hire risk managers to analyze their insurance needs and select the best policies.

Most individuals and businesses consider insurance a necessity, regardless of economic conditions. Therefore, agents are not likely to face unemployment because of a recession.

Earnings

The median annual earnings of salaried insurance sales workers was $31,500 in 1996. The middle 50 percent earned between $21,100 and $49,000 a year. The lowest 10 percent earned $15,000 or less, while the top 10 percent earned over $76,900.

Many independent agents are paid by commission only, whereas sales workers who are employees of an agency may be paid in one of three ways—salary only, salary plus commission, or salary plus bonus. Commissions, however, are the most common form of compensation, especially for experienced agents. The amount of the commission depends on the type and amount of insurance sold, and whether the transaction is a new policy or a renewal. Bonuses are usually awarded when agents meet their sales goals or when an agency's profit goals are met. Some agents involved with financial planning receive an hourly fee for their services rather than a commission.

Company-paid benefits to sales agents generally include continuing education, paid licensing training, group insurance plans, and office space and clerical support services. Some may pay for automobile and transportation expenses, attendance at conventions and meetings, promotion and marketing expenses, and retirement plans. Independent agents working for insurance agencies receive fewer benefits, but their commissions may be higher to help them pay for promotion and marketing expenses. They are typically responsible for their own travel and automobile expenses, life insurance, and retirement plans. In addition, all agents are legally responsible for any mistakes that they make, and independent agents must purchase their own insurance to cover damages from their errors and omissions.

Related Occupations

Other workers who sell financial products or services include real estate agents and brokers, securities and financial services sales representatives, financial advisors, estate planning specialists, and manufacturers' sales workers.

Sources of Additional Information

General occupational information about insurance agents and brokers is available from the home office of many life and

casualty insurance companies. Information on state licensing requirements may be obtained from the department of insurance at any state capital.

For information about insurance sales careers, contact:

❏ Insurance Information Institute, 110 William Street, New York, NY 10038.

For information about insurance sales careers in independent agencies and brokerages, contact:

❏ Independent Insurance Agents of America, 127 S. Peyton St., Alexandria, VA 22314.

For information about life insurance sales careers, contact:

❏ National Association of Life Underwriters, 1922 F St. NW, Washington, DC 20006.

❏ National Association of Professional Insurance Agents, 400 N. Washington St., Alexandria, VA 22314.

For information regarding training for life insurance sales careers, contact:

❏ Life Underwriting Training Council, 7625 Wisconsin Ave., Bethesda, MD 20814.

For information about professional designation programs, contact:

❏ The American College, 270 Bryn Mawr Ave., Bryn Mawr, PA 19010-2195. Homepage: http://www.amercoll.edu

❏ Society of Certified Insurance Counselors, 3630 North Hills Dr., Austin, TX 78731. Phone: (800) 633-2165. Homepage: http://www.scic.com/alliance

❏ The American Institute for Chartered Property and Casualty Underwriters, and the Insurance Institute of America, 720 Providence Rd., P.O. Box 3016, Malvern, PA 19355.

Manufacturers' and Wholesale Sales Representatives

(D.O.T. codes are too numerous to list.)

Significant Points

✴ *Although employers place an emphasis on a strong educational background, many individuals with previous sales experience who do not have a college degree still enter the occupation.*

✴ *Many jobs require a great deal of travel.*

✴ *Many are self-employed manufacturers' agents who work for a commission.*

Nature of the Work

For both manufacturers and wholesalers, sales representatives are an important part of their company's success. Regardless of the type of product they sell, their primary duties are to interest wholesale and retail buyers and purchasing agents in their merchandise and ensure that any questions or concerns of current clients are addressed. They market their company's products to manufacturers, wholesale and retail establishments, government agencies, and other institutions. Sales representatives also provide advice to clients on how to increase sales.

Depending on where they work, sales representatives have different job titles. Many of those working directly for manufacturers are referred to as manufacturers' representatives and those employed by wholesalers generally are called sales representatives. In addition to those employed directly by firms, manufacturers' agents are self-employed sales workers who contract their services to all types of companies. Those selling technical products, for both manufacturers and wholesalers, are usually called industrial sales workers or sales engineers. Many of these titles, however, are used interchangeably.

Manufacturers' and wholesale sales representatives spend much of their time traveling to and visiting with prospective buyers and current clients. During a sales call, they discuss the customers' needs and suggest how their merchandise or services can meet those needs. They may show samples or catalogs that describe items their company stocks and inform customers about prices, availability, and how their products can save money and improve productivity. Because of the vast number of manufacturers and wholesalers selling similar products, they also try to emphasize the unique qualities of the products and services offered by their company. They also take orders and resolve any problems or complaints with the merchandise.

Depending on the products they sell, sales representatives may have additional duties. For example, sales engineers, who are among the most highly trained sales workers, typically sell products whose installation and optimal use require a great deal of technical expertise and support—products such as material handling equipment, numerical-control machinery, and computer systems. In addition to providing information on their firm's products, these workers help prospective and current buyers with technical problems by recommending improved materials and machinery for a firm's manufacturing process, drawing up plans of proposed machinery layouts and estimating cost savings from the use of their equipment. They present this information and negotiate the sale, a process that may take several months. During their presentation, they may use a portable computer so they can have instant access to technical, sales, and other information.

Increasingly, sales representatives who lack technical expertise work as a team with a technical expert. In this arrangement, the duties of a sales representative are to make the preliminary contact with customers, introduce the company's product, and close the sale. The technical expert will attend the sales presentation to explain and answer questions and concerns. In this way, the sales representative is able to spend more time maintaining and soliciting accounts and less time acquiring technical knowledge. After the sale, sales representatives may make frequent follow-up visits to ensure the equipment is functioning properly and may even help train customers' employees to operate and maintain new equipment.

Those selling consumer goods often suggest how and where their merchandise should be displayed. Working with retailers, they may help arrange promotional programs, store displays, and advertising.

Obtaining new accounts is an important part of the job. Sales representatives follow leads suggested by other clients, from advertisements in trade journals, and from participation in trade shows and conferences. At times, they make unannounced visits to potential clients. In addition, they may spend a lot of time meeting with and entertaining prospective clients during evenings and weekends.

Sales representatives also analyze sales statistics, prepare reports, and handle administrative duties, such as filing their expense account reports, scheduling appointments, and making travel plans. They study literature about new and existing products and monitor the sales, prices, and products of their competitors.

In addition to all these duties, manufacturers' agents who operate a sales agency must also manage their business. This requires organizational skills as well as knowledge of accounting, marketing, and administration.

Working Conditions

Some manufacturers' and wholesale sales representatives have large territories and do considerable traveling. Because a sales region may cover several states, they may be away from home for several days or weeks at a time. Others work near their "home base" and do most of their traveling by automobile. Due to the nature of the work and the amount of travel, sales representatives typically work more than 40 hours per week.

Although the hours are long and often irregular, most sales representatives have the freedom to determine their own schedule. As a result, they may be able to arrange their appointments so they can have time off when they want it.

Dealing with different types of people can be demanding but stimulating. In addition, sales representatives often face competition from representatives of other companies as well as from fellow workers. Companies may set goals or quotas that representatives are expected to meet. Because their

earnings depend upon commissions, manufacturers' agents are also under the added pressure to maintain and expand their clientele.

Employment

Manufacturers' and wholesale sales representatives held about 1,557,000 jobs in 1996. Three of every four worked in wholesale trade—mostly for distributors of machinery and equipment, groceries and related products, and motor vehicles and parts. Others were employed in manufacturing and mining. Due to the diversity of products and services sold, employment opportunities are available in every part of the country.

In addition to those working directly for a firm, many sales representatives are self-employed manufacturers' agents who work for a straight commission based on the value of their sales. However, these workers generally gain experience and recognition with a manufacturer or wholesaler prior to going into business for themselves.

Training, Other Qualifications, and Advancement

The background needed for sales jobs varies by product line and market. As the number of college graduates has increased and the job requirements have become more technical and analytical, most firms have placed a greater emphasis on a strong educational background. Nevertheless, many employers still hire individuals with previous sales experience who do not have a college degree. In fact, for some consumer products, sales ability, personality, and familiarity with brands are as important as a degree. On the other hand, firms selling industrial products often require a degree in science or engineering in addition to some sales experience. In general, companies are looking for the best and brightest individuals who display the personality and desire necessary to sell.

Many companies have formal training programs for beginning sales representatives lasting up to two years. However, most businesses are accelerating these programs to reduce costs and expedite the return from training. In some programs, trainees rotate among jobs in plants and offices to learn all phases of production, installation, and distribution of the product. In others, trainees take formal classroom instruction at the plant, followed by on-the-job training under the supervision of a field sales manager.

In some firms, new workers are trained by accompanying more experienced workers on their sales calls. As these workers gain familiarity with the firm's products and clients, they are given increasing responsibility until they are eventually assigned their own territory. As businesses experience greater

competition, increased pressure is placed upon sales representatives to produce faster.

These workers must stay abreast of new merchandise and the changing needs of their customers. They may attend trade shows where new products are displayed or conferences and conventions where they meet with other sales representatives and clients to discuss new product developments. In addition, many companies sponsor meetings of their entire sales force where presentations are made on sales performance, product development, and profitability.

Manufacturers' and wholesale sales representatives should be goal oriented, persuasive, and able to work both as part of a team and independently. A pleasant personality and appearance, the ability to communicate well with people, and problem-solving skills are important as well. In addition, patience and perseverance are needed because completing a sale can take several months. Because these workers may be on their feet for long periods and may have to carry heavy sample cases, some physical stamina is necessary. Sales representatives should also enjoy traveling because much of their time is spent visiting current and prospective clients.

Frequently, promotion takes the form of an assignment to a larger account or territory where commissions are likely to be greater. Experienced sales representatives may move into jobs as sales trainers—workers who train new employees on selling techniques and company policies and procedures. Those who have good sales records and leadership ability may advance to sales supervisor or district manager.

In addition to advancement opportunities within a firm, some go into business for themselves as manufacturers' agents. Others find opportunities in buying, purchasing, advertising, or marketing research.

Job Outlook

Overall, employment of manufacturers' and wholesale sales representatives is expected to grow about as fast as the average for all occupations through the year 2006 due to continued growth in the amount of goods provided that need to be sold. Many job openings will also result from the need to replace workers who transfer to other occupations or leave the labor force.

Unlike many other occupations, technology is not expected to have a dramatic effect on the demand for these workers because sales workers will still be needed to go to the prospective customer in order to demonstrate or illustrate the particulars about the good or service. Technology is expected, however, to make them more effective and productive because it allows them to provide accurate and current information to customers during sales presentations.

Within manufacturing, job opportunities as manufacturers' agents should be a little better than those for sales representatives. Manufacturers are expected to continue outsourcing their sales duties to these workers rather than using in-house or direct selling personnel because agents are more likely to work in a sales area or territory longer than representatives, creating a better working relationship and understanding how customers operate their businesses. Also, by using agents who usually lend their services to more than one company, companies can share costs with the other companies involved with that agent.

Those interested in this occupation should keep in mind that direct selling opportunities in manufacturing are likely to be best for products with strong demand. Furthermore, jobs will be most plentiful in small wholesale and manufacturing firms because a growing number of these companies will rely on wholesalers and manufacturers' agents to market their products as a way to control their costs and expand their customer base.

Employment opportunities and earnings may fluctuate from year to year because sales are affected by changing economic conditions, legislative issues, and consumer preferences. Prospects will be best for those with the appropriate knowledge or technical expertise as well as the personal traits necessary for successful selling.

Earnings

Compensation methods vary significantly by the type of firm and product sold. However, most employers use a combination of salary and commission or salary plus bonus. Commissions are usually based on the amount of sales, whereas bonuses may depend on individual performance, on the performance of all sales workers in the group or district, or on the company's performance.

Median annual earnings of full-time manufacturers' and wholesale sales representatives were about $36,100 in 1996. The middle 50 percent earned between $24,900 and $51,900 per year. The bottom 10 percent earned less than $16,700; the top 10 percent earned more than $75,000 per year. Earnings vary by experience and the type of goods or services sold.

In addition to their earnings, sales representatives are usually reimbursed for expenses such as transportation costs, meals, hotels, and entertaining customers. They often receive benefits such as health and life insurance, a pension plan, vacation and sick leave, personal use of a company car, and "frequent flyer" mileage. Some companies offer incentives such as free vacation trips or gifts for outstanding sales workers.

Unlike those working directly for a manufacturer or wholesaler, manufacturers' agents get paid strictly on commission.

Depending on the type of product they are selling, their experience in the field, and the number of clients, their earnings can be significantly higher or lower than those working in direct sales. In addition, because manufacturers' agents are self-employed, they must pay their own travel and entertainment expenses as well as provide for their own benefits, which can be a significant cost.

Related Occupations

Manufacturers' and wholesale sales representatives must have sales ability and knowledge of the products they sell. Other occupations that require similar skills are retail, services, real estate, insurance, and securities sales workers, as well as wholesale and retail buyers.

Sources of Additional Information

Information on manufacturers' agents is available from:
❏ Manufacturers' Agents National Association, P.O. Box 3467, Laguna Hills, CA 92654-3467.

Career and certification information is available from:
❏ Sales and Marketing Executives International, Statler Office Tower, Suite 977, 1127 Euclid Ave., Cleveland OH, 44115. Homepage: http://www.smei.org
❏ Manufacturers' Representatives Educational Research Foundation, P.O. Box 247, Geneva, IL 60134.

Musicians

(*D.O.T.* 152 except .021)

Significant Points

✷ *Musicians often must supplement their income with earnings from other sources because they can find only part-time or sporadic engagements.*

✷ *Aspiring musicians begin studying an instrument or training their voices at an early age; a bachelor's or higher degree in music or music education is required to teach at the elementary/secondary school or college level.*

✷ *Competition for jobs is keen because the glamour and potentially high earnings in this occupation attract many talented individuals.*

Nature of the Work

Musicians may play musical instruments, sing, compose, arrange, or conduct groups in instrumental or vocal performances. Musicians may perform alone or as part of a group, before live audiences or on radio, or in recording studios, television, or movie productions. While most musicians play for live audiences, some prepare music exclusively for studios or computers.

Some specialize in a particular kind of music or performance. Instrumental musicians play a musical instrument in an orchestra, band, rock group, or jazz group. Some play any of a wide variety of string, brass, woodwind, or percussion instruments or electronic synthesizers; others learn several related instruments, such as the flute and clarinet, often improving their employment opportunities.

Singers interpret music using their knowledge of voice production, melody, and harmony. They sing character parts or perform in their own individual style. Singers are often classified according to their voice range—soprano, contralto, tenor, baritone, or bass—or by the type of music they sing, such as opera, rock, reggae, folk, rap, or country and western.

Composers create original music such as symphonies, operas, sonatas, or popular songs. They transcribe ideas into musical notation using harmony, rhythm, melody, and tonal structure. Many songwriters now compose and edit music using computers. Also, they may play the composition into the computer, which can record and play it back.

Arrangers transcribe and adapt musical composition to a particular style for orchestras, bands, choral groups, or individuals. Components of music—including tempo, volume, and the mix of instruments needed—are arranged to express the composer's message. While some arrangers write directly into a musical composition, others use computer software to make changes. Compositions created with computer software can also be mailed electronically or placed on an Internet site.

Conductors lead instrumental music groups, such as orchestras, dance bands, and various popular ensembles. Conductors audition and select musicians, choose the music to accommodate the talents and abilities of the musicians, and direct rehearsals and performances, applying conducting techniques to achieve desired musical effects.

Choral directors lead choirs and glee clubs, sometimes working with a band or orchestra conductor. Directors audition and select singers and direct them at rehearsals and performances to achieve harmony, rhythm, tempo, shading, and other desired musical effects.

All musicians spend a considerable amount of time practicing, individually and with their band, orchestra, or other musical group.

Working Conditions

Musicians often perform at night and on weekends and spend considerable time in practice and rehearsal. Performances frequently require travel. Because many musicians find only part-time work or experience unemployment between

engagements, they often supplement their income with other types of jobs. In fact, many decide they cannot support themselves as musicians and take permanent, full-time jobs in other occupations, while working only part-time as musicians.

Most instrumental musicians come into contact with a variety of other people, including their colleagues, agents, employers, sponsors, and audiences. They usually work indoors, although some may perform outdoors for parades, concerts, and dances. Certain performances create noise and vibration. In some taverns and restaurants, smoke and odors may be present, and lighting and ventilation may be inadequate.

Employment

An average of about 274,000 musicians held jobs in 1996. Many were between engagements, so that the total number of people employed as musicians during the course of the year might have been greater. Many musicians were self-employed, and nearly three out of five musicians employed in 1996 worked part-time.

Many work in cities in which entertainment and recording activities are concentrated, such as New York, Los Angeles, and Nashville. Classical musicians may perform with professional orchestras or in small chamber music groups like quartets or trios. Musicians may work in opera, musical comedy, and ballet productions. Many are organists who play in churches and synagogues—two out of three musicians who are paid a wage or salary work in religious organizations. Musicians also perform in clubs and restaurants, and for weddings and other events. Well-known musicians and groups give their own concerts, appear live on radio and television, make recordings and music videos, or go on concert tours. The Armed Forces, too, offer careers in their bands and smaller musical groups.

Training, Other Qualifications, and Advancement

Aspiring musicians begin studying an instrument at an early age. They may gain valuable experience playing in a school or community band or orchestra, or with a group of friends. Singers usually start training when their voices mature. Participation in school musicals or in a choir often provides good early training and experience. Musicians need extensive and prolonged training to acquire the necessary skill, knowledge, and ability to interpret music. This training may be obtained through private study with an accomplished musician, in a college or university music program, in a music conservatory, or through practice with a group. For study in an institution, an audition frequently is necessary. Formal courses include musical theory, music interpretation, composition, conducting, and instrumental and voice instruction. Composers,

conductors, and arrangers need advanced training in these subjects as well.

Many colleges, universities, and music conservatories grant bachelor's or higher degrees in music. A master's or doctoral degree is usually required to teach advanced courses in music in colleges and universities; a bachelor's degree may be sufficient to teach basic courses. A degree in music education qualifies graduates for a state certificate to teach music in an elementary or secondary school.

Those who perform popular music must have an understanding of and feeling for the style of music that interests them, but classical training can expand their employment opportunities, as well as their musical abilities. Although voice training is an asset for singers of popular music, many with untrained voices have successful careers. As a rule, musicians take lessons with private teachers when young, and seize every opportunity to make amateur or professional appearances.

Young persons who are considering careers in music should have musical talent, versatility, creative ability, and poise and stage presence to face large audiences. Since quality performance requires constant study and practice, self-discipline is vital. Moreover, musicians who play concert and nightclub engagements must have physical stamina because frequent travel and night performances are required. They must also be prepared to face the anxiety of intermittent employment and rejections when auditioning for work.

Advancement for musicians generally means becoming better known and performing for greater earnings with better known bands and orchestras. Successful musicians often rely on agents or managers to find them performing engagements, negotiate contracts, and plan their careers.

Job Outlook

Competition for musician jobs is keen, and talent alone is no guarantee of success. The glamour and potentially high earnings in this occupation attract many talented individuals. The ability to play several instruments and types of music enhances a musician's employment prospects.

Overall employment of musicians is expected to grow faster than the average for all occupations through the year 2006, reflecting the growing popularity of this form of entertainment. Almost all new wage and salary jobs for musicians will arise in religious organizations, bands, orchestras, and other entertainment groups. A decline in employment is projected for salaried musicians in restaurants and bars, although they comprise a very small proportion of all wage and salary musicians. Bars, which regularly employ musicians, are expected to grow more slowly than eating establishments, where live entertainment is unusual, because consumption of alcoholic beverages outside the home is expected to continue to decline. Overall, most job openings for musicians will arise from the need to replace those who leave the field each year because they are unable to make a living solely as musicians.

Earnings

Earnings often depend on a performer's professional reputation, place of employment, and on the number of hours worked. The most successful musicians can earn far more than the minimum salaries indicated below.

According to the American Federation of Musicians, minimum salaries in major orchestras ranged from about $22,000 to $90,000 per year during the 1996–97 performing season. Each orchestra works out a separate contract with its local union. Top orchestras have a season ranging from 29 to 52 weeks, with most major orchestras working 52 weeks. In regional orchestras, minimum salaries are between $8,000 and $22,000 per year; the season lasts 7 to 48 weeks, with an average of 35 weeks. In contrast, community orchestras have more limited levels of funding and offer salaries that are much lower for seasons of shorter duration.

Musicians employed in motion picture or television recording and those employed by recording companies were paid a minimum ranging from about $120 to $250 per service (three hours of work) in 1996.

Musicians employed by some symphony orchestras work under master wage agreements, which guarantee a season's work up to 52 weeks. Many other musicians may face relatively long periods of unemployment between jobs. Even when employed, however, many work part-time. Thus, their earnings generally are lower than those in many other occupations. Moreover, since they may not work steadily for one employer, some performers cannot qualify for unemployment compensation, and few have typical benefits such as sick leave or vacations with pay. For these reasons, many musicians give private lessons or take jobs unrelated to music to supplement their earnings as performers.

Many musicians belong to a local of the American Federation of Musicians. Professional singers usually belong to a branch of the American Guild of Musical Artists.

Related Occupations

There are many music-related occupations. These include librettists, songwriters, and music therapists. A large number of music teachers work in elementary and secondary schools, music conservatories, and colleges and universities, or are self-employed. Many who teach music also perform.

Technical knowledge of musical instruments is required by instrument repairers, tuners, and copyists. In addition, there are a number of occupations in the business side of music such as booking agents, concert managers, music publishers, and music store owners and managers, as well as salespersons of CDs and cassettes, sheet music, and musical instruments. Others whose work involves music include disc jockeys, music critics, sound and audio technicians, music librarians, and radio and television announcers.

Sources of Additional Information

For a directory of schools, colleges, and universities that offer accredited programs in music and music teacher education, contact:

❑ National Association of Schools of Music, 11250 Roger Bacon Dr., Suite 21, Reston, VA 22091.

Information on careers and employment opportunities for organists is available from:

❑ American Guild of Organists, 475 Riverside Dr., Suite 1260, New York, NY 10115.

For information on careers for bluegrass musicians, contact:

❑ International Bluegrass Music Association, 207 East 2nd St., Owensboro, KY 42303.

Nuclear Medicine Technologists

(*D.O.T.* 078.361-018)

Significant Points

✻ *Relatively few job openings will occur, because the occupation is small.*

✻ *Technologists trained in both nuclear medicine and radiologic technology will have the best prospects.*

Nature of the Work

In nuclear medicine, radionuclides—unstable atoms that emit radiation spontaneously—are used to diagnose and treat disease. Radionuclides are purified and compounded like other drugs to form radiopharmaceuticals. Nuclear medicine technologists administer these radiopharmaceuticals to patients, and then monitor the characteristics and functions of tissues or organs in which they localize. Abnormal areas show higher or lower concentrations of radioactivity than normal.

Nuclear medicine technologists operate cameras that detect and map the radioactive drug in the patient's body to create an image on photographic film. Radiologic technologists also operate diagnostic imaging equipment, but their equipment creates an image by projecting an x ray through the patient.

Nuclear medicine technologists explain test procedures to patients. They prepare a dosage of the radiopharmaceutical and administer it by mouth, injection, or other means. When preparing radiopharmaceuticals, technologists adhere to safety standards that keep the radiation dose to workers and patients as low as possible.

Technologists position patients and start a gamma scintillation camera, or scanner, which creates images of the distribution of a radiopharmaceutical as it localizes in and emits signals from the patient's body. Technologists produce the images on a computer screen or on film for a physician to interpret. Some nuclear medicine studies, such as cardiac function studies, are processed with the aid of a computer.

Nuclear medicine technologists also perform radioimmunoassay studies which assess the behavior of a radioactive substance inside the body. For example, technologists may add radioactive substances to blood or serum to determine levels of hormones or therapeutic drug content.

Technologists keep patient records and record the amount and type of radionuclides received, used, and disposed of.

Working Conditions

Nuclear medicine technologists generally work a 40-hour week. This may include evening or weekend hours in departments which operate on an extended schedule. Opportunities for part-time and shift work are also available. In addition, technologists in hospitals may have on call duty on a rotational basis.

Because technologists are on their feet much of the day, and may lift or turn disabled patients, physical stamina is important.

Although there is potential for radiation exposure in this field, it is kept to a minimum by the use of shielded syringes, gloves, and other protective devices. Technologists also wear badges that measure radiation levels. Because of safety programs, however, badge measurements rarely exceed established safety levels.

Employment

Nuclear medicine technologists held about 13,000 jobs in 1996. Almost nine out of ten jobs were in hospitals. The rest were in physicians' offices and clinics, including imaging centers.

Training, Other Qualifications, and Advancement

Nuclear medicine technology programs range in length from one to four years and lead to a certificate, associate degree, or bachelor's degree. Generally, certificate programs are offered in hospitals; associate programs in community colleges; and bachelor's programs in four-year colleges and in universities. Courses cover physical sciences, the biological effects of radiation exposure, radiation protection and procedures, the use of radiopharmaceuticals, imaging techniques, and computer applications.

One-year certificate programs are for health professionals, especially radiologic technologists and ultrasound technologists wishing to specialize in nuclear medicine. They also attract medical technologists, registered nurses, and others who wish to change fields or specialize. Others interested in the nuclear medicine technology field have three options: a two-year certificate program, a two-year associate program, or a four-year bachelor's program.

The Joint Review Committee on Education Programs in Nuclear Medicine Technology accredits most formal training programs in nuclear medicine technology. In 1997, there were 104 accredited programs.

All nuclear medicine technologists must meet the minimum federal standards on the administration of radioactive drugs and the operation of radiation detection equipment. In addition, about half of all states require technologists to be licensed. Technologists also may obtain voluntary professional certification or registration. Registration or certification is available from the American Registry of Radiologic Technologists and from the Nuclear Medicine Technology Certification Board. Most employers prefer to hire certified or registered technologists.

Technologists may advance to supervisor, then to chief technologist, and to department administrator or director. Some technologists specialize in a clinical area such as nuclear cardiology or computer analysis or leave patient care to take positions in research laboratories. Some become instructors or directors in nuclear medicine technology programs, a step that usually requires a bachelor's degree or a master's in nuclear medicine technology. Others leave the occupation to work as sales or training representatives for medical equipment and radiopharmaceutical manufacturing firms, or as radiation safety officers in regulatory agencies or hospitals.

Job Outlook

Employment of nuclear medicine technologists is expected to grow about as fast as the average for all occupations through the year 2006. The number of openings each year will be very low because the occupation is small. Growth will arise from an increase in the number of middle-aged and older persons who are the primary users of diagnostic procedures, including nuclear medicine tests. Nonetheless, job seekers will face more competition for jobs than in the recent past. In an attempt to employ fewer technologists and lower labor costs, hospitals have begun to merge nuclear medicine and radiologic technology departments. Consequently, opportunities will be best for technologists who can perform both nuclear medicine and radiologic procedures.

Technological innovations may increase the diagnostic uses of nuclear medicine. One example is the use of radiopharmaceuticals in combination with monoclonal antibodies to detect cancer at far earlier stages than is customary today, and without resorting to surgery. Another is the use of radionuclides to examine the heart's ability to pump blood. Wider use of nuclear medical imaging to observe metabolic and biochemical changes for neurology, cardiology, and oncology procedures will also spur some demand for nuclear medicine technologists.

On the other hand, cost considerations will affect the speed with which new applications of nuclear medicine grow. Some promising nuclear medicine procedures, such as positron emission tomography, are extremely costly, and hospitals contemplating them will have to consider equipment costs, reimbursement policies, and the number of potential users.

Earnings

According to a Hay Group survey of acute care hospitals, the median annual base salary of full-time nuclear medicine technologists was $36,100 in January 1997. The middle 50 percent earned between $33,400 and $39,400.

Related Occupations

Nuclear medical technologists operate sophisticated equipment to help physicians and other health practitioners diagnose and treat patients. Radiologic technologists, diagnostic medical sonographers, cardiovascular technologists, electroneurodiagnostic technologists, clinical laboratory technologists, perfusionists, and respiratory therapists also perform similar functions.

Sources of Additional Information

Additional information on a career as a nuclear medicine technologist is available from:
❑ The Society of Nuclear Medicine-Technologist Section, 1850 Samuel Morse Dr., Reston, VA 22090.

For information on a career as a nuclear medicine technologist, enclose a stamped, self-addressed business size envelope with your request to:
❑ American Society of Radiologic Technologists, Customer Service Department, 15000 Central Ave., SE, Albuquerque, NM 87123-3917, or call (800) 444-2778.

For a list of accredited programs in nuclear medicine technology, write to:

❑ Joint Review Committee on Educational Programs in Nuclear Medicine Technology, 350 South 400 East, Suite 200, Salt Lake City, UT 84111-2938.

Information on certification is available from:
❑ Nuclear Medicine Technology Certification Board, 2970 Clairmont Rd., Suite 610, Atlanta, GA 30329.

Paralegals

(*D.O.T.* 119.267-022 and -026)

Significant Points

★ *Paralegals are expected to rank among the 20 fastest growing occupations in the economy as employers recognize that paralegals perform many legal tasks for lower salaries than lawyers.*

★ *Competition for jobs should continue as the growing number of graduates from paralegal education programs keeps pace with employment growth.*

Nature of the Work

Not all legal work requires a law degree. Lawyers are often assisted in their work by paralegals or legal assistants. Paralegals perform many of the same tasks as lawyers, except for those considered to be the practice of law.

Paralegals work for lawyers. Although the lawyers assume responsibility for the legal work, they often delegate many of their tasks to paralegals. Paralegals are prohibited from setting legal fees, giving legal advice, and presenting cases in court.

Paralegals generally do the preparatory work for lawyers involved in closings, hearings, trials, and corporate meetings. Paralegals investigate the facts of cases, ensuring all relevant information is uncovered. They conduct legal research to identify the appropriate laws, judicial decisions, legal articles, and other materials that are relevant to assigned cases. After organizing and analyzing the information, paralegals may prepare written reports that attorneys use in determining how cases should be handled. Should attorneys decide to file lawsuits on behalf of clients, paralegals may help prepare the legal arguments, draft pleadings and motions to be filed with the court, obtain affidavits, and assist attorneys during trials. Paralegals also organize and track files of all documents and correspondence important to cases, and make them available to attorneys.

Paralegals may work in all areas of the law, including litigation, bankruptcy, corporate law, criminal law, employee benefits, patent and copyright law, and real estate. They help draft contracts, mortgages, separation agreements, and trust

instruments. They may also help prepare tax returns and plan estates. Some paralegals coordinate the activities of other law office employees, and keep the financial records for the office.

Paralegals who work for corporations help attorneys with employee contracts, shareholder agreements, stock option plans, and employee benefit plans. They may help prepare and file annual financial reports, maintain corporate minute books and resolutions, and help secure loans for the corporation. Paralegals may also review government regulations to ensure the corporation operates within the law.

The duties of paralegals who work in government vary depending on the agency in which they are employed. Generally, paralegals in government analyze legal material for internal use, maintain reference files, conduct research for attorneys, collect and analyze evidence for agency hearings, and prepare informative or explanatory material on the law, agency regulations, and agency policy for general use by the agency and the public.

Paralegals employed in community legal service projects help the poor, the aged, and others in need of legal assistance. They file forms, conduct research, and prepare documents. When authorized by law, they may represent clients at administrative hearings.

Some paralegals, usually those in small and medium-sized law firms, perform a variety of duties that require a general knowledge of the law. For example, they may research judicial decisions on improper police arrests or help prepare a mortgage contract.

Some paralegals employed by large law firms, government agencies, and corporations specialize in one aspect of the law, including real estate, estate planning, family law, labor law, litigation, and corporate law. Within specialties, functions often are broken down further so paralegals may deal with a specific area. For example, paralegals specializing in labor law may deal exclusively with employee benefits.

A growing number of paralegals use computers in their work. Computer software packages and on-line legal research are increasingly used to search legal literature stored in computer databases and on CD-ROM. The Internet is also used extensively for legal research. In litigation involving many supporting documents, paralegals may use computer databases to organize, index, and retrieve the material. Imaging software allows paralegals to scan documents directly into a database. Paralegals sometimes use billing programs to track hours billed to clients. They may also use computer software packages to perform tax computations and explore the consequences of possible tax strategies for clients.

Working Conditions

Paralegals do most of their work at desks in offices and law libraries. Occasionally, they travel to gather information and perform other duties.

Paralegals employed by corporations and government usually work a standard 40-hour week. Although most paralegals work year round, some are temporarily employed during busy times of the year and then released when the workload diminishes. Paralegals who work for law firms sometimes work very long hours when they are under pressure to meet deadlines. Some law firms reward such loyalty with bonuses and additional time off.

Paralegals handle many routine assignments, particularly when they are inexperienced. Paralegals usually assume more responsible and varied tasks as they gain experience. Furthermore, as new laws and judicial interpretations emerge, paralegals are exposed to new legal problems that make their work more interesting and challenging.

Employment

Paralegals held about 113,000 jobs in 1996. Private law firms employed the vast majority; most of the remainder worked for the various levels of government. Within the federal government, the Department of Justice is the largest employer, followed by the Departments of Treasury and Defense, and the Federal Deposit Insurance Corporation. Other employers include state and local governments, publicly funded legal service projects, banks, real estate development companies, and insurance companies. A small number of paralegals own their own businesses; as freelance legal assistants, they contract their services to attorneys or corporate legal departments.

Training, Other Qualifications, and Advancement

There are several ways to become a paralegal. Employers generally require formal paralegal training obtained through associate or bachelor's degree programs, or certificate programs. Increasingly employers prefer graduates of four-year paralegal programs, or college graduates who have completed short-term paralegal certificate programs. However, the majority of paralegals hold associate degrees. Some employers prefer to train paralegals on the job, promoting experienced legal secretaries or hiring college graduates with no legal experience. Other entrants have experience in a technical field that is useful to law firms, such as a background in tax preparation for tax and estate practice or nursing or health administration for personal injury practice.

Over 800 formal paralegal training programs are offered by four-year colleges and universities, law schools, community and junior colleges, business schools, and proprietary schools. There are currently 214 programs approved by the American Bar Association (ABA). Although this approval is neither required nor sought by many programs, graduation from an ABA-approved program can enhance one's employment opportunities. The requirements for admission to formal training programs vary widely. Some require some college courses or a bachelor's degree; others accept high school graduates or those with legal experience; and a few schools require standardized tests and personal interviews.

Paralegal programs include two-year associate degree programs, four-year bachelor's degree programs, or certificate programs that take only a few months to complete. Many certificate programs only require a high school diploma or GED for admission. Programs typically include general courses on the law and legal research techniques, in addition to courses covering specialized areas of the law, such as real estate, estate planning and probate, litigation, family law, contracts, and criminal law. Many employers prefer applicants with specialized training. Programs increasingly include courses introducing students to the legal applications of computers. Many paralegal training programs include an internship in which students gain practical experience by working for several months in a law office, corporate legal department, or government agency. Experience gained in internships is an asset when seeking a job after graduation.

The quality of paralegal training programs varies; the better programs generally emphasize job placement. Prospective students should examine the experiences of recent graduates of programs in which they are considering enrolling.

Paralegals need not be certified, but the National Association of Legal Assistants has established standards for voluntary certification requiring various combinations of education and experience. Paralegals who meet these standards are eligible to take a two-day examination, given three times each year at several regional testing centers. Those who pass this examination may use the designation Certified Legal Assistant (CLA). This designation is a sign of competence in the field and may enhance employment and advancement opportunities. The Paralegal Advanced Competency Exam, established in 1996 and administered through the National Federation of Paralegal Associations, offers professional recognition to paralegals with a bachelor's degree and at least two years of experience. Those who pass this examination may use the designation Registered Paralegal (RP).

Paralegals must be able to handle legal problems logically and communicate, both orally and in writing, their findings and opinions to their supervising attorney. They must understand legal terminology and have good research and investigative skills. Familiarity with the operation and applications of computers in legal research and litigation support is increasingly important. Paralegals must always stay abreast of new developments in the law that affect their area of practice. Paralegals can participate in continuing legal education seminars to maintain their legal knowledge.

Because paralegals often deal with the public, they must be courteous and uphold the high ethical standards of the legal profession. The National Association of Legal Assistants, the National Federation of Paralegal Associations, and a few states have established ethical guidelines paralegals must follow.

Paralegals are usually given more responsibilities and less supervision as they gain more work experience. In large law firms, corporate legal departments, and government agencies, experienced paralegals may supervise other paralegals and clerical staff, and delegate work assigned by the attorneys. Advancement opportunities include promotion to managerial and other law-related positions within the firm or corporate legal department. However, some paralegals find it easier to move to another law firm when seeking increased responsibility or advancement.

Job Outlook

Competition for jobs should continue as the growing number of graduates from paralegal education programs keeps pace with employment growth. Employment of paralegals is expected to grow much faster than average—ranking among the fastest growing occupations in the economy through the year 2006—as law firms and other employers with legal staffs increasingly hire paralegals to lower the cost, and increase the availability and efficiency, of legal services. While new jobs created by rapid employment growth will create most of the job openings for paralegals in the future, other job openings will arise as people leave the occupation.

Private law firms will continue to be the largest employers of paralegals as a growing population requires additional legal services, especially in areas such as intellectual property, health care law, international law, elder law, sexual harassment, and the environment. The growth of prepaid legal plans should also contribute to the demand for the services of law firms. A growing array of other organizations, such as corporate legal departments, insurance companies, real estate and title insurance firms, and banks will also hire paralegals.

Job opportunities for paralegals will expand even in the public sector. Community legal service programs—which provide assistance to the poor, aged, minorities, and middle-

income families—operate on limited budgets. They will seek to employ additional paralegals in order to minimize expenses and serve the most people. Federal, state, and local government agencies, consumer organizations, and the courts should continue to hire paralegals in increasing numbers.

To a limited extent, paralegal jobs are affected by the business cycle. During recessions, demand declines for some discretionary legal services, such as planning estates, drafting wills, and handling real estate transactions. Corporations are less inclined to initiate litigation when falling sales and profits lead to fiscal belt tightening. As a result, full-time paralegals employed in offices adversely affected by a recession may be laid off or have their work hours reduced. On the other hand, during recessions, corporations and individuals are more likely to face other legal problems, such as bankruptcies, foreclosures, and divorces, that require legal assistance. Paralegals, who provide many of the same legal services at a lower cost, may fare better than lawyers.

Earnings

Earnings of paralegals vary greatly. Salaries depend on education, training, experience, the type and size of employer, and the geographic location of the job. Generally, paralegals who work for large law firms or in large metropolitan areas earn more than those who work for smaller firms or in less populated regions.

According to the National Federation of Paralegal Associations, paralegals had an average annual salary of $32,900 in 1995. Starting salaries of paralegals with one year or less experience averaged $29,300. In addition to a salary, many paralegals received an annual bonus, which averaged about $1,900 in 1995.

The average annual salary of paralegal specialists who work for the federal government was about $44,400 in 1997.

Related Occupations

Several other occupations call for a specialized understanding of the law and the legal system, but do not require the extensive training of a lawyer. Some of these are abstractors, claim examiners, compliance and enforcement inspectors, occupational safety and health workers, patent agents, police officers, and title examiners.

Sources of Additional Information

General information on a career as a paralegal can be obtained from:
❏ Standing Committee on Legal Assistants, American Bar Association, 750 North Lake Shore Dr., Chicago, IL 60611.

For information on certification of paralegals, schools that offer training programs in a specific state, and standards and guidelines for paralegals, contact:
❏ National Association of Legal Assistants, Inc., 1516 South Boston St., Suite 200, Tulsa, OK 74119. Homepage: http://www.nala.org

Information on a career as a paralegal, schools that offer training programs, the Paralegal Advanced Competency Exam, and local paralegal associations can be obtained from:
❏ National Federation of Paralegal Associations, P.O. Box 33108, Kansas City, MO 64114.

Information on careers, training programs, and job postings for paralegals are available at the following Internet site: http://www.paralegals.org

Information on paralegal training programs, including the pamphlet "How to Choose a Paralegal Education Program," may be obtained from:
❏ American Association for Paralegal Education, P.O. Box 40244, Overland Park, KS 66204.

Information on acquiring a job as a paralegal specialist with the federal government may be obtained from the Office of Personnel Management through a telephone-based system. Consult your telephone directory under U.S. government for a local number or call (912) 757-3000 (TDD 912 744-2299). That number is not toll-free and charges may result. Information also is available from their Internet site: http://www.usajobs.opm.gov

Photographers and Camera Operators

(D.O.T. 143)

Significant Points

✴ *Good business sense, imagination, and creativity are essential.*

✴ *Only the most skilled, and those with the best business ability, can maintain a long-term career.*

✴ *A much higher proportion than average are self-employed.*

Nature of the Work

By creatively using lighting, lenses, film, filters, and camera settings, photographers and camera operators produce pictures that record an event, capture a mood, or tell a story. Making commercial quality photographs and movies requires technical expertise and creativity. Producing a successful picture includes choosing and presenting a subject to achieve a particular effect and selecting equipment to accomplish the desired goal. For example, photographers and camera operators may enhance the subject's appearance with lighting or draw attention to a particular aspect of the subject by blurring the background.

Today, many cameras adjust settings like shutter speed and aperture automatically and also let the photographer adjust these settings manually, thus allowing greater creative and technical control over the picture-taking process. In addition to automatic and manual cameras, photographers and camera operators use an array of film, lenses, and equipment—from filters, tripods, and flash attachments to specially constructed motorized vehicles and lighting equipment.

Photography increasingly involves the use of computer technology. A photographer using a traditional silver-halide film camera can take a picture and, once the film is processed and prints are made, use a scanner to transfer the images into digital form. Some photographers prefer to use digital cameras, which use electronic memory rather than a film negative to record an image. The electronic image can be transmitted instantly via a computer modem and telephone line or otherwise downloaded onto a personal computer. Then, using the computer and specialized software, the photographer can manipulate and enhance the scanned or digital image to create a desired effect. The images can be stored on a compact disc (CD) the same way as music. There are some photographers who use this technology to create electronic portfolios, as well.

Some photographers prefer to develop and print their own photographs, especially those who use black and white film or require special effects, but this requires a fully-equipped darkroom and the technical skill to operate it. Other photographers send their film to laboratories for processing. Color film, especially, requires expensive equipment and exacting conditions for correct processing and printing.

Most photographers specialize in portrait, commercial, or news photography. Others specialize in areas such as aerial, police, medical, or scientific photography, which typically involves further specialization in fields like engineering, medicine, biology, or chemistry.

Portrait photographers take pictures of individuals or groups of people and often work in their own studios. Some specialize in weddings or school photographs. Portrait photographers who are business owners arrange for advertising; schedule appointments; set and adjust equipment; develop and retouch negatives; and mount and frame pictures. They also purchase supplies, keep records, bill customers, and may hire and train employees.

Commercial and industrial photographers take pictures of various subjects, such as manufactured articles, models, buildings, merchandise, landscapes, and groups of people. This photography is used in a wide variety of media, including reports, advertisements, and catalogs. Industrial photographers often take still or motion pictures of equipment and machinery, products, workers, and company officials. The pictures are then used for analyzing engineering projects, publicity, or as records of equipment development or deployment, such as the placement of an off-shore oil rig. Companies also use these photographs in publications to report to stockholders or to advertise company products or services. This photography frequently is done on location.

News photographers, also called photojournalists, photograph newsworthy people and places, as well as sporting, political, and community events, for newspapers, journals, magazines, or television. Some photojournalists are salaried staff, while others work independently and are known as freelance photographers.

Self-employed photographers may license the use of their photographs through stock photo agencies. These agencies grant magazines and other customers the right to purchase the use of a photograph, and, in turn, pay the photographer on a commission basis. Stock photo agencies require an application from the photographer and a sizable portfolio. Once accepted, a large number of new submissions are generally required from a photographer each year. Photographers frequently have their photos placed on CDs for this purpose.

Photography also is a fine art medium, and a small portion of photographers sell their photographs as artwork. In addition to technical proficiency, artistic photography requires an even greater emphasis on self-expression and creativity.

Like photographers, camera operators work in a variety of settings. They generally use motion picture or video cameras to film a wide range of subjects, including commercial motion pictures, documentaries, music videos, news events, and training sessions. Some film private ceremonies and special events.

Many video camera operators are employed by independent television stations, local affiliates, or large cable and television networks. They often work in a broadcast studio or cover news events as part of a reporting team. Camera operators employed in the entertainment field use motion picture cameras to film movies, television programs, and commercials. Some camera operators specialize in filming cartoons or special effects for television and movies. Camera operators who work in the entertainment field often meet with directors, actors, and camera assistants to discuss ways of filming and improving scenes.

Working Conditions

Working conditions for photographers and camera operators vary considerably. Photographers employed in government, commercial studios, and advertising agencies usually work a five-day, 40-hour week. News photographers and camera operators often work long, irregular hours and must be available to work on short notice.

Self-employment allows for greater autonomy, freedom of expression, and flexible scheduling. However, income can be uncertain and necessitates a continuous, time-consuming, and sometimes stressful search for new clients. Some self-employed photographers hire an assistant solely for the purpose of seeking additional business.

Portrait photographers often work in their own studios but may also travel to take photographs at schools and other places, as well as at weddings and other events. Press and commercial photographers and camera operators frequently travel locally, can stay overnight on an assignment, or may travel to distant places for long periods of time. Their work may put them in uncomfortable, or even dangerous, surroundings. This is especially true for photojournalists covering natural disasters, civil unrest, or military conflicts.

Some photographers and camera operators must wait long hours in all kinds of weather for an event to take place and stand or walk for long periods while carrying heavy equipment. Photographers often work under severe time restrictions to meet deadlines and satisfy customers. While working on a motion picture production, camera operators are often required to work long and irregular hours. It may also be necessary for camera operators to work in helicopters or on the back of specially equipped vehicles in order to capture a scene or cover a news event.

Employment

Photographers and camera operators held about 154,000 jobs in 1996. About four out of ten were self-employed, a much higher proportion than the average for all occupations. Some self-employed photographers contracted with advertising agencies, magazines, or others to do individual projects at a predetermined fee, while others operated portrait studios or provided photographs to stock photo agencies.

Most salaried photographers worked in portrait or commercial photography studios. Others were employed by newspapers, magazines, advertising agencies, and government agencies. Most camera operators were employed in television broadcasting or at motion picture studios; relatively few were self-employed. Most photographers and camera operators worked in metropolitan areas.

Training, Other Qualifications, and Advancement

Employers usually seek applicants with a good technical understanding of photography who are also imaginative and creative. Entry level positions in photojournalism, as well as in industrial, scientific, or technical photography, are likely to require a college degree in photography, with courses in the specific field being photographed, such as industrial products or botany. Camera operators generally acquire their skills through formal post-secondary training at colleges, photographic institutes, universities, or through on-the-job training. Those in entry-level jobs, including photography and cinematography assistants, learn to set up lights, cameras, and other equipment, and learn to load and unload film. They may receive routine assignments requiring camera adjustments or decisions on what subject matter to capture. With increased experience, they may advance to more demanding assignments. Photography assistants often learn to mix chemicals, develop film, print photographs, and the various other skills necessary to run a photography business.

Individuals interested in photography should subscribe to photographic newsletters and magazines, join camera clubs, and seek employment in camera stores or photo studios. Individuals also should decide on an area of interest and specialize in it. Completing a course of study at a private photographic institute, university, or community college provides many of the necessary skills to be a successful photographer. Summer or part-time work for a photographer, cable or television network, newspaper, or magazine is an excellent way to gain experience and eventual entry into this field.

Courses in photography are offered in many places, including universities, community and junior colleges, vocational-technical institutes, and private trade and technical schools. Courses in cinematography are most often offered by photography institutes and universities. Many photographers enhance their technical expertise by attending seminars.

Basic courses in photography cover equipment, processes, and techniques. Bachelor's degree programs, especially those including business courses, provide a well-rounded education. Art schools offer useful training in design and composition, but may be weak in the commercial aspects of photography.

Photographers who wish to operate their own businesses need business skills as well as talent. These individuals must know how to submit bids; write contracts; hire models, if needed; get permission to take onsite photographs at locations normally not open to the public; obtain releases to use photographs of people; price photographs; know about copyright protection for their work; and keep financial records.

Self-employed photographers should also develop individual styles of photography to differentiate themselves from the competition. Some photographers enter the field by submitting unsolicited photographs to magazines and art directors at advertising agencies.

Both photographers and camera operators need good eyesight, artistic ability, and manual dexterity. They should be patient, accurate, and enjoy working with details. In addition, photographers should be able to work alone or with others, as they frequently deal with clients, graphic designers, and advertising and publishing specialists. Camera operators should have good hand-eye coordination, communication skills, and, if needed, the ability to handhold a camera for extended periods of time.

Commercial photographers must be imaginative and original. Portrait photographers also need the ability to help people relax in front of the camera. Photojournalists must not only be good with a camera, but must also understand the story behind an event, so their pictures match the story. They must be decisive in recognizing a potentially good photograph and act quickly to capture it. This requires journalistic skills and explains why such employers increasingly look for individuals with a four-year degree in photojournalism or journalism with an emphasis on photography.

Different types of filming environments require camera operators to have different strengths. For example, camera operators who want to work on music videos need a good sense of music and rhythm, while those who want to work in news teams must be able to set up quickly and capture the image on the first take whenever possible.

Camera operators are usually hired for a project based on recommendations from individuals such as producers, directors of photography, and camera assistants from previous projects, or through interviews with the producer.

As for career advancement, camera operators can become directors of photography for movie studios, advertising agencies, or television programs. Magazine and news photographers may become photography editors. A few photographers and camera operators become teachers and provide instruction in their own particular area of expertise.

Job Outlook

Photography, particularly commercial photography and photojournalism, is a highly competitive field, because there are more people who want to be photographers than there is employment to support them. Only the most skilled, those with the best business ability, and those who have developed the best reputations in the industry are able to find salaried positions or attract enough work to support themselves as self-employed photographers. Many persons have full-time jobs in other fields and take photographs or videos of weddings and other events on weekends.

Employment of photographers is expected to increase as fast as the average for all occupations through the year 2006. The growing demand for visual images in education, communication, entertainment, marketing, research and development, and other areas should spur demand for photographers. Demand for portrait photographers should increase as the population grows. Also, as advances in telecommunications create new markets and products—electronic newspapers and magazines, for example, which rely heavily on images—the demand for pictures and images is expected to increase over the projection period.

Employment of camera operators is expected to grow as fast as the average for all occupations through the year 2006. Despite businesses making greater use of videos for training films, business meetings, sales campaigns, and public relations work, the growth in employment of camera operators will be restrained as their work and duties in motion pictures and film are expected to be slowly taken over by directors of photography or cinematographers. Expansion of the entertainment industry will create some additional openings, but competition for these jobs will be keen for what generally is regarded as an exciting career field.

Earnings

The median annual earnings for salaried photographers and camera operators who worked full-time were about $30,600 in 1996. The middle 50 percent earned between $21,000 and $46,500. The top 10 percent earned more than $75,100, while the lowest 10 percent earned less than $14,500.

Most salaried photographers work full-time and earn more than the majority of self-employed photographers, many of whom work part-time, but some self-employed photographers have high earnings. Earnings are affected by the number of hours worked, skills, marketing ability, and general business conditions. Because many camera operators who work in film or video do so as freelancers, earnings tend to fluctuate from year to year.

Unlike photojournalists and commercial photographers, very few artistic photographers are successful enough to support themselves solely through this specialty.

Related Occupations

Other jobs requiring visual arts talents include illustrators, visual artists, designers, painters, sculptors, and photo editors.

Sources of Additional Information

Career information on photography is available from:

❏ Professional Photographers of America, Inc., 57 Forsyth St., Suite 1600, Atlanta, GA 30303.

❏ Advertising Photographers of America, 7201 Melrose Ave., Los Angeles, CA 90046.

❏ American Society of Media Photographers, 14 Washington Rd., Suite 502, Princeton Junction, NJ 08550-1033.

General information on news photography careers is available from:

❏ National Press Photographers Association, 3200 Croasdaile Dr., Suite 306, Durham, NC 27705.

Police, Detectives, and Special Agents

(D.O.T. 168.167-010; 372.167-018, .267, .363 and .367-010; 375.133, .137 except -022 and -038, .163, .167 except -018, -026, and -054, .263, .264, .267, .363 through .384; 376.167 and .667-018; 377; and 379.167 and .263-014)

Significant Points

✴ *Police work can be dangerous and stressful.*

✴ *The number of qualified candidates exceeds the number of job openings in federal law enforcement agencies and in most state, local, and special police departments.*

✴ *Opportunities will be best in those urban communities whose departments offer relatively low salaries and where the crime rate is relatively high.*

Nature of the Work

The safety and well being of our nation's citizens greatly depends on the police officers, detectives, and special agents responsible for enforcing statutes, laws, and regulations. Duties vary widely by the size and type of organization but in most jurisdictions, whether on or off duty, law enforcement officers are expected to exercise their authority whenever necessary. And, regardless of where they work or what they do, police, detectives, and special agents must spend considerable time writing reports and maintaining records that are needed when legal actions require them to testify in court.

Police officers who work in small communities and rural areas have general law enforcement duties. In the course of a day's work, they may direct traffic at the scene of a fire, investigate a burglary, or give first aid to an accident victim. In large police departments, by contrast, officers usually are assigned to a specific type of duty. Most officers are detailed to patrol a designated area to prevent crime. Patrols generally cover an area such as business districts or outlying residential neighborhoods. Officers may work alone, but in large agencies they usually patrol with a partner. They attempt to become thoroughly familiar with conditions throughout their patrol area and, while on patrol, remain alert for anything unusual. Suspicious circumstances, such as open windows or lights in vacant buildings, as well as hazards to public safety are noted. They identify, pursue, and arrest suspected criminals, resolve problems within the community, and enforce traffic laws. Officers are becoming more involved in community policing—building partnerships with the citizens of local neighborhoods and mobilizing the public to help the police fight crime.

Some police officers specialize and become experts in chemical and microscopic analysis, firearms identification, handwriting and fingerprint identification. Others may work with special units such as mounted and motorcycle patrol, harbor patrol, canine corps, special weapons and tactics or emergency response teams, or task forces formed to combat specific types of crime.

Detectives and special agents are plainclothes investigators who gather facts and collect evidence for criminal cases. They conduct interviews, examine records, observe the activities of suspects, and participate in raids or arrests.

Some local departments provide security officers, sometimes called bailiffs, to maintain order in courtrooms.

Sheriffs and deputy sheriffs enforce the law on the county level. In metropolitan areas where there are also regular police departments, the sheriff's department may perform specialized duties such as serving legal documents or operating the jail. A sheriffs' duties resemble those of a local or county police chief, but the department is generally on a smaller scale. Most sheriffs' departments employ fewer than 25 sworn officers, and many employ fewer than 10.

State police officers (sometimes called state troopers or highway patrol officers) patrol highways and enforce motor vehicle laws and regulations. They issue traffic citations to motorists who violate the law. At the scene of an accident, they may direct traffic, give first aid, and call for emergency equipment. They also write reports that may be used to determine the cause of the accident. In addition, state police officers may provide services to motorists on the highways, such as calling for road service for drivers with mechanical trouble.

State police also enforce criminal laws. They are frequently called upon to render assistance to officers of other law enforcement agencies. In rural areas that do not have a police force or a local deputy from the sheriff's department, the state police are the primary law enforcement agency, investigating any crimes that occur, such as burglary or assault.

The federal government maintains a high profile in many areas of law enforcement. Federal Bureau of Investigation (FBI) special agents are the government's principal investigators, responsible for investigating violations of more than 260 statutes. Agents may conduct surveillance, monitor court-authorized wiretaps, examine business records to investigate white-collar crime, track the interstate movement of stolen property, collect evidence of espionage activities, or participate in sensitive undercover assignments. Drug Enforcement Administration (DEA) special agents specialize in enforcement of drug laws and regulations. Agents may conduct complex criminal investigations, carry out surveillance of criminals, and infiltrate illicit drug organizations using undercover techniques. U.S. marshals and deputy marshals provide security for federal courts, including judges, witnesses, and prisoners, and apprehend fugitives. U.S. Border Patrol special agents are responsible for protecting more than 8,000 miles of international land and water boundaries. Their primary mission is to detect and prevent the smuggling and unlawful entry of undocumented aliens into the United States and to apprehend those persons found in violation of the immigration laws. Immigration and Naturalization Service (INS) agents facilitate the entry of legal visitors and immigrants to the United States and detain and deport those arriving illegally.

Special agents employed by the U.S. Department of the Treasury work for the Bureau of Alcohol, Tobacco, and Firearms, the U.S. Customs Service, the Internal Revenue Service, and U.S. Secret Service. Bureau of Alcohol, Tobacco, and Firearms special agents investigate violations of federal firearms and explosives laws, as well as federal alcohol and tobacco regulations. Customs agents inspect cargo, collect appropriate duties or fees, and intercept contraband while ensuring that all goods entering the United States comply with United States laws and regulations. Internal Revenue Service special agents collect evidence against individuals and companies that are evading the payment of federal taxes. U.S. Secret Service special agents protect the President, Vice President, and their immediate families, Presidential candidates, ex-Presidents, and foreign dignitaries visiting the United States. Secret Service agents also investigate counterfeiting, the forgery of government checks or bonds, and the fraudulent use of credit cards.

Various other federal agencies employ police and special agents with sworn arrest powers and the authority to carry firearms. These agencies include the U.S. Forest Service under the Department of Agriculture, the National Park Service under the Department of the Interior, and Federal Air Marshals under the Department of Transportation. Other police agencies generally evolved from the need for security for the agency's property and personnel. The largest such agency is the General Services Administration's Federal Protective Service, which provides security for federal buildings and property nationwide.

Working Conditions

Police work can be very dangerous and stressful. In addition to the obvious dangers of confrontations with criminals, the need to be constantly alert and ready to deal appropriately with any situation can be very stressful. Police, detectives, and special agents usually work a 40-hour week, but paid overtime work is common. Shift work is necessary because police protection must be provided around the clock. Junior officers frequently must work weekends, holidays, and nights. Police officers, detectives, and special agents are subject to call at any time their services are needed and may work long hours during investigations. All law enforcement officers are required to file reports of their activities, often involving long hours of paperwork. In most jurisdictions, whether on or off duty, officers are expected to be armed and to exercise their arrest authority whenever necessary.

The jobs of some federal agents such as U.S. Secret Service and DEA special agents require extensive travel, often on very short notice. They frequently relocate a number of times over the course of their career. Some police, detectives, and special agents with agencies such as the U.S. Border Patrol must work outdoors for long periods in all kinds of weather.

Employment

Police, detectives, and special agents held about 704,000 jobs in 1996. About 63 percent of police detectives and investigators were employed by local governments, primarily in cities with more than 25,000 inhabitants. Some cities have very large police forces, while hundreds of small communities employ fewer than 25 officers each. State police agencies employed about 10 percent of all police, detectives, and investigators; various federal agencies employed the other 27 percent.

Training, Other Qualifications, and Advancement

Civil service regulations govern the appointment of police and detectives in practically all state and large city agencies and in many smaller ones. Candidates must be U.S. citizens, usually at least 20 years of age, and must meet rigorous physical and personal qualifications. Eligibility for appointment generally depends on performance in competitive written examinations as well as on education and experience. Physical examinations often include tests of vision, hearing, strength, and agility.

Because personal characteristics such as honesty, judgment, integrity, and a sense of responsibility are especially important in law enforcement work, candidates are interviewed by senior officers, and their character traits and background are investigated. In some agencies, candidates are interviewed by a psychiatrist or a psychologist, or given a personality test. Most applicants are subjected to lie detector examinations or drug testing. Some agencies subject sworn personnel to random drug testing as a condition of continuing employment. Although police, detectives, and special agents work independently, they must perform their duties in accordance with the law and departmental rules. They should enjoy working with people and meeting the public.

In larger police departments, where the majority of law enforcement jobs are found, applicants usually must have at least a high school education. Federal agencies generally require a college degree. A few police departments accept applicants as recruits who have less than a high school education, but the number is declining.

The federal agency with the largest number of special agents is the FBI. To be considered for appointment as an FBI special agent, an applicant either must be a graduate of an accredited law school; be a college graduate with a major in accounting; or be a college graduate with either fluency in a foreign language or three years of full-time work experience. All new agents undergo 16 weeks of training at the FBI academy on the U.S. Marine Corps base in Quantico, Virginia.

Applicants for special agent jobs with the U.S. Department of Treasury's Secret Service and the Bureau of Alcohol, Tobacco, and Firearms must have a bachelor's degree or a minimum of three years' work experience which demonstrates the ability to deal effectively with individuals or groups, among other things. Prospective special agents undergo eight weeks of training at the Federal Law Enforcement Training Center in Glynco, Georgia, and another 8 to 11 weeks of specialized training with their particular agencies.

Applicants for special agent jobs with the U.S. Drug Enforcement Administration (DEA) must have a college degree and either one year of experience conducting criminal investigations, one year of graduate school, or have achieved at least a 2.95 grade point average while in college. DEA special agents undergo 14 weeks of specialized training at the FBI Academy in Quantico, Virginia.

Police departments are encouraging applicants to take postsecondary school training in law enforcement. Many entry level applicants to police jobs have completed some formal postsecondary education and a significant number are college graduates. In 1993, the most recent year for which data are available, 12 percent of local police departments required new

officer recruits to have at least some college education. Many junior colleges, colleges, and universities offer programs in law enforcement or administration of justice. Other courses helpful in preparing for a career in law enforcement include accounting, finance, electrical engineering or computer science, and foreign languages. Physical education and sports are helpful in developing the courage, competitiveness, stamina, and agility needed for law enforcement work. Knowledge of a foreign language is an asset in many agencies.

Some large cities hire high school graduates who are still in their teens as police cadets or trainees. They do clerical work and attend classes, and can be appointed to the regular force at the conclusion of their training, usually in one to two years, upon reaching the minimum age requirement.

Before their first assignments, officers usually go through a period of training. In state and large local departments, recruits get training in their agency's police academy, often for 12 to 14 weeks. In small agencies, recruits often attend a regional or state academy. Training includes classroom instruction in constitutional law and civil rights, state laws and local ordinances, and accident investigation. Recruits also receive training and supervised experience in patrol, traffic control, use of firearms, self-defense, first aid, and handling emergencies.

Police officers usually become eligible for promotion after a probationary period ranging from six months to three years. In a large department, promotion may enable an officer to become a detective or specialize in one type of police work such as laboratory analysis of evidence or working with juveniles. Promotions to corporal, sergeant, lieutenant, and captain usually are made according to a candidate's position on a promotion list, as determined by scores on a written examination and on-the-job performance.

Continuing training helps police officers, detectives, and special agents improve their job performance. Through police department academies, regional centers for public safety employees established by the states, and federal agency training centers, instructors provide annual training in defensive tactics, firearms, use-of-force policies, sensitivity and communications skills, crowd-control techniques, legal developments that affect their work, and advances in law enforcement equipment. Many agencies pay all or part of the tuition for officers to work toward degrees in criminal justice, police science, administration of justice, or public administration, and pay higher salaries to those who earn such a degree.

Job Outlook

The opportunity for public service through law enforcement work is attractive to many. The job is challenging and involves much personal responsibility. Furthermore, in many agencies, law enforcement officers may retire with a pension after 20 or 25 years of service, allowing them to pursue a second career while still in their 40s. Because of relatively attractive salaries and benefits, the number of qualified candidates exceeds the number of job openings in federal law enforcement agencies and in most state, local, and special police departments—resulting in increased hiring standards and selectivity by employers. Competition is expected to remain keen for the higher paying jobs with state and federal agencies and police departments in more affluent areas. Persons having college training in police science, military experience, or both should have the best opportunities. Opportunities will be best in those urban communities whose departments offer relatively low salaries and where the crime rate is relatively high.

Employment of police officers, detectives, and special agents is expected to increase about as fast as the average for all occupations through the year 2006. A more security-conscious society and concern about drug-related crimes should contribute to the increasing demand for police services. At the local and state levels, growth is likely to continue as long as crime remains a serious concern. However, employment growth at the federal level will be tempered by continuing budgetary constraints faced by law enforcement agencies. Turnover in police, detective, and special agent positions is among the lowest of all occupations; nevertheless, the need to replace workers who retire, transfer to other occupations, or stop working for other reasons will be the source of most job openings.

The level of government spending determines the level of employment for police officers, detectives, and special agents. The number of job opportunities, therefore, can vary from year to year and from place to place. Layoffs, on the other hand, are rare because retirements enable most staffing cuts to be handled through attrition. Trained law enforcement officers who lose their jobs because of budget cuts usually have little difficulty finding jobs with other agencies.

Earnings

In 1996, the median salary of nonsupervisory police officers and detectives was about $34,700 a year. The middle 50 percent earned between about $25,700 and $45,300; the lowest 10 percent were paid less than $19,200, while the highest 10 percent earned over $58,500 a year.

Police officers and detectives in supervisory positions had a median salary of about $41,200 a year, also in 1996. The middle 50 percent earned between about $29,200 and $38,400; the lowest 10 percent were paid less than $22,500, while the highest 10 percent earned over $64,500 annually.

Sheriffs and other law enforcement officers had a median annual salary of about $26,700 in 1996. The middle 50 percent earned between about $20,300 and $37,800; the lowest 10 percent were paid less than $15,900, while the highest 10 percent earned over $48,400.

Federal law provides special salary rates to federal employees who serve in law enforcement. Additionally, federal special agents receive availability pay or administratively uncontrolled overtime (AUO)—equal to 25 percent of the agent's grade and step—awarded because of the large amount of overtime that these agents are expected to work. For example, in 1996 FBI agents started at a base salary of $33,800 a year, earning $42,250 a year with availability pay. Other Justice and Treasury Department special agents started at about $25,000 or $30,700 a year, earning $31,300 or $38,400 per year including availability pay, depending on their qualifications. Salaries of federal special agents progress to $55,600 including availability pay, while supervisory agents started at $66,100 including availability pay. Salaries were slightly higher in selected areas where the prevailing local pay level was higher. Because federal agents may be eligible for a special law enforcement benefits package, applicants should ask their recruiter for more information.

Total earnings for local, state, and special police and detectives frequently exceed the stated salary due to payments for overtime, which can be significant. In addition to the common benefits—paid vacation, sick leave, and medical and life insurance—most police and sheriffs' departments provide officers with special allowances for uniforms. In addition, because police officers generally are covered by liberal pension plans, many retire at half-pay after 20 or 25 years of service.

Related Occupations

Police, detectives, and special agents maintain law and order. Workers in related occupations include correctional officers, guards, fire marshals, and inspectors.

Sources of Additional Information

Information about entrance requirements may be obtained from federal, state, and local law enforcement agencies.

Further information about qualifications for employment as an FBI Special Agent is available from the nearest state FBI office; the address and phone number are listed in the local telephone directory.

Further information about qualifications for employment as a DEA Special Agent is available from the nearest DEA office, or call 1-800 DEA-4288.

Information about career opportunities, qualifications, and training to become a deputy marshal is available from:

❑ United States Marshals Service, Employment and Compensation Division, Field Staffing Branch, 600 Army Navy Dr., Arlington, VA 22202.

An overview of career opportunities, qualifications, and training for U.S. Secret Service Special Agents is available from:

❑ U.S. Secret Service, Personnel Division, Room 912, 1800 G St. NW, Washington, DC 20223.

Radio and Television Announcers and Newscasters

(D.O.T. 131.067-010, .262-010; 159.147-010, -014, and -018)

Significant Points

✴ *Competition for announcer and newscaster jobs will continue to be very keen.*

✴ *Jobs at small stations usually have low pay, but offer the best opportunities for beginners.*

✴ *Related unpaid work experience at a campus radio station or as an intern at a commercial station can be very helpful in breaking into the occupation.*

Nature of the Work

Announcers and newscasters are well-known to radio and television audiences. Radio announcers, often called disc jockeys, select and introduce recorded music; present news, sports, weather, and commercials; interview guests; and report on community activities and other matters of interest to their audience. If a written script is required, they may do the research and writing. They often ad-lib much of the commentary. They also may operate the control board, sell commercial time to advertisers, and write commercial and news copy.

Some announcers at large stations usually specialize in sports or weather, or in general news, and may be called newscasters or anchors. Others are news analysts. In small stations, one announcer may do everything.

News anchors, or a pair of co-anchors, present news stories and introduce in-depth videotaped news or live transmissions from on-the-scene reporters. Weathercasters, also called weather reporters or meteorologists, report and forecast weather conditions. They gather information from national satellite weather services, wire services, and other local and regional weather bureaus. Sportscasters select, write, and deliver the sports news. This may include interviews with sports personalities and coverage of games played.

Broadcast news analysts, called commentators, present news stories and also interpret them and discuss how they may affect the nation or listeners.

Show hosts interview guests about their lives, work, or topics of current interest.

Announcers frequently participate in community activities. Sports announcers, for example, may serve as masters of ceremonies at sports club banquets or may be on hand to greet customers at openings of sporting goods stores.

Working Conditions

Announcers and newscasters usually work in well-lighted, air-conditioned, soundproof studios.

The broadcast day is long for radio and TV stations—some are on the air 24 hours a day—so announcers can expect to work unusual hours. Many present early morning shows, when most people are getting ready for work or commuting, or do late night newscasts.

They work within tight schedule constraints, which can be physically and mentally stressful. For many announcers, the intangible rewards—creative work, many personal contacts, and the satisfaction of becoming widely known—far outweigh the disadvantages of irregular and often unpredictable hours, work pressures, and disrupted personal lives.

Employment

Radio and television announcers and newscasters held about 52,000 jobs in 1996. Nearly all were staff announcers, but some were freelance announcers who sold their services for individual assignments to networks and stations, or to advertising agencies and other independent producers.

Training, Other Qualifications, and Advancement

Entry to this occupation is highly competitive. While formal training in broadcast journalism from a college or technical school (private broadcasting school) is valuable, station officials pay particular attention to taped auditions that show an applicant's delivery and—in television—appearance and style on commercials, news, and interviews. Those hired by television stations usually start out as production secretaries, production assistants, researchers, or reporters and are given a chance to move into announcing if they show an aptitude for on-air work. Newcomers to TV broadcasting also may begin as news camera operators. A beginner's chance of landing an on-air newscasting job is remote, except possibly for a small radio station. In radio, newcomers generally start out taping interviews and operating equipment.

Announcers usually begin at a station in a small community and, if qualified, may move to a better paying job in a large city. They also may advance by hosting a regular program as a disc jockey, sportscaster, or other specialist. In the national networks, competition for jobs is particularly intense, and employers look for college graduates with at least several years of successful announcing experience.

Announcers must have a pleasant and well-controlled voice, good timing, excellent pronunciation, and correct English usage. Television announcers need a neat, pleasing appearance as well. Knowledge of theater, sports, music, business, politics, and other subjects likely to be covered in broadcasts improves chances for success. Announcers also must be computer literate because stories are created and edited on the computer. In addition, they should be able to ad-lib all or part of a show and to work under tight deadlines. The most successful announcers attract a large audience by combining a pleasing personality and voice with an appealing style.

High school courses in English, public speaking, drama, foreign languages, and electronics are valuable, and hobbies such as sports and music are additional assets. Students may gain valuable experience at campus radio or TV facilities and at commercial stations serving as interns. For example, even answering the phone on the assignment desk gives the intern the experience of taking calls that may lead to a story. The intern learns what is potentially newsworthy and how to determine priorities. Interns are also favored applicants in the competition for jobs.

Persons considering enrolling in a broadcasting school should contact personnel managers of radio and television stations as well as broadcasting trade organizations to determine the school's reputation for producing suitably trained candidates.

As a result of the Telecommunications Act of 1996, the Federal Communications Commission (FCC) no longer requires anyone who works for a broadcasting station to have a license. Only the station is required to be licensed.

Job Outlook

Competition for jobs as announcers will be very keen because the broadcasting field typically attracts many more job seekers than there are jobs. Small radio stations are more inclined to hire beginners, but the pay is low. Interns generally receive preference for available positions. Because competition for ratings is so intense in major metropolitan areas, large stations will continue to seek announcers and newscasters who have proven that they can attract and retain a large audience.

Newscasters who are knowledgeable in such areas as business, consumer, and health news may have an advantage over others. While specialization is more common at larger stations and the networks, many smaller stations also encourage it

Employment of announcers is expected to decline slightly through the year 2006 due to the lack of growth of new radio and television stations. Openings in this relatively small field will arise from the need to replace those who transfer to other kinds of work or leave the labor force. Many announcers leave the field because they cannot advance to better paying jobs.

Employment in this occupation is not significantly affected by downturns in the economy. If recessions cause advertising revenues to fall, stations tend to cut behind-the-scenes workers rather than announcers and broadcasters.

Earnings

Salaries in broadcasting vary widely. They are higher in television than in radio, higher in larger markets than in small ones, and higher in commercial than in public broadcasting.

According to a survey conducted by the National Association of Broadcasters and the Broadcast Cable Financial Management Association, the average salary for radio news announcers was $31,251 a year in 1996. Salaries ranged from $7,100 in the smallest markets to $102,676 in the largest markets. Sports announcers' average was $43,646, ranging from $10,608 in the smallest to $106,200 in the largest markets.

Among television announcers, news anchors' average salary was $65,520, ranging from $24,935 in the smallest to $199,741 in the largest markets. Weathercasters' average was $52,562, ranging from $25,638 to $103,919. Sportscasters' average was $48,704, ranging from $22,400 to $128,877.

Related Occupations

The success of announcers and news broadcasters depends upon how well they speak to their audiences. Others for whom oral communication skills are vital are interpreters, sales workers, public relations specialists, teachers, and actors.

Sources of Additional Information

For a list of schools that offer programs and courses in broadcasting, contact:

❑ Broadcast Education Association, 1771 N St. NW, Washington, DC 20036.

General information on the broadcasting industry is available from:

❑ National Association of Broadcasters, 1771 N St. NW, Washington, DC 20036.

For information on careers in broadcast news, scholarships, and internships, contact:

❑ Radio-Television News Directors Foundation, 1000 Connecticut Ave. NW, Washington, DC 20036.

Radiologic Technologists

(D.O.T. 078.361-034, .362-026, -046, -054, -058, .364-010)

Significant Points

* *Job seekers may face competition for jobs as hospitals merge radiologic and nuclear medicine departments in an effort to cut costs; radiographers with cross training in nuclear medicine technology will have the best prospects.*

* *Sonographers should experience somewhat better job opportunities than other radiologic technologists, as ultrasound becomes an increasingly attractive alternative to radiologic procedures.*

Nature of the Work

Perhaps the most familiar use of the x ray is the diagnosis of broken bones. However, medical uses of radiation go far beyond that. Radiation is used not only to produce images of the interior of the body, but to treat cancer as well. At the same time, the use of imaging techniques that do not involve x rays, such as ultrasound and magnetic resonance scans, is growing rapidly. The term "diagnostic imaging" embraces these procedures as well as the familiar x ray.

Radiographers produce x-ray films (radiographs) of parts of the human body for use in diagnosing medical problems. They prepare patients for radiologic examinations by explaining the procedure, removing articles such as jewelry, through which x rays cannot pass, and positioning patients so that the correct parts of the body can be radiographed. To prevent unnecessary radiation exposure, technologists surround the exposed area with radiation protection devices, such as lead shields, or limit the size of the x-ray beam. Radiographers position radiographic equipment at the correct angle and height over the appropriate area of a patient's body. Using instruments similar to a measuring tape, technologists may measure the thickness of the section to be radiographed and set controls on the machine to produce radiographs of the appropriate density, detail, and contrast. They place the x-ray film under the part of the patient's body to be examined and make the exposure. They then remove the film and develop it.

Experienced radiographers may perform more complex imaging tests. For fluoroscopies, radiographers prepare a solution of contrast medium for the patient to drink, allowing the radiologist, a physician who interprets x rays, to see soft tissues in the body. Some radiographers who operate computerized tomography scanners to produce cross-sectional views of patients are called CT technologists. Others operate machines that use giant magnets and radiowaves rather than radiation to create an image and are called magnetic resonance imaging (MRI) technologists.

Radiation therapy technologists, also known as radiation therapists, prepare cancer patients for treatment and administer prescribed doses of ionizing radiation to specific body parts. They operate many kinds of equipment, including high-energy linear accelerators with electron capabilities. They position patients under the equipment with absolute accuracy in order to expose affected body parts to treatment while protecting the rest of the body from radiation.

They also check the patient's reactions for radiation side effects such as nausea, hair loss, and skin irritation. They give instructions and explanations to patients who are likely to be very ill. Radiation therapists, in contrast to other radiologic technologists, are likely to see the same patient a number of times during the course of treatment.

Sonographers, also known as ultrasound technologists, direct nonionizing, high frequency sound waves into areas of the patient's body; the equipment then collects reflected echoes to form an image. The image is viewed on a screen and may be recorded on videotape or photographed for interpretation and diagnosis by physicians. Sonographers explain the procedure, record additional medical history, and then position the patient for testing. Viewing the screen as the scan takes place, sonographers look for subtle differences between healthy and pathological areas, decide which images to include, and judge if the images are satisfactory for diagnostic purposes. Sonographers may specialize in neurosonography (the brain), vascular (blood flows), echocardiography (the heart), abdominal (the liver, kidneys, spleen, and pancreas), obstetrics/gynecology (the female reproductive system), and ophthalmology (the eye).

Radiologic technologists must follow physicians' instructions precisely and conform with regulations concerning use of radiation to ensure that they, patients, and coworkers are protected from overexposure.

In addition to preparing patients and operating equipment, radiologic technologists keep patient records and adjust and maintain equipment. They may also prepare work schedules, evaluate equipment purchases, or manage a radiology department.

Working Conditions

Most full-time radiologic technologists work about 40 hours a week; they may have evening, weekend, or on-call hours.

Technologists are on their feet for long periods and may lift or turn disabled patients. They work at radiologic machines but may also do some procedures at patients' bedsides. Some radiologic technologists travel to patients in large vans equipped with sophisticated diagnostic equipment.

Radiation therapists are prone to emotional "burn out" because they treat extremely ill and dying patients on a daily basis. Although potential radiation hazards exist in this occupation, they have been minimized by the use of lead aprons, gloves, and other shielding devices, as well as by instruments that monitor radiation exposure. Technologists wear badges that measure radiation levels in the radiation area, and detailed records are kept on their cumulative lifetime dose.

Employment

Radiologic technologists held about 174,000 jobs in 1996. Most technologists were radiographers. Some were sonographers and radiation therapists. About one radiologic technologist in four worked part-time. More than half of jobs for technologists are in hospitals. Most of the rest are in physicians' offices and clinics, including diagnostic imaging centers.

Training, Other Qualifications, and Advancement

Preparation for this profession is offered in hospitals, colleges and universities, vocational-technical institutes, and the Armed Forces. Hospitals, which employ most radiologic technologists, prefer to hire those with formal training.

Formal training is offered in radiography, radiation therapy, and diagnostic medical sonography (ultrasound). Programs range in length from one to four years and lead to a certificate, associate degree, or bachelor's degree. Two-year programs are most prevalent.

Some one-year certificate programs are for individuals from other health occupations, such as medical technologists and registered nurses, who want to change fields or experienced radiographers who want to specialize in radiation therapy technology or sonography. A bachelor's or master's degree in one of the radiologic technologies is desirable for supervisory, administrative, or teaching positions.

The Joint Review Committee on Education in Radiologic Technology accredits most formal training programs for this field. They accredited 629 radiography programs and 97 radiation therapy programs in 1997. The Joint Review Committee on Education in Diagnostic Medical Sonography accredited 74 programs in sonography in 1997.

Radiography programs require, at a minimum, a high school diploma or the equivalent. High school courses in mathematics, physics, chemistry, and biology are helpful. The programs provide both classroom and clinical instruction in anatomy and physiology, patient care procedures, radiation physics, radiation protection, principles of imaging, medical terminology, positioning of patients, medical ethics, radiobiology, and pathology.

For training programs in radiation therapy and diagnostic medical sonography, applicants with a background in science, or experience in one of the health professions, generally are preferred. Some programs consider applicants with liberal arts backgrounds, however, as well as high school graduates with courses in math and science.

Radiographers and radiation therapists are covered by provisions of the Consumer-Patient Radiation Health and Safety Act of 1981, which aims to protect the public from the hazards of unnecessary exposure to medical and dental radiation by ensuring operators of radiologic equipment are properly trained. The act requires the federal government to set standards that the states, in turn, may use for accrediting training programs and certifying individuals who engage in medical or dental radiography. Because ultrasound does not use ionizing radiation, sonographers are excluded from this act.

In 1997, 36 states and Puerto Rico licensed radiologic technologists. No state requires that sonographers be licensed. Voluntary registration is offered by the American Registry of Radiologic Technologists (ARRT) in both radiography and radiation therapy. The American Registry of Diagnostic Medical Sonographers (ARDMS) certifies the competence of sonographers. To become registered, technologists must be graduates of an accredited program or meet other prerequisites and have passed an examination. Many employers prefer to hire registered technologists.

With experience and additional training, staff technologists may become specialists, performing CT scanning, ultrasound, angiography, and magnetic resonance imaging. Experienced technologists may also be promoted to supervisor, chief radiologic technologist, and—ultimately—department administrator or director. Depending on the institution, courses or a master's degree in business or health administration may be necessary for the director's position. Some technologists progress by becoming instructors or directors in radiologic technology programs; others take jobs as sales representatives or instructors with equipment manufacturers.

With additional education, available at major cancer centers, radiation therapy technologists can specialize as medical radiation dosimetrists. Dosimetrists work with health physicists and oncologists (physicians who specialize in the study and treatment of tumors) to develop treatment plans.

Radiographers and radiation therapists are required to fulfill 24 hours of continuing education every other year and provide documentation to prove that they are complying with these requirements. Sonographers must complete 30 hours of continuing education every three years.

Job Outlook

Job seekers are likely to face competition from many other qualified applicants for most job openings through the year 2006. In an attempt to employ fewer technologists and lower labor costs, hospitals have begun to merge radiologic with nuclear medicine technology departments. Consequently, technologists who can perform both radiologic and nuclear medicine procedures will have the best job opportunities. The streamlining of these departments has led to slower job growth in hospitals at the same time that the number of qualified applicants entering the field has increased. The imbalance between job openings and job seekers has caused competition for jobs to become intense. Though it is unclear how severe the imbalance will remain, it is expected to persist at some level through the year 2006.

Sonographers should experience somewhat better job opportunities than other radiologic technologist occupations. Ultrasound is becoming an increasingly attractive alternative to radiologic procedures. Ultrasound technology is expected to continue to evolve rapidly and spawn many new ultrasound procedures. Furthermore, because radiation is absent from ultrasound procedures, there are no known side effects to patients.

Employment of radiologic technologists is expected to grow faster than the average for all occupations through 2006, as the population grows and ages, increasing the demand for diagnostic imaging and therapeutic technology. For example, radiation therapy will continue to be used—alone or in combination with surgery or chemotherapy—to treat cancer. Although physicians are enthusiastic about the clinical benefits of new technologies, the extent to which they are adopted depends largely on cost and reimbursement considerations. Some promising new technologies may not come into widespread use because they are too expensive and third-party payers may not be willing to pay for their use.

Hospitals will remain the principal employer of radiologic technologists. However, employment is expected to grow most rapidly in offices and clinics of physicians, including diagnostic imaging centers. Health facilities such as these are expected to grow very rapidly through 2006 due to the strong shift toward outpatient care, encouraged by third-party payers and made possible by technological advances that permit more procedures to be performed outside the hospital. Some jobs will also come from the need to replace technologists who leave the occupation.

Earnings

In 1996, median weekly earnings for full-time salaried radiologic technologists were $559. Half earned between $478 and $672; 10 percent earned less than $317; and 10 percent earned more than $849.

According to a Hay Group Survey of acute care hospitals, the median annual base salary of full-time radiologic technologists was $28,800 in January 1997. The middle 50 percent earned between $26,600 and $31,800. Full-time radiation therapy technologists earned a median annual base salary of $37,300; and ultrasound technologists, $36,100.

Related Occupations

Radiologic technologists operate sophisticated equipment to help physicians, dentists, and other health practitioners diagnose and treat patients. Workers in related occupations include radiation dosimetrists, nuclear medicine technologists, cardiovascular technologists and technicians, perfusionists, respiratory therapists, clinical laboratory technologists, and electroneurodiagnostic technologists.

Sources of Additional Information

For career information, enclose a stamped, self-addressed business size envelope with your request to:

❑ American Society of Radiologic Technologists, 15000 Central Ave. SE, Albuquerque, NM 87123-3917.

❑ Society of Diagnostic Medical Sonographers, 12770 Coit Rd., Suite 708, Dallas, TX 75251.

❑ American Healthcare Radiology Administrators, 111 Boston Post Rd., Suite 105, P.O. Box 334, Sudbury, MA 01776.

For the current list of accredited education programs in radiography and radiation therapy technology, write to:

❑ Joint Review Committee on Education in Radiologic Technology, 20 N. Wacker Dr., Suite 600, Chicago, IL 60606-2901.

For a current list of accredited education programs in diagnostic medical sonography, write to:

❑ The Joint Review Committee on Education in Diagnostic Medical Sonography, 7108 S. Alton Way, Building C, Englewood, CO 80112.

Real Estate Agents, Brokers, and Appraisers

(D.O.T. 191.267-010 and 250.157-010, .357-010, -014, and -018)

Significant Points

★ Real estate sales positions should continue to be relatively easy to obtain due to the thousands of people who leave this occupation each year.

★ Real estate agents and brokers must be licensed in every state and in the District of Columbia.

Nature of the Work

The purchase or sale of a home or investment property is not only one of the most important financial events in people's lives, but one of the most complex transactions as well. As a result, people generally seek the help of real estate agents, brokers, and appraisers when trying to buy, sell, or establish a price for real estate.

Real estate agents and brokers have a thorough knowledge of the real estate market in their community. They know which neighborhoods will best fit their clients' needs and budgets. They are familiar with local zoning and tax laws, and know where to obtain financing. Agents and brokers also act as an intermediary in price negotiations between buyers and sellers. Real estate agents are generally independent sales workers who provide their services to a licensed broker on a contract basis. In return, the broker pays the agent a portion of the commission earned from property sold through the firm, by the agent.

Brokers are independent business people who, for a fee, sell real estate owned by others and rent and manage properties. In closing sales, brokers often provide buyers with information on loans to finance their purchase. They also arrange for title searches and for meetings between buyers and sellers when details of the transactions are agreed upon and the new owners take possession. A broker's knowledge, resourcefulness, and creativity in arranging financing that is most favorable to the prospective buyer often mean the difference between success and failure in closing a sale. In some cases, agents assume the responsibilities in closing sales, but in many areas, this is done by lawyers or lenders. Brokers also manage their own offices, advertise properties, and handle other business matters. Some combine other types of work, such as selling insurance or practicing law, with their real estate business.

Before showing properties to potential buyers, the broker or agent has an initial meeting with them to get a feeling for the type of home they would like and can afford. Often, an agent or broker uses a computer to generate lists of properties for sale, their location and description, and to identify available sources of financing. Traditionally, they then take the clients to see a number of homes that are likely to meet their needs and income. Increasingly, however, agents and brokers are able to use computers in their office to give clients a "virtual" tour of properties in which they are interested, allowing them to look at various types of images of the property, including interior and exterior images and floor plans.

Because buying real estate is such an important decision of a person's life, agents may have to meet several times with prospective buyers to discuss available properties. In answering questions, agents emphasize selling points likely to be most important to the buyer. To a young family looking at a house, for example, they may point out the convenient floor plan and the fact that quality schools and shopping centers are close by. To a potential investor seeking the tax advantages of owning a rental property, they may point out the proximity to the city and the ease of finding a renter. If bargaining over price becomes necessary, agents must carefully follow their client's instructions and may have to present counteroffers in order to get the best possible price.

Once the contract has been signed by both parties, the real estate broker or agent must see to it that all special terms of the contract are met before the closing date. For example, if the seller has agreed to a home inspection or a termite and radon inspection, the agent must make sure this is done. Also, if the seller has agreed to any repairs, the broker or agent must see they are made. Increasingly, brokers and agents handle environmental problems by making sure the property they are selling meets environmental regulations. For example, they may be responsible for dealing with problems such as lead paint on the walls. While many details are handled by loan officers, attorneys, or other persons, the agent must check to make sure that they also are completed.

There is more to an agent's and broker's job, however, than just making sales. Because they must have properties to sell, they may spend a significant amount of time obtaining "listings" (owner agreements to place properties for sale with the firm). When listing property for sale, agents and brokers compare the listed property with similar properties that have been sold recently to determine its competitive market price.

Most real estate agents and brokers sell residential property. A few, usually in large firms or small specialized firms, sell commercial, industrial, agricultural, or other types of real estate. Each specialty requires knowledge of that particular type of property and clientele. Selling or leasing business property, for example, requires an understanding of leasing practices, business trends, and location needs. Agents who sell or lease industrial properties must know about transportation, utilities, and labor supply. To sell residential properties, the agent or broker must know the location of schools, religious institutions, shopping facilities, and public transportation, and be familiar with tax rates and insurance coverage.

Because real estate transactions involve substantial financial commitments, parties to the transactions may seek the advice of real estate appraisers, who are objective experts and do not have a vested interest in the property. An appraisal is an unbiased estimate of the quality, value, and best use of a specific property. Appraisals may be used by prospective sellers to set a competitive price, by a lending institution to estimate the market value of a property as a condition for a

mortgage loan, or by local governments to determine the assessed value of a property for tax purposes. Many real estate appraisers are independent fee appraisers or work for real estate appraisal firms, while others are employees of banks, savings and loan associations, mortgage companies, government agencies, or multiservice real estate companies.

During a property inspection, real estate appraisers investigate the quality of the construction, the overall condition of the property, and its functional design. They gather information on properties by taking measurements, interviewing persons familiar with the properties' history, and searching public records of sales, leases, assessments, and other transactions. Appraisers compare the subject property with similar properties for which recent sale prices or rental data are available, to arrive at an estimate of value. They may also estimate the current cost of reproducing any structures on the properties and how much the value of existing structures may have depreciated over time. Appraisers must consider the influence of the location of the properties, potential income, current market conditions, and real estate trends or impending changes that could influence the present and future value of the property. Depending on the purpose of the appraisal, they may estimate the market value of the property, the insurable value, the investment value, or other kinds of value. Appraisers must prepare formal written reports of their findings that meet the standards of The Appraisal Foundation.

Real estate appraisers often specialize in certain types of properties. Most appraise only homes, but others specialize in appraising apartment or office buildings, shopping centers, or a variety of other types of commercial, industrial, or agricultural properties. The amount of time necessary to do an appraisal varies by the type of property—for a residential property it may take a week, whereas for a commercial property, several months may be needed to complete the appraisal.

Working Conditions

Because of advances in telecommunications and the ability to retrieve data on properties over the Internet, a growing number of real estate agents, brokers, and appraisers work out of their homes instead of offices. Even with this convenience, much of their time is spent away from their desk—showing properties to customers, analyzing properties for sale, meeting with prospective clients, researching the state of the market, inspecting properties for appraisal, and performing a wide range of other duties.

Agents, brokers, and appraisers often work more than a standard 40-hour week; nearly one of every four worked 50 hours or more a week in 1996. They often work evenings and weekends to suit the needs of their clients.

Employment

Real estate agents, brokers, and appraisers held about 408,000 jobs in 1996. Many worked part time, combining their real estate activities with other careers. Most real estate agents and brokers were self-employed, working on a commission basis.

Most real estate and appraisal firms are relatively small; indeed, some are a one-person business. Some large real estate firms have several hundred real estate agents operating out of many branch offices. Many brokers have franchise agreements with national or regional real estate organizations. Under this type of arrangement, the broker pays a fee in exchange for the privilege of using the more widely known name of the parent organization. Although franchised brokers often receive help in training salespeople and in running their offices, they bear the ultimate responsibility for the success or failure of the firm.

Persons who are real estate agents, brokers, and appraisers are older, on average, than those in most other occupations. Historically, many homemakers and retired persons were attracted to real estate sales by the flexible and part-time work schedules characteristic of this field and may enter, leave, and later reenter the occupation, depending on the strength of the real estate market, family responsibilities, or other personal circumstances. Recently, however, the high startup costs associated with becoming an agent have made some look elsewhere when looking for part-time work. In addition to those entering or reentering the labor force, some transfer into real estate jobs from a wide range of occupations, including clerical and other sales jobs.

Real estate is sold and appraised in all areas, but employment is concentrated in large urban areas and in smaller but rapidly growing communities.

Training, Other Qualifications, and Advancement

In every state and in the District of Columbia, real estate agents and brokers must be licensed. All states require prospective agents to be a high school graduate, be at least 18 years old, and pass a written test. The examination—more comprehensive for brokers than for agents—includes questions on basic real estate transactions and laws affecting the sale of property. Most states require candidates for the general sales license to complete between 30 and 90 hours of classroom instruction, whereas those seeking the broker's license are required to complete between 60 and 90 hours of formal training in addition to a specified amount of experience in selling real estate (generally one to three years). Some states waive the experience requirements for the broker's license for applicants who have a bachelor's degree in real estate. State licenses generally must be renewed every one or two years, usually without reexamination. Many states, however, require continuing education for license renewal. Prospective agents and brokers should contact the real estate licensing commission of the state(s) in which they wish to work to verify exact licensing requirements.

Federal law requires appraisers of most types of real estate (all property being financed by a federally regulated lender) to be state licensed or certified. In some states, appraisers who are not involved with federally regulated institutions do not have to be certified. State certification requirements for appraisers must meet federal standards, but states are free to set more stringent requirements. Formal courses, appraisal experience, and a satisfactory score on an examination are needed to be certified. Requirements for licensure vary by state, but are somewhat less stringent than for certification. In some states, college education may be substituted for a portion of the experience requirement for licensure.

Individuals enter real estate appraisal from a variety of backgrounds. Traditionally, persons enter from real estate sales, management, and finance positions. However, as real estate transactions have become more complex, involving complicated legal requirements, many firms have turned to college graduates to fill positions. A large number of agents, brokers, and appraisers have some college training, and the number of college graduates selling real estate has risen substantially in recent years. College courses in real estate, finance and business administration, statistics, computer science, economics, and English are helpful. Because many workers start their own company, business courses such as marketing and accounting may be as important as those in real estate or finance.

However, personality traits are equally as important as academic background. Brokers look for applicants who possess a pleasant personality, honesty, and a neat appearance. Maturity, tact, and enthusiasm for the job are required in order to motivate prospective customers in this highly competitive field. Agents should also be well organized and detail oriented, as well as have a good memory for names, faces, and business details, such as taxes, zoning codes, and local land-use regulations. Appraisers should have good judgment, writing, and math skills.

Persons interested in beginning jobs as real estate agents often apply in their own communities, where their knowledge of local neighborhoods is an advantage. A beginner usually learns the practical aspects of the job, including the use of computers to locate or list available properties or identify sources of financing, under the direction of an experienced agent.

Many firms offer formal training programs for both beginners and experienced agents. Larger firms generally offer more extensive programs than smaller firms. Over 1,000 universities, colleges, and junior colleges offer courses in real estate. At some, a student can earn an associate or bachelor's degree with a major in real estate; several offer advanced degrees. Many local real estate associations that are members of the National Association of Realtors sponsor courses covering the fundamentals and legal aspects of the field. Advanced courses in appraisal, mortgage financing, property development and management, and other subjects are also available through various affiliates of the National Association of Realtors.

Many real estate appraisers voluntarily earn professional designations, representing formal recognition of their professional competence and achievements. A number of appraisal organizations have programs that, through a combination of experience, professional education, and examinations, lead to the award of such designations. These professional designations are desirable because requirements for them are more stringent than state standards.

Advancement opportunities for agents often take the form of higher commission rates and more and bigger sales, both of which increase earnings. This occurs as agents gain knowledge and expertise and become more efficient in closing a greater number of transactions. Experienced agents can advance in many large firms to sales or general manager. Persons who have received their broker's license may open their own offices. Others with experience and training in estimating property value may become real estate appraisers, and people familiar with operating and maintaining rental properties may become property managers. Agents, brokers, and appraisers who gain general experience in real estate and a thorough knowledge of business conditions and property values in their localities may enter mortgage financing or real estate investment counseling.

Job Outlook

Employment of real estate agents, brokers, and appraisers is expected to grow more slowly than the average for all occupations through the year 2006. However, a large number of job openings will arise due to replacement needs. Each year, thousands of jobs will become available as workers transfer to other occupations or leave the labor force. Because turnover is high, real estate sales positions should continue to be relatively easy to obtain. Not everyone is successful in this highly competitive field; many beginners become discouraged by their inability to get listings and to close a sufficient number of sales. Lacking financial sustenance and motivation, they subsequently leave the occupation. Well-trained, ambitious people who enjoy selling should have the best chance for success.

Increasing use of electronic information technology may increase the productivity of agents, brokers, and appraisers as

the use of computers, faxes, modems, and databases becomes more commonplace. Some real estate companies are using computer-generated images to show houses to customers without even leaving the office. These devices enable one agent to serve a greater number of customers. Use of this technology may eliminate some of the more marginal agents such as those practicing real estate part time or between jobs. These workers will not be able to compete as easily with full-time agents who have invested in this technology.

Another factor expected to impact the need for agents and brokers is the ability for prospective customers to search for properties that meet their criteria themselves by accessing certain real estate sites on the Internet. While they won't be able to conduct the entire real estate transaction on-line, it does allow the prospective homebuyers the convenience of looking at properties, as well as the ability to find out about issues such as financing, from their own home.

Computer technology has also impacted the need for appraisers. For example, the length of time needed to do a residential appraisal has declined as access to electronic databases has increased, streamlining their work process. Furthermore, specialized computer software programs have allowed lending institutions to derive property values without as much input from appraisers.

Employment growth in this field will stem primarily from increased demand for home purchases and rental units. Shifts in the age distribution of the population over the next decade will result in a growing number of persons in the prime working ages (25 to 54 years old) with careers and family responsibilities. This is the most geographically mobile group in our society, and the one that traditionally makes most of the home purchases. As their incomes rise, they also may be expected to invest in additional real estate.

Employment of real estate agents, brokers, and appraisers is sensitive to swings in the economy. During periods of declining economic activity and tight credit, the volume of sales and the resulting demand for sales workers may decline. During these periods, the earnings of agents, brokers, and appraisers decline, and many work fewer hours or leave the occupation.

Earnings

Commissions on sales are the main source of earnings of real estate agents and brokers—few receive a salary. The rate of commission varies according to the type of property and its value; the percentage paid on the sale of farm and commercial properties or unimproved land usually is higher than that paid for selling a home. Appraisers typically receive a flat fee.

Commissions may be divided among several agents and brokers. The broker and the agent in the firm who obtained the listing generally share their part of the commission when the property is sold; the broker and the agent in the firm who made the sale also generally share their part of the commission. Although an agent's share varies greatly from one firm to another, often it is about half of the total amount received by the firm. The agent who both lists and sells the property maximizes his or her commission.

Real estate agents, brokers, and appraisers who usually worked full time had median annual earnings of $31,500 in 1996. The middle 50 percent earned between $20,500 and $49,700. The top 10 percent earned more than $75,400 and the lowest 10 percent earned less than $12,600.

Income usually increases as an agent gains experience, but individual ability, economic conditions, and the type and location of the property also affect earnings. Sales workers who are active in community organizations and local real estate associations can broaden their contacts and increase their earnings. A beginner's earnings are often irregular because a few weeks or even months may go by without a sale. Although some brokers allow an agent a drawing account against future earnings, this practice is not usual with new employees. The beginner, therefore, should have enough money to live on for about six months or until commissions increase.

Related Occupations

Selling expensive items such as homes requires maturity, tact, and a sense of responsibility. Other sales workers who find these character traits important in their work include motor vehicle sales workers, securities and financial services sales workers, insurance agents and brokers, and manufacturers' representatives. Other appraisers specialize in performing many types of appraisals besides real estate, including aircraft, antiques and fine arts, and business valuations.

Sources of Additional Information

Details on licensing requirements for real estate agents, brokers, and appraisers are available from most local real estate and appraiser organizations or from the state real estate commission or board.

For more information about opportunities in real estate, contact:

❑ National Association of Realtors, Realtor Information Center, 430 North Michigan Ave., Chicago, IL 60611.

Information on careers, and licensing and certification requirements, in real estate appraising is available from:

❑ The Appraisal Foundation, 1029 Vermont Avenue NW, Suite 900, Washington, DC 20005-3517.

Recreation Workers

(*D.O.T.* 153.137-010; 159.124-010; 187.167-238; 195.227-010, -014; 352.167-010)

Significant Points

* ✴ *The recreation field has an unusually large number of part-time, seasonal, and volunteer jobs.*

* ✴ *Educational requirements range from a high school diploma, or sometimes less for many summer jobs, to a graduate degree in parks and recreation or leisure studies for some administrative positions.*

* ✴ *Competition will remain keen for full-time career positions; persons with experience gained in part-time or seasonal recreation jobs, together with formal recreation training, should have the best opportunities.*

Nature of the Work

Many people spend much of their leisure time participating in a wide variety of organized recreation activities, such as aerobics, arts and crafts, water sports, tennis, camping and softball. Recreation programs, as diverse as the people they serve, are offered at local playgrounds and recreation areas, parks, community centers, health clubs, religious organizations, camps, theme parks, and most tourist attractions. Recreation workers plan, organize, and direct these activities.

Recreation workers organize and lead programs and watch over recreational facilities and equipment. They help people pursue their interest in crafts, art, or sports by leading activities. These activities enable people to share common interests in physical and mental activities for entertainment, physical fitness, and self-improvement. Recreation workers organize teams and leagues, and also teach the correct use of equipment and facilities.

In the workplace, recreation workers organize and direct leisure activities and athletic programs for all ages, such as bowling and softball leagues, social functions, travel programs, discount services, and, to an increasing extent, exercise and fitness programs. These activities are generally for adults.

Recreation workers hold a variety of positions at many different levels of responsibility. Recreation leaders are responsible for a recreation program's daily operation, and organize and direct participants. They may lead and give instruction in dance, drama, crafts, games, and sports; schedule use of facilities and keep records of equipment use; and ensure recreation facilities and equipment are used properly. Workers who provide instruction in specialties such as art, music, drama, swimming, or tennis may be called activity specialists. They conduct classes and coach teams in the activity in which they specialize.

Recreation supervisors plan, organize, and manage recreation activities to meet the needs of the population they serve, and supervise recreation leaders. A recreation supervisor serves as a liaison between the director of the park or recreation center and the recreation leaders. A recreation supervisor who has more specialized responsibilities may also direct special activities or events, and oversee a major activity, such as aquatics, gymnastics, or performing arts.

Directors of recreation and parks develop and manage comprehensive recreation programs in parks, playgrounds, and other settings. Directors usually serve as a technical advisor to state and local recreation and park commissions, and may be responsible for recreation and park budgets.

Camp counselors lead and instruct children and teenagers in outdoor-oriented forms of recreation, such as swimming, hiking, horseback riding, and camping. Activities are often intended to enhance campers' appreciation of nature and responsible use of the environment. In addition, counselors provide campers with specialized instruction in activities such as archery, boating, music, drama, gymnastics, tennis, and computers. In resident camps, counselors also provide guidance and supervise daily living and general socialization.

In a related occupation, recreational therapists help individuals recover or adjust to illness, disability, or specific social problems.

Working Conditions

Recreation workers must work while others engage in leisure-time activities. While most recreation workers put in about 40 hours a week, people entering this field, especially camp counselors, should expect some night and weekend work and irregular hours. About three out of ten work part-time, and many jobs are seasonal. The work setting for recreation workers may be anywhere from a cruise ship, to a woodland recreational park, to a playground in the center of a large urban community. Recreation workers often spend much of their time outdoors and may work under a variety of weather conditions. Recreation directors and supervisors may spend most of their time in an office planning programs and special events. Because full-time recreation workers spend more time acting as managers than hands-on activities leaders, they engage in less physical activity. However, as is the case for anyone engaged in physical activity, recreation workers risk suffering an injury, and the work can be physically challenging.

Employment

Recreation workers held about 233,000 jobs in 1996, and many additional workers held summer jobs in this occupation. Of those who held year-round jobs as recreation workers, about half worked in park and recreation departments of municipal and county governments. Nearly two out of ten worked in membership organizations with a civic, social, fraternal, or religious orientation—the Boy Scouts, the YWCA, and Red Cross, for example. About one out of ten was in programs run by social service organizations—senior centers and adult day care programs, or residential care facilities such as halfway houses, group homes, and institutions for delinquent youth. Another one out ten worked for nursing and other personal care facilities.

Other employers included commercial recreation establishments, amusement parks, sports and entertainment centers, wilderness and survival enterprises, tourist attractions, vacation excursion companies, hotels and resorts, summer camps, health and athletic clubs, and apartment complexes.

The recreation field has an unusually large number of part-time, seasonal, and volunteer jobs. These jobs include summer camp counselors, lifeguards, craft specialists, and after-school and weekend recreation program leaders. Teachers and college students take many jobs as recreation workers when school is not in session.

Many unpaid volunteers assist paid recreation workers. The vast majority of volunteers serve as activity leaders at local day-camp programs, or in youth organizations, camps, nursing homes, hospitals, senior centers, YMCAs, and other settings. Some volunteers serve on local park and recreation boards and commissions. Volunteer experience, part-time work during school, or a summer job can lead to a full-time career as a recreation worker.

Training, Other Qualifications, and Advancement

Education needed for recreation worker jobs ranges from a high school diploma, or sometimes less for many summer jobs, to graduate education for some administrative positions in large public recreation systems. Full-time career professional positions usually require a college degree with a major in parks and recreation or leisure studies, but a bachelor's degree in any liberal arts field may be sufficient for some jobs in the private sector. In industrial recreation, or "employee services" as it is more commonly called, companies prefer to hire those with a bachelor's degree in recreation or leisure studies and a background in business administration.

Specialized training or experience in a particular field, such as art, music, drama, or athletics, is an asset for many jobs. Some jobs also require a certification. For example, when teaching or coaching water-related activities, a lifesaving certificate is a prerequisite. Graduates of associate degree programs in parks and recreation, social work, and other human services disciplines also enter some career recreation positions. Occasionally high school graduates are able to enter career positions, but this is not common. Some college students work part-time as recreation workers while earning degrees.

A bachelor's degree and experience are preferred for most recreation supervisor jobs and required for most higher-level administrator jobs. However, increasing numbers of recreation workers who aspire to administrator positions are obtaining master's degrees in parks and recreation or related disciplines Also, many persons in other disciplines, including social work, forestry, and resource management, pursue graduate degrees in recreation.

Programs leading to an associate or bachelor's degree in parks and recreation, leisure studies, or related fields are offered at several hundred colleges and universities. Many also offer master's or doctoral degrees in this field.

In 1997, 93 bachelor's degree programs in parks and recreation were accredited by the National Recreation and Park Association (NRPA). Accredited programs provide broad exposure to the history, theory, and philosophy of park and recreation management. Courses offered include community organization, supervision and administration, recreational needs of special populations, such as older adults or the disabled, and supervised fieldwork. Students may specialize in areas such as therapeutic recreation, park management, outdoor recreation, industrial or commercial recreation, and camp management.

The American Camping Association offers workshops and courses for experienced camp directors at different times and locations throughout the year. Some national youth associations offer training courses for camp directors at the local and regional levels.

Persons planning recreation careers should be outgoing, good at motivating people, and sensitive to the needs of others. Good health and physical fitness are required. Activity planning calls for creativity and resourcefulness. Willingness to accept responsibility and the ability to exercise good judgment are important qualities since recreation personnel often work without close supervision. Part-time or summer recreation work experience while in high school or college may help students decide whether their interests really point to a human services career. Such experience also may increase their leadership skills and understanding of people.

Individuals contemplating careers in recreation at the supervisory or administrative level should develop managerial skills. College courses in management, business administration, accounting, and personnel management are likely to be useful.

Certification for this field is offered by the NRPA National Certification Board. The National Recreation and Parks Association, along with its state chapters, offers certification as a Certified Leisure Professional (CLP) for those with a college degree in recreation, and as a Certified Leisure Technician (CLT) for those with less than four years of college. Other NRPA certifications include Certified Leisure Provisional Professional (CLPP), Certified Playground Inspector (CPI), and Aquatic Facility Operations (AFO) Certification. Continuing education is necessary to remain certified.

Certification is not usually required for employment or advancement in this field, but it is an asset. Employers choosing among qualified job applicants may opt to hire the person with a demonstrated record of professional achievement represented by certification.

Job Outlook

Competition will remain keen for full-time career positions in recreation. All college graduates are eligible for recreation jobs, regardless of major. Also, many high school and junior college graduates are eligible, so the number of full-time career job seekers often greatly exceeds the number of job openings. Opportunities for staff positions should be best for persons with experience gained in part-time or seasonal recreation jobs, together with formal recreation training. Those with graduate degrees should have the best opportunities for supervisory or administrative positions.

Prospects are better for the large number of temporary seasonal jobs. These positions, typically filled by high school or college students, do not generally have formal education requirements and are open to anyone with the desired personal qualities. Employers compete for a share of the vacationing student labor force, and, while salaries in recreation are often lower than those in other fields, the nature of the work and the opportunity to work outdoors are attractive to many. Seasonal employment prospects should be good for applicants with specialized training and certification in an activity like swimming. These workers may obtain jobs as program directors.

Employment of recreation workers is expected to grow faster than the average for all occupations through the year 2006 as growing numbers of people possess both the time and the money to enjoy leisure services. Growth in these jobs will also stem from increased interest in fitness and health and the rising demand for recreational opportunities for older adults in senior centers and retirement communities. However, overall employment in local government—where half of all recreation workers are employed—is expected to grow more slowly than in other industries due to budget constraints, and some local park and recreation departments are expected to do less hiring for permanent, full-time positions than in the past. As a result, this sector's share of recreation worker employment will vary widely by region, since resources as well as priorities for public services differ from one community to another. Thus, hiring prospects for recreation workers will be much better in some park and recreation departments, but worse in others.

Recreation worker jobs should also increase in social services—more recreation workers will be needed to develop and lead activity programs in senior centers, halfway houses, children's homes, and daycare programs for the mentally retarded or developmentally disabled. Similarly, the increasing elderly population will spur job growth in nursing homes and other personal care facilities where recreation activities are becoming more important.

Recreation worker jobs in employee services and recreation will continue to increase as more businesses recognize the benefits to their employees of recreation programs and other services such as wellness programs and elder care. Job growth will also occur in the commercial recreation industry, composed of amusement parks, athletic clubs, camps, sports clinics, and swimming pools, for example.

Earnings

Median annual earnings of recreation workers who worked full-time in 1996 were about $18,700, significantly lower than the median of $25,600 for workers in all occupations. The middle 50 percent earned between about $12,900 and $28,900, while the top 10 percent earned $37,500 or more. However, earnings of recreation directors and others in supervisory or managerial positions can be substantially higher.

Most public and private recreation agencies provide full-time recreation workers with typical benefits; part-time workers receive few, if any, benefits.

Related Occupations

Recreation workers must exhibit leadership and sensitivity in dealing with people. Other occupations that require similar personal qualities include recreational therapists, social workers, parole officers, human relations counselors, school counselors, clinical and counseling psychologists, and teachers.

Sources of Additional Information

For information on jobs in recreation, contact employers such as local government departments of parks and recreation, nursing and personal care facilities, and YMCAs.

Ordering information for materials describing careers and academic programs in recreation is available from:

❑ National Recreation and Park Association, Division of Professional Services, 2775 South Quincy St., Suite 300, Arlington, VA 22206. Homepage: http://www.nrpa.org

For information on careers in employee services and corporate recreation, contact:

❑ National Employee Services and Recreation Association, 2211 York Rd., Suite 207, Oakbrook, IL 60521.

For information on careers in camping and summer counselor opportunities, contact:

❑ American Camping Association, 5000 State Rd. 67 North, Martinsville, IN 46151.

Registered Nurses

(*D.O.T.* 075.124-010 and -014, .127-014, -026, -030 and -034, .137-010 and -014, .264-010 and -014, .364-010, .371-010, .374-014, -018, and -022)

Significant Points

✳ *The largest health care occupation, with over 1.9 million jobs.*

✳ *One of the five occupations projected to have the largest numbers of new jobs.*

✳ *Earnings are above average, particularly for advanced practice nurses who have additional education or training.*

Nature of the Work

Registered nurses (RNs) work to promote health, prevent disease, and help patients cope with illness. They are advocates and health educators for patients, families, and communities. When providing direct patient care, they observe, assess, and record symptoms, reactions, and progress; assist physicians during treatments and examinations; administer medications; and assist in convalescence and rehabilitation. RNs also develop and manage nursing care plans; instruct patients and their families in proper care; and help individuals and groups take steps to improve or maintain their health. While state laws govern the tasks RNs may perform, it is usually the work setting which determines their day-to-day job duties.

Hospital nurses form the largest group of nurses. Most are staff nurses, who provide bedside nursing care and carry out medical regimens. They may also supervise licensed practical nurses and aides. Hospital nurses usually are assigned to one area such as surgery, maternity, pediatrics, emergency room, intensive care, or treatment of cancer patients or may rotate among departments.

Office nurses assist physicians in private practice, clinics, surgicenters, emergency medical centers, and health maintenance organizations (HMOs). They prepare patients for and assist with examinations, administer injections and medications, dress wounds and incisions, assist with minor surgery, and maintain records. Some also perform routine laboratory and office work.

Home health nurses provide periodic services, prescribed by a physician, to patients at home. After assessing patients' home environments, they care for and instruct patients and their families. Home health nurses care for a broad range of patients, such as those recovering from illnesses and accidents, cancer, and child birth. They must be able to work independently and may supervise home health aides.

Nursing home nurses manage nursing care for residents with conditions ranging from a fracture to Alzheimer's disease. Although they generally spend most of their time on administrative and supervisory tasks, RNs also assess residents' medical condition, develop treatment plans, supervise licensed practical nurses and nursing aides, and perform difficult procedures such as starting intravenous fluids. They also work in specialty-care departments, such as long-term rehabilitation units for strokes and head injuries.

Public health nurses work in government and private agencies and clinics, schools, retirement communities and other community settings. They focus on populations, working with individuals, groups, and families to improve the overall health of communities. They also work as partners with communities to plan and implement programs. Public health nurses instruct individuals, families, and other groups in health education, disease prevention, nutrition, and child care. They arrange for immunizations, blood pressure testing, and other health screening. These nurses also work with community leaders, teachers, parents, and physicians in community health education.

Occupational health or industrial nurses provide nursing care at work sites to employees, customers, and others with minor injuries and illnesses. They provide emergency care, prepare accident reports, and arrange for further care if necessary. They also offer health counseling, assist with health examinations and inoculations, and assess work environments to identify potential health or safety problems.

Head nurses or nurse supervisors direct nursing activities. They plan work schedules and assign duties to nurses and aides, provide or arrange for training, and visit patients to observe nurses and to ensure that care is proper. They may also ensure that records are maintained and that equipment and supplies are ordered.

At the advanced level, nurse practitioners provide basic primary health care. They diagnose and treat common acute illnesses and injuries. Nurse practitioners can prescribe medications in most states. Other advanced practice nurses include clinical nurse specialists, certified registered nurse anesthetists, and certified nurse-midwives. Advanced practice nurses have met higher educational and clinical practice requirements beyond the basic nursing education and licensing required of all RNs.

Working Conditions

Most nurses work in well-lighted, comfortable health care facilities. Home health and public health nurses travel to patients' homes and to schools, community centers, and other sites. Nurses may spend considerable time walking and standing. They need emotional stability to cope with human suffering, emergencies, and other stresses. Because patients in hospitals and nursing homes require 24-hour care, nurses in these institutions may work nights, weekends, and holidays. They may also be on call. Office, occupational health, and public health nurses are more likely to work regular business hours. Almost one in ten RNs held more than one job in 1996.

Nursing has its hazards, especially in hospitals, nursing homes, and clinics where nurses may care for individuals with infectious diseases such as hepatitis and AIDS. Nurses must observe rigid guidelines to guard against these and other dangers such as radiation, chemicals used for sterilization of instruments, and anesthetics. In addition, they face back injury when moving patients, shocks from electrical equipment, and hazards posed by compressed gases.

Employment

As the largest health care occupation, registered nurses held about 1,971,000 jobs in 1996. About two out of three jobs were in hospitals, in both inpatient and outpatient departments. Others were in offices and clinics of physicians, home health care agencies, nursing homes, temporary help agencies, schools, and government agencies. About three out of ten RNs worked part-time.

Training, Other Qualifications, and Advancement

In all states, students must graduate from a nursing program and pass a national licensing examination to obtain a nursing license. Nurses may be licensed in more than one state, either by examination or endorsement of a license issued by another state. Licenses must be periodically renewed. Some states require continuing education for licensure renewal.

In 1996, there were over 1,500 entry level RN programs. There are three major educational paths to nursing: associate degree (ADN), diploma, and bachelor of science degree in nursing (BSN). ADN programs, offered by community and junior colleges, take about two years. About two-thirds of all RN graduates in 1995 were from ADN programs. BSN programs, offered by colleges and universities, take four or five years. Nearly one-third of all graduates in 1995 were from these programs. Diploma programs, given in hospitals, last two to three years. Only a small number of graduates come from these programs. Generally, licensed graduates of any of the three program types qualify for entry level positions as staff nurses.

There have been attempts to raise the educational requirements for an RN license to a bachelor's degree and, possibly, create new job titles. These changes, should they occur, will probably be made state by state, through legislation or regulation. Changes in licensure requirements would not affect currently licensed RNs, who would be "grandfathered" in, no matter what their educational preparation. However, individuals considering nursing should carefully weigh the pros and cons of enrolling in a BSN program, since their advancement opportunities are broader. In fact, some career paths are open only to nurses with bachelor's or advanced degrees. A bachelor's degree is generally necessary for administrative positions and is a prerequisite for admission to graduate nursing programs in research, consulting, teaching, or a clinical specialization.

Many ADN and diploma-trained nurses enter bachelor's programs to prepare for a broader scope of nursing practice. They can often find a hospital position and then take advantage of tuition reimbursement programs to work toward a BSN in their spare time.

Nursing education includes classroom instruction and supervised clinical experience in hospitals and other health facilities. Students take courses in anatomy, physiology, microbiology, chemistry, nutrition, psychology and other behavioral sciences, and nursing. Course work also includes liberal arts classes.

Supervised clinical experience is provided in hospital departments such as pediatrics, psychiatry, maternity, and surgery. A growing number of programs include clinical experience in nursing homes, public health departments, home health agencies, and ambulatory clinics.

Nurses should be caring and sympathetic. They must be able to accept responsibility, direct or supervise others, follow orders precisely, and determine when consultation is required.

Experience and good performance can lead to promotion to more responsible positions. Nurses can advance, in management, to assistant head nurse or head nurse. From there, they can advance to assistant director, director, and vice president. Increasingly, management-level nursing positions require a graduate degree in nursing or health services administration. They also require leadership, negotiation skills, and good judgment. Graduate programs preparing executive-level nurses usually last one to two years.

Within patient care, nurses can advance to clinical nurse specialist, nurse practitioner, certified nurse-midwife, or certified registered nurse anesthetist. These positions require one or two years of graduate education, leading in most instances to a master's degree, or to a certificate.

Some nurses move into the business side of health care. Their nursing expertise and experience on a health care team equip them to manage ambulatory, acute, home health, and chronic care services. Some are employed by health care corporations in health planning and development, marketing, and quality assurance.

Job Outlook

Employment of registered nurses is expected to grow faster than the average for all occupations through the year 2006 and, because the occupation is large, many new jobs will result. As nursing school enrollments level off or decline, as they have on a cyclical basis in the past, the number of qualified applicants will fall, reducing reported competition for jobs. There will always be a need for traditional hospital nurses, but a large number of new nurses will be employed in home health, long-term, and ambulatory care.

Faster than average growth will be driven by technological advances in patient care, which permit a greater number of medical problems to be treated, and increasing emphasis on primary care. In addition, the number of older people, who are much more likely than younger people to need medical care, is projected to grow very rapidly. Many job openings also will result from the need to replace experienced nurses who leave the occupation, especially as the average age of the registered nurse population continues to rise.

Employment in hospitals, the largest sector, is expected to grow more slowly than in other health care sectors. While the intensity of nursing care is likely to increase, requiring more nurses per patient, the number of inpatients (those who remain overnight) is not likely to increase much. Also, patients are being released earlier and more procedures are being done on an outpatient basis, both in and outside hospitals. Most rapid growth is expected in hospitals' outpatient facilities, such as same-day surgery, rehabilitation, and chemotherapy.

Employment in home health care is expected to grow the fastest. This is in response to a growing number of older persons with functional disabilities, consumer preference for care in the home, and technological advances which make it possible to bring increasingly complex treatments into the home. The type of care demanded will require nurses who are able to perform complex procedures.

Employment in nursing homes is expected to grow much faster than average due to increases in the number of people in their eighties and nineties, many of whom will require long-term care. In addition, the financial pressure on hospitals to release patients as soon as possible should produce more nursing home admissions. Growth in units to provide specialized long-term rehabilitation for stroke and head injury patients or to treat Alzheimer's victims will also increase employment.

An increasing proportion of sophisticated procedures, which once were performed only in hospitals, are being performed in physicians' offices and clinics, including HMOs, ambulatory surgicenters, and emergency medical centers. Accordingly, employment is expected to grow faster than average in these places as health care in general expands.

In evolving integrated health care networks, nurses may rotate among employment settings. Since jobs in traditional hospital nursing positions are no longer the only option, RNs will need to be flexible. Opportunities will be best for nurses with advanced education and training, such as nurse practitioners.

Earnings

Median weekly earnings of full-time salaried registered nurses were $697 in 1996. The middle 50 percent earned between $571 and $868. The lowest 10 percent earned less than $415; the top 10 percent, more than $1,039.

According to a Hay Group survey of HMOs, group practices, and hospital-based clinics, the median annual base salary of full-time nurse practitioners was $66,800 in May 1996. The middle 50 percent earned between $54,200 and $69,200. Nurse midwives earned about $70,100, and the middle 50 percent earned between $59,300 and $75,700. According to the Hay Group's survey of acute care hospitals, the median annual base salary of full-time nurse anesthetists was $82,000 in January 1997. The middle 50 percent earned between $74,700 and $90,300.

According to the Buck Survey conducted by the American Health Care Association, staff RNs in chain nursing homes had median hourly earnings of $15.85 in 1996. The middle 50 percent earned between $14.03 and $17.73.

Many employers offer flexible work schedules, child care, educational benefits, and bonuses.

Related Occupations

Workers in other health care occupations with responsibilities and duties related to those of registered nurses are occupational therapists, emergency medical technicians, physical therapists, physician assistants, and respiratory therapists.

Sources of Additional Information

The National League for Nursing (NLN) publishes a variety of nursing and nursing education materials, including a list of nursing programs and information on student financial aid. For a complete list of NLN publications, write for a career information brochure. Send your request to:

❏ Communications Department, National League for Nursing, 350 Hudson St., New York, NY 10014. FAX: (212) 989-2272.

For a list of BSN and graduate programs, write to:

❏ American Association of Colleges of Nursing, 1 Dupont Circle NW, Suite 530, Washington, DC 20036. FAX: (202) 785-8320.

Information on registered nurses is also available from:

❏ American Nurses Association, 600 Maryland Ave. SW., Washington, DC 20024-2571.

Respiratory Therapists

(D.O.T. 076.361-014)

Significant Points

✴ *Hospitals will continue to employ more than nine out of ten respiratory therapists, but a growing number will work outside of hospitals under contract to home health agencies and nursing homes.*

✴ *Job opportunities will be best for therapists who work with newborns and infants.*

Nature of the Work

You can live without water for a few days and without food for a few weeks. But without oxygen, you will suffer brain damage within a few minutes and die after about nine minutes. Respiratory therapists, also known as respiratory care practitioners, evaluate, treat, and care for patients with breathing disorders.

In evaluating patients, therapists test the capacity of the lungs and analyze the oxygen and carbon dioxide concentra-

tion as well as the potential of hydrogen (pH), a measure of the acidity or alkalinity level of the blood. To measure lung capacity, therapists have patients breathe into an instrument that measures the volume and flow of oxygen during inhalation and exhalation. By comparing the reading with the norm for the patient's age, height, weight, and sex, respiratory therapists can determine whether lung deficiencies exist. To analyze oxygen, carbon dioxide, and pH levels, therapists draw an arterial blood sample, place it in a blood gas analyzer, and relay the results to a physician.

Respiratory therapists treat all types of patients, ranging from premature infants whose lungs are not fully developed, to elderly people whose lungs are diseased. They provide temporary relief to patients with chronic asthma or emphysema and emergency care for patients who suffered heart failure or a stroke, or are victims of drowning or shock. Respiratory therapists most commonly use oxygen or oxygen mixtures, chest physiotherapy, and aerosol medications. Therapists may place an oxygen mask or nasal cannula on a patient and set the oxygen flow at the level prescribed by a physician to increase a patient's concentration of oxygen. Therapists also connect patients who cannot breathe on their own to ventilators, which deliver pressurized oxygen into the lungs. They insert a tube into a patient's trachea, or windpipe; connect the tube to the ventilator; and set the rate, volume, and oxygen concentration of the oxygen mixture entering the patient's lungs.

Therapists regularly check on patients and equipment. If the patient appears to be having difficulty or if the oxygen, carbon dioxide, or pH level of the blood is abnormal, they change the ventilator setting according to the doctor's order or check equipment for mechanical problems. In home care, therapists teach patients and their families to use ventilators and other life support systems. They visit several times a month to inspect and clean equipment and ensure its proper use and make emergency visits if equipment problems arise.

Respiratory therapists perform chest physiotherapy on patients to remove mucus from their lungs to make it easier for them to breathe. For example, during surgery, anesthesia depresses respiration, so this treatment may be prescribed to help get the patient's lungs back to normal and prevent congestion. Chest physiotherapy also is used on patients suffering from lung diseases that cause mucus to collect in the lungs, such as cystic fibrosis. Therapists place patients in positions to help drain mucus, thump and vibrate patients' rib cages, and instruct them to cough.

Respiratory therapists also administer aerosols—generally liquid medications suspended in a gas that forms a mist which is inhaled—and teach patients how to inhale the aerosol properly to assure its effectiveness.

Therapists are increasingly working under the supervision of nurses and are being asked to perform tasks that fall outside of their traditional role. They are expanding into cardiopulmonary procedures like electrocardiograms and stress testing, but also perform other tasks like drawing blood samples from patients. They also keep records of the materials used and charges to patients. Some therapists teach or supervise other respiratory therapy personnel.

Working Conditions

Respiratory therapists generally work between 35 and 40 hours a week. Because hospitals operate around the clock, therapists may work evenings, nights, or weekends. They spend long periods standing and walking between patients' rooms. In an emergency, they work under a great deal of stress. Gases used by respiratory therapists are potentially hazardous because they are used and stored under pressure. However, adherence to safety precautions and regular maintenance and testing of equipment minimize the risk of injury. As with many health occupations, respiratory therapists run a risk of catching infectious diseases, but careful adherence to proper procedures minimizes this risk, as well.

Employment

Respiratory therapists held about 82,000 jobs in 1996. About nine out of ten jobs were in hospital departments of respiratory care, anesthesiology, or pulmonary medicine. Home health agencies, respiratory therapy clinics, and nursing homes accounted for most of the remaining jobs.

Training, Other Qualifications, and Advancement

Formal training is necessary for entry to this field. Training is offered at the postsecondary level by hospitals, medical schools, colleges and universities, trade schools, vocational-technical institutes, and the Armed Forces. Some programs prepare graduates for jobs as respiratory therapists; other, shorter programs lead to jobs as respiratory therapy technicians. In 1996, 210 programs for respiratory therapists were accredited by the Commission on Accreditation of Allied Health Education Programs (CAAHEP) of the American Medical Association (AMA). Another 158 programs offered CAAHEP-accredited preparation for respiratory therapy technicians.

Formal training programs vary in length and in the credential or degree awarded. Most of the CAAHEP-accredited therapist programs last two years and lead to an associate degree. Some, however, are four-year bachelor's degree programs. Technician programs last about one year and

award certificates. Areas of study for respiratory therapy programs include human anatomy and physiology, chemistry, physics, microbiology, and mathematics. Technical courses deal with procedures, equipment, and clinical tests.

More and more therapists receive on-the-job training, allowing them to administer electrocardiograms and stress tests, as well as draw blood samples from patients.

Therapists should be sensitive to patients' physical and psychological needs. Respiratory care workers must pay attention to detail, follow instructions, and work as part of a team. Operating complicated respiratory therapy equipment requires mechanical ability and manual dexterity.

High school students interested in a career in respiratory care should take courses in health, biology, mathematics, chemistry, and physics. Respiratory care involves basic mathematical problem-solving and an understanding of chemical and physical principles. For example, respiratory care workers must be able to compute medication dosages and calculate gas concentrations.

Forty-seven states license respiratory care personnel. Only Nevada, Delaware, and Washington do not require licensure. The National Board for Respiratory Care offers voluntary certification and registration to graduates of CAAHEP-accredited programs. Two credentials are awarded to respiratory care practitioners who satisfy the requirements: Certified Respiratory Therapy Technician (CRTT) and Registered Respiratory Therapist (RRT). All graduates—those from two- and four-year programs in respiratory therapy, as well as those from one-year technician programs—may take the CRTT examination first. CRTTs who meet education and experience requirements can take a separate examination, leading to the award of the RRT.

Individuals who have completed a four-year program in a nonrespiratory field, but have college-level courses in anatomy, physiology, chemistry, biology, microbiology, physics, and mathematics can become a CRTT after graduating from an AMA-accredited one- or two-year program. After they receive two years of clinical experience, they are eligible to take the registry exam to become an RRT.

Most employers require that applicants for entry-level or generalist positions hold the CRTT or are eligible to take the certification examination. Supervisory positions and those in intensive care specialties, usually require the RRT (or RRT eligibility).

Respiratory therapists advance in clinical practice by moving from care of "general" to "critical" patients, who have significant problems in other organ systems such as the heart or kidneys. Respiratory therapists, especially those with four-year degrees, may also advance to supervisory or managerial positions in a respiratory therapy department. Respiratory therapists in home care and equipment rental firms may become branch manager.

Job Outlook

Job opportunities are expected to remain good. Employment of respiratory therapists is expected to increase much faster than the average for all occupations through the year 2006 because of substantial growth of the middle-aged and elderly population, a development that will heighten the incidence of cardiopulmonary disease.

Older Americans suffer most from respiratory ailments and cardiopulmonary diseases such as pneumonia, chronic bronchitis, emphysema, and heart disease. As their numbers increase, the need for respiratory therapists will increase as well. In addition, advances in treating victims of heart attacks, accident victims, and premature infants (many of whom may be dependent on a ventilator during part of their treatment) will increase the demand for the services of respiratory care practitioners.

Opportunities are expected to be highly favorable for respiratory therapists with cardiopulmonary care skills and experience in working with infants.

Although hospitals will continue to employ the vast majority of therapists, a growing number of therapists can expect to work outside of hospitals under contract to home health agencies and nursing homes.

Earnings

Median weekly earnings for full-time salaried respiratory therapists were $636 in 1996. The middle 50 percent earned between $506 and $767. The lowest 10 percent earned less than $367; the top 10 percent earned more than $978.

According to a Hay Group survey of acute care hospitals, the median annual base salary of full-time respiratory therapists was $32,500 in January 1997. The middle 50 percent earned between $29,300 and $35,000.

Related Occupations

Respiratory therapists, under the supervision of a physician, administer respiratory care and life support to patients with heart and lung difficulties. Other workers who care for, treat, or train people to improve their physical condition include dialysis technicians, registered nurses, occupational therapists, physical therapists, and radiation therapy technologists.

Sources of Additional Information

Information concerning a career in respiratory care is available from:

❑ American Association for Respiratory Care, 11030 Ables Ln., Dallas, TX 75229.

Information on gaining credentials as a respiratory therapy practitioner can be obtained from:

❑ The National Board for Respiratory Care, Inc., 8310 Nieman Rd., Lenexa, KS 66214.

For the current list of CAAHEP-accredited educational programs for respiratory therapy occupations, write to:

❑ Joint Review Committee for Respiratory Therapy Education, 1701 W. Euless Blvd., Suite 300, Euless, TX 76040.

Restaurant and Food Service Managers

(D.O.T. 185.137; 187.161-010 and .167-026, -106, -126, -206, and -210; 319.137-014, -018, and -030)

Significant Points

★ While many jobs are filled by promoting experienced food and beverage preparation and service workers, job opportunities are expected to be best for those with bachelor's or associate degrees in restaurant and institutional food service management.

★ Employment of wage and salary managers is expected to increase more rapidly than self-employed managers, as restaurants increasingly affiliate with national chains rather than being independently owned.

Nature of the Work

Food is consumed outside the home in a variety of settings. Eating places range from institutional cafeterias and fast food to elegant dining establishments. The cuisine, price, and setting where the meals are consumed vary, but managers of these dining facilities share many of the same responsibilities. Efficient and profitable operation of restaurants and institutional food service facilities requires managers and assistant managers to select and appropriately price menu items, use food and other supplies efficiently, and achieve consistent quality in food preparation and service. They also must attend to the various administrative aspects of the business, which includes recruiting, training, and supervising an adequate number of workers.

In most restaurants and institutional food service facilities, the manager is assisted by one or more assistant managers, depending on the size and operating hours of the establishment. In large establishments, as well as in many smaller ones, the management team consists of a general manager, one or more assistant managers, and an executive chef. The

executive chef is responsible for the operation of the kitchen, while the assistant managers oversee service in the dining room and other areas of the operation. In smaller restaurants, the executive chef may be the general manager, and sometimes an owner. In fast-food restaurants and other food service facilities open for long hours, often seven days a week, the manager is aided by several assistant managers, each of whom supervises a shift of workers.

Many restaurants rarely change their menu, while others make frequent alterations. Institutional food service facilities and some restaurants offer a new menu every day. Managers or executive chefs select menu items, taking into account the likely number of customers, and the past popularity of dishes. Other issues taken into consideration when planning a menu include unserved food left over from prior meals that should not be wasted, the need for variety, and the availability of foods due to seasonality and other factors. Managers or executive chefs analyze the recipes of the dishes to determine food, labor, overhead costs and to assign prices to the various dishes. Menus must be developed far enough in advance that supplies can be ordered and received in time.

On a daily basis, managers estimate food consumption, place orders with suppliers, and schedule the delivery of fresh food and beverages. They receive and check the content of deliveries, evaluating the quality of meats, poultry, fish, fruits, vegetables, and baked goods. Managers meet with the sales representatives from restaurant suppliers to place orders replenishing stocks of tableware, linens, paper, cleaning supplies, cooking utensils, and furniture and fixtures. They also arrange for equipment maintenance and repairs, and for a variety of services such as waste removal and pest control.

Managers interview, hire, and, when necessary, fire employees. Many managers report difficulty in hiring experienced food and beverage preparation and service workers. Managers may attend career fairs or arrange for newspaper advertising to expand their pool of applicants. Managers explain the establishment's policies and practices to newly hired workers and oversee their training. Managers schedule the work hours of employees, making sure there are enough workers present to cover peak dining periods. If employees are unable to work, managers may have to fill in for them. Some managers regularly help with cooking, clearing of tables, or other tasks.

Restaurant and food service managers supervise the kitchen and the dining room. They oversee food preparation and cooking, examining the quality and portion sizes to ensure that dishes are prepared and garnished correctly and in a timely manner. They also investigate and resolve customers' complaints about food quality or service. They direct the cleaning of the kitchen and dining areas and the washing of tableware, kitchen utensils, and equipment to maintain company and government sanitation standards. They monitor the actions of their employees and patrons on a continual basis to ensure the health and safety standards and local liquor regulations are obeyed.

Managers have a variety of administrative responsibilities. In larger establishments, much of this work is delegated to a bookkeeper; in smaller establishments, including most fast-food restaurants, managers must keep records of the hours and wages of employees, prepare the payroll, and do paperwork to comply with licensing laws and reporting requirements of tax, wage and hour, unemployment compensation, and Social Security laws. They also maintain the records of supplies and equipment purchased, and ensure that accounts with suppliers are paid on a regular basis. In addition, some managers record the number, type, and cost of items sold to exclude dishes that are unpopular or less profitable.

Many managers are able to ease the burden of recordkeeping and paperwork through the use of computers. Point-of-service (POS) systems are used in many restaurants to increase employee productivity and allow managers to track the sales of specific menu items. Using a POS system, a server keys in the customer's order and the computer immediately sends the order to the kitchen so preparation can begin. The same system totals checks, acts as a cash register and credit card authorizer, and tracks daily sales. To minimize food costs and spoilage, many managers use inventory tracking software to compare the record of daily sales from the POS with a record of present inventory. In some establishments, when supplies needed for the preparation of popular menu items run low, additional inventory can be ordered directly from the supplier using the computer. Computers also allow restaurant and food service managers to more efficiently keep track of employee schedules and pay.

Managers are among the first to arrive and the last to leave. At the conclusion of each day, or sometimes each shift, managers tally the cash and charge receipts received and balance them against the record of sales. They are responsible for depositing the day's receipts at the bank, or securing it in a safe place. Managers are also responsible for locking up, checking that ovens, grills, and lights are off, and switching on alarm systems.

Working Conditions

Evenings and weekends are popular dining periods, making night and weekend work common. Many managers of institutional food service facilities work more conventional hours because factory and office cafeterias are generally open only on weekdays for breakfast and lunch. However, hours are unpredictable, as managers may have to fill in for absent workers on short notice. It is common for restaurant and food service managers to work 50 to 60 hours or more per week.

Managers often experience the pressure of simultaneously coordinating a wide range of activities. When problems occur, it is the responsibility of the manager to resolve them with minimal disruption to customers. The job can be hectic during peak dining hours, and dealing with irate customers or uncooperative employees can be stressful.

Employment

Restaurant and food service managers held about 493,000 jobs in 1996. Most managers were salaried workers, but many others were self-employed. Most worked in restaurants or for contract institutional food service companies, while a smaller number were employed by educational institutions, hospitals, nursing and personal care facilities, and civic, social, and fraternal organizations. Jobs are located throughout the country, with large cities and tourist areas providing more opportunities for more formal dining positions.

Training, Other Qualifications, and Advancement

Many restaurant and food service manager positions are filled by promoting experienced food and beverage preparation and service workers. Waiters, waitresses, chefs, and fast-food workers demonstrating potential for handling increased responsibility sometimes advance to assistant manager or management trainee jobs when openings occur. Executive chefs need extensive experience working as a chef, and general managers need experience working as assistant manager. However, most food service management companies and national or regional restaurant chains also recruit management trainees from two- and four-year college hospitality management programs. Food service and restaurant chains prefer to hire people with degrees in restaurant and institutional food service management, but they often hire graduates with degrees in other fields who have demonstrated interest and aptitude.

A bachelor's degree in restaurant and food service management provides a particularly strong preparation for a career in this occupation. In 1996, more than 160 colleges and universities offered four-year programs in restaurant and hotel management or institutional food service management. For people not interested in pursing a four-year degree, good alternatives are the more than 800 community and junior colleges, technical institutes, and other institutions that offer programs in these fields leading to an associate degree or other formal certification. Both two- and four-year programs

provide instruction in subjects such as nutrition and food planning and preparation, as well as accounting, business law and management, and computer science. Some programs combine classroom and laboratory study with internships that provide on-the-job experience. In addition, many educational institutions offer culinary programs that provide food preparation training which can lead to a career as a cook or chef and provide a foundation for advancement to an executive chef position.

Most employers emphasize personal qualities. Restaurant and food service management can be demanding, so good health and stamina are important. Self-discipline, initiative, and leadership ability are essential. Managers must be able to solve problems and concentrate on details. They need good communication skills to deal with customers and suppliers, as well as to motivate and direct their subordinates. A neat and clean appearance is a must because they often are in close personal contact with the public.

Most restaurant chains and food service management companies have rigorous training programs for their management positions. Through a combination of classroom and on-the-job training, trainees receive instruction and gain work experience in all aspects of the operations of a restaurant or institutional food service facility—food preparation, nutrition, sanitation, security, company policies and procedures, personnel management, recordkeeping, and preparation of reports. Training on use of the restaurant's computer system is increasingly important as well. Often, supplies are ordered electronically and many restaurants use computers to track the popularity of menu items. Usually after six months or a year, trainees receive their first permanent assignment as an assistant manager.

A measure of professional achievement for restaurant and food service managers is to earn the designation of certified Foodservice Management Professional (FMP). Although not a requirement for employment or advancement in the occupation, voluntary certification provides recognition of professional competence, particularly for managers who acquired their skills largely on the job. The Educational Foundation of the National Restaurant Association awards the FMP designation to managers who achieve a qualifying score on a written examination, complete a series of courses that cover a range of food service management topics, and who meet standards of work experience in the field.

Willingness to relocate, usually to a big city, often is essential for advancement to positions with greater responsibility. Managers advance to larger establishments, or regional management positions within restaurant chains. Some eventually open their own eating and drinking establishments. Others

transfer to hotel management positions, because their restaurant management experience provides a good background for food and beverage manager jobs at hotels and resorts.

Job Outlook

Job opportunities are expected to be best for those with a bachelor's or associate degree in restaurant and institutional food service management. Employment of restaurant and food service managers is expected to increase faster than the average for all occupations through the year 2006. In addition to employment growth, the need to replace managers who transfer to other occupations or stop working will create many job openings.

Projected employment growth varies by industry. Eating and drinking places will provide the most new jobs as the number of eating and drinking establishments increases and other industries continue to contract out their food services. Increases in population, personal incomes, and leisure time will continue to produce growth in the number of meals consumed outside the home. To meet the demand for prepared food, more restaurants will be built, and more managers will be employed to supervise them. In addition, the number of manager jobs will increase in eating and drinking places as schools, hospitals, and other businesses contract out more of their food services to institutional food service companies within the eating and drinking industry.

Employment of wage and salary managers in eating and drinking places is expected to increase more rapidly than self-employed managers. New restaurants are increasingly affiliated with national chains rather than being independently owned and operated. As this trend continues, fewer owners will manage restaurants themselves, and more restaurant managers will be employed to run the establishments.

Food service manager jobs are expected to increase in other industries, but growth will be slowed as contracting out becomes more common. Growth in the elderly population should result in more food service manager jobs in nursing homes and other health care institutions, and residential-care and assisted-living facilities.

Employment in eating and drinking establishments is not very sensitive to changes in economic conditions, so restaurant and food service managers are rarely laid off during hard times. However, competition among restaurants is always intense, and many restaurants do not survive.

Earnings

Median earnings for restaurant and food service managers were about $460 a week in 1996. The middle 50 percent earned between about $320 and $630 a week. The lowest paid 10 percent earned $240 a week or less, while the highest paid 10 percent earned over $900 a week.

Earnings of restaurant and food service managers vary greatly according to their responsibilities and the type and size of establishment. Based on a survey conducted by the National Restaurant Association, the median base salary of restaurant managers was about $30,000 in 1995; managers of the largest restaurants and institutional food service facilities often had annual salaries in excess of $50,000. Besides a salary, most managers received an annual bonus or incentive payment based on their performance. In 1995, most bonuses ranged between $2,000 and $10,000.

Executive chefs had a median base salary of $38,000 in 1995. Annual bonus or incentive payments for most executive chefs averaged $3,000.

The median base salary of assistant managers was $23,000 in 1995, but ranged from $21,000 in fast-food restaurants to $27,000 in some of the largest restaurants and food service facilities. Annual bonus or incentive payments for most assistant managers ranged from $1,000 to $4,000.

Manager trainees had a median base salary of $21,000 in 1995, but earned $30,000 in some of the largest restaurants and food service facilities. Annual bonus or incentive payments of most trainees averaged $900.

In addition to typical benefits, most salaried restaurant and food service managers receive free meals and the opportunity for additional training depending on their length of service.

Related Occupations

Restaurant and food service managers direct the activities of businesses which provide a service to customers. Other managers in service-oriented businesses include hotel managers and assistants, health services administrators, retail store managers, and bank managers.

Sources of Additional Information

Information about job opportunities may be obtained from local employers and local offices of the state employment service.

Information about a career as a restaurant and food service manager, two- and four-year college programs in restaurant and food service management, and certification as a Foodservice Management Professional is available from:

❑ The Educational Foundation of the National Restaurant Association, Suite 1400, 250 South Wacker Dr., Chicago, IL 60606.

General information on hospitality careers may be obtained from:

❑ Council on Hotel, Restaurant, and Institutional Education, 1200 17th St. NW, Washington, DC 20036-3097.

For general career information and a directory of accredited private trade and technical schools offering programs in restaurant and food service management, write to:

❑ Accrediting Commission of Career Schools and Colleges of Technology, 2101 Wilson Blvd., Suite 302, Arlington, VA 22201.

Science Technicians

(*D.O.T.* codes are too numerous to list.)

Significant Points

✦ *Science technicians in production jobs often work in eight-hour shifts around the clock.*

✦ *Job opportunities are expected to be very good for qualified graduates of science technician training programs or applied science technology programs who are well-trained on equipment used in laboratories and production facilities.*

Nature of the Work

Science technicians use the principles and theories of science and mathematics to solve problems in research and development and to help invent and improve products and processes. However, their jobs are more practically oriented than those of scientists. Technicians set up, operate, and maintain laboratory instruments, monitor experiments, make observations, calculate and record results, and often develop conclusions. Those who work in production monitor manufacturing processes and may be involved in quality control, testing products for proper proportions of ingredients, purity, or for strength and durability.

As laboratory instrumentation and procedures have become more complex in recent years, the role of science technicians in research and development has expanded. In addition to performing routine tasks, many technicians also develop and adapt laboratory procedures to achieve the best results, interpret data, and devise solutions to problems, under the direction of scientists. The increasing use of robotics to perform many routine tasks has freed technicians to operate more sophisticated laboratory equipment. Science technicians make extensive use of computers, computer-interfaced equipment, robotics, and high-technology industrial applications such as biological engineering.

Most science technicians specialize, learning skills and working in the same disciplines as scientists. Occupational titles, therefore, tend to follow the same structure as scientists. Agricultural technicians work with agricultural scientists

in food, fiber, and animal research, production, and processing. Some conduct tests and experiments to improve the yield and quality of crops or to increase the resistance of plants and animals to disease, insects, or other hazards. Other agricultural technicians do animal breeding and nutrition work.

Biological technicians work with biologists studying living organisms. They may assist scientists who conduct medical research, helping to find a cure for cancer or AIDS, for example. Those who work in pharmaceutical companies help develop and manufacture medicinal and pharmaceutical preparations. Those working in the field of microbiology generally work as lab assistants, studying living organisms and infectious agents. Biological technicians also analyze organic substances such as blood, food, and drugs, and some examine evidence in criminal investigations. Biological technicians working in biotechnology labs use the knowledge and techniques gained from basic research by scientists, including gene splicing and recombinant DNA, and apply these techniques in product development.

Chemical technicians work with chemists and chemical engineers, developing and using chemicals and related products and equipment. Most do research and development, testing, or other laboratory work. For example, they might test packaging for design, integrity of materials, and environmental acceptability; assemble and operate new equipment to develop new products; monitor product quality; or develop new production techniques. Some chemical technicians collect and analyze samples of air and water to monitor pollution levels. Those who focus on basic research might produce compounds through complex organic synthesis. Chemical technicians within chemical plants are also referred to as process technicians. They may operate equipment, monitor plant processes, and analyze plant materials.

Environmental technicians may perform laboratory and field tests to monitor environmental resources and determine the contaminants and sources of pollution. They may collect samples for testing or be involved in abating, controlling, or remediating sources of environmental pollutants. They may be responsible for waste management operations, control and management of hazardous materials inventory, or general activities involving regulatory compliance. There is a growing emphasis on pollution prevention activities.

Nuclear technicians operate nuclear test and research equipment, monitor radiation, and assist nuclear engineers and physicists in research. Some also operate remote control equipment to manipulate radioactive materials or materials to be exposed to radioactivity.

Petroleum technicians measure and record physical and geologic conditions in oil or gas wells using instruments low-

ered into wells or by analysis of the mud from wells. In oil and gas exploration, they collect and examine geological data or test geological samples to determine petroleum and mineral content. Some petroleum technicians, called scouts, collect information about oil and gas well drilling operations, geological and geophysical prospecting, and land or lease contracts.

Other science technicians collect weather information or assist oceanographers.

Working Conditions

Science technicians work under a wide variety of conditions. Most work indoors, usually in laboratories, and have regular hours. Some occasionally work irregular hours to monitor experiments that can't be completed during regular working hours. Production technicians often work in eight-hour shifts around the clock. Others, such as agricultural, petroleum, and environmental technicians, perform much of their work outdoors, sometimes in remote locations.

Some science technicians may be exposed to hazards from equipment, chemicals, or toxic materials. Chemical technicians sometimes work with toxic chemicals or radioactive isotopes; nuclear technicians may be exposed to radiation; and biological technicians sometimes work with disease-causing organisms or radioactive agents. However, there is little risk if proper safety procedures are followed.

Employment

Science technicians held about 228,000 jobs in 1996. Over 35 percent worked in manufacturing, mostly in the chemical industry, but also in the food processing industry. About 16 percent worked in education services and another 15 percent worked in research and testing services. In 1996, the federal government employed about 16,000 science technicians, mostly in the Departments of Defense, Agriculture, and Interior.

Training, Other Qualifications, and Advancement

There are several ways to qualify for a job as a science technician. Most employers prefer applicants who have at least two years of specialized training or an associate degree in applied science or science-related technology. Because employer's preferences vary, however, many science technicians may actually have a bachelor's degree in chemistry or biology, or have taken several science and math courses at four-year colleges.

Many technical and community colleges offer associate degrees in a specific technology or a more general education in science and mathematics. A number of two-year associate degree programs are designed to provide easy transfer to a four-year college or university if desired. Technical institutes generally offer technician training, but provide less theory and general education than technical or community colleges. The length of programs at technical institutes varies, although one-year certificate programs and two-year associate degree programs are common. Some schools offer cooperative-education or internship programs, allowing students the opportunity to work at a local company or other workplace while attending classes in alternate terms. Participation in such programs can significantly enhance a student's employment prospects.

Persons interested in careers as science technicians should take as many high school science and math courses as possible. Science courses taken beyond high school, in an associate or bachelor's program, should be laboratory oriented, with an emphasis on "bench" skills. Because computers and computer-interfaced equipment are often used in research and development laboratories, technicians should have strong computer skills. Communication skills are also important; technicians are often required to report their findings both verbally and in writing. Technicians should also be able to work well with others because teamwork is common.

Prospective science technicians may acquire good career preparation through two-year formal training programs that combine the teaching of scientific principles and theory with practical hands-on application in a laboratory setting with up-to-date equipment. Graduates of four-year bachelor's degree programs in science who have considerable experience in laboratory-based courses, have completed internships, or held summer jobs in laboratories are also well-qualified for science technician positions and are preferred by some employers. However, those with a bachelor's degree who accept technician jobs generally cannot find employment that utilizes their advanced academic education.

Technicians usually begin work as trainees in routine positions under the direct supervision of a scientist or a more experienced technician. Job candidates whose training or educational background encompasses extensive hands-on experience with a variety of laboratory equipment, including computers and related equipment, usually require a much shorter period of on-the-job training. As they gain experience, technicians take on more responsibility and carry out assignments under only general supervision, and some eventually become supervisors.

Job Outlook

Employment of science technicians is expected to increase about as fast as the average for all occupations through the year 2006. Continued growth of scientific and medical research, and development and the production of technical products should stimulate demand for science technicians in all areas. In particular, the growing number of agricultural and medicinal products developed using biotechnology techniques will increase the need for biological technicians. Employment growth will also be fueled by demand for technicians to help regulate waste products, collect air, water, and soil samples to measure levels of pollutants, monitor compliance with environmental regulations, and clean up contaminated sites. However, growth will be moderated somewhat by an expected slowdown in overall employment in the chemical industry.

Job opportunities are expected to be very good for qualified graduates of science technician training programs or applied science technology programs who are well-trained on equipment used in industrial and government laboratories and production facilities. As the instrumentation and techniques used in industrial research, development, and production become more complex, employers are seeking well-trained individuals with highly developed technical and communication skills. In addition to opportunities created by growth, many job openings should arise from the need to replace technicians who retire or leave the labor force for other reasons.

Earnings

Median annual earnings of science technicians were about $27,000 in 1996; the middle 50 percent earned between $19,800 and $37,100. Ten percent earned less than $15,500, and 10 percent earned over $49,500. Median annual earnings were about $31,100 for chemical technicians and about $25,200 for biological technicians in 1996.

In the federal government in 1997, science technicians started at $15,500, $17,400, or $19,500, depending on education and experience. Beginning salaries were slightly higher in selected areas of the country where the prevailing local pay level was higher. The average annual salary for biological science technicians in nonsupervisory, supervisory, and managerial positions employed by the federal government in early 1997 was $28,500; for mathematical technicians, $34,870; for physical science technicians, $35,890; for geodetic technicians, $45,050; for hydrologic technicians, $33,230; and for meteorologic technicians, $41,460.

Related Occupations

Other technicians who apply scientific principles at a level usually taught in two-year associate degree programs include engineering technicians, broadcast technicians, drafters, and health technologists and technicians. Some of the work of agricultural and biological technicians is related to that in agriculture and forestry occupations.

Sources of Additional Information

For information about a career as a chemical technician, contact:

❑ American Chemical Society, Education Division, Career Publications, 1155 16th St. NW, Washington, DC 20036. Homepage: http://www.acs.org

Securities and Financial Services Sales Representatives

(D.O.T. 162.167-034 and -038; 250.257-014, -018, and -022.)

Significant Points

✴ *A college degree and sales ability are among the most important qualifications.*

✴ *Employment is expected to grow much faster than average as investment increases.*

✴ *Many beginning securities sales representatives leave the occupation because they are unable to establish a sufficient clientele; once established, however, these workers have a very strong attachment to their occupation because of high earnings and the considerable investment in training.*

Nature of the Work

Most investors, whether they are individuals with a few hundred dollars to invest or large institutions with millions, use securities sales representatives when buying or selling stocks, bonds, shares in mutual funds, insurance annuities, or other financial products. Securities sales representatives often are called stockbrokers, registered representatives, or account executives.

When an investor wishes to buy or sell securities, sales representatives may relay the order through their firms' offices to the floor of a securities exchange, such as the New York Stock Exchange. There, securities sales representatives known as brokers' floor representatives buy and sell securities. If a security is not traded on an exchange, the sales representative sends the order to the firm's trading department, where it is traded directly with a dealer in an over-the-counter market, such as the NASDAQ computerized trading system. After the transaction has been completed, the sales representative notifies the customer of the final price.

Securities sales representatives also provide many related services for their customers. They may explain the meaning of stock market terms and trading practices; offer financial counseling; devise an individual client financial portfolio,

including securities, life insurance, corporate and municipal bonds, mutual funds, certificates of deposit, annuities, and other investments; and offer advice on the purchase or sale of particular securities.

Not all customers have the same investment goals. Some individuals prefer long-term investments for capital growth or to provide income over the years; others might want to invest in speculative securities that they hope will rise in price quickly. Securities sales representatives furnish information about advantages and disadvantages of an investment based on each person's objectives. They also supply the latest price quotations on any security in which an investor is interested, as well as information on the activities and financial positions of the corporations issuing these securities.

Most securities sales representatives serve individual investors, but others specialize in institutional investors. In institutional investing, most sales representatives concentrate on a specific financial product, such as stocks, bonds, options, annuities, or commodity futures. Some handle the sale of new issues, such as corporate securities issued to finance plant expansion.

The most important part of a sales representative's job is finding clients and building a customer base. Thus, beginning securities sales representatives spend much of their time searching for customers—relying heavily on telephone solicitation. They may meet some clients through business and social contacts. Many sales representatives find it useful to get additional exposure by teaching adult education investment courses or by giving lectures at libraries or social clubs. Brokerage firms may give sales representatives lists of people with whom the firm has done business in the past. Sometimes sales representatives inherit the clients of representatives who have retired.

Financial services sales representatives sell banking and related services. They contact potential customers to explain their services and to ascertain customers' banking and other financial needs. They may discuss services such as deposit accounts, lines of credit, sales or inventory financing, certificates of deposit, cash management, or investment services. They may solicit businesses to participate in consumer credit card programs. At most small and medium-size banks, branch managers and commercial loan officers are responsible for marketing the bank's financial services. As banks offer more and increasingly complex financial services—for example, securities brokerage and financial planning—the job of financial services sales representative is assuming greater importance.

Financial planners, using their knowledge of tax and investment strategies, securities, insurance, pension plans, and real estate, develop and implement financial plans for individuals and businesses. They interview clients to determine their assets, liabilities, cash flow, insurance coverage, tax status, and financial objectives. Then they analyze this information and develop a financial plan tailored to each client's needs.

Working Conditions

Securities sales representatives usually work in offices, where there is much activity. They have access to "quote boards" or computer terminals that continually provide information on the prices of securities. When sales activity increases, due perhaps to unanticipated changes in the economy, the pace can become very hectic.

Established securities sales representatives usually work the same hours as others in the business community. Beginners who are seeking customers may work much longer hours, however. Most securities sales representatives accommodate customers by meeting with them in the evenings or on weekends.

Financial services sales representatives normally work in a comfortable, less stressful office environment. They generally work 40 hours a week. They may spend considerable time outside the office meeting with present and prospective clients, attending civic functions, and participating in trade association meetings. Some financial services sales representatives work exclusively inside banks, providing service to "walk-in" customers.

Employment

Securities and financial services sales representatives held 263,000 jobs in 1996; securities sales representatives accounted for eight out of ten. In addition, a substantial number of people in other occupations sold securities. These include partners and branch office managers in securities firms, as well as insurance agents and brokers offering securities to their customers.

Securities sales representatives are employed by brokerage and investment firms in all parts of the country. Many of these firms are very small. Most sales representatives, however, work for a small number of large firms with main offices in large cities, especially New York.

Financial services sales representatives are employed by banks, savings and loan associations, and other credit institutions.

Training, Other Qualifications, and Advancement

Because securities sales representatives must be well informed about economic conditions and trends, a college education is increasingly important, especially in the larger securities firms. In fact, the overwhelming majority of workers in this occupation are college graduates. Although employers seldom require specialized academic training, courses in business administration, economics, and finance are helpful.

Many employers consider personal qualities and skills more important than academic training. Employers seek applicants who have good sales ability and communication skills, are well groomed, and have a strong desire to succeed. Self-confidence and an ability to handle frequent rejections also are important ingredients for success.

Because maturity and the ability to work independently also are important, many employers prefer to hire those who have achieved success in other jobs. Some firms prefer candidates with sales experience, particularly those who have worked on commission in areas such as real estate or insurance. Therefore, most entrants to this occupation transfer from other jobs. Some begin working as securities sales representatives following retirement from other fields.

Securities sales representatives must meet state licensing requirements, which generally include passing an examination and, in some cases, furnishing a personal bond. In addition, sales representatives must register as representatives of their firm, according to regulations of the securities exchanges where they do business or the National Association of Securities Dealers, Inc. (NASD). Before beginners can qualify as registered representatives, they must pass the General Securities Registered Representative Examination, administered by the NASD, and be an employee of a registered firm for at least four months. Most states require a second examination—the Uniform Securities Agents State Law Examination. These tests measure the prospective representative's knowledge of the securities business, customer protection requirements, and recordkeeping procedures. Many take correspondence courses in preparation for the securities examinations.

Most employers provide on-the-job training to help securities sales representatives meet the requirements for registration. In most firms, this training period takes about four months. Trainees in large firms may receive classroom instruction in securities analysis, effective speaking, and the finer points of selling; take courses offered by business schools and associations; and undergo a period of on-the-job training lasting up to two years. Many firms like to rotate their trainees among various departments in the firm, to give them a broad perspective of the securities business. In small firms, sales representatives often receive training in outside institutions and on the job.

Securities sales representatives must understand the basic characteristics of a wide variety of financial products offered by brokerage firms. Representatives periodically take training, through their firms or outside institutions, to keep abreast of new financial products as they are introduced on the market and to improve their sales techniques. Training in the use of computers is important, as the securities sales business is highly automated.

The principal form of advancement for securities sales representatives is an increase in the number and size of the accounts they handle. Although beginners usually service the accounts of individual investors, eventually they may handle very large institutional accounts, such as those of banks and pension funds. Some experienced sales representatives become branch office managers and supervise other sales representatives while continuing to provide services for their own customers. A few representatives advance to top management positions or become partners in their firms.

Banks and other credit institutions prefer to hire college graduates for financial services sales jobs. A business administration degree with a specialization in finance or a liberal arts degree including courses in accounting, economics, and marketing serves as excellent preparation for this job.

Financial services sales representatives learn through on-the-job training under the supervision of bank officers. Outstanding performance can lead to promotion to managerial positions.

Job Outlook

Due to the highly competitive nature of securities sales work, many beginners leave the occupation because they are unable to establish a sufficient clientele. Once established, however, securities sales representatives have a very strong attachment to their occupation because of high earnings and the considerable investment in training.

The demand for securities sales representatives fluctuates, as the economy expands and contracts. Thus, in an economic downturn, the number of persons seeking jobs usually exceeds the number of openings—sometimes by a great deal. Even during periods of rapid economic expansion, competition for securities sales training positions—particularly in larger firms—is keen, because of potentially high earnings.

Job opportunities for both securities and financial services sales representatives should be best for mature individuals with successful work experience. Opportunities for inexperienced sales representatives should be best in smaller firms.

Employment of securities sales representatives is expected to grow much faster than the average for all occupations through the year 2006, as economic growth, rising personal incomes, and greater inherited wealth increase the funds available for investment. As banks offer increasingly complex

financial services, employment of financial services sales representatives should grow rapidly, even as overall employment in banking declines and more people conduct their banking from home via personal computer.

More individual investors are expected to purchase common stocks, mutual funds, and other financial products after seeking advice from securities sales representatives regarding the increasing array of investment alternatives. Deregulation has enabled brokerage firms to sell certificates of deposit, offer checking and deposit services through cash management accounts, and sell insurance products, such as annuities and life insurance. Growth in the number and size of institutional investors will be strong, as more people enroll in pension plans, set up individual retirement accounts, establish trust funds, and contribute to the endowment funds of colleges and other nonprofit institutions. Additional representatives also will be needed to sell securities issued by new and expanding corporations, by state and local governments financing public improvements, and by foreign governments, whose securities have become attractive to U.S. investors, as international trade expands.

Investors increasingly rely on the growing number of financial planners to assist them in selecting the proper options among a wide variety of financial alternatives. In addition, demand should increase as banks and credit institutions expand the range of financial services they offer and issue more loans for personal and commercial use.

Earnings

In 1996, median annual earnings of securities and financial services sales representatives were $38,800; the middle 50 percent earned between $24,300 and $73,500. Ten percent earned less than $18,100 and 10 percent earned more than $98,400. On average, financial services sales representatives earn considerably less than securities sales representatives.

Trainees usually are paid an hourly wage or salary, until they meet licensing and registration requirements. After candidates are licensed and registered, their earnings depend on commissions from the sale or purchase of stocks and bonds, life insurance, or other securities for customers. Commission earnings are likely to be high when there is much buying and selling and low when there is a slump in market activity. Most firms provide sales representatives with a steady income by paying a "draw against commission"—a minimum salary based on commissions which they can be expected to earn. Securities sales representatives who can provide their clients with the most complete financial services should enjoy the greatest income stability.

Financial services sales representatives usually are paid a salary; some receive a bonus, if they meet certain established goals.

Related Occupations

Similar sales jobs requiring specialized knowledge include insurance agents and real estate agents.

Sources of Additional Information

Information about job opportunities as a securities sales representative may be obtained from the personnel departments of individual securities firms.

For information about job opportunities for financial services sales representatives in various states, contact state bankers' associations or write directly to a particular bank.

Social and Human Service Assistants

(*D.O.T.* 195.367 except -026 and -030)

Significant Points

* *Social and human service assistants rank among the top ten fastest growing occupations.*

* *Job opportunities should be excellent, particularly for applicants with appropriate postsecondary education, but pay is low.*

Nature of the Work

Social and human service assistants is a generic term for people with various job titles, including social service assistant, case management aide, social work assistant, residential counselor, community support worker, alcohol or drug abuse counselor, mental health technician, child-care worker, community outreach worker, life skill counselor, and gerontology aide. They generally work under the direction of professionals from a wide variety of fields, such as nursing, psychiatry, psychology, rehabilitation, or social work. The amount of responsibility and supervision they are given varies a great deal. Some are on their own most of the time and have little direct supervision; others work under close direction.

Social and human service assistants provide direct and indirect client services. They assess clients' needs, establish their eligibility for benefits and services, and help clients obtain them. They examine financial documents such as rent receipts and tax returns to determine whether the client is eligible for food stamps, Medicaid, welfare, and other human service programs. They also arrange for transportation and escorts, if necessary, and provide emotional support. Social and human service assistants monitor and keep case records on clients and report progress to supervisors. Social and human service assistants also may transport or accompany clients to group meal sites, adult day care programs, or doctors' offices; telephone or visit clients' homes to make sure services are being received; or help resolve disagreements, such as those between tenants and landlords. They may also help clients complete applications for financial assistance or assist with daily living needs.

Social and human service assistants play a variety of roles in community settings. They may organize and lead group activities, assist clients in need of counseling or crisis intervention, or administer a food bank or emergency fuel program. In halfway houses, group homes, and government-supported housing programs, they assist adult residents who need supervision in personal hygiene and daily living skills. They review clients' records, ensure they take correct doses of medication, talk with their families, and confer with medical personnel to gain better insight into clients' backgrounds and needs. They also provide emotional support and help clients become involved in community recreation programs and other activities.

In psychiatric hospitals, rehabilitation programs, and outpatient clinics, they may help clients master everyday living skills and teach them how to communicate more effectively and get along better with others. They support the client's participation in the treatment plan, such as individual or group counseling and occupational therapy.

Working Conditions

Working conditions of social and human service assistants vary. They work in offices, group homes, shelters, day programs, sheltered workshops, hospitals, clinics, and in the field visiting clients. Most work a regular 40-hour week, although some work may be in the evening and on weekends. Social and human service assistants in residential settings generally work in shifts because residents need supervision around the clock.

The work, while satisfying, can be emotionally draining. Understaffing and relatively low pay may add to the pressure. Turnover is reported to be high, especially among workers without academic preparation for this field.

Employment

Social and human service assistants held about 178,000 jobs in 1996. About one in three was employed by state and local governments, primarily in public welfare agencies and facilities for mentally disabled and developmentally delayed individuals. Another third worked in private social or human services agencies, offering a variety of services, including adult day care, group meals, crisis intervention, counseling, and job training. Many social and human service assistants supervised residents of group homes and halfway houses. Social and human service assistants also held jobs in clinics, detoxification units, community mental health centers, psychiatric hospitals, day treatment programs, and sheltered workshops.

Training, Other Qualifications, and Advancement

While some employers hire high school graduates, most prefer applicants with some college preparation in human services, social work, or one of the social or behavioral sciences. Some prefer to hire persons with a four-year college degree. The educational attainment of social and human service assistants often influences the kind of work they are assigned and the amount of responsibility entrusted to them. Workers with no more than a high school education are likely to receive on-the-job training to work in direct care services, while those with a college degree might be assigned to do supportive counseling, coordinate program activities, or manage a group home. Employers may also look for experience in other occupations, leadership experience in an organization, or human service volunteer exposure. Some enter the field on the basis of courses in human services, psychology, rehabilitation, social work, sociology, or special education. Most employers provide in-service training such as seminars and workshops.

Because so many human services jobs involve direct contact with people who are vulnerable to exploitation or mistreatment, employers try to select applicants with appropriate personal qualifications. Relevant academic preparation is generally required, and volunteer or work experience is preferred. A strong desire to help others, patience, and understanding are highly valued characteristics. Other important personal traits include communication skills, a strong sense of responsibility, and the ability to manage time effectively. Hiring requirements in group homes tend to be more stringent than in other settings. In some settings, applicants may need a valid driver's license and must meet the Criminal Offense Record Investigation (CORI) requirement. Special licensure or state certifications may also apply.

In 1996, about 380 certificate and associate degree programs in human services or mental health were offered at community and junior colleges, vocational-technical institutes, and other postsecondary institutions. In addition, approximately 400 programs offered a bachelor's degree in human services. Master's degree programs in human services administration are offered as well.

Generally, academic programs in this field educate students for specialized roles. Human services programs have a core cur-

riculum that trains students in observation and recording, interviewing, communication techniques, behavior management, group dynamics, counseling, crisis intervention, case management, and referral. General education courses in liberal arts, sciences, and the humanities are also part of the curriculum. Many degree programs require completion of an internship.

Formal education is almost always necessary for advancement. In general, advancement requires a bachelor's or master's degree in counseling, rehabilitation, social work, or a related field.

Job Outlook

Opportunities for social and human service assistants are expected to be excellent, particularly for applicants with appropriate postsecondary education. The number of social and human service assistants is projected to grow much faster than the average for all occupations between 1996 and the year 2006—ranking among the most rapidly growing occupations. The need to replace workers who retire or stop working for other reasons will create additional job opportunities. These jobs are not attractive to everyone due to the emotionally draining work and relatively low pay, so qualified applicants should have little difficulty finding employment.

Opportunities are expected to be best in job training programs, residential settings, and private social service agencies, which include such services as adult day care and meal delivery programs. Demand for these services will expand with the growing number of older people, who are more likely to need services. In addition, social and human service assistants will continue to be needed to provide services to the mentally disabled and developmentally delayed, those with substance-abuse problems, the homeless, and pregnant teenagers. Faced with rapid growth in the demand for services, but slower growth in resources to provide the services, employers are expected to rely increasingly on social and human service assistants rather than more highly trained workers, such as social workers, who command higher pay.

Job training programs are expected to require additional social and human service assistants as the economy grows and businesses change their mode of production, requiring workers to be retrained. Social and human service assistants help determine workers' eligibility for public assistance programs and help them obtain services while unemployed.

Residential settings should expand also as pressures to respond to the needs of the chronically mentally ill persist. For many years, chronic mental patients have been deinstitutionalized and left to their own devices. Now, more community-based programs, supported independent living sites, and group residences are expected to be established to

house and assist the homeless and chronically mentally ill, and demand for social and human service assistants will increase accordingly.

The number of jobs for social and human service assistants will grow more rapidly than overall employment in state and local governments. State and local governments employ most of their social and human service assistants in corrections and public assistance departments. Corrections departments are growing faster than other areas of government, so social and human service assistants should find that their job opportunities increase along with other corrections jobs. Public assistance programs have been employing more social and human service assistants in an attempt to employ fewer social workers, who are more educated and higher paid.

Earnings

Based on limited information, starting salaries for social and human service assistants ranged from about $15,000 to $24,000 a year in 1997. Experienced workers generally earned between $20,000 and $30,000 annually, depending on their education, experience, and employer.

Related Occupations

Workers in other occupations that require skills similar to those of social and human service assistants include social workers, religious workers, occupational therapy assistants, physical therapy assistants, psychiatric aides, and activity leaders.

Sources of Additional Information

Information on academic programs in human services may be found in most directories of two- and four-year colleges, available at libraries or career counseling centers.

For information on programs and careers in human services, contact:

❑ National Organization for Human Service Education, Brookdale Community College, Lyncroft, NJ 07738.

❑ Council for Standards in Human Service Education, Northern Essex Community College, Haverhill, MA 01830.

Information on job openings may be available from state employment service offices or directly from city, county, or state departments of health, mental health and mental retardation, and human resources.

Visual Artists

(*D.O.T.* 102.261-014; 141.031-010, .061-010, -014, -018, -022, -026, -030, -034, .081-010; 142.061-030, -054; 144; 149.041, .051, .261; 970.131-014, .281-014, .361-018)

Significant Points

* *Nearly 60 percent are self-employed—about seven times the proportion in all professional occupations.*

* *Artists usually develop their skills through a bachelor's degree program or other postsecondary training in art or design.*

* *Keen competition is expected for both salaried jobs and freelance work because the glamorous and exciting image of the graphic and fine arts fields attracts many talented people.*

Nature of the Work

Visual artists communicate ideas, thoughts, and feelings through various methods and materials—including computers, oils, watercolors, acrylics, pastels, magic markers, pencils, pen and ink, silkscreen, plaster, or clay—or other media, such as photographs and sound. They create realistic and abstract works or images of objects, people, nature, topography, or events.

Visual artists generally fall into one of two categories—graphic artists or graphic designers, and fine artists—depending not so much on the medium, but on the artist's purpose in creating a work of art. Graphic artists, many of whom own their own studios, put their artistic skills and vision at the service of commercial clients, such as major corporations, retail stores, and advertising, design, or publishing firms. Fine artists, on the other hand, often create art to satisfy their own need for self-expression, and may display their work in museums, corporate collections, art galleries, and private homes. Some of their work may be done on request from clients, but not as exclusively as graphic artists.

Graphic artists, whether freelancers or employed by a firm, use a variety of print, electronic, and film media to create art that meets a client's needs. Most graphic artists use computer software to design new images; some of this work appears on the Internet and CD-ROM. As computer software becomes increasingly sophisticated, more artists are likely to become involved with this medium. Graphic artists may create promotional displays and marketing brochures for new products, visual designs of annual reports and other corporate literature, or distinctive logos for products or businesses. Artists may be responsible for the overall layout and design of magazines, newspapers, journals, and other publications, and may create graphics for television and computer-generated media. For example, many magazines and newspapers have a homepage on the Internet.

Fine artists may sell their works to stores, commercial art galleries, and museums, or directly to collectors. Commercial galleries may sell artists' works on consignment. The gallery and artist predetermine how much each earns from a sale. Only the most successful fine artists are able to support themselves solely through sale of their works; however, most fine artists hold other jobs as well. Those with teaching certification may teach art in elementary or secondary schools, while those with a master's or Ph.D. degree may teach in colleges or universities. Some fine artists work in arts administration in city, state, or federal arts programs. Others may work as art critics, art consultants, or as directors or representatives in fine art galleries; give private art lessons; or work as curators setting up art exhibits in museums. Sometimes fine artists work in an unrelated field in order to support their careers.

Fine artists usually work independently, choosing whatever subject matter and medium suits them. Usually, they specialize in one or two forms of art. Painters generally work with two-dimensional art forms. Using techniques of shading, perspective, and color mixing, painters produce works depicting realistic scenes or may evoke different moods and emotions, depending on the artist's goals. Artists may combine media and include sound and motion in their works.

Sculptors design three-dimensional art works—either molding and joining materials such as clay, glass, wire, plastic, or metal, or cutting and carving forms from a block of plaster, wood, or stone. Some sculptors combine various materials such as concrete, metal, wood, plastic, and paper.

Printmakers create printed images from designs cut into wood, stone, or metal, or from computer-driven data. The designs may be engraved, as in the case of woodblocking; etched, as in the production of etchings; or derived from computers using advanced color printers.

Painting restorers preserve and restore damaged and faded paintings. They apply solvents and cleaning agents to clean the surfaces, reconstruct or retouch damaged areas, and apply preservatives to protect the paintings. This is very detailed work and is usually reserved for experts in the field.

Illustrators paint or draw pictures for books, magazines, and other publications; films; and paper products, including greeting cards, calendars, wrapping paper, and stationery. Many do a variety of illustrations, while others specialize in a particular style. Some illustrators draw "story boards" for television commercials, movies, and animated features. Story boards present television commercials in a series of scenes similar to a comic strip, so an advertising agency and client (the company doing the advertising) can evaluate proposed commercials. Story boards may also serve as guides to placement of actors and cameras and to other details during the production of commercials. Some work is done electronically, using advanced computer software. This allows ideas to be electronically mailed between clients, or presented on the Internet.

Medical and scientific illustrators combine artistic skills with knowledge of the biological sciences. Medical illustrators draw illustrations of human anatomy and surgical procedures. Scientific illustrators draw illustrations of animals and plants. These illustrations are used in medical and scientific publications, and in audiovisual presentations for teaching purposes. Medical illustrators also work for lawyers, producing exhibits for court cases and doctors. Fashion artists draw illustrations of women's, men's, and children's clothing and accessories for newspapers, magazines, and other media.

Cartoonists draw political, advertising, social, and sports cartoons. Some cartoonists work with others who create the idea or story and write the captions. Most cartoonists, however, have humorous, critical, or dramatic talents in addition to drawing skills.

Animators work in the motion picture and television industries. They draw by hand and use computers to create the large series of pictures which, when transferred to film or tape, form the animated cartoons seen in movies and on television.

Art directors, also called visual journalists, read the material to be printed in periodicals, newspapers, and other printed media, and decide how to best present visually the information in an eye-catching and organized manner. They make decisions about which photographs or art work to use, and oversee production of the printed material. Art directors may also review graphics that will be shown on the Internet.

Working Conditions

Graphic and fine artists generally work in art and design studios located in office buildings or their own studios. While their surroundings are usually well lighted and ventilated, odors from glues, paint, ink, or other materials may be present. They may use computers for extended periods of time.

Graphic artists employed by publishing companies and art and design studios generally work a standard 40-hour week. During busy periods, they may work overtime to meet deadlines. Self-employed graphic artists can set their own hours, but may spend much time and effort selling their services to potential customers or clients and establishing a reputation.

Employment

Visual artists held about 276,000 jobs in 1996. Nearly six out of ten were self-employed. Self-employed artists are either graphic artists who freelance, offering their services to advertising agencies, publishing firms, and other businesses, or fine artists who earn income when they sell a painting or other art work.

Of the artists who were not self-employed, many were graphic artists who worked for advertising agencies, design firms, commercial art and reproduction firms, or printing and publishing firms. Other artists were employed by the motion picture and television industries, wholesale and retail trade establishments, and public relations firms.

Training, Other Qualifications, and Advancement

In the fine arts field, formal training requirements do not exist, but it is very difficult to become skilled enough to make a living, without training. Many colleges and universities offer bachelor's and master's degree programs in fine arts; specialized art schools also offer postsecondary training in this field. In the graphic arts field, demonstrated artistic ability, appropriate training, or other qualifications are needed for success. Evidence of appropriate talent and skill, displayed in an artist's "portfolio," is an important factor used by art and design directors and others in deciding whether to hire or contract out work to an artist. The portfolio is a collection of hand-made, computer-generated, or printed examples of the artist's best work. Assembling a successful portfolio requires skills usually developed in a bachelor's degree program or other postsecondary training in art, design, or visual communications. Internships also provide excellent opportunities for artists to develop and enhance their portfolios. Formal educational programs in art and design also provide training in computer design techniques; computers are widely used in art and design, and knowledge and training in computer techniques are critical for many jobs in these fields.

Recent data from The American Institute of Graphic Arts indicate that over nine out of ten artists have a college degree; among this group, over six out of ten majored in graphic design and nearly two out of ten majored in fine arts. Nearly two out of ten have a master's degree.

The appropriate training and education for prospective medical illustrators is more specific. Medical illustrators must not only demonstrate artistic ability, but must also have a detailed knowledge of living organisms, surgical and medical procedures, and human and sometimes animal anatomy. A four-year bachelor's degree combining art and premedical courses is usually required, followed by a master's degree in medical illustration. This degree is offered in only a few accredited schools in the United States.

Persons hired in advertising agencies or graphic design studios often start with relatively routine work. While doing this work, however, they may observe and practice their skills on the side. Many graphic artists work part-time as freelancers while continuing to hold a full-time job until they get established. Others have enough talent, perseverance, and confidence in their ability to start out freelancing full-time immediately after graduating from art school. Many freelance part-time while still in school in order to develop experience and a portfolio of published work.

The freelance artist develops a set of clients who regularly contract for work. Some successful freelancers are widely recognized for their skill in specialties, such as children's book illustration, design, or magazine illustration. These artists may earn high incomes and can pick and choose the type of work they do.

Fine artists and illustrators advance as their work circulates, and as they establish a reputation for a particular style. The best artists and illustrators continually develop new ideas, and their work constantly evolves over time. Graphic artists may advance to assistant art director, art director, design director, and in some companies, creative director of an art or design department. Some artists may gain enough skill to succeed as a freelancer or may prefer to specialize in a particular area. Some graphic artists become webmasters, maintaining their company's Internet site. Others decide to open their own businesses.

Job Outlook

The glamorous and exciting image of graphic and fine arts fields attracts many talented people with a love for drawing and creative ability. As a result, the supply of aspiring artists will continue to exceed the number of job openings, resulting in keen competition for both salaried jobs and freelance work. Freelance work may be particularly hard to come by, especially at first, and many freelancers earn very little until they acquire experience and establish a good reputation. Fine artists, in particular, may find it difficult to earn a living solely by selling their art work. Nonetheless, graphic arts studios, galleries, and individual clients are always on the lookout for artists who display outstanding talent, creativity, and style. Talented artists who have developed a mastery of artistic techniques and skills, including computer skills, will have the best job prospects.

Employment of visual artists is expected to grow faster than the average for all occupations through the year 2006. Demand for graphic artists should remain strong as producers of information, goods, and services put increasing emphasis on visual appeal in product design, advertising, marketing, and television. The explosive growth of the Internet is expected to provide many additional opportunities for graphic artists. Employment growth for graphic artists, however, may be limited because some firms are turning to employees without formal artistic or design training to operate computer-aided design systems. Employment of fine artists is expected to grow because of population growth, rising incomes, and growth in the number of people who appreciate fine arts.

Demand for artists may also depend on the level of government funding for certain programs. For example, the National Endowment for the Arts offers a variety of grants to artists; however, competition is intense for most awards.

Earnings

Median earnings for salaried visual artists who usually work full-time were about $27,100 a year in 1996. The middle 50 percent earned between $20,000 and $36,400 a year. The top 10 percent earned more than $43,000, and the bottom 10 percent earned less than $15,000.

The Society of Publication Designers estimates that entry-level graphic designers earned between $23,000 and $27,000 annually in 1997.

Earnings for self-employed visual artists vary widely. Those struggling to gain experience and a reputation may be forced to charge close to the minimum wage for their work. Well-established freelancers and fine artists may earn much more than salaried artists. Like other workers, self-employed artists must provide their own benefits.

Related Occupations

Many occupations in the advertising industry, such as account executive or creative director, are related to commercial and graphic art and design. Other workers who apply visual art skills include architects, display workers, landscape architects, photographers, and floral, industrial, and interior designers. Various printing occupations are also related to graphic art, as is the work of art and design teachers. In addition, several occupational options associated with the Internet have emerged—for example, webmaster and Internet page designer. These jobs often require artistic talent as well as computer skills.

Sources of Additional Information

Students interested in careers as illustrators should contact:

❏ The National Association of Schools of Art and Design, 11250 Roger Bacon Dr., Suite 21, Reston, VA 20190.

For information on careers in medical illustration, contact:

❏ The Association of Medical Illustrators, 1819 Peachtree St. NE., Suite 712, Atlanta, GA 30309-1848.

For a list of schools offering degree programs in graphic design, contact:

❏ The American Institute of Graphic Arts, 164 Fifth Ave., New York, NY 10010.

For information on magazine art and design occupations, contact:

❏ The Society of Publication Designers, 60 East 42nd St., Suite 721, New York, NY 10165-1416.

CAREER PLANNING AND JOB SEARCH ADVICE

The Quick Job Search

A Results-Oriented Career Planning and Job Search Minibook

by Mike Farr

While *The Quick Job Search* is short, it covers **all** the major topics needed to explore career options and to conduct an effective job search. The techniques it presents have been proven to reduce the time it takes to find a job and are widely used by job search programs throughout North America.

Major topics include the following:

◆ **Skills Identification:** Includes checklists and activities to help you identify your key skills—essential for career planning, interviewing, and writing resumes.

◆ **Career Planning:** Provides activities to help define your ideal job and a list of the top 250 jobs (85 percent of us work in one of these jobs)—and tips on getting more information on each one.

◆ **Results-Oriented Job Seeking Skills:** Research-based advice on traditional and nontraditional job search methods, with an emphasis on the two most effective techniques: networking and cold contacts.

◆ **Interview Skills, Resumes, Time Management, and More:** Specific techniques on answering problem interview questions, writing a superior resume, setting a daily schedule, getting two interviews a day, and many other innovative and useful techniques.

◆ **Dealing with Job Loss:** Practical and upbeat advice on coping with the stress and discouragement of being unemployed.

◆ **Handling Your Finances While out of Work:** Brief but helpful tips on conserving cash and stretching your resources.

◆ **Sources of Other Information:** Books and other sources of information on occupations, employers, resumes, interviewing skills, industries, and a range of job search topics.

Introduction

I've spent much of the past 20 years of my professional life learning more about career planning and job search methods. My original interest was in helping people find jobs in less time, and in helping them find better jobs. In a broad sense, that is—or should be—the real task of career counseling and job seeking skills. While there is a lot of complexity to these tasks, I have also found some elements of simplicity:

1. If you are going to work, you might as well define what it is you really want to do and are good at.

2. If you are looking for a job, you might as well use techniques that will reduce the time it takes to find one—and that helps you get a better job than otherwise.

This section covers these topics, along with a few others. While I have written much more detailed works on career planning and job seeking, I present the basics of career planning and job seeking in this section. I think that there is enough information here to make a difference for most people, and I hope that it gives you some things to think about, as well as some techniques you have not considered.

About ten years ago, I decided to write something very short but that would cover the most important elements of effective career planning and job seeking. Writing short things is harder for me than writing longer things, since every word has to count. I began by asking myself, "If I only had 30 or so pages, what were the most important things to tell someone?"

The Quick Job Search was the result. While it is a section in this book, it has also been published separately and, in an expanded form, as a book titled *How to Get a Job Now*! It has sold about 300,000 copies in its various forms. I hope you can make good use of it.

Avoid the Temptation; Do the Activities

I already know that you will resist doing the activities included in *The Quick Job Search*. But trust me, doing them is worthwhile. Those who do them will have a better sense of what they are good at, what they want to do, and how to go about doing it. They are more likely to get more interviews and to present themselves better in those interviews. Is this worth giving up a night of TV? Yes, I think so.

Interestingly enough, you will—after reading *The Quick Job Search* and doing its activities—have spent more time on planning your career than most people. And you will know far more than the average job seeker about how to go about finding a job. While you may want to know more, I hope that this is enough to get you started.

> *While this book will teach you techniques to find a better job in less time, job seeking requires you to act, not just learn. So, in going through this book, consider what you can do to put the techniques to work for you. Do the activities. Create a daily plan. Get more interviews. Today, not tomorrow. You see, the sooner and harder you get to work on your job search, the shorter it is likely to be.*

Changing Jobs and Careers Is Often Healthy

Most of us were told from an early age that each career move must be up—involving more money, responsibility, and prestige. Yet research indicates people change careers for many other reasons as well.

In a survey conducted by the Gallup Organization for the National Occupational Information Coordinating Committee, 44 percent of the working adults surveyed expected to be in a different job within three years. This is a very high turnover rate, yet only 41 percent had a definite plan to follow in mapping out their careers.

Logical, ordered careers are found more often with increasing levels of education. For example, while 25 percent of the high school dropouts took the only job available, this was true for only 8 percent of those with at least some college. But you should not assume this means that such occupational stability is healthy. Many adult developmental psychologists believe occupational change is not only normal but may even be necessary for sound adult growth and development. It is common, even normal, to reconsider occupational roles during your twenties, thirties, and forties—even in the absence of economic pressure to do so.

One viewpoint is that a healthy occupational change is one that allows some previously undeveloped aspect of yourself to emerge. The change may be as natural as from clerk to supervisor; or as drastic as from professional musician to airline pilot. Although risk is always a factor when change is involved, reasonable risks are healthy and can raise self-esteem.

But Not Just Any Job Should Do—Nor Any Job Search

Whether you are seeking similar work in another setting or changing careers, you need a workable plan to find the right job. This section will give you the information you need to help you find a good job quickly.

While the techniques are presented here briefly, they are based on my years of experience in helping people find good jobs (not just any job) and to find jobs in less time. The career decision-making section will help you consider the major issues you need to make a good decision about the job you want. The job-seeking skills are ones that have been proven to reduce the amount of time required to find a good job.

Of course, more thorough books have been written on job-seeking techniques, and you may want to look into buying one or more of the better ones to obtain additional information. (A list of such books is included in the bibliography of this book.) But, short as this section is, it DOES present the basic skills to find a good job in less time. The techniques work.

The Six Steps for a Quick and Successful Job Search

You can't just read about getting a job. The best way to get a job is to go out and get interviews! And the best way to get interviews is to make a job out of getting a job.

After many years of experience, I have identified just six basic things you need to do that make a big difference in your job search. Each will be covered in this section.

The Six Steps for a Quick Job Search

1. Know your skills.
2. Have a clear job objective.
3. Know where and how to look for job leads.
4. Spend at least 25 hours a week looking.
5. Get two interviews a day.
6. Follow up on all contacts.

Identify Your Key Skills

One survey of employers found that 90 percent of the people they interviewed did not present the skills they had to do the job they sought. They could not answer the basic question, "Why should I hire you?"

Knowing your skills is essential to do well in an interview. This same knowledge is important in deciding what type of job you will enjoy and do well. For these reasons, I consider identifying your skills an essential part of a successful career plan or job search.

The Three Types of Skills

Most people think of "skills" as job-related skills such as using a computer. But we all have other types of skills that are also important for success on a job—and that are very important to employers. The triangle below presents skills in three groups, and I think that this is a very useful way to consider skills for our purposes.

The Skills Triad

Let's review these three types of skills and identify those that are most important to you.

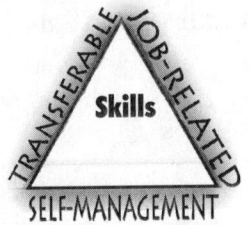

Self-Management Skills

Write down three things about yourself that you think make you a good worker.

Your "Good Worker" Traits

1. _____

2. _____

3. _____

The things you just wrote down are among the most important things for an employer to know about you! They have to do with your basic personality—your ability to adapt to a new environment. They are some of the most important things to emphasize in an interview, yet most job seekers don't realize their importance—and don't mention them.

Review the Self-Management Skills Checklist and put a check mark beside any skills you have. The Key Self-Management Skills are skills that employers find particularly important. If one or more of the Key Self-Management Skills apply to you, mentioning them in an interview can help you greatly.

Self-Management Skills Checklist

Key Self-Management Skills

___ accept supervision	___ hard worker
___ get along with coworkers	___ honest
___ get things done on time	___ productive
___ good attendance	___ punctual

Other Self-Management Skills

___ able to coordinate	___ friendly
___ ambitious	___ good-natured
___ assertive	___ helpful
___ capable	___ humble
___ cheerful	___ imaginative
___ competent	___ independent
___ complete assignments	___ industrious
___ conscientious	___ informal
___ creative	___ intelligent
___ dependable	___ intuitive
___ discreet	___ learn quickly
___ eager	___ loyal
___ efficient	___ mature
___ energetic	___ methodical
___ enthusiastic	___ modest
___ expressive	___ motivated
___ flexible	___ natural
___ formal	___ sense of humor

(continued)

(continued)

___ open-minded
___ optimistic
___ original
___ patient
___ persistent
___ physically strong
___ practice new skills
___ reliable
___ resourceful
___ responsible
___ self-confident

___ sincere
___ solve problems
___ spontaneous
___ steady
___ tactful
___ take pride in work
___ tenacious
___ thrifty
___ trustworthy
___ versatile
___ well-organized

Other Self-Management Skills You Have:

_____

_____

_____

After you are done with the list, circle the five skills you feel are most important and list them in the box that follows.

Note: *Some people find it helpful to complete now the "Essential Job Search Data Worksheet" provided later in this section. It organizes skills and accomplishments from previous jobs and other life experiences.*

Your Top 5 Self-Management Skills ✓

1. _____

2. _____

3. _____

4. _____

5. _____

Transferable Skills

We all have skills that can transfer from one job or career to another. For example, the ability to organize events could be used in a variety of jobs and may be essential for success in certain occupations. Your mission should be to find a job that requires the skills you have and enjoy using.

In the following list, put a check mark beside the skills you have. You may have used them in a previous job or in some nonwork setting.

Transferable Skills Checklist ✓

Key Transferable Skills

___ instruct others
___ manage money, budget
___ manage people
___ meet deadlines
___ meet the public

___ negotiate
___ organize/manage projects
___ public speaking
___ written communication skills

Skills Working with Things

___ assemble things
___ build things
___ construct/repair
___ drive, operate vehicles
___ good with hands

___ observe/inspect
___ operate tools, machines
___ repair things
___ use complex equipment

Skills Working with Data

___ analyze data
___ audit records
___ budget
___ calculate/compute
___ check for accuracy
___ classify things
___ compare
___ compile
___ count
___ detail-oriented

___ evaluate
___ investigate
___ keep financial records
___ locate information
___ manage money
___ observe/inspect
___ record facts
___ research
___ synthesize
___ take inventory

Skills Working with People

___ administer
___ advise
___ care for
___ coach
___ confront others
___ counsel people
___ demonstrate
___ diplomatic
___ help others
___ instruct
___ interview people
___ kind
___ listen
___ negotiate

___ outgoing
___ patient
___ perceptive
___ persuade
___ pleasant
___ sensitive
___ sociable
___ supervise
___ tactful
___ tolerant
___ tough
___ trusting
___ understanding

Skills Working with Words, Ideas

___ articulate
___ communicate verbally
___ correspond with others
___ create new ideas
___ design
___ edit
___ ingenious

___ inventive
___ library research
___ logical
___ public speaking
___ remember information
___ write clearly

(continued)

(continued)

Leadership Skills

___ arrange social functions	___ mediate problems
___ competitive	___ motivate people
___ decisive	___ negotiate agreements
___ delegate	___ plan events
___ direct others	___ results-oriented
___ explain things to others	___ risk-taker
___ influence others	___ run meetings
___ initiate new tasks	___ self-confident
___ make decisions	___ self-motivate
___ manage or direct others	___ solve problems

Creative/Artistic Skills

___ artistic	___ expressive
___ dance, body movement	___ perform, act
___ drawing, art	___ present artistic ideas

Other Similar Skills You Have:

_____

_____

_____

_____

_____

_____

When you are finished, identify the five transferable skills you feel are most important for you to use in your next job and list them in the box below.

Your Top 5 Transferable Skills

1. _____

2. _____

3. _____

4. _____

5. _____

Job-Related Skills

Job content or job-related skills are those you need to do a particular job. A carpenter, for example, needs to know how to use various tools and be familiar with a variety of tasks related to that job.

You may already have a good idea of the type of job that you want. If so, it may be fairly simple for you to identify your job-related skills to emphasize in an interview. But I recommend that you complete at least two other things in this book first:

1. Complete the material that helps you define your job objective more clearly. Doing so will help you clarify just what sort of a job you want and allow you to better select those skills that best support it.

2. Complete the Essential Job Search Data Worksheet that appears later in this book (pages 385-387). It will give you lots of specific skills and accomplishments to consider.

Once you have done these two things, come back and complete the box below. Include the job-related skills you have that you would most like to use in your next job.

Your Top 5 Job-Related Skills

1. _____

2. _____

3. _____

4. _____

5. _____

Begin by Defining Your Ideal Job (You Can Compromise Later)

Too many people look for a job without having a good idea of exactly what they are looking for. Before you go out looking for "a" job, I suggest that you first define exactly what it is you really want—"the" job. Most people think a job objective is the same as a job title, but it isn't. You need to consider other elements of what makes a job satisfying for you. Then, later, you can decide what that job is called and what industry it might be in.

The Eight Factors to Consider in Defining the Ideal Job for You

Following are eight factors to consider when you define your ideal job. Once you know what you want, your task then becomes finding a job that is as close to your ideal job as you can find.

1. What Skills Do You Want to Use?

From the previous skills lists, select the top five skills that you enjoy using and most want to use in your next job.

1. _____

2. _____

3. _____

4. _____

5. _____

2. What Type of Special Knowledge Do You Have?

Perhaps you know how to fix radios, keep accounting records, or cook food. Write down the things you know about from schooling, training, hobbies, family experiences, and other sources. One or more of them could make you a very special applicant in the right setting.

_____

_____

_____

_____

_____

3. With What Types of People Do You Prefer to Work?

Do you like to work with aggressive hardworking folks, creative types, or what?

_____

_____

_____

_____

_____

(continued)

(continued)

4. What Type of Work Environment Do You Prefer?

Do you want to work inside, outside, in a quiet place, a busy place, a clean place, have a window with a nice view, or what? List those things that are important to you.

_____

_____

_____

_____

_____

5. Where Do You Want Your Next Job to Be Located— In What City or Region?

Near a bus line? Close to a child care center? If you are open to live or work anywhere, what would your ideal community be like?

_____

_____

_____

_____

_____

6. How Much Money Do You Hope to Make in Your Next Job?

Many people will take less money if the job is great in other ways—or to survive. Think about the minimum you would take as well as what you would eventually like to earn. Your next job will probably be somewhere between.

_____

_____

_____

_____

_____

(continued)

© 1999 • J. Michael Farr • JIST Works, Inc. • Indianapolis, IN

(continued)

7. How Much Responsibility Are You Willing to Accept?

Usually, the more money you want to make, the more responsibility you must accept. Do you want to work by yourself, be part of a group, or be in charge? If so, at what level?

_____

_____

_____

_____

_____

8. What Things Are Important or Have Meaning to You?

Do you have values that you would prefer to include as a basis of the work you do? For example, some people want to work to help others, clean up our environment, build things, make machines work, gain power or prestige, or care for animals or plants. Think about what is important to you and how you might include this in your next job.

_____

_____

_____

_____

_____

Your Ideal Job

Use the points at left and on previous pages to help you define your ideal job. Think about each one and select the points that are most important to you. Don't worry about a job title yet; just focus on the most important things to include from the previous questions to define your ideal job.

My Ideal Job Objective:

_____

_____

_____

_____

_____

_____

_____

_____

_____

_____

Setting a Specific Job Objective

Whether or not you have a good idea of the type of job you want, it is important to know more about various job options. About 85 percent of all workers work in one of the 250 jobs in the list that follows.

A very simple but effective way for exploring job alternatives is to go through this list and check those about which you want to learn more. Descriptions for many of them can be found in this book. I encourage you to learn more about the jobs that interest you.

If you need help figuring out what type of job to look for, remember that most areas have free or low-cost career counseling and testing services. Contact local government agencies and schools for referrals.

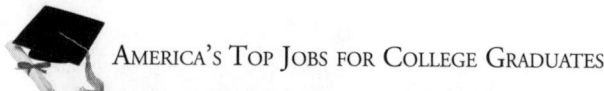

The Top 250 Jobs in Our Workforce

EXECUTIVE, ADMINISTRATIVE, AND MANAGERIAL OCCUPATIONS

Accountants and auditors

Administrative services managers

Budget analysts

Construction and building inspectors

Construction managers

Cost estimators

Education administrators

Employment interviewers

Engineering, science, and computer systems managers

Farmers and farm managers

Financial managers

Funeral directors

General managers and top executives

Government chief executives and legislators

Health services managers

Hotel managers and assistants

Human resources specialists and managers

Industrial production managers

Inspectors and compliance officers, except construction

Insurance underwriters

Loan officers and counselors

Management analysts and consultants

Marketing, advertising, and public relations managers

Property managers

Purchasers and buyers

Restaurant and food service managers

PROFESSIONAL AND TECHNICAL OCCUPATIONS

AIR TRANSPORTATION-RELATED OCCUPATIONS

Aircraft pilots

Air traffic controllers

ENGINEERS AND ENGINEERING TECHNICIANS

ENGINEERS

Aerospace engineers

Chemical engineers

Civil engineers

Electrical and electronics engineers

Industrial engineers

Mechanical engineers

Metallurgical, ceramic, and materials engineers

Mining engineers

Nuclear engineers

Petroleum engineers

ENGINEERING TECHNICIANS

ARCHITECTS, SURVEYORS, AND DRAFTERS

Architects

Drafters

Landscape architects

Surveyors and mapping scientists

COMPUTER, MATHEMATICAL, AND OPERATIONS RESEARCH OCCUPATIONS

Actuaries

Computer programmers

Computer scientists, computer engineers, and systems analysts

Mathematicians

Operations research analysts

Statisticians

SCIENTISTS AND SCIENCE TECHNICIANS

LIFE SCIENTISTS

Agricultural scientists

Biological and medical scientists

Foresters and conservation scientists

PHYSICAL SCIENTISTS

Chemists

Geologists and geophysicists

Meteorologists

Physicists and astronomers

SCIENCE TECHNICIANS

LEGAL OCCUPATIONS

Lawyers and judges

Paralegals

SOCIAL SCIENTISTS

Economists and marketing research analysts

Psychologists

Urban and regional planners

SOCIAL AND RECREATION WORKERS

Recreation workers

Social and human service assistants

Social workers

CLERGY

Protestant ministers

Rabbis

Roman Catholic priests

TEACHERS, COUNSELORS, AND LIBRARY OCCUPATIONS

Adult education teachers

Archivists and curators

College and university faculty

Counselors

Librarians

Library technicians

School teachers–kindergarten, elementary, and secondary

Special education teachers

HEALTH DIAGNOSING PRACTITIONERS

Chiropractors

Dentists

Optometrists

Physicians

Podiatrists

Veterinarians

Health assessment and treating occupations

Dietitians and nutritionists

Occupational therapists

Pharmacists

Physical therapists

Physician assistants

Recreational therapists

Registered nurses

Respiratory therapists

Speech-language pathologists and audiologists

Health technologists and technicians

Cardiovascular technologists and technicians

Clinical laboratory technologists and technicians

Dental hygienists

Dispensing opticians

Electroneurodiagnostic technologists

Emergency medical technicians

Health information technicians

Licensed practical nurses

Nuclear medicine technologists

Radiologic technologists

Surgical technicians

Communications-related occupations

Broadcast technicians

Public relations specialists

Radio and television announcers and newscasters

Reporters and correspondents

Writers and editors

Visual arts occupations

Designers

Photographers and camera operators

Visual artists

Performing arts occupations

Actors, directors, and producers

Dancers and choreographers

Musicians

Marketing and Sales Occupations

Cashiers

Counter and rental clerks

Insurance agents and brokers

Manufacturers' and wholesale sales representatives

Real estate agents, brokers, and appraisers

Retail sales worker supervisors and managers

Retail sales workers

Securities and financial services sales representatives

Services sales representatives

Travel agents

Administrative Support Occupations, Including Clerical

Adjusters, investigators, and collectors

Bank tellers

Clerical supervisors and managers

Computer operators

Court reporters, medical transcriptionists, and stenographers

General office clerks

Information clerks

   Hotel and motel desk clerks

   Interviewing and new accounts clerks

   Receptionists

   Reservation and transportation ticket agents and travel clerks

Loan clerks and credit authorizers, checkers, and clerks

Mail clerks and messengers

Material recording, scheduling, dispatching, and distributing occupations

   Dispatchers

   Stock clerks

   Traffic, shipping, and receiving clerks

Postal clerks and mail carriers

Record clerks

   Billing clerks and billing machine operators

   Bookkeeping, accounting, and auditing clerks

   Brokerage clerks and statement clerks

   File clerks

   Library assistants and bookmobile drivers

   Order clerks

   Payroll and timekeeping clerks

   Personnel clerks

Secretaries

Teacher aides

Telephone operators

Typists, word processors, and data entry keyers

Service Occupations

Food preparation and beverage service occupations

Chefs, cooks, and other kitchen workers

Food and beverage service occupations

Health service occupations

Dental assistants

Medical assistants

Nursing aides and psychiatric aides

Occupational therapy assistants and aides

Physical and corrective therapy assistants and aides

Personal, buildings, and grounds service occupations

Barbers and cosmetologists

Flight attendants

Homemaker-home health aides

Janitors and cleaners and cleaning supervisors

Landscaping, groundskeeping, nursery, greenhouse, and lawn service occupations

Preschool teachers and child-care workers

Private household workers

Veterinary assistants and nonfarm animal caretakers

PROTECTIVE SERVICE OCCUPATIONS

Correctional officers

Firefighting occupations

Guards

Police, detectives, and special agents

Private detectives and investigators

MECHANICS, INSTALLERS, AND REPAIRERS

Aircraft mechanics, including engine specialists

Automotive body repairers

Automotive mechanics

Diesel mechanics

Electronic equipment repairers

    Commercial and industrial electronic equipment repairers

    Communications equipment mechanics

    Computer and office machine repairers

    Electronic home entertainment equipment repairers

    Telephone installers and repairers

Elevator installers and repairers

Farm equipment mechanics

General maintenance mechanics

Heating, air-conditioning, and refrigeration technicians

Home appliance and power tool repairers

Industrial machinery repairers

Line installers and cable splicers

Millwrights

Mobile heavy equipment mechanics

Motorcycle, boat, and small-engine mechanics

Musical instrument repairers and tuners

Vending machine servicers and repairers

CONSTRUCTION TRADES OCCUPATIONS

Bricklayers and stonemasons

Carpet installers

Concrete masons and terrazzo workers

Drywall workers and lathers

Electricians

Glaziers

Insulation workers

Painters and paperhangers

Plasterers

Plumbers and pipefitters

Roofers

Sheetmetal workers

Structural and reinforcing ironworkers

Tilesetters

PRODUCTION OCCUPATIONS

ASSEMBLERS

Precision assemblers

BLUE-COLLAR WORKER SUPERVISORS

FISHING, HUNTING, AND FORESTRY OCCUPATIONS

Fishers, hunters, and trappers

Forestry and logging workers

FOOD PROCESSING OCCUPATIONS

Butchers and meat, poultry, and fish cutters

INSPECTORS, TESTERS, AND GRADERS

METALWORKING AND PLASTIC-WORKING OCCUPATIONS

Boilermakers

Jewelers

Machinists and tool programmers

Metalworking and plastics-working machine operators

Tool and die makers

Welders, cutters, and welding machine operators

PLANT AND SYSTEMS OPERATORS

Electric power generating plant operators and power distributors and dispatchers

Stationary engineers

Water and wastewater treatment plant operators

PRINTING OCCUPATIONS

Bindery workers

Prepress workers

Printing press operators

TEXTILE, APPAREL, AND FURNISHINGS OCCUPATIONS

Apparel workers

Shoe and leather workers and repairers

Textile machinery operators

Upholsterers

WOODWORKING OCCUPATIONS

MISCELLANEOUS PRODUCTION OCCUPATIONS

Dental laboratory technicians

Ophthalmic laboratory technicians

Painting and coating machine operators

Photographic process workers

TRANSPORTATION AND MATERIAL MOVING OCCUPATIONS

Busdrivers

Material moving equipment operators

Rail transportation occupation

Taxi drivers and chauffeurs

Truckdrivers

Water transportation occupations

HANDLERS, EQUIPMENT CLEANERS, HELPERS, AND LABORERS

JOB OPPORTUNITIES IN THE ARMED FORCES

© 1999 • J. Michael Farr • JIST Works, Inc. • Indianapolis, IN

Job Search Methods That Help You Get a Better Job in Less Time

One survey found that 85 percent of all employers don't advertise at all. They hire people they already know, people who find out about the jobs through word of mouth, or people who simply happen to be in the right place at the right time. This is sometimes just luck, but this book will teach you ways to increase your "luck" in finding job openings.

Traditional Job Search Methods Are Not Very Effective

Most job seekers don't know how ineffective some traditional job hunting techniques tend to be.

How People Find Jobs

35%
30%
14%
6%
5%
2%
8%

Heard about opening from someone 35%
Contacted employer directly 30%
Answered want ad 14%
Referred by private employment agency 6%
Referred by state employment agency 5%
Took civil service (government) tests 2%

Other methods (referred by school, union referral, placed ads in journals, etc.) 8%

The chart above shows that fewer than 15 percent of all job seekers get jobs from reading the want ads. Let's take a quick look at want ads and other traditional job search methods.

Help Wanted Ads: As you should remember, only about 15 percent of all people get their jobs through the want ads. Everyone who reads the paper knows about these job openings, so competition for advertised jobs is fierce. Still, some people do get jobs this way, so go ahead and apply. Just be sure to spend most of your time using more effective methods.

The State Employment Service: Each state has a network of local offices to administer unemployment compensation and provide job leads and other services. These services are provided without charge to you or employers. Names vary by state, so it may be called "Job Service," "Department of Labor," "Unemployment Office," or another name.

Nationally, only about 5 percent of all job seekers get their jobs here, and these organizations typically know of only one-tenth (or fewer) of the actual job openings in a region. Still, it is worth a weekly visit. If you ask for the same counselor, you might impress the person enough to remember you and refer you for the better openings.

You should also realize that some of the state employment services provide substantial help in the form of job search workshops and other resources. Look into it; the price is right.

Private Employment Agencies: Recent studies have found that private agencies work reasonably well for those who use them. But there are cautions to consider. For one thing, these agencies work best for entry-level positions or for those with specialized skills that are in demand. Most people who use a private agency usually find their jobs using some other source and their success record is quite modest.

Private agencies also charge a fee either to you (as high as 20 percent of your annual salary!) or to the employer. Most of them call employers asking if they have any openings, something you could do yourself. Unless you have skills that are in high demand, you may do better on your own—and save money. At the least, you should rely on a private agency as only one of the techniques you use and not depend on them too heavily.

Temporary Agencies: These can be a source of quick but temporary jobs to bring in some income as well as give you experience in a variety of settings—something that can help you land full-time jobs later. More and more employers are also using them as a way to evaluate workers for permanent jobs. So consider using these agencies if it makes sense to do so, but make certain that you continue an active search for a full-time job as you do.

Sending Out Resumes: *One survey found that you would have to mail more than 500 unsolicited resumes to get one interview!* A much better approach is to contact the person who might hire you by phone to set up an interview directly; then send a resume. If you insist on sending out unsolicited resumes, do this on weekends—save your "prime time" for more effective job search techniques.

Filling Out Applications: Most applications are used to screen you out. Larger organizations may require them, but remember that your task is to get an interview, not fill out an application. If you do complete them, make them neat and error-free, and do not include anything that could get you screened out. If necessary, leave a problematic section blank. It can always be explained after you get an interview.

Personnel Departments: Hardly anyone gets hired by interviewers in a personnel department. Their job is to screen you and refer the "best" applicants to the person who would actually supervise you. You may need to cooperate with them, but it is often better to go directly to the person who is most likely to supervise you—even if no job opening exists at the moment. And remember that most organizations don't even have a personnel office; only the larger ones do!

The Two Job Search Methods That Work Best

Two-thirds of all people get their jobs using informal methods. These jobs are often not advertised and are part of the "hidden" job market. How do **you** find them?

There are two basic informal job search methods: networking with people you know (which I call warm contacts), and making direct contacts with an employer (which I call cold contacts). They are both based on the most important job search rule of all.

**The Most Important Job Search Rule:
Don't wait until the job is open
before contacting the employer!**

Most jobs are filled by someone the employer meets before the job is formally "open." So the trick is to meet people who can hire you before a job is available! Instead of saying, "Do you have any jobs open?" say, "I realize you may not have any openings now, but I would still like to talk to you about the possibility of future openings."

Develop a Network of Contacts in Five Easy Steps

One study found that 40 percent of all people found their jobs through a lead provided by a friend, a relative, or an acquaintance. Developing new contacts is called "networking," and here's how it works:

1. **Make lists of people you know.** Develop a list of anyone with whom you are friendly; then make a separate list of all your relatives. These two lists alone often add up to 25–100 people or more. Next, think of other groups of people with whom you have something in common, such as former co-workers or classmates; members of your social or sports groups; members of your professional association; former employers; and members of your religious group. You may not know many of these people personally, but most will help you if you ask them.

2. **Contact them in a systematic way.** Each of these people is a contact for you. Obviously, some lists and some people on those lists will be more helpful than others, but almost any one of them could help you find a job lead.

3. **Present yourself well.** Begin with your friends and relatives. Call them and tell them you are looking for a job and need their help. Be as clear as possible about what you are looking for and what skills and qualifications you have. Look

at the sample JIST Card and phone script later in this book for presentation ideas.

4. **Ask them for leads.** It is possible that they will know of a job opening just right for you. If so, get the details and get right on it! More likely, however, they will not, so here are three questions you should ask.

The Three Magic Networking Questions

1. *Do you know of any openings for a person with my skills?* If the answer is no (which it usually is), then ask:

2. *Do you know of someone else who might know of such an opening?* If your contact does, get that name and ask for another one. If he or she doesn't, ask:

3. *Do you know of anyone who might know of someone else who might?* Another good way to ask this is, "Do you know someone who knows lots of people?" If all else fails, this will usually get you a name.

---

5. **Contact these referrals and ask them the same questions.** For each original contact, you can extend your network of acquaintances by hundreds of people. Eventually, one of these people will hire you or refer you to someone who will! This process is called networking, and it does work if you are persistent.

Contact Employers Directly

It takes more courage, but contacting an employer directly is a very effective job search technique. I call these cold contacts because you don't have an existing connection with these contacts. Following are two basic techniques for making cold contacts.

Use the *Yellow Pages* to Find Potential Employers

One effective cold contact technique uses the *Yellow Pages*. You can begin by looking at the index and asking for each entry, "Would an organization of this kind need a person with my skills?" If the answer is "yes," then that type of organization or business is a possible target. You can also rate "yes" entries based on your interest, giving an A to those that seem very interesting, a B to those you are not sure of, and a C to those that don't seem interesting at all.

Next, select a type of organization that got a "yes" response (such as "hotels") and turn to the section of the *Yellow Pages* where they are listed. Then call the organizations listed and ask to speak to the person who is most likely to hire or supervise you. A sample telephone script is included later in this section to give you ideas about what to say.

Drop In Without an Appointment

You can also simply walk in to many potential employers' organizations and ask to speak to the person in charge. This is particularly effective in small businesses, but it works surprisingly well in larger ones too. Remember, you want an interview even if there are no openings now. If your timing is inconvenient, ask for a better time to come back for an interview.

Use the Internet

If you have computer access to the Internet and the World Wide Web, you'll find many useful job search, career planning, and other resources there. As with other job search techniques, you can also waste a lot of time. I've included some information on using the Internet in your job search at the end of this section, so check it out if you are interested.

Most Jobs Are with Small Employers

About 70 percent of all people now work in small businesses—those with 250 or fewer employees. While the largest corporations have reduced the number of employees, small businesses have been creating as many as 80 percent of the new jobs. There are many opportunities to obtain training and promotions in smaller

organizations, too. Many do not even have a personnel department, so nontraditional job search techniques are particularly effective with them.

JIST Cards—an Effective "Mini Resume"

JIST Cards are a job search tool that gets results. Typed, printed, or even neatly written on a 3-by-5-inch card, a JIST Card contains the essential information most employers want to know. Look at the sample cards that follow.

JIST Cards are an effective job search tool! Give them to friends and to each of your network contacts. Attach one to your resume. Enclose one in your thank-you notes before or after an interview. Leave one with employers as a "business card." Use them in many creative ways. Even though they can be typed or even handwritten, it is best to have 100 or more printed so you can put lots of them in circulation. Thousands of job seekers have used them, and they get results!

Sandy Zaremba

Home: (219) 232-7608   **Message:** (219) 234-7465

Position: General Office/Clerical

Over two years' work experience, plus one year of training in office practices. Type 55 wpm, trained in word processing operations, post general ledger, handle payables, receivables, and most accounting tasks. Responsible for daily deposits averaging $5,000. Good interpersonal skills. Can meet strict deadlines and handle pressure well.

Willing to work any hours.

Organized, honest, reliable, and hardworking.

Chris Vorhees

Home: (602) 253-9678

Leave Message: (602) 257-6643

OBJECTIVE: Electronics—installation, maintenance, and sales

SKILLS: Four years' work experience, plus two years advanced training in electronics. A.S. degree in Electronics Engineering Technology. Managed a $300,000/yr. business while going to school full time, with grades in the top 25%. Familiar with all major electronic diagnostic and repair equipment. Hands-on experience with medical, consumer, communications, and industrial electronics equipment and applications. Good problem-solving and communication skills. Customer service oriented.

Willing to do what it takes to get the job done.

Use the Phone to Get Job Leads

Once you have created your JIST Card, it is easy to create a telephone contact "script" based on it. Adapt the basic script to call people you know or your *Yellow Pages* leads. Select *Yellow Pages* index categories that might use a person with your skills and get the numbers of specific organizations in that category. Then ask for the person who is most likely to supervise you and present your phone script.

While it doesn't work every time, most people, with practice, can get one or more interviews in an hour by making these "cold" calls. Here is a phone script based on a JIST Card:

"Hello, my name is Pam Nykanen. I am interested in a position in hotel management. I have four years' experience in sales, catering, and accounting with a 300-room hotel. I also have an associate degree in Hotel Management plus one year of experience with the Bradey Culinary Institute. During my employment, I helped double revenues from meetings and conferences and increased bar revenues by 46 percent. I have good problem-solving skills and am good with people. I am also well-organized, hardworking, and detail-oriented. When may I come in for an interview?"

While this example assumes you are calling someone you don't know, the script can be easily modified for presentation to warm contacts, including referrals. Using the script for making cold calls takes courage, but it does work for most people.

Make Your Job Search a Full-Time Job

On the average, job seekers spend fewer than 15 hours a week actually looking for work. The average length of unemployment varies from three or more months, with some being out of work far longer (older workers and higher earners are two groups who take longer). I believe there is a connection.

Based on many years of experience, I can say that the more time you spend on your job search each week, the less time you are likely to remain unemployed. Of course, using more effective job search methods also helps. Those who follow my advice have proven, over and over, that they get jobs in less than half the average time and they often get better jobs, too. Time management is the key.

Spend at Least 25 Hours a Week Looking for a Job

If you are unemployed and looking for a full-time job, you should look for a job on a full-time basis. It just makes sense to do so, although many do not because of discouragement, lack of good techniques, and lack of structure. Most job seekers have no idea what they are going to do next Thursday–they don't have a plan. The most important thing is to decide how many hours you can commit to your job search, and stay with it. You should spend a minimum of 25 hours a week on hard-core job search activities with no goofing around. Let me walk you through a simple but effective process to help you organize your job search schedule.

Write here how many hours you are willing to spend each week looking for a job: _____

Decide on Which Days You Will Look for Work

Answering the questions below requires you to have a schedule and a plan, just as you had when you were working, right?

Which days of the week will you spend looking for a job?

_____

How many hours will you look each day? _____

At what time will you begin and end your job search on each of these days? _____

_____

Create a Specific Daily Schedule

Having a specific daily job search schedule is very important because most job seekers find it hard to stay productive each day. You already know which job search methods are most effective, and you should plan on spending most of your time using those methods. The sample daily schedule that follows has been very effective for people who have used it, and it will give you ideas for your own. Although you are welcome to create your own daily schedule, I urge you to consider one similar to this one. Why? Because it works.

A Daily Schedule That Works

Time	Activity
7:00 - 8:00 a.m.	Get up, shower, dress, eat breakfast.
8:00 - 8:15 a.m.	Organize work space; review schedule for interviews or follow-ups; update schedule.
8:15 - 9:00 a.m.	Review old leads for follow-up; develop new leads (want ads, *Yellow Pages*, networking lists, etc.).
9:00 - 10:00 a.m.	Make phone calls, set up interviews.
10:00 - 10:15 a.m.	Take a break!
10:15 - 11:00 a.m.	Make more calls.
11:00 - 12:00 p.m.	Make follow-up calls as needed.
12:00 - 1:00 p.m.	Lunch break.
1:00 - 5:00 p.m.	Go on interviews; call cold contacts in the field; research for upcoming interviews at the library.

Do It Now: Get a Schedule Book and Write Down Your Job Search Schedule

This is important: If you are not accustomed to using a daily schedule book or planner, promise yourself that you will get a good one tomorrow. Choose one that allows plenty of space for each day's plan on an hourly basis, plus room for daily "to do" listings. Write in your daily schedule in advance; then add interviews as they come. Get used to carrying it with you and use it!

Redefine What "Counts" as an Interview; Then Get Two a Day

The average job seeker gets about five interviews a month–fewer than two interviews a week. Yet many job seekers using the techniques I suggest get routinely two interviews a day. But to accomplish this, you must redefine what an interview is.

The New Definition of an Interview

An interview is any face-to-face contact with someone who has the authority to hire or supervise a person with your skills—even if the person doesn't have an opening at the time you interview.

With this definition, it is *much* easier to get interviews. You can now interview with all kinds of potential employers, not only those who have a job opening. Many job seekers use the *Yellow Pages* to get two interviews with just one hour of calls by using the telephone contact script discussed earlier. Others simply drop in on potential employers and ask for an unscheduled interview–and they get them. And getting names of others to contact from those you know–networking–is quite effective if you persist.

Getting two interviews a day equals 10 a week and 40 a month. That's 800 percent more interviews than the average job seeker gets. Who do you think will get a job offer quicker? So set out each day to get at least two interviews. It's quite possible to do, now that you know how.

How to Answer Tough Interview Questions

Interviews are where the job search action happens. You have to get them; then you have to do well in them. If you have done your homework, you are getting interviews for jobs that will maximize your skills. That is a good start, but your ability to communicate your skills in the interview makes an enormous difference. This is where, according to employer surveys, most job seekers have problems. They don't effectively communicate the skills they have to do the job, and they answer one or more problem questions poorly.

While thousands of problem interview questions are possible, I have listed just 10 that, if you can answer them well, will prepare you for most interviews.

The Top 10 Problem Questions

1. Why don't you tell me about yourself?

2. Why should I hire you?

3. What are your major strengths?

4. What are your major weaknesses?

5. What sort of pay do you expect to receive?

6. How does your previous experience relate to the jobs we have here?

7. What are your plans for the future?

8. What will your former employer (or references) say about you?

9. Why are you looking for this type of position, and why here?

10. Why don't you tell me about your personal situation?

I don't have the space here to give thorough answers to all of these questions, and there are potentially hundreds more. Instead, let me suggest several techniques that I have developed which you can use to answer almost any interview question.

A Traditional Interview Is Not a Friendly Exchange

Before I present the techniques for answering interview questions, it is important to understand what is going on. In a traditional interview situation, there is a job opening, and you are one of several (or one of a hundred) applicants. In this setting, the employer's task is to eliminate all but one applicant.

Assuming that you got as far as an interview, the interviewer's questions are designed to elicit information that can be used to screen you out. If you are wise, you know that your task is to avoid getting screened out. It's not an open and honest interaction, is it?

This illustrates yet another advantage of nontraditional job search techniques: the ability to talk to an employer before an opening exists. This eliminates the stress of a traditional interview. Employers are not trying to screen you out, and you are not trying to keep them from finding out stuff about you.

Having said that, knowing a technique for answering questions that might be asked in a traditional interview is good preparation for whatever you might run into during your job search.

The Three-Step Process for Answering Interview Questions

I know this might seem too simple, but the Three-Step Process is easy to remember. Its simplicity allows you to evaluate a question and create a good answer. The technique is based on sound principles and has worked for thousands of people, so consider trying it.

Step 1. Understand what is really being asked.

Most questions are really designed to find out about your self-management skills and personality. While they are rarely this blunt, the employer's *real* question is often:

✓ Can I depend on you?

✓ Are you easy to get along with?

✓ Are you a good worker?

✓ Do you have the experience and training to do the job if we hire you?

✓ Are you likely to stay on the job for a reasonable period of time and be productive?

Ultimately, if the employer is not convinced that you will stay and be a good worker, it won't matter if you have the best credentials–he or she won't hire you.

Step 2. Answer the question briefly.

Acknowledge the facts, but...

✓ Present them as an advantage, not a disadvantage.

There are lots of examples in which a specific interview question will encourage you to provide negative information. The classic is the "What are your major weaknesses?" question that I included in my top 10 problem questions list. Obviously, this is a trick question, and many people are just not prepared for it. A good response might be to mention something that is not all that damaging, such as "I have been told that I am a perfectionist, sometimes not delegating as effectively as I might." But your answer is not complete until you continue.

Step 3. Answer the real concern by presenting your related skills.

✓ Base your answer on the key skills that you have identified and that are needed in this job.

✓ Give examples to support your skills statements.

For example, an employer might say to a recent graduate, "We were looking for someone with more experience in this field. Why should we consider you?" Here is one possible answer: "I'm sure there are people who have more experience, but I *do* have more than six years of work experience including three years of advanced training and hands-on experience using the latest methods and techniques. Because my training is recent, I am open to new ideas and am used to working hard and learning quickly."

In the example I presented in Step 2 (about your need to delegate), a good skills statement might be, "I have been working on this problem and have learned to be more willing to let my staff do things, making sure that they have good training and supervision. I've found that their performance improves, and it frees me up to do other things."

Whatever your situation, learn to use it to your advantage. It is essential to communicate your skills during an interview, and the Three-Step Process gives you a technique that can dramatically improve your responses. It works!

Interview Dress and Grooming Rule

If you make a negative first impression, you won't get a second chance to make a good one. So do everything possible to make a good impression.

A Good Rule for Dressing for an Interview

Dress as you think
the boss will dress—*only neater.*

Dress for success! If necessary, get help selecting an interview outfit from someone who dresses well. Pay close attention to your grooming too. Written things like correspondence and resumes must be neat and errorless because they create an impression as well.

Follow Up on All Contacts

People who follow up with potential employers and with others in their network get jobs faster than those who do not.

Four Rules for Effective Follow-Up

1. Send a thank-you note to every person who helps you in your job search.

2. Send the thank-you note within 24 hours after you speak with the person.

3. Enclose JIST Cards with thank-you notes and all other correspondence.

4. Develop a system to keep following up with "good" contacts.

Thank-You Notes Make a Difference

Thank-you notes can be handwritten or typed on quality paper and matching envelopes. Keep them simple, neat, and errorless. Following is a sample:

April 16, 19XX

2234 Riverwood Ave.
Philadelphia, PA 17963

Ms. Sandra Kijek
Henderson & Associates, Inc.
1801 Washington Blvd., Suite 1201
Philadelphia, PA 17963

Dear Ms. Kijek:

Thank you for sharing your time with me so generously today. I really appreciated seeing your state-of-the-art computer equipment.

Your advice has already proved helpful. I have an appointment to meet with Mr. Robert Hopper on Friday as you anticipated.

Please consider referring me to others if you think of someone else who might need a person with my skills.

Sincerely,

William Richardson

William Richardson

Use Job Lead Cards to Organize Your Contacts

Use a simple 3-by-5-inch card to keep essential information on each person in your network. Buy a 3-by-5-inch card file box and tabs for each day of the month. File the cards under the date you want to contact the person, and the rest is easy. I've found that staying in touch with a good contact every other week can pay off big. Here's a sample card to give you ideas to create your own:

ORGANIZATION: _Mutual Health Insurance_

CONTACT PERSON: _Anna Tomey_   PHONE: _317-355-0216_

SOURCE OF LEAD: _Aunt Ruth_

NOTES: _4/10 Called. Anna on vacation. Call back 4/15. 4/15 Interview set 4/20 at 1:30. 4/20 Anna showed me around. They use the same computers we used in school! (Friendly people) Sent thank-you note and JIST Card, call back 5/1. 5/1 Second interview 5/8 at 9 a.m.!_

Resumes: Write a Simple One Now, and a "Better" One Later

You have already learned that sending out resumes and waiting for responses is not an effective job-seeking technique. However, many employers *will* ask you for them, and they are a useful tool in your job search. If you feel that you need a resume, I suggest that you begin with a simple one that you can complete quickly. I've seen too many people spend weeks working on their resume while they could have been out getting interviews instead. If you want a "better" resume, you can work on it on weekends and evenings. So let's begin with the basics.

Basic Tips to Create a Superior Resume

The following tips make sense for any resume format.

Write it yourself. It's okay to look at other resumes for ideas, but write yours yourself. It will force you to organize your thoughts and background.

Make it errorless. One spelling or grammar error will create a negative impressionist (see what I mean?). Get someone else to review your final draft for any errors. Then review it again because these rascals have a way of slipping in.

Make it look good. Poor copy quality, cheap paper, bad type quality, or anything else that creates a poor physical appearance will turn off employers to even the best resume content. Get professional help with design and printing if necessary. Many resume writers and print shops have desktop publishing services and can do it all for you.

Be brief, be relevant. Many good resumes fit on one page and few justify more than two. Include only the most important points. Use short sentences and action words. If it doesn't relate to and support the job objective, cut it!

Be honest. Don't overstate your qualifications. If you end up getting a job you can't handle, it will not be to your advantage. Most employers will see right through it and not hire you.

Be positive. Emphasize your accomplishments and results. This is no place to be too humble or to display your faults.

Be specific. Instead of saying "I am good with people," say "I supervised four people in the warehouse and increased productivity by 30 percent." Use numbers whenever possible, such as the number of people served, percent of sales increase, or dollars saved.

You should also know that everyone feels he or she is a resume expert. Whatever you do, someone will tell you it is wrong. For this reason, it is important to understand that a resume is a job search tool. You should never delay or slow down your job search because your resume is not "good enough." The best approach is to create a simple and acceptable resume as soon as possible, then use it. As time permits, create a better one if you feel you must.

Chronological Resumes

Most resumes use the chronological format. It is a simple format where the most recent experience is listed first, followed by each previous job. This arrangement works fine for someone with work experience in several similar jobs, but not as well for those with limited experience or for career changers.

Look at the two Judith Jones resumes. Both use the chronological approach, but notice that the second one includes some improvements over her first. The improved resume is clearly better, but either would be acceptable to most employers.

Tips for Writing a Simple Chronological Resume

Here are some tips for writing a basic chronological resume.

Name. Use your formal name rather than a nickname if the formal name sounds more professional.

Address. Be complete. Include your zip code and avoid abbreviations. If moving is a possibility, use the address of a friend or relative or be certain to include a forwarding address.

Telephone Number. Employers are most likely to try to reach you by phone, so having a reliable way to be reached is very important. Always include your area code because you never know where your resume might travel. If you don't have an answering machine, get one and make sure you leave it on whenever you are not home. Listen to your message to be sure it presents you in a professional way. Also available are a variety of communication systems: voice

[Sample of a simple chronological resume.]

Judith J. Jones

115 South Hawthorne Avenue
Chicago, Illinois 46204
(312) 653-9217 (home)
(312) 272-7608 (message)

JOB OBJECTIVE

Desire a position in the office management, secretarial, or clerical area. Prefer a position requiring responsibility and a variety of tasks.

EDUCATION AND TRAINING

Acme Business College, Chicago, Illinois
Graduate of a one-year business/secretarial program, 1998

John Adams High School, South Bend, Indiana
Diploma: Business Education

U.S. Army

Financial procedures, accounting functions. Other: Continuing education classes and workshops in Business Communication, Scheduling Systems, and Customer Relations.

EXPERIENCE

1997-1998 — Returned to school to complete and update my business skills. Learned word processing and other new office techniques.

1994-1997 — Claims Processor, Blue Spear Insurance Co., Chicago, Illinois. Handled customer medical claims, filed, miscellaneous clerical duties.

1992-1994 — Sales Clerk, Judy's Boutique, Chicago, Illinois. Responsible for counter sales, display design, and selected tasks.

1990-1992 — Specialist, U.S. Army. Assigned to various stations as a specialist in finance operations. Promoted prior to honorable discharge.

Previous Jobs — Held part-time and summer jobs throughout high school.

PERSONAL

I am reliable, hardworking, and good with people.

---

finish a formal degree or program, list what you did complete. Include any special accomplishments.

Previous Experience. The standard approach is to list employer, job title, dates employed, and responsibilities. But there are better ways of presenting your experience. Look over the "Improved Chronological Resume" for ideas. The improved version emphasizes results, accomplishments, and performance.

Personal Data. Neither of the sample resumes has the standard height, weight, or marital status included on so many resumes. That information is simply not relevant! If you do include some personal information, put it at the bottom and keep it related to the job you want.

References. There is no need to list references. If employers want them, they will ask. If your references are particularly good, it's okay to say so.

Tips for an Improved Chronological Resume

Once you have a simple, errorless, and eye-pleasing resume, get on with your job search. There is no reason to delay! But you may want to create a better one in your spare time (evenings or weekends). If you do, here are some additional tips.

Job Objective. Job objectives often limit the types of jobs for which you will be considered. Instead, think of the type of work you want to do and can do well and describe it in more general terms. Instead of writing "Restaurant Manager," write "Managing a small to mid-sized business" if that is what you are qualified to do.

---

mail, professional answering services, beepers, mobile phones, online e-mail programs, etc. If you do provide an alternative phone number or another way to reach you, just make it clear to the caller what to expect.

Job Objective. This is optional for a very basic resume but is still important to include. Notice that Judy is keeping her options open with her objective. Writing "Secretary" or "Clerical" might limit her to lower-paying jobs or even prevent her from being considered for jobs she might take.

Education and Training. Include any formal training you've had, plus any training that supports the job you seek. If you did not

Education and Training. New graduates should emphasize their recent training and education more than those with five years or so of recent and related work experience. Think about any special accomplishments while in school and include these if they relate to the job. Did you work full time while in school? Did you do particularly well in work-related classes, get an award, or participate in sports?

Skills and Accomplishments. Employers are interested in what you accomplished and did well. Include those things that relate to doing well in the job you seek now. Even "small" things count. Maybe your attendance was perfect, you met a tight

[Sample of an improved chronological resume.]

Judith J. Jones

115 South Hawthorne Avenue
Chicago, Illinois 46204
(312) 653-9217 (home)
(312) 272-7608 (message)

JOB OBJECTIVE

Seeking position requiring excellent management and secretarial skills in an office environment. Position should require a variety of tasks including typing, word processing, accounting/bookkeeping functions, and customer contact.

EDUCATION AND TRAINING

Acme Business College, Chicago, Illinois.
Completed one-year program in Professional Secretarial and Office Management. Grades in top 30 percent of my class. Courses: word processing, accounting theory and systems, time management, basic supervision, and others.

John Adams High School, South Bend, Indiana.
Graduated with emphasis on business and secretarial courses. Won shorthand contest.

Other: Continuing education at my own expense (Business Communications, Customer Relations, Computer Applications, other courses).

EXPERIENCE

1997-1998 — Returned to business school to update skills. Advanced course work in accounting and office management. Learned to operate word processing and PC-based accounting and spreadsheet software. Gained operating knowledge of computers.

1994-1997 — Claims Processor, Blue Spear Insurance Company, Chicago, Illinois. Handled 50 complex medical insurance claims per day—18 percent above department average. Received two merit raises for performance.

1992-1994 — Assistant Manager, Judy's Boutique, Chicago, Illinois. Managed sales, financial records, inventory, purchasing, correspondence, and related tasks during owner's absence. Supervised four employees. Sales increased 15 percent during my tenure.

1990-1992 — Finance Specialist (E4), U.S. Army. Responsible for the systematic processing of 500 invoices per day from commercial vendors. Trained and supervised eight employees. Devised internal system allowing 15 percent increase in invoices processed with a decrease in personnel.

1986-1990 — Various part-time and summer jobs through high school. Learned to deal with customers, meet deadlines, work hard, and other skills.

SPECIAL SKILLS AND ABILITIES

Type 80 words per minute and can operate most office equipment. Good communication and math skills. Accept supervision, able to supervise others. Excellent attendance record.

Promotions. If you were promoted or got good evaluations, say so. A promotion to a more responsible job can be handled as a separate job if this makes sense.

Problem Areas. Employers look for any sign of instability or lack of reliability. It is very expensive to hire and train someone who won't stay or who won't work out. Gaps in employment, jobs held for short periods of time, or a lack of direction in the jobs you've held are all things that employers are concerned about. If you have any legitimate explanation, use it. For example:

"1994–Continued my education at..."

"1995–Traveled extensively throughout the United States."

"1995 to present–Self-employed barn painter and widget maker."

"1995–Had first child, took year off before returning to work."

Use entire years or even seasons of years to avoid displaying a shorter gap you can't explain easily: "Spring 1994–Fall 1995" will not show you as unemployed from October to November, 1995, for example.

Remember that a resume can get you screened out, but it is up to you to get the interview and the job. So, cut out *anything* that is negative in your resume!

deadline, did the work of others during vacations, etc. Be specific and include numbers–even if you have to estimate them.

Job Titles. Many job titles don't accurately reflect the job you did. For example, your job title may have been "Cashier" but you also opened the store, trained new staff, and covered for the boss on vacations. Perhaps "Head Cashier and Assistant Manager" would be more accurate. Check with your previous employer if you are not sure.

[Sample of a simple skills resume.]

ALAN ATWOOD

3231 East Harbor Road
Woodland Hills, California 91367
Home: (818) 447-2111   Message (818) 547-8201

Objective: A responsible position in retail sales

Areas of Accomplishment:

Customer Service
- Communicate well with all age groups.
- Able to interpret customer concerns to help them find the items they want.
- Received 6 Employee of the Month awards in 3 years.

Merchandise Display
- Developed display skills via in-house training and experience.
- Received Outstanding Trainee Award for Christmas toy display.
- Dress mannequins, arrange table displays, and organize sale merchandise.

Stock Control and Marketing
- Maintained and marked stock during department manager's 6-week illness.
- Developed more efficient record-keeping procedures.

Additional Skills
- Operate cash register, IBM-compatible hardware, calculators, and electronic typewriters.
- Punctual, honest, reliable, and a hard-working self-starter.

Experience: Harper's Department Store
Woodland Hills, California
1995 to Present

Education: Central High School
Woodland Hills, California
3.6/4.0 Grade Point Average
Honor Graduate in Distributive Education

Two years retail sales training in Distributive Education. Also courses in Business Writing, Accounting, Typing, and Word Processing.

Skills and Combination Resumes

The functional or "skills" resume emphasizes your most important *skills*, supported by specific examples of how you have used them. This approach allows you to use any part of your life history to support your ability to do the job you seek.

While the skills resume can be very effective, it does require more work to create. And some employers don't like them because they can hide a job seeker's faults (such as job gaps, lack of formal education, or no related work experience) better than a chronological resume.

Still, a skills resume may make sense for you. Look over the sample resumes for ideas. Notice that one resume includes elements of a skills *and* a chronological resume. This is called a "combination" resume—an approach that makes sense if your previous job history or education and training are positive.

[Sample skills resume for someone with substantial experience—but using only one page. Note that no dates are included.]

Ann McLaughlin

Career Objective

Challenging position in programming or related areas that would best utilize expertise in the business environment. This position should have many opportunities for an aggressive, dedicated individual with leadership abilities to advance.

Programming Skills

Include functional program design relating to business issues including payroll, inventory and database management, sales, marketing, accounting, and loan amortization reports. In conjunction with design would be coding, implementation, debugging, and file maintenance. Familiar with distributed network systems including PCs and Macs and working knowledge of DOS, UNIX, COBOL, BASIC, RPG, and FORTRAN. Also familiar with mainframe environments including DEC, Prime, and IBM, including tape and disk file access, organization, and maintenance.

Areas of Expertise

Interpersonal communication strengths, public relations capabilities, plus innovative problem-solving and analytical talents.

Sales

A total of nine years of experience in sales and sales management. Sold security products to distributors and burglar alarm dealers. Increased company's sales from $16,000 to over $70,000 per month. Creatively organized sales programs and marketing concepts. Trained sales personnel in prospecting techniques while training also service personnel in proper installation of burglar alarms. Result: 90 percent of all new business was generated through referrals from existing customers.

Management

Managed burglar alarm company for four years while increasing profits yearly. Supervised office, sales, and installation personnel. Supervised and delegated work to assistants in accounting functions and inventory control. Worked as assistant credit manager, responsible for over $2 million per month in sales. Handled semiannual inventory of five branch stores totaling millions of dollars and supervised 120 people.

Accounting

Balanced all books and prepared tax forms for burglar alarm company. Eight years of experience in credit and collections, with emphasis on collections. Collection rates were over 98% each year; was able to collect a bad debt in excess of $250,000 deemed "uncollectible" by company.

Education

School of Computer Technology, Pittsburgh, PA
Business Applications Programming/TECH EXEC- 3.97 GPA

Robert Morris College, Pittsburgh, PA
Associate degree in Accounting, Minor in Management

2306 Cincinnati Street, Kingsford, PA 15171 (412) 437-6217
Message: (412) 464-1273

[Sample combination resume emphasizing skills and accomplishments within jobs. Note that each position within a company is listed.]

THOMAS P. MARRIN
80 Harrison Avenue
Baldwin L.I., New York 11563
Answering Service: (716) 223-4705

OBJECTIVE:

A middle/upper-level management position with responsibilities including problem solving, planning, organizing, and budget management.

EDUCATION:

University of Notre Dame, B.S. in Business Administration. Course emphasis on accounting, supervision, and marketing. Upper 25% of class. Additional training: Advanced training in time management, organization behavior, and cost control.

MILITARY:

U.S. Army — 2nd Infantry Division, 1985 to 1989, 1st Lieutenant and platoon leader — stationed in Korea and Ft. Knox, Kentucky. Supervised an annual budget of nearly $4 million and equipment valued at over $40 million. Responsible for training, scheduling, and activities of as many as 40 people. Received several commendations. Honorable discharge.

BUSINESS EXPERIENCE:

Wills Express Transit Co., Inc. — Mineola, New York

Promoted to Vice President, Corporate Equipment — 1994 to Present
Controlled purchase, maintenance, and disposal of 1100 trailers and 65 company cars with $6.7 million operating and $8.0 million capital expense responsibilities.

* Scheduled trailer purchases, six divisions.
* Operated 2.3% under planned maintenance budget in company's second best profit year while operating revenues declined 2.5%.
* Originated schedule to correlate drivers' needs with available trailers.
* Developed systematic Purchase and Disposal Plan for company car fleet.
* Restructured Company Car Policy, saving 15% on per car cost.

Promoted to Asst. Vice President, Corporate Operations — 1993 to 1994
Coordinated activities of six sections of Corporate Operations with an operating budget over $10 million.

* Directed implementation of zero-base budgeting.
* Developed and prepared Executive Officer Analyses detailing achievable cost-reduction measures. Resulted in cost reduction of over $600,000 in first two years.
* Designed policy and procedure for special equipment leasing program during peak seasons. Cut capital purchases by over $1 million.

Manager of Communications — 1991 to 1993
Directed and managed $1.4 million communication network involving 650 phones, 150 WATS lines, 3 switchboards, 1 teletype machine, 5 employees.

* Installed computerized WATS Control System. Optimized utilization of WATS lines and pinpointed personal abuse. Achieved payback earlier than originally projected.
* Devised procedures that allowed simultaneous 20% increase in WATS calls and a $75,000/year savings.

Hayfield Publishing Company, Hempstead, New York

Communications Administrator — 1989 to 1991

Managed daily operations of a large Communications Center. Reduced costs and improved services.

© 1999 · J. Michael Farr · JIST Works, Inc. · Indianapolis, IN

The Quick Job Search Review

There are a few thoughts I want to emphasize in closing my brief review of job-seeking skills:

1. Approach your job search as if it were a job itself.

2. Get organized and spend at least 25 hours per week actively looking.

3. Follow up on all the leads you generate and send out lots of thank-you notes and JIST Cards.

4. If you want to get a good job quickly, you must get lots of interviews!

5. Pay attention to all the details; then be yourself in the interview. Remember that employers are people, too. They will hire someone who they feel will do the job well, be reliable, and fit easily into the work environment.

6. When you want the job, tell the employer that you want the job and why. You need to have a good answer to the question "Why should I hire you?" It's that simple.

Essential Job Search Data Worksheet

Completing this worksheet will help you create your resume, fill out applications, and answer interview questions. Take it with you as a reference as you look for a job. Use an erasable pen or pencil so you can make changes. In all sections, emphasize skills and accomplishments that best support your ability to do the job you want. Use extra sheets as needed.

Key Accomplishments

List three accomplishments that best prove your ability to do well in the kind of job you want.

1. _____
   _____

2. _____
   _____

3. _____
   _____

Education/Training

Name of high school(s)/Years attended: _____

_____

_____

_____

Subjects related to job objective: _____

_____

_____

_____

Extracurricular activities/Hobbies/Leisure activities:

_____

_____

_____

_____

Accomplishments/Things you did well: _____

_____

_____

_____

Schools you attended after high school, years attended, degrees/certificates earned: _____

_____

_____

_____

_____

Courses related to job objective: _____

_____

_____

_____

_____

Extracurricular activities/Hobbies/Leisure activities:

_____

_____

_____

_____

Accomplishments/Things you did well: _____

_____

_____

_____

_____

Military training, on-the-job, or informal training, such as from a hobby; dates of training; type of certificate earned: _____

_____

_____

_____

_____

Specific things you can do as a result: _____

_____

_____

_____

Work and Volunteer History

List your most recent job first, followed by each previous job. Include military experience and unpaid work here too, if it makes sense to do so. Use additional sheets to cover *all* your significant jobs or unpaid experiences.

Whenever possible, provide numbers to support what you did: number of people served over one or more years, number of transactions processed, percentage of sales increase, total inventory value you were responsible for, payroll of the staff you supervised, total budget you were responsible for, etc. As much as possible, mention results using numbers because they can be impressive when mentioned in an interview or resume.

Job #1 _____

Name of organization: _____

_____

_____

Address: _____

_____

_____

Phone number: _____

_____

Dates employed: _____

Job title(s): _____

_____

_____

Supervisor's name: _____

_____

Details of any raises or promotions: _____

_____

_____

Machinery or equipment you handled: _____

_____

_____

_____

Special skills this job required: _____

_____

_____

_____

List what you accomplished or did well: _____

_____

_____

Job #2 _____

Name of organization: _____

_____

_____

Address: _____

_____

_____

Phone number: _____

_____

Dates employed: _____

Job title(s): _____

_____

Supervisor's name: _____

_____

Details of any raises or promotions: _____

_____

_____

_____

Machinery or equipment you handled: _____

_____

_____

_____

Special skills this job required: _____

_____

_____

_____

List what you accomplished or did well: _____

_____

_____

_____

Job #3 _____

Name of organization: _____

_____

_____

Address: _____

_____

_____

Phone number: _____

_____

Dates employed: _____

Job title(s): _____

_____

_____

Supervisor's name: _____

_____

Details of any raises or promotions: _____

_____

_____

_____

Machinery or equipment you handled: _____

_____

_____

_____

Special skills this job required: _____

_____

_____

_____

List what you accomplished or did well: _____

_____

_____

_____

References

Contact your references and let them know what type of job you want and why you are qualified. Be sure to review what they will say about you. Because some employers will not give out references by phone or in person, have previous employers write a letter of reference for you in advance. If you worry about a bad reference from a previous employer, negotiate what the employer will say about you or get written references from other people you worked with there. When creating your list of references, be sure to include your reference's name and job title, where he or she works, a business address and phone number, how that person knows you, and what your reference will say about you.

The following material is based on content from a book titled Job Strategies for Professionals *written by a team of authors from the U.S. Employment Service for use by the unemployed. (published by JIST)*

Some Tips for Coping with Job Loss

Being out of work is not fun for most people and is devastating to some. It may help you to know that you are not alone in this experience, and I've included some information here on what to expect and some suggestions for getting through it.

Some Problems You May Experience

Here are some feelings and experiences that you may have after losing your job.

Loss of professional identity: Most of us identify strongly with our careers, and unemployment can often lead to a loss of self-esteem. Being employed garners respect in the community and in the family. When a job is lost, part of your sense of self may be lost as well.

Loss of a network: The loss may be worse when your social life has been strongly linked to the job. Many ongoing "work friendships" are suddenly halted. Old friends and colleagues often don't call because they feel awkward or don't know what to say. Many don't want to be reminded of what could happen to them.

Emotional unpreparedness: If you have never before been unemployed, you may not be emotionally prepared for it and devastated when it happens. It is natural and appropriate to feel this way. You might notice that some people you know don't take their job loss as hard as you have taken it. Studies show that those who change jobs frequently, or who are in occupations prone to cyclic unemployment, suffer far less emotional impact after job loss than those who have been steadily employed and who are unprepared for cutbacks.

Adjusting

You can often adjust to job loss by understanding its psychology. There have been a lot of studies done on how to deal with loss. Psychologists have found that people often have an easier time dealing with loss if they know what feelings they might experience during the "grieving process." Grief doesn't usually overwhelm us all at once; it usually is experienced in stages. The stages of loss or grief may include

Shock–you may not be fully aware of what has happened.

Denial–usually comes next; you cannot believe that the loss is true.

Relief–you may feel a burden has lifted and opportunity awaits.

Anger–often follows; you blame (often without cause) those you think might be responsible, including yourself.

Depression–may set in some time later, when you realize the reality of the loss.

Acceptance–the final stage of the process; you come to terms with the loss and get the energy and desire to move beyond it. The "acceptance" stage is the best place to be when starting a job search, but you might not have the luxury of waiting until this point to begin your search.

Knowing that a normal person will experience some predictable "grieving" reactions can help you deal with your loss in a constructive way. The faster you can begin an active search for a new job, the better off you will be.

Keeping Healthy

Unemployment is a stressful time for most people, and it is important to keep healthy and fit. Try to

✓ **Eat properly.** How you look and your sense of self-esteem can be affected by your eating habits. It is very easy to snack on junk food when you're home all day. Take time to plan your meals and snacks so they are well-balanced and nutritious. Eating properly will help you maintain the good attitude you need during your job search.

✓ **Exercise.** Include some form of exercise as part of your daily activities. Regular exercise reduces stress and depression and can help you get through those tough days.

✓ **Allow time for fun.** When you're planning your time, be sure to build fun and relaxation into your plans. You are allowed to enjoy life even if you are unemployed. Keep a list of activities or tasks that you want to accomplish such as volunteer work, repairs around the house, or hobbies. When free time occurs, you can refer to the list and have lots of things to do.

Family Issues

Unemployment is a stressful time for the entire family. For them, your unemployment means the loss of income and the fear of an uncertain future, and they are also worried about your happiness. Here are some ways you can interact with your family to get through this tough time.

✓ **Do not attempt to "shoulder" your problems alone.** Be open with family members even though it may be hard. Discussions about your job search and the feelings you have allow your family to work as a group and support one another.

✓ **Talk to your family.** Let them know your plans and activities. Share with them how you will be spending your time.

✓ **Listen to your family.** Find out their concerns and suggestions. Maybe there are ways they can assist you.

✓ **Build family spirit.** You will need a great deal of support from your family in the months ahead, but they will also need yours.

✓ **Seek outside help.** Join a family support group. Many community centers, mental health agencies, and colleges have support groups for the unemployed and their families. These groups can provide a place to let off steam and share frustrations. They can also be a place to get ideas on how to survive this difficult period.

Helping Children

If you have children, realize that they can be deeply affected by a parent's unemployment. It is important for them to know what has happened and how it will affect the family. However, try not to overburden them with the responsibility of too many emotional or financial details.

✓ **Keep an open dialogue with your children.** Letting them know what is really going on is vital. Children have a way of imagining the worst, so the facts can actually be far less devastating than what they envision.

✓ **Make sure your children know it's not anyone's fault.** Children may not understand about job loss and may think that *you* did something wrong to cause it. Or they may feel that somehow *they* are responsible or financially burdensome. They need reassurance in these matters, regardless of their age.

✓ **Children need to feel they are helping.** They want to help, and having them do something like taking a cut in allowance, deferring expensive purchases, or getting an after-school job can make them feel as if they are part of the team.

Some experts suggest that it can be useful to alert school counselors to your unemployment so that they can watch the children for problems at school before they become serious.

Coping with Stress

Here are some coping mechanisms that can help you deal with the stress of being unemployed.

✓ **Write down what seems to be causing the stress.** Identify the "stressors"; then think of possible ways to handle each one. Can some demands be altered, lessened, or postponed? Can you live with any of them just as they are? Are there some that you might be able to deal with more effectively?

✓ **Set priorities.** Deal with the most pressing needs or changes first. You cannot handle everything at once.

✓ **Establish a workable schedule.** When you set a schedule for yourself, make sure it is one that can be achieved. As you perform your tasks, you will feel a sense of control and accomplishment.

✓ **Reduce stress.** Learn relaxation techniques or other stress-reduction techniques. This can be as simple as sitting in a chair, closing your eyes, taking a deep breath and breathing out slowly while imagining all the tension going out with your breath. There are a number of other methods, including listening to relaxation tapes, which may help you cope with stress more effectively. Check the additional source material books that offer instruction on these techniques—many of these are available at your public library.

✓ **Avoid isolation.** Keep in touch with your friends, even former coworkers, if you can do that comfortably. Unemployed people often feel a sense of isolation and loneliness. See your friends, talk with them, socialize with them. You are the same person you were before unemployment. The same goes for the activities that you have enjoyed in the past. Evaluate them. Which can you afford to continue? If you find that your old hobbies or activities can't be part of your new budget, maybe you can substitute new activities that are less costly.

✓ **Join a support group.** No matter how understanding or caring your family or friends might be, they may not be able to understand all that you're going through, and you might be able to find help and understanding at a job-seeking support group.

These groups consist of people who are going through the same experiences and emotions as you. Many groups also share tips on job opportunities, as well as feedback on ways to deal more effectively in the job search process. *The National Business Employment Weekly,* available at major newsstands, lists support groups throughout the country. Local churches, YMCAs, YWCAs, and libraries often list or facilitate support groups. A list of self-help organizations—some of which cover the unemployed—is available from the National Self-Help Clearinghouse, 25 West 43rd St., Room 620, New York, NY 10036. The cost is $3, plus a self-addressed, stamped envelope.

Forty Plus is a national nonprofit organization and an excellent source of information about clubs around the country and on issues concerning older employees and the job search process. The address is 15 Park Row, New York, NY 10038. The telephone number is (212) 233-6086.

Keeping Your Spirits Up

Here are some ways you can build your self-esteem and avoid depression.

✓ **List your positives.** Make a list of your positive qualities and your successes. This list is always easier to make when you are feeling good about yourself. Perhaps you can enlist the assistance of a close friend or caring relative, or wait for a sunnier moment.

✓ **Replay your positives.** Once you have made this list, replay the positives in your mind frequently. Associate the replay with an activity you do often; for example, you might review the list in your mind every time you go to the refrigerator!

✓ **Use the list before performing difficult tasks.** Review the list when you are feeling down or to give you energy before you attempt some difficult task.

✓ **Recall successes.** Take time every day to recall a success.

✓ **Use realistic standards.** Avoid the trap of evaluating yourself using impossible standards that come from others. You are in a particular phase of your life; don't dwell on what you think society regards as success. Remind yourself that success will again be yours.

✓ **Know your strengths and weaknesses.** What things do you do well? What skills do you have? Do you need to learn new skills? Everyone has limitations. What are yours? Are there certain job duties that are just not right for you and that you might want to avoid? Balance your limitations against your strong skills so that you don't let the negatives eat at your self-esteem. Incorporate this knowledge into your planning.

✓ **Picture success.** Practice visualizing positive results or outcomes and view them in your mind before the event. Play out the scene in your imagination and picture yourself as successful in whatever you're about to attempt.

✓ **Build success.** Make a "to do" list. Include small, achievable tasks. Divide the tasks on your list and make a list for every day so you will have some "successes" daily.

✓ **Surround yourself with positive people.** Socialize with family and friends who are supportive. You want to be around people who will "pick you up," not "knock you down." You know who your fans are. Try to find time to be around them. It can really make you feel good.

✓ **Volunteer.** Give something of yourself to others through volunteer work. Volunteering will help you feel more worthwhile and may actually give you new skills.

Overcoming Depression

Are you depressed? As hard as it is to be out of work, it also can be a new beginning. A new direction may emerge that will change your life in positive ways. This may be a good time to reevaluate your attitudes and outlook.

✓ **Live in the present.** The past is over and you cannot change it. Learn from your mistakes and use that knowledge to plan for the future; then let the past go. Don't dwell on it or relive it over and over. Don't be overpowered by guilt.

✓ **Take responsibility for yourself.** Try not to complain or blame others. Save your energy for activities that result in positive experiences.

✓ **Learn to accept what you cannot change.** However, realize that in most situations, you do have some control. Your reactions and your behavior are in your control and will often influence the outcome of events.

✓ **Keep the job search under your own command.** This will give you a sense of control and prevent you from giving up and waiting for something to happen. Enlist everyone's aid in your job search, but make sure you do most of the work.

✓ **Talk things out with people you trust.** Admit how you feel. For example, if you realize you're angry, find a positive way to vent it, perhaps through exercise.

✓ **Face your fears.** Try to pinpoint them. "Naming the enemy" is the best strategy for relieving the vague feeling of anxiety. By facing what you actually fear, you can see if your fears are realistic or not.

✓ **Think creatively.** Stay flexible, take risks, and don't be afraid of failure. Try not to take rejection personally. Think of it as information that will help you later in your search. Take criticism as a way to learn more about yourself. Keep plugging away at the job search despite those inevitable setbacks. Most importantly, forget magic. What lies ahead is hard work!

Sources of Professional Help

If your depression won't go away or leads you to self-destructive behaviors such as abuse of alcohol or drugs, you may consider asking a professional for help. Many people who have never sought professional assistance before find that in a time of crisis it really helps to have someone listen and give needed aid. Consult your local mental health clinics, social services agencies, religious organizations, or professional counselors for help for yourself and family members who are affected by your unemployment. Your health insurance may cover some assistance, or, if you do not have insurance, counseling is often available on a "sliding scale" fee, based on income.

Managing Your Finances While Out of Work

As you already know, being unemployed has financial consequences. While the best solution to this is to get a good job in as short a time as possible, you do need to manage your money differently during the time between jobs. Following are some things to think about.

Apply for Benefits Without Delay

Don't be embarrassed to apply for unemployment benefits as soon as possible, even if you're not sure you are eligible. This program is to help you make a transition between jobs, and you helped pay for it by your previous employment. Depending on how long you have worked, you can collect benefits for up to 26 weeks and sometimes even longer. Contact your state labor department or employment security agency for further information. Their addresses and telephone numbers are listed in your phone book.

Prepare Now to Stretch Your Money

Being out of work means lower income and the need to control your expenses. Don't avoid doing this, because the more you plan, the better you can control your finances.

Examine Your Income and Expenses

Create a budget and look for ways to cut expenses. The Monthly Income and Expense Worksheet can help you isolate income and expense categories, but your own budget may be considerably more detailed. I've included two columns for each expense category. Enter in the "Normal" column what you have been spending in that category during the time you were employed. Enter in the "Could Reduce To" column a lower number that you will spend by cutting expenses in that category.

Tips on Conserving Your Cash

While you are unemployed, it is likely that your expenses will exceed your income, and it is essential that you be aggressive in managing your money. Your objective here is very clear: you want to conserve as much cash as possible early on so you can have some for essentials later. Here are some suggestions.

✓ **Begin cutting all nonessential expenses right away.** Don't put this off! There is no way to know how long you will be out of work, and the faster you deal with the financial issues, the better.

✓ **Discuss the situation with other family members.** Ask them to get involved by helping you identify expenses they can cut.

✓ **Look for sources of additional income.** Can you paint houses on weekends? Pick up a temporary job or consulting assignment? Deliver newspapers in the early morning? Can a family member get a job to help out? Any new income will help, and the sooner the better.

✓ **Contact your creditors.** Even if you can make full payments for a while, work out interest-only or reduced-amount payments as soon as possible. When I was unemployed, I went to my creditors right away and asked them to help. They were very cooperative, and most are if you are reasonable with them.

✓ **Register with your local consumer credit counseling organization.** Many areas have free consumer credit counseling organizations that can help you get a handle on your finances and encourage your creditors to cooperate.

✓ **Review your assets.** Make a list of all your assets and their current value. Money in checking, savings, and other accounts is the most available, but you may have additional assets in pension programs, life insurance, and stocks that could be converted to cash if needed. You may also have an extra car that could be sold, equity in your home that could be borrowed against, and other assets that could be sold or used if needed.

✓ **Reduce credit card purchases.** Try to pay for things in cash to save on interest charges and prevent overspending. Be disciplined; you can always use your credit cards later if you are getting desperate for food and other basics.

✓ **Consider cashing in some "luxury" assets.** For example, sell a car or boat you rarely use to generate cash and to save on insurance and maintenance costs.

✓ **Comparison shop** for home/auto/life insurance and other expenses to lower costs.

✓ **Deduct job hunting expenses from your taxes.** Some job hunting expenses may be tax deductible as a "miscellaneous deduction" on your federal income tax return. Keep receipts for employment agency fees, resume expenses, and transportation expenses. If you find work in another city and you must relocate, some moving expenses are tax deductible. Contact an accountant or the IRS for more information.

Monthly Income and Expense Worksheet

Income

Unemployment benefits	_____	Interest/Dividends	_____
Spouse's income	_____	Other income	_____
Severance pay	_____	**TOTALS**	_____

Expenses

	NORMAL	COULD REDUCE TO		NORMAL	COULD REDUCE TO
Mortgage/rent:	_____	_____			
maintenance/ repairs	_____	_____			
Utilities:			**Health insurance:**	_____	_____
electric	_____	_____	other medical/ dental expenses	_____	_____
gas/oil heat	_____	_____	**Tuition:**	_____	_____
water/sewer	_____	_____	other school costs	_____	_____
telephone	_____	_____	**Clothing:**	_____	_____
Food:	_____	_____	**Entertainment:**	_____	_____
restaurants	_____	_____	**Taxes:**	_____	_____
Car payment:	_____	_____	**Job hunting costs:**	_____	_____
fuel	_____	_____	**Other expenses:**	_____	_____
maintenance/ repairs	_____	_____		_____	_____
insurance	_____	_____		_____	_____
Other loan payments:				_____	_____
_____	_____	_____	**TOTALS**	_____	_____

Review Your Health Coverage

You already know that it is dangerous to go without health insurance, so there is no need to lecture you on this, but here are some tips.

✓ **You can probably maintain coverage at your own expense.** Under the COBRA law, if you worked for an employer that provided medical coverage and had 20 or more employees, you may continue your health coverage. However, you must tell your former employer within 60 days of leaving the job.

✓ **Contact professional organizations to which you belong.** They may provide group coverage for their members at low rates.

✓ **Speak to an insurance broker.** If necessary, arrange for health coverage on your own or join a local health maintenance organization (HMO).

✓ **Practice preventive medicine.** The best way to save money on medical bills is to stay healthy. Try not to ignore minor ills. If they persist, phone or visit your doctor.

✓ **Investigate local clinics.** Many local clinics provide services based on a sliding scale. These clinics often provide quality health care at affordable prices. In an emergency, most hospitals will provide you with services on a sliding scale, and most areas usually have one or more hospitals funded locally to provide services to those who can't afford them.

Using the Internet for Career Planning and Job Seeking

This brief review assumes you know how to use the Internet, so I won't get into how it works here. If the Internet and World Wide Web are new to you, I recommend a book titled *Using the Internet and the World Wide Web in Your Job Search* by Fred Jandt and Mary Nemnich. This book covers the basics about how the Internet works, how to get connected, plus a great deal of information on using it for career planning and job seeking.

Some Cautionary Comments

Let me begin by saying that the Internet has its problems as a tool for collecting information or for getting job leads. While the Internet has worked for many in finding job leads, far more users have been disappointed in the results they obtained. The problem is that many users assume that they can simply put their resume in resume databases and that employers will line up to hire them. It sometimes happens, but not often. That is the very same negative experience of people sending out lots of unsolicited resumes to personnel offices, a hopeful approach that has been around since long before computers.

There are two points that I made earlier about job-seeking methods which also apply to using the Internet:

1. It is unwise to rely on just one or two job search methods in conducting your job search.
2. It is essential that you conduct an active rather than a passive approach in your job search.

Just as with sending out lots of unsolicited resumes, simply listing your resume on the Internet is a passive approach that is unlikely to work well for you. Use the Internet in your job search, but plan to use other techniques, including direct contacts with employers.

A Success Story

Now that I have cautioned you regarding its limitations, you should know that the Internet does work very well for some people. To illustrate this, let me share with you a real situation I recently uncovered.

I was doing a series of interviews on jobs for a TV station in a rural area and asked the staff how they got their jobs there. They were all young, and the news anchor had told me that she had only been on the job a few months. It turned out that many of the previous employees had left the station about six months earlier to go to larger markets. That left a remaining recent graduate and new hire in charge but with few staff–and something of an emergency. He had obtained his job by responding to a job posting on a Web site used by broadcasters, so he went ahead and listed on that site all the jobs that were open at his station.

In a few days, new broadcasting graduates from all over the country saw the Internet postings and responded. E-mail went back and forth, and the relatively few willing to come to the station at their expense were invited to interview. Within a few weeks, most of the open positions were filled by young people who had responded on the Internet.

The crises for the TV station ended, and many of those hired told me that they were getting a great opportunity that they did not expect to obtain in any other way. I have to agree. More traditional recruiting methods would have created long delays for the employer and the job seekers. Traditional recruiting would also probably have screened out those with less experience and credentials. These job seekers got these jobs because of their using the Internet. While there were surely people with better credentials, they did not know about or get these jobs.

But note that the ones who got the jobs were those willing to take the chance and travel to the employer at their own expense. They had to be active and take some chances. And they had to be able to make a quick decision to move–something that a young person can more easily do. And they did not simply post their resumes in a resume database somewhere. The winning applicants were proactive in using the Internet to make direct contact with this employer, and then they followed up agressively.

Specific Tips to Increase Your Internet Effectiveness

Here are some things you can do to increase the effectiveness of using the Internet in your job search.

1. **Be as specific as possible in the job you seek**–This is important in using any job search method and even more so in using the Internet. I say this because the Internet is so enor-

mous in its reach that looking for a nonspecific job is simply not an appropriate task. So do your career planning homework and be specific in what you are looking for.

2. **Keep your expectations reasonable**–The people who have the most success on the Internet are those who best understand its limitations. For example, those with technical skills that are in short supply–such as network engineers–will have more employers looking for these skills and more success on the Internet. Keep in mind that many of the advertised jobs are already filled by the time you see them and that thousands of people may apply to those that sound particularly attractive. People do get job leads on the Internet, but be reasonable in your expectations and use a variety of job search methods in addition to the Internet.

3. **Consider your willingness to move**–If you don't want to move, or are willing only to move to certain locations, you should restrict your job search to geographic areas that meet your criteria. Many of the Internet databases allow you to view only those jobs that meet your criteria.

4. **Create a resume that is appropriate for use on the Internet**–With some exceptions, most of the resumes submitted on the Internet end up as simple text files with no graphic elements. Employers can then search a database of resumes for key words or use other searchable criteria. This is why your Internet resume should include a list of key words likely to be used by an employer as search criteria. Additional information on resumes and the Internet can be found in books listed in the bibliography.

5. **Get your resume into the major resume databases used by employers**–Many of the major resume databases allow job seekers to list their resumes for free. Employers are typically charged for advertising their openings or sorting the database for candidates that meet their criteria. Most of these sites are easy to understand and use, and they often provide all sorts of useful information for job seekers. Major sites are listed in the bibliography.

6. **Seek out relevant sites**–Simply getting your resume listed on several Internet sites is often not enough. Many employers do not use these sites, or they use one but not another. Remember the example that I used earlier–those people found out about TV-related jobs from an Internet site that was run by a trade publication for broadcasters. Many professional associations post job openings on their sites or list other sites that would be of interest to that profession. Check out the resources that are available to people in the industries or occupations that interest you, since many of these resources also have Internet sites.

7. **Find specific employer sites**–Some employers have their own Internet sites that list job openings, allow you to apply online, and even provide access to staff who can answer your questions. While this is mostly used by larger technology-oriented companies, many smaller employers and government agencies have set up their own sites to attract candidates.

8. **Use informal chat rooms or request help**–Many Internet sites have interactive chat rooms or allow you to post a message for others to respond to. If you are not familiar with a chat room, it is a way for you to type responses to what someone else types as you are both online. Many sites also have a place for you to leave a message for others to respond to by sending you e-mail messages. Both of these methods allow you to meet potential employers or others in your field who can provide you with the advice or leads you seek.

9. **Use the listings of large Internet browsers or service providers**–While there are thousands of career-related Internet sites, some are better than others. Many sites I list in the bibliography provide links to other sites they recommend. Large service providers such as America Online (www.aol.com) and the Microsoft Network (www.msn.com) provide career-related information and job listings on their sites as well as links to other sites. Most of the larger "search engines" provide links to recommended career-related sites and can be quite useful. Some of the larger such sites include Alta Vista (www.altavista.com), Lycos (www.lycos.com), and Yahoo (www.Yahoo.com).

10. **Don't get ripped off**–Since the Internet has few regulations, many crooks use it as a way to take money from trusting souls. Remember that anyone can set up a site, even if the person does not provide a legitimate service, so be careful before you pay money for anything on the Internet. A general rule is that if it sounds too good to be true, it probably is. For example, if a site "guarantees" that it will find you a job or charges high fees. I recommend you look elsewhere.

Some Useful Internet Sites

There are hundreds and even thousands of Internet sites that provide information on careers or education, list job openings, or provide other career-related information. I've listed just a few of the many in the bibliography at the end of this book. Since most of these sites will list other useful sites, there is enough information in that section of the bibliography to get started.

In Closing

Few people will get a job offer because someone knocks on their door and offers one. The craft of job seeking does involve some luck, but you are far more likely to get lucky if you are out getting interviews. Structure your job search as if it were a full-time job and try not to get discouraged. There are lots of jobs out there, and someone needs what you can do—your job is to find that someone.

I hope this section helps, though you should consider learning more. Career planning and job seeking skills are, I believe, adult survival skills for our new economy. Good luck!

Mike Farr

GOOD ARTICLES FOR COLLEGE GRADUATES AND THOSE CONSIDERING COLLEGE

W hile it's true that money is not everything, it certainly is one thing to consider in planning your career. As I've pointed out earlier in this book, the more education you have, the more you are likely to earn—on the average. But, of course, you are not average.

That's why you should consider a variety of factors in planning your career. Several excellent articles follow that provide accurate and interesting information on earnings of college graduates by their majors, and earnings in different occupations. There are also articles on employment trends for college graduates and on other important topics.

These articles come from various publications from the good people at the U.S. Department of Labor. Don't be concerned that the data referred to in the articles are often from two or more years ago. The articles are more recent than this; the dates simply reflect the time it takes for the data to be analyzed and appear in publications. I hope that you will find one or more of these articles of interest.

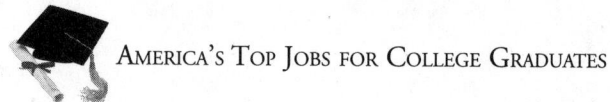

THE OUTLOOK FOR COLLEGE GRADUATES THROUGH 2006

> **Introduction.** This article provides an excellent overview of the advantages of having a college degree. It compares earnings of high school graduates against those with four-year degrees. It should come as no surprise that the earnings difference is enormous. While the projections for those with a college degree are quite positive, the article also points out that such a degree does not guarantee success. I put this article first because it provides a good basis for the more detailed articles that follow in this section.

By Mark Mittelhauser

Popular films and novels have depicted college-educated workers stuck in low-paying, low-status jobs. Although the reality for most college graduates is not as bleak as the media portray, it is true that some graduates will not find jobs that make use of the college-level skills they've developed. The reasons for the frustrating problems these graduates face are complex. Part of their frustration reflects individual circumstances and mismatches between employers and job seekers. But another part is simple mathematics: There are more job seekers with college degrees than there are openings of college-level jobs.

This labor market dilemma for college graduates is not new. In fact, it has existed for more than a decade and is expected to continue. According to the Bureau of Labor Statistics (BLS), there were about 250,000 more college graduates entering the labor force each year between 1986 and 1996 than there were new college-level jobs. This number represents about 1 in 5 of the college-educated entrants to the workforce. The difference between the number of college-educated entrants and college-level job openings from 1996 to 2006 is pro-

jected to remain around 250,000—which means 18 percent of new college graduates may not be able to find college-level jobs.

Why are so many high school students pursuing college degrees if they cannot be assured of college-level jobs upon graduation? The most likely answer is that the labor market favors college graduates—they earn more and experience lower unemployment rates than workers without a degree. In 1996, for example, workers with bachelor's degrees had median annual earnings of about $36,000, while college graduates with more advanced degrees earned around $40,000. In contrast, high school graduates who did not pursue higher education earned about $23,000. Over the course of a lifetime, these differences amount to a significant increase in earnings for those with college degrees. In addition, the college graduate labor force had an unemployment rate of 2.4 percent in 1996, which was less than half the 5.7 percent rate for those with high school diplomas.

Aside from job market indicators, college graduates' labor market experiences are difficult to predict. Aggregate figures, such as those presented above, do not accurately portray the reality of many job seekers. Millions of college graduates are happy in jobs that do not require degrees but offer other desirable characteristics, such as flexible hours or attractive working conditions. Also, some workers with high school diplomas carry out tasks usually associated with college graduates, and many college graduates perform duties that do not require a college degree. In other words, it is difficult to generalize about the employment outlook for such a diverse group of workers.

Developing the Projections

The college graduate outlook presented here is derived from supply and demand estimates of the college-educated labor force. Projections of the demand

---

Mark Mittelhauser is an economist in the Office of Employment Projections, Bureau of Labor Statistics.

for college graduates are calculated using employment projections from the Office of Employment Projections of BLS. Every two years, this office develops projections covering a wide range of variables, including the U.S. labor force, industry output, productivity, and employment by occupation and industry. BLS bases its projections on an analysis of the changing patterns of population growth, consumption, trade, and a host of other variables affecting employment. The most recent projections are discussed in the November 1997 *Monthly Labor Review; Employment Outlook: 1996–2006,* BLS Bulletin 2502; and the winter 1997–98 and spring 1998 issues of the *Occupational Outlook Quarterly.*

Estimates of expected college graduate entrants to the labor force are based on data produced by the U.S. Department of Education's National Center for Education Statistics (NCES). NCES analyzes demographic trends and educational patterns to develop projections of enrollment and completions at various levels of educational attainment. BLS used NCES estimates of bachelor's degrees awarded between 1982 and 1995 and projections through the year 2007 to determine the number of new college-level entrants each year. These figures are published in Projections of Education Statistics to 2007, NCES Bulletin 97-382.

Comparing the number of college-educated job seekers with that of college-level job openings from each of these data sources is complicated because of the variety of entrants and openings. New college graduates constitute the majority of new college-educated entrants to the labor force. But a number of other entrants must also be accounted for, such as immigrants, people recently discharged from military service, and workers returning to the labor force after a long absence. Similarly, economic growth accounts for the majority of openings for college graduates.

College-level jobs also arise in two situations involving occupational change for workers already in the labor force. One is when educational requirements are increased, or upgraded, for occupations that previously did not require workers to have a college degree. The other is when workers with college-level jobs leave the labor force and need to be replaced by workers who have a college degree.

Another difficulty in determining the outlook for college graduates is the classification of college-level jobs. Few occupations exist in which all workers have and need a college degree. Doctors and lawyers clearly fall into this category, but most other occupations include workers with varied training and experience. These occupational requirements are constantly being modified as organizations adapt to changing economic conditions. In addition, job descriptions may be tailored to an individual who fills the position, so requirements for the same job may change from year to year. Finally, it may be difficult to determine which skills were gained in college and which are the result of other types of education or work experience.

The BLS approach for classifying jobs by educational attainment starts with assumptions about broad occupational groups. Remaining consistent with previous analyses, BLS considers workers to be in college-level jobs if they have college degrees and their jobs fall into professional specialty; executive, administrative, and managerial; or technician and related support occupations. For example, 76 percent of professional specialty workers, such as engineers and statisticians, who have college degrees are assumed to need these degrees in their jobs. On the other hand, a college degree is not required to work in some other occupational groups, such as retail sales; services, except police and detective; agricultural, except farm manager; and craft, operator, and laborer positions, except blue-collar worker supervisor. Regardless of their level of education, workers in these groups are assumed to be in jobs that do not require a college degree. For example, none of the nearly 120,000 truck drivers who had a college degree in 1996 was considered to have a job that requires one.

There are many occupations, however, where such classifications are less clear. The educational requirements in these occupations are especially broad or may be constantly changing. As a result, some college graduates who work in these occupations may require a degree to perform their jobs, while others could perform them adequately without one. Police and detective, farm manager, blue-collar worker supervisor, and a number of administrative support workers, such as secretary and bookkeeping and accounting clerk, are among these occupations. BLS determines which of these jobs are "college level" based on data from special supplements to the Current Population Survey (CPS) that indicate whether workers in each occupation need a college degree to perform their job duties. Workers with college degrees who need a college degree are considered to be in college-level jobs, while those who believe they could perform their jobs without a degree are classified as having noncollege-level jobs.

FIGURE 1

College graduates in the labor force, 1996
(thousands)

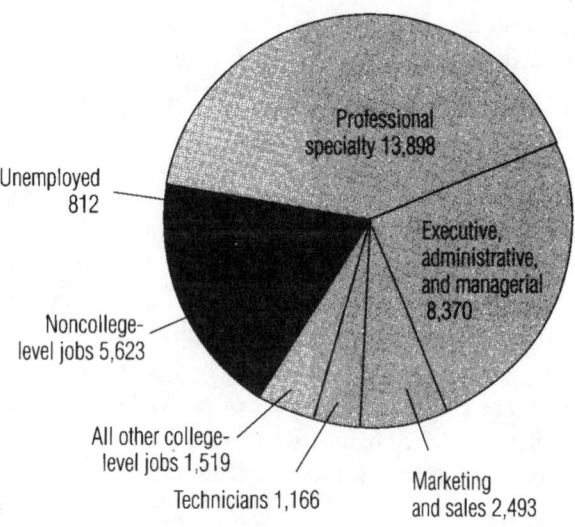

- Professional specialty 13,898
- Unemployed 812
- Executive, administrative, and managerial 8,370
- Noncollege-level jobs 5,623
- All other college-level jobs 1,519
- Technicians 1,166
- Marketing and sales 2,493

The College Graduate Labor Force in 1996

In 1996, about 33 million college graduates were employed in the United States. They worked in a wide range of occupations, but the majority were found in two groups—professional specialty occupations and executive, administrative, and managerial occupations. (See figure 1.) These two groups accounted for two-thirds of college-level employment, with professional specialty occupations providing nearly 14 million jobs and executive, administrative, and managerial occupations supplying another 8.4 million. Engineer, registered nurse, lawyer, teacher, physician, and social worker were among the professional specialty occupations that supplied the most jobs for college graduates. The executive, administrative, and managerial occupations employing the largest number of college graduates were accountant and auditor; marketing, advertising, and public relations manager; medical and health manager; and administrators and officials in public administration.

The balance of the remaining 33 million employed college graduates—about 10 million—were scattered among other occupational groups in 1996. About 3.8 million worked in marketing and sales occupations, where they held jobs such as nonretail commodity sales representatives; first-line supervisors and managers; real estate agents, brokers, and appraisers; and insurance sales agents. Administrative support occupations accounted for an additional 2.6 million workers. Occupations in this group include secretaries; bookkeeping, accounting, and auditing clerks; clerical supervisors and managers; and insurance claims processing workers. The remaining college graduates worked primarily as blue-collar worker supervisors, farm managers, and police or detectives.

Although all of those workers have college degrees, not all were employed in college-level jobs. About 5.6 million, or 17 percent, of them were employed in jobs that did not require a college degree. Many were in administrative support, retail sales, and service occupations, but over a million of these workers were also in production and craft occupations.

Projected Entrants with College Degrees

The most important group of college degree holders to enter the labor market each year is recent college graduates. According to NCES, about 1.19 million people were awarded bachelor's degrees in 1996. The number of college degree earners grew about 20 percent between 1986 and 1996, in spite of a decline in the

FIGURE 2

Bachelor's degrees awarded, 1986–96 and projected 1996–2006
(thousands)

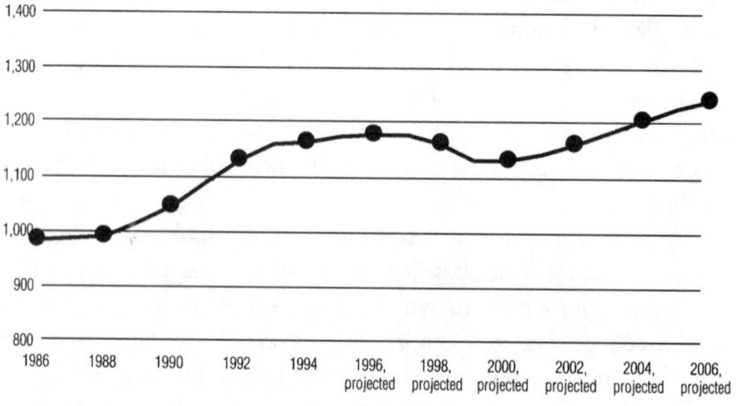

1,400
1,300
1,200
1,100
1,000
900
800

1986 1988 1990 1992 1994 1996, projected 1998, projected 2000, projected 2002, projected 2004, projected 2006, projected

Note: Degrees awarded as of the end of the academic school year (May-June).

traditional college-age population of 18- to 24-year-olds over most of the period. This increase in degree earners was primarily due to growing enrollments of women and of older people.

In contrast, the Census Bureau projects growth in the college-age population between 1997 and 2000 while NCES projects a decline in the number of bachelor's degrees awarded over the same period. The number of bachelor's degree recipients is expected to resume growth in 2001. (See figure 2.) In fact, NCES projects the average number of degree earners each year between 1996 and 2006 will increase to about 1.19 million, up slightly from the 1.10 million recipients annually over the previous 10-year period. Nearly all of this growth is expected to be accounted for by women, who will comprise about 58 percent of all bachelor's degree earners by the year 2006. NCES estimates the number of men receiving bachelor's degrees each year will remain fairly constant between 1996 and 2006.

However, not all of these college graduates will join the labor force during the 1996–2006 period. Some will enter graduate school, start a family, or take a break for various reasons. NCES projects 1.19 million bachelor's degrees will be awarded between 1996 and 2006, a number similar to its projection for the previous decade. Of those recipients, BLS estimates about 1.15 million, or 97 percent, will enter the labor market. This figure is derived from historical patterns of labor force participation among recent college graduates.

In addition to recent college graduates, BLS projects that about 230,000 other degree holders will enter the labor force each year between 1996 and 2006. This number is based on comparisons between historical growth in the college-educated labor force and the annual number of college graduates. These other entrants come from a variety of sources, including recently discharged military personnel, college-educated immigrants, and college degree holders returning to the labor force after a long absence. Not included in this group, however, are college graduates who are unemployed or who hold noncollege-level jobs and may be looking for college-level jobs. It is possible that some of these job seekers might eventually compete with other college graduates in the labor market.

Each year between 1996 and 2006, recent college graduates and other college-educated entrants will make up an estimated 1.38 million college graduates entering the labor force. This will represent an increase of about 6 percent over the 1.3 million who entered the labor force annually during the previous decade.

Projected Job Openings, 1996–2006

The U.S. economy is projected to generate 1.13 million college-level job openings each year between 1996 and 2006, more than 8 percent above the 1.05 million job openings that arose annually over the previous decade. College-level job openings result from employment growth, educational upgrading, and replacement needs. Employment growth is a product of overall economic growth and the shifting demands for goods and services. As the need increases for workers in occupations employing many college graduates, so does the demand for college degree holders throughout the economy. Educational upgrading is an important component of growth that occurs as jobs which previously did not require a college degree for entry begin to require this level of education. Replacement job openings arise as college graduates leave the labor force, and the positions they held become available to other college graduates.

Employment growth. The largest source of new college-level job openings between 1996 and 2006 will continue to be employment growth. Openings due to growth are expected to average 750,000 each year over this 10-year period, accounting for about two-thirds of all college-level openings. As indicated above, the overall growth of the economy is a major determinant of college-level openings resulting from employment growth. Because BLS projects overall annual employment growth to slow from 1.7 percent over the 1986–96 period to 1.3 percent between 1996 and 2006, growth is projected to provide about 75,000 fewer college-level jobs each year during the 1996–2006 period than it did between 1986 and 1996.

The projected slowdown in employment growth is largely due to slower labor force growth, which BLS estimates will decline from 14 percent between 1986 and 1996 to about 11 percent between 1996 and 2006. This slowing in labor force growth reflects demographic trends. As workers in the baby boom population begin to retire and the smaller population of the "baby bust" generation enters the labor market, overall labor force growth will slow. One result of these trends is a projected decline of nearly 3 million in the number of 25- to 34-year-olds between 1996 and 2006. Labor force growth is also influenced by the labor force participation rate of the working-age population. This rate is expected to continue to grow among women, although

FIGURE 3
Employment in college-level jobs, 1996, projected 2006, and projected change, 1996–2006
(number in thousands)

Occupation	1996		2006, projected		Projected change, 1996-2006	
	Number	Percent	Number	Percent	Number	Percent
Total	132,330	100.0	150,940	100.0	18,610	14.1
College-level jobs	27,450	20.8	34,940	23.1	7,490	27.3
Executive, administrative, and managerial	8,370	6.3	10,210	6.8	1,840	22.0
Professional specialty	13,900	10.5	17,930	11.9	4,030	29.0
Technicians and related	1,170	.9	1,600	1.1	430	36.8
Marketing and sales	2,490	1.9	3,250	2.2	760	30.5
Administrative support	1,060	.8	1,420	.9	360	34.0
All other college-level jobs	460	.3	530	.4	70	15.2
Noncollege-level jobs	104,880	79.3	116,000	76.9	11,120	10.6

at a slower rate than in the previous 10 years, while the labor force participation rate of men is projected to continue to decline for all groups under age 45.

The projected slowing of employment growth is expected to have less impact on the college-educated labor force than on other workers in the economy, as growth in college-level jobs is projected to continue outpacing the growth of jobs that typically require lower levels of education. College-level jobs are expected to increase by 27 percent between 1996 and 2006, much faster than the 14 percent expected for all workers. (See figure 3.) As a result, the proportion of college-level jobs relative to all jobs in the economy is expected to rise from around 21 percent in 1996 to slightly over 23 percent in 2006.

One reason college graduates will fare better than workers in other educational groups is the occupational distribution of growth. The major occupational groups that provide college-level jobs are expected to grow more rapidly than the 14-percent increase in employment for the economy as a whole. Professional specialty occupations, the largest source of college-level jobs, will be the fastest-growing occupational group including both college- and noncollege-level jobs. In contrast, the occupational groups expected to grow more slowly than average—

agricultural, craft and other production, and administrative support occupations—employ a relatively small share of college graduates.

As a result of these trends, professional specialty occupations will continue to add more college-level jobs over the projection period than any other occupational group. (See figure 4.) In fact, between 1996 and 2006, professional specialty occupations will account for more than half of all college-level openings due to growth—about 400,000 jobs each year. The occupations that will add the most jobs in this group are computer engineers, computer scientists, and systems analysts. These occupations are expected to be among the fastest growing in the economy. In fact, their combined occupational employment is expected to double over the 1996–2006 period. Other professional specialty occupations projected to provide many job openings are engineers, teachers, registered nurses, therapists, physicians, and social workers. The growth of many of these occupations is the result of the expanding use of computers and increasing need for health care projected as the baby-boom population ages.

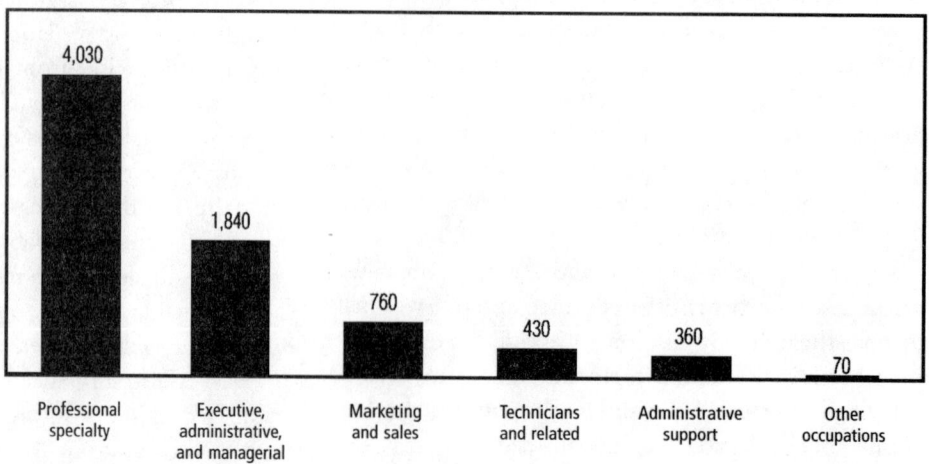

FIGURE 4
Projected college-level job growth by occupational group, 1996–2006
(thousands)

© 1999 • J. Michael Farr • JIST Works, Inc. • Indianapolis, IN

The next largest number of college-level job openings is expected to occur in executive, administrative, and managerial occupations. Employment in college-level jobs within this group is projected to grow annually by 185,000 between 1996 and 2006. Most of the new jobs will arise among managers, including food service and lodging man-agers, financial managers, and marketing, advertising, and public relations managers. Some management support occupations, such as accountants and auditors, management analysts, and personnel, training, and labor relations specialists and managers, will also add new college-level jobs.

The remaining 164,000 college-level job openings arising due to growth each year will be distributed among other major occupational groups. In marketing and sales occupations, the largest source of college-level openings will be sales representatives who sell financial securities, real estate, machines, and a variety of other commodities. The technicians and related support occupations that will add the most college-level jobs are health, engineering, and science technicians, computer programmers, and legal assistants. A number of administrative support occupations, such as clerical supervisors, teacher aides, insurance claims processing workers, and bookkeeping, accounting, and auditing clerks will also add new college-level jobs. Finally, about 8,000 new college-level jobs will arise each year among blue-collar worker supervisors between 1996 and 2006. Agricultural and service occupations are expected to provide limited growth in college-level jobs.

Educational upgrading. Many of the new openings created by growth reflect a related phenomenon—educational upgrading. When organizations restructure or change, they rely on workers in certain occupations to assume new responsibilities. As a result of a reduction of the number of middle managers, for example, firms have shifted some managerial responsibilities to other workers. One result of this trend is that some workers classified as secretaries may now be training new employees, performing research, or working with spreadsheets—tasks often associated with skills developed in college. Along with the new duties may come new titles, such as administrative assistant or administrative aide, but these workers might still be counted as secretaries in government surveys. As educational requirements are upgraded, subsequent job openings are considered to be new openings in college-level jobs.

BLS estimates educational upgrading by tracking changes in educational attainment for occupations which require college degrees. For most of these occupations,

including professional specialty, technician, nonretail sales, and executive, administrative, and managerial occupations, projections of educational upgrading are developed by analyzing the trend of college-educated workers in each occupation. For the remaining occupations with college-level jobs, such as farm managers, secretaries, and police and detectives—those in which it is not assumed college-educated workers need a degree to perform their jobs—estimates are based on analyses of trends in CPS surveys which track degree requirements for each occupation.

Of the 750,000 college-level job openings projected to arise annually between 1996 and 2006 due to economic growth, about 160,000—1 in 5—will result from educational upgrading. This is significantly lower than during the previous 10-year period, in which 250,000 openings were estimated to have arisen annually due to upgrading. Occupational distribution of upgrading is the major reason for this downturn. Upgrading is occurring slowly in the occupational groups that include most college-level jobs, while groups with relatively few college-level jobs are increasingly producing more job openings for college graduates. For example, marketing and sales and administrative support occupations are projected to provide 40 percent of openings due to upgrading between 1996 and 2006, yet these two groups supplied only 13 percent of college-level jobs in 1996.

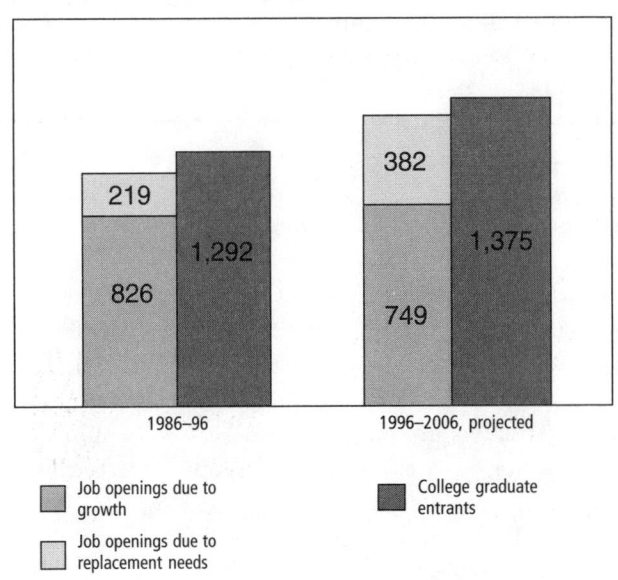

FIGURE 5

College graduates entering the labor force and job openings, 1986–96 and projected 1996–2006

(thousands)

Legend:
- Job openings due to growth
- Job openings due to replacement needs
- College graduate entrants

1986–96: 219, 826, 1,292
1996–2006, projected: 382, 749, 1,375

Replacement openings. Replacement openings are job openings that arise as workers leave the labor force to retire, take a break, return to school, or raise a family. By leaving the labor force, these workers create openings for other college-educated workers. BLS uses data on age distribution and labor market behavior to develop net replacement rates; these rates are used to estimate the number of openings resulting from separations each year and to project the number of labor force entrants needed to replace workers who leave the labor force.

Replacement openings will be an important source of college-level job openings as the baby-boom generation enters age groups with higher rates of retirement. The number of expected openings arising annually from replacement needs is projected to increase from 219,000 over the 1986–96 period to about 380,000 annually between 1996 and 2006. (See figure 5.) Openings due to replacement needs are expected to mirror the distribution of college-level jobs across major occupational groups. Professional specialty and executive, administrative, and managerial occupations will account for about four of every five replacement openings, while other openings will be distributed across the remaining occupational groups.

Job Seekers Exceed Job Openings

Similar to the results of previous BLS studies, the projections outlined above indicate that, between 1996 and 2006, there will be more college degree holders entering the labor force each year than the number of college-level job openings. An average of 1.38 million entrants will be met with approximately 1.13 million college-level job openings each year, a projected annual difference of about 250,000. The size of this difference remains almost unchanged from the previous 10-year period, as the number of both projected entrants and openings is expected to grow at approximately the same rate over the 1996–2006 period.

The proportion of college graduates who do not find employment in college-level jobs—projected to be about 18 percent between 1996 and 2006—will most likely work as sales representatives, first line supervisors, clerks, secretaries, service workers, farm managers, and as various production and blue-collar workers. As mentioned previously, many workers choose these positions because they offer desirable job characteristics. However, some college-educated workers in these positions would rather

have the earnings, status, and other qualities typically associated with college-level jobs.

Degrees, Skills, and Jobs

As the number of new college-educated entrants continues to exceed the available college-level jobs, the job market will continue to frustrate many college graduates. The level of frustration will vary widely based on major field of study, individual aptitude, personal circumstances, and geographic location. Applicants whose majors are in high demand, such as computer engineering, are likely to find jobs more easily and receive higher salaries than job seekers with degrees in other fields, such as philosophy. Similarly, graduates looking for work in areas where the local economy is booming are likely to be more successful than those seeking work in economically depressed areas. More than ever, job seekers need to become familiar with the job market in their chosen fields and tailor their skills to the requirements of employers.

Because of the potential value of a college degree over a worker's lifetime, investment in a college education is still worthwhile. College graduates need to realize, however, that not all college degrees are created equal. An article by Frederic Pryor and David Schaffer in the July 1997 *Monthly Labor Review*, "Wages and the University Educated: A Paradox Resolved," underscores this point. The authors found that the labor market success of college graduates is highly correlated with the skills college graduates bring to the workplace. Graduates with a high level of functional literacy—the ability to read, interpret documents, and perform quantitative calculations in real-life situations—were more likely to be employed in college-level jobs. In contrast, college-educated workers with low functional literacy were more likely to be employed in what were called "high school jobs." The researchers stressed the fact that functional literacy is learned and that success in the labor market is influenced by the efforts of each college graduate.

In a labor market with more college-educated entrants than college-level openings, recent college graduates are well advised to carefully study the changing employment and earnings of the nation's occupations and industries. Although a detailed discussion of specific occupational growth is beyond the scope of this article, the above analysis points to major occupational groups that are expected to provide the most college-level openings between 1996 and 2006. More detailed information on working conditions, employment, train-

ing requirements, earnings, and job outlook for about 250 occupations, covering six of every seven jobs in the economy, is in the *1998–99 Occupational Outlook Handbook*. In addition, the *1998–99 Career Guide to Industries* provides similar information from an industry perspective. These publications are found in most public libraries, career centers, and guidance counselors' offices. The *Handbook* is also accessible online at http://stats.bls.gov/ocohome.htm. As the quest for college-level jobs continues, these publications can help you get a step up on your competition—and there will be plenty of it.

TRENDS IN COLLEGE DEGREES AND MAJORS

Introduction. This article reviews the number of people earning degrees in various fields as well as general trends among those going to college. It does not review the earnings or occupational outcomes of these degrees; you will find this information in several other articles in this section.

By Jonathan W. Kelinson

More people this decade than ever before are getting their college degrees. According to the National Center for Education Statistics (NCES), over 1.6 million bachelor's or higher degrees were conferred by the nation's colleges and universities in academic year 1994–95, the latest year for which data are available. Population growth contributes to the increase, but a comparison of the recent data with those from more than a decade earlier reveals trends in college degrees by educational level and field of study and by college enrollment characteristics.

This article examines trends based on data for bachelor's, master's, first professional, and doctoral degrees awarded between the 1982–83 and 1994–95 academic years, a span of time for which comparable data are available. The first section looks at trends by educational level and field of study, as well as the number of degrees projected to 2005–06. The second section discusses changes based on sex, college enrollment of recent high school graduates, and age and attendance patterns. Where to find related information is noted at the end.

Trends: Past and Projected

Between 1982–83 and 1994–95, the number of degrees granted varied by educational level and field of study. The number awarded in some fields declined or

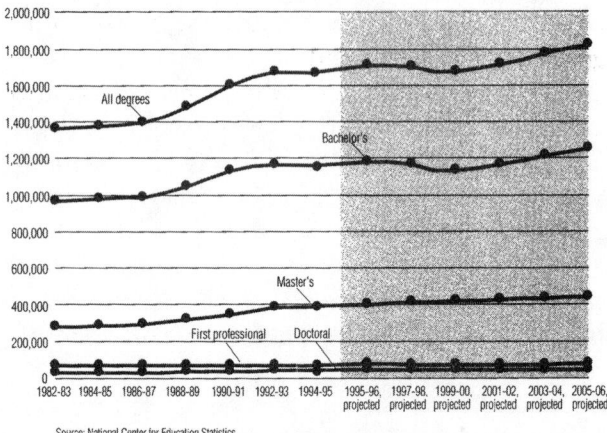

Degrees awarded, all fields of study, 1982–83 to 1994–95 and 1995–96 to 2005–06, projected
(thousands)

Source: National Center for Education Statistics

grew little at the bachelor's level but increased at the master's or doctoral level or both; in other fields, the reverse was true. Projections of degree awards also differ by educational level. (See the above chart.)

Growth by educational level and field of study. Overall, most of the increase in the total number of college degrees conferred during the 1982–83 to 1994–95 period took place from 1987–88 to 1993–94. However, growth differed by educational level. Over the 1982–83 to 1994–95 period, the number of bachelor's degrees granted rose by 20 percent to nearly 1.2 million. The number of master's degrees increased 37 percent, with all of the growth occurring after 1987. The change in doctoral degree awards, though small in number, increased the fastest among the different educational levels—44 percent—primarily during the late 1980s and the mid-1990s. The small number of first professional degrees (dentistry, medicine, and law) increased only slightly, 4 percent, over the period.

Growth in degree awards also varied by field of study at different educational levels. (See the following table.)

Jonathan W. Kelinson is an economist in the Office of Employment Projections, Bureau of Labor Statistics.

Throughout the 1982–83 to 1994–95 period, the Bureau of Labor Statistics (BLS) projected favorable job prospects for occupations requiring a bachelor's or higher degree in technical areas, such as computer science or engineering. Yet most of the bachelor's degree majors increasing their share of the total number of degrees granted between 1982–83 and 1994–95 were in non-technical areas. This includes fields such as psychology, visual and performing arts, and liberal arts and humanities. The number of degrees in areas considered more vocationally oriented, such as business, increased little over the period. The only technical fields that increased their portion of total number of degrees granted were biological and life sciences and health professions. In engineering and physical sciences, the number of degrees decreased significantly.

The trends in degree levels for some fields are interesting, especially for those experiencing a growth in employment and favorable projections for future employment. The number of undergraduate degrees in computer-related fields, for example, retreated from 1982–83 to 1994–95. This decrease occurred despite a three-fold increase between 1982 and 1995 in the number of computer science specialists employed and BLS projections that employment in the field would continue to increase over the next decade. However, the number of master's degrees grew dramatically, nearly doubling from around 5,000 in 1982–83 to more than 10,000 in 1994–95. At the doctoral level, the number more than tripled over the period.

Likewise, engineers recorded contrasting trends in degree patterns during the 1982–83 to 1994–95 period. At the undergraduate level, the number of degrees conferred declined nearly 15,000 from its peak of 77,000 in 1984–85. But at the graduate level, the number of engineering degrees increased steadily, especially toward the end of the period, to account for nearly 13,000 new degrees at both the master's and doctoral levels. That growth represents a 50 percent increase in master's degrees, and the doubling of doctoral degrees signals the largest numerical increase at this level for all fields.

There were similar trends in awards of business degrees. The number of bachelor's degrees increased to a peak of nearly 257,000 in 1992–93 but then retreated close to the 1982–83 level. Meanwhile, the number of master's degrees in business—which represent almost a quarter of all master's degrees—increased 45 percent. Doctoral degrees increased fairly steadily over the period.

The number of undergraduate degrees in health professions, such as nursing and health services admin-istration, declined slightly between 1982–83 and 1988–89, then increased sharply the last few years. The number of master's degrees in health professions, however, increased 83 percent over the period. First professional degrees conferred in health sciences changed little. Pharmacy experienced the largest increase with 2,000, the same number by which dentistry declined.

These four dynamic fields are examined here because of the wide variation in degree awards over the 1982–83 to 1994–95 period, especially at the undergraduate level in computer science, engineering, and business and at the graduate level in health professions. While there are many possible reasons for these variations, one reason common to all four fields is job market conditions.

Overall, the job market was generally favorable throughout the 1970s for college graduates in technical areas, prompting a disproportionate number of students to major in those fields as undergraduates in hopes of securing good jobs upon graduation. In the early 1980s, however, a technology explosion produced the computer and information technology industries and increased the demand for workers with computer science and engineering backgrounds. Jobs were available for those able to do the work regardless of whether they had completed a rigorous technical program, so more students may have opted to give up technical training for other majors.

A similar explanation may apply to business majors at the bachelor's degree level, although without the driving force the information technology boom provided for technology graduates. The perceived advantage of having a bachelor's degree in business might have been sustained over a longer period, until the early 1990s. But with the economy expanding strongly since then, graduates in many different fields now qualify for jobs previously requiring business training.

Finally, trends in awards of degrees in health professions may be attributed to changes in the health care industry affecting the job market. The effects of these changes are most notable at the graduate level because of the increased opportunities created for workers with advanced degrees.

Degree projections. NCES projections of earned degrees between 1995–96 and 2005–06 show relatively little change over present levels. The number of bachelor's degrees is expected to dip slightly in the next few years, then increase gradually. The number of master's degrees is expected to increase modestly over the period, while the number of doctoral and first professional degrees will remain about the same.

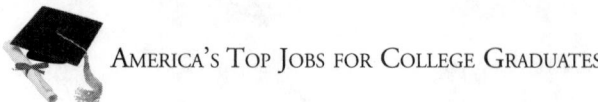

College degrees awarded, selected years 1982-83 to 1994-95, and percent change, 1982-83 to 1994-95

(numbers in thousands)

Field of study and degree [1]	1982-83	1984-85	1986-87	1988-89	1990-91	1992-93	1994-95	Percent change, 1982-83 to 1994-95
Total, all fields	1,366	1,374	1,387	1,437	1,544	1,653	1,681	23
Bachelor's degrees	970	979	991	1,019	1,095	1,165	1,160	20
Agricultural resources	21	18	15	13	18	17	20	-4
Architecture	10	9	9	9	10	9	9	-10
Biological/life sciences	40	38	38	36	40	47	56	40
Business	227	233	241	246	249	257	234	3
Communications	37	40	44	47	52	54	48	30
Computer and information science	25	39	40	30	25	24	24	–
Education	98	88	87	97	111	108	106	8
Engineering	72	77	74	66	62	62	62	-13
Engineering technologies	17	18	19	19	17	16	16	-5
English language and literature/letters	32	33	36	42	52	56	52	63
Foreign languages	11	38	11	12	13	14	14	30
Health professions	65	64	63	59	59	67	80	23
Home/vocational economics	16	15	14	14	15	15	15	-5
Liberal arts and humanities	22	22	24	26	31	33	33	54
Mathematics	13	16	17	16	15	15	14	8
Multidisciplinary/ interdisciplinary studies	14	13	14	15	18	24	26	85
Park, recreation, leisure, and fitness studies	5	5	4	4	4	10	13	147
Philosophy and religion	2	6	6	6	7	8	7	12
Physical sciences and technologies	23	24	20	17	16	18	19	-17
Protective services	13	13	12	15	17	21	24	92
Psychology	40	40	43	49	59	67	72	78
Public administration	14	12	12	13	14	17	19	29
Social sciences and history	95	92	96	108	125	136	128	35
Theology studies and religious vocations	6	6	6	5	5	5	6	-7
Visual and performing arts	40	38	37	38	42	48	49	22
Master's degrees	290	286	289	311	337	370	398	37
Agricultural resources	4	4	4	3	3	4	4	–
Architecture	3	3	3	3	3	4	4	17
Biological/life sciences	6	5	5	5	5	5	5	-4
Business	65	67	67	73	78	90	94	45
Communications	4	3	4	4	4	5	5	47
Computer and information science	5	7	8	9	9	10	10	94
Education	83	75	74	81	87	96	101	22
Engineering	18	21	22	24	24	28	29	52
Engineering technologies	1	1	1	1	1	1	1	108
English language and literature/letters	5	5	5	6	7	8	8	55
Foreign languages	2	2	2	3	3	3	3	27
Health professions	17	17	18	19	21	26	31	83
Home/vocational economics	2	2	2	3	3	3	3	20
Liberal arts and humanities	1	1	2	2	2	3	3	99
Mathematics	4	3	4	4	4	4	4	23
Multidisciplinary/ interdisciplinary studies	2	3	2	3	2	2	2	–
Park, recreation, leisure, and fitness studies	1	1	1	1	–	1	2	189
Philosophy and religion	1	1	1	1	1	1	1	26

Continued
College degrees awarded, selected years 1982-83 to 1994-95, and percent change, 1982-83 to 1994-95
(numbers in thousands)

Physical sciences and technologies	5	6	6	6	5	5	6	9
Protective services	1	1	1	1	1	1	2	31
Psychology	10	10	10	10	11	11	14	39
Public administration	16	16	16	17	18	20	24	46
Social sciences and history	11	11	11	11	12	13	15	32
Theology studies and religious vocations	5	4	5	5	5	5	5	8
Visual and performing arts	9	9	9	8	9	9	10	17
Doctoral degrees	33	34	34	37	40	43	47	44
Agricultural resources	1	1	1	1	1	1	1	10
Biological/life sciences	3	3	3	4	4	4	5	39
Business	1	1	1	1	1	1	1	80
Education	7	7	6	6	6	7	7	-1
Engineering	3	3	4	5	5	6	6	117
English language and literature/ letters	1	1	1	1	1	1	2	58
Foreign languages	1	1	1	1	1	1	1	34
Health professions	1	1	1	1	2	2	2	79
Mathematics	1	1	1	1	1	1	1	68
Physical sciences and technologies	3	3	4	4	4	4	4	37
Psychology	4	3	4	4	4	4	4	6
Social sciences and history	3	3	3	3	3	3	4	27
Theology studies and religious vocations	1	1	1	1	1	1	2	32
First professional [2]	73	75	72	71	72	75	76	4
Total, health sciences	30	30	29	29	28	29	30	2
Chiropractic	3	3	2	3	3	3	3	3
Dentistry	6	5	5	4	4	4	4	-30
Medicine	15	16	15	15	15	16	16	—
Optometry	1	1	1	1	1	1	1	6
Osteopathic	1	1	2	2	1	2	2	41
Pharmacy	1	1	1	1	1	2	2	221
Podiatry	1	1	1	1	1	—	1	-14
Veterinary	2	2	2	2	2	2	2	4
Law	37	37	36	36	38	40	39	7
Theology	6	7	7	6	6	5	6	-8

[1] Information on fields of study with fewer than 5,000 degrees conferred in 1982-83 are not shown separately, but are included in the total for all fields. For doctoral degrees, information is not shown separately if fewer than 500 degrees were conferred.

[2] First professional degrees are the required minimum qualification for entry into some fields. As a result, information for these degrees is included separately from the other degree levels.

— = Fewer than 500 degrees or less than 0.5 percent.

Source: National Center for Education Statistics

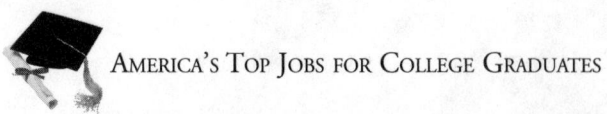

Graduate Characteristics

In addition to showing trends by degree level and field between 1982–83 and 1994–95, NCES data also reveal trends by student characteristic. Noteworthy characteristics for trend analysis are those of sex, length of time between high school graduation and college enrollment, and age and attendance patterns. These factors suggest a move away from previous college enrollment trends, contributing to more students earning a greater number of degrees.

Women graduates. The increases in the number of degrees granted between 1982–83 and 1994–95 are markedly different for men and women. During this period, the total number of degrees earned by women grew 35 percent, compared to a 12 percent increase for men. In 1987-88, women received more degrees than men for the first time—695,636 compared to 690,465, a difference of over 5,000. By 1994–95, women earned 122,000 more degrees than men. At the start of the period, the number of both bachelor's and master's degrees awarded to men and women were about equal. But by 1994–95, women earned about 55 percent of both bachelor's and master's degrees, compared to 45 percent for men.

Overall, the number of first professional degrees increased only 4 percent between 1982–83 and 1994–95. But the number of those degrees earned by women increased 42 percent while decreasing 12 percent for men. Women received 40 percent of all professional degrees in 1994–95, compared to 30 percent at the beginning of the period.

At the doctoral level, the number and share of degrees earned by women also increased. In 1994–95, women's share of doctoral degrees, less than 40 percent, was slightly lower than the proportion earning first professional degrees.

Recent high school graduates. The increase in the proportion of recent high school graduates attending college is another reason the number of degrees conferred expanded between 1982–83 and 1994–95. NCES data show that, a decade after finishing high school, students who enrolled in college immediately afterward were more likely to earn a bachelor's degree than were those who delayed entry. In 1982-83, 51 percent of high school graduates entered a higher education program within one year of graduation. And by 1994–95, this rate increased to 62 percent.

Older and part-time students. Another factor expanding the number of college students working toward a degree was a growth in the numbers of students who did not fall within the traditional college age and who did not attend college full time. Traditionally aged college students, those between the ages of 18 and 24, made up the majority of students on college campuses. But the number of older students increased significantly. For example, in 1985, 15 percent of those attending an institution of higher education were older than 35; this proportion had increased to 21 percent by 1994.

The number of students enrolling in degree programs part time stayed at consistently high levels between 1982–83 and 1994–95. In 1982, a large proportion of students—42 percent—enrolled on a part-time basis; by 1994, that share had risen slightly, to 43 percent.

Related Information

Information about degrees awarded by detailed field of study for 1994–95 is available in *Occupational Projections and Training Data,* 1998 Edition (BLS Bulletin 2501). Completions data and information about changes

[7] The 130 fields included 83 percent of the 8.03 million women in the survey population.

EARNINGS OF COLLEGE GRADUATES IN ALL MAJOR OCCUPATIONS

Introduction. This is a very useful article. It shows you the earnings of those with different levels of education in a variety of major occupations. Many occupations, such as real estate sales occupations, employ college graduates (who earn an average of $36,831 a year) as well as high school graduates (averaging $30,001 a year). The article shows these relative earnings and reviews other interesting points about earnings, education, and occupations.

By Theresa Cosca

You've heard that college graduates benefit financially from extra years of schooling. But how can you be sure an investment in education will pay off? Unfortunately, there are no guarantees because no one knows what the future will bring. Studying data from the recent past can offer some clues, however.

Data from a 1997 Current Population Survey (CPS) show that most 1996 college graduates were employed in higher paying managerial, professional specialty, and high-level sales jobs. These data support the notion that as education increases, so does the likelihood of higher earnings. This article analyzes the median earnings for 1996 college graduates, the kinds of jobs they held, and the proportion of college graduates who earned less than the median for high school graduates.

College Graduate Earnings

One point about college graduate earnings is clear: On average, workers with a bachelor's, master's, doctoral, or professional degree have higher median incomes

and lower unemployment rates than do workers with less education. According to the March 1997 CPS data, median earnings for all college graduates were $40,753 in 1996. This was nearly 75 percent more than the $23,317 median for all high school graduates. The college graduate unemployment rate was 2.4 percent, less than half the 5.7 percent rate for high school graduates.

Education level. One measure of the benefit conferred by higher education is the percent difference in earnings between the median earnings for high school graduates and college graduates, known as the "premium." While the premium for all college graduates averaged 75 percent, it increased with education, as shown in the following tabulation of the median annual earnings of year-round, full-time workers by education level in 1996:

Education level	Median annual earnings	Premium over high school graduates (Percent)	Premium over high school graduates (Dollars)
Professional	$71,868	208	$48,551
Ph.D.	60,827	161	37,510
Master's	46,269	98	22,952
Bachelor's	36,155	55	12,838
High school	23,317	—	—

Medians are a good indicator of what a typical worker might expect in the labor market. However, medians do not tell the whole story. Table 1 presents the variation in earnings by education level between the top and bottom 10 percent of workers, where 80 percent of workers fall. The top 10 percent of all college graduates earned more than $90,144 in 1996. The top 10 percent of workers with a professional degree earned over three times that amount, $316,513. Of these very high earners with professional degrees, most were physicians, lawyers, or high-level executives who have years of education beyond high school. Yet the bottom 10 percent of this highly educated segment of the workforce earned less than $29,800, just above the median for all workers ($27,320).

Theresa Cosca is an economist in the Office of Employment Projections, Bureau of Labor Statistics.

For the remaining education levels, the top 10 percent earned about four times more than the bottom 10 percent. Although median earnings for bachelor's degree holders were $36,155, the bottom 10 percent earned less than $16,698, well below the median for high school graduates ($23,317).

TABLE 1
Distribution of Earnings for College Graduates Who Worked Full- Time, Year Round, by Degree Level, 1996

	9th Decile	Median	1st Decile
Professional degree	$316,513	$71,868	$29,800
Ph.D.	121,320	60,827	27,433
Master's degree	92,782	46,269	23,015
Bachelor's degree	75,132	36,155	16,698
Total, all college graduates	90,144	40,753	18,699

Major occupational group. The typical bachelor's degree holder had median earnings of $36,155, but earnings varied by major occupational group. Table 2 shows median earnings for nine occupational groups; median earnings in four of those groups were higher than those for all bachelor's degree holders. Top earners in the group with the highest paid workers, executive and managerial occupations, made $95,450. Workers in nonretail sales occupations—a group that includes finance and business services sales representatives—were close behind, with the top 10 percent in that group earning more than $91,538.

However, high earnings did not accrue to all workers in a highly paid occupational group. For example, 10 percent of executives and managers earned less than $21,598. The variation was less pronounced for some other occupational groups. For example, earnings for the middle 80 percent of workers in administrative support occupations differed by $35,109, compared to $73,852 for executive and managerial occupations. Within the major occupational groups, the top 10 percent earned anywhere from three to six times more than the bottom 10 percent.

Earnings were highest for workers in college-level jobs. The Bureau of Labor Statistics considers workers to be in college-level jobs if they have college degrees and their jobs are in the professional specialty, executive and managerial, or technician occupational groups. A college degree is not required for a job in some other occupations, such as retail sales; services, except police and detectives; agriculture, except farm managers; and craft, operator, and laborer positions, except blue-collar worker supervisors. Regardless of their level of educa-

tion, workers in these groups are assumed to be in jobs that do not require a college degree, and they tended to have lower earnings.

For workers in other occupational groups, however, educational requirements are less clear. Workers who need a college degree to perform their jobs are considered to be in college-level jobs, while those who could perform their jobs without a degree are classified as having noncollege-level jobs. Among the occupations in these groups are police and detectives, blue-collar worker supervisors, and a number of administrative support workers, such as secretaries and bookkeeping and accounting clerks. Earnings for workers in these occupations vary greatly because of their diverse educational backgrounds.

TABLE 2
Distribution of Earnings for Bachelor's Degree Holders Who Worked Full Time, Year Round, by Occupational Group, 1996

	9th Decile	Median	1st Decile
Executive and managerial	$95,450	$42,045	$21,598
Professional specialty	65,735	36,797	19,662
Technicians	68,862	37,116	20,860
Nonretail sales	91,538	40,118	17,789
Retail sales	77,447	32,366	13,634
Administrative support	48,459	25,963	13,350
Service	55,245	25,924	10,982
Precision production, craft, and repair	68,046	35,159	13,269
Farming, transportation, and machine operators and laborers	47,175	25,654	8,516

Age. Median earnings usually increase with age, as workers amass experience that makes them more valuable to employers. (See table 3.) In 1996, bachelor's degree holders aged 50 to 59 earned a median of $18,000 more than did those aged 20 to 24. Median earnings declined after age 59, as many well-paid workers retired. However, some older workers with high earnings defer retirement; the top 10 percent of workers aged 65 and older earned more than $100,966. Young workers aged 20 to 24 had the least variation in their earnings, with the middle 80 percent making between $10,353 and $37,593.

Young workers are more likely to be in low-paying, entry-level, or temporary jobs. Earnings of workers in the bottom 10 percent peaked between ages 40 and 49, while those in the top 10 percent rose with age. Bachelor's degree graduates with earnings in the top 10 percent earned more than $80,000 annually after age 40. Those in the bottom 10 percent in each age group earned no more than $19,511.

TABLE 3
Distribution of Earnings for Bachelor's Degree Holders Who Worked Full Time, Year Round, by Age Group, 1996

	9th Decile	Median	1st Decile
65 and over	$100,966	$38,313	$14,195
60-64	100,494	39,707	16,030
50-59	91,628	41,165	17,689
40-49	80,074	41,048	19,511
30-39	71,533	38,193	18,635
25-29	50,153	28,577	14,377
20-24	37,593	23,054	10,353

College Graduates Earning Less Than High School Graduates

Another way to characterize college graduate earnings is to compare them to those of high school graduates. In 1996, about 17 percent of college graduates earned less than the median for high school graduates. One-quarter of college graduates earned less than the median for all workers. The proportion remains significant even if workers under age 30, who are more likely to be in low-paying, entry-level, or temporary jobs, are excluded. About 14 percent of the college graduates aged 30 and over earned less than the median for high school graduates.

Workers with the most education were least likely to have lower earnings. (See table 4.) The percentage of workers earning less than $23,317 dropped steadily from 21 percent for bachelor's degree holders to 7 percent for workers with a professional degree. Some high-wage occupations are difficult or impossible to enter without higher education. And within occupations, workers with the most education usually have the highest-paying jobs.

In some occupational groups—such as service, farming, transportation, machine operators and laborers, and administrative support—more than 40 percent of workers with a bachelor's degree earned less than the median for high school graduates. (See table 5.) Only 13 to 14 percent of workers employed in executive and managerial or technical occupations were likely to have lower earnings.

As you might expect, low earnings are most common among younger graduates. Over one-half of young bachelor's degree holders aged 20 to 24 earned less than the median for high school graduates. (See table 6.) But large numbers of older college graduates also have earnings below the median for high school graduates. There are two reasons for this. One is that workers in the old-est age group may retire but continue working in lower-paying jobs to supplement their retirement incomes. The other reason is that higher earning bachelor's degree holders may retire earlier, leaving the relatively lower earners—those who can't afford to retire—in the older age groups.

TABLE 4
Percent of College Graduates Working Full Time, Year Round, Who Earned Less Than the Median for High School Graduates ($23,317), by Degree Level, 1996

Bachelor's degree	21%
Master's degree	11%
Ph.D.	8%
Professional degree	7%

TABLE 5
Percent of Bachelor's Degree Holders Working Full Time, Year Round, Who Earned Less Than the Median for High School Graduates ($23,317), by Occupational Group, 1996

Technicians	14%
Professional specialty	17%
Nonretail sales	17%
Precision production, craft, and repair	24%
Retail sales	26%
Administrative support	42%
Farming, transportation, and machine operators and laborers	45%
Service	46%

TABLE 6
Percent of Bachelor's Degree Holders Working Full Time, Year Round, Who Earned Less Than the Median for High School Graduates ($23,317) by Age Group, 1996

Age 25-29	32%
Age 30-39	18%
Age 40-49	16%
Age 50-59	17%
Age 60-64	16%
Age 65 and over	23%

Detailed Occupations

Earnings often vary by occupation without regard to the education of the worker. Table 7 presents median annual earnings, ranked from highest to lowest, by education level for occupations with at least 100,000 college graduates in 1996. For workers in almost all of the occupations listed, investing in a college degree pays off. Most of the highest-paid workers were employed in college-level professional and managerial occupations. Only 4 of the first 30 occupations listed were not in the professional specialty or executive and managerial occupational groups: production supervisors, securities and financial services sales occupations, police and detectives, and computer programmers.

In all but 9 of the 78 occupations listed in the following table, median earnings for college graduates were higher than the overall median for all high school graduates. All of the lowest-paying occupations were in one of three major occupational groups: administrative support, service, or farming, transportation, and machine operators and laborers.

Only a few high school graduates earned more than the median for all bachelor's degree holders. They were employed in occupations that most often require a college degree, including marketing, advertising and public relations managers, and computer systems analysts and scientists. And although earnings usually increase with education, in a small number of noncollege-level occupations—such as mail and message distributing occupations—more education added little earnings potential.

Beyond the Data

Data in this article are from the March 1997 supplement to the Current Population Survey that collected information on earnings of all workers by education level. In this survey, employed respondents were asked to report their annual earnings, before deductions, for the previous year. The analysis presented here is limited to year-round, full-time workers so the effect of variable schedules on annual earnings does not cloud comparison of earnings. About 3 out of 5 earners aged 16 and older worked year round, full time in 1996. However, less than half of the workers in some occupations—such as prekindergarten and kindergarten teachers, retail sales workers, teacher aides, and waiters and waitresses—worked year round, full time. Most voluntarily chose to forgo year-round, full-time employment for noneconomic reasons, such as to attend school or fulfill personal or family obligations.

The CPS data paint a detailed picture of the earnings success of college graduates. The diversity of their labor market experiences is sometimes masked by medians and broad occupational groupings. General trends can prove informative but should be interpreted with caution. Because educational attainment is only one of many variables determining occupational earnings, individual experiences can vary greatly. Earnings also reflect workers' innate skills and talents. In addition to the factors discussed in this article, other factors affecting compensation include workers' sex, the industry in which occupations are concentrated, job benefits, geographic location, and union affiliation. For some workers, less tangible aspects of a job—flexible hours or the nature of the work itself, for example—are more important than high earnings.

Employers will continue to demand skilled and capable workers who are the best fit for their organization. Data in this article provide only a snapshot of the dynamic labor market for college graduates.

than half the 5.7 percent rate for those with high school diplomas.

TABLE 7

Employment and median annual earnings of college and high school graduates who worked full time, year-round, by occupation and degree level, 1996

Occupation	Total employment[1] (thousands)	Median annual earnings				
		All graduates	Bachelor's degree	Master's degree	Ph.D. or professional degree	High school graduates
Total	124,664	$40,753	$36,155	$46,269	$65,890	$23,317
Physicians	676	92,002	—	—	91,791	—
Dentists	127	80,004	—	—	80,004	—
Lawyers	789	76,803	—	—	77,085	—
Marketing, advertising, and public relations managers	667	60,718	54,087	75,619	—	37,078
Production supervisors	1,224	60,662	61,538	—	—	32,010
Managers and administrators, n.e.c.	7,429	60,138	51,234	76,453	80,980	35,421
Securities and financial services sales occupations	427	56,501	50,512	—	—	30,809
Pharmacists	198	56,003	56,010	—	—	—
Economists	178	55,727	50,478	—	—	—
Electrical and electronic engineers	658	55,127	51,312	61,339	—	—
Mechanical engineers	379	53,430	52,954	61,243	—	—
Civil engineers	232	51,514	50,769	52,307	—	—
Operations and systems researchers and analysts	173	51,003	42,276	—	—	—
Management analysts	315	50,245	51,013	46,312	—	—
Computer systems analysts and scientists	1,227	50,187	46,719	52,788	—	42,365
Industrial engineers	241	49,601	46,541	—	—	—
Postsecondary teachers	918	48,263	22,776	41,345	51,973	—
Chemists, except biochemists	130	47,067	43,270	—	—	—
Financial managers	731	47,037	45,635	64,055	—	30,351
Psychologists	246	46,768	—	37,337	63,840	—
Administrators, education and related fields	724	46,514	36,797	50,462	56,019	17,434
Life scientists	209	46,504	35,012	—	56,863	—
Administrators and officials, public administration	551	46,162	44,325	50,402	—	30,199
Other financial officers	744	46,139	41,775	60,748	—	28,551
Physical and occupational therapists	156	45,744	42,186	—	—	—
Police and detectives, public service	528	45,648	41,005	—	—	33,610
Architects	183	45,495	46,255	—	—	—
Computer programmers	606	44,243	39,589	47,367	—	—
Medicine and health services managers	695	43,369	35,785	55,821	—	24,329
Property and real estate managers	521	42,575	41,852	—	—	25,849
Inspectors and compliance officers	251	41,721	42,530	—	—	—
Registered nurses	1,836	41,675	41,018	47,924	—	—
Sales supervisors and proprietors	4,724	40,308	37,407	55,778	—	26,535
Clinical laboratory technologists and technicians	384	40,255	38,983	—	—	22,046
Editors and reporters	254	40,121	37,349	—	—	—
Mining, manufacturing and wholesale sales representatives	1,403	39,600	39,650	—	—	35,521
Personnel, training, and labor relations specialists	430	38,223	36,042	42,328	—	26,112
Mail and message distributing occupations	935	37,286	36,871	—	—	36,077

(continued)

TABLE 7
(continued)

Employment and median annual earnings of college and high school graduates who worked full time, year-round, by occupation and degree level, 1996

Occupation	Total employment[1] (thousands)	Median annual earnings				
		All graduates	Bachelor's degree	Master's degree	Ph.D. or professional degree	High school graduates
General office supervisors	430	$37,047	$35,117	—	—	$26,058
Accountants and auditors	1,525	36,147	35,320	$46,440	—	24,846
Food service and lodging establishment managers	1,332	35,872	37,292	—	—	20,320
Engineering and related technologists and technicians	888	35,652	33,741	—	—	31,105
Construction supervisors	702	35,532	35,444	—	—	32,776
Managers, service organizations, n.e.c.	566	35,396	29,873	43,267	—	26,441
Insurance adjusters, examiners, and investigators	481	35,313	34,593	—	—	25,466
Insurance sales occupations	593	35,001	32,165	—	—	28,175
Special education teachers	407	34,191	26,691	41,530	—	—
Librarians	221	33,760	—	34,573	—	—
Designers	689	33,052	32,615	—	—	20,651
Educational and vocational counselors	255	32,536	28,412	36,511	—	—
Real estate sales occupations	733	32,475	36,831	—	—	30,001
Legal assistants	297	32,472	31,883	—	—	29,376
Secondary school teachers	1,144	32,465	28,737	37,407	$39,270	—
Authors	158	32,299	26,619	—	—	—
Mechanics and repairers, except supervisors	4,392	32,253	33,615	—	—	27,164
Clergy	355	31,322	24,756	35,199	—	—
Elementary school teachers	1,866	31,272	29,405	36,777	—	—
Production occupations, except supervisors	2,566	30,461	30,076	—	—	27,137
Records processing occupations, except financial	945	29,483	28,125	—	—	20,973
Prekindergarten and kindergarten teachers	526	29,422	25,531	33,267	—	12,577
Material recording, scheduling, and distribution clerks, n.e.c.	1,877	29,366	28,813	—	—	22,438
Construction trades, except supervisors	4,487	28,646	28,688	—	—	26,705
Social workers	800	28,277	25,429	35,685	—	23,543
Machine operators, assemblers, and inspectors	7,708	26,832	26,985	—	—	22,951
Farmers, except horticultural	914	26,553	30,422	—	—	21,258
Retail and personal services sales workers	6,662	26,189	24,863	32,330	—	15,921
Painters, sculptors, craft-artists, and artist printmakers	218	23,993	23,928	—	—	—
Investigators and adjusters, except insurance	930	23,792	25,526	—	—	21,480
Bookkeeping, accounting, and auditing clerks	1,704	23,334	23,128	—	—	20,403
Secretaries	2,883	22,805	22,474	—	—	20,946
Truckdrivers	2,940	21,816	22,168	—	—	28,792
Handlers, equipment cleaners, helpers and laborers	4,561	21,795	23,484	—	—	20,912
Data-entry keyers	676	21,778	21,954	—	—	21,114
Guards and police, except public service	730	21,634	22,284	—	—	16,927
Information clerks	1,764	21,412	21,497	—	—	19,244
General office clerks	781	21,153	21,101	—	—	21,800
Waiters and waitresses	1,356	17,773	18,502	—	—	12,984
Teacher aides	665	13,833	13,944	—	—	11,383

[1]Includes workers at all education levels.
— = Base less than 50,000
n.e.c. = not elsewhere classified

EARNINGS OF COLLEGE GRADUATES— WOMEN COMPARED WITH MEN

Introduction. This article provides data on earnings for both men and women in a variety of major occupations. In most occupations, women seem to earn less than men with similar levels of education. Unfortunately, the data did not try to factor in the effects of many women's responsibilities for raising children. Many women leave the workforce to have and care for children or accept jobs that are more "family" friendly. Men of similar age and education often have more years of work experience as a result, and this factor was not considered in this article. Even so, it provides useful and interesting information on earnings in a variety of occupations—including some where women's average earnings are higher than men's.

By Daniel E. Hecker

Among college graduates aged 25 to 64, women's median annual earnings were 73 percent of men's in 1993. When median earnings of women are compared with those of men of a similar age and with similar levels of education, major fields of study, and occupational characteristics, however, the earnings gap narrowed progressively, although still spanning a wide range: in some cases, women earned nearly as much as, or even more than, men with the same characteristics, while in others, women earned much less. This article uses a 1993 National Science Foundation survey to examine the differences between the earnings of men and women graduates in order to answer the question, How much do women earn compared with men? The short answer to this question is that there are many answers to it: In some fields of study and occupations women do particularly well in relation to men, in others they do not fare so well, and in still others they are in between.

Daniel Hecker is an economist in the Office of Employment Projections, Bureau of Labor Statistics.

Data and Methodology

In 1993, the National Science Foundation surveyed a sample of 215,000 persons under age 75 who reported in the 1990 census that they had a bachelor's or higher degree as of April 1990.[1] Survey sampling rates varied by occupation reported. Data on earnings are considered statistically reliable for scientific and technical major fields of study with an employment of about 3,000 or more and for nonscientific majors with about 6,000 or more. This article includes only data at that level of reliability.

Earnings data from the survey were available only for full-time wage and salary workers. In some occupations, many graduates were self-employed. For these occupations, and for the majors leading to them, the earnings shown may differ from the earnings of all graduates as a whole, and the comparisons between women and men also may differ. Among the occupations most affected in this manner are psychologists; lawyers; writers, artists, and entertainers; salesworkers, except retail; health professionals; and architects.

To limit biases introduced by differences in the age distribution of women and men in specific fields of study, comparisons are made within three age groups: young (25–34), midcareer (35–44), and older (45–64) workers.[2] Earnings are analyzed separately for holders of bachelor's, master's, doctoral, and professional degrees, resulting in comparisons of men's and women's earnings by major field of study for 12 age and degree-level groups.[3] Data were collected for about 150 major fields or subfields of study, as well as 125 occupations. To meet statistical reliability requirements and make the presentation more manageable, some fields or subfields of study and some occupations were aggregated for the analysis presented in this article, reducing the number of fields analyzed to 29 and the number of occupations to 25. Therefore, observed differences in earnings between women and men by major field also may reflect different patterns of majors within each of the 29 groups.

Similarly, differences in earnings within the 25 occupations may reflect differences in occupational patterns.[4]

The methodology used in this article is a variant of that used in many earlier studies;[5] however, the purpose of most of those studies was to calculate the effect of sex discrimination on earnings differences. The analyses examined numerous objective characteristics of women and men associated with earnings and showed how much of the observed earnings differences were attributable to the objective differences, with the remainder assumed to be the result of sex discrimination. By contrast, this article focuses only on two characteristics—major field of study and occupation—and controls for age and degree level. Data are presented so as to highlight the effects on earnings of women's choices of field of study and occupation. Data using other characteristics covered in the National Science Foundation survey that might affect earnings are not examined. Accounting for these could explain more of the observed difference, or they might show that the data presented here understate differences between comparable groups of women and men.[6]

Median Earnings of Women

Median earnings of women compared with those of men of the same age group and degree level.

Some of the differential in earnings between men and women can be accounted for by age and educational attainment. For example, women college graduates aged 25 to 64 had median annual earnings that were 73 percent as high as men's—$34,093, compared with $46,605. In part, this earnings differential is caused by a higher proportion of working women than men being in the young age group and a lower proportion being in the older age group, where earnings tend to peak, reflecting returns to experience. Also, as the following tabulation of the percent distribution of men and women college graduates aged 25 to 64, by age and degree level, in 1993 shows, women were less likely than men to hold doctoral and professional degrees that tend to command high wages, but were more likely to hold master's and bachelor's degrees:

	Men	Women
Age:		
25 to 64	100	100
25 to 34	21	28
35 to 44	37	37
45 to 64	41	35
Degree level:		
All degrees	100	100
Bachelor's degree	62	64
Master's degree	24	30
Doctoral degree	5	3
Professional degree	9	4

Women's median earnings were greater than 73 percent of men's earnings in 9 of 12 comparisons, covering 78 percent of all women. Exceptions were midcareer professional-degree holders, 73 percent; older professional-degree holders, 67 percent; and older bachelor's-degree holders, 65 percent. (See table 1.) Younger women's earnings ranged from 79 percent to 85 percent of men's, midcareer women's from 73 percent to 82 percent, and older women's from 65 percent to 80 percent.

Median earnings of women compared with those of men with the same major field of study and of the same age group and degree level.

When the major field of study was considered, women's earnings were generally even closer to the earnings of men. For example, in all major fields taken as a whole, median earnings for young women graduates with a bachelor's degree were 83 percent as much as the median for young men. Yet, in each of 23 major fields of study with statistically reliable data for both women and men, median earnings of women were more than 83 percent of men's earnings. (See table 1.) Within all 12 age-and-degree-level groups, women's earnings comparisons were greater than the comparisons for all major fields taken as a whole in 117 of 130 major fields, accounting for 96 percent of all employed women in these fields.[7]

The values of the 130 comparisons varied widely. Women's median earnings were 100 percent or more of men's in 11, but these had only 2 percent of women's employment. In about half the comparisons (68, or 52 percent), accounting for almost half (48 percent) of employment in the 130 comparisons, women's earnings were at least 87 percent of men's. However, the proportion of the 130 comparisons meeting this criterion, and of women in these comparisons, varied by age group and by degree level, as shown in the following tabulation:

	Percent of comparisons	Percent of employment
Age:		
25 to 64	52	48
25 to 34	83	68
35 to 44	47	42
45 to 64	35	38
Degree level:		
All levels	52	48
Bachelor's degree	49	35
Master's degree	61	81
Doctoral degree	67	70
Professional degree	0	0

Table 1. Median earnings of women as a percent of men's earnings and percent distribution of employment, by major field of study, degree level, and age group, 1993

Major field of study and degree level	Age 25–34				
	Median annual earnings		Women's earnings as percent of men's in same major	Percent distribution[1]	
	Women	Men		Women	Men
Bachelor's degree					
All major fields	$29,660	$35,694	83	100.0	100.0
Accounting	35,744	39,097	91	7.7	7.8
Agriculture	28,177	31,830	89	1.1	2.3
Architecture/environmental design	31,370	33,048	95	.5	1.1
Biological/life sciences	29,401	33,129	89	2.9	–
Business, except accounting	30,163	34,938	86	21.1	26.3
Chemistry	34,506	35,398	97	.6	.8
Communications	27,317	30,768	89	7.2	5.0
Computer and information sciences	38,966	41,314	94	3.6	6.0
Criminal justice/protective service	26,037	29,401	89	1.2	1.7
Economics	33,597	36,656	92	1.3	2.1
Education, including physical education	24,276	26,366	92	13.0	3.7
Engineering	43,274	43,518	99	2.6	14.5
Engineering-related technologies	36,300	38,688	94	.3	3.3
English language and literature	27,388	28,503	96	3.0	1.4
Foreign languages and linguistics	29,079	28,832	101	1.2	.4
Health/medical technologies	32,526	–		.9	–
History	25,989	30,418	85	1.1	1.7
Liberal arts/general studies	30,672	31,386	98	1.2	.8
Mathematics	35,052	36,828	95	1.3	1.7
Nursing	35,923	–		4.7	–
Pharmacy	47,506	48,979	97	.5	.5
Political science and government	28,507	33,271	86	2.1	2.7
Psychology	26,339	30,657	86	4.3	1.7
Social work	23,333	–		1.3	–
Sociology	25,763	29,142	88	1.6	.8
Theology, philosophy, and religion	–	–		–	–
Visual and performing arts	24,643	25,633	96	5.1	3.3
Master's degree					
All major fields	33,461	42,359	79	100	100
Accounting	–	–		–	–
Agriculture	–	–		–	–
Architecture/environmental design	–	–		–	–
Biological/life sciences	32,296	25,468	127	2.3	1.5
Business, except accounting	43,697	49,066	89	19.3	33.2
Chemistry	–	–		–	–
Communications	32,214	–		2.3	–
Computer and information sciences	47,852	49,352	97	2.5	5.5
Economics	–	–		–	–
Education, including physical education	29,672	29,951	99	32.0	8.4
Engineering	45,824	47,407	97	2.7	18.4
English language and literature	–	–		–	–
Foreign languages and linguistics	–	–		–	–
History	–	–		–	–
Mathematics	39,455	44,319	89	.9	1.6
Psychology	29,517	29,477	100	4.2	2.1
Social work	30,025	31,203	96	4.8	.8
Sociology	–	–		–	–
Theology, philosophy, and religion	–	–		–	–
Visual and performing arts	28,382	29,361	97	2.8	2.5
Doctoral degree					
All major fields	36,285	42,860	85	100.0	100.0
Biological/life sciences	24,422	27,223	90	22.8	14.2
Chemistry	–	–		–	–
Education, including physical education	–	–		–	–
Engineering, mathematics, and computer science	–	–		–	–
English language and literature	–	–		–	–
Foreign languages and linguistics	–	–		–	–
Psychology	–	–		–	–
Sociology	–	–		–	–
Professional degree					
All major fields	40,357	48,320	84	100.0	100.0
Law	43,453	51,494	84	53.3	49.3
Medicine, including dentistry, optometry, osteopathy, podiatry, and veterinary	35,684	41,633	86	37.3	42.9

See footnotes at end of table.

Table 1. Continued—Median earnings of women as a percent of men's earnings and percent distribution of employment, by major field of study, degree level, and age group, 1993

Major field of study and degree level	Age 35–44				
	Median annual earnings		Women's earnings as percent of men's in same major	Percent distribution[1]	
	Women	Men		Women	Men
Bachelor's degree					
All major fields	$32,155	$43,200	74	100.0	100.0
Accounting	39,843	49,502	80	4.9	7.8
Agriculture	28,752	36,578	79	.8	2.4
Architecture/environmental design	46,356	42,602	109	.3	1.3
Biological/life sciences	34,245	41,179	83	3.7	3.8
Business, except accounting	34,638	44,867	77	10.6	23.0
Chemistry	37,501	44,994	83	.5	1.1
Communications	34,102	38,912	88	3.4	3.4
Computer and information sciences	43,757	50,510	87	1.4	2.7
Criminal justice/protective service	31,818	40,149	79	.8	1.5
Economics	49,175	49,378	100	.6	1.8
Education, including physical education	27,988	34,470	81	24.5	7.0
Engineering	49,072	53,287	92	1.3	11.7
Engineering-related technologies	–	–	–	–	–
English language and literature	30,296	38,297	79	4.0	2.0
Foreign languages and linguistics	32,653	33,778	97	1.7	.4
Health/medical technologies	35,526	36,269	98	1.5	.3
History	30,553	38,095	80	1.8	2.8
Liberal arts/general studies	32,073	39,625	81	1.3	.8
Mathematics	37,534	51,580	73	1.6	1.8
Nursing	40,928	44,680	92	6.9	.4
Pharmacy	48,428	50,480	96	.7	.9
Political science and government	31,759	41,023	77	1.4	2.4
Psychology	32,301	40,718	79	4.4	3.1
Social work	28,593	32,174	89	2.1	.4
Sociology	29,532	37,250	79	3.1	1.7
Theology, philosophy, and religion	25,787	31,849	81	.4	1.4
Visual and performing arts	29,604	32,969	90	5.8	3.5
Master's degree					
All major fields	37,579	49,770	76	100.0	100.0
Accounting	50,053	58,435	86	1.1	2.3
Agriculture	33,422	42,145	79	.6	.9
Architecture/environmental design	45,063	44,515	101	.5	1.5
Biological/life sciences	38,695	40,822	95	1.7	1.6
Business, except accounting	51,809	60,386	86	11.3	29.9
Chemistry	–	–	–	–	–
Communications	39,417	53,013	74	1.4	1.3
Computer and information sciences	51,273	57,274	90	1.8	3.8
Economics	38,261	49,955	77	.4	.7
Education, including physical education	35,128	39,237	90	43.7	17.8
Engineering	54,380	59,404	92	1.3	10.9
English language and literature	35,412	34,159	104	1.5	1.1
Foreign languages and linguistics	34,716	–	–	.9	–
History	–	–	–	–	–
Mathematics	31,902	51,773	62	1.0	1.2
Psychology	34,747	38,670	90	4.7	2.8
Social work	33,993	40,064	85	4.1	1.6
Sociology	–	–	–	–	–
Theology, philosophy, and religion	31,487	30,400	104	1.0	4.8
Visual and performing arts	30,523	35,058	87	2.8	2.8
Doctoral degree					
All major fields	43,384	52,991	82	100.0	100.0
Biological/life sciences	40,661	49,271	83	17.1	14.4
Chemistry	59,173	62,706	94	3.8	9.1
Education, including physical education	41,824	47,807	87	16.3	7.8
Engineering, mathematics, and computer science	62,995	62,194	101	4.7	17.6
English language and literature	–	–	–	–	–
Foreign languages and linguistics	–	–	–	–	–
Psychology	44,889	55,155	81	16.0	8.3
Sociology	–	–	–	–	–
Professional degree					
All major fields	59,536	82,017	73	100.0	100.0
Law	57,182	70,164	82	53.2	45.2
Medicine, including dentistry, optometry, osteopathy, podiatry, and veterinary	81,227	100,610	81	34.2	44.0

See footnotes at end of table.

Table 1. Continued—Median earnings of women as a percent of men's earnings and percent distribution of employment, by major field of study, degree level, and age group, 1993

Major field of study and degree level	Age 45–64				
	Median annual earnings		Women's earnings as percent of men's in same major	Percent distribution[1]	
	Women	Men		Women	Men
Bachelor's degree					
All major fields	$32,093	$49,392	65	100.0	100.0
Accounting	35,254	54,745	64	3.4	8.7
Agriculture	–	–	–	–	–
Architecture/environmental design	–	–	–	–	–
Biological/life sciences	32,715	43,260	76	2.6	2.5
Business, except accounting	33,613	50,897	66	7.3	24.5
Chemistry	36,671	52,149	70	.9	1.8
Communications	37,418	49,985	75	1.5	1.9
Computer and information sciences	36,336	51,945	70	.6	.8
Criminal justice/protective service	–	–	–	–	–
Economics	42,743	52,264	82	1.5	.8
Education, including physical education	30,010	38,313	78	34.8	7.6
Engineering	38,707	59,215	65	.5	14.4
Engineering-related technologies	–	–	–	–	–
English language and literature	31,740	43,193	73	6.3	2.0
Foreign languages and linguistics	32,840	37,851	87	2.6	.6
Health/medical technologies	36,038	37,448	96	1.4	.2
History	30,283	42,321	72	2.5	3.3
Liberal arts/general studies	36,807	43,213	85	1.5	.8
Mathematics	34,718	56,389	62	2.2	2.8
Nursing	40,908	–	–	6.3	–
Pharmacy	46,148	51,028	90	.5	1.5
Political science and government	32,255	49,920	65	1.2	2.4
Psychology	32,076	45,514	70	3.2	2.3
Social work	28,953	30,205	96	1.5	.2
Sociology	32,039	45,757	70	3.7	1.8
Theology, philosophy, and religion	33,592	30,516	110	.6	1.8
Visual and performing arts	30,013	36,441	82	5.0	2.1
Master's degree					
All major fields	39,864	51,274	78	100.0	100.0
Accounting	–	–	–	–	–
Agriculture	–	–	–	–	–
Architecture/environmental design	–	–	–	–	–
Biological/life sciences	35,270	43,694	81	1.5	2.1
Business, except accounting	53,703	63,881	84	5.1	24.1
Chemistry	43,304	62,830	69	.5	.7
Communications	42,651	48,091	89	.9	1.0
Computer and information sciences	50,733	64,455	79	.6	1.7
Economics	–	–	–	–	–
Education, including physical education	39,433	45,299	87	52.0	24.8
Engineering	51,144	67,623	76	.3	8.8
English language and literature	36,805	45,352	81	3.3	1.4
Foreign languages and linguistics	40,835	42,036	97	1.7	.6
History	37,523	47,256	79	.8	1.6
Mathematics	42,102	57,842	73	1.2	2.4
Psychology	38,223	43,764	87	5.0	3.1
Social work	38,397	42,153	91	5.2	1.9
Sociology	45,286	44,486	102	.6	.5
Theology, philosophy, and religion	28,249	31,615	89	1.5	5.0
Visual and performing arts	34,520	40,861	84	2.6	2.5
Doctoral degree					
All major fields	49,820	62,247	80	100.0	100.0
Biological/life sciences	57,253	64,814	88	8.6	9.7
Chemistry	–	–	–	–	–
Education, including physical education	49,138	56,479	87	34.3	14.0
Engineering, mathematics, and computer science	–	–	–	–	–
English language and literature	42,273	50,900	83	6.2	3.1
Foreign languages and linguistics	39,220	52,101	75	4.1	2.3
Psychology	51,306	57,221	90	14.5	7.2
Sociology	48,179	49,527	97	3.2	1.5
Professional degree					
All major fields	61,176	91,105	67	100.0	100.0
Law	59,359	85,993	69	51.0	46.0
Medicine, including dentistry, optometry, osteopathy, podiatry, and veterinary	85,825	107,575	80	28.5	43.5

See footnotes at end of table.

In general, the proportions of women earning 87 or more percent of men's earnings increased with degree level, except for those with professional degrees, and decreased with age. Among older women with a bachelor's degree, 23 percent of comparisons met the 87-percent criterion, but these cases included only 8 percent of the women.

In some comparisons, women earned much less than men. For example, among mathematics majors, older women with a bachelor's degree and midcareer women with a master's degree had median earnings only 62 percent as much as men's earnings in the same categories. Younger and midcareer women with a bachelor's degree in computer science engineering, foreign languages, all four health majors, visual arts, and the major field of theology, philosophy, and religion did particularly well in relation to men in those same fields. Women with master's degrees in biological/life sciences, business, and education also did relatively well. Within some fields of study, earnings comparisons varied significantly by degree level. For instance, midcareer women with a bachelor's degree in economics did quite well in comparison to midcareer men with the same degree, but those with a master's degree did poorly, in fact earning much less than women with a bachelor's degree in the subject.

In some majors, comparisons among women varied widely by age group. Older women with bachelor's degrees in four majors—engineering, mathematics, accounting, and chemistry—had earnings comparisons 25 percentage points or more below those of young women with bachelor's degrees in the same four majors. The reason is clear: among men, the earnings of older workers were much greater than those of younger workers, while among women, earnings of older workers were lower than those of younger workers in three out of the aforementioned four majors; only in chemistry were they higher, and even then, just slightly. In fact, in most cases, older women did less well relative to men than did younger women. This is due in part to "vintage" effects that may not be as strong among women in the younger cohort as they age. For example, older women are more likely than younger women to have delayed their entry into the full-time labor force and are less likely to have had the benefit of equal employment opportunity policies when they were young.[8]

Women do better when their major fields are taken into account because women's distribution of employment, by field of study, differs significantly from men's. (See table 1.) What is highly significant is that almost all of the major fields in which men were concentrated had above-average median earnings, while those majors in which women were concentrated were characterized by below-average medians. Men were more likely to have degrees in engineering; engineering technology; computer science; architecture; mathematics; economics; theology, philosophy, and religion; and business, and women were more likely to have degrees in social work, psychology, nursing, medical/health technologies, physical therapy, and education. Notably, among midcareer workers with a bachelor's degree, 24.5 percent of women had majored in the below-average-paying field of education, compared with 7 percent of men. In contrast, only 1.3 percent of women, but 11.7 percent of men, were above-average-paid engineering graduates.

Among younger women, field-of-study patterns were more similar to men's. These patterns reflect women's dramatic shift into business, communications, computer science, and engineering majors and out of education and liberal arts majors (the latter, like education, also preparation for teaching in many cases) during the 1970s and 1980s.[9] Among bachelor's-degree graduates, only 10.7 percent of older, but 28.8 percent of younger, women had a degree in business—either in accounting or in some other business field—while the proportion of men remained unchanged with age, at a third. Younger women were still much more likely than men to have majored in education or social work, however, and much less likely to have majored in engineering or computer science.[10]

Because women were much more likely than men to have a low-paying major, such majors have a greater weight in earnings calculations for all women than for

---

Table 1. Continued—Medium earnings of women as a percent of men's earnings and percent distribution of employment, by major field of study, degree level, and age group, 1993

[1] Because not all major fields of study are shown, percent distribution does not add to 100. The numbers of women and men constituting the 100 percent for all major fields at the four degree levels and in the three age groups are as follows. Bachelor's degree: age 25–34—1,729,000 women, 2,006,300 men; age 35–44—1,832,600 women, 2,918,300 men; age 45–64—1,536,400 women, 2,767,200 men. Master's degree: age 25–34—403,700 women, 427,200 men; age 35–44—913,000 women, 1,069,000 men; age 45–64—1,072,900 women, 1,461,500 men. Doctoral degree: age 25–34—23,700

women, 50,700 men; age 35–44—71,900 women, 181,000 men; age 45–64—114,000 women, 401,800 men. Professional degree: age 25–34—99,800 women, 197,500 men; age 35–44—141,400 women, 463,500 men; age 45–64—91,300 women, 532,800 men.

NOTE: Data are for full-time wage and salary workers only. Dashes indicate data or calculation not considered statistically reliable.

SOURCE: Tabulated by the Bureau of Labor Statistics from a National Science Foundation survey conducted by the Bureau of the Census.

Table 2. Median earnings of women aged 35–44, as a percent of men's earnings, by major field of study, occupation, and degree level, and percent distribution of employment, by occupation, 1993

Major field of study, occupation, and degree level	Median annual earnings		Women's earnings as percent of men's in same major and occupation	Percent distribution[1]	
	Women	Men		Women	Men
Bachelor's degree					
All major fields of study	$32,155	$43,200	74	100.0	100.0
Accounting:					
All occupations[2]	39,843	49,502	80	4.9	7.8
Accountants, auditors, and other financial specialists ..	41,121	47,115	87	59.2	47.6
Clerical and administrative support occupations	22,961	31,284	73	7.1	2.6
Managers, executives, and administrators	49,265	57,800	85	15.5	27.1
Biological/life sciences:					
All occupations	34,245	41,179	83	3.7	3.8
Biological/life scientists	35,468	34,246	104	13.0	7.3
Health technologists and technicians	33,398	34,521	97	15.1	4.8
Managers, executives, and administrators	49,307	52,096	95	9.2	18.6
Business, except accounting:					
All occupations	34,638	44,867	77	10.6	23.0
Accountants, auditors, and other financial specialists ..	35,606	46,384	77	14.0	8.3
Buyers, management analysts, and other management-related occupations	35,208	42,199	83	9.5	9.5
Clerical and administrative support occupations	23,270	29,252	80	16.6	2.9
Computer occupations, excluding engineers	41,756	46,733	89	5.4	4.3
Managers, executives, and administrators	43,624	55,192	79	14.0	27.9
Personnel, training, and labor relations specialists	39,386	47,893	82	5.1	1.4
Sales and marketing occupations, except retail	40,377	48,456	83	17.3	22.6
Communications:					
All occupations	34,102	38,912	88	3.4	3.4
Artists, broadcasters, editors, public relations specialists, and writers	34,198	37,071	92	26.5	25.7
Managers and management-related occupations	42,149	47,120	89	17.2	24.4
Sales and marketing occupations, except retail	49,322	37,878	130	19.8	18.5
Computer and information sciences:					
All occupations	43,757	50,510	87	1.4	2.7
Computer occupations, excluding engineers	43,836	49,967	88	66.0	62.6
Engineers, including computer engineers	48,503	55,783	87	11.2	13.8
Education, including physical education:					
All occupations	27,988	34,470	81	24.5	7.0
Buyers, management analysts, and other management-related occupations	31,450	40,530	78	3.7	6.2
Computer occupations, excluding engineers	38,288	46,576	82	1.6	3.1
Teachers, elementary through grade 12	28,189	30,626	92	50.5	32.4
Managers, executives, and administrators	35,134	48,431	73	4.8	11.2
Sales and marketing occupations, except retail	35,231	47,168	75	4.3	11.5
Engineering:					
All occupations	49,072	53,287	92	1.3	11.7
Engineers, including computer engineers	49,246	53,134	93	48.9	58.3
Mathematics:					
All occupations	37,534	51,580	73	1.6	1.8
Computer occupations, excluding engineers	45,766	52,411	87	29.4	33.0
Psychology:					
All occupations	32,301	40,718	79	4.4	3.1
Clerical, food and other services, and retail sales	25,984	30,658	85	20.1	12.5
Counselors and social workers	27,724	30,409	91	10.7	7.5
Managers, executives, and administrators	44,528	54,227	82	10.3	15.4
Social workers	27,908	30,866	90	9.6	5.8
Visual and performing arts:					
All occupations	29,604	32,969	90	5.8	3.5
Artists, broadcasters, editors, public relations specialists, and writers	32,174	39,004	82	19.6	21.7
Clerical, food and other services, and retail sales	25,375	27,766	91	19.9	11.7
Teachers, elementary through grade 12	30,736	30,930	99	12.9	11.0
Managers, executives, and administrators	38,416	44,457	86	9.4	9.5

See footnotes at end of table.

Table 2. Continued—Median earnings of women aged 35–44, as a percent of men's earnings, by major field of study, occupation, and degree level, and percent distribution of employment, by occupation, 1993

Major field of study, occupation, and degree level	Median annual earnings		Women's earnings as percent of men's in same major and occupation	Percent distribution[1]	
	Women	Men		Women	Men
Master's degree					
All major fields of study	$37,579	$49,770	76	100.0	100.0
Biological/life sciences:					
All occupations	38,695	40,839	95	1.7	1.6
Biological/life scientists	42,126	40,391	104	22.5	33.7
Business, except accounting:					
All occupations	51,824	60,364	86	11.3	29.9
Accountants, auditors, and other financial specialists ..	51,575	57,319	90	18.1	16.8
Buyers, management analysts, and other management-related occupations	57,468	55,919	103	7.3	6.7
Computer occupations, excluding engineers	49,047	57,349	86	4.3	5.5
Managers, executives, and administrators	62,749	69,270	91	27.6	37.3
Sales and marketing occupations, except retail	59,854	63,427	94	11.5	13.3
Computer and information sciences:					
All occupations	51,273	57,274	90	1.8	3.8
Computer occupations, excluding engineers	49,164	55,340	89	49.7	53.6
Engineers, including computer engineers	55,868	61,167	91	21.5	24.7
Education, including physical education:					
All occupations	35,128	39,229	90	43.7	17.8
Counselors, educational and vocational	34,202	36,196	94	5.7	2.8
Teachers, elementary through grade 12	34,511	38,169	90	67.2	49.8
Managers, executives, and administrators	41,731	44,876	93	7.7	23.0
Postsecondary teachers	30,144	33,297	91	2.2	4.6
Engineering:					
All occupations	54,380	59,382	92	1.3	10.9
Engineers, including computer engineers	55,597	58,407	95	54.8	64.4
Psychology:					
All occupations	34,747	38,620	90	4.7	2.8
Counselors and social workers	32,023	34,321	93	26.6	17.7
Social scientists	32,841	32,559	101	17.1	22.1
Social work:					
All occupations	33,993	40,033	85	4.1	1.6
Social workers	33,127	38,532	86	66.0	61.3

[1]The numbers constituting the 100 percent for all major fields of study at the bachelor's-degree level are 1,832,600 women and 2,918,300 men. At the master's-degree level, the numbers are 913,700 women and 1,069,000 men. In each of the major fields, the men's (women's) figure for all occupations is the percent of the total men (women) employed in all major fields of study; the men's (women's) figure for the separate suboccupations is the percent of the men's (women's) all-occupations figure in the major.

[2]Data for all ocupations are from table 1.

NOTE: In occupations with few observations, several occupations were combined. Management-related occupations include two occupational groups: buyers, management analysts, and other management-related occupations; and personnel, training, and labor relations specialists. Data are for full-time wage and salary workers.

SOURCE: Bureau of the Census.

all men; and, correspondingly, high-earnings majors have a lesser weight. As noted earlier, women's calculations also tend to be somewhat more heavily weighted by younger workers and less heavily weighted by those with a doctoral or professional degree. When median earnings of women are compared with those of men of the same age group, degree level, and field of study, they are not weighted and therefore are closer to men's.

A simulation was developed to show what the median earnings for all women would have been if women had the same age, degree-level, and field-of-study distribution as men—that is, the same weights, but with earnings in each field-of-study, age, and degree-level group unchanged. In other words, women would be just as likely as men to have a high-paying or low-paying major, to be in the older or younger age group, and to have a professional or a bachelor's degree.[11] The resulting synthetic distribution of women's earnings has a median of $38,068, 82 percent of the $46,605 earned by men. As was observed earlier, the actual women's median, $34,093, is 73 percent of men's earnings. In other words, adjusting women's age, degree-level, and field-of-study distributions reduces the observed gap in earnings by about 9 percentage points, or approximately one-third.

Median earnings of women compared with those of men with the same occupation and major.

When occupation also was considered, women's median earnings generally were even closer to men's. To make the data more manageable, the analysis was limited to midcareer bachelor's- and master's-degree graduates. Of the 26 bachelor's-degree field comparisons shown in table 1, 10 yielded statistically reliable occupational earnings; of the 16 master's combinations, 7 did. Together, the two degree levels produced a total of 49 major-field and occupation comparisons. (See table 2.) In 38 of these, women did better than in the all-occupation comparisons between women and men; these 38 comparisons accounted for 70 percent of women in the analysis. In one case, namely, holders of master's degrees in education who were employed as teachers, accounting for 20 percent of women in the analysis, women earned the same as did all women education majors.

The preceding comparisons spanned a wide range. In five cases—bachelor's-degree communications majors employed as sales and marketing workers, master's-degree business majors employed as buyers, master's-degree psychology majors employed as social scientists, and

biology majors at both levels employed as biologists—women earned more than men with the same occupation and major.

In some cases, adding the occupational comparison provided very different percentages. Earnings of the sales and marketing workers just noted, at 130 percent of men's earnings, were 42 percentage points above the earnings ratio for all women to all men communications majors, and the bachelor's-degree biologists' men-to-women's earnings ratio was 21 points above that of all biology majors as a whole. On the other hand, bachelor's-degree education majors employed as managers earned only 73 percent as much as men managers, 8 points below the 81 percent for all-women-to-all-men education majors. Women visual and performing arts majors employed as artists, broadcasters, editors, public relations specialists, and writers also had ratios 8 points lower than women in all occupations combined, and accounting majors employed as clerical workers were 7 points lower than women in all occupations combined.

Women generally did even better, when compared to men in the same occupation, because their occupational patterns, like their field-of-study patterns, differed so from men's. Women were less likely than men to be in occupations with above-average earnings, such as sales and marketing workers (except retail) or managers. (See table 2.) Women were more likely than men to be in occupations with below-average earnings, such as teachers, social workers, health technicians, retail sales workers, or clerical, food, and other service workers. Among education majors with bachelor's degrees, women were less than half as likely to be managers as were men, and among master's-degree holders, women were only about a third as likely. At the bachelor's-degree level, women education majors were also much less likely to be in computer or sales and marketing occupations, but were more likely to be elementary-through-12th-grade teachers.

The differences in occupational patterns noted in this article probably reflect different preferences between men and women. However, the anderrepresentation of women in some occupations may also reflect discrimination in hiring and, particularly in the case of managers, promotion. Also, as noted earlier, there may be "vintage" effects that do not fully carry over for younger women as they enter the midcareer group.[12]

The choice of both occupation and major are significant factors in determining a person's earnings. Although women college graduates earned less than men did overall, the earnings gap lessens significantly in most cases when women are compared with men with similar educational backgrounds and similar occupations. This article has highlighted majors and occupations in which women do particularly well, or particularly poorly, in relation to men. Much of the difference between women's and men's earnings, however, is not explained by the data presented. More might be explained by accounting for other objective differences.[13] However, it was not the purpose of the article to do so, or to estimate the difference in men's and women's earnings due to past or existing discrimination in hiring and promotion or to lower pay for equal work.

Footnotes

[1] Individuals who received a bachelor's degree after April 1990 are not included. The survey is the largest one available that has collected detailed information about college graduates' employment characteristics, such as earnings and occupation, by major field of study.

[2] These ranges divide graduates with bachelor's degrees into fairly equal-sized groups. For those with advanced degrees, however, there are fewer in the younger group. The 2–34 age group has fewer workers aged 25 and 26, because the survey population included only individuals who had at least a bachelor's degree three years earlier, at the time of the 1990 census. As a result, the median earnings for this age group are biased upward. Graduates aged 65 and older are excluded, because they are often at least partially retired.

[3] Although the degree-level separations should account for most differences in the quantity of education received, data on college courses taken after achieving the highest degree were not considered. Therefore, those who, for example, had completed all requirements for the doctorate except a dissertation would generally show up as master's degree holders. On-the-job and other nonacademic training, for which there were few data, also may affect earnings.

[4] For example, education comprises 12 subfields plus an "other" category, including education administration, computer teacher education, counselor education, physical education, educational psychology, and elementary teacher education. Also, note that the occupational category of biological and life scientists includes agricultural scientists, biochemists, biological scientists (for instance, botanists and zoologists), forestry or conservation scientists, medical scientists (excluding practitioners), biological and life science technologists and technicians, and an "other" category. Further, there may be differences between women and men in the types of courses taken, even within the same major field. (For a discussion of these differences and a more general discussion of differences in fields of study and occupations entered, see Clifford Adelman, "Lessons of a Generation: Education and Work in the Lives of the High School Class of 1972," *Women at Thirtysomething: Paradoxes of Attainment* (San Francisco, Jossey-Bass, 1994), chapter 2, pp. 36–82.)

[5] See, for example, Alan S. Blinder, "Wage Discrimination: Reduced Form and Structural Estimates," *Journal of Human Resources,* Fall 1973, pp. 436–55; Ronald Oaxaca, "Male-Female Wage Differentials in Urban Labor Markets," *International Economic Review,* October 1973, pp. 693–703; Mary Corcoran and Greg J. Duncan, "Work History, Labor Force Attachment, and Earnings Differences between the Races and Sexes," *Journal of Human Resources,* Winter 1979, pp. 3–20; Thomas N. Daymont and Paul J. Andrisani, "Job Preferences, College Major, and the Gender Gap in Earnings," *Journal of Human Resources,* Summer 1984, pp. 408–28; and Barry Gerhart, "Gender Differences in Current and Starting Salaries: The Role of Performance, College Major, and Job Title," *Industrial and Labor Relations Review,* April 1990, pp. 418–31.

[6] Among the characteristics not examined, but potentially relevant, are having children living at home, marital status, type of employer, type of industry, and geographic location. However, some data on earnings of midcareer bachelor's-degree women without children are presented in footnote 13. Other factors not included in the survey, such as grade-point average in school or hours worked per week, also may be related to annual earnings.

[7] The 130 fields included 83 percent of the 8.03 million women in the survey population.

[8] It is also possible to use data in table 1 to compare earnings of women, by major, to earnings of the median for all men at the same degree level in the same age group. Not surprisingly, women in well-paying majors such as engineering, pharmacy, and business administration (at the master's level) had median earnings greater than those of the median man, and women in education, social work, and other poorly paying majors had earnings much less than those of the median man.

[9] This shift occurred not only because of greater opportunities for women outside of traditional occupations, but also because of the sharp drop in the number of job openings in teaching during the early 1970s.

[10] For further discussion of this point, see Eric Eide, "College Major Choice and Changes in the Gender Wage Gap," *Contemporary Economic Policy,* April 1994, pp. 55–64.

[11] The weighting procedure, with an example using the distribution of midcareer workers with bachelor's degrees in education and engineering, cited several paragraphs earlier, is as follows. Midcareer women with bachelor's degrees in the high-paying field of engineering (median earnings of $49,072) made up less than three-tenths of 1 percent of women college graduates, at all levels, while men in this category made up almost 2.8 percent of all men. Therefore, the earnings of each woman respondent with an engineering major were weighted by a factor of 9.63, increasing the percentage of these women engineering majors to almost 2.8 percent of all women. Midcareer women with bachelor's degrees in low-paying education (median earnings of $27,988) were about 5.6 percent of women college graduates, at all levels, while men in this category were only about 1.7 percent of all men. Therefore, the earnings of each woman respondent with an education major were weighted by a factor of .297, reducing the percentage of these women education majors to about 1.7 percent of all women. Earnings of women respondents with other majors and degree levels, and in other age groups, were similarly weighted.

[12] Most of the women who earned as much as, or more than, the median man with the same major were managers.

[13] For example, women's earnings, and therefore the comparisons with men, are clearly affected by having responsibility for children. For instance, midcareer bachelor's-degree women without children living at home earned $34,293, while all midcareer women with bachelor's degrees had median earnings of $32,155, 74 percent of men's earnings. (See table 2.) Thus, if the earnings of women without children, rather than all women, had been used, then the earnings of midcareer bachelor's-degree women would have been 80 percent. The issue is complex, however, because women without children may be more likely both to have majored in a high-paying field and to be employed in a high-paying occupation. Furthermore, although men's earnings are also affected by the presence of children, for men, having children living at home is associated with *higher,* and not lower, earnings. Furthermore, a question about the number of years of professional work experience was asked in the survey, and the responses might have been used in place of the age-group specification. However, due to respondents' problems interpreting "professional work experience," data on the detailed major field of study were not considered reliable. Nonetheless, a comparison of earnings ratios by age group with earnings ratios by years of professional experience showed only slightly higher ratios for young and midcareer women with bachelor's degrees, but a somewhat higher ratio for older women. This suggests that young and midcareer women had almost as much professional experience as men in the same category, but that older women did not.

THE EMPLOYMENT STATUS OF NEW GRADUATES—ONE YEAR AFTER GRADUATION

Introduction. I included this article because it provides important information on the experiences of new college graduates in the labor force. While it refers to the relatively "old" class of 1993, the data tells us what more recent graduates are likely to experience in their search for jobs. The information on employment outcomes by majors is particularly interesting because it includes the percentages of graduates who went on for advanced degrees as well as the types of jobs they actually obtained.

By Megan Barkume

The number of bachelor's degrees awarded by U.S. colleges and universities rose in 1993 for the 16th straight year to a record 1.17 million. How did these graduates fare in the job market? Did they find work that made use of their academic training? How many enrolled to continue their studies? Did academic performance affect their employment or school enrollment status? What did they earn? These questions are answered by a U.S. Department of Education survey of the class of 1993.

The 1993 survey is the latest in a series of follow-up studies of college graduates one year after graduation. The Department of Education has also conducted surveys for the classes of 1977, 1980, 1984, 1986, and 1990. In addition to information contained in these previous studies, the latest survey looks at the correlation between academic performance and success in the job market. It will also track the graduates over a 12-year period to provide information on their academic enrollment, degree completion, employment, and public service.

This article describes the employment status, continuing education status, effects of academic performance, and earnings of 1993 college graduates as of

Megan Barkume is an economist in the Office of Employment Projections, Bureau of Labor Statistics.

April 1994. The Bureau of Labor Statistics (BLS) has analyzed these data for the graduates as a group and for each of 11 major fields of study:

- Biological sciences
- Business and management
- Education
- Engineering
- Health professions
- History
- Humanities
- Mathematics, computer sciences, and physical sciences
- Psychology
- Public affairs
- Social sciences

Comparisons are also made between professional fields and arts and sciences fields, as defined by the Department of Education.

Employment Status

About 92 percent of the class of 1993 was in the labor force one year after graduation, up from 89 percent for the last comparable class in 1990. (See table 1.) This increase reflects a gain in part-time employment. The proportion of unemployed graduates has been relatively stable between 1977 and 1993.

TABLE 1
Labor Force and Graduate School Status of New Graduates, Selected Years
(percent)

	Class					
	1977	1980	1984	1986	1990	1993
Total in labor force	86	86	86	89	89	92
Employed full time	69	70	71	73	74	73
Employed part time	12	12	12	12	11	14
Unemployed	5	4	3	4	4	5
Not in labor force	14	14	14	11	11	9
Enrolled in graduate school	25	26	23	24	35	27

The class of 1993's labor force participation rate—the proportion of those graduates employed full or part time or seeking work—varied by field. College graduates with a bachelor's degree in professional fields

—business and management, education, engineering, health professions, and public affairs and social services—were usually able to find entry-level work in their field of study. Many graduates in arts and sciences fields—biological sciences; mathematics, computer sciences, and physical sciences; social sciences; history; humanities; and psychology—needed additional education to pursue work in their field.

As a result, graduates with a bachelor's degree in professional fields had a higher labor force participation rate (94 percent) than those with a bachelor's in arts and sciences (87 percent). Table 2 shows the breakdown in employment status by field of study. For example, 85 percent of business and management majors were employed full time, compared to 52 percent of graduates in biological sciences. Education majors had the lowest proportion of graduates unemployed (3 percent), less than half the percentage of biological sciences majors (7 percent). However, both the lowest and highest proportions of part-time workers were within professional fields: Business and management degree graduates had the lowest proportion (8 percent), while education had the highest (21 percent).

TABLE 2
Employment Status of College Graduates, Class of 1993, by Major, in 1994
(percent)

	Unemployed	Out of Labor Force	Full Time	Part Time
All graduates	5	9	14	73
Biological sciences	7	24	17	52
Business and management	4	4	8	85
Education	3	7	21	68
Engineering	6	9	9	76
Health professions	5	7	15	73
History	5	9	14	72
Humanities	5	11	20	64
Mathematics, computer sciences, and physical sciences	5	14	14	68
Psychology	5	14	15	67
Public affairs and social services	5	8	13	75
Social sciences	5	10	13	73

New graduates were surveyed about whether they felt their jobs required a degree, were related to their major, and had career potential. (See table 3.) In general, graduates who majored in professional fields responded more positively to these questions than did arts and sciences graduates. Disciplines such as business, education, engineering, and health professions are closely related to occupations for which a bachelor's degree is sufficient for entry. On the other hand, disciplines such as biological sciences, social sciences, history, and psychology are associated with occupations for which a master's or doctoral degree is usually required. Mathematics, computer sciences, and physical sciences majors had the highest proportion among arts and sciences majors responding that their jobs required a degree, were related to their major, and had career potential.

TABLE 3
Relation of Current Job to Major Field and Career Potential of Job, Class of 1993, by Major Field of Study
(percent)

	4-Year Degree Required	Related to Major Field	Career Potential
All graduates	56	75	72
Biological sciences	49	64	57
Business and management	51	85	77
Education	66	79	75
Engineering	79	87	82
Health professions	73	91	80
History	41	42	67
Humanities	45	58	66
Mathematics, computer sciences, and physical sciences	68	82	75
Psychology	45	57	53
Public affairs and social services	49	72	68
Social sciences	47	57	68

Continuing Education Status

Twenty-six percent of all class of 1993 graduates were continuing their education within one year of receiving their bachelor's degree. Of those, 17 percent were enrolled in graduate or professional school, 4 percent had enrolled in bachelor's or associate degree programs, and about 6 percent were not pursuing a formal credential. (See table 4.) Those with degrees in arts and sciences fields had a higher continuing education enrollment proportion (23 percent) than graduates in professional fields (15 percent).

TABLE 4
Educational Status of College Graduates, Class of 1993, in 1994
(percent)

Enrolled but not pursuing a formal credential	6
Enrolled in bachelor's or associate's degree programs	4
Enrolled in graduate or professional school	17
College graduates not continuing their education	73

Graduates of professional fields and of arts and sciences fields had much different levels of full-time graduate or professional school enrollment. (See table 5.) Less than 9 percent of graduates who majored in professional fields were enrolled, while the proportion for arts and sciences graduates was more than double that. Many arts and sciences graduates took preprofessional programs, such as prelaw and premedicine, or planned to enter occupations for which a master's or doctoral degree is usually required.

TABLE 5
Full-Time Enrollment in Continuing Education, by Major
(percent)

Baccalaureate Degree Major	Full-Time Students in Continuing Education
Total	**26.1**
Professional fields	**8.6**
Business and management	5.0
Education	10.9
Engineering	14.6
Health professions	10.5
Public affairs and social services	8.7
Arts and sciences	**17.5**
Biological sciences	26.6
History	18.2
Humanities	14.2
Mathematics, computer sciences, and physical sciences	20.5
Psychology	18.4
Social sciences	14.4

Other class of 1993 graduates who were not enrolled in school one year after earning their bachelor's degree still planned to continue their education at a later date. Many graduates, for example, said they would delay additional study to gain work experience before returning to school. These graduates planned to resume their education in the future, as indicated in the following tabulation of the educational aspirations of class of 1993 graduates in 1994:

	Percent
No plans	16
Postbaccalaureate certificate	1
Pursue degree	
Master's	59
Doctoral	17
First professional	6
Other	1

Academic Performance

Graduates' employment and enrollment status is also related to their academic performance. (See table 6.)

Class of 1993 graduates with the highest grade point average (GPA) had the lowest unemployment rates; these graduates also were most likely to hold jobs that had definite or possible career potential and were related to their major. In addition, graduates with the best grades were much more likely to be enrolled full time in graduate school and, as a result, to be out of the labor force. Graduates with a GPA of 3.5 or higher, for example, were more than twice as likely to be enrolled in continuing education as those with a GPA of less than 3.0.

TABLE 6
Class of 1993 Employment, Career Potential, and Continuing Education Status in 1994, by GPA
(percent)

	Employment Status				Career Potential		Continuing Education Status		
	Working		Not Working						
	Full Time	Part Time	Unemployed	Not in Labor Force	Definite/ Possible Potential	Job Related to Degree	Enrolled Full Time	Enrolled Part Time	Not Enrolled
3.5 or higher	67	16	4	13	74	79	18	6	77
3.0-3.49	74	13	5	8	72	77	12	6	82
Under 3.0	78	13	5	4	70	70	8	6	87

Earnings

Earnings varied by major and occupation. (See tables 7 and 8.) Graduates who majored in health professions and engineering had the highest average salaries of all graduates; education and psychology graduates earned the least. Earnings data show similar results for the occupations associated with those fields: The highest-paid workers had jobs in engineering and health professions; the lowest earners worked in service occupations such as waiter, child-care worker, nursing aide, and teacher.

TABLE 7
Average Salary of Graduates Employed Full Time, Class of 1993, by Major Field of Study, 1994

	(Thousands of Dollars)
All graduates	$24.2
Biological sciences	22.8
Business and management	27.1
Education	19.3
Engineering	30.9
Health professions	31.3
History	21.0
Humanities	21.3
Mathematics, computer science, and physical science	25.4
Psychology	19.5
Public affairs/social services	22.0
Social science	22.1

TABLE 8
Average Salary of Graduates Employed Full Time, Class of 1993 by Occupation, 1994

	(Thousands of Dollars)
All graduates	$24.2
Administrative, clerical, support	20.2
Business and management	25.4
Computer science, programming	29.7
Engineering	33.3
Health professions	32.4
Mechanic, operator, laborer	22.0
Military, protective services	25.5
Noncomputer technician	26.0
Sales	24.7
School teacher	20.1
Service	16.8
Other professions	23.4

Limitations of the Data

The information in this article should be helpful to individuals selecting a major field of study because it indicates the range of job possibilities for graduates with a degree in the fields discussed. However, the reader should be aware that the data are affected by the size of the sample, the time at which the survey was taken, and the qualifications of candidates other than their academic major—for example, minor fields of study, other courses, extracurricular activities, work experience, grades, quality of the school, and personality traits. Also, the information was collected only a short time after graduation. People are likely to change occupations as they gain experience or additional education.

The results of the survey are based on a nationally representative sample of 10,080 college graduates who received bachelor's degrees between July 1992 and June 1993. Data were collected by a Computer Assisted Telephone Interview (CATI) survey, as well as field interviewing when necessary, between June and October 1994. This sample represents about 1 percent of all bachelor's degree recipients during the same period. The results of a survey covering all graduates might differ.

The following charts profile the 11 major fields for which the survey yielded reliable data. For each field, the charts show the major occupations of the graduates, and the text provides additional information on employment, unemployment, school enrollment, career potential, and earnings.

ONE YEAR LATER
Where is the Class of '93?

Biological Sciences

The biological sciences include majors in zoology, botany, biochemistry, and biophysics. This field had the lowest percentage of graduates employed one year after graduation (69 percent). Of those employed, 52 percent worked full time and 17 percent worked part time. Biological sciences majors also had the highest proportion unemployed (almost 10 percent) among all graduates. But many professional jobs in biological sciences require an advanced degree, and the 35 percent of biological sciences majors enrolled in continuing education one year after graduation is the largest proportion of any field surveyed.

Biological Sciences Majors One Year After Graduation

Profession	Percent
Other professions	17
Administrative and clerical support	17
Noncomputer technician	16
Business and management	9
Sales	9
Mechanic, operator, and laborer	8
School teacher	8
Health professions	7
Service	6
Computer science and programming	3

About 64 percent reported that their jobs were related to biological sciences; about half (49 percent) reported that a four-year degree was required for their job; and 57 percent said their jobs had career potential. The largest percentage of biological sciences graduates held jobs in other professions, including scientists (17 percent) and administrative and clerical support (17 percent) and noncomputer technician jobs (16 percent). Job opportunities for bachelor's degree holders include school teacher and health technician. Biological sciences majors employed full time averaged $22,800 a year.

Business and Management

The business and management field had the highest number of graduates employed one year after graduation (92 percent). Eighty-five percent were employed full time, and 8 percent were employed part time. About 4 percent of business and management majors were unemployed. Relatively few (10 percent) were enrolled in continuing education.

Business and Management Majors One Year After Graduation

Profession	Percent
Business and management	31
Other professions	26
Administrative and clerical support	24
Sales	12
Computer science and programmers	4
Mechanic, operator, and laborer	3

Eighty-five percent of graduates reported holding jobs that were related to business and management; about half (51 percent) said that a four-year degree was required for their job; and 77 percent said that their jobs had career potential. Over 31 percent of graduates were working in business and management occupations. Other professions, including accounting, employed 26 percent of graduates; another 24 percent worked in administrative and clerical support occupations, including bank teller, bookkeeping, real estate appraiser, and insurance adjuster. Business and management majors working full time averaged $27,100 a year.

Education

Graduates in education had a relatively high labor force participation rate (89 percent) one year after graduation, with 68 percent employed full time and 21 percent employed part time. These graduates had the lowest proportion unemployed of all fields (less than 4 percent). Many states require a master's degree for teaching certification. About 19 percent of education graduates were enrolled in continuing education one year after graduation.

Education Majors One Year After Graduation

Profession	Percent
Sales	3
Service	5
Business and management	9
Other professions	13
Administrative and clerical support	13
Teaching	57

Nearly 80 percent of graduates reported being in jobs related to education; 66 percent said that a four-year degree was required for their job; and 75 percent said that their jobs had career potential. The majority of education graduates (57 percent) were employed as school teachers. Some of those were substitute teachers. The next largest category of employment was adminis-trative or clerical support, accounting for 13 percent of graduates. The average annual salary of education majors employed full time was $19,300, the lowest salary of all fields studied; however, most teachers work a 10-month year.

Engineering

Eighty-five percent of engineering graduates were employed one year after graduation, 76 percent of them full time and 9 percent part time. Almost 7 percent of engineering graduates were unemployed, more than double the 3 percent for engineering graduates in the class of 1990. A relatively high proportion (21 percent) was enrolled in continuing education one year after graduation.

Engineering Majors One Year After Graduation

Profession	Percent
Administrative and clerical support	5
Noncomputer technicians	5
Mechanics, operators, and laborers	6
Computer scientists and programmers	8
Other professions	10
Business and management	12
Engineering	54

About 87 percent reported that their jobs were related to their major field; 79 percent said a four-year degree was required for their job; and 82 percent said that their jobs had career potential. Over half of engineering graduates (54 percent) were concentrated in engineering jobs. The proportion of graduates working in other fields ranged from 5 percent in administrative and clerical support to 12 percent in business and management. Engineering graduates employed full time had the second highest salary of all fields studied, $30,900.

Health Professions

Health professions include allied health, such as dental or medical technician, community or mental health, and nurse assisting; physical education or recreation; and other areas of health, such as audiology, dentistry, medicine, nursing, health or hospital administration, and dietetics. About 89 percent of health professions graduates were employed one year after graduation, with 73 percent full time and 15 percent part time. About 5 percent were unemployed.

Health Professions Majors One Year After Graduation

Profession	Percent
Service	4
Other professions	6
Business and management	7
Administrative and clerical support	7
Computer science and programming	8
Noncomputer technician	8
Health professions	60

A high proportion of these workers (91 percent) reported that their jobs were related to their major field; 73 percent said a four-year degree was required for their job; and 80 percent said their jobs had career potential. Seventeen percent of graduates were enrolled in continuing education after graduation. Sixty percent of graduates were employed in health professions one year after graduation. About 10 percent were employed as noncomputer technicians, including medical and dental technicians, hygienists, radiology technicians, and clinical lab technicians. Health professions graduates working full time averaged $31,300, the highest of all fields.

History

Eighty-six percent of all history graduates were employed one year after graduation, 72 percent of them full time and 14 percent part time. About 5 percent of these graduates were unemployed. Nearly a quarter of history graduates were enrolled in continuing education after graduation. This comparatively large number is not surprising, because an advanced degree is usually required to work in this field.

History Majors One Year After Graduation

Profession	Percent
Mechanic, operator, and laborer	4
Service	7
Sales	8
Protective services	9
Other professions	15
Teaching	15
Administrative and clerical support	18
Business and management	24

A relatively low 42 percent of graduates reported having a job related to history. Only 41 percent of graduates reported that a four-year degree was required for their job, and 67 percent of graduates reported that their jobs had career potential. Jobs of history graduates were widely distributed. Nearly a quarter of graduates held jobs in business and management; the next largest group,

18 percent, had administrative and clerical support jobs; and 15 percent were employed as school teachers, possibly to teach history. History graduates working full time had among the lowest salaries of all fields surveyed, $21,300.

Humanities

The humanities field includes foreign languages, philosophy, theology, and the arts. Eighty-four percent of humanities majors were employed one year after graduation, 64 percent full time and 20 percent part time. Of all fields studied, these graduates had one of the highest percentages of part-time workers (20 percent). Over 5 percent were unemployed. About 19 percent of humanities graduates were enrolled in continuing education one year after graduation.

Humanities Majors One Year After Graduation

Profession	Percent
Computer science programming	3
Mechanic, operator, and laborer	5
Service	5
Sales	8
Teaching	11
Business and management	17
Administrative and clerical support	21
Other professions	30

A relatively low 58 percent said they worked in jobs related to their major field; 45 percent reported that a four-year degree was required for their job; and 66 percent said their jobs had career potential. Jobs for humanities majors were widely dispersed, characteristic of majors that do not provide training for a specific profession. The largest portion (30 percent) worked in other professions, including arts and entertainment, the law, as clergy, and in social work, architecture, and accounting. The average salary of humanities graduates working full time was $19,500.

Mathematics, Computer Sciences, and Physical Sciences

A large proportion of mathematics, computer sciences, and physical sciences graduates (82 percent) was employed one year after graduation, 68 percent of them full time and 14 percent part time. The proportion unemployed was nearly 6 percent. Twenty-five percent of mathematics, computer sciences, and physical sciences majors were enrolled in continuing education one year after graduation.

Mathematics, Computer Sciences, and Physical Sciences Majors One Year After Graduation

Profession	Percent
Service	3
Sales	5
Noncomputer technician	5
Mechanic, operator, and laborer	5
Engineering	7
Business and management	8
Other professions	12
Teaching	12
Administrative and clerical support	17
Computer science and programming	26

The majority of graduates in these fields (82 percent) reported that their jobs were related to their major; 68 percent said that a four-year degree was required for their job; and 75 percent said their jobs had career potential. Graduates worked in a wide range of occupations. The largest group, more than a quarter, was employed in computer sciences and programming occupations. The average salary of these graduates working full time was $25,400.

Psychology

Among psychology majors, 81 percent were employed one year after graduation, with 67 percent working full time and 15 percent part time; almost 6 percent were unemployed. As expected, psychology had a high rate of graduate school enrollment (28 percent) because a graduate degree is required for most jobs in this field.

Psychology Majors One Year After Graduation

Profession	Percent
Teaching	3
Mechanic, operator, and laborer	3
Protective services	4
Service	6
Sales	10
Other professions	21
Business and management	26
Administrative and clerical support	27

A fairly low 57 percent said that their jobs were related to psychology; 45 percent said a four-year degree was required for their job; and 53 percent said their jobs had career potential. The majority of workers were split between business and management (26 percent); other professions, including social work, clergy, and science (24 percent); and administrative and clerical support

occupations (22 percent). The others held service, teaching, health professional, sales, and noncomputer technician jobs. The average salary of psychology graduates working full time was $21,600, the second lowest of all fields studied.

Public Affairs and Social Services

The public affairs and social services field includes protective services, social work, and public administration. About 88 percent of graduates were employed one year after graduation, 75 percent full time and 13 percent part time. A relatively low proportion (under 5 percent) was unemployed. Fourteen percent of graduates were enrolled in continuing education one year after graduation.

Public Affairs and Social Services Majors One Year After Graduation

Profession	Percent
Mechanic, operator, and laborer	4
Sales	4
Service	5
Administrative and clerical support	15
Business and management	16
Protective services	22
Other professions	32

Seventy-two percent reported that their jobs were related to their major field; 49 percent reported that a four-year degree was required for their job; and 68 percent said their jobs had career potential. Graduates were fairly widely dispersed. The largest portion, 32 percent, had jobs in other professions, including public relations, radio and television announcing, and social work; the second largest, 22 percent, had jobs in protective services; and the third largest, 16 percent, had jobs in business and management. Public affairs and social services graduates working full time averaged $22,000 a year.

Social Sciences

The social sciences field includes anthropology, archaeology, economics, geography, sociology, political science, and international relations. About 86 percent of graduates were employed one year after graduation, 73 percent full time and 13 percent part time; 5 percent were unemployed. About 19 percent were enrolled in continuing education one year after graduation.

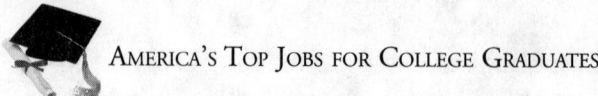
Social Sciences Majors One Year After Graduation

Profession	Percent
Teaching	3
Mechanic, operator, and laborer	3
Protective services	4
Service	6
Sales	10
Other professions	21
Business and management	26
Administrative and clerical support	27

Fifty-seven percent of social science graduates reported that their jobs were related to their major field; 47 percent said that a four-year degree was required for their job; and 68 percent said their jobs had career potential. The majority of graduates held jobs in administrative and support (27 percent) and business and management occupations (26 percent). The average salary of social science majors working full time was $22,100 a year.

THE JOB MARKET FOR PH.D.'S

Introduction. This article is also based on older data, but I included it because of its value to those with or considering advanced degrees. Overall, it points out that, despite difficulties, those with advanced degrees have much higher than average earnings and lower unemployment rates than those with less education. It's a complex picture, and this article does a good job of providing a balanced view.

By Megan Barkume

Will the rigors of years of formal education required to obtain a Doctor of Philosophy (Ph.D.) degree pay off? The prospect of an additional 6 to 10 years of schooling after completing a bachelor's degree is daunting. Still, many people make this long-term commitment.

Ph.D.'s comprise a small part of the workforce. In 1995, about 1.4 million workers—roughly 1 percent of the workforce—held a Ph.D. degree. (See table 1.) Ph.D.'s were older than the labor force as a whole, with a median age of 47 in 1995, compared to 39 for all workers age 20 and over. They were also disproportionately white and male. These workers earned a median salary more than double that for all workers age 20 and over and about 20 percent more than workers with only a bachelor's degree. (See table 2.) Ph.D.'s tended to work longer hours than most workers and also were more likely to hold more than one job. About 8 out of 10 Ph.D. holders worked in professional specialty occupations. Most of the remainder held managerial jobs. (See table 3.)

Historically, Ph.D. programs were designed to prepare teachers and researchers by providing a thorough knowledge of a subject and the skills to conduct research. Colleges and universities have been and still are the primary employers of Ph.D.'s, although nonacademic job opportunities have been growing, particularly for scientists and engineers.

TABLE 1
Profile of Ph.D.'s in the workforce, 1995

	Ph.D.'s		Total employment, age 20 and over	
	Number (thousands)	Percent	Number (thousands)	Percent
Total employment, age 20 and over	1,400	100.0	118,600	100.0
Age				
20-24	3	0.2	12,450	10.5
25-34	187	13.4	32,360	27.3
35-44	436	31.1	34,197	28.8
45-54	462	33.0	24,390	20.6
55-64	230	16.4	11,454	9.7
65-74	70	5.0	3,101	2.6
75-90	13	.9	610	.5
Sex				
Males	1,033	73.6	64,107	54.1
Females	370	26.4	54,456	45.9
Race				
White	1,243	88.7	100,964	85.2
Black	63	4.5	12,710	10.7
Other	48	3.5	4,889	4.1
Class of worker				
Total	1,216	86.7	108,067	91.1
Private	661	47.2	85,821	72.4
Government	455	32.4	18,088	15.3
Self-employed, incorporated	100	7.1	10,365	8.7
Self-employed, unincorporated	186	13.3	10,365	8.7
Without pay	(1)	(2)	131	.1
Number of hours usually worked at main job				
Less than 35	126	9.0	17,354	14.6
35-39	57	4.1	7,296	6.2
40	424	30.2	57,891	48.8
41-49	127	9.1	8,917	7.5
50-59	313	22.3	10,943	9.2
60-69	173	12.3	4,881	4.1
70-99	68	4.9	2,062	1.7
Held more than one job	141	10.1	7,918	6.7

[1] Less than 1.
[2] Less than 0.1.
SOURCE: Current Population Survey, 1995.
NOTE: These data may differ from other published data due to differences in estimating techniques.

TABLE 2
Median annual earnings for workers age 25 and over by education, 1995

Education	Earnings
All workers	**$26,500**
High school graduate	22,500
Associate's degree	27,900
Bachelor's degree	35,700
Master's degree	43,800
Professional degree	52,700
Ph.D. degree	53,200

SOURCE: Current Population Survey, 1995.

TABLE 3
Employment by occupation and industry, 1995

	Employment (thousands)	Percent
Primary occupation		
Executive, administrative, and managerial	224	16
Professional specialty occupations	1,087	77
Engineers	47	3
Mathematical and computer scientists	28	2
Natural scientists	111	8
Health occupations	238	17
Teachers, college and university	329	23
Teachers, except postsecondary	36	3
Other professional specialty	298	21
Technical, sales, and administrative support	60	4
All other occupations	63	4
Industry of main job		
Agriculture, forestry, and fishing; mining; and construction	25,866	2
Manufacturing	103,353	7
Transportation, communications, and public utilities	14,615	1
Wholesale and retail trade	38,237	3
Finance, insurance, and real estate	36,825	3
Business and repair services	26,621	2
Professional and related services	1,063,813	76
Health services	218,484	16
Legal services	104,561	8
Elementary and secondary schools	67,220	5
Colleges and universities	437,386	31
Religious organizations	36,424	3
Research, development, and testing services	56,739	4
Management and public relations services	28,572	2
Miscellaneous professional and related services	26,948	2
Public administration	80,329	6

SOURCE: Current Population Survey, 1995.

How Is the Job Market?

Anecdotal evidence suggests that the current job market for Ph.D.'s is highly competitive. Reports abound of colleges receiving hundreds of applications for each faculty opening, the proliferation of "gypsy" faculty who move from campus to campus holding down part-time jobs, and Ph.D.'s stuck in low-paying postdoctoral appointments with little hope for advancement. Dr. Kerry Grant, Dean of Faculty of Arts and Letters at the University of Buffalo, says, "For years I've told students and parents that the bad news is there are no jobs." But there are. The question is, are there enough?

Some believe that the number of Ph.D's granted is too large for the current job market to bear and that universities should scale down their Ph.D.-granting programs. John Van Alsten, a 36-year-old Ph.D. chemical engineer who works for DuPont, says, "The supply of Ph.D.'s continues to increase and the number of jobs continues to decrease. The problem as I see it is one of a lack of feedback to the universities. There is no incentive whatsoever for them to reduce enrollments; in fact, the only incentive is to increase enrollments. More students provide more research, which brings in more money, which allows them to get more students." And according to Dr. Jack Schuster, a professor of education and public policy at the Claremont Graduate School in California currently working on a research project examining the academic labor market, "There is a widely shared view among doctoral degree-granting institutions that the job outlook is pretty bleak. But there hasn't been a proportionate cutback in Ph.D. programs. Many mechanisms are in place that make it important to sustain the level of graduate students."

Consider the case of one Ph.D. physicist who conducts research in biophysics. After working at the National Institutes of Health (NIH) for seven years, his position was not renewed because of federal government downsizing and a change in the research priorities of his particular program. After spending 14 months looking for jobs—applying for 200 positions and going on seven interviews—he received one offer as an assistant professor, a nontenure-track position at Vanderbilt University in the Department of Physics and Astronomy.

"Unemployment Blues, A Report from the Field" in the September 1994 issue of *Science* portrays a bleak job market for Ph.D.'s. Another *Science* article, in the October 1995 issue, "Is It Time to Begin Ph.D. Population Control?" reports a glut of Ph.D.'s in science and

engineering fields and questions if measures should be taken to restrict doctoral programs. And a controversial 1995 study by William Massey of Stanford University and Charles Goldman of the RAND Corporation predicts a glut of science and engineering Ph.D.'s over the long run, prompting the *New York Times* to state in July 1995, "The holder of a doctoral degree in science or engineering would probably make a better taxi driver or bank teller than someone without a Ph.D. But if a newly minted doctor of science is hoping for a permanent, full-time job in his or her specialty, there is a one in four chance of being disappointed."

Two Views of the Labor Market for Ph.D.'s

In contrast to the bleak picture painted by anecdotes, labor market data show that Ph.D.'s have very low rates of unemployment and part-time employment, and much higher-than-average earnings. Thus, two views of the labor market emerge. On the one hand, anecdotal evidence points to extremely adverse job market conditions, with many Ph.D.'s reporting limited openings and keen competition for jobs. On the other hand, labor market indicators point to favorable employment conditions for Ph.D.'s. Younger Ph.D.'s, with higher unemployment rates and lower earnings than older Ph.D.'s, appear to face less favorable conditions. But this is true for younger workers at every level of educational attainment. Although many Ph.D.'s may have trouble finding employment in their field, data show that the vast majority of them find full-time, high-paying jobs and fare better than most other workers.

A Pessimistic View—Too Many Ph.D.'s?

Ask Ph.D.'s today the most difficult obstacle in obtaining full-time employment, especially in academe, and most will note competition for jobs. Increased competition results from an imbalance in supply and demand for a particular kind of work. Evidence of an oversupply includes recent trends for postdoctoral appointments. However, trends vary widely by field.

Growth in the supply of *Ph.D.'s.* The supply of Ph.D.'s includes both American citizens and foreigners who either studied here or earned their degrees abroad.

National Center for Education Statistics (NCES) data show that the number of Ph.D.'s granted each year has grown rapidly, more than tripling over the 1964–94 period to reach a high of 42,100. (See chart 1.) Women accounted for dramatic growth among Ph.D.'s between 1974 and 1994. The number of Ph.D.'s earned by women grew 150 percent, while men earned 2 percent fewer Ph.D.'s. However, NCES projects that the number of Ph.D. degrees awarded will plateau over the 1994–95 to 2004–05 period, rising only slightly to 43,100.

Chart 1
Ph.D.'s conferred by institutions of higher education, 1964-2005

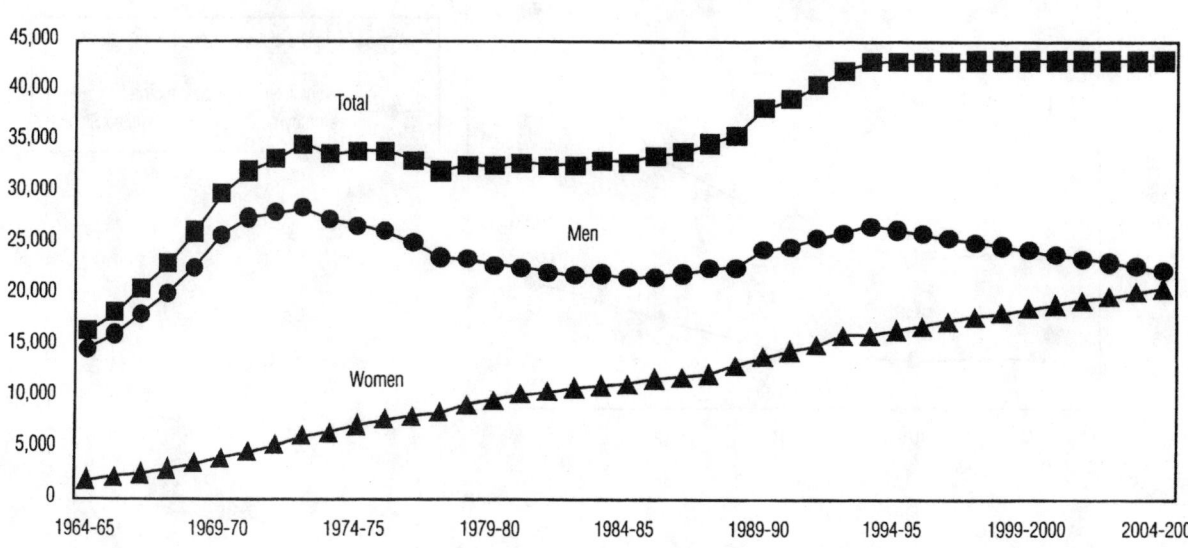

The growing number of non-U.S. citizens earning Ph.D.'s at American universities is another concern. According to the National Research Council (NRC), foreign students accounted for the largest growth among Ph.D.'s over the 1974-94 period, increasing by 153 percent. (See chart 2.) The proportion of Ph.D.'s granted to foreign-born individuals has been rising steadily, from 14 percent in 1964 to 33 percent in 1994. Foreign students are concentrated heavily in science and engineering, earning 61 percent of all Ph.D.'s in engineering and 46 percent of all physical science Ph.D.'s in 1994. And their representation in these fields, compared to American students, continues to grow. China accounts for the largest number of foreign students, followed by Taiwan, Korea, and India.

Although many foreign students return to their native country after earning their degree, most stay to work in the United States, competing with American Ph.D.'s for available jobs. Sixty-two percent, or almost 4,200, of non-U.S. citizens who earned Ph.D.'s in 1994 had postgraduation commitments in the United States.

In addition, immigration legislation grants entry to even more foreign Ph.D. holders. The U.S. Immigration Act of 1990 permits up to an additional 80,000 highly skilled foreign workers entry into the United States yearly, including outstanding professors and researchers. Although the effect of this relatively new legislation is still uncertain, it is likely to increase the supply of foreign Ph.D.'s in the U.S. labor market. In 1992, according to the Department of Justice, about 28,000 outstanding professors and researchers and members of professions with advanced degrees immigrated to the United States under the provisions of this act, a very large number compared to the number of Ph.D.'s awarded that year.

Growing number of postdoctoral appointments. As the supply of Ph.D.'s has grown, more Ph.D.'s are accepting low-paying postdoctoral appointments after graduation, which allow them to continue study or research under a mentor. In 1974, only 15 percent planned postdoctoral study; in 1994, 29 percent did. (See table 4.)

TABLE 4
Ph.D.'s with Postgraduation Employment Commitments by Field, Selected Years, 1974–1994
percent

	1974	1979	1984	1989	1994
All fields	85	80	78	74	71
Physical sciences	64	63	60	53	49
Engineering	90	88	85	80	76
Life sciences	58	46	43	41	36
Social sciences	92	88	87	84	80
Humanities	97	94	96	94	93
Education	98	97	98	97	96
Professional and others	98	97	98	97	96

Chart 2
Ph.D.'s awarded noncitizens and their postdoctoral employment plans, selected years, 1974-1994

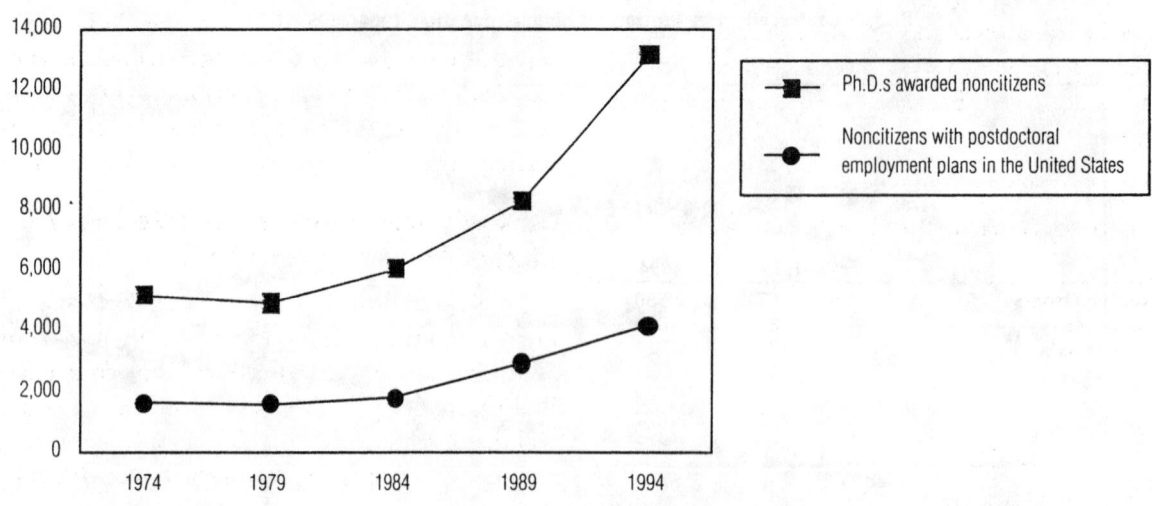

While postdoctoral appointments are becoming more common among humanities, education, and other nonscience graduates, these appointments remain the domain of science and engineering Ph.D.'s. In 1994, 64 percent of life science Ph.D.'s took postdoctoral appointments after graduation, compared to 4 percent of education Ph.D.'s.

The rise in the number of Ph.D.'s obtaining postdoctoral appointments may signal an excess of Ph.D.'s in the job market. Some Ph.D.'s are reported to be taking as many as three or four back-to-back postdoctoral positions because they are finding it difficult to obtain full-time jobs after earning their degree.

Trends in the supply of Ph.D.'s by field. Evidence indicates that enrollment in Ph.D. programs has responded to changing demand in the job market. Fields that have grown rapidly include computer sciences, health sciences, engineering, business and management, and biological sciences. The annual number of doctoral degrees awarded from 1974 to 1994 nearly tripled in health sciences. Both the health and computer science fields gained popularity largely because of the job opportunities they offer outside academe. Humanities—including history, English language and literature, and foreign language and literature—education, mathematics, and some social science fields—such as political science, international relations, and sociology—all lost doctoral students between 1974 and 1994. During this period, the number of doctoral degrees conferred in the humanities and education each dropped 8 percent.

As shown in table 5, the distribution of Ph.D. recipients by major field changed between 1974 and 1994. Representation in physical sciences, engineering, and life sciences increased over the 1974–94 period, while the number of recipients in social sciences, humanities, and education decreased. Earnings were higher in the fields that grew.

TABLE 5
Ph.D. Recipients by Field of Study, 1974 and 1994

	1974	1994
Professional/Others	1,667	2,580
Social sciences	5,882	6,624
Physical sciences	4,976	6,821
Life sciences	4,964	7,734
Humanities	5,170	4,743
Engineering	3,147	5,826
Education	7,241	6,683

The general belief is that Ph.D.'s in the humanities have faced tight job market conditions and intense competition for available jobs for some time, while science and engineering Ph.D.'s have fared better because of at-

tractive job opportunities in government and private industry. The trends regarding the number of degrees granted would tend to confirm this belief. But data also show that 93 percent of recent humanities Ph.D. recipients had definite employment plans after graduation in 1994, compared to only 36 percent of life sciences and 49 percent of physical sciences. (See table 6.)

TABLE 6
Ph.D.'s with Postgraduation Study Commitments by Field, Selected Years, 1974–1994
(percent)

	1974	1979	1984	1989	1994
Professional and others	2	3	2	3	4
Education	2	3	2	3	4
Humanities	3	6	5	6	7
Social sciences	8	12	14	16	20
Life sciences	42	54	57	59	64
Engineering	10	12	15	20	24
Physical science	37	37	41	48	52
All fields	15	20	22	26	29

In recent years, the lack of federal and state government funding for research at universities has restricted the growth of jobs for science and engineering Ph.D.'s. Also, the end of the cold war and the slowdown of the defense industry have restricted job creation in government and private industry. Agencies like NIH, the Department of Energy, and the Department of Agriculture depend heavily on federally funded research and development to hire workers. When this funding is reduced, their capacity for hiring declines accordingly.

Another difficulty facing scientists is the narrowness of specialties within a field. The marketability of these specialized areas changes fairly quickly in response to changes in funding for research. After devoting years to one specific area of study, many new Ph.D. graduates find that their specialty is no longer in demand and that research funding and job opportunities in their area of concentration have declined dramatically or disappeared, forcing them to find employment in other areas.

An Optimistic View—Favorable Labor Market Indicators for Ph.D.'s

Despite growth in the supply of Ph.D.'s, employment statistics show that workers with this level of formal education are faring well. One could conclude that Ph.D.'s are being easily absorbed into the job market and that, even if some Ph.D.'s cannot secure what they consider to be suitable jobs in their specialty, the vast majority are landing full-time, high-paying jobs. Unemployment rates, part-time employment rates, and average earnings all point to this conclusion.

TABLE 7
Work Status of Ph.D.'s by Field, 1993

Field of doctorate	Total Ph.D. labor force	Full-time employed (percent)	Part-time employed (percent)	Postdoctoral appointment (percent)	Unemployed and seeking work (percent)
TOTAL	**565,090**	**89**	**7**	**3**	**1.6**
Sciences	394,060	88	7	4	1.6
Computer and mathematical sciences	28,260	94	4	1	1.1
Computer and information sciences	5,190	96	2	2	1.0
Mathematical sciences	23,070	94	4	1	1.2
Life and related sciences	126,450	85	5	8	1.5
Agricultural and food sciences	15,390	87	6	5	1.9
Biological and health sciences	107,180	85	5	9	1.4
Environmental sciences	3,850	96	4	—	—
Physical and related sciences	100,650	88	5	5	2.1
Chemistry, except biochemistry	52,710	89	5	4	1.8
Geology and oceanography	12,880	87	6	4	3.0
Physics and astronomy	33,930	87	5	6	2.3
Other physical sciences (including earth science)	1,120	88	—	12	—
Social and related sciences	138,680	88	10	1	1.4
Economics	19,690	92	6	<1	1.4
Political and related sciences	14,580	93	5	<1	2.0
Psychology	71,950	85	13	1	1.3
Sociology and anthropology	20,110	90	8	1	1.6
Other social sciences	12,350	92	6	—	1.5
Engineering	76,430	92	4	2	1.7
Aerospace and aeronautical	3,120	91	5	2	2.2
Chemical	11,340	93	4	1	1.8
Civil	7,060	96	4	1	—
Electrical and computer	19,780	93	4	1	1.9
Industrial	1,960	93	3	—	3.0
Mechanical	9,570	92	4	3	1.0
Other engineering	23,580	91	4	3	2.0
Humanities	94,600	89	10	—	1.7
Art history	3,000	82	14	—	4.2
Classics	2,000	87	12	—	1.5
English and American language and literature	23,700	88	11	—	1.5
History	20,100	90	8	—	2.1
Modern language and literature	15,300	89	9	—	1.3
Music	8,700	87	11	—	1.6
Philosophy	7,200	89	9	—	1.9
Other humanities	14,700	88	10	—	1.3

Dashes indicate data are not available.
SOURCE: National Research Council, *Survey of Doctorate Recipients.*

Unemployment rates. NRC data indicate that 1.7 percent of all humanities doctorates in the labor force were unemployed and looking for work in 1993, nearly identical to the 1.7 percent rate for Ph.D. engineers and the 1.6 percent rate for doctoral scientists. (See table 7.) This was substantially lower than the unemployment rate of 6.8 percent for the entire labor force, and 3 percent for professional and managerial workers in 1993. Art history had the highest unemployment rate of any field, 4.2 percent, while computer and information sciences and mechanical engineering had the lowest rates at 1 percent.

As shown in table 8, Ph.D.'s who graduated between 1988 and 1992 enjoyed slightly less favorable labor market conditions than Ph.D.'s overall. Except for engineering and life sciences Ph.D.'s, these graduates were more likely to be unemployed or to be employed in a postdoctoral position than were their predecessors. However, the unemployment rate of humanities Ph.D.'s who graduated between 1988 and 1992 was only 3.3 percent in 1993, almost identical to the 3.2 percent rate experienced by workers with four or more years of postsecondary education and less than half the 6.8 percent rate for all workers combined.

Table 8
Labor Market Status of Recent Ph.D.'s, 1998–92
(percent)

	Involuntarily out-of-field	Unemploy-ment rate	Postdoctoral position
Science and engineering	3.6	1.7	15.5
Computer and mathematical sciences	3.4	1.2	3.5
Engineering	3.4	1.5	6.1
Life sciences	2.3	1.2	31.6
Physical sciences	5.0	2.6	24.6
Social sciences	4.2	2.0	2.5
Humanities	14.2	3.3	.5

SOURCE: National Research Council, *Survey of Doctorate Recipients.*

Part-time employment rate. Part-time employment can reflect a shortage of full-time jobs and indicate underemployment. However, Ph.D.'s in all fields had low part-time employment rates, ranging from 2 percent of computer and information science to 14 percent of art history Ph.D.'s. NRC data indicate that about 40,000 Ph.D.'s were working part time in 1993; of these, about 4,700 humanities Ph.D.'s and 7,700 science and engineering Ph.D.'s indicated that they were holding part-time positions because a suitable full-time job was not available.

Earnings. Salary data also point to a strong labor market for Ph.D.'s. In a tight job market, one would expect to find correspondingly low wages, since workers presumably would be willing to work for lower wages to secure a job. However, as already stated, the median annual earnings for workers with a Ph.D. degree were $53,200 in 1995, higher than earnings for workers at any other level of educational attainment.

Even earnings for Ph.D.'s in the lowest decile ($27,200) were higher than earnings for all workers combined ($26,500). Ph.D.'s in the lowest earnings decile were younger than all Ph.D.'s—with a median age of 41, compared to 47 for Ph.D.'s at all levels of earnings. Also, women made up a larger share of Ph.D.'s in the lowest earnings decile (40 percent) than of Ph.D.'s in all earnings categories (26 percent). But these tendencies— overrepresentation of women and younger workers in lower earnings categories—apply to workers at all levels of educational attainment.

Table 9
Salaries of Ph.D.'s by Field and Employer, 1993

Field	Total	Univer-sities and 4-year colleges	2-year colleges[1]	Other educa-tional institu-tions	Private for profit com-pany	Private not for profit com-pany	Federal Govern-ment	State and local govern-ment
Sciences	$56,500	$50,300	—	$45,800	$70,800	$56,700	$62,200	$48,600
Computer and mathematical sciences	57,800	51,100	—	46,500	75,400	75,900	65,500	—
Life and related sciences	55,000	50,200	—	40,700	68,700	56,700	58,700	49,300
Physical and related sciences	64,100	51,300	—	45,800	72,000	62,900	66,900	47,400
Social and related sciences	52,100	50,000	—	49,000	70,400	53,000	62,600	48,500
Engineering	69,000	61,200	—	36,500	72,800	75,400	70,600	48,200
Humanities	43,700	42,800	44,500	42,900	54,900	43,000	48,900	—

[1]Salaries for scientists and engineers working in 2-year colleges are included under "other educational institutions."
Dashes indicate data are not available.
SOURCE: National Research Council, *Survey of Doctorate Recipients.*

Data from an NRC salary survey reflect similarly high earnings for Ph.D.'s. (See table 9.) Median annual salaries for Ph.D.'s varied by field of doctorate, ranging from $43,700 for humanities Ph.D.'s to $69,000 for engineering Ph.D.'s in 1993.

Salary differentials among fields were more pronounced, reflecting varying opportunities available to workers. For example, faculty members in science, engineering, or business are often able to earn consulting fees from private businesses to supplement their income. Also, faculty in these fields may have opportunities for more lucrative summer employment. Salaries paid by private businesses, industry, and government were generally higher than those paid by educational institutions for most fields.

All these data indicate that Ph.D.'s are finding jobs with high earnings, even though some are not finding jobs in their chosen specialty.

Jobs for Ph.D.'s

The job market for Ph.D.'s is relatively simple and can be divided into two parts: academia and the rest of the economy. Although academe remains the primary employer of Ph.D.'s, the proportion of new Ph.D.'s who obtained academic appointments after graduation declined from 62 percent in 1974 to 52 percent in 1994

Employment Opportunities for Ph.D. Faculty

The expansion of college enrollments in the 1960s increased the demand for new faculty. However, when growth in enrollments began to slow around 1970, colleges and universities greatly reduced their hiring. Consequently, doctoral degree holders in many fields have faced greater competition for available permanent academic jobs since that time.

Current job market for college faculty. Graduates from doctoral programs currently face stiff competition for faculty positions. Budgetary constraints experienced by the nation's institutions of higher education have contributed to a weak academic job market. Although the federal government's share of funding for colleges and universities has held stable since the early 1980s, state support has declined, forcing many institutions to raise tuition and increasingly rely on private funding. The federal government provided about 13 percent of funding for higher education in 1981–82; in 1992–93, that share dropped slightly to 12 percent. Dr. Schuster

notes, "More than cutbacks so far, it's the contemplation of additional cutbacks that has an implication in hiring. The bad news for federal cutbacks is yet to come. The effect right now is psychological." State funding accounted for 30 percent of revenue for higher education in 1981–82; in 1992–93, states were providing 24 percent of that funding. In an effort to cut costs, many colleges and universities have adopted various measures, such as increasing class sizes, cutting low priority programs, and relying more heavily on part-time faculty.

Decreases in research and development and defense budgets have also had an adverse effect on hiring. Along with lower levels of funding, the federal government has become more stringent in controlling costs. In the past, the government allocated block grants to an institution; now, however, institutions are required to clearly justify all expenses.

Like other institutions, the University of Buffalo has been feeling the impact of funding cutbacks for the last several years. Dr. Grant has observed intense competition among departments at his school for available dollars. Funding is being withdrawn, often with little or no planning. He says, "There is no dialog going on between the policy makers and the people being affected by them."

Financial realities are forcing changes in faculty characteristics. There has been erosion of tenure-track positions, and more part-time faculty have been hired to conserve money. "Programs are driven very heavily by pragmatic constraints and much less by innovative teaching and good knowledge," says Dr. Grant. The need to cut costs is leading to the development of a two-tiered faculty, comprising higher paid, full-time, tenured faculty and adjunct faculty, including postgraduates and lecturers with heavy teaching loads, who are paid less.

While reliance on part-time and adjunct faculty is growing, Ph.D.-level faculty remain relatively unaffected. Although NCES data show that the proportion of part-time faculty employed by institutions of higher education increased from 22 percent of all faculty in 1970 to 65 percent in 1991, Current Population Survey data indicate that only 8 percent of Ph.D. level faculty were employed part-time in 1995. Public two-year colleges are the largest employers of part-time faculty, with over half of their teaching staff on part-time contracts. (See table 10.) Two-year colleges also employ far fewer Ph.D. faculty than four-year colleges. At institutions that depend heavily on Ph.D. faculty, such as public and private four-year colleges and universities, employment of part-time faculty is significantly lower.

TABLE 10
Work Status of Faculty by Type of Institution, Fall 1992

	Total	Full time (percent)	Part time (percent)
Public 4-year colleges and universities	320,800	81	19
Public research	124,600	87	13
Public doctoral	67,500	81	19
Public comprehensive	128,700	75	25
Private 4-year colleges and universities	201,000	66	34
Private research	43,300	75	25
Private doctoral	37,100	68	32
Private comprehensive	61,900	59	41
Private liberal arts	58,700	67	33
Public 2-year colleges	230,300	48	52
Other	37,300	65	35

SOURCE: National Center for Education Statistics, *National Study of Postsecondary Faculty.*

It is very rare for part-time positions to offer the possibility of tenure. Although the proportion of full-time faculty who are tenured has barely changed—from 65 percent in 1980 to 64 percent in 1993, according to NCES—growing use of part-time workers is causing some erosion in tenure opportunities, especially for faculty without Ph.D.'s. As more faculty retire, universities are choosing to fill some of these openings with part-time teachers rather than preserving full-time tenure-track positions.

Job outlook for college faculty. Employment forecasts for college faculty must take into account several factors that influence the academic labor market. These factors include college enrollments, faculty retirements, nonacademic employment opportunities, and differences in supply and demand by field. Labor market analysis is complicated by the difficulty of predicting policy changes and their effect on government funding for higher education. However, the supply of Ph.D.'s cannot react quickly to changes in demand due to the length of time required to complete the formal education.

When all these factors are considered, there is reason to believe that the number of job openings for college faculty will increase over the next decade. Two conditions in particular support this conclusion: The projected increase in college enrollments and the expected retirement of many faculty who began their careers in the 1960s or earlier. Also, the projected leveling off of Ph.D.'s awarded over the next 10 to 15 years can only improve job market conditions.

Rising college enrollments are expected to increase demand for college faculty and contribute to job growth. Enrollments rose in the mid-1980s through the early 1990s despite a decline in the traditional college-age population of 18- to 24-year-olds. This resulted from a higher proportion of 18- to 24-year-olds attending college, along with a growing number of part-time, female, and older students. Growth in enrollments should begin to increase after 1996 as the traditional college-age population begins to grow. This will be spurred by the leading edge of the echo generation, the children of the baby boomers, who will be reaching college age. NCES projects that college enrollments will rise from 14.8 million in 1993 to 16.1 million by the year 2005, an increase of 9 percent. Largely because of this growth in enrollment, BLS projects that employment of college faculty will increase by 18 percent between 1994 and 2005, from 823,000 to 972,000, or about 14,000 annually.

BLS data indicate that the annual net replacement rate for college faculty over the 1994–2005 period is 2.7 percent, compared to an average of 2.1 percent for all occupations. The higher rate implies that replacement needs may be a more significant source of job openings for college faculty than for most occupations between 1994 and 2005. BLS estimates that approximately 22,000 positions a year will open up due to net replacement needs over this period, significantly more than the 14,000 positions a year resulting from projected employment growth in the occupation.

Expected replacement needs stem from the large number of faculty hired in the 1960s, most of whom hold full-time, tenured positions, and who will be reaching retirement age in the next 10 to 15 years. The median age of college faculty with a doctorate was 48 in 1995, compared to 42 for faculty with a master's degree and only 38 for all occupations at all education levels. Since the age distribution for college faculty with Ph.D.'s is, as expected, higher than that for faculty with less training, replacement needs are more significant for Ph.D. faculty. While Ph.D.'s made up 39 percent of all college and university faculty in 1995, they represented a disproportionate 52 percent of college faculty in the 55-and-older age group. Thus, retirement among this group over the projection period will leave a greater proportion of Ph.D. faculty positions vacant than faculty positions held by workers with less education.

Although retirement will create openings, there is no guarantee they will be filled by Ph.D.'s in the future. Institutions may choose not to fill these positions or may opt to hire less costly, part-time faculty without a Ph.D., due to budgetary constraints. Thus, even though more openings may become available, it is uncertain how many will be filled as full-time tenured positions. Technological developments, such as satellite transmission of courses, could also reduce the need for faculty, though such developments are unlikely to have much impact in the next decade.

Although the number of openings will rise, competition will remain keen. The total number of openings, 36,000 per year, is far less than the 43,000 new Ph.D.'s that NCES expects to be awarded each year, even without considering the impact of immigration. Competition for jobs is likely to continue due to the expected large pool of available candidates.

Although competition is expected in general, job prospects in certain fields should continue to be favorable. Ph.D.'s in business, engineering, health, and computer science are expected to have favorable job prospects not only because they enjoy better job opportunities outside academe but also because more students are enrolling in these courses at the baccalaureate level.

Job Opportunities Outside Academe

Although doctoral programs have traditionally concentrated on preparing students for academic careers, it is increasingly common for Ph.D.'s to find employment outside university settings. In 1993, less than half of doctoral scientists and engineers worked in educational institutions. (See table 11.) The federal government depends on Ph.D.'s for scientific and engineering research, although demand has been dampened recently by defense cutbacks. And private industry hires large numbers of Ph.D.'s for industrial research and development. The number of recent doctorate recipients accepting postgraduation positions in academe and government dropped over the 1974–94 period, while the number with commitments to work in industry, self-employment, and other areas, such as elementary and secondary schools and nonprofit organizations, increased.

Nonacademic work does offer some benefits; the pay is usually higher in industry than in colleges and universities. Private companies often search for employees with a fairly broad knowledge of a subject area, or areas, that can be applied to a variety of projects. They are interested in workers who can complete projects quickly and develop alternative approaches to a problem. Management and interpersonal skills are highly valued in private industry. Thus, private industry interests are somewhat at odds with training for the traditional

TABLE 11
Employed Ph.D.'s by Sector of Employment, 1993

	Scientists and engineers	Humanities
Total	462,900	93,000
Percent:		
Educational institutions	48	79
2-year college	1	5
4-year college/university	34	67
Research institute	12	3
Elementary/secondary school	1	4
Private for profit company	31	7
Self-employed	6	5
Private not for profit organization	5	6
Government	10	4

SOURCE: National Research Council, *Survey of Doctorate Recipients*.

research Ph.D., which seeks to develop highly specialized knowledge in a defined concentration.

BLS identifies a few science occupations outside education for which a Ph.D. is the main source of training: Biological scientists, medical scientists, physicists and astronomers, and mathematicians. Except for physicists and astronomers, all these occupations are expected to grow over the 1994–2005 period.

For More Information

"Is There Another Degree in Your Future? Choosing Among Professional and Graduate Schools," by Neale Baxter in the Winter 1993–94 issue of the *Occupational Outlook Quarterly*, offers advice to those considering earning a Ph.D. For more information about the specific duties of college faculty, mathematicians, physicists and astronomers, medical scientists, and biological scientists, consult the 1996–97 *Occupational Outlook Handbook*.

Professional societies generally provide information on academic and nonacademic employment opportunities in their fields. Also, special publications on higher education, such as *The Chronicle of Higher Education*, available in libraries, list specific employment opportunities for faculty. Academic Advising Resources on the Internet has sections on graduate schools and jobs in higher education, with links to job announcements from numerous sources. Its Internet address is http://volvo.gslis.utexas.edu:80/~acadres/grad.html.

OCCUPATIONS AND EARNINGS OF WORKERS WITH SOME COLLEGE BUT NO DEGREE

> **Introduction.** I included this last article for those of you who do not yet have but who are considering a four-year college degree. It shows that many occupations have people working in them with various levels of education—and that these people tend to have different earnings. You will also see that many college graduates work in jobs that are also held by those without four-year degrees. Some of these jobs pay above average. Very interesting.

By Daniel Hecker

Workers who have some college education but do not have a degree are more likely than high school graduates but less likely than college graduates to be employed in occupations that usually require a college degree. And they earn more than high school graduates but less than college graduates.

Information about the job market for college graduates is abundant. But little attention is given to another group of workers of nearly equal size—those who have some college education but no degree. A comparison of this group's occupational employment patterns and earnings data with those of workers with a high school diploma and workers with a college degree reveals what you might expect: Some college is better than none, and more is better than less.

In 1996, 17.2 million full-time workers reported having some college but no degree, compared with 17.7 million workers holding a bachelor's degree. These two groups, along with 29.1 million workers with a high school diploma and another 7.8 million workers with an associate's degree, accounted for about 81 percent of all full-time workers aged 22 to 64.

This article examines the occupational employment patterns and earnings data for workers with some college but no degree compared to workers who have a high school diploma and those who have associate and bachelor's degrees. (Information on workers who do not have a high school diploma or who hold advanced degrees—master's, doctoral, and first professional—is not presented here.) The first section explains how the data were developed and defines the groups analyzed. The next section compares occupational patterns and earnings.

Data and Definitions

All data in this article are from the 1996 Current Population Survey (CPS) and are for full-time workers aged 22 to 64. The CPS groups workers by level of education and occupation. The Bureau of Labor Statistics (BLS) analyzes the data further, classifying occupations by the level of education and training usually required for entry into each one. Because occupational patterns and median earnings are different between men and women, data are presented by gender.

CPS Education and Training Categories

The CPS places workers in categories based on their highest level of educational attainment. This article presents data on workers in the following four categories.

Some college, but no degree. Workers with some college but no degree include those who were or still are enrolled in, but have not completed, a bachelor's or associate degree program. This group also includes workers who took or are taking college courses but were never enrolled as degree candidates, as well as workers who have received a certificate of completion for a college program requiring less than the equivalent of two years of full-time study. Individuals in this category can have any number of years of college.

High school graduates. This group includes workers who do not have any academic training beyond high school but may have some posthigh school noncollegiate training received in vocational, trade, correspondence, or Armed Forces schools; in apprenticeships; or in formal employer-sponsored training programs.

Associate degree holders. Workers with an associate degree have completed a college program requiring the equivalent of at least two years of full-time study after high school.

Bachelor's degree holders. These workers have completed a college program requiring the equivalent of at least four or five years of full-time academic study after high school.

Occupational and Training Categories

The CPS places workers in more than 400 detailed occupations. These occupations are combined to form occupational groups. This article presents data by education level and median weekly earnings for the largest detailed occupations and for occupation groups.

In addition, BLS places each detailed occupation in 1 of 11 categories, condensed here into 6, by the level of education and training usually required for entry. These categories range from occupations that require no more than four weeks of on-the-job experience to occupations that usually require a doctoral degree.

Occupations that usually require one year or less of on-the job training. This group includes occupations usually requiring 1 to 12 months of combined on-the-job experience and informal training. Occupations requiring short-term training of a few days to a few weeks are also in this group.

Occupations that usually require long-term on-the-job training. Occupations in this group require more than 12 months of on-the-job training or combined work experience and formal classroom instruction. This category includes craft occupations requiring formal or informal apprenticeships lasting up to four years, as well as those jobs where employers provide formal schooling, such as in police and fire academies or in air traffic control or flight attendant school.

Occupations that usually require skills developed through work experience in a related occupation. Occupations in this category require skills and experience gained in other jobs or developed from hobbies, nonwork activities, or service in the Armed Forces. Examples include supervisors, administrative support occupations; police detectives and investigators; and precision assemblers.

Occupations that usually require completion of vocational training provided in postsecondary vocational schools. This category includes occupations requiring completion of a structured program. Some programs take less than a year to complete and lead to a certificate or diploma. Others last longer than one year but less than four. Occupations in this category include automotive mechanics, licensed practical nurses, and welders and cutters.

Occupations that usually require an associate degree, as described above. Occupations in this category include engineering technologists and technicians, legal assistants, and registered nurses.

Occupations that usually require a bachelor's degree or more education. The largest group in this category includes occupations requiring a bachelor's degree, as defined above. The other groups are occupations usually requiring a bachelor's or higher degree plus work experience; a master's degree, which usually requires one or two years of full-time study beyond the bachelor's degree; a doctoral degree, which usually requires at least three years of full-time study beyond the bachelor's degree; and a first professional degree, which usually requires at least two years of full-time academic study beyond the bachelor's degree. Occupations in this category include teachers, engineers, and lawyers.

Note that according to this classification scheme, no occupations were identified in which the usual education or training was some college but no degree. Also, for most occupations, there is more than one way to qualify for a job. Therefore, some workers without a college degree are employed in occupations that usually require one.

Occupations and Earnings Analysis

Workers with some college but no degree have a better chance than workers with a high school diploma of getting jobs that usually require a college degree. However, workers with some college do not fare as well as college graduates in getting those same jobs.

Earnings follow a similar pattern: Overall, workers with some college earn more than high school graduates but less than college graduates.

TABLE 1
Percent of Employment, by Sex, Level of Education, and Occupational Education and Training Category, 1996

Level of Education	All Training Categories	On-the-job Training of Up to 1 Year	On-the-job Training of More Than 1 Year	Work Experience	Post-secondary Vocational Training	Associate Degree	Bachelor's Degree or More
Men, aged 22–64							
High school diploma	100	43	24	11	6	1	11
Some college, no degree	100	37	25	8	5	2	24
Associate degree	100	26	22	11	8	6	27
Bachelor's degree	100	16	7	11	3	2	62
Women, aged 22–64							
High school diploma	100	60	6	8	11	2	14
Some college, no degree	100	51	4	7	12	4	22
Associate degree	100	36	3	6	14	20	22
Bachelor's degree	100	21	3	6	5	9	57

Employment Patterns

A number of workers with some college were employed in occupational categories usually requiring college-level training. Twenty-four percent of men with some college were in occupations that required a bachelor's degree or more education, compared to only 11 percent of high school graduates. (See table 1.) Not surprisingly, so were 27 percent with an associate degree, and 62 percent with a bachelor's degree. For women with some college, 22 percent were in occupations requiring a bachelor's degree or more, compared to 14 percent of high school graduates, 22 percent with an associate degree, and 57 percent with a bachelor's degree.

In 1996, men with some college were most likely to be in the category of managers not elsewhere classified. (See table 2.) These managers held a variety of jobs in industries such as construction, manufacturing, computer services, and repair services.

Compared to men with only a high school diploma, those with some college were more likely to be managers not elsewhere classified, sales supervisors and proprietors, retail sales workers, and sales representatives. However, this group was less likely than the group with a high school diploma to be machine operators, except precision; truckdrivers; automotive mechanics; and carpenters. Compared to men with an associate degree, those with some college were more likely to be managers not elsewhere classified, sales supervisors and proprietors, and truckdrivers but less likely to be engineers, electricians, and electrical and electronic equipment repairers. Compared to men with a bachelor's degree, they were more likely to be machine operators, except precision; truckdrivers; and carpenters but less likely to be managers not elsewhere classified, sales representatives, and engineers.

Women with some college were more likely to be in a secretarial occupation than in any other. (See table 3.) Compared to female high school graduates, women with some college were more likely to be managers not elsewhere classified, accountants, licensed practical nurses, and secretaries but less likely to be in retail sales, cleaning and building service occupations, and assemblers.

Compared to female associate degree holders, women with some college were more likely to be managers not elsewhere classified, bookkeepers, retail sales workers, and nursing aides but less likely to be registered nurses. Compared to women with a bachelor's degree, they were also more likely to be secretaries or bookkeepers but less likely to be managers not elsewhere classified, accountants, registered nurses, and teachers.

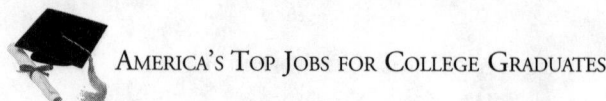

TABLE 2
Percent of Full-Time Employment, by Occupation and Level of Education, Men with Some College Age 22–64,1996

Occupation	Level of Education			
	High School Diploma or Equivalent	Some College, No Degree	Associate Degree	Bachelor's Degree
Managers and administrators, n.e.c.	5.5	9.0	8.0	13.7
Supervisors and proprietors, sales occupations	4.0	6.1	4.4	6.1
Machine operators and tenders, except precision	8.2	4.1	3.3	1.0
Truckdrivers	6.6	3.7	2.5	.7
Sales workers, retail and personal services	2.6	3.3	2.5	2.5
Sales representatives, mining, manufacturing and wholesale	1.2	2.3	1.8	3.8
Sales representatives, finance and business services	.9	2.2	2.2	5.4
Material recording, scheduling, and distribution clerks, n.e.c.	2.4	2.2	1.7	.8
Supervisors, production occupations	2.5	2.1	1.8	.9
Miscellaneous mechanics and repairers	2.0	1.9	2.0	.4
Engineers	.6	1.8	3.7	8.3
Managers, food serving and lodging establishments	1.0	1.7	1.3	1.3
Precision metal working occupations	2.2	1.7	2.0	.1
Janitors and cleaners	2.6	1.6	.9	.4
Carpenters	2.7	1.6	1.2	.4
Writers, artists, entertainers, and athletes	.5	1.5	1.9	2.9
Police and detectives, public service	.7	1.5	1.8	1.1
Electrical and electronic equipment repairers	1.1	1.5	2.4	.6
Electricians	1.7	1.5	2.5	.2
Supervisors, construction occupations	1.5	1.3	.9	.5
Laborers, except construction	2.4	1.3	.7	.3
Mathematical and computer scientists	.3	1.2	1.8	4.0
Engineering technologists and technicians	.6	1.2	3.1	.7
Automobile mechanics	2.0	1.2	2.0	.2
Plumbers, pipefitters, and steamfitters	1.3	1.1	1.1	.1
Assemblers	1.8	1.1	.9	.3
Cooks	1.3	1.0	.9	.3
Industrial machinery repairers	1.4	1.0	1.0	.1
Guards and police, except public service	.9	.9	.9	.4
Machinists	1.3	.9	1.0	-
Computer programmers	.2	.8	.9	1.5
Firefighting occupations	.3	.8	.7	.2
Farm operators and managers	1.3	.8	1.0	.7
Welders and cutters	1.6	.8	.9	.1
Health technologists and technicians	.3	.7	1.4	.6
Sales occupations, other business services	.3	.7	.6	1.2
Mail carriers, postal service	.5	.7	.5	.2
Traffic, shipping, and receiving clerks	1.1	.7	.5	.2
Production inspectors, checkers, and examiners	.6	.7	.4	.2
Construction laborers	1.4	.7	.3	.2
Managers, marketing, advertising, and public relations	.2	.6	.8	1.8
Social, recreation, and religious workers	.2	.6	.5	1.6
Insurance sales occupations	.3	.6	.5	1.5
Correctional institution officers	.5	.6	.6	.1
Groundskeepers and gardeners, except farm	1.1	.6	.3	.3
Bus, truck, and stationary engine mechanics	.9	.6	.8	-
Heating, air conditioning, and refrigeration mechanics	.7	.6	1.0	.1
Industrial truck and tractor equipment operators	1.3	.6	.3	.1
Drafting occupations	.2	.5	1.1	.2
Real estate sales occupations	.2	.5	.5	1.0
Computer operators	.2	.5	.5	.2
Investigators and adjusters, except insurance	.2	.5	.6	.6
Nursing aides, orderlies, and attendants	.4	.5	.4	.1
Supervisors, mechanics and repairers	.5	.5	.7	.1
Painters, construction and maintenance	.8	.5	.3	.2
Power plant, water and other system operators	.7	.5	.5	.2
Busdrivers	.4	.5	.4	.1

n.e.c. = not elsewhere classified
- = Less than 50,000
SOURCE: Current Population Survey

TABLE 3

Percent of Full-Time Employment, by Occupation and Level of Education, Women with Some College Age 22–64, 1996

Occupation	Level of Education			
	High School Diploma or Equivalent	Some College, No Degree	Associate Degree	Bachelor's Degree
Secretaries	7.9	9.2	8.4	2.7
Managers and administrators, n.e.c.	3.5	5.3	4.1	6.4
Bookkeepers, accounting, and auditing clerks	3.4	4.0	2.9	1.3
Supervisors and proprietors, sales occupations	3.9	3.9	3.4	3.3
Sales workers, retail and personal services	5.5	3.6	2.4	1.9
Nursing aides, orderlies, and attendants	3.9	3.3	1.8	.4
Health technologists and technicians	1.5	3.1	6.7	1.9
Material recording, scheduling, and distribution clerks, n.e.c.	2.5	2.3	1.7	.8
Receptionists	1.9	2.2	1.5	.5
Investigators and adjusters, except insurance	1.8	2.2	1.5	1.2
Administrative support occupations, n.e.c	1.7	2.1	1.8	1.1
Accountants and auditors	.8	1.7	2.2	4.4
Data-entry keyers	1.5	1.6	1.3	.4
Typists	1.4	1.5	1.2	.5
General office clerks	1.5	1.5	1.0	.6
Supervisors, administrative support occupations	1.1	1.4	1.0	.8
Licensed practical nurses	.3	1.3	2.6	.2
Managers, medicine and health	.6	1.2	1.9	1.6
Managers, food serving and lodging establishments	1.7	1.2	.7	1.0
Registered nurses	.3	1.2	13.4	6.9
Other financial officers	.7	1.1	1.0	1.1
Management related occupations, n.e.c	.9	1.1	1.2	1.1
Health technologists and technicians, n.e.c.	.8	1.1	1.7	.3
Writers, artists, entertainers, and athletes	.7	1.1	1.4	3.7
Financial managers	.5	1.1	.5	1.4
Insurance adjusters, examiners, and investigators	.7	1.1	.7	.7
Teachers aides	1.0	1.1	.9	.5
Protective service occupations	.8	1.0	.6	.6
Mail and message distributing occupations	1.1	1.0	.5	.4
Social, recreation, and religious workers	.5	.9	1.0	2.8
Family child-care providers	1.1	.9	.7	.4
Officials and administrators, public administration	.6	.9	.6	.9
Mathematical and computer scientists	.3	.8	.9	2.2
Cleaning and building service occupations, except private household	2.8	.8	.6	.2
Sales representatives, mining, manufacturing, and wholesale	.6	.8	.7	1.5
Bank tellers	1.0	.7	.4	.2
Assemblers	2.1	.7	.5	.1
Teachers, prekindergarten and kindergarten	.5	.7	.9	1.8
Legal assistants	.4	.7	1.0	.6
Waiters and waitresses	1.1	.7	.4	.2
Hairdressers and cosmetologists	1.5	.7	1.2	.1
Personnel, training, and labor relations specialists	.4	.7	.5	1.2
Managers, marketing, advertising, and public administration	.2	.6	.5	1.2
Cooks	1.6	.5	.5	.1
Managers, service organizations, n.e.c.	.3	.5	.6	1.2
Clinical laboratory technologists and technicians	.3	.5	1.1	1.0

n.e.c. = not elsewhere classified

SOURCE: Current Population Survey

Earnings

Most workers with some college but no degree earned more than high school graduates and less than workers with an associate or bachelor's degree in 1996. (See table 4.) This financial return associated with attending college is often described in terms of a wage premium—that is, those with some college or a bachelor's degree command an earnings premium over high school graduates of the same age group and sex. The reduction of earnings from not completing a degree is defined as a wage discount.

TABLE 4
Median Weekly Earnings of Full-Time Workers, by Sex and Level of Education, 1996

	Men		Women	
	Median	**Premium or Discount[1]**	**Median**	**Premium or Discount[1]**
All levels	$584	.98	$435	.94
High school graduate or equivalent	504	1.13	361	1.14
Some college, no degree	571	1.00	411	1.00
Associate degree	612	.93	473[2]	.87[2]
Bachelor's degree	767	.74	592	.69

[1] This shows the earnings of workers with some college divided by the earnings of workers in each education group. For example, men with some college earned $1.13 for every $1 earned by high school graduates but earned 93 cents for every $1 earned by associate degree graduates.

[2] For women with associate degrees, except registered nurses, the median was $440 and the index was .93.

Median earnings of men with some college but no degree were 13 percent higher than those of men with just a high school diploma; women with some college earned 14 percent more than their high school counter-

parts did. Compared to associate degree holders, however, men with some college earned 7 percent less, and women with some college earned 13 percent less. The corresponding differences were greater at the bachelor's degree level: Men with some college earned 26 percent less than bachelor's degree holders, and women earned 31 percent less.

Premiums and discounts for those with some college exist for two reasons. First, workers with some college were more likely than high school graduates but less likely than college graduates to be in higher paid occupations. Second, within an occupation, workers with some college usually earned more than their high school graduate coworkers and less than those who had graduated from college.

Effect of differing occupational patterns. Employment data for occupational groups are divided into four categories, each consisting of groups with similar median earnings. The categories for men, ranked by level of earnings from highest to lowest, include:

- Executive, administrative, and managerial occupations; professional specialty occupations; technicians; nonretail sales occupations; and police and firefighters;

- Precision production, mechanics, and construction craft occupations;

- Machine operators, assemblers, and inspectors; transportation and material moving occupations; handlers, equipment cleaners, helpers, and laborers; and farming, forestry, and fishing occupations;

- Administrative support occupations, including clerical; retail sales; and service occupations, except police and firefighters.

Table 5 shows the employment distribution for men in these categories at each educational level.

TABLE 5
Employment Distribution and Median Weekly Earnings of Male Wage and Salary Workers Employed Full Time, by Educational Level and Occupational Group, 1996

	Bachelor's	Associate	Some College	High School Graduate
Executive, professional, technician, nonretail sales, and police and firefighters	78% of employment/ $849 weekly	46% of employment/ $690 weekly	40% of employment/ $673 weekly	20% of employment/ $629 weekly
Precision production, craft, and repair	5% of employment/ $675 weekly	25% of employment/ $653 weekly	22% of employment/ $624 weekly	29% of employment/ $578 weekly
Machine operators, transportation, handlers, and farming	5% of employment /$491 weekly	14% of employment/ $493 weekly	20% of employment/ $479 weekly	34% of employment/ $456 weekly
Administrative support, retail sales, and service, except police and firefighters	11% of employment/ $508 weekly	15% of employment/ $467 weekly	19% of employment/ $424 weekly	17% of employment/ $408 weekly

About 40 percent of men with some college were in the executive occupations group, which had earnings well above the median for all other occupations. In contrast, only 20 percent of men with a high school diploma were in this earnings group. Not surprisingly, so were 46 percent of men with an associate degree and 78 percent of those with a bachelor's degree. The machine operators group, which had median earnings well below that for all men, included only 20 percent of men with some college but 34 percent of high school graduates.

In the other two groups, patterns tended to lower earnings relative to those of men with high school diplomas, but the overall effect was minor. Men with some college were 2 percent more likely to be in the low-paid administrative support occupations. And men with some college were less likely than high school graduates to be in the precision production occupations category, which had median earnings that were somewhat above average.

The categories for women, also ranked by level of earnings, include:

♦ Executive, administrative, and managerial occupations; professional specialty occupations; technicians; and nonretail sales occupations;

♦ Administrative support occupations;

♦ Precision production, craft, and repair occupations; machine operators, assemblers, and inspectors; transportation and material moving occupations; handlers, equipment cleaners, helpers, and laborers; and farming, forestry, and fishing occupations;

♦ Retail sales and service occupations.

Table 6 shows the employment distribution for women in these categories at each educational level.

Thirty-seven percent of women with some college, but only 24 percent of high school graduates, were in the executive occupations category, having the highest median earnings. Also in this category were 52 percent of women with an associate degree, and 77 percent with a bachelor's degree. Only 24 percent of women with some college, but 41 percent of women with high school diplomas, were in the categories having the lowest median earnings, those that include retail sales and precision production occupations. These two groups also had 17 percent of those with an associate degree, and 8 percent with a bachelor's degree.

However, women with some college were more likely than high school graduates to be in below-average earnings category of administrative support occupations.

Occupational earnings and premiums within occupations. Within each occupation, as within occupational groups, workers with some college usually earned more than their high school graduate counterparts but less than those with an associate or a bachelor's degree. Tables 7 and 8 show earnings and earnings premiums or discounts for individual occupations.

Men with some college had higher earnings than those with only a high school diploma in 70 percent of occupations for which there were statistically reliable data; women with some college earned more in 73 percent of occupations as well. Additionally, men with some college earned less than men with an associate degree in 76 percent of the occupations, while women earned less in 71 percent of occupations in the same comparison.

In some occupations, the earnings of workers with some college were the same or lower than those of high school graduates. This is usually because a greater proportion of workers with some college was young, and young workers with little or no experience usually earn less. Data examining occupational patterns only for those

---

TABLE 6
Employment Distribution and Median Weekly Earnings of Female Wage and Salary Workers Employed Full Time, by Educational Level and Occupational Group, 1996

	Bachelor's	Associate	Some College	High School Graduate
Executive, professional, technician, and non retail sales	77% of employment/ $631 weekly	52% of employment/ $566 weekly	37% of employment/ $498 weekly	24% of employment/ $446 weekly
Administrative support	15% of employment/ $438 weekly	31% of employment/ $401 weekly	40% of employment/ $400 weekly	35% of employment/ $392 weekly
Precision production, craft & repair, operators, transportation, handlers, and farming	3% of employment $461 weekly	6% of employment/ $383 weekly	8% of employment/ $357 weekly	18% of employment/ $334 weekly
Retail sales and service	6% of employment/ $378 weekly	11% of employment/ $330 weekly	16% of employment/ $300 weekly	23% of employment/ $278 weekly

---

workers aged 35–64 show that, in almost all cases, workers with some college earned more than high school graduates.

Tables 7 and 8 also show the variation in earnings of workers with some college, depending on the occupation. Note that workers with some college employed in occupations such as nursing aides, and retail sales workers earned less than the median for all high school graduates. Meanwhile, workers with some college employed as engineers, managers, and administrators not elsewhere classified, and financial managers earned premiums of at least 50 percent over the median for high school graduates.

Conclusion

Data in this article show that education pays off for workers with some college but no degree. In 1996, these workers were more likely than high school graduates to be in college-level jobs and to earn substantially more than workers with a high school diploma. Nevertheless, those with some college but no degree were less likely to be in college-level jobs than were workers with an associate or bachelor's degree, and their overall median earnings were below those of their college graduate counterparts.

All differences in occupational patterns and earnings may not be attributable to level of education, however. People who complete just a few college courses may have different personal characteristics from people who do not, perhaps including level of maturity and ambition; verbal, mathematical, or mechanical abilities; or a preference for working with people, data, or things. These differences may affect their occupational choices and earnings. In addition, occupational patterns and earnings may reflect nonacademic training acquired on the job, through postsecondary vocational schools, in the military, or elsewhere. It is clear, however, that completion of some college course work increases one's chances of entering certain occupations and usually increases earnings within that occupation.

Table 7
Median Weekly Earnings of Full-Time Wage and Salary Workers, Men with Some College Compared to Men at Other Educational Levels, 1996

Occupation	Level of Education					Premium or Discount[1] for Workers with Some College, No Degree, Compared to...		
	All Levels	High School Graduate or Equivalents	Some College, No Degree	Associate Degree Recipient	Bachelor's Degree Recipient	High School Graduate	Associate Degree Recipient	Bachelor's Degree Recipient
Total employed	$584	$504	$571	$612	$767	1.13	.93	.74
Writers, artists, entertainers, and athletes	743	585	698	742	747	1.19	.94	.93
Cashiers	303	269	310	-	-	1.15	-	-
Construction laborers	409	414	474	-	-	1.14	-	-
Police and detectives, public service	688	612	695	657	748	1.14	1.06	.93
Managers, food serving and lodging establishments	539	480	542	581	636	1.13	.93	.85
Precision metalworking occupations	603	588	658	682	-	1.12	.96	-
Automotive mechanics	502	508	567	580	-	1.12	.98	-
Carpenters	502	513	569	-	612	1.11	-	.93
Supervisors, production occupations	653	623	685	824	806	1.10	.83	.85
Supervisors and proprietors, sales occupations	614	550	605	594	748	1.10	1.02	.81
Engineers	962	794	876	835	971	1.10	1.05	.90
Plumbers, pipefitters, and steamfitters	603	597	648	-	-	1.09	-	-
Busdrivers	477	480	521	-	-	1.09	-	-
Managers and administrators, n.e.c.	935	726	785	839	1,082	1.08	.94	.73
Electricians	638	619	671	697	-	1.08	.96	-
Guards and police, except public service	370	338	366	-	-	1.08	-	-
Machine operators and tenders, except precision	438	464	499	482	491	1.08	1.04	1.02
Supervisors, construction occupations	676	659	711	-	-	1.08	-	-
Truckdrivers	493	504	541	583	480	1.07	.93	1.13
Power plant, water, and other system operators	635	607	652	-	-	1.07	-	-
Farm occupations, except managerial	293	325	349	-	-	1.07	-	-
Health technologists and technicians	547	474	501	572	620	1.06	.88	.81
Material recording, scheduling, and distribution clerks, n.e.c.	464	463	484	472	527	1.05	1.03	.92
Firefighting occupations	665	632	658	-	-	1.04	-	-
Industrial truck and tractor equipment operators	425	460	478	-	-	1.04	-	-
Groundskeepers and gardeners, except farm	314	329	341	-	-	1.04	-	-
Bus, truck, and stationary engine mechanics	564	565	585	-	-	1.04	-	-
Cooks	300	307	315	309	-	1.03	1.02	-
Electrical and electronic equipment repairers	684	685	706	680	664	1.03	1.04	1.06
Janitors and cleaners	323	350	362	-	-	1.03	-	-
Production inspectors, checkers, and examiners	507	503	520	-	-	1.03	-	-
Assemblers	447	470	481	-	-	1.02	-	-
Farm operators and managers	469	465	475	-	625	1.02	-	.76
Mail carriers, postal service	684	676	690	-	-	1.02	-	-
Industrial machinery repairers	579	588	600	-	-	1.02	-	-
Welders and cutters	488	500	510	-	-	1.02	-	-
Nursing aides, orderlies, and attendants	348	349	353	-	-	1.01	-	-
Mathematical and computer scientists	936	818	819	831	941	1.00	.99	.87
Heating, air conditioning, and refrigeration mechanics	544	559	559	-	-	1.00	-	-
Sales representatives, mining, manufacturing and wholesale trade	728	619	611	697	841	.99	.88	.73
Administrative support occupations, including clerical	506	505	498	515	557	.99	.97	.89
Laborers, except construction	388	404	401	-	-	.99	-	-
Sales workers, retail and personal services	415	410	400	409	543	.98	.98	.74
Insurance, real estate and other services sales workers	732	606	559	639	835	.92	.87	.67
Engineering technologists and technicians	648	660	609	639	711	.92	.95	.86
Painters, construction and maintenance	421	482	430	-	-	.89	-	-
Correctional institution officers	568	612	499	-	-	.82	-	-

[1] This is the earnings of workers with some college divided by earnings in each education group. Thus, men in police and detective occupations with some college earned $1.14 for every $1 earned by high school graduates but 93 cents for every $1 earned by those with a bachelor's degree. Occupations are ranked by index for workers with some college but no degree to that of high school graduates.
n.e.c. = not elsewhere classified
- = Less than 50,000
SOURCE: Current Population Survey

TABLE 8
Median Weekly Earnings of Full-Time Wage and Salary Workers, Men with Some College Compared to Men at Other Educational Levels, 1996

Occupation	Level of Education				Bachelor's Degree Recipient	Premium or Discount[1] for Workers with Some College, No Degree, Compared to...		
	All Levels	High School Graduate or Equivalents	Some College, No Degree	Associate Degree Recipient		High School Graduate	Associate Degree Recipient	Bachelor's Degree Recipient
Total employed	$435	$361	$411	$473	$592	$1.14	.87	.69
Protective service occupations	456	357	501	-	657	1.40	-	.76
Sales representatives, mining, manufacturing, and wholesale trade	589	438	551	-	747	1.26	-	.74
Social, recreation, and religious workers	494	338	417	438	483	1.23	.95	.86
Health technologists and technicians, n.e.c.	417	377	440	476	442	1.17	.92	1.00
Real estate sales occupations	503	447	524	-	548	1.17	-	.96
Health aides, except nursing	314	289	337	-	-	1.17	-	-
Writers, artists, entertainers, and athletes	544	393	449	504	584	1.14	.89	.77
Managers and administrators, n.e.c.	623	495	554	625	756	1.12	.89	.73
Teachers, prekindergarten and kindergarten	370	251	282	-	474	1.12	-	.59
Supervisors, general office	506	470	526	-	-	1.12	-	-
Dental assistants	361	364	405	-	-	1.11	-	-
Teachers aides	273	257	285	-	-	1.11	-	-
Cleaning and building service occupations	272	278	308	-	-	1.11	-	-
Waiters and waitresses	267	265	291	-	287	1.10	-	1.01
Other financial officers	606	522	571	-	622	1.09	-	.92
Assemblers	325	342	374	-	-	1.09	-	-
Farming, forestry, and fishing occupations	268	295	321	-	324	1.09	-	.99
Administrative support occupations, n.e.c.	453	420	456	462	495	1.09	.99	.92
Supervisors and proprietors, sales occupations	424	392	425	494	571	1.08	.86	.74
Nursing aides, orderlies, and attendants	292	291	313	308	-	1.08	1.02	-
Precision production, craft, and repair occupations	384	379	404	430	632	1.07	.94	.64
Secretaries	411	398	425	429	412	1.07	.99	1.03
Accountants and auditors	564	482	508	484	616	1.05	1.05	.82
Managers, medicine and health	613	497	523	610	732	1.05	.86	.71
Transportation and material moving occupations	357	357	369	-	-	1.03	-	-
Financial managers	636	560	578	-	785	1.03	-	.74
Mail and message distributing occupations	542	527	543	-	-	1.03	-	-
Receptionists	344	341	350	344	357	1.03	1.02	.98
Investigators and adjusters, except insurance	406	392	403	393	467	1.03	1.03	.86
Licensed practical nurses	469	460	472	468	-	1.03	1.01	-
Administrators and officials, public administration	639	547	558	-	747	1.02	-	.75
Handlers, equipment cleaners, helpers, and laborers	302	308	314	-	-	1.02	-	-
Sales workers, retail and personal services	277	271	273	348	408	1.01	.78	.67
Insurance sales occupations	483	459	459	-	617	1.00	-	.74
Management related occupations, n.e.c.	508	495	494	-	549	1.00	-	.90
Managers, food serving and lodging establishments	405	389	388	-	511	1.00	-	.76
Typists	407	408	404	-	-	.99	-	-
Bank tellers	317	318	314	-	-	.99	-	-
Bookkeepers, accounting, and auditing clerks	400	401	394	396	437	.98	.99	.90
General office clerks	371	369	361	-	424	.98	-	.85
Insurance adjusters, examiners, and investigators	462	456	446	-	518	.98	-	.86
Computer operators	410	419	407	-	-	.97	-	-
Data-entry keyers	368	377	363	-	-	.96	-	-
Legal assistants	559	571	523	-	-	.92	-	-
Hairdressers and cosmetologists	298	298	271	-	-	.91	-	-

[1] This is the earnings of workers with some college divided by earnings in each education group. Thus, men in police and detective occupations with some college earned $1.40 for every $1 earned by high school graduates but 76 cents for every $1 earned by those with a bachelor's degree. Occupations are ranked by index for workers with some college but no degree to that of high school graduates.

n.e.c. = not elsewhere classified

- = Less than 50,000

SOURCE: Current Population Survey

IMPORTANT LABOR MARKET TRENDS AND DETAILS ON ALL MAJOR INDUSTRIES AND JOBS

This section features articles on labor market and industry trends and helpful data on 500 major jobs. The first article appeared in the introduction to the 1998–99 edition of the *Occupational Outlook Handbook*. It provides an excellent review of important trends in the labor market, including occupations and industries that are growing and declining, the fastest-growing jobs, the importance of education, and many other useful details. The second article gives data on 500 major jobs. This data includes earnings, growth, education needed, unemployment rates, and other details. The last article reviews growth and trends in all major industries.

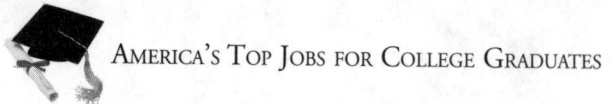

TOMORROW'S JOBS

Making informed career decisions requires reliable information about opportunities in the future. Opportunities result from the relationships between the population, labor force, and the demand for goods and services.

Population ultimately limits the size of the labor force—individuals working or looking for work—which constrains how much can be produced. Demand for various goods and services determines employment in the industries providing them. Occupational employment opportunities, in turn, result from skills needed within specific industries. Opportunities for registered nurses and other health-related specialists, for example, have surged in response to the rapid growth in demand for health services.

Examining the past and anticipating changes in these relationships are the foundation of the Occupational Outlook Program. This section presents highlights of Bureau of Labor Statistics projections of the labor force and occupational and industry employment that can help guide your career plans.

The Labor Force Will Grow More Slowly

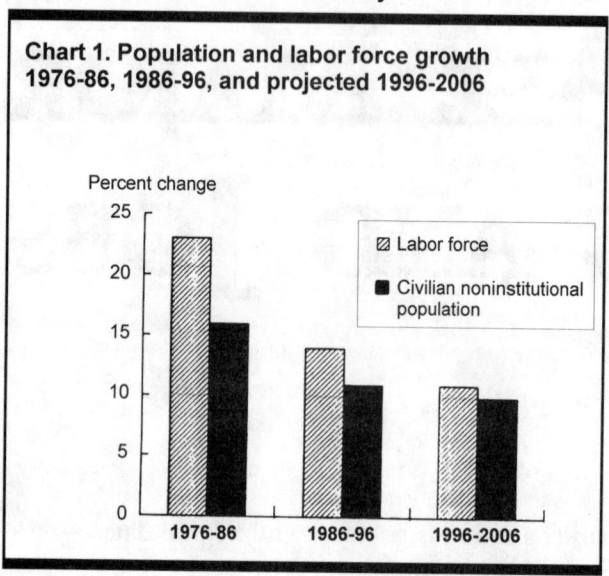

Chart 1. Population and labor force growth 1976-86, 1986-96, and projected 1996-2006

The Labor Force Will Become Increasingly Diverse

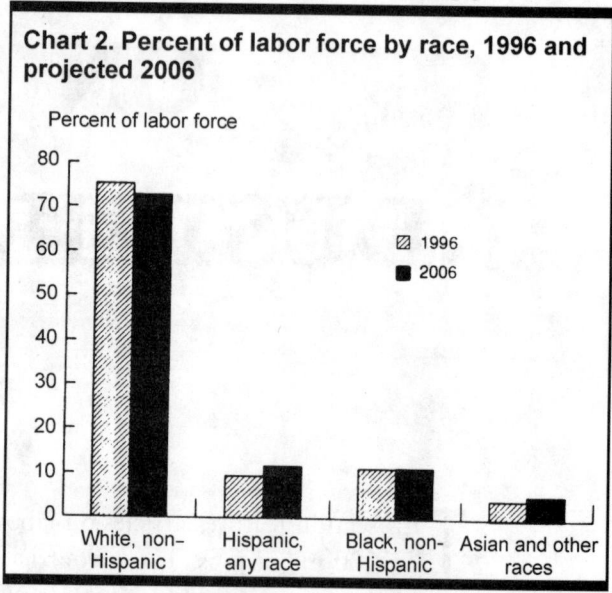

Chart 2. Percent of labor force by race, 1996 and projected 2006

✦ The Bureau of Labor Statistics (BLS) projects that the labor force will grow to 14.9 million between 1996 and 2006. This is 1.2 million less than the previous 10 years reflecting a slower growth in the civilian noninstitutional population 16 years of age and older. Growth was much faster from 1976 to 1986, when the baby boomers were entering the labor force.

✦ The labor force will grow 11 percent between 1996 and 2006, slightly slower than during the 1986–96 period but only half the rate of growth during the 1976–86 period.

✦ As a result of an increase in the percentage of the population working or looking for work, the labor force will continue to grow faster than the population rate.

✦ Between 1996 and 2006, employment will increase by 18.6 million or 14 percent. This is slower than during the 1986–96 period, when the economy added 21 million jobs.

✦ Wage and salary worker employment will account for 94 percent of this increase. In addition, the number of self-employed workers is expected to increase to 11.6 million in 2006, while the number of unpaid family workers will decline.

✦ The labor force growth of Hispanics, Asians, and other races will be faster than for blacks and white non-Hispanics. The projected labor force growth of these ethnic groups stems primarily from immigration.

✦ Despite relatively slow growth, white non-Hispanics will have the largest numerical growth between 1996 and 2006.

✦ Between 1996 and 2006, women's share of the labor force is projected to slowly increase from 46 to 47 percent, continuing a pattern since 1976. The participation rate for women will continue to increase for those 20- to 65-years old.

✦ The number of men in the labor force will grow at a slower rate than in the past, in part reflecting declining employment in well-paid production jobs in manufacturing, and a continued shift in demand for workers from the goods-producing sector to the service-producing sector. Participation rates for men will decline for all age groups below age 45 except for 16–19; the rates for those 16–19 will remain steady at 53 percent. Rates for age groups 45 and above will increase.

The Labor Force Will Become Older

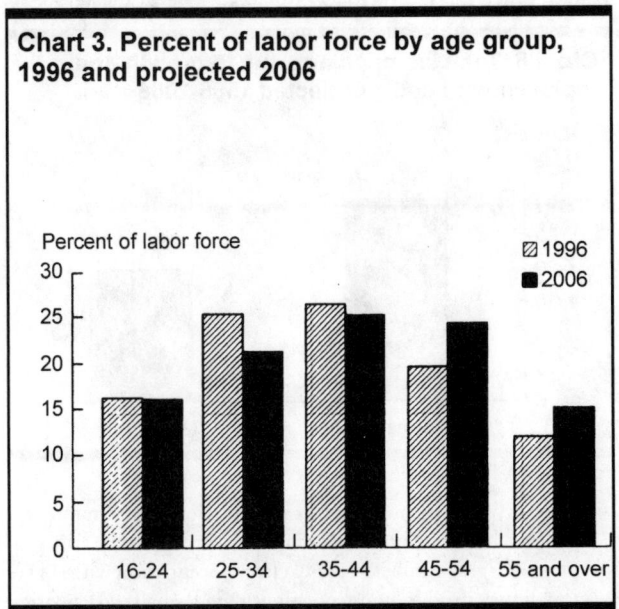

Chart 3. Percent of labor force by age group, 1996 and projected 2006

◆ Workers over age 45 will account for a larger share of the labor force as the baby-boom generation ages.

◆ Two age groups with large numbers of baby boomers will grow by more than 30 percent—people 45 to 54 and those 55 to 64. Only the trailing edge of the baby boomers, those born from 1962 to 1964, will be younger than 45 in 2006.

◆ The very large group of workers aged 35 to 44, which is about one-fourth of the labor force, will change hardly at all during the period. The 25- to 34-year old group will decline by 3 million, a result of falling birth rates in the late 1960s. Those 16 to 24 will increase by more than 3 million, making this group the largest it has been in 25 years.

Industry Employment Growth Is Projected to Be Highly Concentrated in Service-Producing Industries

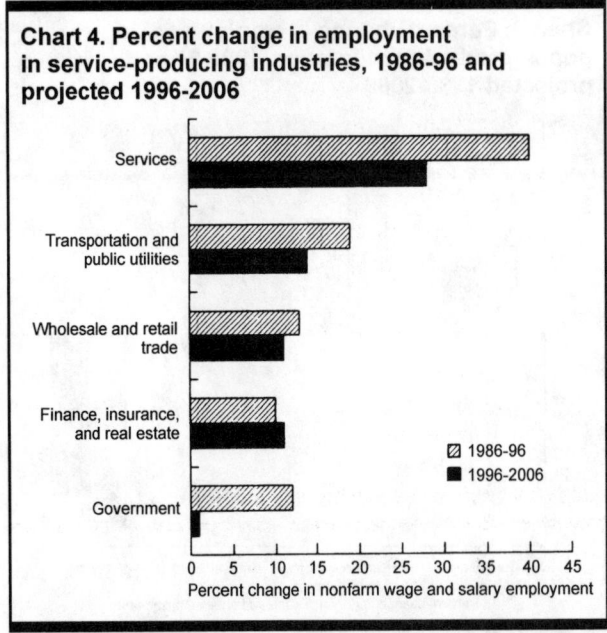

Chart 4. Percent change in employment in service-producing industries, 1986-96 and projected 1996-2006

◆ Employment in service-producing industries will increase faster than average, with growth near 30 percent. Service and retail trade industries will account for 14.8 million out of a total projected growth of 17.5 million wage and salary jobs.

◆ Business, health, and education services will account for 70 percent of the growth within the service industry.

◆ Health care services will increase 30 percent and account for 3.1 million new jobs, the largest numerical increase of any industry from 1996–2006. Factors contributing to continued growth in this industry include the aging population, which will continue to require more services, and the increased use of innovative medical technology for intensive diagnosis and treatment. Patients will increasingly be shifted out of hospitals and into outpatient facilities, nursing homes, and home health care in an attempt to contain costs.

◆ Educational services are projected to increase by 1.8 million jobs between 1996 and 2006. Most jobs will be for teachers, who are projected to account for 1.3 million jobs.

◆ Computer and data processing services will add over 1.3 million jobs from 1996–2006. The 108 percent increase is due to technological advancements and the need for higher skilled workers. The high percent increase makes this the fastest-growing industry over the projection period.

Growth in Goods-Producing Industries Will Be Restrained By Declines in Manufacturing and Mining

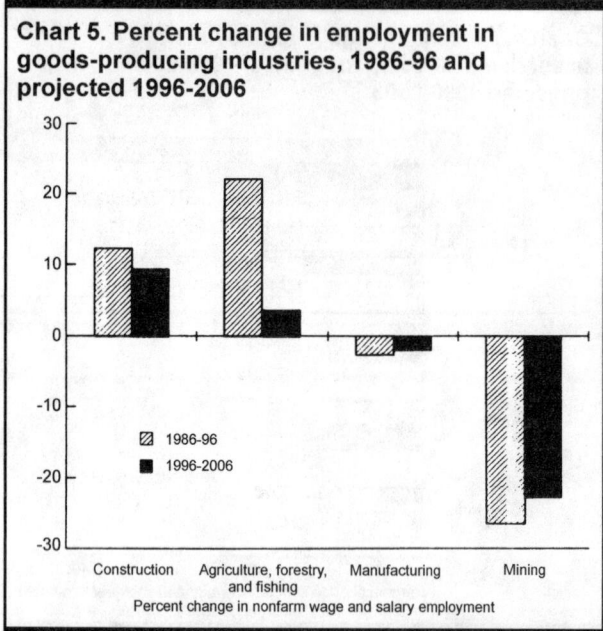

Chart 5. Percent change in employment in goods-producing industries, 1986-96 and projected 1996-2006

Replacement Needs Will Account for Three-Fifths of the 50.6 Million Projected Job Openings Between 1996 and 2006

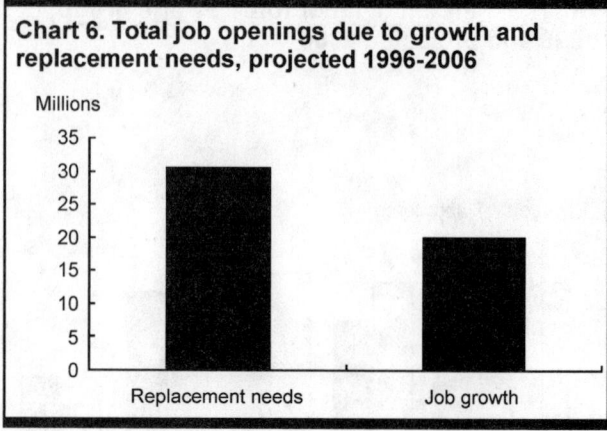

Chart 6. Total job openings due to growth and replacement needs, projected 1996-2006

✦ Projected employment growth in the construction and agriculture industries will be offset by a decline in manufacturing and mining jobs. Manufacturing will account for 13 percent of total wage and salary worker employment in 2006, compared to 15 percent in 1996.

✦ Construction employment will grow one-fourth slower than during the previous 10-year period.

✦ Within the agriculture, forestry, and fishing industry, growth in agriculture services and forestry will more than offset the projected declines in crops, livestock, and livestock related products, and fishing, hunting, and trapping.

✦ Job growth can be measured by percent change and numerical change. The fastest-growing occupations do not necessarily provide the largest number of jobs. A larger occupation with slower growth may produce more openings than a smaller occupation with faster growth.

✦ Job opportunities are enhanced by additional openings resulting from the need to replace workers who leave the occupation. Some workers leave the occupation as they are promoted or change careers; others stop working to return to school, to assume household responsibilities, or retire.

✦ Replacement needs are greater in occupations with low pay and low training requirements with a high proportion of young and part-time workers.

© 1999 • J. Michael Farr • JIST Works, Inc. • Indianapolis, IN

Service and Professional Specialty Occupations Will Provide About Two Out of Every Five Job Openings—Primarily Due to High Replacement Needs

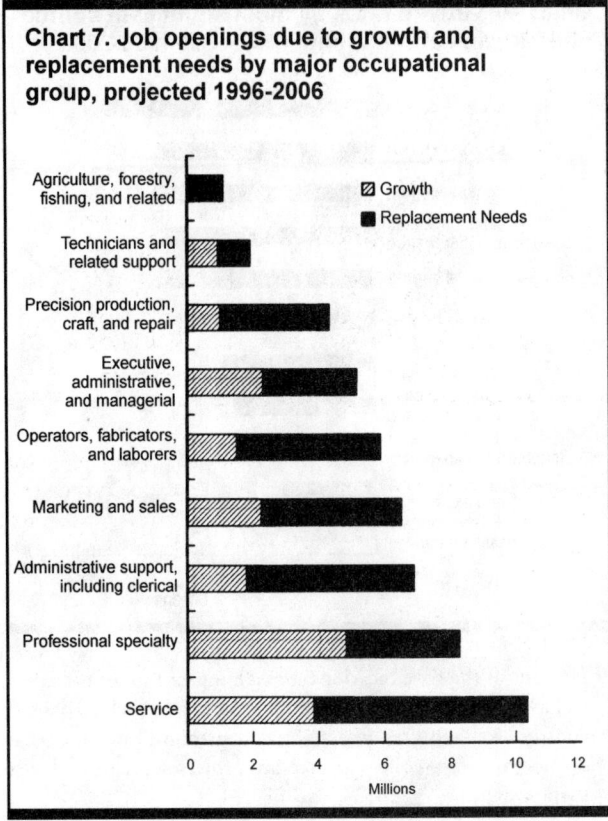

Chart 7. Job openings due to growth and replacement needs by major occupational group, projected 1996-2006

Of the 25 Occupations with Fast Growth, High Pay, and Low Unemployment That Have the Largest Numerical Growth, 18 Require at Least a Bachelor's Degree

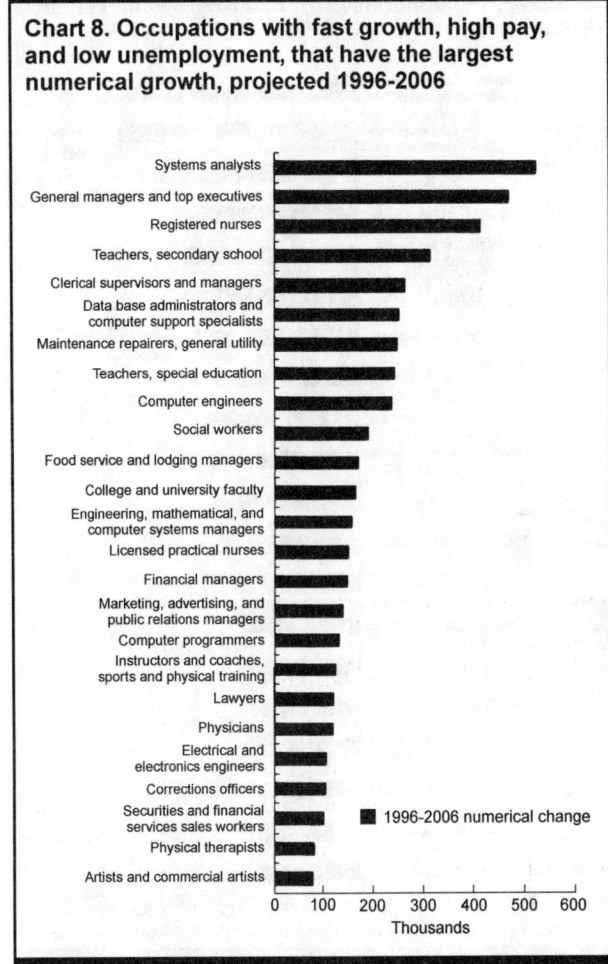

Chart 8. Occupations with fast growth, high pay, and low unemployment, that have the largest numerical growth, projected 1996-2006

✦ Employment in professional specialty occupations is projected to increase at a faster rate and have more job growth than any major occupational group.

✦ Within professional specialty occupations, computer-related occupations and teachers will add 2.3 million new jobs, accounting for 15 percent of all new jobs from 1996 to 2006. Professional specialty occupations comprise the only group that will have a majority of job openings stemming from growth.

✦ Little or no change is expected in employment in agriculture, forestry, fishing, and related occupations. All job openings in this cluster will stem from replacement needs.

✦ Office automation will significantly affect many individual administrative and clerical support occupations. Overall, these occupations will increase more slowly than average, though some are projected to decline.

✦ Precision production, craft, and repair occupations and operators, fabricators, and laborers are projected to grow slower than average due to continuing advances in technology, changes in production methods, and overall decline in manufacturing jobs.

✦ These 25 occupations are somewhat concentrated, with 5 occupations in computer technology, 4 in health care, and 5 in education.

✦ The 25 occupations with fast growth, higher than average pay, and lower than average unemployment that have the largest numerical growth will account for 5 million new jobs, or 27 percent of all job growth.

The Fastest-Growing Occupations Reflect Growth in Computer Technology and Health Care Services

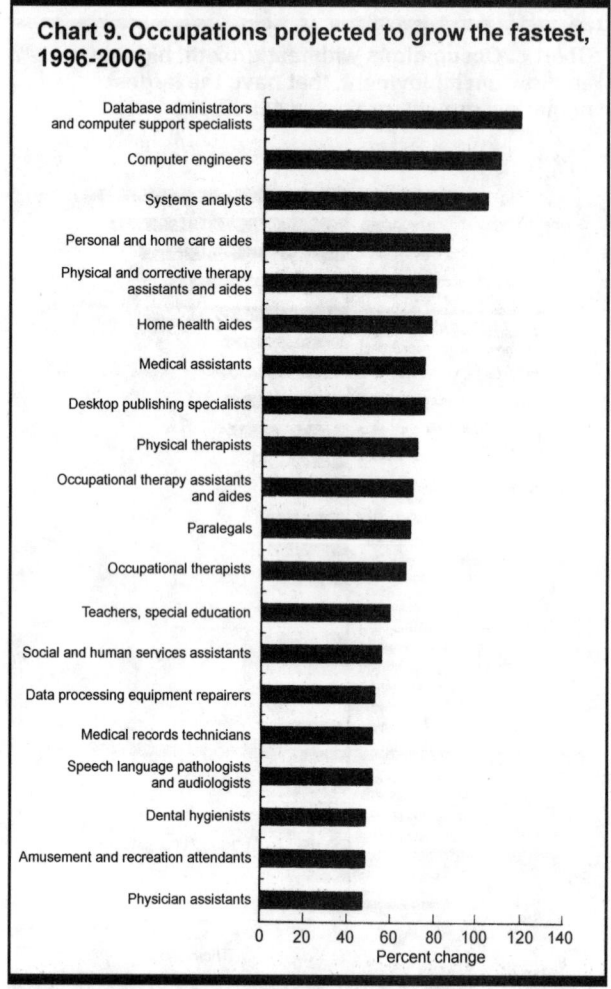

Chart 9. Occupations projected to grow the fastest, 1996-2006

Job Growth Varies Widely by Education and Training Requirements

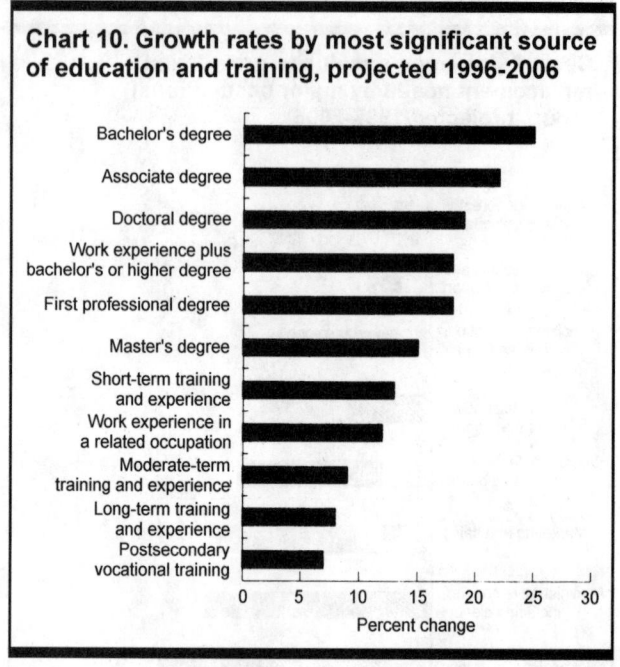

Chart 10. Growth rates by most significant source of education and training, projected 1996-2006

✦ Computer engineers and systems analysts jobs are expected to grow rapidly in order to satisfy expanding needs of scientific research and applications of computer technology. The three fastest-growing occupations are in computer-related fields.

✦ Many of the fastest-growing occupations are concentrated in health services, which are expected to increase more than twice as fast as the whole economy. Personal and home care aides, and home health aides, will be in great demand to provide personal care for an increasing number of elderly people and for persons who are recovering from surgery and other serious health conditions. This is occurring as hospitals and insurance companies require shorter stays for recovery to reduce costs.

✦ Five out of the six education and training categories projected to have the fastest growth require at least a bachelor's degree, and the sixth requires an associate's degree. All categories that do not require a college degree are projected to grow slower than average.

✦ Table 1 presents the fastest-growing occupations and those having the largest numerical increase in employment over the 1996–2006 period, categorized by the level of education and training.

✦ Occupations usually requiring short-term, on-the-job training accounted for 53.5 million jobs in 1996, more than any other education and training category. Occupations requiring a bachelor's degree or more education accounted for 22 percent of all jobs. Occupations in the four education categories not requiring postsecondary education accounted for about 70 percent of all jobs.

✦ Occupations that require a bachelor's degree are projected to grow the fastest, nearly twice as fast as the average for all occupations. All of the 20 occupations with the highest earnings require at least a bachelor's degree. Engineering and health occupations dominate this list.

✦ Education is essential in getting a high-paying job. However, many occupations—for example, registered nurses, blue-collar worker supervisors, electrical and electronic technicians/technologists, automotive mechanics, and carpenters—do not require a college degree, yet offer higher than average earnings.

✦ Labor force groups with lower than average educational attainment in 1996, including Hispanics and blacks, will continue to have difficulty obtaining a share of the high-paying jobs unless they raise their educational attainment. Although high-paying jobs will be available without college training, most jobs that pay above average wages will require a college degree.

Jobs Will Be Available for Job Seekers from Every Education and Training Background

Declining Occupational Employment Stems from Declining Industry Employment and Technological Advancement

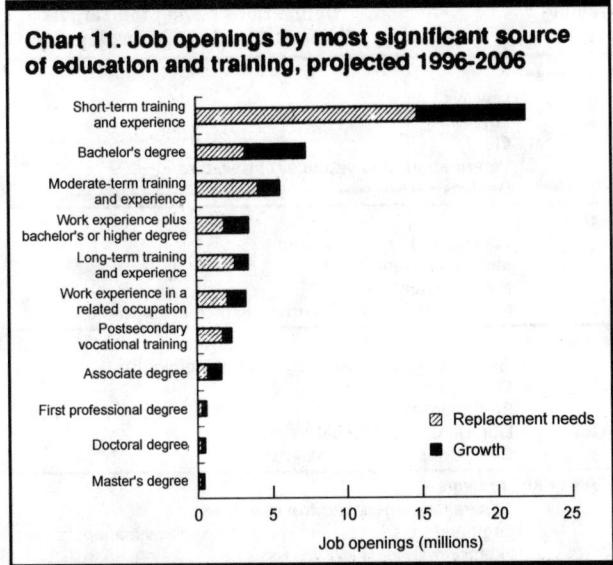

Chart 11. Job openings by most significant source of education and training, projected 1996-2006

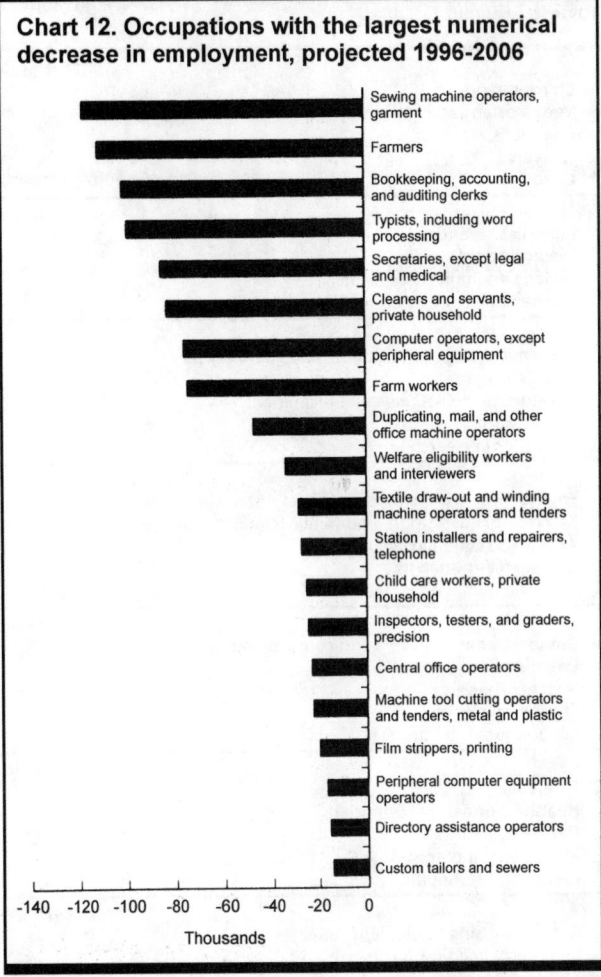

Chart 12. Occupations with the largest numerical decrease in employment, projected 1996-2006

✦ Almost two-thirds of the projected growth will be in occupations that require less than a college degree. However, these positions generally offer the lowest pay and benefits.

✦ Jobs requiring the least education and training—those that can be learned on the job—will provide two of every three openings due to growth and replacement needs; three of every four openings will be in occupations that generally require less than a bachelor's degree.

✦ Manufacturing and agricultural-related jobs, such as sewing machine operators and farmers, are examples of occupations that will lose employment due to declining employment in some goods-producing industries.

✦ Many declining occupations are affected by structural changes, as a result of factors including technological advances and organizational changes. For example, the use of typists and word processors will decline dramatically because of productivity improvements in office automation, and the increased use of word processing equipment by professional and managerial employees.

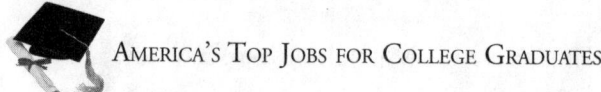

Table 1. Fastest-Growing Occupations and Occupations Having the Largest Numerical Increase in Employment, Projected 1996-2006, by Level of Education and Training

Fastest-Growing Occupations	Education/Training Category	Occupations Having the Largest Numerical Increase in Employment
	First professional degree	
Chiropractors Veterinarians and veterinary inspectors Physicians Lawyers Clergy		Lawyers Physicians Clergy Veterinarians and veterinary inspectors Dentists
	Doctoral degree	
Biological scientists Medical scientists College and university faculty Mathematicians and all other mathematical scientists		College and university faculty Biological scientists Medical scientists Mathematicians and all other mathematical scientists
	Master's degree	
Speech-language pathologists and audiologists Counselors Curators, archivists, museum technicians Psychologists Operations research analysts		Speech-language pathologists and audiologists Counselors Psychologists Librarians, professional Operations research analysts
	Work experience plus bachelor's or higher degree	
Engineering, science, and computer systems managers Marketing, advertising, and public relations managers Artists and commercial artists Management analysts Financial managers		General managers and top executives Engineering, science, and computer systems managers Finance managers Marketing, advertising, and public relations managers Artists and commercial artists
	Bachelor's degree	
Database administrators and computer support specialists Computer engineers Systems analysts Physical therapists Occupational therapists		Systems analysts Teachers, secondary school Database administrators and computer support specialists Teachers, special education Computer engineers
	Associate degree	
Paralegals Health information technicians Dental hygienists Respiratory therapists Cardiology technologists		Registered nurses Paralegals Dental hygienists Radiologic technologists and technicians Health information technicians
	Postsecondary vocational training	
Data processing equipment repairers Emergency medical technicians Manicurists Surgical technologists Medical secretaries		Licensed practical nurses Automotive mechanics Medical secretaries Emergency medical technicians Hairdressers, hairstylists, and cosmetologists
	Work experience	
Food service and lodging managers Teachers and instructors, vocational education and training Lawn service managers Instructors, adult education Nursery and greenhouse managers		Clerical supervisors and managers Marketing and sales worker supervisors Food service and lodging managers Teachers and instructors, vocational education and training Instructors, adult (nonvocational) education
	Long-term training and experience (more than 12 months of on-the-job training)	
Desktop publishing specialists Flight attendants Musicians Correction officers Producers, directors, actors, and entertainers		Cooks, restaurant Correction officers Musicians Police patrol officers Carpenters
	Moderate-term training and experience (1 to 12 months of combined on-the-job experience and informal training)	
Physical and corrective therapy assistants and aides Medical assistants Occupational therapy assistants and aides Social and human services assistants Instructors and coaches, sports and physical training		Medical assistants Instructors and coaches, sports and physical training Social and human services assistants Dental assistants Physical and corrective therapy assistants
	Short-term training and experience (up to 1 month of on-the-job experience)	
Personal and home care aides Home health aides Amusement and recreation attendants Adjustment clerks Bill and account collectors		Cashiers Salespersons, retail Truck drivers, light and heavy Home health aides Teacher aides and educational assistants

DETAILS ON THE TOP 500 JOBS: EARNINGS, PROJECTED GROWTH, EDUCATION REQUIRED, UNEMPLOYMENT RATES, AND OTHER DETAILS

Selected Occupational Data, 1996 and Projected 2006

This article presents data on current and projected employment, employment change, self-employment, and annual average job openings for all national industry-occupation matrix occupations. For most of the categories of occupational information, rankings are presented designating the relative magnitude of data for each detailed occupation. In addition, Table 1 identifies the category of education and training most workers took to become proficient in each detailed occupation.

Data Sources

Table 1 presents information from three sources: 1) the national industry-occupation matrix, 2) the Occupational Employment Statistics (OES) survey, and 3) the Current Population Survey (CPS). The industry-occupation matrix is predominantly based on wage and salary occupational employment data collected from establishments as part of the OES survey. This survey counts jobs. Individuals who hold more than one job are counted at each place they work. The CPS is a monthly survey of about 50,000 households that obtains demographic and labor force information about individuals. Employment information from the CPS counts individuals, not jobs. Data on self-employed and unpaid family workers are derived from the CPS and combined with OES data on wage and salary employment in order to develop total employment estimates.

Occupational data in the industry-occupation matrix are not entirely comparable with those in the CPS because of differences in occupational classification systems, and differences in concepts and methods used in the surveys. Information about worker characteristics that is based on CPS data is applied to industry-occupation matrix occupations based on judgments identifying the most comparable CPS occu-

pations. Comparisons based on CPS occupations with fewer than 50,000 workers in 1996 and some other occupations for which the data appeared unreliable were excluded; data for CPS proxy occupations were substituted. Where possible, larger, closely related CPS occupations were chosen as proxies. For example, data for purchasing agents and buyers, n.e.c. (not elsewhere classified), were used to represent purchasing agents and buyers, farm products. When no detailed occupation could be identified, a summary occupation group was used. For example, data about all therapists were substituted for that of inhalation therapists.

Data Presented

The source of the data for each variable and a brief discussion of its potential use are presented below. Rankings for most data categories identify the relative magnitude of variables in terms of the distribution of employment. For example, 1996 employment and projected 1996–2006 percent change in employment data were assembled for each occupation. Each occupation's employment as a percent of 1996 total employment was calculated. The occupations were sorted by employment change in descending order, and the cumulative percent of 1996 employment for each was determined. Occupations within the group comprising less than 25 percent of total employment are designated VH for a Very High growth rate. Similarly, occupations sorted by descending order of employment change comprising 25–50 percent of employment receive H for High; 50–75 percent, L for Low; and 75–100 percent, VL for Very Low. Occupations were sorted by other data elements and rankings were determined in the same manner.

Employment, 1996 and 2006

(Source: Bureau of Labor Statistics, national industry-occupation matrices for 1996 and 2006.) Employment information is a useful starting point for assessing opportunities because large occupations usually have more openings than small ones regardless of growth or replacement rates.

Employment Change, 1996–2006, Numeric

(Source: Bureau of Labor Statistics, national industry-occupation matrices for 1996 and 2006.) Information on numerical change provides an absolute measure of projected job gains or losses.

Employment Change, 1996-2006, Percent

(Source: Bureau of Labor Statistics, national industry-occupation matrices for 1996 and 2006.) The percent change in employment measures the rate of change. When an occupation grows rapidly, this usually indicates favorable prospects for employment. Moreover, the high demand for workers in a rapidly growing occupation improves chances for advancement and mobility. A modest percentage increase in employment growth can result in many more job openings in a large occupation than in a small occupation that is growing rapidly.

Percent Self-Employed, 1996

(Source: Bureau of Labor Statistics, national industry-occupation matrices for 1996 and 2006.) Individuals who are interested in creating and managing their own business may find it important to know the percentage of self-employed workers. This percentage is calculated from CPS data about unincorporated self-employed persons included in industry-occupation matrix employment data. Unincorporated self-employed persons work for earnings or fees in their own business and, unlike self-employed persons in businesses that are incorporated, do not receive a wage or salary.

Job Openings Due to Growth Plus Total Replacement Needs, 1996–2006

(Source: Bureau of Labor Statistics, *Occupational Outlook Handbook.*) These data provide the broadest measure of opportunities and identify the total number of employees needed annually to enter an occupation. Growth is calculated using data on increases in occupational employment from national industry-occupation matrices for 1996–2006. If employment declines, job openings due growth are zero. Total replacement needs are calculated from 1995–96 CPS data. Data from CPS proxy occupations are used to estimate replacement needs for some matrix occupations. (See Table 2.)

Job Openings Due to Growth Plus Net Replacement Needs, 1996–2006

(Source: Bureau of Labor Statistics, *Occupational Outlook Handbook.*) These data estimate the number of new workers needed annually for an occupation and, if training is required, measure minimum training needs. Growth is calculated using data on increases in occupational employment from national industry-occupation matrices for 1996–2006. If employment declines, job openings due growth are zero. Net replacement needs are calculated from CPS data. Data from CPS proxy occupations estimate replacement needs for some matrix occupations (see Table 2).

Median Hourly Earnings

(Source: 1996 Occupational Employment Statistics survey with some exceptions. These exceptions are that OES data are not available for government chief executives and legislators, and producers, directors, actors, and entertainers. OES data also are not available for private household workers; farm operators and managers; captains and other officers, fishing vessels; and fishers, hunters, and trappers. Hourly 1996 Current Population Survey annual average data for wage and salary employees provide information for the latter group.) Table 1 uses median hourly earnings of workers to compare earnings among different occupations.

Unemployment Rate

(Source: Average of 1994–96 Current Population Survey annual average data.) Some occupations are more susceptible to factors that result in unemployment: Seasonality, fluctuations in economic conditions, and individual business failures. A high unemployment rate indicates that individuals in that occupation are more likely to become unemployed than those in one with a low rate. Data from CPS proxy occupations are used to estimate unemployment rates for some matrix occupations. (See Table 2.)

Percent Part Time

(Source: Average of 1994–96 Current Population Survey annual average data.) It may be important to those persons who prefer part-time work to know the proportion of employees who work fewer than 35 hours per week. Data from CPS proxy occupations are used to estimate the proportion of part-time workers for some matrix occupations. (See Table 2.)

Most Significant Source of Training

(Source: Bureau of Labor Statistics.) Occupations are classified into 1 of 11 categories that describe the education and training needed by most workers to become fully qualified. The categories are first professional degree; doctoral degree; master's degree; work experience in an occupation requiring a bachelor's or higher degree; bachelor's degree; associate degree; postsecondary vocational training; work experience in a related occupation; long-term, on-the-job training; moderate-term, on-the-job training; and short-term, on-the-job training. The following are definitions of these categories.

Occupations that require a first professional degree. The first professional degree is the minimum preparation required for entry into several professions, including law, medicine, dentistry, and the clergy. Completion of this academic program usually requires at least two years of full-time academic study beyond a bachelor's degree.

Occupations that generally require a doctoral degree. The doctoral degree can also be easily related to specific occupations. It normally requires at least three years of full-time academic work beyond the bachelor's degree.

Occupations that generally require a master's degree. Completion of a master's degree program mostly requires one or two years of full-time study beyond the bachelor's degree.

Occupations that generally require work experience in an occupation requiring a bachelor's or higher degree. Most occupations in this category are managerial occupations that require experience in a related nonmanagerial occupation. Jobs in these occupations usually are filled with experienced staff who are promoted into a managerial position, such as engineers who advance to engineering manager. It is very difficult to become a judge without first working as a lawyer, or to become a personnel, training, or labor relations manager without first gaining experience as a specialist in one of these fields.

Occupations that generally require a bachelor's degree. This is a degree program requiring at least four but not more than five years of full-time academic work after high school. The bachelor's degree is considered the minimum training requirement for most professional occupations, such as mechanical engineer, pharmacist, recreational therapist, and landscape architect.

Occupations that generally require an associate degree. Completion of this degree program usually requires at least two years of full-time academic work after high school. Most occupations in this training category are health related, such as registered nurse, respiratory therapist, and radiologic technologist. Also included are science and mathematics technicians and paralegals.

Occupations that generally require completion of vocational training provided in postsecondary vocational schools. Workers normally qualify for jobs by completing vocational training programs or by taking job-related college courses that do not result in a degree. Some programs take less than a year to complete and lead to a certificate or diploma. Others last longer than a year but less than four years. Occupations in this category include some that require only completion of a training program, such as a travel agent, and those that require passing a licensing exam after completion of the program, such as a barber and cosmetologist.

Occupations that generally require skills developed through work experience in a related occupation. Jobs in this category require skills and experience gained in another occupation; this category also includes occupations in which skills may be developed from hobbies or other activities besides current or past employment or from service in the armed forces. Among the occupations are cost estimators, who generally need prior work experience in one of the construction trades; police detectives, who are selected based on their experience as police patrol officers; and lawn service managers, who may be hired based on their experience as groundskeepers.

Long-term, on-the-job training. This category includes occupations that usually require more than 12 months of on-the-job training or combined work experience and formal classroom instruction before workers develop the skills needed for average job performance. This category includes occupations such as electrician, bricklayer, and machinist that normally require formal or informal apprenticeships lasting up to four years. Also included in this type of training are intensive occupation-specific, employer-sponsored programs that workers must successfully complete before they can begin work. These include fire and police academies and schools for air traffic controllers and flight attendants. In other occupations—insurance sales and securities sales, for example—trainees take formal courses, often provided at the job site, to prepare for the required licensing exams. Individuals undergoing training are usually considered employed in the occupation. This group of occupations also includes musicians, athletes, actors, and other entertainers, occupations that require natural ability that must be developed over several years.

Moderate-term, on-the-job training. Workers can achieve average job performance after 1 to 12 months of combined job experience and informal training, which can include observing experienced workers. Individuals undergoing training are normally considered employed in the occupation. This type of training is found among occupations such as dental assistants, drywall installers and finishers, operating engineers, and machine operators. This training relies on trainees watching experienced workers and asking questions. Trainees are given progressively more difficult assignments as they demonstrate their mastery of lower level skills.

Short-term, on-the-job training. Included are occupations like cashier, bank teller, messenger, highway maintenance worker, and veterinary assistant. In these occupations, workers usually can achieve average job performance in just a few days or weeks by working with and observing experienced employees and by asking questions.

Using Ranked Information

Table 1 consolidates 1996 and 2006 projected employment data. Table 1 also provides comparisons of occupational data. It contains rankings of information about current and projected employment, projected job openings, earnings, unemployment rates, and the proportion of part-time workers. Except for the unemployment and part-time categories, a high rating indicates a favorable assessment. A high rating for the unemployment rate is considered undesirable. Unemployment rates in construction occupations, however, are inflated by the nature of the industry and distort comparisons. Workers in these occupations typically incur periods of unemployment after completing a project and before starting work at a new job site.

The rating for the part-time category also should not be used routinely in assessing the desirability of employment because the assessment depends on the perspective of the user. For example, high school students may consider a large proportion of part-time workers desirable because they normally prefer not to work full time. A recent college graduate or anyone seeking full-time employment may reach the opposite conclusion.

The data in Table 1 has many potential uses. At times, users may want to know how a particular occupation, cashiers, for example, compares with others. The "VH" (Very High) rankings in Table 1 for the increase in the number of jobs and for both categories of job openings point out that many jobs are available, certainly a favorable rating. The "VL" (Very Low) ranking for earnings and "VH" (Very High) for unemployment, however, are unfavorable in comparison with other occupations, and these characteristics detract from the desirability of employment in the occupation. Table 1 also shows that cashiers require only short-term, on-the-job training.

Readers may wish to identify occupations with favorable characteristics that job seekers can pursue through a specific type of training. For example, a student may be interested in a scientific or engineering occupation but not care to obtain a four-year college degree. In another instance a planner may wish to ensure that training programs provided by junior colleges in the area are consistent with the needs of the national labor market. For example, the planner could examine information for occupations placed in the associate degree educational and training category.

Although Table 1 contains a great deal of information useful for career guidance, information about occupational comparisons should be used as an aid, not a sole source. After you use the table to identify occupations with favorable prospects, additional information should be obtained from other sources such as the *Occupational Outlook Handbook* and local sources, if available. Consideration should be given to individual aptitudes and preferences, and alternative sources of training available in the local area should be investigated

An electronic version of Table 1 is available on request—call the Chief, Division of Occupational Outlook at (202) 606-5703. The data in Table 1 also are available from the Internet. For access, select the "Employment, Training, & Earnings" button of the "Employment Projections Home Page" (http://stats.bls.gov/emphome.htm) at the BLS site.

Table 1. Occupational employment and job openings data, 1996-2006, and worker characteristics, 1996   (Numbers in thousands)

1996 Matrix Occupation	Employment		Employment change, 1996-2006				Percent self-em-ployed, 1996	Annual average job openings due to growth and total replacement needs, 1996-2006	
			Numeric		Percent				
	1996	2006	Number	Rank	Number	Rank		Number	Rank
Total, all occupations	132,353	150,927	18,574	–	14.0	–	7.9	26,666	–
Executive, administrative, and managerial occupations	13,542	15,866	2,324	–	17.2	–	13.2	1,960	–
Managerial and administrative occupations	9,539	11,262	1,723	–	18.1	–	15.4	1,344	–
Administrative services managers	291	324	33	L	11.3	L	0.0	34	VL
Communication, transportation, and utilities operations managers	156	179	23	L	14.5	H	0.0	19	VL
Construction managers	249	294	45	L	18.0	H	16.1	32	VL
Education administrators	386	430	45	L	11.6	L	7.7	51	L
Engineering, science, and computer systems managers	343	498	155	H	45.2	VH	0.0	58	L
Financial managers	800	946	146	H	18.3	H	1.2	95	L
Food service and lodging managers[1]	589	757	168	H	28.5	VH	35.0	152	L
Funeral directors and morticians[1]	33	33	1	VL	2.0	VL	24.8	4	VL
General managers and top executives	3,210	3,677	467	VH	14.6	H	0.0	393	VH
Government chief executives and legislators[1]	93	95	2	VL	2.2	VL	0.0	7	VL
Industrial production managers	207	202	−5	VL	-2.5	VL	0.0	21	VL
Marketing, advertising, and public relations managers	482	620	138	H	28.5	VH	2.5	93	L
Personnel, training, and labor relations managers	216	254	38	L	17.8	H	0.0	30	VL
Property and real estate managers[1]	271	315	44	L	16.4	H	41.7	42	VL
Purchasing managers	232	251	18	VL	7.8	L	0.0	33	VL
All other managers and administrators[1]	1,981	2,387	406	VH	20.5	H	52.8	281	H
Management support occupations	4,003	4,604	601	–	15.0	–	7.9	615	–
Accountants and auditors	1,002	1,127	125	H	12.4	L	10.8	122	L
Budget analysts	66	73	8	VL	11.7	L	0.0	10	VL
Claims examiners, property and casualty insurance	57	69	13	VL	22.2	VH	0.0	5	VL
Construction and building inspectors	66	76	10	VL	14.5	H	1.9	3	VL
Cost estimators	188	217	29	L	15.5	H	0.0	35	VL
Credit analysts	40	46	6	VL	15.8	H	0.0	7	VL
Employment interviewers, private or public employment service	87	101	14	VL	16.3	H	0.0	19	VL
Inspectors and compliance officers, except construction	163	172	8	VL	5.2	VL	2.3	17	VL
Loan officers and counselors	209	268	59	L	28.1	VH	0.0	39	VL
Management analysts[1]	244	296	52	L	21.2	VH	45.5	15	VL
Personnel, training, and labor relations specialists	328	387	59	L	17.9	H	4.6	74	L
Purchasing agents, except wholesale, retail, and farm products ..	224	238	14	VL	6.4	L	1.4	41	VL
Tax examiners, collectors, and revenue agents	64	66	1	VL	2.3	VL	0.0	5	VL
Underwriters	95	100	6	VL	6.1	L	0.0	4	VL
Wholesale and retail buyers, except farm products	183	183	0	VL	-0.1	VL	6.4	48	L
All other management support workers[1]	988	1,185	198	H	20.0	H	6.4	171	H
Professional specialty occupations	18,173	22,998	4,826	–	26.6	–	8.3	2,539	–
Engineers	1,382	1,632	250	–	18.1	–	3.3	119	–
Aeronautical and astronautical engineers	53	57	4	VL	7.8	L	0.0	2	VL
Chemical engineers[1]	49	57	7	VL	15.0	H	2.2	4	VL
Civil engineers, including traffic engineers	196	231	35	L	17.9	H	6.6	20	VL
Electrical and electronics engineers	367	472	105	H	28.5	VH	3.6	32	VL
Industrial engineers, except safety engineers	115	131	16	VL	13.6	L	3.3	12	VL
Mechanical engineers	228	264	36	L	15.8	H	1.8	10	VL
Metallurgists and metallurgical, ceramic, and materials engineers[1]	18	20	1	VL	6.8	L	0.0	1	VL
Mining engineers, including mine safety engineers[1]	3	3	0	VL	−12.6	VL	0.0	0	VL
Nuclear engineers[1]	14	14	1	VL	5.2	VL	0.0	1	VL
Petroleum engineers[1]	13	11	−2	VL	−14.3	VL	5.4	1	VL
All other engineers[1]	326	373	47	L	14.4	H	3.1	36	VL
Architects and surveyors	212	232	20	–	9.7	–	18.5	27	–
Architects, except landscape and marine	94	113	18	VL	19.6	H	28.1	7	VL
Landscape architects	17	20	3	VL	20.7	H	30.7	1	VL
Surveyors[1]	101	99	−1	VL	-1.4	VL	7.5	18	VL
Life scientists	180	221	41	–	22.6	–	4.6	18	–

[1] One or more Current Population Survey (CPS) based occupations may be used to estimate CPS based data. See Table 2.
NOTE: Rankings are based on employment in all detailed occupations in the National Industry-Occupation Matrix. For details, see "Data presented" section of text. Codes for describing the ranked variables are: VH = Very high, H = High, L = Low, VL = Very low, n. a. = Data not available. A dash indicates data are not applicable.

Table 1. Occupational employment and job openings data, 1996-2006, and worker characteristics, 1996 (Numbers in thousands)

Annual average job openings due to growth and net replacement needs, 1996-2006		Median hourly earnings	Unem-ployment rate	Per-cent part-time	Most significant source of training	1996 Matrix Occupation
Number	Rank					
5,056	–	–	–	–	–	**Total, all occupations**
517	–	–	–	–	–	**Executive, administrative, and managerial occupations**
374						Managerial and administrative occupations
9	VL	VH	VL	VL	Work experience plus degree	Administrative services managers
6	VL	VH	VL	VL	Work experience plus degree	Communication, transportation, and utilities operations managers
10	VL	VH	VL	VL	Bachelor's degree	Construction managers
15	L	VH	VL	L	Work experience plus degree	Education administrators
23	L	VH	VL	VL	Work experience plus degree	Engineering, science, and computer systems managers
30	L	VH	VL	VL	Work experience plus degree	Financial managers
29	L	H	L	L	Work experience in a related occupation	Food service and lodging managers[1]
1	VL	VH	VL	L	Long-term on-the-job-training	Funeral directors and morticians
115	VH	VH	VL	VL	Work experience plus degree	General managers and top executives
2	VL	n. a.	VL	VL	Work experience plus degree	Government chief executives and legislators[1]
4	VL	VH	VL	VL	Bachelor's degree	Industrial production managers
23	L	VH	L	VL	Work experience plus degree	Marketing, advertising, and public relations managers
10	L	VH	L	VL	Work experience plus degree	Personnel, training, and labor relations managers
9	VL	H	L	H	Bachelor's degree	Property and real estate managers[1]
7	VL	VH	VL	VL	Work experience plus degree	Purchasing managers
83	VH	VH	VL	L	Work experience plus degree	All other managers and administrators[1]
143	–	–	–	–	–	Management support occupations
33	H	VH	VL	VL	Bachelor's degree	Accountants and auditors
2	VL	VH	VL	VL	Bachelor's degree	Budget analysts
2	VL	VH	VL	VL	Bachelor's degree	Claims examiners, property and casualty insurance
3	VL	VH	L	VL	Work experience in a related occupation	Construction and building inspectors
5	VL	VH	L	VL	Bachelor's degree	Cost estimators
1	VL	VH	VL	VL	Bachelor's degree	Credit analysts
4	VL	H	L	VL	Bachelor's degree	Employment interviewers, private or public employment service
4	VL	VH	L	VL	Work experience in a related occupation	Inspectors and compliance officers, except construction
10	VL	VH	VL	VL	Bachelor's degree	Loan officers and counselors
8	VL	VH	L	H	Work experience plus degree	Management analysts[1]
15	L	VH	L	VL	Bachelor's degree	Personnel, training, and labor relations specialists
8	VL	VH	L	VL	Bachelor's degree	Purchasing agents, except wholesale, retail, and farm products
1	VL	VH	VL	VL	Bachelor's degree	Tax examiners, collectors, and revenue agents
3	VL	VH	L	VL	Bachelor's degree	Underwriters
5	VL	H	L	H	Bachelor's degree	Wholesale and retail buyers, except farm products
40	H	VH	VL	VL	Bachelor's degree	All other management support workers[1]
829	–	–	–	–	–	**Professional specialty occupations**
58	–	–	–	–	–	Engineers
1	VL	VH	L	VL	Bachelor's degree	Aeronautical and astronautical engineers
2	VL	VH	VL	VL	Bachelor's degree	Chemical engineers[1]
8	VL	VH	VL	VL	Bachelor's degree	Civil engineers, including traffic engineers
20	L	VH	L	VL	Bachelors degree	Electrical and electronics engineers
4	VL	VH	VL	VL	Bachelor's degree	Industrial engineers, except safety engineers
8	VL	VH	VL	VL	Bachelor's degree	Mechanical engineers
1	VL	VH	VL	VL	Bachelor's degree	Metallurgists and metallurgical, ceramic, and materials engineers[1]
0	VL	VH	VL	VL	Bachelor's degree	Mining engineers, including mine safety engineers[1]
0	VL	VH	VL	VL	Bachelor's degree	Nuclear engineers[1]
0	VL	VH	VL	VL	Bachelor's degree	Petroleum engineers[1]
13	L	VH	L	VL	Bachelor's degree	All other engineers[1]
7	–	–	–	–	–	Architects and surveyors
4	VL	VH	L	L	Bachelor's degree	Architects, except landscape and marine
1	VL	VH	L	L	Bachelor's degree	Landscape architects
2	VL	H	L	VL	Postsecondary vocational training	Surveyors[1]
6	–	–	–	–	–	Life scientists

[1]One or more Current Population Survey (CPS) based occupations may be used to estimate CPS based data. See Table 2.
NOTE: Rankings are based on employment in all detailed occupations In the National Industry-Occupation Matrix. For details, see "Data presented" section of text. Codes for describing the ranked variables are: VH = Very high, H = High, L = Low, VL = Very low, n. a. = Data not available. A dash indicates data are not applicable.

Table 1. Occupational employment and job openings data, 1996-2006, and worker characteristics, 1996—Continued   (Numbers in thousands)

1996 Matrix Occupation	Employment		Employment change, 1996-2006				Percent self-em-ployed, 1996	Annual average job openings due to growth and total replacement needs, 1996-2006	
			Numeric		Percent				
	1996	2006	Number	Rank	Number	Rank		Number	Rank
Agricultural and food scientists[1]	24	29	5	VL	19.6	H	8.2	2	VL
Biological scientists	83	103	21	L	25.1	VH	4.7	9	VL
Foresters and conservation scientists[1]	37	43	6	VL	17.4	H	4.9	3	VL
Medical scientists	35	44	9	VL	25.1	VH	1.8	4	VL
All other life scientists	1	1	0	VL	–3.0	VL	0.0	0	VL
Computer, mathematical, and operations research occupations	1,028	2,038	1,010	–	98.2	–	6.0	261	–
Actuaries[1]	16	16	0	VL	1.9	VL	0.0	2	VL
Computer systems analysts, engineers, and scientists	933	1,937	1,004	–	107.6	–	6.3	253	–
Computer engineers and scientists	427	912	485	–	113.4	–	4.8	119	–
Computer engineers	216	451	235	H	109.1	VH	7.0	59	L
Database administrators, computer support specialists, and all other computer scientists	212	461	249	VH	117.8	VH	2.5	60	L
Systems analysts	506	1,025	520	VH	102.8	VH	7.5	133	L
Statisticians[1]	14	14	0	VL	0.7	VL	0.0	1	VL
Mathematicians and all other mathematical scientists[1]	16	17	1	VL	9.1	L	8.1	2	VL
Operations research analysts	50	54	4	VL	7.8	L	3.3	3	VL
Physical scientists	207	242	36	–	17.3	–	5.0	18	–
Chemists	91	108	17	VL	18.3	H	0.0	8	VL
Geologists, geophysicists, and oceanographers[1]	47	54	7	VL	14.6	H	15.0	4	VL
Meteorologists[1]	7	8	1	VL	8.2	L	0.0	1	VL
Physicists and astronomers[1]	18	17	0	VL	–1.6	VL	0.0	1	VL
All other physical scientists[1]	43	55	12	VL	27.5	VH	7.2	4	VL
Social scientists	263	288	24	–	9.2	–	27.6	35	–
Economists	51	60	9	VL	18.6	H	21.7	8	VL
Psychologists	143	154	11	VL	8.0	L	41.0	18	VL
Urban and regional planners[1]	29	31	1	VL	4.7	VL	3.2	4	VL
All other social scientists[1]	41	43	2	VL	5.1	VL	5.5	5	VL
Social, recreational, and religious workers	1,469	1,939	470	–	32.0	–	1.1	257	–
Clergy	208	236	28	L	13.2	L	0.0	20	VL
Directors, religious activities and education[1]	85	115	30	L	35.5	VH	0.0	11	VL
Human services workers[1]	178	276	98	L	55.4	VH	0.0	62	L
Recreation workers	233	285	52	L	22.3	VH	0.0	44	–
Residential counselors	180	254	74	L	41.2	VH	0.0	25	VL
Social workers	585	772	188	H	32.1	VH	2.8	96	L
Lawyers and judicial workers	699	820	120	–	17.2	–	28.0	39	–
Judges, magistrates, and other judicial workers[1]	78	79	2	VL	2.2	VL	0.0	3	VL
Lawyers	622	740	118	H	19.0	H	31.5	36	VL
Teachers, librarians, and counselors	6,565	7,914	1,349	–	20.6	–	2.6	1,000	–
Teachers, preschool and kindergarten	499	596	98	L	19.6	H	1.1	56	L
Teachers, elementary	1,491	1,644	153	H	10.3	L	0.0	170	H
Teachers, secondary school	1,406	1,718	312	VH	22.2	VH	0.0	131	L
Teachers, special education	407	648	241	H	59.1	VH	0.0	49	L
College and university faculty[1]	864	1,026	162	H	18.8	H	0.0	134	L
Other teachers and instructors	878	1,118	240	–	27.3	–	10.6	254	–
Farm and home management advisors	16	10	–6	VL	–38.3	VL	10.0	3	VL
Instructors and coaches, sports and physical training	303	427	123	H	40.7	VH	0.0	96	L
Adult and vocational education teachers	559	682	123	–	21.9	–	16.3	155	–
Instructors, adult (nonvocational) education	248	299	51	L	20.6	H	36.8	68	L
Teachers and instructors, vocational education and training	311	383	72	L	23.0	VH	0.0	87	L
All other teachers and instructors[1]	671	770	99	H	14.8	H	10.0	158	L
Librarians, archivists, curators, and related workers	174	185	10	–	5.9	–	0.0	29	–
Curators, archivists, museum technicians, and restorers[1]	20	23	3	VL	14.7	H	0.0	4	VL
Librarians, professional	154	162	7	VL	4.8	VL	0.0	25	VL
Counselors	175	209	33	L	19.1	H	2.5	19	VL
Health diagnosing occupations	877	1,039	162	–	18.4	–	26.0	43	–
Chiropractors[1]	44	55	12	VL	27.1	VH	56.1	3	VL
Dentists	162	175	13	VL	8.1	L	44.8	3	VL
Optometrists[1]	41	46	5	VL	11.7	L	38.2	2	VL
Physicians	560	678	118	H	21.0	VH	16.2	321	VL

[1]One or more Current Population Survey (CPS) based occupations may be used to estimate CPS based data. See Table 2.
NOTE: Rankings are based on employment in all detailed occupations in the National Industry-Occupation Matrix. For details, see "Data presented" section of text. Codes for describing the ranked variables are: VH = Very high, H = High, L = Low, VL = Very low. n. a. = Data not available. A dash indicates data are not applicable.

Table 1. Occupational employment and job openings data, 1996-2006, and worker characteristics, 1996—Continued (Numbers in thousands)

Annual average job openings due to growth and net replacement needs, 1996-2006		Median hourly earnings	Unemployment rate	Percent part-time	Most significant source of training	1996 Matrix Occupation
Number	Rank					
1	VL	VH	VL	VL	Bachelor's degree	Agricultural and food scientists[1]
3	VL	VH	L	VL	Doctoral degree	Biological scientists
1	VL	VH	VL	VL	Bachelor's degree	Foresters and conservation scientists[1]
1	VL	VH	L	VL	Doctoral degree	Medical scientists
0	VL	VH	L	VL	Doctoral degree	All other life scientists
110	–	–	–	–	–	Computer, mathematical, and operations research occupations
0	VL	VH	VL	VL	Bachelor's degree	Actuaries[1]
107	–	–	–	–	–	Computer systems analysis, engineers, and scientists
52	–	–	–	–	–	Computer engineers and scientists
25	L	VH	VL	VL	Bachelor's degree	Computer engineers
						Database administrators, computer support specialists, and all other computer scientists
27	L	VH	VL	VL	Bachelor's degree	
55	H	VH	VL	VL	Bachelor's degree	Systems analysts
0	VL	VH	VL	VL	Bachelor's degree	Statisticians[1]
0	VL	VH	VL	VL	Doctoral degree	Mathematicians and all other mathematical scientists[1]
2	VL	VH	VL	VL	Master's degree	Operations research analysts
8	–	–	–	–	–	Physical scientists
4	VL	VH	VL	VL	Bachelor's degree	Chemists
2	VL	VH	VL	VL	Bachelor's degree	Geologists, geophysicists, and oceanographers[1]
0	VL	VH	VL	VL	Bachelor's degree	Meteorologists[1]
0	VL	VH	VL	VL	Doctoral degree	Physicists and astronomers
2	VL	VH	VL	VL	Bachelor's degree	All other physical scientists
6	–	–	–	–	–	Social scientists
2	VL	VH	L	VL	Bachelor's degree	Economists
3	VL	VH	VL	H	Master's degree	Psychologists
1	VL	VH	VL	H	Master's degree	Urban and regional planners[1]
1	VL	VH	VL	H	Master's degree	All other social scientists[1]
79	–	–	–	–	–	Social, recreational, and religious workers
7	VL	H	VL	H	First professional degree	Clergy
5	VL	L	VL	VH	Bachelor's degree	Directors, religious activities and education[1]
13	L	L	H	VH	Moderate-term on-the-job-training	Human services workers[1]
15	L	VL	VH	H	Bachelor's degree	Recreation workers
12	L	L	VL	L	Bachelor's degree	Residential counselors
28	L	H	VL	L	Bachelor's degree	Social workers
22	–	–	–	–	–	Lawyers and judicial workers
1	VL	H	VL	L	Work experience plus degree	Judges, magistrates, and other judicial workers[1]
21	L	VH	VL	L	First professional degree	Lawyers
271	–	–	–	–	–	Teachers, librarians, and counselors
19	L	L	L	H	Bachelor's degree	Teachers, preschool and kindergarten
44	H	VH	VL	L	Bachelor's degree	Teachers, elementary
73	VH	VH	VL	L	Bachelor's degree	Teachers, secondary school
30	L	VH	VL	L	Bachelor's degree	Teachers, special education
41	H	VH	L	VH	Doctoral degree	College and university faculty[1]
33	–	–	–	–	–	Other teachers and instructors
0	VL	VH	L	VH	Bachelor's degree	Farm and home management advisors
15	L	L	L	VH	Moderate-term on-the-job-training	Instructors and coaches, sports and physical training
17	–	–	–	–	–	Adult and vocational education teachers
7	VL	H	L	VH	Work experience in a related occupation	Instructors, adult (nonvocational) education
10	VL	VH	L	VH	Work experience in a related occupation	Teachers and instructors, vocational education and training
19	L	VH	L	VH	Master's degree	All other teachers and instructors[1]
5	–	–	–	–	–	Librarians, archivists, curators, and related workers
1	VL	H	VL	H	Master's degree	Curators, archivists, museum technicians, and restorers[1]
5	VL	VH	VL	H	Master's degree	Librarians, professional
7	VL	VH	VL	L	Master's degree	Counselors
30	–	–	–	–	–	Health diagnosing occupations
2	VL	VH	VL	L	First professional degree	Chiropractors[1]
5	VL	VH	VL	H	First professional degree	Dentists
1	VL	VH	VL	L	First professional degree	Optometrists[1]
20	L	VH	VL	L	First professional degree	Physicians

[1]One or more Current Population Survey (CPS) based occupations may be used to estimate CPS based data. See Table 2.
NOTE: Rankings are based on employment in all detailed occupations in the National Industry-Occupation Matrix. For details, see "Data presented" section of text. Codes for describing the ranked variables are: VH = Very high, H = High, L = Low, VL = Very low, n. a. = Data not available. A dash indicates data are not applicable.

Table 1. Occupational employment and job openings data, 1996-2006, and worker characteristics, 1996—Continued (Numbers in thousands)

1996 Matrix Occupation	Employment		Employment change, 1996-2006				Percent self-em-ployed,	Annual average job openings due to growth and total replacement	
			Numeric		Percent				
	1996	2006	Number	Rank	Number	Rank		Number	Rank
Podiatrists[1]	11	12	1	VL	10.1	L	33.6	0	VL
Veterinarians and veterinary inspectors[1]	58	71	13	VL	22.7	VH	35.1	3	VL
Health assessment and treating occupations	2,684	3,393	709	–	26.4	–	2.2	253	–
Dietitians and nutritionists	58	69	11	VL	18.2	H	16.4	9	VL
Pharmacists	172	194	22.	L	12.6	L	4.7	7	VL
Physician assistants[1]	64	93	30	L	46.6	VH	1.2	6	VL
Registered nurses	1,971	2,382	411	VH	20.8	VH	0.7	183	H
Therapists	419	655	236	–	56.3	–	6.7	49	–
Occupational therapists[1]	57	95	38	L	66.1	VH	4.9	7	VL
Physical therapists[1]	115	196	81	L	70.8	VH	7.0	15	VL
Recreational therapists[1]	38	46	8	VL	21.3	VH	26.2	3	VL
Respiratory therapists[1]	82	119	37	L	45.8	VH	0.0	8	VL
Speech-language pathologists and audiologists[1]	87	131	44	L	50.6	VH	6.8	10	VL
All other therapists[1]	40	67	27	L	67.4	VH	3.1	5	VL
Writers, artists, and entertainers	2,606	3,242	636	–	24.4	–	22.0	470	–
Artists and commercial artists	276	354	78	L	28.3	VH	57.3	54	L
Athletes, coaches, umpires, and related workers	42	49	7	VL	15.5	H	31.6	15	VL
Dancers and choreographers[1]	23	30	7	VL	28.0	VH	30.2	5	VL
Designers	342	431	89	–	26.1	–	37.3	58	–
Designers, except interior designers	279	351	72	L	25.7	VH	36.4	48	L
Interior designers	63	80	17	VL	27.5	VH	41.5	11	VL
Musicians	274	366	92	L	33.4	VH	26.8	54	L
Photographers and camera operators	154	180	26	–	16.9	–	41.6	23	–
Camera operators, television, motion picture, video	20	23	3	VL	14.5	H	7.4	3	VL
Photographers	134	157	23	L	17.3	H	46.7	20	VL
Producers, directors, actors, and entertainers[1]	105	130	25	L	23.6	VH	27.3	21	VL
Public relations specialists and publicity writers	110	140	30	L	27.2	VH	4.4	23	VL
Radio and TV announcers and newscasters	52	52	0	VL	–0.6	VL	0.0	11	VL
Reporters and correspondents	60	58	-2	VL	–3.1	VL	8.6	6	VL
Writers and editors, including technical writers	286	347	61	L	21.2	VH	31.6	43	VL
All other professional workers[1]	880	1,104	224	H	25.5	VH	2.2	158	L
Technicians and related support occupations	4,618	5,558	940		20.4		1.5	512	–
Health technicians and technologists	2,301	2,872	571	–	24.8	–	1.1	236	–
Cardiology technologists[1]	17	23	6	VL	34.9	VH	0.0	3	VL
Clinical laboratory technologists and technicians	285	328	42	L	14.9	H	1.8	18	VL
Dental hygienists	133	197	64	L	48.2	VH	0.5	16	VL
Electroneurodiagnostic technologists[1]	6	8	2	VL	24.0	VH	0.0	1	VL
EKG technicians[1]	15	11	-4	VL	–24.2	VL	0.0	1	VL
Emergency medical technicians[1]	150	217	67	L	45.1	VH	0.0	26	VL
Licensed practical nurses	699	848	148	H	21.2	VH	0.4	45	L
Medical records technicians[1]	87	132	44	L	50.9	VH	0.0	12	VL
Nuclear medicine technologists	13	15	2	VL	13.3	L	0.0	1	VL
Opticians, dispensing and measuring	67	76	9	VL	14.1	L	4.0	5	VL
Pharmacy technicians[1]	83	92	9	VL	11.1	L	0.0	10	VL
Psychiatric technicians	66	72	6	VL	9.1	L	0.0	15	VL
Radiologic technologists and technicians	174	224	50	L	28.9	VH	0.4	14	VL
Surgical technologists[1]	49	64	15	VL	31.9	VH	0.0	8	VL
Veterinary technicians and technologists[1]	26	34	7	VL	27.4	VH	0.0	3	VL
All other health professionals and paraprofessionals	430	531	101	H	23.5	VH	3.0	59	L
Engineering and science technicians and technologists	1,236	1,342	106	–	8.6	–	1.0	146	–
Engineering technicians	698	767	70	–	10.0	–	0.7	96	–
Electrical and electronic technicians and technologists	297	341	43	L	14.5	H	0.6	37	VL
All other engineering technicians and technologists[1]	400	427	26	L	6.6	L	0.8	60	L
Drafters	310	317	7	VL	2.3	VL	1.5	30	VL
Science and mathematics technicians[1]	228	258	29	L	12.9	L	1.0	19	VL
Technicians, except health and engineering and science	1,082	1,345	263	–	24.3	–	3.0	130	–
Aircraft pilots and flight engineers	110	125	151	VL	13.8	L	1.4	6	VL

[1]One or more Current Population survey (CPS) based occupations may be used to estimate CPS based data. See Table 2.
NOTE: Rankings are based on employment In all detailed occupations in the National Industry-Occupation Matrix. For details, see "Data presented" section of text. Codes for describing the ranked variables are: VH = Very high, H = High, L = Low, VL = Very low, n. a. = Data not available. A dash indicates data are not applicable.

Table 1. Occupational employment and job openings data, 1996-2006, and worker characteristics, 1996—Continued (Numbers in thousands)

Annual average job openings due to growth and net replacement needs, 1996-2006		Median hourly earnings	Unemployment rate	Percent part-time	Most significant source of training	1996 Matrix Occupation
Number	Rank					
0	VL	VH	VL	L	First professional degree	Podiatrists[1]
2	VL	VH	VL	L	First professional degree	Veterinarians and Veterinary inspectors[1]
109	–	–	–	–	–	Health assessment and treating occupations
2	VL	VH	L	H	Bachelor's degree	Dietitians and nutritionists
6	VL	VH	VL	L	Bachelor's degree	Pharmacists
4	VL	VH	VL	H	Bachelor's degree	Physician assistant[1]
68	H	VH	VL	H	Associate degree	Registered nurses
28	–	–	–	–	–	Therapists
4	VL	VH	VL	H	Bachelor's degree	Occupational therapists[1]
9	VL	VH	VL	H	Bachelor's degree	Physical therapists[1]
1	VL	H	VL	H	Bachelor's degree	Recreational therapists[1]
5	VL	VH	VL	L	Associate degree	Respiratory therapists[1]
5	VL	VH	VL	H	Master's degree	Speech-language pathologists and audiologists[1]
3	VL	H	VL	H	Bachelor's degree	All other therapists[1]
102	–	–	–	–	–	Writers, artists, and entertainers
14	L	H	L	H	Work experience plus degree	Artists and commercial artists
2	VL	L	H	VH	Long-term on-the-job-training	Athletes, coaches, umpires, and related workers
1	VL	H	L	H	Postsecondary vocational training	Dancers and choreographers[1]
15	–	–	–	–	–	Designers
12	L	H	L	H	Bachelor's degree	Designers, except interior designers
3	VL	H	L	H	Bachelor's degree	Interior designers
13	L	H	H	VH	Long-term on-the-job-training	Musicians
5	–	–	–	–	–	Photographers and camera operators
1	VL	L	L	VH	Moderate-term on-the-job-training	Camera operators, television, motion picture, video
4	VL	L	L	VH	Moderate-term on-the-job-training	Photographers
5	VL	n. a.	VH	VH	Long term on-the-job-training	Producers, directors, actors, and entertainers[1]
7	VL	H	L	L	Bachelor's degree	Public relations specialists and publicity writers
2	VL	L	H	VH	Long-term on-the-job-training	Radio and TV announcers and newscasters
2	VL	H	VL	L	Bachelor's degree	Reporters and correspondents
12	L	VH	VL	H	Bachelor's degree	Writers and editors, including technical writers
44	H	H	L	H	Bachelor's degree	All other professional workers[1]
193	–	–	–	–	–	**Technicians and related support occupations**
101	–	–	–	–	–	Health technicians and technologists
1	VL	VH	L	H	Associate degree	Cardiology technologists[1]
7	VL	H	VL	L	Bachelor's degree	Clinical laboratory technologists and technicians
10	L	VH	VL	VH	Associate degree	Dental hygienists
0	VL	H	L	H	Moderate-term on-the-job-training	Electroneurodiagnostic technologists[1]
0	VL	H	L	H	Moderate-term on-the-job-training	EKG technicians[1]
10	VL	L	L	H	Postsecondary vocational training	Emergency medical technicians[1]
30	L	H	L	H	Postsecondary vocational training	Licensed practical nurses
6	VL	L	VL	H	Associate degree	Medical records technicians[1]
0	VL	VH	VL	L	Associate degree	Nuclear medicine technologists
2	VL	L	L	L	Long-term on-the-job-training	Opticians, dispensing and measuring
3	VL	L	L	H	Moderate-term on-the-job-training	Pharmacy technicians[1]
1	VL	L	H	H	Associate degree	Psychiatric technicians
8	VL	H	VL	L	Associate degree	Radiologic technologists and technicians
2	VL	H	L	H	Postsecondary vocational training	Surgical technologists[1]
1	VL	L	H	L	Associate degree	Veterinary technicians and technologists[1]
18	L	H	VL	H	Associate degree	All other health professionals and paraprofessionals[1]
38	–	–	–	–	–	Engineering and science technicians and technologists
23	–	–	–	–	–	Engineering technicians
12	L	VH	L	VL	Associate degree	Electrical and electronic technicians and technologists
11	L	VH	L	VL	Associate degree	All other engineering technicians and technologists[1]
7	VL	H	L	VL	Postsecondary vocational training	Drafters
8	VL	H	L	L	Associate degree	Science and mathematics technicians[1]
54	–	–	–	–	–	Technicians, except health and engineering and science
4	VL	VH	VL	VH	Bachelor's degree	Aircraft pilots and flight engineers

[1]One or more Current Population Survey (CPS) based occupations may be used to estimate CPS based data. See Table 2.
NOTE: Rankings are based on employment in all detailed occupations in the National Industry-Occupation Matrix. For details, see "Data presented" section of text. Codes for describing the ranked variables are: VH = Very high, H = High, L = Low, VL = Very low, n. a. = Data not available. A dash indicates data are not applicable.

Table 1. Occupational employment and job openings data, 1996-2006, and worker characteristics, 1996—Continued (Numbers in thousands)

1996 Matrix Occupation	Employment		Employment change, 1996-2006				Percent self-em-ployed, 1996	Annual average job openings due to growth and total replacement needs, 1996-2006	
			Numeric		Percent				
	1996	2006	Number	Rank	Number	Rank		Number	Rank
Air traffic controllers and airplane dispatchers[1]	29	29	0	VL	−0.3	VL	0.0	2	VL
Broadcast technicians[1]	46	53	7	VL	15.1	H	3.8	4	VL
Computer programmers	568	697	129	H	22.8	VH	3.5	60	L
Legal assistants and technicians, except clerical	221	310	90	–	40.7	–	4.1	42	–
Paralegals	113	189	76	L	67.7	VH	2.1	29	VL
Title examiners and searchers	26	29	3	VL	13.4	L	18.3	4	VL
All other legal assistants, including law clerks	82	92	10	VL	12.1	L	2.4	9	VL
Programmers, numerical, tool, and process control[1]	7	7	0	VL	5.7	L	0.0	1	VL
Technical assistants, library[1]	78	100	22	L	28.0	VH	0.0	11	VL
All other technicians[1]	24	23	0	VL	−2.0	VL	0.0	2	VL
Marketing and sales occupations	14,633	16,897	2,264	–	15.5	–	12.4	4,070	–
Cashiers	3,146	3,677	530	VH	16.8	H	0.5	1,265	VH
Counter and rental clerks	374	458	84	L	22.5	VH	1.9	158	L
Insurance sales workers	409	426	18	VL	4.3	VL	30.1	43	VL
Marketing and sales worker supervisors	2,316	2,562	246	VH	10.6	L	34.3	370	VH
Real estate agents, brokers, and appraisers	408	441	32	–	7.9	–	64.8	52	–
Brokers, real estate	78	89	11	VL	14.1	L	64.8	11	VL
Real estate appraisers	48	54	6	VL	12.1	L	23.5	7	VL
Sales agents, real estate	282	298	16	VL	5.5	VL	71.9	35	VL
Salespersons, retail	4,072	4,481	408	VH	10.0	L	4.5	1,272	VH
Securities and financial services sales workers	263	363	100	H	37.8	VH	24.3	52	L
Travel agents[1]	142	176	34	L	24.0	VH	15.8	19	VL
All other sales and related workers[1]	3,503	4,314	811	VH	23.2	VH	9.5	840	VH
Administrative support occupations, including clerical	24,019	25,825	1,806	–	7.5	–	1.8	4,844	–
Adjusters, investigators, and collectors	1,283	1,605	322	–	25.1	–	0.9	292	–
Adjustment clerks	401	584	183	H	45.5	VH	0.0	129	L
Bill and account collectors	269	381	112	H	41.8	VH	1.1	96	L
Insurance claims and policy processing occupations	466	526	60	–	12.9	–	1.8	58	-
Insurance adjusters, examiners, and Investigators	165	203	38	L	23.1	VH	5.1	15	VL
Insurance claims clerks	121	153	31	L	25.7	VH	0.0	12	VL
Insurance policy processing clerks	179	171	−9	VL	−5.0	VL	0.0	31	VL
Welfare eligibility workers and interviewers	109	76	−34	VL	−30.8	VL	0.0	2	VL
All other adjusters and investigators	38	39	0	VL	1.3	VL	0.0	7	VL
Communications equipment operators	328	295	−33	–	−9.9	–	0.0	74	–
Telephone operators	319	289	−30	–	−9.3	–	0.0	73	–
Central office operators	48	26	−23	VL	−47.0	VL	0.0	9	VL
Directory assistance operators	33	18	−16	VL	−47.1	VL	0.0	6	VL
Switchboard operators	237	246	9	VL	3.7	VL	0.0	58	L
All other communications equipment operators[1]	9	6	−3	VL	−33.7	VL	0.0	2	VL
Computer operators	291	198	−94	–	−32.1	–	2.0	36	–
Computer operators, except peripheral equipment	258	181	−77	VL	−29.8	VL	2.3	32	VL
Peripheral computer equipment operators[1]	33	17	−17	VL	−50.0	VL	0.0	4	VL
Information clerks	1,591	1,958	366	–	23.0	–	1.1	475	–
Hotel desk clerks	144	174	30	L	21.0	VH	0.7	58	L
Interviewing clerks, except personnel and social welfare	98	115	17	VL	17.7	H	1.8	33	VL
New accounts clerks, banking	110	115	5	VL	4.5	VL	0.0	33	VL
Receptionists and Information clerks	1,074	1,392	318	VH	29.7	VH	1.4	336	H
Reservation and transportation ticket agents and travel clerks[1]	166	162	−4	VL	−2.7	VL	0.0	16	VL
Mail clerks and messengers	268	291	23	–	8.6	–	4.1	67	–
Mail clerks, except mail machine operators and postal service	130	137	7	VL	5.7	L	0.0	26	VL
Messengers	138	154	16	VL	11.3	L	7.9	41	VL
Postal clerks and mail carriers	403	443	40	–	9.9	–	0.0	13	–
Postal mail carriers	332	369	37	L	11.2	L	0.0	9	VL
Postal service clerks	71	74	3	VL	3.8	VL	0.0	4	VL
Material recording, scheduling, dispatching, and distributing occupations	3,859	4,084	225	–	5.8	–	0.2	822	–
Dispatchers	234	258	24	–	10.1	–	0.9	44	–

[1]One or more Current Population Survey (CPS) based occupations may be used to estimate CPS based data. See Table 2.
NOTE: Rankings are based on employment in all detailed occupations in the National Industry-Occupation Matrix. For details, see "Data presented" section of text. Codes for describing the ranked variables are: VH = Very high, H = High, L = Low, VL = Very low, n. a. = Data not available. A dash indicates data are not applicable.

Table 1. Occupational employment and job openings data, 1996-2006, and worker characteristics, 1996—Continued (Numbers in thousands)

Annual average job openings due to growth and net replacement needs, 1996-2006		Median hourly earnings	Unemployment rate	Percent part-time	Most significant source of training	1996 Matrix Occupation
Number	Rank					
1	VL	VH	VL	L	Long-term on-the-job-training	Air traffic controllers and airplane dispatchers[1]
2	VL	H	VL	L	Postsecondary vocational training	Broadcast technicians[1]
31	L	VH	VL	VL	Bachelor's degree	Computer programmers
11	–	–	–	–		Legal assistants and technicians, except clerical
9	VL	H	L	L	Associate degree	Paralegals
1	VL	H	L	L	Moderate-term on-the-job-training	Title examiners and searchers
2	VL	H	VL	L	Associate degree	All other legal assistants, including law clerks
0	VL	VH	VL	L	Work experience in a related occupation	Programmers, numerical, tool, and process control[1]
4	VL	L	L	H	Short-term on-the-job-training	Technical assistants, library[1]
1	VL	H	L	H	Moderate-term on-the-job-training	All other technicians[1]
652	–	–	–	–	–	**Marketing and sales occupations**
190	VH	VL	VH	VH	Short-term on-the-job-training	Cashiers
22	L	VL	H	VH	Short-term on-the-job-training	Counter and rental clerks
9	VL	VH	VL	L	Bachelor's degree	Insurance sales workers
62	H	H	VL	L	Work experience in a related occupation	Marketing and sales worker supervisors
10						Real estate agents, brokers, and appraisers
2	VL	VH	VL	H	Work experience in a related occupation	Brokers, real estate
1	VL	VH	VL	H	Bachelor's degree	Real estate appraisers
6	VL	H	VL	H	Postsecondary vocational training	Sales agents, real estate
170	VH	VL	H	VH	Short-term on-the-job-training	Salespersons, retail
12	L	VH	L	L	Bachelor's degree	Securities and financial services sales workers
7	VL	L	L	L	Postsecondary vocational training	Travel agents[1]
170	VH	H	H	H	Moderate-term on-the-job-training	All other sales and related workers[1]
691	–	–	–	–	–	**Administrative support occupations, including clerical**
52	–	–	–	–	–	Adjusters, investigators, and collectors
21	L	L	L	L	Short-term on-the-job-training	Adjustment clerks
17	L	L	L	L	Short-term on-the-job-training	Bill and account collectors
13						Insurance claims and policy processing occupations
6	VL	VH	VL	VL	Long-term on-the-job-training	Insurance adjusters, examiners, and investigators
5	VL	H	VL	VL	Moderate-term on-the-job-training	Insurance claims clerks
2	VL	H	L	L	Moderate-term on-the-job-training	Insurance policy processing clerks
2	VL	H	L	VL	Moderate-term on-the-job-training	Welfare eligibility workers and interviewers
1	VL	H	L	L	Moderate-term on-the-job-training	All other adjusters and investigators
7	–	–	–	–	–	Communications equipment operators
7	–	–	–	–	–	Telephone operators
1	VL	H	H	H	Moderate-term on-the-job-training	Central office operators
1	VL	H	H	H	Moderate-term on-the-job-training	Directory assistance operators
5	VL	L	H	H	Short-term on-the-job-training	Switchboard operators
0	VL	H	H	H	Moderate-term on-the-job-training	All other communications equipment operators[1]
5						Computer operators
4	VL	H	L	L	Moderate-term on-the-job-training	Computer operators, except peripheral equipment
1	VL	L	L	L	Moderate-term on-the-job-training	Peripheral computer equipment operators[1]
73	–	–	–	–	–	Information clerks
9	VL	VL	H	H	Short-term on-the-job-training	Hotel desk clerks
5	VL	L	VH	H	Short-term on-the-job-training	Interviewing clerks, except personnel and social welfare
4	VL	L	VH	H	Work experience in a related occupation	New accounts clerks, banking
52	H	L	H	VH	Short-term on-the-job-training	Receptionists and information clerks
4	VL	H	L	L	Short-term on-the-job-training	Reservation and transportation ticket agents and travel clerks[1]
9	–	–	–	–	–	Mail clerks and messengers
4	VL	L	H	H	Short-term on-the-job-training	Mail clerks, except mail machine operators and postal service
5	VL	L	H	VH	Short-term on-the-job-training	Messengers
13						Postal clerks and mail carriers
12	L	H	VL	VL	Short-term on-the-job-training	Postal mail carriers
2	VL	H	L	VL	Short-term on-the-job-training	Postal service clerks
83	–	–	–	–	–	Material recording, scheduling, dispatching, and distributing occupations
6	–	–	–	–	–	Dispatchers

[1]One or more Current Population Survey (CPS) based occupations may be used to estimate CPS based data. See Table 2.
NOTE: Rankings are based on employment in all detailed occupations in the National Industry-Occupation Matrix. For details, see "Data presented" section of text. Codes for describing the ranked variables are: VH = Very high, H = High, L = Low, VL = Very low, n. a. = Data not available. A dash indicates data are not applicable.

Table 1. Occupational employment and job openings data, 1996-2006, and worker characteristics, 1996—Continued (Numbers in thousands)

1996 Matrix Occupation	Employment		Employment change, 1996-2006				Percent self-employed, 1996	Annual average job openings due to growth and total replacement needs, 1996-2006	
			Numeric		Percent				
	1996	2006	Number	Rank	Number	Rank		Number	Rank
Dispatchers, except police, fire, and ambulance	148	165	17	VL	11.4	L	1.5	29	VL
Dispatchers, police, fire, and ambulance	86	93	7	VL	7.7	L	0.0	16	VL
Meter readers, utilities[1]	55	56	1	VL	2.2	VL	0.0	13	VL
Order fillers, wholesale and retail sales	227	255	28	L	12.1	L	0.0	39	VL
Procurement clerks	56	55	−1	VL	−1.9	VL	0.0	10	VL
Production, planning, and expediting clerks	239	254	15	VL	6.3	L	0.4	63	L
Stock clerks	1,844	1,898	54	L	2.9	VL	0.2	346	H
Traffic, shipping, and receiving clerks	985	1,070	85	L	8.6	L	0.1	251	H
Weighers, measurers, checkers, and samplers, recordkeeping[1]	47	50	3	VL	6.1	L	0.0	11	VL
All other material recording, scheduling, and distribution workers[1]	170	188	17	VL	10.3	L	0.0	45	L
Records processing occupations	3,870	3,887	16	–	0.4	–	5.9	699	–
Advertising clerks[1]	18	18	0	VL	−1.3	VL	0.0	3	VL
Brokerage clerks	76	91	15	VL	19.1	H	0.0	17	VL
Correspondence clerks[1]	31	41	10	VL	30.8	VH	0.0	6	VL
File clerks	293	315	22	L	7.4	L	1.1	125	L
Financial records processing occupations	2,848	2,790	−58	–	−2.0	–	7.7	439	–
Billing, cost, and rate clerks	335	391	55	L	16.5	H	0.6	63	L
Billing, posting, and calculating machine operators[1]	102	100	−1	VL	−1.4	VL	1.3	10	VL
Bookkeeping, accounting, and auditing clerks	2,250	2,147	−102	VL	−4.5	VL	9.5	351	H
Payroll and timekeeping clerks	161	151	−10	VL	−5.9	VL	1.5	14	VL
Library assistants and bookmobile drivers	125	145	19	VL	15.4	H	0.0	35	VL
Order clerks, materials, merchandise, and service	329	338	8	VL	2.6	VL	1.2	51	L
Personnel clerks, except payroll and timekeeping[1]	124	126	2	VL	1.4	VL	0.0	19	VL
Statement clerks	25	25	−1	VL	−2.8	VL	4.1	5	VL
Secretaries, stenographers, and typists	4,153	4,081	−72	–	−1.7	–	2.4	574	–
Secretaries	3,403	3,427	25	–	0.7	–	1.6	466	–
Legal secretaries	284	319	35	L	12.5	L	0.6	44	–
Medical secretaries	239	314	76	L	31.7	VH	0.3	44	L
Secretaries, except legal and medical	2,881	2,794	−87	VL	−3.0	VL	1.9	378	VH
Stenographers and/or court reporters[1]	98	101	4	VL	3.7	VL	27.2	13	VL
Typists, including word processing	653	552	−100	VL	−15.4	VL	2.9	95	L
Other clerical and administrative support workers	7,972	8,983	1,011	–	12.7	–	0.6	1,792	–
Bank tellers	545	550	5	VL	0.8	VL	0.3	108	L
Clerical supervisors and managers	1,369	1,630	262	VH	19.1	H	0.2	202	H
Court clerks	53	57	5	VL	8.7	L	0.0	14	VL
Credit authorizers, credit checkers, and loan and credit clerks	252	256	3	–	1.3	–	0.0	61	–
Credit authorizers	16	10	−6	VL	−38.5	VL	0.0	3	VL
Credit checkers	42	33	−9	VL	−22.2	VL	0.0	8	VL
Loan and credit clerks	181	200	19	VL	10.2	L	0.0	46	L
Loan interviewers	12	13	1	VL	4.5	VL	0.0	3	VL
Customer service representatives, utilities	151	206	55	L	36.3	VH	0.0	32	VL
Data entry keyers, except composing	418	453	35	L	8.3	L	1.3	103	L
Data entry keyers, composing	18	10	−8	VL	−44.6	VL	0.0	3	VL
Duplicating, mail, and other office machine operators[1]	196	149	−47	VL	−24.1	VL	0.0	37	VL
General office clerks	3,111	3,326	215	H	6.9	L	0.5	713	VH
Municipal clerks	22	24	2	VL	9.3	L	0.0	6	VL
Proofreaders and copy markers[1]	26	16	−10	VL	−38.5	VL	7.7	5	VL
Real estate clerks	24	25	2	VL	6.4	L	0.0	5	VL
Statistical clerks	78	65	−13	VL	−17.3	VL	0.0	5	VL
Teacher aides and educational assistants	981	1,352	370	VH	37.7	VH	0.0	296	H
All other clerical and administrative support workers	727	864	137	H	18.8	H	2.5	203	H
Service occupations	21,294	25,147	3,853	–	18.1	–	5.7	6,373	–
Cleaning and building service occupations, except private household	3,545	3,713	168	–	4.7	–	4.6	755	–
Institutional cleaning supervisors	108	115	6	VL	5.7	L	1.8	10	VL

[1]One or more Current Population Survey (CPS) based occupations may be used to estimate CPS based data. See Table 2.
NOTE: Rankings are based on employment in all detailed occupations in the National Industry-Occupation Matrix. For details, see "Data presented" section of text. Codes for describing the ranked variables are: VH = Very high, H = High, L = Low, VL = Very low, n. a. = Data not available. A dash indicates data are not applicable.

Table 1. Occupational employment and job openings data, 1996-2006, and worker characteristics, 1996—Continued (Numbers in thousands)

Annual average job openings due to growth and net replacement needs, 1996-2006		Median hourly earnings	Unemployment rate	Percent part-time	Most significant source of training	1996 Matrix Occupation
Number	Rank					
4	VL	H	L	VL	Moderate-term on-the-job-training	Dispatchers, except police, fire, and ambulance
2	VL	L	L	VL	Moderate-term on-the-job-training	Dispatchers, police, fire, and ambulance
1	VL	H	H	L	Short-term on-the-job-training	Meter readers, utilities[1]
7	VL	L	L	L	Short-term on-the-job-training	Order fillers, wholesale and retail sales
1	VL	L	H	L	Short-term on-the-job-training	Procurement clerks
5	VL	H	L	H	Short-term on-the-job-training	Production, planning, and expediting clerks
33	H	VL	H	L	Short-term on-the-job-training	Stock clerks
23	L	L	H	VL	Short-term on-the-job-training	Traffic, shipping, and receiving clerks
1	VL	L	H	L	Short-term on-the-job-training	Weighers, measurers, checkers, and samplers, recordkeeping[1]
5	VL	L	H	L	Short-term on-the-job-training	All other material recording, scheduling, and distribution workers[1]
89	–	–	–	–	–	Records processing occupations
0	VL	L	L	L	Short-term on-the-job-training	Advertising clerks[1]
2	VL	H	L	L	Moderate-term on-the-job-training	Brokerage clerks
2	VL	L	L	L	Short-term on-the-job-training	Correspondence clerks[1]
13	L	VL	VH	VH	Short-term on-the-job-training	File clerks
54	–	–	–	–	–	Financial records processing occupations
12	L	L	L	L	Short-term on-the-job-training	Billing, cost, and rate clerks
2	VL	L	L	L	Short-term on-the-job-training	Billing, posting, and calculating machine operators[1]
38	H	L	L	VH	Moderate-term on-the-job-training	Bookkeeping, accounting, and auditing clerks
3	VL	H	L	L	Short-term on-the-job-training	Payroll and timekeeping clerks
7	VL	L	H	VH	Short-term on-the-job-training	Library assistants and bookmobile drivers
7	VL	L	L	L	Short-term on-the-job-training	Order clerks, materials, merchandise, and service
3	VL	H	L	VL	Short-term on-the-job-training	Personnel clerks, except payroll and timekeeping[1]
0	VL	L	L	L	Short-term on-the-job-training	Statement clerks
83	–	–	–	–	–	Secretaries, stenographers, and typists
70	–	–	–	–	–	Secretaries
8	VL	H	L	H	Postsecondary vocational training	Legal secretaries
12	L	L	L	H	Postsecondary vocational training	Medical secretaries
50	H	H	L	H	Postsecondary vocational training	Secretaries, except legal and medical
2	VL	H	VL	H	Postsecondary vocational training	Stenographers and/or court reporters[1]
11	L	L	H	H	Moderate-term on-the-job-training	Typists, including word processing
276	–	–	–	–	–	Other clerical and administrative support workers
23	L	L	L	VH	Short-term on-the-job-training	Bank tellers
58	H	H	VL	VL	Work experience in a related occupation	Clerical supervisors and managers
1	VL	L	L	L	Short-term on-the-job-training	Court clerks
4	–	–	–	–	–	Credit authorizers, credit checkers, and loan and credit clerks
0	VL	L	L	L	Short-term on-the-job-training	Credit authorizers
0	VL	L	L	L	Short-term on-the-job-training	Credit checkers
4	VL	L	L	L	Short-term on-the-job-training	Loan and credit clerks
0	VL	H	L	L	Short-term on-the-job-training	Loan interviewers
9	VL	H	L	L	Short-term on-the-job-training	Customer service representatives, utilities
5	VL	L	H	L	Postsecondary vocational training	Data entry keyers, except composing
0	VL	L	H	L	Postsecondary vocational training	Data entry keyers, composing
8	VL	L	H	H	Short-term on-the-job-training	Duplicating, mail, and other office machine operators[1]
92	VH	L	H	H	Short-term on-the-job-training	General office clerks
0	VL	L	L	L	Short-term on-the-job-training	Municipal clerks
1	VL	L	L	H	Short-term on-the-job-training	Proofreaders and copy markers[1]
1	VL	L	H	H	Short-term on-the-job-training	Real estate clerks
1	VL	L	VL	VL	Moderate-term on-the-job-training	Statistical clerks
50	H	VL	L	VH	Short-term on-the-job-training	Teacher aides and educational assistants
22	L	L	L	L	Short-term on-the-job-training	All other clerical and administrative support workers
1,037	–	–	–	–	–	**Service occupations**
87	–	–	–	–	–	Cleaning and building service occupations, except private household
3	VL	L	L	VL	Work experience in a related occupation	Institutional cleaning supervisors

[1]One or more Current Population Survey (CPS) based occupations may be used to estimate CPS based data. See Table 2.
NOTE: Rankings are based on employment in all detailed occupations in the National Industry-Occupation Matrix. For details, see "Data presented" section of text. Codes for describing the ranked variables are: VH = Very high, H = High, L = Low, VL = Very low, n. a. = Data not available. A dash indicates data are not applicable.

Table 1. Occupational employment and job openings data, 1996-2006, and worker characteristics, 1996—Continued (Numbers in thousands)

1996 Matrix Occupation	Employment 1996	Employment 2006	Employment change, 1996-2006 Numeric Number	Numeric Rank	Percent Number	Percent Rank	Percent self-employed, 1996	Annual average job openings due to growth and total replacement needs, 1996-2006 Number	Rank
Janitors and cleaners, including maids and housekeeping cleaners	3,134	3,262	128	H	4.1	VL	4.4	679	VH
Pest controllers and assistants[1]	60	73	13	VL	22.2	VH	10.0	9	VL
All other cleaning and building service workers[1]	3	263	20	L	8.3	L	7.8	56	L
Food preparation and service occupations	6	9,571	1,175	–	14.0	–	0.9	3,301	–
Chefs, cooks, and other kitchen workers	3,402	3,984	583	–	17.1	–	1.6	1,266	–
Cooks, except short order	1,344	1,519	175	–	13.0	–	3.2	432	–
Bakers, bread and pastry	182	231	48	L	26.4	VH	9.1	65	L
Cooks, institution or cafeteria	435	455	21	L	4.7	VL	0.0	131	L
Cooks, restaurant	727	833	106	H	14.6	H	3.7	236	H
Cooks, short order and fast food	804	978	174	H	21.6	VH	1.0	275	H
Food preparation workers[1]	1,253	1,487	234	H	18.7	H	0.1	559	VH
Food and beverage service occupations	4,766	5,296	530	–	11.1	–	0.4	1,934	–
Bartenders	390	392	2	VL	0.4	VL	1.8	82	L
Dining room and cafeteria attendants and bar helpers	439	501	62	L	14.1	L	0.0	211	H
Food counter, fountain, and related workers[1]	1,720	1,963	243	H	14.1	H	0.1	841	VH
Hosts and hostesses, restaurant, lounge, or coffee shop	260	278	18	VL	6.7	L	1.2	89	L
Waiters and waitresses	1,957	2,163	206	H	10.5	L	0.4	711	VH
All other food preparation and service workers	228	290	62	L	27.1	VH	1.3	101	L
Health service occupations	2,167	2,874	706	–	32.6	–	1.6	530	–
Ambulance drivers and attendants, except EMTs	18	25	7	VL	36.5	VH	0.0	4	VL
Dental assistants	202	278	77	L	38.1	VH	0.0	48	L
Medical assistants[1]	225	391	166	H	74.0	VH	0.0	49	L
Nursing aides and psychiatric aides	1,415	1,757	342	–	24.2	–	2.4	363	–
Nursing aides, orderlies, and attendants	1,312	1,645	333	VH	25.4	VH	2.6	340	H
Psychiatric aides	103	112	9	VL	8.6	L	0.0	23	VL
Occupational therapy assistants and aides[1]	16	26	11	VL	68.7	VH	0.0	4	VL
Pharmacy assistants[1]	47	52	5	VL	10.7	L	0.0	7	VL
Physical and corrective therapy assistants and aides	84	151	66	L	78.6	VH	0.0	25	VL
All other health service workers	160	192	33	L	20.4	H	0.0	31	VL
Personal service occupations	2,750	3,875	1,126	–	40.9	–	29.6	837	–
Amusement and recreation attendants	288	426	138	H	47.9	VH	1.1	135	L
Baggage porters and bellhops[1]	38	40	2	VL	5.4	VL	0.0	9	VL
Barbers	59	54	–6	VL	–9.6	VL	74.0	2	VL
Child care workers	830	1,129	299	VH	36.1	VH	57.5	322	H
Cosmetologists and related workers	641	720	78	–	12.2	–	42.0	79	–
Hairdressers, hairstylists, and cosmetologists	586	644	58	L	9.9	L	42.8	71	L
Manicurists	43	62	19	VL	44.7	VH	43.3	7	VL
Shampooers	13	13	1	VL	7.1	L	0.0	1	VL
Flight attendants	132	178	46	L	35.1	VH	0.0	8	VL
Homemaker-home health aides	697	1,247	5501	–	78.8	–	3.0	263	–
Home health aides	495	873	3781	VH	76.5	VH	4.2	180	H
Personal and home care aides[1]	202	374	171	H	84.7	VH	0.0	83	L
Ushers, lobby attendants, and ticket takers[1]	64	82	18	VL	28.4	VH	0.0	19	VL
Private household workers	802	681	–121	–	–15.1	–	0.1	250	–
Child care workers, private households[2]	275	250	–25	VL	–9.0	VL	0.0	117	L
Cleaners and servants, private household[1,2]	505	421	–84	VL	–16.7	VL	0.2	129	L
Cooks, private household[1,2]	8	3	–5	VL	–62.1	VL	0.0	2	VL
Housekeepers and butlers[1,2]	14	7	–7	VL	–50.7	VL	0.0	3	VL
Protective service occupations	2,523	2,980	457	–	18.1	–	0.4	398	–
Firefighting occupations	293	308	16	–	5.3	–	0.0	18	–
Fire fighters	225	238	14	VL	6.1	L	0.0	10	VL
Fire fighting and prevention supervisors[1]	54	54	1	VL	1.1	VL	0.0	7	VL
Fire inspection occupations[1]	14	16	1	VL	9.2	L	0.0	1	VL
Law enforcement occupations	1,024	1,217	193	–	18.9	–	0.0	110	–
Correction officers	320	423	103	H	32.3	VH	0.0	51	L
Police and detectives	704	793	90	–	12.7	–	0.0	59	–
Police and detective supervisors	90	89	–1	VL	–0.7	VL	0.0	10	VL

[1]One or more Current Population Survey (CPS) based occupations may be used to estimate CPS based data. See Table 2.

[2]Current Population Survey data used to determine median weekly earnings ranking.

NOTE: Rankings are based on employment in all detailed occupations in the National Industry-Occupation Matrix. For details, see "Data presented" section of text. Codes for describing the ranked variables are: H = Very high, H = High, L = Low, VL = Very low, n. a. = Data not available. A dash indicates data are not applicable.

© 1999 • J. Michael Farr • JIST Works, Inc. • Indianapolis, IN

Table 1. Occupational employment and job openings data, 1996-2006, and worker characteristics, 1996—Continued (Numbers in thousands)

Annual average job openings due to growth and net replacement needs, 1996-2006		Median hourly earnings	Unemployment rate	Percent part-time	Most significant source of training	1996 Matrix Occupation
Number	Rank					
74	VH	VL	VH	H	Short-term on-the-job-training	Janitors and cleaners, including maids and housekeeping cleaners
2	VL	L	H	L	Moderate-term on-the-job-training	Pest controllers and assistants[1]
7	VL	L	VH	H	Short-term on-the-job-training	All other cleaning and building service workers[1]
479	–	–	–	–	–	Food preparation and service occupations
173	–	–	–	–	–	Chefs, cooks, and other kitchen workers
49	–	–	–	–	–	Cooks, except short order
9	VL	L	VH	VH	Moderate-term on-the-job-training	Bakers, bread and pastry
12	L	VL	VH	VH	Long-term on-the-job-training	Cooks, institution or cafeteria
28	L	VL	VH	VH	Long-term on-the-job-training	Cooks, restaurant
37	H	VL	VH	VH	Short-term on-the-job-training	Cooks, short order and fast food
87	VH	VL	VH	VH	Short-term on-the-job-training	Food preparation workers[1]
290						Food and beverage service occupations
15	L	VL	VH	VH	Short-term on-the-job-training	Bartenders
20	L	VL	VH	VH	Short-term on-the-job-training	Dining room and cafeteria attendants and bar helpers
125	VH	VL	VH	VH	Short-term on-the-job-training	Food counter, fountain, and related workers[1]
9	VL	VL	H	VH	Short-term on-the-job-training	Hosts and hostesses, restaurant, lounge, or coffee shop
120	VH	VL	VH	VH	Short-term on-the-job-training	Waiters and waitresses
15	L	VL	VH	VH	Short-term on-the-job-training	All other food preparation and service workers
106	–	–	–	–	–	Health service occupations
1	VL	VL	L	H	Short-term on-the-job-training	Ambulance drivers and attendants, except EMTs
13	L	L	L	VH	Moderate-term on-the-job-training	Dental assistants
21	L	L	L	H	Moderate-term on-the-job-training	Medical assistants[1]
53	–	–	–	–	–	Nursing aides and psychiatric aides
51	H	VL	H	H	Short-term on-the-job-training	Nursing aides, orderlies, and attendants
2	VL	L	H	H	Short-term on-the-job-training	Psychiatric aides
1	VL	H	L	H	Moderate-term on-the-job-training	Occupational therapy assistants and aides[1]
1	VL	L	L	H	Short-term on-the-job-training	Pharmacy assistants[1]
9	VL	L	L	H	Moderate-term on-the-job-training	Physical and corrective therapy assistants and aides
7	VL	L	L	H	Short-term on-the-job-training	All other health service workers
162	–	–	–	–	–	Personal service occupations
19	L	VL	VH	VH	Short-term on-the-job-training	Amusement and recreation attendants
1	VL	VL	VH	VH	Short-term on-the-job-training	Baggage porters and bellhops[1]
2	VL	L	VL	H	Postsecondary vocational training	Barbers
39	H	VL	H	VH	Short-term on-the-job-training	Child care workers
25	–	–	–	–	–	Cosmetologists and related workers
21	L	VL	VL	VH	Postsecondary vocational training	Hairdressers, hairstylists, and cosmetologists
3	VL	VL	VL	VH	Postsecondary vocational training	Manicurists
0	VL	VL	VL	VH	Short-term on-the-job-training	Shampooers
8	VL	VH	VL	VH	Long-term on-the-job-training	Flight attendants
65	–	–	–	–	–	Homemaker-home health aides
44	H	L	H	H	Short-term on-the-job-training	Home health aides
21	L	VL	H	VH	Short-term on-the-job-training	Personal and home care aides[1]
3	VL	VL	VH	VH	Short-term on-the-job-training	Ushers, lobby attendants, and ticket takers[1]
25	–	–	–	–	–	Private household workers
14	L	VL	VH	VH	Short-term on-the-job-training	Child care workers, private households[2]
11	L	VL	VH	VH	Short-term on-the-job-training	Cleaners and servants, private household[1,2]
0	VL	VL	VH	VH	Moderate-term on-the-job-training	Cooks, private household[1,2]
0	VL	VL	VH	VH	Moderate-term on-the-job-training	Housekeepers and butlers[1,2]
116	–	–	–	–	–	Protective service occupations
13	–	–	–	–	–	Firefighting occupations
10	VL	H	VL	VL	Long-term on-the-job-training	Fire fighters
2	VL	VH	VL	VL	Work experience in a related occupation	Fire fighting and prevention supervisors[1]
1	VL	VH	VL	VL	Work experience in a related occupation	Fire inspection occupations[1]
46	–	–	–	–	–	Law enforcement occupations
15	L	H	VL	VL	Long-term on-the-job-training	Correction officers
31	–	–	–	–	–	Police and detectives
3	VL	VH	VL	VL	Work experience in a related occupation	Police and detective supervisors

[1]One or more Current Population Survey (CPS) based occupations may be used to estimate CPS based data. See Table 2.

[2]Current Population Survey data used to determine median weekly earnings ranking.

NOTE: Rankings are based on employment in all detailed occupations in the National Industry-Occupation Matrix. For details, see "Data presented" section of text. Codes for describing the ranked variables are: VH = Very high, H = High, L = Low, VL = Very low, n. a. = Data not available. A dash indicates data are not applicable.

Table 1. Occupational employment and job openings data, 1996-2006, and worker characteristics, 1996—Continued (Numbers in thousands)

1996 Matrix Occupation	Employment 1996	Employment 2006	Employment change, 1996-2006 Numeric Number	Numeric Rank	Percent Number	Percent Rank	Percent self-employed, 1996	Annual average job openings due to growth and total replacement needs, 1996-2006 Number	Rank
Police detectives and investigators	70	75	5	VL	7.8	L	0.0	6	VL
Police patrol officers	413	486	73	L	17.8	H	0.0	40	VL
Sheriffs and deputy sheriffs	88	96	8	VL	9.3	L	0.0	1	VL
Other law enforcement occupations	43	47	3	VL	7.7	L	0.0	2	VL
Other protective service workers	1,206	1,455	249	–	20.6	–	0.9	270	–
Detectives and investigators, except public	58	69	1.1	VL	18.5	H	17.3	13	VL
Guards	955	1,175	221	H	23.1	VH	0.1	228	H
Crossing guards[1]	61	55	−6	VL	−9.2	VL	0.0	10	VL
All other protective service workers	133	156	23	L	17.2	H	0.0	18	VL
All other service workers[1]	1,112	1,453	341	VH	30.7	VH	9.9	302	H
Agriculture, forestry, fishing, and related occupations	3,785	3,823	37	–	1.0	–	39.0	660	–
Animal caretakers, except farm	130	158	28	L	21.4	VH	26.1	41	VL
Farm operators and managers	1,292	1,175	−118	–	−9.1	–	86.0	126	–
Farmers[2]	1,109	997	−112	VL	−10.1	VL	99.8	115	L
Farm managers[2]	184	178	−6	VL	−3.2	VL	3.2	12	VL
Farm workers	873	798	−75	VL	−8.6	VL	4.2	160	L
Fishers, hunters, and trappers	47	37	−10	–	−20.7	–	72.1	10	–
Captains and other officers, fishing vessels[1,2]	8	7	0	VL	−4.4	VL	47.8	2	VL
Fishers, hunters, and trappers[1,2]	39	30	−9	VL	−23.9	VL	76.9	8	VL
Forestry and logging occupations	122	123	1	–	1.0	–	23.6	19	–
Forest and conservation workers[1]	40	41	1	VL	2.5	VL	3.1	7	VL
Timber cutting and logging occupations	82	82	0	–	0.3	–	33.5	13	–
Fallers and buckers	17	16	−1	VL	−3.5	VL	36.8	2	VL
Logging tractor operators	21	22	1	VL	4.4	VL	6.2	4	VL
Log handling equipment operators	33	34	1	VL	3.1	VL	60.2	5	VL
All other timber cutting and related logging workers	11	10	−1	VL	−10.3	VL	0.0	1	VL
Gardening, nursery, and greenhouse and lawn service occupations	925	1,105	180	–	19.5	–	23.6	225	–
Gardeners, nursery workers and laborers, landscaping and groundskeeping	817	975	158	H	19.4	H	21.5	206	H
Lawn service managers[1]	55	67	12	VL	22.2	VH	64.3	7	VL
Nursery and greenhouse managers[1]	10	12	2	VL	19.1	H	73.6	1	*VL*
Pruners	26	30	4	VL	16.2	H	0.0	6	VL
Sprayers/applicators	18	21	4	VL	21.2	VH	0.0	5	VL
Supervisors, farming, forestry, and agricultural related occupations[1]	88	92	4	VL	4.2	VL	9.0	10	VL
Veterinary assistants	33	42	9	VL	28.0	VH	0.0	11	VL
All other agricultural, forestry, fishing, and related workers[1]	275	293	18	VL	6.5	L	1.7	57	L
Precision production, craft, and repair occupations	14,446	15,448	1,002	–	6.9	–	11.0	1,960	–
Blue collar worker supervisors[1]	1,899	1,947	48	L	2.5	VL	9.9	169	H
Construction trades	3,710	4,014	304	–	8.2	–	22.7	640	–
Bricklayers and stone masons[1]	142	162	19	VL	13.6	L	22.3	27	VL
Carpenters	979	1,038	59	L	6.0	L	31.7	214	H
Carpet installers	64	72	8	VL	12.2	L	60.6	9	VL
Ceiling tile installers and acoustical carpenters	16	18	1	VL	8.7	L	0.0	4	VL
Concrete and terrazzo finishers	137	147	10	VL	7.4	L	8.0	14	VL
Drywall installers and finishers	133	140	7	VL	4.9	VL	29.4	26	VL
Electricians	575	627	52	L	9.1	L	10.6	80	L
Glaziers[1]	36	38	2	VL	5.3	VL	11.6	6	VL
Hard tile setters[1]	29	30	1	VL	4.1	VL	45.1	5	VL
Highway maintenance workers	171	158	−14	VL	−7.9	VL	0.0	19	VL
Insulation workers	65	78	13	VL	19.3	H	1.5	8	VL
Painters and paperhangers, construction and maintenance	444	509	66	L	14.8	H	41.6	86	L
Paving, surfacing, and tamping equipment operators[1]	79	103	24	L	29.9	VH	1.5	18	VL
Pipelayers and pipelaying fitters	62	66	4	VL	5.7	L	10.9	8	VL

[1]One or more Current Population Survey (CPS) based occupations may be used to estimate CPS based data. See Table 2.

[2]Current Population Survey data used to determine median weekly earnings ranking.

NOTE: Rankings are based on employment in all detailed occupations in the National Industry-Occupation Matrix. For details, see "Data presented" section of text. Codes for describing the ranked variables are: VH = Very high, H = High, L = Low, VL = Very low, n. a. = Data not available. A dash indicates data are not applicable.

Table 1. Occupational employment and job openings data, 1996-2006, and worker characteristics, 1996—Continued (Numbers in thousands)

Annual average job openings due to growth and net replacement needs, 1996-2006		Median hourly earnings	Unemployment rate	Percent part-time	Most significant source of training	1996 Matrix Occupation
Number	Rank					
3	VL	VH	VL	VL	Work experience in a related occupation	Police detectives and investigators
22	L	VH	VL	VL	Long-term on-the-job-training	Police patrol officers
2	VL	H	VL	VL	Long-term on-the-job-training	Sheriffs and deputy sheriffs
1	VL	H	VL	VL	Moderate-term on-the-job-training	Other law enforcement occupations
57	–	–	–	–	–	Other protective service workers
2	VL	L	VH	H	Moderate-term on-the-job-training	Detectives and investigators, except public
42	H	VL	VH	H	Short-term on-the-job-training	Guards
2	VL	VL	VH	H	Short-term on-the-job-training	Crossing guards[1]
11	L	L	VH	VH	Short-term on-the-job-training	All other protective service workers
62	H	L	H	H	Work experience in a related occupation	All other service workers[1]
112	–	–	–	–	–	**Agriculture, forestry, fishing, and related occupations**
6	VL	VL	L	VH	Short-term on-the-job-training	Animal caretakers, except farm
25	–	–	–	–	–	Farm operators and managers
21	L	VL	VL	VH	Long-term on-the-job-training	Farmers[2]
4	VL	L	VL	H	Work experience plus degree	Farm managers[2]
24	L	VL	VH	VH	Short-term on-the-job-training	Farm workers
1	–	–	–	–	–	Fishers, hunters, and trappers
0	VL	L	VH	VH	Work experience in a related occupation	Captains and other officers, fishing vessels[1,2]
1	VL	VL	VH	VH	Short-term on-the-job-training	Fishers, hunters, and trappers[1,2]
4	–	–	–	–	–	Forestry and logging occupations
1	VL	L	VH	H	Short-term on-the-job-training	Forest and conservation workers[1]
2	–	–	–	–	–	Timber cutting and logging occupations
1	VL	H	VH	H	Short-term on-the-job-training	Fallers and buckers
1	VL	L	H	VL	Short-term on-the-job-training	Logging tractor operators
1	VL	H	VH	H	Short-term on-the-job-training	Log handling equipment operators
0	VL	H	VH	H	Short-term on-the-job-training	All other timber cutting and related logging workers
40	–	–	–	–	–	Gardening, nursery, and greenhouse and lawn service occupations
36	H	L	VH	VH	Short-term on-the-job-training	Gardeners, nursery workers and laborers, landscaping and groundskeeping
2	VL	H	L	L	Work experience in a related occupation	Lawn service managers[1]
0	VL	L	L	L	Work experience in a related occupation	Nursery and greenhouse managers[1]
1	VL	L	VH	VH	Short-term on-the-job-training	Pruners
1	VL	L	VH	VH	Moderate-term on-the-job-training	Sprayers/applicators
2	VL	H	H	H	Work experience in a related occupation	Supervisors, farming, forestry, and agricutural related occupations[1]
2	VL	VL	L	VH	Short-term on-the-job-training	Veterinary assistants
9	VL	VL	VH	H	Short-term on-the-job-training	All other agricultural, forestry, fishing, and related workers[1]
435	–	–	–	–	–	**Precision production, craft, and repair occupations**
47	H	VH	L	VL	Work experience in a related occupation	Blue collar worker supervisors[1]
113	–	–	–	–	–	Construction trades
4	VL	VH	VH	L	Long-term on-the-job-training	Bricklayers and stone masons[1]
23	L	H	VH	L	Long-term on-the-job-training	Carpenters
3	VL	H	H	H	Moderate-term on-the-job-training	Carpet installers
0	VL	H	VH	L	Moderate-term on-the-job-training	Ceiling tile installers and acoustical carpenters
4	VL	H	VH	L	Long-term on-the-job-training	Concrete and terrazzo finishers
5	VL	H	VH	L	Moderate-term on-the-job-training	Drywall installers and finishers
17	L	VH	H	VL	Long-term on-the-job-training	Electricians
1	VL	H	VH	L	Long-term on-the-job-training	Glaziers[1]
1	VL	VH	VH	H	Long-term on-the-job-training	Hard tile setters[1]
5	VL	H	VH	L	Short-term on-the-job-training	Highway maintenance workers
3	VL	H	VH	VL	Moderate-term on-the-job-training	Insulation workers
16	L	H	VH	L	Moderate-term on-the-job-training	Painters and paperhangers, construction and maintenance
4	VL	H	VH	L	Moderate-term on-the-job-training	Paving, surfacing, and tamping equipment operators[1]
2	VL	H	VH	L	Moderate-term on-the-job-training	Pipelayers and pipelaying fitters

[1]One or more Current Population Survey (CPS) based occupations may be used to estimate CPS based data. See Table 2.

[2]Current Population Survey data used to determine median weekly earnings ranking.

NOTE: Rankings are based on employment in all detailed occupations in the National Industry-Occupation Matrix. For details, see "Data presented" section of text. Codes for describing the ranked variables are: VH = Very high, H = High, L = Low, VL = Very low, n. a. = Data not available. A dash indicates data are not applicable.

Table 1. Occupational employment and job openings data, 1996-2006, and worker characteristics, 1996—Continued (Numbers in thousands)

1996 Matrix Occupation	Employment		Employment change, 1996-2006				Percent self-em-ployed, 1996	Annual average job openings due to growth and total replacement needs, 1996-2006	
	1996	2006	Numeric		Percent				
			Number	Rank	Number	Rank		Number	Rank
Plasterers[1]	32	36	4	VL	13.3	L	22.0	6	VL
Plumbers, pipefitters, and steamfitters	389	406	18	VL	4.5	VL	18.2	53	L
Roofers	138	144	6	VL	4.3	VL	29.5	23	VL
Structural and reinforcing metal workers	67	73	6	VL	9.0	L	2.9	12	VL
All other construction trades workers[1]	150	169	19	VL	12.5	L	13.6	21	VL
Extractive and related workers, including blasters	220	220	0	–	–0.1	–	1.6	16	–
Oil and gas extraction occupations	65	53	–13	–	–19.2	–	0.0	3	–
Roustabouts[1]	28	18	–9	VL	–33.7	VL	0.0	1	VL
All other oil and gas extraction occupations[1]	37	34	–3	VL	–8.4	VL	0.0	2	VL
Mining, quarrying, and tunneling occupations[1]	16	12	–4	VL	–25.8	VL	0.0	1	VL
All other extraction and related workers[1]	138	155	17	VL	12.0	L	2.6	12	VL
Mechanics, installers, and repairers	5,233	5,889	656	–	12.5	–	7.7	717	–
Communications equipment mechanics, installers, and repairers	116	121	5	–	4.3	–	2.7	9	–
Central office and PBX installers and repairers[1]	81	85	4	VL	5.2	VL	3.8	6	VL
Radio mechanics	8	7	–1	VL	–7.2	VL	0.0	1	VL
All other communications equipment mechanics, installers, and repairers[1]	27	28	1	VL	5.1	VL	0.0	3	VL
Electrical and electronic equipment mechanics, installers, and repairers	562	627	66	–	11.7	–	3.2	62	–
Data processing equipment repairers	80	121	42	L	52.3	VH	4.6	21	VL
Electrical powerline installers and repairers	108	111	3	VL	3.0	VL	1.5	6	VL
Electronic home entertainment equipment repairers	33	27	–6	VL	–19.0	VL	14.5	3	VL
Electronics repairers, commercial and industrial equipment	60	67	7	VL	11.8	L	10.6	8	VL
Station installers and repairers, telephone[1]	37	10	–27	VL	–73.5	VL	0.0	1	VL
Telephone and cable TV line installers and repairers[1]	201	242	41	L	20.5	H	0.0	18	VL
All other electrical and electronic equipment mechanics, installers, and repairers	44	50	6	VL	13.0	L	3.5	4	VL
Machinery and related mechanics, installers, and repairers	1,899	2,173	274	–	14.4	–	3.1	261	–
Industrial machinery mechanics[1]	459	489	30	L	6.6	L	2.9	33	VL
Maintenance repairers, general utility	1,362	1,608	246	H	18.0	H	3.2	223	H
Millwrights	78	76	–2	VL	–2.2	VL	0.9	5	VL
Vehicle and mobile equipment mechanics and repairers	1,597	1,764	168	–	10.5	–	15.1	209	–
Aircraft mechanics, including engine specialists	137	155	18	–	13.2	–	1.9	12	–
Aircraft engine specialists[1]	25	27	2	VL	8.9	L	6.3	2	VL
Aircraft mechanics[1]	112	128	16	VL	14.2	H	0.9	10	VL
Automotive body and related repairers	225	254	29	L	12.8	L	19.1	32	VL
Automotive mechanics[1]	775	871	96	L	12.4	L	20.4	112	L
Bus and truck mechanics and diesel engine specialists	266	288	22	L	8.2	L	6.8	22	VL
Farm equipment mechanics[1]	44	37	–7	VL	–15.9	VL	7.1	6	VL
Mobile heavy equipment mechanics	104	111	7	VL	6.5	L	4.8	18	VL
Motorcycle, boat, and small engine mechanics	45	49	3	–	7.1	–	25.8	7	–
Motorcycle repairers[1]	12	13	1	VL	5.7	L	22.1	2	VL
Small engine specialists[1]	34	36	3	VL	7.6	L	27.1	5	VL
Other mechanics, installers, and repairers	1,695	1,814	119	–	7.0	–	4.7	266	–
Bicycle repairers	13	17	4	VL	33.5	VH	0.0	2	VL
Camera and photographic equipment repairers[1]	14	18	3	VL	24.0	VH	53.1	3	VL
Coin and vending machine servicers and repairers	21	19	–1	VL	–6.5	VL	0.0	3	VL
Electric meter installers and repairers[1]	12	8	–4	VL	–33.7	VL	0.0	1	VL
Electromedical and biomedical equipment repairers	10	11	1	VL	11.7	L	0.0	1	VL
Elevator installers and repairers[1]	25	27	2	VL	8.0	L	0.0	4	VL
Heat, air conditioning, and refrigeration mechanics and installers	256	300	44	L	17.0	H	14.9	27	VL
Home appliance and power tool repairers[1]	71	73	2	VL	3.5	VL	8.7	10	VL
Locksmiths and safe repairers[1]	25	29	4	VL	15.0	H	39.0	4	VL
Musical instrument repairers and tuners[1]	9	10	1	VL	7.4	L	51.5	1	VL
Office machine and cash register servicers	62	73	11	VL	17.8	H	4.8	3	VL
Precision instrument repairers[1]	38	38	–1	VL	–2.2	VL	0.0	6	VL
Riggers	9	8	–2	VL	–18.3	VL	0.0	1	VL
Tire repairers and changers	94	101	7	VL	7.0	L	1.7	29	VL

[1]One or more Current Population Survey (CPS) based occupations may be used to estimate CPS based data. See Table 2.
NOTE: Rankings are based on employment in all detailed occupations in the National Industry-Occupation Matrix. For details, see "Data presented" section of text. Codes for describing the ranked variables are: VH = Very high, H = High, L = Low, VL = Very low, n. a. = Data not available. A dash indicates data are not applicable.

Table 1. Occupational employment and job openings data, 1996-2006, and worker characteristics, 1996—Continued (Numbers in thousands)

Annual average job openings due to growth and net replacement needs, 1996-2006		Median hourly earnings	Unemployment rate	Percent part-time	Most significant source of training	1996 Matrix Occupation
Number	Rank					
1	VL	H	VH	L	Long-term on-the-job-training	Plasterers[1]
10	L	VH	H	VL	Long-term on-the-job-training	Plumbers, pipefitters, and steamfitters
5	VL	H	VH	H	Moderate-term on-the-job-training	Roofers
2	VL	VH	VH	VL	Long-term on-the-job-training	Structural and reinforcing metal workers
6	VL	H	VH	L	Moderate-term on-the-job-training	All other construction trades workers[1]
6	–	–	–	–	–	Extractive and related workers, including blasters
1	–	–	–	–	–	Oil and gas extraction occupations
1	VL	L	H	L	Short-term on-the-job-training	Roustabouts[1]
1	VL	L	H	L	Moderate-term on-the-job-training	All other oil and gas extraction occupations[1]
0	VL	H	H	L	Long-term on-the-job-training	Mining, quarrying, and tunneling occupations[1]
4	VL	H	VH	L	Moderate-term on-the-job-training	All other extraction and related workers[1]
190	–	–	–	–	–	Mechanics, installers, and repairers
3	–	–	–	–	–	Communications equipment mechanics, installers, and repairers
2	VL	VH	VL	VL	Postsecondary vocational training	Central office and PBX installers and repairers[1]
0	VL	H	L	VL	Postsecondary vocational training	Radio mechanics
1	VL	VH	L	VL	Postsecondary vocational training	All other communications equipment mechanics, installers, and repairers[1]
22	–	–	–	–	–	Electrical and electronic equipment mechanics, installers, and repairers
7	VL	H	L	VL	Postsecondary vocational training	Data processing equipment repairers
3	VL	VH	VL	VL	Long-term on-the-job-training	Electrical powerline installers and repairers
1	VL	H	L	VL	Postsecondary vocational training	Electronic home entertainment equipment repairers
2	VL	VH	L	VL	Postsecondary vocational training	Electronics repairers, commercial and industrial equipment
1	VL	VH	VL	VL	Postsecondary vocational training	Station installers and repairers, telephone[1]
8	VL	H	VL	VL	Long-term on-the-job-training	Telephone and cable TV line installers and repairers[1]
2	VL	H	L	VL	Postsecondary vocational training	All other electrical and electronic equipment mechanics, installers, and repairers
67	–	–	–	–	–	Machinery and related mechanics, installers, and repairers
13	L	H	L	VL	Long-term on-the-job-training	Industrial machinery mechanics[1]
52	H	L	L	L	Long-term on-the-job-training	Maintenance repairers, general utility
2	VL	VH	H	VL	Long-term on-the-job-training	Millwrights
58	–	–	–	–	–	Vehicle and mobile equipment mechanics and repairers
5	–	–	–	–	–	Aircraft mechanics, including engine specialists
1	VL	H	L	VL	Postsecondary vocational training	Aircraft engine specialists[1]
4	VL	VH	L	VL	Postsecondary vocational training	Aircraft mechanics[1]
10	VL	H	L	L	Long-term on-the-job-training	Automotive body and related repairers
30	L	H	H	L	Postsecondary vocational training	Automotive mechanics[1]
8	VL	H	L	VL	Long-term on-the-job-training	Bus and truck mechanics and diesel engine specialists
1	VL	L	L	VL	Long-term on-the-job-training	Farm equipment mechanics[1]
3	VL	H	L	VL	Long-term on-the-job-training	Mobile heavy equipment mechanics
1	–	–	–	–	–	Motorcycle, boat, and small engine mechanics
0	VL	H	L	L	Long-term on-the-job-training	Motorcycle repairers[1]
1	VL	L	L	L	Long-term on-the-job-training	Small engine specialists[1]
38	–	–	–	–	–	Other mechanics, installers, and repairers
1	VL	VL	L	L	Moderate-term on-the-job-training	Bicycle repairers[1]
1	VL	H	L	VL	Moderate-term on-the-job-training	Camera and photographic equipment repairers[1]
0	VL	L	L	L	Long-term on-the-job-training	Coin and vending machine servicers and repairers
0	VL	VH	L	VL	Long-term on-the-job-training	Electric meter installers and repairers[1]
0	VL	H	L	L	Long-term on-the-job-training	Electromedical and biomedical equipment repairers
1	VL	VH	L	VL	Long-term on-the-job-training	Elevator installers and repairers[1]
10	L	H	L	VL	Long-term on-the-job-training	Heat, air conditioning, and refrigeration mechanics and installers
2	VL	H	L	VL	Long-term on-the-job-training	Home appliance and power tool repairers[1]
1	VL	H	L	VL	Moderate-term on-the-job-training	Locksmiths and safe repairers[1]
0	VL	L	L	VL	Long-term on-the-job-training	Musical instrument repairers and tuners[1]
3	VL	H	VL	VL	Long-term on-the-job-training	Office machine and cash register servicers
1	VL	VH	L	VL	Long-term on-the-job-training	Precision instrument repairers[1]
0	VL	H	L	L	Long-term on-the-job-training	Riggers
4	VL	VL	VH	H	Short-term on-the-job-training	Tire repairers and changers

[1]One or more Current Population Survey (CPS) based occupations may be used to estimate CPS based data. See Table 2.
NOTE: Rankings are based on employment in all detailed occupations in the National Industry-Occupation Matrix. For details, see "Data presented" section of text. Codes for describing the ranked variables are: VH = Very high, H = High, L = Low, VL = Very low, n. a. = Data not available. A dash indicates data are not applicable.

Table 1. Occupational employment and job openings data, 1996-2006, and worker characteristics, 1996—Continued (Numbers in thousands)

1996 Matrix Occupation	Employment		Employment change, 1996-2006				Percent self-em-ployed, 1996	Annual average job openings due to growth and total replacement needs, 1996-2006	
			Numeric		Percent				
	1996	2006	Number	Rank	Number	Rank		Number	Rank
Watchmakers[1]	7	7	0	VL	–5.1	VL	53.5	1	VL
All other mechanics, installers, and repairers[1]	394	467	73	L	18.4	H	1.4	78	L
Production occupations, precision	3,054	3,016	–38	–	–1.2	–	5.2	387	–
Assemblers, precision	380	383	3	–	0.7	–	0.0	61	–
Aircraft assemblers, precision[1]	25	27	2	VL	9.9	L	0.0	3	VL
Electrical and electronic equipment assemblers, precision	194	193	–1	VL	–0.6	VL	0.0	35	VL
Electromechanical equipment assemblers, precision	51	51	0	VL	0.6	VL	0.0	9	VL
Fitters, structural metal, precision[1]	15	12	–3	VL	–18.3	VL	0.0	2	VL
Machine builders and other precision machine assemblers[1]	57	58	1	VL	1.6	VL	0.0	7	VL
All other precision assemblers[1]	38	41	3	VL	8.2	L	0.0	5	VL
Food workers, precision	299	301	2	–	0.6	–	2.3	36	–
Bakers, manufacturing	44	47	3	VL	7.0	L	7.3	9	VL
Butchers and meatcutters	217	205	–12	VL	–5.7	VL	1.2	18	VL
All other precision food and tobacco workers[1]	38	49	1.1	VL	29.3	VH	2.7	8	VL
Inspectors, testers, and graders, precision	634	610	–24	VL	–3.8	VL	0.7	90	L
Metal workers, precision[1]	934	924	–10	–	–1.1	–	3.9	88	–
Boilermakers[1]	18	18	–1	VL	–3.2	VL	5.5	2	VL
Jewelers and silversmiths[1]	32	31	–1	VL	–1.7	VL	36.3	4	VL
Machinists	386	384	–2	VL	–0.5	VL	1.6	35	VL
Sheet metal workers and duct installers[1]	237	236	–1	VL	–0.4	VL	2.9	19	VL
Shipfitters[1]	9	9	0	VL	–0.6	VL	0.0	1	VL
Tool and die makers	134	124	–9	VL	–7.0	VL	0.9	14	VL
All other precision metal workers[1]	117	120	3	VL	2.9	VL	8.6	13	VL
Printing workers, precision	141	124	–17	–	–12.1	–	0.0	24	–
Bookbinders[1]	4	4	–1	VL	–15.0	VL	0.0	1	VL
Prepress printing workers, precision	123	106	–16	–	–13.4	–	0.0	21	–
Compositors and typesetters, precision[1]	6	3	–3	VL	–50.3	VL	0.0	1	VL
Job printers	15	15	1	VL	4.9	VL	0.0	2	VL
Paste-up workers[1]	15	4	–11	VL	–75.0	VL	0.0	2	VL
Desktop publishing specialists[1]	30	53	22	L	73.5	VH	0.0	9	VL
Photoengravers[1]	5	3	–2	VL	–35.8	VL	0.0	1	VL
Camera operators[1]	11	10	–2	VL	–14.9	VL	0.0	2	VL
Film strippers, printing[1]	26	7	–20	VL	–75.0	VL	0.0	3	VL
Platemakers[1]	14	12	–2	VL	–15.1	VL	0.0	2	VL
All other printing workers, precision[1]	13	14	0	VL	1.1	VL	0.0	2	VL
Textile, apparel, and furnishings workers, precision	230	212	–18	–	–7.7	–	30.1	22	–
Custom tailors and sewers	87	73	–15	VL	–16.7	VL	51.5	7	VL
Patternmakers and layout workers, fabric and apparel[1]	14	14	0	VL	–3.3	VL	0.0	1	VL
Shoe and leather workers and repairers, precision[1]	21	17	–4	VL	–20.1	VL	28.5	2	VL
Upholsterers[1]	57	57	0	VL	0.4	VL	28.1	5	VL
All other precision textile, apparel, and furnishings workers[1]	50	51	1	VL	2.8	VL	4.4	8	VL
Woodworkers, precision	229	249	19	–	8.4	–	11.3	37	–
Cabinetmakers and bench carpenters	121	128	7	VL	6.1	L	16.5	20	VL
Furniture finishers[1]	30	33	3	VL	11.5	L	20.2	5	VL
Wood machinists	45	51	6	VL	13.9	L	0.0	8	VL
All other precision woodworkers[1]	33	36	2	VL	6.8	L	0.0	5	VL
Other precision workers	206	213	7	–	3.3	–	7.1	30	–
Dental laboratory technicians, precision	47	48	0	VL	0.7	VL	14.4	4	VL
Optical goods workers, precision	19	19	0	VL	0.4	VL	0.0	1	VL
Photographic process workers, precision	14	14	0	VL	–2.7	VL	28.4	3	VL
All other precision workers	126	133	7	VL	5.4	VL	3.0	22	VL
Plant and system occupations	330	362	32	–	9.9	–	0.0	31	–
Chemical plant and system operators[1]	36	36	0	VL	–0.8	VL	0.0	2	VL
Electric power generating plant operators, distributors, and dispatchers	47	49	2	–	4.3	–	0.0	3	–
Power distributors and dispatchers[1]	15	15	–1	VL	–3.7	VL	0.0	1	VL
Power generating and reactor plant operators[1]	31	34	3	VL	8.3	L	0.0	2	VL
Gas and petroleum plant and system occupations[1]	33	29	–3	VL	–10.5	VL	0.0	2	VL
Stationary engineers	27	26	–2	VL	–5.9	VL	0.0	2	VL

[1]One or more Current Population Survey (CPS) based occupations may be used to estimate CPS based data. See Table 2.
NOTE: Rankings are based on employment in all detailed occupations In the National Industry-Occupation Matrix. For details, see "Data presented" section of text. Codes for describing the ranked variables are: VH = Very high, H = High, L = Low, VL = Very low, n. a. = Data not available, A dash indicates data are not applicable.

Table 1. Occupational employment and job openings data, 1996-2006, and worker characteristics, 1996—Continued (Numbers in thousands)

Annual average job openings due to growth and net replacement needs, 1996-2006		Median hourly earnings	Unem-ployment rate	Per-cent part-time	Most significant source of training	1996 Matrix Occupation
Number	Rank					
0	VL	H	L	VL	Long-term on-the-job-training	Watchmakers[1]
15	L	H	L	VL	Long-term on-the-job-training	All other mechanics, installers, and repairers[1]
68	–	–	–	–	–	Production occupations, precision
9	–	–	–	–	–	Assemblers, precision
1	VL	VH	L	VL	Work experience in a related occupation	Aircraft assemblers, precision[1]
5	VL	L	H	VL	Work experience in a related occupation	Electrical and electronic equipment assemblers, precision
1	VL	L	H	VL	Work experience in a related occupation	Electromechanical equipment assemblers, precision
0	VL	H	L	VL	Work experience in a related occupation	Fitters, structural metal, precision[1]
1	VL	H	L	VL	Work experience in a related occupation	Machine builders and other precision machine assemblers[1]
1	VL	L	L	VL	Work experience in a related occupation	All other precision assemblers[1]
9	–	–	–	–	–	Food workers, precision
1	VL	L	H	H	Moderate-term on-the-job-training	Bakers, manufacturing
6	VL	L	H	VL	Long-term on-the-job-training	Butchers and meatcutters
2	VL	H	H	L	Long-term on-the-job-training	All other precision food and tobacco workers[1]
12	L	L	H	VL	Work experience in a related occupation	Inspectors, testers, and graders, precision
20	–	–	–	–	–	Metal workers, precision[1]
0	VL	VH	L	VL	Long-term on-the-job-training	Boilermakers[1]
1	VL	L	H	H	Postsecondary vocational training	Jewelers and silversmiths[1]
9	VL	H	L	VL	Long-term on-the-job-training	Machinists
5	VL	H	VH	VL	Moderate-term on-the-job-training	Sheet metal workers and duct installers[1]
0	VL	H	L	VL	Long-term on-the-job-training	Shipfitters[1]
2	VL	VH	VL	VL	Long-term on-the-job-training	Tool and die makers
3	VL	H	L	VL	Long-term on-the-job-training	All other precision metal workers[1]
4	–	–	–	–	–	Printing workers, precision
0	VL	H	H	VL	Moderate-term on-the-job-training	Bookbinders[1]
4	–	–	–	–	–	Prepress printing workers, precision
0	VL	L	H	VL	Long-term on-the-job-training	Compositors and typesetters, precision[1]
0	VL	H	L	VL	Long-term on-the-job-training	Job printers
0	VL	L	H	VL	Long-term on-the-job-training	Paste-up workers[1]
3	VL	H	H	VL	Long-term on-the-job-training	Desktop publishing specialists[1]
0	VL	H	H	VL	Long-term on-the-job-training	Photoengravers[1]
0	VL	H	H	VL	Long-term on-the-job-training	Camera operators[1]
0	VL	H	H	VL	Long-term on-the-job-training	Film strippers, printing[1]
0	VL	H	H	VL	Long-term on-the-job-training	Platemakers[1]
0	VL	H	H	VL	Long-term on-the-job-training	All other printing workers, precision[1]
3	–	–	–	–	–	Textile, apparel, and furnishings workers, precision
1	VL	L	H	VH	Work experience in a related occupation	Custom tailors and sewers
0	VL	L	H	H	Long-term on-the-job-training	Patternmakers and layout workers, fabric and apparel[1]
0	VL	L	H	H	Long-term on-the-job-training	Shoe and leather workers and repairers, precision[1]
1	VL	L	L	H	Long-term on-the-job-training	Upholsterers[1]
1	VL	VL	VH	H	Long-term on-the-job-training	All other precision textile, apparel, and furnishings workers[1]
5	–	–	–	–	–	Woodworkers, precision
2	VL	L	L	L	Long-term on-the-job-training	Cabinetmakers and bench carpenters
1	VL	L	L	L	Long-term on-the-job-training	Furniture finishers[1]
1	VL	L	L	L	Long-term on-the-job-training	Wood machinists
1	VL	H	L	L	Long-term on-the-job-training	All other precision woodworkers[1]
6	–	–	–	–	–	Other precision workers
1	VL	H	VL	H	Long-term on-the-job-training	Dental laboratory technicians, precision
0	VL	L	L	L	Long-term on-the-job-training	Optical goods workers, precision
0	VL	L	H	H	Moderate-term on-the-job-training	Photographic process workers, precision
4	VL	L	H	VL	Long-term on-the-job-training	All other precision workers
11	–	–	–	–	–	Plant and system occupations
1	VL	VH	VL	VL	Long-term on-the-job-training	Chemical plant and system operators[1]
1	–	–	–	–	–	Electric power generating plant operators, distributors, and dispatchers
0	VL	VH	VL	VL	Long-term on-the-job-training	Power distributors and dispatchers[1]
1	VL	VH	VL	VL	Long-term on-the-job-training	Power generating and reactor plant operators[1]
1	VL	VH	VL	VL	Long-term on-the-job-training	Gas and petroleum plant and system occupations[1]
1	VL	VH	VL	VL	Long-term on-the-job-training	Stationary engineers

[1]One or more Current Population Survey (CPS) based occupations may be used to estimate CPS based data. See Table 2.

NOTE: Rankings are based on employment in all detailed occupations in the National Industry-Occupation Matrix. For details, see "Data presented" section of text. Codes for describing the ranked variables are: VH = Very high, H = High, L = Low, VL = Very low, n. a. = Data not available. A dash indicates data are not applicable.

Table 1. Occupational employment and job openings data, 1996-2006, and worker characteristics, 1996—Continued (Numbers in thousands)

1996 Matrix Occupation	Employment		Employment change, 1996-2006				Percent self-em-ployed, 1996	Annual average job openings due to growth and total replacement needs, 1996-2006	
	1996	2006	Numeric		Percent				
			Number	Rank	Number	Rank		Number	Rank
Water and liquid waste treatment plant and system operators	98	121	23	L	23.2	VH	0.0	14	VL
All other plant and system operators[1]	88	101	13	VL	14.8	H	0.0	8	VL
Operators, fabricators, and laborers	17,843	19,365	1,522	–	8.5	–	3,5	3,748	–
Machine setters, set-up operators, operators, and tenders	4,898	4,956	58	–	1.2	–	2.0	773	–
Numerical control machine tool operators and tenders, metal and plastic[1]	92	117	25	L	27.4	VH	0.0	21	VL
Combination machine tool setters, set-up operators, operators, and tenders[1]	96	113	17	VL	17.8	H	0.0	20	VL
Machine tool cut and form setters, operators, and tenders, metal and plastic	723	677	–46	–	–6.4	–	0.3	81	–
Drilling and boring machine tool setters and set-up operators, metal and plastic[1]	46	36	–10	VL	–22.0	VL	0.0	7	VL
Grinding machine setters and set-up operators, metal and plastic	63	56	–7	VL	–11.4	VL	3.2	3	VL
Lathe and turning machine tool setters and set-up operators, metal and plastic[1]	71	61	–10	VL	–13.7	VL	0.0	11	VL
Machine forming operators and tenders, metal and plastic	174	168	–6	VL	–3.2	VL	0,0	17	VL
Machine tool cutting operators and tenders, metal and plastic ...	127	105	–22	VL	–17.4	VL	0.0	7	VL
Punching machine setters and set-up operators, metal and plastic	51	47	–4	VL	–8.3	VL	0.0	6	VL
All other machine tool setters, set-up operators, metal and plastic[1]	191	204	13	VL	6.7	L	0.0	29	VL
Metal fabricating machine setters, operators, and related workers	157	162	5	–	3.3	–	0.0	20	–
Metal fabricators, structural metal products[1]	46	50	5	VL	10.6	L	0.0	9	VL
Soldering and brazing machine operators and tenders[1]	11	11	0	VL	0.6	VL	0.0	2	VL
Welding machine setters, operators, and tenders	100	101	0	VL	0.3	VL	0.0	9	VL
Metal and plastic processing machine setters, operators, and related workers	466	528	62	–	13.4	–	0.0	56	–
Electrolytic plating machine operators and tenders, setters and set-up operators, metal and plastic[1]	42	46	4	VL	10.4	L	0.0	5	VL
Foundry mold assembly and shakeout workers	10	10	0	VL	–4.0	VL	0.0	1	VL
Furnace operators and tenders[1]	21	20	–1	VL	–4.6	VL	0.0	2	VL
Heat treating machine operators and tenders, metal and plastic[1]	21	20	–1	VL	–3.7	VL	0.0	2	VL
Metal molding machine operators and tenders, setters and set-up operators	45	49	4	VL	9.1	L	0.0	5	VL
Plastic molding machine operators and tenders, setters and set-up operators	183	216	34	L	18.3	H	0.0	23	VL
All other metal and plastic machine setters, operators, and related workers[1]	144	167	23	L	15.6	H	0.0	18	VL
Printing, binding, and related workers	383	394	11	–	2.9	–	2.8	61	–
Bindery machine operators and set-up operators[1]	81	85	4	VL	4.9	VL	0.0	14	VL
Prepress printing workers, production	19	8	–11	–	–56.2	–	0.0	2	–
Photoengraving and lithographic machine operators and tenders[1]	6	5	–1	VL	–9.5	VL	0.0	1	VL
Typesetting and composing machine operators and tenders[1] ..	14	3	–10	VL	–75.1	VL	0.0	1	VL
Printing press operators	215	226	11	–	5.0	–	5.0	33	–
Letterpress operators	14	9	–5	VL	–34.8	VL	0.0	2	VL
Offset lithographic press operators	76	80	4	VL	5.9	L	6.0	12	VL
Printing press machine setters, operators and tenders	119	129	10	VL	8.6	L	5.1	19	VL
All other printing press setters and set-up operators	6	7	1	VL	14.4	H	0.0	1	VL
Screen printing machine setters and set-up operators	29	31	2	VL	6.1	L	0.0	4	VL
All other printing, binding, and related workers[1]	38	44	5	VL	14.0	L	0.0	7	VL
Textile and related setters, operators, and related workers	933	777	–156	–	–16.7	–	2.8	120	–
Extruding and forming machine operators and tenders, synthetic or glass fibers[1]	22	24	2	VL	9.7	L	0.0	4	VL
Pressing machine operators and tenders, textile, garment, and related materials	78	80	3	VL	3.5	VL	0.0	12	VL

[1]One or more Current Population Survey (CPS) based occupations may be used to estimate CPS based data. See Table 2.
NOTE: Rankings are based on employment in all detailed occupations in the National Industry-Occupation Matrix. For details, see "Data presented" section of text. Codes for describing the ranked variables are: VH = Very high, H = High, L = Low, VL = Very low, n. a. = Data not available. A dash indicates data are not applicable.

Table 1. Occupational employment and job openings data, 1996-2006. and worker characteristics, 1996—Continued (Numbers in thousands)

Annual average job openings due to growth and net replacement needs, 1996-2006		Median hourly earnings	Unemployment rate	Percent part-time	Most significant source of training	1996 Matrix Occupation
Number	Rank					
4	VL	H	VL	VL	Long-term on-the-job-training	Water and liquid waste treatment plant and system operators
4	VL	L	VL	VL	Long-term on-the-job-training	All other plant and system operators[1]
590	–	–	–	–	–	**Operators, fabricators, and laborers**
138	–	–	–	–	–	Machine setters, set-up operators, operators, and tenders
4	VL	H	H	VL	Moderate-term on-the-job-training	Numerical control machine tool operators and tenders, metal and plastic[1]
3	VL	L	H	VL	Moderate-term on-the-job-training	Combination machine tool setters, set-up operators, operators, and tenders[1]
17	–	–	–	–	–	Machine tool cut and form setters, operators, and tenders, metal and plastic
1	VL	H	H	VL	Moderate-term on-the-job-training	Drilling and boring machine tool setters and set-up operators, metal and plastic[1]
1	VL	H	H	VL	Moderate-term on-the-job-training	Grinding machine setters and set-up operators, metal and plastic
1	VL	H	H	VL	Moderate-term on-the-job-training	Lathe and turning machine tool setters and set-up operators, metal and plastic[1]
5	VL	L	H	VL	Moderate-term on-the-job-training	Machine forming operators and tenders, metal and plastic[1]
3	VL	L	L	VL	Moderate-term on-the-job-training	Machine tool cutting operators and tenders, metal and plastic
1	VL	L	H	VL	Moderate-term on-the-job-training	Punching machine setters and set-up operators, metal and plastic
5	VL	H	H	VL	Moderate-term on-the-job-training	All other machine tool setters, set-up operators, metal and plastic[1]
4	–	–	–	–	–	Metal fabricating machine setters, operators, and related workers
1	VL	L	H	VL	Moderate-term on-the-job-training	Metal fabricators, structural metal products[1]
0	VL	L	VL	VL	Moderate-term on-the-job-training	Soldering and brazing machine operators and tenders[1]
3	VL	H	H	VL	Moderate-term on-the-job-training	Welding machine setters, operators, and tenders
20	–	–	–	–	–	Metal and plastic processing machine setters, operators, and related workers
2	VL	L	H	VL	Moderate-term on-the-job-training	Electrolytic plating machine operators and tenders, setters and set-up operators, metal and plastic[1]
0	VL	L	H	VL	Moderate-term on-the-job-training	Foundry mold assembly and shakeout workers
0	VL	H	H	VL	Moderate-term on-the-job-training	Furnace operators and tenders[1]
1	VL	H	H	VL	Moderate-term on-the-job-training	Heat treating machine operators and tenders, metal and plastic[1]
2	VL	H	H	VL	Moderate-term on-the-job-training	Metal molding machine operators and tenders, setters and set-up operators
9	VL	L	H	VL	Moderate-term on-the-job-training	Plastic molding machine operators and tenders, setters and set-up operators
6	VL	L	H	VL	Moderate-term on-the-job-training	All other metal and plastic machine setters, operators. and related workers[1]
8	–	–	–	–	–	Printing, binding, and related workers
2	VL	L	H	VL	Moderate-term on-the-job-training	Bindery machine operators and set-up operators[1]
0	–	–	–	–	–	Prepress printing workers, production
0	VL	L	H	VL	Moderate-term on-the-job-training	Photoengraving and lithographic machine operators and tenders[1]
0	VL	L	H	VL	Moderate-term on-the-job-training	Typesetting and composing machine operators and tenders[1]
5	–	–	–	–	–	Printing press operators
0	VL	H	L	VL	Moderate-term on-the-job-training	Letterpress operators
1	VL	H	L	VL	Moderate-term on-the-job-training	Offset lithographic press operators
3	VL	H	L	VL	Moderate-term on-the-job-training	Printing press machine setters, operators and tenders
0	VL	H	L	VL	Moderate-term on-the-job-training	All other printing press setters and set-up operators
1	VL	L	L	VL	Moderate-term on-the-job-training	Screen printing machine setters and set-up operators
1	VL	L	L	VL	Moderate-term on-the-job-training	All other printing, binding, and related workers[1]
16	–	–	–	–	–	Textile and related setters, operators, and related workers
1	VL	H	VH	L	Moderate-term on-the-job-training	Extruding and forming machine operators and tenders, synthetic or glass fibers[1]
2	VL	VL	VH	H	Moderate-term on-the-job-training	Pressing machine operators and tenders, textile, garment, and related materials

[1]One or more Current Population Survey (CPS) based occupations may be used to estimate CPS based data. See Table 2.
NOTE: Rankings are based on employment in all detailed occupations in the National Industry-Occupation Matrix. For details, see "Data presented" section of text. Codes for describing the ranked variables are: VH = Very high, H = High, L = Low, VL = Very low, n. a. = Data not available. A dash indicates data are not applicable.

Table 1. Occupational employment and job openings data, 1996-2006, and worker characteristics, 1996—Continued   (Numbers in thousands)

1996 Matrix Occupation	Employment		Employment change, 1996-2006				Percent self-em-ployed, 1996	Annual average job openings due to growth and total replacement needs, 1996-2006	
			Numeric		Percent				
	1996	2006	Number	Rank	Number	Rank		Number	Rank
Sewing machine operators, garment	453	334	−118	VL	−26.1	VL	4.7	53	L
Sewing machine operators, non-garment	130	128	−2	VL	−1.9	VL	1.0	17	VL
Textile bleaching and dyeing machine operators and tenders[1] ..	26	28	3	VL	10.0	L	0.0	5	VL
Textile draw-out and winding machine operators and tenders[1] ..	183	155	−28	VL	−15.4	VL	2.2	23	VL
Textile machine setters and set-up operators	41	27	−14	VL	−34.4	VL	0.0	5	VL
Woodworking machine setters, operators, and other related workers	130	118	−12	–	−9.0	–	6.7	41	–
Head sawyers and sawing machine operators and tenders, setters and set-up operators	66	59	−6	VL	−9.7	VL	4.6	23	VL
Woodworking machine operators and tenders, setters and set-up operators[1]	64	59	−5	VL	−8.3	VL	8.9	18	VL
Other machine setters, set-up operators, operators, and tenders	1,919	2,070	151	–	7.9	–	2.6	354	–
Boiler operators and tenders, low pressure	17	14	−4	VL	−20.7	VL	0.0	1	VL
Cement and gluing machine operators and tenders[1]	35	30	−5	VL	−15.5	VL	0.0	6	VL
Chemical equipment controllers, operators and tenders[1]	79	82	3	VL	4.4	VL	0.0	14	VL
Cooking and roasting machine operators and tenders, food and tobacco[1]	30	32	2	VL	7.7	L	0.0	4	VL
Crushing and mixing machine operators and tenders	145	144	0	VL	−0.3	VL	0.0	25	VL
Cutting and slicing machine setters, operators and tenders	95	103	8	VL	8.3	L	6.9	19	VL
Dairy processing equipment operators, including setters[1]	13	12	−2	VL	−13.0	VL	0.0	2	VL
Electronic semiconductor processors	58	65	7	VL	12.3	L	0.0	7	VL
Extruding and forming machine setters, operators and tenders[1]	107	106	−1	VL	−1.3	VL	0.0	19	VL
Furnace, kiln, or kettle operators and tenders[1]	28	25	−3	VL	−9.3	VL	2.6	3	VL
Laundry and dry-cleaning machine operators and tenders, except pressing	180	219	39	L	21.9	VH	12.0	45	L
Motion picture projectionists[1]	8	5	−4	VL	−45.1	VL	0.0	1	VL
Packaging and filling machine operators and tenders	354	410	56	L	15.8	H	0.0	85	L
Painting and coating machine operators	171	185	14	–	8.4	–	6.1	35	–
Coating, painting, and spraying machine operators, tenders, setters, and set-up operators	122	127	5	VL	4.1	VL	1.0	24	VL
Painters, transportation equipment	49	58	9	VL	18.9	H	18.7	11	VL
Paper goods machine setters and set-up operators[1]	51	44	−7	VL	−14.5	VL	0.0	7	VL
Photographic processing machine operators and tenders	49	53	4	VL	8.0	L	0.0	12	VL
Separating and still machine operators and tenders[1]	19	17	−1	VL	−6.0	VL	0.0	3	VL
Shoe sewing machine operators and tenders[1]	11	6	−5	VL	−41.7	VL	0.0	1	VL
Tire building machine operators	14	12	−2	VL	−15.0	VL	0.0	1	VL
All other machine operators, tenders, setters, and set-up operators[1]	454	504	51	L	11.1	L	2.5	63	L
Hand workers, including assemblers and fabricators	2,813	2,898	85	–	3.0	–	3.3	546	–
Cannery workers	66	62	−5	VL	−6.8	VL	0.0	13	VL
Coil winders, tapers, and finishers	22	21	−1	VL	−3.2	VL	0.0	5	VL
Cutters and trimmers, hand[1]	46	48	2	VL	3.9	VL	2.1	9	VL
Electrical and electronic assemblers	229	226	−3	VL	−1.5	VL	0.0	51	L
Grinders and polishers, hand	74	72	−1	VL	−2.0	VL	0.0	12	VL
Machine assemblers	59	57	−2	VL	−3.6	VL	0.0	13	VL
Meat, poultry, and fish cutters and trimmers, hand[1]	151	186	35	L	23.0	VH	0.0	35	VL
Painting, coating, and decorating workers, hand[1]	31	34	3	VL	10.3	L	8.8	6	VL
Pressers, hand	14	13	−2	VL	−12.4	VL	0.0	2	VL
Sewers, hand	13	13	0	VL	0.9	VL	0.0	1	VL
Solderers and brazers[1]	26	32	5	VL	20.7	H	0.0	6	VL
Welders and cutters	352	384	32	L	9.0	L	7.6	37	VL
All other assemblers, fabricators, and hand workers[1]	1,729	1,751	22	L	1.3	VL	3.6	357	H
Transportation and material moving machine and vehicle operators	5,157	5,857	699	–	13.6	–	7.2	837	–
Motor vehicle operators	3,775	4,344	569	–	15.1	–	8.7	624	–
Bus drivers	592	710	117	–	19.8	–	0.3	91	–
Bus drivers, except school	167	192	24	L	14.6	H	1.1	24	VL
Bus drivers, school	425	518	93	L	21.8	VH	0.0	67	L

[1]One or more Current Population Survey (CPS) based occupations may be used to estimate CPS based data. See Table 2.
NOTE: Rankings are based on employment in all detailed occupations in the National Industry-Occupation Matrix. For details, see "Data presented" section of text. Codes for describing the ranked variables are: VH = Very high, H = High, L = Low, VL = Very low. n. a. = Data not available. A dash indicates data are not applicable.

Table 1. Occupational employment and job openings data, 1996-2006, and worker characteristics, 1996—Continued (Numbers in thousands)

Annual average job openings due to growth and net replacement needs, 1996-2006		Median hourly earnings	Unemployment rate	Percent part-time	Most significant source of training	1996 Matrix Occupation
Number	Rank					
7	VL	VL	VH	VL	Moderate-term on-the-job-training	Sewing machine operators, garment
2	VL	VL	VH	VL	Moderate-term on-the-job-training	Sewing machine operators, non-garment
1	VL	L	VH	L	Moderate-term on-the-job-training	Textile bleaching and dyeing machine operators and tenders[1]
3	VL	L	VH	L	Moderate-term on-the-job-training	Textile draw-out and winding machine operators and tenders[1]
1	VL	L	VH	L	Moderate-term on-the-job-training	Textile machine setters and set-up operators
3	–	–	–	–	–	Woodworking machine setters, operators, and other related workers
2	VL	L	VH	VL	Moderate-term on-the-job-training	Head sawyers and sawing machine operators and tenders, setters and set-up operators
1	VL	L	VH	VL	Moderate-term on-the-job-training	Woodworking machine operators and tenders, setters and set-up operators[1]
61	–	–	–	–	–	Other machine setters, set-up operators, operators, and tenders
0	VL	H	VL	VL	Moderate-term on-the-job-training	Boiler operators and lenders, low pressure
1	VL	L	H	VL	Moderate-term on-the-job-training	Cement and gluing machine operators and tenders[1]
2	VL	VH	L	VL	Moderate-term on-the-job-training	Chemical equipment controllers, operators and tenders[1]
1	VL	L	H	VL	Moderate-term on-the-job-training	Cooking and roasting machine operators and tenders, food and tobacco[1]
4	VL	L	H	VL	Moderate-term on-the-job-training	Crushing and mixing machine operators and tenders
3	VL	L	H	VL	Moderate-term on-the-job-training	Cutting and slicing machine sellers, operators and tenders
0	VL	L	L	VL	Moderate-term on-the-job-training	Dairy processing equipment operators, including setters[1]
2	VL	H	H	VL	Moderate-term on-the-job-training	Electronic semiconductor processors
3	VL	L	H	VL	Moderate-term on-the-job-training	Extruding and forming machine setters, operators and tenders[1]
0	VL	H	H	VL	Moderate-term on-the-job-training	Furnace, kiln, or kettle operators and tenders[1]
8	VL	VL	VH	H	Moderate-term on-the-job-training	Laundry and dry-cleaning machine operators and tenders, except pressing
0	VL	VL	H	VL	Short-term on-the-job-training	Motion picture projectionists[1]
12	L	L	VH	VL	Moderate-term on-the-job-training	Packaging and filling machine operators and tenders
6	–	–	–	–	–	Painting and coating machine operators
3	VL	L	H	VL	Moderate-term on-the-job-training	Coating, painting, and spraying machine operators, tenders, setters, and set-up operators
2	VL	H	H	VL	Moderate-term on-the-job-training	Painters, transportation equipment
1	VL	H	H	VL	Moderate-term on-the-job-training	Paper goods machine setters and set-up operators[1]
2	VL	L	H	H	Short-term on-the-job-training	Photographic processing machine operators and tenders
0	VL	H	L	VL	Moderate-term on-the-job-training	Separating and still machine operators and tenders[1]
0	VL	L	VH	VL	Moderate-term on-the-job-training	Shoe sewing machine operators and tenders[1]
0	VL	VH	H	VL	Moderate-term on-the-job-training	Tire building machine operators
14	L	L	H	VL	Moderate-term on-the-job-training	All other machine operators, tenders, setters, and set-up operators[1]
67	–	–	–	–	–	Hand workers, including assemblers and fabricators
1	VL	VL	VH	VL	Short-term on-the-job-training	Cannery workers
0	VL	L	VH	VL	Short-term on-the-job-training	Coil winders, tapers, and finishers
1	VL	L	VH	VL	Short-term on-the-job-training	Cutters and trimmers, hand[1]
5	VL	L	VH	VL	Short-term on-the-job-training	Electrical and electronic assemblers
1	VL	L	H	VH	Short-term on-the-job-training	Grinders and polishers, hand
1	VL	L	VH	VL	Short-term on-the-job-training	Machine assemblers
7	VL	VL	VH	VL	Short-term on-the-job-training	Meat, poultry, and fish cutters and trimmers, hand[1]
1	VL	L	VH	VL	Short-term on-the-job-training	Painting, coating, and decorating workers, hand[1]
0	VL	VL	H	VH	Short-term on-the-job-training	Pressers, hand
0	VL	VL	H	VH	Short-term on-the-job-training	Sewers, hand
1	VL	L	VH	VL	Short-term on-the-job-training	Solderers and brazers[1]
12	L	H	H	VL	Postsecondary vocational training	Welders and cutters
35	H	L	VH	L	Short-term on-the-job-training	All other assemblers, fabricators, and hand workers[1]
156	–	–	–	–	–	Transportation and material moving machine and vehicle operators
113	–	–	–	–	–	Motor vehicle operators
20	–	–	–	–	–	Bus drivers
5	VL	H	L	VH	Moderate-term on-the-job-training	Bus drivers, except school
151	L	L	L	VH	Short-term on-the-job-training	Bus drivers, school

[1]One or more Current Population Survey (CPS) based occupations may be used to estimate CPS based data. See Table 2.
NOTE: Rankings are based on employment in all detailed occupations in the National Industry-Occupation Matrix. For details, see "Data presented" section of text. Codes for describing the ranked variables are: VH = Very high, H = High, L = Low, VL = Very low, n. a. = Data not available. A dash indicates data are not applicable.

Table 1. Occupational employment and job openings data, 1996-2006, and worker characteristics, 1996—Continued (Numbers in thousands)

1996 Matrix Occupation	Employment		Employment change, 1996-2006				Percent self-employed, 1996	Annual average job openings due to growth and total replacement needs, 1996-2006	
			Numeric		Percent				
	1996	2006	Number	Rank	Number	Rank		Number	Rank
Taxi drivers and chauffeurs	106	114	8	VL	7.6	L	32.0	19	VL
Truck drivers	3,050	3,492	442	–	14.5	–	9.6	510	–
Driver/sales workers	331	370	39	L	11.6	L	2.8	28	VL
Truck drivers light and heavy	2,719	3,123	404	VH	14.9	H	10.4	482	VH
All other motor vehicle operators[1]	27	28	1	VL	3.3	VL	0.0	4	VL
Rail transportation workers	83	79	−4	−4.7	–	0.0	6	–	–
Locomotive engineers[1]	27	28	1	VL	3.3	VL	0.0	4	VL
Railroad brake, signal, and switch operators[1]	18	13	−5	VL	−28.2	VL	0.0	1	VL
Railroad conductors and yardmasters[1]	25	25	0	VL	−1.8	VL	0.0	2	VL
Rail yard engineers, dinkey operators, and hostlers[1]	5	4	−1	VL	−19.6	VL	0.0	0	VL
Subway and street car operators[1]	13	14	1	VL	9.2	L	0.0	1	VL
Water transportation and related workers	51	49	−2	–	−3.8	–	7.5	9	–
Able seamen, ordinary seamen, and marine oilers[1]	22	20	−1	VL	−6.2	VL	5.4	4	VL
Captains and pilots, ship[1]	14	13	0	VL	−1.6	VL	10.5	3	VL
Mates, ship, boat, and barge[1]	7	7	0	VL	2.4	VL	0.0	1	VL
Ship engineers[1]	9	8	−1	VL	−6.6	VL	14.4	2	VL
Material moving equipment operators	1,097	1,212	114	–	10.4	–	3.7	171	–
Crane and tower operators	45	45	0	VL	−1.1	VL	0.0	6	VL
Excavation and loading machine operators[1]	97	107	10	VL	10.5	L	18.5	5	VL
Grader, bulldozer, and sewer operators[1]	107	111	5	VL	4.3	VL	5.3	5	VL
Hoist and winch operators[1]	9	10	0	VL	4.8	VL	0.0	1	VL
Industrial truck and tractor operators	479	536	57	L	11.9	L	0.3	96	L
Operating engineers	157	180	23	L	14.4	H	8.9	26	VL
All other material moving equipment operators[1]	202	222	20	L	9.7	L	0.9	32	VL
All other transportation and material moving equipment operators[1]	151	173	22	L	14.5	H	0.0	27	VL
Helpers, laborers, and material movers, hand	4,975	5,654	679	–	13.7	–	1.1	1,591	–
Freight, stock, and material movers, hand[1]	808	849	41	L	5.1	VL	1.8	310	H
Hand packers and packagers	986	1,208	222	H	22.5	VH	0.0	252	H
Helpers, construction trades	546	596	49	L	9.0	L	0.3	161	H
Machine feeders and offbearers	265	263	−2	VL	−0.8	VL	0.0	50	L
Parking lot attendants[1]	68	86	18	VL	26.2	VH	0.0	13	VL
Refuse collectors[1]	116	123	7	VL	6.0	L	0.0	46	L
Service station attendants	174	174	0	VL	0.1	VL	1.7	50	L
Vehicle washers and equipment cleaners	274	343	69	L	25.2	VH	6.6	111	L
All other helpers, laborers, and material movers, hand[1]	1,737	2,012	275	VH	15.8	H	1.1	598	VH

[1]One or more Current Population Survey (CPS) based occupations may be used to estimate CPS based data. See Table 2.
NOTE: Rankings are based on employment in all detailed occupations in the National Industry-Occupation Matrix. For details, see "Data presented" section of text. Codes for describing the ranked variables are: VH = Very high, H = High, L = Low, VL = Very low, n. a. = Data not available. A dash indicates data are not applicable.

Table 1. Occupational employment and job openings data, 1996-2006, and worker characteristics, 1996—Continued (Numbers in thousands)

Annual average job openings due to growth and net replacement needs, 1996-2006		Median hourly earnings	Unemployment rate	Percent part-time	Most significant source of training	1996 Matrix Occupation
Number	Rank					
2	VL	VL	H	H	Short-term on-the-job-training	Taxi drivers and chauffeurs
90	–	–	–	–	–	Truck drivers
12	L	L	L	L	Short-term on-the-job-training	Driver/sales workers
78	VH	H	H	L	Short-term on-the-job-training	Truck drivers light and heavy
1	VL	L	H	H	Short-term on-the-job-training	All other motor vehicle operators[1]
2	–	–	–	–	–	Rail transportation workers
1	VL	H	VL	L	Work experience in a related occupation	Locomotive engineers[1]
0	VL	H	VL	L	Work experience in a related occupation	Railroad brake, signal, and switch operators[1]
1	VL	H	VL	L	Work experience in a related occupation	Railroad conductors and yardmasters[1]
0	VL	VH	VL	L	Work experience in a related occupation	Rail yard engineers, dinkey operators, and hostlers[1]
0	VL	VH	VL	L	Moderate-term on-the-job-training	Subway and streetcar operators[1]
2	–	–	–	–	–	Water transportation and related workers
1	VL	L	VH	H	Short-term on-the-job-training	Able seamen, ordinary seamen, and marine oilers[1]
1	VL	VH	VH	H	Work experience in a related occupation	Captains and pilots, ship[1]
0	VL	H	VH	H	Work experience in a related occupation	Mates, ship, boat, and barge[1]
0	VL	VH	VH	H	Work experience in a related occupation	Ship engineers[1]
34	–	–	–	–	–	Material moving equipment operators
1	VL	H	H	VL	Moderate-term on-the-job-training	Crane and tower operators
3	VL	H	VH	L	Moderate-term on-the-job-training	Excavation and loading machine operators[1]
1	VL	H	VH	L	Moderate-term on-the-job-training	Grader, bulldozer, and scraper operators
0	VL	H	VH	VL	Moderate-term on-the-job-training	Hoist and winch operators[1]
16	L	H	H	VL	Short-term on-the-job-training	Industrial truck and tractor operators
6	VL	VH	VH	VL	Moderate-term on-the-job-training	Operating engineers
7	VL	H	VH	VL	Moderate-term on-the-job-training	All other material moving equipment operators[1]
5	VL	H	H	H	Moderate-term on-the-job-training	All other transportation and material moving equipment operators[1]
229	–	–	–	–	–	Helpers, laborers, and material movers, hand
33	H	L	VH	VH	Short-term on-the-job-training	Freight, stock, and material movers, hand[1]
48	H	VL	VH	L	Short-term on-the-job-training	Hand packers and packagers
24	L	L	VH	H	Short-term on-the-job-training	Helpers, construction trades
7	VL	L	VH	L	Short-term on-the-job-training	Machine feeders and offbearers
3	VL	VL	H	H	Short-term on-the-job-training	Parking lot attendants
5	VL	H	VH	VH	Short-term on-the-job-training	Refuse collectors[1]
7	VL	VL	VH	H	Short-term on-the-job-training	Service station attendants
15	L	VL	VH	H	Short-term on-the-job-training	Vehicle washers and equipment cleaners
86	VH	L	VH	H	Short-term on-the-job-training	All other helpers, laborers, and material movers, hand[1]

[1]One or more Current Population Survey (CPS) based occupations may be used to estimate CPS based data. See Table 2.
NOTE: Rankings are based on employment in all detailed occupations in the National Industry-Occupation Matrix. For details, see "Data presented" section of text. Codes for describing the ranked variables are: VH = Very high, H = High, L = Low, VL = Very low, n. a. = Data not available. A dash indicates data are not applicable.

Table 2. 1996 National industry-occupation matrix occupations which use Current Population Survey proxy occupation data to estimate one or more data elements

1996 Matrix Occupation	Percent part-time and unemployment rate	Replacement needs	
		Total	Net
Executive, administrative, and managerial occupations			
Food service and lodging managers			•
Funeral directors and morticians	•	•	•
Government chief executives and legislators	•	•	•
Property and real estate managers	•		
All other managers and administrators	•	•	•
Management analysts		•	
All other management support workers	•	•	•
Professional specialty occupations			
Chemical engineers		•	
Metallurgists and metallurgical, ceramic, and materials engineers	•	•	•
Mining engineers, including mine safety engineers	•	•	•
Nuclear engineers	•	•	•
Petroleum engineers	•	•	•
All other engineers	•	•	•
Surveyors	•	•	•
Agricultural and food scientists	•	•	•
Foresters and conservation scientists	•	•	•
Actuaries	•	•	•
Statisticians		•	•
Mathematicians and all other mathematical scientists	•	•	•
Geologists, geophysicists, and oceanographers .	•	•	•
Meteorologists	•	•	•
Physicists and astronomers	•	•	•
All other physical scientists	•	•	•
Urban and regional planners		•	•
All other social scientists		•	•
Directors, religious activities and education			•
Human services workers		•	
Judges, magistrates, and other judicial workers ..		•	•
College and university faculty	•	•	•
All other teachers and instructors	•	•	•
Curators, archivists, museum technicians, and restorers	•	•	•
Chiropractors	•	•	•
Optometrists	•	•	•
Podiatrists	•	•	•
Veterinarians and veterinary inspectors		•	•
Physician assistants		•	•
Occupational therapists		•	•
Physical therapists		•	•
Recreational therapists		•	•
Respiratory therapists		•	•
Speech-language pathologists and audiologists .		•	•
All other therapists		•	•
Dancers and choreographers	•	•	•
Producers, directors, actors, and entertainers			•
All other professional workers		•	•
Technicians and related support occupations			
Cardiology technologists			•
Electroneurodiagnostic technologists			•
EKG technicians			•
Emergency medical technicians			•
Medical records technicians	•	•	•
Pharmacy technicians			•
Surgical technologists			•
Veterinary technicians and technologists			•
All other health professionals and paraprofessionals	•	•	•
All other engineering technicians and technologists	•	•	•

1996 Matrix Occupation	Percent part-time and unemployment rate	Replacement needs	
		Total	Net
Science and mathematics technicians		•	•
Air traffic controllers and airplane dispatchers	•	•	•
Broadcast technicians	•	•	•
Programmers, numerical, tool, and process control	•	•	•
Technical assistants, library		•	•
All other technicians	•	•	•
Marketing and sales occupations			
Travel agents			•
All other sales and related workers			•
Administrative support occupations, including clerical			
All other communications equipment operators ..	•	•	•
Peripheral computer equipment operators	•	•	•
Reservation and transportation ticket agents and travel clerks			•
Meter readers, utilities	•	•	•
Weighers, measurers, checkers, and samplers, recordkeeping			•
All other material recording, scheduling, and distribution workers	•	•	•
Advertising clerks	•	•	•
Correspondence clerks	•		•
Billing, posting, and calculating machine operators			•
Personnel clerks, except payroll and timekeeping			
Stenographers and/or court reporters			•
Duplicating, mail, and other office machine operators	•	•	•
Proofreaders and copy markers	•	•	•
Service occupations			
Pest controllers and assistants			•
All other cleaning and building service workers ..	•	•	•
Food preparation workers			•
Food counter, fountain, and related workers			•
Medical assistants			•
Occupational therapy assistants and aides			•
Pharmacy assistants			•
Baggage porters and bellhops	•	•	•
Personal and home care aides			•
Ushers, lobby attendants, and ticket takers	•	•	•
Cleaners and servants, private household	•	•	•
Cooks, private household	•	•	•
Housekeepers and butlers	•	•	•
Fire fighting and prevention supervisors	•	•	•
Fire inspection occupations	•	•	•
Crossing guards	•	•	•
All other service workers		•	•
Agriculture, forestry, fishing, and related occupations			
Captains and other officers, fishing vessels	•	•	•
Fishers, hunters, and trappers	•	•	•
Forest and conservation workers	•	•	•
Lawn service managers	•	•	•
Nursery and greenhouse managers	•	•	•
Supervisors, farming, forestry, and agricutural related occupations	•	•	•
All other agricultural, forestry, fishing, and related workers	•	•	•
Precision production, craft, and repair occupations			
Blue collar worker supervisors	•	•	•

Table 2. 1996 National industry-occupation matrix occupations which use Current Population Survey proxy occupation data to estimate one or more data elements—Continued

1996 Matrix Occupation	Percent part-time and unemployment rate	Replacement needs Total	Replacement needs Net
Bricklayers and stone masons		•	•
Glaziers	•	•	•
Hard tile setters			•
Paving, surfacing, and tamping equipment operators	•	•	•
Plasterers	•	•	•
All other construction trades workers		•	•
Roustabouts		•	•
All other oil and gas extraction occupations	•	•	•
Mining, quarrying, and tunneling occupations	•	•	•
All other extraction and related workers	•	•	•
Central office and PBX installers and repairers		•	
All other communications equipment mechanics, installers, and repairers		•	
Station installers and repairers, telephone		•	
Telephone and cable TV line installers and repairers	•	•	•
Industrial machinery mechanics	•	•	
Aircraft engine specialists		•	
Aircraft mechanics	•	•	•
Automotive mechanics	•	•	
Farm equipment mechanics	•	•	
Motorcycle repairers			•
Small engine specialists			•
Camera and photographic equipment repairers	•	•	•
Electric meter installers and repairers	•	•	•
Elevator installers and repairers	•	•	•
Home appliance and power tool repairers	•	•	•
Locksmiths and safe repairers	•	•	•
Musical instrument repairers and tuners	•	•	•
Precision instrument repairers	•	•	•
Watchmakers	•	•	•
All other mechanics, installers, and repairers	•	•	•
Aircraft assemblers, precision	•	•	•
Fitters, structural metal, precision	•	•	•
Machine builders and other precision machine assemblers	•	•	•
All other precision assemblers	•	•	•
All other precision food and tobacco workers	•	•	
Metal workers, precision			
Boilermakers		•	•
Jewelers and silversmiths		•	•
Sheet metal workers and duct installers	•	•	•
Shipfitters	•	•	•
All other precision metal workers	•	•	•
Bookbinders	•	•	•
Compositors and typesetters, precision	•	•	•
Paste-up workers	•	•	•
Desktop publishing specialists	•	•	•
Photoengravers	•	•	•
Camera operators	•	•	•
Film strippers, printing	•	•	•
Platemakers	•	•	•
All other printing workers, precision	•	•	•
Patternmakers and layout workers, fabric and apparel		•	•
Shoe and leather workers and repairers, precision	•	•	•
Upholsterers			
All other precision textile, apparel, and furnishings workers		•	•
Furniture finishers	•	•	•
All other precision woodworkers	•	•	•
Chemical plant and system operators	•	•	•
Power distributors and dispatchers	•	•	•
Power generating and reactor plant operators	•	•	•
Gas and petroleum plant and system occupations	•	•	•

1996 Matrix Occupation	Percent part-time and unemployment rate	Replacement needs Total	Replacement needs Net
All other plant and system operators	•	•	•
Operators, fabricators, and laborers			
Numerical control machine tool operators and tenders, metal and plastic	•	•	•
Combination machine tool setters, set-up operators, operators, and tenders	•	•	•
Drilling and boring machine tool setters and set-up operators, metal and plastic	•	•	•
Lathe and turning machine tool setters and set-up operators, metal and plastic	•	•	•
All other machine tool setters, set-up operators, metal and plastic	•	•	•
Metal fabricators, structural metal products	•	•	•
Soldering and brazing machine operators and tenders	•	•	•
Electrolytic plating machine operators and tenders, setters and set-up operators, metal and plastic	•	•	•
Furnace operators and tenders		•	
Heat treating machine operators and tenders, metal and plastic	•	•	•
All other metal and plastic machine setters, operators, and related workers	•	•	•
Bindery machine operators and set-up operators	•	•	•
Photoengraving and lithographic machine operators and tenders	•	•	•
Typesetting and composing machine operators and tenders	•	•	•
All other printing, binding, and related workers	•	•	•
Extruding and forming machine operators and tenders, synthetic or glass fibers	•	•	•
Textile bleaching and dyeing machine operators and tenders	•	•	•
Textile draw-out and winding machine operators and tenders	•	•	•
Woodworking machine operators and tenders, setters and set-up operators	•	•	•
Cement and gluing machine operators and tenders	•	•	•
Chemical equipment controllers, operators and tenders		•	•
Cooking and roasting machine operators and tenders, food and tobacco	•	•	•
Dairy processing equipment operators, including setters		•	•
Extruding and forming machine setters, operators and tenders	•	•	•
Furnace, kiln, or kettle operators and tenders			•
Motion picture projectionists			•
Paper goods machine setters and set-up operators	•	•	•
Separating and still machine operators and tenders		•	•
Shoe sewing machine operators and tenders		•	•
All other machine operators, tenders, setters, and set-up operators	•	•	•
Cutters and trimmers, hand	•	•	•
Meat, poultry, and fish cutters and trimmers, hand	•	•	•
Painting, coating, and decorating workers, hand	•	•	•
Solderers and brazers	•	•	•
All other assemblers, fabricators, and hand workers	•	•	•
All other motor vehicle operators	•	•	•
Locomotive engineers	•	•	•
Railroad brake, signal, and switch operators	•	•	•
Railroad conductors and yardmasters	•	•	•
Rail yard engineers, dinkey operators, and hostlers	•	•	•

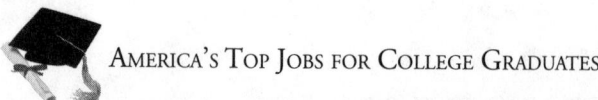

Table 2. 1996 National industry-occupation matrix occupations which use Current Population Survey proxy occupation data to estimate one or more data elements—Continued

1996 Matrix Occupation	Percent part-time and unemployment rate	Replacement needs	
		Total	Net
Subway and streetcar operators			
Able seamen, ordinary seamen, and marine .... oilers	●	●	●
Captains and pilots, ship	●	●	●
Mates, ship, boat, and barge	●	●	●
Ship engineers	●	●	●
Excavation and loading machine operators	●	●	●
Hoist and winch operators	●	●	●

1996 Matrix Occupation	Percent part-time and unemployment rate	Replacement needs	
		Total	Net
All other material moving equipment operators	●	●	●
All other transportation and material moving equipment operators	●	●	●
Freight, stock, and material movers, hand	●	●	●
Parking lot attendants	●	●	●
Refuse collectors	●	●	●
All other helpers, laborers, and material movers, hand	●	●	●

© 1999 • J. Michael Farr • JIST Works, Inc. • Indianapolis, IN

EMPLOYMENT TRENDS WITHIN MAJOR INDUSTRIES

Introduction

While many hundreds of specialized industries exist, more than 70 percent of all workers are employed in just 40 major ones. While space limitations do not allow me to list detailed information on each of these industries, the article that follows provides a good overview of trends within industry types.

The article comes, with minor changes, from the introduction to a book published by the U.S. Department of Labor titled the *Career Guide to Industries*. It includes important information you should consider in making your career plans.

While you may not have thought much about it, the industry you work in is often as important as the career you choose. For example, some industries pay significantly higher wages than others for similar jobs. So, read this article over carefully and consider the possibilities—it can make a big difference.

If you want more information on a specific industry, look for the *Career Guide to Industries* in your library. A more widely available version of the same book, titled *Career Guide to America's Top Industries*, may be available in your library or bookstore. This book is published by JIST.

Here are the industries covered in these books:

Goods-Producing Industries

Agriculture, Mining, and Construction
    Agricultural services
    Construction
    Mining and quarrying
    Oil and gas extraction
Manufacturing
    Aerospace manufacturing
    Apparel and other textile products
    Chemicals manufacturing, except drugs
    Drug manufacturing
    Electronic equipment manufacturing
    Food processing
    Motor vehicle and equipment manufacturing
    Printing and publishing
    Steel manufacturing
    Textile mill products

Service-Producing Industries

Transportation, Communications, and Public Utilities
    Air transportation
    Public utilities
    Radio and television communications
    Telephone communications
    Trucking and warehousing
Wholesale and Retail Trade
    Department, clothing, and accessory stores
    Eating and drinking places
    Grocery stores
    Motor vehicle dealers
    Wholesale trade
Finance and Insurance
    Banking
    Insurance
    Securities and commodities
Services
    Advertising
    Amusement and recreation services
    Child-care services
    Computer and data processing services
    Educational services
    Health services
    Hotels and lodging places
    Management and public relations services
    Motion picture production and distribution
    Personnel supply services
    Social services, except child care
Government
    Federal government
    State and local government

Industry Characteristics: An Overview

The U.S. economy contains industries with increasingly diverse characteristics. For each industry covered in the *Career Guide,* detailed information is provided about specific characteristics: Nature of the industry, working conditions, employment, occupational composition, training and advancement requirements, earnings, and job outlook. This article provides an overview of these characteristics for the economy as a whole.

Nature of the Industry

Industries are defined by the goods and services an industry provides. Because workers in the United States produce such a wide variety of products and services, industries in the U.S. economy vary widely, from steel manufacturers to grocery stores. Although many of these industries are related, each industry contains a unique combination of occupations, production techniques, and business characteristics. Understanding the nature of the industry is important, because it is this unique combination that determines working conditions, educational requirements, and the job outlook for each of the industries discussed in the *Career Guide.*

Industries are comprised of many different places of work, called *establishments,* which range from large factories and office complexes, employing thousands of workers, to small businesses employing only a few workers. Establishments that produce similar goods or services are grouped together into *industries.* Industries that produce related types of goods or services are, in turn, grouped together into *major industry divisions,* which are further categorized as the *goods-producing sector* (agriculture, forestry, and fishing; mining; construction; and manufacturing) or the *service-producing sector* (transportation, communications, and public utilities; wholesale and retail trade; finance and insurance; services; and government).

Distinctions within industries are also varied. Each industry comprises a number of subdivisions that are determined largely by the production processes unique to each industry. An easily recognized example of these subdivisions is in the food processing industry, which is made up of segments that produce meat products, preserved fruits and vegetables, bakery items, beverages, and dairy products—among others. Each of these segments requires workers with varying skills and employs unique production techniques. Another example of these subdivisions is in public utilities, which employs workers in establishments that provide electricity, sanitary services, water, and natural gas. Working conditions and establishment characteristics differ widely in each of these subdivisions.

Currently, there are nearly 7 million business establishments in the United States. The average size of these establishments varies widely across industries. Among industry divisions, manufacturing included many industries having among the highest employment per establishment in 1994. For example, industries manufacturing tobacco, transportation equipment, and primary metals each averaged 100 or more employees per establishment. Nonmanufacturing industries with relatively high employment per establishment included general merchandise stores and metal mining, each with 50 or more workers per establishment.

Most small establishments are in the retail trade and services industries. Other industries that tend to have relatively few employees per establishment included auto repair and parking services, agricultural services, insurance agents and brokers, and real estate; each averaged six or fewer workers per establishment in 1994. On the other hand, educational services had nearly 50 employees per establishment.

Establishments in the United States are predominantly small; 55 percent of all establishments employed fewer than five workers in 1994. Medium to large establishments, however, employ a greater proportion of all workers. For example, establishments that employed 50 or more workers accounted for only 5 percent of all establishments, yet employed 57 percent of all workers. Large establishments—those with more than 500 workers—accounted for only 0.3 percent of all establishments but employed 20 percent of all workers. Percent distribution of employment according to establishment size is shown in Table 1.

Establishment size can play a role in the characteristics of each job. Large establishments offer workers greater occupational mobility and advancement potential, whereas small establishments may provide their employees with broader experience, by requiring them to assume a wider range of responsibilities. Also, small establishments are distributed throughout the nation; every locality has a few small businesses. Large establishments, in contrast, are less common, yet hire more workers.

Table 1. Percent Distribution of Establishments and Employment in All Industries by Establishment Size, 1994

Establishment Size (Number of Workers)	Establishments	Employment
Total	100.0	100.0
1–4	54.9	6.3
5–9	19.8	8.8
10–19	12.2	11.1
20–49	8.1	16.4
50–99	2.7	12.6
100–249	1.6	15.8
250–499	0.4	9.1
500–999	2	6.9
1,000 or more	1	13.0

SOURCE: Department of Commerce, *County Business Patterns,* 1994

Working Conditions

Just as the goods and services of each industry are different, working conditions in industries vary significantly. In some industries, the work setting is quiet, temperature-controlled, and virtually hazard free. Other industries are characterized by noisy, uncomfortable, and sometimes dangerous work environments. Some industries require long workweeks and shift work; in many industries, standard 35- to 40-hour workweeks are common. Still other industries can be seasonal, requiring long hours during busy periods and abbreviated schedules during slower months. These varying conditions usually are determined by production processes, establishment size, and the physical location of work.

One of the most telling indicators of working conditions is an industry's injury and illness rate. Overexertion, contact with dangerous equipment, falls, repetitive motion, and fires are among the most common causes of injury and illness. In 1995, approximately 6.6 million nonfatal injuries and illnesses were reported throughout private industry. Among major industry divisions, manufacturing had the highest rate of injury and illness—11.6 cases for every 100 full-time workers—while finance, insurance, and real estate had the lowest rate—2.6. About 6,000 work-related fatalities were reported in 1995; transportation accidents, violent acts, contact with objects and equipment, falls, and exposure to harmful substances or environments were among the most common causes. Industries with the highest and lowest rates of nonfatal injury and illness are shown in Table 2.

Table 2. Nonfatal Injury and Illness Rates of Selected Industries, 1994

Industry	Cases Per 100 Full-Time Employees
All Industries	**8.1**
High rates	
Motor vehicle manufacturing	23.2
Nursing and personal care facilities	18.2
Food processing	16.3
Sanitary services	14.0
Trucking and warehousing	13.8
Low rates	
Telephone communications	2.4
Insurance	2.3
Banking	2.2
Amusement and recreation services	2.2
Radio and TV broadcasting	1.9

Work schedules are another important reflection of working conditions, and the operational requirements of each industry lead to large differences in hours worked and part-time versus full-time status. The contrast in an average workweek was notable between retail trade and manufacturing—28.8 hours and 41.6 hours, respectively, in 1996. More than 40 percent of workers in retail trade work part time (1 to 34 hours per week), compared to only 10 percent in manufacturing. Industries having relatively high and low percentages of part-time workers are shown in Table 3.

Table 3. Percent of Part-Time Workers in Selected Industries, 1996

Industry	Percent Part Time
All Industries	25.4
Many part-time workers	
Eating and drinking places	51.5
Apparel and accessory stores	48.0
Department stores	40.8
Child day care services	40.2
Personnel supply services	28.9
Few part-time workers	
Chemicals and allied products	8.2
Drug manufacturing	6.5
Motor vehicle manufacturing	6.1
Aircraft and parts	4.6
Guided missiles, space vehicles, and parts	3.5

The low proportion of part-time workers in some manufacturing industries often reflects the continuity of the production processes and the specificity of skills. Once begun, it is costly to halt such processes, since machinery and materials must be tended and moved continuously. For example, the chemical manufacturing industry produces many different chemical products through controlled chemical reactions. These chemical processes require chemical operators to monitor and adjust the flow of materials into and out of the line of production. Production may continue 24 hours a day, 7 days a week, under the watchful eyes of chemical operators working in shifts.

Retail trade and service industries, on the other hand, have seasonal cycles marked by various events, such as school openings or important holidays, that affect hours worked. During busy times of the year, longer hours are common, whereas slack periods lead to cutbacks and shorter workweeks. Jobs in these industries are generally appealing to students and others who desire flexible, part-time schedules.

Employment

The number of wage and salary worker jobs in the United States totaled nearly 122 million in 1996 and is projected to reach almost 140 million by 2006. (See Table 4.) In addition to these workers, the U.S. economy also provided employment for nearly 11 million self-employed workers and about 180,000 unpaid family workers.

Employment is not evenly divided among various industries, as shown in Table 4. The services industry is the largest source of employment, with over 44 million workers, followed by wholesale and retail trade and manufacturing. Among the industries covered in the *Career Guide*, wage and salary employment ranged from 240,000 in steel manufacturing to 10.7 million in educational services. Three industries—educational services, health services, and eating and drinking places—together accounted for about 29 million jobs, or nearly a quarter of the nation's employment.

Although workers of all ages are employed in each industry, certain industries tend to possess workers of distinct age groups. For the reason mentioned above, retail trade employs a relatively high proportion of young workers to fill part-time and temporary positions. The manufacturing sector, on the other hand, has a relatively high median age, because many jobs in this sector require a number of years to learn and also rely on skills that do not easily transfer to other firms. Additionally, manufacturing employment has been declining, providing fewer opportunities for young workers to get jobs. As a result, almost one-third of the workers in retail trade were 24 years of age or younger, whereas only 10 percent of workers in manufacturing were 24 or younger. The age distribution of workers in all industries is contrasted with the distributions in retail trade and manufacturing in Table 5.

Table 4. Wage and Salary Employment in Selected Industries, 1996 and Projected Change, 1996 to 2006
(Employment in Thousands)

Industry	1996 Employment	Percent Distribution	2006 Employment	1996–2006 Employment Change	Percent Change
All Industries	121,685	100.0	139,192	17,507	14.4
Goods-producing	26,547	21.8	26,550	3	0.0
Agriculture, forestry, and fishing	2,026	1.7	2,099	234	3.6
Agricultural services	928	0.8	1,118	190	20.5
Mining	574	.5	443	-69	-22.7
Oil and gas extraction	318	.3	248	-70	-22.1
Mining and quarrying	256	2	196	-61	-23.6
Construction	5,400	4.4	5,900	500	9.3
Manufacturing	18,457	15.2	18,108	-518	-1.9
Food processing	1,693	1.4	1,713	-21	-1.2
Printing and publishing	1,538	1.3	1,501	-37	-2.4
Electronics manufacturing	1,486	1.2	1,451	-35	-2.3
Motor vehicle and equipment manufacturing	963	.8	929	-33	-3.5
Apparel and other textile products manufacturing	864	.7	714	-150	-17.3
Chemicals manufacturing, except drugs	773	.6	751	-22	-2.9
Textile mill products manufacturing	624	.5	588	-36	-5.7
Aerospace manufacturing	550	.5	596	46	8.4
Drug manufacturing	259	.2	319	61	23.5
Steel manufacturing	240	.2	197	-44	-18.2
Service-producing	95,228	78.3	112,643	17,415	18.3
Transportation, communications, and public utilities	6,260	5.1	7,111	789	13.6
Trucking and warehousing	1,641	1.3	1,860	219	13.4
Air transportation	1,122	.9	1,401	279	24.9
Telephone communications	924	.8	940	17	1.8
Public utilities	885	.7	976	91	10.3
Radio and television broadcasting	414	.3	420	6	1.5
Wholesale and retail trade	28,108	23.1	31,103	5,576	10.7
Eating and drinking places	7,499	6.2	8,884	1,384	18.5
Wholesale retail	6,483	5.3	7,228	745	11.5
Department, clothing, and variety stores	3,827	3.1	3,717	-110	-2.9
Grocery stores	3,030	2.5	3,390	360	11.9
Motor vehicle dealers	1,117	.9	1,148	31	2.8
Finance, insurance, and real estate	6,899	5.7	7,561	1,398	10.9
Insurance	2,217	1.8	2,471	254	11.5
Banking	2,024	1.7	1,950	-74	-3.6
Securities and commodities	551	.5	740	189	34.3
Services	44,223	36.3	56,647	15,506	28.1
Educational services	10,692	8.8	12,480	1,789	16.7
Health services	10,507	8.6	13,638	3,131	29.8
Personnel supply services	2,646	2.2	4,039	1,393	52.7
Social services	1,834	1.5	2,727	894	48.7
Hotels and other lodging places	1,716	1.4	1,978	262	15.3
Amusement and recreation services	1,466	1.2	1,998	531	36.3
Computer and data processing services	1,208	1.0	2,509	1,301	107.7
Management and public relations services	874	.7	1,400	527	60.3
Child-care services	569	.5	734	164	28.8
Motion picture production and distribution	247	.2	328	81	32.7
Advertising	242	.2	270	28	11.4
Government	9,738	8.0	10,131	913	4.0
State and local government	6,981	5.7	7,461	480	6.9
Federal government	1,901	1.6	1,790	-111	-5.8

Table 5. Percent Distribution of Industry Sector Employment by Age Group, 1996

Age Group	All Industries	Retail Trade	Manufacturing
Total	100.0	100.0	100.0
16–24	14.7	32.2	9.9
24–54	73.1	77.7	78.4
55 and older	12.2	10.1	11.6

Because employment in some industries is concentrated in one region of the country, job opportunities in these industries should be best in the states in which these establishments are located. Such industries are often located near a source of raw materials upon which the industries rely. For example, oil and gas extraction jobs are concentrated in Texas, Louisiana, and Oklahoma; many textile mill products manufacturing jobs are found in North Carolina, Georgia, and South Carolina; and a significant proportion of motor vehicle and equipment manufacturing jobs are located in Michigan. On the other hand, some industries—such as grocery stores and educational services—have jobs distributed throughout the nation, reflecting population density in different areas.

Occupations in the Industry

As mentioned above, the occupations found in each industry depend on the types of services provided or goods produced. For example, manufacturing companies use machinery and other industrial equipment to fabricate goods, so these companies employ a large number of machine operators and industrial machinery repairers. Other occupations common to the manufacturing sector include assemblers, inspectors, machine setters, and material movers. Retail trade, on the other hand, displays and sells manufactured goods to consumers, so this sector hires numerous sales clerks and other workers, including nearly five out of six cashiers. Major industry divisions and the occupational groups that predominate in each division are shown in Table 6.

The nation's occupational distribution clearly is influenced by its industrial structure, yet there are many occupations (such as general manager or secretary) that are found in all industries. In fact, some of the largest occupations in the U.S. economy are dispersed across many industries. Because nearly every industry relies on administrative support, for example, the executive, ad-ministrative, and managerial occupational group is the largest in the nation. (See Table 7.) Other large occupational groups include services; professional specialty; and operators, fabricators, and laborers.

Training and Advancement

Workers prepare for employment in myriad ways, but the most fundamental form of job training in the United States is a high school education. Fully 87 percent of the nation's workforce possessed a high school diploma, or its equivalent, in 1996. As the premium placed on education in today's economy increases, workers are responding by pursuing additional training. In 1996, the nation's workforce that had some college or an associate's degree totaled 29 percent, while an additional 26 percent had continued in their studies and had attained a bachelor's degree, or higher. In addition to these types of formal education, other sources of qualifying training include formal company training; informal on-the-job training; correspondence courses; the armed forces; and friends, relatives, and other non-work-related training.

Table 6. Industry Divisions and Largest Occupational Concentration, 1996

Industry Division	Largest Occupational Group	Percent of Wage and Salary Jobs
Agriculture, forestry, and fishing	Agriculture and related	70.6
Mining	Precision production	37.2
Construction	Precision production	53.7
Manufacturing	Operators, fabricators, and laborers	45.4
Transportation, communications, and public utilities	Operators, fabricators, and laborers	31.3
Wholesale and retail trade	Marketing and sales	33.3
Finance, insurance, and real estate	Administrative support	49.9
Services	Professional specialty	28.7
Government	Administrative support	27.0

Table 7. Total Employment in Broad Occupational Groups, 1996 and Projected Change, 1996–2006

(Employment in thousands)

Occupational Group	1996 Employment	1996–2006 Percent Change
Total, all occupations	132,353	14.0
Executive, administrative, and managerial	13,542	17.2
Professional specialty	18,173	26.6
Technicians and related support	4,618	20.4
Marketing and sales	14,633	15.5
Administrative support, including clerical	24,019	7.5
Services	21,294	18.1
Agriculture, forestry, fishing, and related	3,785	1.0
Precision production, craft, and repair	14,446	6.9
Operators, fabricators, and laborers	17,843	8.5

Table 9. Industries with the Highest Percentage of Workers Who Have a Bachelor's Degree or Higher, 1996

Industry	Percent
Offices and clinics of health practitioners, not elsewhere classified	77.7
Management and public relations services	71.1
Miscellaneous professional and related services	64.7
Elementary and secondary schools	63.7
Security, commodity brokerage, and investment companies	62.7

Table 10. Industries with the Highest Percentage of Workers Who Have 12 Years or Less of Schooling, or No Diploma, 1996

Industry	Percent
Dairy products stores	40.3
Private households	40.2
Agricultural production, crops	39.8
Meat products	36.4
Apparel and accessories, except knit	35.8

The unique combination of training required to succeed in each industry is determined largely by the industry's occupational composition. For example, machine operators in manufacturing generally need little formal education after high school but sometimes complete considerable on-the-job training. Requirements by major industry division are demonstrated in Table 8. About 66 percent of workers in agriculture, forestry, and fishing; 65 percent in construction; 62 percent in manufacturing; and 56 percent in wholesale and retail trade had a high school diploma or less. On the other hand, 72 percent of workers in government; 69 percent in finance, insurance, and real estate; and 67 percent in services had acquired at least some training at the college level. A more detailed illustration of the variety of training requirements is given in Tables 9 and 10, which show industries having the highest percentages of college graduates and those with workers who have less than 12 years of schooling, or no high school diploma.

Education and training are also important factors in the various advancement paths found in different industries. In general, workers who attain additional on-the-job training or education help their chances of promotion. In much of the manufacturing sector, for example, production workers who receive training in management and computer skills are often more likely to be promoted to supervisors. Other factors that figure prominently in the industries covered in the *Career Guide* include the size of the company or establishment, institutionalized career tracks, and the skills and aptitude of each worker. Advancement paths are unique to each industry, so job seekers should become familiar with the most common paths in the industries in which they are interested.

Table 8. Percent Distribution of Highest Grade Completed or Degree Received by Industry Division, 1996

Industry Division	Bachelor's Degree or Higher	Some College or Associate Degree	High School Graduate or Equivalent	Less Than 12 Years or No Diploma
Agriculture, forestry, and fishing	14	21	35	31
Mining	20	23	42	15
Construction	10	25	44	21
Manufacturing	20	25	40	15
Transportation, communications, and public utilities	20	34	39	8
Wholesale and retail trade	14	30	37	19
Finance, insurance, and real estate	36	33	25	4
Services	39	28	24	9
Government, public administration	36	36	25	3

Earnings

Like other characteristics, earnings differ from industry to industry. These differences are the result of a highly complicated process that relies on a number of factors. For example, wages may vary due to the occupations in the industry, average hours worked, geographical location, industry profits, union affiliation, and educational requirements. In general, to compensate for the higher cost of living, wages are highest in metropolitan areas. And, as would be expected, industries that employ relatively few minimum-wage or part-time workers tend to offer higher earnings.

A good illustration of difference in earnings is shown by comparing earnings of production and nonsupervisory workers in coal mining, averaging $857 a week in 1996, and those of eating and drinking places, where the weekly average was $146. This difference is so large because the coal mining industry employs a relatively highly skilled, highly unionized workforce. On the other hand, eating and drinking places hire many lower-skilled, part-time workers who rely largely on tips, which are not included in the industry earnings data. More differences in industry earnings are highlighted in Table 11. In general, these data understate average earnings for all workers in a given industry, because supervisors are excluded.

Table 11. Average Weekly Earnings of Nongovernment Production or Nonsupervisory Workers in Selected Industries, 1996

Industry	Earnings
All Industries	$407
Industries with high earnings	
Coal mining	857
Computer programming services	822
Crude petroleum and natural gas	810
Motor vehicle production	801
Aerospace manufacturing	800
Steel manufacturing	794
Public utilities	768
Metal mining	764
Motion picture production and services	762
Search and navigation equipment	718
Industries with low earnings	
Individual and family services	282
Residential care	278
Job training and related services	255
Grocery stores	253
Hotels and other lodging places	251
Social services	244
General merchandise stores	231
Child care services	218
Apparel and accessory stores	203
Eating and drinking places	146

Employee benefits, once a minor addition to wages and salaries, continue to grow in diversity and cost. Along with traditional benefits—paid vacations, life and health insurance, and pensions—many employers now offer various benefits to accommodate the needs of a changing labor force—for example, child care; employee assistance programs that provide counseling for personal problems; and wellness programs that encourage exercise, stress management, and self-improvement. Benefits vary among occupational groups, full- and part-time workers, public and private sector workers, regions, unionized and nonunionized workers, and small and large establishments. Data indicate that full-time workers and those in medium-size and large establishments (100 or more workers) receive better benefits than part-time workers and those in small establishments.

Union affiliation may also play a role in earnings and benefits. In 1996, about 16 percent of workers throughout the nation were union members or covered by union contracts. As Table 12 demonstrates, unionization of workers varies widely by industry. Over a third of the workers in government and transportation, communications, and public utilities are union members or are covered by union contracts. This compares with about 4 percent in finance, insurance, and real estate and under 3 percent in agriculture, forestry, and fishing.

Outlook

Total employment in the United States is projected to increase about 14 percent over the 1996–2006 period. Employment growth, however, is only one source of job openings; the total number of openings provided by any industry depends on its current employment level, its growth rate, and its need to replace workers who leave their jobs. Throughout the economy, in fact, replacement needs will create more job openings than employment growth. Employment size is a major determinant of job openings—large industries generally provide more openings than small ones. The occupational composition of an industry is another factor. Industries with a high concentration of professional, technical, and other jobs that require more formal education generally have fewer openings resulting from replacement needs, because these workers tend to leave their occupations less frequently. On the other hand, industries with a high concentration of service, laborer, and other jobs that require little formal education generally have more replacement openings, because these workers are more likely to leave their occupations.

© 1999 • J. Michael Farr • JIST Works, Inc. • Indianapolis, IN

Table 12. Percent of Workers Who Are Union Members or Covered by Union Contracts by Industry Division, 1996

Industry Division	Union Members or Covered by Union Contracts
Total, all industries	16.2
Agriculture, forestry, and fishing	2.5
Mining	14.9
Construction	20.7
Manufacturing	18.4
Transportation, communications, and public utilities	35.3
Wholesale and retail trade	6.3
Finance, insurance, and real estate	0.1
Services	16.2
Government, public administration	37.2

Employment growth is determined largely by changes in worker productivity and the demand for the goods and services produced by an industry. Each industry is affected by a different set of variables that impacts the number and composition of jobs that will be available. Even within an industry, employment in different occupations may grow at different rates. For example, changes in technology, production methods, and business practices in an industry might eliminate some jobs, while creating others. Some industries may be growing rapidly overall, yet opportunities for workers in occupations that are adversely affected by technological change could be stagnant. Similarly, the rate of growth of some occupations may be declining in the economy as a whole, yet may be increasing in a rapidly growing industry.

Employment growth rates will vary widely among industries shown in Table 4. Employment in goods-producing industries is expected to remain constant, as growth in construction and agriculture, forestry, and fishing is expected to be offset by declining employment in mining and manufacturing. Growth in construction employment will be driven by new factory construction, as existing facilities are modernized; by new school construction, reflecting growth in the school-age population; and by infrastructure improvements, such as road and bridge construction. Overall employment in agriculture, forestry, and fishing will grow more slowly than average, with almost all new jobs occurring in the rapidly growing agricultural services industry, which includes landscaping, farm management, veterinary, soil preparation, and crop services.

Employment in mining is expected to decline, due to the spread of labor-saving technology and increased reliance on foreign sources of energy. Manufacturing employment also will decline, as improvements in production technology and rising imports eliminate many production occupations. Due primarily to increasing imports, apparel manufacturing is projected to lose about 150,000 jobs over the 1996–2006 period—more than any other manufacturing industry. Some manufacturing industries with strong domestic markets and export potential, however, are expected to experience increases in employment. Projected growth in drug manufacturing, for example, is based on the increasing domestic demand of an expanding elderly population and continued strong export growth.

Over the 1996–2006 period, growth in overall employment will result primarily from growth in service-producing industries, almost all of which are expected to witness increasing employment. Rising employment in these industries will be driven by service industries—the largest and fastest growing major industry sector—which is projected to provide more than three out of five new jobs across the nation. Health, education, and business services will account for almost 6.5 million of these new jobs. In addition, employment in the nation's fastest growing industry—computer and data processing services—is expected to more than double, adding another 1.3 million jobs. Overall population growth, the rise in the elderly and school age population, and the trend toward contracting out for computer, personnel, and other business services will stimulate job growth in the services sector.

Wholesale and retail trade is expected to add an additional 5.6 million jobs over the coming decade. Nearly 750,000 of these jobs will arise in wholesale trade, driven mostly by growth in trade and the overall economy. Retail trade is expected to add 4.8 million jobs over the 1996–2006 period, resulting largely from increased personal income levels. Eating and drinking places will account for more than 1.3 million of these openings. In contrast to most other industries in the major industry division, employment in department, clothing, and variety stores is expected to decline, as jobs in relatively labor-intensive clothing and accessory stores are displaced by the growth of "mega-retailers" and discount stores.

By 2006, employment in transportation, communications, and public utilities will likely increase by nearly 800,000 new jobs. Trucking and air transportation are expected to add more than half of these jobs, as these industries combined will generate about 500,000 jobs. Trucking industry growth will be fueled by growth in the volume of goods that need to be shipped as the economy expands. Air transportation will expand, as

consumer demand increases, reflecting rising personal income and relatively inexpensive fares resulting from increasing competition. Despite strong growth in demand for telephone services, employment in the telephone communications industry will increase by only about 20,000 jobs, due to labor-saving technology and increased competition. Broadcasting industry employment will not sustain the rapid growth of the past, as the cable television market approaches saturation.

Overall employment growth in finance and insurance is expected to be around 11 percent, adding 1.4 million jobs by 2006. In spite of this growth, employment in banking will decline, as services traditionally offered by commercial banks are increasingly offered by a range of other institutions. Nondepository institutions—including personal and business credit institutions, as well as mortgage banks—are expected to grow at a rapid rate, at the expense of commercial banks. Insurance is expected to add the most jobs—more than 250,000—within this major industry sector.

All 913,000 new government jobs will likely occur in state and local government, reflecting growth in the population and its demand for non-federal public services. The federal government is expected to lose more than 100,000 jobs over the 1996–2006 period, as attempts to balance the federal budget and contract out services to private establishments are felt.

In sum, recent changes in the economy are having far-reaching and complex effects on employment in each of the industries covered in the *Career Guide*. Job seekers would be well-advised to follow these changes closely, keeping track of developments in industries and the variety of occupations which are found in each industry. For more information on specific occupations within industries, consult the *Career Guide's* companion publication, the 1998–1999 *Occupational Outlook Handbook,* which provides detailed information on 250 occupations.

USEFUL CAREER RESOURCES AND INTERNET SITES

Compiled by Mike Farr

T his is not a conventional bibliography. My comments are informal and admittedly biased, and I include only materials I like in some way. I developed this bibliography for a book I wrote titled *The Very Quick Job Search*. Because the bibliography was so well received there, I made a few changes and include it here for your information.

I've been looking at career materials for over 20 years, and it still amazes me how much junk is out there. A good example is resume books that still suggest that sending out many good-looking resumes is the way to get a job. While the advice on creating a resume may be good, the advice on *using* it is—too often—not. I tried to sort the wheat from the chaff, so materials that I do not consider good or useful are not listed.

I emphasize books you are most likely to find in a bookstore or good library. Materials published or distributed by JIST are among those listed, as are some that I have written. Of course, I tend to be enthusiastic about materials I have been involved in, although I try to be objective.

I organize the materials into categories and provide comments on many titles. Within categories, books are not presented in a particular order, although titles published by JIST are listed first. For brevity, I only mention a publisher if it is JIST. I don't provide publication dates, because materials are often updated regularly.

A good bookstore or library should be able to locate a book by its title and author. Most bookstores have a computer that allows them to find any book you want. Ask them to look up a desired title in *Books in Print*. Some materials are rather obscure and not easy to obtain. Others are out of print (it's difficult to keep up with all this), although you may find them through an interlibrary loan program. Ask your librarian to help you locate something you *really* want.

So browse the descriptions that follow. Remember that this an informal list rather than a formal bibliography, but I hope you find it helpful.

General Advice on Finding Career and Job Search Information

As mentioned, many resource materials in this bibliography can be found in a good library. Libraries have more information than I can list, including journals, newspapers, books, CD-ROM databases, Internet access, and other resources. So here are some tips for using the library as your job search friend.

The librarian: Your friendly librarian can be one of your best sources of specific information during your job search. If you can ask the question, he or she can probably give you some ideas on where to find an answer.

Finding Facts Fast: Todd. Perhaps the best book on finding out about anything at the library or elsewhere. Great research aid.

Trade magazines and journals: Most libraries will have one or more professional journals related to a variety of major career areas. Staying current on the publications in your field will help you in the interviewing process. These publications sometimes have job listings.

You Can Get Anything You Want: Dawson.

Develop a Network of Contacts, Including Members of Professional and Trade Associations

You already know hundreds of people, and networking to meet more is covered in many job search books I recommend. Consider joining professional associations related to the job you want. Your membership gives you access to meetings, newsletters, and other information sources. But the biggest benefit is that other members are an excellent source of networking opportunities. They often hire or supervise people with similar skills—or know those who do. You can get access to membership lists and use the contact information to call members in your area or in any part of the country. Make lots of phone contacts, send JIST Cards (described in Section Three), resumes, and thank-you notes—and get lots of interviews!

Directories

People who work in the careers that interest you can tell you which organizations to join. A good library will often have one or more helpful directories including the following:

Career Guide to Professional Associations: Garrett Park Press. Describes more than 2,500 professional associations. The information is more oriented to the job seeker than is the *Encyclopedia of Associations,* but some information may not be current.

Encyclopedia of Associations: Gale Research Company. A listing of more than 22,000 professional, trade, and other nonprofit organizations in the United States, representing more issues than you can imagine. It cross-references them in various helpful ways.

Encyclopedia of Associations—International Organizations: Gale Research. A listing of more than 11,000 organizations in 180 countries. Includes trade, business, and commercial associations, and associations of labor unions.

Professional & Trade Association Job Finder: By career category, details over 1,000 sources of information, referrals, and more.

Newspapers and Professional Journals

While the want ads in newspapers represent relatively few of the available job openings—and allow almost everyone to apply for them—some people do get jobs from want ads. Newspapers also contain other useful employment information. Look for tips on new or expanding businesses and leads for unadvertised job openings. Articles about new or expanding companies can be valuable leads for new job possibilities.

If relocating is a possibility, look at newspapers from other areas. They can serve as a source of job leads as well as indicate some idea of the job market. The major out-of-town newspapers are sold in most large cities and are available in many public libraries.

Some newspapers such as the *New York Times,* the *Chicago Tribune,* and the *Financial Times* are national in scope. The *National Business Employment Weekly,* published by the *Wall Street Journal,* contains much information of interest to professional job seekers. But remember that competition for jobs advertised in these sources is fierce, so don't rely on such publications too heavily.

Review these sources for articles mentioning your target companies. Look for information on new products, expansions, consolidations, relocations, promotions, articles by executives in the companies, annual company earnings, and current problems.

Check back issues of newspapers for old want ads. The ads can provide important information on job duties, salary, and benefits. There may even be a want ad for a job in which you are interested. Perhaps the job

was never filled or the person previously hired has already moved on.

Specialty newspapers such as the *National Business Employment Weekly* have a compilation of the previous week's want ads from the regional editions of the *Wall Street Journal,* plus its own want ads. *National Ad Search* is a weekly tabloid that compiles want ads from 75 key newspapers across the U.S. Expect major competition for jobs listed this widely.

Back issues of major newspapers can be accessed on the Internet, allowing you to sort by key words or for specific geographic areas.

The following is a list of other resources:

Business Newsbank, Newsbank, Inc.: This service provides the narrative of articles from newspapers and business journals from 400 cities. It cross-references information by company name, individual's name, industry, or product category.

New York Times Index: A thorough index of all stories that appear in the *Times.*

Wall Street Journal Index: This is an important source of information on larger business and business trends.

Where the Jobs Are: 1200 Journals with Job/Career Openings: Feingold and Winkler. A unique resource providing tips on responding to journal ads and a cross-reference to specific journals by job type.

Where to Find Business Information: Brownstone and Curruth. Lists and describes the many newsletters, journals, computer databases, books, and other sources of business information.

I provide additional details on using the newspapers under "Getting Information on Specific Employers."

Job Search and Career Planning Books by Yours Truly

I've worked on many job search, career planning, and occupational information books, assessment tests, videos, and software over the years. Some are readily available in bookstores and libraries, while others are used by schools, institutions, and instructors. Most of my materials are published by JIST, and many are included in the various sections of this bibliography, along with brief descriptions.

I feel strongly that only two main issues in the career planning and job search field really matter. The first is that it is essential to select a career that will satisfy you. This involves knowing yourself well enough to select *the* job rather than *a* job. Secondly, if you need to find a job, you might as well find a good one and do it

in as little time as possible. All of my books incorporate these simple principles and tend to be practical and results-oriented. Here is a partial list, should this be of interest to you:

Books You Are Most Likely to Find in Bookstores and Libraries

The Very Quick Job Search—Get a Better Job in Half the Time

How to Get a Job Now!—Six Easy Steps to Getting a Better Job

The Quick Resume & Cover Letter Book

The Quick Interview & Salary Negotiation Book

America's Top Resumes for America's Top Jobs

America's Fastest Growing Jobs

America's Top Jobs® for College Graduates

America's Top Jobs® for People Without a Four-Year Degree

America's Top Medical, Education, and Human Services Jobs

America's Top White-Collar Jobs

Best Jobs for the 21st Century (coauthored with LaVerne Ludden)

Occupational Reference Books

My name appears on several occupational reference books that can be found in libraries. These books are mostly based on information obtained from government sources. I was part of a team that made the information useful. Calling anyone an author of these books is a bit of a stretch, although I spent many hours working on them. These titles include the following:

*The O*NET Dictionary of Occupational Titles*

The Enhanced Occupational Outlook Handbook

The Complete Guide for Occupational Exploration

Materials Used in Schools and Other Programs

One of my life's missions has been to improve the information and training that students and job seekers receive in career and job search programs. Here are some materials I have authored for this use—most are *not* available in bookstores but can be obtained from JIST.

The Quick Job Search: A 32-page book covering the essentials needed for a successful job search. Very short but covers the basics.

The JIST Career Planning and Job Search Course: For instructors, a complete curriculum I wrote to support the use of *The Very Quick Job Search.* It includes lesson plans, over 50 overhead transparencies, and reproducible handout masters.

The JIST Job Search Course: A Young Person's Guide to Getting & Keeping a Good Job: Coauthored by Marie Pavlicko for use by high school students. It has been field tested with thousands of students. Good graphics and easy-to-follow narrative. Accompanying instructor's guide and transparency set.

The Right Job for You: A thorough career planning book that includes lots of information and worksheets.

The Guide for Occupational Exploration Inventory: This is an interest "test" to help with career exploration.

The Work Book: Getting the Job You Want: This is my first job search book. Originally published in 1981, it has been revised several times and has sold over 300,000 copies. It remains popular in postsecondary schools and programs. An instructor's guide is available. Published by McGraw-Hill, Glencoe Division.

Job Finding Fast: A thorough book that includes sections on career decision making as well as job seeking. It was written to support a full course or program at the postsecondary or college level. An instructor's guide is available. Also published by McGraw-Hill, Glencoe Division.

Videos and software: I've written content scripts for numerous job search and career-related videos and have worked on a variety of career-related software.

Etcetera: I've worked on many workbooks and other projects over the years, including several series for youth coauthored with Susan Christophersen (the Living Skills series and the Career and Life Skills series). I have edited or helped to develop many others. It's been work and it's been fun.

Career Materials Published by JIST

I formerly listed career-related books published by JIST in a separate section, but the list became too long. Besides, I only included those JIST books that were likely to be found in a bookstore or library and excluded many videos, assessment tests, instructional materials, and books used in schools and institutions. The JIST books you are most likely to find in a bookstore or library are now included in the various subsections of this bibliography. If you want a more thorough list, contact JIST for a catalog. JIST's Web site (www.JIST.com) provides free chapters of many books and links to other career-related sites.

Information on Occupations and Industries

Hundreds of books provide information on jobs, and most libraries have a basic selection. I suggest you begin with the general career references, and then look for more specific information on jobs that interest you most.

While most people focus their career-planning time on choosing an occupation, I suggest you also consider the industry where you want to work. For example, if you have experience in accounting (a career) and an interest in airplanes (an industry), perhaps accounting-oriented jobs in a flight-related industry such as airports, airplane manufacturing, or air-transportation regulation would be your best fit. I include industry references for this reason and recommend you browse some of them.

Best Sources of Information on Industries

Career Guide to America's Top Industries: Based on information from the U.S. Department of Labor, this book provides details on over 40 major industries. Easy to read and loaded with helpful information, it was written specifically to assist in career planning and job seeking. If you are going to use one book on industries, this is the one I recommend. JIST.

U.S. Industrial Outlook: Based on information from the U.S. Department of Commerce, it provides business forecasts for over 300 industries. Good source of information to review prior to interviews.

Standard Industrial Classification Manual (SIC): A standard reference developed by the U.S. Department of Commerce that lists all industries in an organized way. Accountants, banks, the IRS, and many others use it as a way to codify business. While I would not recommend this as light reading, it is useful for identifying more specialized industries for a job search or career exploration. Available from JIST.

North American Industry Classification System (NAICS): A new system to replace the *SIC Manual* was introduced in 1998 and will be used in Mexico, the United States, and Canada. This book has similar uses to the *SIC Manual.* Available from JIST.

Best Sources of Information on Occupations

Occupational Outlook Handbook: Highly recommended. Published by the U.S. Department of Labor and updated every other year, this book provides descriptions for 250 major jobs covering 87 percent of the workforce. The descriptions are well written and provide information on pay, working conditions, related jobs, projected growth, and more. A very helpful book for exploring career options or for job seeking. Available from JIST.

America's Top 300 Jobs: This is a "bookstore" version of the *Occupational Outlook Handbook* that includes descriptions for all 250 jobs plus additional informa-

tion. JIST.

The Enhanced Occupational Outlook Handbook: Includes all the descriptions in the *Occupational Outlook Handbook* plus 3,000 descriptions of more specialized jobs and 5,000 additional titles. Easy to use. JIST.

*The O*NET Dictionary of Occupational Titles:* This is the first book to provide information on the new O*NET jobs. A new database of occupations called the Occupational Information Network (O*NET) will replace the *Dictionary of Occupational Titles.* This new book provides descriptions for the approximately 1,200 new O*NET jobs plus details on related skills, earnings, abilities, education, and other requirements for each. JIST.

America's Top Jobs series: Each book in this series includes about 100 job descriptions plus a review of job market trends, career planning and job search advice, summary information on hundreds of additional jobs, and useful appendices. The job descriptions are based on those used in the *Occupational Outlook Handbook* and include details on pay, education required, working conditions, and more. All are published by JIST.

America's Fastest Growing Jobs: J. Michael Farr.

America's Top Jobs for College Graduates: J. Michael Farr.

America's Top Jobs for People Without a Four-Year Degree: J. Michael Farr.

America's Top Medical, Education, and Human Services Jobs: J. Michael Farr.

America's Top White-Collar Jobs: J. Michael Farr.

America's Top Military Careers

Best Jobs for the 21st Century: J. Michael Farr and LaVerne Ludden. Lists of jobs for best paying, highest earnings at different education levels and other criteria, plus hundreds of job descriptions. JIST.

The Complete Guide for Occupational Exploration: The U.S. Department of Labor developed the GOE to help people explore careers based on interests. The CGOE narrows broad interests to the many specific jobs within each major category. It lists over 12,000 jobs by occupational cluster, interests, abilities, and traits required for successful performance. You can look up jobs by industry, types of skills or abilities required, values, related home/leisure activities, military experience, education required, or related jobs you have had. JIST.

The Enhanced Guide for Occupational Exploration: Similar to the CGOE, but also provides descriptions for 2,500 jobs. These jobs cover 95 percent of the workforce, and few people will miss those that are not listed. JIST.

Dictionary of Occupational Titles: Published by the U.S. Department of Labor, the DOT provides brief descriptions for 12,741 jobs—more than any other reference. It is a large book, over 1,400 pages, and not particularly easy to use. But it is a standard reference that many other books cross-reference. Available from JIST.

More Career Information Books

Hundreds of books provide information on specific careers. I've selected representative titles, but you will find many others in a good library.

American Almanac of Jobs and Salaries: Wright. Useful data on pay and opportunities for hundreds of jobs.

The Career Connection for College Education—A Guide to College Education & Related Career Opportunities, revised edition: Fred Rowe. Provides information on over 100 college majors and 1,000 occupations that are related to them. Includes information on salaries, course requirements, related high school courses, and other details useful in planning a college major. JIST.

The Career Connection for Technical Education—A Guide to Technical Training & Related Career Opportunities: Fred Rowe. Similar to the above but provides information on 70 technical training majors and 450 related occupations. JIST.

Career Finder—Pathways to Over 1,500 Entry-Level Jobs: Schwartz and Breckner.

Careers without College series: A series of 11 books for those not planning on a four-year college degree. Topics include health care, fashion, cars, office, sports, and others.

Choosing an Airline Career: March.

Discover the Best Jobs for You!: Krannich and Krannich. Explores skills, interests, and specific jobs.

Encyclopedia of Careers: Ferguson Publishing. A series of books providing useful information on all major occupations.

Great Careers: The 4th of July Guide to Careers, Internships, and Volunteer Opportunities in the Non-Profit Sector: An enormous reference of books and programs covering jobs with a social cause.

High-Paying Jobs in 6 Months or Less: For jobs requiring brief training.

High Tech Jobs for Non High Tech Grads: O'Brien. Good ideas for those without technical training.

Jobs Rated Almanac: Krantz. Ranks 250 jobs by pay, benefits, stress, and other criteria.

Occu-Facts: Provides one-page descriptions for over 500 jobs in an easy-to-read format. Jobs are arranged into groups of similar occupations, which encourages its use as a career exploration tool.

Opportunities in...series: A series of books published by VGM Career Horizons. Each covers related jobs in that field, skills required, working conditions, pay, education required, jargon. Some of the careers covered are secretarial; health and medical; office; data processing; computer science; travel; hotel and motel management; cable television; accounting.

Outdoor Careers: Shenk.

Peterson's Engineering, Science and Computer Jobs: An annual update of 900 employers, types of jobs, more.

Professional Careers series: Another series of books on a variety of professional jobs including finance, medicine, law, computers, accounting, business, and others.

Real Estate Careers: Jamic and Rejnis.

The Revised Handbook for Analyzing Jobs: A technical book describing various coding systems used to quantify and categorize jobs. Available from JIST.

The Worker Traits Data Book: Donald Mayall. A technical book that provides coded information on over 12,000 jobs in the *Dictionary of Occupational Titles.* Much of this information is not available elsewhere. JIST.

Worker Trait Group Guide: A simpler version of *The Guide for Occupational Exploration* providing information on clusters of similar jobs. Available from JIST.

Career Planning and Job Search Books

There are innumerable job search and career planning books, and more are published all the time. Most are written by corporate recruiters, headhunters, social workers, academics, and personnel experts who are well intentioned but have little practical experience in determining whether the job search methods they recommend work. Many books provide advice that would, if followed, slow down the job search process.

Generally, I discard books that suggest sending resumes or answering want ads as good job search methods—or that do not include methods appropriate for approaching smaller businesses. The research clearly indicates the importance of these issues, and anyone who is not aware of this should not be considered an expert. So, in my humble opinion, here are some of the better books.

Highly Recommended Career Planning and Job Search Books

This short list includes a few of my books, a few books published by JIST, and a few books I like that are published by others and widely regarded as among the best books on their topics.

The Very Quick Job Search—Get a Better Job in Half the Time: J. Michael Farr. This is my most thorough job search book, and it includes lots of information on career planning and, of course, job seeking. If I had to recommend just one book to a friend who was out of work, this would be it. While written as a "bookstore" book, it is widely used in schools and colleges. There is an accompanying activities book, curriculum, and transparency set. This book has won a variety of awards including best career book of the year. JIST.

How to Get a Job Now!—Six Easy Steps to Getting a Better Job: J. Michael Farr. This short book covers the basics in an interactive format. I included those things I believe most important to know if you want to get a better job in less time. JIST.

Using the Internet and the World Wide Web in Your Job Search: Fred Jandt and Mary Nemnich. For new or more experienced Internet users, it is full of information on getting career information, finding job listings, creating electronic resumes, networking with user groups, and other interesting techniques. Reviews all major career sites. JIST.

The PIE Method for Career Success—A Unique Way to Find Your Ideal Job: Daniel Porot. The PIE method (Pleasure, Information, and Employment) uses a visual and creative format to present career planning and job search techniques. The author is one of Europe's major career consultants, and this book presents his powerful career planning and job seeking concepts in a memorable way. JIST.

Inside Secrets of Finding a Teaching Job: Jack Warner and Clyde Bryan with Diane Warner. Practical advice for new and experienced teachers looking for a new job. JIST.

What Color Is Your Parachute?: Richard N. Bolles. This is the best-selling, career-changing book ever. Well written and entertaining, it is updated each year and includes a useful self-assessment section, "The Quick Job Hunting Map." Bolles is fun to read, and the book is highly recommended.

The Complete Job Search Handbook: All the Skills You Need to Get Any Job, and Have a Good Time Doing It: Howard Figler. A solid book with lots of exercises to assess skills, values, and needs. Procedures for exploring careers and developing a job objective. An excellent book that is loaded with innovative ideas.

Other Career and Job Search Books for a General Audience

Getting the Job You Really Want: J. Michael Farr. Covers career planning and job-seeking topics in a workbook format with lots of activities. Very popular in schools and job search programs and available in bookstores. An instructor's guide is also available. JIST.

Job Search 101—Getting Started on Your Career Path: Pat Morton and Marcia Fox. For college seniors and recent graduates seeking entry-level jobs. JIST.

Job Finding Fast: J. Michael Farr. A thorough career planning and job search workbook used in colleges. An instructor's guide is available. Available from JIST.

Job Strategies for Professionals: Based on advice provided by the U.S. Department of Labor, it provides job search advice for professionals and managers who have lost their jobs. JIST.

Job Rights and Survival Strategies—A Handbook for Terminated Employees: Paul Tobias and Susan Sauter. Covers the legal rights and benefits as well as how to handle these traumatic situations with dignity. Distributed by JIST.

900,000 Plus Jobs Annually: Feingold and Winkler. Reviews 900+ periodicals that list openings and positions wanted in hundreds of fields.

Big Splash in a Small Pond—Finding a Great Job in a Small Company: Resnick and Pechter.

Change Your Job, Change Your Life: Krannich. Reviews jobs trends and job search methods.

Do What You Are—Discover the Perfect Career for You Through the Secrets of Personality Type: Tieger and Barron-Tieger.

Go Hire Yourself an Employer: Richard Irish. Lots of good stuff in this new revision. Covers skills identification, job search, resumes, interviews, the unemployment "blahs," succeeding on the next job, and other topics.

Guerrilla Tactics in the New Job Market: Tom Jackson.

Professional Careers Sourcebook, an Informational Guide for Career Planning: K. Savage and C. Dorgan.

Hardball Job Hunting Tactics: Dick Wright. From a trainer with lots of experience with the hard to employ. Excellent sections on completing applications (a topic not often covered well) and resumes. Brief but good section on job search. Tips for people with various "problems" on how to overcome them.

How to Get Interviews from Classified Job Ads: Elderkin.

Information Interviewing: What It Is and How to Use It in Your Career: Martha Stoodley.

Job & Career Building: Richard Germann and Peter Arnold. A good choice for laid-off professionals, managers, and others with more experience and training.

Job Hunters Sourcebook: Where to Find Employment Leads and Other Job Search Sources: Michelle LeCompte.

Marketing Yourself: The Ultimate Job Seeker's Guide: Dorothy Leeds.

New Network Your Way to Job and Career Success: Ron and Carol Krannich.

Re-Careering in Turbulent Times: Ronald Krannich. Lots of good material including employment trends, selecting a career, getting training and education, communication skills, sources of job leads, interviewing, resumes, relocation, public employment opportunities, and career advancement.

Robert Half on Hiring: Robert Half. Written to help employers select better employees. Most of the advice is based on a series of employer surveys providing unique insight into how employers make hiring decisions.

Selling on the Phone: Porterfield. Self-teaching guide for telemarketing and other sales approaches. Good ideas for reinforcing effective phone skills in the job search.

Starting Over: You in the New Workplace: Jo Danna.

The Complete Job Search Book: Richard Beatty.

The Job Bank Guide to Employment Services: Bob Adams.

The Only Job Hunting Guide You'll Ever Need: Kathryn Ross Petras.

Three Boxes Life and How to Get Out of Them: Richard Bolles. Introduces the concepts of "life/work planning." Very thorough.

Where Do I Go from Here with the Rest of My Life?: John Crystal and Richard Bolles. John Crystal has died, but his techniques and insights into the career planning process helped to start an important movement that came to be called "life/work planning."

Who's Hiring Who: Richard Lathrop. Solid, practical information for job seekers. Good self-assessment sections and excellent resume advice (he calls them "qualifications briefs"). I particularly like this book and respect Lathrop's work.

Specialized Career and Job Search Books

Many books have been written on specialized career and job search topics. For example, there are books to help various segments of our population gain a competitive edge; books on specialized job search methods (such as using the telephone); and books on getting certain types of jobs (such as those with small business or overseas jobs). Some of these materials are not easily categorized into one group, so look through the entire list for things related to your situation—there is probably something in here that fits.

Internet Job Search Books

The Internet is a growing source of information on all topics, but you can also waste a lot of time there unless you know where to look. Here are a few helpful guides to get you started.

Using the Internet and the World Wide Web in Your Job Search: Fred Jandt and Mary Nemnich. A good book for both new and more experienced Internet users. Lists all major career sites and, more importantly, tells you how to use the Internet in effective ways. JIST.

Cyberspace Resume Kit: Nemnich and Jandt. A guide to writing your resume for scanning, e-mail transmission, and resume banks. JIST.

The Quick Internet Guide to Career and College Information: Anne Wolfinger. A timesaving and brief guide for educators, counselors, and employment professionals to the best sites and how to use them. JIST.

Electronic Job Search Revolution: Kennedy and Morrow. Tips on using your computer and online services to get jobs.

Resources for Youth and Parents

An enormous number of materials are available for young people to help them explore career alternatives. I present a few here. Most are not available in bookstores and are available only from the publishers. If you help youth, I suggest you contact JIST and ask for its institutional catalog; it presents materials from a variety of publishers. I also include a few good books for parents to help their kids in their quest for a career (and, of course, to get them out of the house).

Helping Your Child Choose a Career: Luther Otto. One of the most helpful books on the topic for parents, teachers, and even kids. Comprehensive and sensible advice. JIST.

Young Person's Occupational Outlook Handbook: For grades 6–10. Provides information on 250 jobs listed in the *Occupational Outlook Handbook,* plus career exploration advice. JIST.

A Young Person's Guide to Getting & Keeping a Good Job: J. Michael Farr and Marie Pavlicko. A practical workbook for high school students. A separate instructor's guide and overhead transparencies are available. JIST.

Creating Your High School Portfolio: Good activities and content. JIST.

Creating Your High School Resume: Kathryn Kraemer Troutman. A step-by-step guide that helps students to prepare an effective resume for college and career. JIST.

Career and Life Skills series: J. Michael Farr and Susan Christophersen. Four books for grades 7–12 on career preparation. JIST.

Hire Learning series: Patricia Duffy and T. Walter Wannie. Books for high school students on career planning, job seeking, and job success. JIST.

Dream Catchers: Norene Lindsay. A career exploration workbook for grades 5 to 8. JIST.

Pathfinder—Exploring Career & Educational Paths: Norene Lindsay. A workbook for high school students with a separate instructor's guide. JIST.

The Secrets of Getting Better Grades: Brian Marshall and Wendy Ford. Teaches students to study smart, with lots of practical tips for notes, tests, papers, memory, and other techniques. JIST.

Exploring Careers—A Young Person's Guide to Over 300 Jobs: A revision of the original published by the U.S. Department of Labor. An excellent resource for young people, providing details on over 300 jobs in an interesting format. JIST.

Career Coaching Your Kids: Montross et al. Tips on helping your children explore career options. Distributed by JIST.

Career Discovery Encyclopedia: This is a six-volume set for grades 4 and up with reading level at about the 7th grade, appropriate through high school. Excellent, with over 1,000 pages and helpful ways to look up jobs. A school or other good library may have this set.

Children's Dictionary of Occupations. For elementary and middle school students, covers 300 occupations.

Directory of American Youth Organizations: Erickson. Lists more than 500 organizations.

Job Power: The Young People's Job Finding Guide: Haldane and Martin. One of our favorite books for group process ideas on skills identification and selecting a job objective. Simple, direct, useful for any age.

Joyce Lain Kennedy's Career Book: Kennedy and Laramore. A very thorough book, covering just about everything that a young person (or parent) would need to know about career and life decisions. Highly recommended.

Parents with Careers Workbook: Good worksheets and advice on getting organized, child care, home management, single parents, dual careers, time use, and so on.

Summer Jobs for Students: Reviews sources for 20,000 summer jobs and explains how to use the Internet for additional information.

Books for Working Parents and Couples

Home but Not Alone—The Parents' Work-at-Home Handbook: Katherine Murray. A very good book that won an award for being one of the top three business books of the year. Lots of solid tips. JIST.

The Working Parents' Handbook—How to Succeed at Work, Raise Your Kids, Maintain a Home, and Still Have Time for You: Katherine Murray. An entertaining and helpful book providing advice on handling the multiple roles of working parents. Excellent. JIST.

Surviving Your Partner's Job Loss: Jukes and Rosenberg.

The Three Career Couple: Byalick and Saslow. On handling two jobs plus a family.

Books to Help Get Jobs in the Government, Education, and Nonprofit Sector

The Unauthorized Teacher's Survival Guide: Jack Warner and Clyde Bryan with Diane Warner. Great advice for new and experienced teachers, telling you the things you do not learn in teacher's college. JIST.

Inside Secrets of Finding a Teaching Job: Jack Warner and Clyde Bryan with Diane Warner. Helpful techniques for finding a job in teaching, based on years of experience and interviews with many educators. JIST.

Alternative Careers for Teachers: Pollack and Beard. Good ideas on getting a job in another field using transferable skills.

Careers in Local and State Government: Zehring. Where they are, how to apply, take tests, internships, and summer jobs. Job search tips.

Complete Guide to Public Employment: Krannich. Reviews opportunities with federal and local governments, associations, nonprofits, foundations, research, international, and many other institutions. Well done.

Doing Well by Doing Good—The First Complete Guide to Careers in the Non-Profit Sector: McAdam.

Moving Out of Education: A Guide to Career Management & Change: Krannich and Banis. Good tips for this special situation from an ex-educator who moved out.

Take Charge of Your Own Career—A Guide to Federal Employment: Moore and Vanderwey.

Minorities and Immigrants

Best Companies for Minorities: Graham. Profiles of 85 companies.

Career Opportunities for Bilinguals and Multiculturals—A Directory of Resources in Education, Employment and Business: Wertsman. Over 3,500 listings.

Directory of Special Programs for Minority Group Members: Willis L. Johnson. Over 2,800 sources of training, jobs, scholarships, and programs.

Finding a Job in the United States: Friedenberg and Bradley.

Minority Career Guide: Kastre, Kastre, and Edwards.

Minority Organizations—The Directory of Special Programs for Minority Group Members: Oakes. The largest source of information available covering over 5,800 professional organizations and resources.

Stepping Up: Placing Minority Women into Managerial and Professional Jobs: Tips to replicate results of a program that increased the pay, advancement, and retention of minority women.

The Big Book of Minority Opportunities—Directory of Special Programs for Minority Group Members: Oakes. 4,000 source of scholarships, financial aid, and special programs.

The Black Woman's Career Guide: Nivens. Good advice on over 50 good jobs, dress and grooming, skills identification, job search, and more.

The Colorblind Career: Stenson. Success tips for African-American, Hispanic, and Asian-Americans.

Workers Over 40, Displaced Workers, Retirement Issues

Arthur Young's Pre-Retirement Planning Book: Very well done book. Lots of worksheets.

Cracking the Over 50 Job Market: Conner. Good job search advice.

Getting a Job After 50: Morgan. Age discrimination is real and people over 50 need better-than-average job seeking skills to overcome this.

Helping the Dislocated Worker: Ashley and Zahniser. Reviews suggested services and programs—helpful for program planners.

Job Hunting After 50: Strategies for Success: Samuel Ray.

Job Hunting for the 40+ Executive: Birsner. Good advice on the personal and job search needs of middle-aged executives.

Mid Career Job Hunting: Official Handbook of the 40+ Club: E. Patricia Birsner. Solid advice on getting back on track and getting a job.

Retirement Careers: Marsh.

Second Careers—New Ways to Work After 50: Bird. Analyzes career changes of over 6,000 people and how it worked out.

The Over 40 Job Guide: Petras.

People with Disabilities, Disadvantaged Groups, The Homeless

Know-How Is the Key: Dixie Lee Wright. A job search program (student workbook and instructor's guide) for high school through young adult "special needs" students with learning and other disabilities. JIST.

Americans with Disabilities Act Handbook—and Technical Assistance Manual: Government publication providing comprehensive information on the Americans with Disabilities Act (ADA) and how it is interpreted. Available from JIST.

A Helping Hand, A Guide to Customized Support Services for Special Populations: Thorough guide for program operators who emphasize employment—JTPA, older workers, ex-offenders, others.

Bouncing Back from Injury: How to Take Charge of Your Recuperation: Karen Klein and Carla Derrick Hope.

Career Success for People with Physical Disabilities: Kissane. Good advice for job seekers. Lots of exercises.

Complete Guide to Employing Persons with Disabilities: Henry McCarthy. From the National Rehabilitation Information Center; phone (800) 346-2742.

Job Hunting for the Disabled: Adele Lewis and Edith Marks. Interest surveys, programs, job descriptions, and job search tips.

Job Strategies for People with Disabilities: Witt. Good advice as well as lists of resource materials and programs.

Job-Hunting Tips for the So-Called Handicapped or People Who Have Disabilities: Richard N. Bolles.

No One Is Unemployable: Angel and Harney. A good resource for welfare-to-work and ex-offender programs, and other "difficult" populations.

Recovery from Alcohol and Substance Abuse and Coping with Job Loss

Career Knockouts: How to Battle Back: Joyce Lain Kennedy. Avoiding, learning, and even benefiting from job failures.

Clean, Sober and Unemployed: Elliot. Good advice for recovering substance abusers.

Coping with Unemployment: Jud. Dealing with long-term unemployment.

Sacked! Why Good People Get Fired and How to Avoid It: Gould.

Termination Trap: Best Strategies for a Job Going Sour: Cohen. Excellent insights on avoiding or dealing with job loss.

The Career Seekers: Tannenbaum. For anyone recovering from codependency or in a recovery program.

People with Four-Year College, Advanced Degrees, and Technical Training

Finding a Job in Your Field: A Handbook for Ph.D.'s & M.A.'s

Jobs for English Majors and Other Smart People: Good tips for liberal arts grads.

The MBA's Guide to Career Planning: Ed Holton.

The High-Tech Career Book: Collard.

Job Search for the Technical Professional: Moore. For programmers and engineers.

Military/Veterans

Many good materials help vets transition to civilian employment. Following are some specific ones, but many of the career and job search books (such as *America's Top Resumes for America's Top Jobs*) include veterans among their examples.

America's Top Military Careers: Based on Department of Defense information, provides details on 200 enlisted and officer occupations including civilian counterparts. JIST.

The Complete Guide for Occupational Exploration: Among other things, this comprehensive career reference book cross-references military occupations to over 12,000 civilian job titles. JIST.

Jobs and the Military Spouse—Married, Mobile, and Motivated for the New Job Market: Farley.

Resume and Job Hunting Guide for Present and Future Veterans: DePrez. Helpful book with some good techniques.

Veteran's Survival Guide to Good Jobs in Bad Times: Grant's Guides.

You and the Armed Forces: Marrs. Better understand career options and what to expect from military life.

Young Person's Guide to Military Service: Bradley. Covers pros and cons of going into the service. Good sections for minorities and women.

Your Career in the Military: Gordan. Reviews advantages of education and money. Enlistment options and procedures.

Women

More women are in the workforce than ever, and they tend to be better educated than average. But women without advanced education and who are single heads of households are not doing as well. Special advice and resources are clearly needed; here are just a few.

Congratulations! You've Been Fired: Sound Advice for Women Who've Been Terminated, Pink Slipped, Downsized or Otherwise Unemployed: Emily Koltnow and Lynne S. Dumas.

Developing New Horizons for Women: Ruth Helm Osborn. Very good text to improve self-esteem, identify strengths, and develop long-range life and career plans.

Directory of Special Opportunities for Women: Over 1,000 resources for women entering and reentering the workforce. Recommended.

Good Enough for Mothers: Marshall. Balancing work and family.

Homemaker's Complete Guide to Entering the Job Market: Lussier. Useful techniques to transfer homemaking skills to work world and find a job.

Resume Guide for Women of the '90s: Marino.

The Extra Edge: Mitchell. Success strategies for women, based on data from women grads of Harvard Business School.

The Woman's Job Search Handbook: Bloomburg and Holden. Well-done career planning and job search techniques.

Time for a Change: A Woman's Guide to Non-Traditional Occupations: For women considering non-traditional jobs: exercises and narrative, plus a review of 10 growth-oriented jobs.

Winning the Salary Game: Salary Negotiations for Women: Sherry Chastain.

Yes to Career Success!: Hennekins.

International Jobs

If you want to work in another country, you had better do your homework in advance. For example, you should carefully consider personal and family issues that might impede a full adjustment to your host country. Here are some resources to help you consider this option.

Directory of European Industrial and Trade Associations: CBD Research, Kent, England. Lists the industrial and trade associations of Europe.

Directory of European Professional and Learned Societies: CBD Research, Kent, England. Similar in format but deals strictly with learned and professional societies.

Foreign Jobs: The Most Popular Countries: Casewit. Profiles desirable countries and how to get jobs there.

How to Get a Job in Europe—The Insider's Guide: Surrey Books. Gives country-by-country listings of newspapers, business directories, regulations, organizations, and other useful information.

How to Get a Job in the Pacific Rim: Surrey Books. Information similar to above, but for countries bordering the Pacific Ocean.

International agencies: These agencies maintain lists of people available to work as consultants. You might want to register with one or more agencies: World Bank;

U.S. Aid for International Development (USAID); United Nations Development Program; United National Industrial Development Organization.

International Careers: Bob Adams, Inc. Information on finding government, corporate, and nonprofit jobs.

International Jobs: Where They Are, How to Get Them: A Handbook for Over 500 Career Opportunities Around the World: Kocher.

Key British Enterprises: Dun and Bradstreet. Detailed information on the 50,000 British companies that together employ more than a third of the British workforce.

Passport to Overseas Employment—100,000 Job Opportunities Abroad: Information on overseas careers, study, and volunteer programs.

Principal International Businesses: Dun and Bradstreet. While not aimed at the job seeker, it provides details on more than 55,000 companies in 143 countries.

Teaching English Abroad: Griffith.

The Complete Guide to International Jobs and Careers: Your Passport to a World of Exciting and Exotic Employment: Ron and Carol Krannich.

The Peace Corps: Wages are low and living conditions basic, but if you are interested in helping people, the Peace Corps is a possibility.

The U.S. government: Don't overlook government jobs; there are many foreign assignments. A larger library may have the publications *Federal Career Opportunities* or the *Federal News Digest,* which list openings. Federal jobs are listed on the Internet and available through most state employment service offices.

Books on Interviewing and Salary Negotiations

The two most important parts of a job search are getting interviews and doing well in them. I suggest that *the* most important interview question to answer well is "Why should I hire you over someone else?" It takes considerable self-analysis to answer this well. Curling up with a good job search book will help you know that you *do* have good things to say about yourself. Then there is the interview issue of pay, which is where many people lose more money in 30 seconds than at any other time in their lives. Or, worse, they get a job they hate. So here are some good resources on interviewing and salary negotiations, in hopes that they are of help to you.

The Quick Interview & Salary Negotiation Book—Dramatically Improve Your Interviewing Skills in Just a Few Hours!: Mike Farr. A substantial book, but I arranged it so that you can read the first section and do better in interviews later that day. Also covers career planning, job seeking, resumes, pay rates, and other topics of importance for a job seeker. JIST.

101 Dynamite Questions to Ask at Your Job Interview: Fein.

50 Winning Answers to Interview Questions: Albrecht.

American Almanac of Jobs and Salaries: Wright. Covers hundreds of careers in the public and private sector.

American Salaries and Wages Survey: Gale Research. Detailed information on salaries and wages for thousands of jobs, by region. Also gives cost-of-living data, which is helpful in determining what the salary differences really mean.

AMS Office, Professional and Data Processing Salaries Report: Administrative Management Society. Salary distributions for 40 occupations by company size, type of business, and geographic region.

Dynamite Answers to Interview Questions: Ron and Carol Krannich.

Getting to Yes: Negotiating Agreements Without Giving In: Fisher and Ury. Good negotiating tips for anything.

How to Have a Winning Job Interview: Bloch. Good advice in a readable format, with lots of activities.

How to Make $1000 a Minute—Negotiating Your Salaries and Raises: Jack Chapman. Tips on getting more money and benefits during the critical part of a job offer.

Interviewing for Success: Ron and Carol Krannich.

Interviews That Get Results: Vik. Good tips for job seekers.

Knock'em Dead: With Great Answers to Tough Interview Questions: Martin John Yate.

Make Your Job Interview a Success: Biegeleisen. Good checklists, interview answers, grooming tips, and other content.

Out Interviewing the Interviewer: Merman and McLaughlin. Good exercises, case studies, and tips for experienced and not-so-experienced job seekers.

Perks and Parachutes: Tarrant.

Power Interviewing: Job Winning Tactics from Fortune 500 Recruiters: Yeager and Hough.

Ready, Aim, You're Hired!: How to Job-Interview Successfully Anytime, Anywhere with Anyone: Hellman.

State and Metropolitan Area Data Book: Helpful details from the U.S. Department of Commerce providing unemployment rates, average income, employment and population growth, and other details for all major regions—important for those considering a move.

Sweaty Palms—The Neglected Art of Being Interviewed: Anthony Medley. Fun factual tips on illegal questions, problem interviews, appropriate dress and behaviors.

The Evaluation Interview: Richard Fear. Considered a classic for anyone who is, or wants to be, a professional interviewer.

The Five-Minute Interview: Richard H. Beatty.

The Ultimate Interview: How to Get It, Get Ready, and Get the Job You Want: Caple.

When Do I Start?: Clearly written, good content.

White-Collar Pay: Private Goods-Producing Industries: U.S. Department of Labor's Bureau of Labor Statistics. Good source of salary information for white-collar jobs.

Winning the Salary Game: Salary Negotiations for Women: Chastain. Good strategies for men, too.

Books on Resumes and Cover Letters

Hundreds (thousands?) of resume books exist, and most offer bad advice. They often suggest that a good/better/best/perfect resume, sent out to lots of people, will get interviews, but the research clearly indicates that this is not the case. In addition to bad job search advice, many resume books offer unnecessarily rigid advice about the resume itself (that their way is the one enlightened way to do a resume).

In contrast, I believe that resumes are an important tool in the job search but that active job search methods (such as contacting employers by phone) are more effective than passive ones (like sending unsolicited resumes). And I do not believe that one formula exists for a good resume. Like people, resumes can be different. Of course, JIST's resume books are included here; I think they are among the best available.

America's Top Resumes for America's Top Jobs: J. Michael Farr. This is a big book, with 381 sample resumes covering over 200 major jobs. Resumes were selected from submissions by professional resume writers from all over North America. I took this approach to provide a rich array of writing styles, designs, and approaches to solving resume problems. From entry level to very experienced, good examples are here for everyone. JIST.

The Quick Resume & Cover Letter Book—Write and Use an Effective Resume in Only One Day: J. Michael

Farr. Starting with an "instant" resume worksheet and basic formats you can complete in an hour or so, this book then takes you on a tour of everything you need to know about resumes and, more importantly, how to use them in your job search. Lots of good examples plus advice on cover letters, the job search, and related matters. JIST.

The Resume Solution—How to Write (and Use) a Resume That Gets Results: David Swanson. Lots of good advice and examples for creating superior resumes. Very strong on resume design and layout and provides a step-by-step approach that is very easy to follow. JIST.

Gallery of Best Resumes: David Noble. Advice and over 200 examples from professional resume writers. Lots of variety in content and design; an excellent resource. I consider it to be the best resume library, because the resumes are organized into useful categories and are all different. JIST.

Résumé Magic: Susan Britton Whitcomb. Transform your resume with examples and tips from a professional resume writer. JIST.

The Edge Resume & Job Search Strategy: Bill Corbin and Shelby Wright. The only book I know of that includes sample resumes using special papers and die-cut shapes. Unique. Distributed by JIST.

Gallery of Best Resumes for Two-Year Degree Graduates: David Noble. An excellent selection of 229 sample resumes submitted by professional resume writers. Good advice and lots of excellent samples. A very good resource book that organizes resumes by occupational category. JIST.

Professional Resumes for Executives, Managers, and Other Administrators: A New Gallery of Best Resumes by Professional Resume Writers: David Noble. Includes more than 340 resumes, organized by occupation. JIST.

The Federal Resume Guidebook: Kathryn Troutman. A thorough book covering the new procedures for applying for federal government jobs. JIST.

Using WordPerfect in Your Job Search: David Noble. A unique and thorough book that reviews how to use WordPerfect to create effective resumes, correspondence, and other job search documents including scannable and hypertext resumes. JIST.

100 Winning Resumes for $100,000+ Jobs: Enelow.

College Student's Resume Guide: Marino.

Complete Resume Guide: Faux. Some good ideas and examples.

Damn Good Resume Guide: Yana Parker. An irreverent title, but it has many good examples and an easy-to-follow process for creating resumes.

Developing a Professional Vita or Resume: McDaniels. Special resume advice for professionals with advanced education or experience.

Don't Use a Resume: Richard Lathrop. A booklet providing good examples and advice on a special resume that emphasizes skills.

Dynamic Cover Letters: Hanson. A very focused book, just on cover letters.

Dynamite Cover Letters: Ron and Carol Krannich. Good content.

Dynamite Resumes: Ron and Carol Krannich. Lots of good examples and advice.

Encyclopedia of Job-Winning Resumes: Fournier and Spin. Lots of examples in a wide variety of jobs.

High Impact Resumes & Letters: Krannich and Banis. Good job search advice and lots of sample resumes and letters.

How to Write a Winning Resume: Bloch. Good examples for college grads, more experienced job seekers, and professionals.

Job Search Letters That Get Results: Ron and Carol Krannich. Good advice and over 200 sample letters.

Liberal Arts Power: Nadler. How to sell it on your resume.

Ready, Aim, Hired: Developing Your Brand Name Resume: Karson.

Resume Kit: Beatty. Better-than-average advice on putting together effective resumes and cover letters.

Resume Pro: The Professional Guide: Yana Parker. A how-to guide for those who help others write resumes.

Resumes for Computer Professionals: Shanahan. Many examples.

Resumes for Executives and Professionals: Shy and Kind.

Resumes for High School Graduates: VGM editors. An unusual but useful focus.

Resumes for Mid-Career Job Changes: VGM editors.

Resumes for Technicians: Shanahan. Examples, tips for use, and so on.

The No Pain Resume Workbook: Hiyaguha Cohen.

The Perfect Resume: Tom Jackson. Uses a workbook format, making it easy to identify job objective, skills, interests, and achievements. Good examples.

The Resume Catalog—200 Damn Good Resumes: Yana Parker. Organized by job objective. Good.

Writing a Job Winning Resume: John McLaughlin and Stephen Merman. A good book with examples showing how the resume covered a weakness.

Dress and Grooming Advice

One survey of employers found that about 40 percent of job seekers who made it through initial screening and got an interview then created a negative first impression based on dress and grooming. Another study found that candidates who made a negative impression within five minutes had virtually no chance of getting a job offer. So, put the two studies together, and you can see that a big problem exists with first impressions. How you dress and groom is only one issue, of course, but it is one that most people can easily change. So here are some books on that topic.

Always in Style with Color Me Beautiful: Pooser. By a noted color consultant, clothing styles, colors, and makeup for women. Many photos.

Big and Beautiful: Olds. Larger women can be gorgeous, too.

Color Me Beautiful: Jackson. Discover your "seasonal" colors and coordinate your look. Color photos. Well done.

Dress for Success: John Molloy. Some of the advice is dated, but this still gives good research-based help on business attire.

Professional Image: Bixler. One of few on dress, grooming, body language, and details for both men and women.

Red Socks Don't Work: Karpinski. Dressing tips for men in formal corporate environments.

Women's Dress for Success: Molloy. Same thorough approach as for men.

Personal and Career Success and Advancement

There are thousands of personal and career success books and tapes. Some are very good, some are not. I include a selection of the better ones here.

Beat Stress with Strength—A Survival Guide for Work and Life: Stephanie Spera and Sandra Lanto. Includes a personal stress test and many tips for handling stress and achieving balance. JIST.

Career Satisfaction and Success—How to Know and Manage Your Strengths: Bernard Haldane. A complete revision of a classic by a founder of the modern career planning movement. It presents techniques for succeeding on the job and concepts that have changed many

lives for the better, including defining your "motivated skills" and using them as a basis for career planning. JIST.

Dare to Change Your Job and Your Life: Carole Kanchier. Based on interviews with more than 5,000 adults, provides a proven self-help approach to developing a more meaningful career and more fulfilling life. JIST.

Job Savvy—How to Be a Success at Work: LaVerne Ludden. A workbook covering work-appropriate behaviors. JIST.

Jobscape—Career Survival in the New Global Economy: Colin Campbell. A well-written and fascinating book that presents the essential trends shaping the future workforce and how we can best prepare to benefit. JIST.

Networking for Everyone!: Michelle Tullier. More than for the job search, covers creating a network to help you through life—lots of motivational and practical tips. JIST.

Ready, Set, Organize!: Pipi Peterson. Time management strategies for your personal and work lives. Good advice and a fun read. JIST.

SuccessAbilities!—1,001 Practical Ways to Keep Up, Stand Out, and Move Ahead at Work: Paula Ancona. Short and motivational tips from Ancona's nationally syndicated column. JIST.

The Customer Is Usually Wrong!: Fred Jandt. Great tips for handling customers and doing the right thing. JIST.

The Perfect Memo!—Write Your Way to Career Success!: Patricia Westheimer. Good tips and activities for more effective business writing. JIST.

We've Got to Start Meeting Like This!: Roger Mosvick and Robert Nelson. An essential book for getting the most out of meeting time. JIST.

Brushing Up Your Clerical Skills: Steinberg. For new and returning office workers. Exercise on spelling, punctuation, typing, business letters, filing, and more.

Business Protocol: Yager. On-the-job manners.

Do What You Love, The Money Will Follow: Sinetar. For those who seek meaning as our first priority, there is hope that we can also make a living doing the things we really want to do.

Getting Things Done When You Are Not in Charge: Bellman.

How to Jump Start a Stalled Career: Prugh.

How to Make a Habit of Success: Bernard Haldane. Originally published many years ago, it was a best-seller and is still available. Many consider Haldane one of the

founders of the career planning movement that began in the 1950s. This is an important book that has much good advice.

Improve Your Writing for Work: Chesla. Includes lots of samples and activities.

Love Your Work and Success Will Follow: Hirsch. For those who are not happy with their current career.

Moving Up—How to Get High Salaried Jobs: Djeddah. Techniques to get promoted or move out to a new job.

Not Just a Secretary: Morrow and Lebov. Techniques for doing well and getting ahead.

Secretary Today, Manager Tomorrow: How to Turn a Secretarial Job into a Managerial Position: Marrs.

Skills for Success: Scheele. Good advice on getting ahead in all sorts of careers.

Wish Craft: Barbara Sher. An upbeat book that provides activities and advice on setting goals and reaching your full potential.

Working Smart: Zehring. Advice on getting ahead, organizing time, dealing with people, developing leadership skills.

Would You Put That in Writing?: Booher. Good primer for improving your business communications.

Future Trends/Labor Market Information

Jobscape—Career Survival in the New Global Economy: Colin Campbell. A well-written and fascinating book that presents the essential trends shaping the future workforce and how we can best prepare to benefit. JIST.

Work in the New Economy: Robert Wegmann, Robert Chapman, and Miriam Johnson. A very well-researched book on where our economy is going and how we should adapt our career planning and job search methods to get better results. While this is an older book, I consider Wegman's work to be among the best on the topic and much of the advice remains current. JIST.

Emerging Careers: New Occupations for the Year 2000 & Beyond: Based on years of research; details hundreds of new careers. Very good.

Megatrends: Nesbitt. A best-seller that provides a review of where the economy is heading.

The Work Revolution: Schwartz and Neikirk. Thorough and well done. Predicts retraining, education, and other needs of rapid change.

Work Force 2020—Work and Workers in the 21st Century: Richard Judy and Carol D'Amico of the Hudson Institute. A well-researched book predicting likely trends in the workforce.

Work in the 21st Century: Isaac Asimov and others. Anthology of well-done articles on work trends for the future. Stimulating.

Self-Employment, Starting Your Own Business, and Temporary, Part-Time, and Volunteer Jobs

More people are working for themselves; starting small businesses; or working in part time, temporary, or volunteer jobs. There are hundreds of books on these topics, and a good library will have more resources than I can list. Here are a few suggestions.

Self-Employment: From Dream to Reality—An Interactive Workbook for Starting Your Small Business: Linda Gilkerson and Theresia Paauwe. A workbook to encourage "microenterprises," very small business started by those with little money or experience. Unique. JIST.

Mind Your Own Business! Getting Started as an Entrepreneur: LaVerne Ludden and Bonnie Maitlen. A good book for those considering their own business, with lots of good advice. JIST.

Be Your Own Business! The Definitive Guide to Entrepreneurial Success: Marsha Fox and LaVerne Ludden. JIST.

Franchise Opportunities Handbook: LaVerne Ludden. Lists over a thousand franchise companies and provides tips on selecting one that makes sense for a business.

America's New Breed of Entrepreneurs: Presents collective experiences of 48 successful entrepreneurs and how they achieved their goals.

Beginning Entrepreneur: Matthews.

Best Home Businesses for the '90s: Edwards and Edwards.

Directory of Microenterprise Programs: Lists loans and programs for low-income entrepreneurs.

Getting Business to Come to You: Edwards and Edwards. Low-cost marketing tips.

Home Sweet Office: Meade. Telecommunicating from home to a regular job.

How to Build a Successful One Person Business: Bautista.

How to Run Your Own Home Business: Kern and Wolfgram.

How to Start, Run, and Stay in Business: Kishel. Good primer for the school of hard knocks.

Inc. Yourself: How to Profit from Setting Up Your Own Corporation: Shows financial and other advantages, plus how to set up.

Job Sharing Handbook: Smith. Provides guidelines for setting up a shared job, case histories, and so on. Good.

Making It on Your Own—What to Know Before Starting Your Own Business: Feingold.

Opportunities in Your Own Service Business: McKay.

Part-Time Professional: Good information on finding part-time jobs, benefits, negotiating with employers, converting full-time to part-time jobs, and other tips.

Running a One-Person Business: Whitmeyer, Rasberry, Phillips. Practical.

Side by Side: Cuozzo and Graham.

Starting on a Shoe String: Building a Business Without a Bankroll: Goldstein.

Ten Best Opportunities for Starting a Home Business Today: Reed Glenn.

The Mid-Career Entrepreneur: Mancuso.

The Small Business Administration: The U.S. Small Business Administration (SBA) offers loans, training, and planning, and many useful publications. Its toll-free number is 1-800-U ASK SBA. In addition, its Service Corps of Retired Executives (SCORE) provides free help on how to set up and run a small business.

The Temp Track: Justice. Reviews the many opportunities for temporary jobs.

Volunteer America: Kipps. Lists over 1,400 organizations for training, service, and work experience.

Working from Home: Edwards and Edwards.

Places to Live or Move To

Some people will be unhappy wherever they live, but living in a place you like does make life more enjoyable. Here are a few books that provide details.

Best Towns in America: Bayless. Fifty of the U.S.'s most desirable places, plus ways to evaluate all communities.

Country Careers—Successful Ways to Live and Work in the Country: Rojak.

Finding Your Best Place to Live in America: Bowman and Guiliani. Another good book providing information on good places to live.

Greener Pastures Relocation Guide: Finding the Best State in the U.S. for You!

Places Rated Almanac: Richard Boyer and David Savagean. A thorough review of over 270 metropolitan areas with information on housing, education, climate, health services, recreation, arts, transportation, crime, and income.

Getting Information on Specific Employers

There are two basic reasons for you to be interested in specific employers. The first has to do with identifying potential job search targets, and the second is to get more information on an employer prior to an interview.

Some books and businesses "sell" the idea of sending your resume to potential employers as a good thing. Some sell lists in print or computer form so you can mount a big mail campaign. And some sell the idea of having special lists of employers that you can buy from them. I do not think that sending unsolicited resumes to any list is a good idea. While any technique works for some people, you will be better off if your job search is more targeted and involves more direct contact.

You have to begin with knowing the type of job you want and the industries where you will find them. Then and only then can you intelligently begin your search for specific employers.

Free Resources

The yellow pages: The best resource you can get is probably free: It's the *yellow pages* of the phone book. Think about it: It lists all organizations by type and gives you what you need to contact them. All of my job search books tell you how to use the yellow pages as an effective tool in your job search. The yellow pages for regions throughout the country are also available on the Internet, as are many other sources of information on organizations.

Networking: Another free resource of information is networking. If you want to know more about a particular job or place of employment, ask the people who do that kind of work or who work in that place. This is often the only source of information for small organizations not listed in the directories. A good book on networking is *Networking for Everyone! Connecting with People for Career and Job Success* by Michelle Tullier. It provides lots of practical advice for personal and business success and is published by JIST.

Chambers of commerce: Most are not staffed to provide specific information to job seekers, but many do provide information such as new businesses in the area, larger employers, and other details.

Contact the organization directly: For large organizations, contact the human resources or public relations departments. In smaller ones the receptionist or manager may be able to help. Get brochures, an annual report, description of relevant jobs, and anything else that describes the organization.

Annual reports: All publicly owned and many smaller organizations provide annual reports detailing earnings, trends, strategies, and other information. If one is available, it is an excellent source of information.

Books and Directories

A good bookstore or library has many sources of information on specific businesses and other organizations. While many of these resources were not specifically developed for use by job seekers, they can work just fine.

You can use resource materials in several ways. The first is to get information on a specific organization as background for an interview. You can also get names of organizations as well as background information to use in making direct contact lists. With so many potential sources of information, ask a librarian to help you once you have a good idea of what you are looking for.

Following are just a few of the many books and other resources for obtaining information on employers. Some are organized by industry or region or in other ways that may help you. If you use the Internet, more and more information is available there. I suggest you read one of the Internet job search books published by JIST for the most useful sites.

100 Best Companies to Work for in America: Levering and Moscowitz.

America's Corporate Families, The Billion Dollar Directory: Describes 2,500 large corporate "families" and their 28,000 subsidiaries; provides information on each; and cross-references by location, business or product type, and other methods.

America's Fastest Growing Employers: Bob Adams. Lists more than 700 of the fastest-growing companies in the country.

American Business Information Inc. of Omaha, Nebraska: Publishes business directories for many different industries. Phone (402) 593-4600.

Bay Area 500: Hoover. An example of a regional listing, this one provides profiles of the largest companies in the San Francisco area.

Business Newsbank: Newsbank, Inc. This service provides the narrative of articles from newspapers and business journals from 400 cities. Cross-references by company name, individual's name, industry, or product category.

Business Organizations and Agencies Directory: Gale Research Company. Provides useful information to look up by business name and types of activity. Provides contact information.

Business Periodicals Index: Cross-references business articles from over 300 periodicals by subject and company name.

Career Guide—Dun's Employment Opportunities Directory: Aimed specifically at the professional job seeker, lists more than 5,000 major U.S. companies and their personnel directors, career opportunities, and benefits packages.

Chambers of commerce and local business associations: These often publish directories of local companies, available in libraries or by writing to the individual associations.

Contacts Influential: A series of directories providing information on smaller businesses. Allows look up by organization name or type to learn details of its operations and size.

Directory of Executive Recruiters: Joyce Lain Kennedy.

Directory of Executive Search Firms: Lists and cross-references hundreds of these businesses, should they be appropriate for you.

Dun & Bradstreet Million Dollar Directory: Provides information on 180,000 of the largest companies in the country. Gives the type of business, number of employees, and sales volume for each. It also lists the company's top executives.

Hidden Job Market: A Guide to America's 2000 Little-Known Fastest Growing High-Tech Companies: Peterson's Guides. Concentrates on high-tech companies with good growth potential.

Hoover's Handbook of American Business: Profiles more than 750 larger companies.

Hoover's Handbook of Emerging Companies: Spain, Campbell, Talbot. Profiles of 250 entrepreneurial companies.

Job Bank series: Bob Adams Inc. Series of books for job-seeking professionals, each covering a different large city or metropolitan area with details on economic outlook for the covered area, list of major companies, and positions within the company.

Job Hunter's Guide to 100 Great American Cities: Brattle Communications. Lists major employers for 100 of America's largest cities.

Little Known, Fastest Growing High-Tech Companies: Peterson's Guides.

Macrae's State Industrial Directories: Published for northeastern states, but similar volumes are produced for other parts of the country by other publishers. Each book lists thousands of companies, concentrating on those that produce products, rather than services. They include a large number of small firms, in addition to the larger firms listed in many other guides.

Million Dollar Directory: Dun's Marketing Services. Provides general information on over 115,000 businesses.

Moody's Industrial Manual: Provides detailed information on over 3,000 larger organizations.

Moody's Industrial News Reports: Provides articles related to each of the businesses listed in the related directory.

National Business Telephone Directory: Gale Research. An alphabetical listing of companies across the United States, with their addresses and phone numbers. It includes many smaller firms (20 employees minimum).

Peterson's Business and Management Jobs: An annual listing of hundreds of employers plus essential background information on each.

Polk's Directories: R. L. Polk & Co. Each major city has its own Polk Directory created by door-to-door canvass of individuals and businesses in the area. Cross-references by name, address, type of business.

Reference Book of Corporate Management: Dun's Marketing Services. Provides information on the executives and officers of the 6,000 largest U.S. corporations.

Standard & Poor's Register of Corporations, Directors and Executives: Brief information on over 40,000 corporations and their key people cross-referenced by names, types of businesses, and other methods. Lists parent companies with subsidiaries and the interlocking affiliations of directors.

Thomas Register: Lists more than 100,000 companies across the country by name, type of product made, and brand name of product produced.

Yellow pages (the phone book): As I mentioned earlier, your best source is often the yellow pages of the phone book, because it lists virtually all business, government, and not-for-profit organizations in a given area—and even organizes them by type of business! Best of all, this book is free.

Many directories give information about firms in a particular industry. Here are just a few.

The Blue Book of Building and Construction
Directory of Advertising Agencies
Directory of Computer Dealers
McFadden American Bank Directory

School and Training Admissions, Financing, and Survival

Education pays. People with more education and training tend to earn substantially more. Most of the rapidly growing jobs require technical training beyond high school or a four-year college degree. While a four-year college degree makes sense for a lot of people, many occupations with high pay and rapid growth can be learned in two years or less.

More adults are going back to school to upgrade their career skills, and any young person should consider getting as much education and training as possible. Knowledge of computers is now important in most jobs, and, if you have not kept up with the new developments in your field, it is important to do so as soon as possible. Explore a wide variety of training options including technical schools, adult-education classes, workshops, formal college courses, and even classes on the Internet.

You can finance postsecondary training or education in many ways, so don't let a lack of money be a barrier to getting what you need. If you want to do it, seek, and ye shall find a way. Here are some resources.

Back to School: A College Guide for Adults: LaVerne Ludden. A comprehensive guide that includes self-assessment activities and good advice on setting goals, considering various degrees, selecting a college, juggling priorities, and much more. Includes a directory of 1,000 adult-friendly degree programs. JIST.

Ludden's Adult Guide to Colleges and Universities: LaVerne and Marsha Ludden. Good advice for adults going back to school, plus information on more than 1,500 degree programs. Includes many nontraditional programs that can be used to reduce the time required to get a degree. JIST.

Career Connection for College Education—A Guide to College Education and Related Career Opportunities: Fred Rowe. Information on over 100 college majors and 1,000 related occupations. Includes details on salaries, course requirements, related high school courses, and other details useful in planning a college major. JIST.

Career Connection for Technical Education—A Guide to Technical Training and Related Career Opportunities:

Fred Rowe. Similar to the above, this book describes over 60 technical education majors and the careers they lead to. JIST.

Bear's Guide to Finding Money for College: John Bear. Well written, readable, helpful.

But What if I Don't Want to Go to College?: Ungar. Reviews alternative education or training needed for hundreds of jobs.

College 101: Farrar. Primer for getting along in college.

College Admissions Data Handbook: Orchard House. The most thorough and up-to-date source of information on colleges available. Four volumes cover different sections of the country.

College Degrees by Mail: John Bear. Brief descriptions for 100 nonresident schools.

College Degrees You Can Earn from Home: Frey.

College Guide for Students with Learning Disabilities: Sciafini and Lynch. Covers over 500 programs.

College Majors and Careers: A Resource Guide for Effective Life Planning: Phifer. Good information on college majors, skills, related leisure activities, personal attributes, and additional resource materials for major occupational interests.

College Survival Guide: Mayer. Well-done, new student orientation to basics of making it.

Earn College Credit for What You Know: Simosko. On nontraditional college credit programs: types, application procedures, and so on.

Electronic University: A Guide to Distance Learning Programs: Peterson's Guides.

Free Dollars from the Federal Government: Blum.

Free Money for College: A Guide to More Than 1,000 Grants and Scholarships: Blum.

Guide to Non-Traditional College Degrees: John Bear. Fun to read, well done, thorough.

Guide to Technical, Trade, and Business Schools: A four-volume set with thorough profiles of 2,200 accredited schools.

Historically Black Colleges and Universities: Details on all 91 such schools.

How to Apply to American Colleges and Universities: Brennan and Briggs.

Internships: 50,000 On-the-Job Training Opportunities for Students and Adults: Rushing.

Liberal Education and Careers Today: Howard Figler. "I dropped out of pre-med in my junior year of college (a long story) and got a degree in liberal arts—and I turned out OK." Figler makes a case for a liberal arts education with research and advice on why liberal arts is a good way to go.

Major Decisions—A Guide to College Majors: Orchard House. Provides brief descriptions for all college majors.

Minority Student Enrollments in Higher Education: Provides information on 500 schools with the highest minority enrollments.

New Horizons—Education and Career Guide for Adults: Haponski. Methods of seeking and using education to get ahead.

Paying Less for College: Peterson's College Money Handbook: Provides costs, types of aid, and other details from over 1,700 schools.

Person's College Money Handbook.

Peterson's Colleges and Programs for Students with Learning Disabilities: Mangrum and Strichart. Lists over 1,000 colleges with these programs.

Peterson's Internships. Lists 40,000 positions for getting experience as an intern.

Peterson's Scholarships, Grants, and Prizes.

Peterson's Competitive Colleges: Tips on getting into the top 300 schools.

Peterson's Guide to College Admissions: Student workbook on preparing and competing. Well done.

Peterson's Guide to Four-Year Colleges: 1,900 schools and 400 majors. Organized for selection by many criteria, plus tips on applying.

Peterson's Guide to Two-Year Colleges: Details on over 1,400 schools with associate degrees.

Peterson's Independent Study Catalog: Guide to over 12,000 correspondence and Internet courses.

Peterson's National College Databank: With data in over 350 categories, this is a major source of information for colleges of all descriptions.

Tech Prep Guide: Technical, Trade, & Business School Data Handbook: Orchard House. The most thorough reference of its kind, providing information on over 1,600 schools, plus summary information on another 3,000 schools. Four volumes cover different parts of the country.

Time for College—The Adult Student's Guide to Survival and Success: Siebert and Gilpin.

Who Offers Part-Time Degree Programs?: Peterson's Guides. Data on over 2,500 institutions.

Winning Money for College: High school student's guide to scholarship contests.

You Can Make It Without a College Degree: Roesch.

Instructor and Trainer Resources

While you should be able to find books on public speaking in most bookstores and libraries, more specific materials, such as instructor's guides for a job search workshop, are very hard to find. JIST publishes or distributes a variety of these more specialized materials, should you be interested.

Career Exploration Groups: A Facilitator's Guide: Garfield and Nelson. Includes group activities and exercises to aid in self-knowledge, career information, and decision making.

Career Information Service: Norris. One of the few texts for university-level career counseling and development courses. Thorough book for career counselors.

Career Planning Workshop Manual: Instructor's guide for life/work planning workshops. Includes group exercises and worksheets.

Developing Vocational Instruction: Mager and Beach. Easy-to-understand, step-by-step guidelines for developing good curriculum.

How to Organize and Manage a Seminar: What to Do and How to Do It: Murray. Budgets, plans, staffing, promotion, and more. Very good.

Louder & Funnier: A Practical Guide for Overcoming Stage Fright: Nelson. Getting over fear of groups is a major obstacle to success as a trainer or presenter. Excellent.

Making Successful Presentations: Smith. Good for the new or moderately experienced trainer.

Making Vocational Choices: A Theory of Careers: John Holland: There are few career theory books, and this is one of the most influential. In plain and readable English, it presents the research, rationale, and practical uses of his theory of six personality types.

The Business of Public Speaking: Good tips on business aspects of doing presentations.

Where to Start: An Annotated Career Planning Bibliography: Thorough, helpful. Organized by topic.

Work in the New Economy: Robert Wegmann, Robert Chapman, and Miriam Johnson. Well-researched and well-written review of labor market trends and how a job seeker is affected. Though written some time ago, I consider this the best book of its kind. JIST.

Career Interest Tests and Books on Test-Taking

Too many people think a magical, effortless solution exists to their career planning problems. Tests are only tools to provide you with information and can't tell you what to do. I prefer assessment instruments that are self-scored and encourage you to participate in the career decision-making process.

If you have access to a career counselor, ask about taking a career interest test. But remember that it can only provide you with food for thought, not an answer to what you should do. Following are a few of the self-administered and self-scored interest inventories that I like. Most are available from JIST but in packages. Individuals must get them through a counselor, though several inventories are available as a package for individuals on JIST's Internet site at JIST.com. Test-related books are listed after the tests themselves.

Career Exploration Inventory (CEI): John Liptak. Uses a unique past/present and future orientation and results in scores that cross-reference to major occupational interest areas. Includes a large chart of occupational information and an action plan, and recommends sources of additional information. Spanish version available. JIST.

The Guide for Occupational Exploration Inventory (GOEI): J. Michael Farr. Uses an intuitive process to lead to one or more of the 12 career interest areas from the *Guide for Occupational Exploration.* A related information chart then provides substantial information on the jobs in each area, related courses, and leisure activities. Includes an action plan and suggests additional sources of information. JIST.

Leisure/Work Search Inventory (LSI): John Liptak. Ties leisure activities to related jobs, making this a good test for young people with limited work experience or adults looking for more interesting career options. Includes substantial chart of career information, an action plan, and other useful elements. JIST.

Occupational Clues—A Career Interest Survey. A thorough book that includes checklists for values, interests, activities, school subjects. and work experience—all cross-referenced to related job clusters. JIST.

Barriers to Employment Success Inventory (BESI): John Liptak. Self-scored inventory that helps identify barriers to employment—very helpful for programs. JIST.

The Job Search Attitude Inventory: John Liptak. A self-scored assessment that identifies potential problem areas for success in the job search. JIST.

Career Decision-Making System (CDM): Thomas Harrington and Arthur J. O'Shea. A popular interest test that is easy to use, self-scoring, and self-interpreted. Records occupational preferences, school subjects, job values, abilities, plans for future education, and training.

College Majors Finder: Cross-references Holland codes (which can be obtained from the *SDS* and *CDM* described in this section as well as from other devices) to over 900 college majors.

Self-Directed Search (SDS): John L. Holland. Widely used, responses result in recommended jobs in six major clusters. A separate booklet cross-references over 1,100 jobs in a logical manner.

American College Testing Program (ACT): Over 450 pages of skills, reviews, sample questions, study tips, and tips to raise ACT scores.

Book of U.S. Postal Exams: Bautista. Sample exams for 44 job categories.

Career Aptitude Tests: Klein and Outerman. Series of self-scored tests measuring aptitudes against over 250 jobs.

Career Finder: The Pathways to Over 1500 Entry-Level Jobs: Schwartz and Breckner. Checklists result in recommended jobs for more exploration. List salary, openings, and more.

Civil Service Test Tutor: Practice drills and samples for government tests for beginning office jobs such as accounting, file clerk, and telephone operator.

Counselor's Guide to Vocational Guidance Instruments: Kappes and Mastie. Reviews of many tests.

Fairness in Employment Testing: National Academy of Sciences.

Guide to 75 Tests for Special Education: Up-to-date guide covering major tests and how to select, interpret, and use them.

How to Get a Clerical Job in Government: Hundreds of sample questions and answers covering major topics on federal, state, and local exams.

How to Pass Employment Tests: How to do well in tests you may encounter in your job search and in tests given to evaluate advancement potential.

Making the Grade: Study habits and techniques for getting good grades by doing well on all sorts of tests.

Practice for Clerical, Typing, Steno Tests: Sample questions, drills, and exercises to improve scores on most clerical tests.

Practice for the Armed Forces Tests: Drills, sample questions, test-taking tips, and general review for all service tests.

Preparation for the GED: Thorough preparation to increase scores.

Preparation for the SAT: Thorough preparation to increase scores.

Career-Oriented Software

I formerly listed software that you could find for reasonable prices in a retail software store, but changes occur so rapidly that any list is quickly out-of-date. A number of good resume preparation programs are quite helpful in preparing basic resumes, though you won't need them if you have access to a good word processing program and a good resume book. Two good resume programs that have been consistently available are *WinWay Resume on CD-ROM* and *PFS Resume Pro.*

The major word processing programs include resume formats, but they force you to use formats that may not be the best for your situation. David Noble's book *Using WordPerfect in Your Job Search* shows you the many tricks you can do with a powerful word-processing program.

Another category of software that is very helpful in the job search is that of contact management programs such as ACT! or GoldMine. These are designed for individuals like sales people for following up on their contacts and are well suited for follow-up tasks including letters, schedules, and phone calls.

Many career planning, occupational exploration, and related programs are becoming available. Some are poorly done while others seem helpful, so buyer beware.

JIST publishes a variety of software, but the software is priced for multiple users such as schools and other programs, and it is too expensive for individuals. JIST has a free job search program on its Internet site at www.JIST.com if you want to check it out.

To give you an idea of the types of information becoming available, here are some JIST-published programs followed by a few of the many available from other sources:

JIST's Career Explorer CD-ROM: Answering a series of questions about your interests and other factors results in a list of the 20 jobs that best match your responses. The program then allows you to get information on each of these jobs. Takes about 15 minutes.

JIST's Multimedia Occupational Outlook Handbook: Very easy to use, it includes descriptions for the 250 major jobs in the *OOH,* powerful search features, and color images and sounds.

Mike Farr's Get a Job Workshop on CD-ROM: Includes activities, text, video clips, and sound in an interactive format covering setting a job objective, details on all major jobs, identifying skills, job search methods, resumes, job survival, and related topics. JIST.

The Electronic Enhanced Dictionary of Occupational Titles: This is a sophisticated CD-ROM program that includes the complete content of the *Dictionary of Occupational Titles,* the *Occupational Outlook Handbook,* the *Complete Guide for Occupational Exploration,* and additional details on over 12,000 jobs. While it is easy to use, it provides access to detailed technical information on over 12,000 jobs that has not been readily available in the past. JIST.

Young Person's Electronic Occupational Outlook Handbook: A lively and simple-to-use format provides basic information on 250 major jobs.

Free Phone CD-ROM: Toll-free numbers for over 1,000 business categories covering the entire country. Allows lookup by region and other criteria.

Information USA: Provides substantial information on federal jobs, government resources, agencies, grants, loans, scholarships, statistics.

Lovejoy's College Counselor CD-ROM: Provides details on thousands of colleges and technical schools, 2,500 scholarships, and video clips of many schools. Excellent.

Scholarships 101: Information on over 5,000 scholarship sources. Sorts by various criteria and helps write letters asking for additional information.

Select Phone CD-ROM: Includes all listings in the white and yellow pages directories for the entire U.S. Search by name, region, business heading, and so on.

Recommended Web Sites for Career Planning, Job Seeking, Education, and Related Topics

The information available on the Internet and World Wide Web is amazing, and the sites keep getting better. I still prefer old-fashioned books for many uses, but the Internet is clearly superior for certain tasks. If you have not already read Section Three, you should do so now, before you waste lots of hours on the Internet. That sec-tion gives you good advice on career planning and job seeking that will help you decide what, precisely, you want to look for before you dive into the cold, deep waters of the Internet. At the end of that section are a few brief cautions regarding the use of the Internet as well as tips for getting the most from it. Do use caution, as the Internet is addictive to some people. Remember, your objective is to get things done, not to play with your computer.

The selection of Internet sites that follows is based on recommendations in a book by Anne Wolfinger titled *The Quick Internet Guide to Career and College Information,* published by JIST and used here with permission. I shortened comments and deleted sites that were primarily for professional counselors, educators, and the like. JIST's Internet site provides free access to the complete list, including many categories and sites that are not presented here. Anne's book has more detailed comments and many more entries, so you may want to buy the book.

Sites Providing Good Information on Careers, Job Search, Industries, and Related Subjects

These sites do a variety of useful things. Most provide good information as well as links to other career-related sites. Some have job listings or will accept your resume in a database for employers to search. You can start with almost any one of them and eventually get to what you want through links to other sites. With a few exceptions, I've arranged them in alphabetical order.

JIST Works

http://www.jist.com

JIST, the publisher of this book, maintains a site offering free information including career planning and job search advice, downloadable chapters from several books, an interactive job search workshop (based on content provided by yours truly), and direct links to recommended career, education, and job search sites. JIST also has an online bookstore that includes many good books, assessment tests, and other products.

Careers On-Line

http://www.disserv.stu.umn.edu/TC/Grants/COL

This site has job search and employment information for people with disabilities.

Career Resource Center

http://www.careers.org
You'll find more than 11,000 links here to jobs, employers, business, education, and career services on the Web. This site also includes links to bibliographies, software lists, publications, resource evaluations, event calendars, and resources for small businesses and self-employed people. It even lists career resources by geographic location.

Career Resource Homepage, Rensselaer Polytechnic Institute

http://www.rpi.edu/dept/cdc/homepage.html
This lists commercial job databases, resume banks, and employers who post job openings on their own Web sites. There are also links to professional associations, college career services, human resource management resources, alumni services, and various USENET newsgroups.

Career Toolbox

http://www.careertoolbox.com
Sponsored by Chevas Regal, this site features multimedia information on career planning, job search, entrepreneurship, professional development, and money management. While produced for recent college grads, it has useful information for anyone.

Catapult on JobWeb

http://www.jobweb.org/catapult/catapult.htm
From the National Association of Colleges and Employers, this site is aimed at career services professionals working with college students and alumni. It provides links to employment centers, colleges and universities, job search vehicles, industry information, relocation resources, and professional associations.

Definitive Guide to Internet Career Resources

http://phoenix.placement.oakland.edu/
From the Oakland University Career Services Office, this site boasts a thorough listing of career resources.

The Riley Guide: Employment Opportunities and Job Resources on the Internet

http://www.dbm.com/jobguide
One of the best career and job information clearinghouses, this site provides extensive information on using the Internet in your job search. Resources are organized into categories such as arts and humanities, computing and technology, and government jobs, with additional links for state, national, and international resources.

Emory Colossal List of Career Links

http://www.emory.edu/CAREER/Main/Links.html
From the placement office of Emory University, this site is oriented toward its student audience but contains links to and rates career and job search sites.

HomeFair

http://www.homefair.com
If you are relocating, you'll find here useful information on homes and cost of living in hundreds of U.S. and international cities. The site includes a salary calculator and many other resources.

Hoover's Online

http://www.hoovers.com
With information on more than 10,000 companies and a list of 4,000 specific corporate Web addresses, this is a very useful site.

Job Search and Employment Opportunities: Best Bets

http://asa.ugl.lib.umich.edu/chdocs/employment
Best Bets includes only sites that meet the clearinghouse's standards and provides a lengthy description and evaluation of each. Links are organized by field, with additional information for beginners on the Web.

JobHunt

http://www.job-hunt.org
This is a comprehensive roster of sites with descriptions and recommendations, plus job listings and other job resources.

JobSmart

http://jobsmart.org/index.htm

From the Bay Area Library System, this site has links to job banks, job hotlines, career centers, and libraries—plus information on salary surveys, resume writing, the hidden job market, high-tech careers, and career guides.

Military Career Guide Online

http://www.militarycareers.com

From the Department of Defense, this site provides information on 152 enlisted and officer occupations, education, and other benefits. Browse the occupations by category or search occupations that meet your criteria.

National Occupational Information Coordinating Committee (NOICC)

http://www.noicc.gov

A federal agency addressing the needs of vocational education and the career development needs of youth and adults, NOICC provides links to job search assistance sites, career information, education and financial aid sites, and sources of occupational labor market information and educational statistics.

Peace Corps

http://www.peacecorps.gov

This site has comprehensive information on volunteering for the Peace Corps, including application information for agriculture, education, forestry, health, engineering, skilled trades, business, environmental, urban planning, youth development, and more. About 6,500 volunteers now serve in over 90 countries.

Public Register's Annual Report Service (PRARS)

http://www.prars.com

PRARS provides company financials, including annual reports, on more than 3,200 public companies. Listings are organized alphabetically or by industry.

Purdue University Placement Service

http://www.ups.purdue.edu/student/jobsites.htm

You'll find here well-organized links to job search sites, federal government and international job listings, classifieds, newsgroups, resume services, and professional recruiters. The Reference and Resource Material category links to helpful information on career planning, job search, resume writing, interviewing, and more.

What Color Is Your Parachute? Job Hunting Online

http://www.washingtonpost.com/parachute

This site provides an online version of Richard Bolles's *Parachute* book, plus his comments on Internet sites.

Sites with Online Listings of Job Openings, Want Ads, and Resume Banks

In addition to listing job openings, most of these sites provide substantial resources for job seekers. For example, some have interactive resume-writing software, and others offer tips for job seeking or a bookstore offering recommended books. Most allow free posting of your resume to their resume databanks for employers, who pay to view the resumes. They all make it easy to use their services and provide links to other sites that provide specialized information or services.

America's Job Bank

http://www.ajb.dni.us

Run by the U.S. Employment Service, this site lists all the job openings posted at the 1,800 state employment service offices throughout the country, searchable in a variety of ways. Free listings to employers and job seekers.

Best Jobs in the USA Today

http://www.bestjobsusa.com

Best Jobs lists want ads from *USA Today* and from thousands of companies across the nation. Search by state, category, job title, or company name, or enter your own resume. There is no fee for job seekers. The site also features corporate profiles, lists of career fairs, and recent issues of *Employment Review*.

Career City

http://www.careercity.com

Career City features a no-fee resume and job bank and informative articles on resumes and interviewing. Sponsored by Adams Media, the site sells the company's job search and career information books and software.

Career Magazine

http://www.careermag.com

This is an online career resource magazine with articles, job updates, employer profiles, discussion groups, a resume bank, and classified ads. It combines job postings from USENET newsgroups into a database searchable by preferred job locations, skills, and title, with a list ranked by best fit or most recent job postings.

CareerPath

http://www.careerpath.com

CareerPath allows a quick search of want ads from 25 major newspapers across the country. Search by specific newspaper, job category, keyword, or other criteria.

CareerSite

http://www.careersite.com

This unique site lets job seekers and employers create profiles of their credentials or job opportunities. You can search and respond to openings online or wait for CareerSite to e-mail you jobs that match your preferences. CareerSite only sends your resume with your permission and only to employers with matching job needs.

CareerWeb

http://www.cweb.com

CareerWeb features a database of job openings, employer profiles, online career fairs, online bookstores, and links to other career sites. For a fee, CareerWeb will e-mail you openings that meet your preferences.

Federal Jobs Digest

http://www.jobsfed.com

This site claims to list more federal job vacancies than any other source. Organizes job openings by categories such as engineering, science and math, and trade and postal. For a fee, the matching service will analyze which kinds of federal jobs you may be eligible for.

Internet Career Connection

http://www.iccweb.com

This site offers both a job bank and a resume/talent bank. Free to job seekers looking for openings, Internet Career Connection does charge for posting your resume. The site also provides a computerized personality assessment and a list of career resources.

JobBank USA

http://www.jobbankusa.com

JobBank lets you search its own and other job databases for openings, making this a quick way to sort openings from a variety of sites. There is no fee for posting your resume.

JobOptions

http://www.joboptions.com

Formerly known as E.span, JobOptions is one of the larger resume and job banks on the Internet. You can search for job openings, post a confidential resume, and search through a database of thousands of hiring employers. The site also offers well-organized links to career management resources on resume writing, salary surveys, relocation, interviewing, job fairs, working parents, industry information, and continuing education.

JOBTRAK

http://www.jobtrak.com

A job and resume bank with access limited to students and alumni of the more than 400 colleges and universities, JOBTRAK includes employer profiles and full-time and part-time job listings. There is no charge to job seekers.

JobWeb

http://www.jobweb.com

JobWeb contains both job and employer databases with more than 450 employer links you can browse or search.

Online Career Center

http://www.occ.com

This large database of jobs is searchable by type, location, and other criteria, with no charge to job seekers to search the database or post their resumes. Also includes lots of career information.

Monster Board

http://www.monster.com

One of the largest job search sites, Monster Board allows you to search more than 50,000 job openings by location, discipline, or keywords, and delivers results to your personal in-box each time you log in to see your matches. Includes more than 4,000 employer profiles and lots of useful features.

Sites for Choosing a College or Training and for Getting Financial Aid

Many schools have their own Internet sites offering detailed information on programs, student body, activities, admissions requirements, and more. Some of the sites listed here will help you sort through and then link to these schools, while others will help you select programs that meet your criteria or provide other information.

Adventures in Education

http://www.tgslc.org

This site covers financial aid resources with links to educational institutions, financial institutions, scholarship information, government agencies, standardized tests/admissions, and other resources.

Center for All Collegiate Information

http://www.collegiate.net

A clearinghouse for information on postsecondary education, this site links to almost all major college-related sites in a variety of useful ways.

College and University Home Pages

http://www.mit.edu:8001/people/cdemello/univ.html

Linking to more than 3,000 college and university home pages worldwide, this site is sorted alphabetically and geographically. Also links to other school information Web sites around the world.

College Board Online

http://www.collegeboard.org

Run by an association of 3,000 two- and four-year colleges, universities, and education associations, this site offers many services for educators plus good searches for colleges, career searches, and scholarships.

CollegeNET

http://www.collegenet.com

CollegeNet lets you search for two-year and four-year schools and offers links to school home pages, scholarship searches, and education and financial aid resources.

CollegeView

http://www.collegeview.com

Here you can search colleges by criteria including field of study, state, student body size, athletics, and cost. The site also offers multimedia profiles of more than 3,500 colleges, e-mail connections to college admissions offices, and links to college home pages.

fastWEB

http://www.fastweb.com

This is a database of more than 180,000 private-sector scholarships, fellowships, grants, and loans. There is no fee for matching with your profile of skills and abilities.

FinAid: The Financial Aid Information Page

http://www.finaid.org

With links to online scholarship databases and to many other financial aid resources, such as aid for students over 30 and other special groups, this is a good site.

Mapping Your Future

http://www.mapping-your-future.org

The main focus of this site is selecting a postsecondary school and applying for financial aid.

Peterson's Education and Career Center

http://www.petersons.com

You'll find substantial information here on K-12 schools, colleges and universities, graduate study, studying abroad, summer programs, language study, distance learning, financial aid, and other topics. Search colleges alphabetically, geographically, by major, or by keyword.

Project EASI (Easy Access for Students and Institutions)

http://easi.ed.gov/index.html

Run by the U.S. Department of Education to help parents and students get financial aid, this site covers planning for your education, applying and receiving financial aid, and repaying your loan, with links to related Web sites. Free download or online view of *Preparing Your Child for College: A Resource Book for Parents.*

The Princeton Review

http://www.review.com/index.cfm

Search databases for colleges, business schools, law schools, and medical schools; then link to the schools' home pages. This site offers information on admissions, testing, financial aid, and programs. Experts moderate discussion groups on related topics such as the SAT, the GRE, and the bar exam.

National Association of Colleges and Employers (NACE)

http://www.jobweb.org

NACE serves colleges, employer organizations, students, and alumni. The site includes employer/college surveys, salary surveys of newly hired college graduates, a quarterly journal, and a biweekly newsletter.

U.S. News & World Report Colleges & Careers Center

http://www.usnews.com/usnews/edu/home.htm

From *U.S. News & World Report*, this site features college rankings, admissions, articles on careers and self-employment, links to financial aid sites, online discussion forums, a parents' guide, and campus culture information.

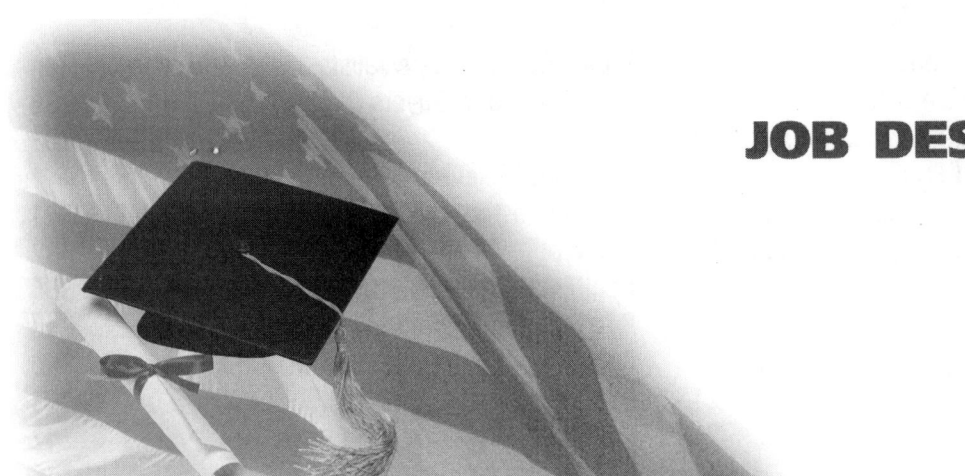

INDEX OF JOB DESCRIPTIONS

© 1999 • J. Michael Farr • JIST Works, Inc. • Indianapolis, IN

Best Jobs for the 21st Century
Expert Reference on the Jobs of Tomorrow
By J. Michael Farr and LaVerne L. Ludden, Ed.D.

Whether you're preparing to enter the job market for the first time or simply wish to remain competitive in your current field, this information-packed reference contains data on the latest employment trends.

✦ Contains over 50 lists of jobs with best pay, high growth, and most openings by numerous categories
✦ Describes 686 jobs with fast growth or high pay
✦ Based on expert analysis of labor and economic trends

ISBN: 1-56370-486-2 • $16.95 • Order Code: J4862

The College Majors Handbook
A Guide to Your Undergraduate College
Investment Decision
By Paul Harrington, Tom Harrington, Neeta Fogg

Are you faced with the college decision? Wondering how to decide on a major? Well, here's a book detailing what *actually* happened to more than 250,000 undergraduates from 60 college majors!

✦ The *only* college planning guide with the perspective of what actually happens to college undergraduates
✦ Identifies jobs in which undergraduates from 60 college majors are employed, their earnings on those jobs, and the projections of employment prospects in those jobs

ISBN: 1-56370-518-4 • $24.95 • Order Code: J5184

Luddens' Adult Guide to Colleges and Universities
A Directory of Thousands of Adult-Friendly
Degree Programs
By LaVerne L. Ludden, Ed.D., Marsha J. Ludden, M.A.

If you're thinking it's too late to go to college, think again! Nearly half of America's college students choose a college *after* they become adults! More than 40% of all college students are over the age of 25 —and the percentage is growing.

✦ Valuable information on more than 1,500 degree programs at more than 400 colleges and universities
✦ Information on nontraditional degrees, flexible schedules, life experience credit, and more!

ISBN: 1-57112-076-9 • $19.95 • Order Code: P0769

Back to School

A College Guide for Adults
By LaVerne L. Ludden, Ed.D.

If you're an adult pondering the college decision, here's a book for you! Written by the former Dean of Graduate and Adult Studies at LeTourneau University.

✦ Offers inside advice on setting objectives, getting financial aid, choosing a college, and juggling priorities
✦ Includes self-assessment exercises to help you focus on college success
✦ Features a valuable directory of 1,000 adult degree programs

ISBN: 1-57112-070-X • $14.95 • Order Code: P070X

Career Satisfaction and Success

A Guide to Job and Personal Freedom
By Bernard Haldane, Ph.D.

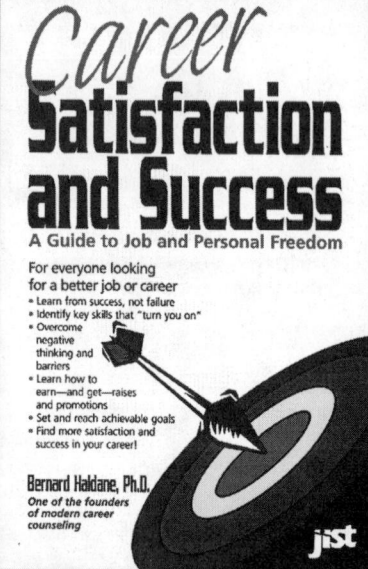

Are you looking for a better job or a more rewarding career? You have more control over your destiny than you may think! Written by one of the founders of modern career counseling, this classic and compelling book will lead you on the path to career and business success! Learn to

✦ Identify and use your "motivated" skills and strengths
✦ Expand your ambitions and capabilities
✦ Explore other career options
✦ Make others aware of your value

ISBN: 1-56370-200-2 • $14.95 • Order Code: J2002

America's Top Resumes for America's Top Jobs®

By J. Michael Farr

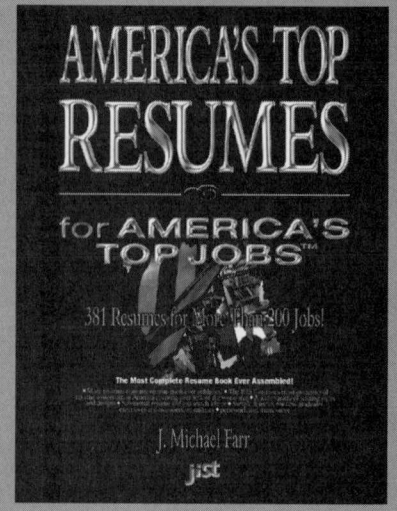

Introducing the ONLY book with sample resumes for all major occupations covering 85% of the workforce! Here you'll find nearly 400 of the best resumes submitted by members of the Professional Association of Resume Writers, grouped according to occupation and annotated by the author to highlight their best features—PLUS career planning and job search advice from Mike Farr!

ISBN: 1-56370-288-6 • $19.95 • Order Code: J2886

The O*NET Dictionary of Occupational Titles

Based on information from the U.S. Department of Labor
Compiled by J. Michael Farr and LaVerne L. Ludden, Ed.D.

JIST is the first publisher to use the U.S. Department of Labor's new O*NET data, which was developed to replace the 1991 edition of the *Dictionary of Occupational Titles*. The O*NET presents a major change in occupational information systems, and this new reference includes

✦ Descriptions of all major jobs—more than 1,100—in the new O*NET database
✦ User-friendly introduction to the O*NET system

ISBN: 1-56370-510-9	ISBN: 1-56370-509-5
$39.95 Softcover	$49.95 Hardcover
Order Code: J5109	Order Code: J5095

Occupational Outlook Handbook

By the U.S. Department of Labor

The *OOH* is the most widely used career exploration resource. This is a quality reprint of the government's *OOH*, only at a less-expensive price. It describes 250 jobs—jobs held by 85% of the American workforce—making the book ideal for students, counselors, teachers, librarians, and job seekers.

✦ Well-written narrative with many charts and photos
✦ Gives DOT numbers for the occupation and related occupations
✦ Sections on nature of the work, working conditions, training, job outlook, earnings

ISBN: 1-56370-464-1	ISBN: 1-56370-475-7
$17.95 Softcover	$22.95 Hardcover
Order Code: J4641	Order Code: J4757

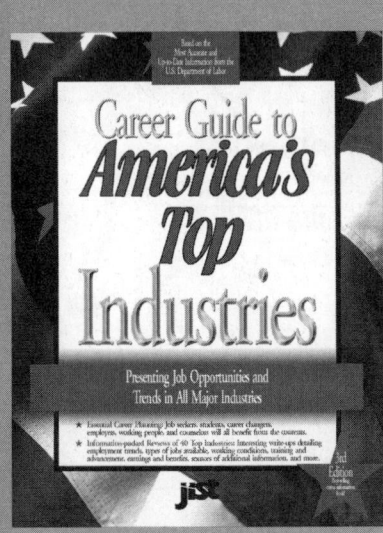

Career Guide to America's Top Industries

Essential Information on Opportunities and Trends in All Major Industries
By the U.S. Department of Labor

Want to know which industries will be leading the pack in the next century? Then be sure to pick up this information-packed review of 40 top industries that account for 75 percent of the jobs in our economy! This book includes

✦ Employment trends
✦ Earnings
✦ Types of jobs available
✦ Working conditions, training and advancement

ISBN: 1-56370-465-X • $16.95 • Order Code: J465X

The Quick Resume & Cover Letter Book

Write and Use an Effective Resume in Only One Day
By J. Michael Farr

A hands-on, total job search guide! The author understands you don't have a lot of valuable time to waste preparing your job search. This award-winning title offers tips on

✦ Writing a "same day resume"
✦ Job searching
✦ Interviewing
✦ Cover and follow-up letters
✦ And much, much more!

ISBN: 1-56370-141-3 • $12.95 • Order Code: RCLQG

The Quick Interview & Salary Negotiation Book

Dramatically Improve Your Interviewing Skills in Just a Few Hours!
By J. Michael Farr

Time is money. And, in just a few hours, you could be on your way to earning more! America's premier job search and career author shares simple, fast, effective techniques for handling unusual and difficult interview situations and negotiating salaries and pay increases. No matter what your level of job experience, you literally cannot afford to miss this book!

ISBN: 1-56370-162-6 • $12.95 • Order Code: J1626

The Very Quick Job Search

Get a Better Job in Half the Time!
By J. Michael Farr

Mike Farr, one of the most important architects of the self-directed job search, has done it again! Nowhere else will you find such excellent, timeless job search information. This award-winning title has been an important resource for more than 150,000 people just like you!

✦ Thorough coverage of all career planning and job search topics—in one book!
✦ Proven, effective advice for *all* job seekers
✦ Latest information on market trends and results-oriented search techniques

ISBN: 1-56370-181-2 • $14.95 • Order Code: J1812

JIST Ordering Information

JIST specializes in publishing the very best results-oriented career and self-directed job search material. Since 1981 we have been a leading publisher in career assessment devices, books, videos, and software. We continue to strive to make our materials the best there are so that people can stay abreast of what's happening in the labor market, and so they can clarify and articulate their skills and experiences for themselves as well as for prospective employers. **Our products are widely available through your local bookstores, wholesalers, and distributors.**

The World Wide Web

For more occupational or book information, get online and see our Web site at **www.jist.com**. Advance information about new products, services, and training events is continually updated.

Quantity Discounts Available!

Quantity discounts are available for businesses, schools, and other organizations.

The JIST Guarantee

We want you to be happy with everything you buy from JIST. If you aren't satisfied with a product, return it to us within 30 days of purchase along with the reason for the return. Please include a copy of the packing list or invoice to guarantee quick credit to your order.

How to Order

For your convenience, the last page of this book contains an order form.

24-Hour Consumer Order Line:
Call toll free 1-800-JIST-USA
Please have your credit card (VISA, MC, or AMEX) information ready!

Mail: Mail your order to
JIST Works, Inc.
720 North Park Avenue
Indianapolis, IN 46202-3490

Fax: Toll free 1-800-JIST-FAX

JIST Order Form

Purchase Order #: _____

Billing Information

Organization Name: _____
Accounting Contact: _____
Street Address: _____
_____
_____
City, State, Zip: _____
Phone Number: (____) _____

Shipping Information (if different from above)

Organization Name: _____
Contact: _____
Street Address: (we *cannot* ship to P.O. boxes) _____
_____
_____
City, State, Zip: _____
Phone Number: (____) _____

Credit Card Purchases: VISA_____ MC_____ AMEX_____
Card Number: _____
Exp. date: _____
Name as on card: _____
Signature: _____

Quantity	Order Code	Product Title	Unit Price	Total
			Subtotal	
			+Sales Tax *Indiana Residents add 5% sales tax.*	
			+Shipping / Handling *Add $3.00 for the first item and an additional $.50 for each item thereafter.*	
			TOTAL	

jist Works, Inc.
720 North Park Avenue
Indianapolis, IN 46202

JIST thanks you for your order!